CODE OF FEDERAL REGULATIONS

Title 16
Commercial Practices

Parts 0 to 999

Revised as of January 1, 2019

Containing a codification of documents
of general applicability and future effect

As of January 1, 2019

Published by the Office of the Federal Register
National Archives and Records Administration
as a Special Edition of the Federal Register

Table of Contents

Cite this Code: CFR

To cite the regulations in this volume use title, part and section number. Thus, 16 CFR 0.1 *refers to title 16, part 0, section 1.*

Explanation

The Code of Federal Regulations is a codification of the general and permanent rules published in the Federal Register by the Executive departments and agencies of the Federal Government. The Code is divided into 50 titles which represent broad areas subject to Federal regulation. Each title is divided into chapters which usually bear the name of the issuing agency. Each chapter is further subdivided into parts covering specific regulatory areas.

Each volume of the Code is revised at least once each calendar year and issued on a quarterly basis approximately as follows:

Title 1 through Title 16..............................as of January 1
Title 17 through Title 27..............................as of April 1
Title 28 through Title 41..............................as of July 1
Title 42 through Title 50..............................as of October 1

The appropriate revision date is printed on the cover of each volume.

LEGAL STATUS

The contents of the Federal Register are required to be judicially noticed (44 U.S.C. 1507). The Code of Federal Regulations is prima facie evidence of the text of the original documents (44 U.S.C. 1510).

HOW TO USE THE CODE OF FEDERAL REGULATIONS

The Code of Federal Regulations is kept up to date by the individual issues of the Federal Register. These two publications must be used together to determine the latest version of any given rule.

To determine whether a Code volume has been amended since its revision date (in this case, January 1, 2019), consult the "List of CFR Sections Affected (LSA)," which is issued monthly, and the "Cumulative List of Parts Affected," which appears in the Reader Aids section of the daily Federal Register. These two lists will identify the Federal Register page number of the latest amendment of any given rule.

EFFECTIVE AND EXPIRATION DATES

Each volume of the Code contains amendments published in the Federal Register since the last revision of that volume of the Code. Source citations for the regulations are referred to by volume number and page number of the Federal Register and date of publication. Publication dates and effective dates are usually not the same and care must be exercised by the user in determining the actual effective date. In instances where the effective date is beyond the cut-off date for the Code a note has been inserted to reflect the future effective date. In those instances where a regulation published in the Federal Register states a date certain for expiration, an appropriate note will be inserted following the text.

OMB CONTROL NUMBERS

The Paperwork Reduction Act of 1980 (Pub. L. 96–511) requires Federal agencies to display an OMB control number with their information collection request.

Many agencies have begun publishing numerous OMB control numbers as amendments to existing regulations in the CFR. These OMB numbers are placed as close as possible to the applicable recordkeeping or reporting requirements.

PAST PROVISIONS OF THE CODE

Provisions of the Code that are no longer in force and effect as of the revision date stated on the cover of each volume are not carried. Code users may find the text of provisions in effect on any given date in the past by using the appropriate List of CFR Sections Affected (LSA). For the convenience of the reader, a "List of CFR Sections Affected" is published at the end of each CFR volume. For changes to the Code prior to the LSA listings at the end of the volume, consult previous annual editions of the LSA. For changes to the Code prior to 2001, consult the List of CFR Sections Affected compilations, published for 1949-1963, 1964-1972, 1973-1985, and 1986-2000.

"[RESERVED]" TERMINOLOGY

The term "[Reserved]" is used as a place holder within the Code of Federal Regulations. An agency may add regulatory information at a "[Reserved]" location at any time. Occasionally "[Reserved]" is used editorially to indicate that a portion of the CFR was left vacant and not accidentally dropped due to a printing or computer error.

INCORPORATION BY REFERENCE

What is incorporation by reference? Incorporation by reference was established by statute and allows Federal agencies to meet the requirement to publish regulations in the Federal Register by referring to materials already published elsewhere. For an incorporation to be valid, the Director of the Federal Register must approve it. The legal effect of incorporation by reference is that the material is treated as if it were published in full in the Federal Register (5 U.S.C. 552(a)). This material, like any other properly issued regulation, has the force of law.

What is a proper incorporation by reference? The Director of the Federal Register will approve an incorporation by reference only when the requirements of 1 CFR part 51 are met. Some of the elements on which approval is based are:

(a) The incorporation will substantially reduce the volume of material published in the Federal Register.

(b) The matter incorporated is in fact available to the extent necessary to afford fairness and uniformity in the administrative process.

(c) The incorporating document is drafted and submitted for publication in accordance with 1 CFR part 51.

What if the material incorporated by reference cannot be found? If you have any problem locating or obtaining a copy of material listed as an approved incorporation by reference, please contact the agency that issued the regulation containing that incorporation. If, after contacting the agency, you find the material is not available, please notify the Director of the Federal Register, National Archives and Records Administration, 8601 Adelphi Road, College Park, MD 20740-6001, or call 202-741-6010.

CFR INDEXES AND TABULAR GUIDES

A subject index to the Code of Federal Regulations is contained in a separate volume, revised annually as of January 1, entitled CFR INDEX AND FINDING AIDS. This volume contains the Parallel Table of Authorities and Rules. A list of CFR titles, chapters, subchapters, and parts and an alphabetical list of agencies publishing in the CFR are also included in this volume.

An index to the text of "Title 3—The President" is carried within that volume.

The Federal Register Index is issued monthly in cumulative form. This index is based on a consolidation of the "Contents" entries in the daily Federal Register.

A List of CFR Sections Affected (LSA) is published monthly, keyed to the revision dates of the 50 CFR titles.

REPUBLICATION OF MATERIAL

There are no restrictions on the republication of material appearing in the Code of Federal Regulations.

INQUIRIES

For a legal interpretation or explanation of any regulation in this volume, contact the issuing agency. The issuing agency's name appears at the top of odd-numbered pages.

For inquiries concerning CFR reference assistance, call 202–741–6000 or write to the Director, Office of the Federal Register, National Archives and Records Administration, 8601 Adelphi Road, College Park, MD 20740-6001 or e-mail *fedreg.info@nara.gov.*

SALES

The Government Publishing Office (GPO) processes all sales and distribution of the CFR. For payment by credit card, call toll-free, 866-512-1800, or DC area, 202-512-1800, M-F 8 a.m. to 4 p.m. e.s.t. or fax your order to 202-512-2104, 24 hours a day. For payment by check, write to: US Government Publishing Office – New Orders, P.O. Box 979050, St. Louis, MO 63197-9000.

ELECTRONIC SERVICES

The full text of the Code of Federal Regulations, the LSA (List of CFR Sections Affected), The United States Government Manual, the Federal Register, Public Laws, Public Papers of the Presidents of the United States, Compilation of Presidential Documents and the Privacy Act Compilation are available in electronic format via *www.govinfo.gov*. For more information, contact the GPO Customer Contact Center, U.S. Government Publishing Office. Phone 202-512-1800, or 866-512-1800 (toll-free). E-mail, *ContactCenter@gpo.gov.*

The Office of the Federal Register also offers a free service on the National Archives and Records Administration's (NARA) World Wide Web site for public law numbers, Federal Register finding aids, and related information. Connect to NARA's web site at *www.archives.gov/federal-register.*

The e-CFR is a regularly updated, unofficial editorial compilation of CFR material and Federal Register amendments, produced by the Office of the Federal Register and the Government Publishing Office. It is available at *www.ecfr.gov.*

OLIVER A. POTTS,
Director,
Office of the Federal Register
January 1, 2019

THIS TITLE

Title 16—COMMERCIAL PRACTICES is composed of two volumes. The first volume contains parts 0–999 and comprises chapter I—Federal Trade Commission. The second volume containing part 1000 to end comprises chapter II—Consumer Product Safety Commission. The contents of these volumes represent all current regulations codified under this title of the CFR as of January 1, 2019.

For this volume, Robert J. Sheehan, III was Chief Editor. The Code of Federal Regulations publication program is under the direction of John Hyrum Martinez, assisted by Stephen J. Frattini.

Title 16—Commercial Practices

(This book contains parts 0 to 999)

CHAPTER I—FEDERAL TRADE COMMISSION

SUBCHAPTER A—ORGANIZATION, PROCEDURES AND RULES OF PRACTICE

SUBCHAPTER C—REGULATIONS UNDER SPECIFIC ACTS OF CONGRESS

SUBCHAPTER D—TRADE REGULATION RULES

CROSS REFERENCES: Animal and Plant Health Inspection Service, Department of Agriculture: 9 CFR Chapter I. Commodity Futures Trading Commission: 17 CFR Chapter I. Consumer Product Safety Commission: 16 CFR Chapter II. Securities and Exchange Commission: 17 CFR Chapter II.

SUPPLEMENTARY PUBLICATIONS: *Federal Trade Commission decisions, Volumes 1–90 Index digest of volumes 1, 2, and 3 of decisions of the Federal Trade Commission with annotation of Federal cases. Mar. 16, 1915–June 30, 1921. Statutes and decisions pertaining to the Federal Trade Commission. 1914–1929, 1930–1938, 1939–1943, 1944–1948, 1949–1955, 1956–1960, 1961–1965, 1966–1970, 1971–1975, 1976, 1977.*

SUBCHAPTER A—ORGANIZATION, PROCEDURES AND RULES OF PRACTICE

PART 0—ORGANIZATION

AUTHORITY: 5 U.S.C. 552(a)(1); 15 U.S.C. 46(g).

SOURCE: 41 FR 54483, Dec. 14, 1976, unless otherwise noted.

§ 0.1 The Commission.

The Federal Trade Commission is an independent administrative agency which was organized in 1915 pursuant to the Federal Trade Commission Act of 1914 (38 Stat. 717, as amended; 15 U.S.C. 41–58). It is responsible for the administration of a variety of statutes which, in general, are designed to promote competition and to protect the public from unfair and deceptive acts and practices in the advertising and marketing of goods and services. It is composed of five members appointed by the President and confirmed by the Senate for terms of seven years.

§ 0.2 Official address.

The principal office of the Commission is at Washington, DC. All communications to the Commission should be addressed to the Federal Trade Commission, 600 Pennsylvania Avenue, NW, Washington, DC 20580, unless otherwise specifically directed. The Commission's Web site address is *www.ftc.gov*.

[63 FR 71582, Dec. 29, 1998, as amended at 65 FR 78408, Dec. 15, 2000]

§ 0.3 Hours.

Principal and field offices are open on each business day from 8:30 a.m. to 5 p.m.

§ 0.4 Laws administered.

The Commission exercises enforcement and administrative authority under the Federal Trade Commission Act (15 U.S.C. 41–58), Clayton Act (15 U.S.C. 12–27), Robinson-Patman Act (15 U.S.C. 13–13b, 21a), Webb-Pomerene (Export Trade) Act (15 U.S.C. 61–66), Packers and Stockyards Act (7 U.S.C. 181–229), Wool Products Labeling Act of 1939 (15 U.S.C. 68–68j), Lanham Trade-Mark Act (15 U.S.C. 1064), Fur Products Labeling Act (15 U.S.C. 69–69j), Textile Fiber Products Identification Act (15 U.S.C. 70–70k), Federal Cigarette Labeling and Advertising Act (15 U.S.C. 1331–1340), Fair Packaging and Labeling Act (15 U.S.C. 1451–1461), Truth in Lending Act (15 U.S.C. 1601–1667f), Fair Credit Reporting Act (15 U.S.C. 1681–1681u), Fair Credit Billing Act (15 U.S.C. 1666–1666j), Equal Credit Opportunity Act (15 U.S.C. 1691–1691f), Fair Debt Collection Practices Act (15 U.S.C. 1692–1692o), Electronic Fund Transfer Act (15 U.S.C. 1693–1693r), Hobby Protection Act (15 U.S.C. 2101–2106), Magnuson-Moss Warranty—Federal Trade Commission Improvement Act (15 U.S.C. 2301–2312, 45–58), Energy Policy and Conservation Act (42 U.S.C. 6201–6422, 15 U.S.C. 2008), Hart-Scott-Rodino Antitrust Improvements Act of 1976 (15 U.S.C. 18a), Petroleum Marketing Practices Act (15 U.S.C. 2801–2841), Comprehensive Smokeless Tobacco Health Education Act of 1986 (15 U.S.C. 4401–4408), Telephone Disclosure and Dispute Resolution Act of 1992 (15 U.S.C. 5701–5724), Telemarketing and Consumer Fraud and Abuse Prevention Act (15 U.S.C. 6101–6108), International Antitrust Enforcement Assistance Act of 1994 (15 U.S.C. 46, 57b–1, 1311–1312, 6201 & note, 6202–6212), Credit Repair Organizations Act (15 U.S.C. 1679–1679j), Children's Online Privacy Protection Act (15 U.S.C. 6501–6506), Identity Theft Assumption and Deterrence Act of 1998 (18

U.S.C. 1028 note), Gramm-Leach-Bliley Act (15 U.S.C. 6801–6809), and other Federal statutes.

[65 FR 78408, Dec. 15, 2000]

§ 0.5 Laws authorizing monetary claims.

The Commission is authorized to entertain monetary claims against it under three statutes. The Federal Tort Claims Act (28 U.S.C. 2671–2680) provides that the United States will be liable for injury or loss of property or personal injury or death caused by the negligent or wrongful acts or omissions of its employees acting within the scope of their employment or office. The Military Personnel and Civilian Employees Claims Act of 1964 (31 U.S.C. 3701, 3721) authorizes the Commission to compensate employees' claims for damage to or loss of personal property incident to their service. The Equal Access to Justice Act (5 U.S.C. 504 and 28 U.S.C. 2412) provides that an eligible prevailing party other than the United States will be awarded fees and expenses incurred in connection with any adversary adjudicative and court proceeding, unless the adjudicative officer finds that the agency was substantially justified or that special circumstances make an award unjust. In addition, eligible parties, including certain small businesses, will be awarded fees and expenses incurred in defending against an agency demand that is substantially in excess of the final decision of the adjudicative officer and is unreasonable when compared with such decision under the facts and circumstances of the case, unless the adjudicative officer finds that the party has committed a willful violation of law or otherwise acted in bad faith, or special circumstances make an award unjust. Questions may be addressed to the Office of the General Counsel, (202) 326–2462.

[63 FR 36340, July 6, 1998]

§ 0.6 [Reserved]

§ 0.7 Delegation of functions.

(a) The Commission, under the authority provided by Reorganization Plan No. 4 of 1961, may delegate, by published order or rule, certain of its functions to a division of the Commission, an individual Commissioner, an administrative law judge, or an employee or employee board, and retains a discretionary right to review such delegated action upon its own initiative or upon petition of a party to or an intervenor in such action.

(b) The Commission delegates its functions, subject to certain limitations, when no quorum is available for the transaction of business. The delegate or delegates are authorized to act in instances in which no party or intervenor would be adversely affected by the delegated action and entitled to seek review by the Commission, as provided by section 1(b) of Reorganization Plan No. 4 of 1961, or in instances in which all such adversely affected parties or intervenors have waived such a right. In actions in which at least one Commissioner is participating, this delegation is to the participating Commissioner or to the body of Commissioners who are participating. In actions in which no Commissioner is available or no Commissioner is participating, the General Counsel in consultation, where appropriate, with the Directors of the Bureaus of Consumer Protection, Competition, and Economics shall exercise this delegated authority without power of redelegation. This delegation does not alter or affect other delegations to Commission staff. This delegation is only authorized for those instances in which the Commission lacks a quorum as set forth in Commission Rule 4.14(b), 16 CFR 4.14(b) (Commission quorum).

[83 FR 7110, Feb. 20, 2018]

§ 0.8 The Chairman.

The Chairman of the Commission is designated by the President, and, subject to the general policies of the Commission, is the executive and administrative head of the agency. He presides at meetings of and hearings before the Commission and participates with other Commissioners in all Commission decisions. Attached to the Office of the Chairman, and reporting directly to him, and through him to the Commission, are the following staff units:

(a) The Office of Public Affairs, which furnishes information concerning Commission activities to news media and the public; and

(b) the Office of Congressional Relations, which coordinates all liaison activities with Congress.

[50 FR 53303, Dec. 31, 1985]

§0.9 Organization structure.

The Federal Trade Commission comprises the following principal units: Office of the Executive Director; Office of the General Counsel; Office of the Secretary; Office of the Inspector General; Office of the Administrative Law Judges; Office of International Affairs; Bureau of Competition; Bureau of Consumer Protection; Bureau of Economics; and the Regional Offices.

[72 FR 9434, Mar. 2, 2007]

§0.10 Office of the Executive Director.

The Executive Director, under the direction of the Chairman, is the chief operating official who develops and implements management and administrative policies, programs and directives for the Commission. The Executive Director works closely with the Bureaus on strategic planning and assessing the management and resource implications of any proposed action. In addition, the Executive Director manages the Commission's facilities and administrative services, financial management, information technology, and human resources.

[65 FR 78408, Dec. 15, 2000]

§0.11 Office of the General Counsel.

The General Counsel is the Commission's chief law officer and adviser, who renders necessary legal services to the Commission, represents the Commission in the Federal and State courts, advises the Commission and other agency officials and staff with respect to questions of law and policy, including advice with respect to legislative matters and ethics, and responds to requests and appeals filed under the Freedom of Information and Privacy Acts and to intra- and intergovernmental access requests.

[65 FR 78408, Dec. 15, 2000]

§0.12 Office of the Secretary.

The Secretary is responsible for the minutes of Commission meetings and is the legal custodian of the Commission's seal, property, papers, and records, including legal and public records. The Secretary, or in the Secretary's absence an Acting Secretary designated by the Commission, signs Commission orders and official correspondence. In addition, the Secretary is responsible for the publication of all Commission actions that appear in the FEDERAL REGISTER and for the publication of *Federal Trade Commission Decisions*.

[65 FR 78408, Dec. 15, 2000]

§0.13 Office of the Inspector General.

The Office of Inspector General (OIG) was established within the Federal Trade Commission in 1989 as required by the Inspector General Act Amendments of 1988 (5 U.S.C. app. 3). The OIG promotes the economy, efficiency and effectiveness of FTC programs and operations. To this end, the OIG independently conducts audits and investigations to find and prevent fraud, waste, and abuse within the agency.

[65 FR 78408, Dec. 15, 2000]

§0.14 Office of Administrative Law Judges.

Administrative law judges are officials to whom the Commission, in accordance with law, delegates the initial performance of statutory fact-finding functions and initial rulings on conclusions of law, to be exercised in conformity with Commission decisions and policy directives and with its Rules of Practice. The administrative law judges also serve as presiding officers assigned to conduct rulemaking proceedings under section 18(a)(1)(B) of the Federal Trade Commission Act as amended and other rulemaking proceedings as directed. The Chief Administrative Law Judge also serves as the Chief Presiding Officer. Administrative law judges are appointed under the authority and subject to the prior approval of the Office of Personnel Management.

[54 FR 19885, May 9, 1989, as amended at 65 FR 78409, Dec. 15, 2000]

§0.15 [Reserved]

§0.16 Bureau of Competition.

The Bureau is responsible for enforcing Federal antitrust and trade regulation laws under section 5 of the Federal Trade Commission Act, the Clayton Act, and a number of other special statutes that the Commission is charged with enforcing. The Bureau's work aims to preserve the free market system and assure the unfettered operation of the forces of supply and demand. Its activities seek to ensure price competition, quality products and services and efficient operation of the national economy. The Bureau carries out its responsibilities by investigating alleged law violations, and recommending to the Commission such further action as may be appropriate. Such action may include injunctive and other equitable relief in Federal district court, complaint and litigation before the agency's administrative law judges, formal nonadjudicative settlement of complaints, trade regulation rules, or reports. The Bureau also conducts compliance investigations and initiates proceedings for civil penalties to assure compliance with final Commission orders dealing with competition and trade restraint matters. The Bureau's activities also include business and consumer education and staff advice on competition laws and compliance, and liaison functions with respect to foreign antitrust and competition law enforcement agencies and organizations, including requests for international enforcement assistance.

[65 FR 78409, Dec. 15, 2000]

§0.17 Bureau of Consumer Protection.

The Bureau investigates unfair or deceptive acts or practices under section 5 of the Federal Trade Commission Act as well as potential violations of numerous special statutes which the Commission is charged with enforcing. It prosecutes before the agency's administrative law judges alleged violations of law after issuance of a complaint by the Commission or obtains through negotiation consented-to orders, which must be accepted and issued by the Commission. In consultation with the General Counsel, the Bureau may also seek injunctive or other equitable relief under section 13(b) of the Federal Trade Commission Act. The Bureau participates in trade regulation rulemaking proceedings under section 18(a)(1)(B) of the Federal Trade Commission Act and other rulemaking proceedings under statutory authority. It investigates compliance with final orders and trade regulation rules and seeks civil penalties or consumer redress for their violation, as well as injunctive and other equitable relief under section 13(b) of the Act. In addition, the Bureau seeks to educate both consumers and the business community about the laws it enforces, and to assist and cooperate with other state, local, foreign, and international agencies and organizations in consumer protection enforcement and regulatory matters. The Bureau also maintains the agency's public reference facilities, where the public may inspect and copy a current index of opinions, orders, statements of policy and interpretations, staff manuals and instructions that affect any member of the public, and other public records of the Commission.

[65 FR 78409, Dec. 15, 2000]

§0.18 Bureau of Economics.

The bureau aids and advises the Commission concerning the economic aspects of all of its functions, and is responsible for the preparation of various economic reports and surveys. The bureau provides economic and statistical assistance to the enforcement bureaus in the investigation and trial of cases.

[41 FR 54483, Dec. 14, 1976. Redesignated at 45 FR 36341, May 29, 1980, and amended at 50 FR 53303, Dec. 31, 1985]

§0.19 The Regional Offices.

(a) These offices are investigatory arms of the Commission, and have responsibility for investigational, trial, compliance, and consumer educational activities as delegated by the Commission. They are under the general supervision of the Office of the Executive Director, and clear their activities through the appropriate operating Bureaus.

(b) The names, geographic areas of responsibility, and addresses of the respective regional offices are as follows:

(1) *Northeast Region* (located in New York City, New York), covering Connecticut, Maine, Massachusetts, New Hampshire, New Jersey, New York, Rhode Island, Vermont, and Puerto Rico. Federal Trade Commission, One Bowling Green, Suite 318, New York, New York 10004.

(2) *Southeast Region* (located in Atlanta, Georgia), covering Alabama, Florida, Georgia, Mississippi, North Carolina, South Carolina, and Tennessee. Federal Trade Commission, Suite 5M35, Midrise Building, 60 Forsyth Street, SW., Atlanta, Georgia 30303.

(3) *East Central Region* (located in Cleveland, Ohio), covering Delaware, District of Columbia, Maryland, Michigan, Ohio, Pennsylvania, Virginia, and West Virginia. Federal Trade Commission, Eaton Center, Suite 200, 1111 Superior Avenue, Cleveland, Ohio 44114.

(4) *Midwest Region* (located in Chicago, Illinois), covering Illinois, Indiana, Iowa, Kansas, Kentucky, Minnesota, Missouri, Nebraska, North Dakota, South Dakota, and Wisconsin. Federal Trade Commission, 55 East Monroe Street, Suite 1860, Chicago, Illinois 60603–5701.

(5) *Southwest Region* (located in Dallas, Texas), covering Arkansas, Louisiana, New Mexico, Oklahoma, and Texas. Federal Trade Commission, 1999 Bryan Street, Suite 2150, Dallas, Texas 75201.

(6) *Northwest Region* (located in Seattle, Washington), covering Alaska, Idaho, Montana, Oregon, Washington, and Wyoming. Federal Trade Commission, 915 Second Avenue, Suite 2896, Seattle, Washington 98174.

(7) *Western Region* (located in San Francisco and Los Angeles, California), covering Arizona, California, Colorado, Hawaii, Nevada, and Utah.

(i) San Francisco Office: Federal Trade Commission, 901 Market Street, Suite 570, San Francisco, California 94103.

(ii) Los Angeles Office: Federal Trade Commission, 10877 Wilshire Boulevard, Suite 700, Los Angeles, California 90024.

(c) Each of the regional offices is supervised by a Regional Director, who is available for conferences with attorneys, consumers, and other members of the public on matters relating to the Commission's activities.

[41 FR 54483, Dec. 14, 1976, as amended at 42 FR 27218, May 27, 1977; 43 FR 754, Jan. 4, 1978; 43 FR 6579, Feb. 15, 1978. Redesignated at 45 FR 36341, May 29, 1980, as amended at 50 FR 53303, Dec. 31, 1985; 63 FR 71582, Dec. 29, 1998; 64 FR 71284, Dec. 21, 1999; 65 FR 78409, Dec. 15, 2000]

§ 0.20 Office of International Affairs.

The Office of International Affairs (OIA) comprises international antitrust, international consumer protection, and international technical assistance. OIA is responsible for designing and implementing the Commission's international program, which provides support and advice to the Bureaus of Competition and Consumer Protection with regard to the international aspects of investigation and prosecution of unlawful conduct. OIA builds cooperative relationships between the Commission and foreign authorities; works closely with Bureau personnel to recommend agency priorities and policies and works, through bilateral relationships and multilateral organizations, to promote those policies internationally; and implements Commission policy and participation in the competition and consumer protection aspects of trade fora and negotiations, such as the U.S. inter-agency delegations negotiating bilateral and multilateral free trade agreements. OIA works with authorized funding sources to develop and implement competition and consumer protection technical assistance programs.

[72 FR 9434, Mar. 2, 2007]

PART 1—GENERAL PROCEDURES

Subpart A—Industry Guidance

ADVISORY OPINIONS

Subpart B—Rules and Rulemaking Under Section 18(a)(1)(B) of the FTC Act

1.7 Scope of rules in this subpart.
1.8 Nature, authority and use of trade regulation rules.
1.9 Petitions to commence trade regulation rule proceedings.
1.10 Advance notice of proposed rulemaking.
1.11 Commencement of a rulemaking proceeding.
1.12 Final notice.
1.13 Rulemaking proceeding.
1.14 Promulgation.
1.15 Amendment or repeal of a rule.
1.16 Petition for exemption from trade regulation rule.
1.17 [Reserved]
1.18 Rulemaking record.
1.19 Modification of a rule by the Commission at the time of judicial review.
1.20 Alternative procedures.

Subpart C—Rules Promulgated Under Authority Other Than Section 18(a)(1)(B) of the FTC Act

1.21 Scope of the rules in this subpart.
1.22 Rulemaking.
1.23 Quantity limit rules.
1.24 Rules applicable to wool, fur, and textile fiber products and rules promulgated under the Fair Packaging and Labeling Act.
1.25 Initiation of proceedings—petitions.
1.26 Procedure.

Subpart D [Reserved]

Subpart E—Export Trade Associations

1.41 Limited antitrust exemption.
1.42 Notice to Commission.
1.43 Recommendations.

Subpart F—Trademark Cancellation Procedure

1.51 Applications.

Subpart G—Injunctive and Condemnation Proceedings

1.61 Injunctions.
1.62 Ancillary court orders pending review.
1.63 Injunctions: Wool, fur, and textile cases.
1.64 Condemnation proceedings.

Subpart H—Administration of the Fair Credit Reporting Act

1.71 Administration.
1.72 Examination, counseling and staff advice.
1.73 Interpretations.

Subpart I—Procedures for Implementation of the National Environmental Policy Act of 1969

1.81 Authority and incorporation of CEQ Regulations.
1.82 Declaration of policy.
1.83 Whether to commence the process for an environmental impact statement.
1.84 Draft environmental impact statements: Availability and comment.
1.85 Final environmental impact statements.
1.86 Supplemental statements.
1.87 NEPA and agency decisionmaking.
1.88 Implementing procedures.
1.89 Effect on prior actions.

Subpart J—Economic Surveys, Investigations, and Reports

1.91 Authority and purpose.

Subpart K—Penalties for Violation of Appliance Labeling Rules

1.92 Scope.
1.93 Notice of proposed penalty.
1.94 Commission proceeding to assess civil penalty.
1.95 Procedures upon election.
1.96 Compromise of penalty.
1.97 Amount of penalty.

Subpart L—Civil Penalty Adjustments Under the Federal Civil Penalties Inflation Adjustment Act of 1990, as Amended

1.98 Adjustment of civil monetary penalty amounts.

Subpart M—Submissions Under the Small Business Regulatory Enforcement Fairness Act

1.99 Submission of rules, guides, interpretations, and policy statements to Congress and the Comptroller General.

Subpart N—Administrative Wage Garnishment

1.100 Administrative wage garnishment.

Subpart O—OMB Control Numbers for Commission Information Collection Requirements

1.101 OMB control numbers assigned pursuant to the Paperwork Reduction Act.
1.102–1.109 [Reserved]

Subpart P—Administrative Debt Collection, Including Administrative Offset

Subpart Q—Tax Refund Offset

Subpart R—Policy With Regard to Indemnification of FTC Employees

AUTHORITY: Sec. 6, 38 Stat. 721 (15 U.S.C. 46), unless otherwise noted.

SOURCE: 32 FR 8444, June 13, 1967, unless otherwise noted.

Subpart A—Industry Guidance

ADVISORY OPINIONS

§ 1.1 Policy.

(a) Any person, partnership, or corporation may request advice from the Commission with respect to a course of action which the requesting party proposes to pursue. The Commission will consider such requests for advice and inform the requesting party of the Commission's views, where practicable, under the following circumstances.

(1) The matter involves a substantial or novel question of fact or law and there is no clear Commission or court precedent; or

(2) The subject matter of the request and consequent publication of Commission advice is of significant public interest.

(b) The Commission has authorized its staff to consider all requests for advice and to render advice, where practicable, in those circumstances in which a Commission opinion would not be warranted. Hypothetical questions will not be answered, and a request for advice will ordinarily be considered inappropriate where:

(1) The same or substantially the same course of action is under investigation or is or has been the subject of a current proceeding involving the Commission or another governmental agency, or

(2) An informed opinion cannot be made or could be made only after extensive investigation, clinical study, testing, or collateral inquiry.

[44 FR 21624, Apr. 11, 1979; 44 FR 23515, Apr. 20, 1979, as amended at 54 FR 14072, Apr. 7, 1989]

§ 1.2 Procedure.

(a) Application. The request for advice or interpretation should be submitted in writing (one original and two copies) to the Secretary of the Commission and should: (1) State clearly the question(s) that the applicant wishes resolved; (2) cite the provision of law under which the question arises; and (3) state all facts which the applicant believes to be material. In addition, the identity of the companies and other persons involved should be disclosed. Letters relating to unnamed companies or persons may not be answered. Submittal of additional facts may be requested prior to the rendering of any advice.

(b) Compliance matters. If the request is for advice as to whether the proposed course of action may violate an outstanding order to cease and desist issued by the Commission, such request will be considered as provided for in § 2.41 of this chapter.

[44 FR 21624, Apr. 11, 1979, as amended at 44 FR 40638, July 12, 1979]

§ 1.3 Advice.

(a) On the basis of the materials submitted, as well as any other information available, and if practicable, the Commission or its staff will inform the requesting party of its views.

(b) Any advice given by the Commission is without prejudice to the right of the Commission to reconsider the questions involved and, where the public interest requires, to rescind or revoke the action. Notice of such rescission or revocation will be given to the requesting party so that he may discontinue the course of action taken pursuant to the Commission's advice. The Commission will not proceed against the requesting party with respect to any action taken in good faith reliance upon the Commission's advice under this section, where all the relevant facts were fully, completely, and accurately presented to the Commission and where such action was promptly discontinued upon notification of rescission or revocation of the Commission's approval.

(c) Advice rendered by the staff is without prejudice to the right of the Commission later to rescind the advice and, where appropriate, to commence an enforcement proceeding.

[44 FR 21624, Apr. 11, 1979]

§ 1.4 Public disclosure.

Written advice rendered pursuant to this section and requests therefor, including names and details, will be placed in the Commission's public record immediately after the requesting party has received the advice, subject to any limitations on public disclosure arising from statutory restrictions, the Commission's rules, and the public interest. A request for confidential treatment of information submitted in connection with the questions should be made separately.

[44 FR 21624, Apr. 11, 1979]

INDUSTRY GUIDES

§ 1.5 Purpose.

Industry guides are administrative interpretations of laws administered by the Commission for the guidance of the public in conducting its affairs in conformity with legal requirements. They provide the basis for voluntary and simultaneous abandonment of unlawful practices by members of industry. Failure to comply with the guides may result in corrective action by the Commission under applicable statutory provisions. Guides may relate to a practice common to many industries or to specific practices of a particular industry.

§ 1.6 How promulgated.

Industry guides[1] are promulgated by the Commission on its own initiative or pursuant to petition filed with the Secretary or upon informal application therefor, by any interested person or group, when it appears to the Commission that guidance as to the legal requirements applicable to particular practices would be beneficial in the public interest and would serve to bring about more widespread and equitable observance of laws administered by the Commission. In connection with the promulgation of industry guides, the Commission at any time may conduct such investigations, make such studies, and hold such conferences or hearings as it may deem appropriate. All or any part of any such investigation, study, conference, or hearing may be conducted under the provisions of subpart A of part 2 of this chapter.

Subpart B—Rules and Rulemaking Under Section 18(a)(1)(B) of the FTC Act

AUTHORITY: 15 U.S.C. 46; 15 U.S.C. 57a; 5 U.S.C. 552; sec. 212(a), Pub. L. 104–121, 110 Stat. 857 (5 U.S.C. 601 note).

§ 1.7 Scope of rules in this subpart.

The rules in this subpart apply to and govern proceedings for the promulgation of rules as provided in section 18(a)(1)(B) of the Federal Trade Commission Act. Such rules shall be known as trade regulation rules. All other rulemaking proceedings shall be governed by the rules in subpart C, except as otherwise required by law or as otherwise specified in this chapter.

[46 FR 26288, May 12, 1981, as amended at 50 FR 53303, Dec. 31, 1985]

§ 1.8 Nature, authority and use of trade regulation rules.

(a) For the purpose of carrying out the provisions of the Federal Trade Commission Act, the Commission is empowered to promulgate trade regulation rules which define with specificity acts or practices which are unfair or

[1] In the past, certain of these have been promulgated and referred to as trade practice rules.

deceptive acts or practices in or affecting commerce. Such rules may include requirements prescribed for the purpose of preventing such acts or practices. A violation of a rule shall constitute an unfair or deceptive act or practice in violation of section 5(a)(1) of that Act, unless the Commission otherwise expressly provides in its rule. However, the respondent in an adjudicative proceeding may show that his conduct does not violate the rule or assert any other defense to which he is legally entitled.

(b) The Commission at any time may conduct such investigations, make such studies and hold such conferences as it may deem necessary. All or any part of any such investigation may be conducted under the provisions of subpart A of part 2 of this chapter.

[46 FR 26288, May 12, 1981]

§ 1.9 Petitions to commence trade regulation rule proceedings.

Trade regulation rule proceedings may be commenced by the Commission upon its own initiative or pursuant to written petition filed with the Secretary by any interested person stating reasonable grounds therefor. If the Commission determines to commence a trade regulation rule proceeding pursuant to the petition, the petitioner shall be mailed a copy of the public notices issued under §§ 1.10, 1.11 and 1.12. Any person whose petition is not deemed by the Commission sufficient to warrant commencement of a rulemaking proceeding shall be notified of that determination and may be given an opportunity to submit additional data.

[46 FR 26288, May 12, 1981, as amended at 50 FR 53303, Dec. 31, 1985]

§ 1.10 Advance notice of proposed rulemaking.

(a) Prior to the commencement of any trade regulation rule proceeding, the Commission shall publish in the FEDERAL REGISTER an advance notice of such proposed proceeding.

(b) The advance notice shall:

(1) Contain a brief description of the area of inquiry under consideration, the objectives which the Commission seeks to achieve, and possible regulatory alternatives under consideration by the Commission; and

(2) Invite the response of interested persons with respect to such proposed rulemaking, including any suggestions or alternative methods for achieving such objectives.

(c) The advance notice shall be submitted to the Committee on Commerce, Science, and Transportation of the Senate and to the Committee on Interstate and Foreign Commerce of the House of Representatives.

(d) The Commission may, in addition to publication of the advance notice, use such additional mechanisms as it considers useful to obtain suggestions regarding the content of the area of inquiry before publication of an initial notice of proposed rulemaking pursuant to § 1.11.

[46 FR 26288, May 12, 1981, as amended at 50 FR 53303, Dec. 31, 1985]

§ 1.11 Commencement of a rulemaking proceeding.

(a) *Initial notice.* A trade regulation rule proceeding shall commence with an initial notice of proposed rulemaking. Such notice shall be published in the FEDERAL REGISTER not sooner than 30 days after it has been submitted to the Committee on Commerce, Science, and Transportation of the Senate and to the Committee on Interstate and Foreign Commerce of the House of Representatives. The initial notice shall include:

(1) The text of the proposed rule including any alternatives which the Commission proposes to promulgate;

(2) Reference to the legal authority under which the rule is proposed;

(3) A statement describing with particularity the reason for the proposed rule;

(4) An invitation to all interested persons to propose issues which meet the criteria of § 1.13(d)(1)(i) for consideration in accordance with § 1.13 (d)(5) and (d)(6);

(5) An invitation to all interested persons to comment on the proposed rule; and

(6) A statement of the manner in which the public may obtain copies of the preliminary regulatory analysis.

(b) *Preliminary regulatory analysis.* Except as otherwise provided by statute, the Commission shall, when commencing a rulemaking proceeding, issue a preliminary regulatory analysis which shall contain:

(1) A concise statement of the need for, and the objectives of, the proposed rule;

(2) A description of any reasonable alternatives to the proposed rule which may accomplish the stated objective of the rule in a manner consistent with applicable law;

(3) For the proposed rule, and for each of the alternatives described in the analysis, a preliminary analysis of the projected benefits and any adverse economic effects and any other effects, and of the effectiveness of the proposed rule and each alternative in meeting the stated objectives of the proposed rule; and

(4) The information required by the Regulatory Flexibility Act, 5 U.S.C. 601–612, and the Paperwork Reduction Act, 44 U.S.C. 3501–3520, if applicable.

[46 FR 26288, May 12, 1981, as amended at 50 FR 53303, Dec. 31, 1985; 63 FR 36340, July 6, 1998]

§ 1.12 Final notice.

A final notice of proposed rulemaking shall be published in the FEDERAL REGISTER and, to the extent practicable, otherwise made available to interested persons. The final notice shall include:

(a) Designated issues, unless there are none, which are to be considered in accordance with § 1.13 (d)(5) and (d)(6);

(b) The time and place of an informal hearing;

(c) Instructions to interested persons seeking to make oral presentations;

(d) A requirement that interested persons who desire to avail themselves of the procedures of § 1.13 (d)(5) and (d)(6) with respect to any issue designated in paragraph (a) of this section must identify their interests with respect to those issues in such manner as may be established by the presiding officer; and

(e) an incorporation by reference of the contents of the initial notice.

[40 FR 33966, Aug. 13, 1975, as amended at 50 FR 53303, Dec. 31, 1985]

§ 1.13 Rulemaking proceeding.

(a) *Written comments.* After commencement of a trade regulation rule proceeding, the Commission shall accept written submissions of data, views, and arguments on all issues of fact, law, and policy. The initial notice shall specify the deadline for filing written comments under this subsection.

(b) *Comments proposing issues subject to the procedures of § 1.13 (d)(5) and (d)(6).* Interested persons may propose issues for consideration in accordance with § 1.13 (d)(5) and (d)(6) until thirty (30) days after the close of the written comment period or such other period as the Commission may establish in the initial notice.

(c) *Presiding officer*—(1) *Assignment.* Upon commencement of a proposed trade regulation rule proceeding, a presiding officer shall be appointed by the Chief Presiding Officer or, when the Commission or one or more of its members serves as presiding officer, by the Commission.

(2) *Powers of the presiding officer.* The presiding officer shall be responsible for the orderly conduct of the rulemaking proceeding and the maintenance of the rulemaking and public records until the close of the postrecord comment period. He shall have all powers necessary to that end including the following:

(i) To publish a final notice in accordance with § 1.12 or issue any other public notice that may be necessary for the orderly conduct of the rulemaking proceeding;

(ii) To designate or modify, issues for consideration in accordance with § 1.13 (d)(5) and (d)(6);

(iii) To set the time and place of the informal hearing and to change any time periods prescribed in this subpart;

(iv) To prescribe rules or issue rulings to avoid unnecessary costs or delay. Such rules or rulings may include, but are not limited to, the imposition of reasonable time limits on each person's oral presentation; and requirements that any examination; including cross-examination, which a person may be entitled to conduct or have conducted be conducted by the presiding officer on behalf of that person in such a manner as the presiding officer determines to be appropriate and to be required for a full and true disclosure with respect to any issue designated for consideration in accordance with § 1.13 (d)(5) and (d)(6);

(v) To make rules and rulings limiting the representation of interested persons for the purpose of examination, including cross-examination, and governing the manner in which such examination is limited, including the selection of a representative from among a group of persons with the same or similar interests;

(vi) To require that oral presentations at the informal hearing or responses to written questions be under oath;

(vii) To require that oral presentations at the informal hearing be submitted in writing in advance of presentation;

(viii) To certify questions to the Commission for its determination; and

(ix) To rule upon all motions or petitions of interested persons, which motions or petitions must be filed with the presiding officer until the close of the postrecord comment period.

(3) *Review of rulings by the presiding officer*—(i) *Review after certification by the presiding officer.* Except as otherwise provided in paragraph (c)(3)(ii) of this section, applications for review of a ruling will not be entertained by the Commission prior to its review of the record pursuant to § 1.14, unless the presiding officer certifies in writing to the Commission that a ruling involves a controlling question of law or policy as to which there is substantial ground for difference of opinion and that an immediate review of the ruling may materially advance the ultimate termination of the proceeding or subsequent review will be an inadequate remedy. Within five (5) days after a ruling by the presiding officer, any interested person may petition the presiding officer for certification of that ruling to the Commission. Certification of a ruling shall not stay the rulemaking proceeding unless the presiding officer or the Commission shall so order. Submissions to the Commission not to exceed fifteen (15) pages may be made within ten (10) days of the presiding officer's certification. All such filings shall be a part of the rulemaking record. The Commission may thereupon, in its discretion, permit the appeal. Commission review, if permitted, will be based on the application for review and any additional submissions, without oral argument or further briefs, unless otherwise ordered by the Commission.

(ii) *Review without certification by the presiding officer.* Within ten (10) days after publication of the final notice, any interested person may petition the Commission for addition, modification or deletion of a designated issue, accompanied by a filing not to exceed fifteen (15) pages. Additional submissions on the issue by other interested persons, not to exceed fifteen (15) pages, may be made within twenty (20) days of the publication of the final notice. The Commission may thereupon, in its discretion, permit the appeal. Commission review, if permitted, will be based on the petition and any additional submissions, without oral argument or further briefs, unless otherwise ordered by the Commission. A petition hereunder shall not stay the rulemaking proceeding unless the presiding officer or the Commission shall so order. All petitions filed under this paragraph shall be a part of the rulemaking record. Notice of the filing of any such petition may be obtained from the Office of the Secretary of the Commission. In the event any designated issue is added or substantially modified by the Commission, interested persons shall be given a further opportunity to identify their interests with respect to those issues.

(4) *Substitution of presiding officer.* In the event of the substitution of a new presiding officer for the one originally appointed, any motion predicated upon such substitution shall be made within five (5) days thereafter.

(5) *Organization.* In the performance of their rulemaking functions, presiding officers shall be responsible to the chief presiding officer who shall not be responsible to any other officer or employee of the Commission.

(6) *Ex parte communications.* Except as required for the disposition of *ex parte* matters as authorized by law, no presiding officer shall consult any person or party with respect to any fact in issue unless such officer gives notice and opportunity for all parties to participate.

(d) *Informal hearings.* An informal hearing with the opportunity for oral presentations on all issues shall be conducted by the presiding officer. In addition, if an issue is designated pursuant to these rules for consideration in accordance with § 1.13(d) (5) and (6), the informal hearing on such issues shall be conducted in accordance with those paragraphs. For all other issues the presiding officer may in his discretion employ, in whole or in part, the procedures of those paragraphs.

(1) *Nature of issues for consideration in accordance with § 1.13* (d)(*5*) *and* (*d*)(*6*)—(i) *Issues that must be considered in accordance with § 1.13(d)*(*5*) *and* (*d*)(*6*). The only issues that must be designated for consideration in accordance with paragraphs (d)(5) and (d)(6) of this section are disputed issues of fact that are determined by the Commission or the presiding officer to be material and necessary to resolve.

(ii) *Issues that may be considered in accordance with § 1.13(d)*(*5*) *and* (*d*)(*6*). The Commission and the presiding officer retain the power to designate any other issues for consideration in accordance with paragraphs (d)(5) and (d)(6) of this section.

(2) *Addition or modification of issues for consideration in accordance with § 1.13(d)(5) and* (*d*)(*6*). The presiding officer may at any time on his own motion or pursuant to a written petition by interested persons, add or modify any issues designated pursuant to § 1.12(a). No such petition shall be considered unless good cause is shown why any such proposed issue was not proposed pursuant to § 1.13(b).

(3) *Identification of interests.* Not later than twenty (20) days after publication of the final notice each interested person who desires to avail himself of the procedures of paragraphs (d)(5) and (d)(6) of this section shall notify the presiding officer in writing of his particular interest with respect to each issue designated for consideration in accordance with those subsections. In the event that new issues are designated, each interested person shall promptly notify the presiding officer of his particular interest with respect to each such issue.

(4) *Examination and cross-examination by the presiding officer.* The presiding officer may conduct any examination, including cross-examination, to which a person may be entitled. For that purpose he may require submission of written requests for presentation of questions to any person making oral presentations and shall determine whether to ask such questions or any other questions. All requests for presentation of questions shall be placed in the rulemaking record.

(5) *Examination, cross-examination, and the presentation of rebuttal submissions by interested persons*—(i) *In general.* The presiding officer shall conduct or allow to be conducted examination, including cross-examination of oral presentations and the presentation of rebuttal submissions relevant to the issues designated for consideration in accordance with paragraphs (d)(5) and (d)(6) of this section. Examination, including, cross-examination, and the presentation of rebuttal submissions, shall be allowed to the extent to which it is appropriate and is required for a full and true disclosure with respect to those issues. Requests for an opportunity to examine, including cross-examine, or to present rebuttal submissions, shall be accompanied by a specific justification therefor. In determining whether or not to grant such requests, the presence of the following circumstances indicate that such requests should be granted:

(A) An issue for examination including cross-examination, or the presentation of rebuttal submissions, is an issue of specific in contrast to legislative fact.

(B) A full and true disclosure with respect to the issue can only be achieved through examination including cross-examination rather than through rebuttal submissions or the presentation of additional oral submissions.

(C) Circumstantial guarantees of the trustworthiness of a presentation do not exist.

(D) The particular presentation is required for the resolution of a designated issue.

(ii) *Selection of representatives for cross-examination.* After consideration of the information supplied in response to the final notice, the presiding officer shall identify groups of persons with the same or similar interests in the proceeding. Any such group may be required to select a single representative for the purpose of examination, including cross-examination. If a group is unable to select a representative then the presiding officer may select a representative of each such group.

(iii) *Inability to select representative for examination, including cross-examination.* No person shall be denied the opportunity to conduct or have conducted, examination, including cross-examination, under paragraph (d)(5)(i) of this section if he is a member of a group as described in paragraph (d)(5)(ii) of this section and is unable to agree upon group representation with other group members after a good faith effort to do so and seeks to present substantial and relevant issues which will not be adequately presented by the group representative. In that event he shall be allowed to conduct or have conducted any examination, including cross-examination, to which he is entitled on issues designated for consideration in accordance with paragraphs (d)(5) and (d)(6) of this section and which affect his particular interest.

(6) *Requests to compel the attendance of persons or the production of documents or to obtain responses to written questions.* During the course of the rulemaking proceeding, the presiding officer shall entertain requests from the Commission's staff or any interested person to compel the attendance of persons or the production of documents or to obtain responses to written questions. Requests to compel the attendance of persons or the production of documents or to obtain responses to written questions shall contain a statement showing the general relevancy of the material, information or presentation, and the reasonableness of the scope of the request, together with a showing that such material, information or presentation is not available by voluntary methods and cannot be obtained through examination, including cross-examination, of oral presentations or the presentation of rebuttal submissions, and is appropriate and required for a full and true disclosure with respect to the issues designated for consideration in accordance with paragraphs (d)(5) and (d)(6) of this section. If the presiding officer determines that a request should be granted, he shall transmit his determination to the Commission which shall determine whether to issue a civil investigative demand under §2.7(b). Information received in response to such a demand may be disclosed in the rulemaking proceeding subject to an *in camera* order under §1.18(b).

(e) *Written transcript.* A verbatim transcript shall be made of the informal hearing which transcript shall be placed in the rulemaking record.

(f) *Staff recommendations.* The staff shall make recommendations to the Commission in a report on the rulemaking record. Such report shall contain its analysis of the record and its recommendations as to the form of the final rule.

(g) *Recommended decision.* After publication of the staff report, the presiding officer shall make a recommended decision based upon his or her findings and conclusions as to all relevant and material evidence, and taking into account the staff report. The recommended decision shall be made by the presiding officer who presided over the rulemaking proceeding except that such recommended decision may be made by another officer if the officer who presided over the proceeding is no longer available to the Commission.

(h) *Postrecord comment.* The staff report and the presiding officer's recommended decision shall be the subject of public comment for a period to be prescribed by the presiding officer at the time the recommended decision is placed in the rulemaking record. The comment period shall be no less than sixty (60) days. The comments shall be confined to information already in the record and may include requests for review by the Commission of determinations made by the presiding officer.

(i) *Commission review of the rulemaking record.* The Commission shall review the rulemaking record to determine what form of rule, if any, it should promulgate. During this review process, the Commission may allow persons who have previously participated in the proceeding to make oral presentations to the Commission, unless it determines with respect to that proceeding that such presentations would not significantly assist it in its deliberations. Presentations shall be confined to information already in the rulemaking record. Requests to participate in an oral presentation must be received by the Commission no later than the close of the comment period under § 1.13(h). The identity of the participants and the format of such presentations will be announced in advance by the Office of Public Information in the Commisison's *Weekly Calendar and Notice of "Sunshine" Meetings* and in accordance with the applicable provisions of 5 U.S.C. 552(b) and § 4.15 of the Commission's Rules of Practice. Such presentations will be transcribed verbatim or summarized at the discretion of the Commission and a copy of the transcript or summary and copies of any written communications and summaries of any oral communications relating to such presentations shall be placed on the rulemaking record.

[40 FR 33966, Aug. 13, 1975, as amended at 43 FR 39084, Sept. 1, 1978; 45 FR 36341, May 29, 1980; 45 FR 78628, Nov. 26, 1980; 46 FR 14888, Mar. 3, 1981; 46 FR 26288, May 12, 1981; 50 FR 53303, Dec. 31, 1985; 54 FR 19886, May 9, 1989]

§ 1.14 Promulgation.

(a) The Commission, after review of the rulemaking record, may issue, modify, or decline to issue any rule. Where it believes that it should have further information or additional views of interested persons, it may withhold final action pending the receipt of such additional information or views. If it determines not to issue a rule, it may adopt and publish an explanation for not doing so.

(1) *Statement of Basis and Purpose.* If the Commission determines to promulgate a rule, it shall adopt a Statement of Basis and Purpose to accompany the rule which shall include:

(i) A statement as to the prevalence of the acts or practices treated by the rule;

(ii) A statement as to the manner and context in which such acts or practices are unfair or deceptive;

(iii) A statement as to the economic effect of the rule, taking into account the effect on small businesses and consumers;

(iv) a statement as to the effect of the rule on state and local laws; and

(v) A statement of the manner in which the public may obtain copies of the final regulatory analysis.

(2) *Final regulatory analysis.* Except as otherwise provided by statute, if the Commission determines to promulgate a final rule, it shall issue a final regulatory analysis relating to the final rule. Each final regulatory analysis shall contain:

(i) A concise statement of the need for, and the objectives of, the final rule;

(ii) A description of any alternatives to the final rule which were considered by the Commission;

(iii) An analysis of the projected benefits and any adverse economic effects and any other effects of the final rule;

(iv) An explanation of the reasons for the determination of the Commission that the final rule will attain its objectives in a manner consistent with applicable law and the reasons the particular alternative was chosen;

(v) A summary of any significant issues raised by the comments submitted during the public comment period in response to the preliminary regulatory analysis, and a summary of the assessment by the Commission of such issues; and

(vi) The information required by the Regulatory Flexibility Act, 5 U.S.C. 601–612, and the Paperwork Reduction Act, 44 U.S.C. 3501–3520, if applicable.

(3) *Small entity compliance guide.* For each rule for which the Commission must prepare a final regulatory flexibility analysis, the Commission will publish one or more guides to assist small entities in complying with the rule. Such guides will be designated as "small entity compliance guides."

(b) In the event the Commission determines, upon its review of the rulemaking record, to propose a revised rule for further proceedings in accordance with this subpart, such proceedings, including the opportunity of interested persons to avail themselves of the procedures of § 1.13 (d)(5) and (d)(6), shall be limited to those portions of the revised rule, the subjects and issues of which were not substantially the subject of comment in response to a previous notice of proposed rulemaking.

(c) The final rule and Statement of Basis and Purpose shall be published in the FEDERAL REGISTER. A rule issued under this subpart shall be deemed promulgated at 3 p.m. Eastern Standard Time on the fourth day after the date on which the final rule and Statement of Basis and Purpose are published in the FEDERAL REGISTER. In the event such day is a Saturday, Sunday or national holiday, then the rule is deemed promulgated at 3 p.m. Eastern Standard Time on the following business day.

[40 FR 33966, Aug. 13, 1975, as amended at 46 FR 26289, May 12, 1981; 50 FR 53304, Dec. 31, 1985; 63 FR 36340, July 6, 1998]

§1.15 Amendment or repeal of a rule.

(a) *Substantive amendment or repeal of a rule.* The procedures for substantive amendment to or repeal of a rule are the same as for the issuance thereof.

(b) *Nonsubstantive amendment of a rule.* The Commission may make a nonsubstantive amendment to a rule by announcing the amendment in the FEDERAL REGISTER.

[46 FR 26289, May 12, 1981]

§1.16 Petition for exemption from trade regulation rule.

Any person to whom a rule would otherwise apply may petition the Commission for an exemption from such rule. The procedures for determining such a petition shall be those of subpart C of these rules.

[40 FR 33966, Aug. 13, 1975]

§1.17 [Reserved]

§1.18 Rulemaking record.

(a) *Definition.* For purposes of these rules the term *rulemaking record* includes the rule, its Statement of Basis and Purpose, the verbatim transcripts of the informal hearing, written submissions, the recommended decision of the presiding officer, and the staff recommendations as well as any public comment thereon, verbatim transcripts or summaries of oral presentations to the Commission any communications placed on the rulemaking record pursuant to §1.18c and any other information which the Commission considers relevant to the rule.

(b) *Public availability.* The rulemaking record shall be publicly available except when the presiding officer, for good cause shown, determines that it is in the public interest to allow any submission to be received *in camera* subject to the provisions of §4.11 of this chapter.

(c) *Communications to Commissioners and Commissioners' personal staffs*—(1) *Communications by outside parties.* Except as otherwise provided in this subpart or by the Commission, after the Commission votes to issue an initial notice of proposed rulemaking, comment on the proposed rule should be directed to the presiding officer pursuant to §1.13. Communications with respect to the merits of that proceeding from any outside party to any Commissioner or Commissioner advisor shall be subject to the following treatment:

(i) *Written communications.* Written communications, including written communications from members of Congress, received within the period for acceptance of initial written comments shall be forwarded promptly to the presiding officer for placement on the rulemaking record. Written communications received after the time period for acceptance of initial written comments but prior to any other deadline for the acceptance of written submissions will be forwarded promptly to the presiding officer, who will determine whether such communications comply with the applicable requirements for written submissions at that stage of the proceeding. Communications that comply with such requirements will be promptly placed on the rulemaking record. Noncomplying communications and all communications received after the time periods for acceptance of written submissions will be placed promptly on the public record.

(ii) *Oral communications.* Oral communications are permitted only when advance notice of such oral communications is published by the Commission's Office of Public Information in its *Weekly Calendar and Notice of "Sunshine" Meetings* and when such oral communications are transcribed verbatim or summarized at the discretion of the Commissioner or Commissioner advisor to whom such oral communications are made and are promptly placed on the rulemaking record together with any written communications and summaries of any oral communications relating to such oral communications. Transcripts or summaries of oral communications which occur after the time period for acceptance of initial written comments but prior to any other deadline for the acceptance of written submissions will be forwarded promptly to the presiding officer together with any written communications and summaries of any oral communications relating to such oral communications. The presiding officer will determine whether such oral communications comply with the applicable requirements for written submissions at that stage of the proceeding. Transcripts or summaries of oral communications that comply with such requirements will be promptly placed on the rulemaking record together with any written communications and summaries of any oral communications relating to such oral communications. Transcripts or summaries of noncomplying oral communications will be promptly placed on the public record together with any written communications and summaries of any oral communications relating to such oral communications. No oral communications are permitted subsequent to the close of the postrecord comment period, except as provided in § 1.13(i). If an oral communication does otherwise occur, the Commissioner or Commissioner advisor will promptly place on the public record either a transcript of the communication or a memorandum setting forth the contents of the communication and the circumstances thereof; such transcript or memorandum will not be part of the rulemaking record.

(iii) *Congressional communications.* The provisions of paragraph (c)(1)(ii) of this section do not apply to communications from members of Congress. Memoranda prepared by the Commissioner or Commissioner advisor setting forth the contents of any oral congressional communications will be placed on the public record. If the communication occurs within the initial comment period and is transcribed verbatim or summarized, the transcript or summary will be promptly placed on the rulemaking record. A transcript or summary of any oral communication which occurs after the time period for acceptance of initial written comments but prior to any other deadline for the acceptance of written submissions will be forwarded promptly to the presiding officer, who will determine whether such oral communication complies with the applicable requirements for written submissions at that stage of the proceeding. Transcripts or summaries of oral communications that comply with such requirements will be promptly placed on the rulemaking record. Transcripts or summaries of noncomplying oral communications will be placed promptly on the public record.

(2) *Communications by certain officers, employees, and agents of the Commission.* Any officer, employee, or agent of the Commission with investigative or other responsibility relating to any rulemaking proceeding within any operating bureau of the Commission is prohibited from communicating or causing to be communicated to any Commissioner or to the personal staff of any Commissioner any fact which is relevant to the merits of such proceeding and which is not on the rulemaking record of such proceeding, unless such communication is made available to the public and is included in the rulemaking record. The provisions of this subsection shall not apply to any communication to the extent such communication is required for the disposition of *ex parte* matters as authorized by law.

(Sec. 6(g), 38 Stat. 721 (15 U.S.C. 46), 80 Stat. 383, as amended (5 U.S.C. 552))

[42 FR 43974, Sept. 1, 1977, as amended at 42 FR 60563, Nov. 28, 1977; 44 FR 16368, Mar. 19, 1979; 44 FR 21005, Apr. 9, 1979; 45 FR 78628, Nov. 26, 1980; 50 FR 53304, Dec. 31, 1985]

§ 1.19 Modification of a rule by the Commission at the time of judicial review.

In the event that a reviewing court determines under section 18(e)(2) of the Federal Trade Commission Act, to allow further submissions and presentations on the rule, the Commission may modify or set aside its rule or make a new rule by reason of the additional submissions and presentations. Such modified or new rule shall then be filed with the court together with an appropriate Statement of Basis and Purpose and the return of such submissions and presentations.

[40 FR 33966, Aug. 13, 1975, as amended at 50 FR 53304, Dec. 31, 1985]

§ 1.20 Alternative procedures.

If the Commission determines at the commencement of a rulemaking proceeding to employ procedures other than those established in the remainder of this subpart, it may do so by announcing those procedures in the FEDERAL REGISTER notice commencing the rulemaking proceeding.

[43 FR 35683, Aug. 11, 1978]

Subpart C—Rules Promulgated Under Authority Other Than Section 18(a)(1)(B) of the FTC Act

AUTHORITY: 15 U.S.C. 46; 5 U.S.C. 552; Sec. 212(a), Pub. L. 104–121, 110 Stat. 857 (5 U.S.C. 601 note).

§ 1.21 Scope of the rules in this subpart.

This subpart sets forth procedures for the promulgation of rules under authority other than section 18(a)(1)(B) of the FTC Act except as otherwise required by law or otherwise specified in the rules of this chapter. This subpart does not apply to the promulgation of industry guides, general statements of policy, rules of agency organization, procedure, or practice, or rules governed by subpart B of this part.

[50 FR 53304, Dec. 31, 1985]

§ 1.22 Rulemaking.

(a) *Nature and authority.* For the purpose of carrying out the provisions of the statutes administered by it, the Commission is empowered to promulgate rules and regulations applicable to unlawful trade practices. Such rules and regulations express the experience and judgment of the Commission, based on facts of which it has knowledge derived from studies, reports, investigations, hearings, and other proceedings, or within official notice, concerning the substantive requirements of the statutes which it administers.

(b) *Scope.* Rules may cover all applications of a particular statutory provision and may be nationwide in effect, or they may be limited to particular areas or industries or to particular product or geographic markets, as may be appropriate.

(c) *Use of rules in adjudicative proceedings.* When a rule is relevant to any issue involved in an ajudicative proceeding thereafter instituted, the Commission may rely upon the rule to resolve such issue, provided that the respondent shall have been given a fair hearing on the applicability of the rule to the particular case.

[40 FR 15232, Apr. 4, 1975]

§ 1.23 Quantity limit rules.

Quantity limit rules are authorized by section 2(a) of the Clayton Act, as amended by the Robinson-Patman Act. These rules have the force and effect of law.

[32 FR 8444, June 13, 1967. Redesignated at 40 FR 15232, Apr. 4, 1975]

§ 1.24 Rules applicable to wool, fur, and textile fiber products and rules promulgated under the Fair Packaging and Labeling Act.

Rules having the force and effect of law are authorized under section 6 of the Wool Products Labeling Act of 1939, section 8 of the Fur Products Labeling Act, section 7 of the Textile Fiber Products Identification Act, and sections 4, 5, and 6 of the Fair Packaging and Labeling Act.

[40 FR 15233, Apr. 4, 1975]

§ 1.25 Initiation of proceedings—petitions.

Proceedings for the issuance of rules or regulations, including proceedings for exemption of products or classes of products from statutory requirements, may be commenced by the Commission upon its own initiative or pursuant to petition filed with the Secretary by any interested person or group stating reasonable grounds therefor. Anyone whose petition is not deemed by the Commission sufficient to warrant the holding of a rulemaking proceeding will be promptly notified of that determination and given an opportunity to submit additional data. Procedures for the amendment or repeal of a rule or regulation are the same as for the issuance thereof.

[32 FR 8444, June 13, 1967. Redesignated at 40 FR 15232, Apr. 4, 1975]

§ 1.26 Procedure.

(a) *Investigations and conferences.* In connection with any rulemaking proceeding, the Commission at any time may conduct such investigations, make such studies, and hold such conferences as it may deem necessary. All or any part of any such investigation may be conducted under the provisions of subpart A of part 2 of this chapter.

(b) *Notice.* General notice of proposed rulemaking will be published in the FEDERAL REGISTER and, to the extent practicable, otherwise made available to interested persons except when the Commission for good cause finds that notice and public procedure relating to the rule are impractical, unnecessary or contrary to the public interest and incorporates such finding and a brief statement of the reasons therefor in the rule. If the rulemaking proceeding was instituted pursuant to petition, a copy of the notice will be served on the petitioner. Such notice will include:

(1) A statement of the time, place, and nature of the public proceedings;

(2) Reference to the authority under which the rule is proposed;

(3) Either the terms or substance of the proposed rule or description of the subjects and issues involved;

(4) An opportunity for interested persons to participate in the proceeding through the submission of written data, views, or arguments; and

(5) A statement setting forth such procedures for treatment of communications from persons not employed by the Commission to Commissioners or Commissioner Advisors with respect to the merits of the proceeding as will incorporate the requirements of § 1.18(c), including the transcription of oral communications required by § 1.18(c)(2), adapted in such form as may be appropriate to the circumstances of the particular proceeding.

(c) *Oral hearings.* Oral hearing on a proposed rule may be held within the discretion of the Commission, unless otherwise expressly required by law. Any such hearing will be conducted by the Commission, a member thereof, or a member of the Commission's staff. At the hearing interested persons may appear and express their views as to the proposed rule and may suggest such amendments, revisions, and additions thereto as they may consider desirable and appropriate. The presiding officer may impose reasonable limitations upon the length of time allotted to any person. If by reason of the limitations imposed the person cannot complete the presentation of his suggestions, he may within twenty-four (24) hours file a written statement covering those relevant matters which he did not orally present.

(d) *Promulgation of rules or orders.* The Commission, after consideration of all relevant matters of fact, law, policy, and discretion, including all relevant matters presented by interested persons in the proceeding, will adopt and publish in the FEDERAL REGISTER an appropriate rule or order, together with a concise general statement of its basis and purpose and any necessary findings, or will give other appropriate public notice of disposition of the proceeding. The FEDERAL REGISTER publication will contain the information required by the Paperwork Reduction Act, 44 U.S.C. 3501–3520, and the Regulatory Flexibility Act, 5 U.S.C. 601–612, if applicable. For each rule for which the Commission must prepare a final regulatory flexibility analysis, the Commission will publish one or more guides to assist small entities in complying with the rule. Such guides will be designated as "small entity compliance guides."

(e) *Effective date of rules.* Except as provided in paragraphs (f) and (g) of this section, the effective date of any rule, or of the amendment, suspension, or repeal of any rule will be as specified in a notice published in the FEDERAL REGISTER, which date will be not less than thirty (30) days after the date of such publication unless an earlier effective date is specified by the Commission upon good cause found and published with the rule.

(f) *Effective date of rules and orders under Fair Packaging and Labeling Act.*

The effective date of any rule or order under the Fair Packaging and Labeling Act will be as specified by order published in the FEDERAL REGISTER, but shall not be prior to the day following the last day on which objections may be filed under paragraph (g) of this section.

(g) *Objections and request for hearing under Fair Packaging and Labeling Act.* On or before the thirtieth (30th) day after the date of publication of an order in the FEDERAL REGISTER pursuant to paragraph (f) of this section, any person who will be adversely affected by the order if placed in effect may file objections thereto with the Secretary of the Commission, specifying with particularity the provisions of the order deemed objectionable, stating the grounds therefor, and requesting a public hearing upon such objections. Objections will be deemed sufficient to warrant the holding of a public hearing only:

(1) If they establish that the objector will be adversely affected by the order;

(2) If they specify with particularity the provisions of the order to which objection is taken; and

(3) If they are supported by reasonable grounds which, if valid and factually supported, may be adequate to justify the relief sought.

Anyone who files objections which are not deemed by the Commission sufficient to warrant the holding of a public hearing will be promptly notified of that determination. As soon as practicable after the time for filing objections has expired, the Commission will publish a notice in the FEDERAL REGISTER specifying those parts of the order which have been stayed by the filing of objections or, if no objections sufficient to warrant the holding of a hearing have been filed, stating that fact.

[32 FR 8444, June 13, 1967. Redesignated at 40 FR 15232, Apr. 4, 1975, as amended at 44 FR 16368, Mar. 19, 1979; 50 FR 53304, Dec. 31, 1985; 63 FR 36340, July 6, 1998]

Subpart D [Reserved]

Subpart E—Export Trade Associations

§1.41 Limited antitrust exemption.

The Export Trade Act authorizes the organization and operation of export trade associations, and extends to them certain limited exemptions from the Sherman Act and the Clayton Act. It also extends the jurisdiction of the Commission under the Federal Trade Commission Act to unfair methods of competition used in export trade against competitors engaged in export trade, even though the acts constituting such unfair methods are done without the territorial jurisdiction of the United States.

§1.42 Notice to Commission.

To obtain the exemptions afforded by the Act, an export trade association is required to file with the Commission, within thirty (30) days after its creation, a verified written statement setting forth the location of its offices and places of business, names, and addresses of its officers, stockholders, or members, and copies of its documents of incorporation or association. On the first day of January of each year thereafter, each association must file a like statement and, when required by the Commission to do so, must furnish to the Commission detailed information as to its organization, business, conduct, practices, management, and relation to other associations, corporations, partnerships, and individuals.

§1.43 Recommendations.

Whenever the Commission has reason to believe that an association has violated the prohibitions of section 2 of the Act, it may conduct an investigation. If, after investigation, it concludes that the law has been violated, it may make to such association recommendations for the readjustment of its business. If the association fails to comply with the recommendations, the Commission will refer its findings and recommendations to the Attorney General for appropriate action.

Subpart F—Trademark Cancellation Procedure

§ 1.51 Applications.

Applications for the institution of proceedings for the cancellation of registration of trade, service, or certification marks under the Trade-Mark Act of 1946 may be filed with the Secretary of the Commission. Such applications shall be in writing, signed by or in behalf of the applicant, and should identify the registration concerned and contain a short and simple statement of the facts constituting the alleged basis for cancellation, the name and address of the applicant, together with all relevant and available information. If, after consideration of the application, or upon its own initiative, the Commission concludes that cancellation of the mark may be warranted, it will institute a proceeding before the Commissioner of Patents for cancellation of the registration.

Subpart G—Injunctive and Condemnation Proceedings

§ 1.61 Injunctions.

In those cases where the Commission has reason to believe that it would be to the interest of the public, the Commission will apply to the courts for injunctive relief, pursuant to the authority granted in section 13 of the Federal Trade Commission Act.

[40 FR 15233, Apr. 4, 1975]

§ 1.62 Ancillary court orders pending review.

Where petition for review of an order to cease and desist has been filed in a U.S. court of appeals, the Commission may apply to the court for issuance of such writs as are ancillary to its jurisdiction or are necessary in its judgment to prevent injury to the public or to competitors pendente lite.

§ 1.63 Injunctions: Wool, fur, and textile cases.

In those cases arising under the Wool Products Labeling Act of 1939, Fur Products Labeling Act, and Textile Fiber Products Identification Act, where it appears to the Commission that it would be to the public interest for it to do so, the Commission will apply to the courts for injunctive relief, pursuant to the authority granted in such Acts.

[32 FR 8444, June 13, 1967, as amended at 41 FR 4814, Feb. 2, 1976]

§ 1.64 Condemnation proceedings.

In those cases arising under the Wool Products Labeling Act of 1939 and Fur Products Labeling Act, and where it appears to the Commission that the public interest requires such action, the Commission will apply to the courts for condemnation, pursuant to the authority granted in such Acts.

[32 FR 8444, June 13, 1967, as amended at 41 FR 4814, Feb. 2, 1976]

Subpart H—Administration of the Fair Credit Reporting Act

AUTHORITY: 84 Stat. 1128, 15 U.S.C. 1681 *et seq.*

§ 1.71 Administration.

The general administration of the Fair Credit Reporting Act (Title VI of the Consumer Credit Protection Act of 1968; enacted October 26, 1970; Pub. L. 91–508, 82 Stat. 146, 15 U.S.C. 1601 *et seq.*) is carried out by the Bureau of Consumer Protection, Division of Credit Practices. Any interested person may obtain copies of the Act and these procedures and rules of practice upon request to the Secretary of the Commission, Washington, DC 20580.

[36 FR 9293, May 22, 1971, as amended at 36 FR 18788, Sept. 22, 1971; 38 FR 32438, Nov. 26, 1973; 46 FR 26290, May 12, 1981]

§ 1.72 Examination, counseling and staff advice.

The Commission maintains a staff to carry out on-the-scene examination of records and procedures utilized to comply with the Fair Credit Reporting Act and to carry out industry counseling. Requests for staff interpretation of the Fair Credit Reporting Act should be directed to the Division of Credit Practices, Bureau of Consumer Protection. Such interpretations represent informal staff opinion which is advisory in nature and is not binding upon the Commission as to any action it may take in the matter. Administrative action to effect correction of minor infractions on a voluntary basis is taken in those cases where such procedure is believed adequate to effect immediate compliance and protect the public interest.

[36 FR 9293, May 22, 1971, as amended at 36 FR 18788, Sept. 22, 1971; 38 FR 32438, Nov. 26, 1973; 46 FR 26290, May 12, 1981]

§ 1.73 Interpretations.

(a) *Nature and purpose.* (1) The Commission issues and causes to be published in the FEDERAL REGISTER interpretations of the provisions of the Fair Credit Reporting Act on its own initiative or pursuant to the application of any person when it appears to the Commission that guidance as to the legal requirements of the Act would be in the public interest and would serve to bring about more widespread and equitable observance of the Act.

(2) The interpretations are not substantive rules and do not have the force or effect of statutory provisions. They are guidelines intended as clarification of the Fair Credit Reporting Act, and, like industry guides, are advisory in nature. They represent the Commission's view as to what a particular provision of the Fair Credit Reporting Act means for the guidance of the public in conducting its affairs in conformity with that Act, and they provide the basis for voluntary and simultaneous abandonment of unlawful practices by members of industry. Failure to comply with such interpretations may result in corrective action by the Commission under applicable statutory provisions.

(b) *Procedure.* (1) Requests for Commission interpretations should be submitted in writing to the Secretary of the Federal Trade Commission stating the nature of the interpretation requested and the reasons and justification therefor. If the request is granted, as soon as practicable thereafter, the Commission will publish a notice in the FEDERAL REGISTER setting forth the text of the proposed interpretation. Comments, views, or objections, together with the grounds therefor, concerning the proposed interpretation may be submitted to the Secretary of the Commission within thirty (30) days of public notice thereof. The proposed interpretation will automatically become final after the expiration of sixty (60) days from the date of public notice thereof, unless upon consideration of written comments submitted as hereinabove provided, the Commission determine to rescind, revoke, modify, or withdraw the proposed interpretation, in which event notification of such determination will be published in the FEDERAL REGISTER.

(2) The issuance of such interpretations is within the discretion of the Commission and the Commission at any time may conduct such investigations and hold such conferences or hearings as it may deem appropriate. Any interpretation issued pursuant to this chapter is without prejudice to the right of the Commission to reconsider the interpretation, and where the public interest requires, to rescind, revoke, modify, or withdraw the interpretation, in which event notification of such action will be published in the FEDERAL REGISTER.

(c) *Applicability of interpretations.* Interpretations issued pursuant to this subpart may cover all applications of a particular statutory provision, or they may be limited in application to a particular industry, as appropriate.

[36 FR 9293, May 22, 1971]

Subpart I—Procedures for Implementation of the National Environmental Policy Act of 1969

AUTHORITY: 15 U.S.C. 46(g), 42 U.S.C. 4321 *et seq.*

SOURCE: 47 FR 3096, Jan. 22, 1982, unless otherwise noted.

§ 1.81 Authority and incorporation of CEQ Regulations.

This subpart is issued pursuant to 102(2) of the National Environmental Policy Act of 1969 (NEPA), as amended (42 U.S.C. 4321 *et seq.*). Pursuant to Executive Order 11514 (March 5, 1970, as amended by Executive Order 11991, May 24, 1977) and the Environmental Quality Improvement Act of 1980, as amended (42 U.S.C. 4371 *et seq.*) the Council on Environmental Quality (CEQ) has issued comprehensive regulations for implementing the procedural provisions of NEPA (40 CFR parts 1500 through 1508) ("CEQ Regulations"). Although it is the Commission's position that these regulations are not binding on it, the Commission's policy is to comply fully with the CEQ Regulations unless it determines in a particular instance or for a category of actions that compliance would not be consistent with the requirements of law. With this caveat, the Commission incorporates into this subpart the CEQ Regulations. The following are supplementary definitions and procedures to be applied in conjunction with the CEQ Regulations.

[47 FR 3096, Jan. 22, 1982, as amended at 50 FR 53304, Dec. 31, 1985]

§ 1.82 Declaration of policy.

(a) Except for actions which are not subject to the requirements of section 102(2)(C) of NEPA, no Commission proposal for a major action significantly affecting the quality of the human environment will be instituted unless an environmental impact statement has been prepared for consideration in the decisionmaking. All relevant environmental documents, comments, and responses as provided in this subpart shall accompany such proposal through all review processes. "Major actions, significantly affecting the quality of the human environment" referred to in this subpart "do not include bringing judicial or administrative civil or criminal enforcement actions" CEQ Regulation (40 CFR 1508.18(a)). In the event that the Commission in an administrative enforcement proceeding actively contemplates the adoption of standards or a form of relief which it determines may have a significant effect on the environment, the Commission will, when consistent with the requirements of law, provide for the preparation of an environmental assessment or an environmental impact statement or such other action as will permit the Commission to assess alternatives with a view toward avoiding or minimizing any adverse effect upon the environment.

(b) No Commission proposal for legislation significantly affecting the quality of the human environment and concerning a subject matter in which the Commission has primary responsibility will be submitted to Congress without an accompanying environmental impact statement.

(c) When the Commission finds that emergency action is necessary and an environmental impact statement cannot be prepared in conformance with the CEQ Regulations, the Commission will consult with CEQ about alternative arrangements in accordance with CEQ Regulation (40 CFR 1506.11).

§ 1.83 Whether to commence the process for an environmental impact statement.

(a) The Bureau responsible for submitting a proposed rule, guide, or proposal for legislation to the Commission for agency action shall, after consultation with the Office of the General Counsel, initially determine whether or not the proposal is one which requires an environmental impact statement. Except for matters where the environmental effects, if any, would appear to be either (1) clearly significant and therefore the decision is made to prepare an environmental impact statement, or (2) so uncertain that environmental analysis would be based on speculation, the Bureau should normally prepare an "environmental assessment" CEQ Regulation (40 CFR 1508.9) for purposes of providing sufficient evidence and analysis for determining whether to prepare an environmental impact statement or a finding of no significant impact. The Bureau should involve environmental agencies to the extent practicable in preparing an assessment. An environmental assessment shall be made available to the public when the proposed action is made public along with any ensuing environmental impact statement or finding of no significant impact.

(b) If the Bureau determines that the proposal is one which requires an environmental impact statement, it shall commence the "scoping process" CEQ Regulation (40 CFR 1501.7) except that the impact statement which is part of a proposal for legislation need not go through a scoping process but shall conform to CEQ Regulation (40 CFR 1506.8). As soon as practicable after its decision to prepare an environmental impact statement and before the scoping process, the Bureau shall publish a notice of intent as provided in CEQ Regulations (40 CFR 1501.7 and 1508.22).

(c) If, on the basis of an environmental assessment, the determination is made not to prepare a statement, a finding of "no significant impact" shall be made in accordance with CEQ Regulation (40 CFR 1508.3) and shall be made available to the public as specified in CEQ Regulation (40 CFR 1506.6).

§ 1.84 Draft environmental impact statements: Availability and comment.

Except for proposals for legislation, environmental impact statements shall be prepared in two stages: Draft statement and final statement.

(a) *Proposed rules or guides.* (1) An environmental impact statement, if deemed necessary, shall be in draft form at the time a proposed rule or guide is published in the FEDERAL REGISTER and shall accompany the proposal throughout the decisionmaking process.

(2) The major decision points with respect to rules and guides are:

(i) Preliminary formulation of a staff proposal;

(ii) The time the proposal is initially published in the FEDERAL REGISTER as a Commission proposal;

(iii) Presiding officer's report (in trade regulation rule proceedings);

(iv) Submission to the Commission of the staff report or recommendation for final action on the proposed guide or rule;

(v) Final decision by the Commission. The decision on whether or not to prepare an environmental impact statement should occur at point (a)(2)(i) of this section. The publication of any draft impact statement should occur at point (a)(2)(ii) of this section. The publication of the final environmental impact statement should occur at point (a)(2)(iv) of this section.

(b) *Legislative proposals.* In legislative matters, a legislative environmental impact statement shall be prepared in accordance with CEQ Regulation (40 CFR 1506.8).

(c) In rule or guide proceedings the draft environmental impact statement shall be prepared in accordance with CEQ Regulation (40 CFR 1502.9) and shall be placed in the public record to which it pertains; in legislative matters, the legislative impact statement shall be placed in a public record to be established, containing the legislative report to which it pertains; these will be available to the public through the Office of the Secretary and will be published in full with the appropriate proposed rule, guide, or legislative report; such statements shall also be filed with the Environmental Protection Agency's (EPA) Office of Environmental Review (CEQ Regulation (40 CFR 1506.9)) for listing in the weekly FEDERAL REGISTER Notice of draft environmental impact statements, and shall be circulated, in accordance with CEQ Regulations (40 CFR 1502.19, 1506.6) to appropriate federal, state and local agencies.

(d) Forty-five (45) days will be allowed for comment on the draft environmental impact statement, calculated from the date of publication in the EPA's weekly FEDERAL REGISTER list of draft environmental impact statements. The Commission may in its discretion grant such longer period as the complexity of the issues may warrant.

§ 1.85 Final environmental impact statements.

(a) After the close of the comment period, the Bureau responsible for the matter will consider the comments received on the draft environmental impact statement and will put the draft statement into final form in accordance with the requirements of CEQ Regulation (40 CFR 1502.9(b)), attaching the comments received (or summaries if response was exceptionally voluminous).

(b) Upon Bureau approval of the final environmental impact statement the final statement will be

(1) Filed with the EPA;

(2) Forwarded to all parties which commented on the draft environmental impact statement and to other interested parties, if practicable;

(3) Placed in the public record of the proposed rule or guide proceeding or legislative matter to which it pertains;

(4) Distributed in any other way which the Bureau in consultation with CEQ deems appropriate.

(c) In rule and guide proceedings, at least thirty (30) days will be allowed for comment on the final environmental impact statement, calculated from the date of publication in the EPA's weekly FEDERAL REGISTER list of final environmental impact statements. In no event will a final rule or guide be promulgated prior to ninety (90) days after notice of the draft environmental impact statement, except where emergency action makes such time period impossible.

§ 1.86 Supplemental statements.

Except for proposals for legislation, as provided in CEQ Regulation (40 CFR 1502.9(c)), the Commission shall publish supplements to either draft or final environmental statements if:

(a) The Commission makes substantial changes in the proposed action that are relevant to environmental concerns; or

(b) There are significant new circumstances or information relevant to environmental concerns and bearing on the proposed action and its impacts. In the course of a trade regulation rule proceeding, the supplement will be placed in the rulemaking record.

§ 1.87 NEPA and agency decisionmaking.

In its final decision on the proposed action or, if appropriate, in its recommendation to Congress, the Commission shall consider all the alternatives in the environmental impact statement and other relevant environmental documents and shall prepare a concise statement which, in accordance with CEQ Regulation § 1505.2, shall:

(a) Identify all alternatives considered by the Commission in reaching its decision or recommendation, specifying the alternatives which were considered to be environmentally preferable;

(b) State whether all practicable means to avoid or minimize environmental harm from the alternative selected have been adopted, and if not, why they were not.

§ 1.88 Implementing procedures.

(a) The General Counsel is designated the official responsible for coordinating the Commission's efforts to improve environmental quality. He will provide assistance to the staff in determining when an environmental impact statement is needed and in its preparation.

(b) The Commission will determine finally whether an action complies with NEPA.

(c) The Directors of the Bureaus of Consumer Protection and Competition will supplement these procedures for their Bureaus to assure that every proposed rule and guide is reviewed to assess the need for an environmental impact statement and that, where need exists, an environmental impact statement is developed to assure timely consideration of environmental factors.

(d) The General Counsel will establish procedures to assure that every legislative proposal on a matter for which the Commission has primary responsibility is reviewed to assess the need for an environmental impact statement and that, where need exists, and environmental impact statement is developed to assure timely consideration of environmental factors.

(e) Parties seeking information or status reports on environmental impact statements and other elements of the NEPA process, should contact the Assistant General Counsel for Litigation and Environmental Policy.

§ 1.89 Effect on prior actions.

It is the policy of the Commission to apply these procedures to the fullest extent possible to proceedings which are already in progress.

Subpart J—Economic Surveys, Investigations and Reports

§ 1.91 Authority and purpose.

General and special economic surveys, investigations, and reports are made by the Bureau of Economics under the authority of the various laws which the Federal Trade Commission administers. The Commission may in any such survey or investigation invoke any or all of the compulsory processes authorized by law.

[32 FR 8444, June 13, 1967. Redesignated at 40 FR 15233, Apr. 4, 1975]

Subpart K—Penalties for Violation of Appliance Labeling Rules

SOURCE: 45 FR 67318, Oct. 10, 1980, unless otherwise noted.

§ 1.92 Scope.

The rules in this subpart apply to and govern proceedings for the assessment of civil penalties for the violation of section 332 of the Energy Policy and Conservation Act, 42 U.S.C. 6302, and the Commission's Rules on Labeling and Advertising of Consumer Appliances, 16 CFR part 305, promulgated under sections 324 and 326 of the Energy Policy and Conservation Act, 42 U.S.C. 6294 and 6296.

§ 1.93 Notice of proposed penalty.

(a) *Notice.* Before issuing an order assessing a civil penalty under this subpart against any person, the Commission shall provide to such person notice of the proposed penalty. This notice shall:

(1) Inform such person of the opportunity to elect in writing within 30 days of receipt of the notice of proposed penalty to have procedures of § 1.95 (in lieu of those of § 1.94) apply with respect to such assessment; and

(2) Include a copy of a proposed complaint conforming to the provision of § 3.11(b) (1) and (2) of the Commission's Rules of Practice, or a statement of the material facts constituting the alleged violation and the legal basis for the proposed penalty; and

(3) Include the amount of the proposed penalty; and

(4) Include a statement of the procedural rules that the Commission will follow if respondent elects to proceed under § 1.94 unless the Commission chooses to follow subparts B, C, D, E, and F of part 3 of this chapter.

(b) *Election.* Within 30 days of receipt of the notice of proposed penalty, the respondent shall, if it wishes to elect to have the procedures of § 1.95 apply, notify the Commission of the election in writing. The notification, to be filed in accordance with § 4.2 of this chapter, may include any factual or legal reasons for which the proposed assessment order should not issue, should be reduced in amount, or should otherwise be modified.

§ 1.94 Commission proceeding to assess civil penalty.

If the respondent fails to elect to have the procedures of § 1.95 apply, the Commission shall determine whether to issue a complaint and thereby commence an adjudicative proceeding in conformance with section 333(d)(2)(A) of the Energy Policy and Conservation Act, 42 U.S.C. 6303(d)(2)(A). If the Commission votes to issue a complaint, the proceeding shall be conducted in accordance with subparts B, C, D, E and F of part 3 of this chapter, unless otherwise ordered in the notice of proposed penalty. In assessing a penalty, the Commission shall take into account the factors listed in § 1.97.

§ 1.95 Procedures upon election.

(a) After receipt of the notification of election to apply the procedures of this section pursuant to § 1.93, the Commission shall promptly assess such penalty as it deems appropriate, in accordance with § 1.97.

(b) If the civil penalty has not been paid within 60 calendar days after the assessment order has been issued under paragraph (a) of this section, the General Counsel, unless otherwise directed, shall institute an action in the appropriate district court of the United States for an order enforcing the assessment of the civil penalty.

(c) Any election to have this section apply may not be revoked except with the consent of the Commission.

§ 1.96 Compromise of penalty.

The Commission may compromise any penalty or proposed penalty at any time, with leave of court when necessary, taking into account the nature and degree of violation and the impact of a penalty upon a particular respondent.

§ 1.97 Amount of penalty.

All penalties assessed under this subchapter shall be in the amount per violation as described in section 333(a) of the Energy Policy and Conservation Act, 42 U.S.C. 6303(a), adjusted for inflation pursuant to § 1.98, unless the Commission otherwise directs. In considering the amount of penalty, the Commission shall take into account:

(a) Respondent's size and ability to pay;

(b) Respondent's good faith;

(c) Any history of previous violations;

(d) The deterrent effect of the penalty action;

(e) The length of time involved before the Commission was made aware of the violation;

(f) The gravity of the violation, including the amount of harm to consumers and the public caused by the violation; and

(g) Such other matters as justice may require.

[32 FR 8444, June 13, 1967, as amended at 61 FR 54548, Oct. 21, 1996]

Subpart L—Civil Penalty Adjustments Under the Federal Civil Penalties Inflation Adjustment Act of 1990, as Amended

AUTHORITY: 28 U.S.C. 2461 note.

§ 1.98 Adjustment of civil monetary penalty amounts.

This section makes inflation adjustments in the dollar amounts of civil monetary penalties provided by law within the Commission's jurisdiction. The following maximum civil penalty amounts apply only to penalties assessed after January 22, 2018, including those penalties whose associated violation predated January 22, 2018.

(a) Section 7A(g)(1) of the Clayton Act, 15 U.S.C. 18a(g)(1)—$41,484;

(b) Section 11(*l*) of the Clayton Act, 15 U.S.C. 21(*l*)—$22,039;

(c) Section 5(*l*) of the FTC Act, 15 U.S.C. 45(*l*)—$41,484;

(d) Section 5(m)(1)(A) of the FTC Act, 15 U.S.C. 45(m)(1)(A)—$41,484;

(e) Section 5(m)(1)(B) of the FTC Act, 15 U.S.C. 45(m)(1)(B)—$41,484;

(f) Section 10 of the FTC Act, 15 U.S.C. 50—$545;

(g) Section 5 of the Webb-Pomerene (Export Trade) Act, 15 U.S.C. 65—$545;

(h) Section 6(b) of the Wool Products Labeling Act, 15 U.SC. 68d(b)—$545;

(i) Section 3(e) of the Fur Products Labeling Act, 15 U.S.C. 69a(e)—$545;

(j) Section 8(d)(2) of the Fur Products Labeling Act, 15 U.S.C. 69f(d)(2)—$545;

(k) Section 333(a) of the Energy Policy and Conservation Act, 42 U.S.C. 6303(a)—$449;

(l) Sections 525(a) and (b) of the Energy Policy and Conservation Act, 42 U.S.C. 6395(a) and (b), respectively—$22,039 and $41,484, respectively;

(m) Section 621(a)(2) of the Fair Credit Reporting Act, 15 U.S.C. 1681s(a)(2)—$3,895;

(n) Section 1115(a) of the Medicare Prescription Drug Improvement and Modernization Act of 2003, Public Law 108–173, 21 U.S.C. 355 note—$14,666;

(o) Section 814(a) of the Energy Independence and Security Act of 2007, 42 U.S.C. 17304—$1,180,566; and

(p) Civil monetary penalties authorized by reference to the Federal Trade Commission Act under any other provision of law within the jurisdiction of the Commission—refer to the amounts set forth in paragraphs (c), (d), (e) and (f) of this section, as applicable.

[83 FR 2903, Jan. 22, 2018]

Subpart M—Submissions Under the Small Business Regulatory Enforcement Fairness Act

AUTHORITY: 5 U.S.C. 801–804.

§ 1.99 Submission of rules, guides, interpretations, and policy statements to Congress and the Comptroller General.

Whenever the Commission issues or substantively amends a rule or industry guide or formally adopts an interpretation or policy statement that constitutes a "rule" within the meaning of 5 U.S.C. 804(3), a copy of the final rule, guide, interpretation or statement, together with a concise description, the proposed effective date, and a statement of whether the rule, guide, interpretation or statement is a "major rule" within the meaning of 5 U.S.C. 804(2), will be transmitted to each House of Congress and to the Comptroller General. The material transmitted to the Comptroller General will also include any additional relevant information required by 5 U.S.C. 801(a)(1)(B). This provision generally applies to rules issued or substantively amended pursuant to § 1.14(c), § 1.15(a), § 1.19, or § 1.26(d); industry guides issued pursuant to §1.6; interpretations and policy statements formally adopted by the Commission; and any rule of agency organization, practice or procedure that substantially affects the rights or obligations of non-agency parties.

[63 FR 36340, July 8, 1998]

Subpart N—Administrative Wage Garnishment

§1.100 Administrative wage garnishment.

(a) *General.* The Commission may use administrative wage garnishment for debts, including those referred to Bureau of the Fiscal Service, Department of Treasury, for cross-servicing. Regulations in 31 CFR 285.11 govern the collection of delinquent nontax debts owed to federal agencies through administrative garnishment of non-Federal wages. Whenever the Bureau of the Fiscal Service collects such a debt for the Commission using administrative wage garnishment, the statutory administrative requirements in 31 CFR 285.11 will govern.

(b) *Hearing official.* Any hearing required to establish the Commission's right to collect a debt through administrative wage garnishment shall be conducted by a qualified individual selected at the discretion of the Chairman of the Commission, as specified in 31 CFR 285.11.

[75 FR 68418, Nov. 8, 2010, as amended at 81 FR 2742, Jan. 19, 2016]

Subpart O—OMB Control Numbers for Commission Information Collection Requirements

AUTHORITY: 44 U.S.C. 3501–3521.

§1.101 OMB control numbers assigned pursuant to the Paperwork Reduction Act.

(a) *Purpose.* This part collects and displays control numbers assigned by the Office of Management and Budget (OMB) pursuant to the Paperwork Reduction Act of 1995 to information collection requirements in rules issued or enforced by the Commission. A response to an information collection is not required unless the collection of information displays a valid OMB control number. This part fulfills the mandate (44 U.S.C. 3507(a)(3), 44 U.S.C. 3512) that agencies display the current control number assigned by the OMB Director to agency information collection requirements and inform affected persons that they need not respond to a collection of information unless it displays a valid control number.

(b) *Display.*

Current OMB control number (all numbers begin with 3084–)	16 CFR part where the information collection requirement is located (or alternate part(s) if issued by another agency, co-enforced by the Federal Trade Commission)
0005	801–803.
0025	453.
0068	306.
0069	305.
0085	12 CFR part 205; 12 CFR part 1005.
0086	12 CFR part 213; 12 CFR part 1013.
0087	12 CFR part 202; 12 CFR part 1002.
0088	12 CFR part 226; 12 CFR part 1026.
0094	309.
0097	310.
0099	301.
0100	300.
0101	303.
0102	308.
0103	423.
0104	425.
0105	432.
0106	435.
0107	436.
0108	455.
0109	460.
0110	500–503.
0111	701.
0112	702.
0113	703.
0117	312.
0121	313.

Current OMB control number (all numbers begin with 3084–)	16 CFR part where the information collection requirement is located (or alternate part(s) if issued by another agency, co-enforced by the Federal Trade Commission)
0127	315.
0128	12 CFR 1022.136; 12 CFR 1022.137.
0131	680; 12 CFR 1022.20.
0132	642; 12 CFR 1022.54.
0137	641; 681.
0142	437.
0144	660; 12 CFR 1022.42; 12 CFR 1022.43.
0145	640; 12 CFR 1022.70.
0150	318.
0156	12 CFR part 1014.
0157	12 CFR part 1015.

[78 FR 65558, Nov. 1, 2013]

§§ 1.102–1.109 [Reserved]

Subpart P—Administrative Debt Collection, Including Administrative Offset

AUTHORITY: 31 U.S.C. 3701 *et seq.*

SOURCE: 81 FR 2742, Jan. 19, 2016, unless otherwise noted.

§ 1.110 Application of Government-wide administrative claims collections standards and adoption of administrative offset regulations.

(a) The Commission shall apply the Federal Claims Collection Standards (FCCS), 31 CFR parts 900–904, in the administrative collection, offset, compromise, suspension, termination, and referral of collection activity for civil claims for money, funds, or property, as defined by 31 U.S.C. 3701(b), unless specific Federal agency statutes or regulations apply to such activities or, as provided for by Title 11 of the United States Code, when the claims involve bankruptcy. The Commission shall also follow Department of Treasury regulations set forth at 31 CFR part 285, as applicable, for administrative debt collection, including centralized offset of federal payments to collect non-tax debts that may be owed to the Commission, 31 CFR 285.5. Nothing in this subpart shall be construed to supersede or require the Commission to provide additional notice or other procedures that may have already been provided or afforded to a debtor in the course of administrative or judicial litigation or otherwise.

(b) For purposes of 31 U.S.C. 3716(b)(1), the Commission adopts without change the regulations on collection by administrative offset set forth at 31 CFR 901.3 and other relevant sections of the FCCS applicable to such offset.

§§ 1.111–1.119 [Reserved]

Subpart Q—Tax Refund Offset

AUTHORITY: 31 U.S.C. 3716 and 3720A, 31 CFR 285.2(c).

SOURCE: 81 FR 2742, Jan. 19, 2016, unless otherwise noted.

§ 1.120 Purpose.

This subpart establishes procedures for the Commission's referral of past-due legally enforceable debts to the Department of the Treasury's Bureau of the Fiscal Service (Fiscal Service) for offset against the tax refund payments of the debtor, consistent with applicable Fiscal Service regulations and definitions set forth in 31 CFR 285.2 and 285.5.

§ 1.121 Notification of intent to collect.

(a) *Notification before tax refund offset.* Reduction of a tax refund payment will be made only after the Commission makes a determination that an amount is owed and past-due and gives or makes a reasonable attempt to give the debtor 60 days written notice of the intent to collect by tax refund offset.

(b) *Contents of notice.* The Commission's notice of intent to collect by tax refund offset will state:

(1) The amount of the debt;

(2) That unless the debt is repaid within 60 days from the date of the notice, the Commission intends to collect the debt by requesting a reduction of any amounts payable to the debtor as a

Federal tax refund payment by an amount equal to the amount of the debt and all accumulated interest and other charges;

(3) That the debtor, within 60 days from the date of the notice, has an opportunity to make a written agreement to repay the amount of the debt, unless such opportunity has previously been provided;

(4) A mailing address for forwarding any written correspondence and a contact name and a telephone number for any questions; and

(5) That the debtor may present evidence to the Commission that all or part of the debt is not past due or legally enforceable by:

(i) Sending a written request for a review of the evidence to the address provided in the notice;

(ii) Stating in the request the amount disputed and the reasons why the debtor believes that the debt is not past due or is not legally enforceable; and

(iii) Including in the request any documents that the debtor wishes to be considered or stating that the additional information will be submitted within the remainder of the 60-day period.

(c) A debtor may dispute the existence or amount of the debt or the terms of repayment, except with respect to debts established by a judicial or administrative order. In those cases, the debtor may not dispute matters or issues already settled, litigated, or otherwise established by such order, including the amount of the debt or the debtor's liability for that debt, except to the extent that the debtor alleges that the amount of the debt does not reflect payments already made to repay the debt in whole or part.

§ 1.122 Commission action as a result of consideration of evidence submitted in response to the notice of intent.

(a) *Consideration of evidence.* If, in response to the notice provided to the debtor under § 1.121, the Commission is notified that the debtor will submit additional evidence, or the Commission receives additional evidence from the debtor within the prescribed time, tax refund offset will be stayed until the Commission can:

(1) Consider the evidence presented by the debtor;

(2) Determine whether all or a portion of the debt is still past due and legally enforceable; and

(3) Notify the debtor of its determination, as set forth in paragraph (b) of this section.

(b) *Commission action on the debt.* (1) If, after considering any additional evidence from the debtor, the Commission determines that the debt remains past-due and legally enforceable, the Commission will notify the debtor of its intent to refer the debt to the Fiscal Service for offset against the debtor's Federal tax refund payment, including whether the amount of the debt remains the same or is modified; or

(2) If, after considering any additional evidence from the debtor, the Commission determines that no part of the debt remains past-due and legally enforceable, the Commission will so notify the debtor and will not refer the debt to the Fiscal Service for offset against the debtor's Federal tax refund payment.

§ 1.123 Change in notification to Bureau of the Fiscal Service.

After the Commission sends the Fiscal Service notification of a debtor's liability for a debt, the Commission will promptly notify the Fiscal Service if the Commission:

(a) Determines that there is a material error or other material change in the information contained in the notification, including in the amount of the debt, subject to any additional due process requirements, where applicable, under this subpart or the Federal Claims Collection Standards, if the amount of debt has increased;

(b) Receives a payment or credits a payment to the account of the debtor named in the notification that reduces the amount of the debt referred to Fiscal Service for offset; or

(c) Otherwise concludes that such notification is appropriate or necessary.

§ 1.124 Interest, penalties, and costs.

To the extent permitted or required by 31 U.S.C. 3717 or other law, regulation, or order, all interest, penalties, and costs applicable to the debt or incurred in connection with its referral for collection by tax refund offset will be assessed on the debt and thus increase the amount of the offset.

§§ 1.125—1.129 [Reserved]

Subpart R—Policy With Regard to Indemnification of FTC Employees

AUTHORITY: 15 U.S.C. 46.

SOURCE: 82 FR 30966, July 5, 2017, unless otherwise noted.

§ 1.130 Policy on employee indemnification.

(a) The Commission may indemnify, in whole or in part, its employees (which for the purpose of this regulation includes former employees) for any verdict, judgment, or other monetary award which is rendered against any such employee, provided that the conduct giving rise to the verdict, judgment, or award was taken within the scope of his or her employment with the Federal Trade Commission and that such indemnification is in the interest of the Federal Trade Commission, as determined as a matter of discretion by the Commission, or its designee.

(b) The Commission may settle or compromise a personal damage claim against its employee by the payment of available funds, at any time, provided the alleged conduct giving rise to the personal damage claim was taken within the scope of employment and that such settlement or compromise is in the interest of the Federal Trade Commission, as determined as a matter of discretion by the Commission, or its designee.

(c) Absent exceptional circumstances, as determined by the Commission or its designee, the Commission will not entertain a request either to agree to indemnify or to settle a personal damage claim before entry of an adverse verdict, judgment, or monetary award.

(d) When an employee of the Federal Trade Commission becomes aware that an action may be or has been filed against the employee in his or her individual capacity as a result of conduct taken within the scope of his or her employment, the employee shall immediately notify his or her supervisor that such an action is pending or threatened. The supervisor shall promptly thereafter notify the Office of the General Counsel. Employees may be authorized to receive legal representation by the Department of Justice in accordance with 28 CFR 50.15.

(e)(1) The employee may, thereafter, request either:

(i) Indemnification to satisfy a verdict, judgment or award entered against the employee; or

(ii) Payment to satisfy the requirements of a settlement proposal.

(2) The employee shall submit a written request, with documentation including copies of the verdict, judgment, award, or settlement proposal, as appropriate, to the head of his or her division or office, who thereupon shall submit to the General Counsel, in a timely manner, a recommended disposition of the request. The General Counsel may also seek the views of the Department of Justice. The failure of an employee to provide notification under paragraph (d) of this section or make a request under this paragraph (e) shall not impair the agency's ability to provide indemnification or payment under this section if it determines it is appropriate to do so.

(f) Any amount paid under this section either to indemnify a Federal Trade Commission employee or to settle a personal damage claim shall be contingent upon the availability of appropriated funds of the Federal Trade Commission.

PART 2—NONADJUDICATIVE PROCEDURES

Subpart A—Inquiries; Investigations; Compulsory Processes

Sec.

Subpart B—Petitions Filed Under Section 7A of the Clayton Act, as Amended, for Review of Requests for Additional Information or Documentary Material

Subpart C—Consent Order Procedure

Subpart D—Reports of Compliance

Subpart E—Requests To Reopen

AUTHORITY: 15 U.S.C. 46.

Subpart A—Inquiries; Investigations; Compulsory Processes

§2.1 How initiated.

Commission investigations and inquiries may be originated upon the request of the President, Congress, governmental agencies, or the Attorney General; upon referrals by the courts; upon complaint by members of the public; or by the Commission upon its own initiative. The Commission has delegated to the Director, Deputy Directors, and Assistant Directors of the Bureau of Competition, the Director, Deputy Directors, and Associate Directors of the Bureau of Consumer Protection and, the Regional Directors and Assistant Regional Directors of the Commission's regional offices, without power of redelegation, limited authority to initiate investigations. The Director of the Bureau of Competition has also been delegated, without power of redelegation, authority to open investigations in response to requests pursuant to an agreement under the International Antitrust Enforcement Assistance Act, 15 U.S.C. 6201 *et seq.*, if the requests do not ask the Commission to use process. Before responding to such a request, the Bureau Director shall transmit the proposed response to the Secretary and the Secretary shall notify the Commission of the proposed response. If no Commissioner objects within three days following the Commission's receipt of such notification, the Secretary shall inform the Bureau Director that he or she may proceed.

[48 FR 41374, Sept. 15, 1983, as amended at 50 FR 53304, Dec. 31, 1985; 65 FR 67259, Nov. 9, 2000]

§2.2 Complaint or request for Commission action.

(a) A complaint or request for Commission action may be submitted via the Commission's web-based complaint site (*https://www.ftccomplaintassistant.gov/*); by a telephone call to 1–877–FTC–HELP (1–877–382–4357); or by a signed statement setting forth the alleged violation of law with such supporting information as is available, and the name and address of the person or persons complained of, filed with the Office of the Secretary in conformity with §4.2(d) of this chapter. No forms or formal procedures are required.

(b) The person making the complaint or request is not regarded as a party to any proceeding that might result from the investigation.

(c) Where the complainant's identity is not otherwise made public, the Commission's policy is not to publish or divulge the name of a complainant except as authorized by law or by the Commission's rules. Complaints or requests submitted to the Commission may, however, be lodged in a database and made available to federal, state, local, and foreign law enforcement agencies that commit to maintain the privacy and security of the information provided. Further, where a complaint is by a consumer or consumer representative concerning a specific consumer product or service, the Commission in the course of a referral of the complaint or request, or in furtherance of an investigation, may disclose the identity of the complainant. In referring any such consumer complaint, the Commission specifically retains its right to take such action as it deems appropriate in the public interest and under any of the statutes it administers.

[77 FR 59305, Sept. 27, 2012]

§ 2.3 Policy as to private controversies.

The Commission acts only in the public interest and does not initiate an investigation or take other action when the alleged violation of law is merely a matter of private controversy and does not tend adversely to affect the public.

[32 FR 8446, June 13, 1967]

§ 2.4 Investigational policy.

Consistent with obtaining the information it needs for investigations, including documentary material, the Commission encourages the just and speedy resolution of investigations. The Commission will therefore employ compulsory process when in the public interest. The Commission encourages cooperation in its investigations. In all matters, whether involving compulsory process or voluntary requests for documents and information, the Commission expects all parties to engage in meaningful discussions with staff to prevent confusion or misunderstandings regarding the nature and scope of the information and material being sought, in light of the inherent value of genuinely cooperative discovery.

[77 FR 59305, Sept. 27, 2012]

§ 2.5 By whom conducted.

Inquiries and investigations are conducted under the various statutes administered by the Commission by Commission representatives designated and duly authorized for the purpose. Such representatives are "examiners" or "Commission investigators" within the meaning of the Federal Trade Commission Act and are authorized to exercise and perform the duties of their office in accordance with the laws of the United States and the regulations of the Commission. Included among such duties is the administration of oaths and affirmations in any matter under investigation by the Commission.

[45 FR 36341, May 29, 1980]

§ 2.6 Notification of purpose.

Any person, partnership, or corporation under investigation compelled or requested to furnish information or documentary material shall be advised of the purpose and scope of the investigation, the nature of the acts or practices under investigation, and the applicable provisions of law. A copy of a Commission resolution, as prescribed under § 2.7(a), shall be sufficient to give persons, partnerships, or corporations notice of the purpose of the investigation. While investigations are generally nonpublic, Commission staff may disclose the existence of an investigation to potential witnesses or other third parties to the extent necessary to advance the investigation.

[77 FR 59305, Sept. 27, 2012]

§ 2.7 Compulsory process in investigations.

(a) *In general.* When the public interest warrants, the Commission may issue a resolution authorizing the use of compulsory process. The Commission or any Commissioner may, pursuant to a Commission resolution, issue a subpoena, or a civil investigative demand, directing the recipient named therein to appear before a designated representative at a specified time and place to testify or to produce documentary material, or both, and in the case of a civil investigative demand, to provide a written report or answers to questions, relating to any matter under investigation by the Commission. For the purposes of this subpart, the term:

(1) Electronically stored information ("ESI") means any writings, drawings, graphs, charts, photographs, sound recordings, images and other data or data compilations stored in any electronic medium from which information can be obtained either directly or, if necessary, after translation by the responding party into a reasonably usable form.

(2) "Documentary material" includes all documents, materials, and information, including ESI, within the meaning of the Federal Rules of Civil Procedure.

(3) "Compulsory process" means any subpoena, CID, access order, or order for a report issued by the Commission.

(4) "Protected status" refers to information or material that may be withheld from production or disclosure on the grounds of any privilege, work product protection, or statutory exemption.

(b) *Civil Investigative Demands.* Civil Investigative Demands ("CIDs") shall be the only form of compulsory process issued in investigations with respect to unfair or deceptive acts or practices under section 5(a)(1) of the Federal Trade Commission Act (hereinafter referred to as "unfair or deceptive acts or practices").

(1) CIDs for the production of documentary material, including ESI, shall describe each class of material to be produced with sufficient definiteness and certainty as to permit such material to be fairly identified, prescribe a return date providing a reasonable period of time within which the material so demanded may be assembled and made available for inspection and copying or reproduction, and identify the Commission's custodian to whom such material shall be made available. Documentary material, including ESI, for which a CID has been issued shall be made available as prescribed in the CID. Such productions shall be made in accordance with the procedures prescribed by section 20(c)(11) of the Federal Trade Commission Act.

(2) CIDs for tangible things, including electronic media, shall describe each class of tangible thing to be produced with sufficient definiteness and certainty as to permit each such thing to be fairly identified, prescribe a return date providing a reasonable period of time within which the things so demanded may be assembled and submitted, and identify the Commission's custodian to whom such things shall be submitted. Submission of tangible things in response to a CID shall be made in accordance with the procedures prescribed by section 20(c)(12) of the Federal Trade Commission Act.

(3) CIDs for written reports or answers to questions shall propound with sufficient definiteness and certainty the reports to be produced or the questions to be answered, prescribe a return date, and identify the Commission's custodian to whom such reports or answers to questions shall be submitted. The submission of written reports or answers to questions in response to a CID shall be made in accordance with the procedures prescribed by section 20(c)(13) of the Federal Trade Commission Act.

(4) CIDs for the giving of oral testimony shall prescribe a date, time, and place at which oral testimony shall commence, and identify the hearing official and the Commission custodian. Oral testimony in response to a CID shall be taken in accordance with the procedures set forth in section 20(c)(14) of the Federal Trade Commission Act.

(c) *Subpoenas.* Except in investigations with respect to unfair or deceptive acts or practices, the Commission may require by subpoena the attendance and testimony of witnesses and the production of documentary material relating to any matter under investigation. Subpoenas for the production of documentary material, including ESI, shall describe each class of material to be produced with sufficient definiteness and certainty as to permit such material to be fairly identified, prescribe a return date providing a reasonable period of time for production, and identify the Commission's custodian to whom such material shall be made available. A subpoena may require the attendance of the witness or the production of documentary material at any place in the United States.

(d) *Special reports.* Except in investigations regarding unfair or deceptive acts or practices, the Commission may issue an order requiring a person, partnership, or corporation to file a written report or answers to specific questions relating to any matter under investigation, study or survey, or under any of the Commission's reporting programs.

(e) *Commission orders requiring access.* Except in investigations regarding unfair or deceptive acts or practices, the Commission may issue an order requiring any person, partnership, or corporation under investigation to grant access to their files, including electronic media, for the purpose of examination and to make copies.

(f) *Investigational hearings.* (1) Investigational hearings may be conducted in the course of any investigation undertaken by the Commission, including rulemaking proceedings under subpart B of part 1 of this chapter, inquiries initiated for the purpose of determining whether a respondent is complying with an order of the Commission or to monitor performance under, and compliance with, a decree entered in suits brought by the United States under the antitrust laws, the development of facts in cases referred by the courts to the Commission as a master in chancery, and investigations made under section 5 of the Webb-Pomerene (Export Trade) Act.

(2) Investigational hearings shall be conducted by one or more Commission employees designated for the purpose of hearing the testimony of witnesses (the "hearing official") and receiving documents and information relating to any subject under investigation. Such hearings shall be under oath or affirmation, stenographically recorded, and the transcript made a part of the record of the investigation. The Commission may, in addition, employ other means to record the hearing.

(3) Unless otherwise ordered by the Commission, investigational hearings shall not be public. For investigational hearings conducted pursuant to a CID for the giving of oral testimony, the hearing official shall exclude from the hearing room all persons other than the person being examined, counsel for the person being examined, Commission staff, and any stenographer or other person recording such testimony. A copy of the transcript shall promptly be forwarded by the hearing official to the Commission custodian designated under § 2.16 of this part. At the discretion of the hearing official, and with the consent of the person being examined (or, in the case of an entity, its counsel), persons other than Commission staff, court reporters, and the hearing official may be present in the hearing room.

(g) *Depositions.* Except in investigations with respect to unfair or deceptive acts or practices, the Commission may order by subpoena a deposition pursuant to section 9 of the Federal Trade Commission Act, of any person, partnership, or corporation, at any stage of an investigation. The deposition shall take place upon notice to the subjects of the investigation, and the examination and cross-examination may proceed as they would at trial. Depositions shall be conducted by a hearing official, for the purpose of hearing the testimony of witnesses and receiving documents and information relating to any subject under investigation. Depositions shall be under oath or affirmation, stenographically recorded, and the transcript made a part of the record of the investigation. The Commission may, in addition, employ other means to record the deposition.

(h) *Testimony from an entity.* Where Commission compulsory process requires oral testimony from an entity, the compulsory process shall describe with reasonable particularity the matters for examination and the entity must designate one or more officers, directors, or managing agents, or designate other persons who consent, to testify on its behalf. Unless a single individual is designated by the entity, the entity must designate in advance and in writing the matters on which each designee will testify. The persons designated must testify about information known or reasonably available to the entity and their testimony shall be binding upon the entity.

(i) *Inspection, copying, testing, and sampling of documentary material, including electronic media.* The Commission, through compulsory process, may require the production of documentary material, or electronic media or other tangible things, for inspection, copying, testing, or sampling.

(j) *Manner and form of production of ESI.* When Commission compulsory process requires the production of ESI, it shall be produced in accordance with the instructions provided by Commission staff regarding the manner and form of production. All instructions shall be followed by the recipient of the process absent written permission to the contrary from a Commission official identified in paragraph (l) of this section. Absent any instructions as to the form for producing ESI, ESI must be produced in the form or forms in which it is ordinarily maintained or in a reasonably usable form.

(k) *Mandatory pre-petition meet and confer process.* Unless excused in writing or granted an extension of no more than 30 days by a Commission official identified in paragraph (l) of this section, a recipient of Commission compulsory process shall meet and confer with Commission staff within 14 days after receipt of process or before the deadline for filing a petition to quash, whichever is first, to discuss compliance and to address and attempt to resolve all issues, including issues relating to protected status and the form and manner in which claims of protected status will be asserted. The initial meet and confer session and all subsequent meet and confer sessions may be in person or by telephone. The recipient must make available personnel with the knowledge necessary for resolution of the issues relevant to compliance with compulsory process. Such personnel could include individuals knowledgeable about the recipient's information or records management systems, individuals knowledgeable about other relevant materials such as organizational charts, and persons knowledgeable about samples of material required to be produced. If any issues relate to ESI, the recipient shall have a person familiar with its ESI systems and methods of retrieval participate in the meeting. The Commission will not consider petitions to quash or limit absent a pre-filing meet and confer session with Commission staff and, absent extraordinary circumstances, will consider only issues raised during the meet and confer process.

(l) *Delegations.* The Directors of the Bureaus of Competition, Consumer Protection, and Economics and the Office of Policy Planning, their Deputy Directors, the Assistant Directors of the Bureaus of Competition and Economics, the Associate Directors of the Bureau of Consumer Protection, the Regional Directors, and the Assistant Regional Directors are all authorized to modify and, in writing, approve the terms of compliance with all compulsory process, including subpoenas, CIDs, reporting programs, orders requiring reports, answers to questions, and orders requiring access. If a recipient of compulsory process has demonstrated satisfactory progress toward compliance, a Commission official identified in this paragraph may, at his or her discretion, extend the time for compliance with Commission compulsory process. The subpoena power conferred by section 329 of the Energy Policy and Conservation Act (42 U.S.C. 6299) and section 5 of the Webb-Pomerene (Export Trade) Act (15 U.S.C. 65) are specifically included within this delegation of authority.

[77 FR 59305, Sept. 27, 2012, as amended at 80 FR 15160, Mar. 23, 2015]

§2.8 [Reserved]

§2.9 Rights of witnesses in investigations.

(a) Any person compelled to submit data to the Commission or to testify in a deposition or investigational hearing shall be entitled to retain a copy or, on payment of lawfully prescribed costs, procure a copy of any document submitted, and of any testimony as stenographically recorded, except that in a nonpublic hearing the witness may for good cause be limited to inspection of the official transcript of the testimony. Upon completion of transcription of the testimony, the witness shall be offered an opportunity to read the transcript. Any changes by the witness shall be entered and identified upon the transcript by the hearing official, together with a statement of the reasons given by the witness for requesting such changes. After the changes are entered, the transcript shall be signed by the witness unless the witness cannot be found, is ill and unavailable, waives in writing his or her right to sign, or refuses to sign. If the transcript is not signed by the witness within 30 days of having been afforded a reasonable opportunity to review it, the hearing official shall sign the transcript and state on the hearing record the fact of the waiver, illness, absence of the witness, or the refusal to sign, together with any reasons given for the failure to sign, as prescribed by section 20(c)(14)(E)(ii) of the Federal Trade Commission Act.

(b) Any witness compelled to appear in person in a deposition or investigational hearing may be accompanied, represented, and advised by counsel, as follows:

(1) In depositions or investigational hearings conducted pursuant to section 9 of the Federal Trade Commission Act, counsel may not consult with the witness while a question directed to a witness is pending, except with respect to issues involving protected status.

(2) Any objection during a deposition or investigational hearing shall be stated concisely on the hearing record in a nonargumentative and nonsuggestive manner. Neither the witness nor counsel shall otherwise object or refuse to answer any question. Following an objection, the examination shall proceed and the testimony shall be taken, except for testimony requiring the witness to divulge information protected by the claim of protected status. Counsel may instruct a witness not to answer only when necessary to preserve a claim of protected status.

(3) The hearing official may elect to recess the deposition or investigational hearing and reconvene the deposition or hearing at a later date to continue a course of inquiry interrupted by any objection made under paragraph (b)(1) or (2) of this section. The hearing official shall provide written notice of the date of the reconvened deposition or hearing to the witness, which may be in the form of an email or facsimile. Failure to reappear or to file a petition to limit or quash in accordance with § 2.10 of this part shall constitute noncompliance with Commission compulsory process for the purposes of a Commission enforcement action under § 2.13 of this part.

(4) In depositions or investigational hearings, immediately following the examination of a witness by the hearing official, the witness or his or her counsel may on the hearing record request that the hearing official permit the witness to clarify any answers. The grant or denial of such request shall be within the discretion of the hearing official and would ordinarily be granted except for good cause stated and explained on the hearing record, and with an opportunity for counsel to undertake to correct the expressed concerns of the hearing official or otherwise to reply.

(5) The hearing official shall conduct the deposition or investigational hearing in a manner that avoids unnecessary delay, and prevents and restrains disorderly or obstructionist conduct. The hearing official shall, where appropriate, report pursuant to § 4.1(e) of this chapter any instance where an attorney, in the course of the deposition or hearing, has allegedly refused to comply with his or her directions, or has allegedly engaged in conduct addressed in § 4.1(e). The Commission may take any action as circumstances may warrant under § 4.1(e) of this chapter.

[77 FR 59307, Sept. 27, 2012]

§ 2.10 Petitions to limit or quash Commission compulsory process.

(a) *In general.* (1) *Petitions.* Any petition to limit or quash any compulsory process shall be filed with the Secretary within 20 days after service of the Commission compulsory process or, if the return date is less than 20 days after service, prior to the return date. Such petition shall set forth all assertions of protected status or other factual and legal objections to the Commission compulsory process, including all appropriate arguments, affidavits, and other supporting documentation. Such petition shall not exceed 5,000 words, including all headings, footnotes, and quotations, but excluding the cover, table of contents, table of authorities, glossaries, copies of the compulsory process order or excerpts thereof, appendices containing only sections of statutes or regulations, the statement required by paragraph (a)(2) of this section, and affidavits and other supporting documentation. Petitions to limit or quash that fail to comply with these provisions shall be rejected by the Secretary pursuant to § 4.2(g) of this chapter.

(2) *Statement.* Each petition filed pursuant to paragraph (a)(1) of this section shall be accompanied by a signed separate statement representing that counsel for the petitioner has conferred with Commission staff pursuant to § 2.7(k) of this part in an effort in good faith to resolve by agreement the issues raised by the petition and has

been unable to reach such an agreement. If some of the issues in controversy have been resolved by agreement, the statement shall, in a non-argumentative manner, specify the issues so resolved and the issues remaining unresolved. The statement shall recite the date, time, and place of each conference between counsel, and the names of all parties participating in each such conference. Failure to include the required statement may result in a denial of the petition.

(3) *Reconvened investigational hearings or depositions.* If the hearing official elects pursuant to §2.9(b)(3) of this part to recess the investigational hearing or deposition and reconvene it at a later date, the witness compelled to reappear may challenge the reconvening by filing with the Secretary a petition to limit or quash the reconvening of the hearing or deposition. Such petition shall be filed within 5 days after receiving written notice of the reconvened hearing; shall set forth all assertions of protected status or other factual and legal objections to the reconvening of the hearing or deposition, including all appropriate arguments, affidavits, and other supporting documentation; and shall be subject to the word count limit in paragraph (a)(1) of this section. Except for good cause shown, the Commission will not consider issues presented and ruled upon in any earlier petition filed by or on behalf of the witness.

(4) *Staff reply.* Commission staff may, without serving the petitioner, provide the Commission a statement that shall set forth any factual and legal response to the petition to limit or quash.

(5) *Extensions of time.* The Directors of the Bureaus of Competition, Consumer Protection, and Economics and the Office of Policy Planning, their Deputy Directors, the Assistant Directors of the Bureaus of Competition and Economics, the Associate Directors of the Bureau of Consumer Protection, the Regional Directors, and the Assistant Regional Directors are delegated, without power of redelegation, the authority to rule upon requests for extensions of time within which to file petitions to limit or quash Commission compulsory process.

(b) *Stay of compliance period.* The timely filing of a petition to limit or quash any Commission compulsory process shall stay the remaining amount of time permitted for compliance as to the portion or portions of the challenged specifications or provisions. If the petition is denied in whole or in part, the ruling by the Commission shall specify new terms for compliance, including a new return date, for the Commission's compulsory process.

(c) *Disposition and review.* The Commission will issue an order ruling on a petition to limit or quash within 40 days after the petition is filed with the Secretary. The order may be served on the petitioner via email, facsimile, or any other method reasonably calculated to provide notice to the petitioner of the order.

(d) *Public disclosure.* All petitions to limit or quash Commission compulsory process and all Commission orders in response to those petitions shall become part of the public records of the Commission, except for information granted confidential treatment under §4.9(c) of this chapter.

[77 FR 59308, Sept. 27, 2012, as amended at 80 FR 15160, Mar. 23, 2015]

§2.11 Withholding requested material.

(a)(1) Any person withholding information or material responsive to an investigational subpoena, CID, access order, or order to file a report issued pursuant to §2.7 of this part, or any other request for production of material issued under this part, shall assert a claim of protected status, as that term is defined in §2.7(a)(4), not later than the date set for the production of the material. The claim of protected status shall include a detailed log of the items withheld, which shall be attested by the lead attorney or attorney responsible for supervising the review of the material and who made the determination to assert the claim. A document, including all attachments, may be withheld or redacted only to the extent necessary to preserve any claim of protected status. The information provided in the log shall be of sufficient detail to enable the Commission staff to assess the validity of the claim for each document, including attachments, without disclosing the protected information. The failure to provide information sufficient to support a claim of protected status may result in a denial of the claim. Absent an instruction as to the form and content of the log, the log shall be submitted in a searchable electronic format, and shall, for each document, including attachments, provide:

(i) Document control number(s);

(ii) The full title (if the withheld material is a document) and the full file name (if the withheld material is in electronic form);

(iii) A description of the material withheld (for example, a letter, memorandum, or email), including any attachments;

(iv) The date the material was created;

(v) The date the material was sent to each recipient (if different from the date the material was created);

(vi) The email addresses, if any, or other electronic contact information to the extent used in the document, from which and to which each document was sent;

(vii) The names, titles, business addresses, email addresses or other electronic contact information, and relevant affiliations of all authors;

(viii) The names, titles, business addresses, email addresses or other electronic contact information, and relevant affiliations of all recipients of the material;

(ix) The names, titles, business addresses, email addresses or other electronic contact information, and relevant affiliations of all persons copied on the material;

(x) The factual basis supporting the claim that the material is protected (for example, that it was prepared by an attorney rendering legal advice to a client in a confidential communication, or prepared by an attorney in anticipation of litigation regarding a specifically identified claim); and

(xi) Any other pertinent information necessary to support the assertion of protected status by operation of law.

(2) Each attorney who is an author, recipient, or person copied on the material shall be identified in the log by an asterisk. The titles, business addresses, email addresses, and relevant affiliations of all authors, recipients, and persons copied on the material may be provided in a legend appended to the log. However, the information required by paragraph (a)(1)(vi) of this section shall be provided in the log.

(b) A person withholding responsive material solely for the reasons described in paragraph (a) of this section shall meet and confer with Commission staff pursuant to §2.7(k) of this part to discuss and attempt to resolve any issues associated with the manner and form in which privilege or protection claims will be asserted. The participants in the meet and confer session may agree to modify the logging requirements set forth in paragraph (a) of this section. The failure to comply with paragraph (a) shall constitute noncompliance subject to judicial enforcement under §2.13(a) of this part.

(c) Unless otherwise provided in the instructions accompanying the compulsory process, and except for information or material subject to a valid claim of protected status, all responsive information and material shall be produced without redaction.

(d)(1)(i) The disclosure of material protected by the attorney-client privilege or as work product shall not operate as a waiver if:

(A) The disclosure is inadvertent;

(B) The holder of the privilege or protection took reasonable steps to prevent disclosure; and

(C) The holder promptly took reasonable steps to rectify the error, including notifying Commission staff of the claim and the basis for it.

(ii) After being so notified, Commission staff must:

(A) Promptly return or destroy the specified material and any copies, not use or disclose the material until any dispute as to the validity of the claim is resolved; and take reasonable measures to retrieve the material from all persons to whom it was disclosed before being notified; or

(B) Sequester such material until such time as an Administrative Law Judge or court may rule on the merits of the claim of privilege or protection in a proceeding or action resulting from the investigation.

(iii) The producing party must preserve the material until the claim of privilege or protection is resolved, the investigation is closed, or any enforcement proceeding is concluded.

(2) When a disclosure is made that waives attorney-client privilege or work product, the waiver extends to an undisclosed communication or information only if:

(i) The waiver is intentional;

(ii) The disclosed and undisclosed information or material concern the same subject matter; and

(iii) They ought in fairness to be considered together.

[77 FR 59308, Sept. 27, 2012]

§2.12 [Reserved]

§2.13 Noncompliance with compulsory processes.

(a) In cases of failure to comply with Commission compulsory processes, appropriate action may be initiated by the Commission or the Attorney General, including actions for enforcement, forfeiture, civil penalties, or criminal sanctions. The Commission may also take any action as the circumstances may warrant under §4.1(e) of this chapter.

(b) The General Counsel, pursuant to delegation of authority by the Commission, without power of redelegation, is authorized, when he or she deems appropriate:

(1) To initiate, on behalf of the Commission, an enforcement proceeding in connection with the failure or refusal of a recipient to comply with, or to obey, a subpoena, a CID, or an access order, if the return date or any extension thereof has passed, or if the recipient breaches any modification regarding compliance;

(2) To approve and have prepared and issued, in the name of the Commission, a notice of default in connection with the failure of a recipient of an order to file a report pursuant to section 6(b) of the Federal Trade Commission Act to timely file that report, if the return date or any extension thereof has passed; to initiate, on behalf of the Commission, an enforcement proceeding; or to request to the Attorney General, on behalf of the Commission, to initiate a civil action in connection with the failure of such recipient to timely file a report, when the return date or any extension thereof has passed;

(3) To initiate, on behalf of the Commission, an enforcement proceeding under section 7A(g)(2) of the Clayton Act (15 U.S.C. 18a(g)(2)) in connection with the failure to substantially comply with any request for the submission of additional information or documentary material under section 7A(e)(1) of the Clayton Act (15 U.S.C. 18a(e)(1)), provided that the General Counsel shall provide notice to the Commission at least 2 days before initiating such action; and

(4) To seek an order of civil contempt in cases where a court order enforcing compulsory process has been violated.

[77 FR 59309, Sept. 27, 2012]

§2.14 Disposition.

(a) When an investigation indicates that corrective action is warranted, and the matter is not subject to a consent settlement pursuant to subpart C of this part, the Commission may initiate further proceedings.

(b) When corrective action is not necessary or warranted in the public interest, the investigation shall be closed. The matter may nevertheless be further investigated at any time if circumstances so warrant.

(c) In matters in which a recipient of a preservation demand, an access letter, or Commission compulsory process has not been notified that an investigation has been closed or otherwise concluded, after a period of twelve months following the last written communication from the Commission staff to the recipient or the recipient's counsel, the recipient is relieved of any obligation to continue preserving information, documentary material, or evidence, for purposes of responding to the Commission's process or the staff's access letter. The "written communication" may be in the form of a letter, an email, or a facsimile.

(d) The Commission has delegated to the Directors of the Bureaus of Competition and Consumer Protection, their Deputy Directors, the Assistant Directors of the Bureau of Competition, the Associate Directors of the Bureau of Consumer Protection, and the Regional Directors, without power of redelegation, limited authority to close investigations.

[77 FR 59309, Sept. 27, 2012]

§ 2.15 Orders requiring witnesses to testify or provide other information and granting immunity.

(a) The Bureau Director, Deputy Directors, and Assistant Directors in the Bureaus of Competition and Economics, the Bureau Director, Deputy Directors and Associate Directors of the Bureau of Consumer Protection, Regional Directors and Assistant Regional Directors are hereby authorized to request, through the Commission's liaison officer, approval from the Attorney General for the issuance of an order requiring a witness to testify or provide other information granting immunity under title 18, section 6002, of the United States Code.

(b) The Commission retains the right to review the exercise of any of the functions delegated under paragraph (a) of this section. Appeals to the Commission from an order requiring a witness to testify or provide other information will be entertained by the Commission only upon a showing that a substantial question is involved, the determination of which is essential to serve the interests of justice. Such appeals shall be made on the record and shall be in the form of a brief not to exceed fifteen (15) pages in length and shall be filed within five (5) days after notice of the complained of action. The appeal shall not operate to suspend the hearing unless otherwise determined by the person conducting the hearing or ordered by the Commission.

(18 U.S.C. 6002, 6004)

[37 FR 5016, Mar. 9, 1972, as amended at 48 FR 41375, Sept. 15, 1983; 61 FR 50645, Sept. 26, 1996]

§ 2.16 Custodians.

(a) *Designation.* The Commission shall designate a custodian and one or more deputy custodians for material to be delivered pursuant to compulsory process in an investigation, a purpose of which is to determine whether any person may have violated any provision of the laws administered by the Commission. The custodian shall have the powers and duties prescribed by section 21 of the FTC Act. Deputy custodians may perform all of the duties assigned to custodians. The appropriate Bureau Directors, Deputy Directors, Associate Directors in the Bureau of Consumer Protection, Assistant Directors in the Bureau of Competition, Regional Directors or Assistant Regional Directors shall take the action required by section 21(b)(7) of the FTC Act if it is necessary to replace a custodian or deputy custodian.

(b) *Copying of custodial documents.* The custodian designated pursuant to section 21 of the Federal Trade Commission Act (subject to the general supervision of the Executive Director) may, from among the material submitted, select the material the copying of which is necessary or appropriate for the official use of the Commission, and shall determine, the number of copies of any such material that are to be reproduced. Copies of material in the physical possession of the custodian may be reproduced by or under the authority of an employee of the Commission designated by the custodian.

(c) Material produced pursuant to the Federal Trade Commission Act, while in the custody of the custodian, shall be for the official use of the Commission in accordance with the Act; but such material shall upon reasonable notice to the custodian be made available for examination by the person who produced such material, or his duly authorized representative, during regular office hours established for the Commission.

[45 FR 36343, May 29, 1980, as amended at 46 FR 26291, May 12, 1981; 48 FR 41376, Sept. 15, 1983; 50 FR 53305, Dec. 31, 1985]

§ 2.17 Statutory delays of notifications and prohibitions of disclosure.

Upon authorization by the Commissioner who issues compulsory process pursuant to § 2.7(a) or, alternatively, upon authorization by the General Counsel, Commission attorneys may seek to delay notifications or prohibit disclosures pursuant to the Right to Financial Privacy Act (12 U.S.C. 3409), the Electronic Communications Privacy Act (18 U.S.C. 2705), or section 7 of the U.S. SAFE WEB Act (15 U.S.C. 57b–2a).

[76 FR 54691, Sept. 2, 2011]

Subpart B—Petitions Filed Under Section 7A of the Clayton Act, as Amended, for Review of Requests for Additional Information or Documentary Material

AUTHORITY: 15 U.S.C. 18a(d), (e).

§ 2.20 Petitions for review of requests for additional information or documentary material.

(a) For purposes of this section, "second request" refers to a request for additional information or documentary material issued under 16 CFR 803.20.

(b) *Second request procedures*—(1) *Notice.* Every request for additional information or documentary material issued under 16 CFR 803.20 shall inform the recipient(s) of the request that the recipient has a right to discuss modifications or clarifications of the request with an authorized representative of the Commission. The request shall identify the name and telephone number of at least one such representative.

(2) *Second request conference.* An authorized representative of the Commission shall invite the recipient to discuss the request for additional information or documentary material soon after the request is issued. At the conference, the authorized representative shall discuss the competitive issues raised by the proposed transaction, to the extent then known, and confer with the recipient about the most effective way to obtain information and documents relating to the competitive issues raised. The conference will ordinarily take place within 5 business days of issuance of the request, unless the recipient declines the invitation or requests a later date.

(3) *Modification of requests.* The authorized representative shall modify the request for additional information or documentary material, or recommend such modification to the responsible Assistant Director of the Bureau of Competition, if he or she determines that a less burdensome request would be consistent with the needs of the investigation. A request for additional information or documentary material may be modified only in writing signed by the authorized representative.

(4) *Review of request decisions.* (i) If the recipient of a request for additional information or documentary material believes that compliance with portions of the request should not be required and the recipient has exhausted reasonable efforts to obtain clarifications or modifications of the request from an authorized representative, the recipient may petition the General Counsel to consider and rule on unresolved issues. Such petition shall be submitted by letter to the General Counsel with a copy to the authorized representative who participated in the second request conference held under paragraph (b)(3) of this section. The petition shall not, without leave of the General Counsel, exceed 500 words, excluding any cover, table of contents, table of authorities, glossaries, proposed form of relief and any appendices containing only sections of statutes or regulations, and shall address petitioner's efforts to obtain modification from the authorized representative.

(ii) Within 2 business days after receiving such a petition, the General Counsel shall set a date for a conference with the petitioner and the authorized representative.

(iii) Such conference shall take place within 7 business days after the General Counsel receives the petition, unless the request recipient agrees to a later date or declines to attend a conference.

(iv) Not later than 3 business days before the date of the conference, the petitioner and the authorized representative may each submit memoranda regarding the issues presented in the petition. Such memoranda shall not, without leave of the General Counsel, exceed 1250 words, excluding any cover, table of contents, table of authorities, glossaries, proposed form of relief and appendices containing only sections of statutes or regulations. Such memoranda shall be delivered to counsel for the other participants on the same day they are delivered to the General Counsel.

(v) The petitioner's memorandum shall include a concise statement of reasons why the request should be modified, together with proposed modifications, or a concise explanation why the recipient believes it has substantially complied with the request for additional information or documentary material.

(vi) The authorized representative's memorandum shall include a concise statement of reasons why the petitioner's proposed modifications are inappropriate or a concise statement of the reasons why the representative believes that the petitioner has not substantially complied with the request for additional information and documentary material.

(vii) The General Counsel shall advise the petitioner and the authorized representative of his or her decision within 3 business days following the conference.

[66 FR 8721, Feb. 1, 2001]

Subpart C—Consent Order Procedure

§ 2.31 Opportunity to submit a proposed consent order.

(a) Where time, the nature of the proceeding, and the public interest permit, any individual, partnership, or corporation being investigated shall be afforded the opportunity to submit through the operating Bureau or Regional Office having responsibility in the matter a proposal for disposition of the matter in the form of a consent order agreement executed by the party being investigated and complying with the requirements of § 2.32, for consideration by the Commission in connection with a proposed complaint submitted by the Commission's staff.

(b) After a complaint has been issued, the consent order procedure described in this part will not be available except as provided in § 3.25(b).

[40 FR 15235, Apr. 4, 1975]

§ 2.32 Agreement.

Every agreement in settlement of a Commission complaint shall contain, in addition to an appropriate proposed order, either an admission of the proposed findings of fact and conclusions of law submitted simultaneously by the Commission's staff or an admission of all jurisdictional facts and an express waiver of the requirement that the Commission's decision contain a statement of findings of fact and conclusions of law. Every agreement also shall waive further procedural steps and all rights to seek judicial review or otherwise to challenge or contest the validity of the order. In addition, where appropriate, every agreement in settlement of a Commission complaint challenging the lawfulness of a proposed merger or acquisition shall also contain a hold-separate or asset-maintenance order. The agreement may state that the signing thereof is for settlement purposes only and does not constitute an admission by any party that the law has been violated as alleged in the complaint. Every agreement shall provide that:

(a) The complaint may be used in construing the terms of the order;

(b) No agreement, understanding, representation, or interpretation not contained in the order or the aforementioned agreement may be used to vary or to contradict the terms of the order;

(c) The order will have the same force and effect and may be altered, modified or set aside in the same manner provided by statute for Commission orders issued on a litigated or stipulated record;

(d) Except as provided by order of the Commission, any order issued pursuant to the agreement will become final upon service;

(e) The agreement will not become a part of the public record unless and until it is accepted by the Commission; and

(f) If the Commission accepts the agreement, further proceedings will be governed by § 2.34.

[64 FR 46268, Aug. 25, 1999]

§ 2.33 Compliance procedure.

The Commission may in its discretion require that a proposed agreement containing an order to cease and desist be accompanied by an initial report signed by the respondent setting forth in precise detail the manner in which the respondent will comply with the order when and if entered. Such report will not become part of the public record unless and until the accompanying agreement and order are accepted by the Commission. At the time any such report is submitted a respondent may request confidentiality for any portion thereof with a precise showing of justification therefor as set out in §4.9(c) and the General Counsel or the General Counsel's designee will dispose of such requests in accordance with that section.

[63 FR 32977, June 17, 1998]

§2.34 Disposition.

(a) *Acceptance of proposed consent agreement.* The Commission may accept or refuse to accept a proposed consent agreement. Except as otherwise provided in paragraph (c) of this section, acceptance does not constitute final approval, but it serves as the basis for further actions leading to final disposition of the matter.

(b) *Effectiveness of hold-separate or asset-maintenance order.* Following acceptance of a consent agreement, the Commission will, if it deems a hold-separate or asset-maintenance order appropriate, issue a complaint and such an order as agreed to by the parties. Such order will be final upon service. The issuance of a complaint under this paragraph will neither commence an adjudicatory proceeding subject to part 3 of this chapter nor subject the consent agreement proceeding to the prohibitions specified in §4.7 of this chapter.

(c) *Public comment.* Promptly after its acceptance of the consent agreement, the Commission will place the order contained in the consent agreement, the complaint, and the consent agreement on the public record for a period of 30 days, or such other period as the Commission may specify, for the receipt of comments or views from any interested person. At the same time, the Commission will place on the public record an explanation of the provisions of the order and the relief to be obtained thereby and any other information that it believes may help interested persons understand the order. The Commission also will publish the explanation in the FEDERAL REGISTER. The Commission retains the discretion to issue a complaint and a Final Decision and Order, incorporating the order contained in a consent agreement, in appropriate cases before seeking public comment. Unless directed otherwise by the Commission, such Decision and Order will be final upon service.

(d) *Comment on initial compliance report.* If respondents have filed an initial report of compliance pursuant to §2.33, the Commission will place that report on the public record, except for portions, if any, granted confidential treatment pursuant to §4.9(c) of this chapter, with the complaint, the order, and the consent agreement.

(e) *Action following comment period.* (1) Following the comment period, on the basis of comments received or otherwise, the Commission may either withdraw its acceptance of the agreement and so notify respondents, in which event it will take such other action as it may consider appropriate, or issue and serve its complaint in such form as the circumstances may require and its decision in disposition of the proceeding.

(2) The Commission, following the comment period, may determine, on the basis of the comments or otherwise, that a Final Decision and Order that was issued in advance of the comment period should be modified. Absent agreement by respondents to the modifications, the Commission may initiate a proceeding to reopen and modify the decision and order in accordance with §3.72(b) of this chapter or commence a new administrative proceeding by issuing a complaint in accordance with §3.11 of this chapter.

[64 FR 46269, Aug. 25, 1999]

Subpart D—Reports of Compliance

§2.41 General compliance obligations and specific obligations regarding acquisitions and divestitures.

(a) In every proceeding in which the Commission has issued an order pursuant to the provisions of section 5 of the Federal Trade Commission Act or section 11 of the Clayton Act, as amended, and except as otherwise specifically provided in any such order, each respondent named in such order shall file with the Commission, within sixty (60) days after service thereof, or within such other time as may be provided by the order or the rules in this chapter, a report in writing, signed by the respondent, setting forth in detail the manner and form of his compliance with the order, and shall thereafter file with the Commission such further signed, written reports of compliance as it may require. An original and one copy of each such report shall be filed with the Secretary of the Commission, and one copy of each such report shall be filed with the Associate Director for Enforcement in the Bureau of Consumer Protection (for consumer protection orders) or with the Assistant Director for Compliance in the Bureau of Competition (for competition orders). Reports of compliance shall be under oath if so requested. Where the order prohibits the use of a false advertisement of a food, drug, device, or cosmetic which may be injurious to health because of results from its use under the conditions prescribed in the advertisement, or under such conditions as are customary or usual, or if the use of such advertisement is with intent to defraud or mislead, or in any other case where the circumstances so warrant, the order may provide for an interim report stating whether and how respondents intend to comply to be filed within ten (10) days after service of the order. Neither the filing of an application for stay pursuant to § 3.56, nor the filing of a petition for judicial review, shall operate to postpone the time for filing a compliance report under the order or this section. If the Commission, or a court, determines to grant a stay of an order, or portion thereof, pending judicial review, or if any order provision is automatically stayed by statute, no compliance report shall be due as to those portions of the order that are stayed unless ordered by the court. Thereafter, as to orders, or portions thereof, that are stayed, the time for filing a report of compliance shall begin to run de novo from the final judicial determination, except that if no petition for certiorari has been filed following affirmance of the order of the Commission by a court of appeals, the compliance report shall be due the day following the date on which the time expires for the filing of such petition. Staff of the Bureaus of Competition and Consumer Protection will review such reports of compliance and may advise each respondent whether the staff intends to recommend that the Commission take any enforcement action. The Commission may, however, institute proceedings, including certification of facts to the Attorney General pursuant to the provisions of section 5(l) of the Federal Trade Commission Act (15 U.S.C. 45(l)) and section 11(l) of the Clayton Act, as amended (15 U.S.C. 21(l)), to enforce compliance with an order, without advising a respondent whether the actions set forth in a report of compliance evidence compliance with the Commission's order or without prior notice of any kind to a respondent.

(b) The Commission has delegated to the Director, the Deputy Directors, and the Assistant Director for Compliance of the Bureau of Competition, and to the Director, the Deputy Directors, and the Associate Director for Enforcement of the Bureau of Consumer Protection the authority to monitor compliance reports and to open and close compliance investigations. With respect to any compliance matter which has received previous Commission consideration as to compliance or in which the Commission or any Commissioner has expressed an interest, any matter proposed to be closed by reason of expense of investigation or testing, or any matter involving substantial questions as to the public interest, Commission policy or statutory construction, the Bureaus shall submit an analysis to the Commission regarding their intended actions.

(c) The Commission has delegated to the Director, Deputy Directors, and Assistant Directors of the Bureau of Competition and to the Director, Deputy Directors, and Associate Directors of the Bureau of Consumer Protection, and to the Regional Directors, the authority, for good cause shown, to extend the time within which reports of compliance with orders to cease and desist may be filed. It is to be noted, however, that an extension of time within which a report of compliance may be filed, or the filing of a report which does not evidence full compliance with the order, does not in any circumstances suspend or relieve a respondent from his obligation under the law with respect to compliance with such order. An order of the Commission to cease and desist becomes final on the date and under the conditions provided in the Federal Trade Commission Act and the Clayton Act. Any person, partnership or corporation against which an order to cease and desist has been issued who is not in full compliance with such order on and after the date provided in these statutes for the order to become final is in violation of such order and is subject to an immediate action for civil penalties. The authority under this paragraph may not be redelegated, except that the Associate Director for Enforcement in the Bureau of Consumer Protection and the Assistant Director for Compliance in the Bureau of Competition may each name a designee under this paragraph.

(d) Any respondent subject to a Commission order may request advice from the Commission as to whether a proposed course of action, if pursued by it, will constitute compliance with such order. The request for advice should be submitted in writing to the Secretary of the Commission and should include full and complete information regarding the proposed course of action. On the basis of the facts submitted, as well as other information available to the Commission, the Commission will inform the respondent whether or not the proposed course of action, if pursued, would constitute compliance with its order. A request ordinarily will be considered inappropriate for such advice:

(1) Where the course of action is already being followed by the requesting party;

(2) Where the same or substantially the same course of action is under investigation or is or has been the subject of a current proceeding, order, or decree initiated or obtained by the Commission or another governmental agency; or

(3) Where the proposed course of action or its effects may be such that an informed decision thereon cannot be made or could be made only after extensive investigation, clinical study, testing or collateral inquiry.

Furthermore, the filing of a request for advice under this paragraph does not in any circumstances suspend or relieve a respondent from his obligation under the law with respect to his compliance with the order. He must in any event be in full compliance on and after the date the order becomes final as prescribed by statute referred to in paragraph (b) of this section. Advice to respondents under this paragraph will be published by the Commission in the same manner and subject to the same restrictions and considerations as advisory opinions under §1.4 of this chapter.

(e) The Commission may at any time reconsider any advice given under this section and, where the public interest requires, rescind or revoke its prior advice. In such event the respondent will be given notice of the Commission's intent to revoke or rescind and will be given an opportunity to submit its views to the Commission. The Commission will not proceed against a respondent for violation of an order with respect to any action which was taken in good faith reliance upon the Commission's advice under this section, where all relevant facts were fully, completely, and accurately presented to the Commission and where such action was promptly discontinued upon notification of rescission or revocation of the Commission's advice.

(f)(1) All applications for approval of proposed divestitures, acquisitions, or similar transactions subject to Commission review under outstanding orders (including modifications to previously approved transactions) shall fully describe the terms of the transaction or modification and shall set forth why the transaction or modification merits Commission approval. Such applications will be placed on the public record, together with any additional applicant submissions that the Commission directs be placed on the public record. The Director of the Bureau of Competition is delegated authority to direct such placement.

(2) The Commission will receive public comment on a prior approval application submitted pursuant to paragraphs (f)(1) or (5) of this section for thirty (30) days. During the comment period, any person may file formal written objections or comments with the Secretary of the Commission, and such objections or comments shall be placed on the public record. In appropriate cases, the Commission may shorten, eliminate, extend, or reopen a comment period.

(3) Responses to applications under this section, together with a statement of supporting reasons, will be published when made, together with responses to any public comments filed under this section.

(4) Persons submitting information that is subject to public record disclosure under this section may request confidential treatment for that information or portions thereof in accordance with § 4.9(c) and the General Counsel or the General Counsel's designee will dispose of such requests in accordance with that section. Nothing in this section requires that confidentiality requests be resolved prior to, or contemporaneously with, the disposition of the application.

(5)(i) Any application to modify either:

(A) An agreement that has been approved by the Commission pursuant to paragraph (f) of this section, or

(B) An agreement incorporated by reference into a final order of the Commission issued in connection with a merger, acquisition, or similar transaction shall be subject to review and approval in the manner described in paragraphs (f)(1) through (4) of this section, except as provided in paragraph (f)(5)(ii) of this section.

(ii) If the application establishes that the proposed modification is purely ministerial, or unlikely under any plausible facts to affect achieving the remedial purposes of the order at issue, the Commission has delegated to the Director, Deputy Directors, and Assistant Director for Compliance of the Bureau of Competition, without power of redelegation, for good cause shown, the authority.

(A) To waive the approval requirement of paragraph (f)(5)(i) of this section; and

(B) To shorten, eliminate, extend or reopen the comment period pursuant to paragraph (f)(2) of this section.

(iii) Any agreement containing a modification approved, or for which the approval requirement is waived, pursuant to this paragraph (f)(5), shall be subject to any outstanding Commission order to the same extent as was the original agreement.

[32 FR 8449, June 13, 1967]

EDITORIAL NOTE: For FEDERAL REGISTER citations affecting § 2.41, see the List of CFR Sections Affected, which appears in the Finding Aids section of the printed volume and at *www.govinfo.gov*.

Subpart E—Requests To Reopen

§ 2.51 Requests to reopen.

(a) *Scope.* Any person, partnership, or corporation subject to a Commission decision containing a rule or order which has become effective, or an order to cease and desist which has become final, may file with the Secretary a request that the Commission reopen the proceeding to consider whether the rule or order, including any affirmative relief provision contained therein, should be altered, modified, or set aside in whole or in part.

(b) *Contents.* A request under this section shall contain a satisfactory showing that changed conditions of law or fact require the rule or order to be altered, modified or set aside, in whole or in part, or that the public interest so requires.

(1) This requirement shall not be deemed satisfied if a request is merely conclusory or otherwise fails to set forth by affidavit(s) specific facts demonstrating in detail:

(i) The nature of the changed conditions and the reasons why they require the requested modifications of the rule or order; or

(ii) The reasons why the public interest would be served by the modification.

(2) Each affidavit shall set forth facts that would be admissible in evidence and shall show that the affiant is competent to testify to the matters stated therein. All information and material that the requester wishes the Commission to consider shall be contained in the request at the time of filing.

(c) *Opportunity for public comment.* A request under this section shall be placed on the public record except for material exempt from public disclosure under rule 4.10(a). Unless the Commission determines that earlier disposition is necessary, the request shall remain on the public record for thirty (30) days after a press release on the request is issued. Bureau Directors are authorized to publish a notice in the FEDERAL

REGISTER announcing the receipt of a request to reopen at their discretion. The public is invited to comment on the request while it is on the public record.

(d) *Determination.* After the period for public comments on a request under this section has expired and no later than one hundred and twenty (120) days after the date of the filing of the request, the Commission shall determine whether the request complies with paragraph (b) of this section and whether the proceeding shall be reopened and the rule or order should be altered, modified, or set aside as requested. In doing so, the Commission may, in its discretion, issue an order reopening the proceeding and modifying the rule or order as requested, issue an order to show cause pursuant to §3.72, or take such other action as is appropriate: *Provided, however,* That any action under §3.72 or otherwise shall be concluded within the specified 120-day period.

(Sec. 6(g), 38 Stat. 721 (15 U.S.C. 46(g)); 80 Stat. 383, as amended, 81 Stat. 54 (5 U.S.C. 552))

[45 FR 36344, May 29, 1980, as amended at 46 FR 26291, May 12, 1981; 47 FR 33251, Aug. 2, 1982; 50 FR 53305, Dec. 31, 1985; 53 FR 40868, Oct. 19, 1988; 65 FR 50637, Aug. 21, 2000]

PART 3—RULES OF PRACTICE FOR ADJUDICATIVE PROCEEDINGS

Subpart A—Scope of Rules; Nature of Adjudicative Proceedings

Subpart B—Pleadings

Subpart C—Prehearing Procedures; Motions; Interlocutory Appeals; Summary Decisions

Subpart D—Discovery; Compulsory Process

Subpart E—Hearings

Subpart F—Decision

Subpart G [Reserved]

Subpart H—Reopening of Proceedings

Subpart I—Recovery of Awards Under the Equal Access to Justice Act in Commission Proceedings

AUTHORITY: 15 U.S.C. 46.

SOURCE: 32 FR 8449, June 13, 1967, unless otherwise noted.

Subpart A—Scope of Rules; Nature of Adjudicative Proceedings

§ 3.1 Scope of the rules in this part; expedition of proceedings.

The rules in this part govern procedure in formal adjudicative proceedings. To the extent practicable and consistent with requirements of law, the Commission's policy is to conduct such proceedings expeditiously. In the conduct of such proceedings the Administrative Law Judge and counsel for all parties shall make every effort at each stage of a proceeding to avoid delay. In the event of a scheduling conflict between a proceeding in which the Commission also has sought or is seeking relief under Section 13(b) of the FTC Act, 15 U.S.C. 53(b), and another proceeding, the proceeding in which the Commission also has sought or is seeking relief under Section 13(b) shall take precedence. The Commission, at any time, or the Administrative Law Judge at any time prior to the filing of his or her initial decision, may, with the consent of the parties, shorten any time limit prescribed by these Rules of Practice.

[74 FR 20208, May 1, 2009]

§ 3.2 Nature of adjudicative proceedings.

Adjudicative proceedings are those formal proceedings conducted under one or more of the statutes administered by the Commission which are required by statute to be determined on the record after opportunity for an agency hearing. The term includes hearings upon objections to orders relating to the promulgation, amendment, or repeal of rules under sections 4, 5 and 6 of the Fair Packaging and Labeling Act, but does not include rulemaking proceedings up to the time when the Commission determines under § 1.26(g) of this chapter that objections sufficient to warrant the holding of a public hearing have been filed. The term also includes proceedings for the assessment of civil penalties pursuant to § 1.94 of this chapter. The term does not include other proceedings such as negotiations for and Commission consideration of the entry of consent orders; investigational hearings as distinguished from proceedings after the issuance of a complaint; requests for extensions of time to comply with final orders or other proceedings involving compliance with final orders; proceedings for the promulgation of industry guides or trade regulation rules; or the promulgation of substantive rules and regulations.

[74 FR 1820, Jan. 13, 2009]

Subpart B—Pleadings

§ 3.11 Commencement of proceedings.

(a) *Complaint.* Except as provided in § 3.13, an adjudicative proceeding is commenced when an affirmative vote is taken by the Commission to issue a complaint.

(b) *Form of complaint.* The Commission's complaint shall contain the following:

(1) Recital of the legal authority and jurisdiction for institution of the proceeding, with specific designation of the statutory provisions alleged to have been violated;

(2) A clear and concise factual statement sufficient to inform each respondent with reasonable definiteness of the type of acts or practices alleged to be in violation of the law;

(3) Where practical, a form of order which the Commission has reason to believe should issue if the facts are found to be as alleged in the complaint; and

(4) Notice of the specific date, time and place for the evidentiary hearing. Unless a different date is determined by the Commission, the date of the evidentiary hearing shall be 5 months from the date of the administrative complaint in a proceeding in which the Commission, in an ancillary proceeding, has sought or is seeking relief pursuant to Section 13(b) of the FTC Act, 15 U.S.C. 53(b), and 8 months from the date of issuance of the administrative complaint in all other proceedings.

[74 FR 1820, Jan. 13, 2009]

§3.12 Answer.

(a) *Time for filing.* A respondent shall file an answer within 14 days after being served with the complaint.

(b) *Content of answer.* An answer shall conform to the following:

(1) *If allegations of complaint are contested.* An answer in which the allegations of a complaint are contested shall contain:

(i) A concise statement of the facts constituting each ground of defense;

(ii) Specific admission, denial, or explanation of each fact alleged in the complaint or, if the respondent is without knowledge thereof, a statement to that effect. Allegations of a complaint not thus answered shall be deemed to have been admitted.

(2) *If allegations of complaint are admitted.* If the respondent elects not to contest the allegations of fact set forth in the complaint, the answer shall consist of a statement that the respondent admits all of the material allegations to be true. Such an answer shall constitute a waiver of hearings as to the facts alleged in the complaint, and together with the complaint will provide a record basis on which the Commission shall issue a final decision containing appropriate findings and conclusions and a final order disposing of the proceeding. In such an answer, the respondent may, however, reserve the right to submit proposed findings of fact and conclusions of law under §3.46.

(c) *Default.* Failure of the respondent to file an answer within the time provided shall be deemed to constitute a waiver of the respondent's right to appear and contest the allegations of the complaint and to authorize the Commission, without further notice to the respondent, to find the facts to be as alleged in the complaint and to enter a final decision containing appropriate findings and conclusions and a final order disposing of the proceeding.

[74 FR 1820, Jan. 13, 2009]

§3.13 Adjudicative hearing on issues arising in rulemaking proceedings under the Fair Packaging and Labeling Act.

(a) *Notice of hearing.* When the Commission, acting under §1.26(g) of this chapter, determines that objections which have been filed are sufficient to warrant the holding of an adjudicative hearing in rulemaking proceedings under the Fair Packaging and Labeling Act, or when the Commission otherwise determines that the holding of such a hearing would be in the public interest, a hearing will be held before an Administrative Law Judge for the purpose of receiving evidence relevant and material to the issues raised by such objections or other issues specified by the Commission. In such case the Commission will publish a notice in the FEDERAL REGISTER containing a statement of:

(1) The provisions of the rule or order to which objections have been filed;

(2) The issues raised by the objections or the issues on which the Commission wishes to receive evidence;

(3) The time and place for hearing, the time to be at least thirty (30) days after publication of the notice; and

(4) The time within which, and the conditions under which, any person who petitioned for issuance, amendment, or repeal of the rule or order, or any person who filed objections sufficient to warrant the holding of the hearing, or any other interested person, may file notice of intention to participate in the proceeding.

(b) *Parties.* Any person who petitions for issuance, amendment, or repeal of a rule or order, and any person who files objections sufficient to warrant the holding of a hearing, and who files timely notice of intention to participate, shall be regarded as a party and shall be individually served with any pleadings filed in the proceeding. Upon written application to the Administrative Law Judge and a showing of good cause, any interested person may be designated by the Administrative Law Judge as a party.

[32 FR 8449, June 13, 1967, as amended at 40 FR 33969, Aug. 13, 1975]

§3.14 Intervention.

(a) Any individual, partnership, unincorporated association, or corporation desiring to intervene in an adjudicative proceeding shall make written application in the form of a motion setting forth the basis therefor. Such application shall be served upon each party to the proceeding in accordance with the provisions of §4.4(b) of this chapter.

The answer filed by any party shall be served upon the applicant in accordance with the provisions of § 4.4(b). The Administrative Law Judge or the Commission may by order permit the intervention to such extent and upon such terms as are provided by law or as otherwise may be deemed proper.

(b) In an adjudicative proceeding where the complaint states that divestiture relief is contemplated, the labor organization[s] representing employees of the respondent[s] may intervene as a matter of right. Applications for such intervention are to be made in accordance with the procedures set forth in paragraph (a) of this section and must be filed within 60 days of the issuance of the complaint. Intervention as a matter of right shall be limited to the issue of the effect, if any, of proposed remedies on employment, with full rights of participation in the proceeding concerning this issue. This paragraph does not affect a labor organization's ability to petition for leave to intervene pursuant to § 3.14(a).

[32 FR 8449, June 13, 1967, as amended at 46 FR 20979, Apr. 8, 1981; 80 FR 25941, May 12, 2015]

§ 3.15 Amendments and supplemental pleadings.

(a) *Amendments*—(1) *By leave.* If and whenever determination of a controversy on the merits will be facilitated thereby, the Administrative Law Judge may, upon such conditions as are necessary to avoid prejudicing the public interest and the rights of the parties, allow appropriate amendments to pleadings or notice of hearing: *Provided, however,* That a motion for amendment of a complaint or notice may be allowed by the Administrative Law Judge only if the amendment is reasonably within the scope of the original complaint or notice. Motions for other amendments of complaints or notices shall be certified to the Commission.

(2) *Conformance to evidence.* When issues not raised by the pleadings or notice of hearing but reasonably within the scope of the original complaint or notice of hearing are tried by express or implied consent of the parties, they shall be treated in all respects as if they had been raised in the pleadings or notice of hearing; and such amendments of the pleadings or notice as may be necessary to make them conform to the evidence and to raise such issues shall be allowed at any time.

(b) *Supplemental pleadings.* The Administrative Law Judge may, upon reasonable notice and such terms as are just, permit service of a supplemental pleading or notice setting forth transactions, occurrences, or events which have happened since the date of the pleading or notice sought to be supplemented and which are relevant to any of the issues involved.

Subpart C—Prehearing Procedures; Motions; Interlocutory Appeals; Summary Decisions

§ 3.21 Prehearing procedures.

(a) *Meeting of the parties before scheduling conference.* As early as practicable before the prehearing scheduling conference described in paragraph (b) of this section, but in any event no later than 5 days after the answer is filed by the last answering respondent, counsel for the parties shall meet to discuss the nature and basis of their claims and defenses and the possibilities for a prompt settlement or resolution of the case. The parties shall also agree, if possible, on—

(1) A proposed discovery plan specifically addressing a schedule for depositions of fact witnesses, the production of documents and electronically stored information, and the timing of expert discovery pursuant to § 3.31A. The parties' agreement regarding electronically stored information should include the scope of and a specified time period for the exchange of such information that is subject to §§ 3.31(b)(2), 3.31(c), and 3.37(a), and the format for the disclosure of such information, consistent with §§ 3.31(c)(3) and 3.37(c);

(2) A preliminary estimate of the time required for the evidentiary hearing; and

(3) Any other matters to be determined at the scheduling conference.

(b) *Scheduling conference.* Not later than 10 days after the answer is filed by the last answering respondent, the Administrative Law Judge shall hold a scheduling conference. At the scheduling conference, counsel for the parties shall be prepared to address:

(1) Their factual and legal theories;

(2) The current status of any pending motions;

(3) A schedule of proceedings that is consistent with the date of the evidentiary hearing set by the Commission;

(4) Steps taken to preserve evidence relevant to the issues raised by the claims and defenses;

(5) The scope of anticipated discovery, any limitations on discovery, and a proposed discovery plan, including the disclosure of electronically stored information;

(6) Issues that can be narrowed by agreement or by motion, suggestions to expedite the presentation of evidence at trial, and any request to bifurcate issues, claims or defenses; and

(7) Other possible agreements or steps that may aid in the just and expeditious disposition of the proceeding and to avoid unnecessary cost.

(c) *Prehearing scheduling order*. (1) Not later than 2 days after the scheduling conference, the Administrative Law Judge shall enter an order that sets forth the results of the conference and establishes a schedule of proceedings that will permit the evidentiary hearing to commence on the date set by the Commission, including a plan of discovery that addresses the deposition of fact witnesses, timing of expert discovery, and the production of documents and electronically stored information, dates for the submission and hearing of motions, the specific method by which exhibits shall be numbered or otherwise identified and marked for the record, and the time and place of a final prehearing conference. The Commission may, upon a showing of good cause, order a later date for the evidentiary hearing than the one specified in the complaint.

(2) The Administrative Law Judge may, upon a showing of good cause, grant a motion to extend any deadline or time specified in this scheduling order other than the date of the evidentiary hearing. Such motion shall set forth the total period of extensions, if any, previously obtained by the moving party. In determining whether to grant the motion, the Administrative Law Judge shall consider any extensions already granted, the length of the proceedings to date, the complexity of the issues, and the need to conclude the evidentiary hearing and render an initial decision in a timely manner. The Administrative Law Judge shall not rule on *ex parte* motions to extend the deadlines specified in the scheduling order, or modify such deadlines solely upon stipulation or agreement of counsel.

(d) *Meeting prior to final prehearing conference*. Counsel for the parties shall meet before the final prehearing conference described in paragraph (e) of this section to discuss the matters set forth therein in preparation for the conference.

(e) *Final prehearing conference*. As close to the commencement of the evidentiary hearing as practicable, the Administrative Law Judge shall hold a final prehearing conference, which counsel shall attend in person, to submit any proposed stipulations as to law, fact, or admissibility of evidence, exchange exhibit and witness lists, and designate testimony to be presented by deposition. At this conference, the Administrative Law Judge shall also resolve any outstanding evidentiary matters or pending motions (except motions for summary decision) and establish a final schedule for the evidentiary hearing.

(f) *Additional prehearing conferences and orders*. The Administrative Law Judge shall hold additional prehearing and status conferences or enter additional orders as may be needed to ensure the just and expeditious disposition of the proceeding and to avoid unnecessary cost. Such conferences shall be held in person to the extent practicable.

(g) *Public access and reporting*. Prehearing conferences shall be public unless the Administrative Law Judge determines in his or her discretion that the conference (or any part thereof) shall be closed to the public. The Administrative Law Judge shall have discretion to determine whether a prehearing conference shall be stenographically reported.

[74 FR 1820, Jan. 13, 2009]

§ 3.22 Motions.

(a) *Presentation and disposition.* Motions filed under § 4.17 of this chapter shall be directly referred to and ruled on by the Commission. Motions to dismiss filed before the evidentiary hearing (other than motions to dismiss under § 3.26(d)), motions to strike, and motions for summary decision shall be directly referred to the Commission and shall be ruled on by the Commission unless the Commission in its discretion refers the motion to the Administrative Law Judge. Except as otherwise provided by an applicable rule, motions not referred to the Administrative Law Judge shall be ruled on by the Commission within 45 days of the filing of the last-filed answer or reply to the motion, if any, unless the Commission determines there is good cause to extend the deadline. If the Commission refers the motion to the Administrative Law Judge, it may set a deadline for the ruling by the Administrative Law Judge, and a party may seek review of the ruling of the Administrative Law Judge in accordance with § 3.23. During the time a proceeding is before an Administrative Law Judge, all other motions shall be addressed to and decided by the Administrative Law Judge, if within his or her authority. The Administrative Law Judge shall certify to the Commission a motion to disqualify filed under § 3.42(g) if the Administrative Law Judge does not disqualify himself or herself within 10 days. The Administrative Law Judge shall certify to the Commission forthwith any other motion upon which he or she has no authority to rule. Rulings containing information granted *in camera* status pursuant to § 3.45 shall be filed in accordance with § 3.45(f). When a motion to dismiss is made at the close of the evidence offered in support of the complaint based upon an alleged failure to establish a *prima facie* case, the Administrative Law Judge shall defer ruling thereon until immediately after all evidence has been received and the hearing record is closed. All written motions shall be filed with the Secretary of the Commission, and all motions addressed to the Commission shall be in writing. The moving party shall also provide a copy of its motion to the Administrative Law Judge at the time the motion is filed with the Secretary.

(b) *Proceedings not stayed.* A motion under consideration by the Commission shall not stay proceedings before the Administrative Law Judge unless the Commission so orders or unless otherwise provided by an applicable rule.

(c) *Content.* All written motions shall state the particular order, ruling, or action desired and the grounds therefor. Memoranda in support of, or in opposition to, any dispositive motion shall not exceed 10,000 words. Memoranda in support of, or in opposition to, any other motion shall not exceed 2,500 words. Any reply in support of a dispositive motion shall not exceed 5,000 words and any reply in support of any other motion authorized by the Administrative Law Judge or the Commission shall not exceed 1,250 words. These word count limitations include headings, footnotes, and quotations, but do not include the cover, table of contents, table of citations or authorities, glossaries, statements with respect to oral argument, any addendums containing statutes, rules or regulations, any certificates of counsel, proposed form of order, and any attachment required by § 3.45(e). Documents that fail to comply with these provisions shall not be filed with the Secretary. Motions must also include the name, address, telephone number, fax number, and e-mail address (if any) of counsel and attach a draft order containing the proposed relief. If a party includes in a motion information that has been granted *in camera* status pursuant to § 3.45(b) or is subject to confidentiality protections pursuant to a protective order, the party shall file 2 versions of the motion in accordance with the procedures set forth in § 3.45(e). The party shall mark its confidential filings with brackets or similar conspicuous markings to indicate the material for which it is claiming confidential treatment. The time period specified by § 3.22(d) within which an opposing party may file an answer will begin to run upon service on that opposing party of the confidential version of the motion.

(d) *Responses.* Within 10 days after service of any written motion, or within such longer or shorter time as may be designated by the Administrative

Law Judge or the Commission, the opposing party shall answer or shall be deemed to have consented to the granting of the relief asked for in the motion. If an opposing party includes in an answer information that has been granted *in camera* status pursuant to §3.45(b) or is subject to confidentiality protections pursuant to a protective order, the opposing party shall file 2 versions of the answer in accordance with the procedures set forth in §3.45(e). The moving party shall have no right to reply, except for dispositive motions or as otherwise permitted by the Administrative Law Judge or the Commission. Reply and surreply briefs to motions other than dispositive motions shall be permitted only in circumstances where the parties wish to draw the Administrative Law Judge's or the Commission's attention to recent important developments or controlling authority that could not have been raised earlier in the party's principal brief. The reply may be conditionally filed with the motion seeking leave to reply. Any reply with respect to a dispositive motion, or any permitted reply to any other motion, shall be filed within 5 days after service of the last answer to that motion.

(e) *Rulings on motions.* Unless otherwise provided by a relevant rule, the Administrative Law Judge shall rule on motions within 14 days after the filing of all motion papers authorized by this section. The Commission, for good cause, may extend the time allowed for a ruling.

(f) *Motions for extensions.* The Administrative Law Judge or the Commission may waive the requirements of this section as to motions for extensions of time; however, the Administrative Law Judge shall have no authority to rule on *ex parte* motions for extensions of time.

(g) *Statement.* Each motion to quash filed pursuant to §3.34(c), each motion to compel or determine sufficiency pursuant to §3.38(a), each motion for sanctions pursuant to §3.38(b), and each motion for enforcement pursuant to §3.38(c) shall be accompanied by a signed statement representing that counsel for the moving party has conferred with opposing counsel in an effort in good faith to resolve by agreement the issues raised by the motion and has been unable to reach such an agreement. If some of the matters in controversy have been resolved by agreement, the statement shall specify the matters so resolved and the matters remaining unresolved. The statement shall recite the date, time, and place of each such conference between counsel, and the names of all parties participating in each such conference. Unless otherwise ordered by the Administrative Law Judge, the statement required by this rule must be filed only with the first motion concerning compliance with the discovery demand at issue.

[74 FR 1821, Jan. 13, 2009, as amended at 80 FR 15160, Mar. 23, 2015]

§3.23 Interlocutory appeals.

(a) *Appeals without a determination by the Administrative Law Judge.* (1) The Commission may, in its discretion, entertain interlocutory appeals where a ruling of the Administrative Law Judge:

(i) Requires the disclosure of records of the Commission or another governmental agency or the appearance of an official or employee of the Commission or another governmental agency pursuant to §3.36, if such appeal is based solely on a claim of privilege: *Provided,* that the Administrative Law Judge shall stay until further order of the Commission the effectiveness of any ruling, whether or not appeal is sought, that requires the disclosure of nonpublic Commission minutes, Commissioner circulations, or similar documents prepared by the Commission, an individual Commissioner, or the Office of the General Counsel;

(ii) Suspends an attorney from participation in a particular proceeding pursuant to §3.42(d); or

(iii) Grants or denies an application for intervention pursuant to the provisions of §3.14.

(2) Appeal from such rulings may be sought by filing with the Commission an application for review within 3 days after notice of the Administrative Law Judge's ruling. An answer may be filed within 3 days after the application for review is filed. The Commission upon its own motion may enter an order staying compliance with a discovery

demand authorized by the Administrative Law Judge pursuant to § 3.36 or placing the matter on the Commission's docket for review. Any order placing the matter on the Commission's docket for review will set forth the scope of the review and the issues which will be considered and will make provision for the filing of memoranda of law if deemed appropriate by the Commission.

(b) *Other interlocutory appeals.* A party may request the Administrative Law Judge to determine that a ruling involves a controlling question of law or policy as to which there is substantial ground for difference of opinion and that an immediate appeal from the ruling may materially advance the ultimate termination of the litigation or subsequent review will be an inadequate remedy. An answer may be filed within 3 days after the request for determination is filed. The Administrative Law Judge shall issue a ruling on the request for determination within 3 days of the deadline for filing an answer. The party may file an application for review with the Commission within 1 day after notice that the Administrative Law Judge has issued the requested determination or 1 day after the deadline has passed for the Administrative Law Judge to issue a ruling on the request for determination and the Administrative Law Judge has not issued his or her ruling. An answer may be filed within 3 days after the application for review is filed.

(c) The application for review shall attach the ruling from which appeal is being taken and any other portions of the record on which the moving party relies. Neither the application for review nor the answer shall exceed 2,500 words. This word count limitation includes headings, footnotes, and quotations, but does not include the cover, table of contents, table of citations or authorities, glossaries, statements with respect to oral argument, any addendums containing statutes, rules or regulations, any certificates of counsel, proposed form of order, and any attachment required by § 3.45(e). The Commission may order additional briefing on the application.

(d) *Ruling on application for review.* Within 3 days after the deadline for filing an answer, the Commission will determine whether to grant the application for review. The denial of an application shall not constitute a ruling on the merits of the ruling that is the subject of the application.

(e) *Proceedings not stayed.* An application for review and appeal hereunder shall not stay proceedings before the Administrative Law Judge unless the Judge or the Commission shall so order.

[74 FR 1822, Jan. 13, 2009, as amended at 80 FR 15160, Mar. 23, 2015]

§ 3.24 Summary decisions.

(a) *Procedure.* (1) Any party may move, with or without supporting affidavits, for a summary decision in the party's favor upon all or any part of the issues being adjudicated. The motion shall be accompanied by a separate and concise statement of the material facts as to which the moving party contends there is no genuine issue for trial. Counsel in support of the complaint may so move at any time after 20 days following issuance of the complaint and any respondent may so move at any time after issuance of the complaint. Any such motion by any party, however, shall be filed in accordance with the scheduling order issued pursuant to § 3.21, but in any case at least 30 days before the date fixed for the hearing.

(2) Any other party may, within 14 days after service of the motion, file opposing affidavits. The opposing party shall include a separate and concise statement of those material facts as to which the opposing party contends there exists a genuine issue for trial, as provided in § 3.24(a)(3). The parties may file memoranda of law in support of, or in opposition to, the motion consistent with § 3.22(c). If a party includes in any such brief or memorandum information that has been granted *in camera* status pursuant to § 3.45(b) or is subject to confidentiality protections pursuant to a protective order, the party shall file 2 versions of the document in accordance with the procedures set forth in § 3.45(e). If the Commission (or, when appropriate, the Administrative Law Judge) determines that there is no genuine issue as to any material fact regarding liability or relief, it shall issue

a final decision and order. In the event that the motion has been referred to the Administrative Law Judge, such determination by the Administrative Law Judge shall constitute his or her initial decision and shall conform to the procedures set forth in §3.51(c). A summary decision, interlocutory in character and in compliance with the procedures set forth in §3.51(c), may be rendered on the issue of liability alone although there is a genuine issue as to relief.

(3) Affidavits shall set forth such facts as would be admissible in evidence and shall show affirmatively that the affiant is competent to testify to the matters stated therein. The Commission (or, when appropriate, the Administrative Law Judge) may permit affidavits to be supplemented or opposed by depositions, answers to interrogatories, or further affidavits. When a motion for summary decision is made and supported as provided in this rule, a party opposing the motion may not rest upon the mere allegations or denials of his or her pleading; the response, by affidavits or as otherwise provided in this rule, must set forth specific facts showing that there is a genuine issue of material fact for trial. If no such response is filed, summary decision, if appropriate, shall be rendered.

(4) Should it appear from the affidavits of a party opposing the motion that it cannot, for reasons stated, present by affidavit facts essential to justify its opposition, the Commission (or, when appropriate, the Administrative Law Judge) may deny the motion for summary decision or may order a continuance to permit affidavits to be obtained or depositions to be taken or discovery to be had or make such other order as is appropriate and a determination to that effect shall be made a matter of record.

(5) If on motion under this rule a summary decision is not rendered upon the whole case or for all the relief asked and a trial is necessary, the Commission (or, when appropriate, the Administrative Law Judge) shall issue an order specifying the facts that appear without substantial controversy and directing further proceedings in the action. The facts so specified shall be deemed established.

(b) *Affidavits filed in bad faith.* (1) Should it appear to the satisfaction of the Commission (or, when appropriate, the Administrative Law Judge) at any time that any of the affidavits presented pursuant to this rule are presented in bad faith, or solely for the purpose of delay, or are patently frivolous, the Commission (or, when appropriate, the Administrative Law Judge) shall enter a determination to that effect upon the record.

(2) If upon consideration of all relevant facts attending the submission of any affidavit covered by paragraph (b)(1) of this section, the Commission (or, when appropriate, the Administrative Law Judge) concludes that action to suspend or remove an attorney from the case is warranted, it shall take action as specified in §3.42(d). If the Administrative Law Judge to whom the Commission has referred a motion for summary decision concludes, upon consideration of all the relevant facts attending the submission of any affidavit covered by paragraph (b)(1) of this section, that the matter should be certified to the Commission for consideration of disciplinary action against an attorney, including reprimand, suspension or disbarment, the Administrative Law Judge shall certify the matter, with his or her findings and recommendations, to the Commission for its consideration of disciplinary action in the manner provided by the Commission's rules. If the Commission has addressed the motion directly, it may consider such disciplinary action without a certification by the Administrative Law Judge.

[74 FR 1822, Jan. 13, 2009]

§3.25 Consent agreement settlements.

(a) The Administrative Law Judge may, in his or her discretion and without suspension of prehearing procedures, hold conferences for the purpose of supervising negotiations for the settlement of the case, in whole or in part, by way of consent agreement.

(b) A proposal to settle a matter in adjudication by consent shall be submitted by way of a motion to withdraw the matter from adjudication for the purpose of considering a proposed settlement. Such motion shall be filed with the Secretary of the Commission, as provided in § 4.2. Any such motion shall be accompanied by a consent proposal; the proposal itself, however, shall not be placed on the public record unless and until it is accepted by the Commission as provided herein. If the consent proposal affects only some of the respondents or resolves only some of the charges in adjudication, the motion required by this paragraph shall so state and shall specify the portions of the matter that the proposal would resolve.

(c) If a consent agreement accompanying the motion has been executed by one or more respondents and by complaint counsel, has been approved by the appropriate Bureau Director, and conforms to § 2.32, and the matter is pending before an Administrative Law Judge, the Secretary shall issue an order withdrawing from adjudication those portions of the matter that the proposal would resolve and all proceedings before the Administrative Law Judge shall be stayed with respect to such portions, pending a determination by the Commission pursuant to paragraph (f) of this section. If a consent proposal is not in the form of a consent agreement executed by a respondent, does not otherwise conform to § 2.32, or has not been executed by complaint counsel, and the matter is pending before the Administrative Law Judge, he or she shall certify the motion and proposal to the Commission upon a written determination that there is a reasonable possibility of settlement. The certification may be accompanied by a recommendation to the Commission as to the disposition of the motion. The Administrative Law Judge shall make a determination as to whether to certify the motion within 5 days after the filing of the motion. The filing of a motion under paragraph (b) of this section and certification thereof to the Commission shall not stay proceedings before the Administrative Law Judge unless the Commission shall so order. Upon certification of such motion, the Commission in its discretion may issue an order withdrawing from adjudication those portions of the matter that the proposal would resolve for the purpose of considering the consent proposal.

(d) If the matter is no longer pending before the Administrative Law Judge, the Commission in its discretion may, upon motion filed under paragraph (b) of this section, issue an order withdrawing from adjudication those portions of the matter that the proposal would resolve for the purpose of considering the consent proposal. Such order may issue whether or not the consent proposal is in the form of a consent agreement executed by a respondent, otherwise conforms to § 2.32, or has been executed by complaint counsel.

(e) The Commission will treat those portions of a matter withdrawn from adjudication pursuant to paragraphs (c) or (d) of this section as being in a nonadjudicative status. Portions not so withdrawn shall remain in an adjudicative status.

(f) After some or all of the allegations in a matter have been withdrawn from adjudication, the Commission may accept a proposed consent agreement, reject it and return the matter or affected portions thereof to adjudication for further proceedings, or take such other action as it may deem appropriate. If an agreement is accepted, it will be disposed of as provided in § 2.34 of this chapter, except that if, following the public comment period provided for in § 2.34, the Commission decides, based on comments received or otherwise, to withdraw its acceptance of the agreement, it will so notify the parties and will return to adjudication any portions of the matter previously withdrawn from adjudication for further proceedings or take such other action it considers appropriate.

(g) This rule will not preclude the settlement of the case by regular adjudicatory process through the filing of an admission answer or submission of the case to the Administrative Law Judge on a stipulation of facts and an agreed order.

[74 FR 20208, May 1, 2009]

§ 3.26 Motions following denial of preliminary injunctive relief.

(a) This section sets forth two procedures by which respondents may obtain consideration of whether continuation of an adjudicative proceeding is in the public interest after a court has denied preliminary injunctive relief in a separate proceeding brought under section 13(b) of the Federal Trade Commission Act, 15 U.S.C. 53(b), in aid of the adjudicative proceeding.

(b) A motion under this section shall be addressed to the Commission and must be filed within 14 days after, but no earlier than:

(1) A district court has denied the Commission's request for a preliminary injunction, if the Commission has not filed a motion for relief pending appeal with the court of appeals within 7 days following the district court's denial of a preliminary injunction; or

(2) A court of appeals has denied a Commission motion for relief pending appeal.

(c) *Withdrawal from adjudication.* Following denial of court relief as specified in paragraph (b) of this section, respondents may move that the adjudicative proceeding be withdrawn from adjudication in order to consider whether the public interest warrants further litigation. Although all respondents must consent to the filing of such a motion, a motion under this paragraph (c) may be filed jointly or separately by each of the respondents in the adjudicative proceeding. At the time respondents file a motion under this paragraph (c), respondents must also electronically transmit a copy to complaint counsel. The Secretary shall issue an order withdrawing the matter from adjudication 2 days after such a motion is filed, except that, if complaint counsel file an objection asserting that the conditions of paragraph (b) of this section have not been met, the Commission shall decide the motion within 10 days after the objection is filed.

(d) *Consideration on the record of a motion to dismiss.* (1) In lieu of a motion to withdraw the adjudicative proceeding from adjudication under paragraph (c) of this section, any respondent may file a motion under this paragraph to dismiss the administrative complaint on the basis that the public interest does not warrant further litigation after a court has denied preliminary injunctive relief to the Commission.

(2) *Stay.* The filing of a motion under this paragraph (d) shall stay the proceeding until 7 days following the disposition of the motion by the Commission, and all deadlines established by these rules shall be tolled for the amount of time the proceeding is so stayed.

(3) *Answer.* Complaint counsel may file a response within 7 days after such motion is filed.

(4) *Ruling by Commission.* Within 30 days after the deadline for filing a response, the Commission shall rule on any motion under this paragraph (d).

(e) *Form.* Memoranda in support of or in opposition to motions authorized by this section shall not exceed 10,000 words. This word count limitation includes headings, footnotes, and quotations, but does not include the cover, table of contents, table of citations or authorities, glossaries, statements with respect to oral argument, any addendums containing statutes, rules or regulations, any certificates of counsel, proposed form of order, and any attachment required by §3.45(e).

(f) *In camera materials.* If any filing includes materials that are subject to confidentiality protections pursuant to an order entered in either the proceeding under section 13(b) or the adjudicative proceeding, such materials shall be treated as *in camera* materials for purposes of this paragraph and the party shall file 2 versions of the document in accordance with the procedures set forth in §3.45(e). The time within which complaint counsel may file an objection or response under this section will begin to run upon service of the *in camera* version of the motion (including any supporting briefs and memoranda).

[80 FR 15161, Mar. 23, 2015]

Subpart D—Discovery; Compulsory Process

§3.31 General discovery provisions.

(a) *Discovery methods.* Parties may obtain discovery by one or more of the following methods: Depositions upon oral examination or written questions; written interrogatories; production of documents or things for inspection and other purposes; and requests for admission. Except as provided in the rules, or unless the Administrative Law Judge orders otherwise, the frequency or sequence of these methods is not limited. The parties shall, to the greatest extent practicable, conduct discovery simultaneously; the fact that a party is conducting discovery shall not operate to delay any other party's discovery. Unless all parties expressly agree otherwise, no discovery shall take place before the issuance of a prehearing scheduling order under § 3.21(c), except for the mandatory initial disclosures required by paragraph (b) of this section.

(b) *Mandatory initial disclosures.* Complaint counsel and respondent's counsel shall, within 5 days of receipt of a respondent's answer to the complaint and without awaiting a discovery request, provide to each other:

(1) The name, and, if known, the address and telephone number of each individual likely to have discoverable information relevant to the allegations of the Commission's complaint, to the proposed relief, or to the defenses of the respondent, as set forth in § 3.31(c)(1); and

(2) A copy of, or a description by category and location of, all documents and electronically stored information including declarations, transcripts of investigational hearings and depositions, and tangible things in the possession, custody, or control of the Commission or respondent(s) that are relevant to the allegations of the Commission's complaint, to the proposed relief, or to the defenses of the respondent, as set forth in § 3.31(c)(1); unless such information or materials are subject to the limitations in § 3.31(c)(2), privileged as defined in § 3.31(c)(4), pertain to hearing preparation as defined in § 3.31(c)(5), pertain to experts as defined in § 3.31A, or are obtainable from some other source that is more convenient, less burdensome, or less expensive. A party shall make its disclosures based on the information then reasonably available to it and is not excused from making its disclosures because it has not fully completed its investigation.

(c) *Scope of discovery.* Unless otherwise limited by order of the Administrative Law Judge or the Commission in accordance with these rules, the scope of discovery under all the rules in this part is as follows:

(1) *In general.* Parties may obtain discovery to the extent that it may be reasonably expected to yield information relevant to the allegations of the complaint, to the proposed relief, or to the defenses of any respondent. Such information may include the existence, description, nature, custody, condition, and location of any books, documents, other tangible things, electronically stored information, and the identity and location of persons having any knowledge of any discoverable matter. Information may not be withheld from discovery on grounds that the information will be inadmissible at the hearing if the information sought appears reasonably calculated to lead to the discovery of admissible evidence.

(2) *Limitations.* Complaint counsel need only search for materials that were collected or reviewed in the course of the investigation of the matter or prosecution of the case and that are in the possession, custody or control of the Bureaus or Offices of the Commission that investigated the matter, including the Bureau of Economics. The Administrative Law Judge may authorize for good cause additional discovery of materials in the possession, custody, or control of those Bureaus or Offices, or authorize other discovery pursuant to § 3.36. Neither complaint counsel, respondent, nor a third party receiving a discovery request under these rules is required to search for materials generated and transmitted between an entity's counsel (including counsel's legal staff or in-house counsel) and not shared with anyone else, or between complaint counsel and non-testifying Commission employees, unless the Administrative Law Judge determines there is good cause to provide such materials. The frequency or extent of use of the discovery methods otherwise permitted under these rules shall be limited by the Administrative Law Judge if he or she determines that:

(i) The discovery sought from a party or third party is unreasonably cumulative or duplicative, or is obtainable from some other source that is more convenient, less burdensome, or less expensive;

(ii) The party seeking discovery has had ample opportunity by discovery in the action to obtain the information sought; or

(iii) The burden and expense of the proposed discovery on a party or third party outweigh its likely benefit.

(3) *Electronically stored information.* A party or third party need not provide discovery of electronically stored information from sources that the party or third party identifies as not reasonably accessible because of undue burden or cost. On a motion to compel discovery, the party or third party from whom discovery is sought must show that the information is not reasonably accessible because of undue burden or cost. If that showing is made, the Administrative Law Judge may nonetheless order discovery if the requesting party shows good cause, considering the limitations of paragraph (c)(2). The Administrative Law Judge may specify conditions for the discovery.

(4) *Privilege.* Discovery shall be denied or limited in order to preserve the privilege of a witness, person, or governmental agency as governed by the Constitution, any applicable act of Congress, or the principles of the common law as they may be interpreted by the Commission in the light of reason and experience.

(5) *Hearing preparations: Materials.* Subject to the provisions of § 3.31A, a party may obtain discovery of documents and tangible things otherwise discoverable under paragraph (c)(1) of this section and prepared in anticipation of litigation or for hearing by or for another party or by or for that other party's representative (including the party's attorney, consultant, or agent) only upon a showing that the party seeking discovery has substantial need of the materials in the preparation of its case and that the party is unable without undue hardship to obtain the substantial equivalent of the materials by other means. In ordering discovery of such materials when the required showing has been made, the Administrative Law Judge shall protect against disclosure of the mental impressions, conclusions, opinions, or legal theories of an attorney or other representative of a party.

(d) *Protective orders; orders to preserve evidence.* In order to protect the parties and third parties against improper use and disclosure of confidential information, the Administrative Law Judge shall issue a protective order as set forth in the appendix to this section. The Administrative Law Judge may also deny discovery or make any other order which justice requires to protect a party or other person from annoyance, embarrassment, oppression, or undue burden or expense, or to prevent undue delay in the proceeding. Such an order may also be issued to preserve evidence upon a showing that there is substantial reason to believe that such evidence would not otherwise be available for presentation at the hearing.

(e) *Supplementation of disclosures and responses.* A party who has made a mandatory initial disclosure under § 3.31(b) or responded to a request for discovery with a disclosure or response is under a duty to supplement or correct the disclosure or response to include information thereafter acquired if ordered by the Administrative Law Judge or in the following circumstances:

(1) A party is under a duty to supplement at appropriate intervals its mandatory initial disclosures under § 3.31(b) if the party learns that in some material respect the information disclosed is incomplete or incorrect and if the additional or corrective information has not otherwise been made known to the other parties during the discovery process or in writing.

(2) A party is under a duty to amend in a timely manner a prior response to an interrogatory, request for production, or request for admission if the party learns that the response is in some material respect incomplete or incorrect.

(f) *Stipulations.* When approved by the Administrative Law Judge, the parties may by written stipulation (1) provide that depositions may be taken before any person, at any time or place, upon any notice, and in any manner and when so taken may be used like other depositions, and (2) modify the procedures provided by these rules for other methods of discovery.

(g) *Disclosure of privileged or protected information or communications; scope of waiver; obligations of receiving party.* (1)(i) The disclosure of privileged or protected information or communications during a part 3 proceeding or during a Commission precomplaint investigation shall not operate as a waiver if:

(A) The disclosure is inadvertent;

(B) The holder of the privilege or protection took reasonable steps to prevent disclosure; and

(C) The holder promptly took reasonable steps to rectify the error, including notifying any party that received the information or communication of the claim and the basis for it.

(ii) After being notified, the receiving party must promptly return, sequester, or destroy the specified information and any copies it has; must not use or disclose the information until the claim is resolved; must take reasonable steps to retrieve the information if the party disclosed it before being notified; and may promptly present the information to the Administrative Law Judge under seal for a determination of the claim. The producing party must preserve the information until the claim is resolved.

(2) The disclosure of privileged or protected information or communications during a part 3 proceeding or during a Commission precomplaint investigation shall waive the privilege or protection as to undisclosed information or communications only if:

(i) The waiver is intentional;

(ii) The disclosed and undisclosed information or communications concern the same subject matter; and

(iii) They ought in fairness to be considered together.

(h) *Restriction on filings.* Unless otherwise ordered by the Administrative Law Judge in his or her discretion, mandatory initial and supplemental disclosures, interrogatories, depositions, requests for documents, requests for admissions, and answers and responses thereto shall be served upon other parties but shall not be filed with the Office of the Secretary, the Administrative Law Judge, or otherwise provided to the Commission, except to support or oppose a motion or to offer as evidence.

APPENDIX A TO § 3.31: STANDARD PROTECTIVE ORDER.

For the purpose of protecting the interests of the parties and third parties in the above-captioned matter against improper use and disclosure of confidential information submitted or produced in connection with this matter:

IT IS HEREBY ORDERED THAT this Protective Order Governing Confidential Material ("Protective Order") shall govern the handling of all Discovery Material, as hereafter defined.

1. As used in this Order, "confidential material" shall refer to any document or portion thereof that contains privileged information, competitively sensitive information, or sensitive personal information. "Sensitive personal information" shall refer to, but shall not be limited to, an individual's Social Security number, taxpayer identification number, financial account number, credit card or debit card number, driver's license number, state-issued identification number, passport number, date of birth (other than year), and any sensitive health information identifiable by individual, such as an individual's medical records. "Document" shall refer to any discoverable writing, recording, transcript of oral testimony, or electronically stored information in the possession of a party or a third party. "Commission" shall refer to the Federal Trade Commission ("FTC"), or any of its employees, agents, attorneys, and all other persons acting on its behalf, excluding persons retained as consultants or experts for purposes of this proceeding.

2. Any document or portion thereof submitted by a respondent or a third party during a Federal Trade Commission investigation or during the course of this proceeding that is entitled to confidentiality under the Federal Trade Commission Act, or any other federal statute or regulation, or under any federal court or Commission precedent interpreting such statute or regulation, as well as any information that discloses the substance of the contents of any confidential materials derived from a document subject to this Order, shall be treated as confidential material for purposes of this Order. The identity of a third party submitting such confidential material shall also be treated as confidential material for the purposes of this Order where the submitter has requested such confidential treatment.

3. The parties and any third parties, in complying with informal discovery requests, disclosure requirements, or discovery demands in this proceeding may designate any responsive document or portion thereof as confidential material, including documents obtained by them from third parties pursuant to discovery or as otherwise obtained.

4. The parties, in conducting discovery from third parties, shall provide to each third party a copy of this Order so as to inform each such third party of his, her, or its rights herein.

5. A designation of confidentiality shall constitute a representation in good faith and after careful determination that the material is not reasonably believed to be already in the public domain and that counsel believes the material so designated constitutes confidential material as defined in Paragraph 1 of this Order.

6. Material may be designated as confidential by placing on or affixing to the document containing such material (in such manner as will not interfere with the legibility thereof), or if an entire folder or box of documents is confidential by placing or affixing to that folder or box, the designation "CONFIDENTIAL—FTC Docket No. XXXX" or any other appropriate notice that identifies this proceeding, together with an indication of the portion or portions of the document considered to be confidential material. Confidential information contained in electronic documents may also be designated as confidential by placing the designation "CONFIDENTIAL—FTC Docket No. XXXX" or any other appropriate notice that identifies this proceeding, on the face of the CD or DVD or other medium on which the document is produced. Masked or otherwise redacted copies of documents may be produced where the portions masked or redacted contain privileged matter, provided that the copy produced shall indicate at the appropriate point that portions have been masked or redacted and the reasons therefor.

7. Confidential material shall be disclosed only to: (a) the Administrative Law Judge presiding over this proceeding, personnel assisting the Administrative Law Judge, the Commission and its employees, and personnel retained by the Commission as experts or consultants for this proceeding; (b) judges and other court personnel of any court having jurisdiction over any appellate proceedings involving this matter; (c) outside counsel of record for any respondent, their associated attorneys and other employees of their law firm(s), provided they are not employees of a respondent; (d) anyone retained to assist outside counsel in the preparation or hearing of this proceeding including consultants, provided they are not affiliated in any way with a respondent and have signed an agreement to abide by the terms of the protective order; and (e) any witness or deponent who may have authored or received the information in question.

8. Disclosure of confidential material to any person described in Paragraph 7 of this Order shall be only for the purposes of the preparation and hearing of this proceeding, or any appeal therefrom, and for no other purpose whatsoever, provided, however, that the Commission may, subject to taking appropriate steps to preserve the confidentiality of such material, use or disclose confidential material as provided by its Rules of Practice; sections 6(f) and 21 of the Federal Trade Commission Act; or any other legal obligation imposed upon the Commission.

9. In the event that any confidential material is contained in any pleading, motion, exhibit or other paper filed or to be filed with the Secretary of the Commission, the Secretary shall be so informed by the Party filing such papers, and such papers shall be filed *in camera*. To the extent that such material was originally submitted by a third party, the party including the materials in its papers shall immediately notify the submitter of such inclusion. Confidential material contained in the papers shall continue to have *in camera* treatment until further order of the Administrative Law Judge, provided, however, that such papers may be furnished to persons or entities who may receive confidential material pursuant to Paragraphs 7 or 8. Upon or after filing any paper containing confidential material, the filing party shall file on the public record a duplicate copy of the paper that does not reveal confidential material. Further, if the protection for any such material expires, a party may file on the public record a duplicate copy which also contains the formerly protected material.

10. If counsel plans to introduce into evidence at the hearing any document or transcript containing confidential material produced by another party or by a third party, they shall provide advance notice to the other party or third party for purposes of allowing that party to seek an order that the document or transcript be granted *in camera* treatment. If that party wishes *in camera* treatment for the document or transcript, the party shall file an appropriate motion with the Administrative Law Judge within 5 days after it receives such notice. Except where such an order is granted, all documents and transcripts shall be part of the public record. Where *in camera* treatment is granted, a duplicate copy of such document or transcript with the confidential material deleted therefrom may be placed on the public record.

11. If any party receives a discovery request in any investigation or in any other proceeding or matter that may require the disclosure of confidential material submitted by another party or third party, the recipient of the discovery request shall promptly notify the submitter of receipt of such request. Unless a shorter time is mandated by an order of a court, such notification shall be in writing and be received by the submitter at least 10 business days before production, and shall include a copy of this Protective Order and a cover letter that will apprise the submitter of its rights hereunder. Nothing

herein shall be construed as requiring the recipient of the discovery request or anyone else covered by this Order to challenge or appeal any order requiring production of confidential material, to subject itself to any penalties for non-compliance with any such order, or to seek any relief from the Administrative Law Judge or the Commission. The recipient shall not oppose the submitter's efforts to challenge the disclosure of confidential material. In addition, nothing herein shall limit the applicability of Rule 4.11(e) of the Commission's Rules of Practice, 16 CFR 4.11(e), to discovery requests in another proceeding that are directed to the Commission.

12. At the time that any consultant or other person retained to assist counsel in the preparation of this action concludes participation in the action, such person shall return to counsel all copies of documents or portions thereof designated confidential that are in the possession of such person, together with all notes, memoranda or other papers containing confidential information. At the conclusion of this proceeding, including the exhaustion of judicial review, the parties shall return documents obtained in this action to their submitters, provided, however, that the Commission's obligation to return documents shall be governed by the provisions of Rule 4.12 of the Rules of Practice, 16 CFR 4.12.

13. The provisions of this Protective Order, insofar as they restrict the communication and use of confidential discovery material, shall, without written permission of the submitter or further order of the Commission, continue to be binding after the conclusion of this proceeding.

[74 FR 1824, Jan. 13, 2009, as amended at 74 FR 20309, May 1, 2009; 76 FR 52251, 52252, Aug. 22, 2011]

§3.31A Expert discovery.

(a) The parties shall serve each other with a list of experts they intend to call as witnesses at the hearing not later than 1 day after the close of fact discovery, meaning the close of discovery except for depositions and other discovery permitted under §3.24(a)(4), and discovery for purposes of authenticity and admissibility of exhibits. Complaint counsel shall serve the other parties with a report prepared by each of its expert witnesses not later than 14 days after the close of fact discovery. Each respondent shall serve each other party with a report prepared by each of its expert witnesses not later than 14 days after the deadline for service of complaint counsel's expert reports. Complaint counsel shall serve respondents with a list of any rebuttal expert witnesses and a rebuttal report prepared by each such witness not later than 10 days after the deadline for service of respondent's expert reports. Aside from any information required by paragraph (c), a rebuttal report shall be limited to rebuttal of matters set forth in a respondent's expert reports. If material outside the scope of fair rebuttal is presented, a respondent may file a motion not later than 5 days after the deadline for service of complaint counsel's rebuttal reports, seeking appropriate relief with the Administrative Law Judge, including striking all or part of the report, leave to submit a surrebuttal report by respondent's experts, or leave to call a surrebuttal witness and to submit a surrebuttal report by that witness.

(b) No party may call an expert witness at the hearing unless he or she has been listed and has provided reports as required by this section. Each side will be limited to calling at the evidentiary hearing 5 expert witnesses, including any rebuttal or surrebuttal expert witnesses. A party may file a motion seeking leave to call additional expert witnesses due to extraordinary circumstances.

(c) Each report shall be signed by the expert and contain a complete statement of all opinions to be expressed and the basis and reasons therefor; the data, materials, or other information considered by the witness in forming the opinions; any exhibits to be used as a summary of or support for the opinions; the qualifications of the witness, including a list of all publications authored by the witness within the preceding 10 years; the compensation to be paid for the study and testimony; and a listing of any other cases in which the witness has testified as an expert at trial or by deposition within the preceding 4 years. A rebuttal or surrebuttal report need not include any information already included in the initial report of the witness.

(d) A party may depose any person who has been identified as an expert whose opinions may be presented at trial. Unless otherwise ordered by the Administrative Law Judge, a deposition of any expert witness shall be conducted after the disclosure of a report prepared by the witness in accordance with paragraph (a) of this section. Depositions of expert witnesses shall be completed not later than 65 days after the close of fact discovery. Upon motion, the Administrative Law Judge may order further discovery by other means, subject to such restrictions as to scope as the Administrative Law Judge may deem appropriate.

(e) A party may not discover facts known or opinions held by an expert who has been retained or specifically employed by another party in anticipation of litigation or preparation for hearing and who is not listed as a witness for the evidentiary hearing. A party may not discover drafts of any report required by this section, regardless of the form in which the draft is recorded, or any communications between another party's attorney and any of that other party's testifying experts, regardless of the form of the communications, except to the extent that the communications:

(1) Relate to compensation for the expert's study or testimony;

(2) Identify facts or data that the other party's attorney provided and that the expert considered in forming the opinions to be expressed; or

(3) Identify assumptions that the other party's attorney provided and that the expert relied on in forming the opinions to be expressed.

(f) The Administrative Law Judge may, upon a finding of good cause, alter the pre-hearing schedule set forth in this section; provided, however, that no such alteration shall affect the date of the evidentiary hearing noticed in the complaint.

[74 FR 1826, Jan. 13, 2009, as amended at 76 FR 52252, Aug. 22, 2011]

§ 3.32 Admissions.

(a) At any time after 30 days after issuance of a complaint, or after publication of notice of an adjudicative hearing in a rulemaking proceeding under § 3.13, any party may serve on any other party a written request for admission of the truth of any matters relevant to the pending proceeding set forth in the request that relate to statements or opinions of fact or of the application of law to fact, including the genuineness of any documents described in the request. Copies of documents shall be served with the request unless they have been or are otherwise furnished or are known to be, and in the request are stated as being, in the possession of the other party. Each matter of which an admission is requested shall be separately set forth.

(b) The matter is admitted unless, within 10 days after service of the request, or within such shorter or longer time as the Administrative Law Judge may allow, the party to whom the request is directed serves upon the party requesting the admission a sworn written answer or objection addressed to the matter. If objection is made, the reasons therefor shall be stated. The answer shall specifically deny the matter or set forth in detail the reasons why the answering party cannot truthfully admit or deny the matter. A denial shall fairly meet the substance of the requested admission, and when good faith requires that a party qualify its answer or deny only a part of the matter of which an admission is requested, the party shall specify so much of it as is true and qualify or deny the remainder. An answering party may not give lack of information or knowledge as a reason for failure to admit or deny unless the party states that it has made reasonable inquiry and that the information known to or readily obtainable by the party is insufficient to enable it to admit or deny. A party who considers that a matter of which an admission has been requested presents a genuine issue for trial may not, on that ground alone, object to the request; the party may deny the matter or set forth reasons why the party cannot admit or deny it.

(c) Any matter admitted under this rule is conclusively established unless the Administrative Law Judge on motion permits withdrawal or amendment of the admission. The Administrative Law Judge may permit withdrawal or amendment when the presentation of the merits of the proceeding will be subserved thereby and the party who obtained the admission fails to satisfy the Administrative Law Judge that withdrawal or amendment will prejudice him in maintaining his action or defense on the merits. Any admission made by a party under this rule is for the purpose of the pending proceeding only and is not an admission by him for any other purpose nor may it be used against him in any other proceeding.

[43 FR 56865, Dec. 4, 1978, as amended at 50 FR 53305, Dec. 31, 1985; 80 FR 15161, Mar. 23, 2015]

§ 3.33 Depositions.

(a) *In general.* Any party may take a deposition of any named person or of a person or persons described with reasonable particularity, provided that such deposition is reasonably expected to yield information within the scope of discovery under § 3.31(c)(1) and subject to the requirements in § 3.36. Such party may, by motion, obtain from the Administrative Law Judge an order to preserve relevant evidence upon a showing that there is substantial reason to believe that such evidence would not otherwise be available for presentation at the hearing. Depositions may be taken before any person having power to administer oaths, either under the law of the United States or of the state or other place in which the deposition is taken, who may be designated by the party seeking the deposition, provided that such person shall have no interest in the outcome of the proceeding. The party seeking the deposition shall serve upon each person whose deposition is sought and upon each party to the proceeding reasonable notice in writing of the time and place at which it will be taken, and the name and address of each person or persons to be examined, if known, and if the name is not known, a description sufficient to identify them. The parties may stipulate in writing or the Administrative Law Judge may upon motion order that a deposition be taken by telephone or other remote electronic means. A deposition taken by such means is deemed taken at the place where the deponent is to answer questions.

(b) The Administrative Law Judge may rule on motion by a party that a deposition shall not be taken upon a determination that such deposition would not be reasonably expected to meet the scope of discovery set forth under § 3.31(c), or that the value of the deposition would be outweighed by the considerations set forth under § 3.43(b). The fact that a witness testifies at an investigative hearing does not preclude the deposition of that witness.

(c)(1) *Notice to corporation or other organization.* A party may name as the deponent a public or private corporation, partnership, association, governmental agency other than the Federal Trade Commission, or any bureau or regional office of the Federal Trade Commission, and describe with reasonable particularity the matters on which examination is requested. The organization so named shall designate one or more officers, directors, or managing agents, or other persons who consent to testify on its behalf, and may set forth, for each person designated, the matters on which he or she will testify. A subpoena shall advise a non-party organization of its duty to make such a designation. The persons so designated shall testify as to matters known or reasonably available to the organization. This subsection does not preclude taking a deposition by any other procedure authorized in these rules.

(2) *Restriction on filings.* Except as provided in § 3.31(h), notices of depositions shall not be filed with the Office of the Secretary or with the Administrative Law Judge, or otherwise provided to the Commission.

(d) *Taking of deposition.* Each deponent shall be duly sworn, and any party shall have the right to question him or her. Objections to questions or to evidence presented shall be in short form, stating the grounds of objections relied upon. The questions propounded and the answers thereto, together with all objections made, shall be recorded and certified by the officer. Thereafter, upon payment of the charges therefor, the officer shall furnish a copy of the deposition to the deponent and to any party.

(e) *Depositions upon written questions.* A party desiring to take a deposition upon written questions shall serve them upon every other party with a notice stating:

(1) The name and address of the person who is to answer them, and

(2) The name or descriptive title and address of the officer before whom the deposition is to be taken.

A deposition upon written questions may be taken of a public or private corporation, partnership, association, governmental agency other than the Federal Trade Commission, or any bureau or regional office of the Federal Trade Commission in accordance with the provisions of § 3.33(c). Within 30 days after the notice and written questions are served, any other party may serve cross questions upon all other parties. Within 10 days after being served with cross questions, the party taking the deposition may serve redirect questions upon all other parties. Within 10 days after being served with redirect questions, any other party may serve recross questions upon all other parties. The content of any question shall not be disclosed to the deponent prior to the taking of the deposition. A copy of the notice and copies of all questions served shall be delivered by the party taking the deposition to the officer designated in the notice, who shall proceed promptly to take the testimony of the deponent in response to the questions and to prepare, certify, and file or mail the deposition, attaching thereto the copy of the notice and the questions received by him or her. When the deposition is filed the party taking it shall promptly give notice thereof to all other parties.

(f) *Correction of deposition.* A deposition may be corrected, as to form or substance, in the manner provided by § 3.44(b). Any such deposition shall, in addition to the other required procedures, be read to or by the deponent and signed by him or her, unless the parties by stipulation waive the signing or the deponent is unavailable or cannot be found or refuses to sign. If the deposition is not signed by the deponent within 30 days of its submission or attempted submission, the officer shall sign it and certify that the signing has been waived or that the deponent is unavailable or that the deponent has refused to sign, as the case may be, together with the reason for the refusal to sign, if any has been given. The deposition may then be used as though signed unless, on a motion to suppress under § 3.33(g)(2)(iv), the Administrative Law Judge determines that the reasons given for the refusal to sign require rejection of the deposition in whole or in part. In addition to and not in lieu of the procedure for formal correction of the deposition, the deponent may enter in the record at the time of signing a list of objections to the transcription of his or her remarks, stating with specificity the alleged errors in the transcript.

(g) *Objections; errors and irregularities*—(1) *Objections to admissibility.* Subject to the provisions of paragraph (g)(2) of this section, objection may be made at the hearing to receiving in evidence any deposition or part thereof for any reason which would require the exclusion of the evidence if the witness were then present and testifying.

(2) *Effect of errors and irregularities in depositions*—(i) *As to notice.* All errors and irregularities in the notice for taking a deposition are waived unless written objection is promptly served upon the party giving the notice.

(ii) *As to disqualification of officer.* Objection to taking a deposition because of disqualification of the officer before whom it is to be taken is waived unless made before the taking of the deposition begins or as soon thereafter as the disqualification becomes known or could be discovered with reasonable diligence.

(iii) *As to taking of deposition.* (A) Objections to the competency of a witness or to the competency, relevancy, or materiality of testimony are not waived by failure to make them before or during the taking of the deposition, unless the ground of the objection is one which might have been obviated or removed if presented at that time.

(B) Errors and irregularities occurring at the oral examination in the manner of taking the deposition, in the form of the questions or answers, in the oath or affirmation, or in the conduct of parties, and errors of any kind which might be obviated, removed, or cured if promptly presented, are waived unless seasonable objection thereto is made at the taking of the deposition.

(C) Objections to the form of written questions are waived unless served in writing upon all parties within the time allowed for serving the succeeding cross or other questions and within 5 days after service of the last questions authorized.

(iv) *As to completion and return of deposition.* Errors and irregularities in the manner in which the testimony is transcribed or the deposition is prepared, signed, certified, endorsed, or otherwise dealt with by the officer are waived unless a motion to suppress the deposition or some part thereof is made with reasonable promptness after such defect is or with due diligence might have been ascertained.

[74 FR 1827, Jan. 13, 2009, as amended at 80 FR 15162, Mar. 23, 2015]

§ 3.34 Subpoenas.

(a) *Subpoenas ad testificandum.* Counsel for a party may sign and issue a subpoena, on a form provided by the Secretary, requiring a person to appear and give testimony at the taking of a deposition to a party requesting such subpoena or to attend and give testimony at an adjudicative hearing.

(b) *Subpoenas duces tecum; subpoenas to permit inspection of premises.* Counsel for a party may sign and issue a subpoena, on a form provided by the Secretary, commanding a person to produce and permit inspection and copying of designated books, documents, or tangible things, or commanding a person to permit inspection of premises, at a time and place therein specified. The subpoena shall specify with reasonable particularity the material to be produced. The person commanded by the subpoena need not appear in person at the place of production or inspection unless commanded to appear for a deposition or hearing pursuant to paragraph (a) of this section. As used herein, the term "documents" includes written materials, electronically stored information, and tangible things. A subpoena *duces tecum* may be used by any party for purposes of discovery, for obtaining documents for use in evidence, or for both purposes, and shall specify with reasonable particularity the materials to be produced.

(c) *Motions to quash; limitation on subpoenas.* Any motion by the subject of a subpoena to limit or quash the subpoena shall be filed within the earlier of 10 days after service thereof or the time for compliance therewith. Such motions shall set forth all assertions of privilege or other factual and legal objections to the subpoena, including all appropriate arguments, affidavits and other supporting documentation, and shall include the statement required by § 3.22(g). Nothing in paragraphs (a) and (b) of this section authorizes the issuance of subpoenas except in accordance with §§ 3.31(c)(2) and 3.36.

[74 FR 1828, Jan. 13, 2009]

§ 3.35 Interrogatories to parties.

(a) *Availability; procedures for use.* (1) Any party may serve upon any other party written interrogatories, not exceeding 25 in number, including all discrete subparts, to be answered by the party served or, if the party served is a public or private corporation, partnership, association or governmental agency, by any officer or agent, who shall furnish such information as is available to the party. For this purpose, information shall not be deemed to be available insofar as it is in the possession of the Commissioners, the General Counsel, the office of Administrative Law Judges, or the Secretary in his or her capacity as custodian or recorder of any such information, or their respective staffs.

(2) Each interrogatory shall be answered separately and fully in writing under oath, unless it is objected to on grounds not raised and ruled on in connection with the authorization, in which event the reasons for objection shall be stated in lieu of an answer. The answers are to be signed by the person making them, and the objections signed by the attorney making them. The party upon whom the interrogatories have been served shall serve a copy of the answers, and objections, if any, within 30 days after the service of the interrogatories. The Administrative Law Judge may allow a shorter or longer time.

(3) Except as provided in § 3.31(h), interrogatories shall not be filed with the Office of the Secretary, the Administrative Law Judge, or otherwise provided to the Commission.

(b) *Scope; use at hearing.* (1) Interrogatories may relate to any matters that can be inquired into under § 3.31(c)(1), and the answers may be used to the extent permitted by the rules of evidence.

(2) An interrogatory otherwise proper is not necessarily objectionable merely

because an answer to the interrogatory involves an opinion or contention that relates to fact or the application of law to fact, but such an interrogatory need not be answered until after designated discovery has been completed, but in no case later than 3 days before the final prehearing conference.

(c) *Option to produce records.* Where the answer to an interrogatory may be derived or ascertained from the records of the party upon whom the interrogatory has been served or from an examination, audit, or inspection of such records, or from a compilation, abstract, or summary based thereon, and the burden of deriving or ascertaining the answer is substantially the same for the party serving the interrogatory as for the party served, it is a sufficient answer to such interrogatory to specify the records from which the answer may be derived or ascertained and to afford to the party serving the interrogatory reasonable opportunity to examine, audit or inspect such records and to make copies, compilations, abstracts or summaries. The specification shall include sufficient detail to permit the interrogating party to identify readily the individual documents from which the answer may be ascertained.

[74 FR 1828, Jan. 13, 2009, as amended at 80 FR 15162, Mar. 23, 2015]

§ 3.36 Applications for subpoenas for records of or appearances by certain officials or employees of the Commission or officials or employees of governmental agencies other than the Commission, and subpoenas to be served in a foreign country.

(a) *Form.* An application for issuance of a subpoena for the production of documents, as defined in § 3.34(b), or for the issuance of a request requiring the production of or access to documents, other tangible things, or electronically stored information for the purposes described in § 3.37(a), in the possession, custody, or control of the Commissioners, the General Counsel, any Bureau or Office not involved in the matter, the office of Administrative Law Judges, or the Secretary in his or her capacity as custodian or recorder of any such information, or their respective staffs, or of a governmental agency other than the Commission or the officials or employees of such other agency, or for the issuance of a subpoena requiring the appearance of a Commissioner, the General Counsel, an official of any Bureau or Office not involved in the matter, an Administrative Law Judge, or the Secretary in his or her capacity as custodian or recorder of any such information, or their respective staffs, or of an official or employee of another governmental agency, or for the issuance of a subpoena to be served in a foreign country, shall be made in the form of a written motion filed in accordance with the provisions of § 3.22(a). No application for records pursuant to § 4.11 of this chapter or the Freedom of Information Act may be filed with the Administrative Law Judge.

(b) *Content.* The motion shall make a showing that:

(1) The material sought is reasonable in scope;

(2) If for purposes of discovery, the material falls within the limits of discovery under § 3.31(c)(1), or, if for an adjudicative hearing, the material is reasonably relevant;

(3) If for purposes of discovery, the information or material sought cannot reasonably be obtained by other means or, if for purposes of compelling a witness to appear at the evidentiary hearing, the movant has a compelling need for the testimony;

(4) With respect to subpoenas to be served in a foreign country, that the party seeking discovery or testimony has a good faith belief that the discovery requested would be permitted by treaty, law, custom, or practice in the country from which the discovery or testimony is sought and that any additional procedural requirements have been or will be met before the subpoena is served; and

(5) If the subpoena requires access to documents or other tangible things, it meets the requirements of § 3.37.

(c) *Execution.* If an Administrative Law Judge issues an order authorizing a subpoena pursuant to this section, the moving party may forward to the Secretary a request for the authorized subpoena, with a copy of the authorizing order attached. Each such subpoena shall be signed by the Secretary; shall have attached to it a copy of the authorizing order; and shall be served by the moving party only in conjunction with a copy of the authorizing order.

[74 FR 1828, Jan. 13, 2009]

§3.37 Production of documents, electronically stored information, and any tangible things; access for inspection and other purposes.

(a) *Availability; procedures for use.* Any party may serve on another party a request: to produce and permit the party making the request, or someone acting on the party's behalf, to inspect and copy any designated documents or electronically stored information, as defined in §3.34(b), or to inspect and copy, test, or sample any tangible things which are within the scope of §3.31(c)(1) and in the possession, custody, or control of the party upon whom the request is served; or to permit entry upon designated land or other property in the possession or control of the party upon whom the order would be served for the purpose of inspection and measuring, surveying, photographing, testing, or sampling the property or any designated object or operation thereon, within the scope of §3.31(c)(1). Each such request shall specify with reasonable particularity the documents or things to be produced or inspected, or the property to be entered. Each such request shall also specify a reasonable time, place, and manner of making the production or inspection and performing the related acts. Each request may specify the form in which electronically stored information is to be produced, but the requested form of electronically stored information must not be overly burdensome or unnecessarily costly to the producing party. A party shall make documents available as they are kept in the usual course of business or shall organize and label them to correspond with the categories in the request. A person not a party to the action may be compelled to produce documents and things or to submit to an inspection as provided in §3.34. Except as provided in §3.31(h), requests under this section shall not be filed with the Office of the Secretary, the Administrative Law Judge, or otherwise provided to the Commission.

(b) *Response; objections.* No more than 30 days after receiving the request, the response of the party upon whom the request is served shall state, with respect to each item or category, that inspection and related activities will be permitted as requested, unless the request is objected to, in which event the reasons for the objection shall be stated. If objection is made to part of an item or category, the part shall be specified and inspection permitted of the remaining parts. The response may state an objection to a requested form for producing electronically stored information. If the responding party objects to a requested form - or if no form was specified in the request - the party must state the form it intends to use. The party submitting the request may move for an order under §3.38(a) with respect to any objection to or other failure to respond to the request or any part thereof, or any failure to permit inspection as requested.

(c) *Production of documents or electronically stored information.* Unless otherwise stipulated or ordered by the Administrative Law Judge, these procedures apply to producing documents or electronically stored information:

(i) A party must produce documents as they are kept in the usual course of business or must organize and label them to correspond to the categories in the request;

(ii) If a request does not specify a form for producing electronically stored information, a party must produce it in a form in which it is ordinarily maintained or in a reasonably usable form; and

(iii) A party need not produce the same electronically stored information in more than one form.

[74 FR 1829, Jan. 13, 2009]

§3.38 Motion for order compelling disclosure or discovery; sanctions.

(a) *Motion for order to compel.* A party may apply by motion to the Administrative Law Judge for an order compelling disclosure or discovery, including a determination of the sufficiency of the answers or objections with respect to the mandatory initial disclosures required by §3.31(b), a request for admission under §3.32, a deposition under §3.33, an interrogatory under §3.35, or a production of documents or things or access for inspection or other purposes under § 3.37. Any memorandum in support of such motion shall be no longer than 2,500 words. Any response to the motion by the opposing party must be filed within 5 days of receipt of service of the motion and shall be no longer than 2,500 words. These word count limitations include headings, footnotes, and quotations, but do not include the cover, table of contents, table of citations or authorities, glossaries, statements with respect to oral argument, any addendums containing statutes, rules or regulations, any certificates of counsel, proposed form of order, and any attachment required by § 3.45(e). The Administrative Law Judge shall rule on a motion to compel within 3 business days of the date in which the response is due. Unless the Administrative Law Judge determines that the objection is justified, the Administrative Law Judge shall order that an initial disclosure or an answer to any requests for admissions, documents, depositions, or interrogatories be served or disclosure otherwise be made.

(b) If a party or an officer or agent of a party fails to comply with any discovery obligation imposed by these rules, upon motion by the aggrieved party, the Administrative Law Judge or the Commission, or both, may take such action in regard thereto as is just, including but not limited to the following:

(1) Order that any answer be amended to comply with the request, subpoena, or order;

(2) Order that the matter be admitted or that the admission, testimony, documents, or other evidence would have been adverse to the party;

(3) Rule that for the purposes of the proceeding the matter or matters concerning which the order or subpoena was issued be taken as established adversely to the party;

(4) Rule that the party may not introduce into evidence or otherwise rely, in support of any claim or defense, upon testimony by such party, officer, agent, expert, or fact witness, or the documents or other evidence, or upon any other improperly withheld or undisclosed materials, information, witnesses, or other discovery;

(5) Rule that the party may not be heard to object to introduction and use of secondary evidence to show what the withheld admission, testimony, documents, or other evidence would have shown;

(6) Rule that a pleading, or part of a pleading, or a motion or other submission by the party, concerning which the order or subpoena was issued, be stricken, or that a decision of the proceeding be rendered against the party, or both.

(c) Any such action may be taken by written or oral order issued in the course of the proceeding or by inclusion in an initial decision of the Administrative Law Judge or an order or opinion of the Commission. It shall be the duty of parties to seek and Administrative Law Judges to grant such of the foregoing means of relief or other appropriate relief as may be sufficient to compensate for withheld testimony, documents, or other evidence. If in the Administrative Law Judge's opinion such relief would not be sufficient, or in instances where a nonparty fails to comply with a subpoena or order, he or she shall certify to the Commission a request that court enforcement of the subpoena or order be sought.

[74 FR 1829, Jan. 13, 2009]

§ 3.38A Withholding requested material.

(a) Any person withholding material responsive to a subpoena issued pursuant to § 3.34 or § 3.36, written interrogatories requested pursuant to § 3.35, a request for production or access pursuant to § 3.37, or any other request for the production of materials under this part, shall assert a claim of privilege or any similar claim not later than the date set for production of the material. Such person shall, if so directed in the subpoena or other request for production, submit, together with such claim, a schedule which describes the nature of the documents, communications, or tangible things not produced or disclosed - and does so in a manner that, without revealing information itself privileged or protected, will enable other parties to assess the claim. The schedule need not describe any material outside the scope of the duty to search set forth in § 3.31(c)(2) except to the extent that the Administrative Law Judge has authorized additional discovery as provided in that paragraph.

(b) A person withholding material for reasons described in § 3.38A(a) shall comply with the requirements of that subsection in lieu of filing a motion to limit or quash compulsory process.

(Sec. 5 of theFTC Act (15 U.S.C. 45))

[74 FR 1830, Jan. 13, 2009]

§ 3.39 Orders requiring witnesses to testify or provide other information and granting immunity.

(a) Where Commission complaint counsel desire the issuance of an order requiring a witness or deponent to testify or provide other information and granting immunity under 18 U.S.C. 6002, Directors and Assistant Directors of Bureaus and Regional Directors and Assistant Regional Directors of Commission Regional Offices who supervise complaint counsel responsible for presenting evidence in support of the complaint are authorized to determine:

(1) That the testimony or other information sought from a witness or deponent, or prospective witness or deponent, may be necessary to the public interest, and

(2) That such individual has refused or is likely to refuse to testify or provide such information on the basis of his or her privilege against self-incrimination; and to request, through the Commission's liaison officer, approval by the Attorney General for the issuance of such order. Upon receipt of approval by the Attorney General (or his or her designee), the Administrative Law Judge is authorized to issue an order requiring the witness or deponent to testify or provide other information and granting immunity when the witness or deponent has invoked his or her privilege against self-incrimination and it cannot be determined that such privilege was improperly invoked.

(b) Requests by counsel other than Commission complaint counsel for an order requiring a witness to testify or provide other information and granting immunity under 18 U.S.C. 6002 may be made to the Administrative Law Judge and may be made *ex parte*. When such requests are made, the Administrative Law Judge is authorized to determine:

(1) That the testimony or other information sought from a witness or deponent, or prospective witness or deponent, may be necessary to the public interest, and

(2) That such individual has refused or is likely to refuse to testify or provide such information on the basis of his or her privilege against self-incrimination; and, upon making such determinations, to request, through the Commission's liaison officer, approval by the Attorney General for the issuance of an order requiring a witness to testify or provide other information and granting immunity; and, after the Attorney General (or his or her designee) has granted such approval, to issue such order when the witness or deponent has invoked his or her privilege against self-incrimination and it cannot be determined that such privilege was improperly invoked.

(18 U.S.C. 6002, 6004)

[74 FR 1830, Jan. 13, 2009]

§ 3.40 Admissibility of evidence in advertising substantiation cases.

(a) If a person, partnership, or corporation is required through compulsory process under section 6, 9 or 20 of the Act issued after October 26, 1977 to submit to the Commission substantiation in support of an express or an implied representation contained in an advertisement, such person, partnership or corporation shall not thereafter be allowed, in any adjudicative proceeding in which it is alleged that the person, partnership, or corporation lacked a reasonable basis for the representation, and for any purpose relating to the defense of such allegation, to introduce into the record, whether directly or indirectly through references contained in documents or oral testimony, any material of any type whatsoever that was required to be but was not timely submitted in response to said compulsory process. *Provided, however*, that a person, partnership, or corporation is not, within the meaning of this section, required through compulsory process to submit substantiation with respect to those portions of said compulsory process to which such person, partnership, or corporation has raised good faith legal objections in a timely motion pursuant to the Commission's Rules of Practice and Procedure, until the Commission denies such motion; or if the person, partnership, or corporation thereafter continues to refuse to comply, until such process has been judicially enforced.

(b) The Administrative Law Judge shall, upon motion, at any stage exclude all material that was required to be but was not timely submitted in response to compulsory process described in paragraph (a) of this section, or any reference to such material, unless the person, partnership, or corporation demonstrates in a hearing, and the Administrative Law Judge finds, that by the exercise of due diligence the material could not have been timely submitted in response to the compulsory process, and that the Commission was notified of the existence of the material immediately upon its discovery. Said findings of the Administrative Law Judge shall be in writing and shall specify with particularity the evidence relied upon. The rules normally governing the admissibility of evidence in Commission proceedings shall in any event apply to any material coming within the above exception.

[42 FR 56500, Oct. 10, 1977; 42 FR 61450, Dec. 5, 1977, as amended at 45 FR 45578, July 7, 1980]

Subpart E—Hearings

§ 3.41 General hearing rules.

(a) *Public hearings.* All hearings in adjudicative proceedings shall be public unless an *in camera* order is entered by the Administrative Law Judge pursuant to § 3.45(b) of this chapter or unless otherwise ordered by the Commission.

(b) *Expedition.* Hearings shall proceed with all reasonable expedition, and, insofar as practicable, shall be held at one place and shall continue, except for brief intervals of the sort normally involved in judicial proceedings, without suspension until concluded. The hearing will take place on the date specified in the notice accompanying the complaint, pursuant to § 3.11(b)(4), and should be limited to no more than 210 hours. The Commission, upon a showing of good cause, may order a later date for the evidentiary hearing to commence or extend the number of hours for the hearing. Consistent with the requirements of expedition:

(1) The Administrative Law Judge may order hearings at more than one place and may grant a reasonable recess at the end of a case-in-chief for the purpose of discovery deferred during the prehearing procedure if the Administrative Law Judge determines that such recess will materially expedite the ultimate disposition of the proceeding.

(2) When actions involving a common question of law or fact are pending before the Administrative Law Judge, the Commission or the Administrative Law Judge may order a joint hearing of any or all the matters in issue in the actions; the Commission or the Administrative Law Judge may order all the actions consolidated; and the Commission or the Administrative Law Judge may make such orders concerning proceedings therein as may tend to avoid unnecessary costs or delay.

(3) When separate hearings will be conducive to expedition and economy, the Commission or the Administrative Law Judge may order a separate hearing of any claim, or of any separate issue, or of any number of claims or issues.

(4) Each side shall be allotted no more than half of the trial time within which to present its opening statements, *in limine* motions, all arguments excluding the closing argument, direct or cross examinations, or other evidence.

(5) Each side shall be permitted to make an opening statement that is no more than 2 hours in duration.

(6) Each side shall be permitted to make a closing argument no later than 5 days after the last filed proposed findings. The closing argument shall last no longer than 2 hours.

(c) *Rights of parties.* Every party, except intervenors, whose rights are determined under § 3.14, shall have the right of due notice, cross-examination, presentation of evidence, objection, motion, argument, and all other rights essential to a fair hearing.

(d) *Adverse witnesses.* An adverse party, or an officer, agent, or employee thereof, and any witness who appears to be hostile, unwilling, or evasive, may be interrogated by leading questions and may also be contradicted and impeached by the party calling him or her.

(e) Requests for an order requiring a witness to testify or provide other information and granting immunity under 18 U.S.C. 6002 shall be disposed of in accordance with § 3.39.

(f) *Collateral federal court actions.* (1) The pendency of a collateral federal court action that relates to the administrative adjudication shall not stay the proceeding:

(i) Unless a court of competent jurisdiction, or the Commission for good cause, so directs; or

(ii) Except as provided in § 3.26.

(2) A stay shall toll any deadlines set by the rules.

[74 FR 1830, Jan. 13, 2009, as amended at 80 FR 15162, Mar. 23, 2015]

§ 3.42 Presiding officials.

(a) *Who presides.* Hearings in adjudicative proceedings shall be presided over by a duly qualified Administrative Law Judge or by the Commission or one or more members of the Commission sitting as Administrative Law Judges; and the term *Administrative Law Judge* as used in this part means and applies to the Commission or any of its members when so sitting.

(b) *How assigned.* The presiding Administrative Law Judge shall be designated by the Chief Administrative Law Judge or, when the Commission or one or more of its members preside, by the Commission, who shall notify the parties of the Administrative Law Judge designated.

(c) *Powers and duties.* Administrative Law Judges shall have the duty to conduct fair and impartial hearings, to take all necessary action to avoid delay in the disposition of proceedings, and to maintain order. They shall have all powers necessary to that end, including the following:

(1) To administer oaths and affirmations;

(2) To issue subpoenas and orders requiring answers to questions;

(3) To take depositions or to cause depositions to be taken;

(4) To compel admissions, upon request of a party or on their own initiative;

(5) To rule upon offers of proof and receive evidence;

(6) To regulate the course of the hearings and the conduct of the parties and their counsel therein;

(7) To hold conferences for settlement, simplification of the issues, or any other proper purpose;

(8) To consider and rule upon, as justice may require, all procedural and other motions appropriate in an adjudicative proceeding, including motions to open defaults;

(9) To make and file initial decisions;

(10) To certify questions to the Commission for its determination;

(11) To reject written submissions that fail to comply with rule requirements, or deny *in camera* status without prejudice until a party complies with all relevant rules; and

(12) To take any action authorized by the rules in this part or in conformance with the provisions of the Administrative Procedure Act as restated and incorporated in title 5, U.S.C.

(d) *Suspension of attorneys by Administrative Law Judge.* The Administrative Law Judge shall have the authority, for good cause stated on the record, to suspend or bar from participation in a particular proceeding any attorney who shall refuse to comply with his directions, or who shall be guilty of disorderly, dilatory, obstructionist, or contumacious conduct, or contemptuous language in the course of such proceeding. Any attorney so suspended or barred may appeal to the Commission in accordance with the provisions of § 3.23(a). The appeal shall not operate to suspend the hearing unless otherwise ordered by the Administrative Law Judge or the Commission; in the event the hearing is not suspended, the attorney may continue to participate therein pending disposition of the appeal.

(e) *Substitution of Administrative Law Judge.* In the event of the substitution of a new Administrative Law Judge for the one originally designated, any motion predicated upon such substitution shall be made within five (5) days thereafter.

(f) *Interference.* In the performance of their adjudicative functions, Administrative Law Judges shall not be responsible to or subject to the supervision or direction of any officer, employee, or agent engaged in the performance of investigative or prosecuting functions for the Commission, and all direction by the Commission to Administrative Law Judges concerning any adjudicative proceedings shall appear in and be made a part of the record.

(g) *Disqualification of Administrative Law Judges.* (1) When an Administrative Law Judge deems himself disqualified to preside in a particular proceeding, he shall withdraw therefrom by notice on the record and shall notify the Director of Administrative Law Judges of such withdrawal.

(2) Whenever any party shall deem the Administrative Law Judge for any reason to be disqualified to preside, or to continue to preside, in a particular proceeding, such party may file with the Secretary a motion addressed to the Administrative Law Judge to disqualify and remove him, such motion to be supported by affidavits setting forth the alleged grounds for disqualification. If the Administrative Law Judge does not disqualify himself within ten (10) days, he shall certify the motion to the Commission, together with any statement he may wish to have considered by the Commission. The Commission shall promptly determine the validity of the grounds alleged, either directly or on the report of another Administrative Law Judge appointed to conduct a hearing for that purpose.

(3) Such motion shall be filed at the earliest practicable time after the participant learns, or could reasonably have learned, of the alleged grounds for disqualification.

(h) *Failure to comply with Administrative Law Judge's directions.* Any party who refuses or fails to comply with a lawfully issued order or direction of an Administrative Law Judge may be considered to be in contempt of the Commission. The circumstances of any such neglect, refusal, or failure, together with a recommendation for appropriate action, shall be promptly certified by the Administrative Law Judge to the Commission. The Commission may make such orders in regard thereto as the circumstances may warrant.

[32 FR 8449, June 13, 1967, as amended at 37 FR 5609, Mar. 17, 1972; 41 FR 8340, Feb. 26, 1976; 43 FR 56868, Dec. 4, 1978; 46 FR 45750, Sept. 15, 1981; 50 FR 53306, Dec. 31, 1985; 66 FR 17629, Apr. 3, 2001; 80 FR 15162, Mar. 23, 2015]

§ 3.43 Evidence.

(a) *Burden of proof.* Counsel representing the Commission, or any person who has filed objections sufficient to warrant the holding of an adjudicative hearing pursuant to § 3.13, shall have the burden of proof, but the proponent of any factual proposition shall be required to sustain the burden of proof with respect thereto.

(b) *Admissibility.* Relevant, material, and reliable evidence shall be admitted. Irrelevant, immaterial, and unreliable evidence shall be excluded. Evidence, even if relevant, may be excluded if its probative value is substantially outweighed by the danger of unfair prejudice, confusion of the issues, or if the evidence would be misleading, or based on considerations of undue delay, waste of time, or needless presentation of cumulative evidence. Evidence that constitutes hearsay may be admitted if it is relevant, material, and bears satisfactory indicia of reliability so that its use is fair. Hearsay is a statement, other than one made by the declarant while testifying at the hearing, offered in evidence to prove the truth of the matter asserted. If otherwise meeting the standards for admissibility described in this paragraph, depositions, investigational hearings, prior testimony in Commission or other proceedings, expert reports, and any other form of hearsay, shall be admissible and shall not be excluded solely on the ground that they are or contain hearsay. However, absent the consent of the parties, before admitting prior testimony (including expert reports) from other proceedings where either the Commission or respondent did not participate, except for other proceedings where the Commission and at least one respondent did participate, the Administrative Law Judge must make a finding upon the motion of a party seeking the admission of such evidence that the prior testimony would not be duplicative, would not present unnecessary hardship to a party or delay to the proceedings, and would aid in the determination of the matter. Statements or testimony by a party-opponent, if relevant, shall be admitted.

(c) *Admissibility of third party documents.* Extrinsic evidence of authenticity as a condition precedent to admissibility of documents received from third parties is not required with respect to the original or a duplicate of a domestic record of regularly conducted activity by that third party that otherwise meets the standards of admissibility described in paragraph (b) if accompanied by a written declaration of its custodian or other qualified person, in a manner complying with any Act of Congress or rule prescribed by the Supreme Court pursuant to statutory authority, certifying that the record:

(1) Was made at or near the time of the occurrence of the matters set forth by, or from information transmitted by, a person with knowledge of those matters;

(2) Was kept in the course of the regularly conducted activity; and

(3) Was made by the regularly conducted activity as a regular practice.

(d) *Presentation of evidence.* (1) A party is entitled to present its case or defense by sworn oral testimony and documentary evidence, to submit rebuttal evidence, and to conduct such cross-examination as, in the discretion of the Commission or the Administrative Law Judge, may be required for a full and true disclosure of the facts.

(2) The Administrative Law Judge shall exercise reasonable control over the mode and order of interrogating witnesses and presenting evidence so as to—

(i) Make the interrogation and presentation effective for the ascertainment of the truth;

(ii) Avoid needless consumption of time; and

(iii) Protect witnesses from harassment or undue embarrassment.

(3) As respondents are in the best position to determine the nature of documents generated by such respondents and which come from their own files, the burden of proof is on the respondent to introduce evidence to rebut a presumption that such documents are authentic and kept in the regular course of business.

(e) *Information obtained in investigations.* Any documents, papers, books, physical exhibits, or other materials or information obtained by the Commission under any of its powers may be disclosed by counsel representing the Commission when necessary in connection with adjudicative proceedings and may be offered in evidence by counsel representing the Commission in any such proceeding

(f) *Official notice.* "Official notice" may be taken of any material fact that is not subject to reasonable dispute in that it is either generally known within the Commission's expertise or capable of accurate and ready determination by resort to sources whose accuracy cannot reasonably be questioned. If official notice is requested or is taken of a material fact not appearing in the evidence in the record, the parties, upon timely request, shall be afforded an opportunity to disprove such noticed fact.

(g) *Objections.* Objections to evidence shall timely and briefly state the grounds relied upon, but the transcript shall not include argument or debate thereon except as ordered by the Administrative Law Judge. Rulings on all objections shall appear in the record.

(h) *Exceptions.* Formal exception to an adverse ruling is not required.

(i) *Excluded evidence.* When an objection to a question propounded to a witness is sustained, the questioner may make a specific offer of what he or she expects to prove by the answer of the witness, or the Administrative Law Judge may, in his or her discretion, receive and report the evidence in full. Rejected exhibits, adequately marked for identification, shall be retained in the record so as to be available for consideration by any reviewing authority.

[74 FR 1831, Jan. 13, 2009, as amended at 76 FR 52252, Aug. 22, 2011]

§ 3.44 Record.

(a) *Reporting and transcription.* Hearings shall be stenographically reported and transcribed by the official reporter of the Commission under the supervision of the Administrative Law Judge, and the original transcript shall be a part of the record and the sole official transcript. Upon a motion by any party, for good cause shown the Administrative Law Judge may order that the live oral testimony of all witnesses be video recorded digitally, at the expense of the moving party, and in such cases the video recording and the written transcript of the testimony shall be made part of the record. If a video recording is so ordered, the moving party shall not pay or retain any person or entity to perform such recording other than the reporter designated by the Commission to transcribe the proceeding, except by order of the Administrative Law Judge upon a finding of good cause. In any order allowing for video recording by a person or entity other than the Commission's designated reporter, the Administrative Law Judge shall prescribe standards and procedures for the video recording to ensure that it is a complete and accurate record of the witnesses' testimony. Copies of the written transcript and video recording are available from the reporter at rates not to exceed the maximum rates fixed by contract between the Commission and the reporter. Copies of a video recording made by a person or entity other than the reporter shall be available at the same rates, or no more than the actual cost of duplication, whichever is higher.

(b) *Corrections.* Corrections of the official transcript may be made only when they involve errors affecting substance and then only in the manner herein provided. Corrections ordered by the Administrative Law Judge or agreed to in a written stipulation signed by all counsel and parties not represented by counsel, and approved by the Administrative Law Judge, shall be included in the record, and such stipulations, except to the extent they are capricious or without substance, shall be approved by the Administrative Law Judge. Corrections shall not be ordered by the Administrative Law Judge except upon notice and opportunity for the hearing of objections. Such corrections shall be made by the official reporter by furnishing substitute type pages, under the usual certificate of the reporter, for insertion in the official record. The original uncorrected pages shall be retained in the files of the Commission.

(c) *Closing of the hearing record.* Upon completion of the evidentiary hearing, the Administrative Law Judge shall issue an order closing the hearing record after giving the parties 3 business days to determine if the record is complete or needs to be supplemented. The Administrative Law Judge shall retain the discretion to permit or order correction of the record as provided in §3.44(b).

[74 FR 1832, Jan. 13, 2009, as amended at 76 FR 52252, Aug. 22, 2011]

§3.45 *In camera* orders.

(a) *Definition.* Except as hereinafter provided, material made subject to an *in camera* order will be kept confidential and not placed on the public record of the proceeding in which it was submitted. Only respondents, their counsel, authorized Commission personnel, and court personnel concerned with judicial review may have access thereto, provided that the Administrative Law Judge, the Commission and reviewing courts may disclose such *in camera* material to the extent necessary for the proper disposition of the proceeding.

(b) *In camera treatment of material.* A party or third party may obtain *in camera* treatment for material, or portions thereof, offered into evidence only by motion to the Administrative Law Judge. Parties who seek to use material obtained from a third party subject to confidentiality restrictions must demonstrate that the third party has been given at least 10 days notice of the proposed use of such material. Each such motion must include an attachment containing a copy of each page of the document in question on which *in camera* or otherwise confidential excerpts appear. The Administrative Law Judge shall order that such material, whether admitted or rejected, be placed *in camera* only after finding that its public disclosure will likely result in a clearly defined, serious injury to the person, partnership, or corporation requesting *in camera* treatment or after finding that the material constitutes sensitive personal information. "Sensitive personal information" shall include, but shall not be limited to, an individual's Social Security number, taxpayer identification number, financial account number, credit card or debit card number, driver's license number, state-issued identification number, passport number, date of birth (other than year), and any sensitive health information identifiable by individual, such as an individual's medical records. For material other than sensitive personal information, a finding that public disclosure will likely result in a clearly defined, serious injury shall be based on the standard articulated in *H.P. Hood & Sons, Inc.*, 58 F.T.C. 1184, 1188 (1961); *see also Bristol-Myers Co.*, 90 F.T.C. 455, 456 (1977), which established a three-part test that was modified by *General Foods Corp.*, 95 F.T.C. 352, 355 (1980). The party submitting material for which *in camera* treatment is sought must provide, for each piece of such evidence and affixed to such evidence, the name and address of any person who should be notified in the event that the Commission intends to disclose *in camera* information in a final decision. No material, or portion thereof, offered into evidence, whether admitted or rejected, may be withheld from the public record unless it falls within the scope of an order issued in accordance with this section, stating the date on which *in camera* treatment will expire, and including:

(1) A description of the material;

(2) A statement of the reasons for granting *in camera* treatment; and

(3) A statement of the reasons for the date on which *in camera* treatment will expire, except in the case of sensitive personal information, which shall be accorded permanent *in camera* treatment unless disclosure or an expiration date is required or provided by law. For *in camera* material other than sensitive personal information, an expiration date may not be omitted except in unusual circumstances, in which event the order shall state with specificity the reasons why the need for confidentiality of the material, or portion thereof at issue is not likely to decrease over time, and any other reasons why such material is entitled to *in camera* treatment for an indeterminate period. If an *in camera* order is silent as to duration, without explanation, then it will expire 3 years after its date of issuance. Material subject to an *in camera* order shall be segregated from the public record and filed in a sealed envelope, or other appropriate container, bearing the title, the docket number of the proceeding, the notation "*In Camera* Record under § 3.45," and the date on which *in camera* treatment expires. If the Administrative Law Judge has determined that *in camera* treatment should be granted for an indeterminate period, the notation should state that fact. Parties are not required to provide documents subject to *in camera* treatment, including documents obtained from third parties, to any individual or entity other than the Administrative Law Judge, counsel for other parties, and, during an appeal, the Commission or a federal court.

(c) *Release of in camera material. In camera* material constitutes part of the confidential records of the Commission and is subject to the provisions of § 4.11 of this chapter.

(d) *Briefs and other submissions referring to in camera or confidential information.* Parties shall not disclose information that has been granted *in camera* status pursuant to § 3.45(b) or is subject to confidentiality protections pursuant to a protective order in the public version of proposed findings, briefs, or other documents. This provision does not preclude references in such proposed findings, briefs, or other documents to *in camera* or other confidential information or general statements based on the content of such information.

(e) *When in camera or confidential information is included in briefs and other submissions.* If a party includes specific information that has been granted *in camera* status pursuant to paragraph (b) of this section or is subject to confidentiality protections pursuant to a protective order in any document filed in a proceeding under this part, the party shall file 2 versions of the document. A complete version shall be marked "*In Camera*" or "Subject to Protective Order," as appropriate, on every page and shall be filed with the Secretary and served by the party on the other parties in accordance with the Commission's rules. Submitters of *in camera* or other confidential material should mark any such material in the complete versions of their submissions in a conspicuous matter, such as with highlighting or bracketing. References to *in camera* or confidential material must be supported by record citations to relevant evidentiary materials and associated Administrative Law Judge *in camera* or other confidentiality rulings to confirm that *in camera* or other confidential treatment is warranted for such material. In addition, the document must include an attachment containing a copy of each page of the document in question on which *in camera* or otherwise confidential excerpts appear, and providing the name and address of any person who should be notified of the Commission's intent to disclose in a final decision any of the *in camera* or otherwise confidential information in the document. Any time period within which these rules allow a party to respond to a document shall run from the date the party is served with the complete version of the document. An expurgated version of the document, marked "Public Record" on every page and omitting the *in camera* and confidential information and attachment that appear in the complete version, shall be filed with the Secretary within 5 days after the filing of the complete version, unless the Administrative Law Judge or the Commission directs otherwise, and shall be served by the party on the other parties in accordance with the rules in this part. The expurgated version shall indicate any omissions with brackets or ellipses, and its pagination and depiction of text on each page shall be identical to that of the *in camera* version.

(f) *When in camera or confidential information is included in rulings or recommendations of the Administrative Law Judge.* If the Administrative Law Judge includes in any ruling or recommendation information that has been granted *in camera* status pursuant to paragraph (b) of this section or is subject to confidentiality protections pursuant to a protective order, the Administrative Law Judge shall file 2 versions of the ruling or recommendation. A complete version shall be marked "*In Camera*" or "Subject to Protective Order," as appropriate, on every page and shall be served upon the parties. The complete version will be placed in the *in camera* record of the proceeding. An expurgated version, to be filed within 5 days after the filing of the complete version, shall omit the *in camera* and confidential information that appears in the complete version, shall be marked "Public Record" on every page, shall be served upon the parties, and shall be included in the public record of the proceeding.

(g) *Provisional in camera rulings.* The Administrative Law Judge may make a provisional grant of *in camera* status to materials if the showing required in §3.45(b) cannot be made at the time the material is offered into evidence but the Administrative Law Judge determines that the interests of justice would be served by such a ruling. Within 20 days of such a provisional grant of *in camera* status, the party offering the evidence or an interested third party must present a motion to the Administrative Law Judge for a final ruling on whether *in camera* treatment of the material is appropriate pursuant to §3.45(b). If no such motion is filed, the Administrative Law Judge may either exclude the evidence, deny *in camera* status, or take such other action as is appropriate.

[74 FR 1832, Jan. 13, 2009, as amended at 76 FR 52253, Aug. 22, 2011; 80 FR 15162, Mar. 3, 2015]

§3.46 Proposed findings, conclusions, and order.

(a) *General.* Within 21 days of the closing of the hearing record, each party may file with the Secretary for consideration of the Administrative Law Judge proposed findings of fact, conclusions of law, and rule or order, together with reasons therefor and briefs in support thereof. Such proposals shall be in writing, shall be served upon all parties, and shall contain adequate references to the record and authorities relied on. If a party includes in the proposals information that has been granted *in camera* status pursuant to §3.45(b), the party shall file 2 versions of the proposals in accordance with the procedures set forth in §3.45(e). Reply findings of fact, conclusions of law, and briefs may be filed by each party within 10 days of service of the initial proposed findings.

(b) *Exhibit index*. The first statement of proposed findings of fact and conclusions of law filed by a party shall include an index listing for each exhibit offered by the party and received in evidence:

(1) The exhibit number, followed by

(2) The exhibit's title or a brief description if the exhibit is untitled;

(3) The transcript page at which the Administrative Law Judge ruled on the exhibit's admissibility or a citation to any written order in which such ruling was made;

(4) The transcript pages at which the exhibit is discussed;

(5) An identification of any other exhibit which summarizes the contents of the listed exhibit, or of any other exhibit of which the listed exhibit is a summary;

(6) A cross-reference, by exhibit number, to any other portions of that document admitted as a separate exhibit on motion by any other party; and

(7) A statement whether the exhibit has been accorded *in camera* treatment, and a citation to the *in camera* ruling.

(c) *Witness index*. The first statement of proposed findings of fact and conclusions of law filed by a party shall also include an index to the witnesses called by that party, to include for each witness:

(1) The name of the witness;

(2) A brief identification of the witness;

(3) The transcript pages at which any testimony of the witness appears; and

(4) A statement whether the witness testimony has been accorded *in camera* treatment, and a citation to the *in camera* ruling.

(d) *Stipulated indices*. As an alternative to the filing of separate indices, the parties are encouraged to stipulate to joint exhibit and witness indices at the time the first statement of proposed findings of fact and conclusions of law is due to be filed.

(e) *Rulings*. The record shall show the Administrative Law Judge's ruling on each proposed finding and conclusion, except when the order disposing of the proceeding otherwise informs the parties of the action taken.

[74 FR 1833, Jan. 13, 2009, as amended at 80 FR 15162, Mar. 23, 2015]

Subpart F—Decision

§ 3.51 Initial decision.

(a) *When filed and when effective*. The Administrative Law Judge shall file an initial decision within 70 days after the filing of the last filed initial or reply proposed findings of fact, conclusions of law and order pursuant to § 3.46, within 85 days of the closing the hearing record pursuant to § 3.44(c) where the parties have waived the filing of proposed findings, or within 14 days after the granting of a motion for summary decision following a referral of such motion from the Commission. The Administrative Law Judge may extend any of these time periods by up to 30 days for good cause. The Commission may further extend any of these time periods for good cause. Except in cases subject to § 3.52(a), once issued, the initial decision shall become the decision of the Commission 30 days after service thereof upon the parties or 30 days after the filing of a timely notice of appeal, whichever shall be later, unless a party filing such a notice shall have perfected an appeal by the timely filing of an appeal brief or the Commission shall have issued an order placing the case on its own docket for review or staying the effective date of the decision.

(b) *Exhaustion of administrative remedies*. An initial decision shall not be considered final agency action subject to judicial review under 5 U.S.C. 704. Any objection to a ruling by the Administrative Law Judge, or to a finding, conclusion or a provision of the order in the initial decision, which is not made a part of an appeal to the Commission shall be deemed to have been waived.

(c) *Content, format for filing*. (1) An initial decision shall be based on a consideration of the whole record relevant to the issues decided, and shall be supported by reliable and probative evidence. The initial decision shall include a statement of findings of fact (with specific page references to principal supporting items of evidence in the record) and conclusions of law, as well as the reasons or basis therefor, upon all the material issues of fact, law, or discretion presented on the record (or those designated under paragraph (c)(2) of this section) and an appropriate rule or order. Rulings containing information granted *in camera* status pursuant to §3.45 shall be filed in accordance with §3.45(f).

(2) The initial decision shall be prepared in a common word processing format, such as WordPerfect or Microsoft Word, and shall be filed by the Administrative Law Judge with the Office of the Secretary in both electronic and paper versions.

(3) When more than one claim for relief is presented in an action, or when multiple parties are involved, the Administrative Law Judge may direct the entry of an initial decision as to one or more but fewer than all of the claims or parties only upon an express determination that there is no just reason for delay and upon an express direction for the entry of initial decision.

(d) *By whom made.* The initial decision shall be made and filed by the Administrative Law Judge who presided over the hearings, except when he or she shall have become unavailable to the Commission.

(e) *Reopening of proceeding by Administrative Law Judge; termination of jurisdiction.* (1) At any time from the close of the hearing record pursuant to §3.44(c) until the filing of his or her initial decision, an Administrative Law Judge may reopen the proceeding for the reception of further evidence for good cause shown.

(2) Except for the correction of clerical errors or pursuant to an order of remand from the Commission, the jurisdiction of the Administrative Law Judge is terminated upon the filing of his or her initial decision with respect to those issues decided pursuant to paragraph (c)(1) of this section.

[74 FR 1834, Jan. 13, 2009]

§3.52 Appeal from initial decision.

(a) *Automatic review of cases in which the Commission sought preliminary relief in federal court; timing.* For proceedings with respect to which the Commission has sought preliminary relief in federal court under 15 U.S.C. 53(b), the Commission will review the initial decision without the filing of a notice of appeal.

(1) In such cases, any party may file objections to the initial decision or order of the Administrative Law Judge by filing its opening appeal brief, subject to the requirements in paragraph (c), within 20 days of the issuance of the initial decision. Any party may respond to any objections filed by another party by filing an answering brief, subject to the requirements of paragraph (d), within 20 days of service of the opening brief. Any party may file a reply to an answering brief, subject to the requirements of paragraph (e), within 5 days of service of the answering brief. Unless the Commission orders that there shall be no oral argument, it will hold oral argument within 10 days after the deadline for the filing of any reply briefs. The Commission will issue its final decision pursuant to §3.54 within 45 days after oral argument. If no oral argument is scheduled, the Commission will issue its final decision pursuant to §3.54 within 45 days after the deadline for the filing of any reply briefs.

(2) If no objections to the initial decision are filed, the Commission may in its discretion hold oral argument within 10 days after the deadline for the filing of objection, and will issue its final decision pursuant to §3.54 within 45 days after oral argument. If no oral argument is scheduled, the Commission will issue its final decision pursuant to §3.54 within 45 days after the deadline for the filing of objections.

(b) *Review in all other cases; timing.* (1) In all cases other than those subject to paragraph (a), any party may file objections to the initial decision or order of the Administrative Law Judge by filing a notice of appeal with the Secretary within 10 days after service of the initial decision. The notice shall specify the party or parties against whom the appeal is taken and shall designate the initial decision and order or part thereof appealed from. If a timely notice of appeal is filed by a party, any other party may thereafter file a notice of appeal within 5 days after service of the first notice, or within 10 days after service of the initial decision, whichever period expires last.

(2) In such cases, any party filing a notice of appeal must perfect its appeal by filing its opening appeal brief, subject to the requirements in paragraph (c), within 30 days of the issuance of the initial decision. Any party may respond to the opening appeal brief by filing an answering brief, subject to the requirements of paragraph (d), within 30 days of service of the opening brief. Any party may file a reply to an answering brief, subject to the requirements of paragraph (e), within 7 days of service of the answering brief. Unless the Commission orders that there shall be no oral argument, it will hold oral argument within 15 days after the deadline for the filing of any reply briefs. The Commission will issue its final decision pursuant to §3.54 within 100 days after oral argument. If no oral argument is scheduled, the Commission will issue its final decision pursuant to §3.54 within 100 days after the deadline for the filing of any reply briefs.

(c) *Appeal brief.* (1) The opening appeal brief shall contain, in the order indicated, the following:

(i) A subject index of the matter in the brief, with page references, and a table of cases (alphabetically arranged), textbooks, statutes, and other material cited, with page references thereto;

(ii) A concise statement of the case, which includes a statement of facts relevant to the issues submitted for review, and a summary of the argument, which must contain a succinct, clear, and accurate statement of the arguments made in the body of the brief, and which must not merely repeat the argument headings;

(iii) A specification of the questions intended to be urged;

(iv) The argument presenting clearly the points of fact and law relied upon in support of the position taken on each question, with specific page references to the record and the legal or other material relied upon; and

(v) A proposed form of order for the Commission's consideration instead of the order contained in the initial decision.

(2) The brief shall not, without leave of the Commission, exceed 14,000 words.

(d) *Answering brief.* The answering brief shall contain a subject index, with page references, and a table of cases (alphabetically arranged), textbooks, statutes, and other material cited, with page references thereto, as well as arguments in response to the appellant's appeal brief. The answering brief shall not, without leave of the Commission, exceed 14,000 words.

(e) *Reply brief.* The reply brief shall be limited to rebuttal of matters in the answering brief and shall not, without leave of the Commission, exceed 7,000 words. The Commission will not consider new arguments or matters raised in reply briefs that could have been raised earlier in the principal briefs. No further briefs may be filed except by leave of the Commission.

(f) *In camera information.* If a party includes in any brief to be filed under this section information that has been granted *in camera* status pursuant to §3.45(b) or is subject to confidentiality provisions pursuant to a protective order, the party shall file 2 versions of the brief in accordance with the procedures set forth in §3.45(e). The time period specified by this section within which a party may file an answering or reply brief will begin to run upon service on the party of the *in camera* or confidential version of a brief.

(g) *Signature.* (1) The original of each brief filed shall have a hand-signed signature by an attorney of record for the party, or in the case of parties not represented by counsel, by the party itself, or by a partner if a partnership, or by an officer of the party if it is a corporation or an unincorporated association.

(2) Signing a brief constitutes a representation by the signer that he or she has read it; that to the best of his or her knowledge, information, and belief, the statements made in it are true; that it is not interposed for delay; that it complies with the applicable word count limitation; and that to the best of his or her knowledge, information, and belief, it complies with all the other rules in this part. If a brief is not signed or is signed with intent to defeat the purpose of this section, it may be stricken as sham and false and the proceeding may go forward as though the brief has not been filed.

(h) *Oral argument.* All oral arguments shall be public unless otherwise ordered by the Commission. Oral arguments will be held in all cases on appeal or review to the Commission, unless the Commission otherwise orders upon its own initiative or upon request of any party made at the time of filing his or her brief. Oral arguments before the Commission shall be reported stenographically, unless otherwise ordered, and a member of the Commission absent from an oral argument may participate in the consideration and decision of the appeal in any case in which the oral argument is stenographically reported.

(i) *Corrections in transcript of oral argument.* The Commission will entertain only joint motions of the parties requesting corrections in the transcript of oral argument, except that the Commission will receive a unilateral motion which recites that the parties have made a good faith effort to stipulate to the desired corrections but have been unable to do so. If the parties agree in part and disagree in part, they should file a joint motion incorporating the extent of their agreement, and, if desired, separate motions requesting those corrections to which they have been unable to agree. The Secretary, pursuant to delegation of authority by the Commission, is authorized to prepare and issue in the name of the Commission a brief "Order Correcting Transcript" whenever a joint motion to correct transcript is received.

(j) *Briefs of amicus curiae.* A brief of an amicus curiae may be filed by leave of the Commission granted on motion with notice to the parties or at the request of the Commission, except that such leave shall not be required when the brief is presented by an agency or officer of the United States; or by a State, territory, commonwealth, or the District of Columbia, or by an agency or officer of any of them. The brief may be conditionally filed with the motion for leave. A motion for leave shall identify the interest of the applicant and state how a Commission decision in the matter would affect the applicant or persons it represents. The motion shall also state the reasons why a brief of an amicus curiae is desirable. Except as otherwise permitted by the Commission, an amicus curiae shall file its brief within the time allowed the parties whose position as to affirmance or reversal the amicus brief will support. The Commission shall grant leave for a later filing only for cause shown, in which event it shall specify within what period such brief must be filed. A motion for an amicus curiae to participate in oral argument will be granted only for extraordinary reasons. An amicus brief may be no more than one-half the maximum length authorized by these rules for a party's principal brief.

(k) *Word count limitation.* The word count limitations in this section include headings, footnotes and quotations, but do not include the cover, table of contents, table of citations or authorities, glossaries, statements with respect to oral argument, any addendums containing statutes, rules or regulations, any certificates of counsel, proposed form of order, and any attachment required by § 3.45(e). Extensions of word count limitations are disfavored, and will only be granted where a party can make a strong showing that undue prejudice would result from complying with the existing limit.

[74 FR 1834, Jan. 13, 2009, as amended at 76 FR 52253, Aug. 22, 2011; 80 FR 15162, Mar. 23, 2015]

§ 3.53 Review of initial decision in absence of appeal.

An order by the Commission placing a case on its own docket for review will set forth the scope of such review and the issues which will be considered and will make provision for the filing of briefs if deemed appropriate by the Commission.

§ 3.54 Decision on appeal or review.

(a) Upon appeal from or review of an initial decision, the Commission will consider such parts of the record as are cited or as may be necessary to resolve the issues presented and, in addition, will, to the extent necessary or desirable, exercise all the powers which it could have exercised if it had made the initial decision.

(b) In rendering its decision, the Commission will adopt, modify, or set aside the findings, conclusions, and rule or order contained in the initial decision, and will include in the decision a statement of the reasons or basis for its action and any concurring and dissenting opinions.

(c) In those cases where the Commission believes that it should have further information or additional views of the parties as to the form and content of the rule or order to be issued, the Commission, in its discretion, may withhold final action pending the receipt of such additional information or views.

(d) The order of the Commission disposing of adjudicative hearings under the Fair Packaging and Labeling Act will be published in the FEDERAL REGISTER and, if it contains a rule or regulation, will specify the effective date thereof, which will not be prior to the ninetieth (90th) day after its publication unless the Commission finds that emergency conditions exist necessitating an earlier effective date, in which event the Commission will specify in the order its findings as to such conditions.

§ 3.55 Reconsideration.

Within fourteen (14) days after completion of service of a Commission decision, any party may file with the Commission a petition for reconsideration of such decision, setting forth the relief desired and the grounds in support thereof. Any petition filed under this subsection must be confined to new questions raised by the decision or final order and upon which the petitioner had no opportunity to argue before the Commission. Any party desiring to oppose such a petition shall file an answer thereto within ten (10) days after service upon him of the petition. The filing of a petition for reconsideration shall not operate to stay the effective date of the decision or order or to toll the running of any statutory time period affecting such decision or order unless specifically so ordered by the Commission.

[32 FR 8449, June 13, 1967, as amended at 61 FR 50650, Sept. 26, 1996]

§ 3.56 Effective date of orders; application for stay.

(a) Other than consent orders, an order to cease and desist under section 5 of the FTC Act becomes effective upon the sixtieth day after service, except as provided in section 5(g)(3) of the FTC Act, and except for divestiture provisions, as provided in section 5(g)(4) of the FTC Act.

(b) Any party subject to a cease and desist order under section 5 of the FTC Act, other than a consent order, may apply to the Commission for a stay of all or part of that order pending judicial review. If, within 30 days after the application was received by the Commission, the Commission either has denied or has not acted on the application, a stay may be sought in a court of appeals where a petition for review of the order is pending.

(c) An application for stay shall state the reasons a stay is warranted and the facts relied upon, and shall include supporting affidavits or other sworn statements, and a copy of the relevant portions of the record. The application shall address the likelihood of the applicant's success on appeal, whether the applicant will suffer irreparable harm if a stay is not granted, the degree of injury to other parties if a stay is granted, and why the stay is in the public interest.

(d) An application for stay shall be filed within 30 days of service of the order on the party. Such application shall be served in accordance with the provisions of § 4.4(b) of this part that are applicable to service in adjudicative proceedings. Any party opposing the application may file an answer within 5 business days after receipt of the application. The applicant may file a reply brief, limited to new matters raised by the answer, within 3 business days after receipt of the answer.

[60 FR 37748, July 21, 1995]

Subpart G [Reserved]

Subpart H—Reopening of Proceedings

§ 3.71 Authority.

Except while pending in a U.S. court of appeals on a petition for review (after the transcript of the record has been filed) or in the U.S. Supreme Court, a proceeding may be reopened by the Commission at any time in accordance with §3.72. Any person subject to a Commission decision containing a rule or order which has become effective, or an order to cease and desist which has become final may file a request to reopen the proceeding in accordance with §2.51.

[44 FR 40637, July 12, 1979]

§3.72 Reopening.

(a) *Before statutory review.* At any time prior to the expiration of the time allowed for filing a petition for review or prior to the filing of the transcript of the record of a proceeding in a U.S. court of appeals pursuant to a petition for review, the Commission may upon its own initiative and without prior notice to the parties reopen the proceeding and enter a new decision modifying or setting aside the whole or any part of the findings as to the facts, conclusions, rule, order, or opinion issued by the Commission in such proceeding.

(b) *After decision has become final.* (1) Whenever the Commission is of the opinion that changed conditions of fact or law or the public interest may require that a Commission decision containing a rule or order which has become effective, or an order to cease and desist which has become final by reason of court affirmance or expiration of the statutory period for court review without a petition for review having been filed, or a Commission decision containing an order dismissing a proceeding, should be altered, modified, or set aside in whole or in part, the Commission will, except as provided in §2.51, serve upon each person subject to such decision (in the case of proceedings instituted under §3.13, such service may be by publication in the FEDERAL REGISTER) an order to show cause, stating the changes it proposes to make in the decision and the reasons they are deemed necessary. Within thirty (30) days after service of such order to show cause, any person served may file an answer thereto. Any person not responding to the order within the time allowed may be deemed to have consented to the proposed changes.

(2) Whenever an order to show cause is not opposed, or if opposed but the pleadings do not raise issues of fact to be resolved, the Commission, in its discretion, may decide the matter on the order to show cause and answer thereto, if any, or it may serve upon the parties (in the case of proceedings instituted under §3.13, such service may be by publication in FEDERAL REGISTER) a notice of hearing, setting forth the date when the cause will be heard. In such a case, the hearing will be limited to the filing of briefs and may include oral argument when deemed necessary by the Commission. When the pleadings raise substantial factual issues, the Commission will direct such hearings as it deems appropriate, including hearings for the receipt of evidence by it or by an Administrative Law Judge. Unless otherwise ordered and insofar as practicable, hearings before an Administrative Law Judge to receive evidence shall be conducted in accordance with subparts B, C, D, and E of part 3 of this chapter. Upon conclusion of hearings before an Administrative Law Judge, the record and the Administrative Law Judge's recommendations shall be certified to the Commission for final disposition of the matter.

(3) *Termination of existing orders*—(i) *Generally.* Notwithstanding the foregoing provisions of this rule, and except as provided in paragraphs (b)(3)(ii) and (iii) of this section, an order issued by the Commission before August 16, 1995, will be deemed, without further notice or proceedings, to terminate 20 years from the date on which the order was first issued, or on January 2, 1996, whichever is later.

(ii) *Exception.* This paragraph applies to the termination of an order issued before August 16, 1995, where a complaint alleging a violation of the order was or is filed (with or without an accompanying consent decree) in federal court by the United States or the Federal Trade Commission while the order remains in force, either on or after August 16, 1995, or within the 20 years preceding that date. If more than one complaint was or is filed while the order remains in force, the relevant complaint for purposes of this paragraph will be the latest filed complaint. An order subject to this paragraph will terminate 20 years from the date on which a court complaint described in this paragraph was or is filed, except as provided in the following sentence. If the complaint was or is dismissed, or a federal court rules or has ruled that the respondent did not violate any provision of the order, and the dismissal or ruling was or is not appealed, or was or is upheld on appeal, the order will terminate according to paragraph (b)(3)(i) of this section as though the complaint was never filed; provided, however, that the order will not terminate between the date that such complaint is filed and the later of the deadline for appealing such dismissal or ruling and the date such dismissal or ruling is upheld on appeal. The filing of a complaint described in this paragraph will not affect the duration of any order provision that has expired, or will expire, by its own terms. The filing of a complaint described in this paragraph also will not affect the duration of an order's application to any respondent that is not named in the complaint.

(iii) *Stay of Termination.* Any party to an order may seek to stay, in whole or part, the termination of the order as to that party pursuant to paragraph (b)(3) (i) or (ii) of this section. Petitions for such stays shall be filed in accordance with the procedures set forth in § 2.51 of these rules. Such petitions shall be filed on or before the date on which the order would be terminated pursuant to paragraph (b)(3) (i) or (ii) of this section. Pending the disposition of such a petition, the order will be deemed to remain in effect without interruption.

(iv) *Orders not terminated.* Nothing in § 3.72(b)(3) is intended to apply to *in camera* orders or other procedural or interlocutory rulings by an Administrative Law Judge or the Commission.

[32 FR 8449, June 13, 1967, as amended at 44 FR 40637, July 12, 1979; 45 FR 21623, Apr. 2, 1980; 60 FR 58515, Nov. 28, 1995]

Subpart I—Recovery of Awards Under the Equal Access to Justice Act in Commission Proceedings

AUTHORITY: 5 U.S.C. 504 and 5 U.S.C. 553(b).

SOURCE: 63 FR 36341, July 6, 1998, unless otherwise noted.

§ 3.81 General provisions.

(a) *Purpose of these rules.* The Equal Access to Justice Act, 5 U.S.C. 504 (called "the Act" in this subpart), provides for the award of attorney fees and other expenses to eligible individuals and entities who are parties to adversary adjudicative proceedings under part 3 of this title. The rules in this subpart describe the parties eligible for awards, how to apply for awards, and the procedures and standards that the Commission will use to make them.

(1) *When an eligible party will receive an award.* An eligible party will receive an award when:

(i) It prevails in the adjudicative proceeding, unless the Commission's position in the proceeding was substantially justified or special circumstances make an award unjust. Whether or not the position of the agency was substantially justified will be determined on the basis of the administrative record as a whole that is made in the adversary proceeding for which fees and other expenses are sought; or

(ii) The agency's demand is substantially in excess of the decision of the adjudicative officer, and is unreasonable when compared with that decision, under all the facts and circumstances of the case. *Demand* means the express final demand made by the agency prior to initiation of the adversary adjudication, but does not include a recitation by the agency of the statutory penalty in the administrative complaint or elsewhere when accompanied by an express demand for a lesser amount.

(b) *When the Act applies.* (1) Section 504(a)(1) of the Act applies to any adversarial adjudicative proceeding pending before the Commission at any time after October 1, 1981. This includes proceedings begun before October 1, 1981, if final Commission action has not been taken before that date.

(2) Section 504(a)(4) applies to any adversarial adjudicative proceeding pending before the Commission at any time on or after March 29, 1996.

(c) *Proceedings covered.* (1) The Act applies to all adjudicative proceedings under part 3 of the rules of practice as defined in §3.2, except hearings relating to the promulgation, amendment, or repeal of rules under the Fair Packaging and Labeling Act.

(2) [Reserved]

(d) *Eligibility of applicants.* (1) To be eligible for an award of attorney fees and other expenses under the Act, the applicant must be a party to the adjudicative proceeding in which it seeks an award. The term *party* is defined in 5 U.S.C. 551(3). The applicant must show that it meets all conditions of eligibility set out in this subpart.

(2) The types of eligible applicants are as follows:

(i) An individual with a net worth of not more than $2 million;

(ii) The sole owner of an unincorporated business who has a net worth of not more than $7 million, including both personal and business interests, and not more than 500 employees;

(iii) A charitable or other tax-exempt organization described in section 501(c)(3) of the Internal Revenue Code (26 U.S.C. 501(c)(3)) with not more than 500 employees;

(iv) A cooperative association as defined in section 15(a) of the Agricultural Marketing Act (12 U.S.C. 1141j(a)) with not more than 500 employees;

(v) Any other partnership, corporation, association, unit of local government, or organization with a net worth of not more than $7 million and not more than 500 employees; and

(vi) For purposes of receiving an award for fees and expenses for defending against an excessive Commission demand, any small entity, as that term is defined under 5 U.S.C. 601.

(3) Eligibility of a party shall be determined as of the date the proceeding was initiated.

(4) An applicant who owns an unincorporated business will be considered as an "individual" rather than a "sole owner of an unincorporated business" if the issues on which the applicant prevails are related primarily to personal interests rather than to business interests.

(5) The employees of an applicant include all persons who regularly perform services for remuneration for the applicant, under the applicant's direction and control. Part-time employees shall be included on a proportional basis.

(6) The net worth and number of employees of the applicant and all of its affiliates shall be aggregated to determine eligibility. Any individual, corporation or other entity that directly or indirectly controls or owns a majority of the voting shares or other interest of the applicant, or any corporation or other entity of which the applicant directly or indirectly owns or controls a majority of the voting shares or other interest, will be considered an affiliate for purposes of this part, unless the Administrative Law Judge determines that such treatment would be unjust and contrary to the purposes of the Act in light of the actual relationship between the affiliated entities. In addition, the Administrative Law Judge may determine that financial relationships of the applicant other than those described in this paragraph constitute special circumstances that would make an award unjust.

(7) An applicant that participates in a proceeding primarily on behalf of one or more other persons or entities that would be ineligible is not itself eligible for an award.

(e) *Standards for awards.* (1) For a prevailing party:

(i) A prevailing applicant will receive an award for fees and expenses incurred after initiation of the adversary adjudication in connection with the entire adversary adjudication, or on a substantive portion of the adversary adjudication that is sufficiently significant and discrete to merit treatment as a separate unit unless the position of the agency was substantially justified. The burden of proof that an award should not be made to an eligible prevailing applicant is on complaint counsel, which may avoid an award by showing that its position had a reasonable basis in law and fact.

(ii) An award to prevailing party will be reduced or denied if the applicant has unduly or unreasonably protracted the proceeding or if special circumstances make an award unjust.

(2) For a party defending against an excessive demand:

(i) An eligible applicant will receive an award for fees and expenses incurred after initiation of the adversary adjudication related to defending against the excessive portion of a Commission demand that is substantially in excess of the decision of the adjudicative officer and is unreasonable when compared with that decision under all the facts and circumstances of the case.

(ii) An award will be denied if the applicant has committed a willful violation of law or otherwise acted in bad faith or if special circumstances make an award unjust.

(f) *Allowable fees and expenses.* (1) Awards will be based on rates customarily charged by persons engaged in the business of acting as attorneys, agents and expert witnesses, even if the services were made available without charge or at a reduced rate to the applicant.

(2) No award for the fee of an attorney or agent under these rules may exceed the hourly rate specified in 5 U.S.C. 504(b)(1)(A). No award to compensate an expert witness may exceed the highest rate at which the Commission paid expert witnesses for similar services at the time the fees were incurred. The appropriate rate may be obtained from the Office of the Executive Director. However, an award may also include the reasonable expenses of the attorney, agent, or witness as a separate item, if the attorney, agent or witness ordinarily charges clients separately for such expenses.

(3) In determining the reasonableness of the fee sought for an attorney, agent or expert witness, the Administrative Law Judge shall consider the following:

(i) If the attorney, agent or witness is in private practice, his or her customary fee for similar services, or, if an employee of the applicant, the fully allocated cost of the services;

(ii) The prevailing rate for similar services in the community in which the attorney, agent or witness ordinarily performs services;

(iii) The time actually spent in the representation of the applicant;

(iv) The time reasonably spent in light of the difficulty or complexity of the issues in the proceeding; and

(v) Such other factors as may bear on the value of the services provided.

(4) The reasonable cost of any study, analysis, engineering report, test, project or similar matter prepared on behalf of a party may be awarded, to the extent that the charge for the service does not exceed the prevailing rate for similar services, and the study or other matter was necessary for preparation of the applicant's case.

(5) Any award of fees or expenses under the Act is limited to fees and expenses incurred after initiation of the adversary adjudication and, with respect to excessive demands, the fees and expenses incurred in defending against the excessive portion of the demand.

(g) *Rulemaking on maximum rates for attorney fees.* If warranted by an increase in the cost of living or by special circumstances (such as limited availability of attorneys qualified to handle certain types of proceedings), the Commission may, upon its own initiative or on petition of any interested person or group, adopt regulations providing that attorney fees may be awarded at a rate higher than the rate specified in 5 U.S.C. 504(b)(1)(A) per hour in some or all the types of proceedings covered by this part. Rulemaking under this provision will be in accordance with Rules of Practice part 1, subpart C of this chapter.

§ 3.82 Information required from applicants.

(a) *Contents of application.* An application for an award of fees and expenses under the Act shall contain the following:

(1) Identity of the applicant and the proceeding for which the award is sought;

(2) A showing that the applicant has prevailed; or, if the applicant has not prevailed, a showing that the Commission's demand was the final demand before initiation of the adversary adjudication and that it was substantially in excess of the decision of the adjudicative officer and was unreasonable when compared with that decision;

(3) Identification of the Commission position(s) that applicant alleges was (were) not substantially justified; or, identification of the Commission's demand that is alleged to be excessive and unreasonable and an explanation as to why the demand was excessive and unreasonable;

(4) A brief description of the type and purpose of the organization or business (unless the applicant is an individual);

(5) A statement of how the applicant meets the criteria of §3.81(d);

(6) The amount of fees and expenses incurred after the initiation of the adjudicative proceeding or, in the case of a claim for defending against an excessive demand, the amount of fees and expenses incurred after the initiation of the adjudicative proceeding attributable to the excessive portion of the demand;

(7) Any other matters the applicant wishes the Commission to consider in determining whether and in what amount an award should be made; and

(8) A written verification under oath or under penalty or perjury that the information provided is true and correct accompanied by the signature of the applicant or an authorized officer or attorney.

(b) *Net worth exhibit.* (1) Each applicant except a qualified tax-exempt organization or cooperative association must provide with its application a detailed exhibit showing the net worth of the application and any affiliates (as defined in §3.81(d)(6)) when the proceeding was initiated. The exhibit may be in any form convenient to the applicant that provides full disclosure of the applicant's and its affiliates' assets and liabilities and is sufficient to determine whether the applicant qualifies under the standards in this part. The Administrative Law Judge may require an applicant to file additional information to determine its eligibility for an award.

(2) Ordinarily, the net worth exhibit will be included in the public record of the proceeding. However, if an applicant objects to public disclosure of information in any portion of the exhibit and believes there are legal grounds for withholding it from disclosure, the applicant may submit that portion of the exhibit directly to the Administrative Law Judge in a sealed envelope labeled "Confidential Financial Information," accompanied by a motion to withhold the information from public disclosure. The motion shall describe the information sought to be withheld and explain, in detail, why it falls within one or more of the specific exemptions from mandatory disclosure under the Freedom of Information Act, 5 U.S.C. 552(b) (1) through (9), why public disclosure of the information would adversely affect the applicant, and why disclosure is not required in the public interest. The material in question shall be served on complaint counsel but need not be served on any other party to the proceeding. If the Administrative Law Judge finds that the information should not be withheld from disclosure, it shall be placed in the public record of the proceeding. Otherwise, any request to inspect or copy the exhibit shall be disposed of in accordance with §4.11.

(c) *Documentation of fees and expenses.* The application shall be accompanied by full documentation of the fees and expenses incurred after initiation of the adversary adjudication, including the cost of any study, analysis, engineering report, test, project or similar matter, for which an award is sought. With respect to a claim for fees and expenses involving an excessive demand, the application shall be accompanied by full documentation of the fees and expenses incurred after initiation of the adversary adjudication, including the cost of any study, analysis, engineering report, test, project or similar matter, for which an award is sought attributable to the portion of the demand alleged to be excessive and unreasonable. A separate itemized statement shall be submitted for each professional firm or individual whose services are covered by the application, showing the hours spent in connection with the proceeding by each individual, a description of the specific services performed, the rate at which each fee has been computed, any expenses for which reimbursement is sought, the total amount claimed, and the total amount paid or payable by the applicant or by any other person or entity for the services provided. The Administrative Law Judge may require the applicant to provide vouchers, receipts, or other substantiation for any expenses claimed.

(d) *When an application may be filed*—(1) For a prevailing party:

(i) An application may be filed not later than 30 days after the Commission has issued an order or otherwise taken action that results in final disposition of the proceeding.

(ii) If review or reconsideration is sought or taken of a decision as to which an applicant believes it has prevailed, proceedings for the award of fees shall be stayed pending final disposition of the underlying controversy.

(2) For a party defending against an excessive demand:

(i) An application may be filed not later than 30 days after the Commission has issued an order or otherwise taken action that results in final disposition of the proceeding.

(ii) If review or reconsideration is sought or taken of a decision as to which an applicant believes the agency's demand was excessive and unreasonable, proceedings for the award of fees and expenses shall be stayed pending final disposition of the underlying controversy.

(3) For purposes of this subpart, *final disposition* means the later of—

(i) The date that the initial decision of the Administrative Law Judge becomes the decision of the Commission pursuant to § 3.51(a);

(ii) The date that the Commission issues an order disposing of any petitions for reconsideration of the Commission's final order in the proceeding; or

(iii) The date that the Commission issues a final order or any other final resolution of a proceeding, such as a consent agreement, settlement or voluntary dismissal, which is not subject to a petition for reconsideration.

§ 3.83 Procedures for considering applicants.

(a) *Filing and service of documents.* Any application for an award or other pleading or document related to an application shall be filed and served on all parties as specified in §§ 4.2 and 4.4(b) of this chapter, except as provided in § 3.82(b)(2) for confidential financial information.

(b) *Answer to application.* (1) Within 30 days after service of an application, complaint counsel may file an answer to the application. Unless complaint counsel requests an extension of time for filing or files a statement of intent to negotiate under paragraph (b)(2) of this section, failure to file an answer within the 30-day period may be treated as a consent to the award requested.

(2) If complaint counsel and the applicant believe that the issues in the fee application can be settled, they may jointly file a statement of their intent to negotiate a settlement. The filing of this statement shall extend the time for filing an answer for an additional 30 days, and further extensions may be granted by the Administrative Law Judge upon request by complaint counsel and the applicant.

(3) The answer shall explain in detail any objections to the award requested and identify the facts relied on in support of complaint counsel's position. If the answer is based on any alleged facts not already in the record of the proceeding, complaint counsel shall include with the answer either supporting affidavits or a request for further proceedings under paragraph (f) of this section.

(c) *Reply.* Within 15 days after service of an answer, the applicant may file a reply. If the reply is based on any alleged facts not already in the record of the proceeding, the applicant shall include with the reply either supporting affidavits or a request for further proceedings under paragraph (f) of this section.

(d) *Comments by other parties.* Any party to a proceeding other than the applicant and complaint counsel may file comments on an application within 30 days after it is served or on an answer within 15 days after it is served. A commenting party may not participate further in proceedings on the application unless the Administrative Law Judge determines that the public interest requires such participation in order to permit full exploration of matters in the comments.

(e) *Settlement.* The applicant and complaint counsel may agree on a proposed settlement of the award before final action on the application. A proposed award settlement entered into in connection with a consent agreement covering the underlying proceeding will be considered in accordance with §3.25. The Commission may request findings of fact or recommendations on the award settlement from the Administrative Law Judge. A proposed award settlement entered into after the underlying proceeding has been concluded will be considered and may be approved or disapproved by the Administrative Law Judge subject to Commission review under paragraph (h) of this section. If an applicant and complaint counsel agree on a proposed settlement of an award before an application has been filed, the application shall be filed with the proposed settlement.

(f) *Further proceedings.* (1) Ordinarily, the determination of an award will be made on the basis of the written record. However, on request of either the applicant or complaint counsel, or on his or her own initiative, the Administrative Law Judge may order further proceedings, such as an informal conference, oral argument, additional written submissions or an evidentiary hearing. Such further proceedings shall be held only when necessary for full and fair resolution of the issues arising from the application, and shall be conducted as promptly as possible.

(2) A request that the Administrative Law Judge order further proceedings under this section shall specifically identify the information sought or the disputed issues and shall explain why the additional proceedings are necessary to resolve the issues.

(g) *Decision.* The Administrative Law Judge shall issue an initial decision on the application within 30 days after closing proceedings on the application.

(1) *For a decision involving a prevailing party:* The decision shall include written findings and conclusions on the applicant's eligibility and status as a prevailing party, and an explanation of the reasons for any difference between the amount requested and the amount awarded. The decision shall also include, if at issue, findings on whether the agency's position was substantially justified, whether the applicant unduly protracted the proceedings, or whether special circumstances make an award unjust.

(2) *For a decision involving an excessive agency demand:* The decision shall include written findings and conclusions on the applicant's eligibility and an explanation of the reasons why the agency's demand was or was not determined to be substantially in excess of the decision of the adjudicative officer and was or was not unreasonable when compared with that decision. That decision shall be based upon all the facts and circumstances of the case. The decision shall also include, if at issue, findings on whether the applicant has committed a willful violation of law or otherwise acted in bad faith, or whether special circumstances make an award unjust.

(h) *Agency review.* Either the applicant or complaint counsel may seek review of the initial decision on the fee application by filing a notice of appeal under §3.52(a), or the Commission may decide to review the decision on its own initiative, in accordance with §3.53. If neither the applicant nor complaint counsel seeks review and the Commission does not take review on its own initiative, the initial decision on the application shall become a final decision of the Commission 30 days after it is issued. Whether to review a decision is a matter within the discretion of the Commission. If review is taken, the Commission will issue a final decision on the application or remand the application to the Administrative Law Judge for further proceedings.

(i) *Judicial review.* Judicial review of final Commission decisions on awards may be sought as provided in 5 U.S.C. 504(c)(2).

(j) *Payment of award.* An applicant seeking payment of an award shall submit to the Secretary of the Commission a copy of the Commission's final decision granting the award, accompanied by a statement that the applicant will not seek review of the decision in the United States courts. The agency will pay the amount awarded to the applicant within 60 days, unless judicial review of the award or of the underlying decision of the adjudicative proceeding has been sought by the applicant or any party to the proceeding.

[63 FR 36341, July 6, 1998, as amended at 76 FR 52253, Aug. 22, 2011; 80 FR 25941, May 6, 2015]

PART 4—MISCELLANEOUS RULES

AUTHORITY: 15 U.S.C. 46.

§ 4.1 Appearances.

(a) *Qualifications*—(1) *Attorneys*—(i) *U.S.-admitted.* Members of the bar of a Federal court or of the highest court of any State or Territory of the United States are eligible to practice before the Commission.

(ii) *European Community (EC)-qualified.* Persons who are qualified to practice law in a Member State of the European Community and authorized to practice before The Commission of the European Communities in accordance with Regulation No. 99/63/EEC are eligible to practice before the Commission.

(iii) Any attorney desiring to appear before the Commission or an Administrative Law Judge may be required to show to the satisfaction of the Commission or the Administrative Law Judge his or her acceptability to act in that capacity.

(2) *Others.* (i) Any individual or member of a partnership involved in any proceeding or investigation may appear on behalf or himself or of such partnership upon adequate identification. A corporation or association may be represented by a bona fide officer thereof upon a showing of adequate authorization.

(ii) At the request of counsel representing any party in an adjudicative proceeding, the Administrative Law Judge may permit an expert in the same discipline as an expert witness to conduct all or a portion of the cross-examination of such witness.

(b) *Restrictions as to former members and employees*—(1) *General prohibition.* Except as provided in this section, or otherwise specifically authorized by the Commission, no former member or employee ("former employee" or "employee") of the Commission may communicate to or appear before the Commission, as attorney or counsel, or otherwise assist or advise behind-the-scenes, regarding a formal or informal proceeding or investigation[1] (except that a former employee who is disqualified solely under paragraph (b)(1)(ii) or paragraph (b)(1)(iv) of this section, is not prohibited from assisting or advising behind-the-scenes) if:

(i) The former employee participated personally and substantially on behalf of the Commission in the same proceeding or investigation in which the employee now intends to participate;

(ii) The participation would begin within two years after the termination of the former employee's service and,

[1] It is important to note that a new "proceeding or investigation" may be considered the same matter as a seemingly separate "proceeding or investigation" that was pending during the former employee's tenure. This is because a "proceeding or investigation" may continue in another form or in part. In determining whether two matters are actually the same, the Commission will consider: the extent to which the matters involve the same or related facts, issues, confidential information and parties; the time elapsed; and the continuing existence of an important Federal interest. See 5 CFR 2637.201(c)(4). For example, where a former employee intends to participate in an investigation of compliance with a Commission order, submission of a request to reopen an order, or a proceeding with respect to reopening an order, the matter will be considered the same as the adjudicative proceeding or investigation that resulted in the order. A former employee who is uncertain whether the matter in which he seeks clearance to participate is wholly separate from any matter that was pending during his tenure should seek advice from the General Counsel or the General Counsel's designee before participating.

within a period of one year prior to the employee's termination, the proceeding or investigation was pending under the employee's official responsibility;

(iii) Nonpublic documents or information pertaining to the proceeding or investigation in question, and of the kind delineated in §4.10(a), came to, or would be likely to have come to, the former employee's attention in the course of the employee's duties, (unless Commission staff determines that the nature of the documents or information is such that no present advantage could thereby be derived); or

(iv) The former employee's participation would begin within one year after the employee's termination and, at the time of termination, the employee was a member of the Commission or a "senior employee" as defined in 18 U.S.C. 207(c).

(2) *Clearance request required.* Any former employee, before participating in a Commission proceeding or investigation (see footnote 1), whether through an appearance before a Commission official or behind-the-scenes assistance, shall file with the Secretary a request for clearance to participate, containing the information listed in §4.1(b)(4) if:

(i) The proceeding or investigation was pending in the Commission while the former employee served;

(ii) A proceeding or investigation from which such proceeding or investigation directly resulted was pending during the former employee's service; or

(iii) Nonpublic documents or information pertaining to the proceeding or investigation in question, and of the kind delineated in §4.10(a), came to or would likely have come to the former employee's attention in the course of the employee's duties, and the employee left the Commission within the previous three years.

NOTE: This requirement applies even to a proceeding or investigation that had not yet been initiated formally when the former employee terminated employment, if the employee had learned nonpublic information relating to the subsequently initiated proceeding or investigation.

(3) *Exceptions.* (i) Paragraphs (b) (1) and (2) of this section do not apply to:

(A) Making a pro se filing of any kind;

(B) Submitting a request or appeal under the Freedom of Information Act, the Privacy Act, or the Government in the Sunshine Act;

(C) Testifying under oath (except that a former employee who is subject to the restrictions contained in paragraph (b)(1)(i) of this section with respect to a particular matter may not, except pursuant to court order, serve as an expert witness for any person other than the United States in that same matter);

(D) Submitting a statement required to be made under penalty of perjury; or

(E) Appearing on behalf of the United States.

(ii) With the exception of subparagraph (b)(1)(iv), paragraphs (b) (1) and (2) of this section do not apply to participating in a Commission rulemaking proceeding, including submitting comments on a matter on which the Commission has invited public comment.

(iii) Paragraph (b)(1)(iv) of this section does not apply to submitting a statement based on the former employee's own special knowledge in the particular area that is the subject of the statement, provided that no compensation is thereby received, other than that regularly provided by law or by §4.5 for witnesses.

(iv) Paragraph (b)(2) of this section does not apply to filing a premerger notification form or participating in subsequent events concerning compliance or noncompliance with Section 7A of the Clayton Act, 15 U.S.C. 18a, or any regulation issued under that section.

(4) *Request contents.* Clearance requests filed pursuant to §4.1(b)(2) shall contain:

(i) The name and matter number (if known) of the proceeding or investigation in question;

(ii) A description of the contemplated participation;

(iii) The name of the Commission office(s) or division(s) in which the former employee was employed and the position(s) the employee occupied;

(iv) A statement whether, while employed by the Commission, the former employee participated in any proceeding or investigation concerning the same company, individual, or industry currently involved in the matter in question;

(v) A certification that while employed by the Commission, the employee never participated personally and substantially in the same matter or proceeding;

(vi) If the employee's Commission employment terminated within the past two years, a certification that the matter was not pending under the employee's official responsibility during any part of the one year before the employee's termination;

(vii) If the employee's Commission employment terminated within the past three years, either a declaration that nonpublic documents or information pertaining to the proceeding or investigation in question, and of the kind delineated in §4.10(a), never came to the employee's attention, or a description of why the employee believes that such nonpublic documents or information could not confer a present advantage to the employee or to the employee's client in the proceeding or investigation in question; and

(viii) A certification that the employee has read, and understands, both the criminal conflict of interest law on post-employment activities (18 U.S.C. 207) and this Rule in their entirety.

(5) *Definitions.* The following definitions apply for purposes of this section:

(i) *Behind-the-scenes* participation includes any form of professional consultation, assistance, or advice to anyone about the proceeding or investigation in question, whether formal or informal, oral or written, direct or indirect.

(ii) *Communicate to or appear before* means making any oral or written communication to, or any formal or informal appearance before, the Commission or any of its members or employees on behalf of any person (except the United States) with the intent to influence.

(iii) *Directly resulted from* means that the proceeding or investigation in question emanated from an earlier phase of the same proceeding or investigation or from a directly linked, antecedent investigation. The existence of some attenuated connection between a proceeding or investigation that was pending during the requester's tenure and the proceeding or investigation in question does not constitute a direct result.

(iv) *Pending under the employee's official responsibility* means that the former employee had the direct administrative or operating authority to approve, disapprove, or otherwise direct official actions in the proceeding or investigation, irrespective of whether the employee's authority was intermediate or final, and whether it was exercisable alone or only in conjunction with others.

(v) *Personal and substantial participation.* A former employee participated in the proceeding or investigation personally if the employee either participated directly or directed a subordinate in doing so. The employee participated substantially if the involvement was significant to the matter or reasonably appeared to be significant. A series of peripheral involvements may be considered insubstantial, while a single act of approving or participating in a critical step may be considered substantial.

(vi) *Present advantage.* Whether exposure to nonpublic information about the proceeding or investigation could confer a present advantage to a former employee will be analyzed and determined on a case-by-case basis. Relevant factors include, *inter alia*, the nature and age of the information, its relation and current importance to the proceeding or investigation in question, and the amount of time that has passed since the employee left the Commission.

(vii) *Proceeding or investigation* shall be interpreted broadly and includes an adjudicative or other proceeding; the consideration of an application; a request for a ruling or other determination; a contract; a claim; a controversy; an investigation; or an interpretive ruling.

(6) *Advice as to whether clearance request is required.* A former employee may ask the General Counsel, either orally or in writing, whether the employee is required to file a request for clearance to participate in a Commission matter pursuant to paragraph (b)(2) of this section. The General

Counsel, or the General Counsel's designee, will make any such determination within three business days.

(7) *Deadline for determining clearance requests.* By the close of the tenth business day after the date on which the clearance request is filed, the General Counsel, or the General Counsel's designee, will notify the requester either that:

(i) The request for clearance has been granted;

(ii) The General Counsel or the General Counsel's designee has decided to recommend that the Commission prohibit the requester's participation; or

(iii) The General Counsel or the General Counsel's designee is, for good cause, extending the period for reaching a determination on the request by up to an additional ten business days.

(8) *Participation of partners or associates of former employees.* (i) If a former employee is prohibited from participating in a proceeding or investigation by virtue of having worked on the matter personally and substantially while a Commission employee, no partner or legal or business associate of that individual may participate except after filing with the Secretary of the Commission an affidavit attesting that:

(A) The former employee will not participate in the proceeding or investigation in any way, directly or indirectly (and describing how the former employee will be screened from participating);

(B) The former employee will not share in any fees resulting from the participation;

(C) Everyone who intends to participate is aware of the requirement that the former employee be screened;

(D) The client(s) have been informed; and

(E) The matter was not brought to the participant(s) through the active solicitation of the former employee.

(ii) If the Commission finds that the screening measures being taken are unsatisfactory or that the matter was brought to the participant(s) through the active solicitation of the former employee, the Commission will notify the participant(s) to cease the representation immediately.

(9) *Effect on other standards.* The restrictions and procedures in this section are intended to apply in lieu of restrictions and procedures that may be adopted by any state or jurisdiction, insofar as such restrictions and procedures apply to appearances or participation in Commission proceedings or investigations. Nothing in this section supersedes other standards of conduct applicable under paragraph (e) of this section. Requests for advice about this section, or about any matter related to other applicable rules and standards of ethical conduct, shall be directed to the Office of the General Counsel.

(c) *Public disclosure.* Any request for clearance filed by a former member or employee pursuant to this section, as well as any written response, are part of the public records of the Commission, except for information exempt from disclosure under §4.10(a) of this chapter. Information identifying the subject of a nonpublic Commission investigation will be redacted from any request for clearance or other document before it is placed on the public record.

(d) *Notice of appearance.* Any attorney desiring to appear before the Commission or an Administrative Law Judge on behalf of a person or party shall file with the Secretary of the Commission a written notice of appearance, stating the basis for eligibility under this section and including the attorney's jurisdiction of admission/qualification, attorney identification number, if applicable, and a statement by the appearing attorney attesting to his/her good standing within the legal profession. No other application shall be required for admission to practice, and no register of attorneys will be maintained.

(e) *Reprimand, suspension, or disbarment of attorneys.* (1)(i) The following provisions govern the evaluation of allegations of misconduct by attorneys practicing before the Commission who are not employed by the Commission.[1] The Commission may publicly

[1] The standards of conduct and disciplinary procedures under this §4.1(e) apply only to outside attorneys practicing before the Commission and not to Commission staff. Allegations of misconduct by Commission employees will be handled pursuant to procedures for employee discipline or pursuant to investigations by the Office of Inspector General.

reprimand, suspend, or disbar from practice before the Commission any such person who has practiced, is practicing, or holds himself or herself out as entitled to practice before the Commission if it finds that such person:

(A) Does not possess the qualifications required by §4.1(a);

(B) Has failed to act in a manner consistent with the rules of professional conduct of the attorney's state(s) of licensure;

(C) Has engaged in obstructionist, contemptuous, or unprofessional conduct during the course of any Commission proceeding or investigation; or

(D) Has knowingly or recklessly given false or misleading information, or has knowingly or recklessly participated in the giving of false information to the Commission or any officer or employee of the Commission.[2]

(ii) An attorney may be responsible for another attorney's violation of this paragraph (e) if the attorney orders, or with knowledge of the specific conduct, ratifies the conduct involved. In addition, an attorney who has direct supervisory authority over another attorney may be responsible for that attorney's violation of this paragraph (e) if the supervisory attorney knew of the conduct at a time when its consequences could have been avoided or mitigated but failed to take reasonable remedial action.

(2) Allegations of attorney misconduct in violation of paragraph (e)(1) of this section may be proffered by any person possessing information concerning the alleged misconduct. Any such allegations may be submitted orally or in writing to a Bureau Officer who will evaluate the sufficiency of the allegations in the first instance to determine whether further action by the Commission is warranted. The Director of the Bureau or office responsible for the matter about which the allegations are made, or the Director's designee, shall serve as the Bureau Officer.

(3) After review and evaluation of the allegations, any supporting materials, and any additional information that the Bureau Officer may acquire, the Bureau Officer, if he or she determines that further action is warranted, shall in writing notify the subject of the complaint of the underlying allegations and potential sanctions available to the Commission under this section, and provide him or her an opportunity to respond to the allegations and provide additional relevant information and material. The Bureau Officer may request that the Commission issue a resolution authorizing the use of compulsory process, and may thereafter initiate the service of compulsory process, to assist in obtaining information for the purpose of making a recommendation to the Commission whether further action may be warranted.

(4) If the Bureau Officer, after review and evaluation of the allegations, supporting material, response by the subject of the allegations, if any, and all additional available information and material, determines that no further action is warranted, he or she may close the matter if the Commission has not issued a resolution authorizing the use of compulsory process. In the event the Bureau Officer determines that further Commission action may be warranted, or if the Commission has issued a resolution authorizing the use of compulsory process, he or she shall make a recommendation to the Commission. The recommendation shall include all relevant information and material as to whether further Commission action, or any other disposition of the matter, may be warranted.

(5) If the Commission has reason to believe, after review of the Bureau Officer's recommendation, that an attorney has engaged in professional misconduct of the type described in paragraph (e)(1) of this section, the Commission may institute administrative disciplinary proceedings proposing public reprimand, suspension, or disbarment of the attorney from practice before the Commission. Except as provided in paragraph (e)(7) of this section, administrative disciplinary proceedings shall be handled in accordance with the following procedures:

(i) The Commission shall serve the respondent attorney with an order to

[2] For purposes of this rule, knowingly giving false or misleading information includes knowingly omitting material facts necessary to make any oral or written statements not misleading in light of the circumstances under which they were made.

show cause why the Commission should not impose sanctions against the attorney. The order to show cause shall specify the alleged misconduct at issue and the possible sanctions. The order to show cause shall be accompanied by all declarations, deposition transcripts, or other evidence the staff wishes the Commission to consider in support of the allegations of misconduct.

(ii) Within 14 days of service of the order to show cause, the respondent may file a response to the allegations of misconduct. If the response disputes any of the allegations of misconduct, it shall do so with specificity and include all materials the respondent wishes the Commission to consider relating to the allegations. If no response is filed, the allegations shall be deemed admitted.

(iii) If, upon considering the written submissions of the respondent, the Commission determines that there remains a genuine dispute as to any material fact, the Commission may order further proceedings to be presided over by an Administrative Law Judge or by one or more Commissioners sitting as Administrative Law Judges (hereinafter referred to collectively as the Administrative Law Judge), or by the Commission. The Commission order shall specify the nature and scope of any proceeding, including whether live testimony will be heard and whether any pre-hearing discovery will be allowed and if so to what extent. The attorney respondent shall be granted due opportunity to be heard in his or her own defense and may be represented by counsel. If the written submissions of the respondent raise no genuine dispute of material fact, the Commission may issue immediately any or all of the sanctions enumerated in the order to show cause provided for in paragraph (e)(5)(i) of this section.

(iv) Commission counsel shall be appointed by the Bureau Officer to prosecute the allegations of misconduct in any administrative disciplinary proceedings instituted pursuant to this rule.

(v) If the Commission assigns the matter to an Administrative Law Judge, the Commission will establish a deadline for an initial decision. The deadline shall not be modified by the Administrative Law Judge except that it may be amended by leave of the Commission.

(vi) Based on the entirety of the record of administrative proceedings, the Administrative Law Judge or the Commission if it reviews the matter in the first instance, shall issue a decision either dismissing the allegations or, if it is determined that the allegations are supported by a preponderance of the evidence, specify an appropriate sanction. An Administrative Law Judge's decision may be appealed to the Commission by either party within 30 days. If the Administrative Law Judge's decision is appealed, the Commission will thereafter issue a scheduling order governing the appeal.

(vii) Investigations and administrative proceedings prior to the hearing on the order to show cause will be nonpublic unless otherwise ordered by the Commission. Any administrative hearing on the order to show cause, and any oral argument on appeal, shall be open to the public unless otherwise ordered for good cause by the Commission or the Administrative Law Judge.

(6) Regardless of any action or determination the Commission may or may not make, the Commission may direct the General Counsel to refer the allegations of misconduct to the appropriate state, territory, or District of Columbia bar or any other appropriate authority for further action.

(7) Upon receipt of notification from any authority having power to suspend or disbar an attorney from the practice of law within any state, territory, or the District of Columbia, demonstrating that an attorney practicing before the Commission is subject to an order of final suspension (not merely temporary suspension pending further action) or disbarment by such authority, the Commission may, without resort to any of the procedures described in this section, enter an order temporarily suspending the attorney from practice before it and directing the attorney to show cause within 30 days from the date of said order why the Commission should not impose further discipline against the attorney. If no response is filed, the attorney will be deemed to have acceded to such further discipline as the Commission deems appropriate. If a response is received, the

Commission may take action or initiate proceedings consistent with paragraph (e)(5) of this section before making a determination whether, and to what extent, to impose further discipline against the attorney.

(8) The disciplinary process described in this section is in addition to, and does not supersede, the authority of the Commission or an Administrative Law Judge to discipline attorneys participating in part 3 proceedings pursuant to §§ 3.24(b)(2) or 3.42(d).

[32 FR 8456, June 13, 1967, as amended at 40 FR 15235, Apr. 4, 1975; 41 FR 16453, Apr. 19, 1976; 46 FR 26295, May 12, 1981; 48 FR 44767, Sept. 30, 1983; 50 FR 50781, Dec. 12, 1985; 50 FR 53306, Dec. 31, 1985; 56 FR 44139, Sept. 27, 1991; 58 FR 40737, July 30, 1993; 63 FR 15758, Apr. 1, 1998; 64 FR 14830, Mar. 29, 1999; 66 FR 13645, Mar. 7, 2001; 66 FR 64143, Dec. 12, 2001; 77 FR 59309, Sept. 27, 2012]

§ 4.2 Requirements as to form, and filing of documents other than correspondence.

(a) *Filing.* (1) All paper and electronic documents filed with the Commission or with an Administrative Law Judge pursuant to part 0, part 1, part 2, or part 3 of this chapter shall be filed with the Secretary of the Commission, except that:

(i) Documents produced in response to compulsory process issued pursuant to part 2 or part 3 of this chapter shall instead be produced to the custodian, deputy custodian, or other person prescribed therein, and in the manner prescribed therein; and

(ii) Comments filed in response to a Commission request for public comment shall instead be filed in the manner prescribed in the FEDERAL REGISTER document or other Commission document containing the request for such comment.

(2) All paper and electronic documents filed with the Commission pursuant to parts 4–999 of this chapter shall be filed with the Secretary of the Commission, except as otherwise provided in such part.

(b) *Title and public or nonpublic status.* All paper and electronic documents filed with the Commission or with an Administrative Law Judge pursuant to any part of this chapter shall clearly show the file or docket number and title of the action in connection with which they are filed. Every page of each such document shall be clearly and accurately labeled "Public", "*In Camera*" or "Confidential".

(c) *Paper and electronic copies of filings before the Commission or an Administrative Law Judge in adjudicative proceedings under part 3 of this chapter.* (1) Each document filed in an adjudicative proceeding under part 3, except documents covered by § 4.2(a)(1)(i), shall be filed with the Secretary of the Commission, shall be in 12-point font with 1-inch margins, and shall comply with the requirements of §§ 4.2(b) and (f) and 4.3(d). Documents may be filed with the Office of the Secretary either electronically or in hard copy.

(i) Documents may be filed electronically by using the Office of the Secretary's electronic filing system and complying with the Secretary's directions for using that system. Documents filed electronically shall be in Adobe portable document format or such other format as the Secretary may direct.

(ii) Documents filed in hard copy shall include a paper original, one paper copy, and an electronic copy in Adobe portable document format or such other format as the Secretary shall direct.

(2) If the document is labeled "*In Camera*" or "Confidential", it must include as an attachment either a motion requesting *in camera* or other confidential treatment, in the form prescribed by § 3.45 of this chapter, or a copy of a Commission, Administrative Law Judge, or federal court order granting such treatment. The document must also include as a separate attachment a set of only those pages of the document on which the *in camera* or otherwise confidential material appears and comply with all other requirements of § 3.45 and any other applicable rules governing *in camera* treatment. A document labeled "*In Camera*" or "Confidential" may be filed electronically using the electronic filing system.

(3) Sensitive personal information, as defined in § 3.45(b) of this chapter, shall not be included in, and must be redacted or omitted from, filings where the filing party determines that such

information is not relevant or otherwise necessary for the conduct of the proceeding.

(4) A copy of each document filed in accordance with this section in an adjudicative proceeding under part 3 of this chapter shall be served by the party filing the document or person acting for that party on all other parties pursuant to §4.4, at or before the time the original is filed.

(d) *Other documents filed with the Commission.* (1) Each document filed with the Commission, and not covered by §4.2(a)(1)(i) or (ii) or §4.2(c), shall be filed with the Secretary of the Commission, and shall be clearly and accurately labeled as required by §4.2(b).

(2) Each such document shall be signed and shall comply with the requirements of §4.2(f). Documents filed under this paragraph (d) shall include a paper original, one paper copy, and an electronic copy in Adobe portable document format, unless the Secretary shall otherwise direct.

(3) Each such document labeled "Public" may be placed on the public record of the Commission at the time it is filed.

(4) If such a document is labeled "Confidential", and it is filed pursuant to §2.10(a), §2.41(f), or §2.51 of this chapter, it will be rejected for filing pursuant to §4.2(g), and will not stay compliance with any applicable obligation imposed by the Commission or the Commission staff, unless the filer simultaneously files:

(i) An explicit request for confidential treatment that includes the factual and legal basis for the request, identifies the specific portions of the document to be withheld from the public record, provides the name and address of the person(s) who should be notified in the event the Commission determines to disclose some or all of the material labeled "Confidential", and otherwise conforms to the requirements of §4.9(c); and

(ii) A redacted public version of the document that is clearly labeled "Public".

(e) *Form.* Paper documents filed with the Secretary of the Commission shall be printed, typewritten, or otherwise processed in permanent form and on good unglazed paper. A motion or other document filed in an adjudicative proceeding under part 3 of this chapter shall contain a caption setting forth the title of the case, the docket number, and a brief descriptive title indicating the purpose of the document.

(f) *Signature.* (1) The original of each document filed shall be signed by an attorney of record for the filing party, or in the case of parties not represented by counsel, by the party itself, or by a partner if a partnership, or by an officer of the party if it is a corporation or an unincorporated association. For documents filed electronically using the Office of the Secretary's electronic filing system, documents must be signed using a scanned signature image, an "s/" followed by the name of the filer using the electronic filing system, or another signature method as the Secretary may direct.

(2) Signing a document constitutes a representation by the signer that he or she has read it; that to the best of his or her knowledge, information, and belief, the statements made in it are true; that it is not interposed for delay; and that to the best of his or her knowledge, information, and belief, it complies with the rules in this part. If a document is not signed or is signed with intent to defeat the purpose of this section, it may be stricken as sham and false and the proceeding may go forward as though the document had not been filed.

(g) *Authority to reject documents for filing.* The Secretary of the Commission may reject a document for filing that fails to comply with the Commission's rules. In cases of extreme hardship, the Secretary may excuse compliance with a rule regarding the filing of documents if the Secretary determines that the non-compliance would not interfere with the functions of the Commission.

[74 FR 1835, Jan. 13, 2009, as amended at 74 FR 20209, May 1, 2009; 76 FR 52253, Aug. 22, 2011; 77 FR 59311, Sept. 27, 2012; 80 FR 25941, May 6, 2015]

§4.3 Time.

(a) *Computation.* Computation of any period of time prescribed or allowed by the rules in this chapter, by order of the Commission or an Administrative

Law Judge, or by any applicable statute, shall begin with the first business day following that on which the act, event, or development initiating such period of time shall have occurred. When the last day of the period so computed is a Saturday, Sunday, or national holiday, or other day on which the office of the Commission is closed, the period shall run until the end of the next following business day. When such period of time, with the intervening Saturdays, Sundays, and national holidays counted, is seven (7) days or less, each of the Saturdays, Sundays, and such holidays shall be excluded from the computation. When such period of time, with the intervening Saturdays, Sundays, and national holidays counted, exceeds seven (7) days, each of the Saturdays, Sundays, and such holidays shall be included in the computation.

(b) *Extensions.* For good cause shown, the Administrative Law Judge may, in any proceeding before him or her: (1) Extend any time limit prescribed or allowed by order of the Administrative Law Judge or the Commission (if the Commission order expressly authorizes the Administrative Law Judge to extend time periods); or (2) extend any time limit prescribed by the rules in this chapter, except those governing motions directed to the Commission, interlocutory appeals and initial decisions and deadlines that the rules expressly authorize only the Commission to extend. Except as otherwise provided by law, the Commission, for good cause shown, may extend any time limit prescribed by the rules in this chapter or by order of the Commission or an Administrative Law Judge, provided, however, that in a proceeding pending before an Administrative Law Judge, any motion on which he or she may properly rule shall be made to the Administrative Law Judge. Notwithstanding the above, where a motion to extend is made after the expiration of the specified period, the motion may be considered where the untimely filing was the result of excusable neglect.

(c) *Additional time after certain kinds of service.* Whenever a party in an adjudicative proceeding under part 3 of this chapter is required or permitted to do an act within a prescribed period after service of a document upon it and the document is served by first-class mail pursuant to § 4.4(a)(2) or (b), 3 days shall be added to the prescribed period. Whenever a party in an adjudicative proceeding under part 3 is required or permitted to do an act within a prescribed period after service of a document upon it and the document is served by electronic delivery pursuant to § 4.4(e), 1 day shall be added to the prescribed period.

(d) *Date of filing.* Documents permitted to be filed using the electronic filing system must be received by 11:59 p.m. Eastern Time to be deemed timely filed that day. All other documents must be received in the Office of the Secretary by 5:00 p.m. Eastern Time to be deemed filed that day, and any such document received after 5:00 p.m. Eastern Time will be deemed filed the following business day.

[32 FR 8456, June 13, 1967, as amended at 42 FR 30150, June 13, 1977; 50 FR 28097, July 10, 1985; 50 FR 53306, Dec. 31, 1985; 66 FR 17633, Apr. 3, 2001; 74 FR 1836, Jan. 13, 2009; 80 FR 25942, May 6, 2015]

§ 4.4 Service.

(a) *By the Commission.* (1) Service of complaints, initial decisions, final orders and other processes of the Commission under 15 U.S.C. 45 may be effected as follows:

(i) *By registered or certified mail.* A copy of the document shall be addressed to the person, partnership, corporation or unincorporated association to be served at his, her or its residence or principal office or place of business, registered or certified, and mailed; service under this provision is complete upon delivery of the document by the Post Office; or

(ii) *By delivery to an individual.* A copy thereof may be delivered to the person to be served, or to a member of the partnership to be served, or to the president, secretary, or other executive officer or a director of the corporation or unincorporated association to be served; service under this provision is complete upon delivery as specified herein; or

(iii) *By delivery to an address.* A copy thereof may be left at the principal office or place of business of the person, partnership, corporation, or unincorporated association, or it may be left at the residence of the person or of a member of the partnership or of an executive officer or director of the corporation, or unincorporated association to be served; service under this provision is complete upon delivery as specified herein.

(2) All documents served by the Commission or Administrative Law Judge in adjudicative proceedings under part 3 of this chapter, other than documents governed by paragraph (a)(1) of this section, may be served by personal delivery (including delivery by courier), by electronic delivery in accordance with §4.4(e), or by first-class mail. Unless otherwise specified in §4.4(e), documents shall be deemed served on the day of personal or electronic delivery or the day of mailing.

(3) All other orders and notices, including subpoenas, orders requiring access, orders to file annual and special reports, and notices of default, may be served by any method reasonably certain to inform the affected person, partnership, corporation or unincorporated association, including any method specified in paragraph (a)(1) of this section, except that civil investigative demands may only be served in the manner provided by section 20(c)(8) of the FTC Act (in the case of service on a partnership, corporation, association, or other legal entity) or section 20(c)(9) of the FTC Act (in the case of a natural person). Service under this provision is complete upon delivery by the Post Office or upon personal delivery (including delivery by courier).

(b) *By parties or third parties in adjudicative proceedings under part 3 of this chapter.* (1) Service of documents by complaint counsel, respondents, or third parties in adjudicative proceedings under part 3 shall be by delivering copies using the following methods.

(i) *Upon complaint counsel.* A copy may be served by personal delivery (including delivery by courier), by electronic delivery in accordance with §4.4(e), or by first-class mail to the lead complaint counsel, with a copy to the Administrative Law Judge.

(ii) *Upon a party other than complaint counsel or upon a third party.* A copy may be served by personal delivery (including delivery by courier), by electronic delivery in accordance with §4.4(e), or by first-class mail, with a copy to the Administrative Law Judge. If the party is an individual or partnership, delivery shall be to such individual or a member of the partnership; if a corporation or unincorporated association, to an officer or agent authorized to accept service of process therefor. Personal delivery includes handing the document to be served to the individual, partner, officer, or agent; leaving it at his or her office with a person in charge thereof; or, if there is no one in charge or if the office is closed or if the party has no office, leaving it at his or her dwelling house or usual place of abode with some person of suitable age and discretion then residing therein.

(2) Unless otherwise specified in §4.4(e), documents served in adjudicative proceedings under part 3 shall be deemed served on the day of personal delivery (including delivery by courier), the day of electronic delivery, or the day of mailing.

(c) *Service upon counsel.* When counsel has appeared in a proceeding on behalf of a party, service upon such counsel of any document, other than a complaint, shall be deemed service upon the party. However, service of those documents specified in paragraph (a)(1) of this section shall be in accordance with paragraphs (a)(1)(i), (ii), and (iii) of this section.

(d) *Proof of service.* In an adjudicative proceeding under part 3, documents presented for filing shall contain proof of service in the form of a statement of the date and manner of service and of the names of the persons served, certified by the person who made service. Proof of service must appear on or be affixed to the documents filed.

(e) *Service by electronic delivery in an adjudicative proceeding under part 3 of this chapter*—(1) *Service through the electronic filing system.* A party may elect, for documents labeled "Public" pursuant to §4.2(b), to be served via the electronic filing system provided by the Office of the Secretary. The electronic filing system cannot be used to serve third parties. For parties that have elected to be served via the electronic filing system:

(i) Service of documents labeled "Public" pursuant to § 4.2(b) may be effected through the electronic filing system;

(ii) Each such party thereby agrees that, for any document served through the electronic filing system, transmission of the notice of electronic filing provided by the electronic filing system shall satisfy the service obligations of the serving party; and

(iii) A document served via the electronic filing system shall be deemed served on the date the notice of electronic filing is transmitted, unless the serving party learns that the notice of electronic filing did not reach the person to be served.

(2) *Service by other methods of electronic delivery.* (i) In the following circumstances, service by other methods of electronic delivery (including service by email) may be effected as the Administrative Law Judge and the Secretary may direct:

(A) The document to be served is labeled "*In Camera*" or "Confidential" pursuant to § 4.2(b);

(B) The party to be served has not elected to be served via the electronic filing system;

(C) The document is to be served upon a third party; or

(D) Service under paragraph (e)(1) of this section is unavailable for technical reasons.

(ii) If documents labeled "*In Camera*" or "Confidential" are being served under this paragraph (e)(2), the documents must be encrypted prior to transit or must be transferred through a secure file transfer protocol. Service of a document under this paragraph (e)(2) shall be complete upon transmission by the serving party, unless the serving party learns that the document did not reach the person to be served.

(f) *Service of process upon the Commission.* Documents served upon the Commission may be served by personal delivery (including delivery by courier) or by first-class mail to the Office of the Secretary of the Commission.

[80 FR 25942, May 6, 2015, as amended at 80 FR 60797, Oct. 8, 2015]

§ 4.5 Fees.

(a) *Deponents and witnesses.* Any person compelled to appear in person in response to subpoena shall be paid the same fees and mileage as are paid witnesses in the courts of the United States.

(b) *Presiding officers.* Officers before whom depositions are taken shall be entitled to the same fees as are paid for like services in the courts of the United States.

(c) *Responsibility.* The fees and mileage referred to in this section shall be paid by the party at whose instance deponents or witnesses appear.

[32 FR 8456, June 13, 1967]

§ 4.6 Cooperation with other agencies.

It is the policy of the Commission to cooperate with other governmental agencies to avoid unnecessary overlapping or duplication of regulatory functions.

[32 FR 8456, June 13, 1967]

§ 4.7 Ex parte communications.

(a) *Definitions.* For purposes of this section, *ex parte communication* means an oral or written communication not on the public record with respect to which reasonable prior notice to all parties is not given, but it shall not include requests for status reports on any matter or proceeding.

(b) *Prohibited ex parte communications.* While a proceeding is in adjudicative status within the Commission, except to the extent required for the disposition of *ex parte* matters as authorized by law:

(1) No person not employed by the Commission, and no employee or agent of the Commission who performs investigative or prosecuting functions in adjudicative proceedings, shall make or knowingly cause to be made to any member of the Commission, or to the Administrative Law Judge, or to any other employee who is or who reasonably may be expected to be involved in the decisional process in the proceeding, an *ex parte* communciation relevant to the merits of that or a factually related proceeding; and

(2) No member of the Commission, the Administrative Law Judge, or any

other employee who is or who reasonably may be expected to be involved in the decisional process in the proceeding, shall make or knowingly cause to be made to any person not employed by the Commission, or to any employee or agent of the Commission who performs investigative or prosecuting functions in adjudicative proceedings, an *ex parte* communication relevant to the merits of that or a factually related proceeding.

(c) *Procedures.* A Commissioner, the Administrative Law Judge or any other employee who is or who may reasonably be expected to be involved in the decisional process who receives or who make or knowingly causes to be made, a communication prohibited by paragraph (b) of this section shall promptly provide to the Secretary of the Commission:

(1) All such written communications;

(2) Memoranda stating the substance of and circumstances of all such oral communications; and

(3) All written responses, and memoranda stating the substance of all oral responses, to the materials described in paragraphs (c) (1) and (2) of this section. The Secretary shall make relevant portions of any such materials part of the public record of the Commission, pursuant to §4.9, and place them in the docket binder of the proceeding to which it pertains, but they will not be considered by the Commission as part of the record for purposes of decision unless introduced into evidence in the proceeding. The Secretary shall also send copies of the materials to or otherwise notify all parties to the proceeding.

(d) *Sanctions.* (1) Upon receipt of an *ex parte* communication knowingly made or knowingly caused to be made by a party and prohibited by paragraph (b) of this section, the Commission, Administrative Law Judge, or other employee presiding over the proceeding may, to the extent consistent with the interests of justice and the policy of the underlying statutes administered by the Commission, require the party to show cause why his claim or interest in the proceeding should not be dismissed, denied, disregarded, or otherwise adversely affected on account of such violation. The Commission may take such action as it considers appropriate, including but not limited to, action under §4.1(e)(2) and 5 U.S.C. 556(d).

(2) A person, not a party to the proceeding who knowingly makes or causes to be made an *ex parte* communication prohibited by paragraph (b) of this section shall be subject to all sanctions provided herein if he subsequently becomes a party to the proceeding.

(e) The prohibitions of this section shall apply in an adjudicative proceeding from the time the Commission votes to issue a complaint pursuant to §3.11, to conduct adjudicative hearings pursuant to §3.13, or to issue an order to show cause pursuant to §3.72(b), or from the time an order by a U.S. court of appeals remanding a Commission decision and order for further proceedings becomes effective, until the time the Commission votes to enter its decision in the proceeding and the time permitted by §3.55 to seek reconsideration of that decision has elapsed. For purposes of this section, an order of remand by a U.S. court of appeals shall be deemed to become effective when the Commission determines not to file a petition for a writ of *certiorari*, or when the time for filing such a petition has expired without a petition having been filed, or when such a petition has been denied. If a petition for reconsideration of a Commission decision is filed pursuant to §3.55, the provisions of this section shall apply until the time the Commission votes to enter an order disposing of the petition. In addition, the prohibitions of this section shall apply with respect to communications concerning an application for stay filed with the Commission pursuant to §3.56 from the time that the application is filed until its disposition.

(f) The prohibitions of paragraph (b) of this section do not apply to a communication occasioned by and concerning a nonadjudicative function of the Commission, including such functions as the initiation, conduct, or disposition of a separate investigation, the issuance of a complaint, or the initiation of a rulemaking or other proceeding, whether or not it involves a party already in an adjudicative proceeding; preparations for judicial review of a Commission order; a proceeding outside the scope of § 3.2, including a matter in state or federal court or before another governmental agency; a nonadjudicative function of the Commission, including but not limited to an obligation under § 4.11 or a communication with Congress; or the disposition of a consent settlement under § 3.25 concerning some or all of the charges involved in a complaint and executed by some or all respondents. The Commission, at its discretion and under such restrictions as it may deem appropriate, may disclose to the public or to respondent(s) in a pending adjudicative proceeding a communication made exempt by this paragraph from the prohibitions of paragraph (b) of this section, however, when the Commission determines that the interests of justice would be served by the disclosure. The prohibitions of paragraph (b) of this section also do not apply to a communication between any member of the Commission, the Administrative Law Judge, or any other employee who is or who reasonably may be expected to be involved in the decisional process, and any employee who has been directed by the Commission or requested by an individual Commissioner or Administrative Law Judge to assist in the decision of the adjudicative proceeding. Such employee shall not, however, have performed an investigative or prosecuting function in that or a factually related proceeding.

[42 FR 43974, Sept. 1, 1977, as amended at 44 FR 40637, July 12, 1979; 46 FR 32435, June 23, 1981; 50 FR 53306, Dec. 31, 1985; 51 FR 36802, Oct. 16, 1986; 57 FR 10805, Mar. 31, 1992; 60 FR 37748, July 21, 1995; 60 FR 67325, Dec. 29, 1995]

§ 4.8 Costs for obtaining Commission records.

(a) *Definitions*. For the purpose of this section:

(1) The term *search* includes all time spent looking, manually or by automated means, for material that is responsive to a request, including page-by-page or line-by-line identification of material within documents.

(2) The term *duplication* refers to the process of making a copy of a document for the purpose of releasing that document in response to a request for Commission records. Such copies can take the form of paper copy, microform, audio-visual materials, or machine readable documentation such as magnetic tape or computer disc. For copies prepared by computer and then saved to a computer disc, the Commission charges the direct costs, including operator time, of production of the disc or other output format. Where paper documents must be scanned in order to comply with a requester's preference to receive the records in an electronic format, the requester shall pay the direct costs associated with scanning those materials. As set out in § 4.8(b), certain requesters do not pay for direct costs associated with duplicating the first 100 pages.

(3) The term *review* refers to the examination of documents located in response to a request to determine whether any portion of such documents may be withheld, and the redaction or other processing of documents for disclosure. Review costs are recoverable from commercial use requesters even if a record ultimately is not disclosed. Review time includes time spent considering formal objections to disclosure made by a business submitter but does not include time spent resolving general legal or policy issues regarding the release of the document.

(4) The term *direct costs* means expenditures that the Commission actually incurs in processing requests. Direct costs include the salary of the employee performing work (the basic rate of pay for the employee plus 16 percent of that rate to cover benefits) and the cost of operating duplicating machinery. Not included in direct costs are overhead expenses such as costs of document review facilities or the costs of heating or lighting such a facility or other facilities in which records are stored. The direct costs of specific services are set forth in § 4.8(b)(6).

(b) *Fees*. User fees pursuant to 31 U.S.C. 9701 and 5 U.S.C. 552(a) shall be charged according to this paragraph, unless the requester establishes the applicability of a public interest fee waiver pursuant to § 4.8(e). The chart summarizes the types of charges that apply to requester categories set out in paragraphs (b)(1)–(b)(3).

Requester categories	Fee charged for all search time	Fee charged for all review time	Duplication charges
Commercial	Fee	Fee	Fee charged for all duplication.
Educational, Non-commercial Scientific Institution, or News Media.	No charge	No charge	No charge for first 100 pages.
All other requesters (including members of the general public).	Fee after two hours	No charge	No charge for first 100 pages.

(1) *Commercial use requesters.* Commercial use requesters will be charged for the direct costs to search for, review, and duplicate documents. A commercial use requester is a requester who seeks information for a use or purpose that furthers the commercial, trade, or profit interests of the requester or the person on whose behalf the request is made.

(2) *Educational requesters, non-commercial scientific institution requesters, and representative of the news media.* Requesters in these categories will be charged for the direct costs to duplicate documents, excluding charges for the first 100 pages.

(i) An *educational institution* is a preschool, a public or private elementary or secondary school, an institution of graduate higher education, an institution of undergraduate higher education, an institution of professional education, and an institution of vocational education, which operates a program or programs of scholarly research. To be in this category, a requester must show that the request is authorized by and is made under the auspices of a qualifying institution and that the records are sought to further the scholarly research of the institution and are not sought for a commercial or an individual use or goal.

(ii) A *non-commercial scientific institution* is an institution that is not operated on a *commercial* basis as that term is referenced in paragraph (b)(1) of this section, and that is operated solely to conduct scientific research the results of which are not intended to promote any particular product or industry.

(iii) A *representative of the news media* is any person or entity that gathers information of potential interest to a segment of the public, uses its editorial skills to turn the raw materials into a distinct work, and distributes that work to an audience. The term "news" means information that is about current events or that would be of current interest to the public. Examples of news media entities include television or radio stations broadcasting to the public at large and publishers of periodicals (but only in those instances where they can qualify as disseminators of news) who make their products available for purchase by or subscription by the general public or free distribution to the general public. These examples are not intended to be all-inclusive. As traditional methods of news delivery evolve (*e.g.*, electronic dissemination of newspapers through telecommunications services), such alternative media shall be considered to be news-media entities. A freelance journalist shall be regarded as working for a news-media entity if the journalist can demonstrate a solid basis for expecting publication through that entity, whether or not the journalist is actually employed by the entity. A publication contract would provide a solid basis for such an expectation, but the past publication record of a requester may also be considered in making such a determination. To qualify for news media status, a request must not be for a nonjournalistic commercial use. A request for records supporting the news dissemination function of the requester is not considered a commercial use.

(3) *Other requesters.* Other requesters not described in paragraphs (b)(1) or (2) will be charged for the direct costs to search for and duplicate documents, except that the first 100 pages of duplication and the first two hours of search time shall be furnished without charge.

(4) *Waiver of small charges.* Notwithstanding the provisions of paragraphs (b)(1), (2), and (3) of this section, charges will be waived if the total

chargeable fees for a request are under $25.00.

(5) *Materials available without charge.* These provisions do not apply to public records, including but not limited to Commission decisions, orders, and other public materials that may be made available to all requesters without charge.

(6)(i) *Schedule of direct costs.* The following uniform schedule of fees applies to records held by all constituent units of the Commission:

Duplication	
Paper to paper copy (up to 8.5″ x 14″)	$0.14 per page.
Converting paper into electronic format (scanning).	Quarter hour rate of operator (Clerical, Other Professional, Attorney/Economist).
Other reproduction (*e.g.*, converting from one electronic format to computer disk or printout, microfilm, microfiche, or microform).	Actual direct cost, including operator time.
Electronic Services	
Compact disc (CD)	$3.00 per disc.
DVD	$3.00 per disc.
Videotape cassette	$2.00 per cassette.
Microfilm Services	
Conversion of existing fiche/film to paper	$0.14 per page.
Other Fees	
Certification	$25.00 each.
Express Mail	U.S. Postal Service Market Rates.
Records maintained at Iron Mountain or Washington National Records Center facilities (records retrieval, refiling, et cetera).	Contract Rates.
Other Services as they arise	Market Rates.

(ii) *Search, review and duplication fees.* Agency staff is divided into three categories: Clerical, attorney/economist, and other professional. Fees for search and review purposes, as well the costs of operating duplication machinery such as converting paper to electronic format (scanning), are assessed on a quarter-hourly basis, and are determined by identifying the category into which the staff member(s) conducting the search or review or duplication procedure belong(s), determining the average quarter-hourly wages of all staff members within that category, and adding 16 percent to reflect the cost of additional benefits accorded to government employees. The exact fees are calculated and announced periodically and are available from the Consumer Response Center, Federal Trade Commission, 600 Pennsylvania Avenue NW., Washington, DC 20580; (202) 326–2222.

(7) *Untimely responses.* (i) Except as provided in paragraphs (b)(7)(ii)–(iv) of this section, search fees for responding to a Freedom of Information Act request will not be assessed for responses that fail to comply with the time limits, as provided at 5 U.S.C. 552(a)(4)(A)(viii), §4.11(a)(1)(ii) and §4.11(a)(3)(ii), if there are no unusual or exceptional circumstances, as those terms are defined by 5 U.S.C. 552(a)(6) and §4.11(a)(1)(ii). Except as provided below, duplication fees will not be assessed for an untimely response, where there are no unusual or exceptional circumstances, made to a requester qualifying for one of the fee categories set forth in paragraph (b)(2) of this section.

(ii) If the Commission has determined that unusual circumstances apply and has provided a timely written notice to the requester in accordance with 5 U.S.C. 552(a)(6)(B), the delay in a response is excused for an additional 10 days. If the Commission fails to comply with the extended time limit, it will not charge search fees (or, for a requester qualifying for one of the fee categories set forth in paragraph (b)(2) of this section, will not charge duplication fees).

(iii) If the Commission has determined that unusual circumstances apply and more than 5,000 pages are necessary to respond to the request, the agency may charge search fees (or, for requesters qualifying for one of the fee categories set forth in paragraph (b)(2) of this section, may charge duplication fees) if timely written notice has been provided to the requester and the agency has discussed with the requester via written mail, electronic mail, or telephone (or made not less than 3 good-faith attempts to do so) how the requester could effectively limit the scope of the request.

(iv) If a court determines that exceptional circumstances exist, the Commission's failure to comply with a time limit shall be excused for the length of time provided by the court order.

(c) *Information to determine fees.* Each request for records shall set forth whether the request is made for either commercial or non-commercial purposes or whether the requester is an educational institution, a noncommercial scientific institution, or a representative of the news media. The deciding official (as designated by the General Counsel) will use this information, any additional information provided by the requester, and any other relevant information to determine the appropriate fee category in which to place the requester. *See* §4.11(a)(3)(i)(A)(3) for procedures on appealing fee category and fee waiver determinations.

(d) *Agreement to pay fees.* (1) Each request that does not contain an application for a fee waiver as set forth in §4.8(e) shall specifically indicate that the requester will either:

(i) Pay, in accordance with §4.8(b), whatever fees may be charged for processing the request; or

(ii) Pay such fees up to a specified amount, whereby the processing of the request would cease once the specified amount has been reached.

(2) Each request that contains an application for a fee waiver shall specifically indicate whether the requester, in the case that the fee waiver is not granted, will:

(i) Pay, in accordance with §4.8(b), whatever fees may be charged for processing the request;

(ii) Pay fees up to a specified amount, whereby the processing of the request would cease once the specified amount has been reached; or

(iii) Not pay fees, whereby the processing of the request will cease at the point fees are to be incurred in accordance with §4.8(b).

(3) If the agreement required by this section is absent, and if the estimated fees exceed $25.00, the requester will be advised of the estimated fees and the request will not be processed until the requester agrees to pay such fees. If the requester does not respond to the notification that the estimated fees exceed $25.00 within 20 calendar days from the date of the notification, the request will be closed.

(e) *Public interest fee waivers*—(1) *Procedures.* A requester may apply for a waiver of fees. The requester shall explain in sufficient detail why a waiver is appropriate under the standards set forth in this paragraph. The application shall also include a statement, as provided by paragraph (d) of this section, of whether the requester agrees to pay costs if the waiver is denied. The deciding official (as designated by the General Counsel) will rule on applications for fee waivers. To appeal the deciding official's determination of the fee waiver, a requester must follow the procedures set forth in §4.11(a)(3).

(2) *Standards.* (i) The first requirement for a fee waiver is that disclosure will likely contribute significantly to public understanding of the operations or activities of the government. This requirement shall be met if the requester establishes that:

(A) The subject matter of the requested information concerns the operations or activities of the Federal government;

(B) The disclosure is likely to contribute to an understanding of these operations or activities;

(C) The understanding to which disclosure is likely to contribute is public understanding, as opposed to the understanding of the individual requester or a narrow segment of interested persons (*e.g.*, by providing specific information about the requester's expertise in the subject area of the request and about the ability and intention to disseminate the information to the public); and

(D) The likely contribution to public understanding will be significant.

(ii) The second requirement for a fee waiver is that the request not be primarily in the commercial interest of the requester. This requirement shall be met if the requester shows either:

(A) That the requester does not have a commercial interest that would be furthered by the requested disclosure; or

(B) If the requester does have a commercial interest that would be furthered by the requested disclosure, that the public interest in disclosure outweighs the identified commercial interest of the requester so that the disclosure is not primarily in the requester's commercial interest.

(f) *Searches that do not yield responsive records.* Charges may be assessed for search time even if the agency fails to locate any responsive records or if it locates only records that are determined to be exempt from disclosure.

(g) *Aggregating requests.* If the deciding official (as designated by the General Counsel) initially, or the General Counsel on appeal, reasonably believes that a requester, or a group of requesters acting in concert, is attempting to evade an assessment of fees by dividing a single request into a series of smaller requests, the requests may be aggregated and fees charged accordingly.

(h) *Advance payment.* If the deciding official (as designated by the General Counsel) initially, or the General Counsel on appeal, estimates or determines that allowable charges that a requester may be required to pay are likely to exceed $250.00, or if the requester has previously failed to pay a fee within 30 days of the date of billing, the requester may be required to pay some or all of the total estimated charge in advance. Further, the requester may be required to pay all unpaid bills, including accrued interest, prior to processing the request.

(i) *Means of payment.* Payment shall be made either electronically through the Department of Treasury's *pay.gov* Web site or by check or money order payable to the Treasury of the United States.

(j) *Interest charges.* The Commission will begin assessing interest charges on an unpaid bill starting on the 31st day following the day on which the bill was sent. Interest will accrue from the date of the billing, and will be calculated at the rate prescribed in 31 U.S.C. 3717.

(k) *Effect of the Debt Collection Act of 1982 (Pub. L. 97–365), as amended by the Debt Collection Improvement Act of 1996 (Pub. L. 104–134).* The Commission will pursue repayment, where appropriate, by employing the provisions of the Debt Collection Act of 1982, as amended by the Debt Collection Improvement Act of 1996, the Federal Claims Collection Standards (FCSS), 31 CFR 900–904, and any other applicable authorities in collecting unpaid fees assessed under this section, including disclosure to consumer reporting agencies and use of collection agencies. The FTC also reserves the legal right to employ other lawful debt collection methods such as alternative dispute resolution and arbitration when appropriate.

[57 FR 10806, Mar. 31, 1992, as amended at 63 FR 45646, Aug. 26, 1998; 64 FR 3012, Jan. 20, 1999; 66 FR 64144, Dec. 12, 2001; 78 FR 15683, Mar. 21, 2014; 82 FR 21686, May 10, 2017]

§ 4.9 The public record.

(a) *General.* (1) Materials on the public record of the Commission are available for public inspection and copying either from the Commission's Web site or upon request.

(2) Materials that are exempt from mandatory public disclosure, or are otherwise not available from the Commission's public record, may be made available only upon request under the

procedures set forth in §4.11, or as provided in §§4.10(d) through (g), 4.13, and 4.15(b)(3), or by the Commission.

(3) *Electronic access to public records.* The majority of recent Commission public records are available for review electronically on the Commission's Web site on the Internet, *www.ftc.gov.* Copies of records that the Commission is required to make available to the public electronically, pursuant to 5 U.S.C. 552(a)(2), may be obtained in that format from *http://www.ftc.gov/foia/readingroom.shtm.*

(4) *Requesting public records*—(i) *Procedures.* Certain older public records may not be available at the FTC Web site. Any person may request copies of such records by contacting the FTC Reading Room by telephone at (202) 326–2222, extension 2. These requests shall specify as clearly and accurately as reasonably possible the records desired. For records that cannot be specified with complete clarity and particularity, requesters shall provide descriptions sufficient to enable qualified Commission personnel to locate the records sought. The Commission, the Supervisor of the Consumer Response Center, the General Counsel, or the deciding official (as designated by the General Counsel) may decide to provide only one copy of any public record and may refuse to provide copies to the requester if the records have been published or are publicly available at places other than the Commission's offices.

(ii) *Costs; agreement to pay costs.* Requesters will be charged search and duplication costs prescribed by Rule 4.8 for requests under this section. All requests shall include a statement of the information needed to determine fees, as provided by §4.8(c), and an agreement to pay fees (or a statement that the requester will not pay fees if a fee waiver is denied), as provided by §4.8(d). Requests may also include an application for a fee waiver, as provided by §4.8(e). Advance payment may be required, as provided by §4.8(h).

(iii) *Records for sale at another government agency.* If requested materials are available for sale at another government agency, the requester will not be provided with copies of the materials but will be advised to obtain them from the selling agency. The U.S. Government Printing Office ("GPO"), the official bookstore for most U.S. Government publications, can be contacted at (202) 512–1800 or toll-free at (866) 512–1800, and at *ContactCenter@gpo.gov.* The GPO's online store can be accessed at *http://bookstore.gpo.gov* and mail orders should be directed to U.S. Government Printing Office, P.O. Box 979050, St. Louis, MO 63197–9000.

(b) *Categories.* Except to the extent material is confidential, as provided in paragraph (c) of this section, the public record of the Commission includes, but is not necessarily limited to:

(1) *Commission Organization and Procedures (16 CFR part 0 and §§4.14 through 4.15, 4.17).* (i) A current index of opinions, orders, statements of policy and interpretations, administrative staff manuals, general instructions and other public records of the Commission;

(ii) A current record of the final votes of each member of the Commission in all matters of public record, including matters of public record decided by notational voting;

(iii) Descriptions of the Commission's organization, including descriptions of where, from whom, and how the public may secure information, submit documents or requests, and obtain copies of orders, decisions and other materials;

(iv) Statements of the Commission's general procedures and policies and interpretations, its nonadjudicative procedures, its rules of practice for adjudicative proceedings, and its miscellaneous rules, including descriptions of the nature and requirements of all formal and informal procedures available, and

(v) Reprints of the principal laws under which the Commission exercises enforcement or administrative responsibilities.

(2) *Industry Guidance (16 CFR 1.1–1.6).* (i) Any advice, advisory opinion or response given and required to be made public under §§1.4 and 2.41 (d) or (f) of this chapter (whether by the Commission or the staff), together with a statement of supporting reasons;

(ii) Industry guides, digests of advisory opinions and compliance advice believed to be of interest to the public generally and other administrative interpretations;

(iii) Transcripts of hearings in all industry guide proceedings, as well as written statements filed with or forwarded to the Commission in connection with these proceedings; and

(iv) Petitions filed with the Secretary of the Commission for the promulgation or issuance, amendment, or repeal of industry guides.

(3) *Rulemaking (16 CFR 1.7 through 1.26).* (i) Petitions filed with the Secretary of the Commission for the promulgation or issuance, amendment, or repeal of rules or regulations within the scope of §§1.7 and 1.21 of this chapter, and petitions for exemptions;

(ii) Notices and advance notices of proposed rulemaking and rules and orders issued in rulemaking proceedings; and

(iii) Transcripts of hearings of all rulemaking proceedings, all other materials that are distributed to the public during these proceedings, and written statements filed with or forwarded to the Commission in connection with these proceedings.

(4) *Investigations.* (i) Petitions to limit or quash compulsory process and the rulings thereon; and

(ii) Closing letters in initial phase and full phase investigations.

(5) *Adjudicative proceedings, stay applications, requests to reopen, and litigated orders. (16 CFR 2.51, 3.1 through 3.24, 3.31 through 3.56, 3.71 through 3.72, 4.7)*—Except for transcripts of matters heard *in camera* pursuant to §3.45 and material filed *in camera* pursuant to §§3.22, 3.24, 3.45, 3.46, 3.51 and 3.52,

(i) The versions of pleadings and transcripts of prehearing conferences to the extent made available under §3.21(e), motions, certifications, orders, and the transcripts of hearings (including public conferences), testimony, oral arguments, and other material made a part thereof, and exhibits and material received in evidence or made a part of the public record in adjudicative proceedings;

(ii) Initial decisions of administrative law judges;

(iii) Orders and opinions in interlocutory matters;

(iv) Final orders and opinions in adjudications, and rulings on stay applications, including separate statements of Commissioners;

(v) Petitions for reconsideration, and answers thereto, filed pursuant to §3.55;

(vi) Applications for stay, answers thereto, and replies, filed pursuant to §3.56;

(vii) Petitions, applications, pleadings, briefs, and other records filed by the Commission with the courts in connection with adjudicative, injunctive, enforcement, compliance, and condemnation proceedings, and in connection with judicial review of Commission actions, and opinions and orders of the courts in disposition thereof;

(viii) Records of *ex parte* communications in adjudicative proceedings and stay applications;

(ix) Petitions to reopen proceedings and orders to determine whether orders should be altered, modified, or set aside in accordance with §2.51; and

(x) Decisions reopening proceedings, and orders to show cause under §3.72.

(6) *Consent agreements (16 CFR 2.31 through 2.34, 3.25).* (i) Agreements containing orders, after acceptance by the Commission pursuant to §§2.34 and 3.25(f) of this chapter;

(ii) Comments and other materials filed or placed on the public record under §§2.34 and 3.25(f) concerning proposed consent agreements and related orders; and

(iii) Decisions and orders issued and served under §§2.34 and 3.25(f), including separate statements of Commissioners.

(7) *Compliance/enforcement (16 CFR 2.33, 2.41).* (i) Reports of compliance filed pursuant to the rules in this chapter or pursuant to a provision in a Commission order and supplemental materials filed in connection with these reports, except for reports of compliance, and supplemental materials filed in connection with Commission orders requiring divestitures or establishment of business enterprises of facilities, which are confidential until the last divestiture or establishment of a business enterprise or facility, as required by a particular order, has been finally approved by the Commission, and staff letters to respondents advising them that their compliance reports do not warrant any further action. At the time each such report is submitted

the filing party may request confidential treatment in accordance with paragraph (c) of this section and the General Counsel or the General Counsel's designee will pass upon such request in accordance with that paragraph;

(ii) Materials required to be made public under 16 CFR 2.41(f) in connection with applications for approval of proposed divestitures, acquisitions or similar transactions subject to Commission review under outstanding orders.

(8) *Access to documents and meetings (16 CFR 4.8, 4.11, 4.13, 4.15).* (i) Letters requesting access to Commission records pursuant to §4.11(a) of this chapter and the Freedom of Information Act, 5 U.S.C. 552, and letters granting or denying such requests (not including access requests and answers thereto from the Congress or other government agencies);

(ii) Announcements of Commission meetings as required under the Sunshine Act, 5 U.S.C. 552b, including records of the votes to close such meetings;

(iii) Summaries or other explanatory materials relating to matters to be considered at open meetings made available pursuant to §4.15(b)(3)

(iv) Commission minutes of open meetings, and, to the extent they are not exempt from mandatory public disclosure under the Sunshine Act or the Freedom of Information Act, portions of minutes or transcripts of closed meetings; and

(v) A guide for requesting records or information from the Commission, including an index of all major information systems, a description of major information and record locator systems maintained by the Commission, and a handbook for obtaining various types and categories of public information.

(9) *Standards of conduct (16 CFR 5.5 through 5.6, 5.10 through 5.26, 5.31, 5.57 through 5.68).* (i) Memoranda to staff elaborating or clarifying standards described in administrative staff manuals and part 5 of this subchapter.

(10) *Miscellaneous (press releases, clearance requests, reports filed by or with the Commission, continuing guaranties, registered identification numbers).* (i) Releases by the Commission's Office of Public Affairs supplying information concerning the activities of the Commission;

(ii) Applications under §4.1(b)(2) of this chapter for clearance or authorization to appear or participate in a proceeding or investigation and of the Commission's responses thereto;

(iii) Continuing guaranties filed under the Wool, Fur, and Textile Acts;

(iv) Published reports by the staff or by the Commission on economic surveys and investigations of general interest;

(v) Filings by the Commission or by the staff in connection with proceedings before other federal agencies or state or local government bodies;

(vi) Registration statements and annual reports filed with the Commission by export trade associations, and bulletins, pamphlets, and reports with respect to such associations released by the Commission;

(vii) The identities of holders of registered identification numbers issued by the Commission pursuant to §1.32 of this chapter;

(viii) The Commission's annual report submitted after the end of each fiscal year, summarizing its work during the year (with copies obtainable from the Superintendent of Documents, U.S. Government Publishing Office, Washington, DC 20402) and any other annual reports made to Congress on activities of the Commission as required by law;

(ix) Records, as determined by the General Counsel or his or her designee, that have been released in response to a request made under the Freedom of Information Act, 5 U.S.C. 552, and which, because of the nature of the subject matter, have become or are likely to become the subject of subsequent requests for substantially the same records, or that have been requested three or more times, except where some or all of those records would be exempt from disclosure under 5 U.S.C. 552 if requested by another party;

(x) A general index of the records referred to under paragraph (b)(10)(ix) of this section;

(xi) Grants of early termination of waiting periods published in accordance with the Hart-Scott-Rodino premerger notification provisions of the Clayton Act, 15 U.S.C. 18a(b)(2);

(xii) Reports on appliance energy consumption or efficiency filed with the Commission pursuant to §305.8 of this chapter;

(xiii) Annual filings by professional boxing sanctioning organizations as required by the Muhammed Ali Boxing Reform Act, 15 U.S.C. 6301 note, 6307a–6307h;

(xiv) All transcripts or other materials that are distributed by staff at public workshops;

(xv) Other documents that the Commission has determined to place on the public record; and

(xvi) Every amendment, revision, substitute, or repeal of any of the foregoing items listed in paragraphs (b)(1) through (10) of this section.

(c) *Confidentiality and in camera material.* (1) Persons submitting material to the Commission described in this section may designate that material or portions of it confidential and request that it be withheld from the public record. All requests for confidential treatment shall be supported by a showing of justification in light of applicable statutes, rules, orders of the Commission or its administrative law judges, orders of the courts, or other relevant authority. The General Counsel or the General Counsel's designee will act upon such request with due regard for legal constraints and the public interest. No such material or portions of material (including documents generated by the Commission or its staff containing or reflecting such material or portions of material) will be placed on the public record until the General Counsel or the General Counsel's designee has ruled on the request for confidential treatment and provided any prior notice to the submitter required by law.

(2) Motions seeking *in camera* treatment of material submitted in connection with a proceeding under part 3 of these rules, except stay applications under §3.56, shall be filed with the Administrative Law Judge who is presiding over the proceeding. Requests for confidential treatment of material submitted in connection with a stay application shall be made in accordance with §4.9(c)(1).

(3) To the extent that any material or portions of material otherwise falling within paragraph (b) of this section contain information that is not required to be made public under §4.10 of this part, the General Counsel or the General Counsel's designee may determine, with due regard for legal constraints and the public interest, to withhold such materials from the public record.

[50 FR 50779, Dec. 12, 1985, as amended at 57 FR 10805, Mar. 31, 1992; 59 FR 34970, July 8, 1994; 60 FR 37749, July 21, 1995; 63 FR 18820, Apr. 16, 1998; 63 FR 32977, June 17, 1998; 63 FR 45647, Aug. 26, 1998; 64 FR 46269, Aug. 25, 1999; 66 FR 17633, Apr. 3, 2001; 66 FR 64144, Dec. 12, 2001; 77 FR 59311, Sept. 27, 2012; 78 FR 13474, Feb. 28, 2013; 80 FR 15162, Mar. 23, 2015; 80 FR 16961, Mar. 31, 2015; 81 FR 93805, Dec. 22, 2016]

EDITORIAL NOTE: At 80 FR 15162, Mar. 23, 2015, in §4.9, paragraph (a)(10)(viii) was revised, however no paragraph (a)(10)(viii) exists, so the amendment could not be incorporated.

§4.10 Nonpublic material.

(a) The following records and other material of the Commission are not required to be made public pursuant to 5 U.S.C. 552.

(1) Records, except to the extent required to be disclosed under other laws or regulations, related solely to the internal personnel rules and practices of the Commission. This exemption applies to internal rules or instructions to Commission personnel which must be kept confidential in order to assure effective performance of the functions and activities for which the Commission is responsible and which do not affect members of the public.

(2) Trade secrets and commercial or financial information obtained from a person and privileged or confidential. As provided in section 6(f) of the Federal Trade Commission Act, 15 U.S.C. 46(f), this exemption applies to competitively sensitive information, such as costs or various types of sales statistics and inventories. It includes trade secrets in the nature of formulas, patterns, devices, and processes of manufacture, as well as names of customers in which there is a proprietary or highly competitive interest.

(3) Interagency or intra-agency memoranda or letters that would not

routinely be available by law to a private party in litigation with the Commission, provided that the deliberative process privilege shall not apply to records created 25 years or more before the date on which the records are requested. This exemption preserves the existing freedom of Commission officials and employees to engage in full and frank communication with each other and with officials and employees of other governmental agencies. This exemption includes records of the deliberations of the Commission except for the record of the final votes of each member of the Commission in every agency proceeding. It includes intraagency and interagency reports, memorandums, letters, correspondence, work papers, and minutes of meetings, as well as staff papers prepared for use within the Commission or between the Commission and other governmental agencies. It also includes information scheduled for public release, but as to which premature release would be contrary to the public interest;

(4) Personnel and medical files and similar files the disclosure of which would constitute a clearly unwarranted invasion of personal privacy except to the extent such files or materials must be disclosed under other laws or regulations. This exemption applies to personnel and medical records and similar records containing private or personal information concerning any individual which, if disclosed to any person other than the individual concerned or his designated legal representative without his permission in writing, would constitute a clearly unwarranted invasion of personal privacy. Examples of files exempt from disclosure include, but are not limited to:

(i) The personnel records of the Commission;

(ii) Files containing reports, records or other material pertaining to individual cases in which disciplinary or other administrative action has been or may be taken, including records of proceedings pertaining to the conduct or performance of duties by Commission personnel;

(5) Records or information compiled for law enforcement purposes, but only to the extent that production of such law enforcement records or information:

(i) Could reasonably be expected to interfere with enforcement proceedings;

(ii) Would deprive a person of a right to a fair trial or an impartial adjudication;

(iii) Could reasonably be expected to constitute an unwarranted invasion of personal privacy;

(iv) Could reasonably be expected to disclose the identity of a confidential source, including a State, local, or foreign agency or authority or any private institution that furnished information on a confidential basis, and, in the case of a record or information compiled by a criminal law enforcement authority in the course of a criminal investigation, or by an agency conducting a lawful national security intelligence investigation, information furnished by a confidential source;

(v) Would disclose techniques and procedures for law enforcement investigations or prosecutions, or would disclose guidelines for law enforcement investigations or prosecutions if such disclosure could reasonably be expected to risk circumvention of the law; or

(vi) Could reasonably be expected to endanger the life or physical safety of any individual.

(6) Information contained in or related to examination, operating, or condition reports prepared by, on behalf of, or for the use of an agency responsible for the regulation or supervision of financial institutions;

(7) Geological and geophysical information and data, including maps, concerning wells; and

(8) Material, as that term is defined in section 21(a) of the Federal Trade Commission Act, which is received by the Commission:

(i) In an investigation, a purpose of which is to determine whether any person may have violated any provision of the laws administered by the Commission; and

(ii) Which is provided pursuant to any compulsory process under the Federal Trade Commission Act, 15 U.S.C. 41, *et seq.*, or which is provided voluntarily in place of compulsory process in such an investigation. See section 21(f) of the Federal Trade Commission Act.

(9) Material, as that term is defined in section 21(a) of the Federal Trade Commission Act, which is received by the Commission pursuant to compulsory process in an investigation, a purpose of which is to determine whether any person may have violated any provision of the laws administered by the Commission. See section 21(b)(3)(C) of the Federal Trade Commission Act.

(10) Such other material of the Commission as may from time to time be designated by the Commission as confidential pursuant to statute or Executive Order. This exempts from disclosure any information that has been designated nonpublic pursuant to criteria and procedures prescribed by Executive Order and that has not been subsequently declassified in accordance with applicable procedures. The exemption also preserves the full force and effect of statutes that restrict public access to specific government records or material.

(11) Material in an investigation or proceeding that involves a possible violation of criminal law, when there is reason to believe that the subject of the investigation or proceeding is not aware of its pendency, and disclosure of the existence of the investigation could reasonably be expected to interfere with enforcement proceedings. When a request is made for records under §4.11(a), the Commission may treat the records as not subject to the requirements of the Freedom of Information Act.

(b) With respect to information contained in transcripts of Commission meetings, the exemptions contained in paragraph (a) of this section, except for paragraphs (a)(3) and (a)(7) of this section, shall apply; in addition, such information will not be made available if it is likely to have any of the effects described in 5 U.S.C. 552b (c)(5), (c)(9), or (c)(10).

(c) Under section 10 of the Federal Trade Commission Act, any officer or employee of the Commission who shall make public any information obtained by the Commission, without its authority, unless directed by a court, shall be deemed guilty of a misdemeanor, and upon conviction thereof, may be punished by a fine not exceeding five thousand dollars ($5,000), or by imprisonment not exceeding 1 year, or by fine and imprisonment, in the discretion of the court.

(d) Except as provided in paragraphs (f) or (g) of this section or in §4.11(b), (c), (d), (i), or (j), no material that is marked or otherwise identified as confidential and that is within the scope of §4.10(a)(8), and no material within the scope of §4.10(a)(9) that is not otherwise public, will be made available without the consent of the person who produced the material, to any individual other than a duly authorized officer or employee of the Commission or a consultant or contractor retained by the Commission who has agreed in writing not to disclose the information. All other Commission records may be made available to a requester under the procedures set forth in §4.11 or may be disclosed by the Commission except where prohibited by law.

(e) Except as provided in paragraphs (f) or (g) of this section or in §4.11(b), (c), (d), (i), or (j), material not within the scope of §4.10(a)(8) or §4.10(a)(9) that is received by the Commission and is marked or otherwise identified as confidential may be disclosed only if it is determined that the material is not within the scope of §4.10(a)(2), and the submitter is provided at least ten days notice of the intent to disclose the material.

(f) Nonpublic material obtained by the Commission may be disclosed to persons other than the submitter in connection with the taking of oral testimony without the consent of the submitter only if the material or transcript is not within the scope of §4.10(a)(2). If the material is marked confidential, the submitter will be provided 10 days' notice of the intended disclosure or will be afforded an opportunity to seek an appropriate protective order.

(g) Material obtained by the Commission:

(1) Through compulsory process and protected by section 21(b) of the Federal Trade Commission Act, 15 U.S.C. 57b–2(b) or voluntarily in lieu thereof and designated by the submitter as confidential and protected by section 21(f) of the Federal Trade Commission

Act, 15 U.S.C. 57b–2(f), and §4.10(d) of this part; or

(2) That is designated by the submitter as confidential, and protected by section 21(c) of the Federal Trade Commission Act, 15 U.S.C. 57b–2(c), and §4.10(e) of this part; or

(3) That is confidential commercial or financial information protected by section 6(f) of the Federal Trade Commission Act, 15 U.S.C. 46(f), and §4.10(a)(2) of this part, may be disclosed in Commission administrative or court proceedings subject to Commission or court protective or *in camera* orders as appropriate. See §§1.18(b) and 3.45.

Prior to disclosure of such material in a proceeding, the submitter will be afforded an opportunity to seek an appropriate protective or *in camera* order. All other material obtained by the Commission may be disclosed in Commission administrative or court proceedings at the discretion of the Commission except where prohibited by law.

(15 U.S.C. 41 *et seq.*)

[38 FR 1731, Jan. 18, 1973, as amended at 40 FR 7629, Feb. 21, 1975; 40 FR 23278, May 29, 1975; 42 FR 13540, Mar. 11, 1977; 46 FR 26291, May 12, 1981; 49 FR 30166, July 27, 1984; 54 FR 7399, Feb. 21, 1989; 57 FR 10807, Mar. 31, 1992; 60 FR 37749, July 21, 1995; 63 FR 38473, July 17, 1998; 65 FR 67259, Nov. 9, 2000; 66 FR 17633, Apr. 3, 2001; 72 FR 28853, May 23, 2007; 81 FR 93805, Dec. 22, 2016]

§4.11 Disclosure requests.

(a) *Freedom of Information Act*—(1) *Initial requests*—(i) *Form and contents; time of receipt.* (A) A request under the provisions of the Freedom of Information Act, 5 U.S.C. 552, as amended, for access to Commission records shall be in writing and transmitted by one of the following means: by the form located on the FTC's FOIA Web site, found at *www.ftc.gov*; by email message to the FOIA email account at *foia@ftc.gov*; by facsimile transmission to (202) 326–2477; or by mail to the following address: Freedom of Information Act Request, Office of the General Counsel, Federal Trade Commission, 600 Pennsylvania Avenue NW., Washington, DC 20580.

(B) Failure to mark the envelope and the request in accordance with paragraph (a)(1)(i)(A) of this section, or the filing of a request for expedited treatment under paragraph (a)(1)(i)(G) of this section, will result in the request (or requests, if expedited treatment has been requested) as received on the date that the processing unit in the Office of General Counsel actually receives the request(s).

(C) *Acknowledgment of requests.* Once a FOIA request is properly received by the processing unit in the Office of the General Counsel, a letter acknowledging the receipt of the request shall be mailed to the requester if processing the request will likely take more than 5 business days.

(D) *Identifiability.* (*1*) A properly filed FOIA request shall reasonably describe the records sought with enough detail to enable the Commission to locate them with a reasonable amount of effort. Whenever possible, the request should include specific information about each record sought such as date, title, name, author, recipient, subject matter of the record, provide information regarding fees pursuant to §4.8(c), and provide sufficient contact information for a response to be sent. Although a mailing address is generally required, an email address can suffice in some instances. The FOIA Office will consider requests to send responses by email.

(*2*) A denial of a request may state that the description required by paragraph (a)(2)(ii)(A) of this section is insufficient to allow identification and location of the records.

(E) *Costs; agreement to pay costs.* Requesters will be charged search, review, duplication and other chargeable direct costs as prescribed by §4.8 for requests under this section. All requests shall include a statement of the information needed to determine fees, as provided by §4.8(c), and an agreement to pay fees (or a statement that the requester will not pay fees if a fee waiver is denied), as provided by §4.8(d). Requests may also include an application for a fee waiver, as provided by §4.8(e). An advance payment may be required in appropriate cases as provided by §4.8(h).

(F) *Failure to agree to pay fees.* If a request does not include an agreement to pay fees, and if the requester is notified of the estimated costs pursuant to §4.8(d)(3), the request will be deemed not to have been received until the requester agrees to pay such fees. If a requester declines to pay fees within 20 calendar days and is not granted a fee waiver, the request will be denied.

(G) *Expedited treatment.* Requests may include an application for expedited treatment. Where such an application is not included with an initial request for access to records under paragraph (a)(1) of this section, the application may be included in any appeal of that request filed under paragraph (a)(3) of this section. Such application, which shall be certified by the requester to be true and correct to the best of such person's knowledge and belief, shall describe the compelling need for expedited treatment, including an explanation as to why a failure to obtain the requested records on an expedited basis could reasonably be expected to pose an imminent threat to the life or physical safety of an individual, or, with respect to a request made by a person primarily engaged in disseminating information, an explanation of the urgency to inform the public concerning actual or alleged Federal Government activity. The deciding official (as designated by the General Counsel) will, within 10 calendar days of receipt of a request for expedited treatment, notify the requester, in writing, of the decision to either grant or deny the request for expedited treatment, and, if the request is denied, advise the requester that this determination may be appealed to the General Counsel.

(H) *Records for sale at another government agency.* If requested materials are available for sale at another government agency, the requester will not be provided with copies of the materials but will be advised to obtain them from the selling agency. The U.S. Government Printing Office ("GPO"), the official bookstore for most U.S. Government publications, can be contacted at (202) 512–1800 (for those in the Washington, DC area), toll-free at (866) 512–1800 and at *ContactCenter@gpo.gov.* The GPO's online store can be accessed at *http://bookstore.gpo.gov* and mail orders should be directed to U.S. Government Printing Office, P.O. Box 979050, St. Louis, MO 63197–9000.

(ii) *Time limit for initial determination.* (A) The deciding official (as designated by the General Counsel) will, within 20 working days of the receipt of a request, or if applicable, the date that a request is properly filed, either grant or deny, in whole or in part, such request, unless the request has been granted expedited treatment in accordance with this section, in which case the request will be processed as soon as practicable. The date that a request is properly filed is the date on which the requester agrees to pay fees necessary for a response, reasonably describes the records sought, and provides sufficient contact information for a response to be sent. Any tolling of the 20-working day period will be done in compliance with the FOIA statute, as amended.

(B) Except in exceptional circumstances as provided in paragraph (a)(1)(ii)(C) of this section, the deciding official (as designated by the General Counsel) may extend the time limit by not more than 10 working days if such extension is:

(*1*) Necessary to search for and collect the records from field facilities or other establishments that are separate from the office processing the request; or

(*2*) Necessary to search for, collect, and appropriately examine a voluminous amount of separate and distinct records which are sought in a single or series of closely related requests; or

(*3*) Necessary for consultation with another agency having a substantial interest in the determination, or for consultation among two or more components of the Commission having substantial subject matter interest therein.

(C) If the deciding official (as designated by the General Counsel) extends the time limit for initial determination pursuant to paragraph (a)(1)(ii)(B) of this section, the requester will be notified in accordance with 5 U.S.C. 552(a)(6)(B). In exceptional circumstances, when the request cannot be processed within the extended time limit, the requester will be so notified and provided an opportunity to limit the scope of the request so that it may be processed within such time limit, or to arrange an alternative time frame for processing the request or a modified request. In exceptional circumstances, when the request cannot be processed within the extended time limit, the Commission will also make available the agency's FOIA Public Liaison to assist in the resolution of any disputes and notify the requester of the right to seek dispute resolution services from the Office of Government Information Services. "Exceptional" circumstances will not include delays resulting from a predictable workload of requests under this section. Unwillingness to make reasonable modifications in the scope of the request or to agree to an alternative time frame may be considered as factors in determining whether exceptional circumstances exist and whether the agency has exercised due diligence in responding to the request.

(D) If the deciding official (as designated by the General Counsel) reasonably believes that requests made by a requester, or a group of requesters acting in concert, actually constitute a single request that would otherwise involve unusual circumstances, as specified in paragraph (a)(1)(ii)(B) of this section, and the requests involve clearly related matters, those multiple requests may be aggregated.

(E) If a request is not granted within the time limits set forth in paragraphs (a)(1)(ii)(A) and (B) of this section, the request shall be deemed to be denied and the requesting party may appeal such denial to the General Counsel in accordance with paragraph (a)(3) of this section.

(iii) *Initial determination.* (A) The deciding official (as designated by the General Counsel) will make reasonable efforts to search, using either manual or electronic means, for documents that exist as of the date of the receipt of a request for the requested records in electronic form or format, except when such efforts would significantly interfere with the operation of the Commission's automated information systems. The deciding official will only withhold information if the agency reasonably foresees that disclosure would harm an interest protected by a FOIA exemption or disclosure is prohibited by law. The deciding official shall consider whether partial disclosure of information is possible whenever there is a determination that a full disclosure of a requested record is not possible and take reasonable steps necessary to segregate and release nonexempt information. Determination letters to a requester shall include the reasons therefor and the right of such person to seek assistance from the FTC's FOIA Public Liaison. Denials will advise the requester that this determination may be appealed to the General Counsel not more than 90 days after the date of the determination if the requester believes either that the records are not exempt, or that the General Counsel should exercise discretion to release such records notwithstanding their exempt status. The deciding official (as designated by the General Counsel) will also provide a reasonable, good-faith estimate of the volume of any materials to which access is denied, unless providing such an estimate would harm an interest protected by an exemption in 5 U.S.C. 552(b) that was cited as a basis for withholding materials. In the case of an adverse determination, FOIA response letters will notify requesters that they may seek dispute resolution services from the FTC's FOIA Public Liaison or from the Office of Government Information Services.

(B) The deciding official (as designated by the General Counsel) is deemed to be the sole official responsible for all denials of initial requests, except denials of access to materials contained in active investigatory files, in which case the Director or Deputy Director of the Bureau or the Director of the Regional Office responsible for the investigation will be the responsible official.

(C) Records to which access has been granted will be made available to the requester in any form or format specified by the requester, if the records are readily reproducible in that form or format, or can be converted to that form or format with a reasonable amount of effort. Certain records which are not easily copied or duplicated, such as tangible exhibits, will be made be available for inspection for a period not to exceed 30 days from date of notification to the requester unless the requester asks for and receives the consent of the deciding official (as designated by the General Counsel) to a longer period. Records assembled pursuant to a request will remain available only during this period and thereafter will be refiled. Appropriate fees may be imposed for any new or renewed request for the same records.

(D) If a requested record cannot be located from the information supplied, or is known to have been destroyed or otherwise disposed of, the requester shall be so notified. The requester will also be notified if a record that is part of an official agency file is lost or missing. If the person so requests, he will also be notified if the record should subsequently be located.

(2) *FOIA Requester Service Center.* If a requester has questions or comments about the FOIA process, the requester should call the FOIA Requester Service Center at (202) 326–2430 to either speak directly to a FOIA Case Officer or leave a voice message. A requester should also ask the FOIA Case Officer to speak with the FOIA Public Liaison if there are concerns about the quality of the service received, or seek mediation resolution assistance during the FOIA response process.

(3) *Appeals to the General Counsel from initial denials*—(i) *Form and contents; time of receipt*—(A)(*1*) If an initial request for expedited treatment is denied, the requester, at any time before the initial determination of the underlying request for records by the deciding official (as designated by the General Counsel) (or, if the request for expedited treatment was filed with any appeal filed under paragraph (a)(3)(i)(A)(*2*) of this section, at any time before the General Counsel's determination on such an appeal), may appeal the denial of expedited treatment to the General Counsel.

(*2*) If an initial request for records is denied in its entirety, the requester may, within 90 days after the adverse determination, appeal such denial to the General Counsel. If an initial request is denied in part, the time for appeal will not expire until 90 days after the date of the final letter notifying the requester that all records to which access has been granted have been made available. In unusual circumstances, the General Counsel or his or her designee may extend the time to appeal.

(*3*) If an initial request for a fee waiver or reduction is denied, the requester may, within 30 days of the date of the letter notifying the requester of that decision, appeal such denial to the General Counsel. In unusual circumstances, the time to appeal may be extended by the General Counsel or his or her designee.

(*4*) The appeal shall be in writing and shall clearly refer to the adverse decision, or portions of the decision, being appealed; the appeal should include a copy of the initial request and a copy of the response to that initial request, if any. The appeal may be: mailed to Freedom of Information Act Appeal, Office of the General Counsel, Federal Trade Commission, 600 Pennsylvania Avenue NW., Washington, DC 20580; submitted by facsimile to (202) 326–3198; or emailed to *FOIAAppeal@ftc.gov.*

(B) If the appeal is mailed, failure to mark the envelope and the appeal in accordance with paragraph (a)(3)(i)(A)(*4*) of this section will result in the appeal (and any request for expedited treatment filed with that appeal) being treated as received on the actual date of receipt by the Office of General Counsel.

(C) Each appeal to the General Counsel that requests him or her to exercise his discretion to release exempt records shall set forth the interest of the requester in the subject matter and the purpose for which the records will be used if the request is granted.

(ii) *Time limit for appeal.* (A)(*1*) Regarding appeals from initial denials of a request for expedited treatment, the General Counsel will either grant or deny the appeal expeditiously;

(*2*) Regarding appeals from initial denials of a request for records, the General Counsel will, within 20 working days of the Office of General Counsel's receipt of such an appeal, either grant or deny it, in whole or in part, unless expedited treatment has been granted in accordance with this section, in which case the appeal will be processed expeditiously.

(B) The General Counsel may, by written notice to the requester in accordance with 5 U.S.C. 552(a)(6)(B), extend the time limit for deciding an appeal by not more than 10 working days pursuant to paragraph (a)(1)(ii)(B) of this section, provided that the amount of any extension utilized during the initial consideration of the request under that paragraph will be subtracted from the amount of additional time otherwise available. Where exceptional circumstances do not permit the processing of the appeal within the extended time limit, the notice and procedures set forth in paragraph (a)(1)(ii)(C) of this section shall apply.

(iii) *Determination of appeal.* (A) The General Counsel has the authority to grant or deny all appeals and to release as an exercise of discretion records exempt from mandatory disclosure under 5 U.S.C. 552(b). In unusual or difficult cases, the General Counsel may, in his or her sole discretion, refer an appeal to the Commission for determination. A denial of an appeal in whole or in part will set forth the basis for the denial; will include a reasonable, good-faith estimate of the volume of any materials to which access is denied, unless providing such an estimate would harm an interest protected by an exemption in 5 U.S.C. 552(b) that was cited as a basis for withholding materials; and will advise the requester that judicial review of the decision is available by civil suit in the district in which the requester resides, or has his principal place of business, or in which the agency records are situated, or in the District of Columbia.

(B) The General Counsel may designate a Deputy General Counsel to make any determination assigned to the General Counsel by paragraph (a) of this section. The General Counsel or the official designated by the General Counsel to make the determination shall be deemed solely responsible for the denial of all appeals, except where an appeal is denied by the Commission. In such instances, the Commission shall be deemed solely responsible for the denial.

(b) *Requests from congressional committees and subcommittees.* Requests from congressional committees and subcommittees for nonpublic material shall be referred to the General Counsel for presentation to the Commission, subject to the provisions in 5 U.S.C. 552(c) and FTC Act 21(b) that neither the Freedom of Information Act, 5 U.S.C. 552, nor the Federal Trade Commission Act, 15 U.S.C. 41, *et seq.*, is authority to withhold information from Congress. Upon receipt of a request from a congressional committee or subcommittee, notice will be given to the submitter of any material marked confidential, or any material within the scope of §4.10(a)(9), that is responsive to the request that the request has been received. No other notice need be provided prior to granting the request. The Commission will inform the committee or subcommittee that the submitter considers such information confidential.

(c) *Requests from Federal and State law enforcement agencies.* Requests from law enforcement agencies of the Federal and State governments for nonpublic records shall be addressed to a liaison officer, where the Commission has appointed such an officer, or if there is none, to the General Counsel. With respect to requests under this paragraph, the General Counsel, the General Counsel's designee, or the appropriate liaison officer is delegated the authority to dispose of them. Alternatively, the General Counsel may refer such requests to the Commission for determination, except that requests must be referred to the Commission for determination where the Bureau having the material sought and the General Counsel do not agree on the disposition. Prior to granting access under this section to any material submitted to the Commission, the General Counsel, the General Counsel's designee, or the liaison officer will obtain from the requester a certification that such information will be maintained in confidence and will be used only for official law enforcement purposes. The certificate will also describe the nature of the law enforcement activity and the anticipated relevance of the information to that activity. A copy of the certificate will be forwarded to the submitter of the information at the time the request is granted unless the agency requests that the submitter not be notified. Requests for material pursuant to compulsory process, or for voluntary testimony, in cases or matters in which the Commission is not a party will be treated in accordance with paragraph (e) of this section.

(d) *Requests from Federal and State agencies for purposes other than law enforcement.* Requests from Federal and State agencies for access to nonpublic records for purposes not related to law enforcement should be addressed to the General Counsel. The General Counsel or the General Counsel's designee is delegated the authority to dispose of requests under this paragraph. Disclosure of nonpublic information will be made consistent with sections 6(f) and 21 of the FTC Act. Requests under this section shall be subject to the fee and fee waiver provisions of §4.8. Requests for material pursuant to compulsory process, or for voluntary testimony, in cases or matters in which the Commission is not a party will be treated in accordance with paragraph (e) of this section.

(e) *Requests for testimony, pursuant to compulsory process or otherwise, and requests for material pursuant to compulsory process, in cases or matters to which the Commission is not a party.* (1) The procedures specified in this section will apply to compulsory process and requests for voluntary testimony directed to Commission employees, except special government employees, that relate in any way to the employees' official duties. These procedures will also apply to compulsory process and requests for voluntary testimony directed to former Commission employees or to current or former special government employees of the Commission that seek nonpublic materials or information acquired during Commission employment. The provisions of paragraph (e)(3) of this section will also apply when requests described above are directed to the Commission. For purposes of this section, the term *testimony* includes any written or oral statement by a witness, such as depositions, affidavits, declarations, and statements at a hearing or trial; the term *nonpublic* includes any material or information which, under §4.10, is not required to be made public; the term *employees*, except where otherwise specified, includes *special government employees* and other Commission employees; and the term *special government employees* includes consultants and other employees as defined by section 202 of title 18 of the United States Code.

(2) Any employee or former employee who is served with compulsory process shall promptly advise the General Counsel of its service, the nature of the material or information sought, and all relevant facts and circumstances. This notification requirement also applies to any employee or former employee whose testimony is sought on a voluntary basis under the conditions set forth in paragraph (e)(1) of this section.

(3) A party who causes compulsory process to be issued to, or who requests testimony by, the Commission or any employee or former employee of the Commission shall furnish a statement to the General Counsel, unless, with respect to a request by a Federal or State agency, the General Counsel determines, as a matter of discretion, to waive this requirement. The statement shall set forth the party's interest in the case or matter, the relevance of the desired testimony or material, and a discussion of whether it is reasonably available from other sources. If testimony is desired, the statement shall also contain a general summary of the testimony and a discussion of whether Commission records could be produced and used in its place. Any authorization for testimony will be limited to the scope of the demand as summarized in such statement.

(4) Absent authorization from the General Counsel, the employee or former employee shall respectfully decline to produce requested material or to disclose requested information. The refusal should be based on this paragraph and on *United States ex rel. Touhy* v. *Ragen*, 340 U.S. 462 (1951).

(5) The General Counsel will consider and act upon compulsory process and requests for voluntary testimony under this section with due regard for statutory restrictions, the Commission's rules and the public interest, taking into account such factors as the need to conserve the time of employees for conducting official business; the need to avoid spending the time and money of the United States for private purposes; the need to maintain impartiality between private litigants in cases where a substantial government

interest is not involved; and the established legal standards for determining whether justification exists for the disclosure of confidential information and material.

(6) Invitations to testify before Congressional committees or subcommittees or to testify before other government bodies on the possible effects of legislative and regulatory proposals are not subject to paragraphs (e)(1) through (5) of this section.

(f) Requests by current or former employees to use nonpublic memoranda as writing samples shall be addressed to the General Counsel. The General Counsel or the General Counsel's designee is delegated the authority to dispose of such requests consistent with applicable nondisclosure provisions, including sections 6(f) and 21 of the FTC Act.

(g) Employees are encouraged to engage in teaching, lecturing, and writing that is not prohibited by law, Executive order, or regulation. However, an employee shall not use information obtained as a result of his Government employment, except to the extent that such information has been made available to the general public or will be made available on request, or when the General Counsel or the General Counsel's designee gives written authorization for the use of nonpublic information on the basis that the use is in the public interest.

(h) The General Counsel (or General Counsel's designee) may authorize a Commission member, other Commission official, or Commission staff to disclose an item or category of information from Commission records not currently available to the public for routine inspection and copying under Rule 4.9(b) where the General Counsel (or General Counsel's designee) determines that such disclosure would facilitate the conduct of official agency business and would not otherwise be prohibited by applicable law, order, or regulation. Requests for such determinations shall be set forth in writing and, in the case of staff requests, shall be forwarded to the General Counsel (or General Counsel's designee) through the relevant Bureau. In unusual or difficult cases, the General Counsel may refer the request to the Commission for determination.

(i) The Director of the Bureau of Competition is authorized, without power of redelegation, to respond to access requests for records and other materials pursuant to an agreement under the International Antitrust Enforcement Assistance Act, 15 U.S.C. 6201 *et seq.* Before responding to such a request, the Bureau Director shall transmit the proposed response to the Secretary and the Secretary shall notify the Commission of the proposed response. If no Commissioner objects within three days following the Commission's receipt of such notification, the Secretary shall inform the Bureau Director that he or she may proceed.

(j)(1) The procedures specified in this section apply to disclosures of certain records to foreign law enforcement agencies in specified circumstances in accordance with the U.S. SAFE WEB Act of 2006. Nothing in this section authorizes the disclosure of material obtained in connection with the administration of the Federal antitrust laws or foreign antitrust laws, as defined in paragraph (j)(5)(i) of this section.

(2) Requests from foreign law enforcement agencies, as defined in paragraph (j)(5)(ii) of this section, for nonpublic records shall be addressed to the Director of the Office of International Affairs or the Director's designee, who shall forward them to the General Counsel with recommendations for disposition after obtaining any required certification described in paragraph (j)(3) of this section and approval of the Bureau of Consumer Protection. With respect to requests under this paragraph, the General Counsel or the General Counsel's designee is delegated the authority to dispose of them. Alternatively, the General Counsel may refer such requests to the Commission for determination, except that requests must be referred to the Commission for determination where the Bureau of Consumer Protection or the Office of International Affairs disagrees with the General Counsel's proposed disposition.

(3) Access under this section to any material subject to the disclosure restrictions in sections 6(f) or 21(b) of the

FTC Act or § 4.10(d) may not be granted unless—

(i) An appropriate official of the foreign law enforcement agency has certified, either by prior agreement or memorandum of understanding or by other written certification, that such material will be maintained in confidence and will be used only for official law enforcement purposes; and

(ii)(A) The foreign law enforcement agency has set forth a bona fide legal basis for its authority to maintain the material in confidence;

(B) The materials are to be used for purposes of investigating, or engaging in enforcement proceedings related to, possible violations of:

(*1*) Foreign laws prohibiting fraudulent or deceptive commercial practices, or other practices substantially similar to practices prohibited by any law administered by the Commission;

(*2*) A law administered by the Commission, if disclosure of the material would further a Commission investigation or enforcement proceeding; or

(*3*) With the approval of the Attorney General, other foreign criminal laws, if such foreign criminal laws are offenses defined in or covered by a criminal mutual legal assistance treaty in force between the government of the United States and the foreign law enforcement agency's government;

(C) The appropriate Federal banking agency, (as defined in section 3(q) of the Federal Deposit Insurance Act (12 U.S.C. 1813(q)) or, in the case of a Federal credit union, the National Credit Union Administration has given its prior approval if the materials to be provided under paragraph (j)(3)(ii)(B) of this section are requested by the foreign law enforcement agency for the purpose of investigating, or engaging in enforcement proceedings based on, possible violations of law by a bank, a savings and loan institution described in section 18(f)(3) of the Federal Trade Commission Act (15 U.S.C. 57a(f)(3)), or a Federal credit union described in section 18(f)(4) of the Federal Trade Commission Act (15 U.S.C. 57a(f)(4)); and

(D) The foreign law enforcement agency is not from a foreign state that the Secretary of State has determined, in accordance with section 6(j) of the Export Administration Act of 1979 (50 U.S.C. App. 2405(j)), has repeatedly provided support for acts of international terrorism, unless and until such determination is rescinded pursuant to section 6(j)(4) of that Act (50 U.S.C. App. 2405(j)(4)).

(4) A copy of the certificate described in paragraph (j)(3) of this section will be forwarded to the submitter of the information at the time the request is granted unless the foreign law enforcement agency requests that the submitter not be notified.

(5) For purposes of this section:

(i) "Federal antitrust laws" and "foreign antitrust laws" are to be interpreted as defined in paragraphs (5) and (7), respectively, of section 12 of the International Antitrust Enforcement Assistance Act of 1994 (15 U.S.C. 6211); and

(ii) "Foreign law enforcement agency" is defined as:

(A) Any agency or judicial authority of a foreign government, including a foreign state, a political subdivision of a foreign state, or a multinational organization constituted by and comprised of foreign states, that is vested with law enforcement or investigative authority in civil, criminal, or administrative matters and

(B) Any multinational organization, to the extent that it is acting on behalf of an entity described in paragraph (j)(5)(i)(A) of this section.

(15 U.S.C. 41 *et seq.*)

[40 FR 7629, Feb. 21, 1975]

EDITORIAL NOTE: For FEDERAL REGISTER citations affecting § 4.11, see the List of CFR Sections Affected, which appears in the Finding Aids section of the printed volume and at *www.govinfo.gov*.

§ 4.12 Disposition of documents submitted to the Commission.

(a) *Material submitted to the Commission.* (1) Any person who has submitted material to the Commission may obtain, on request, the return of material submitted to the Commission which has not been received into evidence:

(i) After the close of the proceeding in connection with which the material was submitted; or

(ii) When no proceeding in which the material may be used has been commenced within a reasonable time after completion of the examination and analysis of all such material and other information assembled in the course of the investigation.

(2) Such request shall be in writing, addressed to the custodian designated pursuant to §2.16 or the Secretary of the Commission in all other circumstances, and shall reasonably describe the material requested. A request for return of material may be filed at any time, but material will not be returned nor will commitments to return material be undertaken prior to the time described in this paragraph.

(b) *Commission-made copies of documents submitted to the Commission.* The Commission will not return to the submitter copies of documents made by the Commission unless, upon a showing of extraordinary circumstances, the Commission determines that return would be required in the public interest.

(c) *Disposition of material not returned.* Subsequent to the time prescribed in paragraph (a) of this section, the staff will examine all submitted material and Commission-made copies of documents located in a reasonable search of the Commission's files and will determine, consistent with the Federal Records Act, 44 U.S.C. 3301, which materials are appropriate for preservation as evidence of the organization, functions, policies, decisions, procedures, operations, or other activities of the Commission or because of the information value of data in them. The Commission will dispose of all material determined not to be appropriate for preservation in accordance with applicable regulations of the National Archives and Records Administration.

[46 FR 26292, May 12, 1981, as amended at 60 FR 37751, July 21, 1995; 78 FR 13474, Feb. 28, 2013]

§4.13 Privacy Act rules.

(a) *Purpose and scope.* (1) This section is promulgated to implement the Privacy Act of 1974 (Pub. L. 93–579, 5 U.S.C. 552a) by establishing procedures whereby an individual can, as to all systems of records maintained by the Commission except those set forth in §4.13(m) as exempt from disclosure, (i) Request notification of whether the Commission maintains a record pertaining to him in any system of records, (ii) request access to such a record or to an accounting of its disclosure, (iii) request that the record be amended or corrected, and (iv) appeal an initial adverse determination of any such request. This section also establishes those systems of records that are specifically exempt from disclosure and from other requirements.

(2) The procedures of this section apply only to requests by an individual as defined in §4.13(b). Except as otherwise provided, they govern only records containing personal information in systems of records for which notice has been published by the Commission in the FEDERAL REGISTER pursuant to section 552a(e)(4) of the Privacy Act of 1974 and which are neither exempt from the provisions of this section nor contained in government-wide systems of personnel records for which notice has been published in the FEDERAL REGISTER by the Office of Personnel Management. Requests for notification, access, and amendment of personnel records which are contained in a system of records for which notice has been given by the Office of Personnel Management are governed by the Office of Personnel Management's notices, 5 CFR part 297. Access to records which are not subject to the requirements of the Privacy Act are governed by §§4.8 through 4.11.

(b) *Definitions.* The following definitions apply to this section only:

(1) *Individual* means a natural person who is a citizen of the United States or an alien lawfully admitted for permanent residence.

(2) *Record* means any item, collection, or grouping of personal information about an individual that is maintained by the Commission, including, but not limited to, his education, financial transactions, medical history, and criminal or employment history and that contains his name, or the identifying number, symbol, or other identifying particular assigned to the individual, such as a finger or voice print or a photograph, but does not include information concerning proprietorships, businesses, or corporations.

(3) *System of records* means a group of any records under the control of the Commission from which information is retrieved by the name of the individual

or by some identifying number, symbol, or other identifying particular assigned to the individual, for which notice has been published by the Commission in the FEDERAL REGISTER pursuant to 5 U.S.C. 552a(e)(4).

(c) *Procedures for requests pertaining to individual records in a record system.* An individual may request access to his or her records or any information pertaining to that individual in a system of records, and notification of whether and to whom the Commission has disclosed a record for which an accounting of disclosures is required to be kept and made available to the individual, using the procedures of this section. Requests for the disclosure of records under this section or to determine whether a system of records contains records pertaining to an individual or to obtain an accounting of disclosures, shall be in writing and if mailed, addressed as follows:

Privacy Act Request, Office of the General Counsel, Federal Trade Commission, 600 Pennsylvania Avenue, NW., Washington, DC 20580.

If requests are presented in person at the Office of the General Counsel, the individual shall be required to execute a written request. All requests shall name the system of records that is the subject of the request, and shall include any additional information specified in the pertinent system notice as necessary to locate the records requested. If the requester wants another person to accompany him or her to review the records, the request shall so state. Nothing in this section will allow an individual access to any information compiled in reasonable anticipation of a civil action or proceeding.

(d) *Times, places, and requirements for identification of individuals making requests.* Verification of identity of persons making written requests to the deciding official (as designated by the General Counsel) ordinarily will not be required. The signature on such requests will be deemed a certification by the signatory that he or she is the individual to whom the record pertains or is the parent or guardian of a minor or the legal guardian of the individual to whom the record pertains. The deciding official (as designated by the General Counsel) may require additional verification of a requester's identity when such information is reasonably necessary to assure that records are not improperly disclosed; provided, however, that no verification of identity will be required if the records sought are publicly available under the Freedom of Information Act.

(e) *Disclosure of requested information to individuals.* Within 10 working days of receipt of a request under §4.13(c), the deciding official (as designated by the General Counsel) will acknowledge receipt of the request. Within 30 working days of the receipt of a request under §4.13(c), the deciding official (as designated by the General Counsel) will inform the requester whether a system of records containing retrievable information pertaining to the requester exists, and if so, either that the request has been granted or that the requested records or information is exempt from disclosure pursuant to §4.13(m). When, for good cause shown, the deciding official (as designated by the General Counsel) is unable to respond within 30 working days of the receipt of the request, that official will notify the requester and inform him or her approximately when a response will be made.

(f) *Special procedures: Medical records.* When the deciding official (as designated by the General Counsel) determines that disclosure of a medical or psychological record directly to a requesting individual could have an adverse effect on the individual, he or she will require the individual to designate a medical doctor to whom the record will be transmitted.

(g) *Request for correction or amendment of record.* An individual to whom access to his records or any information pertaining to him in a system of records has been granted may request that any portion thereof be amended or corrected because he believes it is not accurate, relevant, timely, or complete. An initial request for correction or amendment of a record shall be in writing whether presented in person or by mail, and if by mail, addressed as in §4.13(c). In making a request under this subsection, the requesting party shall state the nature of the information in the record the individual believes to be inaccurate, irrelevant, untimely, or incomplete, the correction or amendment desired, and the reasons therefore.

(h) *Agency review of request for correction or amendment of record.* Whether presented in person or by mail, requests under §4.13(g) will be acknowledged by the deciding official (as designated by the General Counsel) within 10 working days of the receipt of the request if action on the request cannot be completed and the individual notified of the results within that time. Thereafter, the deciding official (as designated by the General Counsel) will promptly either make the requested amendment or correction or inform the requester of his refusal to make the amendment or correction, the reasons for the refusal, and the requester's right to appeal that refusal in accordance with §4.13(i).

(i) *Appeal of initial adverse agency determination.* (1) If an initial request filed under §4.13(c) or §4.13(g) is denied, the requester may appeal that denial to the General Counsel. The appeal shall be in writing and addressed as follows:

Privacy Act Appeal, Office of the General Counsel, Federal Trade Commission, 600 Pennsylvania Avenue, NW., Washington, DC 20580.

Within 30 working days of the receipt of the appeal, the General Counsel will notify the requester of the disposition of that appeal, except that the General Counsel may extend the 30-day period for good cause, in which case, the General Counsel will advise the requester of the approximate date on which review will be completed. In unusual or difficult cases, the General Counsel may, in his or her sole discretion, refer an appeal to the Commission for determination.

(2)(i) If the General Counsel refuses to amend or correct the record in accordance with a request under §4.13(g), the General Counsel will notify the requester of that decision and inform the requester of the right to file with the deciding official (as designated by the General Counsel) a concise statement setting forth the reasons for the requester's disagreement with the General Counsel's determination and the fact that the requester's statement will be treated as set forth in paragraph (i)(2)(ii) of this section. The General Counsel will also inform the requester that judicial review of the decision is available by a civil suit in the district in which the requester resides, or has his principal place of business, or in which the agency records are situated, or in the District of Columbia.

(ii) If the individual files a statement disagreeing with the General Counsel's determination not to amend or correct a record, such disagreement will be clearly noted in the record involved and the individual's statement will be made available to anyone to whom the record has been disclosed after September 27, 1975, or is subsequently disclosed together with, if the General Counsel deems it appropriate, a brief statement of his or her reasons for declining to amend the record.

(j) *Disclosure of record to person other than the individual to whom it pertains.* Except as provided by 5 U.S.C. 552a(b), the written request or prior written consent of the individual to whom a record pertains, or of his parent if a minor, or legal guardian if incompetent, shall be required before such record is disclosed. If the individual elects to inspect a record in person and desires to be accompanied by another person, the deciding official (as designated by the General Counsel) may require the individual to furnish a signed statement authorizing disclosure of his or her record in the presence of the accompanying named person.

(k) *Fees.* No fees will be charged for searching for a record, reviewing it, or for copies of records made by the Commission for its own purposes incident to granting access to a requester. Copies of records to which access has been granted under this section may be obtained by the requester from the deciding official (as designated by the General Counsel) on payment of the reproduction fees provided in §4.8(b)(6).

(l) *Penalties.* Section 552a(i)(3) of the Privacy Act, 5 U.S.C. 552a(i)(3), makes it a misdemeanor, subject to a maximum fine of $5,000, to knowingly and willfully request or obtain any record concerning an individual under false pretenses. Sections 552a(i) (1) and (2) of the Privacy Act, 5 U.S.C. 552a(i) (1) and

(2), provide penalties for violations by agency employees of the Privacy Act or regulations established thereunder. Title 18 U.S.C. 1001, Crimes and Criminal Procedures, makes it a criminal offense, subject to a maximum fine of $10,000 or imprisonment for not more than 5 years or both, to knowingly and willfully make or cause to be made any false or fraudulent statements or representations in any matter within the jurisdiction of any agency of the United States.

(m) *Specific exemptions.* (1) Pursuant to 5 U.S.C. 552a(j)(2), investigatory materials maintained by an agency component in connection with any activity relating to criminal law enforcement in the following systems of records are exempt from all subsections of 5 U.S.C. 552a, except (b), (c)(1) and (2), (e)(4)(A) through (F), (e)(6), (7), (9), (10), and (11), and (i), and from the provisions of this section, except as otherwise provided in 5 U.S.C. 552a(j)(2):

(i) I–7—Office of Inspector General Investigative Files—FTC.

(ii) [Reserved]

(2) Pursuant to 5 U.S.C. 552a(k)(2), investigatory materials compiled for law enforcement purposes in the following systems of records are exempt from subsections (c)(3), (d), (e)(1), (e)(4)(G), (H), and (I), and (f) of 5 U.S.C. 552a, and from the provisions of this section, except as otherwise provided in 5 U.S.C. 552a(k)(2):

(i) I–1—Nonpublic Investigational and Other Nonpublic Legal Program Records—FTC.

(ii) I–2—Disciplinary Action Investigatory Files—FTC.

(iii) I–4—Clearance Application and Response Files—FTC.

(iv) I–5—Matter Management System—FTC.

(v) I–7—Office of Inspector General Investigative Files—FTC.

(vi) I–8—Stenographic Reporting Services Request System—FTC.

(vii) II–3—Worker's Compensation—FTC.

(viii) II–6—Discrimination Complaint System—FTC.

(ix) IV–1—Consumer Information System—FTC.

(x) V–1—Freedom of Information Act Requests and Appeals—FTC.

(xi) V–2—Privacy Act Requests and Appeals—FTC.

(xii) VII–6—Document Management and Retrieval System—FTC.

(3) Pursuant to 5 U.S.C. 552a(k)(5), investigatory materials compiled to determine suitability, eligibility, or qualifications for Federal civilian employment, military service, Federal contracts, or access to classified information, but only where disclosure would reveal the identity of a confidential source of information, in the following systems of records are exempt from subsections (c)(3), (d), (e)(1), (e)(4)(G), (H), and (I), and (f) of 5 U.S.C. 552a, and from the provisions of this section, except as otherwise provided in 5 U.S.C. 552a(k)(5):

(i) II–4—Employment Application-Related Records—FTC.

(ii) II–11—Personnel Security, Identity Management and Access Control Records System—FTC.

[40 FR 40780, Sept. 3, 1975, as amended at 46 FR 26292, May 12, 1981; 48 FR 4280, Jan. 31, 1983; 55 FR 37700, Sept. 13, 1990; 55 FR 38801, Sept. 21, 1990; 57 FR 10808, Mar. 31, 1992; 58 FR 7047, Feb. 4, 1993; 63 FR 45648, Aug. 26, 1998; 64 FR 3014, Jan. 20, 1999; 64 FR 69397, Dec. 13, 1999; 66 FR 64144, Dec. 12, 2001; 67 FR 123, Jan. 2, 2002; 80 FR 15163, Mar. 23, 2015]

§ 4.14 Conduct of business.

(a) Matters before the Commission for consideration may be resolved either at a meeting under § 4.15 or by written circulation. Any Commissioner may direct that a matter presented for consideration be placed on the agenda of a Commission meeting.

(b) A majority of the members of the Commission in office and not recused from participating in a matter (by virtue of 18 U.S.C. 208 or otherwise) constitutes a quorum for the transaction of business in that matter.

(c) Any Commission action, either at a meeting or by written circulation, may be taken only with the affirmative concurrence of a majority of the participating Commissioners, except where a greater majority is required by statute or rule or where the action is taken pursuant to a valid delegation of authority. No Commissioner may delegate the authority to determine his or her vote in any matter requiring Commission action, but authority to report a Commissioner's vote on a particular matter resolved either by written circulation, or at a meeting held in the Commissioner's absence, may be vested in a member of the Commissioner's staff.

[42 FR 13540, Mar. 11, 1977, as amended at 50 FR 53306, Dec. 31, 1985; 70 FR 53297, Sept. 8, 2005]

§4.15 Commission meetings.

(a) *In general.* (1) Meetings of the Commission, as defined in 5 U.S.C. 552b(a)(2), are held at the principal office of the Commission, unless otherwise directed.

(2) *Initial announcements of meetings.* For each meeting, the Commission shall announce:

(i) The time, place and subject matter of the meeting,

(ii) Whether the meeting will be open or closed to the public, and

(iii) The name and phone number of the official who will respond to requests for information about the meeting.

Such announcement shall be made at least one week before the meeting except that where the agency determines pursuant to 5 U.S.C. 552b(e)(1) to call the meeting on less than one week's notice, or where the agency determines to close the meeting pursuant to paragraph (c)(2) of this section, the announcement shall be made at the earliest practicable time.

(3) *Announcements of changes in meetings.* Following the announcement of a meeting, any change in the time, place or subject matter will be announced at the earliest practicable time, and, except with respect to meetings closed under paragraph (c)(2) of this section, any change in the subject matter or decision to open or close a meeting shall be made only as provided in 5 U.S.C. 552b(e)(2).

(4) *Deletions from announcements.* The requirements of paragraphs (a)(2) and (a)(3) of this section do not require the disclosure of any information pertaining to a portion of a closed meeting where such disclosure is likely to concern a matter within the scope of 5 U.S.C. 552b(c).

(5) *Dissemination of notices.* Notices required under paragraphs (a)(2) and (a)(3) of this section will be posted at the principal office of the Commission, recorded on a telephone message device, and, except as to notices of meetings closed under paragraph (c)(2) of this section, submitted to the FEDERAL REGISTER for publication. In addition, notices issued under paragraph (a)(2) of this section one week in advance of the meeting will be sent to all persons and organizations who have requested inclusion on a meeting notice mailing list, and will be issued as a press release to interested media.

(b) *Open meetings.* (1) Commission meetings shall be open to public observation unless the Commission determines that portions may be closed pursuant to 5 U.S.C. 552b(c).

(2) Any person whose interest may be directly affected if a portion of a meeting is open, may request that the Commission close that portion for any of the reasons described in 5 U.S.C. 552b(c). The Commission shall vote on such requests if at least one member desires to do so. Such requests shall be in writing, filed at the earliest practicable time, and describe how the matters to be discussed will have any of the effects enumerated in 5 U.S.C. 552b(c). Requests shall be addressed as follows:

Closed Meeting Request, Office of the General Counsel, Federal Trade Commission, 6th Street and Pennsylvania Avenue NW., Washington, DC 20580.

(3) The Commissioner to whom a matter has been assigned for presentation to the Commission shall have the authority to make available to the public, prior to consideration of that matter at an open meeting, material sufficient to inform the public of the issues likely to be discussed in connection with that matter.

(c) *Closed meetings.* (1) Whenever the Commission votes to close a meeting or series of meetings under these rules, it shall make publicly available within one day notices both of such vote and the General Counsel's determination regarding certification under 5 U.S.C. 552b(f)(1). Such determination by the General Counsel shall be made prior to the Commission vote to close a meeting or series of meetings. Further, except with respect to meetings closed under paragraph (c)(2) of this section, the Commission shall make publicly available within one day a full written explanation of its action in closing any meeting, and a list specifying the names and affiliations of all persons expected to attend, except Commission employees and consultants and any stenographer or court reporter attending for the sole purpose of preparing a verbatim transcript. All Commission employees and consultants may attend nonadjudicative portions of any closed meeting and members of Commissioners' personal staffs, the General Counsel and his staff, and the Secretary and his staff may attend the adjudicative portions of any closed meeting except to the extent the notice of a particular closed meeting otherwise specifically provides. Stenographers or court reporters may attend any closed meeting at which their services are required by the Commission.

(2) If a Commission meeting, or portions thereof, may be closed pursuant to 5 U.S.C. 552b(c)(10), the Commission may, by vote recorded at the beginning of the meeting, or portion thereof, close the portion or portions of the meeting so exempt.

(3) Closed meeting transcripts or minutes required by 5 U.S.C. 552b(f)(1) will be released to the public insofar as they contain information that either is not exempt from disclosure under 5 U.S.C. 552b(c), or, although exempt, should be disclosed in the public interest. The Commission will determine whether to release, in whole or in part, the minutes of its executive sessions to consider oral arguments. With regard to all other closed meetings, the General Counsel or the General Counsel's designee shall determine, in accordance with § 4.9(c), which portions of the transcripts or minutes may be released.

(d) The presiding officer shall be responsible for preserving order and decorum at meetings and shall have all powers necessary to that end.

[42 FR 13541, Mar. 11, 1977; 42 FR 15409, Mar. 22, 1977, as amended at 42 FR 62912, Dec. 14, 1977: 43 FR 1937, Jan. 13, 1978; 43 FR 35684, Aug. 11, 1978; 63 FR 32978, June 17, 1998]

§ 4.16 Privilege against self-incrimination.

Section 2.11 of Pub. L. 91–462 specifically repeals paragraph 7 of section 9 of the Federal Trade Commission Act. Title 18, section 6002, of the United States Code provides that whenever a witness refuses, on the basis of his privilege against self-incrimination, to testify or provide other information in a proceeding before or ancillary to:

(a) A court or grand jury of the United States,

(b) An agency of the United States, or

(c) Either House of Congress, a joint committee of the two Houses, or a committee or a subcommittee of either House, and the person presiding over the proceeding communicates to the witness an order issued under section 6004, the witness may not refuse to comply with the order on the basis of his privilege against self-incrimination; but no testimony or other information compelled under the order (or any information directly or indirectly derived from such testimony or other information) may be used against the witness in any criminal case, except a prosecution for perjury, giving a false statement, or otherwise failing to comply with the order. Title 18, section 6004, of the United States Code provides that:

(1) In the case of any individual who has been or who may be called to testify or provide other information at any proceeding before an agency of the United States, the agency may, with the approval of the Attorney General, issue, in accordance with subsection (b) of section 6004, an order requiring the individual to give testimony or provide other information which he refused to give or provide on the basis of his privilege against self-incrimination, such order to become effective as provided in title 18, section 6002, of the United States Code;

(2) An agency of the United States may issue an order under subsection (a) of section 6004 only if in its judgment

(i) The testimony or other information from such individual may be necessary to the public interest; and

(ii) Such individual has refused or is likely to refuse to testify or provide other information on the basis of his privilege against self-incrimination.

(18 U.S.C. 6002, 6004)

[37 FR 5017, Mar. 9, 1972. Redesignated at 45 FR 36345, May 29, 1980]

§4.17 Disqualification of Commissioners.

(a) *Applicability.* This section applies to all motions seeking the disqualification of a Commissioner from any adjudicative or rulemaking proceeding.

(b) *Procedures.* (1) Whenever any participant in a proceeding shall deem a Commissioner for any reason to be disqualified from participation in that proceeding, such participant may file with the Secretary a motion to the Commission to disqualify the Commissioner, such motion to be supported by affidavits and other information setting forth with particularity the alleged grounds for disqualification.

(2) Such motion shall be filed at the earliest practicable time after the participant learns, or could reasonably have learned, of the alleged grounds for disqualification.

(3)(i) Such motion shall be addressed in the first instance by the Commissioner whose disqualification is sought.

(ii) In the event such Commissioner declines to recuse himself or herself from further participation in the proceeding, the Commission shall determine the motion without the participation of such Commissioner.

(c) *Standards.* Such motion shall be determined in accordance with legal standards applicable to the proceeding in which such motion is filed.

(15 U.S.C. 46(g))

[46 FR 45750, Sept. 15, 1981]

PART 5—STANDARDS OF CONDUCT

Subpart A—Employee Conduct Standards and Financial Conflicts of Interest

Sec.

Subpart B—Financial Disclosure Requirements

Subparts C–D [Reserved]

Subpart E—Disciplinary Actions Concerning Postemployment Conflict of Interest

AUTHORITY: 5 U.S.C. 7301; 5 U.S.C. App. (Ethics in Government Act of 1978); 15 U.S.C. 46(g); E.O. 12674, 54 FR 15159, 3 CFR, 1989 Comp., p. 215, as modified by E.O. 12731, 55 FR 42547, 3 CFR, 1990 Comp., p. 306; 5 CFR part 2635.

SOURCE: 32 FR 13272, Sept. 20, 1967, unless otherwise noted. Redesignated at 41 FR 54483, Dec. 14, 1976.

Subpart A—Employee Conduct Standards and Financial Conflicts of Interest

§5.1 Cross-reference to executive branch-wide regulations.

Commissioners and employees, including special government employees, of the Federal Trade Commission (FTC) are subject to and should refer to the "Standards of Ethical Conduct for Employees of the Executive Branch" at 5 CFR part 2635 ("executive branch-wide Standards of Conduct") and to the FTC regulations at 5 CFR 5701 that supplement the executive branch-wide Standards of Conduct.

[58 FR 15764, Mar. 24, 1993, as amended at 64 FR 42594, Aug. 5, 1999]

§ 5.2 Exemption of insubstantial financial conflicts.

(a) An employee or special Government employee will not be subject to remedial or disciplinary action or to criminal prosecution under 18 U.S.C. 208(a), if he makes a full disclosure in writing to the official responsible for his appointment of the nature and circumstances of the particular matter involved and of his conflicting financial interest relating thereto, and receives in advance a written determination made by such official that the interest is not so substantial as to be deemed likely to affect the integrity of the services which the Government may expect from the employee or special Government employee.

(b) For the purposes of paragraph (a) of this section, the "official responsible for appointment" shall be the Executive Director in all cases where the employee is classified at grade GS–15 or below, or at a comparable pay level, except that each Commissioner shall be the "official responsible for appointment" of advisors in the Commissioner's immediate office.

(c) In all other cases, the Chairman shall be the "official responsible for appointment."

(d) Pursuant to 5 CFR part 2640, certain financial interests are exempted from the provisions of 18 U.S.C. 208(a) as being too remote too inconsequential to affect the integrity of an employee's services.

[58 FR 15764, Mar. 24, 1993, as amended at 63 FR 35130, June 29, 1998]

Subpart B—Financial Disclosure Requirements

§ 5.10 Cross-reference to executive branch-wide regulations.

Commissioners and employees, including special government employees, of the Federal Trade Commission are subject to and should refer to the executive branch-wide financial disclosure regulations at 5 CFR part 2634, and to the procedures for filing and review of financial disclosure reports found in Chapter 3 of the FTC *Administrative Manual*.

[58 FR 15765, Mar. 24, 1993]

Subparts C–D [Reserved]

Subpart E—Disciplinary Actions Concerning Postemployment Conflict of Interest

AUTHORITY: 15 U.S.C. 41 *et seq.*

SOURCE: 46 FR 26050, May 11, 1981, unless otherwise noted.

§ 5.51 Scope and applicability.

These regulations establish procedures for investigating and determining alleged violations of 18 U.S.C. 207 (postemployment restrictions applicable to federal employees) or regulations issued by the Office of Government Ethics, set forth in 5 CFR parts 2637 and 2641, reflecting the views of the Office of Government Ethics and the Department of Justice as to the requirements of 18 U.S.C. 207.

[58 FR 15765, Mar. 24, 1993]

§ 5.52 Nonpublic proceedings.

Any investigation or proceedings held under this part shall be nonpublic unless the respondent specifically requests otherwise, except to the extent required by the Freedom of Information Act (5 U.S.C. 552) or by the Sunshine Act (5 U.S.C. 552b). However, the presiding official's initial decision and any final decision of the Commission shall be placed on the public record, except that information may be designated *in camera* in accordance with § 3.45 of the Commission's Rules of Practice.

§ 5.53 Initiation of investigation.

(a) Investigations under this part may be initiated upon the submission by any person of a written statement to the Secretary setting forth sufficient information to indicate a possible violation of 18 U.S.C. 207 or by the Commission on its own initiative when a possible violation is indicated by information within the Commission's possession.

(b) At the direction of the Commission, the General Counsel shall investigate any alleged violation of 18 U.S.C. 207.

§ 5.54 Referral to the Office of Government Ethics and to the Department of Justice.

(a) The General Counsel shall make a preliminary determination of whether the matter appears frivolous and, if not, shall expeditiously transmit any available information to the Director of the Office of Government Ethics and to the Criminal Division, Department of Justice.

(b) Unless the Department of Justice communicates to the Commission that it does not intend to initiate criminal prosecution, the General Counsel shall coordinate any investigation or proceeding under this part with the Department of Justice in order to avoid prejudicing criminal proceedings.

§ 5.55 Conduct of investigation.

(a) The General Counsel may (1) exercise the authority granted in § 2.5 of the Commission's Rules of Practice to administer oaths and affirmations; and (2) conduct investigational hearings pursuant to part 2 of these rules. He may also recommend that the Commission issue compulsory process in connection with an investigation under this section.

(b) Witnesses in investigations shall have the rights set forth in § 2.9 of the Commission's Rules of Practice.

§ 5.56 Disposition.

(a) Upon the conclusion of an investigation under this part, the General Counsel shall forward to the Commission a summary of the facts disclosed by the investigation along with a recommendation as to whether the Commission should issue an order to show cause pursuant to § 5.57.

(b) When the former government employee involved is an attorney, the General Counsel shall also recommend whether the matter should be referred to the disciplinary committee of the bar(s) of which the attorney is a member.

§ 5.57 Order to show cause.

(a) Upon a Commission determination that there exists reasonable cause to believe a former government employee has violated 18 U.S.C. 207, the Commission may issue an order requiring the former employee to show cause why sanctions should not be imposed.

(b) The show cause order shall contain:

(1) The statutory provisions alleged to have been violated and a clear and concise description of the acts of the former employee that are alleged to constitute the violation;

(2) Notice of the respondent's right to submit an answer and request a hearing, and the time and manner in which the request is to be made; and

(3) A statement of the sanctions that may be imposed pursuant to § 5.67 of this part.

(c) Subsequent to the issuance of an order to show cause, any communications to or from the Commission or any member of the Commission shall be governed by the *ex parte* provisions of § 4.7 of the Commission's Rules of Practice. 16 CFR 4.7.

§ 5.58 Answer and request for a hearing.

(a) An answer and request for a hearing must be filed with the Secretary of the Commission within thirty (30) days after service of the order to show cause.

(b) In the absence of good cause shown, failure to file an answer and request for a hearing within the specified time limit:

(1) Will be deemed a waiver of the respondent's right to contest the allegations of the show cause order or request a hearing and

(2) Shall authorize the Commission to find the facts to be as alleged in the show cause order and enter a final decision providing for the imposition of such sanctions specified in § 5.67 as the Commission deems appropriate.

(c) An answer shall contain (1) a concise statement of the facts or law constituting each ground of defense and (2) specific admission, denial, or explanation of each fact alleged in the show cause order or, if the respondent is without knowledge thereof, a statement to that effect. Any allegations of a complaint not answered in this manner will be deemed admitted.

(d) Hearings shall be deemed waived as to any facts in the show cause order that are specifically admitted or deemed to be admitted as a result of respondent's failure to deny them. Those portions of respondent's answer, together with the show cause order, will provide a record basis for initial decision by the Administrative Law Judge or for final decision by the Commission.

(e) If all material factual allegations of the show cause order are specifically admitted or have been deemed admitted in accordance with paragraph (c) of this section, the Commission will decide the matter on the basis of the allegations set forth in the show cause order and respondent's answer.

§ 5.59 Presiding official.

(a) Upon the receipt of an answer and request for a hearing, the Secretary shall refer the matter to the Chief Administrative Law Judge, who shall appoint an Administrative Law Judge to preside over the hearing and shall notify the respondent and the General Counsel as to the person selected.

(b) The powers and duties of the presiding official shall be as set forth in § 3.42(b) through (h) of the Commission's Rules of Practice.

§ 5.60 Scheduling of hearing.

The presiding official shall fix the date, time and place of the hearing. The hearing shall not be scheduled earlier than fifteen days after receipt of the respondent's answer and request for a hearing. In fixing the time, date and place of the hearing, the presiding official shall give due regard to the respondent's need for adequate time to prepare a defense and an expeditious resolution of allegations that may be damaging to his or her reputation.

§ 5.61 Prehearing procedures; motions; interlocutory appeals; summary decision; discovery; compulsory process.

Because of the nature of the issues involved in proceedings under this part, the Commission anticipates that extensive motions, prehearing proceedings and discovery will not be required in most cases. For this reason, detailed procedures will not be established under this part. However, to the extent deemed warranted by the presiding official, prehearing conferences, motions, interlocutory appeals, summary decisions, discovery and compulsory process shall be permitted and shall be governed, where appropriate, by the provisions set forth in subparts C and D, part 3, of the Commission's Rules of Practice.

§ 5.62 Hearing rights of respondent.

In any hearing under this subpart, the respondent shall have the right:

(a) To be represented by counsel;

(b) To present and cross-examine witnesses and submit evidence;

(c) To present objections, motions, and arguments, oral or written; and

(d) To obtain a transcript of the proceedings on request.

§ 5.63 Evidence; transcript; *in camera* orders; proposed findings of fact and conclusions of law.

Sections 3.43, 3.44, 3.45, and 3.46 of the Commission's Rules of Practice shall govern, respectively, the receipt and objections to admissibility of evidence, the transcript of the hearing, *in camera* orders and the submission and consideration of proposed findings of fact and conclusions of law except that (a) a copy of the hearing transcript shall be provided the respondent; and (b) the Commission has the burden of establishing, by a preponderance of the evidence on the record as a whole, the allegations stated in the order to show cause.

§ 5.64 Initial decision.

Section 3.51 of the Commission's Rules of Practice shall govern the initial decision in proceedings under this subpart, except that the determination of the Administrative Law Judge must be supported by a preponderance of the evidence.

§ 5.65 Review of initial decision.

Appeals from the initial decision of the Administrative Law Judge or review by the Commission in the absence of an appeal shall be governed by §§ 3.52 and 3.53 of the Commission's Rules of Practice except that oral arguments shall be nonpublic subject to the exceptions stated in § 3.52 of this part.

§ 5.66 Commission decision and reconsideration.

The Commission's decision and any reconsideration or reopening of the proceeding shall be governed by §§ 2.51, 3.54, 3.55, 3.71 and 3.72 of the Commission's Rules of Practice, except that (a) if the initial decision is modified or reversed, the Commission shall specify such findings of fact and conclusions of law as are different from those of the presiding official; and (b) references therein to "court of appeals" shall be deemed for purposes of proceedings under this part to refer to "district court."

§ 5.67 Sanctions.

In the case of any respondent who fails to request a hearing after receiving adequate notice of the allegations pursuant to § 5.57 or who is found in the Commission's final decision to have violated 18 U.S.C. 207 (a), (b), or (c), the Commission may order such disciplinary action as it deems warranted, including:

(a) Reprimand;

(b) Suspension from participating in a particular matter or matters before the Commission; or

(c) Prohibiting the respondent from making, with the intent to influence, any formal or informal appearance before, or any oral or written communication to, the Commission or its staff on any matter or business on behalf of any other person (except the United States) for a period not to exceed five (5) years.

§ 5.68 Judicial review.

A respondent against whom the Commission has issued an order imposing disciplinary action under this part may seek judicial review of the Commission's determination in an appropriate United States District Court by filing a petition for such review within sixty (60) days of receipt of notice of the Commission's final decision.

PART 6—ENFORCEMENT OF NONDISCRIMINATION ON THE BASIS OF HANDICAP IN PROGRAMS OR ACTIVITIES CONDUCTED BY THE FEDERAL TRADE COMMISSION

Sec.

AUTHORITY: 29 U.S.C. 794, 794d.

SOURCE: 52 FR 45628, Dec. 1, 1987, unless otherwise noted.

§ 6.101 Purpose.

This part effectuates section 119 of the Rehabilitation, Comprehensive Services, and Developmental Disabilities Amendments of 1978, which amended section 504 of the Rehabilitation Act of 1973 to prohibit discrimination on the basis of handicap in programs or activities conducted by Executive agencies or the United States Postal Service. This part also implements section 508 of the Rehabilitation Act of 1973, as amended, with respect to the accessibility of electronic and information technology developed, procured, maintained, or used by the agency.

[52 FR 45628, Dec. 1, 1987, as amended at 66 FR 51863, Oct. 11, 2001]

§ 6.102 Application.

This part applies to all programs or activities conducted by the Commission except for programs or activities conducted outside the United States that do not involve individuals with handicaps in the United States.

§ 6.103 Definitions.

For purposes of this part, the term—

Auxiliary aids means services or devices that enable persons with impaired sensory, manual, or speaking skills to have an equal opportunity to participate in, and to enjoy the benefits of, programs or activities conducted by the Commission. For example, auxiliary aids useful for persons with impaired vision include readers, Brailled materials, audio recordings, and other similar services and devices. Auxiliary aids useful for persons with impaired hearing include telephone handset amplifiers, telephones compatible with hearing aids, telecommunication devices for deaf persons (TDD's), interpreters, notetakers, written materials, and other similar services and devices.

Commission means the Federal Trade Commission.

Complete complaint means a written statement that contains the complainant's name and address and describes the Commission's alleged discriminatory action in sufficient detail to inform the Commission of the nature and date of the alleged violation of section 504. It shall be signed by the complainant or by someone authorized to do so on his or her behalf. Complaints filed on behalf of classes or third parties shall describe or identify (by name, if possible) the alleged victims of discrimination.

Electronic and information technology includes information technology and any equipment or interconnected system or subsystem of equipment that is used in the creation, conversion, or duplication of data or information. The term includes, but is not limited to, telecommunications products (such as telephones), information kiosks and transaction machines, World Wide Web sites, multimedia, and office equipment such as copiers and fax machines. The term does not include any equipment that contains embedded information technology that is used as an integral part of the product, but the principal function of which is not the acquisition, storage, manipulation, management, movement, control, display, switching, interchange, transmission, or reception of data or information. For example, HVAC (heating, ventilation, and air conditioning) equipment such as thermostats or temperature control devices, and medical equipment where information technology is integral to its operation are not electronic and information technology.

Facility means all or any portion of buildings, structures, equipment, roads, walks, parking lots, rolling stock or other conveyances, or other real or personal property.

Individual with handicaps means any person who has a physical or mental impairment that substantially limits one or more major life activities, has a record of such an impairment, or is regarded as having such an impairment. As used in this definition, the phrase:

(1) *Physical or mental impairment* includes—

(i) Any physiological disorder or condition, cosmetic disfigurement, or anatomical loss affecting one or more of the following body systems: Neurological; musculoskeletal; special sense organs; respiratory, including speech organs; cardiovascular; reproductive; digestive; genitourinary; hemic and lymphatic; skin; and endocrine; or

(ii) Any mental or psychological disorder, such as mental retardation, organic brain syndrome, emotional or mental illness, and specific learning disabilities. The term *physical or mental impairment* includes, but is not limited to, such diseases and conditions as orthopedic, visual, speech, and hearing impairments, cerebral palsy, epilepsy, muscular dystrophy, multiple sclerosis, cancer, heart disease, diabetes, mental retardation, emotional illness, and drug addiction and alcoholism.

(2) *Major life activities* includes functions such as caring for one's self, performing manual tasks, walking, seeing, hearing, speaking, breathing, learning, and working.

(3) *Has a record of such an impairment* means has a history of, or has been misclassified as having, a mental or physical impairment that substantially

limits one or more major life activities.

(4) *Is regarded as having an impairment* means—

(i) Has a physical or mental impairment that does not substantially limit major life activities but is treated by the Commission as constituting such a limitation;

(ii) Has a physical or mental impairment that substantially limits major life activities only as a result of the attitudes of others toward such impairment; or

(iii) Has none of the impairments defined in paragraph (1) of this definition but is treated by the Commission as having such an impairment.

Information technology means any equipment or interconnected system or subsystem of equipment that is used in the automatic acquisition, storage, manipulation, management, movement, control, display, switching, interchange, transmission, or reception of data or information. The term "information technology" includes computers, ancillary equipment, software, firmware and similar procedures, services (including support services), and related resources.

Qualified individual with handicaps means—

(1) With respect to any Commission program or activity under which a person is required to perform services or to achieve a level of accomplishment, an individual with handicaps who meets the essential eligibility requirements and who can achieve the purpose of the program or activity without modifications in the program or activity that the Commission can demonstrate would result in a fundamental alteration in its nature; and

(2) With respect to any other program or activity, an individual with handicaps who meets the essential eligibility requirements for participation in, or receipt of benefits from, that program or activity.

(3) *Qualified handicapped person* as that term is defined for purposes of employment in 29 CFR 1613.702 (f), which is made applicable to this part by §6.140.

Section 504 means section 504 of the Rehabilitation Act of 1973 (Pub. L. 93–112, 87 Stat. 394 (29 U.S.C. 794)), as amended by the Rehabilitation Act Amendments of 1974 (Pub. L. 93–516, 88 Stat. 1617); the Rehabilitation, Comprehensive Services, and Developmental Disabilities Amendments of 1978 (Pub. L. 95–602, 92 Stat. 2955) and the Rehabilitation Act Amendments of 1986 (Pub. L. 99–506, 100 Stat. 1810). As used in this part, section 504 applies only to programs or activities conducted by Executive agencies and not to federally assisted programs.

Section 508 means section 508 of the Rehabilitation Act of 1973, as amended.

[52 FR 45628, Dec. 1, 1987, as amended at 66 FR 51863, Oct. 11, 2001]

§§6.104–6.109 [Reserved]

§6.110 Self-evaluation.

(a) The Commission shall, by February 1, 1989, evaluate its current policies and practices, and the effects thereof, that do not or may not meet the requirements of this part, and, to the extent modification of any such policies and practices is required, the Commission shall proceed to make the necessary modifications.

(b) The Commission shall provide an opportunity to interested persons, including individuals with handicaps or organizations representing individuals with handicaps, to participate in the self-evaluation process by submitting comments (both oral and written).

(c) The Commission shall, for at least three years following completion of the self-evaluation required under paragraph (a) of this section, maintain on file and make available for public inspection:

(1) A description of areas examined and any problems identified, and

(2) A description of any modifications made.

§6.111 Notice.

The Commission shall make available to employees, applicants, participants, beneficiaries, and other interested persons such information regarding the provisions of this part and its applicability to the programs or activities conducted by the Commission, and make such information available to them in such manner as the Chairman or his or her designee finds necessary to apprise such persons of the protections against discrimination assured to them by section 504 and this regulation.

§§ 6.112–6.129 [Reserved]

§ 6.130 General prohibitions against discrimination.

(a) No qualified individual with handicaps shall, on the basis of handicap, be excluded from participation in, be denied the benefits of, or otherwise be subjected to discrimination under any program or activity conducted by the Commission.

(b)(1) The Commission, in providing any aid, benefit, or service, may not, directly or through contractual, licensing, or other arrangements, on the basis of handicap—

(i) Deny a qualified individual with handicaps the opportunity to participate in or benefit from the aid, benefit, or service;

(ii) Afford a qualified individual with handicaps an opportunity to participate in or benefit from the aid, benefit, or service that is not equal to that afforded others;

(iii) Provide a qualified individual with handicaps with an aid, benefit, or service that is not as effective in affording equal opportunity to obtain the same result, to gain the same benefit, or to reach the same level of achievement as that provided to others;

(iv) Provide different or separate aid, benefits, or services to individuals with handicaps or to any class of individuals with handicaps than is provided to others unless such action is necessary to provide qualified individuals with handicaps with aid, benefits, or services that are as effective as those provided to others;

(v) Deny a qualified individual with handicaps the opportunity to participate as a member of planning or advisory boards; or

(vi) Otherwise limit a qualified individual with handicaps in the enjoyment of any right, privilege, advantage, or opportunity enjoyed by others receiving the aid, benefit, or service.

(2) The Commission may not deny a qualified individual with handicaps the opportunity to participate in programs or activities that are not separate or different, despite the existence of permissibly separate or different programs or activities.

(3) The Commission may not, directly or through contractual or other arrangements, utilize criteria or methods of administration the purpose or effect of which would—

(i) Subject qualified individuals with handicaps to discrimination on the basis of handicap; or

(ii) Defeat or substantially impair accomplishment of the objectives of a program or activity with respect to individuals with handicaps.

(4) The Commission may not, in determining the site or location of a facility, make selections the purpose or effect of which would—

(i) Exclude individuals with handicaps from, deny them the benefits of, or otherwise subject them to discrimination under any program or activity conducted by the Commission; or

(ii) Defeat or substantially impair the accomplishment of the objectives of a program or activity with respect to individuals with handicaps.

(5) The Commission, in the selection of procurement contractors, may not use criteria that subject qualified individuals with handicaps to discrimination on the basis of handicap.

(c) The exclusion of nonhandicapped persons from the benefits of a program limited by Federal statute or Executive order to individuals with handicaps or the exclusion of a specific class of individuals with handicaps from a program limited by Federal statute or Executive order to a different class of individuals with handicaps is not prohibited by this part.

(d) The Commission shall administer programs and activities in the most integrated setting appropriate to the needs of qualified individuals with handicaps.

§§ 6.131–6.139 [Reserved]

§ 6.140 Employment.

No qualified individual with handicaps shall, on the basis of handicap, be subjected to discrimination in employment under any program or activity conducted by the Commission. The definitions, requirements and procedures of section 501 of the Rehabilitation Act of 1973 (29 U.S.C. 791), as established by the Equal Employment Opportunity Commission in 29 CFR part 1613, shall apply to employment in federally conducted programs or activities.

§§ 6.141–6.148 [Reserved]

§ 6.149 Program accessibility: Discrimination prohibited.

Except as otherwise provided in § 6.150, no qualified individuals with handicaps shall, because the Commission's facilities are inaccessible to or unusable by individuals with handicaps, be denied the benefits of, be excluded from participation in, or otherwise be subjected to discrimination under any program or activity conducted by the Commission.

§ 6.150 Program accessibility: Existing facilities.

(a) *General.* The Commission shall operate each program or activity so that the program or activity, when viewed in its entirety, is readily accessible to and usable by individuals with handicaps. This paragraph does not—

(1) Necessarily require the Commission to make each of its existing facilities accessible to and usable by individuals with handicaps, or

(2) Require the Commission to take any action that it can demonstrate would result in a fundamental alteration in the nature of a program or activity or in undue financial and administrative burdens. In those circumstances where Commission personnel believe that the proposed action would fundamentally alter the program or activity or would result in undue financial and administrative burdens, the Commission has the burden of proving that compliance with § 6.150(a) would result in such alteration or burdens. The decision that compliance would result in such alteration or burdens must be made by the Chairman or his or her designee after considering all Commission resources available for use in the funding and operation of the conducted program or activity, and must be accompanied by a written statement of the reasons for reaching that conclusion. If an action would result in such an alteration or such burdens, the Commission shall take any other action that would not result in such an alteration or such burdens, but would, nevertheless, ensure that individuals with handicaps receive the benefits and services of the program or activity.

(b) *Methods.* The Commission may comply with the requirements of this section through such means as redesign of equipment, reassignment of services to accessible buildings, assignment of aides to beneficiaries, home visits, delivery of services at alternate accessible sites, alteration of existing facilities and construction of new facilities, use of accessible rolling stock, or any methods that result in making its programs or activities readily accessible to and usable by individuals with handicaps. The Commission is not required to make structural changes in existing facilities where other methods are effective in achieving compliance with this section. The Commission, in making alterations to existing buildings, shall meet accessibility requirements to the extent compelled by the Architectural Barriers Act of 1968, as amended (42 U.S.C. 4151–4157) and any regulations implementing it. In choosing among available methods for meeting the requirements of this section, the Commission shall give priority to those methods that offer programs and activities to qualified individuals with handicaps in the most integrated setting appropriate.

(c) *Time period for compliance.* The Commission shall comply with the obligations established under this section by April 1, 1988, except that where structural changes in facilities are undertaken, such changes shall be made by February 1, 1991, but in any event as expeditiously as possible.

(d) *Transition plan.* In the event that structural changes to facilities will be undertaken to achieve program accessibility, the Commission shall develop, by August 1, 1988, a transition plan setting forth the steps necessary to complete such changes. The Commission shall provide an opportunity to interested persons, including individuals with handicaps or organizations representing individuals with handicaps, to participate in the development of the transition plan by submitting comments (both oral and written). A copy of the transition plan shall be made available for public inspection. The plan shall, at a minimum—

(1) Identify physical obstacles in the Commission's facilities that limit the accessibility of its programs or activities to individuals with handicaps;

(2) Describe in detail the methods that will be used to make the facilities accessible;

(3) Specify the schedule for taking the steps necessary to achieve compliance with this section and, if the time period of the transition plan is longer than one year, identify steps that will be taken during each year of the transition period;

(4) Indicate the official responsible for implementation of the plan; and

(5) Identify the persons or groups with whose assistance the plan was prepared.

§6.151 Program accessibility: New construction and alterations.

Each building or part of a building that is constructed or altered by, on behalf of, or for the use of the Commission shall be designed, constructed, or altered so as to be readily accessible to and usable by individuals with handicaps. The definitions, requirements, and standards of the Architectural Barriers Act (42 U.S.C. 4151–4157), as established in 41 CFR 101–19.600 to 101–19.607, apply to buildings covered by this section.

§6.152 Program accessibility: Electronic and information technology.

(a) When developing, procuring, maintaining, or using electronic and information technology, the Commission shall ensure, unless an undue burden would be imposed on the agency, that the electronic and information technology allows, regardless of the type of medium of the technology:

(1) Individuals with disabilities who are employees to have access to and use of information and data that is comparable to the access to and use of the information and data by employees who are not individuals with disabilities; and

(2) Individuals with disabilities who are members of the public seeking information or services from the Commission to have access to and use of information and data that is comparable to the access to and use of the information and data by members of the public who are not individuals with disabilities.

(b) When the development, procurement, maintenance, or use of electronic and information technology that meets the standards published by the Architectural and Transportation Barriers Compliance Board pursuant to section 508(a)(2) of the Rehabilitation Act of 1973, as amended, would impose an undue burden on the Commission, the Commission shall provide individuals with disabilities covered by paragraph (a) of this section with the information and data involved by an alternative means of access that allows such individuals to use the information and data.

(c) This section shall not apply to any matter legally exempted by section 508, by the standards referenced in paragraph (b) of this section, or by other applicable law or regulation. Nothing in this section shall be construed to limit any right, remedy, or procedure otherwise available under any provision of federal law (including sections 501 through 505 of the Rehabilitation Act of 1973, as amended) that provides greater or equal protection for the rights of individuals with disabilities than section 508.

[66 FR 51863, Oct. 11, 2001]

§§6.153–6.159 [Reserved]

§6.160 Communications.

(a) The Commission shall take appropriate steps to ensure effective communication with applicants, participants, personnel of other Federal entities, and members of the public.

(1) The Commission shall furnish appropriate auxiliary aids where necessary to afford an individual with handicaps an equal opportunity to participate in, and enjoy the benefits of, a program or activity conducted by the Commission.

(i) In determining what type of auxiliary aid is necessary, the Commission shall give primary consideration to the requests of the individual with handicaps.

(ii) The Commission need not provide individually prescribed devices, readers for personal use or study, or other devices of a personal nature.

(2) Where the Commission communicates with applicants and beneficiaries by telephone, telecommunication devices for deaf persons (TDD's), or equally effective telecommunication systems shall be used.

(b) The Commission shall ensure that interested persons, including persons with impaired vision or hearing, can obtain information as to the existence and location of accessible services, activities, and facilities.

(c) The Commission shall provide signs at a primary entrance to each of its inaccessible facilities, directing users to a location at which they can obtain information about accessible facilities. The international symbol for accessibility shall be used at each primary entrance of an accessible facility.

(d) This section does not require the Commission to take any action that it can demonstrate would result in a fundamental alteration in the nature of a program or activity, or in undue financial and administrative burdens. In those circumstances where Commission personnel believe that the proposed action would fundamentally alter the program or activity or would result in undue financial and administrative burdens, the Commission has the burden of proving that compliance with §6.160 would result in such alteration or burdens. The decision that compliance would result in such alteration or burdens must be made by the Chairman or his or her designee after considering all Commission resources available for use in the funding and operation of the conducted program or activity, and must be accompanied by a written statement of the reasons for reaching that conclusion. If an action required to comply with this section would result in such an alteration or such burdens, the Commission shall take any other action that would not result in such an alteration or burdens but would nevertheless ensure that, to the maximum extent possible, individuals with handicaps receive the benefits and services of the program or activity.

§§6.161–6.169 [Reserved]

§6.170 Compliance procedures.

(a) Except as provided in paragraph (b) of this section, this section applies to all allegations of discrimination on the basis of handicap in programs or activities conducted by the Commission.

(b) The Commission shall process complaints alleging violations of section 504 with respect to employment according to the procedures established by the Equal Employment Opportunity Commission in 29 CFR part 1613 pursuant to section 501 of the Rehabilitation Act of 1973 (29 U.S.C. 791). The Commission shall apply the same procedures to process complaints alleging violations of section 508. Complaints alleging a violation of section 508 may not be filed with respect to any exempted matters as described in §6.152(c) of this chapter, and may be filed only with respect to electronic and information technology procured by the Commission on or after June 21, 2001.

(c) Responsibility for implementation and operation of this section is vested in the Director of Equal Employment Opportunity.

(d)(1) A complete complaint under this section may be filed by any person who believes that he or she or any specific class of persons of which he or she is a member has been subjected to discrimination prohibited by this part. The complaint may also be filed by an authorized representative of any such person.

(2) The complaint must be filed within 180 days of the alleged act of discrimination unless the Director of Equal Employment Opportunity extends the time period for good cause.

(3) The complaint must be addressed to the Director of Equal Employment Opportunity, Federal Trade Commission, 600 Pennsylvania Avenue, NW., Washington, DC 20580.

(e) If the Director of Equal Employment Opportunity receives a complaint over which the Commission does not have jurisdiction, he or she shall promptly notify the complainant and shall make reasonable efforts to refer the complaint to the appropriate Government entity.

(f) The Director of Equal Employment Opportunity shall notify the Architectural and Transportation Barriers Compliance Board upon receipt of any complaint alleging that a building or facility that is subject to the Architectural Barriers Act of 1968, as amended (42 U.S.C. 4151–4157) is not readily accessible to and usable by individuals with handicaps.

(g)(1) The Director of Equal Employment Opportunity shall accept and investigate a complete complaint that is filed in accordance with paragraph (d) of this section and over which the Commission has jurisdiction.

(2) If the Director of Equal Employment Opportunity receives a complaint that is not complete (see § 6.103), he or she shall, within 30 days thereafter, notify the complainant that additional information is needed. If the complainant fails to complete the complaint within 30 days of the date of the Director's notice, the Director of Equal Employment Opportunity may dismiss the complaint without prejudice.

(h) Within 180 days of the receipt of a complete complaint over which the Commission has jurisdiction, the Director of Equal Employment Opportunity shall notify the complainant of the results of the investigation in a letter containing—

(1) Findings of fact and conclusions of law;

(2) A description of a remedy for each violation found; and

(3) A notice of the right to appeal to the Commission's General Counsel.

(i)(1) An appeal under this section must be filed within 90 days of the complainant's receipt of the letter under paragraph (h) of this section unless the General Counsel extends the time period for good cause.

(2) The appeal must be addressed to the General Counsel, Federal Trade Commission, 600 Pennsylvania Avenue, NW., Washington, DC 20580.

(3) The appeal shall specify the questions raised by the appeal and the arguments on the points of fact and law relied upon in support of the position taken on each question; and it shall include copies of the complaint filed under paragraph (d) of this section and the letter by the Director of Equal Employment Opportunity under paragraph (h) of this section as well as any other material relied upon in support of the appeal.

(j) The General Counsel shall notify the complainant of the results of the appeal within 60 days of the receipt of the appeal. If the General Counsel determines that additional information is needed from the complainant, the General Counsel shall have 60 days from the date of receipt of the additional information to make a final determination on the appeal. The General Counsel may submit the appeal to the Commission for final determination provided that any final determination of the appeal is made by the Commission within the 60-day period specified by this paragraph.

(k) The time limits specified by paragraphs (h) and (j) of this section may be extended by the Chairman for good cause.

(l) The Commission may delegate its authority for conducting complaint investigations to other Federal agencies, except that the authority for making the final determination may not be delegated.

[52 FR 45628, Dec. 1, 1987, as amended at 66 FR 51864, Oct. 11, 2001]

§§ 6.171–6.999 [Reserved]

PART 14—ADMINISTRATIVE INTERPRETATIONS, GENERAL POLICY STATEMENTS, AND ENFORCEMENT POLICY STATEMENTS

Sec.

AUTHORITY: 15 U.S.C. 41–58.

§ 14.9 Requirements concerning clear and conspicuous disclosures in foreign language advertising and sales materials.

The Federal Trade Commission has noted that, with increasing intensity, advertisers are making special efforts to reach foreign language-speaking consumers. As part of this special effort, advertisements, brochures and sales documents are being printed in foreign languages. In recent years the Commission has issued various cease-and-desist orders as well as rules, guides and other statements, which require affirmative disclosures in connection with certain kinds of representations and business activities. Generally, these disclosures are required to be "clear and conspicuous." Because questions have arisen as to the meaning and application of the phrase "clear and conspicuous" with respect to foreign language advertisements and sales materials, the Commission deems it appropriate to set forth the following enforcement policy statement:

(a) Where cease-and-desist orders as well as rules, guides and other statements require "clear and conspicuous" disclosure of certain information in an advertisement or sales material in a newspaper, magazine, periodical, or other publication that is not in English, the disclosure shall appear in the predominant language of the publication in which the advertisement or sales material appears. In the case of any other advertisement or sales material, the disclosure shall appear in the language of the target audience (ordinarily the language principally used in the advertisement or sales material).

(b) Any respondent who fails to comply with this requirement may be the subject of a civil penalty or other law enforcement proceeding for violating the terms of a Commission cease-and-desist order or rule.

(Sec. 5, 38 Stat. 719, as amended; 15 U.S.C. 45)

[38 FR 21494, Aug. 9, 1973, as amended at 63 FR 34808, June 26, 1998]

§ 14.12 Use of secret coding in marketing research.

(a) The Federal Trade Commission has determined to close its industry-wide investigation of marketing research firms that was initiated in November 1975, to determine if the firms were using questionnaires with invisible coding that could be used to reveal a survey respondent's identity. After a thorough investigation, the Commission has determined that invisible coding has been used by the marketing research industry, but it is neither a commonly used nor widespread practice. Moreover, use of the practice appears to have diminished in recent years. For these reasons, the Commission has determined that further action is not warranted at this time.

(b) However, for the purpose of providing guidance to the marketing research industry, the Commission is issuing the following statement with regard to its future enforcement intentions. The Commission has reason to believe that it is an unfair or deceptive act or practice, violative of section 5 of the Federal Trade Commission Act (15 U.S.C. 45) to induce consumers to provide information about themselves by expressly or implicitly promising that such information is being provided anonymously, when, in fact, a secret or invisible code is used on the survey form or return envelope that allows identification of the consumer who has provided the information.

(c) While the Commission has made no final determination regarding the legality of the foregoing practice, the Commission will take appropriate enforcement action should it discover the practice to be continuing in the future, and in the event that it may be causing substantial consumer injury. Among the circumstances in which the Commission believes that the use of secret coding may cause significant consumer harm are those in which:

(1) A misleading promise of anonymity is used to obtain highly sensitive information about a consumer that such consumer would not choose to disclose if he or she were informed that a code was being used that would allow his or her name to be associated with the response; and

(2) Information of any sort is used for purposes other than those of the market survey.

[43 FR 42742, Sept. 21, 1978]

§ 14.15 In regard to comparative advertising.

(a) *Introduction.* The Commission's staff has conducted an investigation of industry trade associations and the advertising media regarding their comparative advertising policies. In the course of this investigation, numerous industry codes, statements of policy, interpretations and standards were examined. Many of the industry codes and standards contain language that could be interpreted as discouraging the use of comparative advertising. This Policy Statement enunciates the Commission's position that industry self-regulation should not restrain the use by advertisers of truthful comparative advertising.

(b) *Policy Statement.* The Federal Trade Commission has determined that it would be of benefit to advertisers, advertising agencies, broadcasters, and self-regulation entities to restate its current policy concerning comparative advertising.[1] Commission policy in the area of comparative advertising encourages the naming of, or reference to competitiors, but requires clarity, and, if necessary, disclosure to avoid deception of the consumer. Additionally, the use of truthful comparative advertising should not be restrained by broadcasters or self-regulation entities.

(c) The Commission has supported the use of brand comparisions where the bases of comparision are clearly identified. Comparative advertising, when truthful and nondeceptive, is a source of important information to consumers and assists them in making rational purchase decisions. Comparative advertising encourages product improvement and innovation, and can lead to lower prices in the marketplace. For these reasons, the Commission will continue to scrutinize carefully restraints upon its use.

(1) *Disparagement.* Some industry codes which prohibit practices such as "disparagement," "disparagement of competitors," "improper disparagement," "unfairly attaching," "discrediting," may operate as a restriction on comparative advertising. The Commission has previously held that disparaging advertising is permissible so long as it is truthful and not deceptive. In *Carter Products, Inc.*, 60 F.T.C. 782, *modified*, 323 F.2d 523 (5th Cir. 1963), the Commission narrowed an order recommended by the hearing examiner which would have prohibited respondents from disparaging competing products through the use of false or misleading pictures, depictions, or demonstrations, "or otherwise" disparaging such products. In explaining why it eliminated "or otherwise" from the final order, the Commission observed that the phrase would have prevented:

> respondents from making truthful and non-deceptive statements that a product has certain desirable properties or qualities which a competing product or products do not possess. Such a comparison may have the effect of disparaging the competing product, but we know of no rule of law which prevents a seller from honestly informing the public of the advantages of its products as opposed to those of competing products. 60 F.T.C. at 796.

Industry codes which restrain comparative advertising in this manner are subject to challenge by the Federal Trade Commission.

(2) *Substantiation.* On occasion, a higher standard of substantiation by advertisers using comparative advertising has been required by self-regulation entities. The Commission evaluates comparative advertising in the same manner as it evaluates all other advertising techniques. The ultimate question is whether or not the advertising has a tendency or capacity to be false or deceptive. This is a factual issue to be determined on a case-by-case basis. However, industry codes and interpretations that impose a higher standard of substantiation for comparative claims than for unilateral claims are inappropriate and should be revised.

(Sec. 5, 38 Stat. 719, as amended; 15 U.S.C. 45)

[44 FR 47328, Aug. 13, 1979]

§ 14.16 Interpretation of Truth-in-Lending Orders consistent with amendments to the Truth-in-Lending Act and Regulation Z.

Introduction

The Federal Trade Commission (FTC) has determined that there is a need to clarify the compliance responsibilities under the Truth-in-Lending Act (TILA) (Title I, Consumer Credit Protection Act, 15 U.S.C. 1601 *et seq.*), as amended by the Truth-in-Lending Simplification

[1] For purposes of this Policy Statement, comparative advertising is defined as advertising that compares alternative brands on objectively measurable attributes or price, and identifies the alternative brand by name, illustration or other distinctive information.

and Reform Act of 1980 (Pub. L. 96–221, 94 Stat. 168), and under revised Regulation Z (12 CFR part 226, 46 FR 20848), and subsequent amendments to the TILA and Regulation Z, of those creditors and advertisers who are subject to final cease and desist orders that require compliance with provisions of the Truth-in-Lending statute or Regulation Z. Clarification is necessary because the Truth-in-Lending Simplification and Reform Act and revised Regulation Z significantly relaxed prior Truth-in-Lending requirements on which provisions of numerous outstanding orders were based. The Policy Statement provides that the Commission will interpret and enforce Truth-in-Lending provisions of all orders so as to impose no greater or different disclosure obligations on creditors and advertisers named in such orders than are required generally of creditors and advertisers under the TILA and Regulation Z, and subsequent amendments to the TILA and Regulation Z.

Policy Statement

(a) All cease and desist orders issued by the FTC that require compliance with provisions of the Truth-in-Lending Act and Regulation Z (12 CFR part 226) will be interpreted and enforced consistent with the amendments to the TILA incorporated by the Truth-in-Lending Simplification and Reform Act of 1980, and the revision of Regulation Z implementing the same, promulgated on April 1, 1981 by the Board of Governors of the Federal Reserve System (46 FR 20848), and by subsequent amendments to the TILA and Regulation Z. Likewise, the Federal Reserve Board staff commentary to revised Regulation Z (46 FR 50288, October 9, 1981), and subsequent revisions to the Federal Reserve Board staff commentary to Regulation Z, will be considered in interpreting the requirements of existing orders.

(b) After an amendment to Regulation Z becomes effective, compliance with the revised credit disclosure requirements will be considered compliance with the existing order, and:

(1) To the extent that revised Regulation Z deletes disclosure requirements imposed by any Commission order, compliance with these requirements will no longer be required; however,

(2) To the extent that revised Regulation Z imposes additional disclosure or format requirements, a failure to comply with the added requirements will be considered a violation of the TILA.

(c) A creditor or advertiser must continue to comply with all provisions of the order which do not relate to Truth-in-Lending Act requirements or are unaffected by Regulation Z. These provisions are not affected by this policy statement and will remain in full force and effect.

Staff Clarifications

The Commission intends that this Enforcement Policy Statement obviate the need for any creditor or advertiser to file a petition to reopen and modify any affected order under section 2.51 of the Commission's rules of practice (16 CFR 2.51). However, the Commission recognizes that the policy statement may not provide clear guidance to every creditor or advertiser under order. The staff of the Division of Enforcement, Bureau of Consumer Protection, will respond to written requests for clarification of any order affected by this policy statement.

[60 FR 42033, Aug. 15, 1995]

PART 16—ADVISORY COMMITTEE MANAGEMENT

Sec.

AUTHORITY: Federal Advisory Committee Act, 5 U.S.C. App. I Section 8(a).

SOURCE: 51 FR 30055, Aug. 22, 1986, unless otherwise noted.

§ 16.1 Purpose and scope.

(a) The regulations in this part implement the Federal Advisory Committee Act, 5 U.S.C. App. I.

(b) These regulations shall apply to any advisory committee, as defined in paragraph (b) of § 16.2 of this part. However, to the extent that an advisory committee is subject to particular statutory provisions that are inconsistent with the Federal Advisory Committee Act, these regulations do not apply.

§ 16.2 Definitions.

For purposes of this part:

(a) *Administrator* means the Administrator of the General Services Administration.

(b) *Advisory committee*, subject to exclusions described in paragraph (b)(2) of this section, means any committee, board, commission, council, panel, task force, or other similar group, or any subcommittee or other subgroup thereof, which is established or utilized by the Commission for the purpose of obtaining advice or recommendations for the Commission or other agency or officer of the Federal Government on matters that are within the scope of the Commission's jurisdiction.

(1) Where a group provides some advice to the Commission but the group's advisory function is incidental and inseparable from other (e.g., operational or management) functions, the provisions of this part do not apply. However, if the advisory function is separable, the group is subject to this part to the extent that the group operates as an advisory committee.

(2) Groups excluded from the effect of the provisions of this part include:

(i) Any committee composed wholly of full-time officers or employees of the Federal Government;

(ii) Any committee, subcommittee or subgroup that is exclusively operational in nature (e.g., has functions that include making or implementing decisions, as opposed to the offering of advice or recommendations);

(iii) Any inter-agency advisory committee unless specifically made applicable by the establishing authority.

(c) *Commission* means the Federal Trade Commission.

(d) *GSA* means the General Services Administration.

(e) *Secretariat* means the Committee Management Secretariat of the General Services Administration.

(f) *Sunshine Act* means the Government in the Sunshine Act, 5 U.S.C. 552b.

§ 16.3 Policy.

(a) The Commission's policy shall be to:

(1) Establish an advisory committee only when it is essential to the conduct of agency business;

(2) Insure that adequate information is provided to the Congress and the public regarding advisory committees, and that there are adequate opportunities for access by the public to advisory committee meetings;

(3) Insure that the membership of the advisory committee is balanced in terms of the points of view represented and the functions to be performed; and

(4) Terminate an advisory committee whenever the stated objectives of the committee have been accomplished; the subject matter or work of the advisory committee has become obsolete; the cost of operating the advisory committee is excessive in relation to the benefits accruing to the Commission; or the advisory committee is otherwise no longer a necessary or appropriate means to carry out the purposes for which it was established.

(b) No advisory committee may be used for functions that are not solely advisory unless specifically authorized to do so by law. The Commission shall be solely responsible for making policy decisions and determining action to be taken with respect to any matter considered by an advisory committee.

§ 16.4 Advisory Committee Management Officer.

(a) The Commission shall designate the Executive Director as the Advisory Committee Management Officer who shall:

(1) Exercise control and supervision over the establishment, procedures, and accomplishments of the advisory committees established by the Commission;

(2) Assemble and maintain the reports, records, and other papers of any

advisory committee during its existence;

(3) Carry out, on behalf of the Commission, the provisions of the Freedom of Information Act, 5 U.S.C. 552, with respect to such reports, records, and other papers;

(4) Maintain in a single location a complete set for the charters and membership lists of each of the Commission's advisory committees;

(5) Maintain information on the nature, functions, and operations of each of the Commission's advisory committees; and

(6) Provide information on how to obtain copies of minutes of meetings and reports of each of the Commission's advisory committees.

(b) The name of the Advisory Committee Management Officer designated in accordance with this part, and his or her agency address and telephone number, shall be provided to the Secretariat.

§ 16.5 Establishment of advisory committees.

(a) No advisory committee shall be established under this part unless such establishment is:

(1) Specifically authorized by statute; or

(2) Determined as a matter of formal record by the Commission, after consultation with the Administrator, to be in the public interest in connection with the performance of duties imposed on the Commission by law.

(b) In establishing an advisory committee, the Commission shall:

(1) Prepare a proposed charter for the advisory committee in accordance with § 16.6 of this part; and

(2) Submit an original and one copy of a letter to the Administrator requesting concurrence in the Commission's proposal to establish an advisory committee. The letter from the Commission shall describe the nature and purpose of the proposed advisory committee, including an explanation of why establishment of the advisory committee is essential to the conduct of agency business and in the public interest and why the functions of the proposed committee could not be performed by the Commission, by an existing committee, or through other means. The letter shall also describe the Commission's plan to attain balanced membership on the proposed advisory committee in terms of points of view to be represented and functions to be performed. The letter shall be accompanied by two copies of the proposed charter.

(c) Upon the receipt of notification from the Administrator of his or her concurrence or nonconcurrence, the Commission shall notify the Administrator in writing that either:

(1) The advisory committee is being established. The filing of an advisory committee charter as specified in § 16.6 of this part shall be deemed appropriate written notification in this instance; or

(2) The advisory committee is not being established.

(d) If the Commission determines that an advisory committee should be established in accordance with paragraph (c) of this section, the Commission shall publish notice to that effect in the FEDERAL REGISTER at least fifteen days prior to the filing of the advisory committee's charter unless the Administrator authorizes publication of such notice within a shorter period of time. The notice shall identify the name and purpose of the advisory committee, state that the committee is necessary and in the public interest, and identify the name and address of the Commission official to whom the public may submit comments.

(e) The Commission may issue regulations or guidelines as may be necessary to operate and oversee a particular advisory committee.

§ 16.6 Charter.

(a) No advisory committee established, utilized, reestablished or renewed by the Commission under this part shall meet or take any action until its charter has been filed by the Commission with the standing committees of the Senate and House of Representatives having legislative jurisdiction over the Commission.

(b) The charter required by paragraph (a) of this section shall include the following information:

(1) The committee's official designation;

(2) The committee's objectives and the scope of its activity;

(3) The period of time necessary for the committee to carry out its purposes;

(4) The Commission component or official to whom the committee reports;

(5) The agency or official responsible for providing the necessary support for the committee;

(6) A description of the duties for which the committee is responsible, and, if such duties are not solely advisory, a specification of the authority for such functions;

(7) The estimated annual operating cost in dollars and man-years for the committee;

(8) The estimated number and frequency of committee meetings;

(9) The committee's termination date, if less than two years from the date of committee's establishment; and

(10) The date the charter is filed.

(c) A copy of the charter required by paragraph (a) of this section shall also be furnished at the time of filing to the Secretariat and the Library of Congress.

(d) The requirements of this section shall also apply to committees utilized as advisory committees, even though not expressly established for that purpose.

§ 16.7 Meetings.

(a) The Commission shall designate an officer or employee of the Federal Government as the Designated Federal Officer for the advisory committee. The Designated Federal Officer shall attend the meetings of the advisory committee, and shall adjourn committee meetings whenever he or she determines that adjournment is in the public interest. The Commission, in its discretion, may authorize the Designated Federal Officer to chair meetings of the advisory committee.

(b) No meeting of any advisory committee shall be held except at the call of, or with the advance approval of, the Designated Federal Officer and with an agenda approved by such official.

(c) The agenda required by paragraph (b) of this section shall identify, in general terms, matters to be considered at the meeting and shall indicate whether any part of the meeting will concern matters that the General Counsel has determined to be covered by one or more of the exemptions of the Sunshine Act.

(d) Timely notice of each meeting of the advisory committee shall be provided in accordance with § 16.9 of this part.

(e) Subject to the provisions of § 16.8 of this part, each meeting of an advisory committee as defined in § 16.2(b) of this part shall be open to the public. Subcommittees and subgroups that are not utilized by the Commission for the purpose of obtaining advice or recommendations do not constitute advisory committees within the meaning of § 16.2(b) and are not subject to the meeting and other requirements of this part.

(f) Meetings that are completely or partly open to the public shall be held at reasonable times and at places that are reasonably accessible to members of the public. The size of the meeting room shall be sufficient to accommodate members of the public who can reasonably be expected to attend.

(g) Any member of the public shall be permitted to file a written statement with the committee concerning any matter to be considered in a meeting. Interested persons may be permitted by the committee chairman to speak at such meetings in accordance with procedures established by the committee and subject to the time constraints under which the meeting is to be conducted.

(h) No meeting of any advisory committee shall be held in the absence of a quorum. Unless otherwise established by statute or in the charter of the committee, a quorum shall consist of a majority of the committee's authorized membership.

§ 16.8 Closed meetings.

(a) Paragraphs (e), (f), and (g) of § 16.7 of this part, which require that meetings shall be open to the public and that the public shall be afforded an opportunity to participate in such meetings, shall not apply to any advisory committee meeting (or any portion thereof) which the Commission determines is concerned with any matter covered by one or more of the exemptions set forth in paragraph (c) of the Sunshine Act, 5 U.S.C. section 552b(c).

(b) An advisory committee that seeks to have all or part of its meeting closed shall notify the Commission at least thirty days before the scheduled date of the meeting. The notification shall be in writing and shall identify the specific provisions of the Sunshine Act which justify closure. The Commission may waive the thirty-day requirement when a lesser period of time is requested and justified by the advisory committee.

(c) The General Counsel shall review all requests to close meetings and shall advise the Commission on the disposition of each such request.

(d) If the Commission determines that the request is consistent with the policies of the Sunshine Act and the Federal Advisory Committee Act, it shall issue a determination that all or part of the meeting may be closed. A copy of the Commission's determination shall be made available to the public upon request.

(e) The advisory committee shall issue, on an annual basis, a report that sets forth a summary of its activities in meetings closed pursuant to this section, addressing those related matters as would be informative to the public and consistent with the policy of the Sunshine Act and of this part. Notice of the availability of such annual reports shall be published in accordance with § 16.15 of this part.

§ 16.9 Notice of meetings.

(a) Notice of each advisory committee meeting, whether open or closed to the public, shall be published in the FEDERAL REGISTER at least 15 days before the meeting date. Such notice shall include the exact name of the advisory committee as chartered; the time, date, place and purpose of the meeting; and a summary of the meeting agenda. Notice shall also state that the meeting is open to the public or closed in whole or in part, and, if closed, cite the specific exemptions of the Sunshine Act as the basis for closure. The Commission may permit the advisory committee to provide notice of less than fifteen days in extraordinary situations, provided that the reasons for doing so are included in the meeting notice.

(b) In addition to the notice required by paragraph (a) of this section, other forms of notice such as press releases and notices in professional journals may be used to inform interested members of the public of advisory committee meetings.

§ 16.10 Minutes and transcripts of meetings.

(a) Detailed minutes of each advisory committee meeting shall be kept. The minutes shall reflect the time, date and place of the meeting; and accurate summary of each matter that was discussed and each conclusion reached; and a copy of each report or other document received, issued, or approved by the advisory committee. In addition, the minutes shall include a list of advisory committee members and staff and full-time Federal employees who attended the meeting; a list of members of the public who presented oral or written statements; and an estimated number of members of the public who were present at the meeting. The minutes shall describe the extent to which the meeting was open to the public and the nature and extent of any public participation. If it is impracticable to attach to the minutes of the meeting any document received, issued, or approved by the advisory committee, then the minutes shall describe the document in sufficient detail to enable any person who may request the document to identify it readily.

(b) The accuracy of all minutes shall be certified to by the chairperson of the advisory committee.

(c) Minutes need not be kept if a verbatim transcript is made.

§ 16.11 Annual comprehensive review.

(a) The Commission shall conduct an annual comprehensive review of the activities and responsibilities of each advisory committee to determine:

(1) Whether such committee is carrying out its purpose;

(2) Whether, consistent with the provisions of applicable statutes, the responsibilities assigned to it should be revised;

(3) Whether it should be merged with any other advisory committee or committees; or

(4) Whether it should be abolished.

(b) Pertinent factors to be considered in the comprehensive review required by paragraph (a) of this section include the following:

(1) The number of times the committee has met in the past year;

(2) The number of reports or recommendations submitted by the committee;

(3) An evaluation of the substance of the committee's reports or recommendations with respect to the Commission's programs or operations;

(4) An evaluation (with emphasis on the preceding twelve month period of the committee's work) of the history of the Commission's utilization of the committee's recommendations in policy formulation, program planning, decision making, more effective achievement of program objectives, and more economical accomplishment of programs in general.

(5) Whether information or recommendations could be obtained from sources within the Commission or from another advisory committee already in existence;

(6) The degree of duplication of effort by the committee as compared with that of other parts of the Commission or other advisory committees; and

(7) The estimated annual cost of the committee.

(c) The annual review required by this section shall be conducted on a fiscal year basis, and results of the review shall be included in the annual report to the GSA required by § 16.15 of this part. The report shall contain a justification of each advisory committee which the Commission determines should be continued, making reference, as appropriate, to the factors specified in paragraph (b) of this section.

§ 16.12 Termination of advisory committees.

Any advisory committee shall automatically terminate not later than two years after it is established, reestablished, or renewed, unless:

(a) Its duration is otherwise provided by law;

(b) It is renewed in accordance with § 16.13 of this part; or

(c) The Commission terminates it before that time.

§ 16.13 Renewal of advisory committees.

(a) Any advisory committee established under this part may be renewed by appropriate action of the Commission and the filing of a new charter. An advisory committee may be continued by such action for successive two-year periods.

(b) Before it renews an advisory committee in accordance with paragraph (a) of this section, the Commission will inform the Administrator by letter, not more than sixty days nor less than thirty days before the committee expires, of the following:

(1) Its determination that a renewal is necessary and in the public interest;

(2) The reasons for its determination;

(3) The Commission's plan to maintain balanced membership on the committee;

(4) An explanation of why the committee's functions cannot be performed by the Commission or by an existing advisory committee.

(c) Upon receipt of the Administrator's notification of concurrence or nonconcurrence, the Commission shall publish a notice of the renewal in the FEDERAL REGISTER, which shall certify that the renewal of the advisory committee is in the public interest and shall include all the matters set forth in paragraph (b) of this section. The Commission shall cause a new charter to be prepared and filed in accordance with the provisions of §§ 16.5 and 16.6 of this part.

(d) No advisory committee that is required under this section to file a new charter for the purpose of renewal shall take any action, other than preparation and filing of such charter, between the date the new charter is required and the date on which such charter is actually filed.

§ 16.14 Amendments.

(a) The charter of an advisory committee may be amended when the Commission determines that the existing charter no longer accurately describes the committee itself or its goals or procedures. Changes may be minor, such as revising the name of the advisory committee, or may be major, to the extent that they deal with the basic objectives or composition of the committee.

(1) To make a minor amendment to an advisory committee charter, the Commission shall:

(i) Amend the charter language as necessary; and

(ii) File the amended charter in accordance with the provisions of §16.6 of this part.

(2) To make a major amendment to an advisory committee charter, the Commission shall:

(i) Amend the charter language as necessary;

(ii) Submit the proposed amended charter with a letter to the Administrator requesting concurrence in the amended language and an explanation of why the changes are essential and in the public interest; and

(iii) File the amended charter in accordance with the provisions of §16.6 of this part.

(b) Amendment of an existing charter does not constitute renewal of the advisory committee under §16.13 of this part.

§16.15 Reports of advisory committees.

(a) The Commission shall furnish, on a fiscal year basis, a report of the activities of each of its advisory committees to the GSA.

(b) Results of the annual comprehensive review of the advisory committee made under §16.11 shall be included in the annual report.

(c) The Commission shall notify the GSA, by letter, of the termination of, changes in the membership of, or other significant developments with respect to, an advisory committee.

§16.16 Compensation.

(a) *Committee members.* Unless otherwise provided by law, the Commission shall not compensate advisory committee members for their service on an advisory committee. In the exceptional case where the Commission is unable to meet the need for technical expertise or the requirement for balanced membership solely through the appointment of noncompensated members, the Commission may contract for or authorize the advisory committee to contract for the services of a specific consultant who may be appointed as a member of the advisory committee. In such a case, the Commission shall follow the procedures set forth in paragraph (b) of this section.

(b) *Consultants.* Prior to hiring or authorizing the advisory committee to hire a consultant to an advisory committee, the Commission shall determine that the expertise or viewpoint to be offered by the consultant is not otherwise available without cost to the Commission. The compensation to be paid to such consultant may not exceed the maximum rate of pay authorized by 5 U.S.C. section 3109. Hiring of consultants shall be in accordance with OMB Circular A–120 and applicable statutes, regulations, and Executive Orders.

(c) *Staff members.* The Commission may fix the pay of each advisory committee staff member at a rate of the General Schedule, General Management Schedule, or Senior Executive Service in which the Staff member's position would appropriately be placed (5 U.S.C. chapter 51). The Commission may not fix the pay of a staff member at a rate higher than the daily equivalent of the maximum rate for GS–15, unless the Commission has determined that under the General Schedule, General Management Schedule, or Senior Executive Service classification system, the staff member's position would appropriately be placed at a grade higher than GS–15. The Commission shall review this determination annually.

SUBCHAPTER B—GUIDES AND TRADE PRACTICE RULES

PART 17—APPLICATION OF GUIDES IN PREVENTING UNLAWFUL PRACTICES

NOTE: Industry guides are administrative interpretations of laws administered by the Commission for the guidance of the public in conducting its affairs in conformity with legal requirements. They provide the basis for voluntary and simultaneous abandonment of unlawful practices by members of industry. Failure to comply with the guides may result in corrective action by the commission under applicable statutory provisions. Guides may relate to a practice common to many industries or to specific practices of a particular industry.

(Authority: Sec. 6(g), 38 Stat. 722; (15 U.S.C. 46(g))

[44 FR 11176, Feb. 27, 1979]

PART 18—GUIDES FOR THE NURSERY INDUSTRY

AUTHORITY: Secs. 5, 6 FTC Act; 38 Stat. 719, 721; 15 U.S.C. 45, 46.

SOURCE: 44 FR 11177, Feb. 27, 1979, unless otherwise noted.

§ 18.0 Definitions.

Industry products. As used in this part, the term *industry products* includes all types of trees, small fruit plants, shrubs, vines, ornamentals, herbaceous annuals, biennials and perennials, bulbs, corms, rhizomes, and tubers which are offered for sale or sold to the general public. Included are products propagated sexually or asexually and whether grown in a commercial nursery or collected from the wild state. Such products are customarily used for outdoor planting. Not included are florists' or greenhouse plants solely for inside culture or use and annual vegetable plants.

Industry members. Any person, firm, corporation, or organization engaged in the sale, offering for sale, or distribution in commerce of industry products, as defined above.

Lining-out stock. Includes all plant material coming from propagating houses, beds, or frames, and young material such as seedlings rooted or unrooted cuttings, grafts or layers, of suitable size to transplant either in the nursery row or in containers for "growing on."

Nursery-propagated. Reproduced and grown under cultivation, including reproduced and grown under cultivation from plants, seeds or cuttings lawfully collected from the wild state.

Propagated. Reproduced from seeds, cuttings, callus or other plant tissue, spores or other propagules under a controlled environment that is intensely manipulated by human intervention for the purpose of producing selected species or hybrids.

[44 FR 11177, Feb. 27, 1979, as amended at 59 FR 64549, Dec. 14, 1994]

§ 18.1 Deception (general).

(a) It is an unfair or deceptive act or practice to sell, offer for sale, or distribute industry products by any method or under any circumstance or condition that misrepresents directly or by implication to purchasers or prospective purchasers the products with respect to quantity, size, grade, kind, species, age, maturity, condition, vigor, hardiness, number of times transplanted, growth ability, growth characteristics, rate of growth or time required before flowering or fruiting, price, origin or place where grown, or any other material aspect of the industry product.

(b) The inhibitions of this section shall apply to every type of advertisement or method of representation, whether in newspaper, periodical, sales catalog, circular, by tag, label or insignia, by radio or television, by sales representatives, or otherwise.

(c) Among practices inhibited by the foregoing are direct or indirect representations:

(1) That plants have been propagated by grafting or bud selection methods, when such is not the fact.

(2) That industry products are healthy, will grow anywhere without the use of fertilizer, or will survive and produce without special care, when such is not the fact.

(3) That plants will bloom the year round, or will bear an extraordinary number of blooms of unusual size or quality, when such is not the fact.

(4) That an industry product is a new variety, when in fact it is a standard variety to which the industry member has given a new name.

(5) That an industry product cannot be purchased through usual retail outlets, or that there are limited stocks available, when such is not the fact.

(6) That industry products offered for sale will be delivered in time for the next (or any specified) seasonal planting when the industry member is aware of factors which make such delivery improbable.

(7) That the appearance of an industry product as to size, color, contour, foliage, bloom, fruit or other physical characteristic is normal or usual when the appearance so represented is in fact abnormal or unusual.

(8) That the root system of any plant is larger in depth or diameter than that which actually exists, whether accomplished by excessive packaging material, or excessive balling, or other deceptive or misleading practice.

(9) That bulblets are bulbs.

(10) That an industry product is a rare or unusual item when such is not the fact.

[Guide 1]

[44 FR 11177, Feb. 27, 1979, as amended at 59 FR 64549, Dec. 14, 1994; 72 FR 902, Jan. 9, 2007]

§ 18.2 Deception through use of names.

(a) In the sale, offering for sale, or distribution of an industry product, it is an unfair or deceptive act or practice for any industry member to use a name for such product that misrepresents directly or by implication to purchasers or prospective purchasers its true identity.

(b) Subject to the foregoing:

(1) When an industry product has a generally recognized and well-established common name, it is proper to use such name as a designation therefor, either alone or in conjunction with the correct botanical name of the product.

(2) When an industry product has a generally recognized and well-established common name, it is an unfair or deceptive act or practice for an industry member to adopt and use a new name for the product unless such new name is immediately accompanied by the generally recognized and well-established common name, or by the correct botanical name, or by a description of the nature and properties of the product which is of sufficient detail to prevent confusion and deception of purchasers or prospective purchasers as to the true identity of the product.

(3) When an industry product does not have a generally recognized and well-established common name, and a name other than the correct botanical name of the product is applied thereto, such other name shall be immediately accompanied by either the correct botanical name of the product, or a description of the nature and properties of the product which is of sufficient detail as to prevent confusion and deception of purchasers and prospective purchasers as to the true identity of the product.

NOTE: *Industry recommendation.* The industry recommends that in administering the guide in this section the Commission give consideration to the use of plant names listed in such works as Checklist of Woody Ornamental Plants of California, 1977, University of California; Hillier's Manual of Trees and Shrubs, 1971, Hillier & Sons; Manual of Cultivated Conifers, 1965, P. Den Ouden & B. K. Boom; Hortus III, 1976, L. H. Bailey Hortorium; Naming and Registering New Cultivars, 1974, American Association of Nurserymen, Inc.; and to plant name lists periodically published by the plant societies and the horticultural organizations selected as international and national cultivar registration authorities as enumerated in Appendix of Naming and Registering New Cultivars.

[Guide 2]

[44 FR 11177, Feb. 27, 1979, as amended at 59 FR 64549, Dec. 14, 1994]

§ 18.3 Substitution of products.

With respect to industry products offered for sale by an industry member, it is an unfair or deceptive act or practice for any member of the industry:

(a) To ship or deliver industry products which do not conform to representations made prior to securing the order or to specifications upon which the sale is consummated, without advising the purchaser of the substitution and obtaining the purchaser's consent thereto prior to making shipment or delivery, where failure to advise would be misleading to purchasers; or

(b) To falsely represent the reason for making a substitution: *Provided, however*, That nothing in this section is intended to inhibit the shipment of products different from those ordered, prior to obtaining the purchaser's consent to such substitution, when the order is received by the industry member near the close of the planting season for the products ordered and the substitution involved relates but to a product or products the total price of which is comparatively small, and when:

(1) At the commencement of the planting season for the products ordered the industry member had a supply of such products sufficient to meet normal and reasonably expected orders therefor, and such supply has been exhausted; and

(2) The products substituted are of similar variety and of equal or greater value to those ordered by the purchaser and no additional charge is made therefor; and

(3) Notice of the substitution, with adequate identification of the substituted item or items, and with commitment of the industry member to refund any purchase price received for the substituted products if such products are not acceptable to the purchaser and to compensate the purchaser for any expense involved in the return of the substituted products if refund is conditioned on the return thereof, is given the purchaser at the time of his receipt of such products: *And provided further*, That nothing in this section is to be construed as sanctioning the dissemination of an advertisement of an industry product or products or the personal solicitation of orders therefor unless at the time of such dissemination or solicitation the industry member has a supply of such product or products sufficient to meet normal and reasonably expected orders therefor.

[Guide 3]

[44 FR 11177, Feb. 27, 1979, as amended at 59 FR 64549, Dec. 14, 1994]

§ 18.4 Size and grade designations.

(a) In the sale, offering for sale, or distribution of industry products, it is an unfair or deceptive act or practice for an industry member to use any term, designation, number, letter, mark, or symbol as a size or grade designation for any industry product in a manner or under any circumstance that misrepresents directly or by implication to purchasers or prospective purchasers the actual size or grade of such products.

(b) Under this section industry members offering lining-out stock for sale shall specify conspicuously and accurately the size and age of such stock when failure to do so may misrepresent directly or by implication such stock to purchasers or prospective purchasers.

(c) Nothing in this section is to be construed as inhibiting the designation of the size or grade of an industry product by use of a size or grade designation for which a standard has been established which is generally recognized in the industry when the identity of such standard is conjunctively disclosed, the product qualifies for the designation under such standard, and no deception of purchasers or prospective purchasers results in the use of such designation.

NOTE: It is the consensus of the industry that the grade and size standard set forth in the current edition of American Standard for Nursery Stock, ANSI Z60.1, as approved by the American National Standard Institute, Inc., is generally recognized in the industry, and that use of the size and grade designation therein set forth, in accordance with the requirements of the standard for the designations, in the marketing of industry products to which such standard relates, will prevent deception and confusion of purchasers and prospective purchasers of such products.

[Guide 4]

[44 FR 11177, Feb. 27, 1979, as amended at 59 FR 64549, Dec. 14, 1994]

§ 18.5 Deception as to blooming, fruiting, or growing ability.

In the sale, offering for sale, or distribution of industry products, it is an unfair or deceptive act or practice for any industry member to misrepresent directly or by implication to purchasers or prospective purchasers the ability of such products:

(a) To bloom, flower, or fruit within a specified period of time; or

(b) To produce crops within a specified period of time, or to give multiple crops each year, or to produce crops in unfavorable climatic regions; or

(c) To bear fruit through self-pollinization; or

(d) To grow, flourish, and survive irrespective of the climatic conditions, the care exercised in or after planting, or the soil characteristics of the locality in which they are to be planted.

NOTE 1: Under this section, when flower bulbs are of such immaturity as not reasonably to be expected to bloom and flower the first season of their planting, such fact shall be clearly and conspicuously disclosed in all advertisements and sales promotional literature relating to such products: *Provided, however*, That such disclosure need not be made when sales are confined to nurseries and commercial growers for their use as planting stock.

NOTE 2: Under this section, in order to avoid deception of purchasers and prospective purchasers thereof, when rose bushes have been used in a greenhouse for the commercial production of cut flowers, they shall be tagged or labeled so as to clearly, adequately and conspicuously disclose such fact, and such tags and labels shall be so attached thereto as to remain thereon until consummation of consumer sale. A similar disclosure shall be made in all advertising and sales promotional literature relating to such products. And when, by reason of such previous greenhouse use or their condition at the time of removal therefrom or their handling during or subsequent thereto, there is probability that such rose bushes will not satisfactorily thrive and produce flowers when replanted outdoors, or will satisfactorily thrive and produce flowers outdoors only if given special treatment and attention during and after their replanting, such fact shall also be clearly, conspicuously, and nondeceptively disclosed in close conjunction with, and in the same manner as, the aforesaid required disclosure that such products have been used in a greenhouse for the commercial production of cut flowers.

[Guide 5]

[44 FR 11177, Feb. 27, 1979, as amended at 59 FR 64549, Dec. 14, 1994]

§ 18.6 Plants collected from the wild state.

It is an unfair or deceptive act or practice to sell, offer for sale, or distribute industry products collected from the wild state without disclosing that they were collected from the wild state; *provided, however*, that plants propagated in nurseries from plants lawfully collected from the wild state may be designated as "nursery-propagated."

[Guide 6]

[59 FR 64549, Dec. 14, 1994]

§ 18.7 Misrepresentation as to character of business.

(a) In the sale, offering for sale, or distribution of industry products, it is an unfair or deceptive act or practice for any industry member to represent itself directly or by implication to be a grower or propagator of such products, or any portion thereof, or to have any other experience or qualification either relating to the growing or propagation of such products or enabling the industry member to be of assistance to purchasers or prospective purchasers in the selection by them of the kinds or types of products, or the placement thereof, when such is not the fact, or in any other manner to misrepresent directly or by implication the character, nature, or extent of the industry member's business.

NOTE: Among practices subject to the inhibitions of this section is a representation by an industry member to the effect that he is a landscape architect when his training, experience, and knowledge do not qualify him for such representation.

(b) It is also an unfair or deceptive act or practice for an industry member to use the word "guild," "club," "association," "council," "society," "foundation," or any other word of similar import or meaning, as part of a trade name, or otherwise, in such a manner or under such circumstances as to indicate or imply that its business is other than a commercial enterprise operated for profit, unless such be true in fact, or so as to deceive purchasers or prospective purchasers in any other material respect.

[Guide 7]

[59 FR 64549, Dec. 14, 1994]

§ 18.8 Deception as to origin or source of industry products.

(a) It is an unfair or deceptive act or practice to sell, offer for sale, or advertise an industry product by misrepresenting directly or by implication the origin or source of such product to purchasers or prospective purchasers (e.g., by use of the term *Holland* to describe bulbs grown in the U.S.A.); *provided, however*, that when a plant has an accepted common name that incorporates a geographical term and such term has lost its geographical significance as so used, the mere use of such common names does not constitute a misrepresentation as to source or origin (e.g., "Colorado Blue Spruce," "Arizona Cypress," "Black Hills Spruce," "California Privet," "Japanese Barberry," etc.).

(b) It is also an unfair or deceptive act or practice to advertise, sell, or offer for sale an industry product of foreign origin without adequate and non-deceptive disclosure of the name of the foreign country from which it came, where the failure to make such disclosure would be misleading to purchasers or prospective purchasers.

[Guide 8]

[59 FR 64550, Dec. 14, 1994]

PART 20—GUIDES FOR THE REBUILT, RECONDITIONED, AND OTHER USED AUTOMOBILE PARTS INDUSTRY

AUTHORITY: 15 U.S.C. 41–58.

SOURCE: 79 FR 40628, July 14, 2014, unless otherwise noted.

§ 20.0 Scope and purpose of the guides.

(a) The Guides in this part apply to the manufacture, sale, distribution, marketing and advertising (including advertising in electronic format, such as on the Internet) of parts that are not new, and assemblies containing such parts, that were designed for use in automobiles, trucks, motorcycles, tractors, or similar self-propelled vehicles, regardless of whether such parts or assemblies have been cleaned, repaired, reconstructed, or reworked in any other way (industry product or product). Industry products include, but are not limited to, airbags, alternators and generators, anti-lock brake systems, brake cylinders, carburetors, catalytic converters, differentials, engines, fuel injectors, hybrid drive systems and hybrid batteries, navigation and audio systems, power steering pumps, power window motors, rack and pinion units, starters, steering gears, superchargers and turbochargers, tires, transmissions and transaxles, and water pumps.

(b) These guides set forth the Federal Trade Commission's current views about the manufacture, sale, distribution, and advertising of industry products. The guides help businesses avoid making claims that are unfair or deceptive under Section 5 of the FTC Act, 15 U.S.C. 45. They do not confer any rights on any person and do not operate to bind the FTC or the public. The Commission, however, can take action under the FTC Act if a business makes a claim inconsistent with the guides. In any such enforcement action, the Commission must prove that the challenged act or practice is unfair or deceptive in violation of Section 5 of the FTC Act.

§ 20.1 Deception generally.

(a) It is unfair or deceptive to represent, directly or by implication, that any industry product is new or unused when such is not the fact, or to misrepresent the current condition, or extent of previous use, reconstruction, or repair of any industry product.

(b) It is unfair or deceptive to offer for sale or sell any industry product without disclosing, clearly and conspicuously, in advertising, in promotional literature, on invoices, and on the product's packaging that the item is an industry product. Additionally, it is unfair or deceptive to offer for sale or to sell any industry product that appears new or unused without disclosing on the product itself that it is an industry product, using appropriate descriptive terms with sufficient permanency to remain visible for a reasonable time after installation. Examples of appropriate descriptive terms include, but are not limited to "Used," "Secondhand," "Repaired," "Relined," "Reconditioned," "Rebuilt," or "Remanufactured." If the term "recycled" is used, it should be used in a manner consistent with the requirements for that term set forth in the Guides for the Use of Environmental Marketing Claims, 16 CFR 260.7(e). On invoices to the trade only, the disclosure may be by use of any number, mark, or other symbol that is clearly understood by industry members as meaning that the part so marked on the invoices is not new.

(c) It is unfair or deceptive to place any means or instrumentality in the hands of others so that they may mislead consumers as to the previous use of industry products.

§ 20.2 Deception as to the identity of a rebuilder, remanufacturer, reconditioner, reliner, or other reworker.

(a) It is unfair or deceptive to misrepresent the identity of the rebuilder, remanufacturer, reconditioner, reliner or other reworker of an industry product.

(b) If the identity of the original manufacturer of an industry product, or the identity of the manufacturer for which the product was originally made, is revealed and the product was rebuilt, remanufactured, reconditioned, relined, or otherwise reworked by someone else, it is unfair or deceptive to fail to disclose such fact wherever the original manufacturer is identified in advertising or promotional literature concerning the industry product, on the container in which the product is packed, and on the product itself, in close conjunction with, and of the same permanency and conspicuousness as, the disclosure that the product is not new. Examples of such disclosures include:

(1) Disclosure of the identity of the rebuilder: "Rebuilt by John Doe Co."

(2) Disclosure that the industry product was rebuilt by an independent rebuilder: "Rebuilt by an Independent Rebuilder."

(3) Disclosure that the industry product was rebuilt by someone other than the manufacturer identified: "Rebuilt by other than XYZ Motors."

(4) Disclosure that the industry product was rebuilt for the identified manufacturer: "Rebuilt for XYZ Motors."

§ 20.3 Misrepresentation of the terms "rebuilt," "factory rebuilt," "remanufactured," etc.

(a) It is unfair or deceptive to use the word "Rebuilt," or any word of similar import, to describe an industry product which, since it was last subjected to any use, has not been dismantled and reconstructed as necessary, all of its internal and external parts cleaned and made rust and corrosion free, all impaired, defective or substantially worn parts restored to a sound condition or replaced with new, rebuilt (in accord with the provisions of this paragraph) or unimpaired used parts, all missing parts replaced with new, rebuilt or unimpaired used parts, and such rewinding or machining and other operations performed as are necessary to put the industry product in sound working condition.

(b) It is unfair or deceptive to represent an industry product as "Remanufactured" or "Factory Rebuilt" unless the product was rebuilt as described in paragraph (a) of this section at a factory generally engaged in the rebuilding of such products.

PART 23—GUIDES FOR THE JEWELRY, PRECIOUS METALS, AND PEWTER INDUSTRIES

AUTHORITY: 15 U.S.C. 45, 46.

SOURCE: 83 FR 40667, Aug. 16, 2018, unless otherwise noted.

§ 23.0 Scope and application.

(a) The guides in this part apply to jewelry industry products, which include, but are not limited to, the following: Gemstones and their laboratory-created and imitation substitutes; natural and cultured pearls and their imitations; and metallic watch bands not permanently attached to watches. These guides also apply to articles, including optical frames, pens and pencils, flatware, and hollowware, fabricated from precious metals (gold, silver, and platinum group metals), precious metal alloys, and their imitations. These guides also apply to all articles made from pewter. For the purposes of these guides, all articles covered by these guides are defined as "industry products."

(b) These guides apply to persons, partnerships, or corporations, at every level of the trade (including but not limited to manufacturers, suppliers, and retailers) engaged in the business of offering for sale, selling, or distributing industry products.

NOTE TO PARAGRAPH (b): To prevent consumer deception, persons, partnerships, or corporations in the business of appraising, identifying, or grading industry products should utilize the terminology and standards set forth in the guides.

(c) These guides apply to claims and representations about industry products included in labeling, advertising, promotional materials, and all other forms of marketing, whether asserted directly or by implication, through words, symbols, emblems, logos, illustrations, depictions, product brand names, or through any other means.

(d) These guides set forth the Federal Trade Commission's current thinking about claims for jewelry and articles made from precious metals and pewter. The guides help marketers and other industry members avoid making claims that are unfair or deceptive under Section 5 of the FTC Act, 15 U.S.C. 45. They do not confer any rights on any person and do not operate to bind the FTC or the public. The Commission, however, may take action under the FTC Act if a marketer or other industry member makes a claim inconsistent with the guides. In any such enforcement action, the Commission must prove that the challenged act or practice is unfair or deceptive in violation of Section 5 of the FTC Act.

(e) The guides consist of general principles, specific guidance on the use of particular claims for industry products, and examples. Claims may raise issues that are addressed by more than one example and in more than one section of the guides. The examples provide the Commission's views on how reasonable consumers likely interpret certain claims. Industry members may use an alternative approach if the approach satisfies the requirements of Section 5 of the FTC Act. Whether a particular claim is deceptive will depend on the net impression of the advertisement, label, or other promotional material at issue. In addition, although many examples present specific claims and options for qualifying claims, the examples do not illustrate all permissible claims or qualifications under Section 5 of the FTC Act.

§23.1 Deception (general).

It is unfair or deceptive to misrepresent the type, kind, grade, quality, quantity, metallic content, size, weight, cut, color, character, treatment, substance, durability, serviceability, origin, price, value, preparation, production, manufacture, distribution, or any other material aspect of an industry product.

NOTE 1 TO §23.1: If, in the sale or offering for sale of an industry product, any representation is made as to the grade assigned the product, the identity of the grading system used should be disclosed.

NOTE 2 TO §23.1: To prevent deception, any qualifications or disclosures, such as those described in the guides, should be sufficiently clear and prominent. Clarity of language, relative type size and proximity to the claim being qualified, and an absence of contrary claims that could undercut effectiveness, will maximize the likelihood that the qualifications and disclosures are appropriately clear and prominent.

NOTE 3 TO §23.1: An illustration or depiction of a diamond or other gemstone that portrays it in greater than its actual size may mislead consumers, unless a disclosure is made about the item's true size.

§23.2 Misuse of the terms "handmade," "hand-polished," etc.

(a) It is unfair or deceptive to represent, directly or by implication, that any industry product is handmade or hand-wrought unless the entire shaping and forming of such product from raw materials and its finishing and decoration were accomplished by hand labor and manually-controlled methods which permit the maker to control and vary the construction, shape, design, and finish of each part of each individual product.

NOTE TO PARAGRAPH (a): As used herein, "raw materials" include bulk sheet, strip, wire, precious metal clays, ingots, casting grain, and similar items that have not been cut, shaped, or formed into jewelry parts, semi-finished parts, or blanks.

(b) It is unfair or deceptive to represent, directly or by implication, that any industry product is hand-forged, hand-engraved, hand-finished, or hand-polished, or has been otherwise hand-processed, unless the operation described was accomplished by hand labor and manually-controlled methods which permit the maker to control and vary the type, amount, and effect of such operation on each part of each individual product.

§23.3 Misrepresentation as to gold content.

(a) It is unfair or deceptive to misrepresent the presence of gold or gold alloy in an industry product, or the quantity or karat fineness of gold or gold alloy contained in the product, or the karat fineness, thickness, weight ratio, or manner of application of any gold or gold alloy plating, covering, or coating on any surface of an industry product or part thereof.

(b) The following are examples of markings or descriptions that may be misleading:[24]

(1) Use of the word "Gold" or any abbreviation, without qualification, to describe all or part of an industry product, including the surface layer of a coated product, which is not composed throughout of fine (24 karat) gold.

(2) Use of the word "Gold" or any abbreviation to describe all or part of an industry product (including the surface layer of a coated product) composed throughout of an alloy of gold (*i.e.*, gold that is less than 24 karats), unless a correct designation of the karat fineness of the alloy immediately precedes the word "Gold" or its abbreviation, and such fineness designation is of at least equal conspicuousness.

(3) Use of the word "Gold" or any abbreviation to describe all or part of an

[24] See paragraph (c) of this section for examples of acceptable markings and descriptions.

industry product that is not composed throughout of gold or a gold alloy, but is surface-plated or coated with gold alloy, unless the word "Gold" or its abbreviation is adequately qualified to indicate that the product or part is only surface-plated.

(4) Marking, describing, or otherwise representing all or part of an industry product as being plated or coated with gold or gold alloy unless all significant surfaces of the product or part contain a plating or coating of gold or gold alloy that is of reasonable durability.[25]

(5) Use of the term "Gold Plate," "Gold Plated," or any abbreviation to describe all or part of an industry product unless such product or part contains a surface-plating of gold alloy, applied by any process, which is of such thickness and extent of surface coverage that reasonable durability[26] is assured, and unless the term is immediately preceded by a correct designation of the karat fineness of the alloy that is of at least equal conspicuousness as the term used.

(6) Use of the terms "Gold Filled," "Rolled Gold Plate," "Rolled Gold Plated," "Gold Overlay," or any abbreviation to describe all or part of an industry product unless such product or part contains a surface-plating of gold alloy applied by a mechanical process and of such thickness and extent of surface coverage that reasonable durability[27] is assured, and unless the term is immediately preceded by a correct designation of the karat fineness of the alloy that is of at least equal conspicuousness as the term used.

(7) Use of the terms "Gold Plate," "Gold Plated," "Gold Filled," "Rolled Gold Plate," "Rolled Gold Plated," "Gold Overlay," or any abbreviation to describe a product in which the layer of gold plating has been covered with a base metal (such as nickel), which is covered with a thin wash of gold, unless there is a disclosure that the primary gold coating is covered with a base metal, which is gold washed.

(8) Use of the term "Gold Electroplate," "Gold Electroplated," or any abbreviation to describe all or part of an industry product unless such product or part is electroplated with gold or a gold alloy and such electroplating is of such karat fineness, thickness, and extent of surface coverage that reasonable durability[28] is assured, and unless the term is immediately preceded by a correct designation of the karat fineness of the alloy that is of at least equal conspicuousness as the term used.

(9) Use of any name, terminology, or other term to misrepresent that an industry product is equal or superior to, or different than, a known and established type of industry product with reference to its gold content or method of manufacture.

(c) The following are examples of markings and descriptions that are consistent with the principles described above:

(1) An industry product or part thereof, composed throughout of an alloy of gold may be marked and described as "Gold" when such word "Gold," wherever appearing, is immediately preceded by a correct designation of the karat fineness of the alloy, and such karat designation is of equal conspicuousness as the word "Gold" (for example, "14 Karat Gold," "14 K. Gold," "14 Kt. Gold," "9 Karat Gold," or "9 Kt. Gold"). Such product may also be marked and described by a designation of the karat fineness of the gold alloy unaccompanied by the word "Gold" (for example, "14 Karat," "14Kt.," "14 K.," or "9 K.").

NOTE TO PARAGRAPH (c)(1): Use of the term "Gold" or any abbreviation to describe all or part of a product that is composed throughout of gold alloy, but contains a hollow center or interior, may mislead consumers, unless the fact that the product contains a hollow center is disclosed in immediate proximity to the term "Gold" or its abbreviation (for example, "14 Karat Gold-Hollow Center," or "14 K. Gold Tubing," when of a gold

[25] For the purpose of this section, "reasonable durability" means that all areas of the plating are sufficiently thick to assure coverage that reasonable consumers would expect from the surface application. Since industry products include items having surfaces and parts of surfaces that are subject to different degrees of wear, the thickness of the surface application for all items or for different areas of the surface of individual items does not necessarily have to be uniform.

[26] See footnote 2.

[27] See footnote 2.

[28] See footnote 2.

alloy tubing of such karat fineness). Such products should not be marked or described as "solid" or as being solidly of gold or of a gold alloy. For example, when the composition of such a product is 14 karat gold alloy, it should not be described or marked as either "14 Kt. Solid Gold" or as "Solid 14 Kt. Gold."

(2) An industry product or part thereof on which there has been affixed on all significant surfaces by soldering, brazing, welding, or other mechanical means a plating of gold alloy of not less than 10 karat fineness and of reasonable durability[29] may be marked or described as "Gold Plate," "Gold Plated," "Gold Overlay," "Rolled Gold Plate," "Rolled Gold Plated," or an adequate abbreviation, when such plating constitutes at least 1/40th of the weight of the metal in the entire article and when the term is immediately preceded by a designation of the karat fineness of the plating which is of equal conspicuousness as the term used (for example, "14 Kt. Gold Overlay," or "14K. R.G.P."). When such plating constitutes at least 1/20th of the weight of the metal in the entire article, the term "Gold Filled" may be used. The terms "Gold Overlay," "Rolled Gold Plate," and "Rolled Gold Plated" may be used when the karat fineness designation is immediately preceded by a fraction accurately disclosing the portion of the weight of the metal in the entire article accounted for by the plating, and when such fraction is of equal conspicuousness as the term used (for example, "1/40th 12 Kt. Rolled Gold Plate" or "1/40 12 Kt. R.G.P.").

(3) An industry product or part thereof on which there has been affixed on all significant surfaces by an electrolytic process an electroplating of gold, or of a gold alloy of not less than 10 karat fineness, which is of reasonable durability[30] and has a minimum thickness throughout equivalent to 0.175 microns (approximately 7/1,000,000ths of an inch) of fine gold,[31] may be marked or described as "Gold Plate," "Gold Plated," "Gold Electroplate" or "Gold Electroplated," or so abbreviated, if the term is immediately preceded by a designation of the karat fineness of the plating which is of equal conspicuousness as the term used (e.g., "12 Karat Gold Electroplate" or "12K G.E.P."). When the electroplating is of the minimum fineness specified above and of a minimum thickness throughout equivalent to two and one half (2½) microns (or approximately 100/1,000,000ths of an inch) of fine gold, the marking or description may be "Heavy Gold Electroplate" or "Heavy Gold Electroplated." When electroplatings qualify for the term "Gold Electroplate" (or "Gold Electroplated"), or the term "Heavy Gold Electroplate" (or "Heavy Gold Electroplated"), and have been applied by use of a particular kind of electrolytic process, the marking may be accompanied by identification of the process used, as for example, "Gold Electroplated (X Process)" or "Heavy Gold Electroplated (Y Process)."

(d) The provisions of this section relating to markings and descriptions of industry products and parts thereof are subject to the applicable tolerances of the National Stamping Act or any amendment thereof.[32]

NOTE TO PARAGRAPH (d): Exemptions recognized in the assay of karat gold industry products and in the assay of gold filled, gold overlay, and rolled gold plate industry products, and not to be considered in any assay for quality, are listed in the appendix.

§ 23.4 Misuse of the word "vermeil."

(a) It is unfair or deceptive to represent, directly or by implication, that an industry product is "vermeil" if such mark or description misrepresents the product's true composition.

(b) An industry product may be described or marked as "vermeil" if it consists of a base of sterling silver coated or plated on all significant surfaces with gold, or gold alloy of not less than 10 karat fineness, that is of reasonable durability[33] and a minimum

[29] See footnote 2.

[30] See footnote 2.

[31] A product containing 1 micron (otherwise known as 1μ) of 12 karat gold is equivalent to one-half micron of 24-karat gold.

[32] Under the National Stamping Act, articles or parts made of gold or of gold alloy that contain no solder have a permissible tolerance of three parts per thousand. If the part tested contains solder, the permissible tolerance is seven parts per thousand. For full text, see 15 U.S.C. 295, *et seq.*

[33] See footnote 2.

thickness throughout equivalent to two and one half (2½) microns (or approximately 100/1,000,000ths of an inch) of fine gold.

NOTE 1 TO § 23.4: It is unfair or deceptive to use the term "vermeil" to describe a product in which the sterling silver has been covered with a base metal (such as nickel) plated with gold unless there is a disclosure that the sterling silver is covered with a base metal that is plated with gold.

NOTE 2 TO § 23.4: Exemptions recognized in the assay of gold filled, gold overlay, and rolled gold plate industry products are listed in the appendix.

§ 23.5 Misrepresentation as to silver content.

(a) It is unfair or deceptive to misrepresent that an industry product contains silver, or to misrepresent an industry product as having a silver content, plating, electroplating, or coating.

(b) The following are examples of markings or descriptions that may be misleading:

(1) Use of the unqualified word "silver" to mark, describe, or otherwise represent all or part of an industry product, including the surface layer of a coated product, unless an equally conspicuous, accurate quality fineness designation indicating the pure silver content in parts per thousand immediately precedes the term (e.g., "750 silver").

(2) Use of the words "solid silver," "Sterling Silver," "Sterling," or the abbreviation "Ster." to mark, describe, or otherwise represent all or part of an industry product unless it is at least 925/1,000ths pure silver.

(3) Use of the words "coin" or "coin silver" to mark, describe, or otherwise represent all or part of an industry product unless it is at least 900/1,000ths pure silver.

(4) Use of the word "silver" to mark, describe, or otherwise represent all or part of an industry product that is not composed throughout of silver, but has a surface layer or coating of silver, unless the term is adequately qualified to indicate that the product or part is only coated.

(5) Marking, describing, or otherwise representing all or part of an industry product as being plated or coated with silver unless all significant surfaces of the product or part contain a plating or coating of silver that is of reasonable durability.[34]

(c) The provisions of this section relating to markings and descriptions of industry products and parts thereof are subject to the applicable tolerances of the National Stamping Act or any amendment thereof.[35]

NOTE 1 TO § 23.5: The National Stamping Act provides that silver plated articles shall not "be stamped, branded, engraved or imprinted with the word 'sterling' or the word 'coin,' either alone or in conjunction with other words or marks." 15 U.S.C. 297(a).

NOTE 2 TO § 23.5: Exemptions recognized in the assay of silver industry products are listed in the appendix.

§ 23.6 Misuse of the words "platinum," "iridium," "palladium," "ruthenium," "rhodium," and "osmium."

(a) It is unfair or deceptive to use the words "platinum," "iridium," "palladium," "ruthenium," "rhodium," and "osmium," or any abbreviation to mark or describe all or part of an industry product if such marking or description misrepresents the product's true composition. The Platinum Group Metals (PGM) are Platinum, Iridium, Palladium, Ruthenium, Rhodium, and Osmium.

(b) The following are examples of markings or descriptions that may be misleading:[36]

(1) Use of the word "Platinum" or any abbreviation to describe all or part of a product that is not composed throughout of platinum, but has a surface layer or coating of platinum, unless the word "Platinum" or its abbreviation is adequately qualified to indicate that the product or part is only coated.

(2) Marking, describing, or otherwise representing all or part of an industry product as being plated or coated with platinum unless all significant surfaces

[34] See footnote 2.

[35] Under the National Stamping Act, sterling silver articles or parts that contain no solder have a permissible tolerance of four parts per thousand. If the part tested contains solder, the permissible tolerance is ten parts per thousand. For full text, see 15 U.S.C. 294, *et seq.*

[36] See paragraph (c) of this section for examples of acceptable markings and descriptions.

of the product or part contain a plating or coating of platinum that is of reasonable durability.[37]

(3) Use of the word "Platinum" or any abbreviation, without qualification, to describe all or part of an industry product (including the surface layer of a coated product) that is not composed throughout of 950 parts per thousand pure Platinum.

(4) Use of the word "Platinum" or any abbreviation accompanied by a number indicating the parts per thousand of pure Platinum contained in the product without mention of the number of parts per thousand of other PGM contained in the product, to describe all or part of an industry product that is not composed throughout of at least 850 parts per thousand pure platinum, for example, "600Plat."

(5) Use of the word "Platinum" or any abbreviation thereof, to mark or describe any product that is not composed throughout of at least 500 parts per thousand pure Platinum.

(6) Use of the word "Platinum," or any abbreviation accompanied by a number or percentage indicating the parts per thousand of pure Platinum contained in the product, to describe all or part of an industry product that contains at least 500 parts per thousand, but less than 850 parts per thousand, pure Platinum, and does not contain at least 950 parts per thousand PGM (for example, "585 Plat.") without a clear and conspicuous disclosure, immediately following the name or description of such product:

(i) Of the full composition of the product (by name and not abbreviation) and percentage of each metal; and

(ii) That the product may not have the same attributes or properties as traditional platinum products. *Provided, however*, that the marketer need not make disclosure under this paragraph (b)(6)(ii), if the marketer has competent and reliable scientific evidence that such product does not differ materially from any one product containing at least 850 parts per thousand pure Platinum with respect to the following attributes or properties: Durability, luster, density, scratch resistance, tarnish resistance, hypoallergenicity, ability to be resized or repaired, retention of precious metal over time, and any other attribute or property material to consumers.

NOTE TO PARAGRAPH (b)(6): When using percentages to qualify platinum representations, marketers should convert the amount in parts per thousand to a percentage that is accurate to the first decimal place (e.g., "58.5% Platinum, 41.5% Cobalt").

(c) The following are examples of markings and descriptions that are not considered unfair or deceptive:

(1) The following abbreviations for each of the PGM may be used for quality marks on articles: "Plat." or "Pt." for Platinum; "Irid." or "Ir." for Iridium; "Pall." or "Pd." for Palladium; "Ruth." or "Ru." for Ruthenium; "Rhod." or "Rh." for Rhodium; and "Osmi." or "Os." for Osmium.

(2) An industry product consisting of at least 950 parts per thousand pure Platinum may be marked or described as "Platinum."

(3) An industry product consisting of 850 parts per thousand pure Platinum, 900 parts per thousand pure Platinum, or 950 parts per thousand pure Platinum may be marked "Platinum," provided that the Platinum marking is preceded by a number indicating the amount in parts per thousand of pure Platinum (for industry products consisting of 950 parts per thousand pure Platinum, the marking described in §23.7(b)(2) above is also appropriate). Thus, the following markings may be used: "950Pt.," "950Plat.," "900Pt.," "900Plat.," "850Pt.," or "850Plat."

(4) An industry product consisting of at least 950 parts per thousand PGM, and of at least 500 parts per thousand pure Platinum, may be marked "Platinum," provided that the mark of each PGM constituent is preceded by a number indicating the amount in parts per thousand of each PGM (e.g., "600Pt.350Ir.," "600Plat.350Irid.," "550Pt.350Pd.50Ir.," or "550Plat.350Pall.50Irid").

(5) An industry product consisting of at least 500 parts per thousand, but less than 850 parts per thousand, pure Platinum, and not consisting of at least 950 parts per thousand PGM, may be marked or stamped accurately, with a quality marking on the article, using

[37] See footnote 2.

parts per thousand and standard chemical abbreviations (e.g., "585 Pt., 415 Co.").

NOTE TO § 23.6: Exemptions recognized in the assay of platinum industry products are listed in the appendix.

§ 23.7 Disclosure of surface-layer application of rhodium.

It is unfair or deceptive to fail to disclose a surface-layer application of rhodium on products marked or described as precious metal.

§ 23.8 Misrepresentation as to products containing more than one precious metal.

(a) It is unfair or deceptive to misrepresent the relative quantity of each precious metal in a product that contains more than than one precious metal. Marketers should list precious metals in the order of their relative weight in the product from greatest to least (*i.e.*, leading with the predominant metal). Listing precious metals in order of relative weight is not necessary where it is clear to reasonable consumers from context that the metal listed first is not predominant.

(b) The following are examples of markings or descriptions that may be misleading:

(1) Use of the terms "Platinum + Silver" to describe a product that contains more silver than platinum by weight.

(2) Use of the terms "14K/Sterling" to describe a product that contains more silver than gold by weight.

(c) The following are examples of markings and descriptions that are not considered unfair or deceptive:

(1) For a product comprised primarily of silver with a surface-layer application of platinum, "900 platinum over silver."

(2) For a product comprised primarily of silver with visually distinguishable parts of gold, "14k gold-accented silver."

(3) For a product comprised primarily of gold with visually distinguishable parts of platinum, "850 Platinum inset, 14K gold ring."

§ 23.9 Misrepresentation as to content of pewter.

(a) It is unfair or deceptive to mark, describe, or otherwise represent all or part of an industry product as "Pewter" or any abbreviation if such mark or description misrepresents the product's true composition.

(b) An industry product or part thereof may be described or marked as "Pewter" or any abbreviation if it consists of at least 900 parts per 1,000 Grade A Tin, with the remainder composed of metals appropriate for use in pewter.

§ 23.10 Additional guidance for the use of quality marks.

As used in these guides, the term *quality mark* means any letter, figure, numeral, symbol, sign, word, or term, or any combination thereof, that has been stamped, embossed, inscribed, or otherwise placed on any industry product and which indicates or suggests that any such product is composed throughout of any precious metal or any precious metal alloy or has a surface or surfaces on which there has been plated or deposited any precious metal or precious metal alloy. Included are the words "gold," "karat," "carat," "silver," "sterling," "vermeil," "platinum," "iridium," "palladium," "ruthenium," "rhodium," or "osmium," or any abbreviations thereof, whether used alone or in conjunction with the words "filled," "plated," "overlay," or "electroplated," or any abbreviations thereof. Quality markings include those in which the words or terms "gold," "karat," "silver," "vermeil," "platinum" (or platinum group metals), or their abbreviations are included, either separately or as suffixes, prefixes, or syllables.

(a) *Deception as to applicability of marks.* (1) If a quality mark on an industry product is applicable to only part of the product, the part of the product to which it is applicable (or inapplicable) should be disclosed when, absent such disclosure, the location of the mark misrepresents the product or part's true composition.

(2) If a quality mark is applicable to only part of an industry product, but not another part which is of similar

surface appearance, each quality mark should be closely accompanied by an identification of the part or parts to which the mark is applicable.

(b) *Deception by reason of difference in the size of letters or words in a marking or markings.* It is unfair or deceptive to place a quality mark on a product in which the words or letters appear in greater size than other words or letters of the mark, or when different markings placed on the product have different applications and are in different sizes, when the net impression of any such marking would be misleading as to the metallic composition of all or part of the product. (An example of improper marking would be the marking of a gold electroplated product with the word "electroplate" in small type and the word "gold" in larger type, with the result that purchasers and prospective purchasers of the product might only observe the word "gold.")

NOTE 1 TO § 23.10: Legibility of markings. If a quality mark is engraved or stamped on an industry product, or is printed on a tag or label attached to the product, the quality mark should be of sufficient size type as to be legible to persons of normal vision, should be so placed as likely to be observed by purchasers, and should be so attached as to remain thereon until consumer purchase.

NOTE 2 TO § 23.10: Disclosure of identity of manufacturers, processors, or distributors. The National Stamping Act provides that any person, firm, corporation, or association, being a manufacturer or dealer subject to section 294 of the Act, who applies or causes to be applied a quality mark, or imports any article bearing a quality mark "which indicates or purports to indicate that such article is made in whole or in part of gold or silver or of an alloy of either metal" shall apply to the article the trademark or name of such person. 15 U.S.C. 297.

§ 23.11 Misuse of "corrosion proof," "noncorrosive," "corrosion resistant," "rust proof," "rust resistant," etc.

(a) It is unfair or deceptive to:

(1) Use the terms "corrosion proof," "noncorrosive," "rust proof," or any other term of similar meaning to describe an industry product unless all parts of the product will be immune from rust and other forms of corrosion during the life expectancy of the product; or

(2) Use the terms "corrosion resistant," "rust resistant," or any other term of similar meaning to describe an industry product unless all parts of the product are of such composition as to not be subject to material damage by corrosion or rust during the major portion of the life expectancy of the product under normal conditions of use.

(b) Among the metals that may be considered as corrosion (and rust) resistant are: Pure nickel; gold alloys of not less than 10 Kt. fineness; and austenitic stainless steels.

§ 23.12 Definition and misuse of the word "diamond."

(a) A diamond is a mineral consisting essentially of pure carbon crystallized in the isometric system. It is found in many colors. Its hardness is 10; its specific gravity is approximately 3.52; and it has a refractive index of 2.42.

(b) It is unfair or deceptive to use the unqualified word "diamond" to describe or identify any object or product not meeting the requirements specified in the definition of diamond provided above, or which, though meeting such requirements, has not been symmetrically fashioned with at least seventeen (17) polished facets.

NOTE TO PARAGRAPH (b): It is unfair or deceptive to represent, directly or by implication, that industrial grade diamonds or other non-jewelry quality diamonds are of jewelry quality.

(c) The following are examples of descriptions that are not considered unfair or deceptive:

(1) The use of the words "rough diamond" to describe or designate uncut or unfaceted objects or products satisfying the definition of diamond provided above; or

(2) The use of the word "diamond" to describe or designate objects or products satisfying the definition of diamond but which have not been symmetrically fashioned with at least seventeen (17) polished facets when, in immediate conjunction with the word "diamond," there is either a disclosure of the number of facets and shape of the diamond or the name of a type of diamond that denotes shape and that usually has less than seventeen (17) facets (e.g., "rose diamond").

(3) The use of the word "cultured" to describe laboratory-created diamonds that have essentially the same optical, physical, and chemical properties as mined diamonds if the term is qualified by a clear and conspicuous disclosure (for example, the words "laboratory-created," "laboratory-grown," "[manufacturer name]-created," or some other word or phrase of like meaning) conveying that the product is not a mined stone.

NOTE TO PARAGRAPH (c): Additional guidance about imitation and laboratory-created diamond representations and misuse of the words "real," "genuine," "natural," "precious," "semi-precious," and similar terms is set forth in §§ 23.25 and 23.27.

§ 23.13 Misuse of the words "flawless," "perfect," etc.

(a) It is unfair or deceptive to use the word "flawless" to describe any diamond that discloses flaws, cracks, inclusions, carbon spots, clouds, internal lasering, or other blemishes or imperfections of any sort when examined under a corrected magnifier at 10-power, with adequate illumination, by a person skilled in diamond grading.

(b) It is unfair or deceptive to use the word "perfect," or any representation of similar meaning, to describe any diamond unless the diamond meets the definition of "flawless" and is not of inferior color or make.

(c) It is unfair or deceptive to use the words "flawless" or "perfect" to describe a ring or other article of jewelry having a "flawless" or "perfect" principal diamond or diamonds, and supplementary stones that are not of such quality, unless there is a disclosure that the description applies only to the principal diamond or diamonds.

§ 23.14 Disclosure of treatments to diamonds.

A diamond is a gemstone product. Treatments to diamonds should be disclosed in the manner prescribed in § 23.24 of these guides (Disclosure of treatments to gemstones).

§ 23.15 Misuse of the term "blue white."

It is unfair or deceptive to use the term "blue white" or any representation of similar meaning to describe any diamond that under normal, north daylight or its equivalent shows any color or any trace of any color other than blue or bluish.

§ 23.16 Misuse of the term "properly cut," etc.

It is unfair or deceptive to use the terms "properly cut," "proper cut," "modern cut," or any representation of similar meaning to describe any diamond that is lopsided, or is so thick or so thin in depth as to detract materially from the brilliance of the stone.

NOTE TO § 23.16: Stones that are commonly called "fisheye" or "old mine" should not be described as "properly cut," "modern cut," etc.

§ 23.17 Misuse of the words "brilliant" and "full cut."

It is unfair or deceptive to use the unqualified expressions "brilliant," "brilliant cut," or "full cut" to describe, identify, or refer to any diamond except a round diamond that has at least thirty-two (32) facets plus the table above the girdle and at least twenty-four (24) facets below.

NOTE TO § 23.17: Such terms should not be applied to single or rose-cut diamonds. They may be applied to emerald-(rectangular) cut, pear-shaped, heart-shaped, oval-shaped, and marquise-(pointed oval) cut diamonds meeting the above-stated facet requirements when, in immediate conjunction with the term used, the form of the diamond is disclosed.

§ 23.18 Misrepresentation of weight and "total weight."

(a) It is unfair or deceptive to misrepresent the weight of a diamond.

(b) It is unfair or deceptive to use the word "point" or any abbreviation in any representation, advertising, marking, or labeling to describe the weight of a diamond, unless the weight is also stated as decimal parts of a carat (e.g., 25 points or .25 carat).

NOTE TO PARAGRAPH (b): A carat is a standard unit of weight for a diamond and is equivalent to 200 milligrams (1/5 gram). A point is one one-hundredth (1/100) of a carat.

(c) If diamond weight is stated as decimal parts of a carat (e.g., .47

carat), the stated figure should be accurate to the last decimal place. If diamond weight is stated to only one decimal place (e.g., .5 carat), the stated figure should be accurate to the second decimal place (e.g., ".5 carat" could represent a diamond weight between .495–.504).

(d) If diamond weight is stated as fractional parts of a carat, a conspicuous disclosure of the fact that the diamond weight is not exact should be made in close proximity to the fractional representation and a disclosure of a reasonable range of weight for each fraction (or the weight tolerance being used) should also be made.

NOTE TO PARAGRAPH (d): When fractional representations of diamond weight are made, as described in paragraph (d) of this section, in catalogs or other printed materials, the disclosure of the fact that the actual diamond weight is within a specified range should be made conspicuously on every page where a fractional representation is made. Such disclosure may refer to a chart or other detailed explanation of the actual ranges used. For example, "Diamond weights are not exact; see chart on p. X for ranges."

§23.19 Definitions of various pearls.

As used in these guides, the terms set forth below have the following meanings:

(a) *Pearl:* A calcareous concretion consisting essentially of alternating concentric layers of carbonate of lime and organic material formed within the body of certain mollusks, the result of an abnormal secretory process caused by an irritation of the mantle of the mollusk following the intrusion of some foreign body inside the shell of the mollusk, or due to some abnormal physiological condition in the mollusk, neither of which has in any way been caused or induced by humans.

(b) *Cultured pearl:* The composite product created when a nucleus (usually a sphere of calcareous mollusk shell) planted by humans inside the shell or in the mantle of a mollusk is coated with nacre by the mollusk.

(c) *Imitation pearl:* A manufactured product composed of any material or materials that simulate in appearance a pearl or cultured pearl.

(d) *Seed pearl:* A small pearl, as defined in paragraph (a), that measures approximately two millimeters or less.

§23.20 Misuse of the word "pearl."

(a) It is unfair or deceptive to use the unqualified word "pearl" or any other word or phrase of like meaning to describe, identify, or refer to any object or product that is not in fact a pearl, as defined in §23.19(a).

(b) It is unfair or deceptive to use the word "pearl" to describe, identify, or refer to a cultured pearl unless it is immediately preceded, with equal conspicuousness, by the word "cultured" or "cultivated," or by some other word or phrase of like meaning, so as to indicate definitely and clearly that the product is not a pearl.

(c) It is unfair or deceptive to use the word "pearl" to describe, identify, or refer to an imitation pearl unless it is immediately preceded, with equal conspicuousness, by the word "artificial," "imitation," or "simulated," or by some other word or phrase of like meaning, so as to indicate definitely and clearly that the product is not a pearl.

(d) It is unfair or deceptive to use the terms "faux pearl," "fashion pearl," "Mother of Pearl," or any other such term to describe or qualify an imitation pearl product unless it is immediately preceded, with equal conspicuousness, by the word "artificial," "imitation," or "simulated," or by some other word or phrase of like meaning, so as to indicate definitely and clearly that the product is not a pearl.

§23.21 Misuse of terms such as "cultured pearl," "seed pearl," "Oriental pearl," "natura," "kultured," "real," "synthetic," and regional designations.

(a) It is unfair or deceptive to use the term "cultured pearl," "cultivated pearl," or any other word, term, or phrase of like meaning to describe, identify, or refer to any imitation pearl.

(b) It is unfair or deceptive to use the term "seed pearl" or any word, term, or phrase of like meaning to describe, identify, or refer to a cultured or an imitation pearl, without using the appropriate qualifying term "cultured" (e.g., "cultured seed pearl") or "simulated," "artificial," or "imitation" (e.g., "imitation seed pearl").

(c) It is unfair or deceptive to use the term "Oriental pearl" or any word, term, or phrase of like meaning to describe, identify, or refer to any industry product other than a pearl taken from a salt water mollusk and of the distinctive appearance and type of pearls obtained from mollusks inhabiting the Persian Gulf and recognized in the jewelry trade as Oriental pearls.

(d) It is unfair or deceptive to use the word "Oriental" to describe, identify, or refer to any cultured or imitation pearl.

(e) It is unfair or deceptive to use the word "natura," "natural," "nature's," or any word, term, or phrase of like meaning to describe, identify, or refer to a cultured or imitation pearl. It is unfair or deceptive to use the term "organic" to describe, identify, or refer to an imitation pearl, unless the term is qualified in such a way as to make clear that the product is not a natural or cultured pearl.

(f) It is unfair or deceptive to use the term "kultured," "semi-cultured pearl," "cultured-like," "part-cultured," "premature cultured pearl," or any word, term, or phrase of like meaning to describe, identify, or refer to an imitation pearl.

(g) It is unfair or deceptive to use the term "South Sea pearl" unless it describes, identifies, or refers to a pearl that is taken from a salt water mollusk of the Pacific Ocean South Sea Islands, Australia, or Southeast Asia. It is unfair or deceptive to use the term "South Sea cultured pearl" unless it describes, identifies, or refers to a cultured pearl formed in a salt water mollusk of the Pacific Ocean South Sea Islands, Australia, or Southeast Asia.

(h) It is unfair or deceptive to use the term "Biwa cultured pearl" unless it describes, identifies, or refers to cultured pearls grown in fresh water mollusks in the lakes and rivers of Japan.

(i) It is unfair or deceptive to use the word "real," "genuine," "precious," or any word, term, or phrase of like meaning to describe, identify, or refer to any imitation pearl.

(j) It is unfair or deceptive to use the word "synthetic" or similar terms to describe cultured or imitation pearls.

(k) It is unfair or deceptive to use the terms "Japanese Pearls," "Chinese Pearls," "Mallorca Pearls," or any regional designation to describe, identify, or refer to any cultured or imitation pearl, unless the term is immediately preceded, with equal conspicuousness, by the word "cultured," "artificial," "imitation," or "simulated," or by some other word or phrase of like meaning, so as to indicate definitely and clearly that the product is a cultured or imitation pearl.

§ 23.22 Misrepresentation as to cultured pearls.

It is unfair or deceptive to misrepresent the manner in which cultured pearls are produced, the size of the nucleus artificially inserted in the mollusk and included in cultured pearls, the length of time that such products remained in the mollusk, the thickness of the nacre coating, the value and quality of cultured pearls as compared with the value and quality of pearls and imitation pearls, or any other material matter relating to the formation, structure, properties, characteristics, and qualities of cultured pearls.

§ 23.23 Disclosure of treatments to pearls and cultured pearls.

It is unfair or deceptive to fail to disclose that a pearl or cultured pearl has been treated if:

(a) The treatment is not permanent. The seller should disclose that the pearl or cultured pearl has been treated and that the treatment is or may not be permanent;

(b) The treatment creates special care requirements for the pearl or cultured pearl. The seller should disclose that the pearl or cultured pearl has been treated and has special care requirements. It is also recommended that the seller disclose the special care requirements to the purchaser; or

(c) The treatment has a significant effect on the product's value. The seller should disclose that the pearl or cultured pearl has been treated.

NOTE TO § 23.23: The disclosures outlined in this section are applicable to sellers at every level of trade, as defined in § 23.0(b) of these guides, and they may be made at the point of sale prior to sale, except that where a product can be purchased without personally viewing the product (e.g., direct mail catalogs, online services, televised shopping programs), disclosure should be made in the solicitation for, or description of, the product.

§23.24 Disclosure of treatments to gemstones.

It is unfair or deceptive to fail to disclose that a gemstone has been treated if:

(a) The treatment is not permanent. The seller should disclose that the gemstone has been treated and that the treatment is or may not be permanent;

(b) The treatment creates special care requirements for the gemstone. The seller should disclose that the gemstone has been treated and has special care requirements. It is also recommended that the seller disclose the special care requirements to the purchaser; or

(c) The treatment has a significant effect on the stone's value. The seller should disclose that the gemstone has been treated.

NOTE TO §23.24: The disclosures outlined in this section are applicable to sellers at every level of trade, as defined in §23.0(b) of these guides, and they may be made at the point of sale prior to sale, except that where a product can be purchased without personally viewing the product (e.g., direct mail catalogs, online services, televised shopping programs), disclosure should be made in the solicitation for, or description of, the product.

§23.25 Misuse of the words "ruby," "sapphire," "emerald," "topaz," "stone," "birthstone," "gem," "gemstone," etc.

(a) It is unfair or deceptive to use the unqualified words "ruby," "sapphire," "emerald," "topaz," or the name of any other precious or semi-precious stone to describe any product that is not in fact a mined stone of the type described.

(b) It is unfair or deceptive to use the word "ruby," "sapphire," "emerald," "topaz," or the name of any other precious or semi-precious stone, or the word "stone," "birthstone," "gem," "gemstone," or similar term to describe a laboratory-grown, laboratory-created, [manufacturer name]-created, synthetic, imitation, or simulated stone, unless such word or name is immediately preceded with equal conspicuousness by the word "laboratory-grown," "laboratory-created," "[manufacturer name]-created," or some other word or phrase of like meaning, or by the word "imitation" or "simulated," so as to disclose clearly the nature of the product and the fact it is not a mined gemstone.

NOTE 1 TO PARAGRAPH (b): The use of the word "faux" to describe a laboratory-created or imitation stone is not an adequate disclosure that the stone is not a mined stone.

NOTE 2 TO PARAGRAPH (b): Marketers may use the word "cultured" to describe laboratory-created gemstone products that have essentially the same optical, physical, and chemical properties as the named stone if the term (e.g., "cultured ruby") is qualified by a clear and conspicuous disclosure (for example, the words "laboratory-created," "laboratory-grown," "[manufacturer name]-created," or some other word or phrase of like meaning) conveying that the product is not a mined stone. Additional guidance regarding the use of "cultured" to describe a laboratory-created diamond is set forth in §23.12(c)(3).

(c) It is unfair or deceptive to use the word "laboratory-grown," "laboratory-created," "[manufacturer name]-created," "synthetic," or other word or phrase of like meaning with the name of any natural stone to describe any industry product unless such product has essentially the same optical, physical, and chemical properties as the stone named.

(d) It is unfair or deceptive to describe products made with gemstone material and any amount of filler or binder, such as lead glass, in the following way:

(1) With the unqualified word "ruby," "sapphire," "emerald," "topaz," or name of any other precious or semi-precious stone;

(2) As a "treated ruby," "treated sapphire," "treated emerald," "treated topaz," or "treated [gemstone name]";

(3) As a "laboratory-grown [gemstone name]," "laboratory-created [gemstone name]," "[manufacturer name]-created [gemstone name]," "or "synthetic [gemstone name];" or

(4) As a "composite [gemstone name]," "hybrid [gemstone name]," or "manufactured [gemstone name]," unless the term is qualified to disclose clearly and conspicuously that the product: (A) Does not have the same characteristics as the named stone; and

(B) requires special care. It is further recommended that the seller disclose the special care requirements to the purchaser.

§ 23.26 Misrepresentation as to varietal name.

(a) It is unfair or deceptive to mark or describe an industry product with the incorrect varietal name.

(b) The following are examples of markings or descriptions that may be misleading:

(1) Use of the term "yellow emerald" to describe golden beryl or heliodor.

(2) Use of the term "green amethyst" to describe prasiolite.

NOTE TO § 23.26: A varietal name is given for a division of gem species or genus based on a color, type of optical phenomenon, or other distinguishing characteristic of appearance.

§ 23.27 Misuse of the words "real," "genuine," "natural," "precious," etc.

It is unfair or deceptive to use the word "real," "genuine," "natural," "precious," "semi-precious," or similar terms to describe any industry product that is manufactured or produced artificially.

§ 23.28 Misuse of the words "flawless," "perfect," etc.

(a) It is unfair or deceptive to use the word "flawless" as a quality description of any gemstone that discloses blemishes, inclusions, or clarity faults of any sort when examined under a corrected magnifier at 10-power, with adequate illumination, by a person skilled in gemstone grading.

(b) It is unfair or deceptive to use the word "perfect" or any representation of similar meaning to describe any gemstone unless the gemstone meets the definition of "flawless" and is not of inferior color or make.

(c) It is unfair or deceptive to use the word "flawless," "perfect," or any representation of similar meaning to describe any imitation gemstone.

APPENDIX TO PART 23—EXEMPTIONS RECOGNIZED IN THE ASSAY FOR QUALITY OF GOLD ALLOY, GOLD FILLED, GOLD OVERLAY, ROLLED GOLD PLATE, SILVER, AND PLATINUM INDUSTRY PRODUCTS

(a) Exemptions recognized in the industry and not to be considered in any assay for quality of a karat gold industry product include springs, posts, and separable backs of lapel buttons, posts and nuts for attaching interchangeable ornaments, bracelet and necklace snap tongues, metallic parts completely and permanently encased in a nonmetallic covering, field pieces and bezels for lockets,[38] and wire pegs or rivets used for applying mountings and other ornaments, which mountings or ornaments shall be of the quality marked.

NOTE TO PARAGRAPH (a): Exemptions recognized in the industry and not to be considered in any assay for quality of a karat gold optical product include: the hinge assembly (barrel or other special types such as are customarily used in plastic frames); washers, bushings, and nuts of screw assemblies; dowels; springs for spring shoe straps; metal parts permanently encased in a non-metallic covering; and for oxfords,[39] coil and joint springs.

(b) Exemptions recognized in the industry and not to be considered in any assay for quality of a gold filled, gold overlay and rolled gold plate industry product, other than watchcases, include joints, catches, screws, pin stems, pins of scarf pins, hat pins, etc., field pieces and bezels for lockets, posts and separate backs of lapel buttons, bracelet and necklace snap tongues, springs, and metallic parts completely and permanently encased in a nonmetallic covering.

NOTE TO PARAGRAPH (b): Exemptions recognized in the industry and not to be considered in any assay for quality of a gold filled, gold overlay and rolled gold plate optical product include: Screws; the hinge assembly (barrel or other special types such as are customarily used in plastic frames); washers, bushings, tubes and nuts of screw assemblies; dowels; pad inserts; springs for spring shoe straps, cores and/or inner windings of comfort cable temples; metal parts permanently

[38] Field pieces of lockets are those inner portions used as frames between the inside edges of the locket and the spaces for holding pictures. Bezels are the separable inner metal rings to hold the pictures in place.

[39] Oxfords are a form of eyeglasses where a flat spring joins the two eye rims and the tension it exerts on the nose serves to hold the unit in place. Oxfords are also referred to as pince nez.

encased in a nonmetallic covering; and for oxfords, the handle and catch.

(c) Exemptions recognized in the industry and not to be considered in any assay for quality of a silver industry product include screws, rivets, springs, spring pins for wrist watch straps; posts and separable backs of lapel buttons; wire pegs, posts, and nuts used for applying mountings or other ornaments, which mountings or ornaments shall be of the quality marked; pin stems (e.g., of badges, brooches, emblem pins, hat pins, and scarf pins, etc.); levers for belt buckles; blades and skeletons of pocket knives; field pieces and bezels for lockets; bracelet and necklace snap tongues; any other joints, catches, or screws; and metallic parts completely and permanently encased in a nonmetallic covering.

(d) Exemptions recognized in the industry and not to be considered in any assay for quality of an industry product of silver in combination with gold include joints, catches, screws, pin stems, pins of scarf pins, hat pins, etc., posts and separable backs of lapel buttons, springs, bracelet and necklace snap tongues, and metallic parts completely and permanently encased in a nonmetallic covering.

(e) Exemptions recognized in the industry and not to be considered in any assay for quality of a platinum industry product include springs, winding bars, sleeves, crown cores, mechanical joint pins, screws, rivets, dust bands, detachable movement rims, hat pin stems, and bracelet and necklace snap tongues.

PART 24—GUIDES FOR SELECT LEATHER AND IMITATION LEATHER PRODUCTS

Sec.

AUTHORITY: 15 U.S.C. 45, 46.

SOURCE: 61 FR 51583, Oct. 3, 1996, unless otherwise noted.

§ 24.0 Scope and purpose of guides.

(a) The Guides in this part apply to the manufacture, sale, distribution, marketing, or advertising of all kinds or types of leather or simulated-leather trunks, suitcases, traveling bags, sample cases, instrument cases, brief cases, ring binders, billfolds, wallets, key cases, coin purses, card cases, French purses, dressing cases, stud boxes, tie cases, jewel boxes, travel kits, gadget bags, camera bags, ladies' handbags, shoulder bags, purses, pocketbooks, footwear, belts (when not sold as part of a garment) and similar articles (hereinafter, "industry products").

(b) These Guides represent administrative interpretations of laws administered by the Federal Trade Commission for the guidance of the public in conducting its affairs in conformity with legal requirements. These Guides specifically address the application of section 5 of the FTC Act (15 U.S.C. 45) to the manufacture, sale, distribution, marketing, and advertising of industry products listed in paragraph (a) of this section. They provide the basis for voluntary compliance with such laws by members of industry. Conduct inconsistent with the positions articulated in these Guides may result in corrective action by the Commission under section 5 if, after investigation, the Commission has reason to believe that the behavior falls within the scope of conduct declared unlawful by the statute.

§ 24.1 Deception (general).

It is unfair or deceptive to misrepresent, directly or by implication, the kind, grade, quality, quantity, material content, thickness, finish, serviceability, durability, price, origin, size, weight, ease of cleaning, construction, manufacture, processing, distribution, or any other material aspect of an industry product.

§ 24.2 Deception as to composition.

It is unfair or deceptive to misrepresent, directly or by implication, the composition of any industry product or part thereof. It is unfair or deceptive to use the unqualified term "leather" or other unqualified terms suggestive of leather to describe industry products unless the industry product so described is composed in all substantial parts of leather.[1] This section includes, but is not limited to, the following:

[1] For purposes of these Guides, footwear is composed of three parts: the upper, the lining and sock, and the outersole. These three parts are defined as follows: (1) The upper is

Continued

(a) *Imitation or simulated leather.* If all or part of an industry product is made of non-leather material that appears to be leather, the fact that the material is not leather, or the general nature of the material as something other than leather, should be disclosed. For example: Not leather; Imitation leather; Simulated leather; Vinyl; Vinyl coated fabric; or Plastic.

(b) *Embossed or processed leather.* The kind and type of leather from which an industry product is made should be disclosed when all or part of the product has been embossed, dyed, or otherwise processed so as to simulate the appearance of a different kind or type of leather. For example:

(1) An industry product made wholly of top grain cowhide that has been processed so as to imitate pigskin may be represented as being made of Top Grain Cowhide.

(2) Any additional representation concerning the simulated appearance of an industry product composed of leather should be immediately accompanied by a disclosure of the kind and type of leather in the product. For example: Top Grain Cowhide With Simulated Pigskin Grain.

(c) *Backing material.* (1) The backing of any material in an industry product with another kind of material should be disclosed when the backing is not apparent upon casual inspection of the product, or when a representation is made which, absent such disclosure, would be misleading as to the product's composition. For example: Top Grain Cowhide Backed With Vinyl.

(2) The composition of the different backing material should be disclosed if it is visible and consists of non-leather material with the appearance of leather, or leather processed so as to simulate a different kind of leather.

(d) *Misuse of trade names, etc.* A trade name, coined name, trademark, or other word or term, or any depiction or device should not be used if it misrepresents, directly or by implication, that an industry product is made in whole or in part from animal skin or hide, or that material in an industry product is leather or other material. This includes, among other practices, the use of a stamp, tag, label, card, or other device in the shape of a tanned hide or skin or in the shape of a silhouette of an animal, in connection with any industry product that has the appearance of leather but that is not made wholly or in substantial part from animal skin or hide.

(e) *Misrepresentation that product is wholly of a particular composition.* A misrepresentation should not be made, directly or by implication, that an industry product is made wholly of a particular composition. A representation as to the composition of a particular part of a product should clearly indicate the part to which the representation applies.[2] Where a product is made principally of leather but has certain non-leather parts that appear to be leather, the product may be described as made of leather so long as accompanied by clear disclosure of the non-leather parts. For example:

(1) An industry product made of top grain cowhide except for frame covering, gussets, and partitions that are made of plastic but have the appearance of leather may be described as: Top Grain Cowhide With Plastic Frame Covering, Gussets and Partitions; or Top Grain Cowhide With Gussets, Frame Covering and Partitions Made of Non-Leather Material.

(2) An industry product made throughout, except for hardware, of vinyl backed with cowhide may be described as: Vinyl Backed With Cowhide (See also disclosure provision concerning use of backing material in paragraph (c) of this section).

(3) An industry product made of top grain cowhide except for partitions and stay, which are made of plastic-coated fabric but have the appearance of leather, may be described as: Top Grain

---

the outer face of the structural element which is attached to the outersole; (2) the lining and sock are the lining of the upper and the insole, constituting the inside of the footwear article; and (3) the outersole is the bottom part of the footwear article subjected to abrasive wear and attached to the upper.

[2] With regard to footwear, it is sufficient to disclose the presence of non-leather materials in the upper, the lining and sock, or the outersole, provided that the disclosure is made according to predominance of materials. For example, if the majority of the upper is composed of manmade material: Upper of manmade materials and leather.

Cowhide With Partitions and Stay Made of Non-leather Material; or Top Grain Cowhide With Partitions and Stay Made of Plastic-Coated Fabric.

(f) *Ground, pulverized, shredded, reconstituted, or bonded leather.* A material in an industry product that contains ground, pulverized, shredded, reconstituted, or bonded leather and thus is not wholly the hide of an animal should not be represented, directly or by implication, as being leather. This provision does not preclude an accurate representation as to the ground, pulverized, shredded, reconstituted, or bonded leather content of the material. However, if the material appears to be leather, it should be accompanied by either:

(1) An adequate disclosure as described by paragraph (a) of this section; or

(2) If the terms "ground leather," "pulverized leather," "shredded leather," "reconstituted leather," or "bonded leather" are used, a disclosure of the percentage of leather fibers and the percentage of non-leather substances contained in the material. For example: An industry product made of a composition material consisting of 60% shredded leather fibers may be described as: Bonded Leather Containing 60% Leather Fibers and 40% Non-leather Substances.

(g) *Form of disclosures under this section.* All disclosures described in this section should appear in the form of a stamping on the product, or on a tag, label, or card attached to the product, and should be affixed so as to remain on or attached to the product until received by the consumer purchaser. All such disclosures should also appear in all advertising of such products irrespective of the media used whenever statements, representations, or depictions appear in such advertising which, absent such disclosures, serve to create a false impression that the products, or parts thereof, are of a certain kind of composition. The disclosures affixed to products and made in advertising should be of such conspicuousness and clarity as to be noted by purchasers and prospective purchasers casually inspecting the products or casually reading, or listening to, such advertising. A disclosure necessitated by a particular representation should be in close conjunction with the representation.

§ 24.3 Misuse of the terms "waterproof," "dustproof," "warpproof," "scuffproof," "scratchproof," "scuff resistant," and "scratch resistant."

It is unfair or deceptive to:

(a) Use the term "Waterproof" to describe all or part of an industry product unless the designated product or material prevents water from contact with its contents under normal conditions of intended use during the anticipated life of the product or material.

(b) Use the term "Dustproof" to describe an industry product unless the product is so constructed that when it is closed dust cannot enter it.

(c) Use the term "Warpproof" to describe all or part of an industry product unless the designated product or part is such that it cannot warp.

(d) Use the term "Scuffproof," "Scratchproof," or other terms indicating that the product is not subject to wear in any other respect, to describe an industry product unless the outside surface of the product is immune to scratches or scuff marks, or is not subject to wear as represented.

(e) Use the term "Scuff Resistant," "Scratch Resistant," or other terms indicating that the product is resistant to wear in any other respect, unless there is a basis for the representation and the outside surface of the product is meaningfully and significantly resistant to scuffing, scratches, or to wear as represented.

PARTS 25–227 [RESERVED]

PART 233—GUIDES AGAINST DECEPTIVE PRICING

Sec.

AUTHORITY: Secs. 5, 6, 38 Stat. 719, as amended, 721; 15 U.S.C. 45, 46.

SOURCE: 32 FR 15534, Nov. 8, 1967, unless otherwise noted.

§ 233.1 Former price comparisons.

(a) One of the most commonly used forms of bargain advertising is to offer a reduction from the advertiser's own former price for an article. If the former price is the actual, bona fide price at which the article was offered to the public on a regular basis for a reasonably substantial period of time, it provides a legitimate basis for the advertising of a price comparison. Where the former price is genuine, the bargain being advertised is a true one. If, on the other hand, the former price being advertised is not bona fide but fictitious—for example, where an artificial, inflated price was established for the purpose of enabling the subsequent offer of a large reduction—the "bargain" being advertised is a false one; the purchaser is not receiving the unusual value he expects. In such a case, the "reduced" price is, in reality, probably just the seller's regular price.

(b) A former price is not necessarily fictitious merely because no sales at the advertised price were made. The advertiser should be especially careful, however, in such a case, that the price is one at which the product was openly and actively offered for sale, for a reasonably substantial period of time, in the recent, regular course of his business, honestly and in good faith—and, of course, not for the purpose of establishing a fictitious higher price on which a deceptive comparison might be based. And the advertiser should scrupulously avoid any implication that a former price is a selling, not an asking price (for example, by use of such language as, "Formerly sold at $______"), unless substantial sales at that price were actually made.

(c) The following is an example of a price comparison based on a fictitious former price. John Doe is a retailer of Brand X fountain pens, which cost him $5 each. His usual markup is 50 percent over cost; that is, his regular retail price is $7.50. In order subsequently to offer an unusual "bargain", Doe begins offering Brand X at $10 per pen. He realizes that he will be able to sell no, or very few, pens at this inflated price. But he doesn't care, for he maintains that price for only a few days. Then he "cuts" the price to its usual level—$7.50—and advertises: "Terrific Bargain: X Pens, Were $10, Now Only $7.50!" This is obviously a false claim. The advertised "bargain" is not genuine.

(d) Other illustrations of fictitious price comparisons could be given. An advertiser might use a price at which he never offered the article at all; he might feature a price which was not used in the regular course of business, or which was not used in the recent past but at some remote period in the past, without making disclosure of that fact; he might use a price that was not openly offered to the public, or that was not maintained for a reasonable length of time, but was immediately reduced.

(e) If the former price is set forth in the advertisement, whether accompanied or not by descriptive terminology such as "Regularly," "Usually," "Formerly," etc., the advertiser should make certain that the former price is not a fictitious one. If the former price, or the amount or percentage of reduction, is not stated in the advertisement, as when the ad merely states, "Sale," the advertiser must take care that the amount of reduction is not so insignificant as to be meaningless. It should be sufficiently large that the consumer, if he knew what it was, would believe that a genuine bargain or saving was being offered. An advertiser who claims that an item has been "Reduced to $9.99," when the former price was $10, is misleading the consumer, who will understand the claim to mean that a much greater, and not merely nominal, reduction was being offered. [Guide I]

§ 233.2 Retail price comparisons; comparable value comparisons.

(a) Another commonly used form of bargain advertising is to offer goods at prices lower than those being charged by others for the same merchandise in the advertiser's trade area (the area in which he does business). This may be done either on a temporary or a permanent basis, but in either case the advertised higher price must be based upon fact, and not be fictitious or misleading. Whenever an advertiser represents that he is selling below the prices being charged in his area for a particular article, he should be reasonably certain that the higher price he advertises does not appreciably exceed the price at which substantial sales of the article are being made in the area—that is, a sufficient number of sales so that a consumer would consider a reduction from the price to represent a genuine bargain or saving. Expressed another way, if a number of the principal retail outlets in the area are regularly selling Brand X fountain pens at $10, it is not dishonest for retailer Doe to advertise: "Brand X Pens, Price Elsewhere $10, Our Price $7.50".

(b) The following example, however, illustrates a misleading use of this advertising technique. Retailer Doe advertises Brand X pens as having a "Retail Value $15.00, My Price $7.50," when the fact is that only a few small suburban outlets in the area charge $15. All of the larger outlets located in and around the main shopping areas charge $7.50, or slightly more or less. The advertisement here would be deceptive, since the price charged by the small suburban outlets would have no real significance to Doe's customers, to whom the advertisement of "Retail Value $15.00" would suggest a prevailing, and not merely an isolated and unrepresentative, price in the area in which they shop.

(c) A closely related form of bargain advertising is to offer a reduction from the prices being charged either by the advertiser or by others in the advertiser's trade area for other merchandise of like grade and quality—in other words, comparable or competing merchandise—to that being advertised. Such advertising can serve a useful and legitimate purpose when it is made clear to the consumer that a comparison is being made with other merchandise and the other merchandise is, in fact, of essentially similar quality and obtainable in the area. The advertiser should, however, be reasonably certain, just as in the case of comparisons involving the same merchandise, that the price advertised as being the price of comparable merchandise does not exceed the price at which such merchandise is being offered by representative retail outlets in the area. For example, retailer Doe advertises Brand X pen as having "Comparable Value $15.00". Unless a reasonable number of the principal outlets in the area are offering Brand Y, an essentially similar pen, for that price, this advertisement would be deceptive. [Guide II]

§233.3 Advertising retail prices which have been established or suggested by manufacturers (or other nonretail distributors).

(a) Many members of the purchasing public believe that a manufacturer's list price, or suggested retail price, is the price at which an article is generally sold. Therefore, if a reduction from this price is advertised, many people will believe that they are being offered a genuine bargain. To the extent that list or suggested retail prices do not in fact correspond to prices at which a substantial number of sales of the article in question are made, the advertisement of a reduction may mislead the consumer.

(b) There are many methods by which manufacturers' suggested retail or list prices are advertised: Large scale (often nationwide) mass-media advertising by the manufacturer himself; preticketing by the manufacturer; direct mail advertising; distribution of promotional material or price lists designed for display to the public. The mechanics used are not of the essence. This part is concerned with any means employed for placing such prices before the consuming public.

(c) There would be little problem of deception in this area if all products were invariably sold at the retail price set by the manufacturer. However, the widespread failure to observe manufacturers' suggested or list prices, and the advent of retail discounting on a wide scale, have seriously undermined the dependability of list prices as indicators of the exact prices at which articles are in fact generally sold at retail. Changing competitive conditions have created a more acute problem of deception than may have existed previously. Today, only in the rare case are all sales of an article at the manufacturer's suggested retail or list price.

(d) But this does not mean that all list prices are fictitious and all offers of reductions from list, therefore, deceptive. Typically, a list price is a price at which articles are sold, if not everywhere, then at least in the principal retail outlets which do not conduct their business on a discount basis. It will not be deemed fictitious if it is the price at which substantial (that is, not isolated or insignificant) sales are made in the advertiser's trade area (the area in which he does business). Conversely, if the list price is significantly in excess of the highest price at which substantial sales in the trade area are made, there is a clear and serious danger of the consumer being misled by an advertised reduction from this price.

(e) This general principle applies whether the advertiser is a national or regional manufacturer (or other non-retail distributor), a mail-order or catalog distributor who deals directly with the consuming public, or a local retailer. But certain differences in the responsibility of these various types of businessmen should be noted. A retailer competing in a local area has at least a general knowledge of the prices being charged in his area. Therefore, before advertising a manufacturer's list price as a basis for comparison with his own lower price, the retailer should ascertain whether the list price is in fact the price regularly charged by principal outlets in his area.

(f) In other words, a retailer who advertises a manufacturer's or distributor's suggested retail price should be careful to avoid creating a false impression that he is offering a reduction from the price at which the product is generally sold in his trade area. If a number of the principal retail outlets in the area are regularly engaged in making sales at the manufacturer's suggested price, that price may be used in advertising by one who is selling at a lower price. If, however, the list price is being followed only by, for example, small suburban stores, house-to-house canvassers, and credit houses, accounting for only an insubstantial volume of sales in the area, advertising of the list price would be deceptive.

(g) On the other hand, a manufacturer or other distributor who does business on a large regional or national scale cannot be required to police or investigate in detail the prevailing prices of his articles throughout so large a trade area. If he advertises or disseminates a list or preticketed price in good faith (i.e., as an honest estimate of the actual retail price) which does not appreciably exceed the highest price at which substantial sales are made in his trade area, he will not be chargeable with having engaged in a deceptive practice. Consider the following example:

(h) Manufacturer Roe, who makes Brand X pens and sells them throughout the United States, advertises his pen in a national magazine as having a "Suggested Retail Price $10," a price determined on the basis of a market survey. In a substantial number of representative communities, the principal retail outlets are selling the product at this price in the regular course of business and in substantial volume. Roe would not be considered to have advertised a fictitious "suggested retail price." If retailer Doe does business in one of these communities, he would not be guilty of a deceptive practice by advertising, "Brand X Pens, Manufacturer's Suggested Retail Price, $10, Our Price, $7.50."

(i) It bears repeating that the manufacturer, distributor or retailer must in every case act honestly and in good faith in advertising a list price, and not with the intention of establishing a basis, or creating an instrumentality, for a deceptive comparison in any local or other trade area. For instance, a manufacturer may not affix price tickets containing inflated prices as an accommodation to particular retailers who intend to use such prices as the basis for advertising fictitious price reductions. [Guide III]

§ 233.4 Bargain offers based upon the purchase of other merchandise.

(a) Frequently, advertisers choose to offer bargains in the form of additional merchandise to be given a customer on the condition that he purchase a particular article at the price usually offered by the advertiser. The forms which such offers may take are numerous and varied, yet all have essentially the same purpose and effect. Representative of the language frequently employed in such offers are "Free," "Buy One—Get One Free," "2-For-1 Sale," "Half Price Sale," "1¢ Sale," "50% Off," etc. Literally, of course, the seller is not offering anything "free" (i.e., an unconditional gift), or ½ free, or for only 1¢, when he makes such an offer, since the purchaser is required to purchase an article in order to receive the "free" or "1¢" item. It is important, therefore, that where such a form of offer is used, care be taken not to mislead the consumer.

(b) Where the seller, in making such an offer, increases his regular price of the article required to be bought, or decreases the quantity and quality of that article, or otherwise attaches strings (other than the basic condition that the article be purchased in order for the purchaser to be entitled to the "free" or "1¢" additional merchandise) to the offer, the consumer may be deceived.

(c) Accordingly, whenever a "free," "2-for-1," "half price sale," "1¢ sale," "50% off" or similar type of offer is made, all the terms and conditions of the offer should be made clear at the outset. [Guide IV]

§ 233.5 Miscellaneous price comparisons.

The practices covered in the provisions set forth above represent the most frequently employed forms of bargain advertising. However, there are many variations which appear from time to time and which are, in the main, controlled by the same general principles. For example, retailers should not advertise a retail price as a "wholesale" price. They should not represent that they are selling at "factory" prices when they are not selling at the prices paid by those purchasing directly from the manufacturer. They should not offer seconds or imperfect or irregular merchandise at a reduced price without disclosing that the higher comparative price refers to the price of the merchandise if perfect. They should not offer an advance sale under circumstances where they do not in good faith expect to increase the price at a later date, or make a "limited" offer which, in fact, is not limited. In all of these situations, as well as in others too numerous to mention, advertisers should make certain that the bargain offer is genuine and truthful. Doing so will serve their own interest as well as that of the public. [Guide V]

PART 238—GUIDES AGAINST BAIT ADVERTISING

Sec.

AUTHORITY: Secs. 5, 6, 38 Stat. 719, as amended, 721; 15 U.S.C. 45, 46.

SOURCE: 32 FR 15540, Nov. 8, 1967, unless otherwise noted.

§ 238.0 Bait advertising defined.[1]

Bait advertising is an alluring but insincere offer to sell a product or service which the advertiser in truth does not intend or want to sell. Its purpose is to switch consumers from buying the advertised merchandise, in order to sell something else, usually at a higher price or on a basis more advantageous to the advertiser. The primary aim of a bait advertisement is to obtain leads as to persons interested in buying merchandise of the type so advertised.

§ 238.1 Bait advertisement.

No advertisement containing an offer to sell a product should be published when the offer is not a bona fide effort to sell the advertised product. [Guide 1]

§ 238.2 Initial offer.

(a) No statement or illustration should be used in any advertisement which creates a false impression of the grade, quality, make, value, currency of model, size, color, usability, or origin of the product offered, or which may otherwise misrepresent the product in such a manner that later, on disclosure of the true facts, the purchaser may be switched from the advertised product to another.

(b) Even though the true facts are subsequently made known to the buyer, the law is violated if the first

[1] For the purpose of this part "advertising" includes any form of public notice however disseminated or utilized.

contact or interview is secured by deception. [Guide 2]

§ 238.3 Discouragement of purchase of advertised merchandise.

No act or practice should be engaged in by an advertiser to discourage the purchase of the advertised merchandise as part of a bait scheme to sell other merchandise. Among acts or practices which will be considered in determining if an advertisement is a bona fide offer are:

(a) The refusal to show, demonstrate, or sell the product offered in accordance with the terms of the offer,

(b) The disparagement by acts or words of the advertised product or the disparagement of the guarantee, credit terms, availability of service, repairs or parts, or in any other respect, in connection with it,

(c) The failure to have available at all outlets listed in the advertisement a sufficient quantity of the advertised product to meet reasonably anticipated demands, unless the advertisement clearly and adequately discloses that supply is limited and/or the merchandise is available only at designated outlets,

(d) The refusal to take orders for the advertised merchandise to be delivered within a reasonable period of time,

(e) The showing or demonstrating of a product which is defective, unusable or impractical for the purpose represented or implied in the advertisement,

(f) Use of a sales plan or method of compensation for salesmen or penalizing salesmen, designed to prevent or discourage them from selling the advertised product. [Guide 3]

§ 238.4 Switch after sale.

No practice should be pursued by an advertiser, in the event of sale of the advertised product, of "unselling" with the intent and purpose of selling other merchandise in its stead. Among acts or practices which will be considered in determining if the initial sale was in good faith, and not a strategem to sell other merchandise, are:

(a) Accepting a deposit for the advertised product, then switching the purchaser to a higher-priced product,

(b) Failure to make delivery of the advertised product within a reasonable time or to make a refund,

(c) Disparagement by acts or words of the advertised product, or the disparagement of the guarantee, credit terms, availability of service, repairs, or in any other respect, in connection with it,

(d) The delivery of the advertised product which is defective, unusable or impractical for the purpose represented or implied in the advertisement. [Guide 4]

NOTE: *Sales of advertised merchandise.* Sales of the advertised merchandise do not preclude the existence of a bait and switch scheme. It has been determined that, on occasions, this is a mere incidental byproduct of the fundamental plan and is intended to provide an aura of legitimacy to the overall operation.

PART 239—GUIDES FOR THE ADVERTISING OF WARRANTIES AND GUARANTEES

Sec.

AUTHORITY: Secs. 5, 6, 38 Stat. 719 as amended, 721; 15 U.S.C. 45, 46.

SOURCE: 50 FR 18470, May 1, 1985, unless otherwise noted.

§ 239.1 Purpose and scope of the guides.

The Guides for the Advertising of Warranties and Guarantees are intended to help advertisers avoid unfair or deceptive practices in the advertising of warranties or guarantees. The Guides are based upon Commission cases, and reflect changes in circumstances brought about by the Magnuson-Moss Warranty Act (15 U.S.C. 2301 *et seq.*) and the FTC Rules promulgated pursuant to the Act (16 CFR parts 701 and 702). The Guides do not purport to anticipate all possible unfair or deceptive acts or practices in the advertising of warranties or guarantees and the Guides should not be interpreted to limit the Commission's authority to proceed against such acts or practices under section 5 of the Federal Trade Commission Act. The Commission may bring an action under section 5 against any advertiser who misrepresents the product or service offered, who misrepresents the terms or conditions of the warranty offered, or who employs other deceptive or unfair means.

Section 239.2 of the Guides applies only to advertisements for written warranties on consumer products, as "written warranty" and "consumer product" are defined in the Magnuson-Moss Warranty Act, 15 U.S.C. 2301, that are covered by the Rule on Pre-Sale Availability or Written Warranty Terms, 16 CFR part 702. The other sections of the Guides apply to the advertising of any warranty or guarantee.

[50 FR 18470, May 1, 1985; 50 FR 20899, May 21, 1985]

§ 239.2 Disclosures in warranty or guarantee advertising.

(a) If an advertisement mentions a warranty or guarantee that is offered on the advertised product, the advertisement should disclose, with such clarity and prominence as will be noticed and understood by prospective purchasers, that prior to sale, at the place where the product is sold, prospective purchasers can see the written warranty or guarantee for complete details of the warranty coverage.[1]

Examples: The following are examples of disclosures sufficient to convey to prospective purchasers that, prior to sale, at the place where the product is sold, they can see the written warranty or guarantee for complete details of the warranty coverage. These examples are for both print and broadcast advertising. These examples are illustrative, not exhaustive. In each example, the portion of the advertisement that mentions the warranty or guarantee is in regular type and the disclosure is in italics.

A. "The XYZ washing machine is backed by our limited 1 year warranty. *For complete details, see our warranty at a dealer near you.*"

B. "The XYZ bicycle is warranted for 5 years. *Some restrictions may apply. See a copy of our warranty wherever XYZ products are sold.*"

C. "We offer the best guarantee in the business. *Read the details and compare wherever our fine products are sold.*"

D. *"See our full 2 year warranty at the store nearest you."*

E. "Don't take our word—take our warranty. *See our limited 2 year warranty where you shop.*"

(b) If an advertisement in any catalogue, or in any other solicitation[2] for mail order sales or for telephone order sales mentions a warranty or guarantee that is offered on the advertised product, the advertisement should disclose, with such clarity and prominence as will be noticed and understood by prospective purchasers, that prospective purchasers can obtain complete details of the written warranty or guarantee free from the seller upon specific written request or from the catalogue or other solicitation (whichever is applicable).

Examples: The following are examples of disclosures sufficient to convey to consumers how they can obtain complete details of the written warranty or guarantee prior to placing a mail or telephone order. These examples are illustrative, not exhaustive. In each example, the portion of the advertisement that mentions the warranty or guarantee is in regular typeface and the disclosure is in italics.

A. "ABC quality cutlery is backed by our 10 year warranty. *Write to us for a free copy at: (address).*"

B. "ABC power tools are guaranteed. *Read about our limited 90 day warranty in this catalogue.*"

C. *"Write to us for a free copy of our full warranty.* You'll be impressed how we stand behind our product."

[50 FR 20899, May 21, 1985]

[1] In television advertising, the Commission will regard any disclosure of the pre-sale availability of warranties as complying with this Guide if the advertisement makes the necessary disclosure simultaneously with or immediately following the warranty claim and the disclosure is made in the audio portion, or, if in the video portion, it remains on the screen for at least five seconds.

[2] See note 1.

§ 239.3 "Satisfaction Guarantees" and similar representations in advertising; disclosure in advertising that mentions "satisfaction guarantees" or similar representations.

(a) A seller or manufacturer should use the terms "Satisfaction Guarantee," "Money Back Guarantee," "Free Trial Offer," or similar representations in advertising only if the seller or manufacturer, as the case may be, refunds the full purchase price of the advertised product at the purchaser's request.

(b) An advertisement that mentions a "Satisfaction Guarantee" or a similar representation should disclose, with such clarity and prominence as will be noticed and understood by prospective purchasers, any material limitations or conditions that apply to the "Satisfaction Guarantee" or similar representation.

Examples: These examples are for both print and broadcast advertising. These examples are illustrative, not exhaustive.

Example A: (In an advertisement mentioning a satisfaction guarantee that is conditioned upon return of the unused portion within 30 days) "We guarantee your satisfaction. If not completely satisfied with Acme Spot Remover, return the unused portion within 30 days for a full refund."

Example B: (In an advertisement mentioning a money back guarantee that is conditioned upon return of the product in its original packaging) "Money Back Guarantee! Just return the ABC watch in its original package and ABC will fully refund your money."

§ 239.4 "Lifetime" and similar representations.

If an advertisement uses "lifetime," "life," or similar representations to describe the duration of a warranty or guarantee, then the advertisement should disclose, with such clarity and prominence as will be noticed and understood by prospective purchasers, the life to which the representation refers.

Examples: These examples are for both print and broadcast advertising. These examples are illustrative, not exhaustive.

Example A: (In an advertisement mentioning a lifetime guarantee on an automobile muffler where the duration of the guarantee is measured by the life of the car in which it is installed) "Our lifetime guarantee on the Whisper Muffler protects you for as long as your car runs—even if you sell it, trade it, or give it away!"

Example B: (In an advertisement mentioning a lifetime guarantee on a battery where the duration of the warranty is for as long as the original purchaser owns the car in which it was installed) "Our battery is backed by our lifetime guarantee. Good for as long as you own the car!"

§ 239.5 Performance of warranties or guarantees.

A seller or manufacturer should advertise that a product is warranted or guaranteed only if the seller or manufacturer, as the case may be, promptly and fully performs its obligations under the warranty or guarantee.

PART 240—GUIDES FOR ADVERTISING ALLOWANCES AND OTHER MERCHANDISING PAYMENTS AND SERVICES

Sec.

AUTHORITY: Secs. 5, 6, 38 Stat. 719, as amended, 721; 15 U.S.C. 45, 46; 49 Stat. 1526; 15 U.S.C. 13, as amended.

SOURCE: 79 FR 58252, Sept. 29, 2014, unless otherwise noted.

§ 240.1 Purpose of the Guides.

The purpose of these Guides is to provide assistance to businesses seeking to comply with sections 2(d) and (e) of the Robinson-Patman Act (the "Act"). The guides are based on the language of the statute, the legislative history, administrative and court decisions, and the purposes of the Act. Although the Guides are consistent with the case law, the Commission has sought to provide guidance in some areas where no definitive guidance is provided by the case law. The Guides are what their name implies—guidelines for compliance with the law. They do not have the force of law. They do not confer any rights on any person and do not operate to bind the FTC or the public.

§ 240.2 Applicability of the law.

(a) The substantive provisions of section 2(d) and (e) apply only under certain circumstances. Section 2(d) applies only to:

(1) A seller of products

(2) Engaged in interstate commerce

(3) That either directly or through an intermediary

(4) Pays a customer for promotional services or facilities provided by the customer

(5) In connection with the resale (not the initial sale between the seller and the customer) of the seller's products

(6) Where the customer is in competition with one or more of the seller's other customers also engaged in the resale of the seller's products of like grade and quality.

(b) Section 2(e) applies only to:

(1) A seller of products

(2) Engaged in interstate commerce

(3) That either directly or through an intermediary

(4) Furnishes promotional services or facilities to a customer

(5) In connection with the resale (not the initial sale between the seller and the customer) of the seller's products

(6) Where the customer is in competition with one or more of the seller's other customers also engaged in the resale of the seller's products of like grade and quality.

(c) Additionally, section 5 of the FTC Act may apply to buyers of products for resale or to third parties. See § 240.13 of these Guides.

§ 240.3 Definition of seller.

Seller includes any person (manufacturer, wholesaler, distributor, etc.) who sells products for resale, with or without further processing. For example, selling candy to a retailer is a sale for resale without processing. Selling corn syrup to a candy manufacturer is a sale for resale with processing.

§ 240.4 Definition of customer.

A *customer* is any person who buys for resale directly from the seller, or the seller's agent or broker. In addition, a "customer" is any buyer of the seller's product for resale who purchases from or through a wholesaler or other intermediate reseller. The word "customer" which is used in section 2(d) of the Act includes "purchaser" which is used in section 2(e).

Note: There may be some exceptions to this general definition of "customer." For example, the purchaser of distress merchandise would not be considered a "customer" simply on the basis of such purchase. Similarly, a retailer purchasing solely from other retailers, or making sporadic purchases from the seller or one that does not regularly sell the seller's product, or that is a type of retail outlet not usually selling such products (e.g., a hardware store stocking a few isolated food items) will not be considered a "customer" of the seller unless the seller has been put on notice that such retailer is selling its product.

Example 1: A manufacturer sells to some retailers directly and to others through wholesalers. Retailer A purchases the manufacturer's product from a wholesaler and resells some of it to Retailer B. Retailer A is a customer of the manufacturer. Retailer B is not a customer unless the fact that it purchases the manufacturer's product is known to the manufacturer.

Example 2: A manufacturer sells directly to some independent retailers, to the headquarters of chains and of retailer-owned cooperatives, and to wholesalers. The manufacturer offers promotional services or allowances for promotional activity to be performed at the retail level. With respect to such services and allowances, the direct-buying independent retailers, the headquarters of the chains and retailer-owned cooperatives, and the wholesaler's independent retailer customers are customers of the manufacturer. Individual retail outlets of the chains and the members of the retailer-owned cooperatives are not customers of the manufacturer.

Example 3: A seller offers to pay wholesalers to advertise the seller's product in the wholesalers' order books or in the wholesalers' price lists directed to retailers purchasing from the wholesalers. The wholesalers and retailer-owned cooperative headquarters and headquarters of other bona-fide buying groups are customers. Retailers are not customers for purposes of this promotion.

§ 240.5 Definition of competing customers.

Competing customers are all businesses that compete in the resale of the seller's products of like grade and quality at the same functional level of distribution regardless of whether they purchase directly from the seller or through some intermediary.

Example 1: Manufacturer A, located in Wisconsin and distributing shoes nationally, sells shoes to three competing retailers that sell only in the Roanoke, Virginia area. Manufacturer A has no other customers selling in Roanoke or its vicinity. If Manufacturer A offers its promotion to one Roanoke customer, it should include all three, but it can limit the promotion to them. The trade area should be drawn to include retailers who compete.

Example 2: A national seller has direct-buying retailing customers reselling exclusively within the Baltimore area, and other customers within the area purchasing through wholesalers. The seller may lawfully engage in a promotional campaign confined to the Baltimore area, provided that it affords all of its retailing customers within the area the opportunity to participate, including those that purchase through wholesalers.

Example 3: B manufactures and sells a brand of laundry detergent for home use. In one metropolitan area, B's detergent is sold by a grocery store and a discount department store. If these stores compete with each other, any allowance, service or facility that B makes available to the grocery store should also be made available on proportionally equal terms to the discount department store.

§ 240.6 Interstate commerce.

The term "interstate commerce" has not been precisely defined in the statute. In general, if there is any part of a business which is not wholly within one state (for example, sales or deliveries of products, their subsequent distribution or purchase, or delivery of supplies or raw materials), the business may be subject to sections 2(d) and 2(e) of the Act. (The commerce standard for sections 2(d) and (e) is at least as inclusive as the commerce standard for section 2(a).) Sales or promotional offers within the District of Columbia and most United States possessions are also covered by the Act.

§ 240.7 Services or facilities.

The terms "services" and "facilities" have not been exactly defined by the statute or in decisions. One requirement, however, is that the services or facilities be used primarily to promote the resale of the seller's product by the customer. Services or facilities that relate primarily to the original sale are covered by section 2(a). The following list provides some examples—the list is not exhaustive—of promotional services and facilities covered by sections 2(d) and (e):

Cooperative advertising;
Handbills;
Demonstrators and demonstrations;
Catalogues;
Cabinets;
Displays;
Prizes or merchandise for conducting promotional contests;
Special packaging, or package sizes; and
Online advertising.

Example 1: A seller offers a supermarket chain an allowance of $500 per store to stock a new packaged food product and find space for it on the supermarket's shelves and a further allowance of $300 per store for placement of the new product on prime display space, an aisle endcap. The $500 allowance relates primarily to the initial sale of the product to the supermarket chain, and therefore should be assessed under section 2(a) of the Act. In contrast, the $300 allowance for endcap display relates primarily to the resale of the product by the supermarket chain, and therefore should be assessed under section 2(d).

Example 2: During the Halloween season, a seller of multi-packs of individually wrapped candy bars offers to provide those multi-packs to retailers in Halloween-themed packaging. The primary purpose of the special packaging is to promote customers' resale of the candy bars. Therefore, the special packaging is a promotional service or facility covered by section 2(d) or 2(e) of the Act.

Example 3: A seller of liquid laundry detergent ordinarily packages its detergent in containers having a circular footprint. A customer asks the seller to furnish the detergent to it in special packaging having a square footprint, so that the customer can more efficiently warehouse and transship the detergent. Because the purpose of the special packaging is primarily to promote the original sale of the detergent to the customer and not its resale by the customer, the special packaging is not a promotional service or facility covered by section 2(d) or 2(e) of the Act.

§ 240.8 Need for a plan.

A seller who makes payments or furnishes services that come under the Act should do so according to a plan. If there are many competing customers to be considered or if the plan is complex, the seller would be well advised to put the plan in writing. What the plan should include is described in more detail in the remainder of these Guides. Briefly, the plan should make payments or services functionally available to all competing customers on proportionally equal terms. (See § 240.9 of this part.) Alternative terms and conditions should be made available to customers who cannot, in a practical sense, take advantage of any of the plan's offerings. The seller should inform competing customers of the plans available to them, in time for them to decide whether to participate. (See § 240.10 of this part.)

§ 240.9 Proportionally equal terms.

(a) Promotional services and allowances should be made available to all competing customers on proportionally equal terms. No single way to do this is prescribed by law. Any method that treats competing customers on proportionally equal terms may be used. Generally, this can be done most easily by basing the payments made or the services furnished on the dollar volume or on the quantity of the product purchased during a specified period. However, other methods that result in proportionally equal allowances and services being offered to all competing customers are acceptable.

(b) When a seller offers more than one type of service, or payments for more than one type of service, all the services or payments should be offered on proportionally equal terms. The seller may do this by offering all the payments or services at the same rate per unit or amount purchased. Thus, a seller might offer promotional allowances of up to 12 cents a case purchased for expenditures on either newspaper or Internet advertising or handbills.

Example 1: A seller may offer to pay a specified part (e.g., 50 percent) of the cost of local advertising up to an amount equal to a specified percentage (e.g., 5 percent) of the dollar volume of purchases during a specified period of time.

Example 2: A seller may place in reserve for each customer a specified amount of money for each unit purchased, and use it to reimburse these customers for the cost of advertising the seller's product.

Example 3: A seller should not provide an allowance or service on a basis that has rates graduated with the amount of goods purchased, as, for instance, 1 percent of the first $1,000 purchased per month, 2 percent of the second $1,000 per month, and 3 percent of all over that.

Example 4: A seller should not identify or feature one or a few customers in its own advertising without making the same, or if impracticable, alternative services available on proportionally equal terms to customers competing with the identified customer or customers.

Example 5: A seller who makes employees available or arranges with a third party to furnish personnel for purposes of performing work for a customer should make the same offer available on proportionally equal terms to all other competing customers or offer useable and suitable services or allowances on proportionally equal terms to competing customers for whom such services are not useable and suitable.

Example 6: A seller should not offer to pay a straight line rate for advertising if such payment results in a discrimination between competing customers; e.g., the offer of $1.00 per line for advertising in a newspaper that charges competing customers different amounts for the same advertising space. The straight line rate is an acceptable method for allocating advertising funds if the seller offers small retailers that pay more than the lowest newspaper rate an alternative that enables them to obtain the same percentage of their advertising cost as large retailers. If the $1.00 per line allowance is based on 50 percent of the newspaper's lowest contract rate of $2.00 per line, the seller should offer to pay 50 percent of the newspaper advertising cost of smaller retailers that establish, by invoice or otherwise, that they paid more than that contract rate.

Example 7: A seller offers each customer promotional allowances at the rate of one dollar for each unit of its product purchased during a defined promotional period. If Buyer A purchases 100 units, Buyer B 50 units, and Buyer C 25 units, the seller maintains proportional equality by allowing $100 to Buyer A, $50 to Buyer B, and $25 to Buyer C, to be used for the Buyers' expenditures on promotion.

§ 240.10 Availability to all competing customers.

(a) *Functional availability.* (1) The seller should take reasonable steps to ensure that services and facilities are useable in a practical sense by all competing customers. This may require offering alternative terms and conditions under which customers can participate. When a seller provides alternatives in order to meet the availability requirement, it should take reasonable steps to ensure that the alternatives are proportionally equal, and the seller should inform competing customers of the various alternative plans.

(2) The seller should insure that promotional plans or alternatives offered to retailers do not bar any competing retailers from participation, whether they purchase directly from the seller or through a wholesaler or other intermediary.

(3) When a seller offers to competing customers alternative services or allowances that are proportionally equal and at least one such offer is useable in a practical sense by all competing customers, and refrains from taking steps to prevent customers from participating, it has satisfied its obligation to make services and allowances "functionally available" to all customers. Therefore, the failure of any customer to participate in the program does not place the seller in violation of the Act.

Example 1: A manufacturer offers a plan for cooperative advertising on radio, TV, or in newspapers of general circulation. Because the purchases of some of the manufacturer's customers are too small this offer is not useable in a practical sense by them. The manufacturer should offer them alternative(s) on proportionally equal terms that are useable in a practical sense by them. In addition, some competing customers are online retailers that cannot make practical use of radio, TV, or newspaper advertising. The manufacturer should offer them proportionally equal alternatives, such as online advertising, that are useable by them in a practical sense.

Example 2: A seller furnishes demonstrators to large department store customers. The seller should provide alternatives useable in a practical sense on proportionally equal terms to those competing customers who cannot use demonstrators. The alternatives may be services useable in a practical sense that are furnished by the seller, or payments by the seller to customers for their advertising or promotion of the seller's product.

Example 3: A seller offers to pay 75 percent of the cost of advertising in daily newspapers, which are the regular advertising media of the seller's large or chain store customers, but a lesser amount, such as only 50 percent of the cost, or even nothing at all, for advertising in semi-weekly, weekly, or other newspapers or media, such as the Internet, that may be used by small retail customers. Such a plan discriminates against particular customers or classes of customers. To avoid that discrimination, the seller in offering to pay allowances for newspaper advertising should offer to pay the same percent of the cost of newspaper advertising for all competing customers in a newspaper of the customer's choice, or at least in those newspapers that meet the requirements for second class mail privileges. While a small customer may be offered, as an alternative to advertising in daily newspapers, allowances for other media and services such as envelope stuffers, handbills, window banners, Web sites, and the like, the small customer should have the choice to use its promotional allowance for advertising similar to that available to the larger customers, if it can practicably do so.

Example 4: A seller offers short term displays of varying sizes, including some which are useable by each of its competing customers in a practical business sense. The seller requires uniform, reasonable certification of performance by each customer. Because they are reluctant to process the required paper work, some customers do not participate. This fact does not place the seller in violation of the functional availability requirement and it is under no obligation to provide additional alternatives.

(b) *Notice of available services and allowance.:* The seller has an obligation to take steps reasonably designed to provide notice to competing customers of the availability of promotional services and allowances. Such notification should include enough details of the offer in time to enable customers to make an informed judgment whether to participate. When some competing customers do not purchase directly from the seller, the seller must take steps reasonably designed to provide notice to such indirect customers. Acceptable notification may vary. The following is a non-exhaustive list of acceptable methods of notification:

(1) By providing direct notice to customers;

(2) When a promotion consists of providing retailers with display materials, by including the materials within the product shipping container;

(3) By including brochures describing the details of the offer in shipping containers;

(4) By providing information on shipping containers or product packages of the availability and essential features

of an offer, identifying a specific source for further information;

(5) By placing at reasonable intervals in trade publications of general and widespread distribution announcements of the availability and essential features of promotional offers, identifying a specific source for further information; and

(6) If the competing customers belong to an identifiable group on a specific mailing list, by providing relevant information of promotional offers to customers on that list. For example, if a product is sold lawfully only under Government license (alcoholic beverages, etc.), the seller may inform only its customers holding licenses.

(c) A seller may contract with intermediaries or other third parties to provide notice. See § 240.11.

Example 1: A seller has a plan for the retail promotion of its product in Philadelphia. Some of its retailing customers purchase directly and it offers the plan to them. Other Philadelphia retailers purchase the seller's product through wholesalers. The seller may use the wholesalers to reach the retailing customers that buy through them, either by having the wholesalers notify these retailers, or by using the wholesalers' customer lists for direct notification by the seller.

Example 2: A seller that sells on a direct basis to some retailers in an area, and to other retailers in the area through wholesalers, has a plan for the promotion of its product at the retail level. If the seller directly notifies competing direct purchasing retailers, and competing retailers purchasing through the wholesalers, the seller is not required to notify its wholesalers.

Example 3: A seller regularly promotes its product at the retail level and during the year has various special promotional offers. The seller's competing customers include large direct-purchasing retailers and smaller retailers that purchase through wholesalers. The promotions offered can best be used by the smaller retailers if the funds to which they are entitled are pooled and used by the wholesalers on their behalf (newspaper advertisements, for example). If retailers purchasing through a wholesaler designate that wholesaler as their agent for receiving notice of, collecting, and using promotional allowances for them, the seller may assume that notice of, and payment under, a promotional plan to such wholesaler constitutes notice and payment to the retailer. The seller must have a reasonable basis for concluding that the retailers have designated the wholesaler as their agent.

§ 240.11 Wholesaler or third party performance of seller's obligations.

A seller may contract with intermediaries, such as wholesalers, distributors, or other third parties, to perform all or part of the seller's obligations under sections 2(d) and (e). The use of intermediaries does not relieve a seller of its responsibility to comply with the law. Therefore, in contracting with an intermediary, a seller should ensure that its obligations under the law are in fact fulfilled.

§ 240.12 Checking customer's use of payments.

The seller should take reasonable precautions to see that the services the seller is paying for are furnished and that the seller is not overpaying for them. The customer should expend the allowance solely for the purpose for which it was given. If the seller knows or should know that what the seller is paying for or furnishing is not being properly used by some customers, the improper payments or services should be discontinued.

§ 240.13 Customer's and third party liability.

(a) *Customer's liability.* Sections 2(d) and (e) apply to sellers and not to customers. However, where there is likely injury to competition, the Commission may proceed under section 5 of the Federal Trade Commission Act against a customer who knows, or should know, that it is receiving a discriminatory price through services or allowances not made available on proportionally equal terms to its competitors engaged in the resale of a seller's product. Liability for knowingly receiving such a discrimination may result whether the discrimination takes place directly through payments or services, or indirectly through deductions from purchase invoices or other similar means. In addition, the giving or knowing inducement or receipt of proportionally unequal promotional allowances may be challenged under sections 2(a) and 2(f) of the Act, respectively, where no promotional services are performed in return for the payments, or where the payments are not reasonably related to the customer's cost of providing the promotional services. *See, e.g., American Booksellers Ass'n* v. *Barnes & Noble*, 135 F. Supp. 2d 1031 (N.D. Cal. 2001); *but see United Magazine Co.* v. *Murdoch Magazines Distrib., Inc.* 2001 U.S. Dist. Lexis 20878 (S.D.N.Y. 2001). Sections 2(a) and 2(f) of the Act may be enforced by disfavored customers, among others.

Example 1: A customer should not induce or receive advertising allowances for special promotion of the seller's product in connection with the customer's anniversary sale or new store opening when the customer knows or should know that such allowances, or suitable alternatives, are not available on proportionally equal terms to all other customers competing with it in the distribution of the seller's product.

Example 2: Frequently the employees of sellers or third parties, such as brokers, perform in-store services for their grocery retailer customers, such as stocking of shelves, building of displays and checking or rotating inventory, etc. A customer operating a retail grocery business should not induce or receive such services when the customer knows or should know that such services (or usable and suitable alternative services) are not available on proportionally equal terms to all other customers competing with it in the distribution of the seller's product.

Example 3: Where a customer has entered into a contract, understanding, or arrangement for the purchase of advertising with a newspaper or other advertising medium, such as the Internet, that provides for a deferred rebate or other reduction in the price of the advertising, the customer should advise any seller from whom reimbursement for the advertising is claimed that the claimed rate of reimbursement is subject to a deferred rebate or other reduction in price. In the event that any rebate or adjustment in the price is received, the customer should refund to the seller the amount of any excess payment or allowance.

Example 4: A customer should not induce or receive an allowance in excess of that offered in the seller's advertising plan by billing the seller at "vendor rates" or for any other amount in excess of that authorized in the seller's promotional program.

(b) *Third party liability.* Third parties, such as advertising media, may violate section 5 of the Federal Trade Commission Act through double or fictitious rates or billing. An advertising medium, such as the Internet, a newspaper, broadcast station, or printer of catalogues, that publishes a rate schedule containing fictitious rates (or rates that are not reasonably expected to be applicable to a representative number of advertisers), may violate section 5 if the customer uses such deceptive schedule or invoice for a claim for an advertising allowance, payment or credit greater than that to which it would be entitled under the seller's promotional offering. Similarly, an advertising medium that furnishes a customer with an invoice that does not reflect the customer's actual net advertising cost may violate section 5 if the customer uses the invoice to obtain larger payments than it is entitled to receive.

Example 1: A newspaper has a "national" rate and a lower "local" rate. A retailer places an advertisement with the newspaper at the local rate for a seller's product for which the retailer will seek reimbursement under the seller's cooperative advertising plan. The newspaper should not send the retailer two bills, one at the national rate and another at the local rate actually charged.

Example 2: A newspaper has several published rates. A large retailer has in the past earned the lowest rate available. The newspaper should not submit invoices to the retailer showing a high rate by agreement between them unless the invoice discloses that the retailer may receive a rebate and states the amount (or approximate amount) of the rebate, if known, and if not known, the amount of rebate the retailer could reasonably anticipate.

Example 3: A radio station has a flat rate for spot announcements, subject to volume discounts. A retailer buys enough spots to qualify for the discounts. The station should not submit an invoice to the retailer that does not show either the actual net cost or the discount rate.

Example 4: An advertising agent buys a large volume of newspaper advertising space at a low, unpublished negotiated rate. Retailers then buy the space from the agent at a rate lower than they could buy this space directly from the newspaper. The agent should not furnish the retailers invoices showing a rate higher than the retailers actually paid for the space.

§ 240.14 Meeting competition.

A seller charged with discrimination in violation of sections 2(d) and (e) may defend its actions by showing that particular payments were made or services furnished in good faith to meet equally high payments or equivalent services offered or supplied by a competing seller. This defense is available with respect to payments or services offered on an area-wide basis, to those offered to new as well as old customers, and regardless of whether the discrimination has been caused by a decrease or an increase in the payments or services offered. A seller must reasonably believe that its offers are necessary to meet a competitor's offer.

§240.15 Cost justification.

It is no defense to a charge of unlawful discrimination in the payment of an allowance or the furnishing of a service for a seller to show that such payment or service could be justified through savings in the cost of manufacture, sale or delivery.

PART 251—GUIDE CONCERNING USE OF THE WORD "FREE" AND SIMILAR REPRESENTATIONS

§251.1 The guide.

(a) *General.* (1) The offer of "Free" merchandise or service is a promotional device frequently used to attract customers. Providing such merchandise or service with the purchase of some other article or service has often been found to be a useful and valuable marketing tool.

(2) Because the purchasing public continually searches for the best buy, and regards the offer of "Free" merchandise or service to be a special bargain, all such offers must be made with extreme care so as to avoid any possibility that consumers will be misled or deceived. Representative of the language frequently used in such offers are "Free", "Buy 1-Get 1 Free", "2-for-1 Sale", "50% off with purchase of Two", "1¢ Sale", etc. (Related representations that raise many of the same questions include "____ Cents-Off", "Half-Price Sale", "½ Off", etc. See the Commission's "Fair Packaging and Labeling Regulation Regarding 'Cents-Off' and Guides Against Deceptive Pricing.")

(b) *Meaning of "Free"*. (1) The public understands that, except in the case of introductory offers in connection with the sale of a product or service (See paragraph (f) of this section), an offer of "Free" merchandise or service is based upon a regular price for the merchandise or service which must be purchased by consumers in order to avail themselves of that which is represented to be "Free". In other words, when the purchaser is told that an article is "Free" to him if another article is purchased, the word "Free" indicates that he is paying nothing for that article and no more than the regular price for the other. Thus, a purchaser has a right to believe that the merchant will not directly and immediately recover, in whole or in part, the cost of the free merchandise or service by marking up the price of the article which must be purchased, by the substitution of inferior merchandise or service, or otherwise.

(2) The term *regular* when used with the term *price*, means the price, in the same quantity, quality and with the same service, at which the seller or advertiser of the product or service has openly and actively sold the product or service in the geographic market or trade area in which he is making a "Free" or similar offer in the most recent and regular course of business, for a reasonably substantial period of time, i.e., a 30-day period. For consumer products or services which fluctuate in price, the "regular" price shall be the lowest price at which any substantial sales were made during the aforesaid 30-day period. Except in the case of introductory offers, if no substantial sales were made, in fact, at the "regular" price, a "Free" or similar offer would not be proper.

(c) *Disclosure of conditions.* When making "Free" or similar offers all the terms, conditions and obligations upon which receipt and retention of the "Free" item are contingent should be set forth clearly and conspicuously at the outset of the offer so as to leave no reasonable probability that the terms of the offer might be misunderstood. Stated differently, all of the terms, conditions and obligations should appear in close conjunction with the offer of "Free" merchandise or service. For example, disclosure of the terms of the offer set forth in a footnote of an advertisement to which reference is made by an asterisk or other symbol placed next to the offer, is not regarded as making disclosure at the outset. However, mere notice of the existence of a "Free" offer on the main display panel of a label or package is not precluded provided that (1) the notice does not constitute an offer or identify the item being offered "Free", (2) the notice informs the customer of the location, elsewhere on the package or label, where the disclosures required by this section may be found, (3) no purchase or other such material affirmative act is required in order to discover the terms and conditions of the offer, and (4) the notice and the offer are not otherwise deceptive.

(d) *Supplier's responsibilities.* Nothing in this section should be construed as authorizing or condoning the illegal setting or policing of retail prices by a supplier. However, if the supplier knows, or should know, that a "Free" offer he is promoting is not being passed on by a reseller, or otherwise is being used by a reseller as an instrumentality for deception, it is improper for the supplier to continue to offer the product as promoted to such reseller. He should take appropriate steps to bring an end to the deception, inlcuding the withdrawal of the "Free" offer.

(e) *Resellers' participation in supplier's offers.* Prior to advertising a "Free" promotion, a supplier should offer the product as promoted to all competing resellers as provided for in the Commission's "Guides for Advertising Allowances and Other Merchandising Payments and Services." In advertising the "Free" promotion, the supplier should identify those areas in which the offer is not available if the advertising is likely to be seen in such areas, and should clearly state that it is available only through participating resellers, indicating the extent of participation by the use of such terms as "some", "all", "a majority", or "a few", as the case may be.

(f) *Introductory offers.* (1) No "Free" offer should be made in connection with the introduction of a new product or service offered for sale at a specified price unless the offeror expects, in good faith, to discontinue the offer after a limited time and to commence selling the product or service promoted, separately, at the same price at which it was promoted with the "Free" offer.

(2) In such offers, no representation may be made that the price is for one item and that the other is "Free" unless the offeror expects, in good faith, to discontinue the offer after a limited time and to commence selling the product or service promoted, separately, at the same price at which it was promoted with a "Free" offer.

(g) *Negotiated sales.* If a product or service usually is sold at a price arrived at through bargaining, rather than at a regular price, it is improper to represent that another product or service is being offered "Free" with the sale. The same representation is also improper where there may be a regular price, but where other material factors such as quantity, quality, or size are arrived at through bargaining.

(h) *Frequency of offers.* So that a "Free" offer will be special and meaningful, a single size of a product or a single kind of service should not be advertised with a "Free" offer in a trade area for more than 6 months in any 12-month period. At least 30 days should elapse before another such offer is promoted in the same trade area. No more than three such offers should be made in the same area in any 12-month period. In such period, the offeror's sale in that area of the product in the size promoted with a "Free" offer should not exceed 50 percent of the total volume of his sales of the product, in the same size, in the area.

(i) *Similar terms.* Offers of "Free" merchandise or services which may be deceptive for failure to meet the provisions of this section may not be corrected by the substitution of such similar words and terms as "gift", "given without charge", "bonus", or other words or terms which tend to convey the impression to the consuming public that an article of merchandise or service is "Free".

(38 Stat. 717, as amended; 15 U.S.C. 41–58)

[36 FR 21517, Nov. 10, 1971]

PART 254—GUIDES FOR PRIVATE VOCATIONAL AND DISTANCE EDUCATION SCHOOLS

Sec.

AUTHORITY: 38 Stat. 717, as amended; 15 U.S.C. 41–58.

§ 254.0 Scope and application.

(a) The Guides in this part apply to persons, firms, corporations, or organizations engaged in the operation of privately owned schools that offer resident or distance courses, training, or instruction purporting to prepare or qualify individuals for employment in any occupation or trade, or in work requiring mechanical, technical, artistic, business, or clerical skills, or that is for the purpose of enabling a person to improve his appearance, social aptitude, personality, or other attributes. These Guides do not apply to resident primary or secondary schools or institutions of higher education offering at least a 2-year program of accredited college level studies generally acceptable for credit toward a bachelor's degree.

(b) These Guides represent administrative interpretations of laws administered by the Federal Trade Commission for the guidance of the public in conducting its affairs in conformity with legal requirements. These Guides specifically address the application of section 5 of the FTC Act (15 U.S.C. 45) to the advertising, promotion, marketing, and sale of, and the recruitment of students for, courses or programs of instruction offered by private vocational or distance education schools. The Guides provide the basis for voluntary compliance with the law by members of the industry. Practices inconsistent with these Guides may result in corrective action by the Commission under section 5 of the FTC Act if, after investigation, the Commission has reason to believe that the practices fall within the scope of conduct declared unlawful by the statute.

[63 FR 42572, Aug. 10, 1998, as amended at 78 FR 68989, Nov. 18, 2013]

§ 254.1 Definitions.

(a) *Accredited.* A school or program of instruction that has been evaluated and found to meet established criteria by an accrediting agency or association recognized for such purposes by the U.S. Department of Education.

(b) *Approved.* A school or program of instruction that has been recognized by a State or Federal agency as meeting educational standards or other related qualifications as prescribed by that agency for the school or program of instruction to which the term is applied. The term is not and should not be used interchangeably with "Accredited." The term "Approved" is not justified by the mere grant of a corporate charter to operate or license to do business as a school and should not be used unless the represented "approval" has been affirmatively required or authorized by State or Federal law.

(c) *Industry member.* Industry Members are the persons, firms, corporations, or organizations covered by these Guides, as explained in § 254.0(a).

[78 FR 68990, Nov. 19, 2013]

§ 254.2 Deceptive trade or business names.

(a) It is deceptive for an Industry Member to misrepresent, directly or indirectly, expressly or by implication, the nature of the school, its Accreditation, programs of instruction, methods of teaching, or any other material fact through the use of any trade or business name, label, insignia, or designation, or in any other manner.

(b) It is deceptive for an Industry Member to deceptively conceal in any way the fact that it is a school or to misrepresent, directly or indirectly, expressly or by implication, through the use of a trade or business name or in any other manner that:

(1) It is a part of or connected with a branch, bureau, or agency of the U.S. Government, including, but not limited to, the U.S. Department of Education, or of any State, or civil service commission; or

(2) It is an employment agency or an employment agent or authorized training facility for any industry or business.

[78 FR 68990, Nov. 19, 2013]

§ 254.3 Misrepresentation of extent or nature of accreditation or approval.

(a) It is deceptive for an Industry Member to misrepresent, directly or indirectly, expressly or by implication, the nature, extent, or purpose of any Approval by a State or Federal agency or Accreditation by an accrediting agency or association. For example, an Industry Member should not:

(1) Represent, without qualification, that its school is Accredited unless all courses and programs of instruction have been Accredited by an accrediting agency recognized by the U.S. Department of Education. If an Accredited school offers courses or programs of instruction that are not Accredited, all advertisements or promotional materials pertaining to those courses or programs, and making reference to the Accreditation of the school, should clearly and conspicuously disclose that those particular courses or programs are not Accredited.

(2) Represent that its school or program of instruction is Approved, unless the nature, extent, and purpose of that Approval are disclosed.

(3) Misrepresent the extent to which a student successfully completing a course or program of instruction will be able to transfer any credits the student earns to any other postsecondary institution.

(b) It is deceptive for an Industry Member to misrepresent, directly or indirectly, expressly or by implication, that a school or program of instruction has been Approved by a particular industry, or that successful completion of a course or program of instruction qualifies the student for admission to a labor union or similar organization or for receiving a State or Federal license to perform certain functions.

(c) It is deceptive for an Industry Member to misrepresent, directly or indirectly, expressly or by implication, that its courses or programs of instruction are recommended by vocational counselors, high schools, colleges, educational organizations, employment agencies, or members of a particular industry, or that it has been the subject of unsolicited testimonials or endorsements from former students. It is deceptive for an Industry Member to use testimonials or endorsements that do not accurately reflect current practices of the school or current conditions or employment opportunities in the industry or occupation for which students are being trained.

NOTE TO PARAGRAPH (c): The Commission's Guides Concerning Use of Endorsements and Testimonials in Advertising (part 255 of this chapter) provide further guidance in this area.

(d) It is deceptive for an Industry Member to misrepresent, directly or indirectly, expressly or by implication, that its courses or programs of instruction fulfill a requirement that must be completed prior to taking a licensing examination.

[78 FR 68990, Nov. 18, 2013]

§ 254.4 Misrepresentation of facilities, services, qualifications of staff, status, and employment prospects for students after training.

(a) It is deceptive for an Industry Member to misrepresent, directly or indirectly, expressly or by implication, in advertising, promotional materials, recruitment sessions, or in any other manner, the size, location, services, facilities, curriculum, books and materials, or equipment of its school or the number or educational qualifications of its faculty and other personnel. For example, an Industry Member should not:

(1) Misrepresent the qualifications, credentials, experience, or educational background of its instructors, sales representatives, or other employees.

(2) Misrepresent, through statements or pictures, or in any other manner, the nature or efficacy of its courses, training devices, methods, or equipment.

(3) Misrepresent the availability of employment while the student is undergoing instruction or the role of the school in providing or arranging for such employment.

(4) Misrepresent the availability, amount, or nature of any financial assistance available to students, including any Federal student financial assistance. If the cost of training is financed in whole or in part by loans, students should be informed that loans must be repaid whether or not they are successful in completing the program and obtaining employment.

(5) Misrepresent that a private entity providing any financial assistance to the students is part of the Federal government or that loans from the private entity have the same interest rate or repayment terms as loans received from the U.S. Department of Education.

(6) Misrepresent the nature of any relationship between the school or its personnel and any government agency, or that students of the school will receive preferred consideration for employment with any government agency.

(7) Misrepresent that certain individuals or classes of individuals are members of its faculty or advisory board, have prepared instructional materials, or are otherwise affiliated with the school.

(8) Misrepresent the nature and extent of any personal instruction, guidance, assistance, or other service, including placement assistance and assistance overcoming language barriers or learning disabilities, it will provide students either during or after completion of a course.

(9) Misrepresent the extent to which a prospective student will receive credit for courses or a program of instruction already completed at other postsecondary institutions.

(10) Misrepresent the percentage of students who withdraw from a course or program of instruction, or the percentage of students who complete or graduate from a course or program of instruction.

(11) Misrepresent security policies or crime statistics that the school must maintain.

(b) It is deceptive for an Industry Member to misrepresent, directly or indirectly, expressly or by implication, that it is a nonprofit organization or that it is affiliated or otherwise connected with any public institution or private religious or charitable organization.

(c) It is deceptive for an Industry Member that conducts its instruction by correspondence, or other form of distance education, to fail to clearly and conspicuously disclose that fact in all promotional materials.

(d) It is deceptive for an Industry Member to misrepresent, directly or indirectly, expressly or by implication, that a course or program of instruction has been recently revised or instructional equipment is up-to-date, or misrepresent its ability to keep a course or program of instruction current and up-to-date.

(e) It is deceptive for an Industry Member, in promoting any course or program of instruction in its advertising, promotional materials, or in any other manner, to misrepresent, directly or indirectly, expressly or by implication, whether through the use of text, images, endorsements, or by other means, the availability of employment after graduation from a school or program of instruction, the specific type of employment available to a student after graduation from a school or program of instruction, the success that the Industry Member's graduates have realized in obtaining such employment, including the percentage of graduates who have received employment, or the salary or salary range that the Industry Member's graduates have received, or can be expected to receive, in such employment.

NOTE TO PARAGRAPH (e): The Commission's Guides Concerning Use of Endorsements and Testimonials in Advertising (part 255 of this chapter) provide further guidance in this area.

[63 FR 42573, Aug. 10, 1998, as amended at 63 FR 72350, Dec. 31, 1998; 78 FR 68990, Nov. 18, 2013]

§254.5 Misrepresentations of enrollment qualifications or limitations.

(a) It is deceptive for an Industry Member to misrepresent, directly or indirectly, expressly or by implication, the nature or extent of any prerequisites or qualifications for enrollment in a school or program of instruction.

(b) It is deceptive for an Industry Member to misrepresent, directly or indirectly, expressly or by implication, that the lack of a high school education or prior training or experience is not an impediment to successful completion of a course or program of instruction or obtaining employment in the field for which the course or program of instruction provides training.

(c) It is deceptive for an Industry Member to misrepresent, directly or indirectly, expressly or by implication, the time required to complete a course or program of instruction.

(d) It is deceptive for an Industry Member to misrepresent, directly or indirectly, expressly or by implication, a student's likelihood of success in a school or program of instruction, including, but not limited to, misrepresenting the student's score on any admissions test.

[78 FR 68991, Nov. 18, 2013]

§ 254.6 Deceptive use of diplomas, degrees, or certificates.

(a) It is deceptive for an Industry Member to issue a degree, diploma, certificate of completion, or any similar document, that misrepresents, directly or indirectly, expressly or by implication, the subject matter, substance, or content of the course or program of instruction or any other material fact concerning the course or program of instruction for which it was awarded or the accomplishments of the student to whom it was awarded.

(b) It is deceptive for an Industry Member to offer or confer an academic, professional, or occupational degree, if the award of such degree has not been Approved by the appropriate State educational agency or Accredited by a nationally recognized accrediting agency, unless it clearly and conspicuously discloses, in all advertising and promotional materials that contain a reference to such degree, that its award has not been Approved or Accredited by such an agency.

(c) It is deceptive for an Industry Member to offer or confer a high school diploma unless the program of instruction to which it pertains is substantially equivalent to that offered by a resident secondary school, and unless the student is informed, by a clear and conspicuous disclosure in writing prior to enrollment, that the Industry Member cannot guarantee or otherwise control the recognition that will be accorded the diploma by institutions of higher education, other schools, or prospective employers, and that such recognition is a matter solely within the discretion of those entities.

[78 FR 68991, Nov. 18, 2013]

§ 254.7 Deceptive sales practices.

(a) It is deceptive for an Industry Member to use advertisements or promotional materials that misrepresent, directly or indirectly, expressly or by implication, that employment is being offered or that a talent hunt or contest is being conducted. For example, captions such as, "Men/women wanted to train for * * * ," "Help Wanted," "Employment," "Business Opportunities," and words or terms of similar import, may falsely convey that employment is being offered and therefore should be avoided.

(b) It is deceptive for an Industry Member to fail to disclose to a prospective student, prior to enrollment, the total cost of the program of instruction and the school's refund policy if the student does not complete the program of instruction.

(c) It is deceptive for an Industry Member to fail to disclose to a prospective student, prior to enrollment, all requirements for successfully completing the course or program of instruction and the circumstances that would constitute grounds for terminating the student's enrollment prior to completion of the program of instruction.

[78 FR 68991, Nov. 18, 2013]

PART 255—GUIDES CONCERNING USE OF ENDORSEMENTS AND TESTIMONIALS IN ADVERTISING

Sec.

AUTHORITY: 38 Stat. 717, as amended; 15 U.S.C. 41 - 58.

SOURCE: 74 FR 53138, Oct. 15, 2009, unless otherwise noted.

§ 255.0 Purpose and definitions.

(a) The Guides in this part represent administrative interpretations of laws enforced by the Federal Trade Commission for the guidance of the public in conducting its affairs in conformity with legal requirements. Specifically, the Guides address the application of

Section 5 of the FTC Act (15 U.S.C. 45) to the use of endorsements and testimonials in advertising. The Guides provide the basis for voluntary compliance with the law by advertisers and endorsers. Practices inconsistent with these Guides may result in corrective action by the Commission under Section 5 if, after investigation, the Commission has reason to believe that the practices fall within the scope of conduct declared unlawful by the statute. The Guides set forth the general principles that the Commission will use in evaluating endorsements and testimonials, together with examples illustrating the application of those principles. The Guides do not purport to cover every possible use of endorsements in advertising. Whether a particular endorsement or testimonial is deceptive will depend on the specific factual circumstances of the advertisement at issue.

(b) For purposes of this part, an endorsement means any advertising message (including verbal statements, demonstrations, or depictions of the name, signature, likeness or other identifying personal characteristics of an individual or the name or seal of an organization) that consumers are likely to believe reflects the opinions, beliefs, findings, or experiences of a party other than the sponsoring advertiser, even if the views expressed by that party are identical to those of the sponsoring advertiser. The party whose opinions, beliefs, findings, or experience the message appears to reflect will be called the endorser and may be an individual, group, or institution.

(c) The Commission intends to treat endorsements and testimonials identically in the context of its enforcement of the Federal Trade Commission Act and for purposes of this part. The term endorsements is therefore generally used hereinafter to cover both terms and situations.

(d) For purposes of this part, the term product includes any product, service, company or industry.

(e) For purposes of this part, an expert is an individual, group, or institution possessing, as a result of experience, study, or training, knowledge of a particular subject, which knowledge is superior to what ordinary individuals generally acquire.

Example 1: A film critic's review of a movie is excerpted in an advertisement. When so used, the review meets the definition of an endorsement because it is viewed by readers as a statement of the critic's own opinions and not those of the film producer, distributor, or exhibitor. Any alteration in or quotation from the text of the review that does not fairly reflect its substance would be a violation of the standards set by this part because it would distort the endorser's opinion. [*See* § 255.1(b).]

Example 2: A TV commercial depicts two women in a supermarket buying a laundry detergent. The women are not identified outside the context of the advertisement. One comments to the other how clean her brand makes her family's clothes, and the other then comments that she will try it because she has not been fully satisfied with her own brand. This obvious fictional dramatization of a real life situation would not be an endorsement.

Example 3: In an advertisement for a pain remedy, an announcer who is not familiar to consumers except as a spokesman for the advertising drug company praises the drug's ability to deliver fast and lasting pain relief. He purports to speak, not on the basis of his own opinions, but rather in the place of and on behalf of the drug company. The announcer's statements would not be considered an endorsement.

Example 4: A manufacturer of automobile tires hires a well-known professional automobile racing driver to deliver its advertising message in television commercials. In these commercials, the driver speaks of the smooth ride, strength, and long life of the tires. Even though the message is not expressly declared to be the personal opinion of the driver, it may nevertheless constitute an endorsement of the tires. Many consumers will recognize this individual as being primarily a racing driver and not merely a spokesperson or announcer for the advertiser. Accordingly, they may well believe the driver would not speak for an automotive product unless he actually believed in what he was saying and had personal knowledge sufficient to form that belief. Hence, they would think that the advertising message reflects the driver's personal views. This attribution of the underlying views to the driver brings the advertisement within the definition of an endorsement for purposes of this part.

Example 5: A television advertisement for a particular brand of golf balls shows a prominent and well-recognized professional golfer practicing numerous drives off the tee. This would be an endorsement by the golfer even though she makes no verbal statement in the advertisement.

Example 6: An infomercial for a home fitness system is hosted by a well-known entertainer. During the infomercial, the entertainer demonstrates the machine and states that it is the most effective and easy-to-use home exercise machine that she has ever tried. Even if she is reading from a script, this statement would be an endorsement, because consumers are likely to believe it reflects the entertainer's views.

Example 7: A television advertisement for a housewares store features a well-known female comedian and a well-known male baseball player engaging in light-hearted banter about products each one intends to purchase for the other. The comedian says that she will buy him a Brand X, portable, high-definition television so he can finally see the strike zone. He says that he will get her a Brand Y juicer so she can make juice with all the fruit and vegetables thrown at her during her performances. The comedian and baseball player are not likely to be deemed endorsers because consumers will likely realize that the individuals are not expressing their own views.

Example 8: A consumer who regularly purchases a particular brand of dog food decides one day to purchase a new, more expensive brand made by the same manufacturer. She writes in her personal blog that the change in diet has made her dog's fur noticeably softer and shinier, and that in her opinion, the new food definitely is worth the extra money. This posting would not be deemed an endorsement under the Guides.

Assume that rather than purchase the dog food with her own money, the consumer gets it for free because the store routinely tracks her purchases and its computer has generated a coupon for a free trial bag of this new brand. Again, her posting would not be deemed an endorsement under the Guides.

Assume now that the consumer joins a network marketing program under which she periodically receives various products about which she can write reviews if she wants to do so. If she receives a free bag of the new dog food through this program, her positive review would be considered an endorsement under the Guides.

§ 255.1 General considerations.

(a) Endorsements must reflect the honest opinions, findings, beliefs, or experience of the endorser. Furthermore, an endorsement may not convey any express or implied representation that would be deceptive if made directly by the advertiser. [*See* § 255.2(a) and (b) regarding substantiation of representations conveyed by consumer endorsements.

(b) The endorsement message need not be phrased in the exact words of the endorser, unless the advertisement affirmatively so represents. However, the endorsement may not be presented out of context or reworded so as to distort in any way the endorser's opinion or experience with the product. An advertiser may use an endorsement of an expert or celebrity only so long as it has good reason to believe that the endorser continues to subscribe to the views presented. An advertiser may satisfy this obligation by securing the endorser's views at reasonable intervals where reasonableness will be determined by such factors as new information on the performance or effectiveness of the product, a material alteration in the product, changes in the performance of competitors' products, and the advertiser's contract commitments.

(c) When the advertisement represents that the endorser uses the endorsed product, the endorser must have been a bona fide user of it at the time the endorsement was given. Additionally, the advertiser may continue to run the advertisement only so long as it has good reason to believe that the endorser remains a bona fide user of the product. [*See* § 255.1(b) regarding the "good reason to believe" requirement.](d)Advertisers are subject to liability for false or unsubstantiated statements made through endorsements, or for failing to disclose material connections between themselves and their endorsers [*see* § 255.5]. Endorsers also may be liable for statements made in the course of their endorsements.

Example 1: A building contractor states in an advertisement that he uses the advertiser's exterior house paint because of its remarkable quick drying properties and durability. This endorsement must comply with the pertinent requirements of § 255.3 (Expert Endorsements). Subsequently, the advertiser reformulates its paint to enable it to cover exterior surfaces with only one coat. Prior to continued use of the contractor's endorsement, the advertiser must contact the contractor in order to determine whether the contractor would continue to specify the paint and to subscribe to the views presented previously.

Example 2: A television advertisement portrays a woman seated at a desk on which rest five unmarked computer keyboards. An announcer says, "We asked X, an administrative assistant for over ten years, to try these five unmarked keyboards and tell us which one she liked best."The advertisement portrays X typing on each keyboard and then picking the advertiser's brand. The announcer asks her why, and X gives her reasons. This endorsement would probably not represent that X actually uses the advertiser's keyboard at work. In addition, the endorsement also may be required to meet the standards of § 255.3 (expert endorsements).

Example 3: An ad for an acne treatment features a dermatologist who claims that the product is "clinically proven" to work. Before giving the endorsement, she received a write-up of the clinical study in question, which indicates flaws in the design and conduct of the study that are so serious that they preclude any conclusions about the efficacy of the product. The dermatologist is subject to liability for the false statements she made in the advertisement. The advertiser is also liable for misrepresentations made through the endorsement. [*See* Section 255.3 regarding the product evaluation that an expert endorser must conduct.

Example 4: A well-known celebrity appears in an infomercial for an oven roasting bag that purportedly cooks every chicken perfectly in thirty minutes. During the shooting of the infomercial, the celebrity watches five attempts to cook chickens using the bag. In each attempt, the chicken is undercooked after thirty minutes and requires sixty minutes of cooking time. In the commercial, the celebrity places an uncooked chicken in the oven roasting bag and places the bag in one oven. He then takes a chicken roasting bag from a second oven, removes from the bag what appears to be a perfectly cooked chicken, tastes the chicken, and says that if you want perfect chicken every time, in just thirty minutes, this is the product you need. A significant percentage of consumers are likely to believe the celebrity's statements represent his own views even though he is reading from a script. The celebrity is subject to liability for his statement about the product. The advertiser is also liable for misrepresentations made through the endorsement.

Example 5: A skin care products advertiser participates in a blog advertising service. The service matches up advertisers with bloggers who will promote the advertiser's products on their personal blogs. The advertiser requests that a blogger try a new body lotion and write a review of the product on her blog. Although the advertiser does not make any specific claims about the lotion's ability to cure skin conditions and the blogger does not ask the advertiser whether there is substantiation for the claim, in her review the blogger writes that the lotion cures eczema and recommends the product to her blog readers who suffer from this condition. The advertiser is subject to liability for misleading or unsubstantiated representations made through the blogger's endorsement. The blogger also is subject to liability for misleading or unsubstantiated representations made in the course of her endorsement. The blogger is also liable if she fails to disclose clearly and conspicuously that she is being paid for her services. [*See* § 255.5.]

In order to limit its potential liability, the advertiser should ensure that the advertising service provides guidance and training to its bloggers concerning the need to ensure that statements they make are truthful and substantiated. The advertiser should also monitor bloggers who are being paid to promote its products and take steps necessary to halt the continued publication of deceptive representations when they are discovered.

§ 255.2 Consumer endorsements.

(a) An advertisement employing endorsements by one or more consumers about the performance of an advertised product or service will be interpreted as representing that the product or service is effective for the purpose depicted in the advertisement. Therefore, the advertiser must possess and rely upon adequate substantiation, including, when appropriate, competent and reliable scientific evidence, to support such claims made through endorsements in the same manner the advertiser would be required to do if it had made the representation directly, *i.e.*, without using endorsements. Consumer endorsements themselves are not competent and reliable scientific evidence.

(b) An advertisement containing an endorsement relating the experience of one or more consumers on a central or key attribute of the product or service also will likely be interpreted as representing that the endorser's experience is representative of what consumers will generally achieve with the advertised product or service in actual, albeit variable, conditions of use. Therefore, an advertiser should possess and rely upon adequate substantiation for this representation. If the advertiser does not have substantiation that the endorser's experience is representative of what consumers will generally achieve, the advertisement should clearly and conspicuously disclose the generally expected performance in the depicted circumstances, and the advertiser must possess and rely on adequate substantiation for that representation.[105]

(c) Advertisements presenting endorsements by what are represented, directly or by implication, to be "actual consumers" should utilize actual consumers in both the audio and video, or clearly and conspicuously disclose that the persons in such advertisements are not actual consumers of the advertised product.

Example 1: A brochure for a baldness treatment consists entirely of testimonials from satisfied customers who say that after using the product, they had amazing hair growth and their hair is as thick and strong as it was when they were teenagers. The advertiser must have competent and reliable scientific evidence that its product is effective in producing new hair growth.

The ad will also likely communicate that the endorsers' experiences are representative of what new users of the product can generally expect. Therefore, even if the advertiser includes a disclaimer such as, "Notice: These testimonials do not prove our product works. You should not expect to have similar results," the ad is likely to be deceptive unless the advertiser has adequate substantiation that new users typically will experience results similar to those experienced by the testimonialists.

Example 2: An advertisement disseminated by a company that sells heat pumps presents endorsements from three individuals who state that after installing the company's heat pump in their homes, their monthly utility bills went down by $100, $125, and $150, respectively. The ad will likely be interpreted as conveying that such savings are representative of what consumers who buy the company's heat pump can generally expect. The advertiser does not have substantiation for that representation because, in fact, less than 20% of purchasers will save $100 or more. A disclosure such as, "Results not typical" or, "These testimonials are based on the experiences of a few people and you are not likely to have similar results" is insufficient to prevent this ad from being deceptive because consumers will still interpret the ad as conveying that the specified savings are representative of what consumers can generally expect. The ad is less likely to be deceptive if it clearly and conspicuously discloses the generally expected savings and the advertiser has adequate substantiation that homeowners can achieve those results. There are multiple ways that such a disclosure could be phrased, *e.g.*, "the average homeowner saves $35 per month," "the typical family saves $50 per month during cold months and $20 per month in warm months," or "most families save 10% on their utility bills."

Example 3: An advertisement for a cholesterol-lowering product features an individual who claims that his serum cholesterol went down by 120 points and does not mention having made any lifestyle changes. A well-conducted clinical study shows that the product reduces the cholesterol levels of individuals with elevated cholesterol by an average of 15% and the advertisement clearly and conspicuously discloses this fact. Despite the presence of this disclosure, the advertisement would be deceptive if the advertiser does not have adequate substantiation that the product can produce the specific results claimed by the endorser (*i.e.*, a 120-point drop in serum cholesterol without any lifestyle changes).

Example 4: An advertisement for a weight-loss product features a formerly obese woman. She says in the ad, "Every day, I drank 2 WeightAway shakes, ate only raw vegetables, and exercised vigorously for six hours at the gym. By the end of six months, I had gone from 250 pounds to 140 pounds."The advertisement accurately describes the woman's experience, and such a result is within the range that would be generally experienced by an extremely overweight individual who consumed WeightAway shakes, only ate raw vegetables, and exercised as the endorser did. Because the endorser clearly describes the limited and truly exceptional circumstances under which she achieved her results, the ad is not likely to convey that consumers who weigh substantially less or use WeightAway under less extreme circumstances will lose 110 pounds in six months. (If the advertisement simply says that the endorser lost 110

---

[105]The Commission tested the communication of advertisements containing testimonials that clearly and prominently disclosed either "Results not typical" or the stronger "These testimonials are based on the experiences of a few people and you are not likely to have similar results."Neither disclosure adequately reduced the communication that the experiences depicted are generally representative. Based upon this research, the Commission believes that similar disclaimers regarding the limited applicability of an endorser's experience to what consumers may generally expect to achieve are unlikely to be effective.

Nonetheless, the Commission cannot rule out the possibility that a strong disclaimer of typicality could be effective in the context of a particular advertisement. Although the Commission would have the burden of proof in a law enforcement action, the Commission notes that an advertiser possessing reliable empirical testing demonstrating that the net impression of its advertisement with such a disclaimer is non-deceptive will avoid the risk of the initiation of such an action in the first instance.

pounds in six months using WeightAway together with diet and exercise, however, this description would not adequately alert consumers to the truly remarkable circumstances leading to her weight loss.)The advertiser must have substantiation, however, for any performance claims conveyed by the endorsement (e.g., that WeightAway is an effective weight loss product).

If, in the alternative, the advertisement simply features "before" and "after" pictures of a woman who says "I lost 50 pounds in 6 months with WeightAway," the ad is likely to convey that her experience is representative of what consumers will generally achieve. Therefore, if consumers cannot generally expect to achieve such results, the ad should clearly and conspicuously disclose what they can expect to lose in the depicted circumstances (*e.g.*, "most women who use WeightAway for six months lose at least 15 pounds").

If the ad features the same pictures but the testimonialist simply says, "I lost 50 pounds with WeightAway," and WeightAway users generally do not lose 50 pounds, the ad should disclose what results they do generally achieve (*e.g.*, "most women who use WeightAway lose 15 pounds").

Example 5: An advertisement presents the results of a poll of consumers who have used the advertiser's cake mixes as well as their own recipes. The results purport to show that the majority believed that their families could not tell the difference between the advertised mix and their own cakes baked from scratch. Many of the consumers are actually pictured in the advertisement along with relevant, quoted portions of their statements endorsing the product. This use of the results of a poll or survey of consumers represents that this is the typical result that ordinary consumers can expect from the advertiser's cake mix.

Example 6: An advertisement purports to portray a "hidden camera" situation in a crowded cafeteria at breakfast time. A spokesperson for the advertiser asks a series of actual patrons of the cafeteria for their spontaneous, honest opinions of the advertiser's recently introduced breakfast cereal. Even though the words "hidden camera" are not displayed on the screen, and even though none of the actual patrons is specifically identified during the advertisement, the net impression conveyed to consumers may well be that these are actual customers, and not actors. If actors have been employed, this fact should be clearly and conspicuously disclosed.

Example 7: An advertisement for a recently released motion picture shows three individuals coming out of a theater, each of whom gives a positive statement about the movie. These individuals are actual consumers expressing their personal views about the movie. The advertiser does not need to have substantiation that their views are representative of the opinions that most consumers will have about the movie. Because the consumers' statements would be understood to be the subjective opinions of only three people, this advertisement is not likely to convey a typicality message.

If the motion picture studio had approached these individuals outside the theater and offered them free tickets if they would talk about the movie on camera afterwards, that arrangement should be clearly and conspicuously disclosed. [*See* §255.5.]

§255.3 Expert endorsements.

(a) Whenever an advertisement represents, directly or by implication, that the endorser is an expert with respect to the endorsement message, then the endorser's qualifications must in fact give the endorser the expertise that he or she is represented as possessing with respect to the endorsement.

(b) Although the expert may, in endorsing a product, take into account factors not within his or her expertise (*e.g.*, matters of taste or price), the endorsement must be supported by an actual exercise of that expertise in evaluating product features or characteristics with respect to which he or she is expert and which are relevant to an ordinary consumer's use of or experience with the product and are available to the ordinary consumer. This evaluation must have included an examination or testing of the product at least as extensive as someone with the same degree of expertise would normally need to conduct in order to support the conclusions presented in the endorsement. To the extent that the advertisement implies that the endorsement was based upon a comparison, such comparison must have been included in the expert's evaluation; and as a result of such comparison, the expert must have concluded that, with respect to those features on which he or she is expert and which are relevant and available to an ordinary consumer, the endorsed product is at least equal overall to the competitors' products. Moreover, where the net impression created by the endorsement is that the advertised product is superior to other products with respect to any such feature or features, then the expert must in fact have found such superiority. [*See*

§ 255.1(d) regarding the liability of endorsers.]

Example 1: An endorsement of a particular automobile by one described as an "engineer" implies that the endorser's professional training and experience are such that he is well acquainted with the design and performance of automobiles. If the endorser's field is, for example, chemical engineering, the endorsement would be deceptive.

Example 2: An endorser of a hearing aid is simply referred to as "Doctor" during the course of an advertisement. The ad likely implies that the endorser is a medical doctor with substantial experience in the area of hearing. If the endorser is not a medical doctor with substantial experience in audiology, the endorsement would likely be deceptive. A non-medical "doctor" (e.g., an individual with a Ph.D. in exercise physiology) or a physician without substantial experience in the area of hearing can endorse the product, but if the endorser is referred to as "doctor," the advertisement must make clear the nature and limits of the endorser's expertise.

Example 3: A manufacturer of automobile parts advertises that its products are approved by the "American Institute of Science."From its name, consumers would infer that the "American Institute of Science" is a bona fide independent testing organization with expertise in judging automobile parts and that, as such, it would not approve any automobile part without first testing its efficacy by means of valid scientific methods. If the American Institute of Science is not such a bona fide independent testing organization (*e.g.*, if it was established and operated by an automotive parts manufacturer), the endorsement would be deceptive. Even if the American Institute of Science is an independent bona fide expert testing organization, the endorsement may nevertheless be deceptive unless the Institute has conducted valid scientific tests of the advertised products and the test results support the endorsement message.

Example 4: A manufacturer of a non-prescription drug product represents that its product has been selected over competing products by a large metropolitan hospital. The hospital has selected the product because the manufacturer, unlike its competitors, has packaged each dose of the product separately. This package form is not generally available to the public. Under the circumstances, the endorsement would be deceptive because the basis for the hospital's choice—convenience of packaging—is neither relevant nor available to consumers, and the basis for the hospital's decision is not disclosed to consumers.

Example 5: A woman who is identified as the president of a commercial "home cleaning service" states in a television advertisement that the service uses a particular brand of cleanser, instead of leading competitors it has tried, because of this brand's performance. Because cleaning services extensively use cleansers in the course of their business, the ad likely conveys that the president has knowledge superior to that of ordinary consumers. Accordingly, the president's statement will be deemed to be an expert endorsement. The service must, of course, actually use the endorsed cleanser. In addition, because the advertisement implies that the cleaning service has experience with a reasonable number of leading competitors to the advertised cleanser, the service must, in fact, have such experience, and, on the basis of its expertise, it must have determined that the cleaning ability of the endorsed cleanser is at least equal (or superior, if such is the net impression conveyed by the advertisement) to that of leading competitors' products with which the service has had experience and which remain reasonably available to it. Because in this example the cleaning service's president makes no mention that the endorsed cleanser was "chosen," "selected," or otherwise evaluated in side-by-side comparisons against its competitors, it is sufficient if the service has relied solely upon its accumulated experience in evaluating cleansers without having performed side-by-side or scientific comparisons.

Example 6: A medical doctor states in an advertisement for a drug that the product will safely allow consumers to lower their cholesterol by 50 points. If the materials the doctor reviewed were merely letters from satisfied consumers or the results of a rodent study, the endorsement would likely be deceptive because those materials are not what others with the same degree of expertise would consider adequate to support this conclusion about the product's safety and efficacy.

§ 255.4 Endorsements by organizations.

Endorsements by organizations, especially expert ones, are viewed as representing the judgment of a group whose collective experience exceeds that of any individual member, and whose judgments are generally free of the sort of subjective factors that vary from individual to individual. Therefore, an organization's endorsement must be reached by a process sufficient to ensure that the endorsement fairly reflects the collective judgment of the organization. Moreover, if an organization is represented as being expert, then, in conjunction with a proper exercise of its expertise in evaluating the product under § 255.3 (expert endorsements), it must utilize an expert or experts recognized as such by the organization or standards previously adopted by the organization and suitable for judging the relevant merits of such products. [*See* § 255.1(d) regarding the liability of endorsers.]

Example: A mattress seller advertises that its product is endorsed by a chiropractic association. Because the association would be regarded as expert with respect to judging mattresses, its endorsement must be supported by an evaluation by an expert or experts recognized as such by the organization, or by compliance with standards previously adopted by the organization and aimed at measuring the performance of mattresses in general and not designed with the unique features of the advertised mattress in mind.

§ 255.5 Disclosure of material connections.

When there exists a connection between the endorser and the seller of the advertised product that might materially affect the weight or credibility of the endorsement (*i.e.*, the connection is not reasonably expected by the audience), such connection must be fully disclosed. For example, when an endorser who appears in a television commercial is neither represented in the advertisement as an expert nor is known to a significant portion of the viewing public, then the advertiser should clearly and conspicuously disclose either the payment or promise of compensation prior to and in exchange for the endorsement or the fact that the endorser knew or had reason to know or to believe that if the endorsement favored the advertised product some benefit, such as an appearance on television, would be extended to the endorser. Additional guidance, including guidance concerning endorsements made through other media, is provided by the examples below.

Example 1: A drug company commissions research on its product by an outside organization. The drug company determines the overall subject of the research (*e.g.*, to test the efficacy of a newly developed product) and pays a substantial share of the expenses of the research project, but the research organization determines the protocol for the study and is responsible for conducting it. A subsequent advertisement by the drug company mentions the research results as the "findings" of that research organization. Although the design and conduct of the research project are controlled by the outside research organization, the weight consumers place on the reported results could be materially affected by knowing that the advertiser had funded the project. Therefore, the advertiser's payment of expenses to the research organization should be disclosed in this advertisement.

Example 2: A film star endorses a particular food product. The endorsement regards only points of taste and individual preference. This endorsement must, of course, comply with § 255.1; but regardless of whether the star's compensation for the commercial is a $1 million cash payment or a royalty for each product sold by the advertiser during the next year, no disclosure is required because such payments likely are ordinarily expected by viewers.

Example 3: During an appearance by a well-known professional tennis player on a television talk show, the host comments that the past few months have been the best of her career and during this time she has risen to her highest level ever in the rankings. She responds by attributing the improvement in her game to the fact that she is seeing the ball better than she used to, ever since having laser vision correction surgery at a clinic that she identifies by name. She continues talking about the ease of the procedure, the kindness of the clinic's doctors, her speedy recovery, and how she can now engage in a variety of activities without glasses, including driving at night. The athlete does not disclose that, even though she does not appear in commercials for the clinic, she has a contractual relationship with it, and her contract pays her for speaking publicly about her surgery when she can do so. Consumers might not realize that a celebrity discussing a medical procedure in a television interview has been paid for doing so, and knowledge of such payments would likely affect the weight or credibility consumers give to the celebrity's endorsement. Without a clear and conspicuous disclosure that the athlete has been engaged as a spokesperson for the clinic, this endorsement is likely to be deceptive. Furthermore, if consumers are likely to take away from her story that her experience was typical of those who undergo the same procedure at the clinic, the advertiser must have substantiation for that claim.

Assume that instead of speaking about the clinic in a television interview, the tennis player touts the results of her surgery—mentioning the clinic by name—on a social networking site that allows her fans to read in real time what is happening in her life. Given the nature of the medium in which her endorsement is disseminated, consumers might not realize that she is a paid endorser. Because that information might affect the weight consumers give to her endorsement, her relationship with the clinic should be disclosed.

Assume that during that same television interview, the tennis player is wearing clothes bearing the insignia of an athletic wear company with whom she also has an endorsement contract. Although this contract requires that she wear the company's clothes not only on the court but also in public appearances, when possible, she does not mention them or the company during her appearance on the show. No disclosure is required because no representation is being made about the clothes in this context.

Example 4: An ad for an anti-snoring product features a physician who says that he has seen dozens of products come on the market over the years and, in his opinion, this is the best ever. Consumers would expect the physician to be reasonably compensated for his appearance in the ad. Consumers are unlikely, however, to expect that the physician receives a percentage of gross product sales or that he owns part of the company, and either of these facts would likely materially affect the credibility that consumers attach to the endorsement. Accordingly, the advertisement should clearly and conspicuously disclose such a connection between the company and the physician.

Example 5: An actual patron of a restaurant, who is neither known to the public nor presented as an expert, is shown seated at the counter. He is asked for his "spontaneous" opinion of a new food product served in the restaurant. Assume, first, that the advertiser had posted a sign on the door of the restaurant informing all who entered that day that patrons would be interviewed by the advertiser as part of its TV promotion of its new soy protein "steak." This notification would materially affect the weight or credibility of the patron's endorsement, and, therefore, viewers of the advertisement should be clearly and conspicuously informed of the circumstances under which the endorsement was obtained.

Assume, in the alternative, that the advertiser had not posted a sign on the door of the restaurant, but had informed all interviewed customers of the "hidden camera" only after interviews were completed and the customers had no reason to know or believe that their response was being recorded for use in an advertisement. Even if patrons were also told that they would be paid for allowing the use of their opinions in advertising, these facts need not be disclosed.

Example 6: An infomercial producer wants to include consumer endorsements for an automotive additive product featured in her commercial, but because the product has not yet been sold, there are no consumer users. The producer's staff reviews the profiles of individuals interested in working as "extras" in commercials and identifies several who are interested in automobiles. The extras are asked to use the product for several weeks and then report back to the producer. They are told that if they are selected to endorse the product in the producer's infomercial, they will receive a small payment. Viewers would not expect that these "consumer endorsers" are actors who were asked to use the product so that they could appear in the commercial or that they were compensated. Because the advertisement fails to disclose these facts, it is deceptive.

Example 7: A college student who has earned a reputation as a video game expert maintains a personal weblog or "blog" where he posts entries about his gaming experiences. Readers of his blog frequently seek his opinions about video game hardware and software. As it has done in the past, the manufacturer of a newly released video game system sends the student a free copy of the system and asks him to write about it on his blog. He tests the new gaming system and writes a favorable review. Because his review is disseminated via a form of consumer-generated media in which his relationship to the advertiser is not inherently obvious, readers are unlikely to know that he has received the video game system free of charge in exchange for his review of the product, and given the value of the video game system, this fact likely would materially affect the credibility they attach to his endorsement. Accordingly, the blogger should clearly and conspicuously disclose that he received the gaming system free of charge. The manufacturer should advise him at the time it provides the gaming system that this connection should be disclosed, and it should have procedures in place to try to monitor his postings for compliance.

Example 8: An online message board designated for discussions of new music download technology is frequented by MP3 player enthusiasts. They exchange information about new products, utilities, and the functionality of numerous playback devices. Unbeknownst to the message board community, an employee of a leading playback device manufacturer has been posting messages on the discussion board promoting the manufacturer's product. Knowledge of this poster's employment likely would affect the weight or credibility of her endorsement. Therefore, the poster should clearly and conspicuously disclose her relationship to the manufacturer to members and readers of the message board.

Example 9: A young man signs up to be part of a "street team" program in which points are awarded each time a team member talks to his or her friends about a particular advertiser's products. Team members can then exchange their points for prizes, such as concert tickets or electronics. These incentives would materially affect the weight or credibility of the team member's endorsements. They should be clearly and conspicuously disclosed, and the advertiser should take steps to ensure that these disclosures are being provided.

PART 259—GUIDE CONCERNING FUEL ECONOMY ADVERTISING FOR NEW AUTOMOBILES

AUTHORITY: 15 U.S.C. 41–58.

SOURCE: 82 FR 43687, Sept. 19, 2017, unless otherwise noted.

§ 259.1 Purpose.

The Guide in this part contains administrative interpretations of laws enforced by the Federal Trade Commission. Specifically, the Guide addresses the application of Section 5 of the FTC Act (15 U.S.C. 45) to the use of fuel economy information in advertising for new automobiles. This guidance provides the basis for voluntary compliance with the law by advertisers and endorsers. Practices inconsistent with this Guide may result in corrective action by the Commission under Section 5 if, after investigation, the Commission has reason to believe that the practices fall within the scope of conduct declared unlawful by the statute. The Guide sets forth the general principles that the Commission will use in such an investigation together with examples illustrating the application of those principles. The Guide does not purport to cover every possible use of fuel economy in advertising. Whether a particular advertisement is deceptive will depend on the specific advertisement at issue.

§ 259.2 Definitions.

For the purposes of this part, the following definitions shall apply:

Alternative fueled vehicle. Any vehicle that qualifies as a covered vehicle under part 309 of this chapter.

Automobile. Any new passenger automobile, medium duty passenger vehicle, or light truck for which a fuel economy label is required under the Energy Policy and Conservation Act (42 U.S.C. 32901 *et seq.*) or rules promulgated thereunder, the equitable or legal title to which has never been transferred by a manufacturer, distributor, or dealer to an ultimate purchaser or lessee. For the purposes of this part, the terms "vehicle" and "car" have the same meaning as "automobile."

Dealer. Any person located in the United States or any territory thereof engaged in the sale or distribution of new automobiles to the ultimate purchaser.

EPA. The U.S. Environmental Protection Agency.

EPA city fuel economy estimate. The city fuel economy determined in accordance with the city test procedure as defined and determined pursuant to 40 CFR part 600, subpart D.

EPA combined fuel economy estimate. The fuel economy value determined for a vehicle (or vehicles) by harmonically averaging the city and highway fuel economy values, weighted 0.55 and 0.45 respectively, determined pursuant to 40 CFR part 600, subpart D.

EPA driving range estimate. An estimate of the number of miles a vehicle will travel between refueling as defined and determined pursuant to 40 CFR part 600, subpart D.

EPA fuel economy estimate. The average number of miles traveled by an automobile per volume of fuel consumed (*i.e.*, Miles-Per-Gallon ("MPG") rating) as calculated under 40 CFR part 600, subpart D.

EPA highway fuel economy estimate. The highway fuel economy determined in accordance with the highway test procedure as defined and determined pursuant to 40 CFR part 600, subpart D.

Flexible fueled vehicle. Any motor vehicle (or motor vehicle engine) engineered and designed to be operated on any mixture of two or more different fuels.

Fuel. (1) Gasoline and diesel fuel for gasoline- or diesel-powered automobiles;

(2) Electricity for electrically-powered automobiles;

(3) Alcohol for alcohol-powered automobiles;

(4) Natural gas for natural gas-powered automobiles; or

(5) Any other fuel type used in a vehicle for which EPA requires a fuel economy label under 40 CFR part 600, subpart D.

Manufacturer. Any person engaged in the manufacturing or assembling of new automobiles, including any person importing new automobiles for resale and any person who acts for, and is under the control, of such manufacturer, assembler, or importer in connection with the distribution of new automobiles.

Model type. A unique combination of car line, basic engine, and transmission class as defined by 40 CFR part 600, subpart D.

Ultimate purchaser or lessee. The first person, other than a dealer purchasing in his or her capacity as a dealer, who in good faith purchases a new automobile for purposes other than resale or leases such vehicle for his or her personal use.

Vehicle configuration. The unique combination of automobile features, as defined in 40 CFR part 600.

§ 259.3 Qualifications and disclosures.

To prevent deceptive claims, qualifications and disclosures should be clear, prominent, and understandable. To make disclosures clear and prominent, marketers should use plain language and sufficiently large type for a person to see and understand them, should place disclosures in close proximity to the qualified claim, and should avoid making inconsistent statements or using distracting elements that could undercut or contradict the disclosure. The disclosures should also appear in the same format as the claim. For example, for television advertisements, if the fuel economy claim appears in the video, the disclosure recommended by this Guide should appear in the visual format; if the fuel economy claim is audio, the disclosure should be in audio.

§ 259.4 Advertising guidance.

(a) *Misrepresentations.* It is deceptive to misrepresent, directly or by implication, the fuel economy or driving range of an automobile.

(b) *General fuel economy claims.* General unqualified fuel economy claims, which do not reference a specific fuel economy estimate, likely convey a wide range of meanings about a vehicle's fuel economy relative to other vehicles. Such claims, which inherently involve comparisons to other vehicles, can mislead consumers about the vehicle class included in the comparison, as well as the extent to which the advertised vehicle's fuel economy differs from other models. Because it is highly unlikely that advertisers can substantiate all reasonable interpretations of these claims, advertisers making general fuel economy claims should disclose the advertised vehicle's EPA fuel economy estimate in the form of the EPA MPG rating.

Example 1: A new car advertisement states: "This vehicle gets great mileage." The claim is likely to convey a variety of meanings, including that the vehicle has a better MPG rating than all or almost all other cars on the market. However, the advertised vehicle's EPA fuel economy estimates are only slightly better than the average vehicle on the market. Because the advertiser cannot substantiate that the vehicle's rating is better than all or almost all other cars on the market, the advertisement is deceptive. In addition, the advertiser may not be able to substantiate other reasonable interpretations of the claim. To avoid deception, the advertisement should disclose the vehicle's EPA fuel economy estimate (*e.g.*, "EPA-estimated 27 combined MPG").

Example 2: An advertisement states: "This car gets great gas mileage compared to other compact cars." The claim is likely to convey a variety of meanings, including that the vehicle gets better gas mileage than all or almost all other compact cars. However, the vehicle's EPA fuel economy estimates are only slightly better than average compared to other models in its class. Because the advertiser cannot substantiate that the vehicle's rating is better than all or almost all other compact cars, the advertisement is deceptive. In addition, the advertiser may not be able to substantiate other reasonable interpretations of the claim. To address this problem, the advertisement should disclose the vehicle's EPA fuel economy estimate.

(c) *Matching the EPA estimate to the claim.* EPA fuel economy estimates should match the mode of driving claim appearing in the advertisement. If they do not, consumers are likely to associate the stated fuel economy estimate with a different type of driving. Specifically, if an advertiser makes a city or a highway fuel economy claim, it should disclose the corresponding

EPA-estimated city or highway fuel economy estimate. If the advertiser makes both a city and a highway fuel economy claim, it should disclose both the EPA estimated city and highway fuel economy rating. If the advertiser makes a general fuel economy claim without specifically referencing city or highway driving, it should disclose the EPA combined fuel economy estimate, or, alternatively, both the EPA city and highway fuel economy estimates.

Example 1: An automobile advertisement states that model "XYZ gets great gas mileage in town." However, the advertisement does not disclose the EPA city fuel economy estimate. Instead, it only discloses the EPA highway fuel economy estimate, which is higher than the model's city estimate. This claim likely conveys to a significant proportion of reasonable consumers that the highway estimate disclosed in the advertisement applies to city driving. Thus, the advertisement is deceptive to consumers. To remedy this problem, the advertisement should disclose the EPA city fuel economy estimate (*e.g.*, "32 MPG in the city according to the EPA estimate").

Example 2: A new car advertisement states that model "XZA gives you great gas mileage" but only provides the EPA highway fuel economy estimate. Given the likely inconsistency between the general fuel economy claim, which does not reference a specific type of driving, and the disclosed EPA highway estimate, the advertisement is deceptive to consumers. To address this problem, the advertisement should disclose the EPA combined estimate (*e.g.*, "37 MPG for combined driving according to the EPA estimate"), or both the EPA city and highway fuel economy estimates.

Example 3: An advertisement states: "according to EPA estimates, new cars in this class are rated at between 20 and 32 MPG, while the EPA estimate for this car is an impressive 35 MPG highway." The advertisement is likely to imply that the 20 to 32 MPG range and 35 MPG estimate are comparable. In fact, the "20 and 32 MPG" range reflects EPA city estimates. Therefore, the advertisement is deceptive. To address this problem, the advertisement should only provide an apples-to-apples comparison—either using the highway range for the class or using the city estimate for the advertised vehicle.

(d) *Identifying fuel economy and driving range ratings as estimates.* Advertisers citing EPA fuel economy or driving range figures should disclose that these numbers are estimates. Without such disclosures, consumers may incorrectly assume that they will achieve the mileage or range stated in the advertisement. In fact, their actual mileage or range will likely vary for many reasons, including driving conditions, driving habits, and vehicle maintenance. To address potential deception, advertisers may state that the values are "EPA estimate(s)," or use equivalent language that informs consumers that they will not necessarily achieve the stated MPG rating or driving range.

Example 1: An automobile manufacture's Web site states, without qualification, "This car gets 40 MPG on the highway." The claim likely conveys to a significant proportion of reasonable consumers that they will achieve 40 MPG driving this vehicle on the highway. The advertiser based its claim on an EPA highway estimate. However, EPA provides that estimate primarily for comparison purposes—it does not necessarily reflect real world driving results. Therefore, the claim is deceptive. In addition, the use of the term "gets," without qualification, may lead some consumers to believe not only that they can, but will consistently, achieve the stated mileage. To address these problems, the advertisement should clarify that the MPG value is an estimate by stating "EPA estimate" or equivalent language.

(e) *Disclosing EPA test as source of fuel economy and driving range estimates.* Advertisers citing any EPA fuel economy or driving range figures should identify EPA as the source of the test so consumers understand that the estimate is comparable to EPA estimates for competing models. Doing so prevents deception by ensuring that consumers do not associate the claimed ratings with a test other than the EPA-required procedures. Advertisers may avoid deception by stating that the values are "EPA estimate(s)," or equivalent language that identifies the EPA test as the source.

Example 1: A radio commercial for the "XTQ" car states that the vehicle "is rated at an estimated 28 MPG in the city" but does not disclose that an EPA test is the source of this MPG estimate. This advertisement may convey that the source of this test is an entity other than EPA. To avoid deception, the advertisement should state that the MPG figures are EPA estimates.

(f) *Specifying driving modes for fuel economy estimates.* If an advertiser cites an EPA fuel economy estimate, it should identify the particular type of driving associated with the estimate (*i.e.*, estimated city, highway, or combined MPG). Advertisements failing to do so can deceive consumers who incorrectly assume the disclosure applies to a specific type of driving, such as combined or highway, which may not be the driving type the advertiser intended. Thus, such consumers may believe the model's fuel economy rating is higher than it actually is.

Example 1: A television commercial for the car model "ZTA" informs consumers that the ZTA is rated at "25 miles per gallon according to the EPA estimate" but does not disclose whether this number is a highway, city, or combined estimate. The advertisement likely conveys to a significant proportion of reasonable consumers that the 25 MPG figure reflects normal driving (*i.e.*, a combination of city and highway driving), not the highway rating as intended by the advertiser. In fact, the 25 MPG rating is the vehicle's EPA highway estimate. Therefore, the advertisement is deceptive.

(g) *Within vehicle class comparisons.* If an advertisement contains an express comparative fuel economy claim where the relevant comparison is to any group or class, other than all available automobiles, the advertisement should identify the group or class of vehicles used in the comparison. Without such qualifying information, many consumers are likely to assume that the advertisement compares the vehicle to all new automobiles.

Example 1: An advertisement claims that sports car X "outpaces other cars' gas mileage." The claim likely conveys a variety of meanings to a significant proportion of reasonable consumers, including that this vehicle has a higher MPG rating than all or almost all other vehicles on the market. Although the vehicle's MPG rating compares favorably to other sports cars, its fuel economy is only better than roughly half of all new automobiles on the market. Therefore, the claim is deceptive.

(h) *Comparing different model types.* Fuel economy estimates are assigned to specific model types under 40 CFR part 600, subpart D (*i.e.*, unique combinations of car line, basic engine, and transmission class). Therefore, advertisers citing MPG ratings for certain models should ensure that the rating applies to the model type depicted in the advertisement. It is deceptive to state or imply that a rated fuel economy figure applies to a vehicle featured in an advertisement if the estimate does not apply to vehicles of that model type.

Example 1: A manufacturer's advertisement states that model "PDQ" gets "great gas mileage" but depicts the MPG numbers for a similar model type known as the "Econo-PDQ." The advertisement is likely to convey that the claimed MPG rating applies to all types of the PDQ model. However, the "Econo-PDQ" has a better fuel economy rating than other types of the "PDQ" model. Therefore, the advertisement is deceptive.

(i) *"Up to" claims.* Advertisers should avoid using the term "up to" without adequate explanatory language if they intend to communicate that certain versions of a model (*i.e.*, model types) are rated at a stated fuel economy estimate. A significant proportion of reasonable consumers are likely to interpret such claims to mean that the stated MPG can be achieved if the vehicle is driven under certain conditions. Therefore, to address the risk of deception, advertisers should qualify the claim by clearly and prominently disclosing the stated MPG applies to a particular vehicle model type.

Example 1: An advertisement states, without further explanation, that a vehicle model VXR will achieve "up to 40 MPG on the highway." The advertisement is based on a particularly efficient type of this model, with specific options, with an EPA highway estimate of 40 MPG. However, other types of model VXR have lower EPA MPG estimates. A significant proportion of reasonable consumers likely interpret the "up to" claim as applying to all VXR model types. Therefore, the advertisement is deceptive. To address this problem, the advertisement should clearly and prominently disclose that the 40 MPG rating does not apply to all model types of the VXR or use language other than "up to" that better conveys the claim.

(j) *Claims for flexible-fueled vehicles.* Advertisements for flexible-fueled vehicles should not mislead consumers about the vehicle's fuel economy when operated with alternative fuel. If an advertisement for a flexible-fueled vehicle (other than a plug-in hybrid electric vehicle) mentions the vehicle's flexible-fuel capability and makes a fuel economy claim, it should clearly and prominently qualify the claim to identify the type of fuel used. Without such qualification, consumers are likely to take away that the stated fuel economy estimate applies to both gasoline and alternative fuel operation.

Example 1: An automobile advertisement states: "This flex-fuel powerhouse has a 30 MPG highway rating according to the EPA estimate." The advertisement likely implies that the 30 MPG rating applies to both gasoline and alternative fuel operation. In fact, the ethanol EPA estimate for this vehicle is 25 MPG. Therefore, the advertisement is deceptive. To address this problem, the advertisement could clearly and prominently qualify the claim or disclose the MPG ratings for both gasoline and alternative fuel operation.

(k) *General driving range claims.* General unqualified driving range claims, which do not reference a specific driving range estimate, are difficult for consumers to interpret and likely convey a wide range of meanings about a vehicle's range relative to other vehicles. Such claims, which inherently involve comparisons to other vehicles, can mislead consumers about the vehicle class included in the comparison as well as the extent to which the advertised vehicle's driving range differs from other models. Consumers may take away a range of reasonable interpretations from these claims. To avoid possible deception, advertisers making general driving range claims should disclose the advertised vehicle's EPA driving range estimate.

Example 1: An advertisement for an electric vehicle states: "This car has a great driving range." This claim likely conveys a variety of meanings, including that the vehicle has a better driving range than all or almost all other electric vehicles. However, the EPA driving range estimate for this vehicle is only slightly better than roughly half of all other electric vehicles on the market. Because the advertiser cannot substantiate that the vehicle's driving range is better than all or almost all other electric vehicles, the advertisement is deceptive. In addition, the advertiser may not be able to substantiate other reasonable interpretations of the claim. To address this problem, the advertisement should disclose the vehicle's EPA driving range estimate (*e.g.*, "EPA-estimated range of 70 miles per charge").

(l) *Use of non-EPA estimates*—(1) *Disclosure content.* Given consumers' exposure to EPA estimated fuel economy values over the last several decades, fuel economy and driving range estimates derived from non-EPA tests can lead to deception if consumers understand such estimates to be fuel economy ratings derived from EPA-required tests. Accordingly, advertisers should avoid such claims and disclose the EPA fuel economy or driving range estimates. However, if an advertisement includes a claim about a vehicle's fuel economy or driving range based on a non-EPA estimate, advertisers should disclose the EPA estimate and disclose with substantially more prominence than the non-EPA estimate:

(i) That the fuel economy or driving range information is based on a non-EPA test;

(ii) The source of the non-EPA test;

(iii) The EPA fuel economy estimates or EPA driving range estimates for the vehicle; and

(iv) All driving conditions or vehicle configurations simulated by the non-EPA test that are different from those used in the EPA test. Such conditions and variables may include, but are not limited to, road or dynamometer test, average speed, range of speed, hot or cold start, temperature, and design or equipment differences.

(2) *Disclosure format.* The Commission regards the following as constituting "substantially more prominence":

(i) *For visual disclosures on television.* If the fuel economy claims appear only in the visual portion, the EPA figures should appear in numbers twice as large as those used for any other estimate, and should remain on the screen at least as long as any other estimate. Each EPA figure should be broadcast against a solid color background that contrasts easily with the color used for the numbers when viewed on both color and black and white television.

(ii) *For audio disclosures.* For radio and television advertisements in which any other estimate is used only in the audio, equal prominence should be given to the EPA figures. The Commission will regard the following as constituting equal prominence: The EPA estimated city and/or highway MPG should be stated, either before or after each disclosure of such other estimate, at least as audibly as such other estimate.

(iii) *For print and Internet disclosures.* The EPA figures should appear in clearly legible type at least twice as large as that used for any other estimate. The EPA figures should appear against a solid color, and contrasting background. They may not appear in a footnote unless all references to fuel economy appear in a footnote.

Example 1: An Internet advertisement states: "Independent driving experts took the QXT car for a weekend spin and managed to get 55 miles-per-gallon under a variety of driving conditions." It does not disclose the actual EPA fuel economy estimates, nor does it explain how conditions during the "weekend spin" differed from those under the EPA tests. This advertisement likely conveys that the 55 MPG figure is the same or comparable to an EPA fuel economy estimate for the vehicle. This claim is deceptive because it fails to disclose that fuel economy information is based on a non-EPA test, the source of the non-EPA test, the EPA fuel economy estimates for the vehicle, and all driving conditions or vehicle configurations simulated by the non-EPA test that are different from those used in the EPA test.

Example 2: An advertisement states: "The XZY electric car has a driving range of 110 miles per charge in summer conditions according to our expert's test." It provides no additional information regarding this driving range claim. This advertisement likely conveys that this 110-mile driving range figure is comparable to an EPA driving range estimate for the vehicle. The advertisement is deceptive because it does not clearly state that the test is a non-EPA test; it does not provide the EPA estimated driving range; and it does not explain how conditions referred to in the advertisement differed from those under the EPA tests. Without this information, consumers are likely to confuse the claims with range estimates derived from the official EPA test procedures.

PART 260—GUIDES FOR THE USE OF ENVIRONMENTAL MARKETING CLAIMS

Sec.

AUTHORITY: 15 U.S.C. 41–58.

SOURCE: 77 FR 62124, Oct. 11, 2012, unless otherwise noted.

§ 260.1 Purpose, scope, and structure of the guides.

(a) These guides set forth the Federal Trade Commission's current views about environmental claims. The guides help marketers avoid making environmental marketing claims that are unfair or deceptive under Section 5 of the FTC Act, 15 U.S.C. 45. They do not confer any rights on any person and do not operate to bind the FTC or the public. The Commission, however, can take action under the FTC Act if a marketer makes an environmental claim inconsistent with the guides. In any such enforcement action, the Commission must prove that the challenged act or practice is unfair or deceptive in violation of Section 5 of the FTC Act.

(b) These guides do not preempt federal, state, or local laws. Compliance with those laws, however, will not necessarily preclude Commission law enforcement action under the FTC Act.

(c) These guides apply to claims about the environmental attributes of a product, package, or service in connection with the marketing, offering for sale, or sale of such item or service to individuals. These guides also apply to business-to-business transactions. The guides apply to environmental claims in labeling, advertising, promotional materials, and all other forms of marketing in any medium, whether asserted directly or by implication, through words, symbols, logos, depictions, product brand names, or any other means.

(d) The guides consist of general principles, specific guidance on the use of particular environmental claims, and examples. Claims may raise issues that are addressed by more than one example and in more than one section of the guides. The examples provide the Commission's views on how reasonable consumers likely interpret certain claims. The guides are based on marketing to a general audience. However, when a marketer targets a particular segment of consumers, the Commission will examine how reasonable members of that group interpret the advertisement. Whether a particular claim is deceptive will depend on the net impression of the advertisement, label, or other promotional material at issue. In addition, although many examples present specific claims and options for qualifying claims, the examples do not illustrate all permissible claims or qualifications under Section 5 of the FTC Act. Nor do they illustrate the only ways to comply with the guides. Marketers can use an alternative approach if the approach satisfies the requirements of Section 5 of the FTC Act. All examples assume that the described claims otherwise comply with Section 5. Where particularly useful, the Guides incorporate a reminder to this effect.

§260.2 Interpretation and substantiation of environmental marketing claims.

Section 5 of the FTC Act prohibits deceptive acts and practices in or affecting commerce. A representation, omission, or practice is deceptive if it is likely to mislead consumers acting reasonably under the circumstances and is material to consumers' decisions. *See* FTC Policy Statement on Deception, 103 FTC 174 (1983). To determine if an advertisement is deceptive, marketers must identify all express and implied claims that the advertisement reasonably conveys. Marketers must ensure that all reasonable interpretations of their claims are truthful, not misleading, and supported by a reasonable basis before they make the claims. *See* FTC Policy Statement Regarding Advertising Substantiation, 104 FTC 839 (1984). In the context of environmental marketing claims, a reasonable basis often requires competent and reliable scientific evidence. Such evidence consists of tests, analyses, research, or studies that have been conducted and evaluated in an objective manner by qualified persons and are generally accepted in the profession to yield accurate and reliable results. Such evidence should be sufficient in quality and quantity based on standards generally accepted in the relevant scientific fields, when considered in light of the entire body of relevant and reliable scientific evidence, to substantiate that each of the marketing claims is true.

§260.3 General principles.

The following general principles apply to all environmental marketing claims, including those described in §§260.4 through 240.16. Claims should comport with all relevant provisions of these guides.

(a) *Qualifications and disclosures.* To prevent deceptive claims, qualifications and disclosures should be clear, prominent, and understandable. To make disclosures clear and prominent, marketers should use plain language and sufficiently large type, should place disclosures in close proximity to the qualified claim, and should avoid making inconsistent statements or using distracting elements that could undercut or contradict the disclosure.

(b) *Distinction between benefits of product, package, and service.* Unless it is clear from the context, an environmental marketing claim should specify whether it refers to the product, the product's packaging, a service, or just to a portion of the product, package, or service. In general, if the environmental attribute applies to all but minor, incidental components of a product or package, the marketer need not qualify the claim to identify that fact. However, there may be exceptions to this general principle. For example, if a marketer makes an unqualified recyclable claim, and the presence of the incidental component significantly limits the ability to recycle the product, the claim would be deceptive.

Example 1: A plastic package containing a new shower curtain is labeled "recyclable" without further elaboration. Because the context of the claim does not make clear whether it refers to the plastic package or the shower curtain, the claim is deceptive if any part of either the package or the curtain, other than minor, incidental components, cannot be recycled.

Example 2: A soft drink bottle is labeled "recycled." The bottle is made entirely from recycled materials, but the bottle cap is not. Because the bottle cap is a minor, incidental component of the package, the claim is not deceptive.

(c) *Overstatement of environmental attribute.* An environmental marketing claim should not overstate, directly or by implication, an environmental attribute or benefit. Marketers should not state or imply environmental benefits if the benefits are negligible.

Example 1: An area rug is labeled "50% more recycled content than before." The manufacturer increased the recycled content of its rug from 2% recycled fiber to 3%. Although the claim is technically true, it likely conveys the false impression that the manufacturer has increased significantly the use of recycled fiber.

Example 2: A trash bag is labeled "recyclable" without qualification. Because trash bags ordinarily are not separated from other trash at the landfill or incinerator for recycling, they are highly unlikely to be used again for any purpose. Even if the bag is technically capable of being recycled, the claim is deceptive since it asserts an environmental benefit where no meaningful benefit exists.

(d) *Comparative claims.* Comparative environmental marketing claims should be clear to avoid consumer confusion about the comparison. Marketers should have substantiation for the comparison.

Example 1: An advertiser notes that its glass bathroom tiles contain "20% more recycled content." Depending on the context, the claim could be a comparison either to the advertiser's immediately preceding product or to its competitors' products. The advertiser should have substantiation for both interpretations. Otherwise, the advertiser should make the basis for comparison clear, for example, by saying "20% more recycled content than our previous bathroom tiles."

Example 2: An advertiser claims that "our plastic diaper liner has the most recycled content." The diaper liner has more recycled content, calculated as a percentage of weight, than any other on the market, although it is still well under 100%. The claim likely conveys that the product contains a significant percentage of recycled content and has significantly more recycled content than its competitors. If the advertiser cannot substantiate these messages, the claim would be deceptive.

Example 3: An advertiser claims that its packaging creates "less waste than the leading national brand." The advertiser implemented the source reduction several years ago and supported the claim by calculating the relative solid waste contributions of the two packages. The advertiser should have substantiation that the comparison remains accurate.

Example 4: A product is advertised as "environmentally preferable." This claim likely conveys that the product is environmentally superior to other products. Because it is highly unlikely that the marketer can substantiate the messages conveyed by this statement, this claim is deceptive. The claim would not be deceptive if the marketer accompanied it with clear and prominent language limiting the environmental superiority representation to the particular attributes for which the marketer has substantiation, provided the advertisement's context does not imply other deceptive claims. For example, the claim "Environmentally preferable: contains 50% recycled content compared to 20% for the leading brand" would not be deceptive.

§ 260.4 General environmental benefit claims.

(a) It is deceptive to misrepresent, directly or by implication, that a product, package, or service offers a general environmental benefit.

(b) Unqualified general environmental benefit claims are difficult to interpret and likely convey a wide range of meanings. In many cases, such claims likely convey that the product, package, or service has specific and far-reaching environmental benefits and may convey that the item or service has no negative environmental impact. Because it is highly unlikely that marketers can substantiate all reasonable interpretations of these claims, marketers should not make unqualified general environmental benefit claims.

(c) Marketers can qualify general environmental benefit claims to prevent deception about the nature of the environmental benefit being asserted. To avoid deception, marketers should use clear and prominent qualifying language that limits the claim to a specific benefit or benefits. Marketers should not imply that any specific benefit is significant if it is, in fact, negligible. If a qualified general claim conveys that a product is more environmentally beneficial overall because of the particular touted benefit(s), marketers should analyze trade-offs resulting from the benefit(s) to determine if they can substantiate this claim.

(d) Even if a marketer explains, and has substantiation for, the product's specific environmental attributes, this explanation will not adequately qualify a general environmental benefit claim if the advertisement otherwise implies deceptive claims. Therefore, marketers should ensure that the advertisement's context does not imply deceptive environmental claims.

Example 1: The brand name "Eco-friendly" likely conveys that the product has far-reaching environmental benefits and may convey that the product has no negative environmental impact. Because it is highly unlikely that the marketer can substantiate these claims, the use of such a brand name is deceptive. A claim, such as "Eco-friendly: made with recycled materials," would not be deceptive if: (1) The statement "made with recycled materials" is clear and prominent; (2) the marketer can substantiate that the entire product or package, excluding minor, incidental components, is made from recycled material; (3) making the product with recycled materials makes the product more environmentally beneficial overall; and (4) the advertisement's context does not imply other deceptive claims.

Example 2: A marketer states that its packaging is now "Greener than our previous packaging." The packaging weighs 15% less than previous packaging, but it is not recyclable nor has it been improved in any other material respect. The claim is deceptive because reasonable consumers likely would interpret "Greener" in this context to mean that other significant environmental aspects of the packaging also are improved over previous packaging. A claim stating "Greener than our previous packaging" accompanied by clear and prominent language such as, "We've reduced the weight of our packaging by 15%," would not be deceptive, provided that reducing the packaging's weight makes the product more environmentally beneficial overall and the advertisement's context does not imply other deceptive claims.

Example 3: A marketer's advertisement features a picture of a laser printer in a bird's nest balancing on a tree branch, surrounded by a dense forest. In green type, the marketer states, "Buy our printer. Make a change." Although the advertisement does not expressly claim that the product has environmental benefits, the featured images, in combination with the text, likely convey that the product has far-reaching environmental benefits and may convey that the product has no negative environmental impact. Because it is highly unlikely that the marketer can substantiate these claims, this advertisement is deceptive.

Example 4: A manufacturer's Web site states, "Eco-smart gas-powered lawn mower with improved fuel efficiency!" The manufacturer increased the fuel efficiency by 1/10 of a percent. Although the manufacturer's claim that it has improved its fuel efficiency technically is true, it likely conveys the false impression that the manufacturer has significantly increased the mower's fuel efficiency.

Example 5: A marketer reduces the weight of its plastic beverage bottles. The bottles' labels state: "Environmentally-friendly improvement. 25% less plastic than our previous packaging." The plastic bottles are 25 percent lighter but otherwise are no different. The advertisement conveys that the bottles are more environmentally beneficial overall because of the source reduction. To substantiate this claim, the marketer likely can analyze the impacts of the source reduction without evaluating environmental impacts throughout the packaging's life cycle. If, however, manufacturing the new bottles significantly alters environmental attributes earlier or later in the bottles' life cycle, *i.e.*, manufacturing the bottles requires more energy or a different kind of plastic, then a more comprehensive analysis may be appropriate.

§ 260.5 Carbon offsets.

(a) Given the complexities of carbon offsets, sellers should employ competent and reliable scientific and accounting methods to properly quantify claimed emission reductions and to ensure that they do not sell the same reduction more than one time.

(b) It is deceptive to misrepresent, directly or by implication, that a carbon offset represents emission reductions that have already occurred or will occur in the immediate future. To avoid deception, marketers should clearly and prominently disclose if the carbon offset represents emission reductions that will not occur for two years or longer.

(c) It is deceptive to claim, directly or by implication, that a carbon offset represents an emission reduction if the reduction, or the activity that caused the reduction, was required by law.

Example 1: On its Web site, an online travel agency invites consumers to purchase offsets to "neutralize the carbon emissions from your flight." The proceeds from the offset sales fund future projects that will not reduce greenhouse gas emissions for two years. The claim likely conveys that the emission reductions either already have occurred or will occur in the near future. Therefore, the advertisement is deceptive. It would not be deceptive if the agency's Web site stated "Offset the carbon emissions from your flight by funding new projects that will begin reducing emissions in two years."

Example 2: An offset provider claims that its product "will offset your own 'dirty' driving habits." The offset is based on methane capture at a landfill facility. State law requires this facility to capture all methane emitted from the landfill. The claim is deceptive because the emission reduction would have occurred regardless of whether consumers purchased the offsets.

§ 260.6 Certifications and seals of approval.

(a) It is deceptive to misrepresent, directly or by implication, that a product, package, or service has been endorsed or certified by an independent third party.

(b) A marketer's use of the name, logo, or seal of approval of a third-party certifier or organization may be an endorsement, which should meet the criteria for endorsements provided in the FTC's Endorsement Guides, 16 CFR part 255, including Definitions (§ 255.0), General Considerations (§ 255.1), Expert Endorsements (§ 255.3), Endorsements by Organizations (§ 255.4), and Disclosure of Material Connections (§ 255.5).[44]

(c) Third-party certification does not eliminate a marketer's obligation to ensure that it has substantiation for all claims reasonably communicated by the certification.

(d) A marketer's use of an environmental certification or seal of approval likely conveys that the product offers a general environmental benefit (*see* § 260.4) if the certification or seal does not convey the basis for the certification or seal, either through the name or some other means. Because it is highly unlikely that marketers can substantiate general environmental benefit claims, marketers should not use environmental certifications or seals that do not convey the basis for the certification.

(e) Marketers can qualify general environmental benefit claims conveyed by environmental certifications and seals of approval to prevent deception about the nature of the environmental benefit being asserted. To avoid deception, marketers should use clear and prominent qualifying language that clearly conveys that the certification or seal refers only to specific and limited benefits.

Example 1: An advertisement for paint features a "GreenLogo" seal and the statement "GreenLogo for Environmental Excellence." This advertisement likely conveys that: (1) the GreenLogo seal is awarded by an independent, third-party certifier with appropriate expertise in evaluating the environmental attributes of paint; and (2) the product has far-reaching environmental benefits. If the paint manufacturer awarded the seal to its own product, and no independent, third-party certifier objectively evaluated the paint using independent standards, the claim would be deceptive. The claim would not be deceptive if the marketer accompanied the seal with clear and prominent language: (1) indicating that the marketer awarded the GreenLogo seal to its own product; and (2) clearly conveying that the award refers only to specific and limited benefits.

Example 2: A manufacturer advertises its product as "certified by the American Institute of Degradable Materials." Because the advertisement does not mention that the American Institute of Degradable Materials ("AIDM") is an industry trade association, the certification likely conveys that it was awarded by an independent certifier. To be certified, marketers must meet standards that have been developed and maintained by a voluntary consensus standard body.[45] An independent auditor applies these standards objectively. This advertisement likely is not deceptive if the manufacturer complies with § 260.8 of the Guides (Degradable Claims) because the certification is based on independently-developed and -maintained standards and an independent auditor applies the standards objectively.

---

[44] The examples in this section assume that the certifiers' endorsements meet the criteria provided in the Expert Endorsements (§ 255.3) and Endorsements by Organizations (§ 255.4) sections of the Endorsement Guides.

[45] Voluntary consensus standard bodies are "organizations which plan, develop, establish, or coordinate voluntary consensus standards using agreed-upon procedures. * * * A voluntary consensus standards body is defined by the following attributes: (i) Openness, (ii) balance of interest, (iii) due process, (iv) an appeals process, (v) consensus, which is defined as general agreement, but not necessarily unanimity, and includes a process for attempting to resolve objections by interested parties, as long as all comments have been fairly considered, each objector is advised of the disposition of his or her objection(s) and the reasons why, and the consensus members are given an opportunity to change their votes after reviewing the comments." Memorandum for Heads of Executive Departments and Agencies on Federal Participation in the Development and Use of Voluntary Consensus Assessment Activities, February 10, 1998, Circular No. A–119 Revised, Office of Management and Budget at *http://www.whitehouse.gov/omb/circulars_a119*.

Example 3: A product features a seal of approval from "The Forest Products Industry Association," an industry certifier with appropriate expertise in evaluating the environmental attributes of paper products. Because it is clear from the certifier's name that the product has been certified by an industry certifier, the certification likely does not convey that it was awarded by an independent certifier. The use of the seal likely is not deceptive provided that the advertisement does not imply other deceptive claims.

Example 4: A marketer's package features a seal of approval with the text "Certified Non-Toxic." The seal is awarded by a certifier with appropriate expertise in evaluating ingredient safety and potential toxicity. It applies standards developed by a voluntary consensus standard body. Although non-industry members comprise a majority of the certifier's board, an industry veto could override any proposed changes to the standards. This certification likely conveys that the product is certified by an independent organization. This claim would be deceptive because industry members can veto any proposed changes to the standards.

Example 5: A marketer's industry sales brochure for overhead lighting features a seal with the text "EcoFriendly Building Association" to show that the marketer is a member of that organization. Although the lighting manufacturer is, in fact, a member, this association has not evaluated the environmental attributes of the marketer's product. This advertisement would be deceptive because it likely conveys that the EcoFriendly Building Association evaluated the product through testing or other objective standards. It also is likely to convey that the lighting has far-reaching environmental benefits. The use of the seal would not be deceptive if the manufacturer accompanies it with clear and prominent qualifying language: (1) indicating that the seal refers to the company's membership only and that the association did not evaluate the product's environmental attributes; and (2) limiting the general environmental benefit representations, both express and implied, to the particular product attributes for which the marketer has substantiation. For example, the marketer could state: "Although we are a member of the EcoFriendly Building Association, it has not evaluated this product. Our lighting is made from 100 percent recycled metal and uses energy efficient LED technology."

Example 6: A product label contains an environmental seal, either in the form of a globe icon or a globe icon with the text "EarthSmart." EarthSmart is an independent, third-party certifier with appropriate expertise in evaluating chemical emissions of products. While the marketer meets EarthSmart's standards for reduced chemical emissions during product usage, the product has no other specific environmental benefits. Either seal likely conveys that the product has far-reaching environmental benefits, and that EarthSmart certified the product for all of these benefits. If the marketer cannot substantiate these claims, the use of the seal would be deceptive. The seal would not be deceptive if the marketer accompanied it with clear and prominent language clearly conveying that the certification refers only to specific and limited benefits. For example, the marketer could state next to the globe icon: "EarthSmart certifies that this product meets EarthSmart standards for reduced chemical emissions during product usage." Alternatively, the claim would not be deceptive if the EarthSmart environmental seal itself stated: "EarthSmart Certified for reduced chemical emissions during product usage."

Example 7: A one-quart bottle of window cleaner features a seal with the text "Environment Approved," granted by an independent, third-party certifier with appropriate expertise. The certifier granted the seal after evaluating 35 environmental attributes. This seal likely conveys that the product has far-reaching environmental benefits and that Environment Approved certified the product for all of these benefits and therefore is likely deceptive. The seal would likely not be deceptive if the marketer accompanied it with clear and prominent language clearly conveying that the seal refers only to specific and limited benefits. For example, the seal could state: "Virtually all products impact the environment. For details on which attributes we evaluated, go to [a Web site that discusses this product]." The referenced Web page provides a detailed summary of the examined environmental attributes. A reference to a Web site is appropriate because the additional information provided on the Web site is not necessary to prevent the advertisement from being misleading. As always, the marketer also should ensure that the advertisement does not imply other deceptive claims, and that the certifier's criteria are sufficiently rigorous to substantiate all material claims reasonably communicated by the certification.

Example 8: Great Paper Company sells photocopy paper with packaging that has a seal of approval from the No Chlorine Products Association, a non-profit third-party association. Great Paper Company paid the No Chlorine Products Association a reasonable fee for the certification. Consumers would reasonably expect that marketers have to pay for certification. Therefore, there are no material connections between Great Paper Company and the No Chlorine Products Association. The claim would not be deceptive.

§ 260.7 Compostable Claims.

(a) It is deceptive to misrepresent, directly or by implication, that a product or package is compostable.

(b) A marketer claiming that an item is compostable should have competent and reliable scientific evidence that all the materials in the item will break down into, or otherwise become part of, usable compost (e.g., soil-conditioning material, mulch) in a safe and timely manner (*i.e.*, in approximately the same time as the materials with which it is composted) in an appropriate composting facility, or in a home compost pile or device.

(c) A marketer should clearly and prominently qualify compostable claims to the extent necessary to avoid deception if:

(1) The item cannot be composted safely or in a timely manner in a home compost pile or device; or

(2) The claim misleads reasonable consumers about the environmental benefit provided when the item is disposed of in a landfill.

(d) To avoid deception about the limited availability of municipal or institutional composting facilities, a marketer should clearly and prominently qualify compostable claims if such facilities are not available to a substantial majority of consumers or communities where the item is sold.

Example 1: A manufacturer indicates that its unbleached coffee filter is compostable. The unqualified claim is not deceptive, provided the manufacturer has substantiation that the filter can be converted safely to usable compost in a timely manner in a home compost pile or device. If so, the extent of local municipal or institutional composting facilities is irrelevant.

Example 2: A garden center sells grass clipping bags labeled as "Compostable in California Municipal Yard Trimmings Composting Facilities." When the bags break down, however, they release toxins into the compost. The claim is deceptive if the presence of these toxins prevents the compost from being usable.

Example 3: A manufacturer makes an unqualified claim that its package is compostable. Although municipal or institutional composting facilities exist where the product is sold, the package will not break down into usable compost in a home compost pile or device. To avoid deception, the manufacturer should clearly and prominently disclose that the package is not suitable for home composting.

Example 4: Nationally marketed lawn and leaf bags state "compostable" on each bag. The bags also feature text disclosing that the bag is not designed for use in home compost piles. Yard trimmings programs in many communities compost these bags, but such programs are not available to a substantial majority of consumers or communities where the bag is sold. The claim is deceptive because it likely conveys that composting facilities are available to a substantial majority of consumers or communities. To avoid deception, the marketer should clearly and prominently indicate the limited availability of such programs. A marketer could state "Appropriate facilities may not exist in your area," or provide the approximate percentage of communities or consumers for which such programs are available.

Example 5: A manufacturer sells a disposable diaper that states, "This diaper can be composted if your community is one of the 50 that have composting facilities." The claim is not deceptive if composting facilities are available as claimed and the manufacturer has substantiation that the diaper can be converted safely to usable compost in solid waste composting facilities.

Example 6: A manufacturer markets yard trimmings bags only to consumers residing in particular geographic areas served by county yard trimmings composting programs. The bags meet specifications for these programs and are labeled, "Compostable Yard Trimmings Bag for County Composting Programs." The claim is not deceptive. Because the bags are compostable where they are sold, a qualification is not needed to indicate the limited availability of composting facilities.

§ 260.8 Degradable claims.

(a) It is deceptive to misrepresent, directly or by implication, that a product or package is degradable, biodegradable, oxo-degradable, oxo-biodegradable, or photodegradable. The following guidance for degradable claims also applies to biodegradable, oxo-degradable, oxo-biodegradable, and photodegradable claims.

(b) A marketer making an unqualified degradable claim should have competent and reliable scientific evidence that the entire item will completely break down and return to nature (*i.e.*, decompose into elements found in nature) within a reasonably short period of time after customary disposal.

(c) It is deceptive to make an unqualified degradable claim for items entering the solid waste stream if the items do not completely decompose within one year after customary disposal. Unqualified degradable claims for items that are customarily disposed in landfills, incinerators, and recycling facilities are deceptive because these locations do not present conditions in which complete decomposition will occur within one year.

(d) Degradable claims should be qualified clearly and prominently to the extent necessary to avoid deception about:

(1) The product's or package's ability to degrade in the environment where it is customarily disposed; and

(2) The rate and extent of degradation.

Example 1: A marketer advertises its trash bags using an unqualified "degradable" claim. The marketer relies on soil burial tests to show that the product will decompose in the presence of water and oxygen. Consumers, however, place trash bags into the solid waste stream, which customarily terminates in incineration facilities or landfills where they will not degrade within one year. The claim is, therefore, deceptive.

Example 2: A marketer advertises a commercial agricultural plastic mulch film with the claim "Photodegradable," and clearly and prominently qualifies the term with the phrase "Will break down into small pieces if left uncovered in sunlight." The advertiser possesses competent and reliable scientific evidence that within one year, the product will break down, after being exposed to sunlight, into sufficiently small pieces to become part of the soil. Thus, the qualified claim is not deceptive. Because the claim is qualified to indicate the limited extent of breakdown, the advertiser need not meet the consumer expectations for an unqualified photodegradable claim, *i.e.*, that the product will not only break down, but also will decompose into elements found in nature.

Example 3: A marketer advertises its shampoo as "biodegradable" without qualification. The advertisement makes clear that only the shampoo, and not the bottle, is biodegradable. The marketer has competent and reliable scientific evidence demonstrating that the shampoo, which is customarily disposed in sewage systems, will break down and decompose into elements found in nature in a reasonably short period of time in the sewage system environment. Therefore, the claim is not deceptive.

Example 4: A plastic six-pack ring carrier is marked with a small diamond. Several state laws require that the carriers be marked with this symbol to indicate that they meet certain degradability standards if the carriers are littered. The use of the diamond by itself, in an inconspicuous location, does not constitute a degradable claim. Consumers are unlikely to interpret an inconspicuous diamond symbol, without more, as an unqualified photodegradable claim.[46]

Example 5: A fiber pot containing a plant is labeled "biodegradable." The pot is customarily buried in the soil along with the plant. Once buried, the pot fully decomposes during the growing season, allowing the roots of the plant to grow into the surrounding soil. The unqualified claim is not deceptive.

§ 260.9 Free-of claims.

(a) It is deceptive to misrepresent, directly or by implication, that a product, package, or service is free of, or does not contain or use, a substance. Such claims should be clearly and prominently qualified to the extent necessary to avoid deception.

(b) A truthful claim that a product, package, or service is free of, or does not contain or use, a substance may nevertheless be deceptive if:

(1) The product, package, or service contains or uses substances that pose the same or similar environmental risks as the substance that is not present; or

(2) The substance has not been associated with the product category.

(c) Depending on the context, a free-of or does-not-contain claim is appropriate even for a product, package, or service that contains or uses a trace amount of a substance if:

(1) The level of the specified substance is no more than that which would be found as an acknowledged trace contaminant or background level[47];

(2) The substance's presence does not cause material harm that consumers typically associate with that substance; and

[46] The Guides' treatment of unqualified degradable claims is intended to help prevent deception and is not intended to establish performance standards to ensure the degradability of products when littered.

[47] "Trace contaminant" and "background level" are imprecise terms, although allowable manufacturing "trace contaminants" may be defined according to the product area concerned. What constitutes a trace amount or background level depends on the substance at issue, and requires a case-by-case analysis.

(3) The substance has not been added intentionally to the product.

Example 1: A package of t-shirts is labeled "Shirts made with a chlorine-free bleaching process." The shirts, however, are bleached with a process that releases a reduced, but still significant, amount of the same harmful byproducts associated with chlorine bleaching. The claim overstates the product's benefits because reasonable consumers likely would interpret it to mean that the product's manufacture does not cause any of the environmental risks posed by chlorine bleaching. A substantiated claim, however, that the shirts were "bleached with a process that releases 50% less of the harmful byproducts associated with chlorine bleaching" would not be deceptive.

Example 2: A manufacturer advertises its insulation as "formaldehyde free." Although the manufacturer does not use formaldehyde as a binding agent to produce the insulation, tests show that the insulation still emits trace amounts of formaldehyde. The seller has substantiation that formaldehyde is present in trace amounts in virtually all indoor and (to a lesser extent) outdoor environments and that its insulation emits less formaldehyde than is typically present in outdoor environments. Further, the seller has substantiation that the trace amounts of formaldehyde emitted by the insulation do not cause material harm that consumers typically associate with formaldehyde. In this context, the trace levels of formaldehyde emissions likely are inconsequential to consumers. Therefore, the seller's free-of claim would not be deceptive.

§ 260.10 Non-toxic claims.

(a) It is deceptive to misrepresent, directly or by implication, that a product, package, or service is non-toxic. Non-toxic claims should be clearly and prominently qualified to the extent necessary to avoid deception.

(b) A non-toxic claim likely conveys that a product, package, or service is non-toxic both for humans and for the environment generally. Therefore, marketers making non-toxic claims should have competent and reliable scientific evidence that the product, package, or service is non-toxic for humans and for the environment or should clearly and prominently qualify their claims to avoid deception.

Example: A marketer advertises a cleaning product as "essentially non-toxic" and "practically non-toxic." The advertisement likely conveys that the product does not pose any risk to humans or the environment, including household pets. If the cleaning product poses no risk to humans but is toxic to the environment, the claims would be deceptive.

§ 260.11 Ozone-safe and ozone-friendly claims.

It is deceptive to misrepresent, directly or by implication, that a product, package, or service is safe for, or friendly to, the ozone layer or the atmosphere.

Example 1: A product is labeled "ozone-friendly." The claim is deceptive if the product contains any ozone-depleting substance, including those substances listed as Class I or Class II chemicals in Title VI of the Clean Air Act Amendments of 1990, Public Law. 101–549, and others subsequently designated by EPA as ozone-depleting substances. These chemicals include chlorofluorocarbons (CFCs), halons, carbon tetrachloride, 1,1,1-trichloroethane, methyl bromide, hydrobromofluorocarbons, and hydrochlorofluorocarbons (HCFCs).

Example 2: An aerosol air freshener is labeled "ozone-friendly." Some of the product's ingredients are volatile organic compounds (VOCs) that may cause smog by contributing to ground-level ozone formation. The claim likely conveys that the product is safe for the atmosphere as a whole, and, therefore, is deceptive.

§ 260.12 Recyclable claims.

(a) It is deceptive to misrepresent, directly or by implication, that a product or package is recyclable. A product or package should not be marketed as recyclable unless it can be collected, separated, or otherwise recovered from the waste stream through an established recycling program for reuse or use in manufacturing or assembling another item.

(b) Marketers should clearly and prominently qualify recyclable claims to the extent necessary to avoid deception about the availability of recycling programs and collection sites to consumers.

(1) When recycling facilities are available to a substantial majority of consumers or communities where the item is sold, marketers can make unqualified recyclable claims. The term "substantial majority," as used in this context, means at least 60 percent.

(2) When recycling facilities are available to less than a substantial majority of consumers or communities where the item is sold, marketers

should qualify all recyclable claims. Marketers may always qualify recyclable claims by stating the percentage of consumers or communities that have access to facilities that recycle the item. Alternatively, marketers may use qualifications that vary in strength depending on facility availability. The lower the level of access to an appropriate facility is, the more strongly the marketer should emphasize the limited availability of recycling for the product. For example, if recycling facilities are available to slightly less than a substantial majority of consumers or communities where the item is sold, a marketer may qualify a recyclable claim by stating: "This product [package] may not be recyclable in your area," or "Recycling facilities for this product [package] may not exist in your area." If recycling facilities are available only to a few consumers, marketers should use stronger clarifications. For example, a marketer in this situation may qualify its recyclable claim by stating: "This product [package] is recyclable only in the few communities that have appropriate recycling facilities."

(c) Marketers can make unqualified recyclable claims for a product or package if the entire product or package, excluding minor incidental components, is recyclable. For items that are partially made of recyclable components, marketers should clearly and prominently qualify the recyclable claim to avoid deception about which portions are recyclable.

(d) If any component significantly limits the ability to recycle the item, any recyclable claim would be deceptive. An item that is made from recyclable material, but, because of its shape, size, or some other attribute, is not accepted in recycling programs, should not be marketed as recyclable.[48]

Example 1: A packaged product is labeled with an unqualified claim, "recyclable." It is unclear from the type of product and other context whether the claim refers to the product or its package. The unqualified claim likely conveys that both the product and its packaging, except for minor, incidental components, can be recycled. Unless the manufacturer has substantiation for both messages, it should clearly and prominently qualify the claim to indicate which portions are recyclable.

Example 2: A nationally marketed plastic yogurt container displays the Resin Identification Code (RIC)[49] (which consists of a design of arrows in a triangular shape containing a number in the center and an abbreviation identifying the component plastic resin) on the front label of the container, in close proximity to the product name and logo. This conspicuous use of the RIC constitutes a recyclable claim. Unless recycling facilities for this container are available to a substantial majority of consumers or communities, the manufacturer should qualify the claim to disclose the limited availability of recycling programs. If the manufacturer places the RIC, without more, in an inconspicuous location on the container (e.g., embedded in the bottom of the container), it would not constitute a recyclable claim.

Example 3: A container can be burned in incinerator facilities to produce heat and power. It cannot, however, be recycled into another product or package. Any claim that the container is recyclable would be deceptive.

Example 4: A paperboard package is marketed nationally and labeled either "Recyclable where facilities exist" or "Recyclable B Check to see if recycling facilities exist in your area." Recycling programs for these packages are available to some consumers, but not available to a substantial majority of consumers nationwide. Both claims are deceptive because they do not adequately disclose the limited availability of recycling programs. To avoid deception, the marketer should use a clearer qualification, such as one suggested in § 260.12(b)(2).

Example 5: Foam polystyrene cups are advertised as "Recyclable in the few communities with facilities for foam polystyrene cups." A half-dozen major metropolitan areas have established collection sites for recycling those cups. The claim is not deceptive because it clearly discloses the limited availability of recycling programs.

Example 6: A package is labeled "Includes some recyclable material." The package is composed of four layers of different materials, bonded together. One of the layers is made from recyclable material, but the others are not. While programs for recycling the 25 percent of the package that consists of recyclable material are available to a substantial majority of consumers, only a few of

[48] Batteries labeled in accordance with the Mercury-Containing and Rechargeable Battery Management Act, 42 U.S.C. 14322(b), are deemed to be in compliance with these Guides.

[49] The RIC, formerly known as the Society of the Plastics Industry, Inc. (SPI) code, is now covered by ASTM D 7611.

those programs have the capability to separate the recyclable layer from the non-recyclable layers. The claim is deceptive for two reasons. First, it does not specify the portion of the product that is recyclable. Second, it does not disclose the limited availability of facilities that can process multi-layer products or materials. An appropriately qualified claim would be "25 percent of the material in this package is recyclable in the few communities that can process multi-layer products."

Example 7: A product container is labeled "recyclable." The marketer advertises and distributes the product only in Missouri. Collection sites for recycling the container are available to a substantial majority of Missouri residents but are not yet available nationally. Because programs are available to a substantial majority of consumers where the product is sold, the unqualified claim is not deceptive.

Example 8: A manufacturer of one-time use cameras, with dealers in a substantial majority of communities, operates a take-back program that collects those cameras through all of its dealers. The manufacturer reconditions the cameras for resale and labels them "Recyclable through our dealership network." This claim is not deceptive, even though the cameras are not recyclable through conventional curbside or drop-off recycling programs.

Example 9: A manufacturer advertises its toner cartridges for computer printers as "Recyclable. Contact your local dealer for details." Although all of the company's dealers recycle cartridges, the dealers are not located in a substantial majority of communities where cartridges are sold. Therefore, the claim is deceptive. The manufacturer should qualify its claim consistent with § 260.11(b)(2).

Example 10: An aluminum can is labeled "Please Recycle." This statement likely conveys that the can is recyclable. If collection sites for recycling these cans are available to a substantial majority of consumers or communities, the marketer does not need to qualify the claim.

§ 260.13 Recycled content claims.

(a) It is deceptive to misrepresent, directly or by implication, that a product or package is made of recycled content. Recycled content includes recycled raw material, as well as used,[50] reconditioned, and re-manufactured components.

(b) It is deceptive to represent, directly or by implication, that an item contains recycled content unless it is composed of materials that have been recovered or otherwise diverted from the waste stream, either during the manufacturing process (pre-consumer), or after consumer use (post-consumer). If the source of recycled content includes pre-consumer material, the advertiser should have substantiation that the pre-consumer material would otherwise have entered the waste stream. Recycled content claims may—but do not have to—distinguish between pre-consumer and post-consumer materials. Where a marketer distinguishes between pre-consumer and post-consumer materials, it should have substantiation for any express or implied claim about the percentage of pre-consumer or post-consumer content in an item.

(c) Marketers can make unqualified claims of recycled content if the entire product or package, excluding minor, incidental components, is made from recycled material. For items that are partially made of recycled material, the marketer should clearly and prominently qualify the claim to avoid deception about the amount or percentage, by weight, of recycled content in the finished product or package.

(d) For products that contain used, reconditioned, or re-manufactured components, the marketer should clearly and prominently qualify the recycled content claim to avoid deception about the nature of such components. No such qualification is necessary where it is clear to reasonable consumers from context that a product's recycled content consists of used, reconditioned, or re-manufactured components.

Example 1: A manufacturer collects spilled raw material and scraps from the original manufacturing process. After a minimal amount of reprocessing, the manufacturer combines the spills and scraps with virgin material for use in production of the same product. A recycled content claim is deceptive since the spills and scraps are normally reused by industry within the original manufacturing process and would not normally have entered the waste stream.

Example 2: Fifty percent of a greeting card's fiber weight is composed from paper that was diverted from the waste stream. Of this material, 30% is post-consumer and 20% is pre-consumer. It would not be deceptive if the marketer claimed that the card either

[50] The term "used" refers to parts that are not new and that have not undergone any re-manufacturing or reconditioning.

"contains 50% recycled fiber" or "contains 50% total recycled fiber, including 30% post-consumer fiber."

Example 3: A paperboard package with 20% recycled fiber by weight is labeled "20% post-consumer recycled fiber." The recycled content was composed of overrun newspaper stock never sold to customers. Because the newspapers never reached consumers, the claim is deceptive.

Example 4: A product in a multi-component package, such as a paperboard box in a shrink-wrapped plastic cover, indicates that it has recycled packaging. The paperboard box is made entirely of recycled material, but the plastic cover is not. The claim is deceptive because, without qualification, it suggests that both components are recycled. A claim limited to the paperboard box would not be deceptive.

Example 5: A manufacturer makes a package from laminated layers of foil, plastic, and paper, although the layers are indistinguishable to consumers. The label claims that "one of the three layers of this package is made of recycled plastic." The plastic layer is made entirely of recycled plastic. The claim is not deceptive, provided the recycled plastic layer constitutes a significant component of the entire package.

Example 6: A frozen dinner package is composed of a plastic tray inside a cardboard box. It states "package made from 30% recycled material." Each packaging component is one-half the weight of the total package. The box is 20% recycled content by weight, while the plastic tray is 40% recycled content by weight. The claim is not deceptive, since the average amount of recycled material is 30%.

Example 7: A manufacturer labels a paper greeting card "50% recycled fiber." The manufacturer purchases paper stock from several sources, and the amount of recycled fiber in the stock provided by each source varies. If the 50% figure is based on the annual weighted average of recycled material purchased from the sources after accounting for fiber loss during the papermaking production process, the claim is not deceptive.

Example 8: A packaged food product is labeled with a three-chasing-arrows symbol (a Möbius loop) without explanation. By itself, the symbol likely conveys that the packaging is both recyclable and made entirely from recycled material. Unless the marketer has substantiation for both messages, the claim should be qualified. The claim may need to be further qualified, to the extent necessary, to disclose the limited availability of recycling programs and/or the percentage of recycled content used to make the package.

Example 9: In an office supply catalog, a manufacturer advertises its printer toner cartridges "65% recycled." The cartridges contain 25% recycled raw materials and 40% reconditioned parts. The claim is deceptive because reasonable consumers likely would not know or expect that a cartridge's recycled content consists of reconditioned parts. It would not be deceptive if the manufacturer claimed "65% recycled content; including 40% from reconditioned parts."

Example 10: A store sells both new and used sporting goods. One of the items for sale in the store is a baseball helmet that, although used, is no different in appearance than a brand new item. The helmet bears an unqualified "Recycled" label. This claim is deceptive because reasonable consumers likely would believe that the helmet is made of recycled raw materials, when it is, in fact, a used item. An acceptable claim would bear a disclosure clearly and prominently stating that the helmet is used.

Example 11: An automotive dealer, automobile recycler, or other qualified entity recovers a serviceable engine from a wrecked vehicle. Without repairing, rebuilding, remanufacturing, or in any way altering the engine or its components, the dealer attaches a "Recycled" label to the engine, and offers it for sale in its used auto parts store. In this situation, an unqualified recycled content claim likely is not deceptive because reasonable consumers in the automotive context likely would understand that the engine is used and has not undergone any rebuilding.

Example 12: An automobile parts dealer, automobile recycler, or other qualified entity purchases a transmission that has been recovered from a salvaged or end-of-life vehicle. Eighty-five percent of the transmission, by weight, was rebuilt and 15% constitutes new materials. After rebuilding[51] the transmission in accordance with industry practices, the dealer packages it for resale in a box labeled "Rebuilt Transmission," or "Rebuilt Transmission (85% recycled content from rebuilt parts)," or "Recycled Transmission (85% recycled content from rebuilt parts)." Given consumer perception in the automotive context, these claims are not deceptive.

§ 260.14 Refillable claims.

It is deceptive to misrepresent, directly or by implication, that a package is refillable. A marketer should not make an unqualified refillable claim

[51] The term "rebuilding" means that the dealer dismantled and reconstructed the transmission as necessary, cleaned all of its internal and external parts and eliminated rust and corrosion, restored all impaired, defective or substantially worn parts to a sound condition (or replaced them if necessary), and performed any operations required to put the transmission in sound working condition.

unless the marketer provides the means for refilling the package. The marketer may either provide a system for the collection and refill of the package, or offer for sale a product that consumers can purchase to refill the original package.

Example 1: A container is labeled "refillable three times." The manufacturer has the capability to refill returned containers and can show that the container will withstand being refilled at least three times. The manufacturer, however, has established no collection program. The unqualified claim is deceptive because there is no means to return the container to the manufacturer for refill.

Example 2: A small bottle of fabric softener states that it is in a "handy refillable container." In the same market area, the manufacturer also sells a large-sized bottle that consumers use to refill the smaller bottles. The claim is not deceptive because there is a reasonable means for the consumer to refill the smaller container.

§ 260.15 Renewable energy claims.

(a) It is deceptive to misrepresent, directly or by implication, that a product or package is made with renewable energy or that a service uses renewable energy. A marketer should not make unqualified renewable energy claims, directly or by implication, if fossil fuel, or electricity derived from fossil fuel, is used to manufacture any part of the advertised item or is used to power any part of the advertised service, unless the marketer has matched such non-renewable energy use with renewable energy certificates.

(b) Research suggests that reasonable consumers may interpret renewable energy claims differently than marketers may intend. Unless marketers have substantiation for all their express and reasonably implied claims, they should clearly and prominently qualify their renewable energy claims. For instance, marketers may minimize the risk of deception by specifying the source of the renewable energy (e.g., wind or solar energy).

(c) It is deceptive to make an unqualified "made with renewable energy" claim unless all, or virtually all, of the significant manufacturing processes involved in making the product or package are powered with renewable energy or non-renewable energy matched by renewable energy certificates. When this is not the case, marketers should clearly and prominently specify the percentage of renewable energy that powered the significant manufacturing processes involved in making the product or package.

(d) If a marketer generates renewable electricity but sells renewable energy certificates for all of that electricity, it would be deceptive for the marketer to represent, directly or by implication, that it uses renewable energy.

Example 1: A marketer advertises its clothing line as "made with wind power." The marketer buys wind energy for 50% of the energy it uses to make the clothing in its line. The marketer's claim is deceptive because reasonable consumers likely interpret the claim to mean that the power was composed entirely of renewable energy. If the marketer stated, "We purchase wind energy for half of our manufacturing facilities," the claim would not be deceptive.

Example 2: A company purchases renewable energy from a portfolio of sources that includes a mix of solar, wind, and other renewable energy sources in combinations and proportions that vary over time. The company uses renewable energy from that portfolio to power all of the significant manufacturing processes involved in making its product. The company advertises its product as "made with renewable energy." The claim would not be deceptive if the marketer clearly and prominently disclosed all renewable energy sources. Alternatively, the claim would not be deceptive if the marketer clearly and prominently stated, "made from a mix of renewable energy sources," and specified the renewable source that makes up the greatest percentage of the portfolio. The company may calculate which renewable energy source makes up the greatest percentage of the portfolio on an annual basis.

Example 3: An automobile company uses 100% non-renewable energy to produce its cars. The company purchases renewable energy certificates to match the non-renewable energy that powers all of the significant manufacturing processes for the seats, but no other parts, of its cars. If the company states, "The seats of our cars are made with renewable energy," the claim would not be deceptive, as long as the company clearly and prominently qualifies the claim such as by specifying the renewable energy source.

Example 4: A company uses 100% non-renewable energy to manufacture all parts of its product, but powers the assembly process entirely with renewable energy. If the marketer advertised its product as "assembled using renewable energy," the claim would not be deceptive.

Example 5: A toy manufacturer places solar panels on the roof of its plant to generate power, and advertises that its plant is "100%

solar-powered." The manufacturer, however, sells renewable energy certificates based on the renewable attributes of all the power it generates. Even if the manufacturer uses the electricity generated by the solar panels, it has, by selling renewable energy certificates, transferred the right to characterize that electricity as renewable. The manufacturer's claim is therefore deceptive. It also would be deceptive for this manufacturer to advertise that it "hosts" a renewable power facility because reasonable consumers likely interpret this claim to mean that the manufacturer uses renewable energy. It would not be deceptive, however, for the manufacturer to advertise, "We generate renewable energy, but sell all of it to others."

§ 260.16 Renewable materials claims.

(a) It is deceptive to misrepresent, directly or by implication, that a product or package is made with renewable materials.

(b) Research suggests that reasonable consumers may interpret renewable materials claims differently than marketers may intend. Unless marketers have substantiation for all their express and reasonably implied claims, they should clearly and prominently qualify their renewable materials claims. For example, marketers may minimize the risk of unintended implied claims by identifying the material used and explaining why the material is renewable.

(c) Marketers should also qualify any "made with renewable materials" claim unless the product or package (excluding minor, incidental components) is made entirely with renewable materials.

Example 1: A marketer makes the unqualified claim that its flooring is "made with renewable materials." Reasonable consumers likely interpret this claim to mean that the flooring also is made with recycled content, recyclable, and biodegradable. Unless the marketer has substantiation for these implied claims, the unqualified "made with renewable materials" claim is deceptive. The marketer could qualify the claim by stating, clearly and prominently, "Our flooring is made from 100 percent bamboo, which grows at the same rate, or faster, than we use it." The marketer still is responsible for substantiating all remaining express and reasonably implied claims.

Example 2: A marketer's packaging states that "Our packaging is made from 50% plant-based renewable materials. Because we turn fast-growing plants into bio-plastics, only half of our product is made from petroleum-based materials." By identifying the material used and explaining why the material is renewable, the marketer has minimized the risk of unintended claims that the product is made with recycled content, recyclable, and biodegradable. The marketer has adequately qualified the amount of renewable materials in the product.

§ 260.17 Source reduction claims.

It is deceptive to misrepresent, directly or by implication, that a product or package has been reduced or is lower in weight, volume, or toxicity. Marketers should clearly and prominently qualify source reduction claims to the extent necessary to avoid deception about the amount of the source reduction and the basis for any comparison.

Example: An advertiser claims that disposal of its product generates "10% less waste." The marketer does not accompany this claim with a general environmental benefit claim. Because this claim could be a comparison to the advertiser's immediately preceding product or to its competitors' products, the advertiser should have substantiation for both interpretations. Otherwise, the advertiser should clarify which comparison it intends and have substantiation for that comparison. A claim of "10% less waste than our previous product" would not be deceptive if the advertiser has substantiation that shows that the current product's disposal contributes 10% less waste by weight or volume to the solid waste stream when compared with the immediately preceding version of the product.

SUBCHAPTER C—REGULATIONS UNDER SPECIFIC ACTS OF CONGRESS

PART 300—RULES AND REGULATIONS UNDER THE WOOL PRODUCTS LABELING ACT OF 1939

AUTHORITY: 15 U.S.C. 68–68j.

SOURCE: 6 FR 3426, July 15, 1941, unless otherwise noted.

DEFINITIONS

§ 300.1 Terms defined.

(a) The term *Act* means the Wool Products Labeling Act of 1939, 15 U.S.C. 68 *et seq.*, as amended by Public Law 96–242, 94 Stat. 344, and Public Law 109–428, 120 Stat. 2913.

(b) The terms *rule, rules, regulations* and *rules and regulations* mean the rules and regulations prescribed by the Commission pursuant to the Act.

(c) The term *ornamentation* means any fibers or yarns imparting a visibly discernible pattern or design to a yarn or fabric.

(d) The term *fiber trademark* means a word or words used by a person to identify a particular fiber produced or sold by him and to distinguish it from fibers of the same generic class produced or sold by others. Such term shall not include any trademark, product mark, house mark, trade name or other name which does not identify a particular fiber.

(e) The terms *required information* or *information required* mean such information as is required to be disclosed on the required stamp, tag, label or other means of identification under the Act and regulations.

(f) The definitions of terms contained in section 2 of the Act shall be applicable also to such terms when used in rules promulgated under the Act.

(g) The term *United States* means the several States, the District of Columbia, and the territories and possessions of the United States.

(h) The terms *mail order catalog* and *mail order promotional material* mean any materials, used in the direct sale or direct offering for sale of wool products, that are disseminated to ultimate consumers in print or by electronic means, other than by broadcast, and that solicit ultimate consumers to purchase such wool products by mail, telephone, electronic mail, or some other method without examining the actual product purchased.

(i) The terms *label, labels, labeled,* and *labeling* mean the stamp, tag, label, or other means of identification, or authorized substitute therefore, required to be on or affixed to wool products by the Act or Regulations and on which the information required is to appear.

(j) The terms *invoice* and *invoice or other document* have the meaning set forth in § 303.1(h) of this chapter.

(k) The term *trimmings* has the meaning set forth in § 303.12 of this chapter.

[29 FR 6623, May 21, 1964, as amended at 45 FR 44261, July 1, 1980; 50 FR 15105, Apr. 17, 1985; 63 FR 7516, Feb. 13, 1998; 79 FR 32163, June 4, 2014]

LABELING

§ 300.2 General requirement.

Each and every wool product subject to the act shall be marked by a stamp, tag, label, or other means of identification, in conformity with the requirements of the act and the rules and regulations thereunder.

§ 300.3 Required label information.

(a) The marking of wool products under the Act shall be in the form of a stamp, tag, label or other means of identification, showing and displaying upon the product the required information legibly, conspicuously, and nondeceptively. The information required to be shown and displayed upon the product in the stamp, tag, label, or other mark of identification, shall be that which is required by the Act and the rules and regulations thereunder, including the following:

(1) The fiber content of the product specified in section 4(a)(2)(A) of the Act. The generic names and percentages by weight of the constituent fibers present in the wool product, exclusive of permissive ornamentation, shall appear on such label with any percentage of fiber or fibers designated as "other fiber" or "other fibers" as provided by section 4(a)(2)(A)(4) of the Act appearing last

(2) The maximum percentage of the total weight of the wool product of any nonfibrous loading, filling or adulterating matter as prescribed by section 4(a)(2)(B) of the Act.

(3) The name or registered identification number issued by the Commission of the manufacturer of the wool product or the name or registered identification number of one or more persons subject to section 3 of the Act with respect to such wool product.

(4) The name of the country where the wool product was processed or manufactured.

(b) In disclosing the constituent fibers in information required by the Act and regulations in this part or in any non-required information, no fiber present in the amount of less than 5 percent shall be designated by its generic name or fiber trademark but shall be designated as "other fiber," except that the percentage of wool or recycled wool shall always be stated, in accordance with section 4(a)(2)(A) of the Act. When more than one of such fibers, other than wool or recycled wool, are present in amounts of less than 5 percent, they shall be designated in the aggregate as "other fibers." Provided, however, that nothing in this section shall prevent the disclosure of any fiber present in the product which has a clearly established and definite functional significance when present in the amount stated, as for example:

"98% wool
2% nylon."

[29 FR 6623, May 21, 1964, as amended at 45 FR 44261, July 1, 1980; 50 FR 15105, Apr. 17, 1985; 63 FR 7516, Feb. 13, 1998; 79 FR 32163, June 4, 2014]

§ 300.4 Registered identification numbers.

(a) A registered identification number assigned by the Federal Trade Commission under and in accordance with the provisions of this section may be used upon the stamp, tag, label, or other mark of identification required under the Act to be affixed to a wool product, as and for the name of the person to whom such number has been assigned.

(b) Any manufacturer of a wool product or person subject to section 3 of the Act with respect to such wool product, residing in the United States, may apply to the Federal Trade Commission for a registered identification number for use by the applicant on the stamp, tag, label, or other mark of identification required under the Act.

(c) Registered identification numbers shall be used only by the person or firm to whom they are issued, and such numbers are not transferable or assignable. Registered identification numbers shall be subject to cancellation whenever any such number was procured or has been used improperly or contrary to the requirements of the Acts administered by the Federal Trade Commission, and regulations in this part, or when otherwise deemed necessary in the public interest. Registered identification numbers shall be subject to cancellation if the Commission fails to receive prompt notification of any change in name, business address, or legal business status of a person or firm to whom a registered identification number has been assigned, by application duly executed in the form and manner set out in paragraph (e) of this section, reflecting the current name, business address, and legal business status of the person or firm.

(d) Registered identification numbers assigned under this section may be used on labels required in labeling products subject to the provisions of the Fur Products Labeling Act and Textile Fiber Products Identification Act, and numbers previously assigned by the Commission under such Acts may be used as and for the required name in labeling under this Act. When so used by the person or firm to whom assigned, the use of the numbers shall be construed as identifying and binding the applicant as fully and in all respects as though assigned under the specific Act for which it is used.

(e) Requests for a registered identification number, to update information pertaining to an existing number, or to cancel an existing number shall be made through the Commission's Web site at *https://rn.ftc.gov*. Unless otherwise directed by the Commission or its designee, requests made by other means (including but not limited to email) will not be accepted and approved.

[29 FR 6623, May 21, 1964, as amended at 48 FR 12516, Mar. 25, 1983; 63 FR 7516, Feb. 13, 1998; 63 FR 71582, Dec. 28, 1998; 65 FR 75156, Dec. 1, 2000; 82 FR 43691, Sept. 19, 2017]

§ 300.5 Required label and method of affixing.

(a) A label is required to be affixed to each wool product and, where required, to its package or container in a secure manner. Such label shall be conspicuous and shall be of such durability as to remain attached to the product and its package throughout any distribution, sale, resale and until sold and delivered to the ultimate consumer.

(b) Each wool product with a neck must have a label disclosing the country of origin affixed to the inside center of the neck midway between the shoulder seams or in close proximity to another label affixed to the inside center of the neck. The fiber content and RN or name of the company may be disclosed on the same label as the country of origin or on another conspicuous and readily accessible label or labels on the inside or outside of the garment. On all other wool products, the required information shall be disclosed on a conspicuous and readily accessible label or labels on the inside or outside of the product. The country of origin disclosure must always appear on the front side of the label. Other required information may appear either on the front side or the reverse side of a label, provided that the information is conspicuous and readily accessible.

(c) In the case of hosiery products, this section does not require affixing a label to each hosiery product contained in a package if, (1) such hosiery products are intended for sale to the ultimate consumer in such package, (2) such package has affixed to it a label bearing the required information for the hosiery products contained in the package, and (3) the information on the label affixed to the package is equally applicable to each wool product contained therein.

[50 FR 15105, Apr. 17, 1985, as amended at 63 FR 7516, Feb. 13, 1998]

§ 300.6 Labels to be avoided.

Stamps, tags, labels, or other marks of identification, which are insecurely attached, or which in the course of offering the product for sale, selling, reselling, transporting, marketing, or handling incident thereto are likely to become detached, indistinct, obliterated, illegible, mutilated, inaccessible, or inconspicuous, shall not be used.

§ 300.7 English language requirement.

All words, statements and other information required by or under authority of the Act and the rules and regulations thereunder to appear on the stamp, tag, label, or other mark of identification, shall appear in the English language. If the product bears any stamp, tag, label, or mark of identification which contains any of the required information in a language other than English, all of the required information shall appear both in such other language and in the English language.

§ 300.8 Use of fiber trademark and generic names.

(a) Except where another name is required or permitted under the Act or regulations, the respective common generic name of the fiber shall be used when naming fibers in the required information; as for example, "wool," "recycled wool," "cotton," "rayon," "silk," "linen," "acetate," "nylon," "polyester."

(b) The generic names of manufactured fibers as heretofore or hereafter established in § 303.7 of this part (Rule 7) of the regulations promulgated under the Textile Fiber Products Identification Act (72 Stat. 1717; 15 U.S.C. 70) shall be used in setting forth the required fiber content information as to wool products.

(c) A non-deceptive fiber trademark may be used on a label in conjunction with the generic name of the fiber to which it relates. Where such a trademark is placed on a label in conjunction with the required information, the generic name of the fiber must appear in immediate conjunction therewith, and such trademark and generic name must appear in type or lettering of equal size and conspicuousness.

(d) Where a generic name or a fiber trademark is used on any label, whether required or non-required, a full fiber content disclosure with percentages shall be made in accordance with the Act and regulations. Where a generic name or a fiber trademark is used on any hang-tag attached to a wool product that has a label providing required information and the hang-tag provides non-required information, such as a hang-tag stating only a generic fiber name or trademark or providing information about a particular fiber's characteristics, the hang-tag need not provide a full fiber content disclosure; however, if the wool product contains any fiber other than the fiber identified by the generic fiber name or trademark, the hang-tag must disclose clearly and conspicuously that it does not provide the product's full fiber content; for example:

"This tag does not disclose the product's full fiber content." or

"See label for the product's full fiber content."

(e) If a fiber trademark is not used in the required information, but is used elsewhere on the label as nonrequired information, the generic name of the fiber shall accompany the fiber trademark in legible and conspicuous type or lettering the first time the trademark is used.

(f) No fiber trademark or generic name or word, coined word, symbol or depiction which connotes or implies any fiber trademark or generic name shall be used on any label or elsewhere on the product in such a manner as to be false, deceptive, or misleading as to fiber content, or to indicate directly or indirectly that a wool product is composed wholly or in part of a particular fiber, when such is not the case.

(g) The term *fur fiber* may be used to describe the hair or fur fiber or mixtures thereof of any animal or animals other than the sheep, lamb, Angora goat, Cashmere goat, camel, alpaca, llama and vicuna. If the name, symbol, or depiction of any animal producing the hair or fur fiber is used on the stamp, tag, label, or other means of identification applied or affixed to the wool product, the percentage by weight of such hair or fur fiber in the total fiber weight of the wool product shall be separately stated in the required fiber content disclosure: *Provided*, That no such name, symbol or depiction shall be used where such hair or fur fiber is present in the amount of less than five per centum of the total fiber weight. No such name, symbol or depiction shall be used in such a way as to imply in any manner that a wool product contains the fur or hair of an animal when the hair or fur fiber of such animal is not present in the product in the amount of five per centum or more of the total fiber weight. The following are examples of fiber content disclosures under this paragraph:

60% Wool
40% Fur Fiber
or
60% Wool
30% Fur Fiber
10% Angora Rabbit
or
100% Cashgora Hair
or
100% Paco-Vicuna Hair

[29 FR 6624, May 21, 1964, as amended at 45 FR 44261, July 1, 1980; 63 FR 7516, Feb. 13, 1998; 79 FR 32163, June 4, 2014]

§ 300.9 Abbreviations, ditto marks, and asterisks.

(a) In disclosing required information, words or terms shall not be designated by ditto marks or appear in footnotes referred to by asterisks or other symbols in required information, and shall not be abbreviated.

(b) Where the generic name of a textile fiber is required to appear in immediate conjunction with a fiber trademark, a disclosure of the generic name by means of a footnote, to which reference is made by use of an asterisk or other symbol placed next to the fiber trademark, shall not be sufficient in itself to constitute compliance with the Act and regulations.

[29 FR 6624, May 21, 1964]

§ 300.10 Disclosure of information on labels.

(a) Subject to the provisions of § 300.5(b), the required information may appear on any label or labels attached to the product, including the care label required by 16 CFR part 423, provided all the pertinent requirements of the Act and regulations in this part are met and so long as the combination of required information and non-required information is not misleading. All parts of the required information shall be set forth in such a manner as to be clearly legible, conspicuous, and readily accessible to the prospective purchaser. All parts of the required fiber content information shall appear in type or lettering of equal size and conspicuousness.

(b) Subject to the provisions of § 300.8, any non-required information or representations placed on the product shall not minimize, detract from, or conflict with required information and shall not be false, deceptive, or misleading.

[63 FR 7517, Feb. 13, 1998]

§ 300.11 Improper methods of labeling.

The stamp, tag, label, or other mark of identification required under the act, or the required information contained therein, shall not be minimized, rendered obscure or inconspicuous, or be so placed as likely to be unnoticed or unseen by purchasers and purchaser-consumers when the product is offered or displayed for sale or sold to purchasers or the consuming public, by reason of, among others:

(a) Small or indistinct type.

(b) Failure to use letters and numerals of equal size and conspicuousness in naming all fibers and percentages of such fibers as required by the act.

(c) Insufficient background contrast.

(d) Crowding, intermingling, or obscuring with designs, vignettes, or other written, printed or graphic matter.

§ 300.12 Labeling of pairs or products containing two or more units.

(a) Where a wool product consists of two or more parts, units, or items of different fiber content, a separate label containing the required information shall be affixed to each of such parts, units, or items showing the required information as to such part, unit, or item, provided that where such parts, units, or items, are marketed or handled as a single product or ensemble and are sold and delivered to the ultimate consumer as a single product or ensemble, the required information may be set out on a single label in such a manner as to separately show the fiber composition of each part, unit, or item.

(b) Where garments, wearing apparel, or other wool products are marketed or handled in pairs or ensembles of the same fiber content, only one unit of the pair or ensemble need be labeled with the required information when sold and delivered to the ultimate consumer.

(c) Where parts or units of wool products of the types referred to in paragraphs (a) and (b) of this section are sold separately, such parts or units shall be labeled with the information required by the Act and regulations.

[29 FR 6624, May 21, 1964]

§ 300.13 Name or other identification required to appear on labels.

(a) The name required by the Act to be used on labels shall be the name under which the manufacturer of the wool product or other person subject to section 3 of the Act with respect to such product is doing business. Trade names, trade marks or other names which do not constitute the name under which such person is doing business shall not be used for required identification purposes.

(b) Registered identification numbers, as provided for in § 300.4 of this part (Rule 4), may be used for identification purposes in lieu of the required name.

[29 FR 6625, May 21, 1964]

§ 300.14 Substitute label requirement.

When necessary to avoid deception, the name of any person other than the manufacturer of the product appearing on the stamp, tag, label, or other mark of identification affixed to such product shall be accompanied by appropriate words showing that the product was not manufactured by such person; as for example:

Manufactured for: ____________
Distributed by: ____________
____________ Distributors

§ 300.15 Labeling of containers or packaging of wool products.

When wool products are marketed and delivered in a package which is intended to remain unbroken and intact until after delivery to the ultimate consumer, each wool product in the package, except hosiery, and the package shall be labeled with the required information. If the package is transparent to the extent it allows for a clear reading of the required information on the wool product, the package is not required to be labeled.

[50 FR 15106, Apr. 17, 1985]

§ 300.16 Ornamentation.

(a) Where the wool product contains fiber ornamentation not exceeding 5 percent of the total fiber weight of the product and the stated percentages of fiber content of the product are exclusive of such ornamentation, the stamp, tag, label, or other means of identification shall contain a phrase or statement showing such fact; as for example:

50% Wool
25% Recycled Wool
25% Cotton
Exclusive of Ornamentation

The fiber content of such ornamentation may be disclosed where the percentage of the ornamentation in relation to the total fiber weight of the principal fiber or blend of fibers is shown; as for example:

70% Recycled Wool
30% Acetate
Exclusive of 4% Metallic Ornamentation

(b) Where the fiber ornamentation exceeds five per centum it shall be included in the statement of required percentages of fiber content.

(c) Where the ornamentation constitutes a distinct section of the product, sectional disclosure may be made in accordance with § 300.23 of this part (Rule 23).

[29 FR 6625, May 21, 1964, as amended at 45 FR 44261, July 1, 1980]

§ 300.17 Use of the term "all" or "100%."

Where the fabric or product to which the stamp, tag, label, or mark of identification applies is composed wholly of one kind of fiber, either the word *all* or the term *100%* may be used with the correct fiber name; as for example "100% Wool," "All Wool," "100% Recycled Wool," "All Recycled Wool." If any such product is composed wholly of one fiber with the exception of fiber ornamentation not exceeding 5%, such term "all" or "100%" as qualifying the name of the fiber may be used, provided it is immediately followed by the phrase "exclusive of ornamentation," or by a phrase of like meaning; such as, for example:

All Wool—Exclusive of Ornamentation

or

100% Wool—Exclusive of Ornamentation.

[45 FR 44261, July 1, 1980]

§ 300.18 Use of name of specialty fiber.

(a) In setting forth the required fiber content of a product containing any of the specialty fibers named in Section 2(b) of the Act, the name of the specialty fiber present may be used in lieu of the word "wool," provided the percentage of each named specialty fiber is given, and provided further that the name of the specialty fiber so used is qualified by the word "recycled" when the fiber referred to is "recycled wool" as defined in the Act. The following are examples of fiber content designation permitted under this rule:

55% Alpaca—45% Camel Hair
50% Recycled Camel Hair—50% Wool
60% Recycled Alpaca—40% Rayon
35% Recycled Llama—35% Recycled Vicuna—30% Cotton
60% Cotton—40% Recycled Llama.

(b) Where an election is made to use the name of a specialty fiber in lieu of the word "wool" in describing such specialty fiber, such name shall be used at any time reference is made to the specialty fiber either in required or nonrequired information. The name of the specialty fiber or any word, coined word, symbol or depiction connoting or implying the presence of such specialty fiber shall not be used in nonrequired information on the required label or on any secondary or auxiliary label attached to the wool product if the name of such specialty fiber does not appear in the required fiber content disclosure.

[29 FR 6625, May 21, 1964, as amended at 45 FR 44262, July 1, 1980]

§ 300.19 Use of terms "mohair" and "cashmere."

(a)(1) In setting forth the required fiber content of a wool product, the term "cashmere" may be used for such fiber content only if:

(i) Such fiber consists of the fine (dehaired) undercoat fibers produced by a cashmere goat (capra hircus laniger);

(ii) The average diameter of such cashmere fiber does not exceed 19 microns; and

(iii) The cashmere fibers in such wool product contain no more than 3 percent (by weight) of cashmere fibers with average diameters that exceed 30 microns.

(2) The average fiber diameter may be subject to a coefficient of variation around the mean that shall not exceed 24 percent.

(b) In setting forth the required fiber content of a product containing hair of the Angora goat known as mohair or containing cashmere (as defined in paragraph (a) of this section), the term "mohair" or "cashmere," respectively, may be used for such fiber in lieu of the word "wool," provided the respective percentage of each such fiber designated as "mohair" or "cashmere" is given, and provided further that such term "mohair" or "cashmere" where used is qualified by the word "recycled" when the fiber referred to is "recycled wool" as defined in the Act. The following are examples of fiber content designations permitted under this section:

50% mohair-50% wool
60% recycled mohair-40% cashmere
60% cotton-40% recycled cashmere

(c) Where an election is made to use the term "mohair" or "cashmere" in lieu of the term "wool" as permitted by this section, the appropriate designation of "mohair" or "cashmere" shall be used at any time reference is made to such fiber in either required or nonrequired information. The term "mohair" or "cashmere" or any words, coined words, symbols or depictions connoting or implying the presence of such fibers shall not be used in non-required information on the required label or on any secondary or auxiliary label attached to the wool product if the term "mohair" or "cashmere," as the case may be, does not appear in the required fiber content disclosure.

[79 FR 3163, June 4, 2014]

§ 300.20 Use of the terms "virgin" or "new."

The terms "virgin" or "new" as descriptive of a wool product, or any fiber or part thereof, shall not be used when the product, fiber or part so described is not composed wholly of new or virgin fiber which has never been reclaimed from any spun, woven, knitted, felted, braided, bonded, or otherwise manufactured or used product.

[79 FR 32163, June 4, 2014]

§ 300.20a Labeling of very fine wool.

A wool product stamped, tagged, labeled, or otherwise identified in the manner described below is mislabeled:

(a) "Super 80's" or "80's," if the average diameter of wool fiber of such wool product does not average 19.75 microns or finer;

(b) "Super 90's" or "90's," if the average diameter of wool fiber of such wool product does not average 19.25 microns or finer;

(c) "Super 100's" or "100's," if the average diameter of wool fiber of such wool product does not average 18.75 microns or finer;

(d) "Super 110's" or "110's," if the average diameter of wool fiber of such wool product does not average 18.25 microns or finer;

(e) "Super 120's" or "120's," if the average diameter of wool fiber of such wool product does not average 17.75 microns or finer;

(f) "Super 130's" or "130's," if the average diameter of wool fiber of such wool product does not average 17.25 microns or finer;

(g) "Super 140's" or "140's," if the average diameter of wool fiber of such wool product does not average 16.75 microns or finer;

(h) "Super 150's" or "150's," if the average diameter of wool fiber of such wool product does not average 16.25 microns or finer;

(i) "Super 160's" or "160's," if the average diameter of wool fiber of such wool product does not average 15.75 microns or finer;

(j) "Super 170's" or "170's," if the average diameter of wool fiber of such wool product does not average 15.25 microns or finer;

(k) "Super 180's" or "180's," if the average diameter of wool fiber of such wool product does not average 14.75 microns or finer;

(l) "Super 190's" or "190's," if the average diameter of wool fiber of such wool product does not average 14.25 microns or finer;

(m) "Super 200's" or "200's," if the average diameter of wool fiber of such wool product does not average 13.75 microns or finer;

(n) "Super 210's" or "210's," if the average diameter of wool fiber of such wool product does not average 13.25 microns or finer;

(o) "Super 220's" or "220's," if the average diameter of wool fiber of such wool product does not average 12.75 microns or finer;

(p) "Super 230's" or "230's," if the average diameter of wool fiber of such wool product does not average 12.25 microns or finer;

(q) "Super 240's" or "240's," if the average diameter of wool fiber of such wool product does not average 11.75 microns or finer; and

(r) "Super 250's" or "250's," if the average diameter of wool fiber of such wool product does not average 11.25 microns or finer.

[79 FR 32163, June 4, 2014]

§ 300.21 Marking of samples, swatches or specimens.

Where samples, swatches or specimens of wool products subject to the act were used to promote or effect sales of such wool products in commerce, said samples, swatches and specimens, as well as the products themselves, shall be labeled or marked to show their respective fiber contents and other information required by law.

[6 FR 3426, July 15, 1941. Redesignated at 63 FR 7517, Feb. 13, 1998]

§ 300.22 Sectional disclosure of content.

(a) *Permissive.* Where a wool product is composed of two or more sections which are of different fiber composition, the required information as to fiber content may be separated on the same label in such manner as to show the fiber composition of each section.

(b) *Mandatory.* The disclosure as above provided shall be made in all instances where such form of marking is necessary to avoid deception.

[29 FR 6626, May 21, 1964. Redesignated at 63 FR 7517, Feb. 13, 1998]

§ 300.23 Linings, paddings, stiffening, trimmings and facings.

(a) In labeling or marking garments or articles of apparel which are wool products, the fiber content of any linings, paddings, stiffening, trimmings or facings of such garments or articles of apparel shall be given and shall be set forth separately and distinctly in the stamp, tag, label, or other mark of identification of the products.

(1) If such linings, trimmings or facings contain, purport to contain or are represented as containing wool, or recycled wool; or

(2) If such linings are metallically coated, or coated or laminated with any substance for warmth, or if such linings are composed of pile fabrics, or any fabrics incorporated for warmth or represented directly or by implication as being incorporated for warmth, which articles the Commission finds constitute a class of articles which is customarily accompanied by express or implied representations of fiber content; or

(3) If any express or implied representations of fiber content of any of such linings, paddings, stiffening, trimmings or facings are customarily made.

(b) In the case of garments which contain interlinings, the fiber content of such interlinings shall be set forth separately and distinctly as part of the required information on the stamp, tag, label, or other mark of identification of such garment. For purposes of this paragraph (b) the term *interlining* means any fabric or fibers incorporated into a garment or article of wearing apparel as a layer between an outershell and an inner lining.

(c) In the case of wool products which are not garments or articles of apparel, but which contain linings, paddings, stiffening, trimmings, or facings, the stamp, tag, label, or other mark of identification of the product shall show the fiber content of such linings, paddings, stiffening, trimmings or facings, set forth separately and distinctly in such stamp, tag, label, or other mark of identification.

(d) Wool products which are or have been manufactured for sale or sold for use as linings, interlinings, paddings, stiffening, trimmings or facings, but not contained in a garment, article of apparel, or other product, shall be labeled or marked with the required information as in the case of other wool products.

[29 FR 6626, May 21, 1964, as amended at 45 FR 44262, July 1, 1980. Redesignated at 63 FR 7517, Feb. 13, 1998]

§ 300.24 Representations as to fiber content.

(a) Words, coined words, symbols, or depictions which constitute or imply the name or designation of a fiber which is not present in the product shall not appear on labels. Any word or coined word which is phonetically similar to the name or designation of a fiber or which is only a slight variation in spelling from the name or designation of a fiber shall not be used in such a manner as to represent or imply that such fiber is present in the product when the fiber is not present as represented.

(b) Where a word, coined word, symbol, or depiction which connotes or implies the presence of a fiber is used on any label, whether required or non-required, a full fiber content disclosure with percentages shall be made on such label in accordance with the Act and regulations. Where a word, coined word, symbol, or depiction which connotes or implies the presence of a fiber is used on any hang-tag attached to a wool product that has a label providing required information and the hang-tag provides non-required information, such as a hang-tag providing information about a particular fiber's characteristics, the hang-tag need not provide a full fiber content disclosure; however, if the wool product contains any fiber other than the fiber identified on the hang-tag, the hang-tag must disclose clearly and conspicuously that it does not provide the product's full fiber content; for example:

"This tag does not disclose the product's full fiber content." or

"See label for the product's full fiber content."

[29 FR 6626, May 21, 1964, as amended at 50 FR 15106, Apr. 17, 1985. Redesignated at 63 FR 7517, Feb. 13, 1998, as amended at 79 FR 32164, June 4, 2014]

§ 300.25 Country where wool products are processed or manufactured.

(a) In addition to the other information required by the Act and Regulations:

(1) Each imported wool product shall be labeled with the name of the country where such imported product was processed or manufactured;

(2) Each wool product completely made in the United States of materials that were made in the United States shall be labeled using the term *Made in U.S.A.* or some other clear and equivalent term.

(3) Each wool product made in the United States, either in whole or in part of imported materials, shall contain a label disclosing these facts; for example:

"Made in USA of imported fabric"

or

"Knitted in USA of imported yarn" and

(4) Each wool product partially manufactured in a foreign country and partially manufactured in the United States shall contain on a label the following information:

(i) The manufacturing process in the foreign country and in the USA; for example:

"Imported cloth, finished in USA"

or

"Sewn in USA of imported components"

or

"Made in [foreign country], finished in USA"

or

"Scarf made in USA of fabric made in China"

or

"Comforter Filled, Sewn and Finished in the U.S. With Shell Made in China"

or

"Made in [Foreign Country]/fabric made in USA"

or

"Knit in USA, assembled in [Foreign Country]".

(ii) When the U.S. Customs Service requires an origin label on the unfinished product, the manufacturing processes as required in paragraph (a)(4)(i) of this section or the name of the foreign country required by Customs, for example:

"Made in (foreign country)"

(b) For the purpose of determining whether a product should be marked under paragraphs (a) (2), (3), or (4) of this section, a manufacturer needs to consider the origin of only those materials that are covered under the Act and that are one step removed from that manufacturing process. For example, a yarn manufacturer must identify fiber if it is imported, a cloth manufacturer must identify imported yarn and a household product manufacturer must identify imported cloth or imported yarn for household products made directly from yarn, or imported fiber used as filling for warmth.

(c) The term country means the political entity known as a nation. Except for the United States, colonies, possessions or protectorates outside the boundaries of the mother country shall be considered separate countries, and the name thereof shall be deemed acceptable in designating the country where the wool product was processed or manufactured unless the Commission shall otherwise direct.

(d) The country of origin of an imported wool product as determined under the laws and regulations enforced by United States Customs and Border Protection shall be considered to be the country where such wool product was processed or manufactured.

(e) The English name of the country where the imported wool product was processed or manufactured shall be used. The adjectival form of the name of the country will be accepted as the name of the country where the wool product was processed or manufactured, provided the adjectival form of the name does not appear with such other words so as to refer to a kind of species of product. Variant spellings which clearly indicate the English name of the country, such as Brasil for Brazil and Italie for Italy, are acceptable. Abbreviations which unmistakenly indicate the name of a country, such as *Gt. Britain* for *Great Britain*, are acceptable.

(f) Nothing in this rule shall be construed as limiting in any way the information required to be disclosed on labels under the provisions of any Tariff Act of the United States or regulations promulgated thereunder.

[50 FR 15106, Apr. 17, 1985. Redesignated and amended at 63 FR 7517, Feb. 13, 1998; 65 FR 75156, Dec. 1, 2000; 79 FR 32164, June 4, 2014]

§ 300.25a Country of origin in mail order advertising.

When a wool product is advertised in any mail order catalog or mail order promotional material, the description of such product shall contain a clear and conspicuous statement that the product was either made in U.S.A., imported, or both. Other words or phrases with the same meaning may be used. The statement of origin required by this section shall not be inconsistent with the origin labeling of the product being advertised.

[50 FR 15106, Apr. 17, 1985. Redesignated at 63 FR 7517, Feb. 13, 1998]

§ 300.26 Pile fabrics and products composed thereof.

The fiber content of pile fabrics or products made thereof may be stated in the label or mark of identification in such segregated form as will show the fiber content of the face or pile and of the back or base, with the percentages of the respective fibers as they exist in the face or pile and in the back or base: *Provided,* That in such disclosure the respective percentages of the face and the back be given in such manner as will show the ratio between the face and the back. Examples of the form of marking pile fabrics as to fiber content provided for in this section are as follows:

100% Wool Pile
100% Cotton Back
(Back constitutes 60% of fabric and pile 40%)
Pile—60% Recycled Wool, 40% Wool
Back—70% Cotton, 30% Rayon
(Pile constitutes 60% of fabric and back 40%).

[6 FR 3426, July 15, 1941, as amended at 45 FR 44262, July 1, 1980]

§ 300.27 Wool products containing superimposed or added fibers.

Where a wool product is made wholly of one fiber or a blend of fibers with the exception of an additional fiber in minor proportion superimposed or added in certain separate and distinct areas or sections for reinforcing or other useful purposes, the product may be designated according to the fiber content of the principal fiber or blend of fibers, with an excepting naming the superimposed or added fiber, giving the percentage thereof in relation to the total fiber weight of the principal fiber or blend of fibers, and indicating the area or section which contains the superimposed or added fiber. An example of this type of fiber content disclosure, as applied to products having reinforcing fibers added to a particular area or section, is as follows:

55% Recycled Wool
45% Rayon
Except 5% Nylon added to toe and heel

[29 FR 6626, May 21, 1964, as amended at 45 FR 44262, July 1, 1980]

§ 300.28 Undetermined quantities of reclaimed fibers.

(a) Where a wool product is composed in part of various man-made fibers recovered from textile products containing underdetermined qualities of such fibers, the percentage content of the respective fibers recovered from such products may be disclosed on the required stamp, tag, or label, in aggregate form as "man-made fibers" followed by the naming of such fibers in the order of their predominance by weight, as for example:

60% Wool
40% Man-made fibers
Rayon
Acetate
Nylon

(b) Where a wool product is composed in part of wool, or recycled wool and in part of unknown and, for practical purposes, undeterminable non-woolen fibers reclaimed from any spun, woven, knitted, felted, braided, bonded or otherwise manufactured or used product, the required fiber content disclosure may, when truthfully applicable, in lieu of the fiber content disclosure otherwise required by the Act and regulations, set forth (1) the percentages of wool or recycled wool, and (2) the generic names and the percentages of all other fibers whose presence is known or practically ascertainable and (3) the percentage of the unknown and undeterminable reclaimed fibers, designating such reclaimed fibers as "unknown reclaimed fibers" or "undetermined reclaimed fibers," as for example:

75% Recycled Wool—25% Unknown Reclaimed Fibers.

35% recycled Wool—30% Acetate—15% Cotton—20% Undetermined Reclaimed Fibers.

In making the required fiber content disclosure any fibers referred to as "unknown reclaimed fibers" or "undetermined reclaimed fibers" shall be listed last.

(c) The terms *unknown recycled fibers* and *undetermined recycled fibers* may be used in describing the unknown and undeterminable reclaimed fibers referred to in paragraph (b) of this rule in lieu of the terms specified therein, provided, however, That the same standard is used in determining the applicability of the term *recycled* as is used in defining "recycled wool" in section 2(c) of the Act.

(d) For purposes of this rule undetermined or unascertained amounts of wool or recycled wool may be classified and designated as recycled wool.

(e) Nothing contained in this rule shall excuse a full and accurate disclosure of fiber content with correct percentages if the same is known or practically ascertainable, or permit a deviation from the requirements of section 4(a)(2)(A) of the Act with respect to products not labeled under the provisions of this rule or permit a higher classification of wool or recycled wool than that provided by Section 2 of the Act.

[29 FR 6626, May 21, 1964, as amended at 45 FR 44262, July 1, 1980; 45 FR 49542, July 25, 1980]

§300.29 Garments or products composed of or containing miscellaneous cloth scraps.

(a) For wool products which consist of, or are made from, miscellaneous cloth scraps comprising manufacturing by-products and containing various fibers of undetermined percentages, the following form of disclosure as to fiber content of such wool products, where truthfully appliable and with appropriate percentage figure inserted, may be used in the stamp, tag, label, or mark of identification of such product:

(1) Where the product contains chiefly cotton as well as woolen fibers in the minimum percentage designated for recycled wool:

Made of Miscellaneous Cloth Scraps Composed Chiefly of Cotton With Minimum of ____% Recycled Wool.

(2) Where the product contains chiefly rayon as well as woolen fibers in the minimum percentage designated for recycled wool:

Made of Miscellaneous Cloth Scraps Composed Chiefly of Rayon With Minimum of ____% Recycled Wool.

(3) Where the product is composed chiefly of a mixture of cotton and rayon as well as woolen fibers in the minimum percentage designated for recycled wool:

Made of Miscellaneous Cloth Scraps Composed Chiefly of Cotton and Rayon With Minimum of ____% Recycled Wool.

(4) Where the product contains chiefly woolen fibers with the balance of undetermined mixtures of cotton, rayon or other non-woolen fibers:

Made of Miscellaneous Cloth Scraps Containing Cotton, Rayon and Other Non-Woolen Fibers, With Minimum of ____% Recycled Wool.

(b) Where the cotton or rayon content or the non-woolen fiber content mentioned in such forms of disclosure is not known to comprise as much as 50% of the fiber content of the product, the word "chiefly" in the respective form of disclosure specified in this section shall be omitted.

(c) The words "Contents are" may be used in the above-mentioned forms of marking in lieu of the words "Made of" where appropriate to the nature of the product.

(d) For purposes of this rule, undetermined or unascertained amounts of wool or recycled wool which may be contained in the product may be classified and designated as recycled wool.

[6 FR 3426, July 15, 1941, as amended at 45 FR 44262, July 1, 1980]

§ 300.30 Deceptive labeling in general.

Products subject to the act shall not bear, nor have used in connection therewith, any stamp, tag, label, mark or representation which is false, misleading or deceptive in any respect.

MANUFACTURERS' RECORDS

§ 300.31 Maintenance of records.

(a) Pursuant to the provisions of section 6 of the Act, every manufacturer of a wool product subject to the Act, irrespective of whether any guaranty has been given or received, shall maintain records showing the information required by the Act and Regulations with respect to all such wool products made by such manufacturer. Such records shall show:

(1) The fiber content of the product specified in section 4(a)(2)(A) of the Act.

(2) The maximum percentage of the total weight of the wool product of any non-fibrous loading, filling or adulterating matter as prescribed by section 4(a)(2)(B) of the Act.

(3) The name, or registered identification number issued by the Commission, of the manufacturer of the wool product or the name or registered identification number of one or more persons subject to section 3 of the Act with respect to such wool product.

(4) The name of the country where the wool product was processed or manufactured as prescribed by sections 300.25a and/or .25b.

(b) Any person substituting labels shall keep such records as will show the information on the label removed and the name or names of the person or persons from whom the wool product was received.

(c) The purpose of these records is to permit a determination that the requirements of the Act and Regulations have been met and to establish a traceable line of continuity from raw material through processing to finished product. The records shall be preserved for at least three years.

[53 FR 31314, Aug. 18, 1988]

GUARANTIES

§ 300.32 Form of separate guaranty.

(a) The following are suggested forms of separate guaranties under section 9 of the Act which may be used by a guarantor residing in the United States on or as part of an invoice or other document relating to the marketing or handling of any wool products listed and designated therein and showing the date of such invoice or other document and the signature and address of the guarantor:

(1) *General form.*

"We guarantee that the wool products specified herein are not misbranded under the provisions of the Wool Products Labeling Act and rules and regulations thereunder."

(2) *Guaranty based on guaranty.*

"Based upon a guaranty received, we guarantee that the wool products specified herein are not misbranded under the provisions of the Wool Products Labeling Act and rules and regulations thereunder."

NOTE TO PARAGRAPH (a): The printed name and address on the invoice or other document will suffice to meet the signature and address requirements.

(b) The mere disclosure of required information including the fiber content of wool products on a label or on an invoice or other document relating to its marketing or handling shall not be considered a form of separate guaranty.

[79 FR 32164, June 4, 2014]

§ 300.33 Continuing guaranty filed with Federal Trade Commission.

(a)(1) Under section 9 of the Act any person residing in the United States and marketing or handling wool products may file a continuing guaranty with the Federal Trade Commission.

(2) When filed with the Commission a continuing guaranty shall be fully executed in duplicate. Forms for use in preparing continuing guaranties will be supplied by the Commission upon request.

(3) Continuing guaranties filed with the Commission shall continue in effect until revoked. The guarantor shall promptly report any change in business status to the Commission.

(b) The prescribed form for a continuing guaranty is found in §303.38(b) of this chapter. The form is available upon request from the Textile Section, Enforcement Division, Federal Trade Commission, 600 Pennsylvania Avenue, NW, Washington, DC 20580.

(c) Any person who has a continuing guaranty on file with the Commission may, during the effective dates of the guaranty, give notice of such fact by setting forth on the invoice or other document covering the marketing or handling of the product guaranteed the following:

Continuing Guaranty under the Wool Products Labeling Act filed with the Federal Trade Commission.

(d) Any person who falsely represents that he has a continuing guaranty on file with the Federal Trade Commission shall be deemed to have furnished a false guaranty under section 9(b) of the Act.

[29 FR 6627, May 21, 1964, as amended at 48 FR 12517, Mar. 25, 1983; 63 FR 7517, Feb. 13, 1998; 63 FR 71583, Dec. 28, 1998; 79 FR 32164, June 4, 2014]

§300.34 Reference to existing guaranty on labels not permitted.

No representation or suggestion that a wool product is guaranteed under the act by the Government, or any branch thereof shall be made on or in the stamp, tag, label, or other mark of identification, applied or affixed to wool products.

GENERAL

§300.35 Hearings under section 4(d) of the act.

Hearings under section 4(d) of the act will be held when deemed by the Commission to be in the public interest. Interested persons may file applications for such hearings. Such applications shall be filed in quadruplicate and shall contain a detailed technical description of the class or classes of articles or products regarding which applicant requests a determination and announcement by the Commission concerning express or implied representations of fiber content of articles or concerning insignificant or inconsequential textile content of products.

(Sec. 4(d), 54 Stat. 1129; 15 U.S.C. 68b(d))

PART 301—RULES AND REGULATIONS UNDER FUR PRODUCTS LABELING ACT

NAME GUIDE

AUTHORITY: 15 U.S.C. 69 *et seq.*

NAME GUIDE

§ 301.0 Fur products name guide.

Name	Order	Family	Genus-species
Alpaca	Artiodactyla	Camelidae	Lama pacos.
Antelope	Artiodactyla	Bovidae	Hippotragus niger and Antilope cervicapra.
Badger	Carnivora	Mustelidae	Taxida sp. and Meles sp.
Bassarisk	......do	Procyonidae	Bassariscus astutus.
Bear	......do	Ursidae	Ursus sp.
Bear, Polar	......do	......do	Ursus maritimus.
Beaver	Rodentia	Castoridae	Castor canadensis.
Burunduk	......do	Sciuridae	Eutamias asiaticus.
Calf	Artiodactyla	Bovidae	Bos taurus.
Cat, Caracal	Carnivora	Felidae	Caracal caracal.
Cat, Domestic	......do	......do	Felis catus.
Cat, Leopard	......do	......do	Prionailurus bengalensis.
Cat, Lynx	......do	......do	Lynx rufus.
Cat, Manul	......do	......do	Felis manul.
Cat, Margay	......do	......do	Leopardus wiedii.
Cat, Spotted	......do	......do	Felis sp. (South America).
Cat, Wild	......do	......do	Felis catus and Felis lybica.
Cheetah	......do	......do	Acinonyx jubatus.
Chinchilla	Rodentia	Chinchillidae	Chinchilla chinchilla.
Chipmunk	......do	Sciuridae	Tamias sp.
Civet	Carnivora	Viverridae	Viverra sp., Viverricula sp., Paradoxurus sp., and Paguma sp.
Desman	Soricomorpha	Talpidae	Desmana moschata and Galemys pyrenaicus.
Dog	Carnivora	Canidae	Canis familiaris.
Ermine	......do	Mustelidae	Mustela erminea.
Fisher	......do	......do	Martes pennanti.
Fitch	......do	......do	Mustela putorius.
Fox	......do	Canidae	Vulpes vulpes, Vulpes macrotis.
Fox, Blue	......do	......do	Vulpes lagopus.
Fox, Grey	......do	......do	Urocyon cinereoargenteus and Urocyon littoralis.
Fox, Kit	......do	......do	Vulpes velox.
Fox, White	Carnivora	Canidae	Vulpes lagopus.
Genet	......do	Viverridae	Genetta genetta.
Goat	Artiodactyla	Bovidae	Capra hircus.
Guanaco, or its young, the Guanaquito.	......do	Camelidae	Lama guanicoe.
Hamster	Rodentia	Cricetidae	Cricetus cricetus.
Hare	......do	Leporidae	Lepus sp. and Lepus europaeus occidentalis.
Jackal	Carnivora	Canidae	Canis aureus and Canis adustus.
Jackal, Cape	......do	......do	Canis mesomelas.
Jaguar	......do	Felidae	Panthera onca.
Jaguarundi	......do	......do	Herpailurus yagouaroundi.
Kangaroo	Diprotodontia	Macropodidae	Marcopus sp.
Kangaroo-rat	......do	Potoroidae	Bettongia sp.
Kid	Artiodactyla	Bovidae	Capra hircus.
Kinkajou	Carnivora	Procyonidae	Potos flavus.
Koala	Diprotodontia	Phascolarctidae	Phascolarctos cinereus.
Kolinsky	Carnivora	Mustelidae	Mustela sibirica.
Lamb	Artiodactyla	Bovidae	Ovis aries.
Leopard	Carnivora	Felidae	Panthera pardus.

Name	Order	Family	Genus-species
Llama	Artiodactyla	Camelidae	Lama glama.
Lynx	Carnivora	Felidae	Lynx canadensis and Lynx lynx.
Marmot	Rodentia	Sciuridae	Marmota bobak.
Marten, American	Carnivora	Mustelidae	Martes americana and Martes caurina.
Marten, Baum	......do	......do	Martes martes.
Marten, Japanese	......do	......do	Martes melampus.
Marten, Stone	......do	......do	Martes foina.
Mink	......do	......do	Mustela vison and Mustela lutreola.
Mole	Soricomorpha	Talpidae	Talpa sp.
Monkey	Primates	Cercopithecidae	Colobus polykomos.
Muskrat	Rodentia	Muridae	Ondatra zibethicus.
Nutria	......do	Myocastoridae	Myocastor coypus.
Ocelot	Carnivora	Felidae	Leopardus pardalis
Opossum	Didelphimorphia	Didelphidae	Didelphis sp.
Opossum, Australian	Diprotodontia	Phalangeridae	Trichosurus vulpecula.
Opossum, Ringtail	......do	Pseudocheiridae	Pseudocheirus sp.
Opossum, South American.	Didelphimorphia	Didelphidae	Lutreolina crassicaudata.
Opossum, Water	......do	......do	Chironectes minimus.
Otter	Carnivora	Mustelidae	Lontra canadensis, Pteronura brasiliensis, and Lutra lutra.
Otter, Sea	......do	......do	Enhydra lutris.
Pahmi	......do	......do	Helictis moschata and Helictis personata.
Panda	Carnivora	Ailuridae	Ailurus fulgens.
Peschanik	Rodentia	Sciuridae	Spermophilus fulvus.
Pony	Perissodactyla	Equidae	Equus caballus.
Rabbit	Lagomorpha	Leporidae	Oryctolagus cuniculus.
Raccoon	Carnivora	Procyonidae	Procyon lotor and Procyon cancrivorus.
Raccoon, Asiatic	......do	Canidae	Nyctereutes procyonoides.
Raccoon, Mexican	......do	Procyonidae	Nasua sp.
Reindeer	Artiodactyla	Cervidae	Rangifer tarandus.
Sable	Carnivora	Mustelidae	Martes zibellina.
Sable, American	......do	......do	Martes americana and Martes caurina.
Seal, Fur	Carnivora	Otariidae	Callorhinus ursinus.
Seal, Hair	......do	Phocidae	Phoca sp.
Seal, Roc	......do	Otariidae	Otaria flavescens.
Sheep	Artiodactyla	Bovidae	Ovis aries.
Skunk	Carnivora	Mephitidae	Mephitis mephitis, Mephitis macroura, Conepatus semistriatus and Conepatus sp.
Skunk, Spotted	......do	......do	Spilogale sp.
Squirrel	Rodentia	Sciuridae	Sciurus vulgaris.
Squirrel, Flying	......do	......do	Eupetaurus cinereus, Pteromys volans and Petaurista leucogenys.
Suslik	......do	......do	Spermophilus citellus, Spermophilus major rufescens and Spermophilus suslicus.
Vicuna	Artiodactyla	Camelidae	Vicugna vicugna.
Viscacha	Rodentia	Chinchillidae	Lagidium sp.
Wallaby	Diprotodontia	Macropodidae	Wallabia sp., Petrogale sp., and Thylogale sp.
Weasel	Carnivora	Mustelidae	Mustela frenata.
Weasel, Chinese	......do	......do	Mustela sibirica.
Weasel, Japanese	......do	......do	Mustela itatsi (also classified as Mustela sibirica itatsi).
Weasel, Manchurian	Carnivora	Mustelidae	Mustela altaica and Mustela nivalis rixosa.
Wolf	......do	Canidae	Canis lupus.
Wolverine	......do	Mustelidae	Gulo gulo.
Wombat	Diprotodontia	Vombatidae	Vombatus sp.
Woodchuck	Rodentia	Sciuridae	Marmota monax.

[79 FR 30456, May 28, 2014]

REGULATIONS

SOURCE: 17 FR 6075, July 8, 1952, unless otherwise noted.

§301.1 Terms defined.

(a) As used in this part, unless the context otherwise specifically requires:

(1) The term *act* means the *Fur Products Labeling Act* (approved Aug. 8, 1951, Pub. L. 110, 82d Cong., 1st Sess.; 15 U.S.C.A. sec. 69; 65 Stat. 179).

(2) The terms *rule, rules, regulations,* and *rules and regulations,* mean the rules and regulations prescribed by the Commission pursuant to section 8 (b) of the act.

(3) The definitions of terms contained in section 2 of the act shall be applicable also to such terms when used in rules promulgated under the act.

(4) The terms *Fur Products Name Guide* and *Name Guide* mean the register of names of hair, fleece, and fur-bearing animals issued and amended by the Commission pursuant to the provisions of section 7 of the act.

(5) The terms *required information* and *information required* mean the information required to be disclosed on labels, invoices and in advertising under the act and rules and regulations, and such further information as may be permitted by the regulations, when and if used.

(6) The terms *invoice* and *invoice or other document* mean an account, order, memorandum, list, or catalog, which is issued to a purchaser, consignee, bailee, correspondent, agent, or any other person, electronically, in writing, or in some other form capable of being read and preserved in a form that is capable of being accurately reproduced for later reference, whether by transmission, printing, or otherwise, in connection with the marketing or handling of any fur or fur product transported or delivered to such person.

(b) The term *wearing apparel* as used in the definition of a fur product in section 2(d) of the Act means (1) Any articles of clothing or covering for any part of the body; and (2) shall include any assembled furs, used furs, or waste furs, in attached form, including mats, plates or garment shells or furs flat off the board, and furs which have been dyed, tip-dyed, bleached or artificially colored, intended for use as or in wearing apparel: *Provided, however*, That the provisions of section 4(2) of the Act shall not be applicable to those fur products set out in paragraph (b)(2) of this section.

[17 FR 6075, July 8, 1952, as amended at 26 FR 3186, Apr. 14, 1961; 61 FR 67709, Dec. 24, 1996; 65 FR 82270, Dec. 28, 2000; 79 FR 30458, May 28, 2014]

§ 301.2 General requirements.

(a) Each and every fur product, except those exempted under § 301.39 of this part, shall be labeled and invoiced in conformity with the requirements of the act and rules and regulations.

(b) Each and every fur, except those exempted under § 301.39, shall be invoiced in conformity with the requirements of the act and rules and regulations.

(c) Any advertising of fur products or furs, except those exempted under § 301.39, shall be in conformity with the requirements of the act and rules and regulations.

[17 FR 6075, July 8, 1952, as amended at 79 FR 30458, May 28, 2014]

§ 301.3 English language requirements.

All information required under the act and rules and regulations to appear on labels, invoices, and in advertising, shall be set out in the English language. If labels, invoices or advertising matter contain any of the required information in a language other than English, all of the required information shall appear also in the English language. The provisions of this section shall not apply to advertisements in foreign language newspapers or periodicals, but such advertising shall in all other respects comply with the act and regulations.

§ 301.4 Abbreviations or ditto marks prohibited.

In disclosing required information in labeling and advertising, words or terms shall not be abbreviated or designated by the use of ditto marks but shall be spelled out fully, and in invoicing the required information shall not be abbreviated but shall be spelled out fully.

§ 301.5 Use of Fur Products Name Guide.

(a) The Fur Products Name Guide (§ 301.0 of this part) is set up in four columns under the headings of Name, Order, Family and Genus-Species. The applicable animal name appearing in the column headed "Name" shall be used in the required information in labeling, invoicing and advertising of fur products and furs. The scientific names appearing under the columns headed Order, Family, and Genus-Species are furnished for animal identification purposes and shall not be used.

(b) Where the name of the animal appearing in the Name Guide consists of two separate words the second word shall precede the first in designating the name of the animal in the required information; as for example: "Fox, Black" shall be disclosed as "Black Fox."

§ 301.6 Animals not listed in Fur Products Name Guide.

(a) All furs are subject to the act and regulations regardless of whether the name of the animal producing the fur appears in the Fur Products Name Guide.

(b) Where fur is obtained from an animal not listed in the Fur Products Name Guide it shall be designated in the required information by the true English name of the animal or in the absence of a true English name, by the name which properly identifies such animal in the United States.

§ 301.7 Describing furs by certain breed names prohibited.

If the fur of an animal is described in any manner by its breed, species, strain or coloring, irrespective of former usage, such descriptive matter shall not contain the name of another animal either in the adjective form or otherwise nor shall such description (subject to any exception contained in this part or animal names appearing in the Fur Products Name Guide) contain a name in an adjective form or otherwise which connotes a false geographic origin of the animal. For example, such designations as "Sable Mink," "Chinchilla Rabbit," and "Aleutian Mink" shall not be used.

§ 301.8 Use of terms "Persian Lamb," "Broadtail Lamb," and "Persian-broadtail Lamb" permitted.

(a) The term *Persian Lamb* may be used to describe the skin of the young lamb of the Karakul breed of sheep or top-cross breed of such sheep, having hair formed in knuckled curls.

(b) The term *Broadtail Lamb* may be used to describe the skin of the prematurely born, stillborn, or very young lamb of the Karakul breed of sheep or top-cross breed of such sheep, having flat light-weight fur with a moire pattern.

(c) The term *Persian-broadtail Lamb* may be used to describe the skin of the very young lamb of the Karakul breed of sheep or top-cross breed of such sheep, having hair formed in flattened knuckled curls with a moire pattern.

(d) The terms "Persian Lamb", "Broadtail Lamb", or "Persian-broadtail Lamb" shall not be used to describe: (1) The so-called Krimmer, Bessarabian, Rumanian, Shiraz, Salzfelle, Metis, Dubar, Meshed, Caracul, Iranian, Iraqi, Chinese, Mongolian, Chekiang, or Indian lamb skins, unless such lamb skins conform with the requirements set out in paragraph (a), (b), or (c) of this section respectively; or (2) any other lamb skins having hair in a wavy or open curl pattern.

§ 301.9 Use of terms "Mouton Lamb" and "Shearling Lamb" permitted.

(a) The term *Mouton Lamb* may be used to describe the skin of a lamb which has been sheared, the hair straightened, chemically treated, and thermally set to produce a moisture repellant finish; as for example:

Dyed Mouton Lamb

(b) The term *Shearling Lamb* may be used to describe the skin of a lamb which has been sheared and combed.

[17 FR 6075, July 8, 1952, as amended at 26 FR 3186, Apr. 14, 1961]

§ 301.10 Use of term "Broadtail-processed Lamb" permitted.

The term *Broadtail-processed Lamb* may be used to describe the skin of a lamb which has been sheared, leaving a moire hair pattern on the pelt having the appearance of the true fur pattern of "Broadtail Lamb"; as for example:

Dyed Broadtail-processed Lamb
Fur origin: Argentina

§ 301.11 Fictitious or non-existing animal designations prohibited.

No trade names, coined names, nor other names or words descriptive of a fur as being the fur of an animal which is in fact fictitious or non-existent shall be used in labeling, invoicing or advertising of a fur or fur product.

§ 301.12 Country of origin of imported furs.

(a)(1) In the case of furs imported into the United States from a foreign country, the country of origin of such furs shall be set forth as a part of the information required by the act in invoicing and advertising.

(2) In the case of fur products imported into the United States from a foreign country, or fur products made from furs imported into the United States from a foreign country, the country of origin of the furs contained in such products shall be set forth as a part of the information required by the act in labeling, invoicing and advertising.

(b) The term *country* means the political entity known as a nation. Colonies, possessions or protectorates outside the boundaries of the mother country shall be considered separate countries and the name thereof shall be deemed acceptable in designating the "country of origin" unless the Commission shall otherwise direct.

(c) The country in which the animal producing the fur was raised, or if in a feral state, was taken, shall be considered the "country of origin."

(d) When furs are taken within the territorial waters of a country, such country shall be considered the "country of origin." Furs taken outside such territorial waters, or on the high seas, shall have as their country of origin the country having the nearest mainland.

(e)(1) The English name of the country of origin shall be used. Abbreviations which unmistakably indicate the name of a country, such as "Gt. Britain" for "Great Britain," are acceptable. Abbreviations such as "N.Z." for "New Zealand" are not acceptable.

(2) The name of the country of origin, when used as a part of the required information in labeling shall be preceded by the term *fur origin;* as for example:

Dyed Muskrat
Fur Origin: Russia

or

Dyed China Mink
Fur Origin: China

(3) In addition to the required disclosure of country of origin the name of the country may also appear in adjective form in connection with the name of the animal; as for example:

Tip-dyed Canadian American Sable
Fur Origin: Canada

or

Russian Sable
Fur Origin: Russia

(f) Nothing in this section shall be construed as limiting in any way the information required to be disclosed on labels under the provisions of any Tariff Act of the United States or regulations prescribed by the Secretary of the Treasury.

[17 FR 6075, July 8, 1952, as amended at 26 FR 3186, Apr. 14, 1961; 61 FR 67709, Dec. 24, 1996]

§ 301.13 Fur products having furs with different countries of origin.

When a fur product is composed of furs with different countries of origin the names of such countries shall be set forth in the required information in the order of predominance by surface areas of the furs in the fur product.

§ 301.14 Country of origin of used furs.

When the country of origin of used furs is unknown, and no representations are made directly or by implication with respect thereto, this fact shall be set out as a part of the required information in lieu of the country of origin as "Fur origin: Unknown."

§ 301.15 Designation of section producing domestic furs permitted.

In the case of furs produced in the United States the name of the section or area producing the furs used in the fur product may be set out in connection with the name of the animal; as for example:

Dyed Fur Seal
Fur origin: Alaska

or

Dyed Muskrat
Fur origin: Minnesota

§ 301.16 Disclosure of origin of certain furs raised or taken in United States.

If the name of any animal set out in the Fur Products Name Guide or term permitted by the regulations to be used in connection therewith connotes foreign origin and such animal is raised or taken in the United States, furs obtained therefrom shall be described in disclosing the required information as having the United States as the country of origin; as for example:

Dyed Persian Lamb

Fur origin: United States
or
Mexican Raccoon
Fur origin: United States

§ 301.17 Misrepresentation of origin of furs.

No misleading nor deceptive statements as to the geographical or zoological origin of the animal producing a fur shall be used directly or indirectly in labeling, invoicing or advertising furs or fur products.

§ 301.18 Passing off domestic furs as imported furs prohibited.

No domestic furs nor fur products shall be labeled, invoiced or advertised in such a manner as to represent directly or by implication that they have been imported.

§ 301.19 Pointing, dyeing, bleaching or otherwise artificially coloring.

(a) Where a fur or fur product is pointed or contains or is composed of bleached, dyed or otherwise artificially colored fur, such facts shall be disclosed as a part of the required information in labeling, invoicing and advertising.

(b) The term *pointing* means the process of inserting separate hairs into furs or fur products for the purpose of adding guard hairs, either to repair damaged areas or to simulate other furs.

(c) The term *bleaching* means the process for producing a lighter shade of a fur, or removing off-color spots and stains by a bleaching agent.

(d) The term *dyeing* (which includes the processes known in the trade of tipping the hair or fur, feathering, and beautifying) means the process of applying dyestuffs to the hair or fur, either by immersion in a dye bath or by application of the dye by brush, feather, spray, or otherwise, for the purpose of changing the color of the fur or hair, or to accentuate its natural color. When dyestuff is applied by immersion in a dye bath or by application of the dye by brush, feather, or spray, it may respectively be described as "vat dyed", "brush dyed", "feather dyed", or "spray dyed", as the case may be. When dyestuff is applied only to the ends of the hair or fur, by feather or otherwise, it may also be described as "tip-dyed". The application of dyestuff to the leather or the skin (known in the trade as "tipping", as distinguished from tip-dyeing the hair or fur as above described) and which does not affect a change of, nor accentuate the natural color of the hair or fur, shall not be considered as "dyeing". When fluorescent dye is applied to a fur or fur product it may be described as "brightener added".

(e) The term *artificial coloring* means any change or improvement in color of a fur or fur product in any manner other than by pointing, bleaching, dyeing, or tip-dyeing, and shall be described in labeling, invoicing and advertising as "color altered" or "color added".

(f) The term *blended* shall not be used as a part of the required information to describe the pointing, bleaching, dyeing, tip-dyeing, or otherwise artificially coloring of furs.

(g) Where a fur or fur product is not pointed, bleached, dyed, tip-dyed, or otherwise artificially colored it shall be described as "natural".

(h) Where any fur or fur product is dressed, processed or treated with a solution or compound containing any metal and such compound or solution effects any change or improvement in the color of the hair, fleece or fur fiber, such fur or fur product shall be described in labeling, invoicing and advertising as "color altered" or "color added".

(i)(1) Any person dressing, processing or treating a fur pelt in such a manner that it is required under paragraph (e) or (h) of this section to be described as "color altered" or "color added" shall place a black stripe at least one half inch (1.27 cm) in width across the leather side of the skin immediately above the rump or place a stamp with a solid black center in the form of either a two inch (5.08 cm) square or a circle at least two inches (5.08 cm) in diameter on the leather side of the pelt and shall use black ink for all other stamps or markings on the leather side of the pelt.

(2) Any person dressing, processing or treating a fur pelt which after processing is considered natural under paragraph (g) of this section shall place a white stripe at least one half inch

(1.27 cm) in width across the leather side of the skin immediately above the rump or place a stamp with a solid white center in the form of either a two inch (5.08 cm) square or a circle at least two inches (5.08 cm) in diameter on the leather side of the pelt and shall use white ink for all other stamps or markings on the leather side of the pelt.

(3) Any person dressing, processing or treating a fur pelt in such a manner that it is considered dyed under paragraph (d) of this section shall place a yellow stripe at least one half inch (1.27 cm) in width across the leather side immediately above the rump or place a stamp with a solid yellow center in the form of either a two inch (5.08 cm) square or a circle at least two inches (5.08 cm) in diameter on the leather side of the pelt and shall use yellow ink for all other stamps or markings on the leather side of the pelt.

(4) In lieu of the marking or stamping otherwise required by paragraphs (i) (1), (2), and (3) of this section, any person dressing, processing or treating a fur pelt so as to be subject to the stamping or marking requirements of this paragraph may stamp the leather side of the pelt with the appropriate truthful designation "dyed", "color altered", "color added", or "natural", as the case may be, in such manner that the stamp will not be obliterated or mutilated by further processing and will remain clearly legible until the finished fur product reaches the ultimate consumer.

(5) Where, after assembling, fur garment shells, mats, plates or other assembled furs are processed or treated in such a manner as to fall within the stamping or marking provisions of this paragraph, such assembled furs, in lieu of the stamping or marking of each individual pelt or piece, may be appropriately stamped on the leather side as provided in this paragraph in such a manner that the stamp will remain on the finished fur product and clearly legible until it reaches the ultimate consumer and will not be mutilated or obliterated by further processing.

(j) Any person who shall process a fur pelt in such a manner that after such processing it is no longer considered as natural shall clearly, conspicuously and legibly stamp on the leather side of the pelt and on required invoices relating thereto a lot number or other identifying number which relates to such records of the processor as will show the source and disposition of the pelts and the details of the processing performed. Such person shall also stamp his name or registered identification number on the leather side of the pelt.

(k) Any person who possesses fur pelts of a type which are always considered as dyed under paragraph (d) of this section after processing or any person who processes fur pelts which are always natural at the time of sale to the ultimate consumer, which pelts for a valid reason cannot be marked or stamped as provided in this section, may file an affidavit with the Federal Trade Commission's Bureau of Consumer Protection setting forth such facts as will show that the pelts are always dyed or natural as the case may be and that the stamping of such pelts cannot be reasonably accomplished. If the Bureau of Consumer Protection is satisfied that the public interest will be protected by the filing of the affidavit, it may accept such affidavit and advise the affiant that marking of the fur pelts themselves as provided in this section will be unnecessary until further notice. Any person filing such an affidavit shall promptly notify the Commission of any change in circumstances with respect to its operations.

(l) Any person subject to this section who incorrectly marks or fails to mark fur pelts as provided in paragraphs (i) and (j) of this section shall be deemed to have misbranded such products under section 4(l) of the Act. Any person subject to this section who furnishes a false or misleading affidavit under paragraph (k) of this section or fails to give the notice required by paragraph (k) of this section shall be deemed to have neglected and refused to maintain the records required by section 8(d) of the Act.

[17 FR 6075, July 8, 1952, as amended at 26 FR 3186, Apr. 14, 1961; 34 FR 381, Jan. 10, 1969; 36 FR 5689, Mar. 26, 1971; 41 FR 2636, Jan. 19, 1976; 53 FR 31314, Aug. 18, 1988; 61 FR 67709, Dec. 24, 1996; 79 FR 30458, May 28, 2014]

§ 301.20 Fur products composed of pieces.

(a) Where fur products, or fur mats and plates, are composed in whole or in substantial part of paws, tails, bellies, gills, ears, throats, heads, scrap pieces, or waste fur, such fact shall be disclosed as a part of the required information in labeling, invoicing, and advertising. Where a fur product is made of the backs of skins, such fact may be set out in labels, invoices, and advertising.

(b) Where fur products, or fur mats and plates, are composed wholly or substantially of two or more of the parts set out in paragraph (a) of this section or one or more of such parts and other fur, disclosure in respect thereto shall be made by naming such parts or other fur in order of predominance by surface area.

(c) The terms *substantial part* and *substantially* mean ten per centum (10 percent) or more in surface area.

(d) The term *assembled* shall not be used in lieu of the terms set forth in paragraph (a) of this section to describe fur products or fur mats and plates composed of such parts.

[17 FR 6075, July 8, 1952, as amended at 79 FR 30458, May 28, 2014]

§ 301.21 Disclosure of used furs.

(a) When fur in any form has been worn or used by an ultimate consumer it shall be designated "used fur" as a part of the required information in invoicing and advertising.

(b) When fur products or fur mats and plates are composed in whole or in part of used fur, such fact shall be disclosed as a part of the required information in labeling, invoicing and advertising; as for example:

Leopard
Used Fur
or
Dyed Muskrat
Contains Used Fur

§ 301.22 Disclosure of damaged furs.

(a) The term *damaged fur*, as used in this part, means a fur, which, because of a known or patent defect resulting from natural causes or from processing, is of such a nature that its use in a fur product would decrease the normal life and durability of such product.

(b) When damaged furs are used in a fur product, full disclosure of such fact shall be made as a part of the required information in labeling, invoicing, or advertising such product; as for example:

Mink
Fur origin: Canada
Contains Damaged Fur

§ 301.23 Second-hand fur products.

When a fur product has been used or worn by an ultimate consumer and is subsequently marketed in its original, reconditioned, or rebuilt form with or without the addition of any furs or used furs, the requirements of the act and regulations in respect to labeling, invoicing and advertising of such product shall be applicable thereto, subject, however, to the provisions of § 301.14 of this part as to country of origin requirement, and in addition, as a part of the required information such product shall be designated "Second-hand", "Reconditioned-Second-hand", or "Rebuilt-Second-hand", as the case may be.

§ 301.24 Repairing, restyling and remodeling fur products for consumer.

When fur products owned by and to be returned to the ultimate-consumer are repaired, restyled or remodeled and used fur or fur is added thereto, labeling of the fur product shall not be required. However, the person adding such used fur or fur to the fur product, or who is responsible therefor, shall give to the owner an invoice disclosing the information required under the act and regulations respecting the used fur or fur added to the fur product, subject, however, to the provisions of § 301.14 of this part as to country of origin requirements.

§ 301.25 Name required to appear on labels and invoices.

The name required by the act to be used on labels and invoices shall be the full name under which the person is doing business, and no trade-mark, trade name nor other name which does not constitute such full name shall be used in lieu thereof.

§ 301.26 Registered identification numbers.

(a) Registered numbers for use as the required identification in lieu of the name on fur product labels as provided in section 4(2)(E) of the Act will be issued by the Commission to qualified persons residing in the United States upon receipt of an application duly executed on the Commission's Web site at *https://rn.ftc.gov* or by such means as the Commission or its designee may direct.

(b)(1) Registered identification numbers shall be used only by the person or concern to whom they are issued, and such numbers are not transferable or assignable.

(2) Registered identification numbers shall be subject to cancellation if the Federal Trade Commission fails to receive prompt notification of any change in name, business address, or legal business status of a person or firm to whom a registered identification number has been assigned, by application duly executed in the form and manner set out in paragraph (d) of this section, reflecting the current name, business address, and legal business status of the person or firm.

(3) Registered identification numbers shall be subject to cancellation whenever any such number was procured or has been used improperly or contrary to the requirements of the act and regulations, or when otherwise deemed necessary in the public interest.

(c) Registered identification numbers assigned under this rule may be used on labels required in labeling products subject to the provisions of the Wool Products Labeling Act and Textile Fiber Products Identification Act, and numbers previously assigned or to be assigned by the Commission under such Acts may be used as and for the required name in labeling under this Act. When so used by the person or firm to whom assigned, the use of the numbers shall be construed as identifying and binding the applicant as fully and in all respects as though assigned under the specific Act for which it is used.

(d) Requests for a registered identification number, to update information pertaining to an existing number, or to cancel an existing number shall be made through the Commission's Web site at *https://rn.ftc.gov*. Unless otherwise directed by the Commission or its designee, requests made by other means (including but not limited to email) will not be accepted and approved.

[17 FR 6075, July 8, 1952, as amended at 26 FR 3187, Apr. 14, 1961; 48 FR 12516, Mar. 25, 1983; 63 FR 7517, Feb. 13, 1998; 63 FR 71583, Dec. 28, 1998; 82 FR 43691, Sept. 19, 2017]

§ 301.27 Labels and method of affixing.

At all times during the marketing of a fur product the required label shall be conspicuous and of such durability as to remain attached to the product throughout any distribution, sale, or resale, and until sold and delivered to the ultimate consumer.

[79 FR 30458, May 28, 2014]

§ 301.28 [Reserved]

§ 301.29 Requirements in respect to disclosure on label.

(a) The required information shall be set forth in such a manner as to be clearly legible, conspicuous, and readily accessible to the prospective purchaser, and all parts of the required information shall be set out in letters of equal size and conspicuousness. All of the required information with respect to the fur product shall be set out on one side of the label. The label may include any nonrequired information which is true and non-deceptive and which is not prohibited by the act and regulations, but in all cases the animal name used shall be that set out in the Name Guide.

(b) The required information may be set out in hand printing provided it conforms to the requirements of paragraph (a) of this section, and is set out in indelible ink in a clear, distinct, legible and conspicuous manner. Handwriting shall not be used in setting out any of the required information on the label.

[17 FR 6075, July 8, 1952, as amended at 26 FR 3187, Apr. 14, 1961; 79 FR 30458, May 28, 2014]

§ 301.30 [Reserved]

§ 301.31 Labeling of fur products consisting of two or more units.

(a) The label shall be attached to and appear upon each garment or separate article of wearing apparel subject to the act irrespective of whether two or more garments or articles may be sold or marketed together or in combination with each other.

(b) In the case of fur products that are marketed or handled in pairs or ensembles, only one label is required if all units in the pair or group are of the same fur and have the same country of origin. The information set out on the label must be applicable to each unit and supply the information required under the act and rules and regulations.

[17 FR 6075, July 8, 1952, as amended at 79 FR 30458, May 28, 2014]

§ 301.32 Fur product containing material other than fur.

(a) Where a fur product contains a material other than fur the content of which is required to be disclosed on labels under other statutes administered by the Commission, such information may be set out on the same side of the label and in immediate conjunction with the information required under this Act; as for example:

100% Wool
Interlining—100% Recycled Wool
Trim—Dyed Muskrat
Fur Origin: Canada

or

Body: 100% Cotton
Lining: 100% Nylon
Collar: Dyed Mouton Lamb
Fur Origin: Argentina

(b) Information which may be desirable or necessary to fully inform the purchaser of other material content of a fur product may be set out on the same side of the label as used for disclosing the information required under the Act and rules and regulations; as for example:

Body—Leather
Trim—Dyed Mink

[26 FR 3187, Apr. 14, 1961, as amended at 45 FR 44263, July 1, 1980]

§ 301.33 Labeling of samples.

Where samples of furs or fur products subject to the act are used to promote or effect sales of fur products, said samples, as well as the fur products purchased therefrom, shall be labeled to show the information required under the act and regulations.

§ 301.34 Misbranded or falsely invoiced fur products.

(a) If a person subject to section 3 of the Act with respect to a fur product finds that a fur product is misbranded he shall correct the label or replace same with a substitute containing the required information.

(b) If a person subject to section 3 of the Act with respect to a fur or fur product finds that the invoice issued to him is false or deceptive, he shall, in connection with any invoice issued by him in relation to such fur or fur product correctly set forth all of the information required by the Act and regulations in relation to such fur or fur product.

[26 FR 3187, Apr. 14, 1961]

§ 301.35 Substitution of labels.

(a) Persons authorized under the provisions of section 3(e) of the act to substitute labels affixed to fur products may do so, provided the substitute label is complete and carries all the information required under the act and rules and regulations in the same form and manner as required in respect to the original label. The substitute label need not, however, show the name or registered number appearing on the original label if the name or registered number of the person who affixes the substitute appears thereon.

(b) The original label may be used as a substitute label provided the name or registered number of the person making the substitution is inserted thereon without interfering with or obscuring in any manner other required information. In connection with such substitution the name or registered number as well as any record numbers appearing on the original label may be removed.

(c) Persons substituting labels under the provision of this section shall maintain the records required under § 301.41 of this part.

[17 FR 6075, July 8, 1952, as amended at 79 FR 30458, May 28, 2014]

§ 301.36 Sectional fur products.

(a) Where a fur product is composed of two or more sections containing different animal furs the required information with respect to each section shall be separately set forth in labeling, invoicing or advertising; as for example:

Dyed Rabbit
Fur origin: France
Trimming: Dyed Mouton-processed Lamb
Fur origin: Argentina

or

Body: Dyed Kolinsky
Fur origin: Russia
Tail: Dyed Mink
Fur origin: Canada

(b) The provisions of this section shall not be interpreted so as to require the disclosure of very small amounts of different animal furs added to complete a fur product or skin such as the ears, snoot, or under part of the jaw.

§ 301.37 Manner of invoicing furs and fur products.

(a) In the invoicing of furs and fur products, all of the required information shall be set out in a clear, legible, distinct and conspicuous manner. The invoice shall be issued at the time of the sale or other transaction involving furs or fur products, but the required information need not be repeated in subsequent periodic statements of account respecting the same furs or fur products.

(b) Non-required information or representations appearing in the invoicing of furs and fur products shall in no way be false or deceptive nor include any names, terms or representations prohibited by the act and regulations. Nor shall such information or representations be set forth or used in such manner as to interfere with the required information.

§ 301.38 Advertising of furs and fur products.

(a)(1) In advertising furs or fur products, all parts of the required information shall be stated in close proximity with each other and, if printed, in legible and conspicuous type of equal size.

(2) Non-required information or representations appearing in the advertising of furs and fur products shall in no way be false or deceptive nor include any names, terms or representations prohibited by the act and regulations. Nor shall such information or representations be set forth or used in such manner as to interfere with the required information.

(b)(1) In general advertising of a group of fur products composed in whole or in part of imported furs having various countries of origin, the disclosure of such countries of origin may, by reference, be made through the use of the following statement in the advertisement in a clear and conspicuous manner:

Fur products labeled to show country of origin of imported furs

(2) The provisions of this paragraph shall not be applicable in the case of catalogue, mail order, or other types of advertising which solicit the purchase of fur products in such a manner that the purchaser or prospective purchaser would not have the opportunity of viewing the product and attached label prior to delivery thereof.

(c) In advertising of an institutional type referring only to the general nature or kind of business conducted or to the general classification of the types or kinds of furs or fur products manufactured or handled, and which advertising is not intended to aid, promote, or assist directly or indirectly in the sale or offering for sale of any specific fur products or furs, the required information need not be set forth: *Provided, however,* That if reference is made in the advertisement to a color of the fur which was caused by dyeing, bleaching or other artificial coloring, such facts shall be disclosed in the advertising, and provided further, that when animal names are used in such advertising, such names shall be those set forth in the Fur Products Name Guide. For example, the kind of advertising contemplated by this paragraph is as follows:

X Fur Company
Famous for its Black Dyed Persian Lamb Since 1900

or

X Company
Manufacturers of Fine Muskrat Coats, Capes and Stoles

§ 301.39 Exempted fur products.

The requirements of the act and regulations in this part do not apply to fur products that consist of fur obtained from an animal through trapping or hunting and that are sold in a face-to-face transaction at a place such as a residence, craft fair, or other location used on a temporary or short-term basis, by the person who trapped or hunted the animal, where the revenue from the sale of apparel or fur products is not the primary source of income of such person.

[79 FR 30458, May 28, 2014]

§ 301.40 [Reserved]

§ 301.41 Maintenance of records.

(a) Pursuant to section 3(e) and section 8(d)(1), of the Act, each manufacturer or dealer in fur products or furs (including dressers, dyers, bleachers and processors), irrespective of whether any guaranty has been given or received, shall maintain records showing all of the required information relative to such fur products or furs in such manner as will readily identify each fur or fur product manufactured or handled. Such records shall show:

(1) That the fur product contains or is composed of natural, pointed, bleached, dyed, tip-dyed or otherwise artificially colored fur, when such is the fact;

(2) That the fur product contains used fur, when such is the fact;

(3) The name or names (as set forth in the Fur Products Name Guide) of the animal or animals that produced the fur;

(4) That the fur product is composed in whole or in substantial part of paws, tails, bellies, gills, ears, throats, heads, scrap pieces, or waste fur, when such is the fact;

(5) The name of the country of origin of any imported furs used in the fur products;

(6) The name, or other identification issued and registered by the Commission, of one or more of the persons who manufacture, import, sell, advertise, offer, transport or distribute the fur product in commerce.

(b) The purpose of the records is to permit a determination that the requirements of the Act and Regulations have been met and to establish a traceable line of continuity from raw material through processing to finished product. The records shall be preserved for at least three years.

[53 FR 31315, Aug. 18, 1988, as amended at 79 FR 30458, May 28, 2014]

§ 301.42 Deception as to nature of business.

When necessary to avoid deception, the name of any person other than the manufacturer of the fur product appearing on the label or invoice shall be accompanied by appropriate words showing that the fur product was not manufactured by such person; as for example:

Distributed by ____________

or

____________ Wholesalers

§ 301.43 Use of deceptive trade or corporate names, trademarks or graphic representations prohibited.

No person shall use in labeling, invoicing or advertising any fur or fur product a trade name, corporate name, trademark or other trade designation or graphic representation which misrepresents directly or by implication to purchasers, prospective purchasers or the consuming public:

(a) The character of the product including method of construction;

(b) The name of the animal producing the fur;

(c) The method or manner of distribution; or

(d) The geographical or zoological origin of the fur.

[61 FR 67710, Dec. 24, 1996]

§ 301.44 Misrepresentation of prices.

(a) No person shall, with respect to a fur or fur product, advertise such fur or fur product at alleged wholesale prices or at alleged manufacturers cost or less, unless such representations are true in fact; nor shall any person advertise a fur or fur product at prices purported to be reduced from what are in fact fictitious prices, nor at a purported reduction in price when such purported reduction is in fact fictitious.

(b) No person shall, with respect to a fur or fur product, advertise such fur or fur product with comparative prices and percentage savings claims except on the basis of current market values or unless the time of such compared price is given.

(c) No person shall, with respect to a fur or fur product, advertise such fur or fur product as being "made to sell for", being "worth" or "valued at" a certain price, or by similar statements, unless such claim or representation is true in fact.

(d) No person shall, with respect to a fur or fur product, advertise such fur or fur product as being of a certain value or quality unless such claims or representations are true in fact.

(e) Persons making pricing claims or representations of the types described in paragraphs (a), (b), (c) and (d) of this section shall maintain full and adequate records disclosing the facts upon which such claims or representations are based.

(f) No person shall, with respect to a fur or fur product, advertise such fur or fur product by the use of an illustration which shows such fur or fur product to be a higher priced product than the one so advertised.

(g) No person shall, with respect to a fur or fur product, advertise such fur or fur product as being "bankrupt stock", "samples", "show room models", "Hollywood Models", "Paris Models", "French Models", "Parisian Creations", "Furs Worn by Society Women", "Clearance Stock", "Auction Stock", "Stock of a business in a state of liquidation", or similar statements, unless such representations or claims are true in fact.

§ 301.45 Representations as to construction of fur products.

(a) No misleading nor deceptive statements as to the construction of fur products shall be used directly or indirectly in labeling, invoicing or advertising such products. (For example, a fur product made by the skin-on-skin method should not be represented as having been made by the letout method.)

(b) Where a fur product is made by the method known in the trade as letting-out, or is made of fur which has been sheared or plucked, such facts may be set out in labels, invoices and advertising.

§ 301.46 Reference to guaranty by Government prohibited.

No representation nor suggestion that a fur or fur product is guaranteed under the act by the Government, or any branch thereof, shall be made in the labeling, invoicing or advertising in connection therewith.

§ 301.47 Form of separate guaranty.

The following is a suggested form of separate guaranty under section 10 of the Act which may be used by a guarantor residing in the United States, on and as part of an invoice or other document in which the merchandise covered is listed and specified and which shows the date of such document and the signature and address of the guarantor:

We guarantee that the fur products or furs specified herein are not misbranded nor falsely nor deceptively advertised or invoiced under the provisions of the Fur Products Labeling Act and rules and regulations thereunder.

NOTE TO § 301.47. The printed name and address on the invoice or other document will suffice to meet the signature and address requirements.

[79 FR 30458, May 28, 2014]

§ 301.48 Continuing guaranties.

(a)(1) Under section 10 of the Act any person residing in the United States and handling fur or fur products may file a continuing guaranty with the Federal Trade Commission. When filed with the Commission a continuing guaranty shall be fully executed in duplicate. Forms for use in preparing continuing guaranties shall be supplied by the Commission upon request.

(2) Continuing guaranties filed with the Commission shall continue in effect until revoked. The guarantor shall promptly report any change in business status to the Commission.

(3) The prescribed form for a continuing guaranty is found in § 303.38(b) of this chapter. The form is available upon request from the Textile Section, Enforcement Division, Federal Trade Commission, 600 Pennsylvania Avenue, NW, Washington, DC 20580.

(b) Any person who has a continuing guaranty on file with the Commission may, during the effective dates of the guaranty, give notice of such fact by setting forth on the invoice or other document covering the marketing or handling of the product guaranteed the following: "Continuing guaranty under the Fur Products Labeling Act filed with the Federal Trade Commission."

(c) Any person who falsely represents in writing that he has a continuing guaranty on file with the Federal Trade Commission when such is not a fact shall be deemed to have furnished a false guaranty under section 10(b) of the Act.

[26 FR 3188, Apr. 14, 1961, as amended at 48 FR 12517, Mar. 25, 1983; 63 FR 7517, Feb. 13, 1998; 63 FR 71583, Dec. 28, 1998; 79 FR 30458, May 28, 2014]

§ 301.48a Guaranties not received in good faith.

A guaranty shall not be deemed to have been received in good faith within the meaning of section 10(a) of the Act:

(a) Unless the recipient of such guaranty shall have examined the required label, required invoice and advertisement relating to the fur product or fur so guaranteed;

(b) If the recipient of the guaranty has knowledge that the fur or fur product guaranteed is misbranded, falsely invoiced or falsely advertised.

[26 FR 3188, Apr. 14, 1961]

§ 301.49 Deception in general.

No furs nor fur products shall be labeled, invoiced, or advertised in any manner which is false, misleading or deceptive in any respect.

PART 303—RULES AND REGULATIONS UNDER THE TEXTILE FIBER PRODUCTS IDENTIFICATION ACT

Sec.

AUTHORITY: 15 U.S.C. 70 *et seq.*

SOURCE: 24 FR 4480, June 2, 1959, unless otherwise noted.

§ 303.1 Terms defined.

As used in this part, unless the context otherwise specifically requires:

(a) The term *Act* means the *Textile Fiber Products Identification Act* (approved September 2, 1958, 85th Congress, 2d Sess.; 15 U.S.C. 70, 72 Stat. 1717).

(b) The terms *rule, rules, regulations,* and *rules and regulations* mean the rules and regulations prescribed by the Commission pursuant to section 7(c) of the Act.

(c) The definition of terms contained in section 2 of the Act shall be applicable also to such terms when used in rules promulgated under the Act.

(d) The term *United States* means the several States, the District of Columbia, and the Territories and possessions of the United States.

(e) The terms *required information* and *information required* mean such information as is required to be disclosed on labels or invoices and in advertising under the Act and regulations.

(f) The terms *label, labels, labeled,* and *labeling* mean the stamp, tag, label, or other means of identification, or authorized substitute therefor, required to be on or affixed to textile fiber products by the Act and regulations and on which the information required is to appear.

(g) The terms *marketing or handling* and *marketed or handled,* when applied to textile fiber products, mean any one or all of the transactions set forth in section 3 of the Act.

(h) The terms *invoice* and *invoice or other document* mean an account, order, memorandum, list, or catalog, which is issued to a purchaser, consignee, bailee, correspondent, agent, or any other person, electronically, in writing, or in some other form capable of being read and preserved in a form that is capable of being accurately reproduced for later reference, whether by transmission, printing, or otherwise, in connection with the marketing or handling of any textile fiber product transported or delivered to such person.

(i) The term *outer coverings of furniture, mattresses, and box springs* means those coverings as are permanently incorporated in such articles.

(j) The term *wearing apparel* means any costume or article of clothing or covering for any part of the body worn or intended to be worn by individuals.

(k) The term *beddings* means sheets, covers, blankets, comforters, pillows, pillowcases, quilts, bedspreads, pads, and all other textile fiber products used or intended to be used on or about a bed or other place for reclining or sleeping but shall not include furniture, mattresses or box springs.

(l) The term *headwear* means any textile fiber product worn exclusively on or about the head or face by individuals.

(m) The term *backings,* when applied to floor coverings, means that part of a floor covering to which the pile, face, or outer surface is woven, tufted, hooked, knitted, or otherwise attached, and which provides the structural base of the floor covering. The term *backing* shall also include fabrics attached to the structural base of the floor covering in such a way as to form a part of such structural base, but shall not include the pile, face, or outer surface of the floor covering or any part thereof.

(n) The term *elastic material* means a fabric composed of yarn consisting of an elastomer or a covered elastomer.

(o) The term *coated fabric* means any fabric which is coated, filled, impregnated, or laminated with a continuous-film-forming polymeric composition in such a manner that the weight added to the base fabric is at least 35 percent of the weight of the fabric before coating, filling, impregnation, or lamination.

(p) The term *upholstered product* means articles of furniture containing stuffing and shall include mattresses and box springs.

(q) The term *ornamentation* means any fibers or yarns imparting a visibly discernible pattern or design to a yarn or fabric.

(r) The term *fiber trademark* means a word or words used by a person to identify a particular fiber produced or sold by him and to distinguish it from fibers of the same generic class produced or sold by others. Such term shall not include any trade mark, product mark, house mark, trade name or other name which does not identify a particular fiber.

(s) The term *wool* means the fiber from the fleece of the sheep or lamb or hair of the Angora or Cashmere goat (and may include the so-called specialty fibers from the hair of the camel, alpaca, llama, and vicuna) which has never been reclaimed from any woven or felted wool product.

(t) The term *recycled wool* means (1) the resulting fiber when wool has been woven or felted into a wool product which, without ever having been utilized in any way by the ultimate consumer, subsequently has been made into a fibrous state, or (2) the resulting fiber when wool or reprocessed wool has been spun, woven, knitted, or felted into a wool product which, after having been used in any way by the ultimate consumer, subsequently has been made into a fibrous state.

(u) The terms *mail order catalog* and *mail order promotional material* mean any materials, used in the direct sale or direct offering for sale of textile products, that are disseminated to ultimate consumers in print or by electronic means, other than by broadcast, and that solicit ultimate consumers to purchase such textile products by mail, telephone, electronic mail, or some other method without examining the actual product purchased.

[24 FR 4480, June 2, 1959, as amended at 45 FR 44263, July 1, 1980; 50 FR 15106, Apr. 17, 1985; 63 FR 7517, Feb. 13, 1998; 79 FR 18770, Apr. 4, 2014]

§ 303.2 General requirements.

(a) Each textile fiber product, except those exempted or excluded under section 12 of the Act, shall be labeled or invoiced in conformity with the requirements of the Act and regulations.

(b) Any advertising of textile fiber products subject to the Act shall be in conformity with the requirements of the Act and regulations.

(c) The requirements of the Act and regulations shall not be applicable to products required to be labeled under the Wool Products Labeling Act of 1939 (Pub. L. 76–850, 15 U.S.C. 68, 54 Stat. 1128).

(d) Any person marketing or handling textile fiber products who shall cause or direct a processor or finisher to label, invoice, or otherwise identify any textile fiber product with required information shall be responsible under the Act and regulations for any failure of compliance with the Act and regulations by reason of any statement or omission in such label, invoice, or other means of identification utilized in accordance with his direction: *Provided*, That nothing herein shall relieve the processor or finisher of any duty or liability to which he may be subject under the Act and regulations.

§ 303.3 Fibers present in amounts of less than 5 percent.

(a) Except as permitted in sections 4(b)(1) and 4(b)(2) of the Act, as amended, no fiber present in the amount of less than 5 percent of the total fiber weight shall be designated by its generic name or fiber trademark in disclosing the constituent fibers in required information, but shall be designated as "other fiber." When more than one of such fibers are present in a product, they shall be designated in the aggregate as "other fibers." Provided, however, that nothing in this section shall be construed as prohibiting the disclosure of any fiber present in a textile fiber product which has a clearly established and definite functional significance when present in the amount contained in such product, as for example:

96 percent Acetate
4 percent Spandex.

(b) In making such disclosure, all of the provisions of the Act and regulations in this part setting forth the manner and form of disclosure of fiber content information, including the provisions of §§ 303.17 and 303.41 of this part relating to the use of generic names and fiber trademarks, shall be applicable.

[63 FR 7518, Feb. 13, 1998]

§ 303.4 English language requirement.

All required information shall be set out in the English language. If the required information appears in a language other than English, it also shall appear in the English language. The provisions of this section shall not apply to advertisements in foreign language newspapers or periodicals, but such advertising shall in all other respects comply with the Act and regulations.

§ 303.5 Abbreviations, ditto marks, and asterisks prohibited.

(a) In disclosing required information, words or terms shall not be designated by ditto marks or appear in footnotes referred to by asterisks or other symbols in required information, and shall not be abbreviated except as permitted in § 303.33(e) of this part.

(b) Where the generic name of a textile fiber is required to appear in immediate conjunction with a fiber trademark in advertising, labeling, or invoicing, a disclosure of the generic name by means of a footnote, to which reference is made by use of an asterisk or other symbol placed next to the fiber trademark, shall not be sufficient in itself to constitute compliance with the Act and regulations.

[24 FR 4480, June 2, 1959, as amended at 65 FR 75156, Dec. 1, 2000]

§ 303.6 Generic names of fibers to be used.

(a) Except where another name is permitted under the Act and regulations, the respective generic names of all fibers present in the amount of 5 per centum or more of the total fiber weight of the textile fiber product shall be used when naming fibers in the required information; as for example: "cotton," "rayon," "silk," "linen," "nylon," etc.

(b) Where a textile fiber product contains the hair or fiber of a fur-bearing animal present in the amount 5 per centum or more of the total fiber weight of the product, the name of the animal producing such fiber may be used in setting forth the required information, provided the name of such animal is used in conjunction with the words "fiber," "hair," or "blend;" as for example:

80 percent Rabbit hair.
20 percent Nylon.

or

80 percent Silk.
20 percent Mink fiber.

(c) The term *fur fiber* may be used to describe the hair or fur fiber or mixtures thereof of any animal or animals other than the sheep, lamb, Angora goat, Cashmere goat, camel, alpaca, llama or vicuna where such hair or fur fiber or mixture is present in the amount of 5 per centum or more of the total fiber weight of the textile fiber product and no direct or indirect representations are made as to the animal or animals from which the fiber so designated was obtained; as for example:

60 percent Cotton.
40 percent Fur fiber.

or

50 percent Nylon.
30 percent Mink hair.
20 percent Fur fiber.

(d) Where textile fiber products subject to the Act contain (1) wool or (2) recycled wool in amounts of five per centum or more of the total fiber weight, such fibers shall be designated and disclosed as wool or recycled wool as the case may be.

[24 FR 4480, June 2, 1959, as amended at 45 FR 44263, July 1, 1980]

§ 303.7 Generic names and definitions for manufactured fibers.

Pursuant to the provisions of section 7(c) of the Act, the Commission hereby establishes the generic names for manufactured fibers, together with their respective definitions, set forth in this section, and the generic names for manufactured fibers, together with their respective definitions, set forth in International Organization for Standardization ISO 2076:2010(E), "Textiles—Man-made fibres—Generic names." International Organization for Standardization ISO 2076:2010(E), "Textiles—Man-made fibres—Generic names, Fifth edition, 2010–01–15 is incorporated by reference into this section with the approval of the Director of the Federal Register under 5 U.S.C. 552(a) and 1 CFR part 51. To enforce any edition other than that specified in this section, the Federal Trade Commission must publish notice of change in the FEDERAL REGISTER and the material must be available to the public. All approved material is available for inspection at the Federal Trade Commission, 600 Pennsylvania Ave. NW., Room 130, Washington, DC 20580, (202) 326–2222, and is available from the American National Standards Institute, 11 West 42nd St., 13th floor, New York, NY 10036. It is also available for inspection at the National Archives and Records

Administration (NARA). For information on the availability of this material at NARA, call 202–741–6030, or go to:*http://www.archives.gov/federal_register/code_of_federal_regulations/ibr_locations.html.*

(a) *Acrylic.* A manufactured fiber in which the fiber-forming substance is any long chain synthetic polymer composed of at least 85 percent by weight of acrylonitrile units

$$(-CH_2-\underset{CN}{\underset{|}{CH}}-).$$

(b) *Modacrylic.* A manufactured fiber in which the fiber-forming substance is any long chain synthetic polymer composed of less than 85 percent but at least 35 percent by weight of acrylonitrile units

$$(-CH_2-\underset{CN}{\underset{|}{CH}}-),$$

except fibers qualifying under paragraph (j)(2) of this section and fibers qualifying under paragraph (q) of this section. (Sec. 7, 72 Stat. 1717; 15 U.S.C. section 70e)

(c) *Polyester.* A manufactured fiber in which the fiber-forming substance is any long chain synthetic polymer composed of at least 85% by weight of an ester of a substituted aromatic carboxylic acid, including but not restricted to substituted terephthalate units,

$$p(-R-O-\underset{O}{\underset{\|}{C}}-C_6H_4-\underset{O}{\underset{\|}{C}}-O-),$$

and para substituted hydroxy-benzoate units,

$$p(-R-O-C_6H_4-\underset{O}{\underset{\|}{C}}-O-).$$

(1) Where the fiber is formed by the interaction of two or more chemically distinct polymers (of which none exceeds 85% by weight), and contains ester groups as the dominant functional unit (at least 85% by weight of the total polymer content of the fiber), and which, if stretched at least 100%, durably and rapidly reverts substantially to its unstretched length when the tension is removed, the term *elasterell-p* may be used as a generic description of the fiber.

(2) Where the glycol used to form the ester consists of at least ninety mole percent 1,3-propanediol, the term "*triexta*" may be used as a generic description of the fiber.

(d) *Rayon.*A manufactured fiber composed of regenerated cellulose, as well as manufactured fibers composed of regenerated cellulose in which substituents have replaced not more than 15% of the hydrogens of the hydroxyl groups. Where the fiber is composed of cellulose precipitated from an organic solution in which no substitution of the hydroxyl groups takes place and no chemical intermediates are formed, the term *lyocell* may be used as a generic description of the fiber.

(e) *Acetate.* A manufactured fiber in which the fiber-forming substance is cellulose acetate. Where not less than 92 percent of the hydroxyl groups are acetylated, the term triacetate may be used as a generic description of the fiber.

(f) *Saran.* A manufactured fiber in which the fiber-forming substance is any long chain synthetic polymer composed of at least 80 percent by weight of vinylidene chloride units $(-CH_9-CCl_2-)$.

(g) *Azlon.* A manufactured fiber in which the fiber-forming substance is composed of any regenerated naturally occurring proteins.

(h) *Nytril.* A manufactured fiber containing at least 85 percent of a long chain polymer of vinylidene dinitrile $(-CH_2-C(CN)_2-)$ where the vinylidene dinitrile content is no less than every other unit in the polymer chain.

(i) *Nylon.* A manufactured fiber in which the fiber-forming substance is a long-chain synthetic polyamide in which less than 85 percent of the amide

$$\left(-\underset{\underset{\displaystyle O}{\|}}{C}-NH-\right)$$

linkages are attached directly to two aromatic rings.

(j) *Rubber*. A manufactured fiber in which the fiber-forming substance is comprised of natural or synthetic rubber, including the following categories:

(1) A manufactured fiber in which the fiber-forming substance is a hydrocarbon such as natural rubber, polyisoprene, polybutadiene, copolymers of dienes and hydrocarbons, or amorphous (noncrystalline) polyolefins.

(2) A manufactured fiber in which the fiber-forming substance is a copolymer of acrylonitrile and a diene (such as butadiene) composed of not more than 50 percent but at least 10 percent by weight of acrylonitrile units

$$(-CH_2-\underset{\underset{\displaystyle CN}{|}}{CH}-)$$

The term *lastrile* may be used as a generic description for fibers falling within this category.

(3) A manufactured fiber in which the fiber-forming substance is a polychloroprene or a copolymer of chloroprene in which at least 35 percent by weight of the fiber-forming substance is composed of chloroprene units

$$(-CH_2-\underset{\underset{\displaystyle Cl}{|}}{C}=CH-CH_2-).$$

(k) *Spandex*. A manufactured fiber in which the fiber-forming substance is a long chain synthetic polymer comprised of at least 85 percent of a segmented polyurethane.

(l) *Vinal*. A manufactured fiber in which the fiber-forming substance is any long chain synthetic polymer composed of at least 50 percent by weight of vinyl alcohol units ($-CH_2-CHOH-$), and in which the total of the vinyl alcohol units and any one or more of the various acetal units is at least 85 percent by weight of the fiber.

(m) *Olefin*. A manufactured fiber in which the fiber-forming substance is any long chain synthetic polymer composed of at least 85 percent by weight of ethylene, propylene, or other olefin units, except amorphous (noncrystalline) polyolefins qualifying under paragraph (j)(1) of this section [Rule 7]. Where the fiber-forming substance is a cross-linked synthetic polymer, with low but significant crystallinity, composed of at least 95 percent by weight of ethylene and at least one other olefin unit, and the fiber is substantially elastic and heat resistant, the term *lastol* may be used as a generic description of the fiber.

(n) *Vinyon*. A manufactured fiber in which the fiber-forming substance is any long chain synthetic polymer composed of at least 85 percent by weight of vinyl chloride units ($-CH_2-CHCl-$).

(o) *Metallic*. A manufactured fiber composed of metal, plastic-coated metal, metal-coated plastic, or a core completely covered by metal.

(p) *Glass*. A manufactured fiber in which the fiber-forming substance is glass.

(q) *Anidex*. A manufactured fiber in which the fiber-forming substance is any long chain synthetic polymer composed of at least 50 percent by weight of one or more esters of a monohydric alcohol and acrylic acid, $CH_2{=}CH$—COOH.

(r) *Novoloid*. A manufactured fiber containing at least 85 percent by weight of a cross-linked novolac.

(s) *Aramid*. A manufactured fiber in which the fiber-forming substance is a long-chain synthetic polyamide in which at least 85 percent of the amide

$$\left(-\underset{\underset{\displaystyle O}{\|}}{C}-NH-\right)$$

linkages are attached directly to two aromatic rings.

(t) *Sulfar*. A manufactured fiber in which the fiber-forming substance is a long chain synthetic polysulfide in which at least 85% of the sulfide (—S—) linkages are attached directly to two (2) aromatic rings.

(u) *PBI*. A manufactured fiber in which the fiber-forming substance is a long chain aromatic polymer having reoccurring imidazole groups as an integral part of the polymer chain.

(v) *Elastoester*. A manufactured fiber in which the fiber-forming substance is a long-chain synthetic polymer composed of at least 50% by weight of aliphatic polyether and at least 35% by weight of polyester, as defined in 16 CFR 303.7(c).

(w) *Melamine*. A manufactured fiber in which the fiber-forming substance is a synthetic polymer composed of at least 50% by weight of a cross-linked melamine polymer.

(x) *Fluoropolymer*. A manufactured fiber containing at least 95% of a long-chain polymer synthesized from aliphatic fluorocarbon monomers.

(y) *PLA*. A manufactured fiber in which the fiber-forming substance is composed of at least 85% by weight of lactic acid ester units derived from naturally occurring sugars.

(Sec. 6, 72 Stat. 1717; 15 U.S.C. 70e)

[24 FR 4480, June 2, 1959; 24 FR 5737, July 17, 1959]

EDITORIAL NOTE: For FEDERAL REGISTER citations affecting § 303.7, see the List of CFR Sections Affected, which appears in the Finding Aids section of the printed volume and at *www.govinfo.gov*.

§ 303.8 Procedure for establishing generic names for manufactured fibers.

(a) Prior to the marketing or handling of a manufactured fiber for which no generic name has been established or otherwise recognized by the Commission, the manufacturer or producer thereof shall file a written application with the Commission, requesting the establishment of a generic name for such fiber, stating therein:

(1) The reasons why the applicant's fiber should not be identified by one of the generic names established by the Commission in § 303.7 of this part;

(2) The chemical composition of the fiber, including the fiber-forming substances and respective percentages thereof, together with samples of the fiber;

(3) Suggested names for consideration as generic, together with a proposed definition for the fiber;

(4) Any other information deemed by the applicant to be pertinent to the application, including technical data in the form of test methods;

(5) The earliest date on which the application proposes to market or handle the fiber in commerce for other than developmental or testing purposes.

(b) Upon receipt of the application, the Commission will, within sixty (60) days, either deny the application or assign to the fiber a numerical or alphabetical symbol for temporary use during further consideration of such application.

(c) After taking the necessary procedure in consideration of the application, the Commission in due course shall establish a generic name or advise the applicant of its refusal to grant the application and designate the proper existing generic name for the fiber.

[24 FR 4480, June 2, 1959, as amended at 63 FR 7518, Feb. 13, 1998]

§ 303.9 Use of fur-bearing animal names and symbols prohibited.

(a) The advertising or the labeling of a textile fiber product shall not contain any names, words, depictions, descriptive matter, or other symbols which connote or signify a fur-bearing animal, unless such product or the part thereof in connection with which the names, words, depictions, descriptive matter, or other symbols are used is a fur product within the meaning of the Fur Products Labeling Act.

(b) Subject to the provisions of paragraph (a) of this section and § 303.6 of this part, a textile fiber product shall not be described or referred to in any manner in an advertisement or label with:

(1) The name or part of the name of a fur-bearing animal, whether as a single word or a combination word, or any coined word which is phonetically similar to a fur-bearing animal name, or which is only a slight variation in spelling of a fur-bearing animal name or part of the name. As for example, such terms as "Ermine," "Mink," "Persian," "Broadtail," "Beaverton," "Marmink," "Sablelon," "Lam," "Pershian," "Minx," or similar terms shall not be used.

(2) Any word or name symbolic of a fur-bearing animal by reason of conventional usage or by reason of its

close relationship with fur-bearing animals. As for example, such terms as "guardhair," "underfur," and "mutation," or similar terms, shall not be used.

(c) Nothing contained herein shall prevent:

(1) The nondeceptive use of animal names or symbols in referring to a textile fiber product where the fur of such animal is not commonly or commercially used in fur products, as that term is defined in the Fur Products Labeling Act, as for example "kitten soft", "Bear Brand", etc.

(2) The nondeceptive use of a trademark or trade name containing the name, symbol, or depiction of a fur-bearing animal unless:

(i) The textile fiber product in connection with which such trademark or trade name is used simulates a fur or fur product; or

(ii) Such trademark or trade name is used in any advertisement of a textile fiber product together with any depiction which has the appearance of a fur or fur product; or

(iii) The use of such trademark or trade name is prohibited by the Fur Products Labeling Act.

[24 FR 4480, June 2, 1959, as amended at 28 FR 722, Jan. 16, 1963]

§ 303.10 Fiber content of special types of products.

(a) Where a textile product is made wholly of elastic yarn or material, with minor parts of non-elastic material for structural purposes, it shall be identified as to the percentage of the elastomer, together with the percentage of all textile coverings of the elastomer and all other yarns or materials used therein.

Where a textile fiber product is made in part of elastic material and in part of other fabric, the fiber content of such fabric shall be set forth sectionally by percentages as in the case of other fabrics. In such cases the elastic material may be disclosed by describing the material as elastic followed by a listing in order of predominance by weight of the fibers used in such elastic, including the elastomer, where such fibers are present by 5 per centum or more with the designation "other fiber" or "other fibers" appearing last when fibers required to be so designated are present. An example of labeling under this paragraph is:

Front and back non-elastic sections:
50 percent Acetate.
50 percent Cotton.
Elastic: Rayon, cotton, nylon, rubber.

(b) Where drapery or upholstery fabrics are manufactured on hand-operated looms for a particular customer after the sale of such fabric has been consummated, and the amount of the order does not exceed 100 yards (91.44 m) of fabric, the required fiber content disclosure may be made by listing the fibers present in order of predominance by weight with any fiber or fibers required to be designated as "other fiber" or "other fibers" appearing last, as for example:

Rayon
Wool
Acetate
Metallic
Other fibers

(c)(1) Where a manufactured textile fiber is essentially a physical combination or mixture of two or more chemically distinct constituents or components combined at or prior to the time of extrusion, which components if separately extruded would each fall within different existing definitions of textile fibers as set forth in § 303.7 of this part (Rule 7), the fiber content disclosure as to such fiber, shall for all purposes under the regulations in this part

(i) Disclose such fact in the required fiber content information by appropriate nondeceptive descriptive terminology, such as "biconstituent fiber" or "multiconstituent fiber,"

(ii) Set out the components contained in the fiber by the appropriate generic name specified in § 303.7 of this part (Rule 7) in the order of their predominance by weight, and

(iii) Set out the respective percentages of such components by weight.

(2) If the components of such fibers are of a matrix-fibril configuration, the term *matrix-fibril fiber* or *matrix fiber* may be used in setting forth the information required by this paragraph.

(3) Examples of proper fiber content designations under this paragraph are:

100% Biconstituent Fiber

(65% Nylon, 35% Polyester)
80% Matrix Fiber (60% Nylon, 40% Polyester)
15% Polyester
5% Rayon

(4) All of the provisions as to fiber content disclosures contained in the Act and regulations, including the provisions relative to fiber content tolerances and disclosures of fibers present in amounts of less than 5 percentum of the total fiber weight, shall also be applicable to the designations and disclosures prescribed by this paragraph.

[25 FR 7044, July 26, 1960, as amended at 30 FR 14253, Nov. 13, 1965; 34 FR 12134 July 19, 1969; 61 FR 11544, Mar. 21, 1996]

§ 303.11 Floor coverings containing backings, fillings, and paddings.

In disclosing the required fiber content information as to floor coverings containing exempted backings, fillings, or paddings, the disclosure shall be made in such manner as to indicate that it relates only to the face, pile, or outer surface of the floor covering and not to the backing, filling, or padding. Examples of the form of marking these types of floor coverings as to fiber content are as follows:

100% Cotton Pile
Face—60% Rayon, 40% Cotton
Outer Surface—100% Wool

§ 303.12 Trimmings of household textile articles.

(a) Pursuant to section 12 of the Act, trimmings incorporated in articles of wearing apparel and other household textile articles are exempt from the Act and regulations, except for decorative trim, decorative patterns and designs, and elastic materials in findings exceeding the surface area thresholds described in paragraphs (a)(3) and (b) of this section. Trimmings may, among other forms of trim, include:

(1) Rickrack, tape, belting, binding, braid, labels (either required or non-required), collars, cuffs, wrist bands, leg bands, waist bands, gussets, gores, welts, and findings, including superimposed garters in hosiery, and elastic materials and threads inserted in or added to the basic product or garment in minor proportion for holding, reinforcing or similar structural purposes;

(2) Decorative trim, whether applied by embroidery, overlay, applique, or attachment; and

(3) Decorative patterns or designs which are an integral part of the fabric out of which the household textile article is made. *Provided*, that such decorative trim or decorative pattern or design, as specified in paragraphs (a)(2) and (3) of this section, does not exceed 15 percent of the surface area of the household textile article. If no representation is made as to the fiber content of the decorative trim or decoration, as provided for in paragraphs (a)(2) and (3) of this section, and the fiber content of the decorative trim or decoration differs from the fiber content designation of the basic fabric, the fiber content designation of the basic fabric shall be followed by the statement "exclusive of decoration."

(b) The term *findings* may also include elastic material which constitutes a part of the basic fabric or material out of which the household textile article is made, where such elastic material does not exceed 20 percent of the surface area of the household textile article: *Provided*, That the required information as to fiber content of products subject to this paragraph is followed by the statement "exclusive of elastic."

[24 FR 4480, June 2, 1959, as amended at 79 FR 18770, Apr. 4, 2014]

§ 303.13 Sale of remnants and products made of remnants.

(a) In disclosing the required fiber content information as to remnants of fabric which are for practical purposes of unknown or undeterminable fiber content:

(1) The fiber content disclosure of such remnants of fabrics may be designated in the required information as "remnants of undetermined fiber content."

(2) Where such remnants of fabrics are displayed for sale at retail, a conspicuous sign may, in lieu of individual labeling, be used in immediate conjunction with such display, stating with respect to required fiber content disclosure that the goods are "remnants of undetermined fiber content."

(3) Where textile fiber products are made of such remnants, the required

fiber content information of the products may be disclosed as "made of remnants of undetermined fiber content." If any representations as to fiber content are made with respect to such remnants, the provisions of this paragraph shall not apply.

(b) Where remnants of fabrics are marketed or handled in bales, bundles, or packages and are all of the same fiber content or are designated in the manner permitted by paragraph (a) of this section, the individual remnants need not be labeled if the bales, bundles, or packages containing such remnants are labeled with the required information including fiber content percentages or the designation permitted by paragraph (a) of this section.

(c) Where remnants of fabrics of the same fiber content are displayed for sale at retail, a conspicuous sign may, in lieu of individual labeling, be used in immediate conjunction with such display, stating the fiber content information with respect to such remnants; as for example: "remnants, 100 percent cotton," "remnants, 50 percent rayon, 50 percent acetate," etc.

§ 303.14 Products containing unknown fibers.

(a) Where a textile fiber product is made from miscellaneous scraps, rags, odd lots, secondhand materials, textile by-products, or waste materials of unknown, and for practical purposes, undeterminable fiber content, the required fiber content disclosure may, when truthfully applicable, in lieu of the fiber content disclosure otherwise required by the Act and regulations, indicate that such product is composed of miscellaneous scraps, rags, odd lots, textile by-products, secondhand materials (in case of secondhand materials, words of like import may be used) or waste materials, as the case may be, of unknown or undetermined fiber content, as for example:

Made of miscellaneous scraps of undetermined fiber content
100% unknown fibers—rags
All undetermined fibers—textile by-products
100% miscellaneous odd lots of undetermined fiber content
Secondhand materials—fiber content unknown
Made of unknown fibers—waste materials

(b) Where a textile fiber product is made in part from miscellaneous scraps, rags, odd lots, textile by-products, second-hand materials or waste materials of unknown and, for practical purposes, undeterminable fiber content together with a percentage of known or determinable fibers, the required fiber content disclosure may, when truthfully applicable, in lieu of the fiber content disclosure otherwise required by the Act and regulations, indicate the percentage of miscellaneous scraps, rags, odd lots, secondhand materials (in case of secondhand materials, words of like import may be used), textile by-products, or waste materials of unknown or undetermined fiber content and the percentage of known fibers, as for example:

45% Rayon
30% Acetate
25% Miscellaneous scraps of undetermined fiber content.

60% Cotton
40% Unknown fibers—waste materials.

40% Acrylic
20% Modacrylic
40% Undetermined fibers—odd lots.

50% Polyester
30% Cotton
20% Textile by-products of undetermined fiber content.

50% Rayon
50% Secondhand materials—fiber content unknown.

45% Acetate
30% Cotton
25% Miscellaneous rags—undetermined fiber content.

(c) No representation as to fiber content shall be made as to any textile product or any portion of a textile fiber product designated as composed of unknown or undetermined fibers. If any such representation is made, a full and complete fiber content disclosure shall be required.

(d) Nothing contained in this section shall excuse a full disclosure as to fiber content if the same is known or practically ascertainable.

[25 FR 4317, May 14, 1960]

§ 303.15 Required label and method of affixing.

(a) A label is required to be affixed to each textile product and, where required, to its package or container in a secure manner. Such label shall be conspicuous and shall be of such durability as to remain attached to the product and its package throughout any distribution, sale, resale and until sold and delivered to the ultimate consumer.

(b) Each textile fiber product with a neck must have a label disclosing the country of origin affixed to the inside center of the neck midway between the shoulder seams or in close proximity to another label affixed to the inside center of the neck. The fiber content and RN or name of the company may be disclosed on the same label as the country of origin or on another conspicuous and readily accessible label or labels on the inside or outside of the garment. On all other textile products, the required information shall be disclosed on a conspicuous and readily accessible label or labels on the inside or outside of the product. The country of origin disclosure must always appear on the front side of the label. Other required information may appear either on the front side or the reverse side of a label, provided that the information is conspicuous and readily accessible.

(c) In the case of hosiery products, this section shall not be construed as requiring the affixing of a label to each hosiery product contained in a package if,

(1) Such hosiery products are intended for sale to the ultimate consumer in such package,

(2) Such package has affixed to it a label bearing the required information for the hosiery products contained in the package, and

(3) The information on the label affixed to the package is equally applicable to each textile fiber product contained therein.

(d) Socks provided for in subheading 6115.92.90, 6115.93.90, 6115.99.18, 6111.20.60, 6111.30.50, or 6111.90.50 of the Harmonized Tariff Schedule of the United States, as in effect on September 1, 2003, shall be marked, as legibly, indelibly, and permanently as the nature of the article or package will permit, to disclose the English name of the country of origin. This disclosure shall appear on the front of the package, adjacent to the size designation of the product, and shall be set forth in such a manner as to be clearly legible, conspicuous, and readily accessible to the ultimate consumer. *Provided, however,* any package that contains several different types of goods and includes socks classified under subheading 6115.92.90, 6115.93.90, 6115.99.18, 6111.20.60, 6111.30.50, or 6111.90.50 of the Harmonized Tariff Schedule of the United States, as in effect on September 1, 2003, shall not be subject to the requirements of this subsection.

[50 FR 15106, Apr. 17, 1985, as amended at 63 FR 7518, Feb. 13, 1998; 70 FR 73369, Dec. 12, 2005]

§ 303.16 Arrangement and disclosure of information on labels.

(a) Subject to the provisions of § 303.15(b), information required by the Act and regulations in this part may appear on any label or labels attached to the textile fiber product, including the care label required by 16 CFR part 423, provided all the pertinent requirements of the Act and regulations in this part are met and so long as the combination of required information and non-required information is not misleading. The required information shall include the following:

(1) The generic names and percentages by weight of the constituent fibers present in the textile fiber product, excluding permissive ornamentation, in amounts of 5 percent or more and any fibers disclosed in accordance with § 303.3(a) shall appear in order of predominance by weight with any percentage of fiber or fibers required to be designated as "other fiber" or "other fibers" appearing last.

(2) The name, provided for in § 303.19, or registered identification number issued by the Commission, of the manufacturer or of one or more persons marketing or handling the textile fiber product.

(3) The name of the country where such product was processed or manufactured, as provided for in § 303.33.

(b) All parts of the required information shall be set forth in such a manner as to be clearly legible, conspicuous, and readily accessible to the prospective purchaser. All parts of the fiber content information shall appear in type or lettering of equal size and conspicuousness.

(c) Subject to the provisions of § 303.17, any non-required information or representations placed on the product shall not minimize, detract from, or conflict with required information and shall not be false, deceptive, or misleading.

(d) Non-deceptive terms which are properly and truthfully descriptive of a fiber may be used in conjunction with the generic name of such fiber; as for example: "100 percent cross-linked rayon," "100 percent solution dyed acetate," "100 percent combed cotton," "100 percent nylon 66," etc.

[24 FR 4480, June 2, 1959, as amended at 25 FR 4317, May 14, 1960; 30 FR 14254, Nov. 13, 1965; 30 FR 15313, Dec. 11, 1965; 50 FR 15107, Apr. 17, 1985; 53 FR 31315, Aug. 18, 1988; 63 FR 7518, Feb. 13, 1998]

§ 303.17 Use of fiber trademarks and generic names on labels.

(a) A non-deceptive fiber trademark may be used on a label in conjunction with the generic name of the fiber to which it relates. Where such a trademark is placed on a label in conjunction with the required information, the generic name of the fiber must appear in immediate conjunction therewith, and such trademark and generic name must appear in type or lettering of equal size and conspicuousness.

(b) Where a generic name or a fiber trademark is used on any label providing required information, a full fiber content disclosure shall be made in accordance with the Act and regulations the first time the generic name or fiber trademark appears on the label. Where a fiber generic name or trademark is used on any hang-tag attached to a textile fiber product that has a label providing required information and the hang-tag provides non-required information, such as a hang-tag stating only a fiber generic name or trademark or providing information about a particular fiber's characteristics, the hang-tag need not provide a full fiber content disclosure; however, if the textile fiber product contains any fiber other than the fiber identified by the fiber generic name or trademark, the hang-tag must disclose clearly and conspicuously that it does not provide the product's full fiber content; for example:

"This tag does not disclose the product's full fiber content."

or

"See label for the product's full fiber content."

(c) If a fiber trademark is not used in the required information, but is used elsewhere on the label as non-required information, the generic name of the fiber shall accompany the fiber trademark in legible and conspicuous type or lettering the first time the trademark is used.

(d) No fiber trademark or generic name shall be used in non-required information on a label in such a manner as to be false, deceptive, or misleading as to fiber content, or to indicate directly or indirectly that a textile fiber product is composed wholly or in part of a particular fiber, when such is not the case.

[24 FR 4480, June 2, 1959, as amended at 79 FR 18771, Apr. 4, 2014]

§ 303.18 Terms implying fibers not present.

Words, coined words, symbols or depictions, (a) which constitute or imply the name or designation of a fiber which is not present in the product, (b) which are phonetically similar to the name or designation of such a fiber, or (c) which are only a slight variation of spelling from the name or designation of such a fiber shall not be used in such a manner as to represent or imply that such fiber is present in the product.

[30 FR 13693, Oct. 28, 1965]

§ 303.19 Name or other identification required to appear on labels.

(a) The name required by the Act to be used on labels shall be the name under which the person is doing business. Where a person has a word trademark, used as a house mark, registered in the United States Patent Office, such word trademark may be used on labels in lieu of the name otherwise required. No trademark, trade names, or other names except those provided for above shall be used for required identification purposes.

(b) Registered identification numbers, as provided for in § 303.20 of this part, may be used for identification purposes in lieu of the required name.

[24 FR 4480, June 2, 1959, as amended at 83 FR 3071, Jan. 23, 2018]

§303.20 Registered identification numbers.

(a) Registered numbers for use as the required identification in lieu of the name on textile fiber product labels, as provided in section 4(b)(3) of the Act, will be issued by the Commission to qualified persons residing in the United States upon receipt of an application duly executed on the Commission's Web site at *https://rn.ftc.gov* or by such means as the Commission or its designee may direct.

(b)(1) Registered identification numbers shall be used only by the person or concern to whom they are issued, and such numbers are not transferable or assignable.

(2) Registered identification numbers shall be subject to cancellation whenever any such number was procured or has been used improperly or contrary to the requirements of the Acts administered by the Federal Trade Commission, and regulations promulgated thereunder, or when otherwise deemed necessary in the public interest.

(3) Registered identification numbers shall be subject to cancellation if the Commission fails to receive prompt notification of any change in name, business address, or legal business status of a person or firm to whom a registered identification number has been assigned, by application duly executed on the Commission's Web site at *https://rn.ftc.gov* or by such means as the Commission or its designee may direct.

(c) Registered identification numbers assigned under this section may be used on labels required in labeling products subject to the provisions of the Wool Products Labeling Act and Fur Products Labeling Act, and numbers previously assigned by the Commission under such Acts may be used as and for the required name in labeling under this Act. When so used by the person or firm to whom assigned, the use of the numbers shall be construed as identifying and binding the applicant as fully and in all respects as though assigned under the specific Act for which it is used.

(d) Requests for a registered identification number, to update information pertaining to an existing number, or to cancel an existing number shall be made through the Commission's Web site at *https://rn.ftc.gov*. Unless otherwise directed by the Commission or its designee, requests made by other means (including but not limited to email) will not be accepted and approved.

[82 FR 43692, Sept. 19, 2017]

§303.21 Marking of samples, swatches, or specimens and products sold therefrom.

(a) Where samples, swatches, or specimens of textile fiber products subject to the Act are used to promote or effect sales of such textile fiber products, the samples, swatches, or specimens, as well as the products themselves, shall be labeled to show their respective fiber contents and other required information: *Provided*, That such samples, swatches or specimens need not be labeled:

(1) If the samples, swatches, or specimens are less than two square inches (12.9 cm^2) in area and the information otherwise required to appear on the label is clearly, conspicuously, and non-deceptively disclosed on accompanying promotional matter in accordance with the Act and regulations.

(2) If the samples, swatches, or specimens are keyed to a catalogue to which reference is necessary in order to complete the sale of the textile fiber products, and which catalogue at the necessary point of reference clearly, conspicuously, and non-deceptively discloses the information otherwise required to appear on the label in accordance with the Act and regulations; or

(3) If such samples, swatches, or specimens are not used to effect sales to ultimate consumers and are not in the form intended for sale or delivery to, or for use by, the ultimate consumer, and are accompanied by an invoice or other document showing the required information.

(b) Where properly labeled samples, swatches, or specimens are used to effect the sale of articles of wearing apparel or other household textile articles which are manufactured specifically for a particular customer after the sale is consummated, the articles of wearing apparel or other household textile articles need not be labeled if they are of the same fiber content as the samples, swatches, or specimens from which the sale was effected and an invoice or other document accompanies them showing the information otherwise required to appear on the label.

[24 FR 4480, June 2, 1959, as amended at 61 FR 11544, Mar. 21, 1996; 79 FR 18771, Apr. 4, 2014]

§ 303.22 Products containing linings, interlinings, fillings, and paddings.

In disclosing the required information as to textile fiber products, the fiber content of any linings, interlinings, fillings, or paddings shall be set forth separately and distinctly if such linings, interlinings, fillings, or paddings are incorporated in the product for warmth rather than for structural purposes, or if any express or implied representations are made as to their fiber content. Examples are as follows:

100% Nylon
Interlining: 100% Rayon
Covering: 100% Rayon
Filling: 100% Cotton.

§ 303.23 Textile fiber products containing superimposed or added fibers.

Where a textile fiber product is made wholly of one fiber or a blend of fibers with the exception of an additional fiber in minor proportion superimposed or added in certain separate and distinct areas or sections for reinforcing or other useful purposes, the product may be designated according to the fiber content of the principal fiber or blend of fibers, with an exception naming the superimposed or added fiber, giving the percentage thereof in relation to the total fiber weight of the principal fiber or blend of fibers, and indicating the area or section which contains the superimposed or added fiber. Examples of this type of fiber content disclosure, as applied to products having reinforcing fibers added to a particular area or section, are as follows:

55% Cotton
45% Rayon
Except 5% Nylon added to toe and heel.

All Cotton except 1% Nylon added to neckband.

§ 303.24 Pile fabrics and products composed thereof.

The fiber content of pile fabrics or products composed thereof may be stated on the label in such segregated form as will show the fiber content of the face or pile and of the back or base, with percentages of the respective fibers as they exist in the face or pile and in the back or base: *Provided*, That in such disclosure the respective percentages of the face and back be given in such manner as will show the ratio between the face and the back. Examples of the form of marking pile fabric as to fiber content provided for in this section are as follows:

100% Nylon Pile
100% Cotton Back
(Back constitutes 60% of fabric and pile 40%).
Face—60% Rayon, 40% Nylon
Back—70% Cotton, 30% Rayon
(Face constitutes 60% of fabric and back 40%).

§ 303.25 Sectional disclosure of content.

(a) *Permissive*. Where a textile fiber product is composed of two or more sections which are of different fiber composition, the required information as to fiber content may be separated in the same label in such manner as to show the fiber composition of each section.

(b) *Mandatory*. The disclosure as above provided shall be made in all instances where such form of marking is necessary to avoid deception.

§ 303.26 Ornamentation.

(a)(1) Where the textile fiber product contains fiber ornamentation not exceeding five per centum of the total fiber weight of the product and the stated percentages of the fiber content are exclusive of such ornamentation, the label or any invoice used in lieu thereof shall contain a phrase or statement showing such fact; as for example:

60% Cotton
40% Rayon
Exclusive of Ornamentation;

or

All Cotton
Exclusive of Ornamentation.

(2) The fiber content of such ornamentation may be disclosed where the percentage of the ornamentation in relation to the total fiber weight of the principal fiber or blend of fibers is shown; as for example:

70% Nylon
30% Acetate
Exclusive of 4% Metallic Ornamentation;

or

100% Rayon
Exclusive of 3% Silk Ornamentation.

(b) Where the fiber ornamentation exceeds five per centum, it shall be included in the statement of required percentages of fiber content.

(c) Where the ornamentation constitutes a distinct section of the product, sectional disclosure may be made in accordance with § 303.25 of this part.

§ 303.27 Use of the term "All" or "100%."

Where a textile fiber product or part thereof is comprised wholly of one fiber, other than any fiber ornamentation, decoration, elastic, or trimming as to which fiber content disclosure is not required, either the word *All* or the term *100%* may be used in labeling, together with the correct generic name of the fiber and any qualifying phrase, when required; as for example: "100% Cotton," "All Rayon, Exclusive of Ornamentation," "100% Acetate, Exclusive of Decoration," "All Nylon, Exclusive of Elastic," etc.

§ 303.28 Products contained in packages.

When textile products are marketed and delivered in a package which is intended to remain unbroken and intact until after delivery to the ultimate consumer, each textile product in the package, except hosiery, and the package shall be labeled with the required information. If the package is transparent to the extent it allows for a clear reading of the required information on the textile product, the package is not required to be labeled.

[50 FR 15107, Apr. 17, 1985]

§ 303.29 Labeling of pairs or products containing two or more units.

(a) Where a textile fiber product consists of two or more parts, units, or items of different fiber content, a separate label containing the required information shall be affixed to each of such parts, units or items showing the required information as to such part, unit, or item: *Provided*, That where such parts, units, or items are marketed or handled as a single product or ensemble and are sold and delivered to the ultimate consumer as a single product or ensemble, the required information may be set out on a single label in such a manner as to separately show the fiber composition of each part, unit, or item.

(b) Where garments, wearing apparel, or other textile fiber products are marketed or handled in pairs or ensembles of the same fiber content, only one unit of the pair or ensemble need be labeled with the required information when sold and delivered to the ultimate consumer.

[24 FR 4480, June 2, 1959, as amended at 25 FR 4318, May 14, 1960]

§ 303.30 Textile fiber products in form for consumer.

A textile fiber product shall be considered to be in the form intended for sale or delivery to, or for use by, the ultimate consumer when the manufacturing or processing of the textile fiber product is substantially complete. The fact that minor or insignificant details of the manufacturing or processing have not been completed shall not excuse the labeling of such products as to the required information. For example, a garment must be labeled even though such matters as the finishing of a hem or cuff or the affixing of buttons thereto remain to be completed.

§ 303.31 Invoice in lieu of label.

Where a textile fiber product is not in the form intended for sale, delivery to, or for use by the ultimate consumer, an invoice or other document may be used in lieu of a label, and such invoice or other document shall show, in addition to the name and address of the person issuing the invoice or other document, the fiber content of such product as provided in the Act and regulations as well as any other required information.

[79 FR 18771, Apr. 4, 2014]

§ 303.32 Products containing reused stuffing.

Any upholstered product, mattress, or cushion which contains stuffing which has been previously used as stuffing in any other upholstered product, mattress, or cushion shall have securely attached thereto a substantial tag or label, at least 2 inches (5.08 cm) by 3 inches (7.62 cm) in size, and statements thereon conspicuously stamped or printed in the English language and in plain type not less than ⅓ inch (8.38 mm) high, indicating that the stuffing therein is composed in whole or in part of "reused stuffing," "secondhand stuffing," "previously used stuffing," or "used stuffing."

[61 FR 11544, Mar. 21, 1996]

§ 303.33 Country where textile fiber products are processed or manufactured.

(a) In addition to the other information required by the Act and Regulations:

(1) Each imported textile fiber product shall be labeled with the name of the country where such imported product was processed or manufactured;

(2) Each textile fiber product completely made in the United States of materials that were made in the United States shall be labeled using the term *Made in U.S.A.* or some other clear and equivalent term.

(3) Each textile fiber product made in the United States, either in whole or in part of imported materials, shall contain a label disclosing these facts; for example:

Made in USA of imported fabric

or

Knitted in USA of imported yarn

and

(4) Each textile fiber product partially manufactured in a foreign country and partially manufactured in the United States shall contain on a label the following information:

(i) The manufacturing process in the foreign country and in the USA; for example:

"Imported cloth, finished in USA"

or

"Sewn in USA of imported components"

or

"Made in [foreign country], finished in USA"

or

"Scarf made in USA of fabric made in China"

or

"Comforter Filled, Sewn and Finished in the U.S. With Shell Made in China"

or

"Made in [Foreign Country]/fabric made in USA"

or

"Knit in USA, assembled in [Foreign Country]".

(ii) When the U.S. Customs Service requires an origin label on the unfinished product, the manufacturing processes as required in paragraph (a)(4)(i) of this section or the name of the foreign country required by Customs, for example:

"Made in (foreign country)"

(b) For the purpose of determining whether a product should be marked under paragraphs (a) (2), (3), or (4) of this section, a manufacturer needs to consider the origin of only those materials that are covered under the Act and that are one step removed from that manufacturing process. For example, a yarn manufacturer must identify fiber if it is imported, a cloth manufacturer must identify imported yarn and a household product manufacturer must identify imported cloth or imported yarn for household products made directly from yarn, or imported fiber used as filling for warmth.

(c) The term *country* means the political entity known as a nation. Except for the United States, colonies, possessions or protectorates outside the boundaries of the mother country shall be considered separate countries, and the name thereof shall be deemed acceptable in designating the country where the textile fiber product was processed or manufactured unless the Commission shall otherwise direct.

(d) The country of origin of an imported textile fiber product as determined under the laws and regulations enforced by United States Customs and Border Protection shall be considered to be the country where such textile fiber product was processed or manufactured.

(e) The English name of the country where the imported textile fiber product was processed or manufactured shall be used. The adjectival form of the name of the country will be accepted as the name of the country where the textile fiber product was processed or manufactured, provided the adjectival form of the name does not appear with such other words so as to refer to a kind or species of product. Variant spellings which clearly indicate the English name of the country, such as Brasil for Brazil and Italie for Italy, are acceptable. Abbreviations which unmistakably indicate the name of a country, such as "Gt. Britain" for "Great Britain," are acceptable.

(f) Nothing in this section shall be construed as limiting in any way the information required to be disclosed on labels under the provisions of any Tariff Act of the United States or regulations promulgated thereunder.

[24 FR 4480, June 2, 1959, as amended at 50 FR 15107, Apr. 17, 1985; 63 FR 7521, Feb. 13, 1998; 65 FR 75158, Dec. 1, 2000; 79 FR 18771, Apr. 4, 2014]

§ 303.34 Country of origin in mail order advertising.

When a textile fiber product is advertised in any mail order catalog or mail order promotional material, the description of such product shall contain a clear and conspicuous statement that the product was either made in U.S.A., imported, or both. Other words or phrases with the same meaning may be used. The statement of origin required by this section shall not be inconsistent with the origin labeling of the product being advertised.

[50 FR 15107, Apr. 17, 1985]

§ 303.35 Use of terms "virgin" or "new."

The terms *virgin* or *new* as descriptive of a textile fiber product, or any fiber or part thereof, shall not be used when the product, fiber or part so described is not composed wholly of new or virgin fiber which has never been reclaimed from any spun, woven, knitted, felted, bonded, or similarly manufactured product.

[79 FR 18771, Apr. 4, 2014]

§ 303.36 Form of separate guaranty.

(a) The following are suggested forms of separate guaranties under section 10 of the Act which may be used by a guarantor residing in the United States on or as part of an invoice or other document relating to the marketing or handling of any textile fiber products listed and designated therein, and showing the date of such invoice or other document and the signature and address of the guarantor.

(1) *General form.* We guarantee that the textile fiber products specified herein are not misbranded nor falsely nor deceptively advertised or invoiced under the provisions of the Textile Fiber Products Identification Act and rules and regulations thereunder.

(2) *Guaranty based on guaranty.* Based upon a guaranty received, we guaranty that the textile fiber products specified herein are not misbranded nor falsely nor deceptively advertised or invoiced under the provisions of the Textile Fiber Products Identification Act and rules and regulations thereunder.

NOTE: The printed name and address on the invoice or other document will suffice to meet the signature and address requirements.

(b) The mere disclosure of required information including the fiber content of a textile fiber product on a label or on an invoice or other document relating to its marketing or handling shall not be considered a form of separate guaranty.

[24 FR 4480, June 2, 1959, as amended at 79 FR 18771, Apr. 4, 2014]

§ 303.37 Form of continuing guaranty from seller to buyer.

Under section 10 of the Act, a seller residing in the United States may give a buyer a continuing guaranty to be applicable to all textile fiber products sold or to be sold. The following is the prescribed form of continuing guaranty from seller to buyer:

We, the undersigned, guaranty that all textile fiber products now being sold or which may hereafter be sold or delivered to ______________ are not, and will not be misbranded or falsely or deceptively advertised or invoiced under the provisions of the Textile Fiber Products Identification Act and rules and regulations thereunder. We acknowledge that furnishing a false guaranty is an unlawful unfair and deceptive act or practice pursuant to the Federal Trade Commission Act, and certify that we will actively monitor and ensure compliance with the Textile Fiber Products Identification Act and rules and regulations thereunder during the duration of this guaranty.

Dated, signed, and certified this ____ day of ____, 20__, at ______________ (City), ______________ (State or Territory) ______________ (name under which business is conducted.)

I certify that the information supplied in this form is true and correct.

____

Signature of Proprietor, Principal Partner, or Corporate Official

____

Name (Print or Type) and Title

[79 FR 18771, Apr. 4, 2014]

§ 303.38 Continuing guaranty filed with Federal Trade Commission.

(a)(1) Under section 10 of the act any person residing in the United States and marketing or handling textile fiber products may file a continuing guaranty with the Federal Trade Commission. When filed with the Commission a continuing guaranty shall be fully executed in duplicate. Forms for use in preparing continuing guaranties will be supplied by the Commission upon request.

(2) Continuing guaranties filed with the Commission shall continue in effect until revoked. The guarantor shall promptly report any change in business status to the Commission.

(b) Prescribed form for a continuing guaranty:

CONTINUING GUARANTY FOR FIBER & FUR PRODUCTS

BUSINESS INFORMATION

1. Legal Name of Guarantor Firm

2. Name under which Guarantor Firm does business, if different from legal name

3. Type of Company: ☐ Proprietorship ☐ Partnership ☐ Corporation

4. Address of Principal Office or Place of Business *(Include Zip Code)*

OPTIONAL INFORMATION:

Web Address:

Telephone Number: Fax Number:

UNDER WHICH LAW IS THE CONTINUING GUARANTY TO BE FILED?

5. Put an "X" in the appropriate boxes.

☐ **Under the Textile Fiber Products Identification Act** (15 U.S.C. §§ 70-70k): The company named above, which manufacturers, markets, or handles textile fiber products: (1) guarantees that any textile fiber product it sells, ships, or delivers will not be misbranded or falsely or deceptively advertised or invoiced; (2) acknowledges that furnishing a false guaranty is an unlawful unfair and deceptive act or practice pursuant to the Federal Trade Commission Act; and (3) certifies that it will actively monitor and ensure compliance with the Textile Fiber Products Identification Act and the Rules and Regulations issued under the Act during the duration of the guaranty.

☐ **Under the Wool Products Labeling Act** (15 U.S.C. §§ 68-68j): The company named above, which manufacturers, markets, or handles wool products: (1) guarantees that any wool product it sells, ships, or delivers will not be misbranded; (2) acknowledges that furnishing a false guaranty is an unlawful unfair and deceptive act or practice pursuant to the Federal Trade Commission Act; and (3) certifies that it will actively monitor and ensure compliance with the Wool Products Labeling Act and the Rules and Regulations issued under the Act during the duration of the guaranty.

☐ **Under the Fur Products Labeling Act** (15 U.S.C. §§ 69-69k): The company named above, which manufacturers, markets, or handles fur products: (1) guarantees that any fur product it sells, ships, or delivers will not be misbranded or falsely or deceptively advertised or invoiced; (2) acknowledges that furnishing a false guaranty is an unlawful unfair and deceptive act or practice pursuant to the Federal Trade Commission Act; and (3) certifies that it will actively monitor and ensure compliance with the Fur Products Labeling Act and the Rules and Regulations issued under the Act during the duration of the guaranty.

CERTIFICATION

I hereby certify that the information provided on this form is true and correct.

6. Signature of proprietor, principal partner, or corporate official

7. Name *(Please print or type)*

8. Title

9. City and State where signed

10. Date

INSTRUCTIONS

The Textile Fiber Products Identification Act, the Wool Products Labeling Act, and the Fur Products Labeling Act provide that any marketer or manufacturer of fiber or fur products covered by those Acts may file a continuing guaranty with the Federal Trade Commission. The person signing and certifying the guaranty must reside in the United States. Use this form to file such guaranties with the Federal Trade Commission.

In completing this form, please observe the following:

(a) All appropriate blanks on the form should be filled in. Include your Zip Code in item 4.

(b) In item 6, signature of proprietor, partner, or corporate official of guarantor firm.

(c) Send two completed, signed original copies to:

Federal Trade Commission
Division of Enforcement
600 Pennsylvania Ave., NW
Washington, DC 20580

(d) Do not fax application - mail signed originals only.

Length of Guaranty:
Continuing guaranties continue in effect until revoked.

Changes:
The guarantor must immediately notify the Commission in writing of any change in business status. Any change in the address of the guarantor's principal office and place of business must also be promptly reported.

DO NOT USE THIS SPACE
Filed______________ 20___
FEDERAL TRADE COMMISSION

FTC Form 31-A (rev. 09/13)

(c) Any person who has a continuing guaranty on file with the Commission may, during the effective dates of the guaranty, give notice of such fact by setting forth on the invoice or other document covering the marketing or handling of the product guaranteed the following: Continuing guaranty under the Textile Fiber Products Identification Act filed with the Federal Trade Commission.

(d) Any person who falsely represents in writing that he has a continuing guaranty on file with the Federal Trade Commission when such is not a fact shall be deemed to have furnished a false guaranty under section 10(b) of the Act.

[24 FR 4486, June 2, 1959, as amended at 48 FR 12517, Mar. 25, 1983; 63 FR 7521, Feb. 18, 1998; 63 FR 71585, Dec. 28, 1998; 79 FR 18772, Apr. 4, 2014]

§ 303.39 Maintenance of records.

(a) Pursuant to the provisions of section 6 of the Act, every manufacturer of a textile fiber product subject to the Act, irrespective of whether any guaranty has been given or received, shall maintain records showing the information required by the Act and Regulations with respect to all such textile fiber products made by such manufacturer. Such records shall show:

(1) The generic names and percentages by weight of the constituent fibers present in the textile fiber product, exclusive of permissive ornamentation, in amounts of five per centum or more.

(2) The name, provided for in § 303.19, or registered identification number issued by the Commission, of the manufacturer or of one or more persons marketing or handling the textile fiber product.

(3) The name of the country where such product was processed or manufactured as provided for in § 303.33.

The purpose of the records is to permit a determination that the requirements of the Act and Regulations have been met and to establish a traceable line of continuity from raw material through processing to finished product.

(b) Any person substituting a stamp, tag, label, or other identification pursuant to section 5(b) of the Act shall keep such records as will show the information set forth on the stamp, tag, label, or other identification that he removed and the name or names of the person or persons from whom such textile fiber product was received.

(c) The records required to be maintained pursuant to the provisions of this rule shall be preserved for at least three years.

[24 FR 4480, June 2, 1959, as amended at 53 FR 31315, Aug. 18, 1988]

§ 303.40 Use of terms in written advertisements that imply presence of a fiber.

The use of terms in written advertisements, including advertisements disseminated through the Internet and similar electronic media, that are descriptive of a method of manufacture, construction, or weave, and that by custom and usage are also indicative of a textile fiber or fibers, or the use of terms in such advertisements that constitute or connote the name or presence of a fiber or fibers, shall be deemed to be an implication of fiber content under section 4(c) of the Act, except that the provisions of this section shall not be applicable to non-deceptive shelf or display signs in retail stores indicating the location of textile fiber products and not intended as advertisements.

[63 FR 7523, Feb. 13, 1998]

§ 303.41 Use of fiber trademarks and generic names in advertising.

(a) In advertising textile fiber products, the use of a fiber trademark or a generic fiber name shall require a full disclosure of the fiber content information required by the Act and regulations in at least one instance in the advertisement.

(b) Where a fiber trademark is used in advertising textile fiber products containing more than one fiber, other than permissible ornamentation, such fiber trademark and the generic name of the fiber must appear in the required fiber content information in immediate proximity and conjunction with each other in plainly legible type or lettering of equal size and conspicuousness.

(c) Where a fiber trademark is used in advertising textile fiber products containing only one fiber, other than permissive ornamentation, such fiber trademark and the generic name of the fiber must appear in immediate proximity and conjunction with each other in plainly legible and conspicuous type or lettering at least once in the advertisement.

(d) Where a fiber trademark or generic name is used in non-required information in advertising, such fiber trademark or generic name, shall not be used in such a manner as to be false, deceptive, or misleading as to fiber content, or to indicate, directly or indirectly, that a textile fiber product is composed wholly or in part of a particular fiber, when such is not the case.

[24 FR 4480, June 2, 1959, as amended at 79 FR 18774, Apr. 4, 2014]

§ 303.42 Arrangement of information in advertising textile fiber products.

(a) Where a textile fiber product is advertised in such manner as to require disclosure of the information required by the Act and regulations, all parts of the required information shall be stated in immediate conjunction with each other in legible and conspicuous type or lettering of equal size and prominence. In making the required disclosure of the fiber content of the product, the generic names of fibers present in an amount 5 percent or more of the total fiber weight of the product, together with any fibers disclosed in accordance with § 303.3(a), shall appear in order of predominance by weight, to be followed by the designation "other fiber" or "other fibers" if a fiber or fibers required to be so designated are present. The advertisement need not state the percentage of each fiber.

(b) Non-required information or representations shall in no way be false, deceptive, or misleading as to fiber content and shall not include any names, terms, or representations prohibited by the Act and regulations. Such non-required information or representations shall not be set forth or so used as to interfere with, minimize, or detract from the required information.

(c) Non-deceptive terms which are properly and truthfully descriptive of a fiber may be used in conjunction with the generic name of such fiber; as for example: "cross-linked rayon," "solution dyed acetate," "combed cotton," "nylon 66," etc.

[24 FR 4480, June 2, 1959, as amended at 30 FR 14254, Nov. 13, 1965; 30 FR 15313, Dec. 11, 1965; 63 FR 7523, Feb. 13, 1998; 79 FR 18774, Apr. 4, 2014]

§ 303.43 Fiber content tolerances.

(a) A textile fiber product which contains more than one fiber shall not be deemed to be misbranded as to fiber content percentages if the percentages by weight of any fibers present in the total fiber content of the product, exclusive of permissive ornamentation, do not deviate or vary from the percentages stated on the label in excess of 3 percent of the total fiber weight of the product. For example, where the label indicates that a particular fiber is present in the amount of 40 percent, the amount of such fiber present may vary from a minimum of 37 percent of the total fiber weight of such product to a maximum of 43 percent of the total fiber weight of such product.

(b) Where the percentage of any fiber or fibers contained in a textile fiber product deviates or varies from the percentage stated on the label by more than the tolerance or variation provided in paragraph (a) of this section, such product shall be misbranded unless the person charged proves that the entire deviation or variation from the fiber content percentages stated on the label resulted from unavoidable variations in manufacture and despite the exercise of due care.

(c) Where representations are made to the effect that a textile fiber product is composed wholly of one fiber, the tolerance provided in section 4(b)(2) of the Act and paragraph (a) of this section shall not apply, except as to permissive ornamentation where the textile fiber product is represented to be composed of one fiber "exclusive of ornamentation."

§ 303.44 Products not intended for uses subject to the Act.

Textile fiber products intended for uses not within the scope of the Act and regulations or intended for uses in other textile fiber products which are exempted or excluded from the Act shall not be subject to the labeling and invoicing requirements of the Act and regulations: *Provided*, an invoice or other document covering the marketing or handling of such products is given, which indicates that the products are not intended for uses subject to the Textile Fiber Products Identification Act.

[79 FR 18774, Apr. 4, 2014]

§ 303.45 Coverage and exclusions from the Act.

(a) The following textile fiber products are subject to the Act and regulations in this part, unless excluded from the Act's requirements in paragraph (b) of this section:

(1) Articles of wearing apparel;

(2) Handkerchiefs;

(3) Scarfs;

(4) Beddings;

(5) Curtains and casements;

(6) Draperies;

(7) Tablecloths, napkins, and doilies;

(8) Floor coverings;

(9) Towels;

(10) Wash cloths and dish cloths;

(11) Ironing board covers and pads;

(12) Umbrellas and parasols;

(13) Batts;

(14) Products subject to section 4(h) of the Act;

(15) Flags with heading or more than 216 square inches (13.9 dm^2) in size;

(16) Cushions;

(17) All fibers, yarns and fabrics (including narrow fabrics except packaging ribbons);

(18) Furniture slip covers and other covers or coverlets for furniture;

(19) Afghans and throws;

(20) Sleeping bags;

(21) Antimacassars and tidies;

(22) Hammocks; and

(23) Dresser and other furniture scarfs.

(b) Pursuant to section 12(b) of the Act, all textile fiber products other than those identified in paragraph (a) of this section, and the following textile fiber products, are excluded from the Act's requirements:

(1) Belts, suspenders, arm bands, permanently knotted neckties, garters, sanitary belts, diaper liners, labels (either required or non-required) individually and in rolls, looper clips intended for handicraft purposes, book cloth, artists' canvases, tapestry cloth, and shoe laces.

(2) All textile fiber products manufactured by the operators of company stores and offered for sale and sold exclusively to their own employees as ultimate consumers.

(3) Coated fabrics and those portions of textile fiber products made of coated fabrics.

(4) Secondhand household textile articles which are discernibly secondhand or which are marked to indicate their secondhand character.

(5) Non-woven products of a disposable nature intended for one-time use only.

(6) All curtains, casements, draperies, and table place mats, or any portions thereof otherwise subject to the Act, made principally of slats, rods, or strips, composed of wood, metal, plastic, or leather.

(7) All textile fiber products in a form ready for the ultimate consumer procured by the military services of the United States which are bought according to specifications, but shall not include those textile fiber products sold and distributed through post exchanges, sales commissaries, or ship stores; provided, however, that if the military services sell textile fiber products for nongovernmental purposes the information with respect to the fiber content of such products shall be furnished to the purchaser thereof who shall label such products in conformity with the Act and regulations before such products are distributed for civilian use.

(8) All hand woven rugs made by Navajo Indians which have attached thereto the "Certificate of Genuineness" supplied by the Indian Arts and Crafts Board of the United States Department of Interior. The term Navajo Indian means any Indian who is listed on the register of the Navajo Indian Tribe or is eligible for listing thereon.

(c) The exclusions provided for in paragraph (b) of this section shall not be applicable:

(1) if any representations as to the fiber content of such products are made on any label or in any advertisement without making a full and complete fiber content disclosure on such label or in such advertisement in accordance with the Act and regulations in this part with the exception of those products excluded by paragraph (b)(5) of this section; or

(2) If any false, deceptive, or misleading representations are made as to the fiber content of such products.

(d) The exclusions from the Act provided in paragraph (b) of this section are in addition to the exemptions from the Act provided in section 12(a) of the Act and shall not affect or limit such exemptions.

[79 FR 18774, Apr. 4, 2014]

PART 304—RULES AND REGULATIONS UNDER THE HOBBY PROTECTION ACT

Sec.

AUTHORITY: 15 U.S.C. 2101 *et seq.*

SOURCE: 40 FR 5496, Feb. 6, 1975, unless otherwise noted.

§ 304.1 Terms defined.

(a) *Act* means the Hobby Protection Act (approved November 29, 1973; Pub. L. 93–167, 87 Stat. 686, (15 U.S.C. 2101 *et seq.*)).

(b) *Commerce* has the same meanings as such term has under the Federal Trade Commission Act.

(c) *Commission* means the Federal Trade Commission.

(d) *Imitation numismatic item* means an item which purports to be, but in fact is not, an original numismatic item or which is a reproduction, copy, or counterfeit of an original numismatic item. Such term includes an original numismatic item which has been altered or modified in such a manner that it could reasonably purport to be an original numismatic item other than the one which was altered or modified. The term shall not include any re-issue or re-strike of any original numismatic item by the United States or any foreign government.

(e) *Imitation political item* means an item which purports to be, but in fact is not, an original political item, or which is a reproduction, copy or counterfeit of an original item.

(f) *Original numismatic item* means anything which has been a part of a coinage or issue which has been used in exchange or has been used to commemorate a person, object, place, or event. Such term includes coins, tokens, paper money, and commemorative medals.

(g) *Original political item* means any political button, poster, literature, sticker, or any advertisement produced for use in any political cause.

(h) *Person* means any individual, group, association, partnership, or any other business entity.

(i) *Regulations* means any or all regulations prescribed by the Federal Trade Commission pursuant to the Act.

(j) *United States* means the States, the District of Columbia, and the Commonwealth of Puerto Rico.

(k) *Diameter of a reproduction* means the length of the longest possible straight line connecting two points on the perimeter of the reproduction.

[40 FR 5496, Feb. 6, 1975, as amended at 53 FR 38942, Oct. 4, 1988]

§ 304.2 General requirement.

Imitation political or numismatic items subject to the Act shall be marked in conformity with the requirements of the Act and the regulations promulgated thereunder. Any violation of these regulations shall constitute a violation of the Act and of the Federal Trade Commission Act.

§ 304.3 Applicability.

Any person engaged in the manufacturing, or importation into the United States for introduction into or distribution in commerce, of imitation political or imitation numismatic items shall be subject to the requirements of the Act and the regulations promulgated thereunder. Any person engaged in the sale in commerce of imitation numismatic items shall be subject to the requirements of the Act and the regulations promulgated thereunder. It shall be a violation of the Act and the regulations promulgated thereunder for a person to provide substantial assistance or support to any manufacturer, importer, or seller of imitation numismatic items, or to any manufacturer or importer of imitation political items, if that person knows or should have known that the manufacturer, importer, or seller is engaged in any practice that violates the Act and the regulations promulgated thereunder.

[81 FR 70938, Oct. 14, 2016]

§ 304.4 Application of other law or regulation.

The provisions of these regulations are in addition to, and not in substitution for or limitation of, the provisions of any other law or regulation of the United States (including the existing statutes and regulations prohibiting the reproduction of genuine currency) or of the law or regulation of any State.

§ 304.5 Marking requirements for imitation political items.

(a) An imitation political item which is manufactured in the United States, or imported into the United States for introduction into or distribution in commerce, shall be plainly and permanently marked with the calendar year in which such item was manufactured.

(b) The calendar year shall be marked upon the item legibly, conspicuously and nondeceptively, and in accordance with the further requirements of these regulations.

(1) The calendar year shall appear in arabic numerals, shall be based upon the Gregorian calendar and shall consist of four digits.

(2) The calendar year shall be marked on either the obverse or the reverse surface of the item. It shall not be marked on the edge of the item.

(3) An imitation political item of incusable material shall be incused with the calendar year in sans-serif numerals. Each numeral shall have a vertical dimension of not less than two millimeters (2.0 mm) and a minimum depth of three-tenths of one millimeter (0.3 mm) or one-half (½) the thickness of the reproduction, whichever is the lesser. The minimum total horizontal dimension for the four numerals composing the calendar year shall be six millimeters (6.0 mm).

(4) An imitation political button, poster, literature, sticker, or advertisement composed of nonincusable material shall be imprinted with the calendar year in sans-serif numerals. Each numeral shall have a vertical dimension of not less than two millimeters (2.0 mm). The minimum total horizontal dimension of the four numerals composing the calendar year shall be six millimeters (6.0 mm).

§ 304.6 Marking requirements for imitation numismatic items.

(a) An imitation numismatic item which is manufactured in the United States, or imported into the United States for introduction into or distribution in commerce, shall be plainly and permanently marked "COPY".

(b) The word "COPY" shall be marked upon the item legibly, conspicuously, and nondeceptively, and in accordance with the further requirements of these regulations.

(1) The word "COPY" shall appear in capital letters, in the English language.

(2) The word "COPY" shall be marked on either the obverse or the reverse surface of the item. It shall not be marked on the edge of the item.

(3) An imitation numismatic item of incusable material shall be incused with the word "COPY" in sans-serif letters having a vertical dimension of not less than two millimeters (2.0 mm) or not less than one-sixth of the diameter of the reproduction, and a minimum depth of three-tenths of one millimeter (0.3 mm) or to one-half (½) the thickness of the reproduction, whichever is the lesser. The minimum total horizontal dimension of the word "COPY" shall be six millimeters (6.0 mm) or not less than one-half of the diameter of the reproduction.

(4) An imitation numismatic item composed of nonincusable material shall be imprinted with the word "COPY" in sans-serif letters having a vertical dimension of not less than two millimeters (2.0 mm) or not less than one-sixth of the diameter of the reproduction. The minimum total horizontal dimension of the word "COPY" shall be six millimeters (6.0 mm) or not less than one-half of the diameter of the reproduction.

[40 FR 5496, Feb. 6, 1975, as amended at 53 FR 38942, Oct. 4, 1988]

PART 305—ENERGY AND WATER USE LABELING FOR CONSUMER PRODUCTS UNDER THE ENERGY POLICY AND CONSERVATION ACT ("ENERGY LABELING RULE")

AUTHORITY: 42 U.S.C. 6294.

SOURCE: 52 FR 46894, Dec. 10, 1987, unless otherwise noted.

SCOPE

§ 305.1 Scope of the regulations in this part.

The rule in this part establishes requirements for consumer appliance products, as hereinafter described, in commerce, as "commerce" is defined in the Energy Policy and Conservation Act, 42 U.S.C. 6291, with respect to:

(a) Labeling and/or marking the products with information required by this part indicating their operating cost (or different useful measure of energy consumption) and related information, disclosing their water use rate and related information, or stating their compliance with applicable standards under section 325 of the Energy Policy and Conservation Act, 42 U.S.C. 6295;

(b) Including in printed matter displayed or distributed at the point of sale of such products, or including in any catalog from which the products may be purchased, information concerning their water use or their energy consumption;

(c) Including on the labels, separately attaching to the products, or shipping with the products, additional information relating to energy consumption, energy efficiency, or energy cost; and

(d) Making representations, in writing or in broadcast advertising, respecting the water use, energy consumption, or energy efficiency of the products, or the cost of water used or energy consumed by the products.

[52 FR 46894, Dec. 10, 1987, as amended at 54 FR 28034, July 5, 1989]

DEFINITIONS

§ 305.2 Definitions.

(a) *Act* means the Energy Policy and Conservation Act (Pub. L. 94–163), and amendments thereto.

(b) *ANSI* means the American National Standards Institute and, as used herein, is the prefix for national standards and codes adopted by ANSI.

(c) *ASME* means the American Society of Mechanical Engineers and, as used herein, is the prefix for national standards and codes adopted by ASME.

(d) *Average lamp efficacy* means the lamp efficacy readings taken over a statistically significant period of manufacture with the readings averaged over that period.

(e) *Ballast efficacy factor* means the relative light output divided by the power input of a fluorescent lamp ballast, as measured under test conditions specified in American National Standards Institute (ANSI) standard C82.2–1984, or as may be prescribed by the Secretary of Energy. Copies of ANSI standard C82.2–1984 may be obtained from the American National Standards Institute, 11 West 42nd St., New York, NY 10036.

(f) *Base* for lamps means the portion of the lamp which screws into the socket.

(g) *Bulb shape* means the shape of the lamp, especially the glass portion.

(h) *Catalog* means printed material, including material disseminated over the Internet, which contains the terms of sale, retail price, and instructions for ordering, from which a retail consumer can order a covered product.

(i) *Color rendering index* or *CRI* for lamps means the measure of the degree of color shift objects undergo when illuminated by a light source as compared with the color of those same objects when illuminated by a reference source of comparable color temperature.

(j) *Commission* means the Federal Trade Commission.

(k) *Consumer product* means any article (other than an automobile, as "automobile" is defined in 15 U.S.C. 2001(1) [sec. 501(1) of the Motor Vehicle Information and Cost Savings Act]) of a type—

(1) Which in operation consumes, or is designed to consume, energy or, with respect to showerheads, faucets, water closets, and urinals, water; and

(2) Which, to any significant extent, is distributed in commerce for personal use or consumption by individuals; without regard to whether such article or such type is in fact distributed in commerce for personal use or consumption by an individual, except that such term includes fluorescent lamp ballasts, metal halide lamp fixtures, general service fluorescent lamps, medium base compact fluorescent lamps, general service incandescent lamps (including incandescent reflector lamps), showerheads, faucets, water closets, and urinals distributed in commerce for personal or commercial use or consumption.

(l) *Consumer appliance product* means any of the following consumer products, excluding those products designed solely for use in recreational vehicles and other mobile equipment:

(1) Refrigerators, refrigerator-freezers, and freezers that can be operated by alternating current electricity, excluding—

(i) Any type designed to be used without doors; and

(ii) Any type which does not include a compressor and condenser unit as an integral part of the cabinet assembly.

(2) Dishwashers.

(3) Water heaters.

(4) Room air conditioners.

(5) Clothes washers.

(6) Clothes dryers.

(7) Central air conditioners and central air conditioning heat pumps.

(8) Furnaces.

(9) Direct heating equipment.

(10) Pool heaters.

(11) Kitchen ranges and ovens.

(12) Television sets.

(13) Fluorescent lamp ballasts.

(14) General service fluorescent lamps.

(15) Medium base compact fluorescent lamps.

(16) General service incandescent lamps, including incandescent reflector lamps.

(17) Showerheads.

(18) Faucets.

(19) Water closets.

(20) Urinals.

(21) Metal halide lamp fixtures.

(22) Ceiling fans.

(23) Any other type of consumer product that the Department of Energy classifies as a covered product under section 322(b) of the Act (42 U.S.C. 6292).

(m) *Correlated color temperature* for lamps means the absolute temperature of a blackbody whose chromaticity most nearly resembles that of the light source.

(n) *Covered product* means any consumer product or consumer appliance product described in § 305.3 of this part.

(o) *Distributor* means a person (other than a manufacturer or retailer) to whom a consumer appliance product is delivered or sold for purposes of distribution in commerce.

(p) *Energy efficiency rating* means the following product-specific energy usage descriptors: *annual fuel utilization efficiency (AFUE)* for furnaces; *combined energy efficiency ratio (CEER)* for room air conditioners; *seasonal energy efficiency ratio (SEER)* for the cooling function of central air conditioners and heat pumps; *heating seasonal performance factor (HSPF)* for the heating function of heat pumps; *airflow efficiency* for ceiling fans; and, *thermal efficiency (TE)* for pool heaters, as these descriptors are determined in accordance with tests prescribed under section 323 of the Act (42 U.S.C. 6293). These product-specific energy usage descriptors shall be used in satisfying all the requirements of this part.

(q) *Estimated annual energy consumption and estimated annual operating cost*—(1) *Estimated annual energy consumption* means the energy or (for products described in sections 305.3(n)–(q)) water that is likely to be consumed annually in representative use of a consumer product, as determined in accordance with tests prescribed under section 323 of the Act (42 U.S.C. 6293).

(i) *Kilowatt-hour use per year*, or *kWh/yr.*, means estimated annual energy consumption expressed in kilowatt-hours of electricity.

(ii) *Therm use per year*, or *therms/yr.*, means estimated annual energy consumption expressed in therms of natural gas.

(iii) *Gallon use per year*, or *gallons/yr.*, means estimated annual energy consumption expressed in gallons of propane or No. 2 heating oil.

(2) *Estimated annual operating cost* means the aggregate retail cost of the energy that is likely to be consumed annually in representative use of a consumer product, as determined in accordance with tests prescribed under section 323 of the Act (42 U.S.C. 6293).

(r) *Flow restricting or controlling spout end device* means an aerator used in a faucet.

(s) *Flushometer valve* means a valve attached to a pressured water supply pipe and so designed that, when actuated, it opens the line for direct flow into the fixture at a rate and quantity to operate properly the fixture, and then gradually closes to provide trap reseal in the fixture in order to avoid water hammer. The pipe to which this device is connected is in itself of sufficient size that, when opened, will allow the device to deliver water at a sufficient rate of flow for flushing purposes.

(t) *IES* means the Illuminating Engineering Society of North America and, as used herein, is the prefix for test procedures adopted by IES.

(u) *Lamp efficacy* means the light output of a lamp divided by its wattage, expressed in lumens per watt (LPW).

(v) *Lamp type* means all lamps designated as having the same electrical and lighting characteristics and made by one manufacturer.

(w) *Life* and *lifetime* for lamps mean length of operating time of a statistically large group of lamps between first use and failure of 50 percent of the group.

(x) *Light output* for lamps means the total luminous flux (power) of a lamp in lumens.

(y) *Luminaire* means a complete lighting unit consisting of a fluorescent lamp or lamps, together with parts designed to distribute the light, to position and protect such lamps, and to connect such lamps to the power supply through the ballast.

(z) *Manufacturer* means any person who manufactures, produces, assembles, or imports a consumer appliance product. Assembly operations which are solely decorative are not included.

(aa) *New covered product*, as used in § 305.4, means a covered product the title of which has not passed to a purchaser who buys the product for purposes other than resale or leasing for a period in excess of one year.

(bb) *Private labeler* means an owner of a brand or trademark on the label of a consumer appliance product which bears a private label.

(cc) *Range of comparability* means a group of models within a class of covered products, each model of which satisfies approximately the same consumer needs.

(dd) *Range of energy efficiency ratings* means the range of energy efficiency ratings for all models within a designated range of comparability.

(ee) *Range of estimated annual energy cost* means the range of estimated annual energy cost per year of all models within a designated range of comparability.

(ff) *Retailer* means a person to whom a consumer appliance product is delivered or sold, if such delivery or sale is for purposes of sale or distribution in commerce to purchasers who buy such product for purposes other than resale. The term *retailer* includes purchasers of appliances who install such appliances in newly constructed or newly rehabilitated housing, or mobile homes, with the intent to sell the covered appliances as part of the sale of such housing or mobile homes.

(gg) *Water use* means the quantity of water flowing through a showerhead, faucet, water closet, or urinal at point of use, determined in accordance with test procedures under section 323 of the Act, 42 U.S.C. 6293.

(hh) *Wattage* for lamps means the total electrical power consumed by a lamp in watts, after an initial seasoning period and including, for fluorescent lamps, arc watts plus cathode watts.

[72 FR 49965, Aug. 29, 2007, as amended at 73 FR 39225, July 9, 2008; 73 FR 63066, Oct. 23, 2008; 83 FR 7596, Feb. 22, 2018]

§ 305.3 Description of covered products.

(a) *Refrigerators and refrigerator-freezers.* (1) *Electric refrigerator* means a cabinet designed for the refrigerated storage of food, designed to be capable of achieving storage temperatures above 32 °F (0 °C) and below 39 °F (3.9 °C), and having a source of refrigeration requiring single phase, alternating current electric energy input only. An electric refrigerator may include a compartment for the freezing and storage of food at temperatures below 32 °F (0 °C), but does not provide a separate low temperature compartment designed for the freezing and storage of food at temperatures below 8 °F (−13.3 °C).

(2) *Electric refrigerator-freezer* means a cabinet which consists of two or more compartments with at least one of the compartments designed for the refrigerated storage of food and designed to be capable of achieving storage temperatures above 32 °F (0 °C) and below 39 °F (3.9 °C), and with at least one of the compartments designed for the freezing and storage of food at temperatures below 8 °F (−13.3 °C) which may be adjusted by the user to a temperature of 0 °F (−17.8 °C) or below. The source of refrigeration requires single phase, alternating current electric energy input only.

(b) *Freezer* means a cabinet designed as a unit for the freezing and storage of food at temperatures of 0 °F. or below, and having a source of refrigeration requiring single phase, alternating current electric energy input only.

(c) *Dishwasher* means a cabinetlike appliance which, with the aid of water and detergent, washes, rinses, and dries (when a drying process is included) dishware, glassware, eating utensils and most cooking utensils by chemical, mechanical, and/or electrical means and discharges to the plumbing drainage system.

(1) *Water Heating Dishwasher* means a dishwasher which is designed for heating cold inlet water (nominal 50 °F.) or a dishwasher for which the manufacturer recommends operation with a nominal inlet water temperature of 120 °F. and may operate at either of these inlet water temperatures by providing internal water heating to above 120 °F. in at least one wash phase of the normal cycle.

(2) [Reserved]

(d) *Water heater* means a product which utilizes oil, gas, or electricity to heat potable water for use outside the heater upon demand, including—

(1) Storage type units which heat and store water at a thermostatically controlled temperature, including gas storage water heaters with an input of 75,000 Btu per hour or less, oil storage water heaters with an input of 105,000 Btu per hour or less, and electric storage water heaters with an input of 12 kilowatts or less;

(2) Instantaneous type units which heat water but contain no more than one gallon of water per 4,000 Btu per hour of input, including gas instantaneous water heaters with an input of 200,000 Btu per hour or less, oil instantaneous water heaters with an input of 210,000 Btu per hour or less, and electric instantaneous water heaters with an input of 12 kilowatts or less; and

(3) Heat pump type units, with a maximum current rating of 24 amperes at a voltage no greater than 250 volts, which are products designed to transfer thermal energy from one temperature level to a higher temperature level for the purpose of heating water, including all ancillary equipment such as fans, storage tanks, pumps, or controls necessary for the device to perform its function.

(e) *Room air conditioner* means a consumer product, other than a packaged terminal air conditioner, which is powered by a single phase electric current and which is an encased assembly designed as a unit for mounting in a window or through the wall for the purpose of providing delivery of conditioned air to an enclosed space. It includes a prime source of refrigeration and may include a means for ventilating and heating.

(f) *Clothes washer* means a consumer product designed to clean clothes, utilizing a water solution of soap and/or detergent and mechanical agitation or other movement, and must be one of the following classes: automatic clothes washers, semi-automatic clothes washers, and other clothes washers.

(1) *Automatic clothes washer* means a class of clothes washer which has a control system capable of scheduling a pre-selected combination of operations, such as regulation of water fill level, and performance of wash, rinse, drain and spin functions, without the need for the user to intervene subsequent to the initiation of machine operation. Some models may require user intervention to initiate these different segments of the cycle after the machine has begun operation, but they do not require the user to intervene to regulate the water temperature by adjusting the external water faucet valves.

(2) *Semi-automatic clothes washer* means a class of clothes washer that is the same as an automatic clothes washer except that the user must intervene to regulate the water temperature by adjusting the external water faucet valves.

(3) *Other clothes washer* means a class of clothes washer which is not an automatic or semi-automatic clothes washer.

(g) *Furnaces*. (1) *Furnace* means a product which utilizes only single-phase electric current, or single-phase electric current or DC current in conjunction with natural gas, propane, or home heating oil, and which—

(i) Is designed to be the principal heating sources for the living space of a residence;

(ii) Is not contained within the same cabinet with a central air conditioner whose rated cooling capacity is above 65,000 Btu per hour;

(iii) Is an electric central furnace, electric boiler, forced-air central furnace, gravity central furnace, or low pressure steam or hot water boiler; and

(iv) Has a heat input rate of less than 300,000 Btu per hour for electric boilers and low pressure steam or hot water boilers and less than 225,000 Btu per hour for forced-air central furnaces, gravity central furnaces, and electric central furnaces.

(2) *Electric central furnace* means a furnace designed to supply heat through a system of ducts with air as the heating medium, in which heat is generated by one or more electric resistance heating elements and the heated air is circulated by means of a fan or blower.

(3) *Forced air central furnace* means a gas or oil burning furnace designed to supply heat through a system of ducts with air as the heating medium. The heat generated by combustion of gas or oil is transferred to the air within a casing by conduction through heat exchange surfaces and is circulated through the duct system by means of a fan or blower.

(4) *Gravity central furnace* means a gas fueled furnace which depends primarily on natural convection for circulation of heated air and which is designed to be used in conjunction with a system of ducts.

(5) *Electric boiler* means an electrically powered furnace designed to supply low pressure steam or hot water for space heating application. A low pressure steam boiler operates at or below 15 pounds per square inch gauge (psig) steam pressure; a hot water boiler operates at or below 160 psig water pressure and 250 °F. water temperature.

(6) *Low pressure steam or hot water boiler* means an electric, gas or oil burning furnace designed to supply low pressure steam or hot water for space heating application. A low pressure steam boiler operates at or below 15 pounds psig steam pressure; a hot water boiler operates at or below 160 psig water pressure and 250 °F. water temperature.

(7) *Outdoor furnace or boiler* is a furnace or boiler normally intended for installation out-of-doors or in an unheated space (such as an attic or a crawl space).

(8) *Weatherized warm air furnace or boiler* means a furnace or boiler designed for installation outdoors, approved for resistance to wind, rain, and snow, and supplied with its own venting system.

(h) *Central air conditioner* means a product, other than a packaged terminal air conditioner, which is powered by single phase electric current, air cooled, rated below 65,000 Btu per hour, not contained within the same cabinet as a furnace, the rated capacity of which is above 225,000 Btu per hour, and is a heat pump or a cooling only unit.

(1) *Condenser-evaporator coil combination* means a condensing unit made by one manufacturer and one of several evaporator coils, either manufactured

by the same manufacturer or another manufacturer, intended to be combined with that particular condensing unit.

(2) *Condensing unit* means a component of a "central air conditioner" which is designed to remove heat absorbed by the refrigerant and to transfer it to the outside environment, and which consists of an outdoor coil, compressor(s), and air moving device.

(3) *Evaporator coil* means a component of a central air conditioner which is designed to absorb heat from an enclosed space and transfer the heat to a refrigerant.

(4) *Single package unit* means any central air conditioner in which all the major assemblies are enclosed in one cabinet.

(5) *Split system* means any central air conditioner in which one or more of the major assemblies are separate from the others.

(i) *Heat pump* means a product, other than a packaged terminal heat pump, which consists of one or more assemblies, powered by single phase electric current, rated below 65,000 Btu per hour, utilizing an indoor conditioning coil, compressor, and refrigerant-to-outdoor air heat exchanger to provide air heating, and may also provide air cooling, dehumidifying, humidifying, circulating, and air cleaning.

(j) *Fluorescent lamp ballast* means a device which is used to start and operate fluorescent lamps by providing a starting voltage and current and limiting the current during normal operation.

(k) *Fluorescent lamp:* (1) Means a low pressure mercury electric-discharge source in which a fluorescing coating transforms some of the ultra-violet energy generated by the mercury discharge into light, including only the following:

(i) Any straight-shaped lamp (commonly referred to as 4-foot medium bi-pin lamps) with medium bi-pin bases of nominal overall length of 48 inches and rated wattage of 28 or more;

(ii) Any U-shaped lamp (commonly referred to as 2-foot U-shaped lamps) with medium bi-pin bases of nominal overall length between 22 and 25 inches and rated wattage of 28 or more;

(iii) Any rapid start lamp (commonly referred to as 8-foot high output lamps) with recessed double contact bases of nominal overall length of 96 inches and 0.800 nominal amperes, as defined in ANSI C78.1–1978 and related supplements (copies of ANSI C78.1–1978 and related supplements may be obtained from the American National Standards Institute, 11 West 42nd St., New York, NY 10036); and

(iv) Any instant start lamp (commonly referred to as 8-foot slimline lamps) with single pin bases of nominal overall length of 96 inches and rated wattage of 52 or more, as defined in ANSI C78.3–1978 (R1984) and related supplement ANSI C78.3a–1985 (copies of ANSI C78.3–1978 (R1984) and related supplement ANSI C78.3a–1985 may be obtained from the American National Standards Institute, 11 West 42nd St., New York, NY 10036); but

(2) *Fluorescent lamp* does not mean any lamp excluded by the Department of Energy, by rule, as a result of a determination that standards for such lamp would not result in significant energy savings because such lamp is designed for special applications or has special characteristics not available in reasonably substitutable lamp types; and

(3) *General service fluorescent lamp* means a fluorescent lamp which can be used to satisfy the majority of fluorescent applications, but does not mean any lamp designed and marketed for the following nongeneral lighting applications:

(i) Fluorescent lamps designed to promote plant growth;

(ii) Fluorescent lamps specifically designed for cold temperature installations;

(iii) Colored fluorescent lamps;

(iv) Impact-resistant fluorescent lamps;

(v) Reflectorized or aperture lamps;

(vi) Fluorescent lamps designed for use in reprographic equipment;

(vii) Lamps primarily designed to produce radiation in the ultra-violet region of the spectrum; and

(viii) Lamps with a color rendering index of 82 or greater.

(l) *General service lamp* means:

(1) A lamp that is:

(i) A medium base compact fluorescent lamp;

(ii) A general service incandescent lamp;

(iii) A general service light-emitting diode (LED or OLED) lamp; or

(iv) Any other lamp that the Secretary of Energy determines is used to satisfy lighting applications traditionally served by general service incandescent lamps.

(2) Exclusions. The term *general service lamp* does not include—

(i) Any lighting application or bulb shape described in paragraphs (n)(3)(ii)(A) through (T) of this section; and

(ii) Any general service fluorescent lamp.

(m) *Medium base compact fluorescent lamp* means an integrally ballasted fluorescent lamp with a medium screw base, a rated input voltage range of 115 to 130 volts and which is designed as a direct replacement for a general service incandescent lamp; however, the term does not include—

(1) Any lamp that is:

(i) Specifically designed to be used for special purpose applications; and

(ii) Unlikely to be used in general purpose applications, such as the applications described in the definition of "General Service Incandescent Lamp" in paragraph (n)(3)(ii) of this section; or

(2) Any lamp not described in the definition of "General Service Incandescent Lamp" in this section and that is excluded by the Department of Energy, by rule, because the lamp is—

(i) Designed for special applications; and

(ii) Unlikely to be used in general purpose applications.

(n) *Incandescent lamp:*

(1) Means a lamp in which light is produced by a filament heated to incandescence by an electric current, including only the following:

(i) Any lamp (commonly referred to as lower wattage nonreflector general service lamps, including any tungsten halogen lamp) that has a rated wattage between 30 and 199 watts, has an E26 medium screw base, has a rated voltage or voltage range that lies at least partially within 115 and 130 volts, and is not a reflector lamp;

(ii) Any lamp (commonly referred to as a reflector lamp) which is not colored or designed for rough or vibration service applications, that contains an inner reflective coating on the outer bulb to direct the light, an R, PAR, ER, BR, BPAR, or similar bulb shapes with E26 medium screw bases, a rated voltage or voltage range that lies at least partially within 115 and 130 volts, a diameter which exceeds 2.25 inches, and has a rated wattage that is 40 watts or higher;

(iii) Any general service incandescent lamp (commonly referred to as a high- or higher wattage lamp) that has a rated wattage above 199 watts (above 205 watts for a high wattage reflector lamp); but

(2) *Incandescent lamp* does not mean any lamp excluded by the Secretary of Energy, by rule, as a result of a determination that standards for such lamp would not result in significant energy savings because such lamp is designed for special applications or has special characteristics not available in reasonably substitutable lamp types;

(3) *General service incandescent lamp* means:

(i) In general, a standard incandescent, halogen, or reflector type lamp that—

(A) Is intended for general service applications;

(B) Has a medium screw base;

(C) Has a lumen range of not less than 310 lumens and not more than 2,600 lumens; and

(D) Is capable of being operated at a voltage range at least partially within 110 and 130 volts.

(ii) *Exclusions.* The term "general service incandescent lamp" does not include the following incandescent lamps:

(A) An appliance lamp as defined at 42 U.S.C. 6291(30);

(B) A black light lamp;

(C) A bug lamp;

(D) A colored lamp as defined at 42 U.S.C. 6291(30);

(E) An infrared lamp;

(F) A left hand thread lamp;

(G) A marine lamp;

(H) A marine signal service lamp;

(I) A mine service lamp;

(J) A plant light lamp;

(K) A rough service lamp as defined at 42 U.S.C. 6291(30);

(L) A shatter resistant lamp (including a shatter-proof lamp and a shatter-protected lamp);

(M) A sign service lamp;

(N) A silver bowl lamp;

(O) A showcase lamp;

(P) A traffic signal lamp;

(Q) A vibration service lamp as defined at 42 U.S.C. 6291(30);

(R) A G shape lamp (as defined in ANSI C78.20–2003 and C79.1–2002) with a diameter of 5 inches or more;

(S) A T shape lamp (as defined in ANSI C78.20–2003 and C79.1–2002) and that uses not more than 40 watts or has a length of more than 10 inches; or

(T) A B, BA, CA, F, G16–1/2, G–25, G–30, S, or M–14 lamp (as defined in ANSI C79.1–2002 and ANSI C78.20–2003) of 40 watts or less.

(4) *Incandescent reflector lamp* means a lamp described in paragraph (n)(1)(ii) of this section; and

(5) *Tungsten halogen lamp* means a gas filled tungsten filament incandescent lamp containing a certain proportion of halogens in an inert gas.

(o) *Light emitting diode (LED)* means a p n junction solid state device the radiated output of which is a function of the physical construction, material used, and exciting current of the device. The output of a light emitting diode may be in B

(1) The infrared region;

(2) The visible region; or

(3) The ultraviolet region.

(p) *Organic light emitting diode (OLED)* means a thin-film light-emitting device that typically consists of a series of organic layers between 2 electrical contacts (electrodes).

(q) *General service light-emitting diode (LED or OLED)* lamp means any light emitting diode (LED or OLED) lamp that:

(1) Is a consumer product;

(2) Is intended for general service applications;

(3) Has a medium screw base;

(4) Has a lumen range of not less than 310 lumens and not more than 2,600 lumens; and

(5) Is capable of being operated at a voltage range at least partially within 110 and 130 volts.

(r) *Showerhead* means a component or set of components distributed in commerce for attachment to a single supply fitting, for spraying water onto a bather, typically from an overhead position, excluding safety shower showerheads.

(s) *Faucet* means a lavatory faucet, kitchen faucet, metering faucet, or replacement aerator for a lavatory or kitchen faucet.

(t) *Water closet* means a plumbing fixture having a water-containing receptor which receives liquid and solid body waste and, upon actuation, conveys the waste through an exposed integral trap seal into a gravity drainage system, except such term does not include fixtures designed for installation in prisons.

(u) *Urinal* means a plumbing fixture which receives only liquid body waste and, on demand, conveys the waste through a trap seal into a gravity drainage system, except such term does not include fixtures designed for installation in prisons.

(v) *Pool heater* means an appliance designed for heating nonpotable water contained at atmospheric pressure, including heating water in swimming pools, spas, hot tubs and similar applications.

(w) *Metal halide lamp fixture* means a light fixture for general lighting application that is designed to be operated with a metal halide lamp and a ballast for a metal halide lamp and that is subject to and complies with Department of Energy efficiency standards issued pursuant to 42 U.S.C. 6295.

(1) *Metal halide ballast* means a ballast used to start and operate metal halide lamps.

(2) *Metal halide lamp* means a high intensity discharge lamp in which the major portion of the light is produced by radiation of metal halides and their products of dissociation, possibly in combination with metallic vapors.

(x) Ceiling fan means a nonportable device that is suspended from a ceiling for circulating air via the rotation of fan blades, excluding large-diameter and high-speed small diameter fans as defined in appendix U of subpart B of 10 CFR part 430. The requirements of this part are otherwise limited to those ceiling fans for which the Department of Energy has adopted and published test procedures for measuring energy usage.

(y) *Television* means a product that is designed to produce dynamic video, contains an internal TV tuner encased within the product housing, and is capable of receiving dynamic visual content from wired or wireless sources including but not limited to: broadcast and similar services for terrestrial, cable, satellite, and/or broadband transmission of analog and/or digital signals; and/or display-specific data connections, such as HDMI, Component video, S-video, Composite video; and/or media storage devices such as a USB flash drive, memory card, or a DVD; and/or network connections, usually using Internet Protocol, typically carried over Ethernet or Wi-Fi. The requirements of this part are limited to those televisions for which the Department of Energy has adopted and published test procedures for measuring energy use.

(z) *Specialty consumer lamp* means

(1) Any lamp that:

(i) Is not included under the definition of general service lamp in this part;

(ii) Has a lumen range between 310 lumens and no more than 2,600 lumens or a rated wattage between 30 and 199;

(iii) Has one of the following bases:

(A) A medium screw base;

(B) A candelabra screw base;

(C) A GU–10 base; or

(D) A GU–24 base; and

(iv) Is capable of being operated at a voltage range at least partially within 110 and 130 volts.

(2) *Inclusions*. The term *specialty consumer lamp* includes, but is not limited to, the following lamps if such lamps meet the conditions listed in paragraph (1):

(i) vibration-service lamps as defined at 42 U.S.C. 6291(30)(AA);

(ii) rough service lamps as defined at 42 U.S.C. 6291(30)(X);

(iii) appliance lamps as defined at 42 U.S.C. 6291(30)(T); and

(iv) shatter resistant lamps (including a shatter proof lamp and a shatter protected lamp) as defined in 42 U.S.C. 6291(30)(Z).

(3) *Exclusions*. The term *specialty consumer lamp* does not include:

(i) A black light lamp;

(ii) A bug lamp;

(iii) A colored lamp;

(iv) An infrared lamp;

(v) A left-hand thread lamp;

(vi) A marine lamp;

(vii) A marine signal service lamp;

(viii) A mine service lamp;

(ix) A sign service lamp;

(x) A silver bowl lamp;

(xi) A showcase lamp;

(xii) A traffic signal lamp;

(xiii) A G-shape lamp with diameter of 5 inches or more;

(xiv) A C7, M–14, P, RP, S, or T shape lamp;

(xv) A intermediate screw-base lamp; and

(xvi) A plant light lamp.

[52 FR 46894, Dec. 10, 1987, as amended at 59 FR 34031, 34032, July 1, 1994; 59 FR 49563, Sept. 28, 1994; 59 FR 67525, Dec. 29, 1994; 71 FR 4984, Jan. 31, 2006; 72 FR 49966, Aug. 29, 2007; 73 FR 63067, Oct. 23, 2008; 76 FR 79057, Dec. 21, 2011; 76 FR 1050, Jan. 6, 2011; 78 FR 2207, Jan. 10, 2013; 79 FR 19466, Apr. 9, 2014; 80 FR 67298, Nov. 2, 2015; 81 FR 63646, Sept. 15, 2016; 81 FR]

GENERAL

§ 305.4 Prohibited acts.

(a) It shall be unlawful and subject to the enforcement penalties of section 333 of the Act, as adjusted for inflation pursuant to § 1.98 of this chapter, for each unit of any new covered product to which the part applies:

(1) For any manufacturer or private labeler knowingly to distribute in commerce any new covered product unless such covered product is marked and/or labeled in accordance with this part with a marking, label, hang tag, or energy fact sheet which conforms to the provisions of the Act and this part.

(2) For any manufacturer, distributor, retailer, or private labeler knowingly to remove or render illegible any marking or label required to be provided with such product by this part.

(3) For any manufacturer or private labeler knowingly to distribute in commerce any new covered product, if there is not included (i) on the label, (ii) separately attached to the product, or (iii) shipped with the product, additional information relating to energy consumption or energy efficiency which conforms to the requirements in this part.

(b) Subject to enforcement penalties assessed per model per day of violation pursuant to 42 U.S.C. 6303 and adjusted for inflation by § 1.98 of this chapter, it shall be unlawful for any manufacturer or private labeler knowingly to:

(1) Refuse a request by the Commission or its designated representative for access to, or copying of, records required to be supplied under this part.

(2) Refuse to make reports or provide upon request by the Commission or its designated representative any information required to be supplied under this part.

(3) Refuse upon request by the Commission or its designated representative to permit a representative designated by the Commission to observe any testing required by this part while such testing is being conducted or to inspect the results of such testing. This section shall not limit the Commission from requiring additional testing under this part.

(4) Refuse, when requested by the Commission or its designated representative, to supply at the manufacturer's expense, no more than two of each model of each covered product to any laboratory designated by the Commission for the purpose of ascertaining whether the information in catalogs or set out on the label or marked on the product as required by this part is accurate. This action will be taken only after review of a manufacturer's testing records and an opportunity to revalidate test data has been extended to the manufacturer.

(5) Distribute in commerce any catalog containing a listing for a covered product without the information required by § 305.20 of this part. This subsection shall also apply to distributors and retailers.

(6) Fail to make a label for a covered product available on a publicly accessible Web site in accordance with § 305.6. This provision applies only to manufacturers.

(c) Pursuant to section 333(c) of the Act, it shall be an unfair or deceptive act or practice in violation of section 5(a)(1) of the Federal Trade Commission Act (15 U.S.C. 45(a)(1)) for any manufacturer, distributor, retailer, or private labeler in or affecting commerce to display or distribute at point of sale any printed material applicable to a covered product under this rule if such printed material does not contain the information required by § 305.19. This requirement does not apply to any broadcast advertisement or to any advertisement in a newspaper, magazine, or other periodical.

(d)(1) It shall be an unfair or deceptive act or practice in violation of section 5(a)(1) of the Federal Trade Commission Act, 15 U.S.C. 45(a)(1), for any manufacturer, distributor, retailer or private labeler to make any representation in or affecting commerce, in writing (including a representation on a label) or in any broadcast advertisement, with respect to the energy use or efficiency or, in the case of showerheads, faucets, water closets, and urinals, water use of a covered product to which a test procedure is applicable under section 323 of the Act, 42 U.S.C. 6293, or the cost of energy consumed by such product, unless such product has been tested in accordance with such test procedure and such representation fairly discloses the results of such testing.

(2) Effective 180 days after an amended or new test procedure applicable to a covered product is prescribed or established under section 323(b) of the Act, 42 U.S.C. 6293(b), it shall be an unfair or deceptive act or practice in violation of section 5(a)(1) of the Federal Trade Commission Act, 15 U.S.C. 45(a)(1), for any manufacturer, distributor, retailer or private labeler to make any representation in or affecting commerce, in writing (including a representation on a label) or in any broadcast advertisement, with respect to the energy use or efficiency or, in the case of showerheads, faucets, water closets and urinals, water use of such product, or cost of energy consumed by such product, unless the product has been tested in accordance with such amended or new test procedures and such representation fairly discloses the results of such testing. This requirement is not limited to consumer appliance products covered by the labeling requirements of this part.

(3) Any manufacturer, distributor, retailer, or private labeler may file a petition with the Commission not later

than sixty (60) days before the expiration of the period involved for an extension of the 180 day period. If the Commission finds that the requirements would impose an undue hardship on the petitioner, the Commission may extend the 180 day period with respect to the petitioner up to an additional 180 days.

(e) This part shall not apply to:

(1) Any covered product if it is manufactured, imported, sold, or held for sale for export from the United States, so long as such product is not in fact distributed in commerce for use in the United States, and such covered product or the container thereof bears a stamp or label stating that such covered product is intended for export.

(2) Any covered product, other than central air conditioners, pulse combustion and condensing furnaces, fluorescent lamp ballasts, showerheads, faucets, water closets, urinals, pool heaters, instantaneous water heaters, heat pump water heaters, general service fluorescent lamps, medium base compact fluorescent lamps, and general service incandescent lamps (including incandescent reflector lamps), if the manufacture of the product was completed prior to May 19, 1980. Any central air conditioner or any pulse combustion or condensing furnace if its manufacture was completed prior to June 7, 1988. Any fluorescent lamp ballast if its manufacture was completed prior to January 1, 1990. Any showerhead, faucet, water closet or urinal if its manufacture was completed prior to October 24, 1994. Any pool heater, instantaneous water heater, or heat pump water heater if its manufacture was completed prior to December 29, 1994. Any general service fluorescent lamp, medium base compact fluorescent lamp, or general service incandescent lamp (including any incandescent reflector lamp), if its manufacture was completed prior to May 15, 1995.

(3) Any catalog or point-of-sale printed material pertaining to any covered products that were manufactured prior to May 19, 1980; any catalog or point-of-sale printed material pertaining to any central air conditioners or pulse combustion or condensing furnaces manufactured prior to June 7, 1988; any catalog or point-of-sale printed material pertaining to any fluorescent lamp ballasts manufactured prior to June 23, 1989; any catalog or point-of-sale printed material pertaining to any showerheads, faucets, water closets or urinals manufactured prior to October 24, 1994; any catalog or point-of-sale printed material pertaining to any pool heaters, instantaneous water heaters, or heat pump water heaters manufactured prior to December 29, 1994; or any catalog or point-of-sale printed material pertaining to general service fluorescent lamps, medium base compact fluorescent lamps, or general service incandescent lamps (including incandescent reflector lamps), that were manufactured prior to May 15, 1995; except that any representations respecting the energy consumption, energy efficiency, or water use of any covered product or other consumer appliance product, or respecting the cost of energy consumed or water used by such product, are subject to the requirements of paragraph (d) of this section.

(4) Televisions manufactured before May 10, 2011.

(f) As used in paragraphs (a) and (b) of this section, the term *knowingly* means:

(1) The having of actual knowledge, or

(2) The presumed having of knowledge deemed to be possessed by a reasonable person who acts in the circumstances, including knowledge obtainable upon the exercise of due care.

[52 FR 46894, Dec. 10, 1987, as amended at 54 FR 28035, July 5, 1989; 58 FR 54964, Oct. 25, 1993; 59 FR 49563, Sept. 28, 1994; 59 FR 67526, Dec. 29, 1994; 61 FR 54549, Oct. 21, 1996; 72 FR 49966, Aug. 29, 2007; 76 FR 1050, Jan. 6, 2011; 78 FR 2207, Jan. 10, 2013]

TESTING

§ 305.5 Determinations of estimated annual energy consumption, estimated annual operating cost, and energy efficiency rating, water use rate, and other required disclosure content.

(a) Unless otherwise stated in paragraphs (b) and (c) of this section, the content of any disclosures required by this part must be determined in accordance with the testing and sampling provisions required by the Department of Energy as set forth in subpart B to

10 CFR part 430, 10 CFR part 431, and 10 CFR 429.11.

(b) For any representations required by this part but not subject to Department of Energy requirements and not otherwise specified in this section, manufacturers and private labelers of any covered product must possess and rely upon a reasonable basis consisting of competent and reliable scientific tests and procedures substantiating the representation.

(c) Representations for ceiling fans under § 305.13 and televisions under § 305.17 must be derived from applicable procedures in 10 CFR parts 429, 430, and 431.

[78 FR 2207, Jan. 10, 2013, as amended at 79 FR 19467, Apr. 9, 2014; 83 FR 7596, Feb. 22, 2018]

§ 305.6 Duty to provide labels on Web sites.

For each covered product that a manufacturer distributes in commerce after July 15, 2013, which is required by this part to bear an EnergyGuide or Lighting Facts label, the manufacturer must make a copy of the label available on a publicly accessible Web site in a manner that allows catalog sellers to hyperlink to the label or download it for use in Web sites or paper catalogs. The label for each specific model must remain on the Web site for six months after production of that model ceases.

[78 FR 2208, Jan. 10, 2013]

§ 305.7 Determinations of capacity.

The capacity of covered products shall be determined as follows:

(a) *Refrigerators and refrigerator-freezers.* The capacity shall be the total refrigerated volume (VT) in cubic feet, rounded to the nearest one-tenth of a cubic foot, as determined according to appendix A to 10 CFR part 430, subpart B.

(b) *Freezers.* The capacity shall be the total refrigerated volume (VT) in cubic feet, rounded to the nearest one-tenth of a cubic foot, as determined according to appendix B to 10 CFR part 430, subpart B.

(c) *Dishwashers.* The capacity shall be the place-setting capacity, determined according to appendix C to 10 CFR part 430, subpart B.

(d) *Water heaters.* The capacity shall be the rated storage volume and first hour rating (for storage-type models), and gallons per minute (for instantaneous-type models), as determined according to appendix E to 10 CFR part 430, subpart B.

(e) *Pool heaters.* The capacity shall be the heating capacity in Btu's per hour, rounded to the nearest 1,000 Btu's per hour, as determined according to appendix P to 10 CFR part 430, subpart B.

(f) *Room air conditioners.* The capacity shall be the cooling capacity in Btu's per hour, as determined according to appendix F to 10 CFR part 430, subpart B, but rounded to the nearest value ending in hundreds that will satisfy the relationship that the value of CEER used in representations equals the rounded value of capacity divided by the value of input power in watts. If a value ending in hundreds will not satisfy this relationship, the capacity may be rounded to the nearest value ending in 50 that will.

(g) *Clothes washers.* The capacity shall be the tub capacity as determined according to Department of Energy test procedures in 10 CFR part 430, subpart B, expressed in terms of "Capacity (tub volume)" in cubic feet, rounded to the nearest one-tenth of a cubic foot, and the capacity class designations "standard" or "compact."

(h) *Furnaces.* The capacity shall be the heating capacity in Btu's per hour, rounded to the nearest 1,000 Btu's per hour, as determined according to appendix N to 10 CFR part 430, subpart B.

(i) *Central air conditioners, cooling.* The capacity shall be the cooling capacity in Btu's per hour, as determined according to appendix M to 10 CFR part 430, subpart B, rounded to the nearest 100 Btu's per hour for capacities less than 20,000 Btu's per hour; to the nearest 200 Btu's per hour for capacities between 20,000 and 37,999 Btu's per hour; and to the nearest 500 Btu's per hour for capacities between 38,000 and 64,999 Btu's per hour.

(j) *Central air conditioners, heating.* The capacity shall be the heating capacity in Btu's per hour, as determined according to appendix M to 10 CFR part 430, subpart B, rounded to the nearest

100 Btu's per hour for capacities less than 20,000 Btu's per hour; to the nearest 200 Btu's per hour for capacities between 20,000 and 37,999 Btu's per hour; and to the nearest 500 Btu's per hour for capacities between 38,000 and 64,999 Btu's per hour.

(k) *Fluorescent lamp ballasts*. The capacity shall be the ballast input voltage, as determined according to appendix Q to 10 CFR part 430, subpart B.

(l) *Ceiling fans*. The capacity shall be the airflow in cubic feet per minute as determined according to appendix U of 10 CFR part 430, subpart B.

[59 FR 34033, July 1, 1994, as amended at 59 FR 49564, Sept. 28, 1994; 70 FR 3875, Jan. 27, 2005; 73 FR 63067, Oct. 23, 2008; 78 FR 43981, July 23, 2013; 79 FR 77870, Dec. 29, 2014; 80 FR 67299, Nov. 2, 2015; 81 FR 7202, Feb. 11, 2016; 81 FR 63646, Sept. 15, 2016; 83 FR 7596, Feb. 22, 2018]

§ 305.8 Submission of data.

(a)(1) Except as provided in paragraphs (a)(2) through (4) of this section, each manufacturer of a covered product subject to the disclosure requirements of this part and subject to Department of Energy certification requirements in 10 CFR part 429 shall submit annually a report for each model in current production containing the same information that must be submitted to the Department of Energy pursuant to 10 CFR part 429 for that product, and that the Department has identified as public information pursuant to 10 CFR part 429. In lieu of submitting the required information to the Commission as required by this section, manufacturers may submit such information to the Department of Energy via the CCMS at *https://regulations.doe.gov/ccms* as provided by 10 CFR 429.12.

(2) Manufacturers of ceiling fans shall submit annually a report containing the brand name, model number, diameter (in inches), wattage excluding any lights, airflow (capacity) for each basic model in current production, and starting serial number, date code or other means of identifying the date of manufacture with the first submission for each basic model. In lieu of submitting the required information to the Commission as required by this section, manufacturers may submit such information to the Department of Energy via the Compliance and Certification Management System (CCMS) at *https://regulations.doe.gov/ccms* as provided by 10 CFR 429.12.

(3) Manufacturers of televisions shall submit annually a report containing the brand name; model number; screen size (diagonal in inches); power (in watts) consumed in on mode, standby-passive mode, in standby-active mode, low mode, and off mode; and annual energy consumption (kWh/year) for each basic model in current production. The report should also include a starting serial number, date code, or other means of identifying the date of manufacture with the first submission for each basic model. In lieu of submitting the required information to the Commission as required by this section, manufacturers may submit such information to the Department of Energy via the Compliance and Certification Management System (CCMS) at *https://regulations.doe.gov/ccms* as provided by 10 CFR 429.12.

(4) This section does not require reports for general service light-emitting diode (LED or OLED) lamps or specialty consumer lamps.

(5) After September 15, 2017, manufacturers must begin submitting a Web site address for the online EnergyGuide labels covered by § 305.6(a) in new model and annual reports required by this section. Manufacturers may accomplish this by either submitting a specific link to a URL for each label, a link to a PDF download for each label, or a link to a Web site that takes users directly to a searchable database of the covered labels from which the label image or download may be accessed using the model number as certified to DOE pursuant to 10 CFR part 429 and the model number advertised in product literature. Such label information must be submitted either at the time the model is certified to DOE pursuant to 10 CFR part 429 or at some time on or before the annual report date immediately following such certification. In lieu of submitting the required information to the Commission, manufacturers may submit such information to the Department of Energy via the CCMS at *https://regulations.doe.gov/ccms*

as provided by 10 CFR 429.12. The requirements in this paragraph do not apply to Lighting Facts labels.

(b)(1) All data required by §305.8(a) except serial numbers shall be submitted to the Commission annually, on or before the following dates:

Product category	Deadline for data submission
Refrigerators	Aug. 1
Refrigerators-freezers	Aug. 1
Freezers	Aug. 1
Central air conditioners	July 1
Heat pumps	July 1
Dishwashers	June 1
Water heaters	May 1
Room air conditioners	July 1
Furnaces	May 1
Pool heaters	May 1
Clothes washers	Oct. 1
Fluorescent lamp ballasts	Mar. 1
Showerheads	Mar. 1
Faucets	Mar. 1
Water closets	Mar. 1
Ceiling fans	Mar. 1
Urinals	Mar. 1
Metal halide lamp fixtures	Sept. 1
General service fluorescent lamps	Mar. 1
Medium base compact fluorescent lamps	Mar. 1
General service incandescent lamps	Mar. 1
Televisions	June 1

(2) All revisions to such data (both additions to and deletions from the preceding data) shall be submitted to the Commission as part of the next annual report period.

(c) All information required by paragraphs (a)(1) through (3) of this section must be submitted for new models prior to any distribution of such model. Models subject to design or retrofit alterations which change the data contained in any annual report shall be reported in the manner required for new models. Models which are discontinued shall be reported in the next annual report.

[52 FR 46894, Dec. 10, 1987]

EDITORIAL NOTE: For FEDERAL REGISTER citations affecting §305.8, see the List of CFR Sections Affected, which appears in the Finding Aids section of the printed volume and at *www.govinfo.gov*.

§305.10 Ranges of comparability on the required labels.

(a) *Range of estimated annual energy costs or energy efficiency ratings.* The range of estimated annual operating costs or energy efficiency ratings for each covered product (except televisions, ceiling fans, fluorescent lamp ballasts, lamps, metal halide lamp fixtures, showerheads, faucets, water closets and urinals) shall be taken from the appropriate appendix to this part in effect at the time the labels are affixed to the product. The Commission shall publish revised ranges in the FEDERAL REGISTER in 2022. When the ranges are revised, all information disseminated after 90 days following the publication of the revision shall conform to the revised ranges. Products that have been labeled prior to the effective date of a modification under this section need not be relabeled.

(b) *Representative average unit energy cost.* The Representative Average Unit Energy Cost to be used on labels as required by §305.11 and disclosures as required by §305.20 are listed in appendices K1 and K2 to this part. The Commission shall publish revised Representative Average Unit Energy Cost figures in the FEDERAL REGISTER in 2022. When the cost figures are revised, all information disseminated after 90 days following the publication of the revision shall conform to the new cost figure.

(c) *Operating Costs or Efficiency Ratings Outside Current Range.* When the estimated annual operating cost or energy efficiency rating of a given model of a covered product falls outside the limits of the current range for that product, which could result from the introduction of a new or changed model, the manufacturer shall:

(1) Omit placement of such product on the scale that appears as required by §§305.11 and 305.12 of this part, and

(2) Add one of the two sentences below, as appropriate, in the space just below the scale on the label, as follows:

The estimated yearly energy cost of this model was not available at the time the range was published.

The energy efficiency rating of this model was not available at the time the range was published.

(3) For refrigerator and refrigerator-freezer labels:

(i) If the model's energy cost falls outside of either or both ranges on the label, include the language in paragraph (c)(2) of this section.

(ii) If the model's energy cost only falls outside of the range for models with similar features, but is within the range for all models, include the product on the scale and place a triangle below the dollar value.

(iii) If the model's energy cost falls outside of both ranges of comparability, omit the triangle beneath the yearly operating cost value.

[72 FR 49967, Aug. 29, 2007, as amended at 73 FR 63067, Oct. 23, 2008; 76 FR 1050, Jan. 6, 2011; 78 FR 43981, July 23, 2013; 81 FR 7202, Feb. 11, 2016; 83 FR 7596, Feb. 22, 2018]

Required Disclosures

§ 305.11 Labeling for refrigerators, refrigerator-freezers, freezers, dishwashers, clothes washers, water heaters, room air conditioners, and pool heaters.

(a) *Layout.* All energy labels for refrigerators, refrigerator-freezers, freezers, dishwashers, clothes washers, water heaters, pool heaters, and room air conditioners shall use one size, similar colors, and typefaces with consistent positioning of headline, copy, and charts to maintain uniformity for immediate consumer recognition and readability. Trim size dimensions for all labels shall be as follows: width must be between 5¼ inches and 5½ inches (13.34 cm. and 13.97 cm.); length must be between 7⅜ inches (18.73 cm.) and 7⅝ (19.37 cm.). Copy is to be set between 27 picas and 29 picas and copy page should be centered (right to left and top to bottom). Depth is variable but should follow closely the prototype labels appearing at the end of this part illustrating the basis layout. All positioning, spacing, type sizes, and line widths should be similar to and consistent with the prototype and sample labels in appendix L to this part.

(b) *Type style and setting.* The Arial series typeface or equivalent shall be used exclusively on the label. Specific sizes and faces to be used are indicated on the prototype labels. No hyphenation should be used in setting headline or copy text. Positioning and spacing should follow the prototypes closely. Generally, text must be set flush left with two points leading except where otherwise indicated. See the prototype labels for specific directions.

(c) *Colors.* The basic colors of all labels covered by this section shall be process yellow or equivalent and process black. The label shall be printed full bleed process yellow. All type and graphics shall be print process black.

(d) *Label types.* Except as indicated in paragraph (d)(3) of this section, the labels must be affixed to the product in the form of an adhesive label or a hang tag as follows:

(1) *Adhesive labels.* All adhesive labels should be applied so they can be easily removed without the use of tools or liquids, other than water, but should be applied with an adhesive with an adhesion capacity sufficient to prevent their dislodgment during normal handling throughout the chain of distribution to the retailer or consumer. The paper stock for pressure-sensitive or other adhesive labels shall have a basic weight of not less than 58 pounds per 500 sheets (25″ x 38″) or equivalent, exclusive of the release liner and adhesive. A minimum peel adhesion capacity for the adhesive of 12 ounces per square inch is suggested, but not required if the adhesive can otherwise meet the above standard. In lieu of a label with adhesive backing, manufacturers may adhere the label with adhesive tape, provided the tape is affixed along the entire top and bottom of the label.

(2) *Hang tags.* Labels may be affixed to the product in the form of a hang tag using cable ties or double strings connected through reinforced punch holes, or with attachment and label material of equivalent or greater strength and durability. If paper stock is used for hang tags, it shall have a basic weight of not less than 110 pounds per 500 sheets (25½″ x 30½″ index). When materials are used to attach the hang tags to appliance products, the materials shall be of sufficient strength to insure that if gradual pressure is applied to the hang tag by pulling it away from where it is affixed to the product, the hang tag will tear before the material used to affix the hang tag to the product breaks.

(3) *Package labels for certain products.* Labels for electric instantaneous water heaters shall be printed on or affixed to the product's packaging in a conspicuous location. Labels for room air conditioners produced on or after October 1, 2019 shall be printed on or affixed

to the principal display panel of the product's packaging.

(e) *Placement*—(1) *Adhesive labels.* Manufacturers shall affix adhesive labels to the covered products in such a position that it is easily read by a consumer examining the product. The label should be generally located on the upper-right-front corner of the product's front exterior. However, some other prominent location may be used as long as the label will not become dislodged during normal handling throughout the chain of distribution to the retailer or consumer. The top of the label should not exceed 74 inches from the base of taller products. The label can be displayed in the form of a flap tag adhered to the top of the appliance and bent (folded at 90°) to hang over the front, as long as this can be done with assurance that it will be readily visible.

(2) *Hang tags.* A hang tag shall be affixed to the interior of the product in such a position that it can be easily read by a consumer examining the product. A hang tag can be affixed in any position that meets this requirement as long as the label will not become dislodged during normal handling throughout the chain of distribution to the retailer or consumer.

(f) *Label content.* (1) Headlines and texts, as illustrated in the prototype and sample labels in appendix L to this part, are standard for all labels.

(2) Name of manufacturer or private labeler shall, in the case of a corporation, be deemed to be satisfied only by the actual corporate name, which may be preceded or followed by the name of the particular division of the corporation. In the case of an individual, partnership, or association, the name under which the business is conducted shall be used. Inclusion of the name of the manufacturer or private labeler is optional at the discretion of the manufacturer or private labeler.

(3) Model number(s) will be the designation given by the manufacturer or private labeler.

(4) Capacity or size is that determined in accordance with § 305.7. For refrigerators, refrigerator-freezers, and freezers, the capacity provided on the label shall be the model's total refrigerated volume (VT) as determined in accordance with § 305.7 and the model description must be consistent with the categories described in Appendices A and B to this part. Capacity for storage water heaters shall be presented in both rated storage volume ("tank size (storage capacity)") and first hour rating as indicated on the sample label in appendix L to this part.

(5) Unless otherwise indicated in this paragraph, estimated annual operating costs for refrigerators, refrigerator-freezers, freezers, clothes washers, dishwashers, room air conditioners, and water heaters are as determined in accordance with §§ 305.5 and 305.10. Thermal efficiencies for pool heaters are as determined in accordance with § 305.5. Labels for clothes washers and dishwashers must disclose estimated annual operating cost for both electricity and natural gas as illustrated in the sample labels in appendix L to this part. Labels for dual-mode refrigerator-freezers that can operate as either a refrigerator or a freezer must reflect the estimated energy cost of the model's most energy intensive configuration.

(6) Unless otherwise indicated in this paragraph, ranges of comparability for estimated annual operating costs or thermal efficiencies, as applicable, are found in the appropriate appendices accompanying this part.

(7) Placement of the labeled product on the scale shall be proportionate to the lowest and highest estimated annual operating costs or thermal efficiencies, as applicable.

(8) Labels for refrigerators, refrigerator-freezers, freezers, dishwashers, clothes washers, and water heaters must contain the model's estimated annual energy consumption as determined in accordance with § 305.5 and as indicated on the sample labels in appendix L. Labels for room air conditioners, and pool heaters must contain the model's energy efficiency rating or thermal efficiency, as applicable, as determined in accordance with § 305.5 and as indicated on the sample labels in appendix L to this part.

(9) Labels must contain a statement as illustrated in the prototype labels in appendix L and specified as follows by product type:

(i) Labels for refrigerators and refrigerator-freezers must contain a statement as illustrated in the prototype labels in appendix L and specified as follows (fill in the blanks with the appropriate energy cost figure):

Your cost will depend on your utility rates and use.

Both cost ranges based on models of similar size capacity.

[Insert statement required by § 305.11(f)(9)(iii)].

Estimated energy cost based on a national average electricity cost of ____ cents per kWh.

ftc.gov/energy.

(ii) For refrigerators, refrigerator-freezers, and freezers and clothes washers the label shall contain the text and graphics illustrated in sample labels 1 and 2 of appendix L, including the statement:

Compare ONLY to other labels with yellow numbers.

Labels with yellow numbers are based on the same test procedures.

(iii) For refrigerators and refrigerator-freezers, the following sentence shall be included as part of the statement required by paragraph (f)(9)(i) of this section:

(A) For models covered under appendix A1, the sentence shall read:

Models with similar features have automatic defrost and no freezer.

(B) For models covered under appendix A2, the sentence shall read:

Models with similar features have manual defrost.

(C) For models covered under appendix A3, the sentence shall read:

Models with similar features have partial automatic defrost.

(D) For models covered under appendix A4, the sentence shall read:

Models with similar features have automatic defrost, top-mounted freezer, and no through-the-door ice.

(E) For models covered under appendix A5, the sentence shall read:

Models with similar features have automatic defrost, side-mounted freezer, and no through-the-door ice.

(F) For models covered under appendix A6, the sentence shall read:

Models with similar features have automatic defrost, bottom-mounted freezer, and no through-the-door ice.

(G) For models covered under appendix A7, the sentence shall read:

Models with similar features have automatic defrost, bottom-mounted freezer and through-the-door ice.

(H) For models covered under appendix A8, the sentence shall read:

Models with similar features have automatic defrost, side-mounted freezer, and through-the-door ice.

(iv) Labels for freezers must contain a statement as illustrated in the prototype labels in appendix L and specified as follows (fill in the blanks with the appropriate energy cost figure):

Your cost will depend on your utility rates and use.

[Insert statement required by § 305.11(f)(10)(v)].

Estimated energy cost based on a national average electricity cost of ____ cents per kWh.

ftc.gov/energy.

(v) For freezers, the following sentence shall be included as part of the statement required by paragraph (f)(9)(iv) of this section:

(A) For models covered under appendix B1, the sentence shall read:

Cost range based only on upright freezer models of similar capacity with manual defrost.

(B) For models covered under appendix B2, the sentence shall read:

Cost range based only on upright freezer models of similar capacity with automatic defrost.

(C) For models covered under appendix B3, the sentence shall read:

Cost range based only on chest and other freezer models of similar capacity.

(vi) For room air conditioners covered under appendix E, the statement will read as follows (fill in the blanks with the appropriate model type, year, energy type, and energy cost figure):

Your costs will depend on your utility rates and use.

Cost range based only on models [of similar capacity without reverse cycle and with louvered sides; of similar capacity without reverse cycle and without louvered sides; with reverse cycle and with louvered sides; or with reverse cycle and without louvered sides].

Estimated annual energy cost is based on a national average electricity cost of ___cents per kWh and a seasonal use of 8 hours use per day over a 3 month period.

For more information, visit *www.ftc.gov/energy*.

(vii) For water heaters covered by appendices D1, D2, and D3, the statement will read as follows (fill in the blanks with the appropriate fuel type, and energy cost figures):

Your costs will depend on your utility rates and use.

Cost range based only on models fueled by [natural gas, oil, propane, or electricity] with a [very small, low, medium, or high] first hour rating [fewer than 18 gallons, 18–50.9 gallons, 51–74.9 gallons, or greater than 75 gallons].

Estimated energy cost is based on a national average [electricity, natural gas, propane, or oil] cost of [___ cents per kWh or $___ per therm or gallon].

Estimated yearly energy use: ___ [kWh or therms].

ftc.gov/energy.

(viii) For instantaneous water heaters (appendices D4 and D5), the statement will read as follows (fill in the blanks with the appropriate model type, and the energy cost figures):

Your costs will depend on your utility rates and use.

Cost range based only on [electric models or models fueled by natural gas] with a [very small, low, medium, or high] gallons per minute rating [0 to 1.6, 1.7 to 2.7, 2.8 to 4.0, or greater than 4.0].

Estimated energy cost is based on a national average [electricity, natural gas, or propane] cost of [___ cents per kWh or $___ per therm or gallon].

Estimated yearly energy use: ___ [kWh or therms].

ftc.gov/energy.

(ix) For dishwashers covered by appendices C1 and C2, the statement will read as follows (fill in the brackets with the appropriate capacity and the energy cost figures):

Your costs will depend on your utility rates and use.

Cost range based only on [compact/standard] capacity models.

Estimated energy cost is based on four washloads a week, and a national average electricity cost of [___] cents per kWh and natural gas cost of $[___] per therm.

For more information, visit *www.ftc.gov/energy*.

(x) For clothes washers covered by appendices F1 and F2 of this part, the statement will read as follows (fill in the blanks with the appropriate capacity and energy cost figures):

Your costs will depend on your utility rates and use.

Cost range based only on [compact/standard] capacity models.

Estimated energy cost is based on six wash loads a week and a national average electricity cost of ___ cents per kWh and natural gas cost of $ ___ per therm. *ftc.gov/energy*.

(xi) For pool heaters covered under appendices J1 and J2, the statement will read as follows:

Efficiency range based only on models fueled by [natural gas or oil].

For more information, visit *www.ftc.gov/energy*.

(10) The following statement shall appear on each label as illustrated in the prototype and sample labels in appendix L of this part:

Federal law prohibits removal of this label before consumer purchase.

(11) No marks or information other than that specified in this part shall appear on or directly adjoining this label except that:

(i) A part or publication number identification may be included on this label, as desired by the manufacturer. If a manufacturer elects to use a part or publication number, it must appear in the lower right-hand corner of the label and be set in 6-point type or smaller.

(ii) The energy use disclosure labels required by the governments of Canada or Mexico may appear directly adjoining this label, as desired by the manufacturer.

(iii) The manufacturer or private labeler may include the ENERGY STAR logo on the bottom right corner of the label for certified products. The logo must be 1 inch by 1 inch in size. Only manufacturers that have signed a Memorandum of Understanding with the Department of Energy or the Environmental Protection Agency may add the ENERGY STAR logo to labels on certified covered products; such manufacturers may add the ENERGY STAR logo to labels only on those covered products that are contemplated by the Memorandum of Understanding.

[72 FR 49967, Aug. 29, 2007, as amended at 78 FR 2208, Jan. 10, 2013; 78 FR 43981, July 23, 2013; 80 FR 67299, Nov. 2, 2015; 81 FR 7202, Feb. 11, 2016; 81 FR 63646, Sept. 15, 2016; 82 FR 29235, June 28, 2017; 83 FR 7596, Feb. 22, 2018]

§ 305.12 Labeling for central air conditioners, heat pumps, and furnaces.

(a) *Layout.* All energy labels for central air conditioners, heat pumps, and furnaces (including boilers) shall use one size, similar colors, and typefaces with consistent positioning of headline, copy, and charts to maintain uniformity for immediate consumer recognition and readability. Trim size dimensions for all labels shall be as follows: width must be between 5¼ inches and 5½ inches (13.34 cm. and 13.97 cm.); length must be between 7⅜ inches (18.78 cm.) and 7⅝ (19.34 cm.). Copy is to be set between 27 picas and 29 picas and copy page should be centered (right to left and top to bottom). Depth is variable but should follow closely the prototype labels appearing at the end of this part illustrating the basic layout. All positioning, spacing, type sizes, and line widths should be similar to and consistent with the prototype and sample labels in appendix L.

(b) *Type style and setting.* The Arial series typeface or equivalent shall be used exclusively on the label. Specific sizes and faces to be used are indicated on the prototype labels. No hyphenation should be used in setting headline or copy text. Positioning and spacing should follow the prototypes closely. Generally, text must be set flush left with two points leading except where otherwise indicated. See the prototype labels for specific directions.

(c) *Colors.* The basic colors of all labels covered by this section shall be process yellow or equivalent and process black. The label shall be printed full bleed process yellow. All type and graphics shall be print process black.

(d) *Label type.* The labels must be affixed in the form of an adhesive label, unless otherwise indicated by this section. All adhesive labels should be applied with an adhesive with an adhesion capacity sufficient to prevent their dislodgment during normal handling throughout the chain of distribution to the retailer or consumer. The paper stock for pressure-sensitive or other adhesive labels shall have a basic weight of not less than 58 pounds per 500 sheets (25''x38'') or equivalent, exclusive of the release liner and adhesive. A minimum peel adhesion capacity for the adhesive of 12 ounces per square inch is suggested, but not required if the adhesive can otherwise meet the above standard.

(e) *Placement.* (1) Manufacturers shall affix adhesive labels to the covered products in such a position that they are easily read by persons examining the products. The labels should be generally located on the upper-right-front corner of each product's front exterior. However, other prominent locations may be used as long as labels will not become dislodged during normal handling throughout the chain of distribution to retailers or consumers. Tops of the labels should not exceed 74 inches from the base of taller products. Labels can be displayed in the form of a flap tag adhered to the top of the appliance and bent (folded at 90°) to hang over the front, as long as this can be done with assurance that it will be readily visible. Labels for split-system central air conditioners should be affixed to the condensing unit.

(2) In addition to the requirements of paragraph (e)(1), for split-system and single-package central air conditioners, and all non-weatherized and mobile home furnaces manufactured on or after the compliance date of regional efficiency standards issued by the Department of Energy for those products in 10 CFR part 430, manufacturers shall affix labels to covered product packages or the products themselves in positions that allow persons examining the packaged products to read the labels easily. Labels on packaging must be affixed via adhesive or another means sufficient to prevent their dislodgment during normal handling throughout the chain of distribution to the retailer or consumer. Labels for split-system central air conditioners should be affixed to condensing units' packages or condensing units consistent with this paragraph.

(f) *Content of furnace labels: Content of labels for non-weatherized furnaces, weatherized furnaces, mobile home furnaces, electric furnaces, and boilers.* (1) Headlines and texts, as illustrated in the prototype and sample labels in appendix L to this part.

(2) Name of manufacturer or private labeler shall, in the case of a corporation, be deemed to be satisfied only by the actual corporate name, which may be preceded or followed by the name of the particular division of the corporation. In the case of an individual, partnership, or association, the name under which the business is conducted shall be used. Inclusion of the name of the manufacturer or private labeler is optional at the discretion of the manufacturer or private labeler.

(3) The model's basic model number. The label may include multiple model numbers on a single label for models as long as the models share the same efficiency ratings and capacities and the presentation of such information is clear and prominent.

(4) The model's capacity. Inclusion of capacity is optional at the discretion of the manufacturer or private labeler.

(5) The annual fuel utilization efficiency (AFUE) for furnace models as determined in accordance with § 305.5.

(6) Ranges of comparability consisting of the lowest and highest annual fuel utilization efficiency (AFUE) ratings for all furnaces of the model's type consistent with the sample labels in appendix L.

(7) Placement of the labeled product on the scale shall be proportionate to the lowest and highest annual fuel utilization efficiency ratings forming the scale.

(8) The following statement shall appear in bold print on furnace labels adjacent to the range(s) as illustrated in the sample labels in appendix L:

For energy cost info, visit *productinfo.energy.gov.*

(9) The following statement shall appear at the top of the label as illustrated in the sample labels in appendix L to this part:

Federal law prohibits removal of this label before consumer purchase.

(10) No marks or information other than that specified in this part shall appear on or directly adjoining this label except that:

(i) A part or publication number identification may be included on this label, as desired by the manufacturer. If a manufacturer elects to use a part or publication number, it must appear in the lower right-hand corner of the label and be set in 6-point type or smaller.

(ii) The energy use disclosure labels required by the governments of Canada or Mexico may appear directly adjoining this label, as desired by the manufacturer.

(iii) The manufacturer may include the ENERGY STAR logo on the label for certified products in a location consistent with the sample labels in appendix L to this part. The logo must be no larger than 1 inch by 3 inches in size. Only manufacturers that have signed a Memorandum of Understanding with the Department of Energy or the Environmental Protection Agency may add the ENERGY STAR logo to labels on qualifying covered products; such manufacturers may add the ENERGY STAR logo to labels only on those covered products that are contemplated by the Memorandum of Understanding.

(11) Manufacturers of boilers shipped with more than one input nozzle to be installed in the field must label such boilers with the AFUE of the system when it is set up with the nozzle that results in the lowest AFUE rating.

(12) Manufacturers that ship out boilers that may be set up as either steam or hot water units must label the boilers with the AFUE rating derived by conducting the required test on the boiler as a hot water unit.

(13) Manufacturers of oil furnaces must label their products with the AFUE rating associated with the furnace's input capacity set by the manufacturer at shipment. The oil furnace label may also contain a chart, as illustrated in sample label 9B in appendix L to this part, indicating the efficiency rating at up to three additional input capacities offered by the manufacturer. Consistent with paragraph (f)(10)(iii) of this section, labels for oil furnaces may include the ENERGY STAR logo only if the model qualifies for that program

on all input capacities displayed on the label.

(14) Manufacturers of models that qualify as both furnaces and central air conditioners or heat pumps under DOE requirements may combine the disclosures required by this section on one label for models that meet all applicable DOE regional efficiency standards.

(g) *Content of central air conditioner labels: Content of labels for central air conditioners and heat pumps.* (1) Headlines and texts, as illustrated in the prototype and sample labels in appendix L to this part.

(2) Name of manufacturer or private labeler shall, in the case of a corporation, be deemed to be satisfied only by the actual corporate name, which may be preceded or followed by the name of the particular division of the corporation. In the case of an individual, partnership, or association, the name under which the business is conducted shall be used. Inclusion of the name of the manufacturer or private labeler is optional at the discretion of the manufacturer or private labeler.

(3) The model's basic model number. The label may include multiple model numbers on a single label for models as long as the models share the same efficiency ratings and capacities and the presentation of such information is clear and prominent.

(4) The model's capacity. Inclusion of capacity is optional at the discretion of the manufacturer or private labeler for all models except split-system labels, which may not disclose capacity.

(5) The seasonal energy efficiency ratio (SEER) for the cooling function of central air conditioners as determined in accordance with § 305.5. For the heating function, the heating seasonal performance factor (HSPF) shall be calculated for heating Region IV for the standardized design heating requirement nearest the capacity measured in the High Temperature Test in accordance with § 305.5. In addition, as illustrated in the sample labels in appendix L to this part, the ratings for any split-system air conditioner condenser evaporator coil combinations shall be the minimum rating of all condenser-evaporator coil combinations certified to the Department of Energy pursuant to 10 CFR part 430. The ratings for any split-system heat pump condenser-evaporator coil combinations shall include the low and high ratings of all condenser-evaporator coil combinations certified to the Department of Energy pursuant to 10 CFR part 430.

(6)(i) Each cooling-only central air conditioner label shall contain a range of comparability consisting of the lowest and highest SEER for all cooling-only central air conditioners consistent with sample label 7A in appendix L to this part.

(ii) Each heat pump label, except as noted in paragraph (g)(6)(iii) of this section, shall contain two ranges of comparability. The first range shall consist of the lowest and highest seasonal energy efficiency ratios for the cooling side of all heat pumps consistent with sample label 8 in appendix L to this part. The second range shall consist of the lowest and highest heating seasonal performance factors for the heating side of all heat pumps consistent with sample label 8 in appendix L to this part.

(iii) Each heating-only heat pump label shall contain a range of comparability consisting of the lowest and highest heating seasonal performance factors for all heating-only heat pumps following the format of sample label 8 in appendix L to this part.

(7) Placement of the labeled product on the scale shall be proportionate to the lowest and highest efficiency ratings forming the scale.

(8) The following statement shall appear on the label in bold print as indicated in the sample labels in appendix L to this part.

For energy cost info, visit *productinfo.energy.gov.*

(9) All labels on split-system condenser units must contain one of the following three statements:

(i) For labels disclosing only the seasonal energy efficiency ratio for cooling, the statement should read:

* Your air conditioner's efficiency rating may be better depending on the coil your contractor installs.

(ii) For labels disclosing both the seasonal energy efficiency ratio for cooling and the heating seasonal performance factor for heating, the statement should read:

This system's efficiency ratings depend on the coil your contractor installs with this unit. The heating efficiency rating varies slightly in different geographic regions. Ask your contractor for details.

(iii) For labels disclosing only the heating seasonal performance factor for heating, the statement should read:

This system's efficiency rating depends on the coil your contractor installs with this unit. The efficiency rating varies slightly in different geographic regions. Ask your contractor for details.

(10) The following statement shall appear at the top of the label as illustrated in the sample labels in appendix L of this part:

Federal law prohibits removal of this label before consumer purchase.

(11) For any single-package air conditioner with a minimum Energy Efficiency Ratio (EER) of at least 11.0, any split system central air conditioner with a rated cooling capacity of at least 45,000 Btu/h and minimum efficiency ratings of at least 14 SEER and 11.7 EER, and any split-system central air conditioners with a rated cooling capacity less than 45,000 Btu/h and minimum efficiency ratings of at least 14 SEER and 12.2 EER, the label must contain the following regional standards information:

(i) A statement that reads:

Notice Federal law allows this unit to be installed in all U.S. states and territories.

(ii) For split systems, a statement that reads:

Energy Efficiency Ratio (EER): The installed system's minimum EERis ____.

(iii) For single-package air conditioners, a statement that reads:

Energy Efficiency Ratio (EER): This model's EER is [____].

(12) For any split system central air conditioner with a rated cooling capacity of at least 45,000 Btu/h and minimum efficiency ratings of at least 14 SEER but lower than 11.7 EER, and any split-system central air conditioners with a rated cooling capacity less than 45,000 Btu/h and minimum efficiency ratings of at least 14 SEER but lower than 12.2 EER, the label must contain the following regional standards information.

(i) A statement that reads:

Notice Federal law allows this unit to be installed only in: AK, AL, AR, CO, CT, DC, DE, FL, GA, HI, ID, IL, IA, IN, KS, KY, LA, MA, ME, MD, MI, MN, MO, MS, MT, NC, ND, NE., NH, NJ, NY, OH, OK, OR, PA, RI, SC, SD, TN, TX, UT, VA, VT, WA, WV, WI, WY and U.S. territories. Federal law prohibits installation of this unit in other states.

(ii) A map appropriate for the model and accompanying text as illustrated in the sample label 7 in appendix L of this part.

(iii) A statement that reads:

Energy Efficiency Ratio (EER): The installed system's minimum EERis ____.

(13) For any split system central air conditioner with a minimum rated efficiency rating less than 14 SEER, the label must contain the following regional standards information:

(i) A statement that reads:

Notice Federal law allows this unit to be installed only in: AK, CO, CT, ID, IL, IA, IN, KS, MA, ME, MI, MN, MO, MT, ND, NE., NH, NJ, NY, OH, OR, PA, RI, SD, UT, VT, WA, WV, WI, WY, and U.S. Territories. Federal law prohibits installation of this unit in other states.

(ii) A map appropriate for the model and accompanying text as illustrated in the sample label 7 in appendix L of this part.

(iii) A statement that reads:

Energy Efficiency Ratio (EER): The installed system's minimum EER is ____.

(14) For any single-package air conditioner with a minimum EER below 11.0, the label must contain the following regional standards information:

(i) A statement that reads:

Notice Federal law allows this unit to be installed only in: AK, AL, AR, CO, CT, DC, DE, FL, GA, HI, ID, IL, IA, IN, KS, KY, LA, MA, ME, MD, MI, MN, MO, MS, MT, NC, ND, NE., NH, NJ, NY, OH, OK, OR, PA, RI, SC, SD, TN, TX, UT, VA, VT, WA, WV, WI, WY and U.S. territories. Federal law prohibits installation of this unit in other states.

(ii) A map appropriate for the model and accompanying text as illustrated in the sample label 7 in appendix L of this part.

(15) No marks or information other than that specified in this part shall appear on or directly adjoining this label except that:

(i) A part or publication number identification may be included on this label, as desired by the manufacturer. If a manufacturer elects to use a part or publication number, it must appear in the lower right-hand corner of the label and be set in 6-point type or smaller.

(ii) The energy use disclosure labels required by the governments of Canada or Mexico may appear directly adjoining this label, as desired by the manufacturer.

(iii) The manufacturer may include the ENERGY STAR logo on the label for certified products in a location consistent with the sample labels in appendix L to this part. The logo must be no larger than 1 inch by 3 inches in size. Only manufacturers that have signed a Memorandum of Understanding with the Department of Energy or the Environmental Protection Agency may add the ENERGY STAR logo to labels on qualifying covered products; such manufacturers may add the ENERGY STAR logo to labels only on those covered products that are contemplated by the Memorandum of Understanding.

[72 FR 49969, Aug. 29, 2007, as amended at 78 FR 2208, Jan. 10, 2013; 78 FR 8374, Feb. 6, 2013; 78 FR 43982, July 23, 2013; 79 FR 77870, Dec. 29, 2014; 81 FR 63648, Sept. 15, 2016; 83 FR 7596, Feb. 22, 2018]

§ 305.13 Labeling for ceiling fans.

(a) *Ceiling fans*—(1) *Content.* Any covered product that is a ceiling fan, except for large diameter and high-speed small diameter fans as defined in 10 CFR part 430, shall be labeled clearly and conspicuously on the package's principal display panel with the following information on the label consistent with the sample label in appendix L to this part:

(i) Headlines, including the title "EnergyGuide," and text as illustrated in the sample label in appendix L to this part;

(ii) The product's estimated yearly energy cost based on 6.4 hours use per day and 12 cents per kWh;

(iii) The product's airflow expressed in cubic feet per minute and determined pursuant to § 305.5;

(iv) The product's energy use expressed in watts and determined pursuant to § 305.5 as indicated in the sample label in appendix L of this part;

(v) The statement "Based on 12 cents per kWh and 6.4 hours use per day";

(vi) The statement "Your cost depends on rates and use";

(vii) The statement "All estimates based on typical use, excluding lights";

(viii) The statement "The higher the airflow, the more air the fan will move";

(ix) The statement "Airflow Efficiency: ____Cubic Feet Per Minute Per Watt";

(x) The address *ftc.gov/energy;*

(xi) For fans less than 19 inches in diameter, the label shall display a cost range of $10 to $50 along with the statement underneath the range "Cost Range of Similar Models (18″ or smaller)";

(xii) For fans from 19 or more inches and less than or equal to 84 inches in diameter, the label shall display a cost range of $3 to $34 along with the statement underneath the range "Cost Range of Similar Models (19″–84″).

(xiii) Placement of the labeled product on the scale proportionate to the lowest and highest estimated annual energy costs as illustrated in the Sample Labels in appendix L. When the estimated annual energy cost of a given model falls outside the limits of the current range for that product, the manufacturer shall place the product at the end of the range closest to the model's energy cost.

(xiv) The ENERGY STAR logo as illustrated on the ceiling fan label illustration in Appendix L for qualified products, if desired by the manufacturer. Only manufacturers that have signed a Memorandum of Understanding with the Department of Energy or the Environmental Protection Agency may add the ENERGY STAR logo to labels on qualifying covered products; such manufacturers may add the ENERGY STAR logo to labels only on those products that are covered by the Memorandum of Understanding;

(2) *Label size, color, and text font.* The label shall be four inches wide and

three inches high. The label colors shall be black text on a process yellow or other neutral contrasting background. The text font shall be Arial or another equivalent font. The label's text size, format, content, and the order of the required disclosures shall be consistent with the ceiling fan label illustration of appendix L of this part.

(3) *Placement.* The ceiling fan label shall be printed on or affixed to the principal display panel of the product's packaging.

(4) *Additional information.* No marks or information other than that specified in this part shall appear on this label, except a model name, number, or similar identifying information.

(5) *Labeling for "multi-mount" fans.* For "multi-mount" fan models that can be installed either extended from the ceiling or flush with the ceiling, the label content must reflect the lowest efficiency (cubic feet per minute per watt) configuration. Manufacturers may provide a second label depicting the efficiency at the other configuration.

(b) [Reserved]

[73 FR 63068, Oct. 23, 2008, as amended at 81 FR 63649, Sept. 15, 2016; 81 FR 74917, Oct. 28, 2016; 82 FR 29236, June 28, 2017]

§305.14 Energy information disclosures for heating and cooling equipment.

The following provisions apply to any covered central air conditioner, heat pump, or furnace.

(a) *Manufacturer duty to provide labels.* For any covered central air conditioner, heat pump, or furnace model that a manufacturer distributes in commerce, the manufacturer must make a copy of the EnergyGuide label available on a publicly accessible Web site in a manner that allows catalog sellers and consumers to hyperlink to the label or download it for their use. The labels must remain on the Web site for six months after the manufacturer ceases the model's production.

(b) *Distribution.* (1) Manufacturers and private labelers must provide to distributors and retailers, including assemblers, EnergyGuide labels for covered central air conditioners, heat pumps, and furnaces (including boilers) they sell to them. The label may be provided in paper or electronic form (including Internet-based access). Distributors must give this information to retailers, including assemblers, they supply.

(2) Retailers, including assemblers, who sell covered central air conditioners, heat pumps, and furnaces (including boilers) to consumers must show the labels for the products they offer to customers and let them read the labels before the customers agree to purchase the product. For example, the retailer may display labeled units in their store or direct consumers to the labels in a binder or computer at a counter or service desk.

(3) Retailers, including installers and assemblers, who negotiate or make sales at a place other than their regular places of business, including sales over the telephone or through electronic communications, must show the labels for the products they offer to customers and let them read the labels before the customers agree to purchase the product. If the labels are on a Web site, retailers, including assemblers, who negotiate or make sales at a place other than their regular places of business, may choose to provide customers with instructions to access such labels in lieu of showing them a paper version of the information. Retailers who choose to use the Internet for the required label disclosures must provide customers the opportunity to read such information prior to sale of the product.

(c) *Oil furnace labels.* If an installer installs an oil furnace with an input capacity different from that set by the manufacturer and the manufacturer identifies alternative capacities on the label, the installer must permanently mark the appropriate box on the EnergyGuide label displaying the installed input capacity and the associated AFUE as illustrated in Sample Labels in appendix L to this part.

[81 FR 63650, Sept. 15, 2016]

§305.15 Labeling for lighting products.

(a) *Fluorescent lamp ballasts and luminaires*—(1) *Contents.* Fluorescent lamp ballasts that are "covered products," as defined in §305.2(n), and to which standards are applicable under section 325 of the Act, shall be marked conspicuously, in color-contrasting ink, with a capital letter "E" printed within a circle. Packaging for such fluorescent lamp ballasts, as well as packaging for luminaires into which they are incorporated, shall also be marked conspicuously with a capital letter "E" printed within a circle. For purposes of this section, the encircled capital letter "E" will be deemed "conspicuous," in terms of size, if it is as large as either the manufacturer's name or another logo, such as the "UL," "CBM" or "ETL" logos, whichever is larger, that appears on the fluorescent lamp ballast, the packaging for such ballast or the packaging for the luminaire into which the covered ballast is incorporated, whichever is applicable for purpose of labeling.

(2) *Product labeling.* The encircled capital letter "E" on fluorescent lamp ballasts must appear conspicuously, in color-contrasting ink, (i.e., in a color that contrasts with the background on which the encircled capital letter "E" is placed) on the surface that is normally labeled. It may be printed on the label that normally appears on the fluorescent lamp ballast, printed on a separate label, or stamped indelibly on the surface of the fluorescent lamp ballast.

(3) *Package labeling.* For purposes of labeling under this section, packaging for such fluorescent lamp ballasts and the luminaires into which they are incorporated consists of the plastic sheeting, or "shrink-wrap," covering pallet loads of fluorescent lamp ballasts or luminaires as well as any containers in which such fluorescent lamp ballasts or the luminaires into which they are incorporated are marketed individually or in small numbers. The encircled capital letter "E" on packages containing fluorescent lamp ballasts or the luminaires into which they are incorporated must appear conspicuously, in color-contrasting ink, on the surface of the package on which printing or a label normally appears. If the package contains printing on more than one surface, the label must appear on the surface on which the product inside the package is described. The encircled capital letter "E" may be printed on the surface of the package, printed on a label containing other information, printed on a separate label, or indelibly stamped on the surface of the package. In the case of pallet loads containing fluorescent lamp ballasts or the luminaires into which they are incorporated, the encircled capital letter "E" must appear conspicuously, in color-contrasting ink, on the plastic sheeting, unless clear plastic sheeting is used and the encircled capital letter "E" is legible underneath this packaging. The encircled capital letter "E" must also appear conspicuously on any documentation that would normally accompany such a pallet load. The encircled capital letter "E" may appear on a label affixed to the sheeting or may be indelibly stamped on the sheeting. It may be printed on the documentation, printed on a separate label that is affixed to the documentation or indelibly stamped on the documentation.

(b) *General service lamps.* Except as provided in paragraph (f) of this section, any covered product that is a general service lamp shall be labeled as follows:

(1) *Principal display panel content.* The principal display panel of the product package shall be labeled clearly and conspicuously with the following information:

(i) The light output of each lamp included in the package, expressed as "Brightness" in average initial lumens rounded to the nearest five; and

(ii) The estimated annual energy cost of each lamp included in the package, expressed as "Estimated Energy Cost" in dollars and based on usage of 3 hours per day and 11 cents ($0.11) per kWh.

(2) *Principal display panel format.* The light output (brightness) and energy cost shall appear in that order and with equal clarity and conspicuousness on the principal display panel of the product package. The format, terms, specifications, and minimum sizes shall follow the specifications and minimum sizes displayed in Prototype Label 5 in appendix L of this part.

(3) *Lighting Facts label content.* The side or rear display panel of the product package shall be labeled clearly and conspicuously with a Lighting Facts label that contains the following information in the following order:

(i) The light output of each lamp included in the package, expressed as

"Brightness" in average initial lumens rounded to the nearest five;

(ii) The estimated annual energy cost of each lamp included in the package based on the average initial wattage, a usage rate of 3 hours per day and 11 cents ($0.11) per kWh and explanatory text as illustrated in Prototype Label 6 in appendix L of this part;

(iii) The life, as defined in § 305.2(w), of each lamp included in the package, expressed in years rounded to the nearest tenth (based on 3 hours operation per day);

(iv) The correlated color temperature of each lamp included in the package, as measured in degrees Kelvin and expressed as "Light Appearance" and by a number and a marker in the form of a scale as illustrated in Prototype Label 6 to appendix L of this part placed proportionately on the scale where the left end equals 2,600 K and the right end equals 6,600 K;

(v) The wattage, as defined in § 305.2(hh), for each lamp included in the package, expressed as energy used in average initial wattage;

(vi) The ENERGY STAR logo as illustrated in Prototype Label 6 to appendix L of this part for certified products, if desired by the manufacturer or private labeler. Only manufacturers or private labelers that have signed a Memorandum of Understanding with the Department of Energy or the Environmental Protection Agency may add the ENERGY STAR logo to labels on certified covered products; such manufacturers or private labelers may add the ENERGY STAR logo to labels only on those products that are covered by the Memorandum of Understanding;

(vii) The design voltage of each lamp included in the package, if other than 120 volts;

(viii) For any general service lamp containing mercury, the following statement: "Contains Mercury For more on clean up and safe disposal, visit *epa.gov/cfl.*" The manufacturer may also print an "Hg[Encircled]" symbol on the label after the term "Contains Mercury"; and

(ix) No marks or information other than that specified in this part shall appear on the Lighting Facts label.

(4) *Standard Lighting Facts label format.* Except as provided in paragraph (b)(5) of this section, information specified in paragraph (b)(3) of this section shall be presented on covered lamp packages in the format, terms, explanatory text, specifications, and minimum sizes as shown in Prototype Labels 6 in appendix L of this part and consistent in format and orientation with Sample Labels 10, 11, or 12 in appendix L. The text and lines shall be all black or one color type, printed on a white or other neutral contrasting background whenever practical.

(i) The Lighting Facts information shall be set off in a box by use of hairlines and shall be all black or one color type, printed on a white or other neutral contrasting background whenever practical.

(ii) All information within the Lighting Facts label shall utilize:

(A) Arial or an equivalent type style;

(B) Upper and lower case letters;

(C) Leading as indicated in Prototype Label 6 in appendix L of this part;

(D) Letters that never touch;

(E) The box and hairlines separating information as illustrated in Prototype Labels 6 in appendix L of this part; and

(F) The minimum font sizes and line thicknesses as illustrated in Prototype Label 6 in appendix L of this part.

(5) *Lighting Facts format for small packages.* If the total surface area of the product package available for labeling is less than 24 square inches and the package shape or size cannot accommodate the standard label required by paragraph (b)(4) of this section, manufacturers may provide the information specified in paragraph (b)(3) of this section using a smaller, linear label following the format, terms, explanatory text, specifications, and minimum sizes illustrated in Prototype Label 7 in appendix L of this part.

(6) *Bilingual labels.* The information required by paragraphs (b)(1) through (5) of this section may be presented in a second language either by using separate labels for each language or in a bilingual label with the English text in the format required by this section immediately followed by the text in the second language. Sample Label 13 in appendix L of this part provides an example of a bilingual Lighting Facts label. All required information must be included in both languages. Numeric

characters that are identical in both languages need not be repeated.

(7) *Product labeling.* Any general service lamp shall be labeled legibly on the product with the following information:

(i) The lamp's average initial lumens, expressed as a number rounded to the nearest five, adjacent to the word "lumens," both provided in minimum 8 point font; and

(ii) For general service lamps containing mercury, the following statement: "Mercury disposal: *epa.gov/cfl*" in minimum 8 point font.

(c) *Specialty consumer lamps.* (1) Any specialty consumer lamp that is a vibration-service lamp as defined at 42 U.S.C. 6291, rough service lamp as defined at 42 U.S.C. 6291(30), appliance lamp as defined at 42 U.S.C. 6291(30); or shatter resistant lamp (including a shatter proof lamp and a shatter protected lamp) must be labeled pursuant to the requirements in paragraphs (b)(1) through (7) of this section.

(2) *Specialty consumer lamp Lighting Facts label content.* All specialty consumer lamps not covered by paragraph (c)(1) of this section shall be labeled pursuant to the requirements of paragraphs (b)(1) through (7) of this section or as follows:

(i) The principal display panel of the product package shall be labeled clearly and conspicuously with the following information consistent with the Prototype Labels in Appendix L:

(A) The light output of each lamp included in the package, expressed as "Brightness" in average initial lumens rounded to the nearest five;

(B) The estimated annual energy cost of each lamp included in the package, expressed as "Estimated Energy Cost" in dollars and based on usage of 3 hours per day and 11 cents ($0.11) per kWh; and

(C) The life, as defined in § 305.2(w), of each lamp included in the package, expressed in years rounded to the nearest tenth (based on 3 hours operation per day).

(ii)(A) If the lamp contains mercury, the principal display panel shall contain the following statement in minimum 10 point font: "Contains Mercury For more on clean up and safe disposal, visit epa.gov/cfl."

(B) The manufacturer may also print an "Hg[Encircled]" symbol on package after the term "Contains Mercury."

(iii) If the lamp contains mercury, the lamp shall be labeled legibly on the product with the following statement: "Mercury disposal: epa.gov/cfl" in minimum 8 point font.

(iv) If the required disclosures for a lamp covered by paragraph (c)(2) of this section will not be legible on the front panel of a single-card, blister package due to the small size of the panel, the manufacturer or private labeler may print the statement "Lighting Facts see back" on the principal display panel consistent with the sample label in Appendix L as long as the Lighting Facts label required by paragraph (b)(3) of this section appears on the rear panel.

(v) No marks or information other than that specified in this part shall appear on the Lighting Facts label.

(3) *Specialty Lighting Facts label format.* Information specified in paragraph (c)(2) of this section shall be presented on covered lamp packages in the format, terms, explanatory text, specifications, and minimum sizes as shown in the Prototype Labels of appendix L and consistent in format and orientation with Sample Labels in Appendix L of this part. The text and lines shall be all black or one color type, printed on a white or other neutral contrasting background whenever practical.

(i) The Lighting Facts information shall be set off in a box by use of hairlines and shall be all black or one color type, printed on a white or other neutral contrasting background whenever practical.

(ii) All information within the Lighting Facts label shall utilize:

(A) Arial or an equivalent type style;

(B) Upper and lower case letters;

(C) Leading as indicated in the Prototype Labels in Appendix L of this part;

(D) Letters that never touch;

(E) The box and hairlines separating information as illustrated in the Prototype Labels in appendix L of this part; and

(F) The minimum font sizes and line thicknesses as illustrated in Prototype Labels in Appendix L of this part.

(iii) For small package labels covered by (c)(2)(iv) of this section, the words "Lighting Facts see back" shall appear on the primary display panel in a size and format specified in appendix L of this part.

(4) *Bilingual labels.* The information required by paragraph (c) of this section may be presented in a second language either by using separate labels for each language or in a bilingual label with the English text in the format required by this section immediately followed by the text in the second language. All required information must be included in both languages. Numeric characters that are identical in both languages need not be repeated.

(d) For lamps that do not meet the definition of general service lamp or specialty consumer lamp, manufacturers and private labelers have the discretion to label with the Lighting Facts label as long as they comply with all requirements applicable to specialty consumer lamps in this part.

(e)(1) Any covered incandescent lamp that is subject to and does not comply with the January 1, 2012 or January 1, 2013 efficiency standards specified in 42 U.S.C. 6295 or the DOE standards at 10 CFR 430.32(n)(5) effective July 14, 2012 shall be labeled clearly and conspicuously on the principal display panel of the product package with the following information in lieu of the labeling requirements specified in paragraph (b):

(2) The light output, energy usage and life ratings of any product covered by paragraph (c)(1) of this section shall appear in that order and with equal clarity and conspicuousness on the product's principal display panel. The light output, energy usage and life ratings shall be disclosed in terms of "lumens," "watts," and "hours" respectively, with the lumens, watts, and hours rating numbers each appearing in the same type style and size and with the words "lumens," "watts," and "hours" each appearing in the same type style and size. The words "light output," "energy used," and "life" shall precede and have the same conspicuousness as both the rating numbers and the words "lumens," "watts," and "hours," except that the letters of the words "lumens," "watts," and "hours" shall be approximately 50% of the sizes of those used for the words "light output," "energy used," and "life," respectively.

(f)(1) The required disclosures of any covered product that is a general service lamp or specialty consumer lamp shall be measured at 120 volts, regardless of the lamp's design voltage. If a lamp's design voltage is 125 volts or 130 volts, the disclosures of the wattage, light output, energy cost, and life ratings shall in each instance be:

(i) At 120 volts and followed by the phrase "at 120 volts." In such case, the labels for such lamps also may disclose the lamp's wattage, light output, energy cost, and life at the design voltage (*e.g.*, "Light Output 1710 Lumens at 125 volts"); or

(ii) At the design voltage and followed by the phrase "at (125 volts/130 volts)" if the ratings at 120 volts are disclosed clearly and conspicuously on another panel of the package, and if all panels of the package that contain a claimed light output, energy cost, wattage or lifeclearly and conspicuously identify the lamp as "(125 volt/130 volt)," and if the principal display panel clearly and conspicuously discloses the following statement:

This product is designed for (125/130) volts. When used on the normal line voltage of 120 volts, the light output and energy efficiency are noticeably reduced. See (side/back) panel for 120 volt ratings.

(2) For any covered product that is an incandescent reflector lamp, the required disclosures of light output shall be given for the lamp's total forward lumens.

(3) For any covered product that is a compact fluorescent lamp, the required light output disclosure shall be measured at a base-up position; but, if the manufacturer or private labeler has reason to believe that the light output at a base-down position would be more than 5% different, the label also shall disclose the light output at the base-down position or, if no test data for the base-down position exist, the fact that at a base-down position the light output might be more than 5% less.

(4) For any covered product that is a general service lamp or specialty consumer lamp and operates at discrete, multiple light levels (*e.g.*, 800, 1600, and 2500 lumens), the light output, energy cost, and wattage disclosures required by this section must be provided at each of the lamp's levels of light output and the lamp's life provided on the basis of the shortest lived operating mode. The multiple numbers shall be separated by a "/" (*e.g.*, 800/1600/2500 lumens) if they appear on the same line on the label.

(5) A manufacturer or private labeler who distributes general service fluorescent lamps, general service lamps, or specialty consumer lamp without labels attached to the lamps or without labels on individual retail-sale packaging for one or more lamps may meet the package disclosure requirements of this section by making the required disclosures, in the manner and form required by those paragraphs, on the bulk shipping cartons that are to be used to display the lamps for retail sale.

(6) Any manufacturer or private labeler who makes any representation, other than those required by this section, on a package of any covered product that is a general service fluorescent lamp, general service lamp, or specialty consumer lamp regarding the cost of operation or life of such lamp shall clearly and conspicuously disclose in close proximity to such representation the assumptions upon which it is based, including, *e.g.*, purchase price, unit cost of electricity, hours of use, patterns of use. If those assumptions differ from those required for the cost and life information on the Lighting Facts label (11 cents per kWh and 3 hours per day), the manufacturer or private labeler must also disclose, with equal clarity and conspicuousness and in close proximity to, the same representation based on the assumptions for cost and life required on the Lighting Facts label.

(g)(1) Any covered product that is a general service fluorescent lamp or an incandescent reflector lamp shall be labeled clearly and conspicuously with a capital letter "E" printed within a circle and followed by an asterisk. The label shall also clearly and conspicuously disclose, either in close proximity to that asterisk or elsewhere on the label, the following statement:

*[The encircled "E"] means this bulb meets Federal minimum efficiency standards.

(i) If the statement is not disclosed on the principal display panel, the asterisk shall be followed by the following statement:

See [Back,Top, Side] panel for details.

(ii) For purposes of this paragraph, the encircled capital letter "E" shall be clearly and conspicuously disclosed in color-contrasting ink on the label of any covered product that is a general service fluorescent lamp and will be deemed "conspicuous," in terms of size, if it appears in typeface at least as large as either the manufacturer's name or logo or another logo disclosed on the label, such as the "UL" or "ETL" logos, whichever is larger.

(2) Instead of labeling any covered product that is a general service fluorescent lamp with the encircled "E" and with the statement described in paragraph (e)(1) of this section, a manufacturer or private labeler who would not otherwise put a label on such a lamp may meet the disclosure requirements of that paragraph by permanently marking the lamp clearly and conspicuously with the encircled "E."

(3) Any cartons in which any covered products that are general service fluorescent lamps and general service lamps are shipped within the United States or imported into the United States shall disclose clearly and conspicuously the following statement:

These lamps comply with Federal energy efficiency labeling requirements.

(h) *Metal halide lamp fixtures and metal halide ballasts*—(1) *Contents.* Metal halide ballasts contained in a metal halide lamp fixture covered by this Part shall be marked conspicuously, in color-contrasting ink, with a capital letter "E" printed within a circle. Packaging for metal halide lamp fixtures covered by this part shall also be marked conspicuously with a capital letter "E" printed within a circle. For purposes of this section, the encircled capital letter "E" will be deemed "conspicuous," in terms of size, if it is as large as either the manufacturer's name or another logo, such as the "UL," "CBM" or "ETL" logos, whichever is larger, that appears on the metal halide ballast, or the packaging for the metal halide lamp fixture, whichever is applicable for purposes of labeling.

(2) *Product labeling.* The encircled capital letter "E" on metal halide ballasts must appear conspicuously, in color-contrasting ink (i.e., in a color that contrasts with the background on which the encircled capital letter "E" is placed) on the surface that is normally labeled. It may be printed on the label that normally appears on the metal halide ballast, printed on a separate label, or stamped indelibly on the surface of the metal halide ballast.

(3) *Package labeling.* For purposes of labeling under this section, packaging for metal halide lamp fixtures consists of the plastic sheeting, or "shrink-wrap," covering pallet loads of metal halide lamp fixtures as well as any containers in which such metal halide lamp fixtures are marketed individually or in small numbers. The encircled capital letter "E" on packages containing metal halide lamp fixtures must appear conspicuously, in color-contrasting ink, on the surface of the package on which printing or a label normally appears. If the package contains printing on more than one surface, the label must appear on the surface on which the product inside the package is described. The encircled capital letter "E" may be printed on the surface of the package, printed on a label containing other information, printed on a separate label, or indelibly stamped on the surface of the package. In the case of pallet loads containing metal halide lamp fixtures, the encircled capital letter "E" must appear conspicuously, in color-contrasting ink, on the plastic sheeting, unless clear plastic sheeting is used and the encircled capital letter "E" is legible underneath this packaging.

[72 FR 49971, Aug. 29, 2007, as amended at 73 FR 63068, Oct. 23, 2008; 75 FR 41714, July 19, 2010; 76 FR 20236, Apr. 12, 2011; 78 FR 2209, Jan. 10, 2013; 82 FR 67299, Nov. 2, 2017; 83 FR 14583, Apr. 5, 2018]

§305.16 Labeling and marking for plumbing products.

(a) *Showerheads and faucets.* Showerheads and faucets shall be marked and labeled as follows:

(1) Each showerhead and flow restricting or controlling spout end device shall bear a permanent legible marking indicating the flow rate, expressed in gallons per minute (gpm) or gallons per cycle (gpc), and the flow rate value shall be the actual flow rate or the maximum flow rate specified by the standards established in subsection (j) of section 325 of the Act, 42 U.S.C. 6295(j). Except where impractical due to the size of the fitting, each flow rate disclosure shall also be given in liters per minute (L/min) or liters per cycle (L/cycle). For purposes of this section, the marking indicating the flow rate will be deemed "legible," in terms of placement, if it is located in close proximity to the manufacturer's identification marking.

(2) Each showerhead and faucet shall bear a permanent legible marking to identify the manufacturer. This marking shall be the trade name, trademark, or other mark known to identify the manufacturer. Such marking shall be located where it can be seen after installation.

(3) The package for each showerhead and faucet shall disclose the manufacturer's name and the model number.

(4) The package or any label attached to the package for each showerhead or faucet shall contain at least the following: The flow rate expressed in gallons per minute (gpm) or gallons per cycle (gpc), and the flow rate value shall be the actual flow rate or the maximum flow rate specified by the standards established in subsection (j) of section 325 of the Act, 42 U.S.C. 6295(j). Each flow rate disclosure shall also be given in liters per minute (L/min) or liters per cycle (L/cycle).

(b) *Water closets and urinals.* Water closets and urinals shall be marked and labeled as follows:

(1) Each such fixture (and flushometer valve associated with such fixture) shall bear a permanent legible marking indicating the flow rate, expressed in gallons per flush (gpf), and the water use value shall be the actual water use or the maximum water use

specified by the standards established in subsection (k) of section 325 of the Act, 42 U.S.C. 6295(k). Except where impractical due to the size of the fixture, each flow rate disclosure shall also be given in liters per flush (Lpf). For purposes of this section, the marking indicating the flow rate will be deemed "legible," in terms of placement, if it is located in close proximity to the manufacturer's identification marking.

(2) Each water closet (and each component of the water closet if the fixture is comprised of two or more components) and urinal shall be marked with the manufacturer's name or trademark or, in the case of private labeling, the name or registered trademark of the customer for whom the unit was manufactured. This mark shall be legible, readily identified, and applied so as to be permanent. The mark shall be located so as to be visible after the fixture is installed, except for fixtures built into or for a counter or cabinet.

(3) The package, and any labeling attached to the package, for each water closet and urinal shall disclose the flow rate, expressed in gallons per flush (gpf), and the water use value shall be the actual water use or the maximum water use specified by the standards established in subsection (k) of section 325 of the Act, 42 U.S.C. 6295(k). Each flow rate disclosure shall also be given in liters per flush (Lpf).

(4) With respect to any gravity tank-type white 2-piece toilet offered for sale or sold before January 1, 1997, which has a water use greater than 1.6 gallons per flush (gpf), any printed matter distributed or displayed in connection with such product (including packaging and point-of-sale material, catalog material, and print advertising) shall include, in a conspicuous manner, the words "For Commercial Use Only."

(5) With respect to any gravity tank-type white 2-piece toilet offered for sale or sold before January 1, 1997, which has a water use greater than 1.6 gallons per flush (gpf), any printed matter distributed or displayed in connection with such product (including packaging and point-of-sale material, catalog material, and print advertising) shall include, in a conspicuous manner, the words "For Commercial Use Only."

(c) *Annual operating cost claims for covered plumbing products.* Until such time as the Commission has prescribed a format and manner of display for labels conveying estimated annual operating costs of covered showerheads, faucets, water closets, and urinals or ranges of estimated annual operating costs for the types or classes of such plumbing products, the Act prohibits manufacturers from making such representations on the labels of such covered products. 42 U.S.C. 6294(c)(8). If, before the Commission has prescribed such a format and manner of display for labels of such products, a manufacturer elects to provide for any such product a label conveying such a claim, it shall submit the proposed claim to the Commission so that a format and manner of display for a label may be prescribed.

[73 FR 49973, Aug. 29, 2007, as amended at 82 FR 29236, June 28, 2017; 83 FR 7597, Feb. 22, 2018]

§ 305.17 Television labeling.

(a) *Layout.* All energy labels for televisions shall use one of three shapes: a vertical rectangle, a horizontal rectangle, and a triangle as detailed in Prototype Labels in appendix L. All label size, positioning, spacing, type sizes, positioning of headline, copy, and line widths must be consistent with the prototype and sample labels in appendix L. The minimum label size for the vertical rectangle label is 1.5″ × 5.5″. The minimum size for the horizontal rectangle label is 1.5″ × 5.23″. The minimum size for the triangle label is 4.5″ × 4.5″ (right angle sides).

(b) *Type style and setting.* The Arial series typeface or equivalent shall be used exclusively on the label. Prototype Labels in appendix L contain specific directions for type style and setting and indicate the specific sizes, leading, faces, positioning, and spacing to be used. No hyphenations should be used in setting headline or copy text.

(c) *Colors.* The basic colors of all labels and icons covered by this section shall be process yellow or equivalent and process black. The label shall be printed full bleed process yellow. All type and graphics shall be printed process black.

(d) *Label types.* Except as provided in paragraph (i), the labels must be affixed to the product in the form of either an adhesive label, cling label, or alternative label as follows:

(1) *Adhesive label.* All adhesive labels shall be applied so they can be easily removed without the use of tools or liquids, other than water, but shall be applied with an adhesive with an adhesion capacity sufficient to prevent their dislodgment during normal handling throughout the chain of distribution to the retailer and consumer. The paper stock for pressure-sensitive or other adhesive labels shall have a basic weight of not less than 58 pounds per 500 sheets (25 × 38) or equivalent, exclusive of the release liner and adhesive. A minimum peel adhesion capacity for the adhesive of 12 ounces per square inch is suggested, but not required if the adhesive can otherwise meet the above standard.

(2) *Cling label.* Labels may be affixed, using the screen's static charge, to the product in the form of a cling label. The cling label shall be affixed in a manner that prevents dislodgment during normal handling throughout the chain of distribution to the retailer and consumer.

(3) *Alternative label.* In lieu of an adhesive or cling label, labels may be affixed using an alternative method to secure the label to the product as long as the method will prevent dislodgment during normal handling throughout the chain of distribution to the retailer and consumer. The label may not be affixed using a hang tag as described in §305.11(d)(2). The label shall consist of paper stock having a basic weight of not less than 110 pounds per 500 sheets (25 ½″ × 30 ½″) or other material of equivalent durability.

(e) *Placement*—(1) *In general.* Except as provided in paragraph (i), all labels must be clear and conspicuous to consumers viewing the television screen from the front.

(2) *Adhesive label.* The adhesive label shall be in the shape of a horizontal or vertical rectangle and shall be located on the bezel in the bottom right-hand corner of the television. The horizontal rectangular label shall be located on the far right of the bottom bezel and the vertical rectangular label shall be located on the bottom of the right-hand bezel. Another location on the bezel may be used if the television's configuration prevents such placement.

(3) *Cling label.* The cling label shall be in the shape of a triangle and shall be located in the bottom right-hand corner of the screen.

(4) *Alternative label.* The alternative label shall be in the shape of either a horizontal rectangle, vertical rectangle, or triangle. It shall be visible from the front of the television and located in the bottom right-hand corner of the television. Another prominent location visible from the front of the television may be used if the television's configuration or the mechanism to secure the alternative label prevents such placement.

(f) *Label content.* The television label shall contain the following information:

(1) Headlines, texts, and statements as illustrated in the prototype and sample labels in appendix L to this part.

(2) Name of manufacturer or private labeler. This requirement shall, in the case of a corporation, be satisfied only by the actual corporate name, which may be preceded or followed by the name of a particular division of the corporation. In the case of an individual, partnership, or association, the name under which the business is conducted shall be used.

(3) Model number(s) as designated by the manufacturer or private labeler.

(4) Estimated annual energy costs determined in accordance with §305.5 of this part and based on a usage rate of 5 hours in on mode and 19 hours in standby (sleep) mode per day and an electricity cost rate of 12 cents per kWh.

(5) The applicable ranges of comparability for estimated annual energy costs based on the labeled product's diagonal screen size, according to the following table:

Screen size (diagonal)	Annual energy cost ranges for televisions	
	Low	High
16–20″ (16.0 to 20.49″)	$3	$4
21–23″ (20.5 to 23.49″)	4	5
24–29″ (23.5 to 29.49″)	4	7

Screen size (diagonal)	Annual energy cost ranges for televisions	
	Low	High
30–34″ (29.5 to 34.49″)	6	13
35–39″ (34.5 to 39.49″)	7	13
40–44″ (39.5 to 44.49″)	5	21
45–49″ (44.5 to 49.49″)	6	24
50–54″ (49.5 to 54.49″)	8	34
55–59″ (54.5 to 59.49″)	8	34
60–64″ (59.5 to 64.49″)	12	48
65–69″ (64.5 to 69.49″)	10	51
69.5″ or greater	15	97

(6) Placement of the labeled product on the scale proportionate to the lowest and highest estimated annual energy costs as illustrated in Prototype and Sample Labels in appendix L. When the estimated annual energy cost of a given television model falls outside the limits of the current range for that product, the manufacturer shall place the product at the end of the range closest to the model's energy cost.

(7) The model's estimated annual energy consumption as determined in accordance with §305.5 and based on a usage rate of 5 hours in on mode and 19 hours in sleep (standby) mode per day.

(8) No marks or information other than that specified in this part shall appear on or directly adjoining this label except that:

(i) A manufacturer may include a part or publication number identification on the label, as long as it appears in the lower right-hand corner of the label and is set in 6-point type or smaller.

(ii) The manufacturer may include the ENERGY STAR logo on the label as illustrated in Sample Labels in appendix L. The logo must be 0.375″ wide. Only manufacturers that have signed a Memorandum of Understanding with the Department of Energy or the Environmental Protection Agency covering the televisions to be labeled may add the ENERGY STAR logo to those labels.

(g) *Distribution of labels.* Consistent with §305.6 of this part, for each covered television that a manufacturer distributes in commerce which is required by this part to bear an EnergyGuide label, the manufacturer must make a copy of the label available on a publicly accessible Web site in a manner that allows catalog sellers to hyperlink to the label or download it for use in Web sites or paper catalogs. The label for each specific model must remain on the Web site for six months after production of the model ceases.

[76 FR 1050, Jan. 6, 2011, as amended at 78 FR 2209, Jan. 10, 2013; 78 FR 43982, July 23, 2013; 79 FR 19467, Apr. 9, 2014; 80 FR 16260, Mar. 27, 2015]

§305.18 [Reserved]

§305.19 Promotional material displayed or distributed at point of sale.

(a)(1) Any manufacturer, distributor, retailer or private labeler who prepares printed material for display or distribution at point of sale concerning a covered product (except fluorescent lamp ballasts, metal halide lamp fixtures, general service fluorescent lamps, general service lamps, showerheads, faucets, water closets or urinals) shall clearly and conspicuously include in such printed material the following required disclosure:

> Before purchasing this appliance, read important information about its estimated annual energy consumption, yearly operating cost, or energy efficiency rating that is available from your retailer.

(2) Any manufacturer, distributor, retailer or private labeler who prepares printed material for display or distribution at point of sale concerning a covered product that is a fluorescent lamp ballast or metal halide lamp fixture to which standards are applicable under section 325 of the Act, shall disclose conspicuously in such printed material, in each description of such product, an encircled capital letter "E".

(3) Any manufacturer, distributer, retailer, or private labeler who prepares printed material for display or distribution at point of sale concerning a covered product that is a general service fluorescent lamp, general service lamps, and who makes any representation in such promotional material regarding the cost of operation of such lamp shall clearly and conspicuously disclose in close proximity to such representation the assumptions upon which it is based, including, e.g., purchase price, unit cost of electricity, hours of use, and patterns of use.

(4) Any manufacturer, distributor, retailer, or private labeler who prepares printed material for display or distribution at point-of-sale concerning a covered product that is a showerhead, faucet, water closet, or urinal shall clearly and conspicuously include in such printed material the product's water use, expressed in gallons and liters per minute (gpm and L/min) or per cycle (gpc and L/cycle) or gallons and liters per flush (gpf and Lpf) as specified in § 305.11(f).

(b) This section shall not apply to:

(1) Written warranties.

(2) Use and care manuals, installation instructions, or other printed material containing primarily post-purchase information for the purchaser.

(3) Printed material containing only the identification of a covered product, pricing information and/or non-energy related representations concerning that product.

(4) Any printed material distributed prior to the effective date listed in § 305.4(e).

[59 FR 34036, July 1, 1994, as amended at 59 FR 67530, Dec. 29, 1994; 60 FR 14211, Mar. 16, 1995. Redesignated at 72 FR 49971, Aug. 29, 2007, as amended at 72 FR 49974, Aug. 29, 2007; 73 FR 39226, July 9, 2008; 75 FR 41716, July 19, 2010]

§ 305.20 Paper catalogs and Web sites.

(a) Covered products offered for sale on the Internet. Any manufacturer, distributor, retailer, or private labeler who advertises a covered product on an Internet Web site in a manner that qualifies as a catalog under this Part shall disclose energy information as follows:

(1) *Content.*—(i) *Products required to bear EnergyGuide or Lighting Facts labels.* All Web sites advertising covered refrigerators, refrigerator-freezers, freezers, room air conditioners, clothes washers, dishwashers, ceiling fans, pool heaters, central air conditioners, heat pumps, furnaces, general service lamps, specialty consumer lamps (for products offered for sale after May 2, 2018), and televisions must display, for each model, a recognizable and legible image of the label required for that product by this part. The Web site may hyperlink to the image of the label using the sample EnergyGuide and Lighting Facts icons depicted in appendix L of this part. The Web site must hyperlink the image in a way that does not require consumers to save the hyperlinked image in order to view it.

(ii) *Products not required to bear EnergyGuide or Lighting Facts labels.* All Web sites advertising covered showerheads, faucets, water closets, urinals, general service fluorescent lamps, fluorescent lamp ballasts, and metal halide lamp fixtures must include the following disclosures for each covered product. For plumbing products, the Web site may hyperlink to the disclosures using a prominent link labeled "Water Usage" or a similar description which facilitates the disclosure of the covered product's rated water usage.

(A) Showerheads, faucets, water closets, and urinals. The product's water use, expressed in gallons and liters per minute (gpm and L/min) or per cycle (gpc and L/cycle) or gallons and liters per flush (gpf and Lpf) as specified in § 305.16.

(B) General service fluorescent lamps, fluorescent lamp ballasts, and metal halide lamp fixtures. A capital letter "E" printed within a circle.

(2) *Format.* The required Web site disclosures, whether label image, icon, or text, must appear clearly and conspicuously and in close proximity to the covered product's price on each Web page that contains a detailed description of the covered product and its price. The label and hyperlink icon must conform to the prototypes in appendix L, but may be altered in size to accommodate the Web page's design, as long as they remain clear and conspicuous to consumers viewing the page.

(b) Covered products offered for sale in paper catalogs. Any manufacturer, distributor, retailer, or private labeler that advertises a covered product in a paper publication that qualifies as a catalog under this Part shall disclose energy information as follows:

(1) *Content.* (i) Products required to bear EnergyGuide or Lighting Facts labels. All paper catalogs advertising covered products required by this Part to bear EnergyGuide or Lighting Facts labels illustrated in appendix L (refrigerators, refrigerator-freezers, freezers,

room air conditioners, clothes washers, dishwashers, ceiling fans, pool heaters, central air conditioners, heat pumps, furnaces, general service fluorescent lamps, general service lamps, and televisions) must either display an image of the full label prepared in accordance with this Part, or make a text disclosure as follows:

(A) *Refrigerator, refrigerator-freezer, and freezer.* The capacity of the model determined in accordance with § 305.7, the estimated annual operating cost determined in accordance with § 305.5 and appendix K of this Part, and a disclosure stating "Your energy cost depends on your utility rates and use. The estimated cost is based on ____ cents per kWh. For more information, visit *www.ftc.gov/energy.*"

(B) *Room air conditioners and water heaters.* The capacity of the model determined in accordance with § 305.7, the estimated annual operating cost determined in accordance with § 305.5 and appendix K of this Part, and a disclosure stating "Your operating costs will depend on your utility rates and use. The estimated operating cost is based on a [electricity, natural gas, propane, or oil] cost of [$ ____ per kWh, therm, or gallon]. For more information, visit *www.ftc.gov/energy.*"

(C) *Clothes washers and dishwashers.* The capacity of the model for clothes washers determined in accordance with § 305.7 and the estimated annual operating cost for clothes washers and dishwashers determined in accordance with § 305.5 and appendix K, and a disclosure stating "Your energy cost depends on your utility rates and use. The estimated cost is based on [4 washloads a week for dishwashers, or 8 washloads a week for clothes washers] and __ cents per kWh for electricity and $__ per therm for natural gas. For more information, visit *www.ftc.gov/energy.*"

(D) *General service fluorescent lamps or general service lamps.* All the information concerning that lamp required by § 305.15 of this part to be disclosed on the lamp's package, and, for general service lamps, a disclosure stating "Your energy cost depends on your utility rates and use. The estimated cost and life is based on 11 cents per kWh and 3 hours of use per day. For more information, visit *www.ftc.gov/energy.*" For the "Light Appearance" disclosure required by § 305.15(b)(3)(iv), the catalog need only disclose the lamp's correlated color temperature in Kelvin (e.g., 2700 K). General service fluorescent lamps or incandescent reflector lamps must also include a capital letter "E" printed within a circle and the statement described in § 305.15(d)(1).

(E) *Ceiling fans.* All the information required by § 305.13.

(F) *Televisions.* The estimated annual operating cost determined in accordance with § 305.5 and a disclosure stating "Your energy cost depends on your utility rates and use. The estimated cost is based on 12 cents per kWh and 5 hours of use per day. For more information, visit *www.ftc.gov/energy.*"

(G) *Central air conditioners, heat pumps, and furnaces (including boilers), and pool heaters.* The capacity of the model determined in accordance with § 305.7 and the energy efficiency or thermal efficiency ratings determined in accordance with § 305.5 on each page that lists the covered product.

(ii) Products not required to bear EnergyGuide or Lighting Facts labels. All paper catalogs advertising covered products not required by this Part to bear labels with specific design characteristics illustrated in appendix L (showerheads, faucets, water closets, urinals, fluorescent lamp ballasts, and metal halide lamp fixtures) must make a text disclosure for each covered product identical to those required for Internet disclosures under § 305.20(a)(1)(ii).

(2) *Format.* The required disclosures, whether text, label image, or icon, must appear clearly and conspicuously on each page that contains a detailed description of the covered product and its price. If a catalog displays an image of the full label, the size of the label may be altered to accommodate the catalog's design, as long as the label remains clear and conspicuous to consumers. For text disclosures made pursuant to § 305.20(b)(1)(i) and (ii), the required disclosure may be displayed once per page per type of product if the catalog offers multiple covered products of the same type on a page, as

long as the disclosure remains clear and conspicuous.

[78 FR 2209, Jan. 10, 2013, as amended at 80 FR 67300, Nov. 2, 2015; 82 FR 29236, June 28, 2017]

ADDITIONAL REQUIREMENTS

§ 305.21 Test data records.

(a) Test data shall be kept on file by the manufacturer of a covered product for a period of two years after production of that model has been terminated.

(b) Upon notification by the Commission or its designated representative, a manufacturer or private labeler shall provide, within 30 days of the date of such request, the underlying test data from which the water use or energy consumption rate, the energy efficiency rating, the estimated annual cost of using each basic model, or the light output, energy usage, correlated color temperature, and life ratings and, for fluorescent lamps, the color rendering index, for each basic model or lamp type were derived.

[52 FR 46894, Dec. 10, 1987, as amended at 59 FR 67530, Dec. 29, 1994. Redesignated at 72 FR 49971, Aug. 29, 2007, as amended at 75 FR 41717, July 19, 2010]

§ 305.22 Required testing by designated laboratory.

Upon notification by the Commission or its designated representative, a manufacturer of a covered product shall supply, at the manufacturer's expense, no more than two of each model of each product to a laboratory, which will be identified by the Commission or its designated representative in the notice, for the purpose of ascertaining whether the estimated annual energy consumption, the estimated annual operating cost, or the energy efficiency rating, or the light output, energy usage and life ratings or, for general service fluorescent lamps, the color rendering index, disclosed on the label or fact sheet or in an industry directory, or, as required in a catalog, or the representation made by the label that the product is in compliance with applicable standards in section 325 of the Act, 42 U.S.C. 6295, is accurate. Such a procedure will only be followed after the Commission or its staff has examined the underlying test data provided by the manufacturer as required by § 305.21(b) and after the manufacturer has been afforded the opportunity to reverify test results from which the estimated annual energy consumption, the estimated annual operating cost, or the energy efficiency rating for each basic model was derived, or the light output, energy usage and life ratings or, for general service fluorescent lamps, the color rendering index, for each basic model or lamp type was derived. A representative designated by the Commission shall be permitted to observe any reverification procedures required by this part, and to inspect the results of such reverification. The Commission will pay the charges for testing by designated laboratories.

[59 FR 67530, Dec. 29, 1994. Redesignated at 72 FR 49971, Aug. 29, 2007, as amended at 72 FR 49974, Aug. 29, 2007]

EFFECT OF THIS PART

§ 305.23 Effect on other law.

This regulation supersedes any State regulation to the extent required by section 327 of the Act. Pursuant to the Act, all State regulations that require the disclosure for any covered product of information with respect to energy consumption, other than the information required to be disclosed in accordance with this part, are superseded.

[52 FR 46894, Dec. 10, 1987. Redesignated at 72 FR 49971, Aug. 29, 2007]

§ 305.24 Stayed or invalid parts.

If any section or portion of a section of this part is stayed or held invalid, the remainder of the part will not be affected.

[52 FR 46894, Dec. 10, 1987. Redesignated at 59 FR 34036, July 1, 1994, and further redesignated at 72 FR 49974, Aug. 29, 2007]

§ 305.25 [Reserved]

APPENDIX A1 TO PART 305—REFRIGERATORS WITH AUTOMATIC DEFROST

RANGE INFORMATION

Manufacturer's rated total refrigerated volume in cubic feet	Range of estimated annual operating costs (dollars/year)	
	Low	High
Less than 10.5	$18	$39
10.5 to 12.4	30	34
12.5 to 14.4	34	36
14.5 to 16.4	(*)	(*)
16.5 to 18.4	34	40
18.5 to 20.4	40	41
20.5 to 22.4	37	48
22.5 to 24.4	45	50
24.5 to 26.4	(*)	(*)
26.5 to 28.4	(*)	(*)
28.5 and over	(*)	(*)

(*) No data.

[81 FR 63650, Sept. 15, 2016]

APPENDIX A2 TO PART 305—REFRIGERATORS AND REFRIGERATOR-FREEZERS WITH MANUAL DEFROST

RANGE INFORMATION

Manufacturer's rated total refrigerated volume in cubic feet	Range of estimated annual operating costs (dollars/year)	
	Low	High
Less than 10.5	$24	$41
10.5 to 12.4	(*)	(*)
12.5 to 14.4	30	30
14.5 to 16.4	(*)	(*)
16.5 to 18.4	(*)	(*)
18.5 to 20.4	(*)	(*)
20.5 to 22.4	(*)	(*)
22.5 to 24.4	(*)	(*)
24.5 to 26.4	(*)	(*)
26.5 to 28.4	(*)	(*)
28.5 and over	(*)	(*)

(*) No data.

[81 FR 63650, Sept. 15, 2016]

APPENDIX A3 TO PART 305—REFRIGERATOR-FREEZERS WITH PARTIAL AUTOMATIC DEFROST

RANGE INFORMATION

Manufacturer's rated total refrigerated volume in cubic feet	Range of estimated annual operating costs (dollars/year)	
	Low	High
Less than 10.5	$25	$44
10.5 to 12.4	(*)	(*)
12.5 to 14.4	(*)	(*)
14.5 to 16.4	(*)	(*)
16.5 to 18.4	(*)	(*)
18.5 to 20.4	(*)	(*)
20.5 to 22.4	(*)	(*)
22.5 to 24.4	(*)	(*)
24.5 to 26.4	(*)	(*)
26.5 to 28.4	(*)	(*)
28.5 and over	(*)	(*)

(*) No data.

[81 FR 63650, Sept. 15, 2016]

APPENDIX A4 TO PART 305—REFRIGERATOR-FREEZERS WITH AUTOMATIC DEFROST WITH TOP-MOUNTED FREEZER WITHOUT THROUGH-THE-DOOR ICE SERVICE

RANGE INFORMATION

Manufacturer's rated total refrigerated volume in cubic feet	Range of estimated annual operating costs (dollars/year)	
	Low	High
Less than 10.5	$36	$53
10.5 to 12.4	37	51
12.5 to 14.4	40	55
14.5 to 16.4	40	57
16.5 to 18.4	43	59
18.5 to 20.4	45	62
20.5 to 22.4	46	63
22.5 to 24.4	56	66
24.5 to 26.4	(*)	(*)
26.5 to 28.4	(*)	(*)
28.5 and over	(*)	(*)

(*) No data.

[81 FR 63650, Sept. 15, 2016]

APPENDIX A5 TO PART 305—REFRIGERATOR-FREEZERS WITH AUTOMATIC DEFROST WITH SIDE-MOUNTED FREEZER WITHOUT THROUGH-THE-DOOR ICE SERVICE

RANGE INFORMATION

Manufacturer's rated total refrigerated volume in cubic feet	Range of estimated annual operating costs (dollars/year)	
	Low	High
Less than 10.5	$25	$70
10.5 to 12.4	(*)	(*)
12.5 to 14.4	(*)	(*)
14.5 to 16.4	37	37
16.5 to 18.4	(*)	(*)
18.5 to 20.4	(*)	(*)
20.5 to 22.4	63	86
22.5 to 24.4	67	90
24.5 to 26.4	69	93
26.5 to 28.4	85	96
28.5 and over	86	101

(*) No data.

[81 FR 63650, Sept. 15, 2016]

APPENDIX A6 TO PART 305—REFRIGERATOR-FREEZERS WITH AUTOMATIC DEFROST WITH BOTTOM-MOUNTED FREEZER WITHOUT THROUGH-THE-DOOR ICE SERVICE

RANGE INFORMATION

Manufacturer's rated total refrigerated volume in cubic feet	Range of estimated annual operating costs (dollars/year)	
	Low	High
Less than 10.5	$19	$62
10.5 to 12.4	38	63
12.5 to 14.4	49	65
14.5 to 16.4	52	72
16.5 to 18.4	54	73
18.5 to 20.4	54	75
20.5 to 22.4	58	79
22.5 to 24.4	71	83
24.5 to 26.4	64	81

RANGE INFORMATION—Continued

Manufacturer's rated total refrigerated volume in cubic feet	Range of estimated annual operating costs (dollars/year)	
	Low	High
26.5 to 28.4	77	84
28.5 and over	78	86

[81 FR 63650, Sept. 15, 2016]

APPENDIX A7 TO PART 305—REFRIGERATOR-FREEZERS WITH AUTOMATIC DEFROST WITH BOTTOM-MOUNTED FREEZER WITH THROUGH-THE-DOOR ICE SERVICE

RANGE INFORMATION

Manufacturer's rated total refrigerated volume in cubic feet	Range of estimated annual operating costs (dollars/year)	
	Low	High
Less than 10.5	(*)	(*)
10.5 to 12.4	(*)	(*)
12.5 to 14.4	(*)	(*)
14.5 to 16.4	(*)	(*)
16.5 to 18.4	(*)	(*)
18.5 to 20.4	$77	$83
20.5 to 22.4	79	87
22.5 to 24.4	80	91
24.5 to 26.4	76	93
26.5 to 28.4	74	95
28.5 and over	78	103

(*) No data.

[81 FR 63650, Sept. 15, 2016]

APPENDIX A8 TO PART 305—REFRIGERATOR-FREEZERS WITH AUTOMATIC DEFROST WITH SIDE-MOUNTED FREEZER WITH THROUGH-THE-DOOR ICE SERVICE

RANGE INFORMATION

Manufacturer's rated total refrigerated volume in cubic feet	Range of estimated annual operating costs (dollars/year)	
	Low	High
Less than 10.5	(*)	(*)
10.5 to 12.4	(*)	(*)
12.5 to 14.4	(*)	(*)
14.5 to 16.4	(*)	(*)
16.5 to 18.4	(*)	(*)
18.5 to 20.4	$78	$78
20.5 to 22.4	72	94
22.5 to 24.4	81	98
24.5 to 26.4	73	99
26.5 to 28.4	89	104
28.5 and over	82	107

(*) No data.

[81 FR 63650, Sept. 15, 2016]

Appendix A9 to Part 305—All Refrigerators and Refrigerator-Freezers

RANGE INFORMATION

Manufacturer's rated total refrigerated volume in cubic feet	Range of estimated annual operating costs (dollars/year)	
	Low	High
Less than 10.5	$18	$70
10.5 to 12.4	30	63
12.5 to 14.4	30	65
14.5 to 16.4	37	72
16.5 to 18.4	34	73
18.5 to 20.4	40	83
20.5 to 22.4	37	94
22.5 to 24.4	45	98
24.5 to 26.4	64	99
26.5 to 28.4	74	104
28.5 and over	78	107

[81 FR 63653, Sept. 15, 2016]

Appendix B1 to Part 305—Upright Freezers With Manual Defrost

RANGE INFORMATION

Manufacturer's rated total refrigerated volume in cubic feet	Range of estimated annual operating costs (dollars/year)	
	Low	High
Less than 5.5	$26	$36
5.5 to 7.4	37	38
7.5 to 9.4	30	30
9.5 to 11.4	31	31
11.5 to 13.4	38	38
13.5 to 15.4	40	40
15.5 to 17.4	43	43
17.5 to 19.4	(*)	(*)
19.5 to 21.4	48	48
21.5 to 23.4	(*)	(*)
23.5 to 25.4	(*)	(*)
25.5 to 27.4	(*)	(*)
27.5 to 29.4	(*)	(*)
29.5 and over	(*)	(*)

(*) No data.

[81 FR 63653, Sept. 15, 2016]

Appendix B2 To Part 305—Upright Freezers With Automatic Defrost

RANGE INFORMATION

Manufacturer's rated total refrigerated volume in cubic feet	Range of estimated annual operating costs (dollars/year)	
	Low	High
Less than 5.5	$32	$32
5.5 to 7.4	(*)	(*)
7.5 to 9.4	53	59
9.5 to 11.4	59	59
11.5 to 13.4	57	67
13.5 to 15.4	47	73
15.5 to 17.4	52	74
17.5 to 19.4	54	71
19.5 to 21.4	57	76
21.5 to 23.4	81	87
23.5 to 25.4	(*)	(*)
25.5 to 27.4	(*)	(*)
27.5 to 29.4	(*)	(*)

RANGE INFORMATION—Continued

Manufacturer's rated total refrigerated volume in cubic feet	Range of estimated annual operating costs (dollars/year)	
	Low	High
29.5 and over	(*)	(*)

(*) No data.

[81 FR 63653, Sept. 15, 2016]

APPENDIX B3 TO PART 305—CHEST FREEZERS AND ALL OTHER FREEZERS

RANGE INFORMATION

Manufacturer's rated total refrigerated volume in cubic feet	Range of estimated annual operating costs (dollars/year)	
	Low	High
Less than 5.5	$16	$27
5.5 to 7.4	24	30
7.5 to 9.4	23	31
9.5 to 11.4	25	30
11.5 to 13.4	(*)	(*)
13.5 to 15.4	35	36
15.5 to 17.4	33	37
17.5 to 19.4	40	40
19.5 to 21.4	(*)	(*)
21.5 to 23.4	46	46
23.5 to 25.4	(*)	(*)
25.5 to 27.4	(*)	(*)
27.5 to 29.4	(*)	(*)
29.5 and over	(*)	(*)

(*) No data.

[81 FR 63653, Sept. 15, 2016]

APPENDIX C1 TO PART 305—COMPACT DISHWASHERS

RANGE INFORMATION

"Compact" includes countertop dishwasher models with a capacity of fewer than eight (8) place settings. Place settings shall be in accordance with appendix C to 10 CFR part 430, subpart B. Load patterns shall conform to the operating normal for the model being tested.

Capacity	Range of estimated annual energy costs (dollars/year)	
	Low	High
Compact	$17	$27

[83 FR 7597, Feb. 22, 2018]

APPENDIX C2 TO PART 305—STANDARD DISHWASHERS

RANGE INFORMATION

"Standard" includes dishwasher models with a capacity of eight (8) or more place settings. Place settings shall be in accordance with appendix C to 10 CFR part 430, subpart B. Load patterns shall conform to the operating normal for the model being tested.

Capacity	Range of estimated annual energy costs (dollars/year)	
	Low	High
Standard	$26	$40

[83 FR 7597, Feb. 22, 2018]

APPENDIX D1 TO PART 305—WATER HEATERS—GAS

RANGE INFORMATION

Capacity (first hour rating in gallons)	Range of estimated annual energy costs (dollars/year)			
First hour rating	Natural gas ($/year)		Propane ($/year)	
	Low	High	Low	High
"Very Small"—less than 18	*	*	*	*
"Low"—18 to 50.9	$154	$155	*	*
"Medium"—51 to 74.9	177	206	437	560
"High"—over 75	225	297	506	732

* No data.

[81 FR 63654, Sept. 15, 2016]

APPENDIX D2 TO PART 305—WATER HEATERS ELECTRIC

RANGE INFORMATION

Capacity (first hour rating in gallons)	Range of estimated annual energy costs (dollars/year)	
First hour rating	Low	High
"Very Small"—less than 18	*	*
"Low"—18 to 50.9	$93	$295
"Medium"—51 to 74.9	120	423
High"—over 75	191	252

*No data.

[81 FR 63654, Sept. 15, 2016]

APPENDIX D3 TO PART 305—WATER HEATERS—OIL

RANGE INFORMATION

Capacity (first hour rating in gallons)	Range of estimated annual energy costs (dollars/year)	
First hour rating	Low	High
"Very Small"—less than 18	*	*
"Low"—18 to 50.9	*	*
"Medium"—51 to 74.9	*	*
High"—over 75	$649	$730

*No data.

[81 FR 63654, Sept. 15, 2016]

Appendix D4 to Part 305—Water Heaters—Instantaneous-Gas

Range Information

Capacity	Range of estimated annual energy costs (dollars/year)			
Capacity (maximum flow rate); gallons per minute (gpm)	Natural gas ($/year)		Propane ($/year)	
	Low	High	Low	High
"Very Small"—less than 1.6	*	*	*	*
"Low"—1.7 to 2.7	*	*	*	*
"Medium"—2.8 to 3.9	$130	$151	$321	$372
"High"—over 4.0	195	230	485	567

*No data.

[81 FR 63654, Sept. 15, 2016]

Appendix D5 to Part 305—Water Heaters—Instantaneous—Electric

Range Information

Capacity	Range of estimated annual energy costs (dollars/year)	
	Low	High
Capacity (maximum flow rate); gallons per minute (gpm):		
"Very Small"—less than 1.6	$72	$74
"Low"—1.7 to 2.7	*	*
"Medium"—2.8 to 3.9	*	*
"High"—over 4.0	*	*

[82 FR 29236, June 28, 2017]

Appendix E to Part 305—Room Air Conditioners

Range Information

Manufacturer's rated cooling capacity in Btu's/hr	Range of estimated annual energy costs (dollars/year)	
	Low	High
Without Reverse Cycle and with Louvered Sides:		
Less than 6,000 Btu	$40	$53
6,000 to 7,999 Btu	48	72
8,000 to 13,999 Btu	65	127
14,000 to 19,999 Btu	115	182
20,000 and more Btu	189	386
Without Reverse Cycle and without Louvered Sides:		
Less than 6,000 Btu	(*)	(*)
6,000 to 7,999 Btu	58	80
8,000 to 13,999 Btu	69	147
14,000 to 19,999 Btu	117	158
20,000 and more Btu	(*)	(*)
With Reverse Cycle and with Louvered Sides	68	238
With Reverse Cycle, without Louvered Sides	(*)	(*)

*No sufficient data submitted.

[83 FR 7597, Feb. 22, 2018]

APPENDIX F1 TO PART 305—STANDARD CLOTHES WASHERS

RANGE INFORMATION

"Standard" includes all household clothes washers with a tub capacity of 1.6 cu. ft. or more.

Capacity	Range of estimated annual operating costs (dollars/year)	
	Low	High
Standard	$8	$51

[81 FR 7202, Feb. 11, 2016]

APPENDIX F2 TO PART 305—COMPACT CLOTHES WASHERS

RANGE INFORMATION

"Compact" includes all household clothes washers with a tub capacity of less than 1.6 cu. ft.

Capacity	Range of estimated annual operating costs (dollars/year)	
	Low	High
Compact	$10	$24

[81 FR 7202, Feb. 11, 2016]

APPENDIX G1 TO PART 305—FURNACES—GAS

Furnace type	Range of annual fuel utilization efficiencies (AFUEs)	
	Low	High
Non-Weatherized Gas Furnaces—All Capacities	80.0	98.7
Weatherized Gas Furnaces—All Capacities	81.0	95.0

[83 FR 7598, Feb. 22, 2018]

APPENDIX G2 TO PART 305—FURNACES— ELECTRIC

Furnace type	Range of annual fuel utilization efficiencies (AFUEs)	
	Low	High
Electric Furnaces—All Capacities	100.0	100.0

[83 FR 7598, Feb. 22, 2018]

APPENDIX G3 TO PART 305—FURNACES—OIL

Type	Range of annual fuel utilization efficiencies (AFUEs)	
	Low	High
Non-Weatherized Oil Furnaces—All Capacities	83.0	96.7
Weatherized Oil Furnaces—All Capacities	78.0	83.0

[83 FR 7598, Feb. 22, 2018]

APPENDIX G4 TO PART 305—MOBILE HOME FURNACES—GAS

Type	Range of annual fuel utilization efficiencies (AFUEs)	
	Low	High
Mobile Home Gas Furnaces—All Capacities	80.0	97.3

[83 FR 7598, Feb. 22, 2018]

APPENDIX G5 TO PART 305—MOBILE HOME FURNACES—OIL

Type	Range of annual fuel utilization efficiencies (AFUEs)	
	Low	High
Mobile Home Oil Furnaces—All Capacities	80.0	87.0

[83 FR 7598, Feb. 22, 2018]

APPENDIX G6 TO PART 305—BOILERS (GAS)

Type	Range of annual fuel utilization efficiencies (AFUEs)	
	Low	High
Gas Boilers (except steam)—All Capacities	82.0	96.8
Gas Boilers (steam)—All Capacities	80.4	83.4

[83 FR 7598, Feb. 22, 2018]

APPENDIX G7 TO PART 305—BOILERS (OIL)

Type	Range of annual fuel utilization efficiencies (AFUEs)	
	Low	High
Oil Boilers—All Capacities	82.0	90.0

[83 FR 7598, Feb. 22, 2018]

APPENDIX G8 TO PART 305—BOILERS (ELECTRIC)

Type	Range of annual fuel utilization efficiencies (AFUEs)	
	Low	High
Electric Boilers—All Capacities	100	100

[83 FR 7598, Feb. 22, 2018]

APPENDIX H TO PART 305—COOLING PERFORMANCE FOR CENTRAL AIR CONDITIONERS

Manufacturer's rated cooling capacity (btu's/hr)	Range of SEER's	
	Low	High
Single Package Units		
Central Air Conditioners (Cooling Only): All capacities	14	20
Heat Pumps (Cooling Function): All capacities	14	18.1
Split System Units		
Central Air Conditioner models allowed only in northern states (listed in 305.12(g)(13)) (Cooling Only): All capacities	13	26
Central Air Conditioner models allowed in all states (Cooling Only): All capacities	14	26

Manufacturer's rated cooling capacity (btu's/hr)	Range of SEER's	
	Low	High
Heat Pumps (Cooling Function): All capacities	14	30.5
Small-duct, high-velocity Systems	12	12.5
Space-Constrained Products		
Central Air Conditioners (Cooling Only): All capacities	12	14
Heat Pumps (Cooling Function): All capacities	12	14

[81 FR 63656, Sept. 15, 2016]

Appendix I to Part 305—Heating Performance and Cost for Central Air Conditioners

Manufacturer's rated heating capacity (Btu's/hr.)	Range of HSPF's	
	Low	High
Single Package Units		
Heat Pumps (Heating Function): All capacities	8.0	9.2
Split System Units		
Heat Pumps (Heating Function): All capacities	8.2	13.5
Small-duct, high-velocity Systems	7.2	7.2
Space-Constrained Products		
Heat Pumps (Heating Function): All capacities	7.4	7.6

[79 FR 52550, Sept. 4, 2014]

Appendix J1 to Part 305—Pool Heaters—Gas

Range Information

Manufacturer's rated heating capacities	Range of thermal efficiencies (percent)			
	Natural Gas		Propane	
	Low	High	Low	High
All capacities	82.0	96.0	82.0	96.0

[83 FR 7599, Feb. 22, 2018]

Appendix J2 to Part 305—Pool Heaters—Oil

Range Information

Manufacturer's rated heating capacities	Range of thermal efficiencies (percent)	
	Low	High
All capacities	(*)	(*)

*No data submitted.

[83 FR 7599, Feb. 22, 2018]

APPENDIX K1 TO PART 305—REPRESENTATIVE AVERAGE UNIT ENERGY COSTS FOR REFRIGERATORS, REFRIGERATOR–FREEZERS, FREEZERS, CLOTHES WASHERS, AND WATER HEATER LABELS

This Table contains the representative unit energy costs that must be utilized to calculate estimated annual energy cost disclosures required under §§ 305.11 and 305.20 for refrigerators, refrigerator-freezers, freezers, clothes washers, and water heaters. This Table is based on information published by the U.S. Department of Energy in 2013.

Type of energy	In commonly used terms	As required by DOE test procedure
Electricity	¢12.00/kWh [2] [3]	$.1200/kWh.
Natural Gas	$1.09/therm [4] or $11.12/MCF [5] [6]	$0.0000109/Btu.
No. 2 Heating Oil	$3.80/gallon [7]	$0.00002740/Btu.
Propane	$2.41/gallon [8]	$0.00002639/Btu.
Kerosene	$4.21/gallon [9]	$0.00003119/Btu.

[1] Btu stands for British thermal unit.
[2] kWh stands for kiloWatt hour.
[3] 1 kWh = 3,412 Btu.
[4] 1 therm = 100,000 Btu. Natural gas prices include taxes.
[5] MCF stands for 1,000 cubic feet.
[6] For the purposes of this table, 1 cubic foot of natural gas has an energy equivalence of 1,023 Btu.
[7] For the purposes of this table, 1 gallon of No. 2 heating oil has an energy equivalence of 138,690 Btu.
[8] For the purposes of this table, 1 gallon of liquid propane has an energy equivalence of 91,333 Btu.
[9] For the purposes of this table, 1 gallon of kerosene has an energy equivalence of 135,000 Btu.

[83 FR 7600, Feb. 22, 2018]

APPENDIX K2 TO PART 305—REPRESENTATIVE AVERAGE UNIT ENERGY COSTS FOR DISHWASHER AND ROOM AIR CONDITIONER LABELS

This Table contains the representative unit energy costs that must be utilized to calculate estimated annual energy cost disclosures required under §§ 305.11 and 305.20 for dishwashers and room air conditioners. This Table is based on information published by the U.S. Department of Energy in 2017.

Type of energy	In commonly used terms	As required by DOE test procedure
Electricity	¢13.00/kWh [2] [3]	$.1300/kWh.
Natural Gas	$1.05/therm [4] or $10.86/MCF [5] [6]	$0.00001052/Btu.
No. 2 Heating Oil	$2.59/gallon [7]	$0.00001883/Btu.
Propane	$1.53/gallon [8]	$0.00001672/Btu.
Kerosene	$3.01/gallon [9]	$0.00002232/Btu.

[1] Btu stands for British thermal units.
[2] kWh stands for kilowatt hour.
[3] kWh = 3,412 Btu.
[4] therm = 100,000 Btu.
[5] MCF stands for 1,000 cubic feet.
[6] For the purposes of this table, one cubic foot of natural gas has an energy equivalence of 1,032 Btu.
[7] For the purposes of this table, one gallon of No. 2 heating oil has an energy equivalence of 137,561 Btu.
[8] For the purposes of this table, one gallon of liquid propane has an energy equivalence of 91,333 Btu.
[9] For the purposes of this table, one gallon of kerosene has an energy equivalence of 135,000 Btu.

[83 FR 7600, Feb. 22, 2018]

APPENDIX L TO PART 305—SAMPLE LABELS

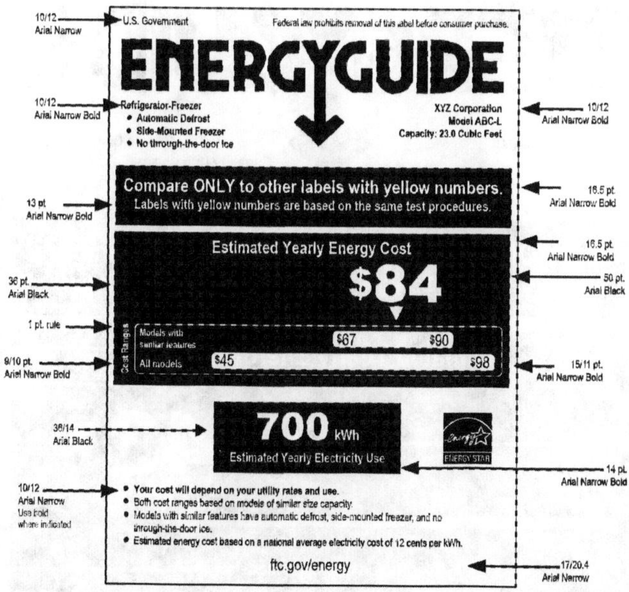

Prototype Label 1 – Refrigerator-Freezer

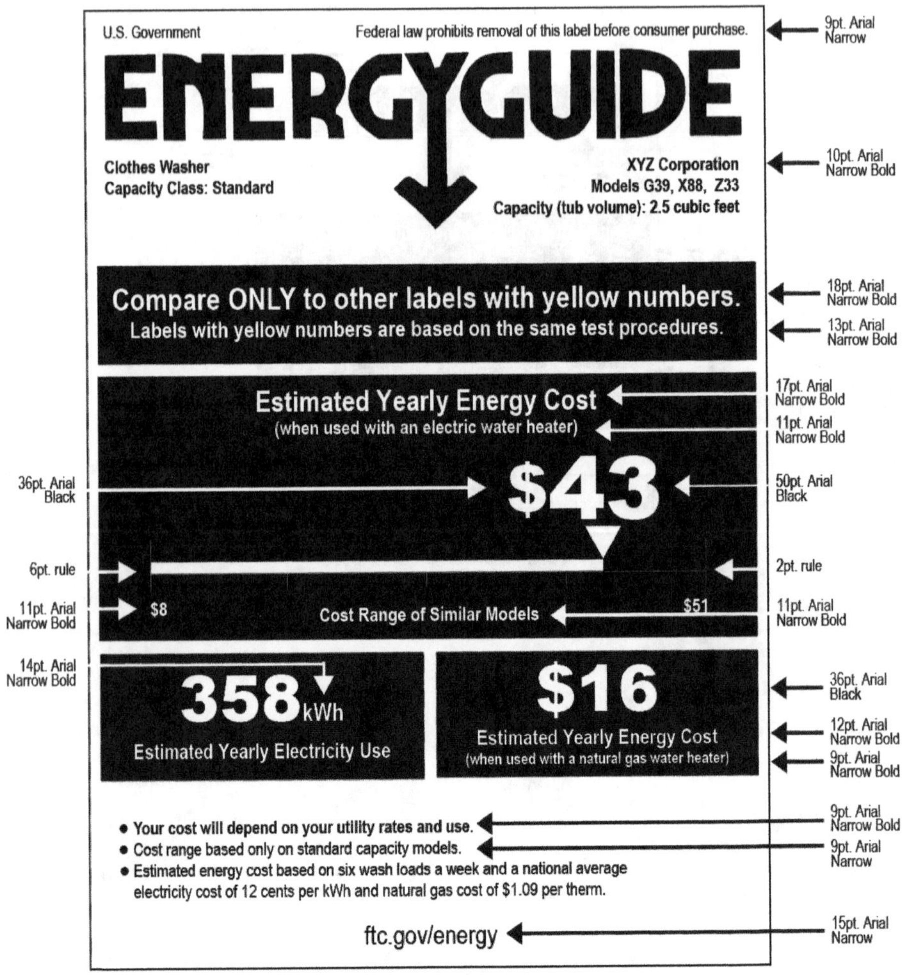

Prototype Label 2 – Clothes Washer

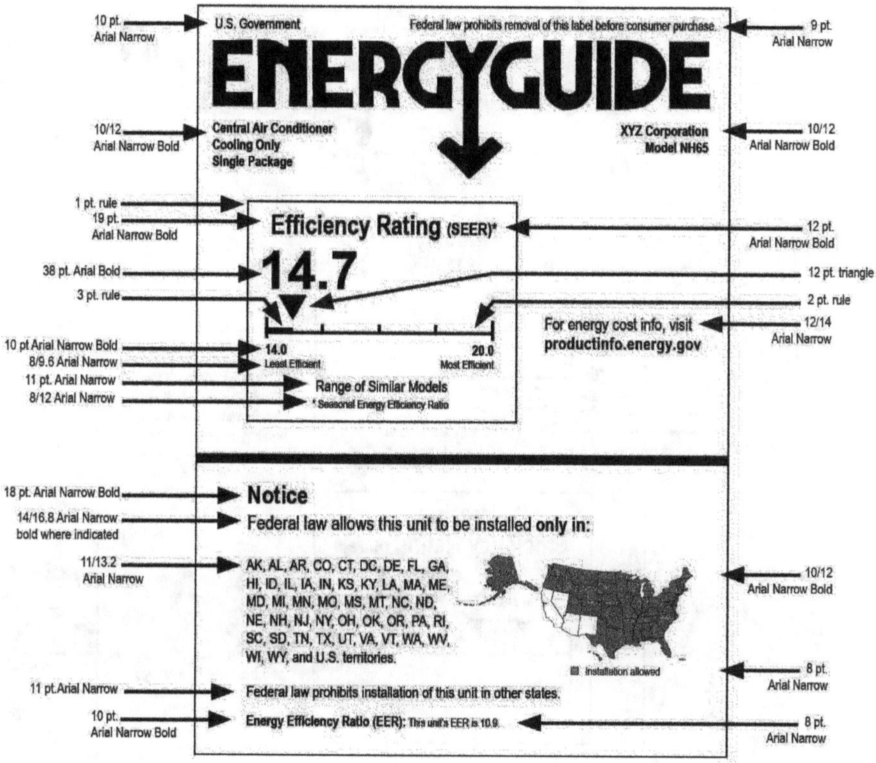

Prototype Label 3 – Single-Package Central Air Conditioner

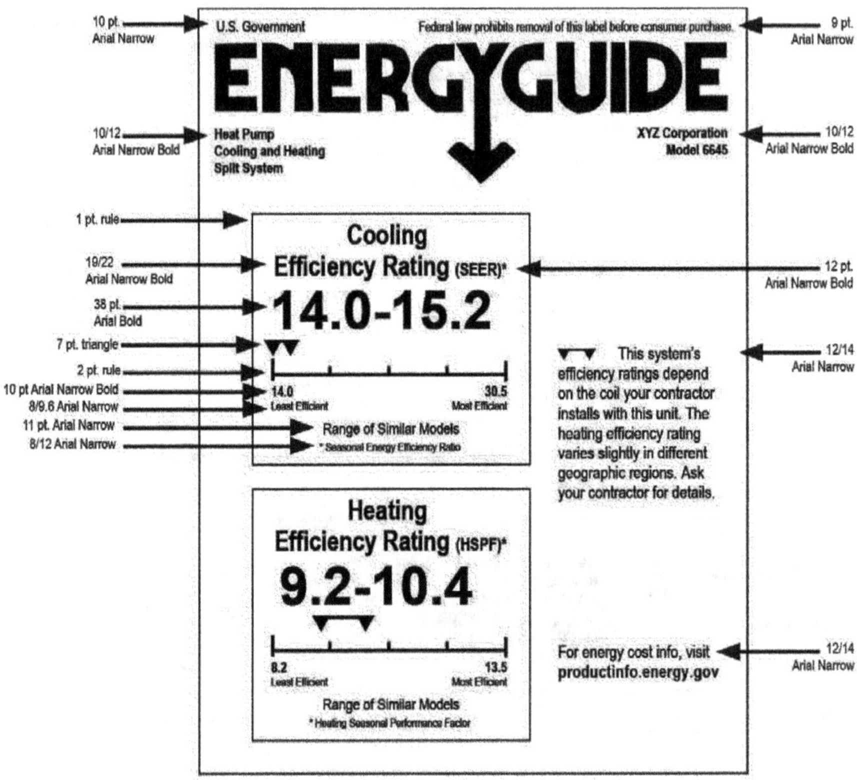

Prototype Label 4 – Split-system Heat Pump

* Typeface is Arial or equivalent type style. Type is black or one color printed on a white or other neutral contrasting background.

8 point type with 1.6 points of leading and 0.5 point rule 2 points below

20 point type with 3 points of leading

Dollar symbol is 11 point type with 3.5 point baseline shift

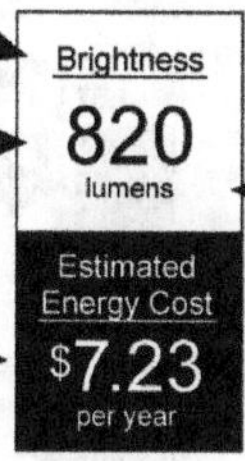

Label is enclosed by 0.5 point box rule with 5 points of text measure

7 point type with 1.4 points of leading

Dark-filled rectangle is 0.8" x 0.75"

18 point type with 1 point of leading

* Minimum size for vertical label is 0.8" x 1.5". Scale label and all text proportionally.

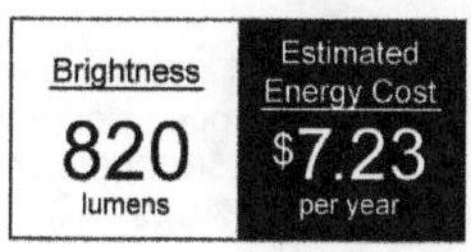

* Minimum size for vertical label is 1.6" x 0.75". Scale label and all text proportionally.

PROTOTYPE LABEL 5

FRONT PACKAGE DISCLOSURE FOR GENERAL SERVICE LAMPS

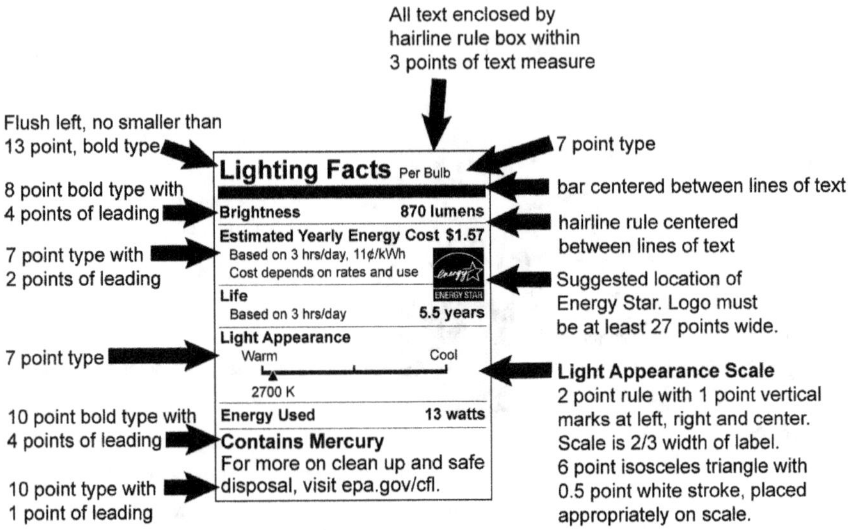

* Typeface is Arial or equivalent type style. Type sizes shown are minimum allowable. Use bold or heavy typeface where indicated. Type is black or one color printed on a white or other neutral contrasting background. Pursuant to § 305.15(b)(3)(vi), the Energy Star logo may appear only on qualified lamps. Pursuant to § 305.15(b)(3)(viii), the mercury disclosure is required only for lamps containing mercury.

PROTOTYPE LABEL 6

LIGHTING FACTS LABEL FOR GENERAL SERVICE LAMPS (STANDARD FORMAT)

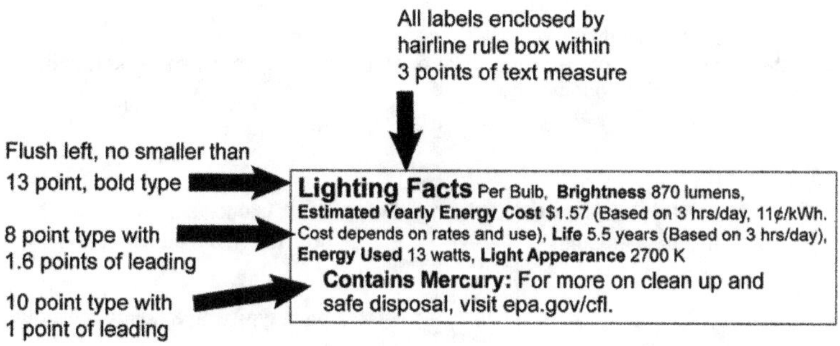

* Typeface is Arial or equivalent type style. Type sizes shown are minimum allowable. Use bold or heavy typeface where indicated. Type is black or one color printed on a white or other neutral contrasting background. Pursuant to § 305.15(b)(3)(viii), the mercury disclosure is required only for lamps containing mercury.

PROTOTYPE LABEL 7

LIGHTING FACTS LABEL FOR GENERAL SERVICE LAMPS CONTAINING MERCURY (LINEAR FORMAT)

* Typeface is Arial or equivalent type style.
* Type is black or one color printed on a white or other neutral contrasting background.
* Scale label and all text proportionally.

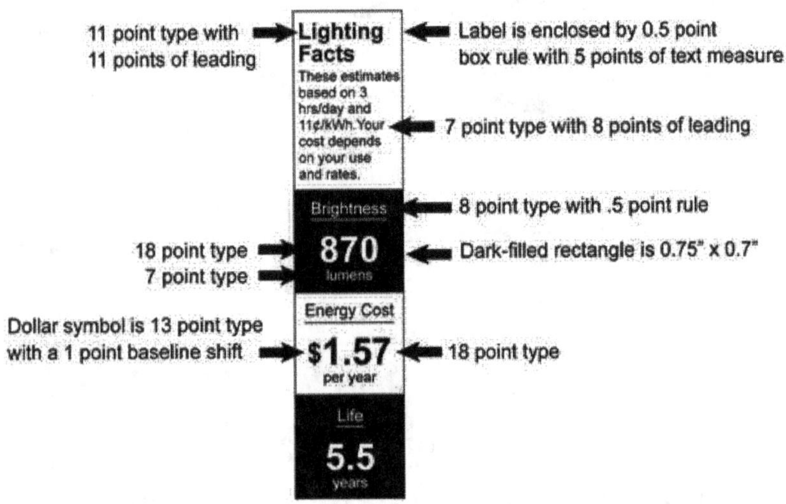

Prototype Label 7A

Lighting Facts Label Alternative for Specialty Consumer Lamps

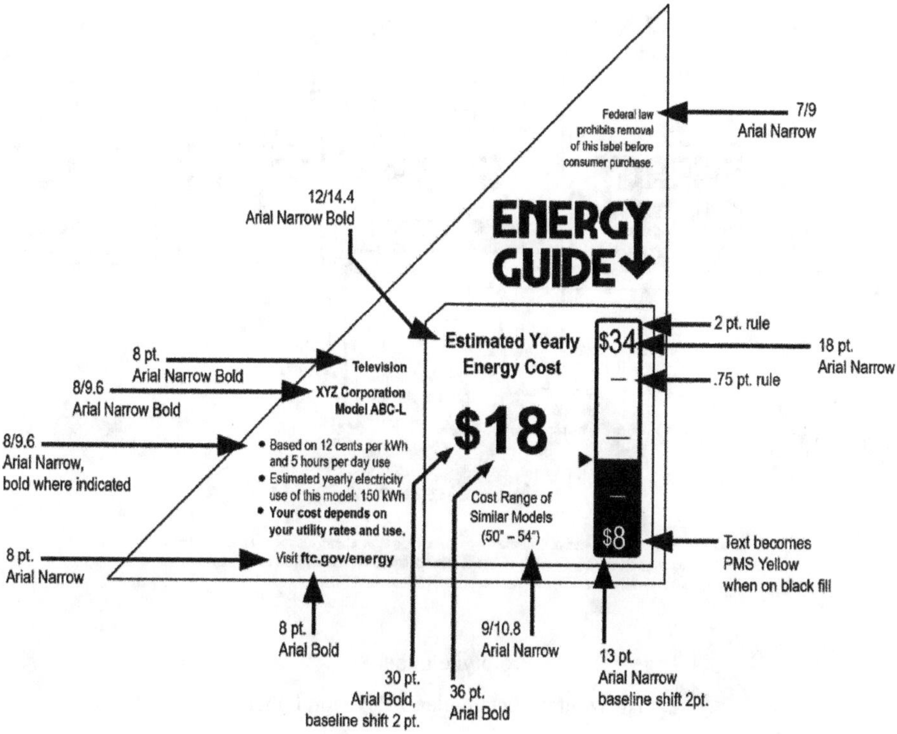

Minimum label size right angle triangle 4.5" x 4.5"

* Typeface is Arial Narrow and Arial or equivalent type style. Type sizes shown are minimum allowable. Use bold or heavy typeface where indicated. Type is black printed on process yellow or equivalent color background. Energy Star logo, if applicable, must be at least 0.36" wide.

Prototype Label 8

Triangular Television Label

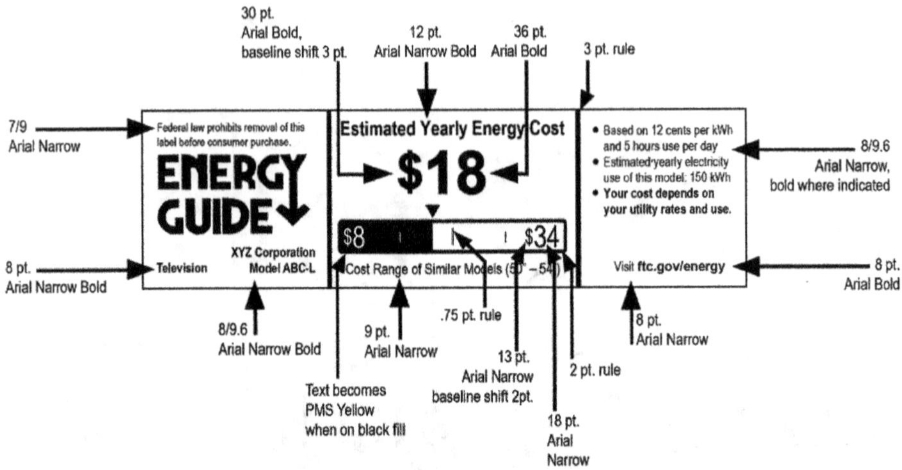

Minimum label size 1.5" x 5.25

* Typeface is Arial Narrow and Arial or equivalent type style. Type sizes shown are minimum allowable. Use bold or heavy typeface where indicated. Type is black printed on process yellow or equivalent color background. Energy Star logo, if applicable, must be at least 0.36" wide.

Prototype Label 9

Horizontal Rectangular Television Label

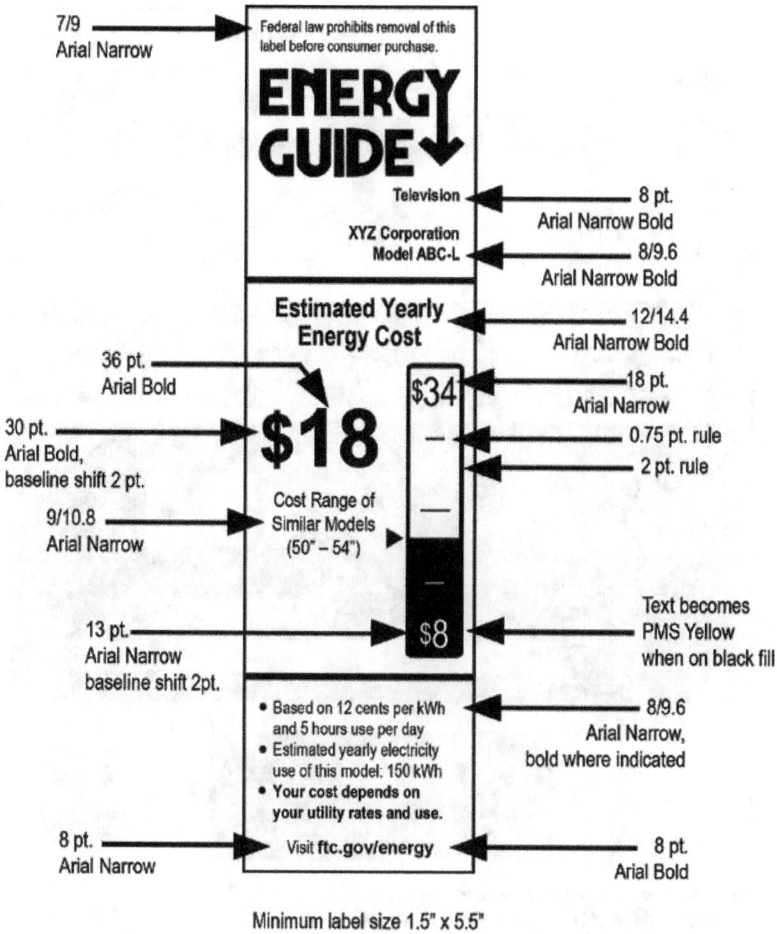

* Typeface is Arial Narrow and Arial or equivalent type style. Type sizes shown are minimum allowable. Use bold or heavy typeface where indicated. Type is black printed on process yellow or equivalent color background. Energy Star logo, if applicable, must be at least 0.36" wide.

Prototype Label 10

Vertical Rectangular Television Label

Sample Label 1 – Refrigerator-Freezer

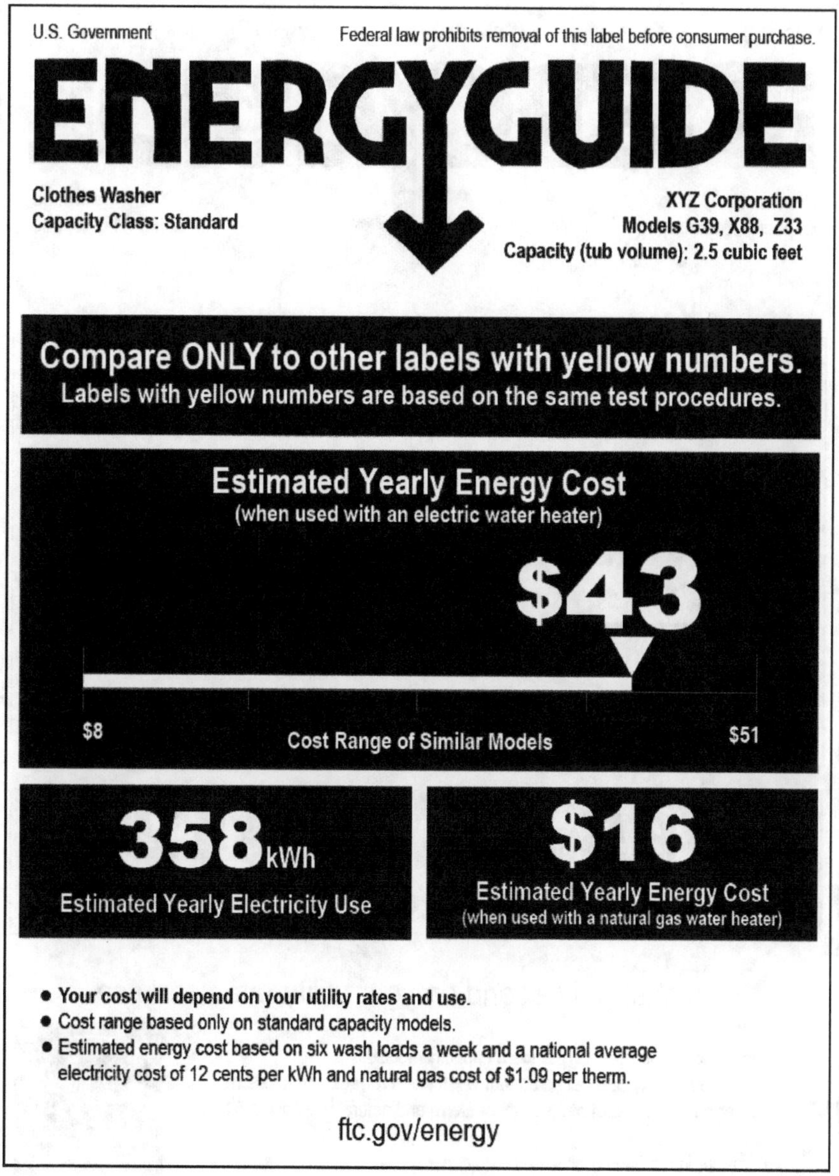

Sample Label 2 – Clothes Washer

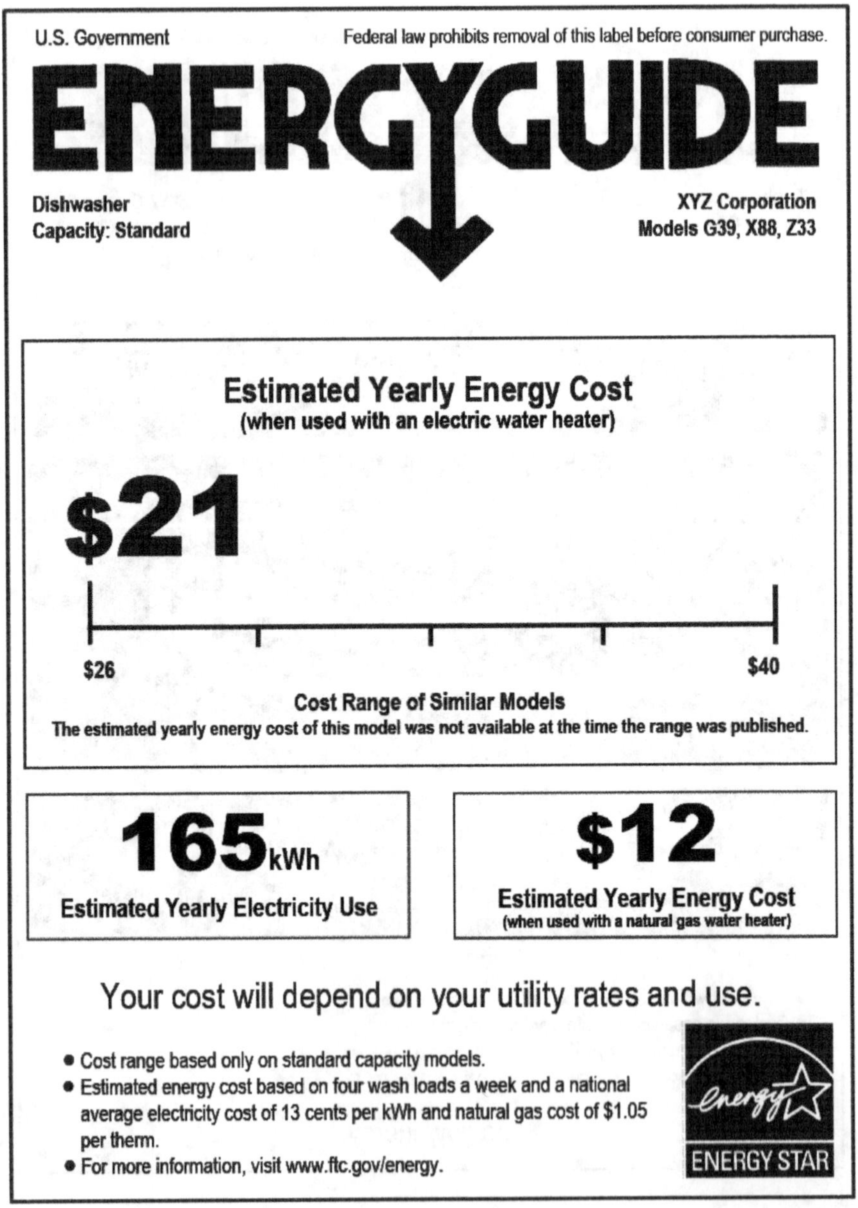

Sample Label 3 -- Dishwasher

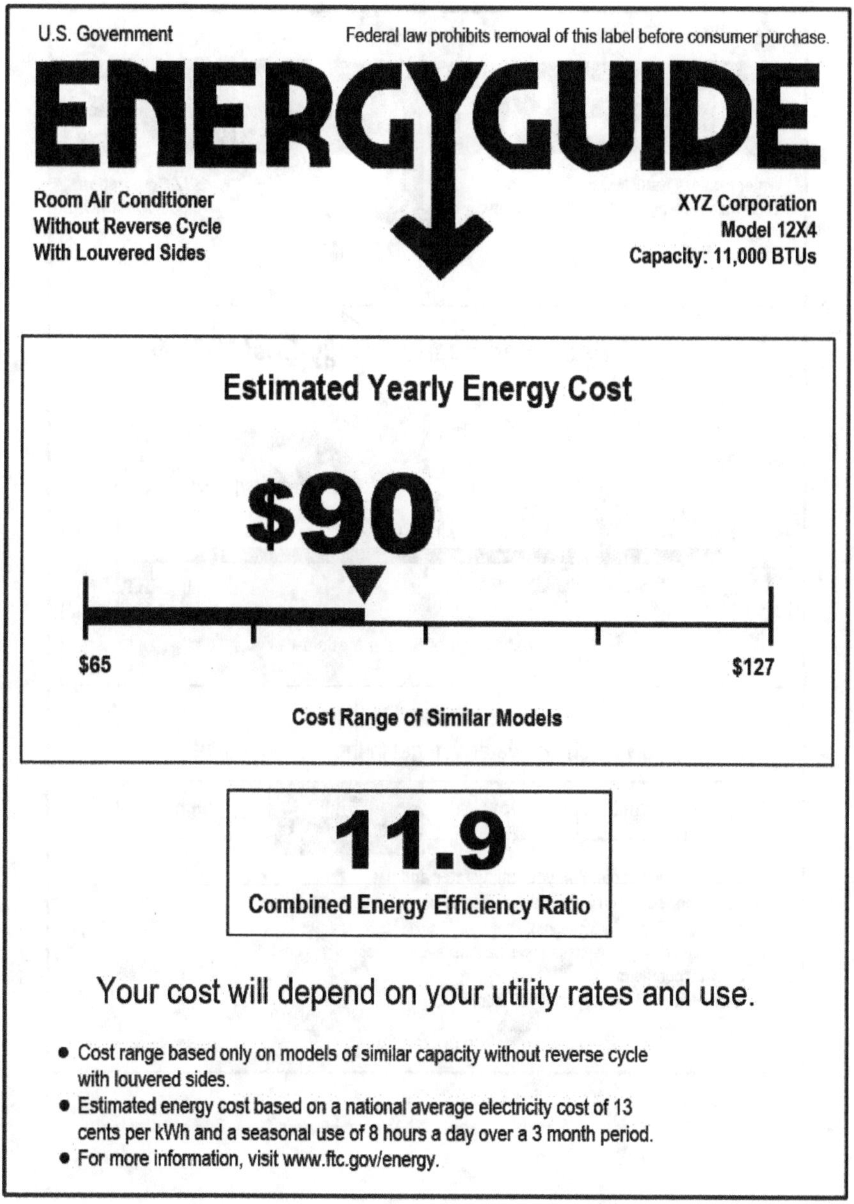

U.S. Government

Federal law prohibits removal of this label before consumer purchase.

ENERGYGUIDE

Room Air Conditioner
Without Reverse Cycle
With Louvered Sides

XYZ Corporation
Model 12X4
Capacity: 11,000 BTUs

Estimated Yearly Energy Cost

$90

$65

$127

Cost Range of Similar Models

11.9

Combined Energy Efficiency Ratio

Your cost will depend on your utility rates and use.

- Cost range based only on models of similar capacity without reverse cycle with louvered sides.
- Estimated energy cost based on a national average electricity cost of 13 cents per kWh and a seasonal use of 8 hours a day over a 3 month period.
- For more information, visit www.ftc.gov/energy.

Sample Label 4 – Room Air Conditioner

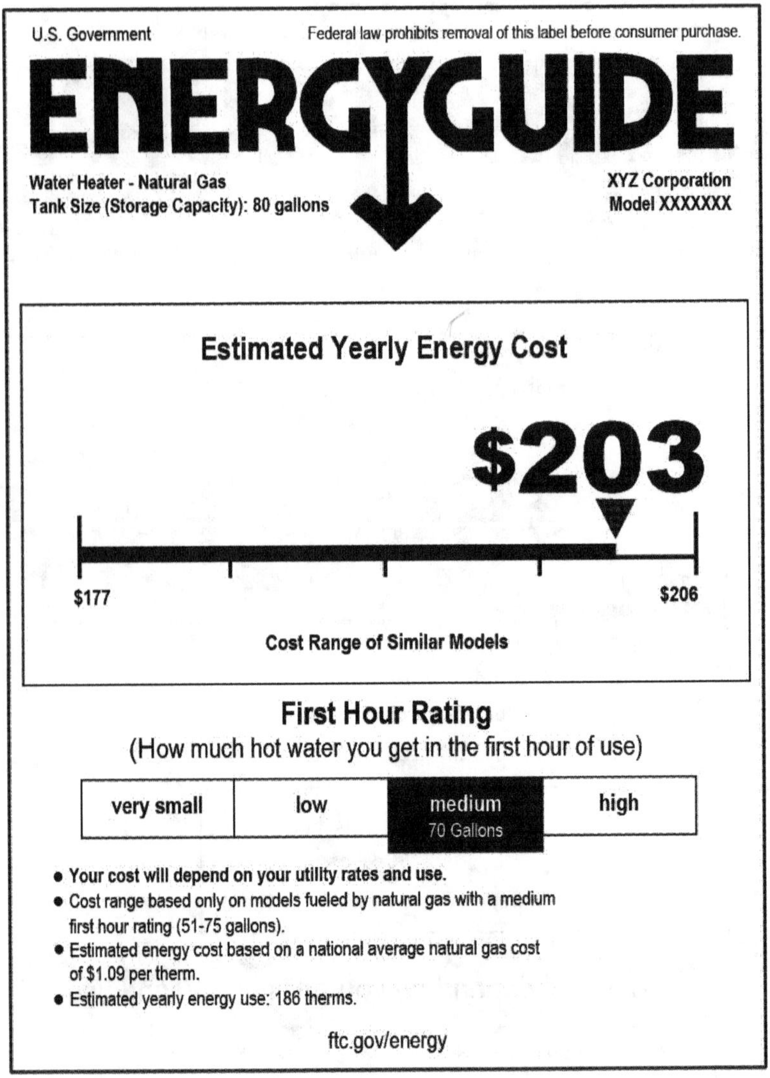

Sample Label 5 – Water Heater

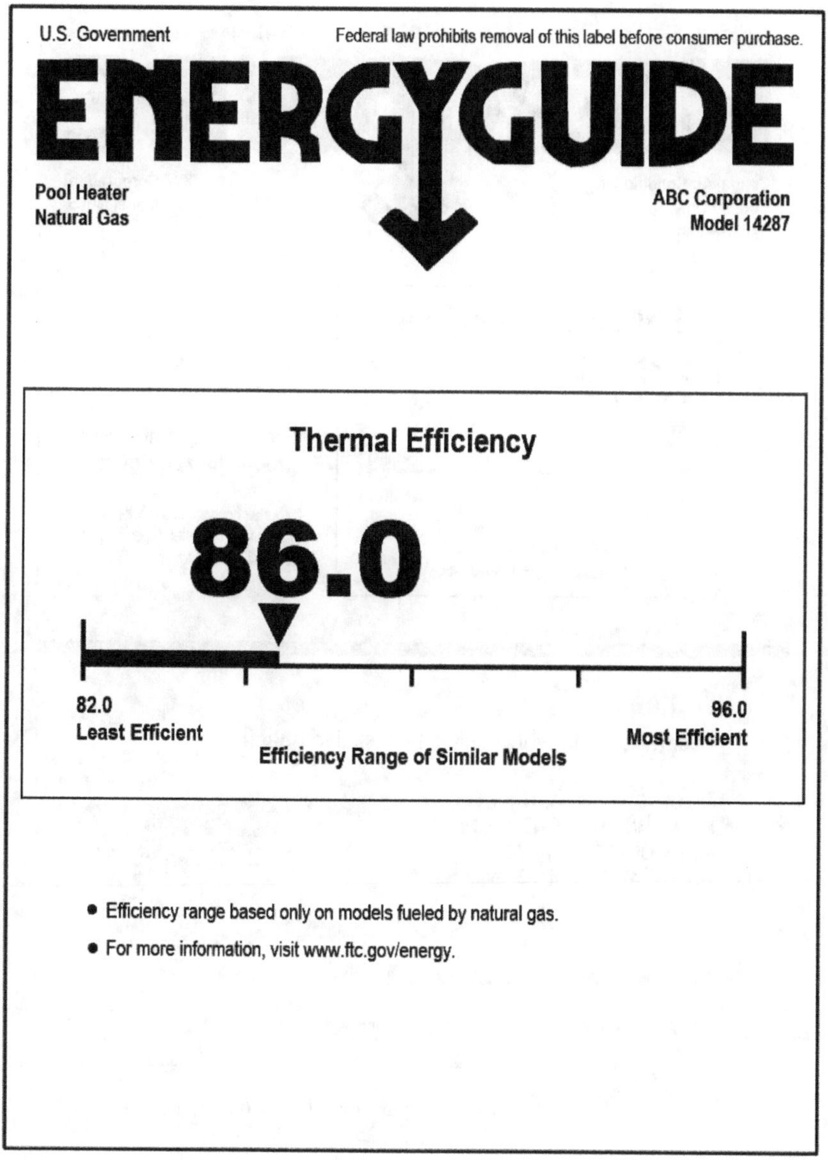

Sample Label 6 -- Pool Heater

U.S. Government

Federal law prohibits removal of this label before consumer purchase.

ENERGYGUIDE

Central Air Conditioner
Cooling Only
Split System

XYZ Corporation
Model NH65

Efficiency Rating (SEER)**

13.7*

13.0 Least Efficient — 26.0 Most Efficient

Range of Similar Models

** Seasonal Energy Efficiency Ratio

For energy cost info, visit
productinfo.energy.gov

* Your air conditioner's efficiency rating may be better depending on the coil your contractor installs.

Notice

Federal law allows this unit to be installed **only in:**

AK, CO, CT, ID, IL, IA, IN, KS, MA, ME, MI, MN, MO, MT, ND, NE, NH, NJ, NY, OH, OR, PA, RI, SD, UT, VT, WA, WV, WI, WY, and U.S. territories.

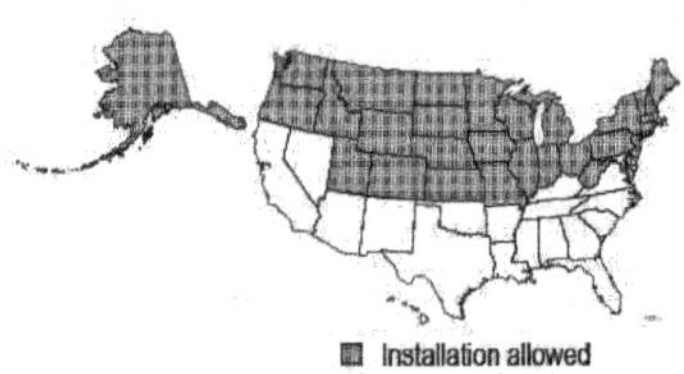

Federal law prohibits installation of this unit in other states.

Energy Efficiency Ratio (EER): The installed system's minimum EER is 12.7.

Sample Label 7 – Split-system Central Air Conditioner

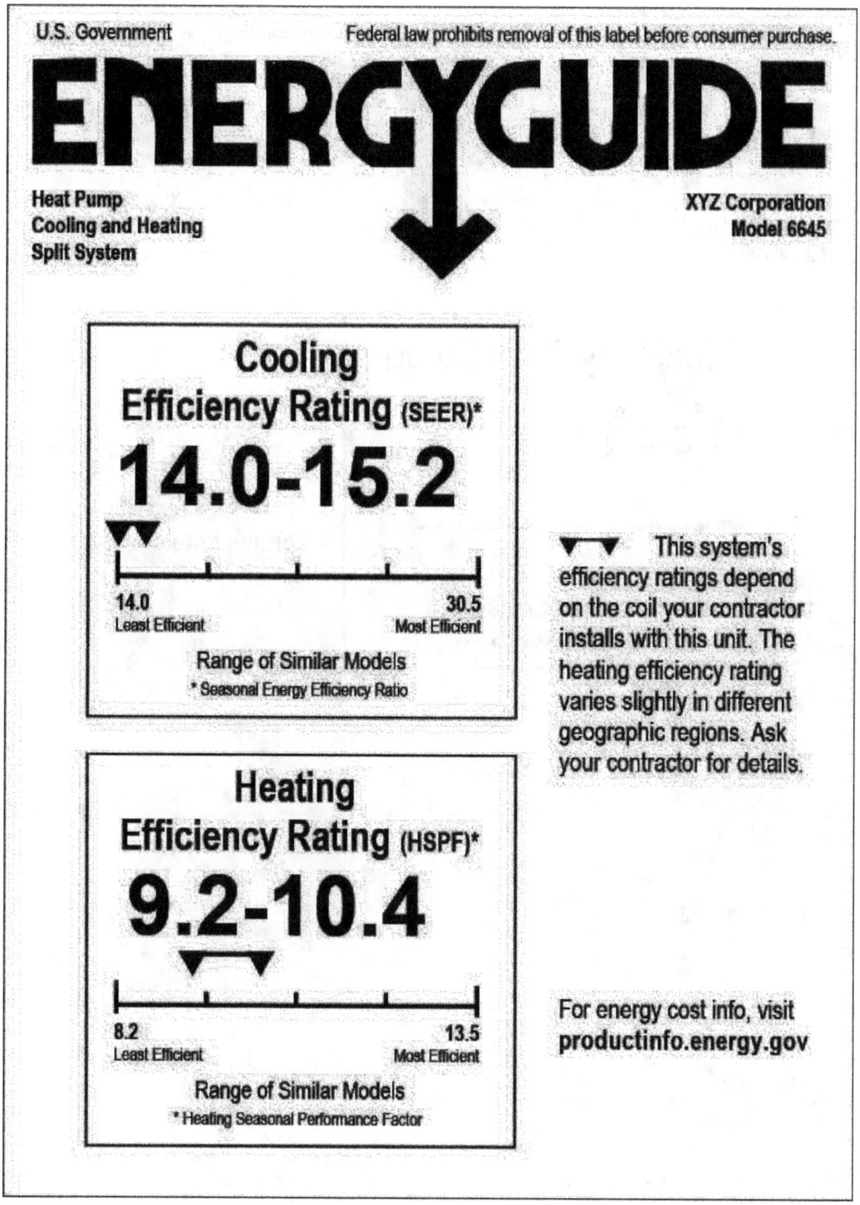

Sample Label 8 – Split-system Heat Pump

U.S. Government

Federal law prohibits removal of this label before consumer purchase.

ENERGYGUIDE

Furnace
Non-weatherized
Natural Gas

XYZ Corporation
Model TJ81

Efficiency Rating (AFUE)*

83.1

80.0 Least Efficient

98.7 Most Efficient

Range of Similar Models

* Annual Fuel Utilization Efficiency

For energy cost info, visit
productinfo.energy.gov

Sample Label 9 – Non-weatherized Gas Furnace

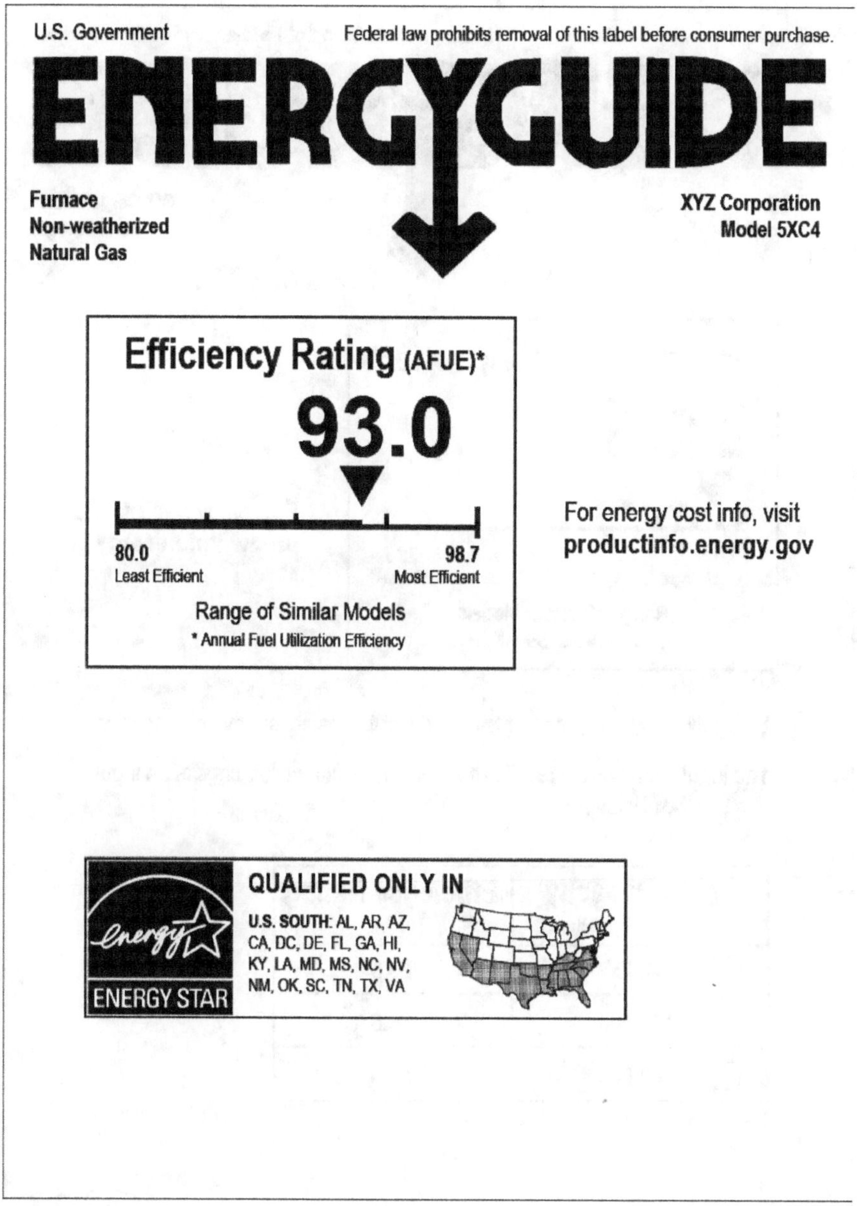

Sample Label 9A – Non-weatherized Gas Furnace (ENERGY STAR certified)

U.S. Government

Federal law prohibits removal of this label before consumer purchase.

ENERGYGUIDE

Furnace
Non-weatherized
Oil

XYZ Corporation
Model GX40

Efficiency Rating (AFUE)*

84.1

83.0 Least Efficient — 96.7 Most Efficient

Range of Similar Models

*Annual Fuel Utilization Efficiency

For energy cost info, visit
productinfo.energy.gov

Your efficiency rating depends on the input capacity set by your installer.

The input capacity is 119,000 Btu/h unless your installer checks an input capacity box below.

Input Capacity set by installer (Btu/h)	**Efficiency Rating** (AFUE)
☐ 84,000	85.5
☐ 105,000	84.8
☐ 140,000	83.5

Sample Label 9B – Non-weatherized Oil Furnaces

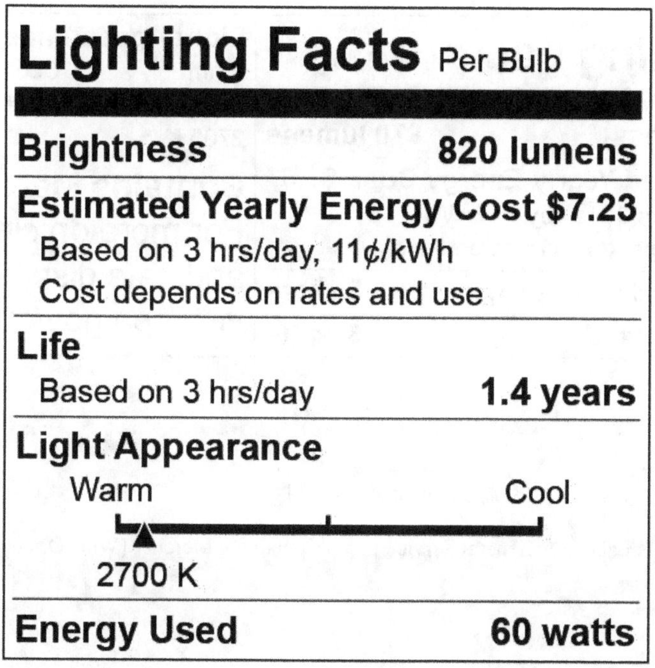

Sample Label 10

Lighting Facts Label for General Service Lamp Not Containing Mercury

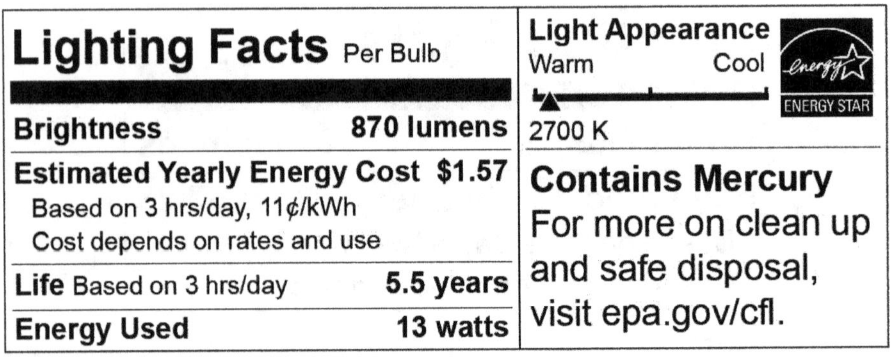

Sample Label 11

Lighting Facts Label For General Service Lamp Containing Mercury (Wide Orientation)

Lighting Facts
Per Bulb

Brightness	**870 lumens**
Estimated Yearly Energy Cost Based on 3 hrs/day, 11¢/kWh. Cost depends on rates and use.	**$1.57** ENERGY STAR
Life Based on 3 hrs/day	**5.5 years**
Light Appearance Warm — Cool 2700 K	
Energy Used	**13 watts**

Contains Mercury
For more on clean up and safe disposal, visit epa.gov/cfl.

Sample Label 12

Lighting Facts Label For General Service Lamp Containing Mercury (Tall Orientation)

Sample Label 13

Lighting Facts Label For General Service Lamp Containing Mercury (Bilingual Example)

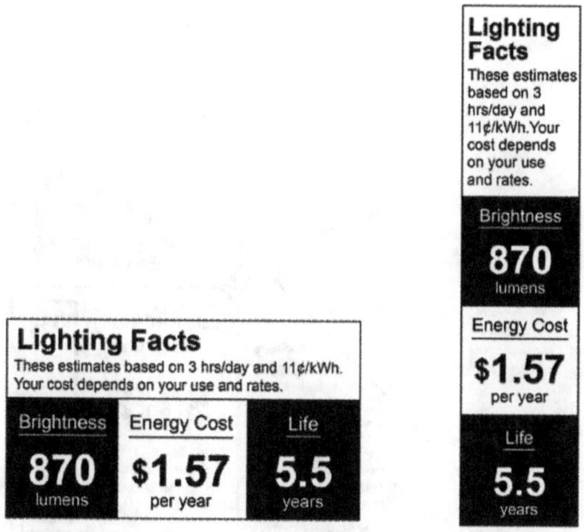

Sample Label 13C

Lighting Facts Label Alternative for Specialty Consumer Lamps

Sample Label 13D

Icon for Specialty Consumer Lamp Packages that Meet the Requirements of section 305.15(c)(2)(iv)

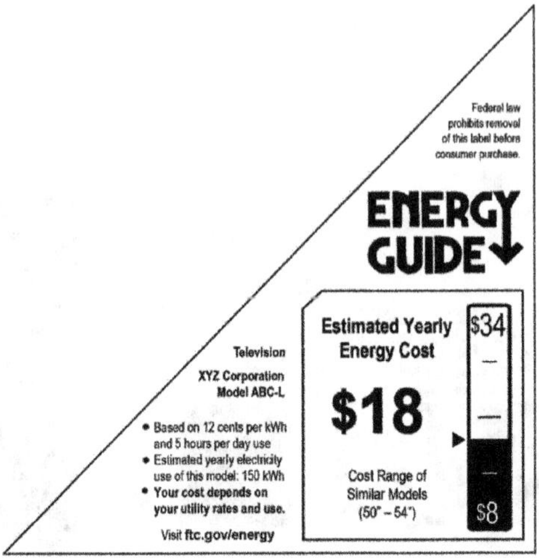

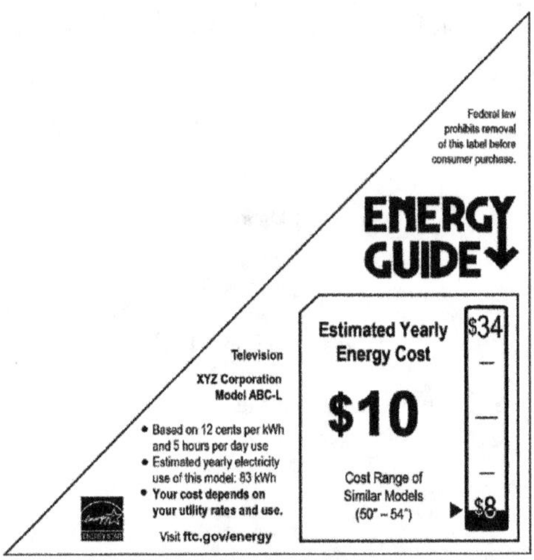

Sample Label 14
Triangular Television Labels

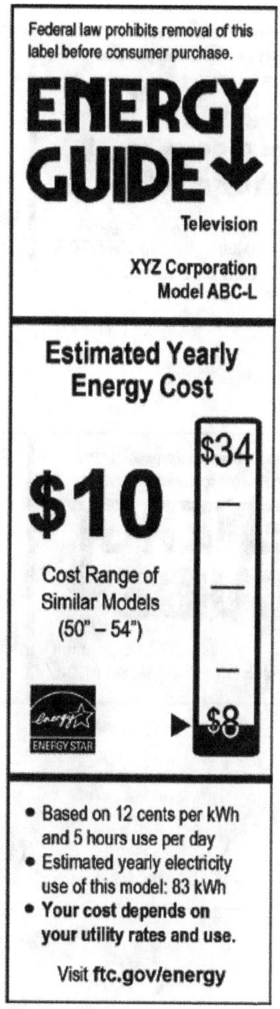

Sample Label 15

Vertical Television Labels

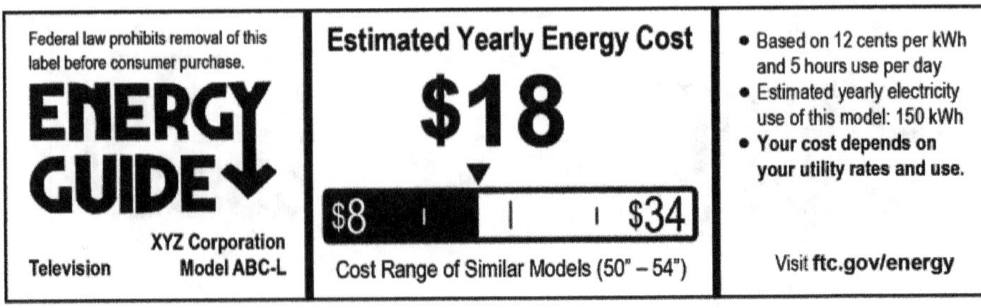

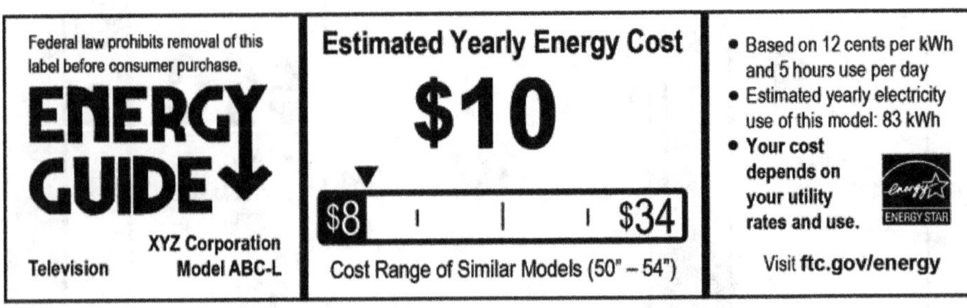

Sample Label 16

Horizontal Television Labels

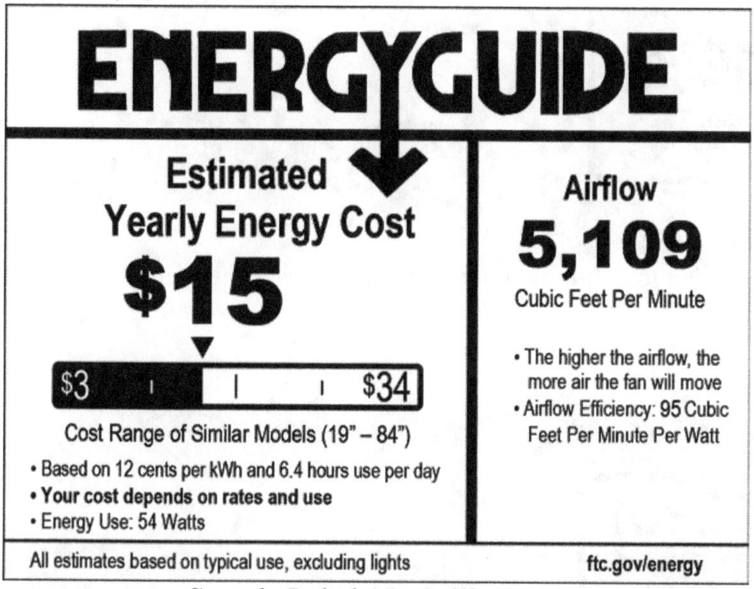

Sample Label 17- Ceiling Fan

Sample Label Icon (for use on television retail websites before January 1, 2014)

Sample Label Icon (for use on all retail websites after January 1, 2014)

Sample Label Icon (for use on all retail websites after January 1, 2014)

[59 FR 25212, May 13, 1994; 59 FR 34053, July 1, 1994. Redesignated at 59 FR 49565, Sept. 28, 1994]

EDITORIAL NOTE: For FEDERAL REGISTER citations affecting appendix L, see the List of CFR Sections Affected, which appears in the Finding Aids section of the printed volume and at *www.govinfo.gov*.

PART 306—AUTOMOTIVE FUEL RATINGS, CERTIFICATION AND POSTING

GENERAL

DUTIES OF REFINERS, IMPORTERS, AND PRODUCERS

AUTHORITY: 15 U.S.C. 2801 *et seq.;* 42 U.S.C. 17021.

SOURCE: 44 FR 19169, Mar. 30, 1979, unless otherwise noted.

GENERAL

§ 306.0 Definitions.

As used in this part:

(a) *Octane rating* means the rating of the anti-knock characteristics of a grade or type of gasoline as determined by dividing by 2 the sum of the research octane number plus the motor octane number.

(b) *Research octane number and motor octane number.* These terms have the meanings given such terms in the specifications of ASTM D4814–15a, Standard Specification for Automotive Spark-Ignition Engine Fuel, (incorporated by reference, see § 306.13) and, with respect to any grade or type of gasoline, are determined in accordance with one of the following test methods or protocols:

(1) ASTM D2699–15a, Standard Test Method for Research Octane Number of Spark-Ignition Engine Fuel, and ASTM D2700–14, Standard Test Method for Motor Octane Number of Spark-Ignition Engine Fuel, (both incorporated by reference, see § 306.13) or

(2) ASTM D2885–13, Standard Test Method for Determination of Octane Number of Spark-Ignition Engine Fuels by On-Line Direct Comparison Technique, (incorporated by reference, see § 306.13).

(c) *Refiner* means any person engaged in the production or importation of automotive fuel.

(d) *Producer* means any person who purchases component elements and combines them to produce and market automotive fuel.

(e) *Distributor* means any person who receives automotive fuel and distributes such automotive fuel to another person other than the ultimate purchaser.

(f) *Retailer* means any person who markets automotive fuel to the general public for ultimate consumption.

(g) *Ultimate purchaser* means, with respect to any item, the first person who purchases such item for purposes other than resale.

(h) *Person,* for purposes of applying any provision of the Federal Trade Commission Act, 15 U.S.C. 41 *et seq.*, with respect to any provision of this part, includes a partnership and a corporation.

(i) *Automotive fuel* means liquid fuel of a type distributed for use as a fuel in any motor vehicle, and the term includes, but is not limited to:

(1) Gasoline, an automotive spark-ignition engine fuel, which includes, but is not limited to, gasohol (generally a mixture of approximately 90 percent unleaded gasoline and 10 percent ethanol) and fuels developed to comply with the Clean Air Act, 42 U.S.C. 7401 *et seq.*, such as reformulated gasoline and oxygenated gasoline; and

(2) Alternative liquid automotive fuels, including, but not limited to:

(i) Methanol, denatured ethanol, and other alcohols;

(ii) Mixtures containing 85 percent or more by volume of methanol and/or other alcohols (or such other percentage, as provided by the Secretary of the United States Department of Energy, by rule), with gasoline or other fuels;

(iii) Ethanol flex fuels;

(iv) Liquefied natural gas;

(v) Liquefied petroleum gas;

(vi) Coal-derived liquid fuels;

(vii) Biodiesel;

(viii) Biomass-based diesel;

(ix) Biodiesel blends containing more than 5 percent biodiesel by volume; and

(x) Biomass-based diesel blends containing more than 5 percent biomass-based diesel by volume.

(3) Biodiesel blends and biomass-based diesel blends that contain less than or equal to 5 percent biodiesel by

volume and less than or equal to 5 percent biomass-based diesel by volume, and that meet ASTM D975–07b, Standard Specification for Diesel Fuel Oils (incorporated by reference, see § 306.13), are not automotive fuels covered by the requirements of this part.

NOTE TO PARAGRAPH (i): Provided, however, that biodiesel blends and biomass-based diesel blends that contain less than or equal to 5 percent biodiesel by volume and less than or equal to 5 percent biomass-based diesel by volume, and that meet ASTM D975–09b, Standard Specification for Diesel Fuel Oils (incorporated by reference, see § 306.13), are not automotive fuels covered by the requirements of this part.

(j) *Automotive fuel rating* means—

(1) For gasoline, the octane rating.

(2) For an alternative liquid automotive fuel other than biodiesel, biomass-based diesel, biodiesel blends, biomass-based diesel blends, and ethanol flex fuels, the commonly used name of the fuel with a disclosure of the amount, expressed as the minimum percentage by volume, of the principal component of the fuel. A disclosure of other components, expressed as the minimum percentage by volume, may be included, if desired.

(3) For biomass-based diesel, biodiesel, biomass-based diesel blends with more than 5 percent biomass-based diesel, and biodiesel blends with more than 5 percent biodiesel, a disclosure of the biomass-based diesel or biodiesel component, expressed as the percentage by volume.

(4) For ethanol flex fuels, a disclosure of the ethanol component, expressed as the percentage by volume and the text "Use Only in Flex-Fuel Vehicles/May Harm Other Engines."

(k) *Biomass-based diesel* means a diesel fuel substitute produced from nonpetroleum renewable resources that meets the registration requirements for fuels and fuel additives established by the Environmental Protection Agency under 42 U.S.C. 7545, and includes fuel derived from animal wastes, including poultry fats and poultry wastes, and other waste materials, or from municipal solid waste and sludges and oils derived from wastewater and the treatment of wastewater, except that the term does not include biodiesel as defined in this part.

(l) Biodiesel means the monoalkyl esters of long chain fatty acids derived from plant or animal matter that meet: The registration requirements for fuels and fuel additives under 40 CFR part 79; and the requirements of ASTM D6751–10, Standard Specification for Biodiesel Fuel Blend Stock (B100) for Middle Distillate Fuels, (incorporated by reference, see § 306.13).

(m) *Biodiesel blend* means a blend of petroleum-based diesel fuel with biodiesel.

(n) *Biomass-based diesel blend* means a blend of petroleum-based diesel fuel with biomass-based diesel.

(o) *Ethanol flex fuels* means a mixture of gasoline and ethanol containing more than 10 percent but not greater than 83 percent ethanol by volume.

[58 FR 41372, Aug. 3, 1993, as amended at 69 FR 18803, Apr. 9, 2004; 73 FR 40162, July 11, 2008; 76 FR 19690, Apr. 8, 2011; 81 FR 2062, Jan. 14, 2016]

§ 306.1 What this rule does.

This rule deals with the certification and posting of automotive fuel ratings in or affecting commerce as "commerce" is defined in the Federal Trade Commission Act, 15 U.S.C. 41 *et seq.* It applies to persons, partnerships, and corporations. If you are covered by this regulation, breaking any of its rules is an unfair or deceptive act or practice under section 5 of that Act. You can be fined up to $10,000 (plus an adjustment for inflation, under § 1.98 of this chapter) each time you break a rule.

[58 FR 41373, Aug. 3, 1993, as amended at 61 FR 54549, Oct. 21, 1996; 61 FR 55840, Oct. 29, 1996]

§ 306.2 Who is covered.

You are covered by this rule if you are a refiner, importer, producer, distributor, or retailer of automotive fuel.

[58 FR 41373, Aug. 3, 1993]

§ 306.3 Stayed or invalid parts.

If any part of this rule is stayed or held invalid, the rest of it will stay in force.

[44 FR 19169, Mar. 30, 1979. Redesignated at 58 FR 41372, Aug. 3, 1993]

§ 306.4 Preemption.

The Petroleum Marketing Practices Act ("PMPA"), 15 U.S.C. 2801 *et seq.*, as amended, is the law that directs the FTC to enact this rule. Section 204 of PMPA, 15 U.S.C. 2824, provides:

(a) To the extent that any provision of this title applies to any act or omission, no State or any political subdivision thereof may adopt or continue in effect, except as provided in subsection (b), any provision of law or regulation with respect to such act or omission, unless such provision of such law or regulation is the same as the applicable provision of this title.

(b) A State or political subdivision thereof may provide for any investigative or enforcement action, remedy, or penalty (including procedural actions necessary to carry out such investigative or enforcement actions, remedies, or penalties) with respect to any provision of law or regulation permitted by subsection (a).

[58 FR 41373, Aug. 3, 1993]

DUTIES OF REFINERS, IMPORTERS AND PRODUCERS

§ 306.5 Automotive fuel rating.

If you are a refiner, importer, or producer, you must determine the automotive fuel rating of all automotive fuel before you transfer it. You can do that yourself or through a testing lab.

(a) To determine the automotive fuel rating of gasoline, add the research octane number and the motor octane number and divide by two, as explained by ASTM D4814–15a, Standard Specifications for Automotive Spark-Ignition Engine Fuel, (incorporated by reference, see § 306.13). To determine the research octane and motor octane numbers, you may do one of the following:

(1) Use ASTM D2699–15a, Standard Test Method for Research Octane Number of Spark-Ignition Engine Fuel (incorporated by reference, see § 306.13), to determine the research octane number, and ASTM D2700–14, Standard Test Method for Motor Octane Number of Spark-Ignition Engine Fuel (incorporated by reference, see § 306.13), to determine the motor octane number; or

(2) Use the test method set forth in ASTM D2885–13, Standard Test Method for Determination of Octane Number of Spark-Ignition Engine Fuels by On-Line Direct Comparison Technique (incorporated by reference, see § 306.13).

(b) To determine automotive fuel ratings for alternative liquid automotive fuels other than ethanol flex fuels, biodiesel blends, and biomass-based diesel blends, you must possess a reasonable basis, consisting of competent and reliable evidence, for the percentage by volume of the principal component of the alternative liquid automotive fuel that you must disclose. In the case of biodiesel blends, you must possess a reasonable basis, consisting of competent and reliable evidence, for the percentage of biodiesel contained in the fuel. In the case of biomass-based diesel blends, you must possess a reasonable basis, consisting of competent and reliable evidence, for the percentage of biomass-based diesel contained in the fuel. In the case of ethanol flex fuels, you must possess a reasonable basis, consisting of competent and reliable evidence, for the percentage of ethanol contained in the fuel. You also must have a reasonable basis, consisting of competent and reliable evidence, for the minimum percentages by volume of other components that you choose to disclose.

[81 FR 2063, Jan. 14, 2016]

§ 306.6 Certification.

In each transfer you make to anyone who is not a consumer, you must certify the automotive fuel rating of the automotive fuel consistent with your determination. You can do this in either of two ways:

(a) Include a delivery ticket or other paper with each transfer of automotive fuel. It may be an invoice, bill of lading, bill of sale, terminal ticket, delivery ticket, or any other written proof of transfer. It must contain at least these four items:

(1) Your name;

(2) The name of the person to whom the automotive fuel is transferred;

(3) The date of the transfer;

(4) The automotive fuel rating. Octane rating numbers may be rounded off to a whole or half number equal to or less than the number determined by you.

(b) Give the person a letter or other written statement. This letter must include the date, your name, the other person's name, and the automotive fuel rating of any automotive fuel you will transfer to that person from the date of the letter onwards. Octane rating numbers may be rounded to a whole or half number equal to or less than the number determined by you. This letter of certification will be good until you transfer automotive fuel with a lower automotive fuel rating, except that a letter certifying the fuel rating of biomass-based diesel, biodiesel, a biomass-based diesel blend, a biodiesel blend, or an ethanol flex fuel will be good only until you transfer those fuels with a different automotive fuel rating, whether the rating is higher or lower. When this happens, you must certify the automotive fuel rating of the new automotive fuel either with a delivery ticket or by sending a new letter of certification.

(c) When you transfer automotive fuel to a common carrier, you must certify the automotive fuel rating of the automotive fuel to the common carrier, either by letter or on the delivery ticket or other paper.

[58 FR 41373, Aug. 3, 1993, as amended at 59 FR 48798, Sept. 23, 1994; 73 FR 40163, July 11, 2008; 76 FR 19691, Apr. 8, 2011; 81 FR 2063, Jan. 14, 2016]

§ 306.7 Recordkeeping.

You must keep records of how you determined automotive fuel ratings for one year. They must be available for inspection by Federal Trade Commission and Environmental Protection Agency staff members, or by people authorized by FTC or EPA.

[58 FR 41374, Aug. 3, 1993]

DUTIES OF DISTRIBUTORS

§ 306.8 Certification.

If you are a distributor, you must certify the automotive fuel rating of the automotive fuel in each transfer you make to anyone who is not a consumer.

(a) In the case of gasoline, if you do not blend the gasoline with other gasoline, you must certify the gasoline's octane rating consistent with the octane rating certified to you. If you blend the gasoline with other gasoline, you must certify consistent with your determination of the average, weighted by volume, of the octane ratings certified to you for each gasoline in the blend, or consistent with the lowest octane rating certified to you for any gasoline in the blend. Whether you blend gasoline or not, you may choose to certify the octane rating of the gasoline consistent with your determination of the octane rating according to the method in § 306.5. In cases involving gasoline, the octane rating may be rounded to a whole or half number equal to or less than the number certified to you or determined by you.

(b) If you do not blend alternative liquid automotive fuels, you must certify consistent with the automotive fuel rating certified to you. If you blend alternative liquid automotive fuels, you must possess a reasonable basis, consisting of competent and reliable evidence, for the automotive fuel rating that you certify for the blend.

(c) You may certify either by using a delivery ticket with each transfer of automotive fuel, as outlined in § 306.6(a), or by using a letter of certification, as outlined in § 306.6(b).

(d) When you transfer automotive fuel to a common carrier, you must certify the automotive fuel rating of the automotive fuel to the common carrier, either by letter or on the delivery ticket or other paper. When you receive automotive fuel from a common carrier, you also must receive from the common carrier a certification of the automotive fuel rating of the automotive fuel, either by letter or on the delivery ticket or other paper.

[58 FR 41374, Aug. 3, 1993, as amended at 59 FR 48798, Sept. 23, 1994]

§ 306.9 Recordkeeping.

You must keep for one year any delivery tickets or letters of certification on which you based your automotive fuel rating certifications. You must also keep for one year records of any automotive fuel rating determinations you made according to § 306.5. They must be available for inspection by Federal Trade Commission and Environmental Protection Agency staff members, or by persons authorized by FTC or EPA.

[58 FR 41374, Aug. 3, 1993]

DUTIES OF RETAILERS

§ 306.10 Automotive fuel rating posting.

(a) If you are a retailer, you must post the automotive fuel rating of all automotive fuel you sell to consumers. You must do this by putting at least one label on each face of each dispenser through which you sell automotive fuel. If you are selling two or more kinds of automotive fuel with different automotive fuel ratings from a single dispenser, you must put separate labels for each kind of automotive fuel on each face of the dispenser. Provided, however, that you do not need to post the automotive fuel rating of a mixture of gasoline and ethanol containing more than 10 but not more than 15 percent ethanol if the face of the dispenser is labeled in accordance with 40 CFR 80.1501.

(b)(1) The label, or labels, must be placed conspicuously on the dispenser so as to be in full view of consumers and as near as reasonably practical to the price per unit of the automotive fuel.

(2) You may petition for an exemption from the placement requirements by writing the Secretary of the Federal Trade Commission, Washington, DC 20580. You must state the reasons that you want the exemption.

(c) In the case of gasoline, if you do not blend the gasoline with other gasoline, you must post the octane rating of the gasoline consistent with the octane rating certified to you. If you blend the gasoline with other gasoline, you must post consistent with your determination of the average, weighted by volume, of the octane ratings certified to you for each gasoline in the blend, or consistent with the lowest octane rating certified to you for any gasoline in the blend. Whether you blend gasoline or not, you may choose to post the octane rating of the gasoline consistent with your determination of the octane rating according to the method in § 306.5. In cases involving gasoline, the octane rating must be shown as a whole or half number equal to or less than the number certified to you or determined by you.

(d) If you do not blend alternative liquid automotive fuels, you must post consistent with the automotive fuel rating certified to you. If you blend alternative liquid automotive fuels, you must possess a reasonable basis, consisting of competent and reliable evidence, for the automotive fuel rating that you post for the blend.

(e)(1) You must maintain and replace labels as needed to make sure consumers can easily see and read them.

(2) If the labels you have are destroyed or are unusable or unreadable for some unexpected reason, you can satisfy the law by posting a temporary label as much like the required label as possible. You must still get and post the required label without delay.

(f) The following examples of automotive fuel rating disclosures for some presently available alternative liquid automotive fuels are meant to serve as illustrations of compliance with this part, but do not limit the Rule's coverage to only the mentioned fuels:

(1) "Methanol/Minimum ___% Methanol"

(2) "___% Ethanol/Use Only in Flex-Fuel Vehicles/May Harm Other engines"

(3) "M85/Minimum ___% Methanol"

(4) "LPG/Minimum ___% Propane" or "LPG/Minimum ___% Propane and ___% Butane"

(5) "LNG/Minimum ___% Methane"

(6) "B20 Biodiesel Blend/contains biomass-based diesel or biodiesel in quantities between 5 percent and 20 percent"

(7) "20% Biomass-Based Diesel Blend/contains biomass-based diesel or biodiesel in quantities between 5 percent and 20 percent"

(8) "B100 Biodiesel/contains 100 percent biodiesel"

(9) "100% Biomass-Based Diesel/contains 100 percent biomass-based diesel"

(g) When you receive automotive fuel from a common carrier, you also must receive from the common carrier a certification of the automotive fuel rating of the automotive fuel, either by letter or on the delivery ticket or other paper.

[58 FR 41374, Aug. 3, 1993, as amended at 59 FR 48798, Sept. 23, 1994; 73 FR 40163, July 11, 2008; 81 FR 2063, Jan. 14, 2016]

§ 306.11 Recordkeeping.

You must keep for one year any delivery tickets or letters of certification on which you based your posting of automotive fuel ratings. You also must keep for one year records of any automotive fuel rating determinations you made according to § 306.5. These records may be kept at the retail outlet or at another, reasonably close location. They must be available for inspection by Federal Trade Commission and Environmental Protection Agency staff members or by persons authorized by FTC or EPA.

[58 FR 41374, Aug. 3, 1993]

LABEL SPECIFICATIONS

§ 306.12 Labels.

All labels must meet the following specifications:

(a) *Layout*—(1) *For gasoline labels.* The label is 3 inches (7.62 cm) wide × 2½ inches (6.35 cm) long. The illustrations appearing at the end of this rule are prototype labels that demonstrate the proper layout. "Helvetica Black" or equivalent type is used throughout except for the octane rating number on octane labels, which is in Franklin gothic type. All type is centered. Spacing of the label is ¼ inch (.64 cm) between the top border and the first line of text, ⅛ inch (.32 cm) between the first and second line of text, ¼ inch (.64 cm) between the octane rating and the line of text above it. All text and numerals are centered within the interior borders.

(2) *For alternative liquid automotive fuel labels (one principal component), other than biodiesel, biomass-based diesel, biodiesel blends, or biomass-based diesel blends.* The label is 3 inches (7.62 cm) wide × 2½ inches (6.35 cm) long. "Helvetica Black" or equivalent type is used throughout. All type is centered. The band at the top of the label contains the name of the fuel. This band should measure 1 inch (2.54 cm) deep. Spacing of the fuel name is ¼ inch (.64 cm) from the top of the label and 3/16 inch (.48 cm) from the bottom of the black band, centered horizontally within the black band. The first line of type beneath the black band is ⅛ inch (.32 cm) from the bottom of the black band. All type below the black band is centered horizontally, with ⅛ inch (.32 cm) between each line. The bottom line of type is 3/16 inch (.48 cm) from the bottom of the label. All type should fall no closer than 3/16 inch (.48 cm) from the side edges of the label. If you wish to change the dimensions of this one principal component label to accommodate a fuel descriptor that is longer than shown in the sample labels, you must petition the Federal Trade Commission. You can do this by writing to the Secretary of the Federal Trade Commission, Washington, DC 20580. You must state the size and contents of the label that you wish to use, and the reasons that you want to use it.

(3) *For alternative liquid automotive fuel labels (two components).* The label is 3 inches (7.62 cm) wide × 2½ inches (6.35 cm) long. "Helvetica Black" or equivalent type is used throughout. All type is centered. The band at the top of the label contains the name of the fuel. This band should measure 1 inch (2.54 cm) deep. Spacing of the fuel name is ¼ inch (.64 cm) from the top of the label and 3/16 inch (.48 cm) from the bottom of the black band, centered horizontally within the black band. The first line of type beneath the black band is 3/16 inch (.48 cm) from the bottom of the black band. All type below the black band is centered horizontally, with ⅛ inch (.32 cm) between each line. The bottom line of type is ¼ inch (.64 cm) from the bottom of the label. All type should fall no closer than 3/16 inch (.48 cm) from the side edges of the label. If you wish to change the dimensions of this two component label to accommodate additional fuel components, you must petition the Federal Trade Commission. You can do this by writing to the Secretary of the Federal Trade Commission, Washington, DC 20580. You must state the size and contents of the label that you wish to use, and the reasons that you want to use it.

(4) *For ethanol flex fuels.* (i) The label is 3 inches (7.62 cm) wide x 2½ inches (6.35 cm) long. "Helvetica Black" or equivalent type is used throughout. The band at the top of the label contains one of the following:

(A) *For all ethanol flex* fuels. The numerical value representing the volume percentage of ethanol in the fuel followed by the percentage sign and then by the term "ETHANOL"; or

(B) *For ethanol flex fuels containing more than 10 percent and no greater than 50 percent ethanol by volume.* The numerical value representing the volume percentage of ethanol in the fuel, rounded to the nearest multiple of 10, followed by the percentage sign and then the term "ETHANOL"; or

(C) *For ethanol flex fuels containing more than 50 percent and no greater than 83 percent ethanol by volume.* The numerical value representing the volume percentage of ethanol in the fuel, rounded to the nearest multiple of 10, followed by the percentage sign and then the term "ETHANOL" or the phrase, "51%–83% ETHANOL."

(ii) The band should measure 1 inch (2.54 cm) deep. The type in the band is centered both horizontally and vertically. The percentage disclosure and the word "ETHANOL" are in 24 point font. In the case of labels including the phrase, "51%–83% ETHANOL," the percentage disclosure is in 18 point font, and the word "ETHANOL" is in 24 point font and at least ⅛ inch (.32 cm) below the percentage disclosure. The type below the black band is centered vertically and horizontally. The first line is the text: "USE *ONLY* IN." It is in 16 point font, except for the word "*ONLY*," which is in 26 point font. The word "*ONLY*" is underlined with a 2 point (or thicker) underline. The second line is in 16 point font, at least ⅛ inch (.32 cm) below the first line, and is the text: "FLEX-FUEL VEHICLES." The third line is in 10 point font, at least ⅛ inch (.32 cm) below the first line, and is the text "MAY HARM OTHER ENGINES."

(5) *For biodiesel blends containing more than 5 percent and no greater than 20 percent biodiesel by volume.* (i) The label is 3 inches (7.62 cm) wide × 2½ inches (6.35 cm) long. "Helvetica Black" or equivalent type is used throughout. All type is centered. The band at the top of the label contains either:

(A) The capital letter "B" followed immediately by the numerical value representing the volume percentage of biodiesel in the fuel (e.g., "B20") and then by the term "Biodiesel Blend"; or

(B) The term "Biodiesel Blend."

(ii) The band should measure 1 inch (2.54 cm) deep. Spacing of the text in the band is ¼ inch (.64 cm) from the top of the label and 3/16 inch (.48 cm) from the bottom of the black band, centered horizontally within the black band. Directly underneath the black band, the label shall read "contains biomass-based diesel or biodiesel in quantities between 5 percent and 20 percent." The script underneath the black band must be centered horizontally, with ⅛ inch (.32 cm) between each line. The bottom line of type is ¼ inch (.64 cm) from the bottom of the label. All type should fall no closer than 3/16 inch (.48 cm) from the side edges of the label.

(6) *For biomass-based diesel blends containing more than 5 percent and no greater than 20 percent biomass-based diesel by volume.* (i) The label is 3 inches (7.62 cm) wide × 2½ inches (6.35 cm) long. "Helvetica Black" or equivalent type is used throughout. All type is centered. The band at the top of the label contains either:

(A) The numerical value representing the volume percentage of biomass-based diesel in the fuel followed immediately by the percentage symbol (*e.g.*, "20%") and then by the term "Biomass-Based Diesel Blend"; or

(B) The term "Biomass-Based Diesel Blend."

(ii) The band should measure 1 inch (2.54 cm) deep. Spacing of the text in the band is ¼ inch (.64 cm) from the top of the label and 3/16 inch (.48 cm) from the bottom of the black band, centered horizontally within the black band. Directly underneath the black band, the label shall read "contains biomass-based diesel or biodiesel in quantities between 5 percent and 20 percent." The script underneath the black band must be centered horizontally, with ⅛ inch (.32 cm) between each line. The bottom line of type is ¼ inch (.64 cm) from the bottom of the label. All type should fall no closer than 3/16 inch (.48 cm) from the side edges of the label.

(7) *For biodiesel blends containing more than 20 percent biodiesel by volume.* The requirements are the same as in paragraph (a)(4) of this section, except that the black band at the top of the label

shall contain the capital letter "B" followed immediately by the numerical value representing the volume percentage of biodiesel in the fuel (e.g., "B–70") and then the term "Biodiesel Blend." In addition, the words directly underneath the black band shall read "contains more than 20 percent biomass-based diesel or biodiesel."

(8) *For biomass-based diesel blends containing more than 20 percent biomass-based diesel by volume.* The requirements are the same as in paragraph (a)(5) of this section, except that the black band at the top of the label shall contain the numerical value representing the volume percentage of biomass-based diesel in the fuel followed immediately by the percentage symbol (e.g., "70%") and then the term "Biomass-Based Diesel Blend." In addition, the words directly underneath the black band shall read "contains more than 20 percent biomass-based diesel or biodiesel."

(9) *For 100% biodiesel.* The requirements are the same as in paragraph (a)(4) of this section, except that the black band at the top of the label shall contain the phrase "B-100 Biodiesel." In addition, the words directly underneath the black band shall read "contains 100 percent biodiesel."

(10) *For 100% biomass-based diesel.* The requirements are the same as in paragraph (a)(5) of this section, except that the black band at the top of the label shall contain the phrase "100% Biomass-Based Diesel." In addition, the words directly underneath the black band shall read "contains 100 percent biomass-based diesel."

(b) *Type size and setting*—(1) *For gasoline labels.* The Helvetica series or equivalent type is used for all numbers and letters with the exception of the octane rating number. Helvetica is available in a variety of phototype setting systems, by linotype, and in a variety of computer desk-top and phototype setting systems. Its name may vary, but the type must conform in style and thickness to the sample provided here. The line "Minimum Octane Rating" is set in 12 point Helvetica Bold, all capitals, with letterspace set at 12½ points. The line "(R + M)/2 METHOD" is set in 10 point Helvetica Bold, all capitals, with letterspace set at 10½ points. The octane number is set in 96 point Franklin gothic condensed with ⅛ inch (.32 cm) space between the numbers.

(2) *For alternative liquid automotive fuel labels (one principal component).* Except as provided above, labels should conform to the following specifications. All type should be set in upper case (all caps) "Helvetica Black" or equivalent type throughout. Helvetica Black is available in a variety of computer desk-top and phototype setting systems. Its name may vary, but the type must conform in style and thickness to the sample provided here. The spacing between letters and words should be set as "normal." The type for the fuel name is 50 point (½ inch (1.27 cm) cap height) "Helvetica Black," knocked out of a 1 inch (2.54 cm) deep band. The type for the words "MINIMUM" and the principal component is 24 point (¼ inch (.64 cm) cap height). The type for percentage is 36 point (⅜ inch (.96 cm) cap height).

(3) *For alternative liquid automotive fuel labels (two components).* All type should be set in upper case (all caps) "Helvetica Black" or equivalent type throughout. Helvetica Black is available in a variety of computer desk-top and phototype setting systems. Its name may vary, but the type must conform in style and thickness to the sample provided here. The spacing between letters and words should be set as "normal." The type for the fuel name is 50 point (½ inch (1.27 cm) cap height) "Helvetica Black," knocked out of a 1 inch (2.54 cm) deep band. All other type is 24 point (¼ inch (.64 cm) cap height).

(c) *Colors*—(1) *For gasoline labels.* The basic color on all octane labels is process yellow. All type is process black. All borders are process black. All colors must be non-fade.

(2) *For alternative liquid automotive fuel labels other than biodiesel and biodiesel blends.* The background color on all the labels is Orange: PMS 1495 or its equivalent. The knock-out type within the black band is Orange: PMS 1495 or its equivalent. All other type is process black. All borders are process black. All colors must be non-fade.

(3) *For biodiesel and biodiesel blends.* The background color on all the labels is Blue: PMS 277 or its equivalent. The

knock-out type within the black band is Blue: PMS 277 or its equivalent. All other type is process black. All borders are process black. All colors must be non-fade.

(d) *Contents.* Examples of the contents are shown in the sample labels. The proper octane rating for each gasoline must be shown. The proper automotive fuel rating for each alternative liquid automotive fuel must be shown. No marks or information other than that called for by this rule may appear on the labels.

(e) *Special label protection.* All labels must be capable of withstanding extremes of weather conditions for a period of at least one year. They must be resistant to automotive fuel, oil, grease, solvents, detergents, and water.

(f) *Illustrations of labels.* Labels should meet the specifications in this section, and should look like these examples, except the black print should be on the appropriately colored background.

M-85

MINIMUM
85%
METHANOL

LPG

MINIMUM
90% PROPANE
2% BUTANE

LPG

MINIMUM
90%
PROPANE

E-100

MINIMUM
95%
ETHANOL

B-100 Biodiesel
contains 100 percent biodiesel

100% Biomass-Based Diesel
contains 100 percent biomass-based diesel

B-20 Biodiesel Blend
contains biomass-based diesel or biodiesel in quantities between 5 percent and 20 percent

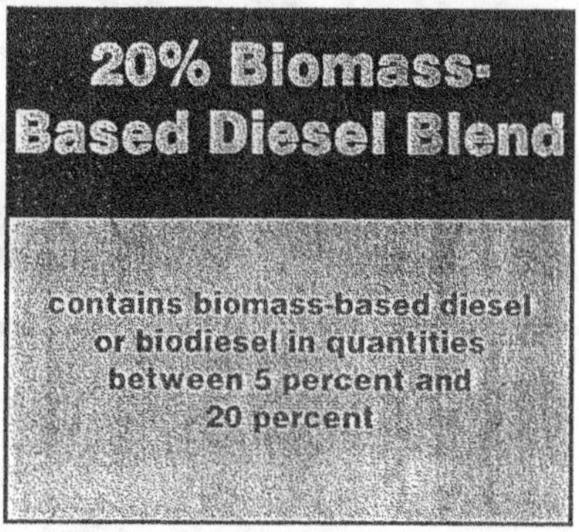
20% Biomass-Based Diesel Blend
contains biomass-based diesel or biodiesel in quantities between 5 percent and 20 percent

[58 FR 41375, Aug. 3, 1993, as amended at 73 FR 40163, July 11, 2008; 76 FR 19691, Apr. 8, 2011; 81 FR 2063, Jan. 14, 2016]

EDITORIAL NOTE: At 81 FR 2063, Jan. 14, 2016, § 306.12 was amended by removing the illustration of the "E–100" label, however, since the label is part of a larger illustration, it could not be removed.

§ 306.13 Incorporation by reference.

(a) Certain material is incorporated by reference into this part with the approval of the Director of the Federal Register under 5 U.S.C. 552(a) and 1 CFR part 51. You may inspect all approved material at the FTC Library, (202) 326–2395, Federal Trade Commission, Room H–630, 600 Pennsylvania Avenue NW., Washington, DC 20580, and at the National Archives and Records Administration ("NARA"). For information on the availability of this material at NARA, call 202–741–6030, or go to: *http://www.archives.gov/federal-register/cfr/ibr-locations.html.*

(b) ASTM International (ASTM), 100 Barr Harbor Drive, West Conshohocken, PA 19428 telephone: 1–877–909–2786; Internet address: *http://www.astm.org.*

(1) ASTM D975–07b, Standard Specification for Diesel Fuel Oils, published July 2007; IBR approved for § 306.0(i).

(2) ASTM D975–09b, Standard Specification for Diesel Fuel Oils, published August 2009; IBR approved for § 306.0(i).

(3) ASTM D2699–15a, Standard Test Method for Research Octane Number of Spark-Ignition Engine Fuel, published November 2015; IBR approved for §§ 306.0(b) and 306.5(a).

(4) ASTM D2700–14, Standard Test Method for Motor Octane Number of Spark-Ignition Engine Fuel, published November 2014; IBR approved for §§ 306.0(b) and 306.5(a).

(5) ASTM D2885–13, Standard Test Method for Determination of Octane Number of Spark-Ignition Engine Fuels by On-Line Direct Comparison Technique, published July 2013; IBR approved for §§ 306.0(b) and 306.5(a).

(6) ASTM D4814–15a, Standard Specification for Automotive Spark-Ignition Engine Fuel, published August 2015; IBR approved for §§ 306.0(b) and 306.5(a).

(7) ASTM D6751–10, Standard Specification for Biodiesel Fuel Blend Stock (B100) for Middle Distillate Fuels, published October 2010; IBR approved for § 306.0(l).

[81 FR 2064, Jan. 14, 2016]

APPENDIX A TO PART 306—SUMMARY OF LABELING REQUIREMENTS FOR BIODIESEL FUELS

(Part 1 of 2)

Fuel type	Blends of 5 percent or less	Blends of more than 5 but not more than 20 percent		
		Header	Text	Color
Biodiesel	No label required	Either "B-XX Biodiesel Blend" or "Biodiesel Blend"	contains biomass-based diesel or biodiesel in quantities between 5 percent and 20 percent	Blue
Biomass-Based Diesel	No label required	Either "XX% Biomass-Based Diesel Blend" or "Biomass-Based Diesel Blend"	contains biomass-based diesel or biodiesel in quantities between 5 percent and 20 percent	Orange

(Part 2 of 2)

Fuel type	Blends of more than 20 percent			Pure (100%) Biodiesel or Biomass-Based diesel		
	Header	Text	Color	Header	Text	Color
Biodiesel	B-XX Biodiesel Blend	contains more than 20 percent biomass-based diesel or biodiesel	Blue	B-100 Biodiesel	contains 100 percent biodiesel	Blue
Biomass-Based Diesel	XX% Biomass-Based Diesel Blend	contains more than 20 percent biomass-based diesel or biodiesel	Orange	100% Biomass-Based Diesel	contains 100 percent biomass-based diesel	Orange

[73 FR 40164, July 11, 2008]

PART 307 [RESERVED]

PART 308—TRADE REGULATION RULE PURSUANT TO THE TELEPHONE DISCLOSURE AND DISPUTE RESOLUTION ACT OF 1992

Sec.

AUTHORITY: Pub. L. 102–556, 106 Stat. 4181 (15 U.S.C. 5701, *et seq.*)

SOURCE: 58 FR 42400, Aug. 9, 1993, unless otherwise noted.

§ 308.1 Scope of regulations in this part.

This rule implements titles II and III of the Telephone Disclosure and Dispute Resolution Act of 1992, to be codified in relevant part at 15 U.S.C. 5711–14, 5721–24.

§ 308.2 Definitions.

(a) *Bona fide educational service* means any pay-per-call service dedicated to providing information or instruction relating to education, subjects of academic study, or other related areas of school study.

(b) *Commission* means the Federal Trade Commission.

(c) *Pay-per-call service* has the meaning provided in section 228 of the Communications Act of 1934, 47 U.S.C. 228.[1]

(d) *Person* means any individual, partnership, corporation, association, government or governmental subdivision or agency, or other entity.

(e)(1) *Presubscription or comparable arrangement* means a contractual agreement in which

(i) The service provider clearly and conspicuously discloses to the consumer all material terms and conditions associated with the use of the service, including the service provider's name and address, a business telephone number which the consumer may use to obtain additional information or to register a complaint, and the rates for the service;

(ii) The service provider agrees to notify the consumer of any future rate changes;

(iii) The consumer agrees to utilize the service on the terms and conditions disclosed by the service provider; and

(iv) The service provider requires the use of an identification number or other means to prevent unauthorized access to the service by nonsubscribers.

(2) Disclosure of a credit card or charge card number, along with authorization to bill that number, made during the course of a call to a pay-per-call service shall constitute a presubscription or comparable arrangement if the credit or charge card is subject to the dispute resolution requirements of the Fair Credit Billing Act and the Truth in Lending Act, as amended. No other action taken by the consumer during the course of a call to a pay-per-call service can be construed as creating a presubscription or comparable arrangement.

(f) *Program-length commercial* means any commercial or other advertisement fifteen (15) minutes in length or longer or intended to fill a television or radio broadcasting or cablecasting time slot of fifteen (15) minutes in length or longer.

(g) *Provider of pay-per-call services* means any person who sells or offers to sell a pay-per-call service. A person who provides only transmission services or billing and collection services shall not be considered a provider of pay-per-call services.

---

[1] Section 228 of the Communications Act of 1934 states:

(1) The term *pay-per-call services* means any service—

(A) In which any person provides or purports to provide—

(i) Audio information or audio entertainment produced or packaged by such person;

(ii) Access to simultaneous voice conversation services; or

(iii) Any service, including the provision of a product, the charges for which are assessed on the basis of the completion of the call;

(B) For which the caller pays a per-call or per-time-interval charge that is greater than, or in addition to, the charge for transmission of the call; and

(C) Which is accessed through use of a 900 telephone number or other prefix or area code designated by the (Federal Communications) Commission in accordance with subsection (b)(5) (47 U.S.C. 228(b)(5)).

(2) Such term does not include directory services provided by a common carrier or its affiliate or by a local exchange carrier or its affiliate, or any service the charge for which is tariffed, or any service for which users are assessed charges only after entering into a presubcription or comparable arrangement with the provider of such service.

(h) *Reasonably understandable volume* means at an audible level that renders the message intelligible to the receiving audience, and, in any event, at least the same audible level as that principally used in the advertisement or the pay-per-call service.

(i) *Service bureau* means any person, other than a common carrier, who provides, among other things, access to telephone service and voice storage to pay-per-call service providers.

(j) *Slow and deliberate manner* means at a rate that renders the message intelligible to the receiving audience, and, in any event, at a cadence or rate no faster than that principally used in the advertisement or the pay-per-call service.

(k) *Sweepstakes,* including games of chance, means a game or promotional mechanism that involves the elements of a prize and chance and does not require consideration.

§308.3 Advertising of pay-per-call services.

(a) *General requirements.* The following requirements apply to disclosures required in advertisements under §§308.3 (b)–(d), and (f):

(1) The disclosures shall be made in the same language as that principally used in the advertisement.

(2) Television video and print disclosures shall be of a color or shade that readily contrasts with the background of the advertisement.

(3) In print advertisements, disclosures shall be parallel with the base of the advertisement.

(4) Audio disclosures, whether in television or radio, shall be delivered in a slow and deliberate manner and in a reasonably understandable volume.

(5) Nothing contrary to, inconsistent with, or in mitigation of, the required disclosures shall be used in any advertisement in any medium; nor shall any audio, video or print technique be used that is likely to detract significantly from the communication of the disclosures.

(6) In any program-length commercial, required disclosures shall be made at least three times (unless more frequent disclosure is otherwise required) near the beginning, middle and end of the commercial.

(b) *Cost of the call.* (1) The provider of pay-per-call services shall clearly and conspicuously disclose the cost of the call, in Arabic numerals, in any advertisement for the pay-per-call service, as follows:

(i) If there is a flat fee for the call, the advertisement shall state the total cost of the call.

(ii) If the call is billed on a time-sensitive basis, the advertisement shall state the cost per minute and any minimum charges. If the length of the program can be determined in advance, the advertisement shall also state the maximum charge that could be incurred if the caller listens to the complete program.

(iii) If the call is billed on a variable rate basis, the advertisement shall state, in accordance with §§308.3(b)(1) (i) and (ii), the cost of the initial portion of the call, any minimum charges, and the range of rates that may be charged depending on the options chosen by the caller.

(iv) The advertisement shall disclose any other fees that will be charged for the service.

(v) if the caller may be transferred to another pay-per-call service, the advertisement shall disclose the cost of the other call, in accordance with §§308.3(b)(1) (i), (ii), (iii), and (iv).

(2) For purposes of §308.3(b), disclosures shall be made "clearly and conspicuously" as set forth in §308.3(a) and as follows:

(i) In a television or videotape advertisement, the video disclosure shall appear adjacent to each video presentation of the pay-per-call number. However, in an advertisement displaying more than one pay-per-call number with the same cost, the video disclosure need only appear adjacent to the largest presentation of the pay-per-call number. Each letter or numeral of the video disclosure shall be, at a minimum, one-half the size of each letter or numeral of the pay-per-call number to which the disclosure is adjacent. In addition, the video disclosure shall appear on the screen for the duration of the presentation of the pay-per-call number. An audio disclosure shall be made at least once, simultaneously with a video presentation of the disclosure. However, no audio presentation of the disclosure is required in: (A) An advertisement fifteen (15) seconds or less in length in which the pay-per-call number is not presented in the audio portion, or (B) an advertisement in which there is no audio presentation of information regarding the pay-per-call service, including the pay-per-call number. In an advertisement in which the pay-per-call number is presented *only* in the audio portion, the cost of the call shall be delivered immediately following the first and last delivery of the pay-per-call number, except that in a program-length commercial, the disclosure shall be delivered immediately following each delivery of the pay-per-call number.

(ii) In a print advertisement, the disclosure shall be placed adjacent to each presentation of the pay-per-call number. However, in an advertisement displaying more than one pay-per-call number with the same cost, the disclosure need only appear adjacent to the largest presentation of the pay-per-call number. Each letter or numeral of the disclosure shall be, at a minimum, one-half the size of each letter or numeral of the pay-per-call number to which the disclosure is adjacent.

(iii) In a radio advertisement, the disclosure shall be made at least once, and shall be delivered immediately following the first delivery of the pay-per-call number. In a program-length commercial, the disclosure shall be delivered immediately following each delivery of the pay-per-call number.

(c) *Sweepstakes; games of chance.* (1) The provider of pay-per-call services that advertises a prize or award or a service or product at no cost or for a reduced cost, to be awarded to the winner of any sweepstakes, including games of chance, shall clearly and conspicuously disclose in the advertisement the odds of being able to receive the prize, award, service, or product at no cost or reduced cost. If the odds are not calculable in advance, the advertisement shall disclose the factors used in calculating the odds. Either the advertisement or the preamble required by § 308.5(a) for such service shall clearly and conspicuously disclose that no call to the pay-per-call service is required to participate, and shall also disclose the existence of a free alternative method of entry, and either instructions on how to enter, or a local or toll-free telephone number or address to which consumers may call or write for information on how to enter the sweepstakes. Any description or characterization of the prize, award, service, or product that is being offered at no cost or reduced cost shall be truthful and accurate.

(2) For purposes of § 308.3(c), disclosures shall be made "clearly and conspicuously" as set forth in § 308.3(a) and as follows:

(i) In a television or videotape advertisement, the disclosures may be made in either the audio or video portion of the advertisement. If the disclosures are made in the video portion, they shall appear on the screen in sufficient size and for sufficient time to allow consumers to read and comprehend the disclosures.

(ii) In a print advertisement, the disclosures shall appear in a sufficient size and prominence and such location to be readily noticeable, readable and comprehensible.

(d) *Federal programs.* (1) The provider of pay-per-call services that advertises a pay-per-call service that is not operated or expressly authorized by a Federal agency, but that provides information on a Federal program, shall clearly and conspicuously disclose in the advertisement that the pay-per-call service is not authorized, endorsed, or approved by any Federal agency. Advertisements providing information on a Federal program shall include, but not be limited to, advertisements that contain a seal, insignia, trade or brand name, or any other term or symbol that reasonably could be interpreted or construed as implying any Federal government connection, approval, or endorsement.

(2) For purposes of § 308.3(d), disclosures shall be made "clearly and conspicuously" as set forth in § 308.3(a) and as follows:

(i) In a television or videotape advertisement, the disclosure may be made in either the audio or video portion of the advertisement. If the disclosure is made in the video portion, it shall appear on the screen in sufficient size and for sufficient time to allow consumers to read and comprehend the disclosure.

The disclosure shall begin within the first fifteen (15) seconds of the advertisement.

(ii) In a print advertisement, the disclosure shall appear in a sufficient size and prominence and such location to be readily noticeable, readable and comprehensible. The disclosure shall appear in the top one-third of the advertisement.

(iii) In a radio advertisement, the disclosure shall begin within the first fifteen (15) seconds of the advertisement.

(e) *Prohibition on advertising to children.* (1) The provider of pay-per-call services shall not direct advertisements for such pay-per-call services to children under the age of 12, unless the service is a bona fide educational service.

(2) For the purposes of this regulation, advertisements directed to children under 12 shall include: any pay-per-call advertisement appearing during or immediately adjacent to programming for which competent and reliable audience composition data demonstrate that more than 50% of the audience is composed of children under 12, and any pay-per-call advertisement appearing in a periodical for which competent and reliable readership data demonstrate that more than 50% of the readership is composed of children under 12.

(3) For the purposes of this regulation, if competent and reliable audience composition or readership data does not demonstrate that more than 50% of the audience or readership is composed of children under 12, then the Commission shall consider the following criteria in determining whether an advertisement is directed to children under 12:

(i) Whether the advertisement appears in a publication directed to children under 12, including, but not limited to, books, magazines and comic books;

(ii) Whether the advertisement appears during or immediately adjacent to television programs directed to children under 12, including, but not limited to, children's programming as defined by the Federal Communications Commission, animated programs, and after-school programs;

(iii) Whether the advertisement appears on a television station or channel directed to children under 12;

(iv) Whether the advertisement is broadcast during or immediately adjacent to radio programs directed to children under 12, or broadcast on a radio station directed to children under 12;

(v) Whether the advertisement appears on the same video as a commercially-prepared video directed to children under 12, or preceding a movie directed to children under 12 shown in a movie theater;

(vi) Whether the advertisement or promotion appears on product packaging directed to children under 12; and

(vii) Whether the advertisement, regardless of when or where it appears, is directed to children under 12 in light of its subject matter, visual content, age of models, language, characters, tone, message, or the like.

(f) *Advertising to individuals under the age of 18.* (1) The provider of pay-per-call services shall ensure that any pay-per-call advertisement directed primarily to individuals under the age of 18 shall contain a clear and conspicuous disclosure that all individuals under the age of 18 must have the permission of such individual's parent or legal guardian prior to calling such pay-per-call service.

(2) For purposes of § 308.3(f), disclosures shall be made "clearly and conspicuously" as set forth in § 308.3(a) and as follows:

(i) In a television or videotape advertisement, each letter or numeral of the video disclosure shall be, at a minimum, one-half the size of each letter or numeral of the largest presentation of the pay-per-call number. The video disclosure shall appear on the screen for sufficient time to allow consumers to read and comprehend the disclosure. An audio disclosure shall be made at least once, simultaneously with a video presentation of the disclosure. However, no audio presentation of the disclosure is required in: (A) An advertisement fifteen (15) seconds or less in length in which the pay-per-call number is not presented in the audio portion, or (B) an advertisement in which there is no audio presentation of information regarding the pay-per-call service, including the pay-per-call number.

(ii) In a print advertisement, each letter or numeral of the disclosure shall be, at a minimum, one-half the size of each letter or numeral of the largest presentation of the pay-per-call number.

(3) For the purposes of this regulation, advertisements directed primarily to individuals under 18 shall include: Any pay-per-call advertisement appearing during or immediately adjacent to programming for which competent and reliable audience composition data demonstrate that more than 50% of the audience is composed of individuals under 18, and any pay-per-call advertisement appearing in a periodical for which competent and reliable readership data demonstrate that more than 50% of the readership is composed of individuals under 18.

(4) For the purposes of this regulation, if competent and reliable audience composition or readership data does not demonstrate that more than 50% of the audience or readership is composed of individuals under 18, then the Commission shall consider the following criteria in determining whether an advertisement is directed primarily to individuals under 18:

(i) Whether the advertisement appears in publications directed primarily to individuals under 18, including, but not limited to, books, magazines and comic books;

(ii) Whether the advertisement appears during or immediately adjacent to television programs directed primarily to individuals under 18, including, but not limited to, mid-afternoon weekday television shows;

(iii) Whether the advertisement is broadcast on radio stations that are directed primarily to individuals under 18;

(iv) Whether the advertisement appears on a cable or broadcast television station directed primarily to individuals under 18;

(v) Whether the advertisement appears on the same video as a commercially-prepared video directed primarily to individuals under 18, or preceding a movie directed primarily to individuals under 18 shown in a movie theater; and

(vi) Whether the advertisement, regardless of when or where it appears, is directed primarily to individuals under 18 in light of its subject matter, visual content, age of models, language, characters, tone, massage, or the like.

(g) *Electronic tones in advertisements.* The provider of pay-per-call services is prohibited from using advertisements that emit electronic tones that can automatically dial a pay-per-call service.

(h) *Telephone solicitations.* The provider of pay-per-call services shall ensure that any telephone message that solicits calls to the pay-per-call service discloses the cost of the call in a slow and deliberate manner and in a reasonably understandable volume, in accordance with §§ 308.3(b)(1)(i)-(v).

(i) *Referral to toll-free telephone numbers.* The provider of pay-per-call services is prohibited from referring in advertisements to an 800 telephone number, or any other telephone number advertised as or widely understood to be toll-free, if that number violates the prohibition concerning toll-free numbers set forth in § 308.5(i).

§ 308.4 Special rule for infrequent publications.

(a) The provider of any pay-per-call service that advertises a pay-per-call service in a publication that meets the requirements set forth in § 308.4(c) may include in such advertisement, in lieu of the cost disclosures required by § 308.3(b), a clear and conspicuous disclosure that a call to the advertised pay-per-call service may result in a substantial charge.

(b) The provider of any pay-per-call service that places an alphabetical listing in a publication that meets the requirements set forth in § 308.4(c) is not required to make any of the disclosures required by §§ 308.3 (b), (c), (d) and (f) in the alphabetical listing, provided that such listing does not contain any information except the name, address and telephone number of the pay-per-call provider.

(c) The publication referred to in § 308.4 (a) and (b) must be:

(1) Widely distributed;

(2) Printed annually or less frequently; and

(3) One that has an established policy of not publishing specific prices in advertisements.

§ 308.5 Pay-per-call service standards.

(a) *Preamble message.* The provider of pay-per-call services shall include, in each pay-per-call message, an introductory disclosure message ("preamble") in the same language as that principally used in the pay-per-call message, that clearly, in a slow and deliberate manner and in a reasonably understandable volume:

(1) Identifies the name of the provider of the pay-per-call service and describes the service being provided;

(2) Specifies the cost of the service as follows:

(i) If there is a flat fee for the call, the preamble shall state the total cost of the call;

(ii) If the call is billed on a time-sensitive basis, the preamble shall state the cost per minute and any minimum charges; if the length of the program can be determined in advance, the preamble shall also state the maximum charge that could be incurred if the caller listens to the complete program;

(iii) If the call is billed on a variable rate basis, the preamble shall state, in accordance with §§ 308.5(a)(2) (i) and (ii), the cost of the initial portion of the call, any minimum charges, and the range of rates that may be charged depending on the options chosen by the caller;

(iv) Any other fees that will be charged for the service shall be disclosed, as well as fees for any other pay-per-call service to which the caller may be transferred;

(3) Informs the caller that charges for the call begin, and that to avoid charges the call must be terminated, three seconds after a clearly discernible signal or tone indicating the end of the preamble;

(4) Informs the caller that anyone under the age of 18 must have the permission of parent or legal guardian in order to complete the call; and

(5) Informs the caller, in the case of a pay-per-call service that is not operated or expressly authorized by a Federal agency but that provides information on a Federal program, or that uses a trade or brand name or any other term that reasonably could be interpreted or construed as implying any Federal government connection, approval or endorsement, that the pay-per-call service is not authorized, endorsed, or approved by any Federal agency.

(b) *No charge to caller for preamble message.* The provider of pay-per-call services is prohibited from charging a caller any amount whatsoever for such a service if the caller hangs up at any time prior to three seconds after the signal or tone indicating the end of the preamble described in § 308.5(a). However, the three-second delay, and the message concerning such delay described in § 308.5(a)(3), is not required if the provider of pay-per-call services offers the caller an affirmative means (such as pressing a key on a telephone keypad) of indicating a decision to incur the charges.

(c) *Nominal cost calls.* The preamble described in § 308.5(a) is not required when the entire cost of the pay-per-call service, whether billed as a flat rate or on a time sensitive basis, is $2.00 or less.

(d) *Data service calls.* The preamble described in § 308.5(a) is not required when the entire call consists of the non-verbal transmission of information.

(e) *Bypass mechanism.* The provider of pay-per-call services that offers to frequent callers or regular subscribers to such services the option of activating a bypass mechanism to avoid listening to the preamble during subsequent calls shall not be deemed to be in violation of § 308.5(a), *provided that* any such bypass mechanism shall be disabled for a period of no less than 30 days immediately after the institution of an increase in the price for the service or a change in the nature of the service offered.

(f) *Billing limitations.* The provider of pay-per-call services is prohibited from billing consumers in excess of the amount described in the preamble for those services and from billing for any services provided in violation of any section of this rule.

(g) *Stopping the assessment of time-based charges.* The provider of pay-per-call services shall stop the assessment of time-based charges immediately upon disconnection by the caller.

(h) *Prohibition on services to children.* The provider of pay-per-call services shall not direct such services to children under the age of 12, unless such service is a bona fide educational service. The Commission shall consider the following criteria in determining whether a pay-per-call service is directed to children under 12:

(1) Whether the pay-per-call service is advertised in the manner set forth in §§ 308.3(e) (2) and (3); and

(2) Whether the pay-per-call service, regardless of when or where it is advertised, is directed to children under 12, in light of its subject matter, content, language, featured personality, characters, tone, message, or the like.

(i) *Prohibition concerning toll-free numbers.* Any person is prohibited from using an 800 number or other telephone number advertised as or widely understood to be toll-free in a manner that would result in:

(1) The calling party being assessed, by virtue of completing the call, a charge for the call;

(2) The calling party being connected to an access number for, or otherwise transferred to, a pay-per-call service;

(3) The calling party being charged for information conveyed during the call unless the calling party has a presubscription or comparable arrangement to be charged for the information; or

(4) The calling party being called back collect for the provision of audio or data information services, simultaneous voice conversation services, or products.

(j) *Disclosure requirements for billing statements.* The provider of pay-per-call services shall ensure that any billing statement for such provider's charges shall:

(1) Display any charges for pay-per-call services in a portion of the consumer's bill that is identified as not being related to local and long distance telephone charges;

(2) For each charge so displayed, specify the type of service, the amount of the charge, and the date, time, and, for calls billed on a time-sensitive basis, the duration of the call; and

(3) Display the local or toll-free telephone number where consumers can obtain answers to their questions and information on their rights and obligations with regard to their use of pay-per-call services, and can obtain the name and mailing address of the provider of pay-per-call services.

(k) *Refunds to consumers.* The provider of pay-per-call services shall be liable for refunds or credits to consumers who have been billed for pay-per-call services, and who have paid the charges for such services, pursuant to pay-per-call programs that have been found to have violated any provision of this rule or any other Federal rule or law.

(l) *Service bureau liability.* A service bureau shall be liable for violations of the rule by pay-per-call services using its call processing facilities where it knew or should have known of the violation.

§ 308.6 Access to information.

Any common carrier that provides telecommunication services to any provider of pay-per-call services shall make available to the Commission, upon written request, any records and financial information maintained by such carrier relating to the arrangements (other than for the provision of local exchange service) between such carrier and any provider of pay-per-call services.

§ 308.7 Billing and collection for pay-per-call services.

(a) *Definitions.* For the purposes of this section, the following definitions shall apply:

(1) *Billing entity* means any person who transmits a billing statement to a customer for a telephone-billed purchase, or any person who assumes responsibility for receiving and responding to billing error complaints or inquiries.

(2) *Billing error* means any of the following:

(i) A reflection on a billing statement of a telephone-billed purchase that was not made by the customer nor made from the telephone of the customer who was billed for the purchase or, if made, was not in the amount reflected on such statement.

(ii) A reflection on a billing statement of a telephone-billed purchase for which the customer requests additional clarification, including documentary evidence thereof.

(iii) A reflection on a billing statement of a telephone-billed purchase that was not accepted by the customer or not provided to the customer in accordance with the stated terms of the transaction.

(iv) A reflection on a billing statement of a telephone-billed purchase for a call made to an 800 or other toll free telephone number.

(v) The failure to reflect properly on a billing statement a payment made by the customer or a credit issued to the customer with respect to a telephone-billed purchase.

(vi) A computation error or similar error of an accounting nature on a billing statement of a telephone-billed purchase.

(vii) Failure to transmit a billing statement for a telephone-billed purchase to a customer's last known address if that address was furnished by the customer at least twenty days before the end of the billing cycle for which the statement was required.

(viii) A reflection on a billing statement of a telephone-billed purchase that is not identified in accordance with the requirements of §308.5(j).

(3) *Customer* means any person who acquires or attempts to acquire goods or services in a telephone-billed purchase, or who receives a billing statement for a telephone-billed purchase charged to a telephone number assigned to that person by a providing carrier.

(4) *Preexisting agreement* means a "presubscription or comparable arrangement," as that term is defined in §308.2(e).

(5) *Providing carrier* means a local exchange or interexchange common carrier providing telephone services (other than local exchange services) to a vendor for a telephone-billed purchase that is the subject of a billing error complaint or inquiry.

(6) *Telephone-billed purchase* means any purchase that is completed solely as a consequence of the completion of the call or a subsequent dialing, touch tone entry, or comparable action of the caller. Such term does not include:

(i) A purchase by a caller pursuant to a preexisting agreement with a vendor;

(ii) Local exchange telephone services or interexchange telephone services or any service that the Federal Communications Commission determines by rule—

(A) Is closely related to the provision of local exchange telephone services or interexchange telephone services; and

(B) Is subject to billing dispute resolution procedures required by Federal or state statute or regulation; or

(iii) The purchase of goods or services that is otherwise subject to billing dispute resolution procedures required by Federal statute or regulation.

(7) *Vendor* means any person who, through the use of the telephone, offers goods or services for a telephone-billed purchase.

(b) *Initiation of billing review.* A customer may initiate a billing review with respect to a telephone-billed purchase by providing the billing entity with notice of a billing error no later than 60 days after the billing entity transmitted the first billing statement that contains a charge for such telephone-billed purchase. If the billing error is the reflection on a billing statement of a telephone-billed purchase not provided to the customer in accordance with the stated terms of the transaction, the 60-day period shall begin to run from the date the goods or services are delivered or, if not delivered, should have been delivered, if such date is later than the date the billing statement was transmitted. A billing error notice shall:

(1) Set forth or otherwise enable the billing entity to identify the customer's name and the telephone number to which the charge was billed;

(2) Indicate the customer's belief that the statement contains a billing error and the type, date, and amount of such; and

(3) Set forth the reasons for the customer's belief, to the extent possible, that the statement contains a billing error.

(c) *Disclosure of method of providing notice; presumption if oral notice is permitted.* A billing entity shall clearly and conspicuously[2] disclose on each

[2] The standard for "clear and conspicuous" as used in this section shall be the standard enunciated by the Board of Governors of the Federal Reserve System in its Official Staff

Continued

billing statement or on other material accompanying the billing statement the method (oral or written) by which the customer may provide notice to initiate review of a billing error in the manner set forth in § 308.7(b). If oral notice is permitted, any customer who orally communicates an allegation of a billing error to a billing entity shall be presumed to have properly initiated a billing review in accordance with the requirements of § 308.7(b).

(d) *Response to customer notice.* A billing entity that receives notice of a billing error as described in § 308.7(b) shall:

(1) Send a written acknowledgement to the customer including a statement that any disputed amount need not be paid pending investigation of the billing error. This shall be done no later than forty (40) days after receiving the notice, unless the action required by § 308.7(d)(2) is taken within such 40-day period; and

(2)(i) Correct the billing error and credit the customer's account for any disputed amount and any related charges, and notify the customer of the correction. The billing entity also shall disclose to the customer that collection efforts may occur despite the credit, and shall provide the names, mailing addresses, and business telephone numbers of the vendor and providing carrier, as applicable, that are the subject of the telephone-billed purchase, or provide the customer with a local or toll-free telephone number that the customer may call to obtain this information directly. However, the billing entity is not required to make the disclosure concerning collection efforts if the vendor, its agent, or the providing carrier, as applicable, will not collect or attempt to collect the disputed charge; or

(ii) Transmit an explanation to the customer, after conducting a reasonable investigation (including, where appropriate, contacting the vendor or providing carrier),[3] setting forth the reasons why it has determined that no billing error occurred or that a different billing error occurred from that asserted, make any appropriate adjustments to the customer's account, and, if the customer so requests, provide a written explanation and copies of documentary evidence of the customer's indebtedness.

(3) The action required by § 308.7(d)(2) shall be taken no later than two complete billing cycles of the billing entity (in no event later than ninety (90) days) after receiving the notice of the billing error and before taking any action to collect the disputed amount, or any part thereof. After complying with § 308.7(d)(2), the billing entity shall:

(i) If it is determined that any disputed amount is in error, promptly notify the appropriate providing carrier or vendor, as applicable, of its disposition of the customer's billing error and the reasons therefor; and

(ii) Promptly notify the customer in writing of the time when payment is due of any portion of the disputed amount determined not to be in error, which time shall be the longer of ten (10) days or the number of days the customer is ordinarily allowed (whether by custom, contract or state law) to pay undisputed amounts, and that failure to pay such amount may be reported to a credit reporting agency or subject the customer to a collection action, if that in fact may happen.

(e) *Withdrawal of billing error notice.* A billing entity need not comply with the requirements of § 308.7(d) if the customer has, after giving notice of a billing error and before the expiration of the time limits specified therein, agreed that the billing statement was correct or agreed to withdraw voluntarily the billing error notice.

Commentary on Regulation Z, which requires simply that the disclosures be in a reasonably understandable form. See 12 CFR part 226, Supplement I, Comment 226.5(a)(1)–1.

[3] If a customer submits a billing error notice alleging either the nondelivery of goods or services or that information appearing on a billing statement has been reported incorrectly to the billing entity, the billing entity shall not deny the assertion unless it conducts a reasonable investigation and determines that the goods or services were actually delivered as agreed or that the information was correct. There shall be a rebuttable presumption that goods or services were actually delivered to the extent that a vendor or providing carrier produces documents prepared and maintained in the ordinary course of business showing the date on, and the place to, which the goods or services were transmitted or delivered.

(f) *Limitation on responsibility for billing error.* After complying with the provisions of §308.7(d), a billing entity has no further responsibility under that section if the customer continues to make substantially the same allegation with respect to a billing error.

(g) *Customer's right to withhold disputed amount; limitation on collection action.* Once the customer has submitted notice of a billing error to a billing entity, the customer need not pay, and the billing entity, providing carrier, or vendor may not try to collect, any portion of any required payment that the customer reasonably believes is related to the disputed amount until the billing entity receiving the notice has complied with the requirements of §308.7(d). The billing entity, providing carrier, or vendor are not prohibited from taking any action to collect any undisputed portion of the bill, or from reflecting a disputed amount and related charges on a billing statement, provided that the billing statement clearly states that payment of any disputed amount or related charges is not required pending the billing entity's compliance with §308.7(d).

(h) *Prohibition on charges for initiating billing review.* A billing entity, providing carrier, or vendor may not impose on the customer any charge related to the billing review, including charges for documentation or investigation.

(i) *Restrictions on credit reporting*—(1) *Adverse credit reports prohibited.* Once the customer has submitted notice of a billing error to a billing entity, a billing entity, providing carrier, vendor, or other agent may not report or threaten directly or indirectly to report adverse information to any person because of the customer's withholding payment of the disputed amount or related charges, until the billing entity has met the requirements of §308.7(d) and allowed the customer as many days thereafter to make payment as prescribed by §308.7(d)(3)(ii).

(2) *Reports on continuing disputes.* If a billing entity receives further notice from a customer within the time allowed for payment under §308.7(i)(1) that any portion of the billing error is still in dispute, a billing entity, providing carrier, vendor, or other agent may not report to any person that the customer's account is delinquent because of the customer's failure to pay that disputed amount unless the billing entity, providing carrier, vendor, or other agent also reports that the amount is in dispute and notifies the customer in writing of the name and address of each person to whom the vendor, billing entity, providing carrier, or other agent has reported the account as delinquent.

(3) *Reporting of dispute resolutions required.* A billing entity, providing carrier, vendor, or other agent shall report in writing any subsequent resolution of any matter reported pursuant to §308.7(i)(2) to all persons to whom such matter was initially reported.

(j) *Forfeiture of right to collect disputed amount.* Any billing entity, providing carrier, vendor, or other agent who fails to comply with the requirements of §§308.7(c), (d), (g), (h), or (i) forfeits any right to collect from the customer the amount indicated by the customer, under §308.7(b)(2), to be in error, and any late charges or other related charges thereon, up to $50 per transaction.

(k) *Prompt notification of returns and crediting of refunds.* When a vendor other than the billing entity accepts the return of property or forgives a debt for services in connection with a telephone-billed purchase, the vendor shall, within seven (7) business days from accepting the return or forgiving the debt, either:

(1) Mail or deliver a cash refund directly to the customer's address, and notify the appropriate billing entity that the customer has been given a refund, or

(2) Transmit a credit statement to the billing entity through the vendor's normal channels for billing telephone-billed purchases. The billing entity shall, within seven (7) business days after receiving a credit statement, credit the customer's account with the amount of the refund.

(l) *Right of customer to assert claims or defenses.* Any billing entity or providing carrier who seeks to collect charges from a customer for a telephone-billed purchase that is the subject of a dispute between the customer and the vendor shall be subject to all claims (other than tort claims) and defenses arising out of the transaction and relating to the failure to resolve the dispute that the customer could assert against the vendor, if the customer has made a good faith attempt to resolve the dispute with the vendor or providing carrier (other than the billing entity). The billing entity or providing carrier shall not be liable under this paragraph for any amount greater than the amount billed to the customer for the purchase (including any related charges).

(m) *Retaliatory actions prohibited.* A billing entity, providing carrier, vendor, or other agent may not accelerate any part of the customer's indebtedness or restrict or terminate the customer's access to pay-per-call services solely because the customer has exercised in good faith rights provided by this section.

(n) *Notice of billing error rights*—(1) *Annual statement.* (i) A billing entity shall mail or deliver to each customer, with the first billing statement for a telephone-billed purchase mailed or delivered after the effective date of these regulations, a statement of the customer's billing rights with respect to telephone-billed purchases. Thereafter the billing entity shall mail or deliver the billing rights statement at least once per calendar year to each customer to whom it has mailed or delivered a billing statement for a telephone-billed purchase during the previous twelve months. The billing rights statement shall disclose that the rights and obligations of the customer and the billing entity, set forth therein, are provided under the federal Telephone Disclosure and Dispute Resolution Act. The statement shall describe the procedure that the customer must follow to notify the billing entity of a billing error and the steps that the billing entity must take in response to the customer's notice. If the customer is permitted to provide oral notice of a billing error, the statement shall disclose that a customer who orally communicates an allegation of a billing error is presumed to have provided sufficient notice to initiate a billing review. The statement shall also disclose the customer's right to withhold payment of any disputed amount, and that any action to collect any disputed amount will be suspended, pending completion of the billing review. The statement shall further disclose the customer's rights and obligations if the billing entity determines that no billing error occurred, including what action the billing entity may take if the customer continues to withhold payment of the disputed amount. Additionally, the statement shall inform the customer of the billing entity's obligation to forfeit any disputed amount (up to $50 per transaction) if the billing entity fails to follow the billing and collection procedures prescribed by § 308.7 of this rule.

(ii) A billing entity that is a common carrier may comply with § 308.7(n)(1)(i) by, within 60 days after the effective date of these regulations, mailing or delivering the billing rights statement to all of its customers and, thereafter, mailing or delivering the billing rights statement at least once per calendar year, at intervals of not less than 6 months nor more than 18 months, to all of its customers.

(2) *Alternative summary statement.* As an alternative to § 308.7(n)(1), a billing entity may mail or deliver, on or with each billing statement, a statement that sets forth the procedure that a customer must follow to notify the billing entity of a billing error. The statement shall also disclose the customer's right to withhold payment of any disputed amount, and that any action to collect any disputed amount will be suspended, pending completion of the billing review.

(3) *General disclosure requirements.* (i) The disclosures required by § 308.7(n)(1) shall be made clearly and conspicuously on a separate statement that the customer may keep.

(ii) The disclosures required by § 308.7(n)(2) shall be made clearly and conspicuously and may be made on a separate statement or on the customer's billing statement. If any of the disclosures are provided on the back of the billing statement, the billing entity shall include a reference to those disclosures on the front of the statement.

(iii) At the billing entity's option, additional information or explanations may be supplied with the disclosures required by § 308.7(n), but none shall be stated, utilized, or placed so as to mislead or confuse the customer or contradict, obscure, or detract attention from the information required to be disclosed. The disclosures required by § 308.7(n) shall appear separately and above any other disclosures.

(o) *Multiple billing entities*. If a telephone-billed purchase involves more than one billing entity, only one set of disclosures need by given, and the billing entities shall agree among themselves which billing entity must comply with the requirements that this regulation imposes on any or all of them. The billing entity designated to receive and respond to billing errors shall remain the only billing entity responsible for complying with the terms of § 308.7(d). If a billing entity other than the one designated to receive and respond to billing errors receives notice of a billing error as described in § 308.7(b), that billing entity shall either: (1) Promptly transmit to the customer the name, mailing address, and business telephone number of the billing entity designated to receive and respond to billing errors; or (2) transmit the billing error notice within fifteen (15) days to the billing entity designated to receive and respond to billing errors. The time requirements in § 308.7(d) shall not begin to run until the billing entity designated to receive and respond to billing errors receives notice of the billing error, either from the customer or from the billing entity to whom the customer transmitted the notice.

(p) *Multiple customers*. If there is more than one customer involved in a telephone-billed purchase, the disclosures may be made to any customer who is primarily liable on the account.

§ 308.8 Severability.

The provisions of this rule are separate and severable from one another. If any provision is stayed or determined to be invalid, it is the Commission's intention that the remaining provisions shall continue in effect.

§ 308.9 Rulemaking review.

No later than four years after the effective date of this Rule, the Commission shall initiate a rulemaking review proceeding to evaluate the operation of the rule.

PART 309—LABELING REQUIREMENTS FOR ALTERNATIVE FUELS AND ALTERNATIVE FUELED VEHICLES

Subpart A—General

AUTHORITY: 42 U.S.C. 13232(a).

SOURCE: 60 FR 26955, May 19, 1995, unless otherwise noted.

Subpart A—General

§ 309.1 Definitions.

As used in subparts B and C of this part:

(a) *Acquisition* includes either of the following:

(1) Acquiring the beneficial title to a covered vehicle; or

(2) Acquiring a covered vehicle for transportation purposes pursuant to a contract or similar arrangement for a period of 120 days or more.

(b) *Aftermarket conversion system* means any combination of hardware which allows a vehicle or engine to operate on a fuel other than the fuel which the vehicle or engine was originally certified to use.

(c) *Alternative fuel* means

(1) Methanol, denatured ethanol, and other alcohols;

(2) Mixtures containing 85 percent or more by volume of methanol, denatured ethanol, and/or other alcohols (or such other percentage, but not less than 70 percent, as determined by the Secretary, by rule, to provide for requirements relating to cold start, safety, or vehicle functions), with gasoline or other fuels;

(3) Natural gas;

(4) Liquefied petroleum gas;

(5) Hydrogen;

(6) Coal-derived liquid fuels;

(7) Fuels (other than alcohol) derived from biological materials;

(8) Electricity (including electricity from solar energy); and

(9) Any other fuel the Secretary determines, by rule, is substantially not petroleum and would yield substantial energy security benefits and substantial environmental benefits.

(d)(1) *Consumer* in subpart C means an individual, corporation, partnership, association, State, municipality, political subdivision of a State, and any agency, department, or instrumentality of the United States.

(2) *Consumer or ultimate purchaser* in subpart B means, with respect to any non-liquid alternative vehicle fuel (including electricity), the first person who purchases such fuel for purposes other than resale.

(e) *Conventional fuel* means gasoline or diesel fuel.

(f) *Covered vehicle* means either of the following:

(1) A dedicated or dual fueled passenger car (or passenger car derivative) capable of seating 12 passengers or less; or

(2) A dedicated or dual fueled motor vehicle (other than a passenger car or passenger car derivative) with a gross vehicle weight rating less than 8,500 pounds which has a vehicle curb weight of less than 6,000 pounds and which has a basic vehicle frontal area of less than 45 square feet, which is:

(i) Designed primarily for purposes of transportation of property or is a derivation of such a vehicle; or

(ii) Designed primarily for transportation of persons and has a capacity of more than 12 persons; or

(3) Any vehicle that is—

(i) A new qualified fuel cell motor vehicle (as defined in 26 U.S.C. 30B(b)(3));

(ii) A new advanced lean burn technology motor vehicle (as defined in 26 U.S.C. 30B(c)(3));

(iii) A new qualified hybrid motor vehicle (as defined in 26 U.S.C. 30B(d)(3)); or

(iv) Any other type of vehicle that the Administrator of the Environmental Protection Agency demonstrates to the Secretary would achieve a significant reduction in petroleum consumption.

(g) *Dedicated* means designed to operate solely on alternative fuel.

(h) *Distributor* means any person, except a common carrier, who receives non-liquid alternative vehicle fuel (other than electricity) and distributes such fuel to another person other than the consumer. It also means any person, except a common carrier, who receives an electric vehicle fuel dispensing system and distributes such system to a retailer.

(i) *Dual fueled* means capable of operating on alternative fuel and capable of operating on conventional fuel.

(j) *Electric charging system equipment* means equipment that includes an electric battery charger and is used for dispensing electricity to consumers for the purpose of recharging batteries in an electric vehicle.

(k) *Electric vehicle* ("EV") means a vehicle designed to operate exclusively on electricity stored in a rechargeable battery, multiple batteries, or battery pack.

(l) *Electric vehicle fuel dispensing system* means electric charging system equipment or an electrical energy dispensing system.

(m) *Electrical energy dispensing system* means equipment that does not include an electric charger and is used for dispensing electricity to consumers for the purpose of recharging batteries in an electric vehicle that contains an on-board electric battery charger.

(n) *Emission certification standard* means the emission standard to which a covered vehicle has been certified pursuant to 40 CFR parts 86 and 88.

(o) *Estimated cruising range* for non-EVs means a manufacturer's reasonable estimate of the number of miles a new covered vehicle will travel between refueling, expressed as a lower estimate (i.e., minimum estimated cruising range) and an upper estimate (i.e., maximum estimated cruising range), as determined by § 309.22. Estimated cruising range for EVs means a manufacturer's reasonable estimate of the number of miles a new covered EV will travel between recharging, expressed as a single estimate, as determined by § 309.22.

(p) *Fuel dispenser* means:

(1) For non-liquid alternative vehicle fuels (other than electricity), the dispenser through which a retailer sells the fuel to consumers.

(2) For electric vehicle fuel dispensing systems, the dispenser through which a retailer dispenses electricity to consumers for the purpose of recharging batteries in an electric vehicle.

(q) *Fuel rating* means:

(1) For non-liquid alternative vehicle fuels (other than electricity), including, but not limited to, compressed natural gas and hydrogen gas, the commonly used name of the fuel with a disclosure of the amount, expressed as a minimum molecular percentage, of the principal component of the fuel. A disclosure of other components, expressed as a minimum molecular percentage, may be included, if desired.

(2) For electric vehicle fuel dispensing systems, a common identifier (such as, but not limited to, "electricity," "electric charging system," "electric charging station") with a disclosure of the system's kilowatt ("kW") capacity, voltage, whether the voltage is alternating current ("ac") or direct current ("dc"), amperage, and whether the system is conductive or inductive.

(r) *Manufacturer* means the person who obtains a certificate of conformity that the vehicle complies with the standards and requirements of 40 CFR parts 86 and 88.

(s) *Manufacturer of an electric vehicle fuel dispensing system* means any person who manufactures or assembles an electric vehicle fuel dispensing system that is distributed specifically for use by retailers in dispensing electricity to consumers for the purpose of recharging batteries in an electric vehicle.

(t) *New covered vehicle* means a covered vehicle which has not been acquired by a consumer.

(u) *New vehicle dealer* means a person who is engaged in the sale or leasing of new covered vehicles.

(v) *New vehicle label* means a window sticker containing the information required by § 309.20(e).

(w) *Non-liquid alternative fueled vehicle* means a vehicle capable of operating on a non-liquid alternative vehicle fuel.

(x) *Non-liquid alternative vehicle fuel* means alternative fuel used for the purpose of powering a non-liquid alternative fueled vehicle, including, but not limited to, compressed natural gas ("CNG"), hydrogen gas ("hydrogen"), electricity, and any other non-liquid vehicle fuel the Secretary determines, by rule, is substantially not petroleum and would yield substantial energy benefits and substantial environmental benefits.

(y) *Person* means an individual, partnership, corporation, or any other business organization.

(z) *Producer* means any person who purchases component elements and combines them to produce and market non-liquid alternative vehicle fuel (other than electricity).

(aa) *Refiner* means any person engaged in the production or importation of non-liquid alternative vehicle fuel (other than electricity).

(bb) *Retailer* means any person who offers for sale, sells, or distributes non-liquid alternative vehicle fuel (including electricity) to consumers.

(cc) *Secretary* means the Secretary of the United States Department of Energy.

(dd) *Vehicle fuel tank capacity* means the tank's usable capacity (i.e., the volume of fuel that can be pumped into the tank through the filler pipe with the vehicle on a level surface and with the unusable capacity already in the tank). The term does not include unusable capacity (i.e., the volume of fuel left at the bottom of the tank when the vehicle's fuel pump can no longer draw fuel from the tank), the vapor volume of the tank (i.e., the space above the fuel tank filler neck), or the volume of the fuel tank filler neck.

[60 FR 26955, May 19, 1995, as amended at 78 FR 23835, Apr. 23, 2013]

§ 309.2 What this part does.

This part establishes labeling requirements for non-liquid alternative vehicle fuels, and for certain vehicles powered in whole or in part by alternative fuels.

§ 309.3 Stayed or invalid portions.

If any portion of this part is stayed or held invalid, the rest of it will stay in force.

§ 309.4 Preemption.

Inconsistent state and local regulations are preempted to the extent they would frustrate the purposes of this part.

Subpart B—Requirements for Alternative Fuels

DUTIES OF IMPORTERS, PRODUCERS, AND REFINERS OF NON-LIQUID ALTERNATIVE VEHICLE FUELS (OTHER THAN ELECTRICITY) AND OF MANUFACTURERS OF ELECTRIC VEHICLE FUEL DISPENSING SYSTEMS

§ 309.10 Alternative vehicle fuel rating.

(a) If you are an importer, producer, or refiner of non-liquid alternative vehicle fuel (other than electricity), you must determine the fuel rating of all non-liquid alternative vehicle fuel (other than electricity) before you transfer it. You can do that yourself or through a testing lab. To determine fuel ratings, you must possess a reasonable basis, consisting of competent and reliable evidence, for the minimum percentage of the principal component of the non-liquid alternative vehicle fuel (other than electricity) that you must disclose, and for the minimum percentages of other components that you choose to disclose. For the purposes of this section, fuel ratings for the minimum percentage of the principal component of compressed natural gas are to be determined in accordance with test methods set forth in American Society for Testing and Materials ("ASTM") D 1945–91, "Standard Test Method for Analysis of Natural Gas by Gas Chromatography." For the purposes of this section, fuel ratings for the minimum percentage of the principal component of hydrogen gas are to be determined in accordance with test methods set forth in ASTM D 1946–90, "Standard Practice for Analysis of Reformed Gas by Gas Chromatography." This incorporation by reference was approved by the Director of the Federal Register in accordance with 5 U.S.C. 552(a) and 1 CFR part 51. Copies of D 1945–91 and D 1946–90 may be obtained from the American Society for Testing and Materials, 1916 Race Street, Philadelphia, PA 19103, or may be inspected at the Federal Trade Commission, Public Reference Room, room 130, 600 Pennsylvania Avenue, NW, Washington, DC, or at the National Archives and Records Administration (NARA). For information on the availability of this material at NARA, call 202–741–6030, or go to: *http://www.archives.gov/federal_register/code_of_federal_regulations/ibr_locations.html.*

(b) If you are a manufacturer of electric vehicle fuel dispensing systems, you must determine the fuel rating of the electric charge delivered by the electric vehicle fuel dispensing system before you transfer such systems. To determine the fuel rating of the electric vehicle fuel dispensing system, you must possess a reasonable basis, consisting of competent and reliable evidence, for the following output information you must disclose: kilowatt ("kW") capacity, voltage, whether the voltage is alternating current ("ac") or direct current ("dc"), amperage, and whether the system is conductive or inductive.

[60 FR 26955, May 19, 1995, as amended at 69 FR 18803, Apr. 9, 2004]

§309.11 Certification.

(a) For non-liquid alternative vehicle fuel (other than electricity), in each transfer you make to anyone who is not a consumer, you must certify the fuel rating of the non-liquid alternative vehicle fuel (other than electricity) consistent with your determination. You can do this in either of two ways:

(1) Include a delivery ticket or other paper with each transfer of non-liquid alternative vehicle fuel (other than electricity). It may be an invoice, bill of lading, bill of sale, terminal ticket, delivery ticket, or any other written proof of transfer. It must contain at least these four items:

(i) Your name;

(ii) The name of the person to whom the non-liquid alternative vehicle fuel (other than electricity) is transferred;

(iii) The date of the transfer; and

(iv) The fuel rating.

(2) Give the person a letter or written statement. This letter must include the date, your name, the other person's name, and the fuel rating of any non-liquid alternative vehicle fuel (other than electricity) you will transfer to that person from the date of the letter onwards. This letter of certification will be good until you transfer non-liquid alternative vehicle fuel (other than electricity) with a lower percentage of the principal component, or of any other component disclosed in the certification. When this happens, you must certify the fuel rating of the new non-liquid alternative vehicle fuel (other than electricity) either with a delivery ticket or by sending a new letter of certification.

(b) For electric vehicle fuel dispensing systems, in each transfer you make to anyone who is not a consumer, you must certify the fuel rating of the electric vehicle fuel dispensing system consistent with your determination. You can do this in either of two ways:

(1) Include a delivery ticket or other paper with each transfer of an electric vehicle fuel dispensing system. It may be an invoice, bill of lading, bill of sale, delivery ticket, or any other written proof of transfer. It must contain at least these five items:

(i) Your name;

(ii) The name of the person to whom the electric vehicle fuel dispensing system is transferred;

(iii) The date of the transfer;

(iv) The model number, serial number, or other identifier of the electric vehicle fuel dispensing system; and

(v) The fuel rating.

(2) Make the required certification by placing clearly and conspicuously on the electric vehicle fuel dispensing system a permanent legible marking or permanently attached label that discloses the manufacturer's name, the model number, serial number, or other identifier of the system, and the fuel rating. Such marking or label must be located where it can be seen after installation of the system. The marking or label will be deemed "legible," in terms of placement, if it is located in close proximity to the manufacturer's identification marking. This marking or label must be in addition to, and not a substitute for, the label required to be posted on the electric vehicle fuel dispensing system by the retailer.

(c) When you transfer non-liquid alternative vehicle fuel (other than electricity), or an electric vehicle fuel dispensing system, to a common carrier, you must certify the fuel rating of the non-liquid alternative vehicle fuel (other than electricity) or electric vehicle fuel dispensing system to the common carrier, either by letter or on the delivery ticket or other paper, or by a permanent marking or label attached to the electric vehicle fuel dispensing system by the manufacturer.

§309.12 Recordkeeping.

You must keep for one year records of how you determined fuel ratings. The records must be available for inspection by Federal Trade Commission staff members, or by people authorized by FTC.

DUTIES OF DISTRIBUTORS OF NON-LIQUID ALTERNATIVE VEHICLE FUELS (OTHER THAN ELECTRICITY) AND OF ELECTRIC VEHICLE FUEL DISPENSING SYSTEMS

§309.13 Certification.

(a) If you are a distributor of non-liquid alternative vehicle fuel (other than electricity), you must certify the fuel rating of the fuel in each transfer you make to anyone who is not a consumer. You may certify either by using a delivery ticket or other paper with each transfer of fuel, as outlined in § 309.11(a)(1), or by using a letter of certification, as outlined in § 309.11(a)(2).

(b) If you are a distributor of electric vehicle fuel dispensing systems, you must certify the fuel rating of the system in each transfer you make to anyone who is not a consumer. You may certify by using a delivery ticket or other paper with each transfer, as outlined in § 309.11(b)(1), or by using the permanent marking or permanent label attached to the system by the manufacturer, as outlined in § 309.11(b)(2).

(c) If you do not blend non-liquid alternative vehicle fuels (other than electricity), you must certify consistent with the fuel rating certified to you. If you blend non-liquid alternative vehicle fuel (other than electricity), you must possess a reasonable basis, consisting of competent and reliable evidence, as required by § 309.10(a), for the fuel rating that you certify for the blend.

(d) When you transfer non-liquid alternative vehicle fuel (other than electricity), or an electric vehicle fuel dispensing system, to a common carrier, you must certify the fuel rating of the non-liquid alternative vehicle fuel (other than electricity) or electric vehicle fuel dispensing system to the common carrier, either by letter or on the delivery ticket or other paper, or by a permanent marking or label attached to the electric vehicle fuel dispensing system by the manufacturer. When you receive non-liquid alternative vehicle fuel (other than electricity), or an electric vehicle fuel dispensing system, from a common carrier, you also must receive from the common carrier a certification of the fuel rating of the non-liquid alternative vehicle fuel (other than electricity) or electric vehicle fuel dispensing system, either by letter or on the delivery ticket or other paper, or by a permanent marking or label attached to the electric vehicle fuel dispensing system by the manufacturer.

§ 309.14 Recordkeeping.

You must keep for one year any delivery tickets, letters of certification, or other paper on which you based your fuel rating certifications for non-liquid alternative vehicle fuels (other than electricity) and for electric vehicle fuel dispensing systems. You also must keep for one year records of any fuel rating determinations you made according to § 309.10. If you rely for your certification on a permanent marking or permanent label attached to the electric vehicle fuel dispensing system by the manufacturer, you must not remove or deface the permanent marking or label. The records must be available for inspection by Federal Trade Commission staff members, or by persons authorized by FTC.

Duties of Retailers

§ 309.15 Posting of non-liquid alternative vehicle fuel rating.

(a) If you are a retailer who offers for sale or sells non-liquid alternative vehicle fuel (other than electricity) to consumers, you must post the fuel rating of each non-liquid alternative vehicle fuel. If you are a retailer who offers for sale or sells electricity to consumers through an electric vehicle fuel dispensing system, you must post the fuel rating of the electric vehicle fuel dispensing system you use. You must do this by putting at least one label on the face of each fuel dispenser through which you sell non-liquid alternative vehicle fuel. If you are selling two or more kinds of non-liquid alternative vehicle fuels with different fuel ratings from a single fuel dispenser, you must put separate labels for each kind of non-liquid alternative vehicle fuel on the face of the fuel dispenser.

(b)(1) The label, or labels, must be placed conspicuously on the fuel dispenser so as to be in full view of consumers and as near as reasonably practical to the price per unit of the non-liquid alternative vehicle fuel.

(2) You may petition for an exemption from the placement requirements by writing the Secretary of the Federal Trade Commission, Washington, DC 20580. You must state the reasons that you want the exemption.

(c) If you do not blend non-liquid alternative vehicle fuels (other than electricity), you must post consistent with the fuel rating certified to you. If you blend non-liquid alternative vehicle fuel (other than electricity), you must possess a reasonable basis, consisting of competent and reliable evidence, as required by § 309.10(a), for the fuel rating that you post for the blend.

(d)(1) You must maintain and replace labels as needed to make sure consumers can easily see and read them.

(2) If the labels you have are destroyed or are unusable or unreadable for some unexpected reason, you may satisfy this part by posting a temporary label as much like the required label as possible. You must still get and post the required label without delay.

(e) The following examples of fuel rating disclosures for CNG and hydrogen are meant to serve as illustrations of compliance with this part, but do not limit the rule's coverage to only the mentioned non-liquid alternative vehicle fuels (other than electricity):

(1) "CNG"

"Minimum"
"XXX%"
"Methane"

(2) "Hydrogen"

"Minimum"
"XXX%"
"Hydrogen"

(f) The following example of fuel rating disclosures for electric vehicle fuel dispensing systems is meant to serve as an illustration of compliance with this part:

"Electricity"
"XX kW"
"XXX vac/XX amps"
"Inductive"

(g) When you receive non-liquid alternative vehicle fuel (other than electricity), or an electric vehicle fuel dispensing system, from a common carrier, you also must receive from the common carrier a certification of the fuel rating of the non-liquid alternative vehicle fuel (other than electricity) or electric vehicle fuel dispensing system, either by letter or on the delivery ticket or other paper, or by a permanent marking or label attached to the electric vehicle fuel dispensing system by the manufacturer.

§ 309.16 Recordkeeping.

You must keep for one year any delivery tickets, letters of certification, or other paper on which you based your posting of fuel ratings for non-liquid alternative vehicle fuels. You also must keep for one year records of any fuel rating determinations you made according to § 309.10. If you rely for your posting on a permanent marking or permanent label attached to the electric vehicle fuel dispensing system by the manufacturer, you must not remove or deface the permanent marking or label. The required records, other than the permanent marking or label on the electric vehicle fuel dispensing system, may be kept at the retail outlet or at a reasonably close location. The records, including the permanent marking or label on each electric vehicle fuel dispensing system, must be available for inspection by Federal Trade Commission staff members or by persons authorized by FTC.

LABEL SPECIFICATIONS

§ 309.17 Labels.

All labels must meet the following specifications:

(a) *Layout:*

(1) *Non-liquid alternative vehicle fuel (other than electricity) labels with disclosure of principal component only.* The label is 3″ (7.62 cm) wide × 2½″ (6.35 cm) long. "Helvetica black" type is used throughout. All type is centered. The band at the top of the label contains the name of the fuel. This band should measure 1″ (2.54 cm) deep. Spacing of the fuel name is ¼″ (.64 cm) from the top of the label and 3⁄16″ (.48 cm) from the bottom of the black band, centered horizontally within the black band. The first line of type beneath the black band is ⅛″ (.32 cm) from the bottom of the black band. All type below the black band is centered horizontally, with ⅛″ (.32 cm) between lines. The bottom line of type is 3⁄16″ (.48 cm) from the bottom of the label. All type should fall no closer than 3⁄16″ (.48 cm) from the side edges of the label. If you wish to change the format of this single component label, you must petition the Federal Trade Commission. You can do this by writing to the Secretary of the

Federal Trade Commission, Washington, DC 20580. You must state the size and contents of the label that you wish to use, and the reasons that you want to use it.

(2) *Non-liquid alternative vehicle fuel (other than electricity) labels with disclosure of two components.* The label is 3″ (7.62 cm) wide × 2½″ (6.35 cm) long. "Helvetica black" type is used throughout. All type is centered. The band at the top of the label contains the name of the fuel. This band should measure 1″ (2.54 cm) deep. Spacing of the fuel name is ¼″ (.64 cm) from the top of the label and 3⁄16″ (.48 cm) from the bottom of the black band, centered horizontally within the black band. The first line of type beneath the black band is 3⁄16″ (.48 cm) from the bottom of the black band. All type below the black band is centered horizontally, with ⅛″ (.32 cm) between lines. The bottom line of type is ¼″ (.64 cm) from the bottom of the label. All type should fall no closer than 3⁄16″ (.48 cm) from the side edges of the label. If you wish to change the format of this two component label, you must petition the Federal Trade Commission. You can do this by writing to the Secretary of the Federal Trade Commission, Washington, DC 20580. You must state the size and contents of the label that you wish to use, and the reasons that you want to use it.

(3) *Electric vehicle fuel dispensing system labels.* The label is 3″ (7.62 cm) wide × 2½″ (6.35 cm) long. "Helvetica black" type is used throughout. All type is centered. The band at the top of the label contains the common identifier of the fuel. This band should measure 1″ (2.54 cm) deep. Spacing of the common identifier is ¼″ (.64 cm) from the top of the label and 3⁄16″ (.48 cm) from the bottom of the black band, centered horizontally within the black band. The first line of type beneath the black band is 3⁄16″ (.48 cm) from the bottom of the black band. All type below the black band is centered horizontally, with ⅛″ (.32 cm) between lines. The bottom line of type is ¼″ (.64 cm) from the bottom of the label. All type should fall no closer than 3⁄16″ (.48 cm) from the side edges of the label.

(b) *Type size and setting:*

(1) *Labels for non-liquid alternative vehicle fuels (other than electricity) with disclosure of principal component only.* All type should be set in upper case (all caps) "Helvetica Black" throughout. Helvetica Black is available in a variety of computer desk-top and phototypesetting systems. Its name may vary, but the type must conform in style and thickness to the sample provided here. The spacing between letters and words should be set as "normal." The type for the fuel name is 50 point (½″ (1.27 cm) cap height) knocked out of a 1″ (2.54 cm) deep band. The type for the words "MINIMUM" and the principal component is 24 pt. (¼″ (.64 cm) cap height). The type for percentage is 36 pt. (⅜″ (.96 cm) cap height).

(2) *Labels for non-liquid alternative vehicle fuels (other than electricity) with disclosure of two components.* All type should be set in upper case (all caps) "Helvetica Black" throughout. Helvetica Black is available in a variety of computer desk-top and phototypesetting systems. Its name may vary, but the type must conform in style and thickness to the sample provided here. The spacing between letters and words should be set as "normal." The type for the fuel name is 50 point (½″ 1.27 cm) cap height) knocked out of a 1″ (2.54 cm) deep band. All other type is 24 pt. (¼″ (.64 cm) cap height).

(3) *Labels for electric vehicle fuel dispensing systems.* All type should be set in upper case (all caps) "Helvetica Black" throughout. Helvetica Black is available in a variety of computer desk-top and photo-typesetting systems. Its name may vary, but the type must conform in style and thickness to the sample provided here. The spacing between letters and words should be set as "normal." The type for the common identifier is 50 point (½″ 1.27 cm) cap height) knocked out of a 1″ (2.54 cm) deep band. All other type is 24 pt. (¼″ (.64 cm) cap height).

(c) *Colors:* The background color on the labels for all non-liquid alternative vehicle fuels (including electricity), and the color of the knock-out type within the black band, is Orange: PMS 1495. All other type is process black. All borders are process black. All colors must be non-fade.

(d) *Contents.* Examples of the contents are shown in Figures 1 through 3. The proper fuel rating for each non-liquid alternative vehicle fuel (including electricity) must be shown. No marks or information other than that called for by this part may appear on the labels.

(e) *Special label protection.* All labels must be capable of withstanding extremes of weather conditions for a period of at least one year. They must be resistant to vehicle fuel, oil, grease, solvents, detergents, and water.

(f) *Illustrations of labels.* Labels must meet the specifications in this section and look like Figures 1 through 3 of appendix A, except the black print should be on the appropriately colored background.

Subpart C—Requirements for Alternative Fueled Vehicles

§ 309.20 Labeling requirements for new covered vehicles.

(a) Before offering a new covered vehicle for acquisition to consumers, manufacturers shall affix or cause to be affixed, and new vehicle dealers shall maintain or cause to be maintained, fuel economy labels as required by 40 CFR part 600. For dual fueled vehicles, such labels must include driving range information for alternative fuel and gasoline operation and be otherwise consistent with provisions in 40 CFR part 600.

(b) If an aftermarket conversion system is installed on a vehicle by a person other than the manufacturer prior to such vehicle's being acquired by a consumer, the manufacturer shall provide that person with the vehicle's fuel economy label prepared pursuant to 40 CFR part 600 and ensure that new fuel economy vehicle labels are affixed to such vehicles as required by paragraph (a) of this section.

[78 FR 23835, Apr. 23, 2013]

§ 309.21 Recordkeeping.

Manufacturers required to comply this subpart shall establish, maintain, and retain copies of all data, reports, records, and procedures used to meet the requirements of this subpart for three years after the end of the model year to which they relate. They must be available for inspection by Federal Trade Commission staff members, or by people authorized by the Federal Trade Commission.

[60 FR 26955, May 19, 1995. Redesignated at 78 FR 23835, Apr. 23, 2013]

APPENDIX A TO PART 309—FIGURES FOR PART 309

Figure 1

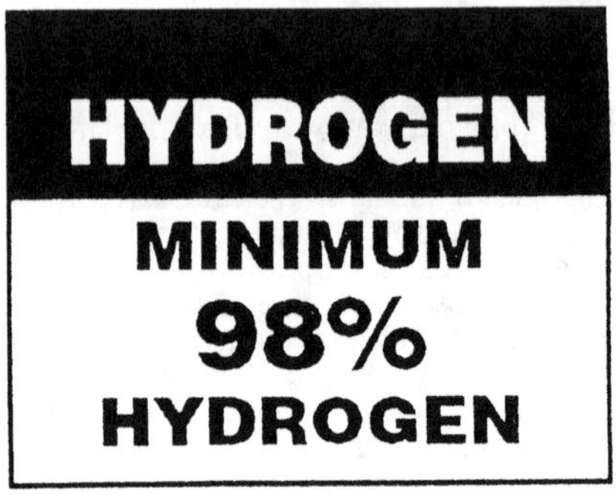

Figure 2

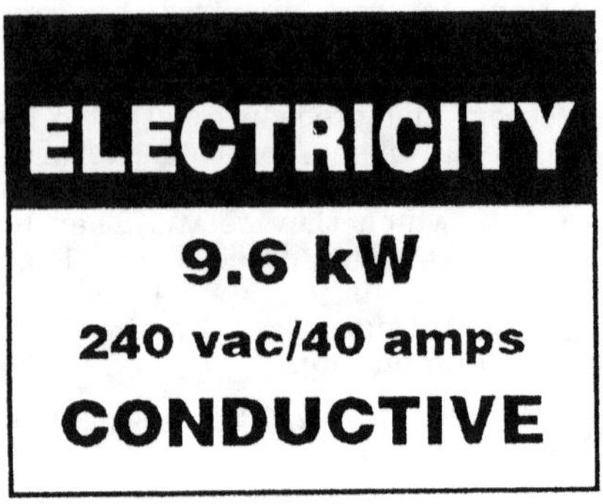

Figure 3

[60 FR 26955, May 19, 1995, as amended at 69 FR 55339, Sept. 14, 2004; 78 FR 23835, Apr. 23, 2013]

PART 310—TELEMARKETING SALES RULE 16 CFR PART 310

Sec.

AUTHORITY: 15 U.S.C. 6101–6108.

SOURCE: 75 FR 48516, Aug. 10, 2010, unless otherwise noted.

§ 310.1 Scope of regulations in this part.

This part implements the Telemarketing and Consumer Fraud and Abuse Prevention Act, 15 U.S.C. 6101-6108, as amended.

§ 310.2 Definitions.

(a) *Acquirer* means a business organization, financial institution, or an agent of a business organization or financial institution that has authority from an organization that operates or licenses a credit card system to authorize merchants to accept, transmit, or process payment by credit card through the credit card system for money, goods or services, or anything else of value.

(b) *Attorney General* means the chief legal officer of a state.

(c) *Billing information* means any data that enables any person to access a customer's or donor's account, such as a credit card, checking, savings, share or similar account, utility bill, mortgage loan account, or debit card.

(d) *Caller identification service* means a service that allows a telephone subscriber to have the telephone number, and, where available, name of the calling party transmitted contemporaneously with the telephone call, and displayed on a device in or connected to the subscriber's telephone.

(e) *Cardholder* means a person to whom a credit card is issued or who is authorized to use a credit card on behalf of or in addition to the person to whom the credit card is issued.

(f) *Cash-to-cash money transfer* means the electronic (as defined in section 106(2) of the Electronic Signatures in Global and National Commerce Act (15 U.S.C. 7006(2)) transfer of the value of cash received from one person to another person in a different location that is sent by a money transfer provider and received in the form of cash. For purposes of this definition, *money transfer provider* means any person or financial institution that provides cash-to-cash money transfers for a person in the normal course of its business, whether or not the person holds an account with such person or financial institution. The term *cash-to-cash money transfer* includes a remittance transfer, as defined in section 919(g)(2) of the Electronic Fund Transfer Act ("EFTA"), 15 U.S.C. 1693a, that is a cash-to-cash transaction; however it does not include any transaction that is:

(1) An electronic fund transfer as defined in section 903 of the EFTA;

(2) Covered by Regulation E, 12 CFR 1005.20, pertaining to gift cards; or

(3) Subject to the Truth in Lending Act, 15 U.S.C. 1601 *et seq.*

(g) *Cash reload mechanism* is a device, authorization code, personal identification number, or other security measure that makes it possible for a person to convert cash into an electronic (as defined in section 106(2) of the Electronic Signatures in Global and National Commerce Act (15 U.S.C. 7006(2)) form that can be used to add funds to a general-use prepaid card, as defined in Regulation E, 12 CFR 1005.2, or an account with a payment intermediary. For purposes of this definition, a cash reload mechanism is not itself a general-use prepaid debit card or a swipe reload process or similar method in which funds are added directly onto a person's own general-use prepaid card or account with a payment intermediary.

(h) *Charitable contribution* means any donation or gift of money or any other thing of value.

(i) *Commission* means the Federal Trade Commission.

(j) *Credit* means the right granted by a creditor to a debtor to defer payment of debt or to incur debt and defer its payment.

(k) *Credit card* means any card, plate, coupon book, or other credit device existing for the purpose of obtaining money, property, labor, or services on credit.

(l) *Credit card sales draft* means any record or evidence of a credit card transaction.

(m) *Credit card system* means any method or procedure used to process credit card transactions involving credit cards issued or licensed by the operator of that system.

(n) *Customer* means any person who is or may be required to pay for goods or services offered through telemarketing.

(o) *Debt relief service* means any program or service represented, directly or by implication, to renegotiate, settle, or in any way alter the terms of payment or other terms of the debt between a person and one or more unsecured creditors or debt collectors, including, but not limited to, a reduction in the balance, interest rate, or fees owed by a person to an unsecured creditor or debt collector.

(p) *Donor* means any person solicited to make a charitable contribution.

(q) *Established business relationship* means a relationship between a seller and a consumer based on:

(1) the consumer's purchase, rental, or lease of the seller's goods or services or a financial transaction between the

consumer and seller, within the eighteen (18) months immediately preceding the date of a telemarketing call; or

(2) the consumer's inquiry or application regarding a product or service offered by the seller, within the three (3) months immediately preceding the date of a telemarketing call.

(r) *Free-to-pay conversion* means, in an offer or agreement to sell or provide any goods or services, a provision under which a customer receives a product or service for free for an initial period and will incur an obligation to pay for the product or service if he or she does not take affirmative action to cancel before the end of that period.

(s) *Investment opportunity* means anything, tangible or intangible, that is offered, offered for sale, sold, or traded based wholly or in part on representations, either express or implied, about past, present, or future income, profit, or appreciation.

(t) *Material* means likely to affect a person's choice of, or conduct regarding, goods or services or a charitable contribution.

(u) *Merchant* means a person who is authorized under a written contract with an acquirer to honor or accept credit cards, or to transmit or process for payment credit card payments, for the purchase of goods or services or a charitable contribution.

(v) *Merchant agreement* means a written contract between a merchant and an acquirer to honor or accept credit cards, or to transmit or process for payment credit card payments, for the purchase of goods or services or a charitable contribution.

(w) *Negative option feature* means, in an offer or agreement to sell or provide any goods or services, a provision under which the customer's silence or failure to take an affirmative action to reject goods or services or to cancel the agreement is interpreted by the seller as acceptance of the offer.

(x) *Outbound telephone call* means a telephone call initiated by a telemarketer to induce the purchase of goods or services or to solicit a charitable contribution.

(y) *Person* means any individual, group, unincorporated association, limited or general partnership, corporation, or other business entity.

(z) *Preacquired account information* means any information that enables a seller or telemarketer to cause a charge to be placed against a customer's or donor's account without obtaining the account number directly from the customer or donor during the telemarketing transaction pursuant to which the account will be charged.

(aa) *Prize* means anything offered, or purportedly offered, and given, or purportedly given, to a person by chance. For purposes of this definition, chance exists if a person is guaranteed to receive an item and, at the time of the offer or purported offer, the telemarketer does not identify the specific item that the person will receive.

(bb) *Prize promotion* means:

(1) A sweepstakes or other game of chance; or

(2) An oral or written express or implied representation that a person has won, has been selected to receive, or may be eligible to receive a prize or purported prize.

(cc) *Remotely created payment order* means any payment instruction or order drawn on a person's account that is created by the payee or the payee's agent and deposited into or cleared through the check clearing system. The term includes, without limitation, a "remotely created check," as defined in Regulation CC, Availability of Funds and Collection of Checks, 12 CFR 229.2(fff), but does not include a payment order cleared through an Automated Clearinghouse (ACH) Network or subject to the Truth in Lending Act, 15 U.S.C. 1601 *et seq.*, and Regulation Z, 12 CFR part 1026.

(dd) *Seller* means any person who, in connection with a telemarketing transaction, provides, offers to provide, or arranges for others to provide goods or services to the customer in exchange for consideration.

(ee) *State* means any state of the United States, the District of Columbia, Puerto Rico, the Northern Mariana Islands, and any territory or possession of the United States.

(ff) *Telemarketer* means any person who, in connection with telemarketing, initiates or receives telephone calls to or from a customer or donor.

(gg) *Telemarketing* means a plan, program, or campaign which is conducted to induce the purchase of goods or services or a charitable contribution, by use of one or more telephones and which involves more than one interstate telephone call. The term does not include the solicitation of sales through the mailing of a catalog which: contains a written description or illustration of the goods or services offered for sale; includes the business address of the seller; includes multiple pages of written material or illustrations; and has been issued not less frequently than once a year, when the person making the solicitation does not solicit customers by telephone but only receives calls initiated by customers in response to the catalog and during those calls takes orders only without further solicitation. For purposes of the previous sentence, the term "further solicitation" does not include providing the customer with information about, or attempting to sell, any other item included in the same catalog which prompted the customer's call or in a substantially similar catalog.

(hh) *Upselling* means soliciting the purchase of goods or services following an initial transaction during a single telephone call. The upsell is a separate telemarketing transaction, not a continuation of the initial transaction. An "external upsell" is a solicitation made by or on behalf of a seller different from the seller in the initial transaction, regardless of whether the initial transaction and the subsequent solicitation are made by the same telemarketer. An "internal upsell" is a solicitation made by or on behalf of the same seller as in the initial transaction, regardless of whether the initial transaction and subsequent solicitation are made by the same telemarketer.

[75 FR 48516, Aug. 10, 2010, as amended at 80 FR 77557, Dec. 14, 2015]

§310.3 Deceptive telemarketing acts or practices.

(a) *Prohibited deceptive telemarketing acts or practices.* It is a deceptive telemarketing act or practice and a violation of this Rule for any seller or telemarketer to engage in the following conduct:

(1) Before a customer consents to pay[659] for goods or services offered, failing to disclose truthfully, in a clear and conspicuous manner, the following material information:

(i) The total costs to purchase, receive, or use, and the quantity of, any goods or services that are the subject of the sales offer;[660]

(ii) All material restrictions, limitations, or conditions to purchase, receive, or use the goods or services that are the subject of the sales offer;

(iii) If the seller has a policy of not making refunds, cancellations, exchanges, or repurchases, a statement informing the customer that this is the seller's policy; or, if the seller or telemarketer makes a representation about a refund, cancellation, exchange, or repurchase policy, a statement of all material terms and conditions of such policy;

(iv) In any prize promotion, the odds of being able to receive the prize, and, if the odds are not calculable in advance, the factors used in calculating the odds; that no purchase or payment is required to win a prize or to participate in a prize promotion and that any purchase or payment will not increase the person's chances of winning; and the no-purchase/no-payment method of participating in the prize promotion with either instructions on how to participate or an address or local or toll-free telephone number to which customers may write or call for information on how to participate;

[659] When a seller or telemarketer uses, or directs a customer to use, a courier to transport payment, the seller or telemarketer must make the disclosures required by §310.3(a)(1) before sending a courier to pick up payment or authorization for payment, or directing a customer to have a courier pick up payment or authorization for payment. In the case of debt relief services, the seller or telemarketer must make the disclosures required by §310.3(a)(1) before the consumer enrolls in an offered program.

[660] For offers of consumer credit products subject to the Truth in Lending Act, 15 U.S.C. 1601 *et seq.*, and Regulation Z, 12 CFR 226, compliance with the disclosure requirements under the Truth in Lending Act and Regulation Z shall constitute compliance with §310.3(a)(1)(i) of this Rule.

(v) All material costs or conditions to receive or redeem a prize that is the subject of the prize promotion;

(vi) In the sale of any goods or services represented to protect, insure, or otherwise limit a customer's liability in the event of unauthorized use of the customer's credit card, the limits on a cardholder's liability for unauthorized use of a credit card pursuant to 15 U.S.C. 1643;

(vii) If the offer includes a negative option feature, all material terms and conditions of the negative option feature, including, but not limited to, the fact that the customer's account will be charged unless the customer takes an affirmative action to avoid the charge(s), the date(s) the charge(s) will be submitted for payment, and the specific steps the customer must take to avoid the charge(s); and

(viii) In the sale of any debt relief service:

(A) the amount of time necessary to achieve the represented results, and to the extent that the service may include a settlement offer to any of the customer's creditors or debt collectors, the time by which the debt relief service provider will make a bona fide settlement offer to each of them;

(B) to the extent that the service may include a settlement offer to any of the customer's creditors or debt collectors, the amount of money or the percentage of each outstanding debt that the customer must accumulate before the debt relief service provider will make a bona fide settlement offer to each of them;

(C) to the extent that any aspect of the debt relief service relies upon or results in the customer's failure to make timely payments to creditors or debt collectors, that the use of the debt relief service will likely adversely affect the customer's creditworthiness, may result in the customer being subject to collections or sued by creditors or debt collectors, and may increase the amount of money the customer owes due to the accrual of fees and interest; and

(D) to the extent that the debt relief service requests or requires the customer to place funds in an account at an insured financial institution, that the customer owns the funds held in the account, the customer may withdraw from the debt relief service at any time without penalty, and, if the customer withdraws, the customer must receive all funds in the account, other than funds earned by the debt relief service in compliance with § 310.4(a)(5)(i)(A) through (C).

(2) Misrepresenting, directly or by implication, in the sale of goods or services any of the following material information:

(i) The total costs to purchase, receive, or use, and the quantity of, any goods or services that are the subject of a sales offer;

(ii) Any material restriction, limitation, or condition to purchase, receive, or use goods or services that are the subject of a sales offer;

(iii) Any material aspect of the performance, efficacy, nature, or central characteristics of goods or services that are the subject of a sales offer;

(iv) Any material aspect of the nature or terms of the seller's refund, cancellation, exchange, or repurchase policies;

(v) Any material aspect of a prize promotion including, but not limited to, the odds of being able to receive a prize, the nature or value of a prize, or that a purchase or payment is required to win a prize or to participate in a prize promotion;

(vi) Any material aspect of an investment opportunity including, but not limited to, risk, liquidity, earnings potential, or profitability;

(vii) A seller's or telemarketer's affiliation with, or endorsement or sponsorship by, any person or government entity;

(viii) That any customer needs offered goods or services to provide protections a customer already has pursuant to 15 U.S.C. 1643;

(ix) Any material aspect of a negative option feature including, but not limited to, the fact that the customer's account will be charged unless the customer takes an affirmative action to avoid the charge(s), the date(s) the charge(s) will be submitted for payment, and the specific steps the customer must take to avoid the charge(s); or

(x) Any material aspect of any debt relief service, including, but not limited to, the amount of money or the percentage of the debt amount that a customer may save by using such service; the amount of time necessary to achieve the represented results; the amount of money or the percentage of each outstanding debt that the customer must accumulate before the provider of the debt relief service will initiate attempts with the customer's creditors or debt collectors or make a bona fide offer to negotiate, settle, or modify the terms of the customer's debt; the effect of the service on a customer's creditworthiness; the effect of the service on collection efforts of the customer's creditors or debt collectors; the percentage or number of customers who attain the represented results; and whether a debt relief service is offered or provided by a non-profit entity.

(3) Causing billing information to be submitted for payment, or collecting or attempting to collect payment for goods or services or a charitable contribution, directly or indirectly, without the customer's or donor's express verifiable authorization, except when the method of payment used is a credit card subject to protections of the Truth in Lending Act and Regulation Z,[661] or a debit card subject to the protections of the Electronic Fund Transfer Act and Regulation E.[662] Such authorization shall be deemed verifiable if any of the following means is employed:

(i) Express written authorization by the customer or donor, which includes the customer's or donor's signature;[663]

(ii) Express oral authorization which is audio-recorded and made available upon request to the customer or donor, and the customer's or donor's bank or other billing entity, and which evidences clearly both the customer's or donor's authorization of payment for the goods or services or charitable contribution that are the subject of the telemarketing transaction and the customer's or donor's receipt of all of the following information:

(A) An accurate description, clearly and conspicuously stated, of the goods or services or charitable contribution for which payment authorization is sought;

(B) The number of debits, charges, or payments (if more than one);

(C) The date(s) the debit(s), charge(s), or payment(s) will be submitted for payment;

(D) The amount(s) of the debit(s), charge(s), or payment(s);

(E) The customer's or donor's name;

(F) The customer's or donor's billing information, identified with sufficient specificity such that the customer or donor understands what account will be used to collect payment for the goods or services or charitable contribution that are the subject of the telemarketing transaction;

(G) A telephone number for customer or donor inquiry that is answered during normal business hours; and

(H) The date of the customer's or donor's oral authorization; or

(iii) Written confirmation of the transaction, identified in a clear and conspicuous manner as such on the outside of the envelope, sent to the customer or donor via first class mail prior to the submission for payment of the customer's or donor's billing information, and that includes all of the information contained in §§ 310.3(a)(3)(ii)(A)-(G) and a clear and conspicuous statement of the procedures by which the customer or donor can obtain a refund from the seller or telemarketer or charitable organization in the event the confirmation is inaccurate; provided, however, that this means of authorization shall not be deemed verifiable in instances in which goods or services are offered in a transaction involving a free-to-pay conversion and preacquired account information.

(4) Making a false or misleading statement to induce any person to pay for goods or services or to induce a charitable contribution.

---

[661] Truth in Lending Act, 15 U.S.C. 1601 *et seq.*, and Regulation Z, 12 CFR part 226.

[662] Electronic Fund Transfer Act, 15 U.S.C. 1693 *et seq.*, and Regulation E, 12 CFR part 205.

[663] For purposes of this Rule, the term "signature" shall include an electronic or digital form of signature, to the extent that such form of signature is recognized as a valid signature under applicable federal law or state contract law.

(b) *Assisting and facilitating.* It is a deceptive telemarketing act or practice and a violation of this Rule for a person to provide substantial assistance or support to any seller or telemarketer when that person knows or consciously avoids knowing that the seller or telemarketer is engaged in any act or practice that violates §§ 310.3(a), (c) or (d), or § 310.4 of this Rule.

(c) *Credit card laundering.* Except as expressly permitted by the applicable credit card system, it is a deceptive telemarketing act or practice and a violation of this Rule for:

(1) A merchant to present to or deposit into, or cause another to present to or deposit into, the credit card system for payment, a credit card sales draft generated by a telemarketing transaction that is not the result of a telemarketing credit card transaction between the cardholder and the merchant;

(2) Any person to employ, solicit, or otherwise cause a merchant, or an employee, representative, or agent of the merchant, to present to or deposit into the credit card system for payment, a credit card sales draft generated by a telemarketing transaction that is not the result of a telemarketing credit card transaction between the cardholder and the merchant; or

(3) Any person to obtain access to the credit card system through the use of a business relationship or an affiliation with a merchant, when such access is not authorized by the merchant agreement or the applicable credit card system.

(d) *Prohibited deceptive acts or practices in the solicitation of charitable contributions.* It is a fraudulent charitable solicitation, a deceptive telemarketing act or practice, and a violation of this Rule for any telemarketer soliciting charitable contributions to misrepresent, directly or by implication, any of the following material information:

(1) The nature, purpose, or mission of any entity on behalf of which a charitable contribution is being requested;

(2) That any charitable contribution is tax deductible in whole or in part;

(3) The purpose for which any charitable contribution will be used;

(4) The percentage or amount of any charitable contribution that will go to a charitable organization or to any particular charitable program;

(5) Any material aspect of a prize promotion including, but not limited to: the odds of being able to receive a prize; the nature or value of a prize; or that a charitable contribution is required to win a prize or to participate in a prize promotion; or

(6) A charitable organization's or telemarketer's affiliation with, or endorsement or sponsorship by, any person or government entity.

[75 FR 48516, Aug. 10, 2010, as amended at 80 FR 77558, Dec. 14, 2015]

§ 310.4 Abusive telemarketing acts or practices.

(a) *Abusive conduct generally.* It is an abusive telemarketing act or practice and a violation of this Rule for any seller or telemarketer to engage in the following conduct:

(1) Threats, intimidation, or the use of profane or obscene language;

(2) Requesting or receiving payment of any fee or consideration for goods or services represented to remove derogatory information from, or improve, a person's credit history, credit record, or credit rating until:

(i) The time frame in which the seller has represented all of the goods or services will be provided to that person has expired; and

(ii) The seller has provided the person with documentation in the form of a consumer report from a consumer reporting agency demonstrating that the promised results have been achieved, such report having been issued more than six months after the results were achieved. Nothing in this Rule should be construed to affect the requirement in the Fair Credit Reporting Act, 15 U.S.C. 1681, that a consumer report may only be obtained for a specified permissible purpose;

(3) Requesting or receiving payment of any fee or consideration from a person for goods or services represented to recover or otherwise assist in the return of money or any other item of value paid for by, or promised to, that person in a previous transaction, until seven (7) business days after such money or other item is delivered to that person. This provision shall not

apply to goods or services provided to a person by a licensed attorney;

(4) Requesting or receiving payment of any fee or consideration in advance of obtaining a loan or other extension of credit when the seller or telemarketer has guaranteed or represented a high likelihood of success in obtaining or arranging a loan or other extension of credit for a person;

(5)(i) Requesting or receiving payment of any fee or consideration for any debt relief service until and unless:

(A) The seller or telemarketer has renegotiated, settled, reduced, or otherwise altered the terms of at least one debt pursuant to a settlement agreement, debt management plan, or other such valid contractual agreement executed by the customer;

(B) The customer has made at least one payment pursuant to that settlement agreement, debt management plan, or other valid contractual agreement between the customer and the creditor or debt collector; and

(C) To the extent that debts enrolled in a service are renegotiated, settled, reduced, or otherwise altered individually, the fee or consideration either:

(*1*) Bears the same proportional relationship to the total fee for renegotiating, settling, reducing, or altering the terms of the entire debt balance as the individual debt amount bears to the entire debt amount. The individual debt amount and the entire debt amount are those owed at the time the debt was enrolled in the service; or

(*2*) Is a percentage of the amount saved as a result of the renegotiation, settlement, reduction, or alteration. The percentage charged cannot change from one individual debt to another. The amount saved is the difference between the amount owed at the time the debt was enrolled in the service and the amount actually paid to satisfy the debt.

(ii) Nothing in §310.4(a)(5)(i) prohibits requesting or requiring the customer to place funds in an account to be used for the debt relief provider's fees and for payments to creditors or debt collectors in connection with the renegotiation, settlement, reduction, or other alteration of the terms of payment or other terms of a debt, provided that:

(A) The funds are held in an account at an insured financial institution;

(B) The customer owns the funds held in the account and is paid accrued interest on the account, if any;

(C) The entity administering the account is not owned or controlled by, or in any way affiliated with, the debt relief service;

(D) The entity administering the account does not give or accept any money or other compensation in exchange for referrals of business involving the debt relief service; and

(E) The customer may withdraw from the debt relief service at any time without penalty, and must receive all funds in the account, other than funds earned by the debt relief service in compliance with §310.4(a)(5)(i)(A) through (C), within seven (7) business days of the customer's request.

(6) Disclosing or receiving, for consideration, unencrypted consumer account numbers for use in telemarketing; provided, however, that this paragraph shall not apply to the disclosure or receipt of a customer's or donor's billing information to process a payment for goods or services or a charitable contribution pursuant to a transaction;

(7) Causing billing information to be submitted for payment, directly or indirectly, without the express informed consent of the customer or donor. In any telemarketing transaction, the seller or telemarketer must obtain the express informed consent of the customer or donor to be charged for the goods or services or charitable contribution and to be charged using the identified account. In any telemarketing transaction involving preacquired account information, the requirements in paragraphs (a)(7)(i) through (ii) of this section must be met to evidence express informed consent.

(i) In any telemarketing transaction involving preacquired account information and a free-to-pay conversion feature, the seller or telemarketer must:

(A) Obtain from the customer, at a minimum, the last four (4) digits of the account number to be charged;

(B) Obtain from the customer his or her express agreement to be charged for the goods or services and to be charged using the account number pursuant to paragraph (a)(7)(i)(A) of this section; and,

(C) Make and maintain an audio recording of the entire telemarketing transaction.

(ii) In any other telemarketing transaction involving preacquired account information not described in paragraph (a)(7)(i) of this section, the seller or telemarketer must:

(A) At a minimum, identify the account to be charged with sufficient specificity for the customer or donor to understand what account will be charged; and

(B) Obtain from the customer or donor his or her express agreement to be charged for the goods or services and to be charged using the account number identified pursuant to paragraph (a)(7)(ii)(A) of this section;

(8) Failing to transmit or cause to be transmitted the telephone number, and, when made available by the telemarketer's carrier, the name of the telemarketer, to any caller identification service in use by a recipient of a telemarketing call; provided that it shall not be a violation to substitute (for the name and phone number used in, or billed for, making the call) the name of the seller or charitable organization on behalf of which a telemarketing call is placed, and the seller's or charitable organization's customer or donor service telephone number, which is answered during regular business hours;

(9) Creating or causing to be created, directly or indirectly, a remotely created payment order as payment for goods or services offered or sold through telemarketing or as a charitable contribution solicited or sought through telemarketing; or

(10) Accepting from a customer or donor, directly or indirectly, a cash-to-cash money transfer or cash reload mechanism as payment for goods or services offered or sold through telemarketing or as a charitable contribution solicited or sought through telemarketing.

(b) *Pattern of calls.* (1) It is an abusive telemarketing act or practice and a violation of this Rule for a telemarketer to engage in, or for a seller to cause a telemarketer to engage in, the following conduct:

(i) Causing any telephone to ring, or engaging any person in telephone conversation, repeatedly or continuously with intent to annoy, abuse, or harass any person at the called number;

(ii) Denying or interfering in any way, directly or indirectly, with a person's right to be placed on any registry of names and/or telephone numbers of persons who do not wish to receive outbound telephone calls established to comply with paragraph (b)(1)(iii)(A) of this section, including, but not limited to, harassing any person who makes such a request; hanging up on that person; failing to honor the request; requiring the person to listen to a sales pitch before accepting the request; assessing a charge or fee for honoring the request; requiring a person to call a different number to submit the request; and requiring the person to identify the seller making the call or on whose behalf the call is made;

(iii) Initiating any outbound telephone call to a person when:

(A) That person previously has stated that he or she does not wish to receive an outbound telephone call made by or on behalf of the seller whose goods or services are being offered or made on behalf of the charitable organization for which a charitable contribution is being solicited; or

(B) That person's telephone number is on the "do-not-call" registry, maintained by the Commission, of persons who do not wish to receive outbound telephone calls to induce the purchase of goods or services unless the seller or telemarketer:

(*1*) Can demonstrate that the seller has obtained the express agreement, in writing, of such person to place calls to that person. Such written agreement shall clearly evidence such person's authorization that calls made by or on behalf of a specific party may be placed to that person, and shall include the telephone number to which the calls may be placed and the signature[664] of that person; or

[664] For purposes of this Rule, the term "signature" shall include an electronic or digital form of signature, to the extent that such form of signature is recognized as a

(*2*) Can demonstrate that the seller has an established business relationship with such person, and that person has not stated that he or she does not wish to receive outbound telephone calls under paragraph (b)(1)(iii)(A) of this section; or

(iv) Abandoning any outbound telephone call. An outbound telephone call is "abandoned" under this section if a person answers it and the telemarketer does not connect the call to a sales representative within two (2) seconds of the person's completed greeting.

(v) Initiating any outbound telephone call that delivers a prerecorded message, other than a prerecorded message permitted for compliance with the call abandonment safe harbor in § 310.4(b)(4)(iii), unless:

(A) In any such call to induce the purchase of any good or service, the seller has obtained from the recipient of the call an express agreement, in writing, that:

(i) The seller obtained only after a clear and conspicuous disclosure that the purpose of the agreement is to authorize the seller to place prerecorded calls to such person;

(ii) The seller obtained without requiring, directly or indirectly, that the agreement be executed as a condition of purchasing any good or service;

(iii) Evidences the willingness of the recipient of the call to receive calls that deliver prerecorded messages by or on behalf of a specific seller; and

(iv) Includes such person's telephone number and signature;[665] and

(B) In any such call to induce the purchase of any good or service, or to induce a charitable contribution from a member of, or previous donor to, a non-profit charitable organization on whose behalf the call is made, the seller or telemarketer:

(i) Allows the telephone to ring for at least fifteen (15) seconds or four (4) rings before disconnecting an unanswered call; and

(ii) Within two (2) seconds after the completed greeting of the person called, plays a prerecorded message that promptly provides the disclosures required by § 310.4(d) or (e), followed immediately by a disclosure of one or both of the following:

(A) In the case of a call that could be answered in person by a consumer, that the person called can use an automated interactive voice and/or keypress-activated opt-out mechanism to assert a Do Not Call request pursuant to § 310.4(b)(1)(iii)(A) at any time during the message. The mechanism must:

(1) Automatically add the number called to the seller's entity-specific Do Not Call list;

(2) Once invoked, immediately disconnect the call; and

(3) Be available for use at any time during the message; and

(B) In the case of a call that could be answered by an answering machine or voicemail service, that the person called can use a toll-free telephone number to assert a Do Not Call request pursuant to § 310.4(b)(1)(iii)(A). The number provided must connect directly to an automated interactive voice or keypress-activated opt-out mechanism that:

(1) Automatically adds the number called to the seller's entity-specific Do Not Call list;

(2) Immediately thereafter disconnects the call; and

(3) Is accessible at any time throughout the duration of the telemarketing campaign; and

(iii) Complies with all other requirements of this part and other applicable federal and state laws.

(C) Any call that complies with all applicable requirements of this paragraph (v) shall not be deemed to violate § 310.4(b)(1)(iv) of this part.

(D) This paragraph (v) shall not apply to any outbound telephone call that delivers a prerecorded healthcare message made by, or on behalf of, a covered entity or its business associate, as those terms are defined in the HIPAA Privacy Rule, 45 CFR 160.103.

(2) It is an abusive telemarketing act or practice and a violation of this Rule for any person to sell, rent, lease, purchase, or use any list established to comply with § 310.4(b)(1)(iii)(A), or

---

valid signature under applicable federal law or state contract law.

[665] For purposes of this Rule, the term "signature" shall include an electronic or digital form of signature, to the extent that such form of signature is recognized as a valid signature under applicable federal law or state contract law.

maintained by the Commission pursuant to § 310.4(b)(1)(iii)(B), for any purpose except compliance with the provisions of this Rule or otherwise to prevent telephone calls to telephone numbers on such lists.

(3) A seller or telemarketer will not be liable for violating § 310.4(b)(1)(ii) and (iii) if it can demonstrate that, as part of the seller's or telemarketer's routine business practice:

(i) It has established and implemented written procedures to comply with § 310.4(b)(1)(ii) and (iii);

(ii) It has trained its personnel, and any entity assisting in its compliance, in the procedures established pursuant to § 310.4(b)(3)(i);

(iii) The seller, or a telemarketer or another person acting on behalf of the seller or charitable organization, has maintained and recorded a list of telephone numbers the seller or charitable organization may not contact, in compliance with § 310.4(b)(1)(iii)(A);

(iv) The seller or a telemarketer uses a process to prevent telemarketing to any telephone number on any list established pursuant to § 310.4(b)(3)(iii) or 310.4(b)(1)(iii)(B), employing a version of the "do-not-call" registry obtained from the Commission no more than thirty-one (31) days prior to the date any call is made, and maintains records documenting this process;

(v) The seller or a telemarketer or another person acting on behalf of the seller or charitable organization, monitors and enforces compliance with the procedures established pursuant to § 310.4(b)(3)(i); and

(vi) Any subsequent call otherwise violating paragraph (b)(1)(ii) or (iii) of this section is the result of error and not of failure to obtain any information necessary to comply with a request pursuant to paragraph (b)(1)(iii)(A) of this section not to receive further calls by or on behalf of a seller or charitable organization.

(4) A seller or telemarketer will not be liable for violating § 310.4(b)(1)(iv) if:

(i) The seller or telemarketer employs technology that ensures abandonment of no more than three (3) percent of all calls answered by a person, measured over the duration of a single calling campaign, if less than 30 days, or separately over each successive 30-day period or portion thereof that the campaign continues.

(ii) The seller or telemarketer, for each telemarketing call placed, allows the telephone to ring for at least fifteen (15) seconds or four (4) rings before disconnecting an unanswered call;

(iii) Whenever a sales representative is not available to speak with the person answering the call within two (2) seconds after the person's completed greeting, the seller or telemarketer promptly plays a recorded message that states the name and telephone number of the seller on whose behalf the call was placed[666]; and

(iv) The seller or telemarketer, in accordance with § 310.5(b)-(d), retains records establishing compliance with § 310.4(b)(4)(i)-(iii).

(c) *Calling time restrictions.* Without the prior consent of a person, it is an abusive telemarketing act or practice and a violation of this Rule for a telemarketer to engage in outbound telephone calls to a person's residence at any time other than between 8:00 a.m. and 9:00 p.m. local time at the called person's location.

(d) *Required oral disclosures in the sale of goods or services.* It is an abusive telemarketing act or practice and a violation of this Rule for a telemarketer in an outbound telephone call or internal or external upsell to induce the purchase of goods or services to fail to disclose truthfully, promptly, and in a clear and conspicuous manner to the person receiving the call, the following information:

(1) The identity of the seller;

(2) That the purpose of the call is to sell goods or services;

(3) The nature of the goods or services; and

(4) That no purchase or payment is necessary to be able to win a prize or participate in a prize promotion if a prize promotion is offered and that any purchase or payment will not increase the person's chances of winning. This disclosure must be made before or in conjunction with the description of the prize to the person called. If requested

[666] This provision does not affect any seller's or telemarketer's obligation to comply with relevant state and federal laws, including but not limited to the TCPA, 47 U.S.C. 227, and 47 CFR part 64.1200.

by that person, the telemarketer must disclose the no-purchase/no-payment entry method for the prize promotion; provided, however, that, in any internal upsell for the sale of goods or services, the seller or telemarketer must provide the disclosures listed in this section only to the extent that the information in the upsell differs from the disclosures provided in the initial telemarketing transaction.

(e) *Required oral disclosures in charitable solicitations.* It is an abusive telemarketing act or practice and a violation of this Rule for a telemarketer, in an outbound telephone call to induce a charitable contribution, to fail to disclose truthfully, promptly, and in a clear and conspicuous manner to the person receiving the call, the following information:

(1) The identity of the charitable organization on behalf of which the request is being made; and

(2) That the purpose of the call is to solicit a charitable contribution.

[75 FR 48516, Aug. 10, 2010, as amended at 76 FR 58716, Sept. 22, 2011; 80 FR 77559, Dec. 14, 2015]

§ 310.5 Recordkeeping requirements.

(a) Any seller or telemarketer shall keep, for a period of 24 months from the date the record is produced, the following records relating to its telemarketing activities:

(1) All substantially different advertising, brochures, telemarketing scripts, and promotional materials;

(2) The name and last known address of each prize recipient and the prize awarded for prizes that are represented, directly or by implication, to have a value of $25.00 or more;

(3) The name and last known address of each customer, the goods or services purchased, the date such goods or services were shipped or provided, and the amount paid by the customer for the goods or services;[667]

(4) The name, any fictitious name used, the last known home address and telephone number, and the job title(s) for all current and former employees directly involved in telephone sales or solicitations; provided, however, that if the seller or telemarketer permits fictitious names to be used by employees, each fictitious name must be traceable to only one specific employee; and

(5) All verifiable authorizations or records of express informed consent or express agreement required to be provided or received under this Rule.

(b) A seller or telemarketer may keep the records required by § 310.5(a) in any form, and in the same manner, format, or place as they keep such records in the ordinary course of business. Failure to keep all records required by § 310.5(a) shall be a violation of this Rule.

(c) The seller and the telemarketer calling on behalf of the seller may, by written agreement, allocate responsibility between themselves for the recordkeeping required by this Section. When a seller and telemarketer have entered into such an agreement, the terms of that agreement shall govern, and the seller or telemarketer, as the case may be, need not keep records that duplicate those of the other. If the agreement is unclear as to who must maintain any required record(s), or if no such agreement exists, the seller shall be responsible for complying with §§ 310.5(a)(1)-(3) and (5); the telemarketer shall be responsible for complying with § 310.5(a)(4).

(d) In the event of any dissolution or termination of the seller's or telemarketer's business, the principal of that seller or telemarketer shall maintain all records as required under this section. In the event of any sale, assignment, or other change in ownership of the seller's or telemarketer's business, the successor business shall maintain all records required under this section.

§ 310.6 Exemptions.

(a) Solicitations to induce charitable contributions via outbound telephone calls are not covered by § 310.4(b)(1)(iii)(B) of this Rule.

(b) The following acts or practices are exempt from this Rule:

[667] For offers of consumer credit products subject to the Truth in Lending Act, 15 U.S.C. 1601 *et seq.*, and Regulation Z, 12 CFR 226, compliance with the recordkeeping requirements under the Truth in Lending Act, and Regulation Z, shall constitute compliance with § 310.5(a)(3) of this Rule.

(1) The sale of pay-per-call services subject to the Commission's Rule entitled "Trade Regulation Rule Pursuant to the Telephone Disclosure and Dispute Resolution Act of 1992," 16 CFR part 308, *provided*, however, that this exemption does not apply to the requirements of §§ 310.4(a)(1), (a)(7), (b), and (c);

(2) The sale of franchises subject to the Commission's Rule entitled "Disclosure Requirements and Prohibitions Concerning Franchising," ("Franchise Rule") 16 CFR part 436, and the sale of business opportunities subject to the Commission's Rule entitled "Disclosure Requirements and Prohibitions Concerning Business Opportunities," ("Business Opportunity Rule") 16 CFR part 437, *provided*, however, that this exemption does not apply to the requirements of §§ 310.4(a)(1), (a)(7), (b), and (c);

(3) Telephone calls in which the sale of goods or services or charitable solicitation is not completed, and payment or authorization of payment is not required, until after a face-to-face sales or donation presentation by the seller or charitable organization, *provided*, however, that this exemption does not apply to the requirements of §§ 310.4(a)(1), (a)(7), (b), and (c);

(4) Telephone calls initiated by a customer or donor that are not the result of any solicitation by a seller, charitable organization, or telemarketer, *provided*, however, that this exemption does not apply to any instances of upselling included in such telephone calls;

(5) Telephone calls initiated by a customer or donor in response to an advertisement through any medium, other than direct mail solicitation, *provided*, however, that this exemption does not apply to:

(i) Calls initiated by a customer or donor in response to an advertisement relating to investment opportunities, debt relief services, business opportunities other than business arrangements covered by the Franchise Rule or Business Opportunity Rule, or advertisements involving offers for goods or services described in § 310.3(a)(1)(vi) or § 310.4(a)(2) through (4);

(ii) The requirements of § 310.4(a)(9) or (10); or

(iii) Any instances of upselling included in such telephone calls;

(6) Telephone calls initiated by a customer or donor in response to a direct mail solicitation, including solicitations via the U.S. Postal Service, facsimile transmission, electronic mail, and other similar methods of delivery in which a solicitation is directed to specific address(es) or person(s), that clearly, conspicuously, and truthfully discloses all material information listed in § 310.3(a)(1), for any goods or services offered in the direct mail solicitation, and that contains no material misrepresentation regarding any item contained in § 310.3(d) for any requested charitable contribution; *provided*, however, that this exemption does not apply to:

(i) Calls initiated by a customer in response to a direct mail solicitation relating to prize promotions, investment opportunities, debt relief services, business opportunities other than business arrangements covered by the Franchise Rule or Business Opportunity Rule, or goods or services described in § 310.3(a)(1)(vi) or § 310.4(a)(2) through (4);

(ii) The requirements of § 310.4(a)(9) or (10); or

(iii) Any instances of upselling included in such telephone calls; and

(7) Telephone calls between a telemarketer and any business to induce the purchase of goods or services or a charitable contribution by the business, except calls to induce the retail sale of nondurable office or cleaning supplies; *provided*, however, that §§ 310.4(b)(1)(iii)(B) and 310.5 shall not apply to sellers or telemarketers of nondurable office or cleaning supplies.

[75 FR 48516, Aug. 10, 2010, as amended at 80 FR 77559, Dec. 14, 2015]

§ 310.7 Actions by states and private persons.

(a) Any attorney general or other officer of a state authorized by the state to bring an action under the Telemarketing and Consumer Fraud and Abuse Prevention Act, and any private person who brings an action under that Act, shall serve written notice of its action on the Commission, if feasible, prior to its initiating an action under this Rule. The notice shall be sent to the Office of the Director, Bureau of Consumer Protection, Federal Trade Commission, Washington, DC 20580, and shall include a copy of the state's or private person's complaint and any other pleadings to be filed with the court. If prior notice is not feasible, the state or private person shall serve the Commission with the required notice immediately upon instituting its action.

(b) Nothing contained in this Section shall prohibit any attorney general or other authorized state official from proceeding in state court on the basis of an alleged violation of any civil or criminal statute of such state.

§310.8 Fee for access to the National Do Not Call Registry.

(a) It is a violation of this Rule for any seller to initiate, or cause any telemarketer to initiate, an outbound telephone call to any person whose telephone number is within a given area code unless such seller, either directly or through another person, first has paid the annual fee, required by §310.8(c), for access to telephone numbers within that area code that are included in the National Do Not Call Registry maintained by the Commission under §310.4(b)(1)(iii)(B); provided, however, that such payment is not necessary if the seller initiates, or causes a telemarketer to initiate, calls solely to persons pursuant to §§310.4(b)(1)(iii)(B)(i) or (ii), and the seller does not access the National Do Not Call Registry for any other purpose.

(b) It is a violation of this Rule for any telemarketer, on behalf of any seller, to initiate an outbound telephone call to any person whose telephone number is within a given area code unless that seller, either directly or through another person, first has paid the annual fee, required by §310.8(c), for access to the telephone numbers within that area code that are included in the National Do Not Call Registry; provided, however, that such payment is not necessary if the seller initiates, or causes a telemarketer to initiate, calls solely to persons pursuant to §§310.4(b)(1)(iii)(B)(i) or (ii), and the seller does not access the National Do Not Call Registry for any other purpose.

(c) The annual fee, which must be paid by any person prior to obtaining access to the National Do Not Call Registry, is $63 for each area code of data accessed, up to a maximum of $17,406; *provided*, however, that there shall be no charge to any person for accessing the first five area codes of data, and *provided further*, that there shall be no charge to any person engaging in or causing others to engage in outbound telephone calls to consumers and who is accessing area codes of data in the National Do Not Call Registry if the person is permitted to access, but is not required to access, the National Do Not Call Registry under this Rule, 47 CFR 64.1200, or any other Federal regulation or law. No person may participate in any arrangement to share the cost of accessing the National Do Not Call Registry, including any arrangement with any telemarketer or service provider to divide the costs to access the registry among various clients of that telemarketer or service provider.

(d) Each person who pays, either directly or through another person, the annual fee set forth in paragraph (c) of this section, each person excepted under paragraph (c) from paying the annual fee, and each person excepted from paying an annual fee under §310.4(b)(1)(iii)(B), will be provided a unique account number that will allow that person to access the registry data for the selected area codes at any time for the twelve month period beginning on the first day of the month in which the person paid the fee ("the annual period"). To obtain access to additional area codes of data during the first six months of the annual period, each person required to pay the fee under paragraph (c) of this section must first pay $63 for each additional area code of data not initially selected. To obtain access to additional area codes of data during the second six months of the annual period, each person required to pay the fee under paragraph (c) of this section must first pay $32 for each additional area code of data not initially selected. The payment of the additional fee will permit the person to access the additional area codes of data for the remainder of the annual period.

(e) Access to the National Do Not Call Registry is limited to telemarketers, sellers, others engaged in or causing others to engage in telephone calls to consumers, service providers acting on behalf of such persons, and any government agency that has law enforcement authority. Prior to accessing the National Do Not Call Registry, a person must provide the identifying information required by the operator of the registry to collect the fee, and must certify, under penalty of law, that the person is accessing the registry solely to comply with the provisions of this Rule or to otherwise prevent telephone calls to telephone numbers on the registry. If the person is accessing the registry on behalf of sellers, that person also must identify each of the sellers on whose behalf it is accessing the registry, must provide each seller's unique account number for access to the national registry, and must certify, under penalty of law, that the sellers will be using the information gathered from the registry solely to comply with the provisions of this Rule or otherwise to prevent telephone calls to telephone numbers on the registry.

[75 FR 48516, Aug. 10, 2010; 75 FR 51934, Aug. 24, 2010, as amended at 77 FR 51697, Aug. 27, 2012; 78 FR 53643, Aug. 30, 2013; 79 FR 51478, Aug. 29, 2014; 80 FR 77560, Dec. 14, 2016; 81 FR 59845, Aug. 31, 2016; 82 FR 39534, Aug. 21, 2017; 83 FR 46640, Sept. 14, 2018]

§310.9 Severability.

The provisions of this Rule are separate and severable from one another. If any provision is stayed or determined to be invalid, it is the Commission's intention that the remaining provisions shall continue in effect.

PART 311—TEST PROCEDURES AND LABELING STANDARDS FOR RECYCLED OIL

Sec.

AUTHORITY: 42 U.S.C. 6363(d).

SOURCE: 60 FR 55421, Oct. 31, 1995, unless otherwise noted.

§311.1 Definitions.

As used in this part:

(a) *Manufacturer* means any person who re-refines or otherwise processes used oil to remove physical or chemical impurities acquired through use or who blends such re-refined or otherwise processed used oil with new oil or additives.

(b) *New oil* means any synthetic oil or oil that has been refined from crude oil and which has not been used and may or may not contain additives. Such term does not include used oil or recycled oil.

(c) *Processed used* oil means re-refined or otherwise processed used oil or blend of oil, consisting of such re-refined or otherwise processed used oil and new oil or additives.

(d) *Recycled oil* means processed used oil that the manufacturer has determined, pursuant to section 311.4 of this part, is substantially equivalent to new oil for use as engine oil.

(e) *Used oil* means any synthetic oil or oil that has been refined from crude oil, which has been used and, as a result of such use, has been contaminated by physical or chemical impurities.

(f) *Re-refined oil* means used oil from which physical and chemical contaminants acquired through use have been removed.

§311.2 Stayed or invalid parts.

If any part of this rule is stayed or held invalid, the rest of it will remain in force.

§311.3 Preemption.

No law, regulation, or order of any State or political subdivision thereof may apply, or remain applicable, to any container of recycled oil, if such law, regulation, or order requires any container of recycled oil, which container bears a label in accordance with the terms of §311.5 of this part, to bear any label with respect to the comparative characteristics of such recycled oil with new oil that is not identical to that permitted by §311.5 of this part.

§ 311.4 Testing.

To determine the substantial equivalency of processed used oil with new oil for use as engine oil, manufacturers or their designees must use the test procedures in API 1509, Engine Oil Licensing and Certification System, Seventeenth Edition, September 2012 (Addendum 1, October 2014, Errata, March 2015). The Director of the Federal Register approves this incorporation by reference in accordance with 5 U.S.C. 552(a) and 1 CFR part 51. You may obtain a copy from API, 1220 L Street NW, Washington, DC 20005; telephone: 202–682–8000; internet address: *https://www.api.org*. You may inspect a copy at the FTC Library, 202–326–2395, Federal Trade Commission, Room H–630, 600 Pennsylvania Avenue NW, Washington, DC 20580. It is also available for inspection at the National Archives and Records Administration (NARA). For information on the availability of this material at NARA, call 202–741–6030 or go to *http://www.archives.gov/federal_register/code_of_federal_regulations/ibr_locations.html*.

[83 FR 48216, Sept. 24, 2018]

§ 311.5 Labeling.

A manufacturer or other seller may represent, on a label on a container of processed used oil, that such oil is substantially equivalent to new oil for use as engine oil only if the manufacturer has determined that the oil is substantially equivalent to new oil for use as engine oil in accordance with the NIST test procedures prescribed under § 311.4 of this part, and has based the representation on that determination.

§ 311.6 Prohibited acts.

It is unlawful for any manufacturer or other seller to represent, on a label on a container of processed used oil, that such oil is substantially equivalent to new oil for use as engine oil unless the manufacturer or other seller has based such representation on the manufacturer's determination that the processed used oil is substantially equivalent to new oil for use as engine oil in accordance with the NIST test procedures prescribed under § 311.4 of this part. Violations will be subject to enforcement through civil penalties (as adjusted for inflation pursuant to § 1.98 of this chapter), imprisonment, and/or injunctive relief in accordance with the enforcement provisions of Section 525 of the Energy Policy and Conservation Act (42 U.S.C. 6395).

[60 FR 55421, Oct. 31, 1995, as amended at 65 FR 69666, Nov. 20, 2000]

PART 312—CHILDREN'S ONLINE PRIVACY PROTECTION RULE

Sec.

AUTHORITY: 15 U.S.C. 6501–6508.

SOURCE: 78 FR 4008, Jan. 17, 2013, unless otherwise noted.

§ 312.1 Scope of regulations in this part.

This part implements the Children's Online Privacy Protection Act of 1998, (15 U.S.C. 6501, *et seq.*,) which prohibits unfair or deceptive acts or practices in connection with the collection, use, and/or disclosure of personal information from and about children on the Internet.

§ 312.2 Definitions.

Child means an individual under the age of 13.

Collects or *collection* means the gathering of any personal information from a child by any means, including but not limited to:

(1) Requesting, prompting, or encouraging a child to submit personal information online;

(2) Enabling a child to make personal information publicly available in identifiable form. An operator shall not be considered to have collected personal information under this paragraph if it takes reasonable measures to delete all or virtually all personal information from a child's postings before they are made public and also to delete such information from its records; or

(3) Passive tracking of a child online.

Commission means the Federal Trade Commission.

Delete means to remove personal information such that it is not maintained in retrievable form and cannot be retrieved in the normal course of business.

Disclose or disclosure means, with respect to personal information:

(1) The release of personal information collected by an operator from a child in identifiable form for any purpose, except where an operator provides such information to a person who provides support for the internal operations of the Web site or online service; and

(2) Making personal information collected by an operator from a child publicly available in identifiable form by any means, including but not limited to a public posting through the Internet, or through a personal home page or screen posted on a Web site or online service; a pen pal service; an electronic mail service; a message board; or a chat room.

Federal agency means an agency, as that term is defined in Section 551(1) of title 5, United States Code.

Internet means collectively the myriad of computer and telecommunications facilities, including equipment and operating software, which comprise the interconnected world-wide network of networks that employ the Transmission Control Protocol/Internet Protocol, or any predecessor or successor protocols to such protocol, to communicate information of all kinds by wire, radio, or other methods of transmission.

Obtaining verifiable consent means making any reasonable effort (taking into consideration available technology) to ensure that before personal information is collected from a child, a parent of the child:

(1) Receives notice of the operator's personal information collection, use, and disclosure practices; and

(2) Authorizes any collection, use, and/or disclosure of the personal information.

Online contact information means an email address or any other substantially similar identifier that permits direct contact with a person online, including but not limited to, an instant messaging user identifier, a voice over internet protocol (VOIP) identifier, or a video chat user identifier.

Operator means any person who operates a Web site located on the Internet or an online service and who collects or maintains personal information from or about the users of or visitors to such Web site or online service, or on whose behalf such information is collected or maintained, or offers products or services for sale through that Web site or online service, where such Web site or online service is operated for commercial purposes involving commerce among the several States or with 1 or more foreign nations; in any territory of the United States or in the District of Columbia, or between any such territory and another such territory or any State or foreign nation; or between the District of Columbia and any State, territory, or foreign nation. This definition does not include any nonprofit entity that would otherwise be exempt from coverage under Section 5 of the Federal Trade Commission Act (15 U.S.C. 45). Personal information is *collected or maintained on behalf of* an operator when:

(1) It is collected or maintained by an agent or service provider of the operator; or

(2) The operator benefits by allowing another person to collect personal information directly from users of such Web site or online service.

Parent includes a legal guardian.

Person means any individual, partnership, corporation, trust, estate, cooperative, association, or other entity.

Personal information means individually identifiable information about an individual collected online, including:

(1) A first and last name;

(2) A home or other physical address including street name and name of a city or town;

(3) Online contact information as defined in this section;

(4) A screen or user name where it functions in the same manner as online contact information, as defined in this section;

(5) A telephone number;

(6) A Social Security number;

(7) A persistent identifier that can be used to recognize a user over time and across different Web sites or online services. Such persistent identifier includes, but is not limited to, a customer number held in a cookie, an Internet Protocol (IP) address, a processor or device serial number, or unique device identifier;

(8) A photograph, video, or audio file where such file contains a child's image or voice;

(9) Geolocation information sufficient to identify street name and name of a city or town; or

(10) Information concerning the child or the parents of that child that the operator collects online from the child and combines with an identifier described in this definition.

Release of personal information means the sharing, selling, renting, or transfer of personal information to any third party.

Support for the internal operations of the Web site or online service means:

(1) Those activities necessary to:

(i) Maintain or analyze the functioning of the Web site or online service;

(ii) Perform network communications;

(iii) Authenticate users of, or personalize the content on, the Web site or online service;

(iv) Serve contextual advertising on the Web site or online service or cap the frequency of advertising;

(v) Protect the security or integrity of the user, Web site, or online service;

(vi) Ensure legal or regulatory compliance; or

(vii) Fulfill a request of a child as permitted by §312.5(c)(3) and (4);

(2) So long as The information collected for the activities listed in paragraphs (1)(i)–(vii) of this definition is not used or disclosed to contact a specific individual, including through behavioral advertising, to amass a profile on a specific individual, or for any other purpose.

Third party means any person who is not:

(1) An operator with respect to the collection or maintenance of personal information on the Web site or online service; or

(2) A person who provides support for the internal operations of the Web site or online service and who does not use or disclose information protected under this part for any other purpose.

Web site or online service directed to children means a commercial Web site or online service, or portion thereof, that is targeted to children.

(1) In determining whether a Web site or online service, or a portion thereof, is directed to children, the Commission will consider its subject matter, visual content, use of animated characters or child-oriented activities and incentives, music or other audio content, age of models, presence of child celebrities or celebrities who appeal to children, language or other characteristics of the Web site or online service, as well as whether advertising promoting or appearing on the Web site or online service is directed to children. The Commission will also consider competent and reliable empirical evidence regarding audience composition, and evidence regarding the intended audience.

(2) A Web site or online service shall be deemed directed to children when it has actual knowledge that it is collecting personal information directly from users of another Web site or online service directed to children.

(3) A Web site or online service that is directed to children under the criteria set forth in paragraph (1) of this definition, but that does not target children as its primary audience, shall not be deemed directed to children if it:

(i) Does not collect personal information from any visitor prior to collecting age information; and

(ii) Prevents the collection, use, or disclosure of personal information from visitors who identify themselves as under age 13 without first complying with the notice and parental consent provisions of this part.

(4) A Web site or online service shall not be deemed directed to children solely because it refers or links to a commercial Web site or online service directed to children by using information location tools, including a directory, index, reference, pointer, or hypertext link.

§ 312.3 Regulation of unfair or deceptive acts or practices in connection with the collection, use, and/or disclosure of personal information from and about children on the Internet.

General requirements. It shall be unlawful for any operator of a Web site or online service directed to children, or any operator that has actual knowledge that it is collecting or maintaining personal information from a child, to collect personal information from a child in a manner that violates the regulations prescribed under this part. Generally, under this part, an operator must:

(a) Provide notice on the Web site or online service of what information it collects from children, how it uses such information, and its disclosure practices for such information (§ 312.4(b));

(b) Obtain verifiable parental consent prior to any collection, use, and/or disclosure of personal information from children (§ 312.5);

(c) Provide a reasonable means for a parent to review the personal information collected from a child and to refuse to permit its further use or maintenance (§ 312.6);

(d) Not condition a child's participation in a game, the offering of a prize, or another activity on the child disclosing more personal information than is reasonably necessary to participate in such activity (§ 312.7); and

(e) Establish and maintain reasonable procedures to protect the confidentiality, security, and integrity of personal information collected from children (§ 312.8).

§ 312.4 Notice.

(a) *General principles of notice.* It shall be the obligation of the operator to provide notice and obtain verifiable parental consent prior to collecting, using, or disclosing personal information from children. Such notice must be clearly and understandably written, complete, and must contain no unrelated, confusing, or contradictory materials.

(b) *Direct notice to the parent.* An operator must make reasonable efforts, taking into account available technology, to ensure that a parent of a child receives direct notice of the operator's practices with regard to the collection, use, or disclosure of personal information from children, including notice of any material change in the collection, use, or disclosure practices to which the parent has previously consented.

(c) *Content of the direct notice to the parent*—(1) *Content of the direct notice to the parent under § 312.5(c)(1) (Notice to Obtain Parent's Affirmative Consent to the Collection, Use, or Disclosure of a Child's Personal Information).* This direct notice shall set forth:

(i) That the operator has collected the parent's online contact information from the child, and, if such is the case, the name of the child or the parent, in order to obtain the parent's consent;

(ii) That the parent's consent is required for the collection, use, or disclosure of such information, and that the operator will not collect, use, or disclose any personal information from the child if the parent does not provide such consent;

(iii) The additional items of personal information the operator intends to collect from the child, or the potential opportunities for the disclosure of personal information, should the parent provide consent;

(iv) A hyperlink to the operator's online notice of its information practices required under paragraph (d) of this section;

(v) The means by which the parent can provide verifiable consent to the collection, use, and disclosure of the information; and

(vi) That if the parent does not provide consent within a reasonable time from the date the direct notice was sent, the operator will delete the parent's online contact information from its records.

(2) *Content of the direct notice to the parent under § 312.5(c)(2) (Voluntary Notice to Parent of a Child's Online Activities Not Involving the Collection, Use or Disclosure of Personal Information).* Where an operator chooses to notify a parent of a child's participation in a Web site or online service, and where such site or service does not collect any personal information other than the parent's online contact information, the direct notice shall set forth:

(i) That the operator has collected the parent's online contact information from the child in order to provide notice to, and subsequently update the parent about, a child's participation in a Web site or online service that does not otherwise collect, use, or disclose children's personal information;

(ii) That the parent's online contact information will not be used or disclosed for any other purpose;

(iii) That the parent may refuse to permit the child's participation in the Web site or online service and may require the deletion of the parent's online contact information, and how the parent can do so; and

(iv) A hyperlink to the operator's online notice of its information practices required under paragraph (d) of this section.

(3) *Content of the direct notice to the parent under § 312.5(c)(4) (Notice to a Parent of Operator's Intent to Communicate with the Child Multiple Times).* This direct notice shall set forth:

(i) That the operator has collected the child's online contact information from the child in order to provide multiple online communications to the child;

(ii) That the operator has collected the parent's online contact information from the child in order to notify the parent that the child has registered to receive multiple online communications from the operator;

(iii) That the online contact information collected from the child will not be used for any other purpose, disclosed, or combined with any other information collected from the child;

(iv) That the parent may refuse to permit further contact with the child and require the deletion of the parent's and child's online contact information, and how the parent can do so;

(v) That if the parent fails to respond to this direct notice, the operator may use the online contact information collected from the child for the purpose stated in the direct notice; and

(vi) A hyperlink to the operator's online notice of its information practices required under paragraph (d) of this section.

(4) *Content of the direct notice to the parent required under § 312.5(c)(5) (Notice to a Parent In Order to Protect a Child's Safety).* This direct notice shall set forth:

(i) That the operator has collected the name and the online contact information of the child and the parent in order to protect the safety of a child;

(ii) That the information will not be used or disclosed for any purpose unrelated to the child's safety;

(iii) That the parent may refuse to permit the use, and require the deletion, of the information collected, and how the parent can do so;

(iv) That if the parent fails to respond to this direct notice, the operator may use the information for the purpose stated in the direct notice; and

(v) A hyperlink to the operator's online notice of its information practices required under paragraph (d) of this section.

(d) *Notice on the Web site or online service.* In addition to the direct notice to the parent, an operator must post a prominent and clearly labeled link to an online notice of its information practices with regard to children on the home or landing page or screen of its Web site or online service, *and,* at each area of the Web site or online service where personal information is collected from children. The link must be in close proximity to the requests for information in each such area. An operator of a general audience Web site or online service that has a separate children's area must post a link to a notice of its information practices with regard to children on the home or landing page or screen of the children's area. To be complete, the online notice of the Web site or online service's information practices must state the following:

(1) The name, address, telephone number, and email address of all operators collecting or maintaining personal

information from children through the Web site or online service. *Provided that:* The operators of a Web site or online service may list the name, address, phone number, and email address of one operator who will respond to all inquiries from parents concerning the operators' privacy policies and use of children's information, as long as the names of all the operators collecting or maintaining personal information from children through the Web site or online service are also listed in the notice;

(2) A description of what information the operator collects from children, including whether the Web site or online service enables a child to make personal information publicly available; how the operator uses such information; and, the operator's disclosure practices for such information; and

(3) That the parent can review or have deleted the child's personal information, and refuse to permit further collection or use of the child's information, and state the procedures for doing so.

§ 312.5 Parental consent.

(a) *General requirements.* (1) An operator is required to obtain verifiable parental consent before any collection, use, or disclosure of personal information from children, including consent to any material change in the collection, use, or disclosure practices to which the parent has previously consented.

(2) An operator must give the parent the option to consent to the collection and use of the child's personal information without consenting to disclosure of his or her personal information to third parties.

(b) *Methods for verifiable parental consent.* (1) An operator must make reasonable efforts to obtain verifiable parental consent, taking into consideration available technology. Any method to obtain verifiable parental consent must be reasonably calculated, in light of available technology, to ensure that the person providing consent is the child's parent. (2) Existing methods to obtain verifiable parental consent that satisfy the requirements of this paragraph include:

(i) Providing a consent form to be signed by the parent and returned to the operator by postal mail, facsimile, or electronic scan;

(ii) Requiring a parent, in connection with a monetary transaction, to use a credit card, debit card, or other online payment system that provides notification of each discrete transaction to the primary account holder;

(iii) Having a parent call a toll-free telephone number staffed by trained personnel;

(iv) Having a parent connect to trained personnel via video-conference;

(v) Verifying a parent's identity by checking a form of government-issued identification against databases of such information, where the parent's identification is deleted by the operator from its records promptly after such verification is complete; or

(vi) *Provided that,* an operator that does not "disclose" (as defined by § 312.2) children's personal information, may use an email coupled with additional steps to provide assurances that the person providing the consent is the parent. Such additional steps include: Sending a confirmatory email to the parent following receipt of consent, or obtaining a postal address or telephone number from the parent and confirming the parent's consent by letter or telephone call. An operator that uses this method must provide notice that the parent can revoke any consent given in response to the earlier email.

(3) *Safe harbor approval of parental consent methods.* A safe harbor program approved by the Commission under § 312.11 may approve its member operators' use of a parental consent method not currently enumerated in paragraph (b)(2) of this section where the safe harbor program determines that such parental consent method meets the requirements of paragraph (b)(1) of this section.

(c) *Exceptions to prior parental consent.* Verifiable parental consent is required prior to any collection, use, or disclosure of personal information from a child *except* as set forth in this paragraph:

(1) Where the sole purpose of collecting the name or online contact information of the parent or child is to provide notice and obtain parental consent under § 312.4(c)(1). If the operator has not obtained parental consent after

a reasonable time from the date of the information collection, the operator must delete such information from its records;

(2) Where the purpose of collecting a parent's online contact information is to provide voluntary notice to, and subsequently update the parent about, the child's participation in a Web site or online service that does not otherwise collect, use, or disclose children's personal information. In such cases, the parent's online contact information may not be used or disclosed for any other purpose. In such cases, the operator must make reasonable efforts, taking into consideration available technology, to ensure that the parent receives notice as described in § 312.4(c)(2);

(3) Where the sole purpose of collecting online contact information from a child is to respond directly on a one-time basis to a specific request from the child, and where such information is not used to re-contact the child or for any other purpose, is not disclosed, and is deleted by the operator from its records promptly after responding to the child's request;

(4) Where the purpose of collecting a child's and a parent's online contact information is to respond directly more than once to the child's specific request, and where such information is not used for any other purpose, disclosed, or combined with any other information collected from the child. In such cases, the operator must make reasonable efforts, taking into consideration available technology, to ensure that the parent receives notice as described in § 312.4(c)(3). An operator will not be deemed to have made reasonable efforts to ensure that a parent receives notice where the notice to the parent was unable to be delivered;

(5) Where the purpose of collecting a child's and a parent's name and online contact information, is to protect the safety of a child, and where such information is not used or disclosed for any purpose unrelated to the child's safety. In such cases, the operator must make reasonable efforts, taking into consideration available technology, to provide a parent with notice as described in § 312.4(c)(4);

(6) Where the purpose of collecting a child's name and online contact information is to:

(i) Protect the security or integrity of its Web site or online service;

(ii) Take precautions against liability;

(iii) Respond to judicial process; or

(iv) To the extent permitted under other provisions of law, to provide information to law enforcement agencies or for an investigation on a matter related to public safety; and where such information is not be used for any other purpose;

(7) Where an operator collects a persistent identifier and no other personal information and such identifier is used for the sole purpose of providing support for the internal operations of the Web site or online service. In such case, there also shall be no obligation to provide notice under § 312.4; or

(8) Where an operator covered under paragraph (2) of the definition of *Web site or online service directed to children* in § 312.2 collects a persistent identifier and no other personal information from a user who affirmatively interacts with the operator and whose previous registration with that operator indicates that such user is not a child. In such case, there also shall be no obligation to provide notice under § 312.4.

§ 312.6 Right of parent to review personal information provided by a child.

(a) Upon request of a parent whose child has provided personal information to a Web site or online service, the operator of that Web site or online service is required to provide to that parent the following:

(1) A description of the specific types or categories of personal information collected from children by the operator, such as name, address, telephone number, email address, hobbies, and extracurricular activities;

(2) The opportunity at any time to refuse to permit the operator's further use or future online collection of personal information from that child, and to direct the operator to delete the child's personal information; and

(3) Notwithstanding any other provision of law, a means of reviewing any personal information collected from

the child. The means employed by the operator to carry out this provision must:

(i) Ensure that the requestor is a parent of that child, taking into account available technology; and

(ii) Not be unduly burdensome to the parent.

(b) Neither an operator nor the operator's agent shall be held liable under any Federal or State law for any disclosure made in good faith and following reasonable procedures in responding to a request for disclosure of personal information under this section.

(c) Subject to the limitations set forth in § 312.7, an operator may terminate any service provided to a child whose parent has refused, under paragraph (a)(2) of this section, to permit the operator's further use or collection of personal information from his or her child or has directed the operator to delete the child's personal information.

§ 312.7 Prohibition against conditioning a child's participation on collection of personal information.

An operator is prohibited from conditioning a child's participation in a game, the offering of a prize, or another activity on the child's disclosing more personal information than is reasonably necessary to participate in such activity.

§ 312.8 Confidentiality, security, and integrity of personal information collected from children.

The operator must establish and maintain reasonable procedures to protect the confidentiality, security, and integrity of personal information collected from children. The operator must also take reasonable steps to release children's personal information only to service providers and third parties who are capable of maintaining the confidentiality, security and integrity of such information, and who provide assurances that they will maintain the information in such a manner.

§ 312.9 Enforcement.

Subject to sections 6503 and 6505 of the Children's Online Privacy Protection Act of 1998, a violation of a regulation prescribed under section 6502 (a) of this Act shall be treated as a violation of a rule defining an unfair or deceptive act or practice prescribed under section 18(a)(1)(B) of the Federal Trade Commission Act (15 U.S.C. 57a(a)(1)(B)).

§ 312.10 Data retention and deletion requirements.

An operator of a Web site or online service shall retain personal information collected online from a child for only as long as is reasonably necessary to fulfill the purpose for which the information was collected. The operator must delete such information using reasonable measures to protect against unauthorized access to, or use of, the information in connection with its deletion.

§ 312.11 Safe harbor programs.

(a) *In general.* Industry groups or other persons may apply to the Commission for approval of self-regulatory program guidelines ("safe harbor programs"). The application shall be filed with the Commission's Office of the Secretary. The Commission will publish in the FEDERAL REGISTER a document seeking public comment on the application. The Commission shall issue a written determination within 180 days of the filing of the application.

(b) *Criteria for approval of self-regulatory program guidelines.* Proposed safe harbor programs must demonstrate that they meet the following performance standards:

(1) Program requirements that ensure operators subject to the self-regulatory program guidelines ("subject operators") provide substantially the same or greater protections for children as those contained in §§ 312.2 through 312.8, and 312.10.

(2) An effective, mandatory mechanism for the independent assessment of subject operators' compliance with the self-regulatory program guidelines. At a minimum, this mechanism must include a comprehensive review by the safe harbor program, to be conducted not less than annually, of each subject operator's information policies, practices, and representations. The assessment mechanism required under this paragraph can be provided by an independent enforcement program, such as a seal program.

(3) Disciplinary actions for subject operators' non-compliance with self-regulatory program guidelines. This performance standard may be satisfied by:

(i) Mandatory, public reporting of any action taken against subject operators by the industry group issuing the self-regulatory guidelines;

(ii) Consumer redress;

(iii) Voluntary payments to the United States Treasury in connection with an industry-directed program for violators of the self-regulatory guidelines;

(iv) Referral to the Commission of operators who engage in a pattern or practice of violating the self-regulatory guidelines; or

(v) Any other equally effective action.

(c) *Request for Commission approval of self-regulatory program guidelines.* A proposed safe harbor program's request for approval shall be accompanied by the following:

(1) A detailed explanation of the applicant's business model, and the technological capabilities and mechanisms that will be used for initial and continuing assessment of subject operators' fitness for membership in the safe harbor program;

(2) A copy of the full text of the guidelines for which approval is sought and any accompanying commentary;

(3) A comparison of each provision of §§312.2 through 312.8, and 312.10 with the corresponding provisions of the guidelines; and

(4) A statement explaining:

(i) How the self-regulatory program guidelines, including the applicable assessment mechanisms, meet the requirements of this part; and

(ii) How the assessment mechanisms and compliance consequences required under paragraphs (b)(2) and (b)(3) provide effective enforcement of the requirements of this part.

(d) *Reporting and recordkeeping requirements.* Approved safe harbor programs shall:

(1) By July 1, 2014, and annually thereafter, submit a report to the Commission containing, at a minimum, an aggregated summary of the results of the independent assessments conducted under paragraph (b)(2) of this section, a description of any disciplinary action taken against any subject operator under paragraph (b)(3) of this section, and a description of any approvals of member operators' use of a parental consent mechanism, pursuant to §312.5(b)(3);

(2) Promptly respond to Commission requests for additional information; and

(3) Maintain for a period not less than three years, and upon request make available to the Commission for inspection and copying:

(i) Consumer complaints alleging violations of the guidelines by subject operators;

(ii) Records of disciplinary actions taken against subject operators; and

(iii) Results of the independent assessments of subject operators' compliance required under paragraph (b)(2) of this section.

(e) *Post-approval modifications to self-regulatory program guidelines.* Approved safe harbor programs must submit proposed changes to their guidelines for review and approval by the Commission in the manner required for initial approval of guidelines under paragraph (c)(2) of this section. The statement required under paragraph (c)(4) of this section must describe how the proposed changes affect existing provisions of the guidelines.

(f) *Revocation of approval of self-regulatory program guidelines.* The Commission reserves the right to revoke any approval granted under this section if at any time it determines that the approved self-regulatory program guidelines or their implementation do not meet the requirements of this part. Safe harbor programs that were approved prior to the publication of the Final Rule amendments must, by March 1, 2013, submit proposed modifications to their guidelines that would bring them into compliance with such amendments, or their approval shall be revoked.

(g) *Operators' participation in a safe harbor program.* An operator will be deemed to be in compliance with the requirements of §§312.2 through 312.8, and 312.10 if that operator complies with Commission-approved safe harbor program guidelines. In considering whether to initiate an investigation or bring an enforcement action against a subject operator for violations of this part, the Commission will take into account the history of the subject operator's participation in the safe harbor program, whether the subject operator has taken action to remedy such non-compliance, and whether the operator's non-compliance resulted in any one of the disciplinary actions set forth in paragraph (b)(3).

[78 FR 4008, Jan. 17, 2013, as amended at 78 FR 76986, Dec. 20, 2013]

§ 312.12 Voluntary Commission Approval Processes.

(a) *Parental consent methods.* An interested party may file a written request for Commission approval of parental consent methods not currently enumerated in § 312.5(b). To be considered for approval, a party must provide a detailed description of the proposed parental consent methods, together with an analysis of how the methods meet § 312.5(b)(1). The request shall be filed with the Commission's Office of the Secretary. The Commission will publish in the FEDERAL REGISTER a document seeking public comment on the request. The Commission shall issue a written determination within 120 days of the filing of the request; and

(b) *Support for internal operations of the Web site or online service.* An interested party may file a written request for Commission approval of additional activities to be included within the definition of support for internal operations. To be considered for approval, a party must provide a detailed justification why such activities should be deemed support for internal operations, and an analysis of their potential effects on children's online privacy. The request shall be filed with the Commission's Office of the Secretary. The Commission will publish in the FEDERAL REGISTER a document seeking public comment on the request. The Commission shall issue a written determination within 120 days of the filing of the request.

§ 312.13 Severability.

The provisions of this part are separate and severable from one another. If any provision is stayed or determined to be invalid, it is the Commission's intention that the remaining provisions shall continue in effect.

PART 313—PRIVACY OF CONSUMER FINANCIAL INFORMATION

AUTHORITY: 15 U.S.C. 6801 *et seq.*

SOURCE: 65 FR 33677, May 24, 2000, unless otherwise noted.

§313.1 Purpose and scope.

(a) *Purpose.* This part governs the treatment of nonpublic personal information about consumers by the financial institutions listed in paragraph (b) of this section. This part:

(1) Requires a financial institution in specified circumstances to provide notice to customers about its privacy policies and practices;

(2) Describes the conditions under which a financial institution may disclose nonpublic personal information about consumers to nonaffiliated third parties; and

(3) Provides a method for consumers to prevent a financial institution from disclosing that information to most nonaffiliated third parties by "opting out" of that disclosure, subject to the exceptions in §§313.13, 313.14, and 313.15.

(b) *Scope.* This part applies only to nonpublic personal information about individuals who obtain financial products or services primarily for personal, family or household purposes from the institutions listed below. This part does not apply to information about companies or about individuals who obtain financial products or services for business, commercial, or agricultural purposes. This part applies to those "financial institutions" and "other persons" over which the Federal Trade Commission ("Commission") has enforcement authority pursuant to Section 505(a)(7) of the Gramm-Leach-Bliley Act. An entity is a "financial institution" if its business is engaging in a financial activity as described in Section 4(k) of the Bank Holding Company Act of 1956, 12 U.S.C. 1843(k), which incorporates by reference activities enumerated by the Federal Reserve Board in 12 CFR 211.5(d) and 12 CFR 225.28. The "financial institutions" subject to the Commission's enforcement authority are those that are not otherwise subject to the enforcement authority of another regulator under Section 505 of the Gramm-Leach-Bliley Act. More specifically, those entities include, but are not limited to, mortgage lenders, "pay day" lenders, finance companies, mortgage brokers, account servicers, check cashers, wire transferors, travel agencies operated in connection with financial services, collection agencies, credit counselors and other financial advisors, tax preparation firms, non-federally insured credit unions, and investment advisors that are not required to register with the Securities and Exchange Commission. They are referred to in this part as "You." The "other persons" to whom this part applies are third parties that are not financial institutions, but that receive nonpublic personal information from financial institutions with whom they are not affiliated. Nothing in this part modifies, limits, or supersedes the standards governing individually identifiable health information promulgated by the Secretary of Health and Human Services under the authority of sections 262 and 264 of the Health Insurance Portability and Accountability Act of 1996, 42 U.S.C. 1320d–1320d–8. Any institution of higher education that complies with the Federal Educational Rights and Privacy Act ("FERPA"), 20 U.S.C. 1232g, and its implementing regulations, 34 CFR part 99, and that is also a financial institution subject to the requirements of this part, shall be deemed to be in compliance with this part if it is in compliance with FERPA.

§313.2 Model privacy form and examples.

(a) *Model privacy form.* Use of the model privacy form in appendix A of this part, consistent with the instructions in appendix A, constitutes compliance with the notice content requirements of §§313.6 and 313.7 of this part, although use of the model privacy form is not required.

(b) *Examples.* The examples in this part are not exclusive. Compliance with an example, to the extent applicable, constitutes compliance with this part.

[74 FR 62965, Dec. 1, 2009]

§313.3 Definitions.

As used in this part, unless the context requires otherwise:

(a) *Affiliate* means any company that controls, is controlled by, or is under common control with another company.

(b)(1) *Clear and conspicuous* means that a notice is reasonably understandable and designed to call attention to the nature and significance of the information in the notice.

(2) *Examples*—(i) *Reasonably understandable.* You make your notice reasonably understandable if you:

(A) Present the information in the notice in clear, concise sentences, paragraphs, and sections;

(B) Use short explanatory sentences or bullet lists whenever possible;

(C) Use definite, concrete, everyday words and active voice whenever possible;

(D) Avoid multiple negatives;

(E) Avoid legal and highly technical business terminology whenever possible; and

(F) Avoid explanations that are imprecise and readily subject to different interpretations.

(ii) *Designed to call attention.* You design your notice to call attention to the nature and significance of the information in it if you:

(A) Use a plain-language heading to call attention to the notice;

(B) Use a typeface and type size that are easy to read;

(C) Provide wide margins and ample line spacing;

(D) Use boldface or italics for key words; and

(E) In a form that combines your notice with other information, use distinctive type size, style, and graphic devices, such as shading or sidebars, when you combine your notice with other information.

(iii) *Notices on web sites.* If you provide a notice on a web page, you design your notice to call attention to the nature and significance of the information in it if you use text or visual cues to encourage scrolling down the page if necessary to view the entire notice and ensure that other elements on the web site (such as text, graphics, hyperlinks, or sound) do not distract attention from the notice, and you either:

(A) Place the notice on a screen that consumers frequently access, such as a page on which transactions are conducted; or

(B) Place a link on a screen that consumers frequently access, such as a page on which transactions are conducted, that connects directly to the notice and is labeled appropriately to convey the importance, nature and relevance of the notice.

(c) *Collect* means to obtain information that you organize or can retrieve by the name of an individual or by identifying number, symbol, or other identifying particular assigned to the individual, irrespective of the source of the underlying information.

(d) *Company* means any corporation, limited liability company, business trust, general or limited partnership, association, or similar organization.

(e)(1) *Consumer* means an individual who obtains or has obtained a financial product or service from you that is to be used primarily for personal, family, or household purposes, or that individual's legal representative.

(2) *Examples*—(i) An individual who applies to you for credit for personal, family, or household purposes is a consumer of a financial service, regardless of whether the credit is extended.

(ii) An individual who provides nonpublic personal information to you in order to obtain a determination about whether he or she may qualify for a loan to be used primarily for personal, family, or household purposes is a consumer of a financial service, regardless of whether the loan is extended.

(iii) An individual who provides nonpublic personal information to you in connection with obtaining or seeking to obtain financial, investment, or economic advisory services is a consumer, regardless of whether you establish a continuing advisory relationship.

(iv) If you hold ownership or servicing rights to an individual's loan that is used primarily for personal, family, or household purposes, the individual is your consumer, even if you hold those rights in conjunction with one or more other institutions. (The individual is also a consumer with respect to the other financial institutions involved.) An individual who has a loan in which you have ownership or servicing rights is your consumer, even if you, or another institution with those rights, hire an agent to collect on the loan.

(v) An individual who is a consumer of another financial institution is not your consumer solely because you act as agent for, or provide processing or other services to, that financial institution.

(vi) An individual is not your consumer solely because he or she has designated you as trustee for a trust.

(vii) An individual is not your consumer solely because he or she is a beneficiary of a trust for which you are a trustee.

(viii) An individual is not your consumer solely because he or she is a participant or a beneficiary of an employee benefit plan that you sponsor or for which you act as a trustee or fiduciary.

(f) *Consumer reporting agency* has the same meaning as in section 603(f) of the Fair Credit Reporting Act (15 U.S.C. 1681a(f)).

(g) *Control* of a company means:

(1) Ownership, control, or power to vote 25 percent or more of the outstanding shares of any class of voting security of the company, directly or indirectly, or acting through one or more other persons;

(2) Control in any manner over the election of a majority of the directors, trustees, or general partners (or individuals exercising similar functions) of the company; or

(3) The power to exercise, directly or indirectly, a controlling influence over the management or policies of the company.

(h) *Customer* means a consumer who has a customer relationship with you.

(i)(1) *Customer relationship* means a continuing relationship between a consumer and you under which you provide one or more financial products or services to the consumer that are to be used primarily for personal, family, or household purposes.

(2) *Examples*—(i) *Continuing relationship.* A consumer has a continuing relationship with you if the consumer:

(A) Has a credit or investment account with you;

(B) Obtains a loan from you;

(C) Purchases an insurance product from you;

(D) Holds an investment product through you, such as when you act as a custodian for securities or for assets in an Individual Retirement Arrangement;

(E) Enters into an agreement or understanding with you whereby you undertake to arrange or broker a home mortgage loan, or credit to purchase a vehicle, for the consumer;

(F) Enters into a lease of personal property on a non-operating basis with you;

(G) Obtains financial, investment, or economic advisory services from you for a fee;

(H) Becomes your client for the purpose of obtaining tax preparation or credit counseling services from you;

(I) Obtains career counseling while seeking employment with a financial institution or the finance, accounting, or audit department of any company (or while employed by such a financial institution or department of any company);

(J) Is obligated on an account that you purchase from another financial institution, regardless of whether the account is in default when purchased, unless you do not locate the consumer or attempt to collect any amount from the consumer on the account;

(K) Obtains real estate settlement services from you; or

(L) Has a loan for which you own the servicing rights.

(ii) *No continuing relationship.* A consumer does not, however, have a continuing relationship with you if:

(A) The consumer obtains a financial product or service from you only in isolated transactions, such as using your ATM to withdraw cash from an account at another financial institution; purchasing a money order from you; cashing a check with you; or making a wire transfer through you;

(B) You sell the consumer's loan and do not retain the rights to service that loan;

(C) You sell the consumer airline tickets, travel insurance, or traveler's checks in isolated transactions;

(D) The consumer obtains one-time personal or real property appraisal services from you; or

(E) The consumer purchases checks for a personal checking account from you.

(j) *Federal functional regulator* means:

(1) The Board of Governors of the Federal Reserve System;

(2) The Office of the Comptroller of the Currency;

(3) The Board of Directors of the Federal Deposit Insurance Corporation;

(4) The Director of the Office of Thrift Supervision;

(5) The National Credit Union Administration Board; and

(6) The Securities and Exchange Commission.

(k)(1) *Financial institution* means any institution the business of which is engaging in financial activities as described in section 4(k) of the Bank Holding Company Act of 1956 (12 U.S.C. 1843(k)). An institution that is significantly engaged in financial activities is a financial institution.

(2) *Examples of financial institution.* (i) A retailer that extends credit by issuing its own credit card directly to consumers is a financial institution because extending credit is a financial activity listed in 12 CFR 225.28(b)(1) and referenced in section 4(k)(4)(F) of the Bank Holding Company Act and issuing that extension of credit through a proprietary credit card demonstrates that a retailer is significantly engaged in extending credit.

(ii) A personal property or real estate appraiser is a financial institution because real and personal property appraisal is a financial activity listed in 12 CFR 225.28(b)(2)(i) and referenced in section 4(k)(4)(F) of the Bank Holding Company Act.

(iii) An automobile dealership that, as a usual part of its business, leases automobiles on a nonoperating basis for longer than 90 days is a financial institution with respect to its leasing business because leasing personal property on a nonoperating basis where the initial term of the lease is at least 90 days is a financial activity listed in 12 CFR 225.28(b)(3) and referenced in section 4(k)(4)(F) of the Bank Holding Company Act.

(iv) A career counselor that specializes in providing career counseling services to individuals currently employed by or recently displaced from a financial organization, individuals who are seeking employment with a financial organization, or individuals who are currently employed by or seeking placement with the finance, accounting or audit departments of any company is a financial institution because such career counseling activities are financial activities listed in 12 CFR 225.28(b)(9)(iii) and referenced in section 4(k)(4)(F) of the Bank Holding Company Act.

(v) A business that prints and sells checks for consumers, either as its sole business or as one of its product lines, is a financial institution because printing and selling checks is a financial activity that is listed in 12 CFR 225.28(b)(10)(ii) and referenced in section 4(k)(4)(F) of the Bank Holding Company Act.

(vi) A business that regularly wires money to and from consumers is a financial institution because transferring money is a financial activity referenced in section 4(k)(4)(A) of the Bank Holding Company Act and regularly providing that service demonstrates that the business is significantly engaged in that activity.

(vii) A check cashing business is a financial institution because cashing a check is exchanging money, which is a financial activity listed in section 4(k)(4)(A) of the Bank Holding Company Act.

(viii) An accountant or other tax preparation service that is in the business of completing income tax returns is a financial institution because tax preparation services is a financial activity listed in 12 CFR 225.28(b)(6)(vi) and referenced in section 4(k)(4)(G) of the Bank Holding Company Act.

(ix) A business that operates a travel agency in connection with financial services is a financial institution because operating a travel agency in connection with financial services is a financial activity listed in 12 CFR 211.5(d)(15) and referenced in section 4(k)(4)(G) of the Bank Holding Company Act.

(x) An entity that provides real estate settlement services is a financial institution because providing real estate settlement services is a financial activity listed in 12 CFR 225.28(b)(2)(viii) and referenced in section 4(k)(4)(F) of the Bank Holding Company Act.

(xi) A mortgage broker is a financial institution because brokering loans is a financial activity listed in 12 CFR 225.28(b)(1) and referenced in section 4(k)(4)(F) of the Bank Holding Company Act.

(xii) An investment advisory company and a credit counseling service are each financial institutions because providing financial and investment advisory services are financial activities referenced in section 4(k)(4)(C) of the Bank Holding Company Act.

(3) *Financial institution* does not include:

(i) Any person or entity with respect to any financial activity that is subject to the jurisdiction of the Commodity Futures Trading Commission under the Commodity Exchange Act (7 U.S.C. 1 *et seq.*);

(ii) The Federal Agricultural Mortgage Corporation or any entity chartered and operating under the Farm Credit Act of 1971 (12 U.S.C. 2001 *et seq.*); or

(iii) Institutions chartered by Congress specifically to engage in securitizations, secondary market sales (including sales of servicing rights) or similar transactions related to a transaction of a consumer, as long as such institutions do not sell or transfer nonpublic personal information to a nonaffiliated third party other than as permitted by §§313.14 and 313.15 of this part.

(iv) Entities that engage in financial activities but that are not significantly engaged in those financial activities.

(4) *Examples of entities that are not significantly engaged in financial activities.* (i) A retailer is not a financial institution if its only means of extending credit are occasional "lay away" and deferred payment plans or accepting payment by means of credit cards issued by others.

(ii) A retailer is not a financial institution merely because it accepts payment in the form of cash, checks, or credit cards that it did not issue.

(iii) A merchant is not a financial institution merely because it allows an individual to "run a tab."

(iv) A grocery store is not a financial institution merely because it allows individuals to whom it sells groceries to cash a check, or write a check for a higher amount than the grocery purchase and obtain cash in return.

(l)(1) *Financial product or service* means any product or service that a financial holding company could offer by engaging in a financial activity under section 4(k) of the Bank Holding Company Act of 1956 (12 U.S.C. 1843(k)).

(2) *Financial service* includes your evaluation or brokerage of information that you collect in connection with a request or an application from a consumer for a financial product or service.

(m)(1) *Nonaffiliated third party* means any person except:

(i) Your affiliate; or

(ii) A person employed jointly by you and any company that is not your affiliate (but *nonaffiliated third party* includes the other company that jointly employs the person).

(2) *Nonaffiliated third party* includes any company that is an affiliate by virtue of your or your affiliate's direct or indirect ownership or control of the company in conducting merchant banking or investment banking activities of the type described in section 4(k)(4)(H) or insurance company investment activities of the type described in section 4(k)(4)(I) of the Bank Holding Company Act (12 U.S.C. 1843(k)(4)(H) and (I)).

(n)(1) *Nonpublic personal information* means:

(i) Personally identifiable financial information; and

(ii) Any list, description, or other grouping of consumers (and publicly available information pertaining to them) that is derived using any personally identifiable financial information that is not publicly available.

(2) *Nonpublic personal information* does not include:

(i) Publicly available information, except as included on a list described in paragraph (n)(1)(ii) of this section; or

(ii) Any list, description, or other grouping of consumers (and publicly available information pertaining to them) that is derived without using any personally identifiable financial information that is not publicly available.

(3) *Examples of lists*—(i) Nonpublic personal information includes any list of individuals' names and street addresses that is derived in whole or in part using personally identifiable financial information (that is not publicly available), such as account numbers.

(ii) Nonpublic personal information does not include any list of individuals' names and addresses that contains only publicly available information, is not derived, in whole or in part, using personally identifiable financial information that is not publicly available, and is not disclosed in a manner that indicates that any of the individuals on the list is a consumer of a financial institution.

(o)(1) *Personally identifiable financial information* means any information:

(i) A consumer provides to you to obtain a financial product or service from you;

(ii) About a consumer resulting from any transaction involving a financial product or service between you and a consumer; or

(iii) You otherwise obtain about a consumer in connection with providing a financial product or service to that consumer.

(2) *Examples*—(i) *Information included.* Personally identifiable financial information includes:

(A) Information a consumer provides to you on an application to obtain a loan, credit card, or other financial product or service;

(B) Account balance information, payment history, overdraft history, and credit or debit card purchase information;

(C) The fact that an individual is or has been one of your customers or has obtained a financial product or service from you;

(D) Any information about your consumer if it is disclosed in a manner that indicates that the individual is or has been your consumer;

(E) Any information that a consumer provides to you or that you or your agent otherwise obtain in connection with collecting on, or servicing, a credit account;

(F) Any information you collect through an Internet "cookie" (an information collecting device from a web server); and

(G) Information from a consumer report.

(ii) *Information not included.* Personally identifiable financial information does not include:

(A) A list of names and addresses of customers of an entity that is not a financial institution; and

(B) Information that does not identify a consumer, such as aggregate information or blind data that does not contain personal identifiers such as account numbers, names, or addresses.

(p)(1) *Publicly available information* means any information that you have a reasonable basis to believe is lawfully made available to the general public from:

(i) Federal, State, or local government records;

(ii) Widely distributed media; or

(iii) Disclosures to the general public that are required to be made by Federal, State, or local law.

(2) *Reasonable basis.* You have a reasonable basis to believe that information is lawfully made available to the general public if you have taken steps to determine:

(i) That the information is of the type that is available to the general public; and

(ii) Whether an individual can direct that the information not be made available to the general public and, if so, that your consumer has not done so.

(3) *Examples*—(i) *Government records.* Publicly available information in government records includes information in government real estate records and security interest filings.

(ii) *Widely distributed media.* Publicly available information from widely distributed media includes information from a telephone book, a television or radio program, a newspaper, or a web site that is available to the general public on an unrestricted basis. A web site is not restricted merely because an Internet service provider or a site operator requires a fee or a password, so long as access is available to the general public.

(iii) *Reasonable basis*—(A) You have a reasonable basis to believe that mortgage information is lawfully made available to the general public if you have determined that the information is of the type included on the public record in the jurisdiction where the mortgage would be recorded.

(B) You have a reasonable basis to believe that an individual's telephone number is lawfully made available to the general public if you have located the telephone number in the telephone book or the consumer has informed you that the telephone number is not unlisted.

(q) *You* includes each "financial institution" (but excludes any "other person") over which the Commission has enforcement jurisdiction pursuant to section 505(a)(7) of the Gramm-Leach-Bliley Act.

Subpart A—Privacy and Opt Out Notices

§313.4 Initial privacy notice to consumers required.

(a) *Initial notice requirement.* You must provide a clear and conspicuous notice that accurately reflects your privacy policies and practices to:

(1) *Customer.* An individual who becomes your customer, not later than when you establish a customer relationship, except as provided in paragraph (e) of this section; and

(2) *Consumer.* A consumer, before you disclose any nonpublic personal information about the consumer to any nonaffiliated third party, if you make such a disclosure other than as authorized by §§313.14 and 313.15.

(b) *When initial notice to a consumer is not required.* You are not required to provide an initial notice to a consumer under paragraph (a) of this section if:

(1) You do not disclose any nonpublic personal information about the consumer to any nonaffiliated third party, other than as authorized by §§313.14 and 313.15; and

(2) You do not have a customer relationship with the consumer.

(c) *When you establish a customer relationship*—(1) *General rule.* You establish a customer relationship when you and the consumer enter into a continuing relationship.

(2) *Special rule for loans.* You establish a customer relationship with a consumer when you originate a loan to the consumer for personal, family, or household purposes. If you subsequently transfer the servicing rights to that loan to another financial institution, the customer relationship transfers with the servicing rights.

(3)(i) *Examples of establishing customer relationship.* You establish a customer relationship when the consumer:

(A) Opens a credit card account with you;

(B) Executes the contract to obtain credit from you or purchase insurance from you;

(C) Agrees to obtain financial, economic, or investment advisory services from you for a fee; or

(D) Becomes your client for the purpose of your providing credit counseling or tax preparation services, or to obtain career counseling while seeking employment with a financial institution or the finance, accounting, or audit department of any company (or while employed by such a company or financial institution);

(E) Provides any personally identifiable financial information to you in an effort to obtain a mortgage loan through you;

(F) Executes the lease for personal property with you;

(G) Is an obligor on an account that you purchased from another financial institution and whom you have located and begun attempting to collect amounts owed on the account; or

(H) Provides you with the information necessary for you to compile and provide access to all of the consumer's on-line financial accounts at your Web site.

(ii) *Examples of loan rule.* You establish a customer relationship with a consumer who obtains a loan for personal, family, or household purposes when you:

(A) Originate the loan to the consumer and retain the servicing rights; or

(B) Purchase the servicing rights to the consumer's loan.

(d) *Existing customers.* When an existing customer obtains a new financial product or service from you that is to be used primarily for personal, family, or household purposes, you satisfy the initial notice requirements of paragraph (a) of this section as follows:

(1) You may provide a revised privacy notice, under §313.8, that covers the customer's new financial product or service; or

(2) If the initial, revised, or annual notice that you most recently provided to that customer was accurate with respect to the new financial product or service, you do not need to provide a new privacy notice under paragraph (a) of this section.

(e) *Exceptions to allow subsequent delivery of notice.* (1) You may provide the initial notice required by paragraph (a)(1) of this section within a reasonable time after you establish a customer relationship if:

(i) Establishing the customer relationship is not at the customer's election; or

(ii) Providing notice not later than when you establish a customer relationship would substantially delay the customer's transaction and the customer agrees to receive the notice at a later time.

(2) *Examples of exceptions*—(i) *Not at customer's election.* Establishing a customer relationship is not at the customer's election if you acquire a customer's loan, or the servicing rights, from another financial institution and the customer does not have a choice about your acquisition.

(ii) *Substantial delay of customer's transaction.* Providing notice not later than when you establish a customer relationship would substantially delay the customer's transaction when:

(A) You and the individual agree over the telephone to enter into a customer relationship involving prompt delivery of the financial product or service; or

(B) You establish a customer relationship with an individual under a program authorized by Title IV of the Higher Education Act of 1965 (20 U.S.C. 1070 *et seq.*) or similar student loan programs where loan proceeds are disbursed promptly without prior communication between you and the customer.

(iii) *No substantial delay of customer's transaction.* Providing notice not later than when you establish a customer relationship would not substantially delay the customer's transaction when the relationship is initiated in person at your office or through other means by which the customer may view the notice, such as through a web site.

(f) *Delivery.* When you are required to deliver an initial privacy notice by this section, you must deliver it according to §313.9. If you use a short-form initial notice for non-customers according to §313.6(d), you may deliver your privacy notice according to §313.6(d)(3).

§313.5 Annual privacy notice to customers required.

(a)(1) *General rule.* You must provide a clear and conspicuous notice to customers that accurately reflects your privacy policies and practices not less than annually during the continuation of the customer relationship. *Annually* means at least once in any period of 12 consecutive months during which that relationship exists. You may define the 12-consecutive-month period, but you must apply it to the customer on a consistent basis.

(2) *Example.* You provide a notice annually if you define the 12-consecutive-month period as a calendar year and provide the annual notice to the customer once in each calendar year following the calendar year in which you provided the initial notice. For example, if a customer opens an account on any day of year 1, you must provide an annual notice to that customer by December 31 of year 2.

(b)(1) *Termination of customer relationship.* You are not required to provide an annual notice to a former customer.

(2) *Examples.* Your customer becomes a former customer when:

(i) In the case of a closed-end loan, the customer pays the loan in full, you charge off the loan, or you sell the loan without retaining servicing rights;

(ii) In the case of a credit card relationship or other open-end credit relationship, you sell the receivables without retaining servicing rights;

(iii) In the case of credit counseling services, the customer has failed to make required payments under a debt management plan, has been notified that the plan is terminated, and you no longer provide any statements or notices to the customer concerning that relationship;

(iv) In the case of mortgage or vehicle loan brokering services, your customer has obtained a loan through you (and you no longer provide any statements or notices to the customer concerning that relationship), or has ceased using your services for such purposes;

(v) In the case of tax preparation services, you have provided and received payment for the service and no longer provide any statements or notices to the customer concerning that relationship;

(vi) In the case of providing real estate settlement services, at the time the customer completes execution of all documents related to the real estate closing, you have received payment, or you have completed all of your responsibilities with respect to the settlement, including filing documents on the public record, whichever is later.

(vii) In cases where there is no definitive time at which the customer relationship has terminated, you have not communicated with the customer about the relationship for a period of 12 consecutive months, other than to provide annual privacy notices or promotional material.

(c) *Special rule for loans.* If you do not have a customer relationship with a consumer under the special rule for loans in § 313.4(c)(2), then you need not provide an annual notice to that consumer under this section.

(d) *Delivery.* When you are required to deliver an annual privacy notice by this section, you must deliver it according to § 313.9.

§ 313.6 Information to be included in privacy notices.

(a) *General rule.* The initial, annual, and revised privacy notices that you provide under §§ 313.4, 313.5, and 313.8 must include each of the following items of information that applies to you or to the consumers to whom you send your privacy notice, in addition to any other information you wish to provide:

(1) The categories of nonpublic personal information that you collect;

(2) The categories of nonpublic personal information that you disclose;

(3) The categories of affiliates and nonaffiliated third parties to whom you disclose nonpublic personal information, other than those parties to whom you disclose information under §§ 313.14 and 313.15;

(4) The categories of nonpublic personal information about your former customers that you disclose and the categories of affiliates and nonaffiliated third parties to whom you disclose nonpublic personal information about your former customers, other than those parties to whom you disclose information under §§ 313.14 and 313.15;

(5) If you disclose nonpublic personal information to a nonaffiliated third party under § 313.13 (and no exception under § 313.14 or § 313.15 applies to that disclosure), a separate statement of the categories of information you disclose and the categories of third parties with whom you have contracted;

(6) An explanation of the consumer's right under § 313.10(a) to opt out of the disclosure of nonpublic personal information to nonaffiliated third parties, including the method(s) by which the consumer may exercise that right at that time;

(7) Any disclosures that you make under section 603(d)(2)(A)(iii) of the Fair Credit Reporting Act (15 U.S.C. 1681a(d)(2)(A)(iii)) (that is, notices regarding the ability to opt out of disclosures of information among affiliates);

(8) Your policies and practices with respect to protecting the confidentiality and security of nonpublic personal information; and

(9) Any disclosure that you make under paragraph (b) of this section.

(b) *Description of nonaffiliated third parties subject to exceptions.* If you disclose nonpublic personal information to third parties as authorized under §§ 313.14 and 313.15, you are not required to list those exceptions in the initial or annual privacy notices required by §§ 313.4 and 313.5. When describing the categories with respect to those parties, it is sufficient to state that you make disclosures to other nonaffiliated companies for your everyday business purposes, such as to process transactions, maintain account(s), respond to court orders and legal investigations, or report to credit bureaus.

(c) *Examples*—(1) *Categories of nonpublic personal information that you collect.* You satisfy the requirement to categorize the nonpublic personal information that you collect if you list the following categories, as applicable:

(i) Information from the consumer;

(ii) Information about the consumer's transactions with you or your affiliates;

(iii) Information about the consumer's transactions with nonaffiliated third parties; and

(iv) Information from a consumer reporting agency.

(2) *Categories of nonpublic personal information you disclose*—(i) You satisfy the requirement to categorize the nonpublic personal information that you disclose if you list the categories described in paragraph (e)(1) of this section, as applicable, and a few examples to illustrate the types of information in each category.

(ii) If you reserve the right to disclose all of the nonpublic personal information about consumers that you collect, you may simply state that fact without describing the categories or examples of the nonpublic personal information you disclose.

(3) *Categories of affiliates and nonaffiliated third parties to whom you disclose.* You satisfy the requirement to categorize the affiliates and nonaffiliated third parties to whom you disclose nonpublic personal information if you list them using the following categories, as applicable, and a few applicable examples to illustrate the significant types of third parties covered in each category.

(i) Financial service providers, followed by illustrative examples such as mortgage bankers, securities broker-dealers, and insurance agents.

(ii) Non-financial companies, followed by illustrative examples such as retailers, magazine publishers, airlines, and direct marketers; and

(iii) Others, followed by examples such as nonprofit organizations.

(4) *Disclosures under exception for service providers and joint marketers.* If you disclose nonpublic personal information under the exception in §313.13 to a nonaffiliated third party to market products or services that you offer alone or jointly with another financial institution, you satisfy the disclosure requirement of paragraph (a)(5) of this section if you:

(i) List the categories of nonpublic personal information you disclose, using the same categories and examples you used to meet the requirements of paragraph (a)(2) of this section, as applicable; and

(ii) State whether the third party is:

(A) A service provider that performs marketing services on your behalf or on behalf of you and another financial institution; or

(B) A financial institution with whom you have a joint marketing agreement.

(5) *Simplified notices.* If you do not disclose, and do not wish to reserve the right to disclose, nonpublic personal information about customers or former customers to affiliates or nonaffiliated third parties except as authorized under §§313.14 and 313.15, you may simply state that fact, in addition to the information you must provide under paragraphs (a)(1), (a)(8), (a)(9), and (b) of this section.

(6) *Confidentiality and security.* You describe your policies and practices with respect to protecting the confidentiality and security of nonpublic personal information if you do both of the following:

(i) Describe in general terms who is authorized to have access to the information; and

(ii) State whether you have security practices and procedures in place to ensure the confidentiality of the information in accordance with your policy. You are not required to describe technical information about the safeguards you use.

(d) *Short-form initial notice with opt out notice for non-customers*—(1) You may satisfy the initial notice requirements in §§313.4(a)(2), 313.7(b), and 313.7(c) for a consumer who is not a customer by providing a short-form initial notice at the same time as you deliver an opt out notice as required in §313.7.

(2) A short-form initial notice must:

(i) Be clear and conspicuous;

(ii) State that your privacy notice is available upon request; and

(iii) Explain a reasonable means by which the consumer may obtain that notice.

(3) You must deliver your short-form initial notice according to §313.9. You are not required to deliver your privacy notice with your short-form initial notice. You instead may simply provide the consumer a reasonable means to obtain your privacy notice. If a consumer who receives your short-form notice requests your privacy notice, you must deliver your privacy notice according to §313.9.

(4) *Examples of obtaining privacy notice.* You provide a reasonable means by which a consumer may obtain a copy of your privacy notice if you:

(i) Provide a toll-free telephone number that the consumer may call to request the notice; or

(ii) For a consumer who conducts business in person at your office, maintain copies of the notice on hand that you provide to the consumer immediately upon request.

(e) *Future disclosures.* Your notice may include:

(1) Categories of nonpublic personal information that you reserve the right to disclose in the future, but do not currently disclose; and

(2) Categories of affiliates or nonaffiliated third parties to whom you reserve the right in the future to disclose, but to whom you do not currently disclose, nonpublic personal information.

(f) *Model privacy form.* Pursuant to §313.2(a) of this part, a model privacy form that meets the notice content requirements of this section is included in appendix A of this part.

[65 FR 33677, May 24, 2000, as amended at 74 FR 62965, Dec. 1, 2009]

§313.7 Form of opt out notice to consumers; opt out methods.

(a)(1) *Form of opt out notice.* If you are required to provide an opt out notice under §313.10(a), you must provide a clear and conspicuous notice to each of your consumers that accurately explains the right to opt out under that section. The notice must state:

(i) That you disclose or reserve the right to disclose nonpublic personal information about your consumer to a nonaffiliated third party;

(ii) That the consumer has the right to opt out of that disclosure; and

(iii) A reasonable means by which the consumer may exercise the opt out right.

(2) *Examples*—(i) *Adequate opt out notice.* You provide adequate notice that the consumer can opt out of the disclosure of nonpublic personal information to a nonaffiliated third party if you:

(A) Identify all of the categories of nonpublic personal information that you disclose or reserve the right to disclose, and all of the categories of nonaffiliated third parties to which you disclose the information, as described in §313.6(a) (2) and (3) and state that the consumer can opt out of the disclosure of that information; and

(B) Identify the financial products or services that the consumer obtains from you, either singly or jointly, to which the opt out direction would apply.

(ii) *Reasonable opt out means.* You provide a reasonable means to exercise an opt out right if you:

(A) Designate check-off boxes in a prominent position on the relevant forms with the opt out notice;

(B) Include a reply form that includes the address to which the form should be mailed; or

(C) Provide an electronic means to opt out, such as a form that can be sent via electronic mail or a process at your web site, if the consumer agrees to the electronic delivery of information; or

(D) Provide a toll-free telephone number that consumers may call to opt out.

(iii) *Unreasonable opt out means.* You *do not* provide a reasonable means of opting out if:

(A) The only means of opting out is for the consumer to write his or her own letter to exercise that opt out right; or

(B) The only means of opting out as described in any notice subsequent to the initial notice is to use a check-off box that you provided with the initial notice but did not include with the subsequent notice.

(iv) *Specific opt out means.* You may require each consumer to opt out through a specific means, as long as that means is reasonable for that consumer.

(b) *Same form as initial notice permitted.* You may provide the opt out notice together with or on the same written or electronic form as the initial notice you provide in accordance with §313.4.

(c) *Initial notice required when opt out notice delivered subsequent to initial notice.* If you provide the opt out notice later than required for the initial notice in accordance with §313.4, you must also include a copy of the initial notice with the opt out notice in writing or, if the consumer agrees, electronically.

(d) *Joint relationships.* (1) If two or more consumers jointly obtain a financial product or service from you, you may provide a single opt out notice, unless one or more of those consumers requests a separate opt out notice. Your opt out notice must explain how you will treat an opt out direction by a joint consumer (as explained in paragraph (d)(5)(ii)of this section).

(2) Any of the joint consumers may exercise the right to opt out. You may either:

(i) Treat an opt out direction by a joint consumer as applying to all of the associated joint consumers; or

(ii) Permit each joint consumer to opt out separately.

(3) If you permit each joint consumer to opt out separately, you must permit one of the joint consumers to opt out on behalf of all of the joint consumers.

(4) You may not require *all* joint consumers to opt out before you implement *any* opt out direction.

(5) *Example.* If John and Mary have a joint credit card account with you and arrange for you to send statements to John's address, you may do any of the following, but you must explain in your opt out notice which opt out policy you will follow:

(i) Send a single opt out notice to John's address, but you must accept an opt out direction from either John or Mary.

(ii) Treat an opt out direction by either John or Mary as applying to the entire account. If you do so, and John opts out, you may not require Mary to opt out as well before implementing John's opt out direction.

(iii) Permit John and Mary to make different opt out directions. If you do so,

(A) You must permit John and Mary to opt out for each other;

(B) If both opt out, you must permit both to notify you in a single response (such as on a form or through a telephone call); and

(C) If John opts out and Mary does not, you may only disclose nonpublic personal information about Mary, but not about John and not about John and Mary jointly.

(e) *Time to comply with opt out.* You must comply with a consumer's opt out direction as soon as reasonably practicable after you receive it.

(f) *Continuing right to opt out.* A consumer may exercise the right to opt out at any time.

(g) *Duration of consumer's opt out direction.* (1) A consumer's direction to opt out under this section is effective until the consumer revokes it in writing or, if the consumer agrees, electronically.

(2) When a customer relationship terminates, the customer's opt out direction continues to apply to the nonpublic personal information that you collected during or related to that relationship. If the individual subsequently establishes a new customer relationship with you, the opt out direction that applied to the former relationship does not apply to the new relationship.

(h) *Delivery.* When you are required to deliver an opt out notice by this section, you must deliver it according to § 313.9.

(i) *Model privacy form.* Pursuant to § 313.2(a) of this part, a model privacy form that meets the notice content requirements of this section is included in appendix A of this part.

[65 FR 33677, May 24, 2000, as amended at 74 FR 62966, Dec. 1, 2009]

§ 313.8 Revised privacy notices.

(a) *General rule.* Except as otherwise authorized in this part, you must not, directly or through any affiliate, disclose any nonpublic personal information about a consumer to a nonaffiliated third party other than as described in the initial notice that you provided to that consumer under § 313.4, unless:

(1) You have provided to the consumer a clear and conspicuous revised notice that accurately describes your policies and practices;

(2) You have provided to the consumer a new opt out notice;

(3) You have given the consumer a reasonable opportunity, before you disclose the information to the nonaffiliated third party, to opt out of the disclosure; and

(4) the consumer does not opt out.

(b) *Examples*—(1) Except as otherwise permitted by §§ 313.13, 313.14, and 313.15, you must provide a revised notice before you:

(i) Disclose a new category of nonpublic personal information to any nonaffiliated third party;

(ii) Disclose nonpublic personal information to a new category of nonaffiliated third party; or

(iii) Disclose nonpublic personal information about a former customer to a nonaffiliated third party if that former customer has not had the opportunity to exercise an opt out right regarding that disclosure.

(2) A revised notice is not required if you disclose nonpublic personal information to a new nonaffiliated third party that you adequately described in your prior notice.

(c) *Delivery.* When you are required to deliver a revised privacy notice by this section, you must deliver it according to §313.9.

§313.9 Delivering privacy and opt out notices.

(a) *How to provide notices.* You must provide any privacy notices and opt out notices, including short-form initial notices, that this part requires so that each consumer can reasonably be expected to receive actual notice in writing or, if the consumer agrees, electronically.

(b)(1) *Examples of reasonable expectation of actual notice.* You may reasonably expect that a consumer will receive actual notice if you:

(i) Hand-deliver a printed copy of the notice to the consumer;

(ii) Mail a printed copy of the notice to the last known address of the consumer;

(iii) For the consumer who conducts transactions electronically, clearly and conspicuously post the notice on the electronic site and require the consumer to acknowledge receipt of the notice as a necessary step to obtaining a particular financial product or service;

(iv) For an isolated transaction with the consumer, such as an ATM transaction, post the notice on the ATM screen and require the consumer to acknowledge receipt of the notice as a necessary step to obtaining the particular financial product or service.

(2) *Examples of unreasonable expectation of actual notice.* You may *not,* however, reasonably expect that a consumer will receive actual notice of your privacy policies and practices if you:

(i) Only post a sign in your branch or office or generally publish advertisements of your privacy policies and practices;

(ii) Send the notice via electronic mail to a consumer who does not obtain a financial product or service from you electronically.

(c) *Annual notices only.* You may reasonably expect that a customer will receive actual notice of your annual privacy notice if:

(1) The customer uses your web site to access financial products and services electronically and agrees to receive notices at the web site and you post your current privacy notice continuously in a clear and conspicuous manner on the web site; or

(2) The customer has requested that you refrain from sending any information regarding the customer relationship, and your current privacy notice remains available to the customer upon request.

(d) *Oral description of notice insufficient.* You may not provide any notice required by this part solely by orally explaining the notice, either in person or over the telephone.

(e) *Retention or accessibility of notices for customers*—(1) For customers only, you must provide the initial notice required by §313.4(a)(1), the annual notice required by §313.5(a), and the revised notice required by §313.8 so that the customer can retain them or obtain them later in writing or, if the customer agrees, electronically.

(2) *Examples of retention or accessibility.* You provide a privacy notice to the customer so that the customer can retain it or obtain it later if you:

(i) Hand-deliver a printed copy of the notice to the customer;

(ii) Mail a printed copy of the notice to the last known address of the customer; or

(iii) Make your current privacy notice available on a web site (or a link to another web site) for the customer who obtains a financial product or service electronically and agrees to receive the notice at the web site.

(f) *Joint notice with other financial institutions.* You may provide a joint notice from you and one or more of your affiliates or other financial institutions, as identified in the notice, as long as the notice is accurate with respect to you and the other institutions.

(g) *Joint relationships.* If two or more consumers jointly obtain a financial product or service from you, you may satisfy the initial, annual, and revised notice requirements of §§313.4(a), 313.5(a), and 313.8(a) by providing one notice to those consumers jointly, unless one or more of those consumers requests separate notices.

Subpart B—Limits on Disclosures

§313.10 Limits on disclosure of nonpublic personal information to nonaffiliated third parties.

(a)(1) *Conditions for disclosure.* Except as otherwise authorized in this part, you may not, directly or through any affiliate, disclose any nonpublic personal information about a consumer to a nonaffiliated third party unless:

(i) You have provided to the consumer an initial notice as required under §313.4;

(ii) You have provided to the consumer an opt out notice as required in §313.7;

(iii) You have given the consumer a reasonable opportunity, before you disclose the information to the nonaffiliated third party, to opt out of the disclosure; and

(iv) The consumer does not opt out.

(2) *Opt out definition.* Opt out means a direction by the consumer that you not disclose nonpublic personal information about that consumer to a nonaffiliated third party, other than as permitted by §§313.13, 313.14, and 313.15.

(3) *Examples of reasonable opportunity to opt out.* You provide a consumer with a reasonable opportunity to opt out if:

(i) *By mail.* You mail the notices required in paragraph (a)(1) of this section to the consumer and allow the consumer to opt out by mailing a form, calling a toll-free telephone number, or any other reasonable means within 30 days from the date you mailed the notices.

(ii) *By electronic means.* A customer opens an on-line account with you and agrees to receive the notices required in paragraph (a)(1) of this section electronically, and you allow the customer to opt out by any reasonable means within 30 days after the date that the customer acknowledges receipt of the notices in conjunction with opening the account.

(iii) *Isolated transaction with consumer.* For an isolated transaction, such as the purchase of a money order by a consumer, you provide the consumer with a reasonable opportunity to opt out if you provide the notices required in paragraph (a)(1) of this section at the time of the transaction and request that the consumer decide, as a necessary part of the transaction, whether to opt out before completing the transaction.

(b) *Application of opt out to all consumers and all nonpublic personal information*—(1) You must comply with this section, regardless of whether you and the consumer have established a customer relationship

(2) Unless you comply with this section, you may not, directly or through any affiliate, disclose any nonpublic personal information about a consumer that you have collected, regardless of whether you collected it before or after receiving the direction to opt out from the consumer.

(c) *Partial opt out.* You may allow a consumer to select certain nonpublic personal information or certain nonaffiliated third parties with respect to which the consumer wishes to opt out.

§313.11 Limits on redisclosure and reuse of information.

(a)(1) *Information you receive under an exception.* If you receive nonpublic personal information from a nonaffiliated financial institution under an exception in §313.14 or §313.15 of this part, your disclosure and use of that information is limited as follows:

(i) You may disclose the information to the affiliates of the financial institution from which you received the information;

(ii) You may disclose the information to your affiliates, but your affiliates may, in turn, disclose and use the information only to the extent that you may disclose and use the information; and

(iii) You may disclose and use the information pursuant to an exception in §313.14 or §313.15 in the ordinary course of business to carry out the activity covered by the exception under which you received the information.

(2) *Example.* If you receive a customer list from a nonaffiliated financial institution in order to provide account processing services under the exception in §313.14(a), you may disclose that information under any exception in §313.14 or §313.15 in the ordinary course of business in order to provide those services. You could also disclose that information in response to a properly authorized subpoena. You could not disclose that information to a third party for marketing purposes or use that information for your own marketing purposes.

(b)(1) *Information you receive outside of an exception.* If you receive nonpublic personal information from a nonaffiliated financial institution other than under an exception in §313.14 or §313.15 of this part, you may disclose the information only:

(i) To the affiliates of the financial institution from which you received the information;

(ii) To your affiliates, but your affiliates may, in turn, disclose the information only to the extent that you can disclose the information; and

(iii) To any other person, if the disclosure would be lawful if made directly to that person by the financial institution from which you received the information.

(2) *Example.* If you obtain a customer list from a nonaffiliated financial institution outside of the exceptions in §§313.14 and 313.15:

(i) You may use that list for your own purposes; and

(ii) You may disclose that list to another nonaffiliated third party only if the financial institution from which you purchased the list could have lawfully disclosed the list to that third party. That is, you may disclose the list in accordance with the privacy policy of the financial institution from which you received the list, as limited by the opt out direction of each consumer whose nonpublic personal information you intend to disclose, and you may disclose the list in accordance with an exception in §313.14 or §313.15, such as to your attorneys or accountants.

(c) *Information you disclose under an exception.* If you disclose nonpublic personal information to a nonaffiliated third party under an exception in §313.14 or 313.15 of this part, the third party may disclose and use that information only as follows:

(1) The third party may disclose the information to your affiliates;

(2) The third party may disclose the information to its affiliates, but its affiliates may, in turn, disclose and use the information only to the extent that the third party may disclose and use the information; and

(3) The third party may disclose and use the information pursuant to an exception in §313.14 or §313.15 in the ordinary course of business to carry out the activity covered by the exception under which it received the information.

(d) *Information you disclose outside of an exception.* If you disclose nonpublic personal information to a nonaffiliated third party other than under an exception in §313.14 or §313.15 of this part, the third party may disclose the information only:

(1) To your affiliates;

(2) To its affiliates, but its affiliates, in turn, may disclose the information only to the extent the third party can disclose the information; and

(3) To any other person, if the disclosure would be lawful if you made it directly to that person.

§313.12 Limits on sharing account number information for marketing purposes.

(a) *General prohibition on disclosure of account numbers.* You must not, directly or through an affiliate, disclose, other than to a consumer reporting agency, an account number or similar form of access number or access code for a consumer's credit card account, deposit account, or transaction account to any nonaffiliated third party for use in telemarketing, direct mail marketing, or other marketing through electronic mail to the consumer.

(b) *Exceptions.* Paragraph (a) of this section does not apply if you disclose an account number or similar form of access number or access code:

(1) To your agent or service provider solely in order to perform marketing for your own products or services, as long as the agent or service provider is not authorized to directly initiate charges to the account; or

(2) To a participant in a private label credit card program or an affinity or similar program where the participants in the program are identified to the customer when the customer enters into the program.

(c) *Examples*—(1) *Account number.* An account number, or similar form of access number or access code, does not include a number or code in an encrypted form, as long as you do not provide the recipient with a means to decode the number or code.

(2) *Transaction account.* A transaction account is an account other than a deposit account or a credit card account. A transaction account does not include an account to which third parties cannot initiate charges.

Subpart C—Exceptions

§313.13 Exception to opt out requirements for service providers and joint marketing.

(a) *General rule.* (1) The opt out requirements in §§313.7 and 313.10 do not apply when you provide nonpublic personal information to a nonaffiliated third party to perform services for you or functions on your behalf, if you:

(i) Provide the initial notice in accordance with §313.4; and

(ii) Enter into a contractual agreement with the third party that prohibits the third party from disclosing or using the information other than to carry out the purposes for which you disclosed the information, including use under an exception in §313.14 or §313.15 in the ordinary course of business to carry out those purposes.

(2) *Example.* If you disclose nonpublic personal information under this section to a financial institution with which you perform joint marketing, your contractual agreement with that institution meets the requirements of paragraph (a)(1)(ii) of this section if it prohibits the institution from disclosing or using the nonpublic personal information except as necessary to carry out the joint marketing or under an exception in §313.14 or §313.15 in the ordinary course of business to carry out that joint marketing.

(b) *Service may include joint marketing.* The services a nonaffiliated third party performs for you under paragraph (a) of this section may include marketing of your own products or services or marketing of financial products or services offered pursuant to joint agreements between you and one or more financial institutions.

(c) *Definition of joint agreement.* For purposes of this section, joint agreement means a written contract pursuant to which you and one or more financial institutions jointly offer, endorse, or sponsor a financial product or service.

§313.14 Exceptions to notice and opt out requirements for processing and servicing transactions.

(a) *Exceptions for processing transactions at consumer's request.* The requirements for initial notice in §313.4(a)(2), for the opt out in §§313.7 and 313.10, and for service providers and joint marketing in §313.13 do not apply if you disclose nonpublic personal information as necessary to effect, administer, or enforce a transaction that a consumer requests or authorizes, or in connection with:

(1) Servicing or processing a financial product or service that a consumer requests or authorizes;

(2) Maintaining or servicing the consumer's account with you, or with another entity as part of a private label credit card program or other extension of credit on behalf of such entity; or

(3) A proposed or actual securitization, secondary market sale (including sales of servicing rights), or similar transaction related to a transaction of the consumer.

(b) *Necessary to effect, administer, or enforce a transaction* means that the disclosure is:

(1) Required, or is one of the lawful or appropriate methods, to enforce

your rights or the rights of other persons engaged in carrying out the financial transaction or providing the product or service; or

(2) Required, or is a usual, appropriate or acceptable method:

(i) To carry out the transaction or the product or service business of which the transaction is a part, and record, service, or maintain the consumer's account in the ordinary course of providing the financial service or financial product;

(ii) To administer or service benefits or claims relating to the transaction or the product or service business of which it is a part;

(iii) To provide a confirmation, statement, or other record of the transaction, or information on the status or value of the financial service or financial product to the consumer or the consumer's agent or broker;

(iv) To accrue or recognize incentives or bonuses associated with the transaction that are provided by you or any other party;

(v) To underwrite insurance at the consumer's request or for reinsurance purposes, or for any of the following purposes as they relate to a consumer's insurance: account administration, reporting, investigating, or preventing fraud or material misrepresentation, processing premium payments, processing insurance claims, administering insurance benefits (including utilization review activities), participating in research projects, or as otherwise required or specifically permitted by Federal or State law;

(vi) In connection with:

(A) The authorization, settlement, billing, processing, clearing, transferring, reconciling or collection of amounts charged, debited, or otherwise paid using a debit, credit, or other payment card, check, or account number, or by other payment means;

(B) The transfer of receivables, accounts, or interests therein; or

(C) The audit of debit, credit, or other payment information.

§313.15 Other exceptions to notice and opt out requirements.

(a) *Exceptions to opt out requirements.* The requirements for initial notice in §313.4(a)(2), for the opt out in §§313.7 and 313.10, and for service providers and joint marketing in §313.13 do not apply when you disclose nonpublic personal information:

(1) With the consent or at the direction of the consumer, provided that the consumer has not revoked the consent or direction;

(2)(i) To protect the confidentiality or security of your records pertaining to the consumer, service, product, or transaction;

(ii) To protect against or prevent actual or potential fraud, unauthorized transactions, claims, or other liability;

(iii) For required institutional risk control or for resolving consumer disputes or inquiries;

(iv) To persons holding a legal or beneficial interest relating to the consumer; or

(v) To persons acting in a fiduciary or representative capacity on behalf of the consumer;

(3) To provide information to insurance rate advisory organizations, guaranty funds or agencies, agencies that are rating you, persons that are assessing your compliance with industry standards, and your attorneys, accountants, and auditors;

(4) To the extent specifically permitted or required under other provisions of law and in accordance with the Right to Financial Privacy Act of 1978 (12 U.S.Cet seq.), to law enforcement agencies (including a federal functional regulator, the Secretary of the Treasury, with respect to 31 U.S.C. Chapter 53, Subchapter II (Records and Reports on Monetary Instruments and Transactions) and 12 U.S.C. Chapter 21 (Financial Recordkeeping), a State insurance authority, with respect to any person domiciled in that insurance authority's State that is engaged in providing insurance, and the Federal Trade Commission), self-regulatory organizations, or for an investigation on a matter related to public safety;

(5)(i) To a consumer reporting agency in accordance with the Fair Credit Reporting Act (15 U.S.C. 1681 *et seq.*), or

(ii) From a consumer report reported by a consumer reporting agency;

(6) In connection with a proposed or actual sale, merger, transfer, or exchange of all or a portion of a business or operating unit if the disclosure of

nonpublic personal information concerns solely consumers of such business or unit; or

(7)(i) To comply with Federal, State, or local laws, rules and other applicable legal requirements;

(ii) To comply with a properly authorized civil, criminal, or regulatory investigation, or subpoena or summons by Federal, State, or local authorities; or

(iii) To respond to judicial process or government regulatory authorities having jurisdiction over you for examination, compliance, or other purposes as authorized by law.

(b) *Examples of consent and revocation of consent.* (1) A consumer may specifically consent to your disclosure to a nonaffiliated insurance company of the fact that the consumer has applied to you for a mortgage so that the insurance company can offer homeowner's insurance to the consumer.

(2) A consumer may revoke consent by subsequently exercising the right to opt out of future disclosures of nonpublic personal information as permitted under § 313.7(f).

Subpart D—Relation to Other Laws; Effective Date

§ 313.16 Protection of Fair Credit Reporting Act.

Nothing in this part shall be construed to modify, limit, or supersede the operation of the Fair Credit Reporting Act (15 U.S.C. 1681 *et seq.*), and no inference shall be drawn on the basis of the provisions of this part regarding whether information is transaction or experience information under section 603 of that Act.

§ 313.17 Relation to State laws.

(a) *In general.* This part shall not be construed as superseding, altering, or affecting any statute, regulation, order, or interpretation in effect in any State, except to the extent that such State statute, regulation, order, or interpretation is inconsistent with the provisions of this part, and then only to the extent of the inconsistency.

(b) *Greater protection under State law.* For purposes of this section, a State statute, regulation, order, or interpretation is not inconsistent with the provisions of this part if the protection such statute, regulation, order, or interpretation affords any consumer is greater than the protection provided under this part, as determined by the Commission on its own motion or upon the petition of any interested party, after consultation with the applicable federal functional regulator or other authority.

§ 313.18 Effective date; transition rule.

(a) *Effective date*—(1) *General rule.* This part is effective November 13, 2000. In order to provide sufficient time for you to establish policies and systems to comply with the requirements of this part, the Commission has extended the time for compliance with this part until July 1, 2001.

(2) *Exception.* This part is not effective as to any institution that is significantly engaged in activities that the Federal Reserve Board determines, after November 12, 1999, (pursuant to its authority in Section 4(k)(1–3) of the Bank Holding Company Act), are activities that a financial holding company may engage in, until the Commission so determines.

(b)(1) *Notice requirement for consumers who are your customers on the compliance date.* By July 1, 2001, you must have provided an initial notice, as required by § 313.4, to consumers who are your customers on July 1, 2001.

(2) *Example.* You provide an initial notice to consumers who are your customers on July 1, 2001, if, by that date, you have established a system for providing an initial notice to all new customers and have mailed the initial notice to all your existing customers.

(c) *Two-year grandfathering of service agreements.* Until July 1, 2002, a contract that you have entered into with a nonaffiliated third party to perform services for you or functions on your behalf satisfies the provisions of § 313.13(a)(1) of this part, even if the contract does not include a requirement that the third party maintain the confidentiality of nonpublic personal information, as long as you entered into the contract on or before July 1, 2000.

Appendix A to Part 313—Model Privacy Form

A. The Model Privacy Form

Version 1: Model Form With No Opt-Out.

Rev. [insert date]

FACTS	WHAT DOES [NAME OF FINANCIAL INSTITUTION] DO WITH YOUR PERSONAL INFORMATION?
Why?	Financial companies choose how they share your personal information. Federal law gives consumers the right to limit some but not all sharing. Federal law also requires us to tell you how we collect, share, and protect your personal information. Please read this notice carefully to understand what we do.
What?	The types of personal information we collect and share depend on the product or service you have with us. This information can include: ■ Social Security number and [income] ■ [account balances] and [payment history] ■ [credit history] and [credit scores] When you are *no longer* our customer, we continue to share your information as described in this notice.
How?	All financial companies need to share customers' personal information to run their everyday business. In the section below, we list the reasons financial companies can share their customers' personal information; the reasons [name of financial institution] chooses to share; and whether you can limit this sharing.

Reasons we can share your personal information	Does [name of financial institution] share?	Can you limit this sharing?
For our everyday business purposes— such as to process your transactions, maintain your account(s), respond to court orders and legal investigations, or report to credit bureaus		
For our marketing purposes— to offer our products and services to you		
For joint marketing with other financial companies		
For our affiliates' everyday business purposes— information about your transactions and experiences		
For our affiliates' everyday business purposes— information about your creditworthiness		
For our affiliates to market to you		
For nonaffiliates to market to you		

Questions?	Call [phone number] or go to [website]

Page 2

Who we are	
Who is providing this notice?	[insert]
What we do	
How does [name of financial institution] protect my personal information?	To protect your personal information from unauthorized access and use, we use security measures that comply with federal law. These measures include computer safeguards and secured files and buildings. [insert]
How does [name of financial institution] collect my personal information?	We collect your personal information, for example, when you ■ [open an account] or [deposit money] ■ [pay your bills] or [apply for a loan] ■ [use your credit or debit card] [We also collect your personal information from other companies.] OR [We also collect your personal information from others, such as credit bureaus, affiliates, or other companies.]
Why can't I limit all sharing?	Federal law gives you the right to limit only ■ sharing for affiliates' everyday business purposes—information about your creditworthiness ■ affiliates from using your information to market to you ■ sharing for nonaffiliates to market to you State laws and individual companies may give you additional rights to limit sharing. [See below for more on your rights under state law.]
Definitions	
Affiliates	Companies related by common ownership or control. They can be financial and nonfinancial companies. ■ *[affiliate information]*
Nonaffiliates	Companies not related by common ownership or control. They can be financial and nonfinancial companies. ■ *[nonaffiliate information]*
Joint marketing	A formal agreement between nonaffiliated financial companies that together market financial products or services to you. ■ *[joint marketing information]*
Other important information	
[insert other important information]	

Version 2: Model Form with Opt-Out by Telephone and/or Online.

Rev. [insert date]

FACTS	WHAT DOES [NAME OF FINANCIAL INSTITUTION] DO WITH YOUR PERSONAL INFORMATION?
Why?	Financial companies choose how they share your personal information. Federal law gives consumers the right to limit some but not all sharing. Federal law also requires us to tell you how we collect, share, and protect your personal information. Please read this notice carefully to understand what we do.
What?	The types of personal information we collect and share depend on the product or service you have with us. This information can include: ■ Social Security number and [income] ■ [account balances] and [payment history] ■ [credit history] and [credit scores]
How?	All financial companies need to share customers' personal information to run their everyday business. In the section below, we list the reasons financial companies can share their customers' personal information; the reasons [name of financial institution] chooses to share; and whether you can limit this sharing.

Reasons we can share your personal information	Does [name of financial institution] share?	Can you limit this sharing?
For our everyday business purposes— such as to process your transactions, maintain your account(s), respond to court orders and legal investigations, or report to credit bureaus		
For our marketing purposes— to offer our products and services to you		
For joint marketing with other financial companies		
For our affiliates' everyday business purposes— information about your transactions and experiences		
For our affiliates' everyday business purposes— information about your creditworthiness		
For our affiliates to market to you		
For nonaffiliates to market to you		

To limit our sharing	■ Call **[phone number]**—our menu will prompt you through your choice(s) or ■ Visit us online: **[website]** **Please note:** If you are a *new* customer, we can begin sharing your information [30] days from the date we sent this notice. When you are *no longer* our customer, we continue to share your information as described in this notice. However, you can contact us at any time to limit our sharing.
Questions?	Call [phone number] or go to [website]

Page 2

Who we are	
Who is providing this notice?	[insert]

What we do	
How does [name of financial institution] protect my personal information?	To protect your personal information from unauthorized access and use, we use security measures that comply with federal law. These measures include computer safeguards and secured files and buildings. [insert]
How does [name of financial institution] collect my personal information?	We collect your personal information, for example, when you ■ [open an account] or [deposit money] ■ [pay your bills] or [apply for a loan] ■ [use your credit or debit card] [We also collect your personal information from other companies.] **OR** [We also collect your personal information from others, such as credit bureaus, affiliates, or other companies.]
Why can't I limit all sharing?	Federal law gives you the right to limit only ■ sharing for affiliates' everyday business purposes—information about your creditworthiness ■ affiliates from using your information to market to you ■ sharing for nonaffiliates to market to you State laws and individual companies may give you additional rights to limit sharing. [See below for more on your rights under state law.]
What happens when I limit sharing for an account I hold jointly with someone else?	[Your choices will apply to everyone on your account.] **OR** [Your choices will apply to everyone on your account—unless you tell us otherwise.]

Definitions	
Affiliates	Companies related by common ownership or control. They can be financial and nonfinancial companies. ■ *[affiliate information]*
Nonaffiliates	Companies not related by common ownership or control. They can be financial and nonfinancial companies. ■ *[nonaffiliate information]*
Joint marketing	A formal agreement between nonaffiliated financial companies that together market financial products or services to you. ■ *[joint marketing information]*

Other important information
[insert other important information]

Version 3: Model Form with Mail-In Opt-Out Form.

Rev. [insert date]

FACTS	WHAT DOES [NAME OF FINANCIAL INSTITUTION] DO WITH YOUR PERSONAL INFORMATION?
Why?	Financial companies choose how they share your personal information. Federal law gives consumers the right to limit some but not all sharing. Federal law also requires us to tell you how we collect, share, and protect your personal information. Please read this notice carefully to understand what we do.
What?	The types of personal information we collect and share depend on the product or service you have with us. This information can include: ■ Social Security number and [income] ■ [account balances] and [payment history] ■ [credit history] and [credit scores]
How?	All financial companies need to share customers' personal information to run their everyday business. In the section below, we list the reasons financial companies can share their customers' personal information; the reasons [name of financial institution] chooses to share; and whether you can limit this sharing.

Reasons we can share your personal information	Does [name of financial institution] share?	Can you limit this sharing?
For our everyday business purposes— such as to process your transactions, maintain your account(s), respond to court orders and legal investigations, or report to credit bureaus		
For our marketing purposes— to offer our products and services to you		
For joint marketing with other financial companies		
For our affiliates' everyday business purposes— information about your transactions and experiences		
For our affiliates' everyday business purposes— information about your creditworthiness		
For our affiliates to market to you		
For nonaffiliates to market to you		

To limit our sharing	■ Call [phone number]—our menu will prompt you through your choice(s) ■ Visit us online: [website] or ■ Mail the form below **Please note:** If you are a *new* customer, we can begin sharing your information [30] days from the date we sent this notice. When you are *no longer* our customer, we continue to share your information as described in this notice. However, you can contact us at any time to limit our sharing.
Questions?	Call [phone number] or go to [website]

✂

Mail-in Form		
Leave Blank OR [If you have a joint account, your choice(s) will apply to everyone on your account unless you mark below. ❑ Apply my choices only to me]	Mark any/all you want to limit: ❑ Do not share information about my creditworthiness with your affiliates for their everyday business purposes. ❑ Do not allow your affiliates to use my personal information to market to me. ❑ Do not share my personal information with nonaffiliates to market their products and services to me. Name ______ Address ______ City, State, Zip ______ [Account #] ______	**Mail to:** [Name of Financial Institution] [Address1] [Address2] [City], [ST] [ZIP]

Version 4. Optional Mail-in Form.

Mail-in Form		
Leave Blank OR [If you have a joint account, your choice(s) will apply to everyone on your account unless you mark below. ❑ Apply my choices only to me]	**Mark any/all you want to limit:** ❑ Do not share information about my creditworthiness with your affiliates for their everyday business purposes. ❑ Do not allow your affiliates to use my personal information to market to me. ❑ Do not share my personal information with nonaffiliates to market their products and services to me.	
	Name	
	Address	
	City, State, Zip	
	[Account #]	

Mail To: [Name of Financial Institution], [Address1] [Address2], [City], [ST] [ZIP]

1. How the Model Privacy Form is Used

(a) The model form may be used, at the option of a financial institution, including a group of financial institutions that use a common privacy notice, to meet the content requirements of the privacy notice and opt-out notice set forth in §§313.6 and 313.7 of this part.

(b) The model form is a standardized form, including page layout, content, format, style, pagination, and shading. Institutions seeking to obtain the safe harbor through use of the model form may modify it only as described in these Instructions.

(c) Note that disclosure of certain information, such as assets, income, and information from a consumer reporting agency, may give rise to obligations under the Fair Credit Reporting Act [15 U.S.C. 1681–1681x] (FCRA), such as a requirement to permit a consumer to opt out of disclosures to affiliates or designation as a consumer reporting agency if disclosures are made to nonaffiliated third parties.

(d) The word "customer" may be replaced by the word "member" whenever it appears in the model form, as appropriate.

2. The Contents of the Model Privacy Form

The model form consists of two pages, which may be printed on both sides of a single sheet of paper, or may appear on two separate pages. Where an institution provides a long list of institutions at the end of the model form in accordance with Instruction C.3(a)(1), or provides additional information in accordance with Instruction C.3(c), and such list or additional information exceeds the space available on page two of the model form, such list or additional information may extend to a third page.

(a) *Page One.* The first page consists of the following components:

(1) Date last revised (upper right-hand corner).

(2) Title.

(3) Key frame (Why?, What?, How?).

(4) Disclosure table ("Reasons we can share your personal information").

(5) "To limit our sharing" box, as needed, for the financial institution's opt-out information.

(6) "Questions" box, for customer service contact information.

(7) Mail-in opt-out form, as needed.

(b) *Page Two.* The second page consists of the following components:

(1) Heading (Page 2).

(2) Frequently Asked Questions ("Who we are" and "What we do").

(3) Definitions.

(4) "Other important information" box, as needed.

3. The Format of the Model Privacy Form

The format of the model form may be modified only as described below.

(a) *Easily readable type font.* Financial institutions that use the model form must use an easily readable type font. While a number of factors together produce an easily readable type font, institutions are required to use a minimum of 10-point font (unless otherwise expressly permitted in these Instructions) and sufficient spacing between the lines of type.

(b) *Logo.* A financial institution may include a corporate logo on any page of the notice, so long as it does not interfere with the readability of the model form or the space constraints of each page.

(c) *Page size and orientation.* Each page of the model form must be printed on paper in portrait orientation, the size of which must be sufficient to meet the layout and minimum font size requirements, with sufficient white space on the top, bottom, and sides of the content.

(d) *Color.* The model form must be printed on white or light color paper (such as cream) with black or other contrasting ink color. Spot color may be used to achieve visual interest, so long as the color contrast is distinctive and the color does not detract from the readability of the model form. Logos may also be printed in color.

(e) *Languages.* The model form may be translated into languages other than English.

C. Information Required in the Model Privacy Form

The information in the model form may be modified only as described below:

1. Name of the Institution or Group of Affiliated Institutions Providing the Notice

Insert the name of the financial institution providing the notice or a common identity of affiliated institutions jointly providing the notice on the form wherever [name of financial institution] appears.

2. Page One

(a) *Last revised date.* The financial institution must insert in the upper right-hand corner the date on which the notice was last revised. The information shall appear in minimum 8-point font as "rev. [month/year]" using either the name or number of the month, such as "rev. July 2009" or "rev. 7/09".

(b) *General instructions for the "What?" box.* (1) The bulleted list identifies the types of personal information that the institution collects and shares. All institutions must use the term "Social Security number" in the first bullet.

(2) Institutions must use five (5) of the following terms to complete the bulleted list: income; account balances; payment history; transaction history; transaction or loss history; credit history; credit scores; assets; investment experience; credit-based insurance scores; insurance claim history; medical information; overdraft history; purchase history; account transactions; risk tolerance; medical-related debts; credit card or other debt; mortgage rates and payments; retirement assets; checking account information; employment information; wire transfer instructions.

(c) *General instructions for the disclosure table.* The left column lists reasons for sharing or using personal information. Each reason correlates to a specific legal provision described in paragraph C.2(d) of this Instruction. In the middle column, each institution must provide a "Yes" or "No" response that accurately reflects its information sharing policies and practices with respect to the reason listed on the left. In the right column, each institution must provide in each box one of the following three (3) responses, as applicable, that reflects whether a consumer can limit such sharing: "Yes" if it is required to or voluntarily provides an opt-out; "No" if it does not provide an opt-out; or "We don't share" if it answers "No" in the middle column. Only the sixth row ("For our affiliates to market to you") may be omitted at the option of the institution. *See* paragraph C.2(d)(6) of this Instruction.

(d) *Specific disclosures and corresponding legal provisions.* (1) *For our everyday business purposes.* This reason incorporates sharing information under §§313.14 and 313.15 and with service providers pursuant to §313.13 of this part other than the purposes specified in paragraphs C.2(d)(2) or C.2(d)(3) of these Instructions.

(2) *For our marketing purposes.* This reason incorporates sharing information with service providers by an institution for its own marketing pursuant to §313.13 of this part. An institution that shares for this reason may choose to provide an opt-out.

(3) *For joint marketing with other financial companies.* This reason incorporates sharing information under joint marketing agreements between two or more financial institutions and with any service provider used in connection with such agreements pursuant to §313.13 of this part. An institution that shares for this reason may choose to provide an opt-out.

(4) *For our affiliates' everyday business purposes—information about transactions and experiences.* This reason incorporates sharing information specified in sections 603(d)(2)(A)(i) and (ii) of the FCRA. An institution that shares for this reason may choose to provide an opt-out.

(5) *For our affiliates' everyday business purposes—information about creditworthiness.* This reason incorporates sharing information pursuant to section 603(d)(2)(A)(iii) of the FCRA. An institution that shares for this reason must provide an opt-out.

(6) *For our affiliates to market to you.* This reason incorporates sharing information specified in section 624 of the FCRA. This reason may be omitted from the disclosure table when: the institution does not have affiliates (or does not disclose personal information to its affiliates); the institution's affiliates do not use personal information in a manner that requires an opt-out; or the institution provides the affiliate marketing notice separately. Institutions that include this reason must provide an opt-out of indefinite duration. An institution that is required to provide an affiliate marketing opt-out, but does not include that opt-out in the

model form under this part, must comply with section 624 of the FCRA and 16 CFR parts 680 and 698 with respect to the initial notice and opt-out and any subsequent renewal notice and opt-out. An institution not required to provide an opt-out under this subparagraph may elect to include this reason in the model form.

(7) *For nonaffiliates to market to you.* This reason incorporates sharing described in §§ 313.7 and 313.10(a) of this part. An institution that shares personal information for this reason must provide an opt-out.

(e) *To limit our sharing:* A financial institution must include this section of the model form *only* if it provides an opt-out. The word "choice" may be written in either the singular or plural, as appropriate. Institutions must select one or more of the applicable opt-out methods described: telephone, such as by a toll-free number; a Web site; or use of a mail-in opt-out form. Institutions may include the words "toll-free" before telephone, as appropriate. An institution that allows consumers to opt out online must provide either a specific Web address that takes consumers directly to the opt-out page or a general Web address that provides a clear and conspicuous direct link to the opt-out page. The opt-out choices made available to the consumer who contacts the institution through these methods must correspond accurately to the "Yes" responses in the third column of the disclosure table. In the part titled "Please note" institutions may insert a number that is 30 or greater in the space marked "[30]." Instructions on voluntary or state privacy law opt-out information are in paragraph C.2(g)(5) of these Instructions.

(f) *Questions box.* Customer service contact information must be inserted as appropriate, where [phone number] or [Web site] appear. Institutions may elect to provide either a phone number, such as a toll-free number, or a Web address, or both. Institutions may include the words "toll-free" before the telephone number, as appropriate.

(g) *Mail-in opt-out form.* Financial institutions must include this mail-in form *only* if they state in the "To limit our sharing" box that consumers can opt out by mail. The mail-in form must provide opt-out options that correspond accurately to the "Yes" responses in the third column in the disclosure table. Institutions that require customers to provide only name and address may omit the section identified as "[account #]." Institutions that require additional or different information, such as a random opt-out number or a truncated account number, to implement an opt-out election should modify the "[account #]" reference accordingly. This includes institutions that require customers with multiple accounts to identify each account to which the opt-out should apply. An institution must enter its opt-out mailing address: In the far right of this form (*see* version 3); or below the form (*see* version 4). The reverse side of the mail-in opt-out form must not include any content of the model form.

(1) *Joint accountholder.* Only institutions that provide their joint accountholders the choice to opt out for only one accountholder, in accordance with paragraph C.3(a)(5) of these Instructions, must include in the far left column of the mail-in form the following statement: "If you have a joint account, your choice(s) will apply to everyone on your account unless you mark below. ☐ Apply my choice(s) only to me." The word "choice" may be written in either the singular or plural, as appropriate. Financial institutions that provide insurance products or services, provide this option, and elect to use the model form may substitute the word "policy" for "account" in this statement. Institutions that do not provide this option may eliminate this left column from the mail-in form.

(2) *FCRA Section 603(d)(2)(A)(iii) opt-out.* If the institution shares personal information pursuant to section 603(d)(2)(A)(iii) of the FCRA, it must include in the mail-in opt-out form the following statement: "☐ Do not share information about my creditworthiness with your affiliates for their everyday business purposes."

(3) *FCRA Section 624 opt-out.* If the institution incorporates section 624 of the FCRA in accord with paragraph C.2(d)(6) of these Instructions, it must include in the mail-in opt-out form the following statement: "☐ Do not allow your affiliates to use my personal information to market to me."

(4) *Nonaffiliate opt-out.* If the financial institution shares personal information pursuant to § 313.10(a) of this part, it must include in the mail-in opt-out form the following statement: "☐ Do not share my personal information with nonaffiliates to market their products and services to me."

(5) *Additional opt-outs.* Financial institutions that use the disclosure table to provide opt-out options beyond those required by Federal law must provide those opt-outs in this section of the model form. A financial institution that chooses to offer an opt-out for its own marketing in the mail-in opt-out form must include one of the two following statements: "☐ Do not share my personal information to market to me." *or* "☐ Do not use my personal information to market to me." A financial institution that chooses to offer an opt-out for joint marketing must include the following statement: "☐ Do not share my personal information with other financial institutions to jointly market to me."

(h) *Barcodes.* A financial institution may elect to include a barcode and/or "tagline" (an internal identifier) in 6-point font at the bottom of page one, as needed for information internal to the institution, so long as these do not interfere with the clarity or text of the form.

3. Page Two

(a) *General Instructions for the Questions.* Certain of the Questions may be customized as follows:

(1) *"Who is providing this notice?"* This question may be omitted where only one financial institution provides the model form and that institution is clearly identified in the title on page one. Two or more financial institutions that jointly provide the model form must use this question to identify themselves as required by §313.9(f) of this part. Where the list of institutions exceeds four (4) lines, the institution must describe in the response to this question the general types of institutions jointly providing the notice and must separately identify those institutions, in minimum 8-point font, directly following the "Other important information" box, or, if that box is not included in the institution's form, directly following the "Definitions." The list may appear in a multi-column format.

(2) *"How does [name of financial institution] protect my personal information?"* The financial institution may only provide additional information pertaining to its safeguards practices following the designated response to this question. Such information may include information about the institution's use of cookies or other measures it uses to safeguard personal information. Institutions are limited to a maximum of 30 additional words.

(3) *"How does [name of financial institution] collect my personal information?"* Institutions must use five (5) of the following terms to complete the bulleted list for this question: Open an account; deposit money; pay your bills; apply for a loan; use your credit or debit card; seek financial or tax advice; apply for insurance; pay insurance premiums; file an insurance claim; seek advice about your investments; buy securities from us; sell securities to us; direct us to buy securities; direct us to sell your securities; make deposits or withdrawals from your account; enter into an investment advisory contract; give us your income information; provide employment information; give us your employment history; tell us about your investment or retirement portfolio; tell us about your investment or retirement earnings; apply for financing; apply for a lease; provide account information; give us your contact information; pay us by check; give us your wage statements; provide your mortgage information; make a wire transfer; tell us who receives the money; tell us where to send the money; show your government-issued ID; show your driver's license; order a commodity futures or option trade. Institutions that collect personal information from their affiliates and/or credit bureaus must include after the bulleted list the following statement: "We also collect your personal information from others, such as credit bureaus, affiliates, or other companies." Institutions that do not collect personal information from their affiliates or credit bureaus but do collect information from other companies must include the following statement instead: "We also collect your personal information from other companies." Only institutions that do not collect any personal information from affiliates, credit bureaus, or other companies can omit both statements.

(4) *"Why can't I limit all sharing?"* Institutions that describe state privacy law provisions in the *"Other important information"* box must use the bracketed sentence: "See below for more on your rights under state law." Other institutions must omit this sentence.

(5) *"What happens when I limit sharing for an account I hold jointly with someone else?"* Only financial institutions that provide opt-out options must use this question. Other institutions must omit this question. Institutions must choose one of the following two statements to respond to this question: "Your choices will apply to everyone on your account." or "Your choices will apply to everyone on your account—unless you tell us otherwise." Financial institutions that provide insurance products or services and elect to use the model form may substitute the word "policy" for "account" in these statements.

(b) *General Instructions for the Definitions.* The financial institution must customize the space below the responses to the three definitions in this section. This specific information must be in italicized lettering to set off the information from the standardized definitions.

(1) *Affiliates.* As required by §313.6(a)(3) of this part, where [*affiliate information*] appears, the financial institution must:

(i) If it has no affiliates, state: "[*name of financial institution*] *has no affiliates*";

(ii) If it has affiliates but does not share personal information, state: *"[name of financial institution] does not share with our affiliates"*; or

(iii) If it shares with its affiliates, state, as applicable: *"Our affiliates include companies with a [common corporate identity of financial institution] name; financial companies such as [insert illustrative list of companies]; nonfinancial companies, such as [insert illustrative list of companies;] and others, such as [insert illustrative list]."*

(2) *Nonaffiliates.* As required by §313.6(c)(3) of this part, where [*nonaffiliate information*] appears, the financial institution must:

(i) If it does not share with nonaffiliated third parties, state: *"[name of financial institution] does not share with nonaffiliates so they can market to you"*; or

(ii) If it shares with nonaffiliated third parties, state, as applicable: *"Nonaffiliates we share with can include [list categories of companies such as mortgage companies, insurance companies, direct marketing companies, and nonprofit organizations]."*

(3) *Joint Marketing.* As required by §313.13 of this part, where [*joint marketing*] appears, the financial institution must:

(i) If it does not engage in joint marketing, state: "*[name of financial institution] doesn't jointly market*"; or

(ii) If it shares personal information for joint marketing, state, as applicable: "*Our joint marketing partners include [list categories of companies such as credit card companies].*"

(c) *General instructions for the "Other important information" box.* This box is optional. The space provided for information in this box is not limited. Only the following types of information can appear in this box.

(1) State and/or international privacy law information; and/or

(2) Acknowledgment of receipt form.

[74 FR 62966, Dec. 1, 2009]

PART 314—STANDARDS FOR SAFEGUARDING CUSTOMER INFORMATION

Sec.

AUTHORITY: 15 U.S.C. 6801(b), 6805(b)(2).

SOURCE: 67 FR 36493, May 23, 2002, unless otherwise noted.

§314.1 Purpose and scope.

(a) *Purpose.* This part, which implements sections 501 and 505(b)(2) of the Gramm-Leach-Bliley Act, sets forth standards for developing, implementing, and maintaining reasonable administrative, technical, and physical safeguards to protect the security, confidentiality, and integrity of customer information.

(b) *Scope.* This part applies to the handling of customer information by all financial institutions over which the Federal Trade Commission ("FTC" or "Commission") has jurisdiction. This part refers to such entities as "you." This part applies to all customer information in your possession, regardless of whether such information pertains to individuals with whom you have a customer relationship, or pertains to the customers of other financial institutions that have provided such information to you.

§314.2 Definitions.

(a) *In general.* Except as modified by this part or unless the context otherwise requires, the terms used in this part have the same meaning as set forth in the Commission's rule governing the Privacy of Consumer Financial Information, 16 CFR part 313.

(b) *Customer information* means any record containing nonpublic personal information as defined in 16 CFR 313.3(n), about a customer of a financial institution, whether in paper, electronic, or other form, that is handled or maintained by or on behalf of you or your affiliates.

(c) *Information security program* means the administrative, technical, or physical safeguards you use to access, collect, distribute, process, protect, store, use, transmit, dispose of, or otherwise handle customer information.

(d) *Service provider* means any person or entity that receives, maintains, processes, or otherwise is permitted access to customer information through its provision of services directly to a financial institution that is subject to this part.

§314.3 Standards for safeguarding customer information.

(a) *Information security program.* You shall develop, implement, and maintain a comprehensive information security program that is written in one or more readily accessible parts and contains administrative, technical, and physical safeguards that are appropriate to your size and complexity, the nature and scope of your activities, and the sensitivity of any customer information at issue. Such safeguards shall include the elements set forth in §314.4 and shall be reasonably designed to achieve the objectives of this part, as set forth in paragraph (b) of this section.

(b) *Objectives.* The objectives of section 501(b) of the Act, and of this part, are to:

(1) Insure the security and confidentiality of customer information;

(2) Protect against any anticipated threats or hazards to the security or integrity of such information; and

(3) Protect against unauthorized access to or use of such information that could result in substantial harm or inconvenience to any customer.

§314.4 Elements.

In order to develop, implement, and maintain your information security program, you shall:

(a) Designate an employee or employees to coordinate your information security program.

(b) Identify reasonably foreseeable internal and external risks to the security, confidentiality, and integrity of customer information that could result in the unauthorized disclosure, misuse, alteration, destruction or other compromise of such information, and assess the sufficiency of any safeguards in place to control these risks. At a minimum, such a risk assessment should include consideration of risks in each relevant area of your operations, including:

(1) Employee training and management;

(2) Information systems, including network and software design, as well as information processing, storage, transmission and disposal; and

(3) Detecting, preventing and responding to attacks, intrusions, or other systems failures.

(c) Design and implement information safeguards to control the risks you identify through risk assessment, and regularly test or otherwise monitor the effectiveness of the safeguards' key controls, systems, and procedures.

(d) Oversee service providers, by:

(1) Taking reasonable steps to select and retain service providers that are capable of maintaining appropriate safeguards for the customer information at issue; and

(2) Requiring your service providers by contract to implement and maintain such safeguards.

(e) Evaluate and adjust your information security program in light of the results of the testing and monitoring required by paragraph (c) of this section; any material changes to your operations or business arrangements; or any other circumstances that you know or have reason to know may have a material impact on your information security program.

§314.5 Effective date.

(a) Each financial institution subject to the Commission's jurisdiction must implement an information security program pursuant to this part no later than May 23, 2003.

(b) Two-year grandfathering of service contracts. Until May 24, 2004, a contract you have entered into with a nonaffiliated third party to perform services for you or functions on your behalf satisfies the provisions of §314.4(d), even if the contract does not include a requirement that the service provider maintain appropriate safeguards, as long as you entered into the contract not later than June 24, 2002.

PART 315—CONTACT LENS RULE

AUTHORITY: Pub. L. 108–164, secs. 1–12; 117 Stat. 2024 (15 U.S.C. 7601–7610).

SOURCE: 69 FR 40508, July 2, 2004, unless otherwise noted.

§315.1 Scope of regulations in this part.

This part, which shall be called the "Contact Lens Rule," implements the Fairness to Contact Lens Consumers Act, codified at 15 U.S.C. 7601–7610, which requires that rules be issued to address the release, verification, and sale of contact lens prescriptions. This part specifically governs contact lens prescriptions and related issues. Part 456 of Title 16 governs the availability of eyeglass prescriptions and related issues (the Ophthalmic Practice Rules (Eyeglass Rule)).

§ 315.2 Definitions.

For purposes of this part, the following definitions shall apply:

Business hour means an hour between 9 a.m. and 5 p.m., during a weekday (Monday through Friday), excluding Federal holidays. "Business hour" also may include, at the seller's option, a prescriber's regular business hours on Saturdays, provided that the seller has actual knowledge of these hours. "Business hour" shall be determined based on the time zone of the prescriber.

"Eight (8) business hours" shall be calculated from the time the prescriber receives the prescription verification information from the seller, and shall conclude when eight (8) business hours have elapsed. For verification requests received by a prescriber during non-business hours, the calculation of "eight (8) business hours" shall begin at 9 a.m. on the next weekday that is not a Federal holiday or, if applicable, on Saturday at the beginning of the prescriber's actual business hours.

Commission means the Federal Trade Commission.

Contact lens means any contact lens for which State or Federal law requires a prescription.

Contact lens fitting means the process that begins after an initial eye examination for contact lenses and ends when a successful fit has been achieved or, in the case of a renewal prescription, ends when the prescriber determines that no change in the existing prescription is required, and such term may include:

(1) An examination to determine lens specifications;

(2) Except in the case of a renewal of a contact lens prescription, an initial evaluation of the fit of the contact lens on the eye; and

(3) Medically necessary follow-up examinations.

Contact lens prescription means a prescription, issued in accordance with State and Federal law, that contains sufficient information for the complete and accurate filling of a prescription for contact lenses, including the following:

(1) The name of the patient;

(2) The date of examination;

(3) The issue date and expiration date of prescription;

(4) The name, postal address, telephone number, and facsimile telephone number of prescriber;

(5) The power, material or manufacturer or both of the prescribed contact lens;

(6) The base curve or appropriate designation of the prescribed contact lens;

(7) The diameter, when appropriate, of the prescribed contact lens; and

(8) In the case of a private label contact lens, the name of the manufacturer, trade name of the private label brand, and, if applicable, trade name of equivalent brand name.

Direct communication means completed communication by telephone, facsimile, or electronic mail.

Issue date means the date on which the patient receives a copy of the prescription at the completion of a contact lens fitting.

Ophthalmic goods are contact lenses, eyeglasses, or any component of eyeglasses.

Ophthalmic services are the measuring, fitting, and adjusting of ophthalmic goods subsequent to an eye examination.

Prescriber means, with respect to contact lens prescriptions, an ophthalmologist, optometrist, or other person permitted under State law to issue prescriptions for contact lenses in compliance with any applicable requirements established by the Food and Drug Administration. "Other person," for purposes of this definition, includes a dispensing optician who is permitted under State law to issue prescriptions and who is authorized or permitted under State law to perform contact lens fitting services.

Private label contact lenses mean contact lenses that are sold under the label of a seller where the contact lenses are identical to lenses made by the same manufacturer but sold under the labels of other sellers.

§ 315.3 Availability of contact lens prescriptions to patients.

(a) *In general.* When a prescriber completes a contact lens fitting, the prescriber:

(1) Whether or not requested by the patient, shall provide to the patient a

copy of the contact lens prescription; and

(2) Shall, as directed by any person designated to act on behalf of the patient, provide or verify the contact lens prescription by electronic or other means.

(b) *Limitations.* A prescriber may not:

(1) Require the purchase of contact lenses from the prescriber or from another person as a condition of providing a copy of a prescription under paragraph (a)(1) or (a)(2) of this section or as a condition of verification of a prescription under paragraph (a)(2) of this section;

(2) Require payment in addition to, or as part of, the fee for an eye examination, fitting, and evaluation as a condition of providing a copy of a prescription under paragraph (a)(1) or (a)(2) of this section or as a condition of verification of a prescription under paragraph (a)(2) of this section; or

(3) Require the patient to sign a waiver or release as a condition of releasing or verifying a prescription under paragraph (a)(1) or (a)(2) of this section.

§315.4 Limits on requiring immediate payment.

A prescriber may require payment of fees for an eye examination, fitting, and evaluation before the release of a contact lens prescription, but only if the prescriber requires immediate payment in the case of an examination that reveals no requirement for ophthalmic goods. For purposes of the preceding sentence, presentation of proof of insurance coverage for that service shall be deemed to be a payment.

§315.5 Prescriber verification.

(a) *Prescription requirement.* A seller may sell contact lenses only in accordance with a contact lens prescription for the patient that is:

(1) Presented to the seller by the patient or prescriber directly or by facsimile; or

(2) Verified by direct communication.

(b) *Information for verification.* When seeking verification of a contact lens prescription, a seller shall provide the prescriber with the following information through direct communication:

(1) The patient's full name and address;

(2) The contact lens power, manufacturer, base curve or appropriate designation, and diameter when appropriate;

(3) The quantity of lenses ordered;

(4) The date of patient request;

(5) The date and time of verification request;

(6) The name of a contact person at the seller's company, including facsimile and telephone numbers; and

(7) If the seller opts to include the prescriber's regular business hours on Saturdays as "business hours" for purposes of paragraph (c)(3) of this section, a clear statement of the prescriber's regular Saturday business hours.

(c) *Verification events.* A prescription is verified under paragraph (a)(2) of this section only if one of the following occurs:

(1) The prescriber confirms the prescription is accurate by direct communication with the seller;

(2) The prescriber informs the seller through direct communication that the prescription is inaccurate and provides the accurate prescription; or

(3) The prescriber fails to communicate with the seller within eight (8) business hours after receiving from the seller the information described in paragraph (b) of this section. During these eight (8) business hours, the seller shall provide a reasonable opportunity for the prescriber to communicate with the seller concerning the verification request.

(d) *Invalid prescription.* If a prescriber informs a seller before the deadline under paragraph (c)(3) of this section that the contact lens prescription is inaccurate, expired, or otherwise invalid, the seller shall not fill the prescription. The prescriber shall specify the basis for the inaccuracy or invalidity of the prescription. If the prescription communicated by the seller to the prescriber is inaccurate, the prescriber shall correct it, and the prescription shall then be deemed verified under paragraph (c)(2) of this section.

(e) *No alteration of prescription.* A seller may not alter a contact lens prescription. Notwithstanding the preceding sentence, a seller may substitute for private label contact lenses specified on a prescription identical contact lenses that the same company manufactures and sells under different labels.

(f) *Recordkeeping requirement—verification requests.* A seller shall maintain a record of all direct communications referred to in paragraph (a) of this section. Such record shall consist of the following:

(1) For prescriptions presented to the seller: the prescription itself, or the facsimile version thereof (including an email containing a digital image of the prescription), that was presented to the seller by the patient or prescriber.

(2) For verification requests by the seller:

(i) If the communication occurs via facsimile or e-mail, a copy of the verification request, including the information provided to the prescriber pursuant to paragraph (b) of this section, and confirmation of the completed transmission thereof, including a record of the date and time the request was made;

(ii) If the communication occurs via telephone, a log:

(A) Describing the information provided pursuant to paragraph (b) of this section,

(B) Setting forth the date and time the request was made,

(C) Indicating how the call was completed, and

(D) Listing the names of the individuals who participated in the call.

(3) For communications from the prescriber, including prescription verifications:

(i) If the communication occurs via facsimile or e-mail, a copy of the communication and a record of the time and date it was received;

(ii) If the communication occurs via telephone, a log describing the information communicated, the date and time that the information was received, and the names of the individuals who participated in the call.

(4) The records required to be maintained under this section shall be maintained for a period of not less than three years, and these records must be available for inspection by the Federal Trade Commission, its employees, and its representatives.

(g) *Recordkeeping requirement—Saturday business hours.* A seller that exercises its option to include a prescriber's regular Saturday business hours in the time period for verification specified in §315.5(c)(3) shall maintain a record of the prescriber's regular Saturday business hours and the basis for the seller's actual knowledge thereof. Such records shall be maintained for a period of not less than three years, and these records must be available for inspection by the Federal Trade Commission, its employees, and its representatives.

§315.6 Expiration of contact lens prescriptions.

(a) *In general.* A contact lens prescription shall expire:

(1) On the date specified by the law of the State in which the prescription was written, if that date is one year or more after the issue date of the prescription;

(2) Not less than one year after the issue date of the prescription if such State law specifies no date or specifies a date that is less than one year after the issue date of the prescription; or

(3) Notwithstanding paragraphs (a)(1) and (a)(2) of this section, on the date specified by the prescriber, if that date is based on the medical judgment of the prescriber with respect to the ocular health of the patient.

(b) *Special rules for prescriptions of less than one year.* (1) If a prescription expires in less than one year, the specific reasons for the medical judgment referred to in paragraph (a)(3) of this section shall be documented in the patient's medical record with sufficient detail to allow for review by a qualified professional in the field.

(2) The documentation described in the paragraph above shall be maintained for a period of not less than three years, and it must be available for inspection by the Federal Trade Commission, its employees, and its representatives.

(3) No prescriber shall include an expiration date on a prescription that is less than the period of time that he or she recommends for a reexamination of the patient that is medically necessary.

§315.7 Content of advertisements and other representations.

Any person who engages in the manufacture, processing, assembly, sale, offering for sale, or distribution of contact lenses may not represent, by advertisement, sales presentation, or otherwise, that contact lenses may be obtained without a prescription.

§315.8 Prohibition of certain waivers.

A prescriber may not place on a prescription, or require the patient to sign, or deliver to the patient, a form or notice waiving or disclaiming the liability or responsibility of the prescriber for the accuracy of the eye examination. The preceding sentence does not impose liability on a prescriber for the ophthalmic goods and services dispensed by another seller pursuant to the prescriber's correctly verified prescription.

§315.9 Enforcement.

Any violation of this Rule shall be treated as a violation of a rule under section 18 of the Federal Trade Commission Act, 15 U.S.C. 57a, regarding unfair or deceptive acts or practices, and the Commission will enforce this Rule in the same manner, by the same means, and with the same jurisdiction, powers, and duties as are available to it pursuant to the Federal Trade Commission Act, 15 U.S.C. 41 *et seq.*

§315.10 Severability.

The provisions of this part are separate and severable from one another. If any provision is stayed or determined to be invalid, it is the Commission's intention that the remaining provisions shall continue in effect.

§315.11 Effect on state and local laws.

(a) State and local laws and regulations that establish a prescription expiration date of less than one year or that restrict prescription release or require active verification are preempted.

(b) Any other State or local laws or regulations that are inconsistent with the Act or this part are preempted to the extent of the inconsistency.

PART 316—CAN-SPAM RULE

Sec.

AUTHORITY: 15 U.S.C. 7701-7713.

SOURCE: 73 FR 29677, May 21, 2008, unless otherwise noted.

§316.1 Scope.

This part implements the Controlling the Assault of Non-Solicited Pornography and Marketing Act of 2003 ("CAN-SPAM Act"), 15 U.S.C. 7701-7713.

§316.2 Definitions.

(a) The definition of the term "affirmative consent" is the same as the definition of that term in the CAN-SPAM Act, 15 U.S.C. 7702(1).

(b) "Character" means an element of the American Standard Code for Information Interchange ("ASCII") character set.

(c) The definition of the term "commercial electronic mail message" is the same as the definition of that term in the CAN-SPAM Act, 15 U.S.C. 7702(2).

(d) The definition of the term "electronic mail address" is the same as the definition of that term in the CAN-SPAM Act, 15 U.S.C. 7702(5).

(e) The definition of the term "electronic mail message" is the same as the definition of that term in the CAN-SPAM Act, 15 U.S.C. 7702(6).

(f) The definition of the term "initiate" is the same as the definition of that term in the CAN-SPAM Act, 15 U.S.C. 7702(9).

(g) The definition of the term "Internet" is the same as the definition of that term in the CAN-SPAM Act, 15 U.S.C. 7702(10).

(h) "Person" means any individual, group, unincorporated association, limited or general partnership, corporation, or other business entity.

(i) The definition of the term "procure" is the same as the definition of that term in the CAN-SPAM Act, 15 U.S.C. 7702(12).

(j) The definition of the term "protected computer" is the same as the definition of that term in the CAN-SPAM Act, 15 U.S.C. 7702(13).

(k) The definition of the term "recipient" is the same as the definition of that term in the CAN-SPAM Act, 15 U.S.C. 7702(14).

(l) The definition of the term "routine conveyance" is the same as the definition of that term in the CAN-SPAM Act, 15 U.S.C. 7702(15).

(m) The definition of the term "sender" is the same as the definition of that term in the CAN-SPAM Act, 15 U.S.C. 7702(16), *provided that,* when more than one person's products, services, or Internet website are advertised or promoted in a single electronic mail message, each such person who is within the Act's definition will be deemed to be a "sender," except that, only one person will be deemed to be the "sender" of that message if such person: (A) is within the Act's definition of "sender"; (B) is identified in the "from" line as the sole sender of the message; and (C) is in compliance with 15 U.S.C. 7704(a)(1), 15 U.S.C. 7704(a)(2), 15 U.S.C. 7704(a)(3)(A)(i), 15 U.S.C. 7704(a)(5)(A), and 16 CFR 316.4.

(n) The definition of the term "sexually oriented material" is the same as the definition of that term in the CAN-SPAM Act, 15 U.S.C. 7704(d)(4).

(o) The definition of the term "transactional or relationship messages" is the same as the definition of that term in the CAN-SPAM Act, 15 U.S.C. 7702(17).

(p) "Valid physical postal address" means the sender's current street address, a Post Office box the sender has accurately registered with the United States Postal Service, or a private mailbox the sender has accurately registered with a commercial mail receiving agency that is established pursuant to United States Postal Service regulations.

§ 316.3 Primary purpose.

(a) In applying the term "commercial electronic mail message" defined in the CAN-SPAM Act, 15 U.S.C. 7702(2), the "primary purpose" of an electronic mail message shall be deemed to be commercial based on the criteria in paragraphs (a)(1) through (3) and (b) of this section:[1]

(1) If an electronic mail message consists exclusively of the commercial advertisement or promotion of a commercial product or service, then the "primary purpose" of the message shall be deemed to be commercial.

(2) If an electronic mail message contains both the commercial advertisement or promotion of a commercial product or service as well as transactional or relationship content as set forth in paragraph (c) of this section, then the "primary purpose" of the message shall be deemed to be commercial if:

(i) A recipient reasonably interpreting the subject line of the electronic mail message would likely conclude that the message contains the commercial advertisement or promotion of a commercial product or service; or

(ii) The electronic mail message's transactional or relationship content as set forth in paragraph (c) of this section does *not* appear, in whole or in substantial part, at the beginning of the body of the message.

(3) If an electronic mail message contains both the commercial advertisement or promotion of a commercial product or service as well as other content that is not transactional or relationship content as set forth in paragraph (c) of this section, then the "primary purpose" of the message shall be deemed to be commercial if:

(i) A recipient reasonably interpreting the subject line of the electronic mail message would likely conclude that the message contains the commercial advertisement or promotion of a commercial product or service; or

(ii) A recipient reasonably interpreting the body of the message would likely conclude that the primary purpose of the message is the commercial

[1] The Commission does not intend for these criteria to treat as a "commercial electronic mail message" anything that is not commercial speech.

advertisement or promotion of a commercial product or service. Factors illustrative of those relevant to this interpretation include the placement of content that is the commercial advertisement or promotion of a commercial product or service, in whole or in substantial part, at the beginning of the body of the message; the proportion of the message dedicated to such content; and how color, graphics, type size, and style are used to highlight commercial content.

(b) In applying the term "transactional or relationship message" defined in the CAN-SPAM Act, 15 U.S.C. 7702(17), the "primary purpose" of an electronic mail message shall be deemed to be transactional or relationship if the electronic mail message consists exclusively of transactional or relationship content as set forth in paragraph (c) of this section.

(c) Transactional or relationship content of email messages under the CAN-SPAM Act is content:

(1) To facilitate, complete, or confirm a commercial transaction that the recipient has previously agreed to enter into with the sender;

(2) To provide warranty information, product recall information, or safety or security information with respect to a commercial product or service used or purchased by the recipient;

(3) With respect to a subscription, membership, account, loan, or comparable ongoing commercial relationship involving the ongoing purchase or use by the recipient of products or services offered by the sender, to provide —

(i) Notification concerning a change in the terms or features;

(ii) Notification of a change in the recipient's standing or status; or

(iii) At regular periodic intervals, account balance information or other type of account statement;

(4) To provide information directly related to an employment relationship or related benefit plan in which the recipient is currently involved, participating, or enrolled; or

(5) To deliver goods or services, including product updates or upgrades, that the recipient is entitled to receive under the terms of a transaction that the recipient has previously agreed to enter into with the sender.

§316.4 Requirement to place warning labels on commercial electronic mail that contains sexually oriented material.

(a) Any person who initiates, to a protected computer, the transmission of a commercial electronic mail message that includes sexually oriented material must:

(1) Exclude sexually oriented materials from the subject heading for the electronic mail message and include in the subject heading the phrase "SEXUALLY-EXPLICIT: " in capital letters as the first nineteen (19) characters at the beginning of the subject line;[2]

(2) Provide that the content of the message that is initially viewable by the recipient, when the message is opened by any recipient and absent any further actions by the recipient, include only the following information:

(i) The phrase "SEXUALLY-EXPLICIT: " in a clear and conspicuous manner;[3]

(ii) Clear and conspicuous identification that the message is an advertisement or solicitation;

(iii) Clear and conspicuous notice of the opportunity of a recipient to decline to receive further commercial electronic mail messages from the sender;

(iv) A functioning return electronic mail address or other Internet-based mechanism, clearly and conspicuously displayed, that

(A) A recipient may use to submit, in a manner specified in the message, a reply electronic mail message or other form of Internet-based communication requesting not to receive future commercial electronic mail messages from that sender at the electronic mail address where the message was received; and

(B) Remains capable of receiving such messages or communications for

---

[2] The phrase "SEXUALLY-EXPLICIT" comprises 17 characters, including the dash between the two words. The colon (:) and the space following the phrase are the 18th and 19th characters.

[3] This phrase consists of nineteen (19) characters and is identical to the phrase required in 316.5(a)(1) of this Rule.

no less than 30 days after the transmission of the original message;

(v) Clear and conspicuous display of a valid physical postal address of the sender; and

(vi) Any needed instructions on how to access, or activate a mechanism to access, the sexually oriented material, preceded by a clear and conspicuous statement that to avoid viewing the sexually oriented material, a recipient should delete the email message without following such instructions.

(b) *Prior affirmative consent.* Paragraph (a) does not apply to the transmission of an electronic mail message if the recipient has given prior affirmative consent to receipt of the message.

§ 316.5 Prohibition on charging a fee or imposing other requirements on recipients who wish to opt out.

Neither a sender nor any person acting on behalf of a sender may require that any recipient pay any fee, provide any information other than the recipient's electronic mail address and opt-out preferences, or take any other steps except sending a reply electronic mail message or visiting a single Internet Web page, in order to:

(a) Use a return electronic mail address or other Internet-based mechanism, required by 15 U.S.C. 7704(a)(3), to submit a request not to receive future commercial electronic mail messages from a sender; or

(b) Have such a request honored as required by 15 U.S.C. 7704(a)(3)(B) and (a)(4).

§ 316.6 Severability.

The provisions of this Part are separate and severable from one another. If any provision is stayed or determined to be invalid, it is the Commission's intention that the remaining provisions shall continue in effect.

PART 317—PROHIBITION OF ENERGY MARKET MANIPULATION RULE

AUTHORITY: 42 U.S.C. 17301-17305; 15 U.S.C. 41-58.

SOURCE: 74 FR 40701, Aug. 12, 2009, unless otherwise noted.

§ 317.1 Scope.

This part implements Subtitle B of Title VIII of The Energy Independence and Security Act of 2007 ("EISA"), Pub. L. 110-140, 121 Stat. 1723 (December 19, 2007), codified at 42 U.S.C. 17301-17305. This Rule applies to any person over which the Federal Trade Commission has jurisdiction under the Federal Trade Commission Act, 15 U.S.C. 41 *et seq.*

§ 317.2 Definitions.

The following definitions shall apply throughout this Rule:

(a) *Crude oil* means any mixture of hydrocarbons that exists:

(1) In liquid phase in natural underground reservoirs and that remains liquid at atmospheric pressure after passing through separating facilities; or

(2) As shale oil or tar sands requiring further processing for sale as a refinery feedstock.

(b) *Gasoline* means:

(1) Finished gasoline, including, but not limited to, conventional, reformulated, and oxygenated blends; and

(2) Conventional and reformulated gasoline blendstock for oxygenate blending.

(c) *Knowingly* means that the person knew or must have known that his or her conduct was fraudulent or deceptive.

(d) *Person* means any individual, group, unincorporated association, limited or general partnership, corporation, or other business entity.

(e) *Petroleum distillates* means:

(1) Jet fuels, including, but not limited to, all commercial and military specification jet fuels; and

(2) Diesel fuels and fuel oils, including, but not limited to, No. 1, No. 2, and No. 4 diesel fuel, and No. 1, No. 2, and No. 4 fuel oil.

(f) *Wholesale* means:

(1) All purchases or sales of crude oil or jet fuel; and

(2) All purchases or sales of gasoline or petroleum distillates (other than jet fuel) at the terminal rack or upstream of the terminal rack level.

§ 317.3 Prohibited practices.

It shall be unlawful for any person, directly or indirectly, in connection with the purchase or sale of crude oil, gasoline, or petroleum distillates at wholesale, to:

(a) Knowingly engage in any act, practice, or course of business—including the making of any untrue statement of material fact—that operates or would operate as a fraud or deceit upon any person; or

(b) Intentionally fail to state a material fact that under the circumstances renders a statement made by such person misleading, provided that such omission distorts or is likely to distort market conditions for any such product.

§ 317.4 Preemption.

The Federal Trade Commission does not intend, through the promulgation of this Rule, to preempt the laws of any state or local government, except to the extent that any such law conflicts with this Rule. A law is not in conflict with this Rule if it affords equal or greater protection from the prohibited practices set forth in § 317.3.

§ 317.5 Severability.

The provisions of this Rule are separate and severable from one another. If any provision is stayed or determined to be invalid, it is the Commission's intention that the remaining provisions shall continue in effect.

PART 318—HEALTH BREACH NOTIFICATION RULE

Sec.

AUTHORITY: Public Law 111-5, 123 Stat. 115 (2009).

SOURCE: 74 FR 42980, Aug. 25, 2009, unless otherwise noted.

§ 318.1 Purpose and scope.

(a) This part, which shall be called the "Health Breach Notification Rule," implements section 13407 of the American Recovery and Reinvestment Act of 2009. It applies to foreign and domestic vendors of personal health records, PHR related entities, and third party service providers, irrespective of any jurisdictional tests in the Federal Trade Commission (FTC) Act, that maintain information of U.S. citizens or residents. It does not apply to HIPAA-covered entities, or to any other entity to the extent that it engages in activities as a business associate of a HIPAA-covered entity.

(b) This part preempts state law as set forth in section 13421 of the American Recovery and Reinvestment Act of 2009.

§ 318.2 Definitions.

(a) *Breach of security* means, with respect to unsecured PHR identifiable health information of an individual in a personal health record, acquisition of such information without the authorization of the individual. Unauthorized acquisition will be presumed to include unauthorized access to unsecured PHR identifiable health information unless the vendor of personal health records, PHR related entity, or third party service provider that experienced the breach has reliable evidence showing that there has not been, or could not reasonably have been, unauthorized acquisition of such information.

(b) *Business associate* means a business associate under the Health Insurance Portability and Accountability Act, Public Law 104-191, 110 Stat. 1936, as defined in 45 CFR 160.103.

(c) *HIPAA*-covered entity means a covered entity under the Health Insurance Portability and Accountability Act, Public Law 104-191, 110 Stat. 1936, as defined in 45 CFR 160.103.

(d) *Personal health record* means an electronic record of PHR identifiable health information on an individual that can be drawn from multiple sources and that is managed, shared, and controlled by or primarily for the individual.

(e) *PHR identifiable health information* means "individually identifiable health information," as defined in section

1171(6) of the Social Security Act (42 U.S.C. 1320d(6)), and, with respect to an individual, information:

(1) That is provided by or on behalf of the individual; and

(2) That identifies the individual or with respect to which there is a reasonable basis to believe that the information can be used to identify the individual.

(f) *PHR related entity* means an entity, other than a HIPAA-covered entity or an entity to the extent that it engages in activities as a business associate of a HIPAA-covered entity, that:

(1) Offers products or services through the Web site of a vendor of personal health records;

(2) Offers products or services through the Web sites of HIPAA-covered entities that offer individuals personal health records; or

(3) Accesses information in a personal health record or sends information to a personal health record.

(g) *State* means any of the several States, the District of Columbia, Puerto Rico, the Virgin Islands, Guam, American Samoa and the Northern Mariana Islands.

(h) *Third party service provider* means an entity that:

(1) Provides services to a vendor of personal health records in connection with the offering or maintenance of a personal health record or to a PHR related entity in connection with a product or service offered by that entity; and

(2) Accesses, maintains, retains, modifies, records, stores, destroys, or otherwise holds, uses, or discloses unsecured PHR identifiable health information as a result of such services.

(i) *Unsecured* means PHR identifiable information that is not protected through the use of a technology or methodology specified by the Secretary of Health and Human Services in the guidance issued under section 13402(h)(2) of the American Reinvestment and Recovery Act of 2009.

(j) *Vendor of personal health records* means an entity, other than a HIPAA-covered entity or an entity to the extent that it engages in activities as a business associate of a HIPAA-covered entity, that offers or maintains a personal health record.

§318.3 Breach notification requirement.

(a) *In general.* In accordance with §§318.4, 318.5, and 318.6, each vendor of personal health records, following the discovery of a breach of security of unsecured PHR identifiable health information that is in a personal health record maintained or offered by such vendor, and each PHR related entity, following the discovery of a breach of security of such information that is obtained through a product or service provided by such entity, shall:

(1) Notify each individual who is a citizen or resident of the United States whose unsecured PHR identifiable health information was acquired by an unauthorized person as a result of such breach of security; and

(2) Notify the Federal Trade Commission.

(b) *Third party service providers.* A third party service provider shall, following the discovery of a breach of security, provide notice of the breach to an official designated in a written contract by the vendor of personal health records or the PHR related entity to receive such notices or, if such a designation is not made, to a senior official at the vendor of personal health records or PHR related entity to which it provides services, and obtain acknowledgment from such official that such notice was received. Such notification shall include the identification of each customer of the vendor of personal health records or PHR related entity whose unsecured PHR identifiable health information has been, or is reasonably believed to have been, acquired during such breach. For purposes of ensuring implementation of this requirement, vendors of personal health records and PHR related entities shall notify third party service providers of their status as vendors of personal health records or PHR related entities subject to this Part.

(c) *Breaches treated as discovered.* A breach of security shall be treated as discovered as of the first day on which such breach is known or reasonably should have been known to the vendor of personal health records, PHR related entity, or third party service provider, respectively. Such vendor, entity, or third party service provider shall be deemed to have knowledge of a breach if such breach is known, or reasonably should have been known, to any person, other than the person committing the breach, who is an employee, officer, or other agent of such vendor of personal health records, PHR related entity, or third party service provider.

§ 318.4 Timeliness of notification.

(a) *In general.* Except as provided in paragraph (c) of this section and § 318.5(c), all notifications required under §§ 318.3(a)(1), 318.3(b), and 318.5(b) shall be sent without unreasonable delay and in no case later than 60 calendar days after the discovery of a breach of security.

(b) *Burden of proof.* The vendor of personal health records, PHR related entity, and third party service provider involved shall have the burden of demonstrating that all notifications were made as required under this Part, including evidence demonstrating the necessity of any delay.

(c) *Law enforcement exception.* If a law enforcement official determines that a notification, notice, or posting required under this Part would impede a criminal investigation or cause damage to national security, such notification, notice, or posting shall be delayed. This paragraph shall be implemented in the same manner as provided under 45 CFR 164.528(a)(2), in the case of a disclosure covered under such section.

§ 318.5 Methods of notice.

(a) *Individual notice.* A vendor of personal health records or PHR related entity that discovers a breach of security shall provide notice of such breach to an individual promptly, as described in § 318.4, and in the following form:

(1) Written notice, by first-class mail to the individual at the last known address of the individual, or by email, if the individual is given a clear, conspicuous, and reasonable opportunity to receive notification by first-class mail, and the individual does not exercise that choice. If the individual is deceased, the vendor of personal health records or PHR related entity that discovered the breach must provide such notice to the next of kin of the individual if the individual had provided contact information for his or her next of kin, along with authorization to contact them. The notice may be provided in one or more mailings as information is available.

(2) If, after making reasonable efforts to contact all individuals to whom notice is required under § 318.3(a), through the means provided in paragraph (a)(1) of this section, the vendor of personal health records or PHR related entity finds that contact information for ten or more individuals is insufficient or out-of-date, the vendor of personal health records or PHR related entity shall provide substitute notice, which shall be reasonably calculated to reach the individuals affected by the breach, in the following form:

(i) Through a conspicuous posting for a period of 90 days on the home page of its Web site; or

(ii) In major print or broadcast media, including major media in geographic areas where the individuals affected by the breach likely reside. Such a notice in media or web posting shall include a toll-free phone number, which shall remain active for at least 90 days, where an individual can learn whether or not the individual's unsecured PHR identifiable health information may be included in the breach.

(3) In any case deemed by the vendor of personal health records or PHR related entity to require urgency because of possible imminent misuse of unsecured PHR identifiable health information, that entity may provide information to individuals by telephone or other means, as appropriate, in addition to notice provided under paragraph (a)(1) of this section.

(b) *Notice to media.* A vendor of personal health records or PHR related entity shall provide notice to prominent media outlets serving a State or jurisdiction, following the discovery of a breach of security, if the unsecured PHR identifiable health information of 500 or more residents of such State or jurisdiction is, or is reasonably believed to have been, acquired during such breach.

(c) *Notice to FTC.* Vendors of personal health records and PHR related entities shall provide notice to the Federal Trade Commission following the discovery of a breach of security. If the breach involves the unsecured PHR identifiable health information of 500 or more individuals, then such notice shall be provided as soon as possible and in no case later than ten business days following the date of discovery of the breach. If the breach involves the unsecured PHR identifiable health information of fewer than 500 individuals, the vendor of personal health records or PHR related entity may maintain a log of any such breach, and submit such a log annually to the Federal Trade Commission no later than 60 calendar days following the end of the calendar year, documenting breaches from the preceding calendar year. All notices pursuant to this paragraph shall be provided according to instructions at the Federal Trade Commission's Web site.

§ 318.6 Content of notice.

Regardless of the method by which notice is provided to individuals under § 318.5 of this part, notice of a breach of security shall be in plain language and include, to the extent possible, the following:

(a) A brief description of what happened, including the date of the breach and the date of the discovery of the breach, if known;

(b) A description of the types of unsecured PHR identifiable health information that were involved in the breach (such as full name, Social Security number, date of birth, home address, account number, or disability code);

(c) Steps individuals should take to protect themselves from potential harm resulting from the breach;

(d) A brief description of what the entity that suffered the breach is doing to investigate the breach, to mitigate harm, and to protect against any further breaches; and

(e) Contact procedures for individuals to ask questions or learn additional information, which shall include a toll-free telephone number, an email address, Web site, or postal address.

§ 318.7 Enforcement.

A violation of this part shall be treated as an unfair or deceptive act or practice in violation of a regulation under § 18(a)(1)(B) of the Federal Trade Commission Act (15 U.S.C. 57a(a)(1)(B)) regarding unfair or deceptive acts or practices.

§ 318.8 Effective date.

This part shall apply to breaches of security that are discovered on or after September 24, 2009.

§ 318.9 Sunset.

If new legislation is enacted establishing requirements for notification in the case of a breach of security that apply to entities covered by this part, the provisions of this part shall not apply to breaches of security discovered on or after the effective date of regulations implementing such legislation.

PART 320—DISCLOSURE REQUIREMENTS FOR DEPOSITORY INSTITUTIONS LACKING FEDERAL DEPOSIT INSURANCE

AUTHORITY: 12 U.S.C. 1831t; 15 U.S.C. 41 *et seq.*

SOURCE: 77 FR 22203, Apr. 13, 2012, unless otherwise noted.

§ 320.1 Cross-reference.

The rules formerly at 16 CFR part 320 have been republished by the Consumer Financial Protection Bureau at 12 CFR part 1009, "Disclosure Requirements for Depository Institutions Lacking Federal Deposit Insurance (Regulation I)."

PART 321—MORTGAGE ACTS AND PRACTICES—ADVERTISING

AUTHORITY: Pub. L. 111–8, section 626, 123 Stat. 524, as amended by Pub. L. 111–24, section 511, 123 Stat. 1734.

SOURCE: 77 FR 22203, Apr. 13, 2012, unless otherwise noted.

§ 321.1 Cross-reference.

The rules formerly at 16 CFR part 321 have been republished by the Consumer Financial Protection Bureau at 12 CFR part 1014, "Mortgage Acts and Practices Advertising (Regulation N)."

PART 322—MORTGAGE ASSISTANCE RELIEF SERVICES

AUTHORITY: Pub. L. 111–8, section 626, 123 Stat. 524, as amended by Pub. L. 111–24, section 511, 123 Stat. 1734.

SOURCE: 77 FR 22203, Apr. 13, 2012, unless otherwise noted.

§ 322.1 Cross-reference.

The rules formerly at 16 CFR part 322 have been republished by the Consumer Financial Protection Bureau at 12 CFR part 1015, "Mortgage Assistance Relief Services (Regulation O)."

SUBCHAPTER D—TRADE REGULATION RULES

PART 408—UNFAIR OR DECEPTIVE ADVERTISING AND LABELING OF CIGARETTES IN RELATION TO THE HEALTH HAZARDS OF SMOKING

CROSS REFERENCE: For a statement of basis and purpose of Trade Regulation Rule, see 29 FR 8325 of July 2, 1964.

[30 FR 9485, July 29, 1965]

PART 410—DECEPTIVE ADVERTISING AS TO SIZES OF VIEWABLE PICTURES SHOWN BY TELEVISION RECEIVING SETS

EFFECTIVE DATE NOTE: At 83 FR 50487, Oct. 9, 2019, part 410 was removed, effective Jan. 7, 2019.

§ 410.1 The Rule.

In connection with the sale of television receiving sets, in commerce, as "commerce" is defined in the Federal Trade Commission Act, it is an unfair method of competition and an unfair and deceptive act or practice to use any figure or size designation to refer to the size of the picture shown by a television receiving set or the picture tube contained therein unless such indicated size is the actual size of the viewable picture area measured on a single plane basis. If the indicated size is other than the horizontal dimension of the actual viewable picture area such size designation shall be accompanied by a statement, in close connection and conjunction therewith, clearly and conspicuously showing the manner of measurement.

NOTE 1: For the purposes of this part, measurement of the picture area on a single plane basis refers to a measurement of the distance between the outer extremities (sides) of the picture area which does not take into account the curvature of the tube.

NOTE 2: Any referenced or footnote disclosure of the manner of measurement by means of the asterisk or some similar symbol does not satisfy the "close connection and conjunction" requirement of this part.

Examples of proper size descriptions when a television receiving set shows a 20-inch picture measured diagonally, a 19-inch picture measured horizontally, a 15-inch picture measured vertically, and a picture area of 262 square inches include:

"20 inch (50.80 cm) picture measured diagonally" or
"20 inch (50.80 cm) diagonal"
"19 inch × 15 inch (48.26 cm × 38.10 cm) picture" or
"19 inch (48.26 cm) picture" or
"19 inch (48.26 cm)" or
"262 square inch (1,690.32 cm. sq.) picture."

Examples of improper size descriptions of a television set showing a picture of the size described above include:

"21 inch (53.34 cm) set" or
"21 inch (53.34 cm) diagonal set" or
"21 inch (53.34 cm) over-all diagonal" or "Brand Name 21."

NOTE 3: The numbers in parentheses reflect the metric equivalent of the English measurements. They are provided for information purposes only, and are not required to be included in the disclosures.

(38 Stat. 717, as amended, 15 U.S.C. 41–58)

[36 FR 21518, Nov. 10, 1971; 36 FR 22286, Nov. 24, 1971, as amended at 59 FR 54812, Nov. 2, 1994]

PART 423—CARE LABELING OF TEXTILE WEARING APPAREL AND CERTAIN PIECE GOODS AS AMENDED

AUTHORITY: 38 Stat. 717, as amended; (15 U.S.C. 41, *et seq.*)

SOURCE: 48 FR 22743, May 20, 1983; 48 FR 24869, June 3, 1983, unless otherwise noted.

§423.1 Definitions.

(a) *Care label* means a permanent label or tag, containing regular care information and instructions, that is attached or affixed in such a manner that it will not become separated from the product and will remain legible during the useful life of the product.

(b) *Certain Piece Goods* means textile products sold by the piece from bolts or rolls for the purpose of making home sewn textile wearing apparel. This includes remnants, the fiber content of which is known, that are cut by or for a retailer but does not include manufacturers' remnants, up to ten yards long, that are clearly and conspicuously marked *pound goods* or *fabrics of undetermined origin* (i.e., fiber content is not known and cannot be easily ascertained) and trim, up to five inches wide.

(c) *Dryclean* means a commercial process by which soil is removed from products or specimens in a machine which uses any common organic solvent (e.g. petroleum, perchlorethylene, fluorocarbon). The process may also include adding moisture to the solvent, up to 75% relative humidity, hot tumble drying up to 160 degrees F (71 degrees C) and restoration by steam press or steam-air finishing.

(d) *Machine Wash* means a process by which soil is removed from products in a specially designed machine using water, detergent or soap and agitation. When no temperature is given, e.g., *warm* or *cold*, hot water up to 145 degrees F (63 degrees C) can be regularly used.

(e) *Regular Care* means customary and routine care, not spot care.

(f) *Textile Product* means any commodity, woven, knit or otherwise made primarily of fiber, yarn or fabric and intended for sale or resale, requiring care and maintenance to effectuate ordinary use and enjoyment.

(g) *Textile Wearing Apparel* means any finished garment or article of clothing made from a textile product that is customarily used to cover or protect any part of the body, including hosiery, excluding footwear, gloves, hats or other articles used exclusively to cover or protect the head or hands.

[48 FR 22743, May 20, 1983; 48 FR 24869, June 3, 1983, as amended at 65 FR 47275, Aug. 2, 2000]

§423.2 Terminology.

(a) Any appropriate terms may be used on care labels or care instructions so long as they clearly and accurately describe regular care procedures and otherwise fulfill the requirements of this regulation.

(b) Any appropriate symbols may be used on care labels or care instructions, in addition to the required appropriate terms so long as the terms fulfill the requirements of this part. See §423.8(g) for conditional exemption allowing the use of symbols without terms.

(c) The terminology set forth in appendix A may be used to fulfill the requirements of this regulation.

[48 FR 22743, May 20, 1983; 48 FR 24869, June 3, 1983; 62 FR 29008, May 29, 1997]

§423.3 What this regulation does.

This regulation requires manufacturers and importers of textile wearing apparel and certain piece goods, in or affecting commerce, as "commerce" is defined in the Federal Trade Commission Act, to provide regular care instructions at the time such products are sold to purchasers through the use of care labels or other methods described in this rule.

§423.4 Who is covered.

Manufacturers and importers of textile wearing apparel and certain piece goods are covered by this regulation. This includes any person or organization that directs or controls the manufacture or importation of covered products.

§423.5 Unfair or deceptive acts or practices.

(a) *Textile wearing apparel and certain piece goods.* In connection with the sale, in or affecting commerce, of textile wearing apparel and certain piece goods, it is an unfair or deceptive act or practice for a manufacturer or importer:

(1) To fail to disclose to a purchaser, prior to sale, instructions which prescribe a regular care procedure necessary for the ordinary use and enjoyment of the product;

(2) To fail to warn a purchaser, prior to sale, when the product cannot be cleaned by any cleaning procedure, without being harmed;

(3) To fail to warn a purchaser, prior to sale, when any part of the prescribed regular care procedure, which a consumer or professional cleaner could reasonably be expected to use, would harm the product or others being cleaned with it;

(4) To fail to provide regular care instructions and warnings, except as to piece goods, in a form that can be referred to by the consumer throughout the useful life of the product;

(5) To fail to possess, prior to sale, a reasonable basis for all regular care information disclosed to the purchaser.

(b) *Violations of this regulation.* The Commission has adopted this regulation to prevent the unfair or deceptive acts or practices, defined in paragraph (a) of this section. Each manufacturer or importer covered by this regulation must comply with the requirements in §§ 423.2 and 423.6 through 423.8 of this regulation. Any manufacturer or importer who complies with the requirements of §§ 423.2 and 423.6 through 423.8 does not violate this regulation.

(Approved by the Office of Management and Budget under control number 3084–0046)

§ 423.6 Textile wearing apparel.

This section applies to textile wearing apparel.

(a) Manufacturers and importers must attach care labels so that they can be seen or easily found when the product is offered for sale to consumers. If the product is packaged, displayed, or folded so that customers cannot see or easily find the label, the care information must also appear on the outside of the package or on a hang tag fastened to the product.

(b) Care labels must state what regular care is needed for the ordinary use of the product. In general, labels for textile wearing apparel must have either a washing instruction or a drycleaning instruction. If a washing instruction is included, it must comply with the requirements set forth in paragraph (b)(1) of this section. If a drycleaning instruction is included, it must comply with the requirements set forth in paragraph (b)(2) of this section. If either washing or drycleaning can be used on the product, the label need have only one of these instructions. If the product cannot be cleaned by any available cleaning method without being harmed, the label must so state. [For example, if a product would be harmed both by washing and by drycleaning, the label might say "Do not wash—do not dryclean," or "Cannot be successfully cleaned."] The instructions for washing and drycleaning are as follows:

(1) Washing, drying, ironing, bleaching and warning instructions must follow these requirements:

(i) *Washing.* The label must state whether the product should be washed by hand or machine. The label must also state a water temperature—in terms such as *cold, warm,* or *hot*—that may be used. However, if the regular use of hot water up to 145 degrees F (63 degrees C) will not harm the product, the label need not mention any water temperature. [For example, *Machine wash* means hot, warm or cold water can be used.]

(ii) *Drying.* The label must state whether the product should be dried by machine or by some other method. If machine drying is called for, the label must also state a drying temperature that may be used. However, if the regular use of a high temperature will not harm the product, the label need not mention any drying temperature. [For example, *Tumble dry* means that a high, medium, or low temperature setting can be used.]

(iii) *Ironing.* Ironing must be mentioned on a label only if it will be needed on a regular basis to preserve the appearance of the product, or if it is required under paragraph (b)(1)(v) of this section, *Warnings.* If ironing is mentioned, the label must also state an ironing temperature that may be used. However, if the regular use of a hot iron will not harm the product, the label need not mention any ironing temperature.

(iv) *Bleaching.* (A) If all commercially available bleaches can safely be used on a regular basis, the label need not mention bleaching.

(B) If all commercially available bleaches would harm the product when used on a regular basis, the label must say "No bleach" or "Do not bleach."

(C) If regular use of chlorine bleach would harm the product, but regular use of a non-chlorine bleach would not, the label must say "Only non-chlorine bleach, when needed."

(v) *Warnings.* (A) If there is any part of the prescribed washing procedure which consumers can reasonably be expected to use that would harm the product or others being washed with it in one or more washings, the label must contain a warning to this effect. The warning must use words "Do not," "No," "Only," or some other clear wording. [For example, if a shirt is not colorfast, its label should state "Wash with like colors" or "Wash separately." If a pair of pants will be harmed by ironing, its label should state "Do not iron."]

(B) Warnings are not necessary for any procedure that is an alternative to the procedure prescribed on the label. [For example, if an instruction states "Dry flat," it is not necessary to give the warning "Do not tumble dry."]

(2) *Drycleaning*—(i) *General.* If a drycleaning instruction is included on the label, it must also state at least one type of solvent that may be used. However, if all commercially available types of solvent can be used, the label need not mention any types of solvent. The terms "Drycleanable" or "Commercially Dryclean" may not be used in an instruction. [For example, if drycleaning in perchlorethylene would harm a coat, the label might say "Professionally dryclean: fluorocarbon or petroleum."]

(ii) *Warnings.* (A) If there is any part of the drycleaning procedure which consumers or drycleaners can reasonably be expected to use that would harm the product or others being cleaned with it, the label must contain a warning to this effect. The warning must use the words "Do not," "No," "Only," or some other clear wording. [For example, the drycleaning process normally includes moisture addition to solvent up to 75% relative humidity, hot tumble drying up to 160 degrees F and restoration by steam press or steam-air finish. If a product can be drycleaned in all solvents but steam should not be used, its label should state "Professionally dryclean. No steam."]

(B) Warnings are not necessary to any procedure which is an alternative to the procedure prescribed on the label. [For example, if an instruction states "Professionally dryclean, fluorocarbon," it is not necessary to give the warning "Do not use perchlorethylene."]

(c) A manufacturer or importer must establish a reasonable basis for care information by processing prior to sale:

(1) Reliable evidence that the product was not harmed when cleaned reasonably often according to the instructions on the label, including instructions when silence has a meaning. [For example, if a shirt is labeled "Machine wash. Tumble dry. Cool iron.," the manufacturer or importer must have reliable proof that the shirt is not harmed when cleaned by machine washing (in hot water), with any type of bleach, tumble dried (at a high setting), and ironed with a cool iron]; or

(2) Reliable evidence that the product or a fair sample of the product was harmed when cleaned by methods warned against on the label. However, the manufacturer or importer need not have proof of harm when silence does not constitute a warning. [For example, if a shirt is labeled "Machine wash warm. Tumble dry medium", the manufacturer need not have proof that the shirt would be harmed if washed in hot water or dried on high setting]; or

(3) Reliable evidence, like that described in paragraph (c)(1) or (2) of this section, for each component part of the product in conjunction with reliable evidence for the garment as a whole; or

(4) Reliable evidence that the product or a fair sample of the product was successfully tested. The tests may simulate the care suggested or warned against on the label; or

(5) Reliable evidence of current technical literature, past experience, or the industry expertise supporting the care information on the label; or

(6) Other reliable evidence.

[48 FR 22743, May 20, 1983; 48 FR 24869, June 3, 1983, as amended at 65 FR 47275, Aug. 2, 2000]

§ 423.7 Certain piece goods.

This section applies to certain piece goods.

(a) Manufacturers and importers of certain piece goods must provide care information clearly and conspicuously on the end of each bolt or roll.

(b) Care information must say what regular care is needed for the ordinary use of the product, pursuant to the instructions set forth in § 423.6. Care information on the end of the bolt need only address information applicable to the fabric.

§ 423.8 Exemptions.

(a) Any item of textile wearing apparel, without pockets, that is totally reversible (i.e., the product is designed to be used with either side as the outer part or face) is exempt from the care label requirement.

(b) Manufacturers or importers can ask for an exemption from the care label requirement for any other textile wearing apparel product or product line, if the label would harm the appearance or usefulness of the product. The request must be made in writing to the Secretary of the Commission. The request must be accompanied by a labeled sample of the product and a full statement explaining why the request should be granted.

(c) If an item is exempt from care labeling under paragraph (a) or (b), of this section the consumers still must be given the required care information for the product. However, the care information can be put on a hang tag, on the package, or in some other conspicuous place, so that consumers will be able to see the care information before buying the product.

(d) Manufacturers and importers of products covered by § 423.5 are exempt from the requirement for a permanent care label if the product can be cleaned safely under the harshest procedures. This exemption is available only if there is reliable proof that all of the following washing and drycleaning procedures can safely be used on a product:

(1) Machine washing in hot water;

(2) Machine drying at a high setting;

(3) Ironing at a hot setting;

(4) Bleaching with all commercially available bleaches;

(5) Drycleaning with all commercially available solvents. In such case, the statement "wash or dry clean, any normal method" must appear on a hang tag, on the package, or in some other conspicuous place, so that consumers will be able to see the statement before buying the product.

If a product meets the requirements outlined above, it is automatically exempt from the care label requirement. It is not necessary to file a request for this exemption.

(e) Manufacturers and importers need not provide care information with products sold to institutional buyers for commercial use.

(f) All exemption granted under § 423.1(c) (1) or (2) or the Care Labeling Rule issued on December 9, 1971, will continue to be in effect if the product still meets the standards on which the original exemption was based. Otherwise, the exemption is automatically revoked.

(g) The symbol system developed by the American Society for Testing and Materials (ASTM) and designated as ASTM Standard D5489–96c Guide to Care Symbols for Care Instructions on Consumer Textile Products may be used on care labels or care instructions in lieu of terms so long as the symbols fulfill the requirements of this part. In addition, symbols from the symbol system designated as ASTM Standard D5489–96c may be combined with terms so long as the symbols and terms used fulfill the requirements of this part. Provided, however, that for the 18-month period beginning on July 1, 1997, such symbols may be used on care labels in lieu of terms only if an explanation of the meaning of the symbols used on the care label in terms is attached to, or provided with, the item of textile wearing apparel. This incorporation by reference was approved by the Director of the Federal Register in accordance with 5 U.S.C. 552(a) and 1 CFR part 51. Copies of ASTM Standard D5489–96c Guide to Care Symbols for Care Instructions on Textile Products may be obtained from the American

Society for Testing and Materials, 100 Barr Harbor Drive, West Conshohocken, PA 19428, or may be inspected at the Federal Trade Commission, room 130, 600 Pennsylvania Avenue, NW., Washington, DC, or at the National Archives and Records Administration (NARA). For information on the availability of this material at NARA, call 202-741-6030, or go to: *http://www.archives.gov/federal_register/code_of_federal_regulations/ibr_locations.html.*

(15 U.S.C. 41–58)

[48 FR 22743, May 20, 1983; 48 FR 24869, June 3, 1983, as amended at 62 FR 29008, May 29, 1997; 69 FR 18803, Apr. 9, 2004]

§ 423.9 Conflict with flammability standards.

If there is a conflict between this regulation and any regulations issued under the Flammable Fabrics Act, the Flammable Fabics regulation govern over this one.

§ 423.10 Stayed or invalid parts.

If any part of this regulation is stayed or held invalid, the rest of it will stay in force.

Appendix A to Part 423—Glossary of Standard Terms

1. *Washing, Machine Methods:*

a. "Machine wash"—a process by which soil may be removed from products or specimens through the use of water, detergent or soap, agitation, and a machine designed for this purpose. When no temperature is given, e.g., "warm" or "cold," hot water up to 145 degrees F (63 degrees C) can be regularly used.

b. "Hot"—initial water temperature ranging from 112 to 145 degrees F [45 to 63 degrees C].

c. "Warm"—initial water temperature ranging from 87 to 111 degrees F [31 to 44 degrees C].

d. "Cold"—initial water temperature up to 86 degrees F [30 degrees C].

e. "Do not have commercially laundered"—do not employ a laundry which uses special formulations, sour rinses, extermely large loads or extermely high temperatures or which otherwise is employed for commercial, industrial or institutional use. Employ laundering methods designed for residential use or use in a self-service establishment.

f. "Small load"—smaller than normal washing load.

g. "Delicate cycle" or "gentle cycle"—slow agitation and reduced time.

h. "Durable press cycle" or "permanent press cycle"—cool down rinse or cold rinse before reduced spinning.

i. "Separately"—alone.

j. "With like colors"—with colors of similar hue and intensity.

k. "Wash inside out"—turn product inside out to protect face of fabric.

l. "Warm rinse"—initial water temperature setting 90° to 110 °F (32° to 43 °C).

m. "Cold rinse"—initial water temperature setting same as cold water tap up to 85 °F (29 °C).

n. "Rinse thoroughly"—rinse several times to remove detergent, soap, and bleach.

o. "No spin" or "Do not spin"—remove material start of final spin cycle.

p. "No wring" or "Do not wring"—do not use roller wringer, nor wring by hand.

2. *Washing, Hand Methods:*

a. "Hand wash"—a process by which soil may be manually removed from products or specimens through the use of water, detergent or soap, and gentle squeezing action. When no temperature is given, e.g., "warm" or "cold", hot water up to 150 °F (66 °C) can be regularly used.

b. "Warm"—initial water temperature 90° to 110 °F (32° to 43 °C) (hand comfortable).

c. "Cold"—initial water temperature same as cold water tap up to 85 °F (29 °C).

d. "Separately"—alone.

e. "With like colors"—with colors of similar hue and intensity.

f. "No wring or twist"—handle to avoid wrinkles and distortion.

g. "Rinse thoroughly"—rinse several times to remove detergent, soap, and bleach.

h. "Damp wipe only"—surface clean with damp cloth or sponge.

3. *Drying, All Methods:*

a. "Tumble dry"—use machine dryer. When no temperature setting is given, machine drying at a hot setting may be regularly used.

b. "Medium"—set dryer at medium heat.

c. "Low"—set dryer at low heat.

d. "Durable press" or "Permanent press"—set dryer at permanent press setting.

e. "No heat"—set dryer to operate without heat.

f. "Remove promptly"—when items are dry, remove immediately to prevent wrinkling.

g. "Drip dry"—hang dripping wet with or without hand shaping and smoothing.

h. "Line dry"—hang damp from line or bar in or out of doors.

i. "Line dry in shade"—dry away from sun.

j. "Line dry away from heat"—dry away from heat.

k. "Dry flat"—lay out horizontally for drying.

l. "Block to dry"—reshape to original dimensions while drying.

m. "Smooth by hand"—by hand, while wet, remove wrinkles, straighten seams and facings.

4. *Ironing and Pressing:*

a. "Iron"—Ironing is needed. When no temperature is given iron at the highest temperature setting may be regularly used.

b. "Warm iron"—medium temperature setting.

c. "Cool iron"—lowest temperature setting.

d. "Do not iron"—item not to be smoothed or finished with an iron.

e. "Iron wrong side only"—article turned inside out for ironing or pressing.

f. "No steam" or "Do not steam"—steam in any form not to be used.

g. "Steam only"—steaming without contact pressure.

h. "Steam press" or "Steam iron"—use iron at steam setting.

i. "Iron damp"—articles to be ironed should feel moist.

j. "Use press cloth"—use a dry or a damp cloth between iron and fabric.

5. *Bleaching:*

a. "Bleach when needed"—all bleaches may be used when necessary.

b. "No bleach" or "Do not bleach"—no bleaches may be used.

c. "Only non-chlorine bleach, when needed"—only the bleach specified may be used when necessary. Chlorine bleach may not be used.

6. *Washing or Drycleaning:*

a. "Wash or dryclean, any normal method"—can be machine washed in hot water, can be machine dried at a high setting, can be ironed at a hot setting, can be bleached with all commercially available bleaches and can be drycleaned with all commercially available solvents.

7. *Drycleaning, All Procedures:*

a. "Dryclean"—a process by which soil may be removed from products or specimens in a machine which uses any common organic solvent (for example, petroleum, perchlorethylene, fluorocarbon) located in any commercial establishment. The process may include moisture addition to solvent up to 75% relative humidity, hot tumble drying up to 160 °F (71 °C) and restoration by steam press or steam-air finishing.

b. "Professionally dryclean"—use the drycleaning process but modified to ensure optimum results either by a drycleaning attendant or through the use of a drycleaning machine which permits such modifications or both. Such modifications or special warnings must be included in the care instruction.

c. "Petroleum", "Fluorocarbon", or "Perchlorethylene"—employ solvent(s) specified to dryclean the item.

d. "Short cycle"—reduced or minimum cleaning time, depending upon solvent used.

e. "Minimum extraction"—least possible extraction time.

f. "Reduced moisture" or "Low moisture"—decreased relative humidity.

g. "No tumble" or "Do not tumble"—do not tumble dry.

h. "Tumble warm"—tumble dry up to 120 °F (49 °C).

i. "Tumble cool"—tumble dry at room temperature.

j. "Cabinet dry warm"—cabinet dry up to 120 °F (49 °C).

k. "Cabinet dry cool"—cabinet dry at room temperature.

l. "Steam only"—employ no contact pressure when steaming.

m. "No steam" or "Do not steam"—do not use steam in pressing, finishing, steam cabinets or wands.

8. *Leather and Suede Cleaning:*

a. "Leather clean"—have cleaned only by a professional cleaner who uses special leather or suede care methods.

[48 FR 22743, May 20, 1983; 48 FR 24868, June 3, 1983; 48 FR 27225, June 14, 1983, as amended at 65 FR 47275, Aug. 2, 2000]

PART 424—RETAIL FOOD STORE ADVERTISING AND MARKETING PRACTICES

AUTHORITY: 15 U.S.C. 41–58.

§ 424.1 Unfair or deceptive acts or practices.

In connection with the sale or offering for sale by retail food stores of food, grocery products or other merchandise to consumers in or affecting commerce as "commerce" is defined in section 4 of the Federal Trade Commission Act, 15 U.S.C. 44, it is an unfair or deceptive act or practice in violation of section 5(a)(1) of the Federal Trade Commission Act, 15 U.S.C. 45(a)(1), to offer any such products for sale at a stated price, by means of an advertisement disseminated in an area served by any stores which are covered by the advertisement, if those stores do not have the advertised products in stock and readily available to customers during the effective period of the advertisement, unless the advertisement clearly and adequately discloses that supplies of the advertised products are limited or the advertised products are available only at some outlets.

[54 FR 35467, Aug. 28, 1989, as amended at 79 FR 70056, Nov. 25, 2014]

§424.2 Defenses.

No violation of §424.1 shall be found if:

(a) The advertised products were ordered in adequate time for delivery in quantities sufficient to meet reasonably anticipated demand;

(b) The food retailer offers a "raincheck" for the advertised products;

(c) The food retailer offers at the advertised price or at a comparable price reduction a similar product that is at least comparable in value to the advertised product; or

(d) The food retailer offers other compensation at least equal to the advertised value.

[54 FR 35467, Aug. 28, 1989, as amended at 79 FR 70056, Nov. 25, 2014]

PART 425—USE OF PRENOTIFICATION NEGATIVE OPTION PLANS

§425.1 The rule.

(a) In connection with the sale, offering for sale, or distribution of goods and merchandise in or affecting commerce, as "commerce" is defined in the Federal Trade Commission Act, it is an unfair or deceptive act or practice, for a seller in connection with the use of any negative option plan to fail to comply with the following requirements:

(1) Promotional material shall clearly and conspicuously disclose the material terms of the plan, including:

(i) That aspect of the plan under which the subscriber must notify the seller, in the manner provided for by the seller, if he does not wish to purchase the selection;

(ii) Any obligation assumed by the subscriber to purchase a minimum quantity of merchandise;

(iii) The right of a contract-complete subscriber to cancel his membership at any time;

(iv) Whether billing charges will include an amount for postage and handling;

(v) A disclosure indicating that the subscriber will be provided with at least ten (10) days in which to mail any form, contained in or accompanying an announcement identifying the selection, to the seller;

(vi) A disclosure that the seller will credit the return of any selections sent to a subscriber, and guarantee to the Postal Service or the subscriber postage to return such selections to the seller when the announcement and form are not received by the subscriber in time to afford him at least ten (10) days in which to mail his form to the seller;

(vii) The frequency with which the announcements and forms will be sent to the subscriber and the maximum number of announcements and forms which will be sent to him during a 12-month period.

(2) Prior to sending any selection, the seller shall mail to its subscribers, within the time specified by paragraph (a)(3) of this section:

(i) An announcement identifying the selection;

(ii) A form, contained in or accompanying the announcement, clearly and conspicuously disclosing that the subscriber will receive the selection identified in the announcement unless he instructs the seller that he does not want the selection, designating a procedure by which the form may be used for the purpose of enabling the subscriber so to instruct the seller, and specifying either the return date or the mailing date.

(3) The seller shall mail the announcement and form either at least twenty (20) days prior to the return date or at least fifteen (15) days prior to the mailing date, or provide a mailing date at least ten (10) days after receipt by the subscriber, provided, however, that whichever system the seller chooses for mailing the announcement and form, such system must provide the subscriber with at least ten (10) days in which to mail his form.

(b) In connection with the sale or distribution of goods and merchandise in or affecting commerce, as "commerce" is defined in the Federal Trade Commission Act, it shall constitute an unfair or deceptive act or practice for a seller in connection with the use of any negative option plan to:

(1) Refuse to credit, for the full invoiced amount thereof, the return of any selection sent to a subscriber, and to guarantee to the Postal Service or the subscriber postage adequate to return such selection to the seller, when:

(i) The selection is sent to a subscriber whose form indicating that he does not want to receive the selection was received by the seller by the return date or was mailed by the subscriber by the mailing date;

(ii) Such form is received by the seller after the return date, but has been mailed by the subscriber and postmarked at least 3 days prior to the return date;

(iii) Prior to the date of shipment of such selection, the seller has received from a contract-complete subscriber, a written notice of cancellation of membership adequately identifying the subscriber; however, this provision is applicable only to the first selection sent to a canceling contract-complete subscriber after the seller has received written notice of cancellation. After the first selection shipment, all selection shipments thereafter are deemed to be unordered merchandise pursuant to section 3009 of the Postal Reorganization Act of 1970, as adopted by the Federal Trade Commission in its public notice, dated September 11, 1970;

(iv) The announcement and form are not received by the subscriber in time to afford him at least ten (10) days in which to mail his form.

(2) Fail to notify a subscriber known by the seller to be within any of the circumstances set forth in paragraphs (b)(1)(i) through (iv) of this section, that if the subscriber elects, the subscriber may return the selection with return postage guaranteed and receive a credit to his account.

(3) Refuse to ship within 4 weeks after receipt of an order merchandise due subscribers as introductory and bonus merchandise, unless the seller is unable to deliver the merchandise originally offered due to unanticipated circumstances beyond the seller's control and promptly makes a reasonably equivalent alternative offer. However, where the subscriber refuses to accept alternatively offered introductory merchandise, but instead insists upon termination of his membership due to the seller's failure to provide the subscriber with his originally requested introductory merchandise, or any portion thereof, the seller must comply with the subscriber's request for cancellation of membership, provided the subscriber returns to the seller any introductory merchandise which already may have been sent him.

(4) Fail to terminate promptly the membership of a properly identified contract-complete subscriber upon his written request.

(5) Ship, without the express consent of the subscriber, substituted merchandise for that ordered by the subscriber.

(c) For the purposes of this part:

(1) *Negative option plan* refers to a contractual plan or arrangement under which a seller periodically sends to subscribers an announcement which identifies merchandise (other than annual supplements to previously acquired merchandise) it proposes to send to subscribers to such plan, and the subscribers thereafter receive and are billed for the merchandise identified in each such announcement, unless by a date or within a time specified by the seller with respect to each such announcement the subscribers, in conformity with the provisions of such plan, instruct the seller not to send the identified merchandise.

(2) *Subscriber* means any person who has agreed to receive the benefits of, and assume the obligations entailed in, membership in any negative option plan and whose membership in such negative option plan has been approved and accepted by the seller.

(3) *Contract-complete subscriber* refers to a subscriber who has purchased the minimum quantity of merchandise required by the terms of membership in a negative option plan.

(4) *Promotional material* refers to an advertisement containing or accompanying any device or material which a prospective subscriber sends to the seller to request acceptance or enrollment in a negative option plan.

(5) *Selection* refers to the merchandise identified by a seller under any negative option plan as the merchandise which the subscriber will receive and be billed for, unless by the date, or

within the period specified by the seller, the subscriber instructs the seller not to send such merchandise.

(6) *Announcement* refers to any material sent by a seller using a negative option plan in which the selection is identified and offered to subscribers.

(7) *Form* refers to any form which the subscriber returns to the seller to instruct the seller not to send the selection.

(8) *Return date* refers to a date specified by a seller using a negative option plan as the date by which a form must be received by the seller to prevent shipment of the selection.

(9) *Mailing date* refers to the time specified by a seller using a negative option plan as the time by or within which a form must be mailed by a subscriber to prevent shipment of the selection.

(38 Stat. 717, as amended; 15 U.S.C. 41–58)

[38 FR 4896; Feb. 22, 1973; 38 FR 6991, Mar. 15, 1973, as amended at 63 FR 44562, Aug. 20, 1998]

PART 429—RULE CONCERNING COOLING-OFF PERIOD FOR SALES MADE AT HOMES OR AT CERTAIN OTHER LOCATIONS

Sec.

AUTHORITY: Sections 1–23, FTC Act, 15 U.S.C. 41–58.

§429.0 Definitions.

For the purposes of this part the following definitions shall apply:

(a) *Door-to-Door Sale*—A sale, lease, or rental of consumer goods or services in which the seller or his representative personally solicits the sale, including those in response to or following an invitation by the buyer, and the buyer's agreement or offer to purchase is made at a place other than the place of business of the seller (*e.g.*, sales at the buyer's residence or at facilities rented on a temporary or short-term basis, such as hotel or motel rooms, convention centers, fairgrounds and restaurants, or sales at the buyer's workplace or in dormitory lounges), and which has a purchase price of $25 or more if the sale is made at the buyer's residence or a purchase price of $130 or more if the sale is made at locations other than the buyer's residence, whether under single or multiple contracts. The term *door-to-door sale* does not include a transaction:

(1) Made pursuant to prior negotiations in the course of a visit by the buyer to a retail business establishment having a fixed permanent location where the goods are exhibited or the services are offered for sale on a continuing basis; or

(2) In which the consumer is accorded the right of rescission by the provisions of the Consumer Credit Protection Act (15 U.S.C. 1635) or regulations issued pursuant thereto; or

(3) In which the buyer has initiated the contact and the goods or services are needed to meet a bona fide immediate personal emergency of the buyer, and the buyer furnishes the seller with a separate dated and signed personal statement in the buyer's handwriting describing the situation requiring immediate remedy and expressly acknowledging and waiving the right to cancel the sale within 3 business days; or

(4) Conducted and consummated entirely by mail or telephone; and without any other contact between the buyer and the seller or its representative prior to delivery of the goods or performance of the services; or

(5) In which the buyer has initiated the contact and specifically requested the seller to visit the buyer's home for the purpose of repairing or performing maintenance upon the buyer's personal property. If, in the course of such a visit, the seller sells the buyer the right to receive additional services or goods other than replacement parts necessarily used in performing the maintenance or in making the repairs, the sale of those additional goods or services would not fall within this exclusion; or

(6) Pertaining to the sale or rental of real property, to the sale of insurance, or to the sale of securities or commodities by a broker-dealer registered with the Securities and Exchange Commission.

(b) *Consumer Goods or Services*—Goods or services purchased, leased, or rented primarily for personal, family, or household purposes, including courses of instruction or training regardless of the purpose for which they are taken.

(c) *Seller*—Any person, partnership, corporation, or association engaged in the door-to-door sale of consumer goods or services.

(d) *Place of Business*—The main or permanent branch office or local address of a seller.

(e) *Purchase Price*—The total price paid or to be paid for the consumer goods or services, including all interest and service charges.

(f) *Business Day*—Any calendar day except Sunday or any federal holiday (e.g., New Year's Day, Presidents' Day, Martin Luther King's Birthday, Memorial Day, Independence Day, Labor Day, Columbus Day, Veterans' Day, Thanksgiving Day, and Christmas Day.)

[60 FR 54186, Oct. 20, 1995, as amended at 80 FR 1332, Jan. 9, 2015]

§429.1 The Rule.

In connection with any door-to-door sale, it constitutes an unfair and deceptive act or practice for any seller to:

(a) Fail to furnish the buyer with a fully completed receipt or copy of any contract pertaining to such sale at the time of its execution, which is in the same language, e.g., Spanish, as that principally used in the oral sales presentation and which shows the date of the transaction and contains the name and address of the seller, and in immediate proximity to the space reserved in the contract for the signature of the buyer or on the front page of the receipt if a contract is not used and in bold face type of a minimum size of 10 points, a statement in substantially the following form:

"You, the buyer, may cancel this transaction at any time prior to midnight of the third business day after the date of this transaction. See the attached notice of cancellation form for an explanation of this right."

The seller may select the method of providing the buyer with the duplicate notice of cancellation form set forth in paragraph (b) of this section, *provided however*, that in the event of cancellation the buyer must be able to retain a complete copy of the contract or receipt. Furthermore, if both forms are not attached to the contract or receipt, the seller is required to alter the last sentence in the statement above to conform to the actual location of the forms.

(b) Fail to furnish each buyer, at the time the buyer signs the door-to-door sales contract or otherwise agrees to buy consumer goods or services from the seller, a completed form in duplicate, captioned either "NOTICE OF RIGHT TO CANCEL" or "NOTICE OF CANCELLATION," which shall (where applicable) contain in ten point bold face type the following information and statements in the same language, e.g., Spanish, as that used in the contract.

NOTICE OF CANCELLATION

[enter date of transaction]

____

(Date)

You may CANCEL this transaction, without any Penalty or Obligation, within THREE BUSINESS DAYS from the above date.

If you cancel, any property traded in, any payments made by you under the contract or sale, and any negotiable instrument executed by you will be returned within TEN BUSINESS DAYS following receipt by the seller of your cancellation notice, and any security interest arising out of the transaction will be cancelled.

If you cancel, you must make available to the seller at your residence, in substantially as good condition as when received, any goods delivered to you under this contract or sale, or you may, if you wish, comply with the instructions of the seller regarding the return shipment of the goods at the seller's expense and risk.

If you do make the goods available to the seller and the seller does not pick them up within 20 days of the date of your Notice of Cancellation, you may retain or dispose of the goods without any further obligation. If you fail to make the goods available to the seller, or if you agree to return the goods to the seller and fail to do so, then you remain liable for performance of all obligations under the contract.

To cancel this transaction, mail or deliver a signed and dated copy of this Cancellation Notice or any other written notice, or send a telegram, to [*Name of seller*], at [*address of seller's place of business*] NOT LATER THAN MIDNIGHT OF [*date*].

I HEREBY CANCEL THIS TRANSACTION.
(Date) ____________
(Buyer's signature) ____________

(c) Fail, before furnishing copies of the "Notice of Cancellation" to the buyer, to complete both copies by entering the name of the seller, the address of the seller's place of business, the date of the transaction, and the date, not earlier than the third business day following the date of the transaction, by which the buyer may give notice of cancellation.

(d) Include in any door-to-door contract or receipt any confession of judgment or any waiver of any of the rights to which the buyer is entitled under this section including specifically the buyer's right to cancel the sale in accordance with the provisions of this section.

(e) Fail to inform each buyer orally, at the time the buyer signs the contract or purchases the goods or services, of the buyer's right to cancel.

(f) Misrepresent in any manner the buyer's right to cancel.

(g) Fail or refuse to honor any valid notice of cancellation by a buyer and within 10 business days after the receipt of such notice, to: (i) Refund all payments made under the contract or sale; (ii) return any goods or property traded in, in substantially as good condition as when received by the seller; (iii) cancel and return any negotiable instrument executed by the buyer in connection with the contract or sale and take any action necessary or appropriate to terminate promptly any security interest created in the transaction.

(h) Negotiate, transfer, sell, or assign any note or other evidence of indebtedness to a finance company or other third party prior to midnight of the fifth business day following the day the contract was signed or the goods or services were purchased.

(i) Fail, within 10 business days of receipt of the buyer's notice of cancellation, to notify the buyer whether the seller intends to repossess or to abandon any shipped or delivered goods.

[37 FR 22934, Oct. 26, 1972, as amended at 38 FR 30105, Nov. 1, 1973; 38 FR 31828, Nov. 19, 1973; 53 FR 45459, Nov. 10, 1988; 60 FR 54186, Oct. 20, 1995]

§ 429.2 Effect on State laws and municipal ordinances.

(a) The Commission is cognizant of the significant burden imposed upon door-to-door sellers by the various and often inconsistent State laws that provide the buyer the right to cancel a door-to-door sales transaction. However, it does not believe that this constitutes sufficient justification for preempting all of the provisions of such laws and the ordinances of the political subdivisions of the various States. The rulemaking record in this proceeding supports the view that the joint and coordinated efforts of both the Commission and State and local officials are required to insure that consumers who have purchased from a door-to-door seller something they do not want, do not need, or cannot afford, be accorded a unilateral right to rescind, without penalty, their agreements to purchase those goods or services.

(b) This part will not be construed to annul, or exempt any seller from complying with, the laws of any State or the ordinances of a political subdivision thereof that regulate door-to-door sales, except to the extent that such laws or ordinances, if they permit door-to-door selling, are directly inconsistent with the provisions of this part. Such laws or ordinances which do not accord the buyer, with respect to the particular transaction, a right to cancel a door-to-door sale that is substantially the same or greater than that provided in this part, which permit the imposition of any fee or penalty on the buyer for the exercise of such right, or which do not provide for giving the buyer a notice of the right to cancel the transaction in substantially the same form and manner provided for in this part, are among those which will be considered directly inconsistent.

[60 FR 54187, Oct. 20, 1995]

§ 429.3 Exemptions.

(a) The requirements of this part do not apply for sellers of automobiles, vans, trucks or other motor vehicles sold at auctions, tent sales or other temporary places of business, provided that the seller is a seller of vehicles with a permanent place of business.

(b) The requirements of this part do not apply for sellers of arts or crafts sold at fairs or similar places.

[60 FR 54187, Oct. 20, 1995]

PART 432—POWER OUTPUT CLAIMS FOR AMPLIFIERS UTILIZED IN HOME ENTERTAINMENT PRODUCTS

Sec.

AUTHORITY: 38 Stat. 717, as amended; (15 U.S.C. 41–58).

SOURCE: 39 FR 15387, May 3, 1974, unless otherwise noted.

§ 432.1 Scope.

(a) Except as provided in paragraph (b) of this section, this part shall apply whenever any power output (in watts or otherwise), power band or power frequency response, or distortion capability or characteristic is represented, either expressly or by implication, in connection with the advertising, sale, or offering for sale, in commerce as "commerce" is defined in the Federal Trade Commission Act, of sound power amplification equipment manufactured or sold for home entertainment purposes, such as for example, radios, record and tape players, radio-phonograph and/or tape combinations, component audio amplifiers, self-powered speakers for computers, multimedia systems and sound systems, and the like.

(b) Representations shall be exempt from this part if all representations of performance characteristics referred to in paragraph (a) of this section clearly and conspicuously disclose a manufacturer's rated power output and that rated output does not exceed two (2) watts (per channel or total).

(c) It is an unfair method of competition and an unfair or deceptive act or practice within the meaning of section 5(a)(1) of the Federal Trade Commission Act (15 U.S.C. 45(a)(1)) to violate any applicable provision of this part.

[39 FR 15387, May 3, 1974, as amended at 63 FR 37235, July 9, 1998]

§ 432.2 Required disclosures.

(a) Whenever any direct or indirect representation is made of the power output, power band or power frequency response, or distortion characteristics of sound power amplification equipment, the following disclosure shall be made clearly, conspicuously, and more prominently than any other representations or disclosures permitted under this part: The manufacturer's rated minimum sine wave continuous average power output, in watts, per channel (if the equipment is designed to amplify two or more channels simultaneously) at an impedance of 8 ohms, or, if the amplifier is not designed for an 8-ohm impedance, at the impedance for which the amplifier is primarily designed, measured with all associated channels fully driven to rated per channel power. *Provided*, however, when measuring maximum per channel output of self-powered combination speaker systems that employ two or more amplifiers dedicated to different portions of the audio frequency spectrum, such as those incorporated into combination subwoofer-satellite speaker systems, only those channels dedicated to the same audio frequency spectrum should be considered associated channels that need be fully driven simultaneously to rated per channel power.

(b) In addition, whenever any direct or indirect representation is made of the power output, power band or power frequency response, or distortion characteristics of sound power amplification equipment in any product brochure or manufacturer specification sheet, the following disclosures also shall be made clearly, conspicuously, and more prominently than any other representations or disclosures permitted under this part:

(1) The manufacturer's rated power band or power frequency response, in Hertz (Hz), for the rated power output required to be disclosed in paragraph (a) of this section; and

(2) The manufacturer's rated percentage of maximum total harmonic distortion at any power level from 250 mW to

the rated power output, and its corresponding rated power band or power frequency response.

[65 FR 81239, Dec. 22, 2000]

§ 432.3 Standard test conditions.

For purposes of performing the tests necessary to make the disclosures required under § 432.2 of this part:

(a) The power line voltage shall be 120 volts AC (230 volts when the equipment is made for foreign sale or use, unless a different nameplate rating is permanently affixed to the product by the manufacturer in which event the latter figure would control), RMS, using a sinusoidal wave containing less than 2 percent total harmonic content. In the case of equipment designed for battery operation only, tests shall be made with the battery power supply for which the particular equipment is designed and such test voltage must be disclosed under the required disclosures of § 432.2 of this part. If capable of both AC and DC battery operation, testing shall be with AC line operation;

(b) The AC power line frequency for domestic equipment shall be 60 Hz and 50 Hz for equipment made for foreign sale or use;

(c) The amplifier shall be preconditioned by simultaneously operating all channels at one-eighth of rated power output for one hour using a sinusoidal wave at a frequency of 1,000 Hz; *provided, however*, that for amplifiers utilized as a component in a self-powered subwoofer system, the sinusoidal wave used as a preconditioning signal may be any frequency within the amplifier's intended operating bandwidth that will allow the amplifier to be driven to one-eighth of rated power for one hour;

(d) The preconditioning and testing shall be in still air and an ambient temperature of at least 77 °F (25 °C);

(e) Rated power shall be obtainable at all frequencies within the rated power band without exceeding the rated maximum percentage of total harmonic distortion after input signals at said frequencies have been continuously applied at full rated power for not less than five (5) minutes at the amplifier's auxiliary input, or if not provided, at the phono input.

(f) At all times during warm-up and testing, tone loudness-contour and other controls shall be preset for the flattest response.

[39 FR 15387, May 3, 1974, as amended at 65 FR 81240, Dec. 22, 2000]

§ 432.4 Optional disclosures.

Other operating characteristics and technical specifications not required in § 432.2 of this part may be disclosed: *Provided:*

(a) That any other power output is rated by the manufacturer, is expressed in minimum watts per channel, and such power output representation(s) complies with the provisions of § 432.2 of this part; except that if a peak or other instantaneous power rating, such as music power or peak power, is represented under this section, the maximum percentage of total harmonic distortion (see § 432.2(d) of this part) may be disclosed only at such rated output: *And provided further,*

(b) That all disclosures or representations made under this section are less conspicuously, and prominently made than the disclosures required in § 432.2 of this part; and

(c) The rating and testing methods or standards used in determining such representations are disclosed, and well known and generally recognized by the industry at the time the representations or disclosures are made, are neither intended nor likely to deceive or confuse the consumers and are not otherwise likely to frustrate the purpose of this part.

NOTE 1: For the purpose of paragraph (b) of this section, optional disclosures will not be considered less prominent if they are either bold faced or are more than two-thirds the height of the disclosures required by § 432.2.

NOTE 2: Use of the asterisk in effecting any of the disclosures required by § 432.2 and permitted by § 432.4 shall not be deemed conspicuous disclosure.

[39 FR 15387, May 3, 1974; 39 FR 17838, May 21, 1974]

§ 432.5 Prohibited disclosures.

No performance characteristics to which this part applies shall be represented or disclosed if they are not obtainable as represented or disclosed when the equipment is operated by the consumer in the usual and normal manner without the use of extraneous aids.

§ 432.6 Liability for violation.

If the manufacturer or, in the case of foreign made products, the importer or domestic sales representative of a foreign manufacturer, of any product covered by this part furnishes the information required or permitted under this part, then any other seller of the product shall not be deemed to be in violation of § 432.5 of this part due to his reliance upon or transmittal of the written representations of the manufacturer or importer if such seller has been furnished by the manufacturer, importer, or sales representative a written certification attesting to the accuracy of the representations to which this part applies: *And provided further,* That such seller is without actual knowledge of the violation contained in said written certification.

PART 433—PRESERVATION OF CONSUMERS' CLAIMS AND DEFENSES

Sec.

AUTHORITY: 38 Stat. 717, as amended; (15 U.S.C. 41, *et seq.*)

§ 433.1 Definitions.

(a) *Person.* An individual, corporation, or any other business organization.

(b) *Consumer.* A natural person who seeks or acquires goods or services for personal, family, or household use.

(c) *Creditor.* A person who, in the ordinary course of business, lends purchase money or finances the sale of goods or services to consumers on a deferred payment basis; *Provided,* such person is not acting, for the purposes of a particular transaction, in the capacity of a credit card issuer.

(d) *Purchase money loan.* A cash advance which is received by a consumer in return for a "Finance Charge" within the meaning of the Truth in Lending Act and Regulation Z, which is applied, in whole or substantial part, to a purchase of goods or services from a seller who (1) refers consumers to the creditor or (2) is affiliated with the creditor by common control, contract, or business arrangement.

(e) *Financing a sale.* Extending credit to a consumer in connection with a "Credit Sale" within the meaning of the Truth in Lending Act and Regulation Z.

(f) *Contract.* Any oral or written agreement, formal or informal, between a creditor and a seller, which contemplates or provides for cooperative or concerted activity in connection with the sale of goods or services to consumers or the financing thereof.

(g) *Business arrangement.* Any understanding, procedure, course of dealing, or arrangement, formal or informal, between a creditor and a seller, in connection with the sale of goods or services to consumers or the financing thereof.

(h) *Credit card issuer.* A person who extends to cardholders the right to use a credit card in connection with purchases of goods or services.

(i) *Consumer credit contract.* Any instrument which evidences or embodies a debt arising from a "Purchase Money Loan" transaction or a "financed sale" as defined in paragraphs (d) and (e) of this section.

(j) *Seller.* A person who, in the ordinary course of business, sells or leases goods or services to consumers.

[40 FR 53506, Nov. 18, 1975]

§ 433.2 Preservation of consumers' claims and defenses, unfair or deceptive acts or practices.

In connection with any sale or lease of goods or services to consumers, in or affecting commerce as "commerce" is defined in the Federal Trade Commission Act, it is an unfair or deceptive act or practice within the meaning of section 5 of that Act for a seller, directly or indirectly, to:

(a) Take or receive a consumer credit contract which fails to contain the following provision in at least ten point, bold face, type:

NOTICE

ANY HOLDER OF THIS CONSUMER CREDIT CONTRACT IS SUBJECT TO ALL CLAIMS AND DEFENSES WHICH THE DEBTOR COULD ASSERT AGAINST THE SELLER OF GOODS OR SERVICES OBTAINED PURSUANT HERETO OR WITH THE PROCEEDS HEREOF. RECOVERY HEREUNDER BY THE DEBTOR SHALL NOT EXCEED AMOUNTS PAID BY THE DEBTOR HEREUNDER.

or,

(b) Accept, as full or partial payment for such sale or lease, the proceeds of any purchase money loan (as purchase money loan is defined herein), unless any consumer credit contract made in connection with such purchase money loan contains the following provision in at least ten point, bold face, type:

NOTICE

ANY HOLDER OF THIS CONSUMER CREDIT CONTRACT IS SUBJECT TO ALL CLAIMS AND DEFENSES WHICH THE DEBTOR COULD ASSERT AGAINST THE SELLER OF GOODS OR SERVICES OBTAINED WITH THE PROCEEDS HEREOF. RECOVERY HEREUNDER BY THE DEBTOR SHALL NOT EXCEED AMOUNTS PAID BY THE DEBTOR HEREUNDER.

[40 FR 53506, Nov. 18, 1975; 40 FR 58131, Dec. 15, 1975]

§433.3 Exemption of sellers taking or receiving open end consumer credit contracts before November 1, 1977 from requirements of §433.2(a).

(a) Any seller who has taken or received an open end consumer credit contract before November 1, 1977, shall be exempt from the requirements of 16 CFR part 433 with respect to such contract provided the contract does not cut off consumers' claims and defenses.

(b) *Definitions*. The following definitions apply to this exemption:

(1) All pertinent definitions contained in 16 CFR 433.1.

(2) Open end consumer credit contract: a consumer credit contract pursuant to which "open end credit" is extended.

(3) "Open end credit": consumer credit extended on an account pursuant to a plan under which a creditor may permit an applicant to make purchases or make loans, from time to time, directly from the creditor or indirectly by use of a credit card, check, or other device, as the plan may provide. The term does not include negotiated advances under an open-end real estate mortgage or a letter of credit.

(4) Contract which does not cut off consumers' claims and defenses: A consumer credit contract which does not constitute or contain a negotiable instrument, or contain any waiver, limitation, term, or condition which has the effect of limiting a consumer's right to assert against any holder of the contract all legally sufficient claims and defenses which the consumer could assert against the seller of goods or services purchased pursuant to the contract.

[42 FR 19490, Apr. 14, 1977, as amended at 42 FR 46510, Sept. 16, 1977]

PART 435—MAIL, INTERNET, OR TELEPHONE ORDER MERCHANDISE

Sec.

AUTHORITY: 15 U.S.C. 57a.

SOURCE: 79 FR 55619, Sept. 17, 2014, unless otherwise noted.

§435.1 Definitions.

For purposes of this part:

(a) *Mail, Internet, or telephone order sales* shall mean sales in which the buyer has ordered merchandise from the seller by mail, via the Internet, or by telephone, regardless of the method of payment or the method used to solicit the order.

(b) *Prompt refund* shall mean:

(1) Where a refund is made pursuant to paragraph (d)(1), (d)(2)(ii), (d)(2)(iii), or (d)(3) of this section, a refund sent by any means at least as fast and reliable as first class mail within seven (7) working days of the date on which the buyer's right to refund vests under the provisions of this part. Provided, however, that where the seller cannot provide a refund by the same method payment was tendered, *prompt refund* shall mean a refund sent in the form of cash, check, or money order, by any means at least as fast and reliable as first class mail, within seven (7) working days of the date on which the seller

discovers it cannot provide a refund by the same method as payment was tendered;

(2) Where a refund is made pursuant to paragraph (d)(2)(i) of this section, a refund sent by any means at least as fast and reliable as first class mail within one (1) billing cycle from the date on which the buyer's right to refund vests under the provisions of this part.

(c) *Receipt of a properly completed order* shall mean, where the buyer tenders full or partial payment in the proper amount in the form of cash, check, or money order; authorization from the buyer to charge an existing charge account; or other payment methods, the time at which the seller receives both said payment and an order from the buyer containing all of the information needed by the seller to process and ship the order. Provided, however, that where the seller receives notice that a payment by means other than cash or credit as tendered by the buyer has been dishonored or that the buyer does not qualify for a credit sale, *receipt of a properly completed order* shall mean the time at which:

(1) The seller receives notice that a payment by means other than cash or credit in the proper amount tendered by the buyer has been honored;

(2) The buyer tenders cash in the proper amount; or

(3) The seller receives notice that the buyer qualifies for a credit sale.

(d) *Refund* shall mean:

(1) Where the buyer tendered full payment for the unshipped merchandise in the form of cash, check, or money order, a return of the amount tendered in the form of cash, check, or money order sent to the buyer;

(2) Where there is a credit sale:

(i) And the seller is a creditor, a copy of a credit memorandum or the like or an account statement sent to the buyer reflecting the removal or absence of any remaining charge incurred as a result of the sale from the buyer's account;

(ii) And a third party is the creditor, an appropriate credit memorandum or the like sent to the third party creditor which will remove the charge from the buyer's account and a copy of the credit memorandum or the like sent to the buyer that includes the date that the seller sent the credit memorandum or the like to the third party creditor and the amount of the charge to be removed, or a statement from the seller acknowledging the cancellation of the order and representing that it has not taken any action regarding the order which will result in a charge to the buyer's account with the third party;

(iii) And the buyer tendered partial payment for the unshipped merchandise in the form of cash, check, or money order, a return of the amount tendered in the form of cash, check, or money order sent to the buyer.

(3) Where the buyer tendered payment for the unshipped merchandise by any means other than those enumerated in paragraph (d)(1) or (2) of this section:

(i) Instructions sent to the entity that transferred payment to the seller instructing that entity to return to the buyer the amount tendered in the form tendered and a statement sent to the buyer setting forth the instructions sent to the entity, including the date of the instructions and the amount to be returned to the buyer; or

(ii) A return of the amount tendered in the form of cash, check, or money order sent to the buyer; or

(iii) A statement from the seller sent to the buyer acknowledging the cancellation of the order and representing that the seller has not taken any action regarding the order which will access any of the buyer's funds.

(e) *Shipment* shall mean the act by which the merchandise is physically placed in the possession of the carrier.

(f) *Telephone* refers to any direct or indirect use of the telephone to order merchandise, regardless of whether the telephone is activated by, or the language used is that of human beings, machines, or both.

(g) The *time of solicitation* of an order shall mean that time when the seller has:

(1) Mailed or otherwise disseminated the solicitation to a prospective purchaser;

(2) Made arrangements for an advertisement containing the solicitation to appear in a newspaper, magazine or the like or on radio or television which

cannot be changed or cancelled without incurring substantial expense; or

(3) Made arrangements for the printing of a catalog, brochure or the like which cannot be changed without incurring substantial expense, in which the solicitation in question forms an insubstantial part.

§435.2 Mail, Internet, or telephone order sales.

In connection with mail, Internet, or telephone order sales in or affecting commerce, as "commerce" is defined in the Federal Trade Commission Act, it constitutes an unfair method of competition, and an unfair or deceptive act or practice for a seller:

(a)(1) To solicit any order for the sale of merchandise to be ordered by the buyer through the mail, via the Internet, or by telephone unless, at the time of the solicitation, the seller has a reasonable basis to expect that it will be able to ship any ordered merchandise to the buyer:

(i) Within that time clearly and conspicuously stated in any such solicitation; or

(ii) If no time is clearly and conspicuously stated, within thirty (30) days after receipt of a properly completed order from the buyer. Provided, however, where, at the time the merchandise is ordered the buyer applies to the seller for credit to pay for the merchandise in whole or in part, the seller shall have fifty (50) days, rather than thirty (30) days, to perform the actions required in this paragraph (a)(1)(ii).

(2) To provide any buyer with any revised shipping date, as provided in paragraph (b) of this section, unless, at the time any such revised shipping date is provided, the seller has a reasonable basis for making such representation regarding a definite revised shipping date.

(3) To inform any buyer that it is unable to make any representation regarding the length of any delay unless:

(i) The seller has a reasonable basis for so informing the buyer; and

(ii) The seller informs the buyer of the reason or reasons for the delay.

(4) In any action brought by the Federal Trade Commission, alleging a violation of this part, the failure of a respondent-seller to have records or other documentary proof establishing its use of systems and procedures which assure the shipment of merchandise in the ordinary course of business within any applicable time set forth in this part will create a rebuttable presumption that the seller lacked a reasonable basis for any expectation of shipment within said applicable time.

(b)(1) Where a seller is unable to ship merchandise within the applicable time set forth in paragraph (a)(1) of this section, to fail to offer to the buyer, clearly and conspicuously and without prior demand, an option either to consent to a delay in shipping or to cancel the buyer's order and receive a prompt refund. Said offer shall be made within a reasonable time after the seller first becomes aware of its inability to ship within the applicable time set forth in paragraph (a)(1) of this section, but in no event later than said applicable time.

(i) Any offer to the buyer of such an option shall fully inform the buyer regarding the buyer's right to cancel the order and to obtain a prompt refund and shall provide a definite revised shipping date, but where the seller lacks a reasonable basis for providing a definite revised shipping date the notice shall inform the buyer that the seller is unable to make any representation regarding the length of the delay.

(ii) Where the seller has provided a definite revised shipping date which is thirty (30) days or less later than the applicable time set forth in paragraph (a)(1) of this section, the offer of said option shall expressly inform the buyer that, unless the seller receives, prior to shipment and prior to the expiration of the definite revised shipping date, a response from the buyer rejecting the delay and cancelling the order, the buyer will be deemed to have consented to a delayed shipment on or before the definite revised shipping date.

(iii) Where the seller has provided a definite revised shipping date which is more than thirty (30) days later than the applicable time set forth in paragraph (a)(1) of this section or where the seller is unable to provide a definite revised shipping date and therefore informs the buyer that it is unable to make any representation regarding the length of the delay, the offer of said option shall also expressly inform the buyer that the buyer's order will automatically be deemed to have been cancelled unless:

(A) The seller has shipped the merchandise within thirty (30) days of the applicable time set forth in paragraph (a)(1) of this section, and has received no cancellation prior to shipment; or

(B) The seller has received from the buyer within thirty (30) days of said applicable time, a response specifically consenting to said shipping delay. Where the seller informs the buyer that it is unable to make any representation regarding the length of the delay, the buyer shall be expressly informed that, should the buyer consent to an indefinite delay, the buyer will have a continuing right to cancel the buyer's order at any time after the applicable time set forth in paragraph (a)(1) of this section by so notifying the seller prior to actual shipment.

(iv) Nothing in this paragraph shall prohibit a seller who furnishes a definite revised shipping date pursuant to paragraph (b)(1)(i) of this section, from requesting, simultaneously with or at any time subsequent to the offer of an option pursuant to paragraph (b)(1) of this section, the buyer's express consent to a further unanticipated delay beyond the definite revised shipping date in the form of a response from the buyer specifically consenting to said further delay. Provided, however, that where the seller solicits consent to an unanticipated indefinite delay the solicitation shall expressly inform the buyer that, should the buyer so consent to an indefinite delay, the buyer shall have a continuing right to cancel the buyer's order at any time after the definite revised shipping date by so notifying the seller prior to actual shipment.

(2) Where a seller is unable to ship merchandise on or before the definite revised shipping date provided under paragraph (b)(1)(i) of this section and consented to by the buyer pursuant to paragraph (b)(1)(ii) or (iii) of this section, to fail to offer to the buyer, clearly and conspicuously and without prior demand, a renewed option either to consent to a further delay or to cancel the order and to receive a prompt refund. Said offer shall be made within a reasonable time after the seller first becomes aware of its inability to ship before the said definite revised date, but in no event later than the expiration of the definite revised shipping date. Provided, however, that where the seller previously has obtained the buyer's express consent to an unanticipated delay until a specific date beyond the definite revised shipping date, pursuant to paragraph (b)(1)(iv) of this section or to a further delay until a specific date beyond the definite revised shipping date pursuant to paragraph (b)(2) of this section, that date to which the buyer has expressly consented shall supersede the definite revised shipping date for purposes of paragraph (b)(2) of this section.

(i) Any offer to the buyer of said renewed option shall provide the buyer with a new definite revised shipping date, but where the seller lacks a reasonable basis for providing a new definite revised shipping date, the notice shall inform the buyer that the seller is unable to make any representation regarding the length of the further delay.

(ii) The offer of a renewed option shall expressly inform the buyer that, unless the seller receives, prior to the expiration of the old definite revised shipping date or any date superseding the old definite revised shipping date, notification from the buyer specifically consenting to the further delay, the buyer will be deemed to have rejected any further delay, and to have cancelled the order if the seller is in fact unable to ship prior to the expiration of the old definite revised shipping date or any date superseding the old definite revised shipping date. Provided, however, that where the seller offers the buyer the option to consent to an indefinite delay the offer shall expressly inform the buyer that, should the buyer so consent to an indefinite delay, the buyer shall have a continuing right to cancel the buyer's order at any time after the old definite revised shipping date or any date superseding the old definite revised shipping date.

(iii) Paragraph (b)(2) of this section shall not apply to any situation where a seller, pursuant to the provisions of paragraph (b)(1)(iv) of this section, has previously obtained consent from the buyer to an indefinite extension beyond the first revised shipping date.

(3) Wherever a buyer has the right to exercise any option under this part or to cancel an order by so notifying the seller prior to shipment, to fail to furnish the buyer with adequate means, at the seller's expense, to exercise such option or to notify the seller regarding cancellation.

(4) Nothing in paragraph (b) of this section shall prevent a seller, where it is unable to make shipment within the time set forth in paragraph (a)(1) of this section or within a delay period consented to by the buyer, from deciding to consider the order cancelled and providing the buyer with notice of said decision within a reasonable time after it becomes aware of said inability to ship, together with a prompt refund.

(c) To fail to deem an order cancelled and to make a prompt refund to the buyer whenever:

(1) The seller receives, prior to the time of shipment, notification from the buyer cancelling the order pursuant to any option, renewed option or continuing option under this part;

(2) The seller has, pursuant to paragraph (b)(1)(iii) of this section, provided the buyer with a definite revised shipping date which is more than thirty (30) days later than the applicable time set forth in paragraph (a)(1) of this section or has notified the buyer that it is unable to make any representation regarding the length of the delay and the seller:

(i) Has not shipped the merchandise within thirty (30) days of the applicable time set forth in paragraph (a)(1) of this section, and

(ii) Has not received the buyer's express consent to said shipping delay within said thirty (30) days;

(3) The seller is unable to ship within the applicable time set forth in paragraph (b)(2) of this section, and has not received, within the said applicable time, the buyer's consent to any further delay;

(4) The seller has notified the buyer of its inability to make shipment and has indicated its decision not to ship the merchandise;

(5) The seller fails to offer the option prescribed in paragraph (b)(1) of this section and has not shipped the merchandise within the applicable time set forth in paragraph (a)(1) of this section.

(d) In any action brought by the Federal Trade Commission, alleging a violation of this part, the failure of a respondent-seller to have records or other documentary proof establishing its use of systems and procedures which assure compliance, in the ordinary course of business, with any requirement of paragraph (b) or (c) of this section will create a rebuttable presumption that the seller failed to comply with said requirement.

§435.3 Limited applicability.

(a) This part shall not apply to:

(1) Subscriptions, such as magazine sales, ordered for serial delivery, after the initial shipment is made in compliance with this part;

(2) Orders of seeds and growing plants;

(3) Orders made on a collect-on-delivery (C.O.D.) basis;

(4) Transactions governed by the Federal Trade Commission's Trade Regulation Rule entitled "Use of Prenotification Negative Option Plans," 16 CFR Part 425.

(b) By taking action in this area:

(1) The Federal Trade Commission does not intend to preempt action in the same area, which is not inconsistent with this part, by any State, municipal, or other local government. This part does not annul or diminish any rights or remedies provided to consumers by any State law, municipal ordinance, or other local regulation, insofar as those rights or remedies are equal to or greater than those provided by this part. In addition, this part does not supersede those provisions of any State law, municipal ordinance, or other local regulation which impose obligations or liabilities upon sellers, when sellers subject to this part are not in compliance therewith.

(2) This part does supersede those provisions of any State law, municipal ordinance, or other local regulation which are inconsistent with this part to the extent that those provisions do not provide a buyer with rights which are equal to or greater than those rights granted a buyer by this part.

This part also supersedes those provisions of any State law, municipal ordinance, or other local regulation requiring that a buyer be notified of a right which is the same as a right provided by this part but requiring that a buyer be given notice of this right in a language, form, or manner which is different in any way from that required by this part. In those instances where any State law, municipal ordinance, or other local regulation contains provisions, some but not all of which are partially or completely superseded by this part, the provisions or portions of those provisions which have not been superseded retain their full force and effect.

(c) If any provision of this part, or its application to any person, partnership, corporation, act or practice is held invalid, the remainder of this part or the application of the provision to any other person, partnership, corporation, act or practice shall not be affected thereby.

PART 436—DISCLOSURE REQUIREMENTS AND PROHIBITIONS CONCERNING FRANCHISING

AUTHORITY: 15 U.S.C. 41-58.

SOURCE: 72 FR 15544, Mar. 30, 2007, unless otherwise noted.

Subpart A—Definitions

§ 436.1 Definitions.

Unless stated otherwise, the following definitions apply throughout part 436:

(a) *Action* includes complaints, cross claims, counterclaims, and third-party complaints in a judicial action or proceeding, and their equivalents in an administrative action or arbitration.

(b) *Affiliate* means an entity controlled by, controlling, or under common control with, another entity.

(c) *Confidentiality clause* means any contract, order, or settlement provision that directly or indirectly restricts a current or former franchisee from discussing his or her personal experience as a franchisee in the franchisor's system with any prospective franchisee. It does not include clauses that protect franchisor's trademarks or other proprietary information.

(d) *Disclose*, *state*, *describe*, and *list* each mean to present all material facts accurately, clearly, concisely, and legibly in plain English.

(e) *Financial performance representation* means any representation, including any oral, written, or visual representation, to a prospective franchisee, including a representation in the general media, that states, expressly or by implication, a specific level or range of actual or potential sales, income, gross profits, or net profits. The term includes a chart, table, or mathematical calculation that shows possible results based on a combination of variables.

(f) *Fiscal year* refers to the franchisor's fiscal year.

(g) *Fractional franchise* means a franchise relationship that satisfies the following criteria when the relationship is created:

(1) The franchisee, any of the franchisee's current directors or officers, or any current directors or officers of a parent or affiliate, has more than two years of experience in the same type of business; and

(2) The parties have a reasonable basis to anticipate that the sales arising from the relationship will not exceed 20% of the franchisee's total dollar volume in sales during the first year of operation.

(h) *Franchise* means any continuing commercial relationship or arrangement, whatever it may be called, in which the terms of the offer or contract specify, or the franchise seller promises or represents, orally or in writing, that:

(1) The franchisee will obtain the right to operate a business that is identified or associated with the franchisor's trademark, or to offer, sell, or distribute goods, services, or commodities that are identified or associated with the franchisor's trademark;

(2) The franchisor will exert or has authority to exert a significant degree of control over the franchisee's method of operation, or provide significant assistance in the franchisee's method of operation; and

(3) As a condition of obtaining or commencing operation of the franchise, the franchisee makes a required payment or commits to make a required payment to the franchisor or its affiliate.

(i) *Franchisee* means any person who is granted a franchise.

(j) *Franchise seller* means a person that offers for sale, sells, or arranges for the sale of a franchise. It includes the franchisor and the franchisor's employees, representatives, agents, subfranchisors, and third-party brokers who are involved in franchise sales activities. It does not include existing franchisees who sell only their own outlet and who are otherwise not engaged in franchise sales on behalf of the franchisor.

(k) *Franchisor* means any person who grants a franchise and participates in the franchise relationship. Unless otherwise stated, it includes subfranchisors. For purposes of this definition, a "subfranchisor" means a person who functions as a franchisor by engaging in both pre-sale activities and post-sale performance.

(l) *Leased department* means an arrangement whereby a retailer licenses or otherwise permits a seller to conduct ≤business from the retailer's location where the seller purchases no goods, services, or commodities directly or indirectly from the retailer, a person the retailer requires the seller to do business with, or a retailer-affiliate if the retailer advises the seller to do business with the affiliate.

(m) *Parent* means an entity that controls another entity directly, or indirectly through one or more subsidiaries.

(n) *Person* means any individual, group, association, limited or general partnership, corporation, or any other entity.

(o) *Plain English* means the organization of information and language usage understandable by a person unfamiliar with the franchise business. It incorporates short sentences; definite, concrete, everyday language; active voice; and tabular presentation of information, where possible. It avoids legal jargon, highly technical business terms, and multiple negatives.

(p) *Predecessor* means a person from whom the franchisor acquired, directly or indirectly, the major portion of the franchisor's assets.

(q) *Principal business address* means the street address of a person's home office in the United States. A principal business address cannot be a post office box or private mail drop.

(r) *Prospective franchisee* means any person (including any agent, representative, or employee) who approaches or is approached by a franchise seller to discuss the possible establishment of a franchise relationship.

(s) *Required payment* means all consideration that the franchisee must pay to the franchisor or an affiliate, either by contract or by practical necessity, as a condition of obtaining or commencing operation of the franchise. A required payment does not include payments for the purchase of reasonable amounts of inventory at bona fide wholesale prices for resale or lease.

(t) *Sale of a franchise* includes an agreement whereby a person obtains a franchise from a franchise seller for value by purchase, license, or otherwise. It does not include extending or renewing an existing franchise agreement where there has been no interruption in the franchisee's operation of the business, unless the new agreement contains terms and conditions that differ materially from the original agreement. It also does not include the transfer of a franchise by an existing franchisee where the franchisor has had no significant involvement with the prospective transferee. A franchisor's approval or disapproval of a transfer alone is not deemed to be significant involvement.

(u) *Signature* means a person's affirmative step to authenticate his or her identity. It includes a person's handwritten signature, as well as a person's use of security codes, passwords, electronic signatures, and similar devices to authenticate his or her identity.

(v) *Trademark* includes trademarks, service marks, names, logos, and other commercial symbols.

(w) *Written* or *in writing* means any document or information in printed form or in any form capable of being preserved in tangible form and read. It includes: type-set, word processed, or handwritten document; information on computer disk or CD-ROM; information sent via email; or information posted on the Internet. It does not include mere oral statements.

Subpart B—Franchisors' Obligations

§ 436.2 Obligation to furnish documents.

In connection with the offer or sale of a franchise to be located in the United States of America or its territories, unless the transaction is exempted under subpart E of this part, it is an unfair or deceptive act or practice in violation of Section 5 of the Federal Trade Commission Act:

(a) For any franchisor to fail to furnish a prospective franchisee with a copy of the franchisor's current disclosure document, as described in subparts C and D of this part, at least 14 calendar-days before the prospective franchisee signs a binding agreement with, or makes any payment to, the franchisor or an affiliate in connection with the proposed franchise sale.

(b) For any franchisor to alter unilaterally and materially the terms and conditions of the basic franchise agreement or any related agreements attached to the disclosure document without furnishing the prospective franchisee with a copy of each revised agreement at least seven calendar-days before the prospective franchisee signs the revised agreement. Changes to an agreement that arise out of negotiations initiated by the prospective franchisee do not trigger this seven calendar-day period.

(c) For purposes of paragraphs (a) and (b) of this section, the franchisor has furnished the documents by the required date if:

(1) A copy of the document was hand-delivered, faxed, emailed, or otherwise delivered to the prospective franchisee by the required date;

(2) Directions for accessing the document on the Internet were provided to the prospective franchisee by the required date; or

(3) A paper or tangible electronic copy (for example, computer disk or CD-ROM) was sent to the address specified by the prospective franchisee by first-class United States mail at least three calendar days before the required date.

Subpart C—Contents of a Disclosure Document

§ 436.3 Cover page.

Begin the disclosure document with a cover page, in the order and form as follows:

(a) The title "FRANCHISE DISCLOSURE DOCUMENT" in capital letters and bold type.

(b) The franchisor's name, type of business organization, principal business address, telephone number, and, if applicable, email address and primary home page address.

(c) A sample of the primary business trademark that the franchisee will use in its business.

(d) A brief description of the franchised business.

(e) The following statements:

(1) The total investment necessary to begin operation of a [franchise system name] franchise is [the total amount of Item 7 (§ 436.5(g))]. This includes [the total amount in Item 5 (§ 436.5(e))] that must be paid to the franchisor or affiliate.

(2) This disclosure document summarizes certain provisions of your franchise agreement and other information in plain English. Read this disclosure document and all accompanying agreements carefully. You must receive this disclosure document at least 14 calendar-days before you sign a binding agreement with, or make any payment to, the franchisor or an affiliate in connection with the proposed franchise sale. [The following sentence in bold type] NOTE, HOWEVER, THAT NO GOVERNMENTAL AGENCY HAS VERIFIED THE INFORMATION CONTAINED IN THIS DOCUMENT.

(3) The terms of your contract will govern your franchise relationship. Don't rely on the disclosure document alone to understand your contract. Read all of your contract carefully. Show your contract and this disclosure document to an advisor, like a lawyer or an accountant.

(4) Buying a franchise is a complex investment. The information in this disclosure document can help you make up your mind. More information on franchising, such as "*A Consumer's Guide to Buying a Franchise*," which can help you understand how to use this disclosure document, is available from the Federal Trade Commission. You can contact the FTC at 1-877-FTC-HELP or by writing to the FTC at 600 Pennsylvania Avenue, NW., Washington, D.C. 20580. You can also visit the FTC's home page at *www.ftc.gov* for additional information. Call your state agency or visit your public library for other sources of information on franchising.

(5) There may also be laws on franchising in your state. Ask your state agencies about them.

(6) [The issuance date].

(f) A franchisor may include the following statement between the statements set out at paragraphs (e)(2) and (3) of this section: "You may wish to receive your disclosure document in another format that is more convenient for you. To discuss the availability of disclosures in different formats, contact [name or office] at [address] and [telephone number]."

(g) Franchisors may include additional disclosures on the cover page, on a separate cover page, or addendum to comply with state pre-sale disclosure laws.

§ 436.4 Table of contents.

Include the following table of contents. State the page where each disclosure Item begins. List all exhibits by letter, as shown in the following example.

TABLE OF CONTENTS

1. The Franchisor and any Parents, Predecessors, and Affiliates
2. Business Experience
3. Litigation
4. Bankruptcy
5. Initial Fees
6. Other Fees
7. Estimated Initial Investment
8. Restrictions on Sources of Products and Services
9. Franchisee's Obligations
10. Financing
11. Franchisor's Assistance, Advertising, Computer Systems, and Training
12. Territory
13. Trademarks
14. Patents, Copyrights, and Proprietary Information
15. Obligation to Participate in the Actual Operation of the Franchise Business
16. Restrictions on What the Franchisee May Sell
17. Renewal, Termination, Transfer, and Dispute Resolution
18. Public Figures
19. Financial Performance Representations
20. Outlets and Franchisee Information
21. Financial Statements
22. Contracts
23. Receipts

EXHIBITS

A. Franchise Agreement

§ 436.5 Disclosure items.

(a) *Item 1: The Franchisor, and any Parents, Predecessors, and Affiliates.* Disclose:

(1) The name and principal business address of the franchisor; any parents; and any affiliates that offer franchises in any line of business or provide products or services to the franchisees of the franchisor.

(2) The name and principal business address of any predecessors during the 10-year period immediately before the close of the franchisor's most recent fiscal year.

(3) The name that the franchisor uses and any names it intends to use to conduct business.

(4) The identity and principal business address of the franchisor's agent for service of process.

(5) The type of business organization used by the franchisor (for example, corporation, partnership) and the state in which it was organized.

(6) The following information about the franchisor's business and the franchises offered:

(i) Whether the franchisor operates businesses of the type being franchised.

(ii) The franchisor's other business activities.

(iii) The business the franchisee will conduct.

(iv) The general market for the product or service the franchisee will offer. In describing the general market, consider factors such as whether the market is developed or developing, whether the goods will be sold primarily to a certain group, and whether sales are seasonal.

(v) In general terms, any laws or regulations specific to the industry in which the franchise business operates.

(vi) A general description of the competition.

(7) The prior business experience of the franchisor; any predecessors listed in § 436.5(a)(2) of this part; and any affiliates that offer franchises in any line of business or provide products or services to the franchisees of the franchisor, including:

(i) The length of time each has conducted the type of business the franchisee will operate.

(ii) The length of time each has offered franchises providing the type of business the franchisee will operate.

(iii) Whether each has offered franchises in other lines of business. If so, include:

(A) A description of each other line of business.

(B) The number of franchises sold in each other line of business.

(C) The length of time each has offered franchises in each other line of business.

(b) *Item 2: Business Experience.* Disclose by name and position the franchisor's directors, trustees, general partners, principal officers, and any other individuals who will have management responsibility relating to the sale or operation of franchises offered by this document. For each person listed in this section, state his or her principal positions and employers during the past five years, including each position's starting date, ending date, and location.

(c) *Item 3: Litigation.* (1) Disclose whether the franchisor; a predecessor; a parent or affiliate who induces franchise sales by promising to back the franchisor financially or otherwise guarantees the franchisor's performance; an affiliate who offers franchises under the franchisor's principal trademark; and any person identified in § 436.5(b) of this part:

(i) Has pending against that person:

(A) An administrative, criminal, or material civil action alleging a violation of a franchise, antitrust, or securities law, or alleging fraud, unfair or deceptive practices, or comparable allegations.

(B) Civil actions, other than ordinary routine litigation incidental to the business, which are material in the context of the number of franchisees and the size, nature, or financial condition of the franchise system or its business operations.

(ii) Was a party to any material civil action involving the franchise relationship in the last fiscal year. For purposes of this section, "franchise relationship" means contractual obligations between the franchisor and franchisee directly relating to the operation of the franchised business (such as royalty payment and training obligations). It does not include actions involving suppliers or other third parties, or indemnification for tort liability.

(iii) Has in the 10-year period immediately before the disclosure document's issuance date:

(A) Been convicted of or pleaded nolo contendere to a felony charge.

(B) Been held liable in a civil action involving an alleged violation of a franchise, antitrust, or securities law, or involving allegations of fraud, unfair or deceptive practices, or comparable allegations. "Held liable" means that, as a result of claims or counterclaims, the person must pay money or other consideration, must reduce an indebtedness by the amount of an award, cannot enforce its rights, or must take action adverse to its interests.

(2) Disclose whether the franchisor; a predecessor; a parent or affiliate who guarantees the franchisor's performance; an affiliate who has offered or sold franchises in any line of business within the last 10 years; or any other person identified in § 436.5(b) of this part is subject to a currently effective injunctive or restrictive order or decree resulting from a pending or concluded action brought by a public agency and relating to the franchise or to a Federal, State, or Canadian franchise, securities, antitrust, trade regulation, or trade practice law.

(3) For each action identified in paragraphs (c)(1) and (2) of this section, state the title, case number or citation, the initial filing date, the names of the parties, the forum, and the relationship of the opposing party to the franchisor (for example, competitor, supplier, lessor, franchisee, former franchisee, or class of franchisees). Except as provided in paragraph (c)(4) of this section, summarize the legal and factual nature of each claim in the action, the relief sought or obtained, and any conclusions of law or fact.[1] In addition, state:

(i) For pending actions, the status of the action.

(ii) For prior actions, the date when the judgment was entered and any damages or settlement terms.[2]

(iii) For injunctive or restrictive orders, the nature, terms, and conditions of the order or decree.

(iv) For convictions or pleas, the crime or violation, the date of conviction, and the sentence or penalty imposed.

(4) For any other franchisor-initiated suit identified in paragraph (c)(1)(ii) of this section, the franchisor may comply with the requirements of paragraphs (c)(3)(i) through (iv) of this section by listing individual suits under one common heading that will serve as the case summary (for example, "royalty collection suits").

(d) *Item 4: Bankruptcy.* (1) Disclose whether the franchisor; any parent; predecessor; affiliate; officer, or general partner of the franchisor, or any other individual who will have management responsibility relating to the sale or operation of franchises offered by this document, has, during the 10-year period immediately before the date of this disclosure document:

(i) Filed as debtor (or had filed against it) a petition under the United States Bankruptcy Code ("Bankruptcy Code").

(ii) Obtained a discharge of its debts under the Bankruptcy Code.

(iii) Been a principal officer of a company or a general partner in a partnership that either filed as a debtor (or had filed against it) a petition under the Bankruptcy Code, or that obtained a discharge of its debts under the Bankruptcy Code while, or within one year after, the officer or general partner held the position in the company.

(2) For each bankruptcy, state:

[1] Franchisors may include a summary opinion of counsel concerning any action if counsel consent to use the summary opinion and the full opinion is attached to the disclosure document.

[2] If a settlement agreement must be disclosed in this Item, all material settlement terms must be disclosed, whether or not the agreement is confidential. However, franchisors need not disclose the terms of confidential settlements entered into before commencing franchise sales. Further, any franchisor who has historically used only the Franchise Rule format, or who is new to franchising, need not disclose confidential settlements entered prior to the effective date of this Rule.

(i) The current name, address, and principal place of business of the debtor.

(ii) Whether the debtor is the franchisor. If not, state the relationship of the debtor to the franchisor (for example, affiliate, officer).

(iii) The date of the original filing and the material facts, including the bankruptcy court, and the case name and number. If applicable, state the debtor's discharge date, including discharges under Chapter 7 and confirmation of any plans of reorganization under Chapters 11 and 13 of the Bankruptcy Code.

(3) Disclose cases, actions, and other proceedings under the laws of foreign nations relating to bankruptcy.

(e) *Item 5: Initial Fees.* Disclose the initial fees and any conditions under which these fees are refundable. If the initial fees are not uniform, disclose the range or formula used to calculate the initial fees paid in the fiscal year before the issuance date and the factors that determined the amount. For this section, "initial fees" means all fees and payments, or commitments to pay, for services or goods received from the franchisor or any affiliate before the franchisee's business opens, whether payable in lump sum or installments. Disclose installment payment terms in this section or in § 436.5(j) of this part.

(f) *Item 6: Other Fees.* Disclose, in the following tabular form, all other fees that the franchisee must pay to the franchisor or its affiliates, or that the franchisor or its affiliates impose or collect in whole or in part for a third party. State the title "OTHER FEES" in capital letters using bold type. Include any formula used to compute the fees.[3]

ITEM 6 TABLE

OTHER FEES

Column 1 Type of fee	Column 2 Amount	Column 3 Due Date	Column 4 Remarks

(1) In column 1, list the type of fee (for example, royalties, and fees for lease negotiations, construction, remodeling, additional training or assistance, advertising, advertising cooperatives, purchasing cooperatives, audits, accounting, inventory, transfers, and renewals).

(2) In column 2, state the amount of the fee.

(3) In column 3, state the due date for each fee.

(4) In column 4, include remarks, definitions, or caveats that elaborate on the information in the table. If remarks are long, franchisors may use footnotes instead of the remarks column. If applicable, include the following information in the remarks column or in a footnote:

(i) Whether the fees are payable only to the franchisor.

(ii) Whether the fees are imposed and collected by the franchisor.

(iii) Whether the fees are non-refundable or describe the circumstances when the fees are refundable.

(iv) Whether the fees are uniformly imposed.

(v) The voting power of franchisor-owned outlets on any fees imposed by cooperatives. If franchisor-owned outlets have controlling voting power, disclose the maximum and minimum fees that may be imposed.

(g) *Item 7: Estimated Initial Investment.* Disclose, in the following tabular form, the franchisee's estimated initial investment. State the title "YOUR ESTIMATED INITIAL INVESTMENT" in capital letters using bold type. Franchisors may include additional expenditure tables to show expenditure variations caused by differences such as in site location and premises size.

[3] If fees may increase, disclose the formula that determines the increase or the maximum amount of the increase. For example, a percentage of gross sales is acceptable if the franchisor defines the term "gross sales."

ITEM 7 TABLE:
YOUR ESTIMATED INITIAL INVESTMENT

Column 1 Type of expenditure	Column 2 Amount	Column 3 Method of payment	Column 4 When due	Column 4 To whom payment is to be made
Total.				

(1) In column 1:

(i) List each type of expense, beginning with pre-opening expenses. Include the following expenses, if applicable. Use footnotes to include remarks, definitions, or caveats that elaborate on the information in the Table.

(A) The initial franchise fee.

(B) Training expenses.

(C) Real property, whether purchased or leased.

(D) Equipment, fixtures, other fixed assets, construction, remodeling, leasehold improvements, and decorating costs, whether purchased or leased.

(E) Inventory to begin operating.

(F) Security deposits, utility deposits, business licenses, and other prepaid expenses.

(ii) List separately and by name any other specific required payments (for example, additional training, travel, or advertising expenses) that the franchisee must make to begin operations.

(iii) Include a category titled "Additional funds— [initial period]" for any other required expenses the franchisee will incur before operations begin and during the initial period of operations. State the initial period. A reasonable initial period is at least three months or a reasonable period for the industry. Describe in general terms the factors, basis, and experience that the franchisor considered or relied upon in formulating the amount required for additional funds.

(2) In column 2, state the amount of the payment. If the amount is unknown, use a low-high range based on the franchisor's current experience. If real property costs cannot be estimated in a low-high range, describe the approximate size of the property and building and the probable location of the building (for example, strip shopping center, mall, downtown, rural, or highway).

(3) In column 3, state the method of payment.

(4) In column 4, state the due date.

(5) In column 5, state to whom payment will be made.

(6) Total the initial investment, incorporating ranges of fees, if used.

(7) In a footnote, state:

(i) Whether each payment is non-refundable, or describe the circumstances when each payment is refundable.

(ii) If the franchisor or an affiliate finances part of the initial investment, the amount that it will finance, the required down payment, the annual interest rate, rate factors, and the estimated loan repayments. Franchisors may refer to §436.5(j) of this part for additional details.

(h) *Item 8: Restrictions on Sources of Products and Services.* Disclose the franchisee's obligations to purchase or lease goods, services, supplies, fixtures, equipment, inventory, computer hardware and software, real estate, or comparable items related to establishing or operating the franchised business either from the franchisor, its designee, or suppliers approved by the franchisor, or under the franchisor's specifications. Include obligations to purchase imposed by the franchisor's written agreement or by the franchisor's practice.[4] For each applicable obligation, state:

(1) The good or service required to be purchased or leased.

---

[4] Franchisors may include the reason for the requirement. Franchisors need not disclose in this Item the purchase or lease of goods or services provided as part of the franchise without a separate charge (such as initial training, if the cost is included in the franchise fee). Describe such fees in Item 5 of this section. Do not disclose fees already described in §436.5(f) of this part.

(2) Whether the franchisor or its affiliates are approved suppliers or the only approved suppliers of that good or service.

(3) Any supplier in which an officer of the franchisor owns an interest.

(4) How the franchisor grants and revokes approval of alternative suppliers, including:

(i) Whether the franchisor's criteria for approving suppliers are available to franchisees.

(ii) Whether the franchisor permits franchisees to contract with alternative suppliers who meet the franchisor's criteria.

(iii) Any fees and procedures to secure approval to purchase from alternative suppliers.

(iv) The time period in which the franchisee will be notified of approval or disapproval.

(v) How approvals are revoked.

(5) Whether the franchisor issues specifications and standards to franchisees, subfranchisees, or approved suppliers. If so, describe how the franchisor issues and modifies specifications.

(6) Whether the franchisor or its affiliates will or may derive revenue or other material consideration from required purchases or leases by franchisees. If so, describe the precise basis by which the franchisor or its affiliates will or may derive that consideration by stating:

(i) The franchisor's total revenue.[5]

(ii) The franchisor's revenues from all required purchases and leases of products and services.

(iii) The percentage of the franchisor's total revenues that are from required purchases or leases.

(iv) If the franchisor's affiliates also sell or lease products or services to franchisees, the affiliates' revenues from those sales or leases.

(7) The estimated proportion of these required purchases and leases by the franchisee to all purchases and leases by the franchisee of goods and services in establishing and operating the franchised businesses.

(8) If a designated supplier will make payments to the franchisor from franchisee purchases, disclose the basis for the payment (for example, specify a percentage or a flat amount). For purposes of this disclosure, a "payment" includes the sale of similar goods or services to the franchisor at a lower price than to franchisees.

(9) The existence of purchasing or distribution cooperatives.

(10) Whether the franchisor negotiates purchase arrangements with suppliers, including price terms, for the benefit of franchisees.

(11) Whether the franchisor provides material benefits (for example, renewal or granting additional franchises) to a franchisee based on a franchisee's purchase of particular products or services or use of particular suppliers.

(i) *Item 9: Franchisee's Obligations.* Disclose, in the following tabular form, a list of the franchisee's principal obligations. State the title "FRANCHISEE'S OBLIGATIONS" in capital letters using bold type. Cross-reference each listed obligation with any applicable section of the franchise or other agreement and with the relevant disclosure document provision. If a particular obligation is not applicable, state "Not Applicable." Include additional obligations, as warranted.

ITEM 9 TABLE:

FRANCHISEE'S OBLIGATIONS

[In bold] **This table lists your principal obligations under the franchise and other agreements. It will help you find more detailed information about your obligations in these agreements and in other items of this disclosure document.**

Obligation	Section in agreement	Disclosure document item
a. Site selection and acquisition/lease		
b. Pre-opening purchase/leases		

[5] Take figures from the franchisor's most recent annual audited financial statement required in § 436.5(u) of this part. If audited statements are not yet required, or if the entity deriving the income is an affiliate, disclose the sources of information used in computing revenues.

ITEM 9 TABLE:—Continued

FRANCHISEE'S OBLIGATIONS

[In bold] **This table lists your principal obligations under the franchise and other agreements. It will help you find more detailed information about your obligations in these agreements and in other items of this disclosure document.**

Obligation	Section in agreement	Disclosure document item
c. Site development and other pre-opening requirements		
d. Initial and ongoing training		
e. Opening		
f. Fees		
g. Compliance with standards and policies/operating manual		
h. Trademarks and proprietary information		
i. Restrictions on products/services offered		
j. Warranty and customer service requirements		
k. Territorial development and sales quotas		
l. Ongoing product/service purchases		
m. Maintenance, appearance, and remodeling requirements		
n. Insurance		
o. Advertising		
p. Indemnification		
q. Owner's participation/management/staffing		
r. Records and reports		
s. Inspections and audits		
t. Transfer		
u. Renewal		
v. Post-termination obligations		
w. Non-competition covenants		
x. Dispute resolution		
y. Other (describe)		

(j) *Item 10: Financing.* (1) Disclose the terms of each financing arrangement, including leases and installment contracts, that the franchisor, its agent, or affiliates offer directly or indirectly to the franchisee.[6] The franchisor may summarize the terms of each financing arrangement in tabular form, using footnotes to provide additional information. For a sample Item 10 table, see appendix A of this part. For each financing arrangement, state:

(i) What the financing covers (for example, the initial franchise fee, site acquisition, construction or remodeling, initial or replacement equipment or fixtures, opening or ongoing inventory or supplies, or other continuing expenses).[7]

[6] Indirect offers of financing include a written arrangement between a franchisor or its affiliate and a lender, for the lender to offer financing to a franchisee; an arrangement in which a franchisor or its affiliate receives a benefit from a lender in exchange for financing a franchise purchase; and a franchisor's guarantee of a note, lease, or other obligation of the franchisee.

[7] Include sample copies of the financing documents as an exhibit to §436.5(v) of this

Continued

(ii) The identity of each lender providing financing and their relationship to the franchisor (for example, affiliate).

(iii) The amount of financing offered or, if the amount depends on an actual cost that may vary, the percentage of the cost that will be financed.

(iv) The rate of interest, plus finance charges, expressed on an annual basis. If the rate of interest, plus finance charges, expressed on an annual basis, may differ depending on when the financing is issued, state what that rate was on a specified recent date.

(v) The number of payments or the period of repayment.

(vi) The nature of any security interest required by the lender.

(vii) Whether a person other than the franchisee must personally guarantee the debt.

(viii) Whether the debt can be prepaid and the nature of any prepayment penalty.

(ix) The franchisee's potential liabilities upon default, including any:

(A) Accelerated obligation to pay the entire amount due;

(B) Obligations to pay court costs and attorney's fees incurred in collecting the debt;

(C) Termination of the franchise; and

(D) Liabilities from cross defaults such as those resulting directly from non-payment, or indirectly from the loss of business property.

(x) Other material financing terms.

(2) Disclose whether the loan agreement requires franchisees to waive defenses or other legal rights (for example, confession of judgment), or bars franchisees from asserting a defense against the lender, the lender's assignee or the franchisor. If so, describe the relevant provisions.

(3) Disclose whether the franchisor's practice or intent is to sell, assign, or discount to a third party all or part of the financing arrangement. If so, state:

(i) The assignment terms, including whether the franchisor will remain primarily obligated to provide the financed goods or services; and

(ii) That the franchisee may lose all its defenses against the lender as a result of the sale or assignment.

(4) Disclose whether the franchisor or an affiliate receives any consideration for placing financing with the lender. If such payments exist:

(i) Disclose the amount or the method of determining the payment; and

(ii) Identify the source of the payment and the relationship of the source to the franchisor or its affiliates.

(k) *Item 11: Franchisor's Assistance, Advertising, Computer Systems, and Training.* Disclose the franchisor's principal assistance and related obligations of both the franchisor and franchisee as follows. For each obligation, cite the section number of the franchise agreement imposing the obligation. Begin by stating the following sentence in bold type: "EXCEPT AS LISTED BELOW, [THE FRANCHISOR] IS NOT REQUIRED TO PROVIDE YOU WITH ANY ASSISTANCE."

(1) Disclose the franchisor's pre-opening obligations to the franchisee, including any assistance in:

(i) Locating a site and negotiating the purchase or lease of the site. If such assistance is provided, state:

(A) Whether the franchisor generally owns the premises and leases it to the franchisee.

(B) Whether the franchisor selects the site or approves an area in which the franchisee selects a site. If so, state further whether and how the franchisor must approve a franchisee-selected site.

(C) The factors that the franchisor considers in selecting or approving sites (for example, general location and neighborhood, traffic patterns, parking, size, physical characteristics of existing buildings, and lease terms).

(D) The time limit for the franchisor to locate or approve or disapprove the site and the consequences if the franchisor and franchisee cannot agree on a site.

(ii) Conforming the premises to local ordinances and building codes and obtaining any required permits.

(iii) Constructing, remodeling, or decorating the premises.

(iv) Hiring and training employees.

---

part. Cite the section and name of the document containing the financing terms and conditions.

(v) Providing for necessary equipment, signs, fixtures, opening inventory, and supplies. If any such assistance is provided, state:

(A) Whether the franchisor provides these items directly or only provides the names of approved suppliers.

(B) Whether the franchisor provides written specifications for these items.

(C) Whether the franchisor delivers or installs these items.

(2) Disclose the typical length of time between the earlier of the signing of the franchise agreement or the first payment of consideration for the franchise and the opening of the franchisee's business. Describe the factors that may affect the time period, such as ability to obtain a lease, financing or building permits, zoning and local ordinances, weather conditions, shortages, or delayed installation of equipment, fixtures, and signs.

(3) Disclose the franchisor's obligations to the franchisee during the operation of the franchise, including any assistance in:

(i) Developing products or services the franchisee will offer to its customers.

(ii) Hiring and training employees.

(iii) Improving and developing the franchised business.

(iv) Establishing prices.

(v) Establishing and using administrative, bookkeeping, accounting, and inventory control procedures.

(vi) Resolving operating problems encountered by the franchisee.

(4) Describe the advertising program for the franchise system, including the following:

(i)The franchisor's obligation to conduct advertising, including:

(A) The media the franchisor may use.

(B) Whether media coverage is local, regional, or national.

(C) The source of the advertising (for example, an in-house advertising department or a national or regional advertising agency).

(D) Whether the franchisor must spend any amount on advertising in the area or territory where the franchisee is located.

(ii) The circumstances when the franchisor will permit franchisees to use their own advertising material.

(iii) Whether there is an advertising council composed of franchisees that advises the franchisor on advertising policies. If so, disclose:

(A) How members of the council are selected.

(B) Whether the council serves in an advisory capacity only or has operational or decision-making power.

(C) Whether the franchisor has the power to form, change, or dissolve the advertising council.

(iv) Whether the franchisee must participate in a local or regional advertising cooperative. If so, state:

(A) How the area or membership of the cooperative is defined.

(B) How much the franchisee must contribute to the fund and whether other franchisees must contribute a different amount or at a different rate.

(C) Whether the franchisor-owned outlets must contribute to the fund and, if so, whether those contributions are on the same basis as those for franchisees.

(D) Who is responsible for administering the cooperative (for example, franchisor, franchisees, or advertising agency).

(E) Whether cooperatives must operate from written governing documents and whether the documents are available for the franchisee to review.

(F) Whether cooperatives must prepare annual or periodic financial statements and whether the statements are available for review by the franchisee.

(G) Whether the franchisor has the power to require cooperatives to be formed, changed, dissolved, or merged.

(v) Whether the franchisee must participate in any other advertising fund. If so, state:

(A) Who contributes to the fund.

(B) How much the franchisee must contribute to the fund and whether other franchisees must contribute a different amount or at a different rate.

(C) Whether the franchisor-owned outlets must contribute to the fund and, if so, whether it is on the same basis as franchisees.

(D) Who administers the fund.

(E) Whether the fund is audited and when it is audited.

(F) Whether financial statements of the fund are available for review by the franchisee.

(G) How the funds were used in the most recently concluded fiscal year, including the percentages spent on production, media placement, administrative expenses, and a description of any other use.

(vi) If not all advertising funds are spent in the fiscal year in which they accrue, how the franchisor uses the remaining amount, including whether franchisees receive a periodic accounting of how advertising fees are spent.

(vii) The percentage of advertising funds, if any, that the franchisor uses principally to solicit new franchise sales.

(5) Disclose whether the franchisor requires the franchisee to buy or use electronic cash registers or computer systems. If so, describe the systems generally in non-technical language, including the types of data to be generated or stored in these systems, and state the following:

(i) The cost of purchasing or leasing the systems.

(ii) Any obligation of the franchisor, any affiliate, or third party to provide ongoing maintenance, repairs, upgrades, or updates.

(iii) Any obligations of the franchisee to upgrade or update any system during the term of the franchise, and, if so, any contractual limitations on the frequency and cost of the obligation.

(iv) The annual cost of any optional or required maintenance, updating, upgrading, or support contracts.

(v) Whether the franchisor will have independent access to the information that will be generated or stored in any electronic cash register or computer system. If so, describe the information that the franchisor may access and whether there are any contractual limitations on the franchisor's right to access the information.

(6) Disclose the table of contents of the franchisor's operating manual provided to franchisees as of the franchisor's last fiscal year-end or a more recent date. State the number of pages devoted to each subject and the total number of pages in the manual as of this date. This disclosure may be omitted if the franchisor offers the prospective franchisee the opportunity to view the manual before buying the franchise.

(7) Disclose the franchisor's training program as of the franchisor's last fiscal year-end or a more recent date.

(i) Describe the training program in the following tabular form. Title the table "TRAINING PROGRAM" in capital letters and bold type.

ITEM 11 TABLE

TRAINING PROGRAM

Column 1 Subject	Column 2 Hours of Classroom Training	Column 3 Hours of On-The-Job Training	Column 4 Location

(A) In column 1, state the subjects taught.

(B) In column 2, state the hours of classroom training for each subject.

(C) In column 3, state the hours of on-the-job training for each subject.

(D) In column 4, state the location of the training for each subject.

(ii) State further:

(A) How often training classes are held and the nature of the location or facility where training is held (for example, company, home, office, franchisor-owned store).

(B) The nature of instructional materials and the instructor's experience, including the instructor's length of experience in the field and with the franchisor. State only experience relevant to the subject taught and the franchisor's operations.

(C) Any charges franchisees must pay for training and who must pay travel and living expenses of the training program enrollees.

(D) Who may and who must attend training. State whether the franchisee or other persons must complete the program to the franchisor's satisfaction. If successful completion is required, state how long after signing the agreement or before opening the business the training must be completed. If training is not mandatory, state the percentage of new franchisees that enrolled in the training program during the preceding 12 months.

(E) Whether additional training programs or refresher courses are required.

(l) *Item 12: Territory*. Disclose:

(1) Whether the franchise is for a specific location or a location to be approved by the franchisor.

(2) Any minimum territory granted to the franchisee (for example, a specific radius, a distance sufficient to encompass a specified population, or another specific designation).

(3) The conditions under which the franchisor will approve the relocation of the franchised business or the franchisee's establishment of additional franchised outlets.

(4) Franchisee options, rights of first refusal, or similar rights to acquire additional franchises.

(5) Whether the franchisor grants an exclusive territory.

(i) If the franchisor does not grant an exclusive territory, state: "You will not receive an exclusive territory. You may face competition from other franchisees, from outlets that we own, or from other channels of distribution or competitive brands that we control."

(ii) If the franchisor grants an exclusive territory, disclose:

(A) Whether continuation of territorial exclusivity depends on achieving a certain sales volume, market penetration, or other contingency, and the circumstances when the franchisee's territory may be altered. Describe any sales or other conditions. State the franchisor's rights if the franchisee fails to meet the requirements.

(B) Any other circumstances that permit the franchisor to modify the franchisee's territorial rights (for example, a population increase in the territory giving the franchisor the right to grant an additional franchise in the area) and the effect of such modifications on the franchisee's rights.

(6) For all territories (exclusive and non-exclusive):

(i) Any restrictions on the franchisor from soliciting or accepting orders from consumers inside the franchisee's territory, including:

(A) Whether the franchisor or an affiliate has used or reserves the right to use other channels of distribution, such as the Internet, catalog sales, telemarketing, or other direct marketing sales, to make sales within the franchisee's territory using the franchisor's principal trademarks.

(B) Whether the franchisor or an affiliate has used or reserves the right to use other channels of distribution, such as the Internet, catalog sales, telemarketing, or other direct marketing, to make sales within the franchisee's territory of products or services under trademarks different from the ones the franchisee will use under the franchise agreement.

(C) Any compensation that the franchisor must pay for soliciting or accepting orders from inside the franchisee's territory.

(ii) Any restrictions on the franchisee from soliciting or accepting orders from consumers outside of his or her territory, including whether the franchisee has the right to use other channels of distribution, such as the Internet, catalog sales, telemarketing, or other direct marketing, to make sales outside of his or her territory.

(iii) If the franchisor or an affiliate operates, franchises, or has plans to operate or franchise a business under a different trademark and that business sells or will sell goods or services similar to those the franchisee will offer, describe:

(A) The similar goods and services.

(B) The different trademark.

(C) Whether outlets will be franchisor owned or operated.

(D) Whether the franchisor or its franchisees who use the different trademark will solicit or accept orders within the franchisee's territory.

(E) The timetable for the plan.

(F) How the franchisor will resolve conflicts between the franchisor and franchisees and between the franchisees of each system regarding territory, customers, and franchisor support.

(G) The principal business address of the franchisor's similar operating business. If it is the same as the franchisor's principal business address stated in §436.5(a) of this part, disclose whether the franchisor maintains (or plans to maintain) physically separate offices and training facilities for the similar competing business.

(m) *Item 13: Trademarks.* (1) Disclose each principal trademark to be licensed to the franchisee. For this Item, "principal trademark" means the primary trademarks, service marks, names, logos, and commercial symbols the franchisee will use to identify the franchised business. It may not include every trademark the franchisor owns.

(2) Disclose whether each principal trademark is registered with the United States Patent and Trademark Office. If so, state:

(i) The date and identification number of each trademark registration.

(ii) Whether the franchisor has filed all required affidavits.

(iii) Whether any registration has been renewed.

(iv) Whether the principal trademarks are registered on the Principal or Supplemental Register of the United States Patent and Trademark Office.

(3) If the principal trademark is not registered with the United States Patent and Trademark Office, state whether the franchisor has filed any trademark application, including any "intent to use" application or an application based on actual use. If so, state the date and identification number of the application.

(4) If the trademark is not registered on the Principal Register of the United States Patent and Trademark Office, state: "We do not have a federal registration for our principal trademark. Therefore, our trademark does not have many legal benefits and rights as a federally registered trademark. If our right to use the trademark is challenged, you may have to change to an alternative trademark, which may increase your expenses."

(5) Disclose any currently effective material determinations of the United States Patent and Trademark Office, the Trademark Trial and Appeal Board, or any state trademark administrator or court; and any pending infringement, opposition, or cancellation proceeding. Include infringement, opposition, or cancellation proceedings in which the franchisor unsuccessfully sought to prevent registration of a trademark in order to protect a trademark licensed by the franchisor. Describe how the determination affects the ownership, use, or licensing of the trademark.

(6) Disclose any pending material federal or state court litigation regarding the franchisor's use or ownership rights in a trademark. For each pending action, disclose:[8]

(i) The forum and case number.

(ii) The nature of claims made opposing the franchisor's use of the trademark or by the franchisor opposing another person's use of the trademark.

(iii) Any effective court or administrative agency ruling in the matter.

(7) Disclose any currently effective agreements that significantly limit the franchisor's rights to use or license the use of trademarks listed in this section in a manner material to the franchise. For each agreement, disclose:

(i) The manner and extent of the limitation or grant.

(ii) The extent to which the agreement may affect the franchisee.

(iii) The agreement's duration.

(iv) The parties to the agreement.

(v) The circumstances when the agreement may be canceled or modified.

(vi) All other material terms.

(8) Disclose:

(i) Whether the franchisor must protect the franchisee's right to use the principal trademarks listed in this section, and must protect the franchisee against claims of infringement or unfair competition arising out of the franchisee's use of the trademarks.

(ii) The franchisee's obligation to notify the franchisor of the use of, or claims of rights to, a trademark identical to or confusingly similar to a trademark licensed to the franchisee.

(iii) Whether the franchise agreement requires the franchisor to take affirmative action when notified of these uses or claims.

(iv) Whether the franchisor or franchisee has the right to control any

[8] The franchisor may include an attorney's opinion relative to the merits of litigation or of an action if the attorney issuing the opinion consents to its use. The text of the disclosure may include a summary of the opinion if the full opinion is attached and the attorney issuing the opinion consents to the use of the summary.

administrative proceedings or litigation involving a trademark licensed by the franchisor to the franchisee.

(v) Whether the franchise agreement requires the franchisor to participate in the franchisee's defense and/or indemnify the franchisee for expenses or damages if the franchisee is a party to an administrative or judicial proceeding involving a trademark licensed by the franchisor to the franchisee, or if the proceeding is resolved unfavorably to the franchisee.

(vi) The franchisee's rights under the franchise agreement if the franchisor requires the franchisee to modify or discontinue using a trademark.

(9) Disclose whether the franchisor knows of either superior prior rights or infringing uses that could materially affect the franchisee's use of the principal trademarks in the state where the franchised business will be located. For each use of a principal trademark that the franchisor believes is an infringement that could materially affect the franchisee's use of a trademark, disclose:

(i) The nature of the infringement.

(ii) The locations where the infringement is occurring.

(iii) The length of time of the infringement (to the extent known).

(iv) Any action taken or anticipated by the franchisor.

(n) *Item 14: Patents, Copyrights, and Proprietary Information.* (1) Disclose whether the franchisor owns rights in, or licenses to, patents or copyrights that are material to the franchise. Also, disclose whether the franchisor has any pending patent applications that are material to the franchise. If so, state:

(i) The nature of the patent, patent application, or copyright and its relationship to the franchise.

(ii) For each patent:

(A) The duration of the patent.

(B) The type of patent (for example, mechanical, process, or design).

(C) The patent number, issuance date, and title.

(iii) For each patent application:

(A) The type of patent application (for example, mechanical, process, or design).

(B) The serial number, filing date, and title.

(iv) For each copyright:

(A) The duration of the copyright.

(B) The registration number and date.

(C) Whether the franchisor can and intends to renew the copyright.

(2) Describe any current material determination of the United States Patent and Trademark Office, the United States Copyright Office, or a court regarding the patent or copyright. Include the forum and matter number. Describe how the determination affects the franchised business.

(3) State the forum, case number, claims asserted, issues involved, and effective determinations for any material proceeding pending in the United States Patent and Trademark Office or any court.[9]

(4) If an agreement limits the use of the patent, patent application, or copyright, state the parties to and duration of the agreement, the extent to which the agreement may affect the franchisee, and other material terms of the agreement.

(5) Disclose the franchisor's obligation to protect the patent, patent application, or copyright; and to defend the franchisee against claims arising from the franchisee's use of patented or copyrighted items, including:

(i) Whether the franchisor's obligation is contingent upon the franchisee notifying the franchisor of any infringement claims or whether the franchisee's notification is discretionary.

(ii) Whether the franchise agreement requires the franchisor to take affirmative action when notified of infringement.

(iii) Who has the right to control any litigation.

(iv) Whether the franchisor must participate in the defense of a franchisee or indemnify the franchisee for expenses or damages in a proceeding involving a patent, patent application, or copyright licensed to the franchisee.

(v) Whether the franchisor's obligation is contingent upon the franchisee modifying or discontinuing the use of

[9] If counsel consents, the franchisor may include a counsel's opinion or a summary of the opinion if the full opinion is attached.

the subject matter covered by the patent or copyright.

(vi) The franchisee's rights under the franchise agreement if the franchisor requires the franchisee to modify or discontinue using the subject matter covered by the patent or copyright.

(6) If the franchisor knows of any patent or copyright infringement that could materially affect the franchisee, disclose:

(i) The nature of the infringement.

(ii) The locations where the infringement is occurring.

(iii) The length of time of the infringement (to the extent known).

(iv) Any action taken or anticipated by the franchisor.

(7) If the franchisor claims proprietary rights in other confidential information or trade secrets, describe in general terms the proprietary information communicated to the franchisee and the terms for use by the franchisee. The franchisor need only describe the general nature of the proprietary information, such as whether a formula or recipe is considered to be a trade secret.

(o) *Item 15: Obligation to Participate in the Actual Operation of the Franchise Business.* (1) Disclose the franchisee's obligation to participate personally in the direct operation of the franchisee's business and whether the franchisor recommends participation. Include obligations arising from any written agreement or from the franchisor's practice.

(2) If personal "on-premises" supervision is not required, disclose the following:

(i) If the franchisee is an individual, whether the franchisor recommends on-premises supervision by the franchisee.

(ii) Limits on whom the franchisee can hire as an on-premises supervisor.

(iii) Whether an on-premises supervisor must successfully complete the franchisor's training program.

(iv) If the franchisee is a business entity, the amount of equity interest, if any, that the on-premises supervisor must have in the franchisee's business.

(3) Disclose any restrictions that the franchisee must place on its manager (for example, maintain trade secrets, covenants not to compete).

(p) *Item 16: Restrictions on What the Franchisee May Sell.* Disclose any franchisor-imposed restrictions or conditions on the goods or services that the franchisee may sell or that limit access to customers, including:

(1) Any obligation on the franchisee to sell only goods or services approved by
the franchisor.

(2) Any obligation on the franchisee to sell all goods or services authorized by the franchisor.

(3) Whether the franchisor has the right to change the types of authorized goods or services and whether there are limits on the franchisor's right to make changes.

(q) *Item 17: Renewal, Termination, Transfer, and Dispute Resolution.* Disclose, in the following tabular form, a table that cross-references each enumerated franchise relationship item with the applicable provision in the franchise or related agreement. Title the table "THE FRANCHISE RELATIONSHIP" in capital letters and bold type.

(1) Describe briefly each contractual provision. If a particular item is not applicable, state "Not Applicable."

(2) If the agreement is silent about one of the listed provisions, but the franchisor unilaterally offers to provide certain benefits or protections to franchisees as a matter of policy, use a footnote to describe the policy and state whether the policy is subject to change.

(3) In the summary column for Item 17(c), state what the term "renewal" means for your franchise system, including, if applicable, a statement that franchisees may be asked to sign a contract with materially different terms and conditions than their original contract.

ITEM 17 TABLE:

THE FRANCHISE RELATIONSHIP

[In bold] **This table lists certain important provisions of the franchise and related agreements. You should read these provisions in the agreements attached to this disclosure document.**

Provision	Section in franchise or other agreement	Summary
a. Length of the franchise term		
b. Renewal or extension of the term		
c. Requirements for franchisee to renew or extend		
d. Termination by franchisee		
e. Termination by franchisor without cause		
f. Termination by franchisor with cause		
g. "Cause" defined—curable defaults		
h. "Cause" defined—non-curable defaults		
i. Franchisee's obligations on termination/non-renewal		
j. Assignment of contract by franchisor		
k. "Transfer" by franchisee—defined		
l. Franchisor approval of transfer by franchisee		
m. Conditions for franchisor approval of transfer		
n. Franchisor's right of first refusal to acquire franchisee's business		
o. Franchisor's option to purchase franchisee's business		
p. Death or disability of franchisee		
q. Non-competition covenants during the term of the franchise		
r. Non-competition covenants after the franchise is terminated or expires		
s. Modification of the agreement		
t. Integration/merger clause		
u. Dispute resolution by arbitration or mediation		
v. Choice of forum		
w. Choice of law		

(r) *Item 18: Public Figures.* Disclose:

(1) Any compensation or other benefit given or promised to a public figure arising from either the use of the public figure in the franchise name or symbol, or the public figure's endorsement or recommendation of the franchise to prospective franchisees.

(2) The extent to which the public figure is involved in the management or control of the franchisor. Describe the public figure's position and duties in the franchisor's business structure.

(3) The public figure's total investment in the franchisor, including the amount the public figure contributed in services performed or to be performed. State the type of investment (for example, common stock, promissory note).

(4) For purposes of this section, a public figure means a person whose name or physical appearance is generally known to the public in the geographic area where the franchise will be located.

(s) *Item 19: Financial Performance Representations.* (1) Begin by stating the following:

> The FTC's Franchise Rule permits a franchisor to provide information about the actual or potential financial performance of its franchised and/or franchisor-owned outlets, if there is a reasonable basis for the information, and if the information is included in the disclosure document. Financial performance information that differs from that included in Item 19 may be given only if: (1) a franchisor provides the actual records of an existing outlet you are considering buying; or (2) a franchisor supplements the information provided in this Item 19, for example, by providing information about possible performance at a particular location or under particular circumstances.

(2) If a franchisor does not provide any financial performance representation in Item 19, also state:

> We do not make any representations about a franchisee's future financial performance or the past financial performance of company-owned or franchised outlets. We also do not authorize our employees or representatives to make any such representations either orally or in writing. If you are purchasing an existing outlet, however, we may provide you with the actual records of that outlet. If you receive any other financial performance information or projections of your future income, you should report it to the franchisor's management by contacting [name, address, and telephone number], the Federal Trade Commission, and the appropriate state regulatory agencies.

(3) If the franchisor makes any financial performance representation to prospective franchisees, the franchisor must have a reasonable basis and written substantiation for the representation at the time the representation is made and must state the representation in the Item 19 disclosure. The franchisor must also disclose the following:

(i) Whether the representation is an historic financial performance representation about the franchise system's existing outlets, or a subset of those outlets, or is a forecast of the prospective franchisee's future financial performance.

(ii) If the representation relates to past performance of the franchise system's existing outlets, the material bases for the representation, including:

(A) Whether the representation relates to the performance of all of the franchise system's existing outlets or only to a subset of outlets that share a particular set of characteristics (for example, geographic location, type of location (such as free standing vs. shopping center), degree of competition, length of time the outlets have operated, services or goods sold, services supplied by the franchisor, and whether the outlets are franchised or franchisor-owned or operated).

(B) The dates when the reported level of financial performance was achieved.

(C) The total number of outlets that existed in the relevant period and, if different, the number of outlets that had the described characteristics.

(D) The number of outlets with the described characteristics whose actual financial performance data were used in arriving at the representation.

(E) Of those outlets whose data were used in arriving at the representation, the number and percent that actually attained or surpassed the stated results.

(F) Characteristics of the included outlets, such as those characteristics noted in paragraph (3)(ii)(A) of this section, that may differ materially from those of the outlet that may be offered to a prospective franchisee.

(iii) If the representation is a forecast of future financial performance, state the material bases and assumptions on which the projection is based. The material assumptions underlying a forecast include significant factors upon which a franchisee's future results are expected to depend. These factors include, for example, economic or market conditions that are basic to a franchisee's operation, and encompass matters affecting, among other things, a franchisee's sales, the cost of goods or services sold, and operating expenses.

(iv) A clear and conspicuous admonition that a new franchisee's individual financial results may differ from the result stated in the financial performance representation.

(v) A statement that written substantiation for the financial performance representation will be made available to the prospective franchisee upon reasonable request.

(4) If a franchisor wishes to disclose only the actual operating results for a specific outlet being offered for sale, it need not comply with this section, provided the information is given only to potential purchasers of that outlet.

(5) If a franchisor furnishes financial performance information according to this section, the franchisor may deliver to a prospective franchisee a supplemental financial performance representation about a particular location or variation, apart from the disclosure document. The supplemental representation must:

(i) Be in writing.

(ii) Explain the departure from the financial performance representation in the disclosure document.

(iii) Be prepared in accordance with the requirements of paragraph (s)(3)(i)-(iv) of this section.

(iv) Be furnished to the prospective franchisee.

(t) *Item 20: Outlets and Franchisee Information.* (1) Disclose, in the following tabular form, the total number of franchised and company-owned outlets for each of the franchisor's last three fiscal years. For purposes of this section, "outlet" includes outlets of a type substantially similar to that offered to the prospective franchisee. A sample Item 20(1) Table is attached as appendix B to this part.

ITEM 20 TABLE NO. 1

Systemwide Outlet Summary

For years [ ] to [ ]

Column 1 Outlet Type	Column 2 Year	Column 3 Outlets at the Start of the Year	Column 4 Outlets at the End of the Year	Column 5 Net Change
Franchised	2004			
	2005			
	2006			
Company-Owned	2004			
	2005			
	2006			
Total Outlets	2004			
	2005			
	2006			

(i) In column 1, include three outlet categories titled "franchised," "company-owned, and "total outlets."

(ii) In column 2, state the last three fiscal years.

(iii) In column 3, state the total number of each type of outlet operating at the beginning of each fiscal year.

(iv) In column 4, state the total number of each type of outlet operating at the end of each fiscal year.

(v) In column 5, state the net change, and indicate whether the change is positive or negative, for each type of outlet during each fiscal year.

(2) Disclose, in the following tabular form, the number of franchised and company-owned outlets and changes in the number and ownership of outlets located in each state during each of the last three fiscal years. Except as noted, each change in ownership shall be reported only once in the following tables. If multiple events occurred in the process of transferring ownership of an outlet, report the event that occurred last in time. If a single outlet changed ownership two or more times during the same fiscal year, use footnotes to describe the types of changes involved

and the order in which the changes occurred.

(i) Disclose, in the following tabular form, the total number of franchised outlets transferred in each state during each of the franchisor's last three fiscal years. For purposes of this section, "transfer" means the acquisition of a controlling interest in a franchised outlet, during its term, by a person other than the franchisor or an affiliate. A sample Item 20(2) Table is attached as appendix C to this part.

ITEM 20 TABLE NO. 2

Transfers of Outlets from Franchisees to New Owners (other than the Franchisor)

For years [ ] to [ ]

Column 1 State	Column 2 Year	Column 3 Number of Transfers
	2004	
	2005	
	2006	
	2004	
	2005	
	2006	
Total	2004	
	2005	
	2006	

(A) In column 1, list each state with one or more franchised outlets.

(B) In column 2, state the last three fiscal years.

(C) In column 3, state the total number of completed transfers in each state during each fiscal year.

(ii) Disclose, in the following tabular form, the status of franchisee-owned outlets located in each state for each of the franchisor's last three fiscal years. A sample Item 20(3) Table is attached as appendix D to this part.

ITEM 20 TABLE NO. 3

Status of Franchised Outlets

For years [ ] to [ ]

Column 1 State	Column 2 Year	Column 3 Outlets at Start of Year	Column 4 Outlets Opened	Column 5 Terminations	Column 6 Non-Renewals	Column 7 Reacquired by Franchisor	Column 8 Ceased Operations-Other Reasons	Column 9 Outlets at End of the Year
	2004							
	2005							
	2006							
	2004							
	2005							
	2006							
Totals	2004							
	2005							
	2006							

(A) In column 1, list each state with one or more franchised outlets.

(B) In column 2, state the last three fiscal years.

(C) In column 3, state the total number of franchised outlets in each state at the start of each fiscal year.

(D) In column 4, state the total number of franchised outlets opened in each state during each fiscal year. Include both new outlets and existing company-owned outlets that a franchisee purchased from the franchisor. (Also report the number of existing company-owned outlets that are sold to a franchisee in Column 7 of Table 4).

(E) In column 5, state the total number of franchised outlets that were terminated in each state during each fiscal year. For purposes of this section, "termination" means the franchisor's termination of a franchise agreement prior to the end of its term and without providing any consideration to the franchisee (whether by payment or forgiveness or assumption of debt).

(F) In column 6, state the total number of non-renewals in each state during each fiscal year. For purposes of this section, "non-renewal" occurs when the franchise agreement for a franchised outlet is not renewed at the end of its term.

(G) In column 7, state the total number of franchised outlets reacquired by the franchisor in each state during each fiscal year. For purposes of this section, a "reacquisition" means the franchisor's acquisition for consideration (whether by payment or forgiveness or assumption of debt) of a franchised outlet during its term. (Also report franchised outlets reacquired by the franchisor in column 5 of Table 4).

(H) In column 8, state the total number of outlets in each state not operating as one of the franchisor's outlets at the end of each fiscal year for reasons other than termination, non-renewal, or reacquisition by the franchisor.

(I) In column 9, state the total number of franchised outlets in each state at the end of the fiscal year.

(iii) Disclose, in the following tabular form, the status of company-owned outlets located in each state for each of the franchisor's last three fiscal years. A sample Item 20(4) Table is attached as appendix E to this part.

ITEM 20 TABLE NO. 4

Status of Company-Owned Outlets

For years [ ] to [ ]

Column 1 State	Column 2 Year	Column 3 Outlets at Start of Year	Column 4 Outlets Opened	Column 5 Outlets Reacquired From Franchisee	Column 6 Outlets Closed	Column 7 Outlets Sold to Franchisee	Column 8 Outlets at End of the Year
	2004						
	2005						
	2006						
	2004						
	2005						
	2006						
Totals	2004						
	2005						
	2006						

(A) In column 1, list each state with one or more company-owned outlets.

(B) In column 2, state the last three fiscal years.

(C) In column 3, state the total number of company-owned outlets in each state at the start of the fiscal year.

(D) In column 4, state the total number of company-owned outlets opened in each state during each fiscal year.

(E) In column 5, state the total number of franchised outlets reacquired from franchisees in each state during each fiscal year.

(F) In column 6, state the total number of company-owned outlets closed in each state during each fiscal year. Include both actual closures and instances when an outlet ceases to operate under the franchisor's trademark.

(G) In column 7, state the total number of company-owned outlets sold to franchisees in each state during each fiscal year.

(H) In column 8, state the total number of company-owned outlets operating in each state at the end of each fiscal year.

(3) Disclose, in the following tabular form, projected new franchised and company-owned outlets. A sample Item 20(5) Table is attached as appendix F to this part.

ITEM 20 TABLE NO. 5

Projected Openings As Of [Last Day of Last Fiscal Year]

Column 1 State	Column 2 Franchise Agreements Signed But Outlet Not Opened	Column 3 Projected New Franchised Outlet In The Next Fiscal Year	Column 4 Projected New Company-Owned Outlet In the Next Fiscal Year
Total			

(i) In column 1, list each state where one or more franchised or company-owned outlets are located or are projected to be located.

(ii) In column 2, state the total number of franchise agreements that had been signed for new outlets to be located in each state as of the end of the previous fiscal year where the outlet had not yet opened.

(iii) In column 3, state the total number of new franchised outlets in each state projected to be opened during the next fiscal year.

(iv) In column 4, state the total number of new company-owned outlets in each state that are projected to be opened during the next fiscal year.

(4) Disclose the names of all current franchisees and the address and telephone number of each of their outlets. Alternatively, disclose this information for all franchised outlets in the state, but if these franchised outlets total fewer than 100, disclose this information for franchised outlets from contiguous states and then the next closest states until at least 100 franchised outlets are listed.

(5) Disclose the name, city and state, and current business telephone number, or if unknown, the last known home telephone number of every franchisee who had an outlet terminated, canceled, not renewed, or otherwise voluntarily or involuntarily ceased to do business under the franchise agreement during the most recently completed fiscal year or who has not communicated with the franchisor within 10 weeks of the disclosure document issuance date.[10] State in immediate conjunction with this information: "If you buy this franchise, your contact information may be disclosed to other buyers when you leave the franchise system."

(6) If a franchisor is selling a previously-owned franchised outlet now under its control, disclose the following additional information for that outlet for the last five fiscal years. This information may be attached as an addendum to a disclosure document, or, if disclosure has already been made, then in a supplement to the previously furnished disclosure document.

(i) The name, city and state, current business telephone number, or if unknown, last known home telephone number of each previous owner of the outlet;

(ii) The time period when each previous owner controlled the outlet;

(iii) The reason for each previous change in ownership (for example, termination, non-renewal, voluntary transfer, ceased operations); and

(iv) The time period(s) when the franchisor retained control of the outlet (for example, after termination, non-renewal, or reacquisition).

(7) Disclose whether franchisees signed confidentiality clauses during the last three fiscal years. If so, state

[10] Franchisors may substitute alternative contact information at the request of the former franchisee, such as a home address, post office address, or a personal or business email address.

the following: "In some instances, current and former franchisees sign provisions restricting their ability to speak openly about their experience with [name of franchise system]. You may wish to speak with current and former franchisees, but be aware that not all such franchisees will be able to communicate with you." Franchisors may also disclose the number and percentage of current and former franchisees who during each of the last three fiscal years signed agreements that include confidentiality clauses and may disclose the circumstances under which such clauses were signed.

(8) Disclose, to the extent known, the name, address, telephone number, email address, and Web address (to the extent known) of each trademark-specific franchisee organization associated with the franchise system being offered, if such organization:

(i) Has been created, sponsored, or endorsed by the franchisor. If so, state the relationship between the organization and the franchisor (for example, the organization was created by the franchisor, sponsored by the franchisor, or endorsed by the franchisor).

(ii) Is incorporated or otherwise organized under state law and asks the franchisor to be included in the franchisor's disclosure document during the next fiscal year. Such organizations must renew their request on an annual basis by submitting a request no later than 60 days after the close of the franchisor's fiscal year. The franchisor has no obligation to verify the organization's continued existence at the end of each fiscal year. Franchisors may also include the following statement: "The following independent franchisee organizations have asked to be included in this disclosure document."

(u) *Item 21*: *Financial Statements*. (1) Include the following financial statements prepared according to United States generally accepted accounting principles, as revised by any future United States government mandated accounting principles, or as permitted by the Securities and Exchange Commission. Except as provided in paragraph (u)(2) of this section, these financial statements must be audited by an independent certified public accountant using generally accepted United States auditing standards. Present the required financial statements in a tabular form that compares at least two fiscal years.

(i) The franchisor's balance sheet for the previous two fiscal year-ends before the disclosure document issuance date.

(ii) Statements of operations, stockholders equity, and cash flows for each of the franchisor's previous three fiscal years.

(iii) Instead of the financial disclosures required by paragraphs (u)(1)(i) and (ii) of this section, the franchisor may include financial statements of any of its affiliates if the affiliate's financial statements satisfy paragraphs (u)(1)(i) and (ii) of this section and the affiliate absolutely and unconditionally guarantees to assume the duties and obligations of the franchisor under the franchise agreement. The affiliate's guarantee must cover all of the franchisor's obligations to the franchisee, but need not extend to third parties. If this alternative is used, attach a copy of the guarantee to the disclosure document.

(iv) When a franchisor owns a direct or beneficial controlling financial interest in a subsidiary, its financial statements should reflect the financial condition of the franchisor and its subsidiary.

(v) Include separate financial statements for the franchisor and any subfranchisor, as well as for any parent that commits to perform post-sale obligations for the franchisor or guarantees the franchisor's obligations. Attach a copy of any guarantee to the disclosure document.

(2) A start-up franchise system that does not yet have audited financial statements may phase-in the use of audited financial statements by providing, at a minimum, the following statements at the indicated times:

(i) The franchisor' first partial or full fiscal year selling franchises.	An unaudited opening balance sheet.

(ii) The franchisor' second fiscal year selling franchises.	Audited balance sheet opinion as of the end of the first partial or full fiscal year selling franchises.
(iii) The franchisor' third and subsequent fiscal years selling franchises.	All required financial statements for the previous fiscal year, plus any previously disclosed audited statements that still must be disclosed according to paragraphs (u)(1)(i) and (ii) of this section.

(iv) Start-up franchisors may phase-in the disclosure of audited financial statements, provided the franchisor:

(A) Prepares audited financial statements as soon as practicable.

(B) Prepares unaudited statements in a format that conforms as closely as possible to audited statements.

(C) Includes one or more years of unaudited financial statements or clearly and conspicuously discloses in this section that the franchisor has not been in business for three years or more, and cannot include all financial statements required in paragraphs (u)(1)(i) and (ii) of this section.

(v) *Item 22: Contracts.* Attach a copy of all proposed agreements regarding the franchise offering, including the franchise agreement and any lease, options, and purchase agreements.

(w) *Item 23: Receipts.* Include two copies of the following detachable acknowledgment of receipt in the following form as the last pages of the disclosure document:

(1) State the following:

RECEIPT

This disclosure document summarizes certain provisions of the franchise agreement and other information in plain language. Read this disclosure document and all agreements carefully.

If [name of franchisor] offers you a franchise, it must provide this disclosure document to you 14 calendar-days before you sign a binding agreement with, or make a payment to, the franchisor or an affiliate in connection with the proposed franchise sale.

If [name of franchisor] does not deliver this disclosure document on time or if it contains a false or misleading statement, or a material omission, a violation of federal law and state law may have occurred and should be reported to the Federal Trade Commission, Washington, D.C. 20580 and [state agency].

(2) Disclose the name, principal business address, and telephone number of each franchise seller offering the franchise.

(3) State the issuance date.

(4) If not disclosed in paragraph (a) of this section, state the name and address of the franchisor's registered agent authorized to receive service of process.

(5) State the following:

I received a disclosure document dated ________ that included the following Exhibits:

(6) List the title(s) of all attached Exhibits.

(7) Provide space for the prospective franchisee's signature and date.

(8) Franchisors may include any specific instructions for returning the receipt (for example, street address, email address, facsimile telephone number).

Subpart D—Instructions

§ 436.6 Instructions for preparing disclosure documents.

(a) It is an unfair or deceptive act or practice in violation of Section 5 of the FTC Act for any franchisor to fail to include the information and follow the instructions for preparing disclosure documents set forth in subpart C (basic disclosure requirements) and subpart D (updating requirements) of part 436. The Commission will enforce this provision according to the standards of liability under Sections 5, 13(b), and 19 of the FTC Act.

(b) Disclose all required information clearly, legibly, and concisely in a single document using plain English. The disclosures must be in a form that permits each prospective franchisee to store, download, print, or otherwise maintain the document for future reference.

(c) Respond fully to each disclosure Item. If a disclosure Item is not applicable, respond negatively, including a reference to the type of information required to be disclosed by the Item. Precede each disclosure Item with the appropriate heading.

(d) Do not include any materials or information other than those required or permitted by part 436 or by state law not preempted by part 436. For the sole purpose of enhancing the prospective franchisee's ability to maneuver through an electronic version of a disclosure document, the franchisor may include scroll bars, internal links, and search features. All other features (e.g., multimedia tools such as audio, video, animation, pop-up screens, or links to external information) are prohibited.

(e) Franchisors may prepare multi-state disclosure documents by including non-preempted, state-specific information in the text of the disclosure document or in Exhibits attached to the disclosure document.

(f) Subfranchisors shall disclose the required information about the franchisor, and, to the extent applicable, the same information concerning the subfranchisor.

(g) Before furnishing a disclosure document, the franchisor shall advise the prospective franchisee of the formats in which the disclosure document is made available, any prerequisites for obtaining the disclosure document in a particular format, and any conditions necessary for reviewing the disclosure document in a particular format.

(h) Franchisors shall retain, and make available to the Commission upon request, a sample copy of each materially different version of their disclosure documents for three years after the close of the fiscal year when it was last used.

(i) For each completed franchise sale, franchisors shall retain a copy of the signed receipt for at least three years.

§436.7 Instructions for updating disclosures.

(a) All information in the disclosure document shall be current as of the close of the franchisor's most recent fiscal year. After the close of the fiscal year, the franchisor shall, within 120 days, prepare a revised disclosure document, after which a franchise seller may distribute only the revised document and no other disclosure document.

(b) The franchisor shall, within a reasonable time after the close of each quarter of the fiscal year, prepare revisions to be attached to the disclosure document to reflect any material change to the disclosures included, or required to be included, in the disclosure document. Each prospective franchisee shall receive the disclosure document and the quarterly revisions for the most recent period available at the time of disclosure.

(c) If applicable, the annual update shall include the franchisor's first quarterly update, either by incorporating the quarterly update information into the disclosure document itself, or through an addendum.

(d) When furnishing a disclosure document, the franchise seller shall notify the prospective franchisee of any material changes that the seller knows or should have known occurred in the information contained in any financial performance representation made in Item 19 (section 436.5(s)).

(e) Information that must be audited pursuant to §436.5(u) of this part need not be audited for quarterly revisions; provided, however, that the franchisor states in immediate conjunction with the information that such information was not audited.

Subpart E—Exemptions

§436.8 Exemptions.

(a) The provisions of part 436 shall not apply if the franchisor can establish any of the following:

(1) The total of the required payments, or commitments to make a required payment, to the franchisor or an affiliate that are made any time from before to within six months after commencing operation of the franchisee's business is less than $570.

(2) The franchise relationship is a fractional franchise.

(3) The franchise relationship is a leased department.

(4) The franchise relationship is covered by the Petroleum Marketing Practices Act, 15 U.S.C. 2801.

(5)(i) The franchisee's initial investment, excluding any financing received from the franchisor or an affiliate and excluding the cost of unimproved land, totals at least $1,143,100 and the prospective franchisee signs an acknowledgment verifying the grounds for the exemption. The acknowledgment shall state: "The franchise sale is for more than $1,143,100—excluding the cost of unimproved land and any financing received from the franchisor or an affiliate— and thus is exempted from the Federal Trade Commission's Franchise Rule disclosure requirements, pursuant to 16 CFR 436.8(a)(5)(i)";[11] or

(ii) The franchisee (or its parent or any affiliates) is an entity that has been in business for at least five years and has a net worth of at least $5,715,500.

(6) One or more purchasers of at least a 50% ownership interest in the franchise: within 60 days of the sale, has been, for at least two years, an officer, director, general partner, individual with management responsibility for the offer and sale of the franchisor's franchises or the administrator of the franchised network; or within 60 days of the sale, has been, for at least two years, an owner of at least a 25% interest in the franchisor.

(7) There is no written document that describes any material term or aspect of the relationship or arrangement.

(b) For purposes of the exemptions set forth in this section, the Commission shall adjust the size of the monetary thresholds every fourth year based upon the Consumer Price Index. For purposes of this section, "Consumer Price Index" means the Consumer Price Index for all urban consumers published by the Department of Labor.

[72 FR 15544, Mar. 30, 2007, as amended at 77 FR 36150, June 18, 2012; 81 FR 31501, May 19, 2016]

Subpart F—Prohibitions

§ 436.9 Additional prohibitions.

It is an unfair or deceptive act or practice in violation of Section 5 of the Federal Trade Commission Act for any franchise seller covered by part 436 to:

(a) Make any claim or representation, orally, visually, or in writing, that contradicts the information required to be disclosed by this part.

(b) Misrepresent that any person:

(1) Purchased a franchise from the franchisor or operated a franchise of the type offered by the franchisor.

(2) Can provide an independent and reliable report about the franchise or the experiences of any current or former franchisees.

(c) Disseminate any financial performance representations to prospective franchisees unless the franchisor has a reasonable basis and written substantiation for the representation at the time the representation is made, and the representation is included in Item 19 (§ 436.5(s)) of the franchisor's disclosure document. In conjunction with any such financial performance representation, the franchise seller shall also:

(1) Disclose the information required by §§ 436.5(s)(3)(ii)(B) and (E) of this part if the representation relates to the past performance of the franchisor's outlets.

(2) Include a clear and conspicuous admonition that a new franchisee's individual financial results may differ from the result stated in the financial performance representation.

(d) Fail to make available to prospective franchisees, and to the Commission upon reasonable request, written substantiation for any financial performance representations made in Item 19 (§ 436.5(s)).

(e) Fail to furnish a copy of the franchisor's disclosure document to a prospective franchisee earlier in the sales process than required under § 436.2 of this part, upon reasonable request.

(f) Fail to furnish a copy of the franchisor's most recent disclosure document and any quarterly updates to a prospective franchisee, upon reasonable request, before the prospective franchisee signs a franchise agreement.

(g) Present for signing a franchise agreement in which the terms and conditions differ materially from those presented as an attachment to the disclosure document, unless the franchise seller informed the prospective franchisee of the differences at least seven days before execution of the franchise agreement.

(h) Disclaim or require a prospective franchisee to waive reliance on any representation made in the disclosure

[11] The large franchise exemption applies only if at least one individual prospective franchisee in an investor-group qualifies for the exemption by investing at the threshold level stated in this section.

document or in its exhibits or amendments. Provided, however, that this provision is not intended to prevent a prospective franchisee from voluntarily waiving specific contract terms and conditions set forth in his or her disclosure document during the course of franchise sale negotiations.

(i) Fail to return any funds or deposits in accordance with any conditions disclosed in the franchisor's disclosure document, franchise agreement, or any related document.

Subpart G—Other Provisions

§ 436.10 Other laws and rules.

(a) The Commission does not approve or express any opinion on the legality of any matter a franchisor may be required to disclose by part 436. Further, franchisors may have additional obligations to impart material information to prospective franchisees outside of the disclosure document under Section 5 of the Federal Trade Commission Act. The Commission intends to enforce all applicable statutes and rules.

(b) The FTC does not intend to preempt the franchise practices laws of any state or local government, except to the extent of any inconsistency with part 436. A law is not inconsistent with part 436 if it affords prospective franchisees equal or greater protection, such as registration of disclosure documents or more extensive disclosures.

§ 436.11 Severability.

If any provision of this part is stayed or held invalid, the remainder will stay in force.

APPENDIX A TO PART 436—SAMPLE ITEM 10 TABLE—SUMMARY OF FINANCING OFFERED

SUMMARY OF FINANCING OFFERED

Item Financed	Source of Financing	Down Payment	Amount Financed	Term (Yrs)	Interest Rate	Monthly Payment	Prepay Penalty	Security Required	Liability Upon Default	Loss of Legal Right on Default
Initial Fee										
Land/Constr										
Leased Space										
Equip. Lease										
Equip. Purchase										
Opening Inventory										
Other Financing										

APPENDIX B TO PART 436—SAMPLE ITEM 20(1) TABLE—SYSTEMWIDE OUTLET SUMMARY

Systemwide Outlet Summary
For years 2004 to 2006

Column 1 Outlet Type	Column 2 Year	Column 3 Outlets at the Start of the Year	Column 4 Outlets at the End of the Year	Column 5 Net Change
Franchised	2004	859	1,062	+ 203
	2005	1,062	1,296	+ 234
	2006	1,296	2,720	+ 1,424
Company Owned	2004	125	145	+ 20

Systemwide Outlet Summary
For years 2004 to 2006

Column 1 Outlet Type	Column 2 Year	Column 3 Outlets at the Start of the Year	Column 4 Outlets at the End of the Year	Column 5 Net Change
	2005	145	76	-69
	2006	76	141	+ 65
Total Outlets	2004	984	1,207	+ 223
	2005	1,207	1,372	+ 165
	2006	1,372	2,861	+ 1,489

APPENDIX C TO PART 436—SAMPLE ITEM 20(2) TABLE—TRANSFERS OF FRANCHISED OUTLETS

Transfers of Franchised Outlets from Franchisees to New Owners (other than the Franchisor)
For years 2004 to 2006

Column 1 State	Column 2 Year	Column 3 Number of Transfers
NC	2004	1
	2005	0
	2006	2
SC	2004	0

Transfers of Franchised Outlets from Franchisees to New Owners (other than the Franchisor)
For years 2004 to 2006

Column 1 State	Column 2 Year	Column 3 Number of Transfers
	2005	0
	2006	2
Total	2004	1
	2005	0
	2006	4

APPENDIX D TO PART 436—SAMPLE ITEM 20(3) TABLE—STATUS OF FRANCHISE OUTLETS

Status of Franchise Outlets
For years 2004 to 2006

Column 1 State	Column 2 Year	Column 3 Outlets at Start of Year	Column 4 Outlets Opened	Column 5 Terminations	Column 6 Non-Renewals	Column 7 Reacquired by Franchisor	Column 8 Ceased Operations-Other Reasons	Column 9 Outlets at End of the Year
AL	2004	10	2	1	0	0	1	10
	2005	11	5	0	1	0	0	15
	2006	15	4	1	0	1	2	15
AZ	2004	20	5	0	0	0	0	25
	2005	25	4	1	0	0	2	26
	2006	26	4	0	0	0	0	30
Totals	2004	30	7	1	0	0	1	35
	2005	36	9	1	1	0	2	41
	2006	41	8	1	0	1	2	45

APPENDIX E TO PART 436—SAMPLE ITEM 20(4) TABLE—STATUS OF COMPANY-OWNED OUTLETS

Status of Company-Owned Outlets
For years 2004 to 2006

Column 1 State	Column 2 Year	Column 3 Outlets at Start of Year	Column 4 Outlets Opened	Column 5 Outlets Reacquired From Franchisees	Column 6 Outlets Closed	Column 7 Outlets Sold to Franchisees	Column 8 Outlets at End of the Year
NY	2004	1	0	1	0	0	2
	2005	2	2	0	1	0	3
	2006	3	0	0	3	0	0
OR	2004	4	0	1	0	0	5
	2005	5	0	0	2	0	3
	2006	3	0	0	0	1	2
Totals	2004	5	0	2	0	0	7
	2005	7	2	0	3	0	6
	2006	6	0	0	3	1	2

APPENDIX F TO PART 436—SAMPLE ITEM 20(5) TABLE—PROJECTED NEW FRANCHISED OUTLETS

Projected New Franchised Outlets
As of December 31, 2006

Column 1 State	Column 2 Franchise Agreements Signed But Outlet Not Opened	Column 3 Projected New Franchised Outlets in the Next Fiscal Year	Column 4 Projected New Company-Owned Outlets in the Current Fiscal Year
CO	2	3	1
NM	0	4	2
Total	2	7	3

PART 437—BUSINESS OPPORTUNITY RULE

AUTHORITY: 15 U.S.C. 41–58.

SOURCE: 76 FR 76860, Dec. 8, 2012, unless otherwise noted.

§437.1 Definitions.

The following definitions shall apply throughout this part:

(a) *Action* means a criminal information, indictment, or proceeding; a civil complaint, cross claim, counterclaim, or third party complaint in a judicial action or proceeding; arbitration; or any governmental administrative proceeding, including, but not limited to, an action to obtain or issue a cease and desist order, an assurance of voluntary compliance, and an assurance of discontinuance.

(b) *Affiliate* means an entity controlled by, controlling, or under common control with a business opportunity seller.

(c) *Business opportunity* means a commercial arrangement in which:

(1) A seller solicits a prospective purchaser to enter into a new business; and

(2) The prospective purchaser makes a required payment; and

(3) The seller, expressly or by implication, orally or in writing, represents that the seller or one or more designated persons will:

(i) Provide locations for the use or operation of equipment, displays, vending machines, or similar devices, owned, leased, controlled, or paid for by the purchaser; or

(ii) Provide outlets, accounts, or customers, including, but not limited to, Internet outlets, accounts, or customers, for the purchaser's goods or services; or

(iii) Buy back any or all of the goods or services that the purchaser makes, produces, fabricates, grows, breeds, modifies, or provides, including but not limited to providing payment for such services as, for example, stuffing envelopes from the purchaser's home.

(d) *Designated person* means any person, other than the seller, whose goods or services the seller suggests, recommends, or requires that the purchaser use in establishing or operating a new business.

(e) *Disclose* or *state* means to give information in writing that is clear and conspicuous, accurate, concise, and legible.

(f) *Earnings claim* means any oral, written, or visual representation to a prospective purchaser that conveys, expressly or by implication, a specific level or range of actual or potential sales, or gross or net income or profits. Earnings claims include, but are not limited to:

(1) Any chart, table, or mathematical calculation that demonstrates possible results based upon a combination of variables; and

(2) Any statements from which a prospective purchaser can reasonably infer that he or she will earn a minimum level of income (e.g., "earn enough to buy a Porsche," "earn a six-figure income," or "earn your investment back within one year").

(g) *Exclusive territory* means a specified geographic or other actual or implied marketing area in which the seller promises not to locate additional purchasers or offer the same or similar goods or services as the purchaser through alternative channels of distribution.

(h) *General media* means any instrumentality through which a person may communicate with the public, including, but not limited to, television, radio, print, Internet, billboard, Web site, commercial bulk email, and mobile communications.

(i) *Material* means likely to affect a person's choice of, or conduct regarding, goods or services.

(j) *New business* means a business in which the prospective purchaser is not currently engaged, or a new line or type of business.

(k) *Person* means an individual, group, association, limited or general partnership, corporation, or any other business entity.

(l) *Prior business* means:

(1) A business from which the seller acquired, directly or indirectly, the major portion of the business' assets; or

(2) Any business previously owned or operated by the seller, in whole or in part.

(m) *Providing locations, outlets, accounts, or customers* means furnishing the prospective purchaser with existing or potential locations, outlets, accounts, or customers; requiring, recommending, or suggesting one or more locators or lead generating companies; providing a list of locator or lead generating companies; collecting a fee on behalf of one or more locators or lead generating companies; offering to furnish a list of locations; or otherwise assisting the prospective purchaser in obtaining his or her own locations, outlets, accounts, or customers, *provided, however*, that advertising and general advice about business development and training shall not be considered as "providing locations, outlets, accounts, or customers."

(n) *Purchaser* means a person who buys a business opportunity.

(o) *Quarterly* means as of January 1, April 1, July 1, and October 1.

(p) *Required payment* means all consideration that the purchaser must pay to the seller or an affiliate, either by contract or by practical necessity, as a condition of obtaining or commencing operation of the business opportunity. Such payment may be made directly or indirectly through a third party. A required payment does not include payments for the purchase of reasonable amounts of inventory at bona fide wholesale prices for resale or lease.

(q) *Seller* means a person who offers for sale or sells a business opportunity.

(r) *Signature* or *signed* means a person's affirmative steps to authenticate his or her identity.

It includes a person's handwritten signature, as well as an electronic or digital form of signature to the extent that such signature is recognized as a valid signature under applicable federal law or state contract law.

(s) *Written* or *in writing* means any document or information in printed form or in any form capable of being downloaded, printed, or otherwise preserved in tangible form and read. It includes: type-set, word processed, or handwritten documents; information on computer disk or CD–ROM; information sent via email; or information posted on the Internet. It does not include mere oral statements.

§ 437.2 The obligation to furnish written documents.

In connection with the offer for sale, sale, or promotion of a business opportunity, it is a violation of this Rule and an unfair or deceptive act or practice in violation of Section 5 of the Federal Trade Commission Act ("FTC Act") for any seller to fail to furnish a prospective purchaser with the material information required by §§ 437.3(a) and 437.4(a) of this part in writing at least seven calendar days before the earlier of the time that the prospective purchaser:

(a) Signs any contract in connection with the business opportunity sale; or

(b) Makes a payment or provides other consideration to the seller, directly or indirectly through a third party.

§ 437.3 The disclosure document.

In connection with the offer for sale, sale, or promotion of a business opportunity, it is a violation of this Rule and an unfair or deceptive act or practice in violation of Section 5 of the FTC Act, for any seller to:

(a) Fail to disclose to a prospective purchaser the following material information in a single written document in the form and using the language set forth in appendix A to this part; or if the offer for sale, sale, or promotion of a business opportunity is conducted in Spanish, in the form and using the language set forth in appendix B to this part; or if the offer for sale, sale, or promotion of a business opportunity is conducted in a language other than English or Spanish, using the form and an accurate translation of the language set forth in appendix A to this part:

(1) *Identifying information.* State the name, business address, and telephone number of the seller, the name of the salesperson offering the opportunity, and the date when the disclosure document is furnished to the prospective purchaser.

(2) *Earnings claims.* If the seller makes an earnings claim, check the "yes" box and attach the earnings statement required by § 437.4. If not, check the "no" box.

(3) *Legal actions.* (i) If any of the following persons has been the subject of any civil or criminal action for misrepresentation, fraud, securities law violations, or unfair or deceptive practices, including violations of any FTC Rule, within the 10 years immediately preceding the date that the business opportunity is offered, check the "yes" box:

(A) The seller;

(B) Any affiliate or prior business of the seller; or

(C) Any of the seller's officers, directors, sales managers, or any individual who occupies a position or performs a function similar to an officer, director, or sales manager of the seller.

(ii) If the "yes" box is checked, disclose all such actions in an attachment to the disclosure document. State the full caption of each action (names of the principal parties, case number, full name of court, and filing date). For each action, the seller may also provide a brief accurate statement not to exceed 100 words that describes the action.

(iii) If there are no actions to disclose, check the "no" box.

(4) *Cancellation or refund policy.* If the seller offers a refund or the right to cancel the purchase, check the "yes" box. If so, state all material terms and conditions of the refund or cancellation policy in an attachment to the disclosure document. If no refund or cancellation is offered, check the "no" box.

(5) *References.* (i) State the name, state, and telephone number of all purchasers who purchased the business opportunity within the last three years. If more than 10 purchasers purchased the business opportunity within the last three years, the seller may limit the disclosure by stating the name, state, and telephone number of at least the 10 purchasers within the past three years who are located nearest to the prospective purchaser's location. Alternatively, a seller may furnish a prospective buyer with a list disclosing all purchasers nationwide within the last three years. If choosing this option, insert the words "See Attached List" without removing the list headings or the numbers 1 through 10, and attach a list of the references to the disclosure document.

(ii) Clearly and conspicuously, and in immediate conjunction with the list of references, state the following: "If you buy a business opportunity from the seller, your contact information can be disclosed in the future to other buyers."

(6) *Receipt.* Attach a duplicate copy of the disclosure document to be signed and dated by the purchaser. The seller may inform the prospective purchaser how to return the signed receipt (for example, by sending to a street address, email address, or facsimile telephone number).

(b) Fail to update the disclosures required by paragraph (a) of this section at least quarterly to reflect any changes in the required information, including, but not limited to, any changes in the seller's refund or cancellation policy, or the list of references; *provided, however,* that until a seller has 10 purchasers, the list of references must be updated monthly.

§ 437.4 Earnings claims.

In connection with the offer for sale, sale, or promotion of a business opportunity, it is a violation of this Rule and an unfair or deceptive act or practice in violation of Section 5 of the FTC Act, for the seller to:

(a) Make any earnings claim to a prospective purchaser, unless the seller:

(1) Has a reasonable basis for its claim at the time the claim is made;

(2) Has in its possession written materials that substantiate its claim at the time the claim is made;

(3) Makes the written substantiation available upon request to the prospective purchaser and to the Commission; and

(4) Furnishes to the prospective purchaser an earnings claim statement. The earnings claim statement shall be a single written document and shall state the following information:

(i) The title "EARNINGS CLAIM STATEMENT REQUIRED BY LAW" in capital, bold type letters;

(ii) The name of the person making the earnings claim and the date of the earnings claim;

(iii) The earnings claim;

(iv) The beginning and ending dates when the represented earnings were achieved;

(v) The number and percentage of all persons who purchased the business opportunity prior to the ending date in paragraph (a)(4)(iv) of this section who achieved at least the stated level of earnings;

(vi) Any characteristics of the purchasers who achieved at least the represented level of earnings, such as their location, that may differ materially from the characteristics of the prospective purchasers being offered the business opportunity; and

(vii) A statement that written substantiation for the earnings claim will be made available to the prospective purchaser upon request.

(b) Make any earnings claim in the general media, unless the seller:

(1) Has a reasonable basis for its claim at the time the claim is made;

(2) Has in its possession written material that substantiates its claim at the time the claim is made;

(3) States in immediate conjunction with the claim:

(i) The beginning and ending dates when the represented earnings were achieved; and

(ii) The number and percentage of all persons who purchased the business opportunity prior to the ending date in paragraph (b)(3)(i) of this section who achieved at least the stated level of earnings.

(c) Disseminate industry financial, earnings, or performance information unless the seller has written substantiation demonstrating that the information reflects, or does not exceed, the typical or ordinary financial, earnings, or performance experience of purchasers of the business opportunity being offered for sale.

(d) Fail to notify any prospective purchaser in writing of any material changes affecting the relevance or reliability of the information contained in an earnings claim statement before the prospective purchaser signs any contract or makes a payment or provides other consideration to the seller, directly or indirectly, through a third party.

§ 437.5 Sales conducted in Spanish or other languages besides English.

(a) If the seller conducts the offer for sale, sale, or promotion of a business opportunity in Spanish, the seller must provide the disclosure document required by § 437.3(a) in the form and language set forth in appendix B to this part, and the disclosures required by §§ 437.3(a) and 437.4 must be made in Spanish.

(b) If the seller conducts the offer for sale, sale, or promotion of a business opportunity in a language other than English or Spanish, the seller must provide the disclosure document required by § 437.3(a) using the form and an accurate translation of the language set forth in appendix A to this part, and the disclosures required by §§ 437.3(a) and 437.4 must be made in that language.

§ 437.6 Other prohibited practices.

In connection with the offer for sale, sale, or promotion of a business opportunity, it is a violation of this part and an unfair or deceptive act or practice in violation of Section 5 of the FTC Act for any seller, directly or indirectly through a third party, to:

(a) Disclaim, or require a prospective purchaser to waive reliance on, any statement made in any document or attachment that is required or permitted to be disclosed under this Rule;

(b) Make any claim or representation, orally, visually, or in writing, that is inconsistent with or contradicts the information required to be disclosed by §§ 437.3 (basic disclosure document) and 437.4 (earnings claims document) of this Rule;

(c) Include in any disclosure document or earnings claim statement any materials or information other than what is explicitly required or permitted by this Rule. For the sole purpose of enhancing the prospective purchaser's ability to maneuver through an electronic version of a disclosure document or earnings statement, the seller may include scroll bars and internal links. All other features (e.g., multimedia tools such as audio, video, animation, or pop-up screens) are prohibited;

(d) Misrepresent the amount of sales, or gross or net income or profits a prospective purchaser may earn or that prior purchasers have earned;

(e) Misrepresent that any governmental entity, law, or regulation prohibits a seller from:

(1) Furnishing earnings information to a prospective purchaser; or

(2) Disclosing to prospective purchasers the identity of other purchasers of the business opportunity;

(f) Fail to make available to prospective purchasers, and to the Commission upon request, written substantiation for the seller's earnings claims;

(g) Misrepresent how or when commissions, bonuses, incentives, premiums, or other payments from the seller to the purchaser will be calculated or distributed;

(h) Misrepresent the cost, or the performance, efficacy, nature, or central characteristics of the business opportunity or the goods or services offered to a prospective purchaser;

(i) Misrepresent any material aspect of any assistance offered to a prospective purchaser;

(j) Misrepresent the likelihood that a seller, locator, or lead generator will find locations, outlets, accounts, or customers for the purchaser;

(k) Misrepresent any term or condition of the seller's refund or cancellation policies;

(l) Fail to provide a refund or cancellation when the purchaser has satisfied the terms and conditions disclosed pursuant to §437.3(a)(4);

(m) Misrepresent a business opportunity as an employment opportunity;

(n) Misrepresent the terms of any territorial exclusivity or territorial protection offered to a prospective purchaser;

(o) Assign to any purchaser a purported exclusive territory that, in fact, encompasses the same or overlapping areas already assigned to another purchaser;

(p) Misrepresent that any person, trademark or service mark holder, or governmental entity, directly or indirectly benefits from, sponsors, participates in, endorses, approves, authorizes, or is otherwise associated with the sale of the business opportunity or the goods or services sold through the business opportunity;

(q) Misrepresent that any person:

(1) Has purchased a business opportunity from the seller or has operated a business opportunity of the type offered by the seller; or

(2) Can provide an independent or reliable report about the business opportunity or the experiences of any current or former purchaser.

(r) Fail to disclose, with respect to any person identified as a purchaser or operator of a business opportunity offered by the seller:

(1) Any consideration promised or paid to such person. Consideration includes, but is not limited to, any payment, forgiveness of debt, or provision of equipment, services, or discounts to the person or to a third party on the person's behalf; or

(2) Any personal relationship or any past or present business relationship other than as the purchaser or operator of the business opportunity being offered by the seller.

§437.7 Record retention.

To prevent the unfair and deceptive acts or practices specified in this Rule, business opportunity sellers and their principals must prepare, retain, and make available for inspection by Commission officials copies of the following documents for a period of three years:

(a) Each materially different version of all documents required by this Rule;

(b) Each purchaser's disclosure receipt;

(c) Each executed written contract with a purchaser; and

(d) All substantiation upon which the seller relies for each earnings claim from the time each such claim is made.

§437.8 Franchise exemption.

The provisions of this Rule shall not apply to any business opportunity that constitutes a "franchise," as defined in the Franchise Rule, 16 CFR part 436; *provided, however,* that the provisions of this Rule shall apply to any such franchise if it is exempted from the provisions of part 436 because, either:

(a) Under §436.8(a)(1), the total of the required payments or commitments to make a required payment, to the franchisor or an affiliate that are made any time from before to within six months after commencing operation of the franchisee's business is less than $500, or

(b) Under §436.8(a)(7), there is no written document describing any material term or aspect of the relationship or arrangement.

§437.9 Outstanding orders; preemption.

(a) A business opportunity required by prior FTC or court order to follow the Franchise Rule, 16 CFR part 436, may petition the Commission to amend the order or to stipulate to an amendment of the court order so that the business opportunity may follow the provisions of this part.

(b) The FTC does not intend to preempt the business opportunity sales practices laws of any state or local government, except to the extent of any conflict with this part. A law is not in conflict with this Rule if it affords prospective purchasers equal or greater protection, such as registration of disclosure documents or more extensive disclosures. All such disclosures, however, must be made in a separate state disclosure document.

§437.10 Severability.

The provisions of this part are separate and severable from one another. If any provision is stayed or determined to be invalid, the remaining provisions shall continue in effect.

APPENDIX A to PART 437

DISCLOSURE OF IMPORTANT INFORMATION ABOUT BUSINESS OPPORTUNITY

Required by the Federal Trade Commission, Rule 16 C.F.R. Part 437

Name of Seller: Address:

Phone: Salesperson: Date:

[Name of Seller] has completed this form, which provides important information about the business opportunity it is offering you. The Federal Trade Commission, an agency of the federal government, requires that [Name of Seller] complete this form and give it to you. However, the Federal Trade Commission has not seen this completed form or checked that the information is true. **Make sure that this information is the same as what the salesperson told you about this opportunity.**

LEGAL ACTIONS: Has [Name of Seller] or any of its key personnel been the subject of a civil or criminal action involving misrepresentation, fraud, securities law violation, or unfair or deceptive practices, including violations of any FTC Rule, within the past 10 years?

☐ **YES** → *If the answer is yes,* [Name of Seller] *must attach a list of all such legal actions to this form.*

☐ **NO**

CANCELLATION OR REFUND POLICY: Does [Name of Seller] offer a cancellation or refund policy?

☐ **YES** → *If the answer is yes,* [Name of Seller] *must attach a statement describing this policy to this form.*

☐ **NO**

EARNINGS: Has [Name of Seller] or its salesperson discussed how much money purchasers of this business opportunity can earn or have earned? In other words, have they stated or implied that purchasers can earn a specific level of sales, income, or profit?

☐ **YES** → *If the answer is yes,* [Name of Seller] *must attach an Earnings Claims Statement to this form. Read this statement carefully. You may wish to show this information to an advisor or accountant.*

☐ **NO**

REFERENCES: In the section below, [Name of Seller] must provide you with contact information for at least 10 people who have purchased a business opportunity from them. If fewer than 10 are listed, this is the total list of all purchasers. **You may wish to contact the people below to compare their experiences with what [Name of Seller] told you about the business opportunity.**

Note: If you purchase a business opportunity from [Name of Seller], your contact information can be disclosed in the future to other potential buyers.

	Name	State	Telephone Number		Name	State	Telephone Number
1.				6.			
2.				7.			
3.				8.			
4.				9.			
5.				10			

Signature: ______________________________ Date: ______________

By signing above, you are acknowledging that you have received this form. This is not a purchase contract. To give you enough time to research this opportunity, the Federal Trade Commission requires that after you receive this form, [Name of Seller] must wait at least seven calendar days before asking you to sign a purchase contract or make any payments.

For more information about business opportunities in general: Visit the FTC's website at www.ftc.gov/bizopps or call 1-877-FTC-HELP (877-382-4357). You can also contact your state's Attorney General.

APPENDIX B to PART 437

DIVULGACIÓN DE INFORMACIÓN IMPORTANTE SOBRE OPORTUNIDAD DE NEGOCIO
Formulario requerido por la Comisión Federal de Comercio (FTC)
Regla 16 de la Parte 437 del Código de Regulaciones Federales

Nombre del Vendedor: Domicilio:
Teléfono: Representante de Ventas: Fecha:

[Nombre del Vendedor] completó el presente formulario y en el mismo le suministra información importante sobre la oportunidad de negocio que le está ofreciendo. La Comisión Federal de Comercio (*Federal Trade Commission*, FTC), una agencia del gobierno federal, le requiere a la compañía [Nombre del Vendedor] que complete el presente formulario y que se lo entregue a usted. Pero la FTC no ha visto este formulario completado por la compañía ni ha verificado que la información indicada sea veraz. **Asegúrese de que la información contenida en el presente formulario coincida con lo que le dijo el representante de ventas respecto de esta oportunidad.**

ACCIONES LEGALES: ¿La compañía [Nombre del Vendedor] o alguno de los principales miembros de su personal ha sido sujeto de una acción civil o penal, que involucre falsedad, fraude, infracción de las leyes de títulos y valores, o prácticas desleales o engañosas, incluyendo infracciones de las Reglas o Normas de la FTC, dentro de los 10 últimos años?

☐ **SI** → *Si la respuesta es afirmativa,* [Nombre del Vendedor] *debe adjuntar al formulario una lista completa de dichas acciones legales.*
☐ **NO**

POLÍTICA DE CANCELACIÓN O REINTEGRO: ¿Ofrece [Nombre del Vendedor] una política de cancelación o reintegro?

☐ **SÍ** → *Si la respuesta es afirmativa,* [Nombre del Vendedor] *debe adjuntar al formulario una declaración con la descripción de dicha política.*
☐ **NO**

INGRESOS: ¿La compañía [Nombre del Vendedor] o alguno de sus representantes de ventas ha manifestado la cantidad de dinero que pueden ganar o que han ganado los compradores de esta oportunidad de negocio? ¿Dicho en otras palabras, han expresado de manera explícita o implícita que los compradores pueden alcanzar un nivel específico de ventas, o ganar un nivel específico de ingresos?

☐ **SÍ** → *Si la respuesta es afirmativa,* [Nombre del Vendedor] *debe adjuntar a este formulario una Declaración de los Ingresos Proclamados. Lea esta declaración atentamente. Puede que desee analizar esta información con un asesor o contador.*
☐ **NO**

REFERENCIAS: En esta sección del formulario, [Nombre del Vendedor] debe listar la información de contacto de por lo menos 10 personas que le hayan comprado una oportunidad de negocio. Si le suministran los datos de menos de 10 personas, es porque ésa es la lista completa de todos los compradores. **Puede que desee comunicarse con las personas listadas a continuación para comparar sus respectivas experiencias con lo que le dijo [Nombre del Vendedor] sobre la oportunidad de negocio que le está ofreciendo.**

Nota: Si usted compra una oportunidad de negocio de [Nombre del Vendedor], podrá divulgarse su información de contacto a otros posibles compradores.

	Nombre	Estado	Número de Teléfono		Nombre	Estado	Número de Teléfono
1.				6.			
2.				7.			
3.				8.			
4.				9.			
5.				10.			

Firma: ______________________ Fecha: ____________

Por medio de su firma, usted acusa recibo del presente formulario. Esto no es un contrato de compra. La Comisión Federal de Comercio (FTC) establece que con el fin de concederle el tiempo necesario para que usted investigue esta oportunidad, [Nombre del Vendedor] debe esperar un mínimo de siete días naturales o corridos a partir de la fecha en que le entregue este formulario antes de pedirle que firme un contrato de compra o que efectúe un pago.

Para más información sobre oportunidades de negocio en general: Visite el sitio Web de la FTC www.ftc.gov/bizopps o llame al 1-877-FTC-HELP (877-382-4357). Usted también puede establecer contacto con el Fiscal General de su estado de residencia.

PART 444—CREDIT PRACTICES

Sec.

AUTHORITY: Sec. 18(a), 88 Stat. 2193, as amended 93 Stat. 95 (15 U.S.C. 57a); 80 Stat. 383, as amended, 81 Stat. 54 (5 U.S.C. 552).

SOURCE: 49 FR 7789, Mar. 1, 1984, unless otherwise noted.

§ 444.1 Definitions.

(a) *Lender.* A person who engages in the business of lending money to consumers within the jurisdiction of the Federal Trade Commission.

(b) *Retail installment seller.* A person who sells goods or services to consumers on a deferred payment basis or pursuant to a lease-purchase arrangement within the jurisdiction of the Federal Trade Commission.

(c) *Person.* An individual, corporation, or other business organization.

(d) *Consumer.* A natural person who seeks or acquires goods, services, or money for personal, family, or household use.

(e) *Obligation.* An agreement between a consumer and a lender or retail installment seller.

(f) *Creditor.* A lender or a retail installment seller.

(g) *Debt.* Money that is due or alleged to be due from one to another.

(h) *Earnings.* Compensation paid or payable to an individual or for his or her account for personal services rendered or to be rendered by him or her, whether denominated as wages, salary, commission, bonus, or otherwise, including periodic payments pursuant to a pension, retirement, or disability program.

(i) *Household goods.* Clothing, furniture, appliances, one radio and one television, linens, china, crockery, kitchenware, and personal effects (including wedding rings) of the consumer and his or her dependents, provided that the following are not included within the scope of the term *household goods:*

(1) Works of art;

(2) Electronic entertainment equipment (except one television and one radio);

(3) Items acquired as antiques; and

(4) Jewelry (except wedding rings).

(j) *Antique.* Any item over one hundred years of age, including such items that have been repaired or renovated without changing their original form or character.

(k) *Cosigner.* A natural person who renders himself or herself liable for the obligation of another person without compensation. The term shall include any person whose signature is requested as a condition to granting credit to another person, or as a condition for forbearance on collection of another person's obligation that is in default. The term shall not include a spouse whose signature is required on a credit obligation to perfect a security interest pursuant to State law. A person who does not receive goods, services, or money in return for a credit obligation does not receive compensation within the meaning of this definition. A person is a cosigner within the meaning of this definition whether or not he or she is designated as such on a credit obligation.

§ 444.2 Unfair credit practices.

(a) In connection with the extension of credit to consumers in or affecting commerce, as commerce is defined in the Federal Trade Commission Act, it is an unfair act or practice within the meaning of Section 5 of that Act for a lender or retail installment seller directly or indirectly to take or receive from a consumer an obligation that:

(1) Constitutes or contains a cognovit or confession of judgment (for purposes other than executory process in the State of Louisiana), warrant of attorney, or other waiver of the right to notice and the opportunity to be heard in the event of suit or process thereon.

(2) Constitutes or contains an executory waiver or a limitation of exemption from attachment, execution, or other process on real or personal property held, owned by, or due to the consumer, unless the waiver applies solely to property subject to a security interest executed in connection with the obligation.

(3) Constitutes or contains an assignment of wages or other earnings unless:

(i) The assignment by its terms is revocable at the will of the debtor, or

(ii) The assignment is a payroll deduction plan or preauthorized payment plan, commencing at the time of the transaction, in which the consumer authorizes a series of wage deductions as a method of making each payment, or

(iii) The assignment applies only to wages or other earnings already earned at the time of the assignment.

(4) Constitutes or contains a nonpossessory security interest in household goods other than a purchase money security interest.

(b) [Reserved]

§444.3 Unfair or deceptive cosigner practices.

(a) In connection with the extension of credit to consumers in or affecting commerce, as commerce is defined in the Federal Trade Commission Act, it is:

(1) A deceptive act or practice within the meaning of section 5 of that Act for a lender or retail installment seller, directly or indirectly, to misrepresent the nature or extent of cosigner liability to any person.

(2) An unfair act or practice within the meaning of section 5 of that Act for a lender or retail installment seller, directly or indirectly, to obligate a cosigner unless the cosigner is informed prior to becoming obligated, which in the case of open end credit shall mean prior to the time that the agreement creating the cosigner's liability for future charges is executed, of the nature of his or her liability as cosigner.

(b) Any lender or retail installment seller who complies with the preventive requirements in paragraph (c) of this section does not violate paragraph (a) of this section.

(c) To prevent these unfair or deceptive acts or practices, a disclosure, consisting of a separate document that shall contain the following statement and no other, shall be given to the cosigner prior to becoming obligated, which in the case of open end credit shall mean prior to the time that the agreement creating the cosigner's liability for future charges is executed:

NOTICE TO COSIGNER

You are being asked to guarantee this debt. Think carefully before you do. If the borrower doesn't pay the debt, you will have to. Be sure you can afford to pay if you have to, and that you want to accept this responsibility.

You may have to pay up to the full amount of the debt if the borrower does not pay. You may also have to pay late fees or collection costs, which increase this amount.

The creditor can collect this debt from you without first trying to collect from the borrower. The creditor can use the same collection methods against you that can be used against the borrower, such as suing you, garnishing your wages, etc. If this debt is ever in default, that fact may become a part of *your* credit record.

This notice is not the contract that makes you liable for the debt.

§444.4 Late charges.

(a) In connection with collecting a debt arising out of an extension of credit to a consumer in or affecting commerce, as commerce is defined in the Federal Trade Commission Act, it is an unfair act or practice within the meaning of section 5 of that Act for a creditor, directly or indirectly, to levy or collect any deliquency charge on a payment, which payment is otherwise a full payment for the applicable period and is paid on its due date or within an applicable grace period, when the only delinquency is attributable to late fee(s) or delinquency charge(s) assessed on earlier installment(s).

(b) For purposes of this section, *collecting a debt* means any activity other than the use of judicial process that is intended to bring about or does bring about repayment of all or part of a consumer debt.

§444.5 State exemptions.

(a) If, upon application to the Federal Trade Commission by an appropriate State agency, the Federal Trade Commission determines that:

(1) There is a State requirement or prohibition in effect that applies to any transaction to which a provision of this rule applies; and

(2) The State requirement or prohibition affords a level of protection to consumers that is substantially equivalent to, or greater than, the protection afforded by this rule;

Then that provision of the rule will not be in effect in that State to the extent specified by the Federal Trade Commission in its determination, for as long as the State administers and enforces the State requirement or prohibition effectively.

(b) [Reserved]

PART 453—FUNERAL INDUSTRY PRACTICES

AUTHORITY: 15 U.S.C. 57a(a); 15 U.S.C. 46(g); 5 U.S.C. 552.

SOURCE: 59 FR 1611, Jan. 11, 1994, unless otherwise noted.

§ 453.1 Definitions.

(a) *Alternative container.* An "alternative container" is an unfinished wood box or other non-metal receptacle or enclosure, without ornamentation or a fixed interior lining, which is designed for the encasement of human remains and which is made of fiberboard, pressed-wood, composition materials (with or without an outside covering) or like materials.

(b) *Cash advance item.* A "cash advance item" is any item of service or merchandise described to a purchaser as a "cash advance," "accommodation," "cash disbursement," or similar term. A cash advance item is also any item obtained from a third party and paid for by the funeral provider on the purchaser's behalf. Cash advance items may include, but are not limited to: cemetery or crematory services; pallbearers; public transportation; clergy honoraria; flowers; musicians or singers; nurses; obituary notices; gratuities and death certificates.

(c) *Casket.* A "casket" is a rigid container which is designed for the encasement of human remains and which is usually constructed of wood, metal, fiberglass, plastic, or like material, and ornamented and lined with fabric.

(d) *Commission.* "Commission" refers to the Federal Trade Commission.

(e) *Cremation.* "Cremation" is a heating process which incinerates human remains.

(f) *Crematory.* A "crematory" is any person, partnership or corporation that performs cremation and sells funeral goods.

(g) *Direct cremation.* A "direct cremation" is a disposition of human remains by cremation, without formal viewing, visitation, or ceremony with the body present.

(h) *Funeral goods.* "Funeral goods" are the goods which are sold or offered for sale directly to the public for use in connection with funeral services.

(i) *Funeral provider.* A "funeral provider" is any person, partnership or corporation that sells or offers to sell funeral goods and funeral services to the public.

(j) *Funeral services.* "Funeral services" are any services which may be used to:

(1) Care for and prepare deceased human bodies for burial, cremation or other final disposition; and

(2) arrange, supervise or conduct the funeral ceremony or the final disposition of deceased human bodies.

(k) *Immediate burial.* An "immediate burial" is a disposition of human remains by burial, without formal viewing, visitation, or ceremony with the body present, except for a graveside service.

(l) *Memorial service.* A "memorial service" is a ceremony commemorating the deceased without the body present.

(m) *Funeral ceremony.* A "funeral ceremony" is a service commemorating the deceased with the body present.

(n) *Outer burial container.* An "outer burial container" is any container which is designed for placement in the grave around the casket including, but not limited to, containers commonly known as burial vaults, grave boxes, and grave liners.

(o) *Person.* A "person" is any individual, partnership, corporation, association, government or governmental subdivision or agency, or other entity.

(p) *Services of funeral director and staff.* The "services of funeral director and staff" are the basic services, not to be included in prices of other categories in § 453.2(b)(4), that are furnished by a funeral provider in arranging any funeral, such as conducting the arrangements conference, planning the funeral, obtaining necessary permits, and placing obituary notices.

§453.2 Price disclosures.

(a) *Unfair or deceptive acts or practices.* In selling or offering to sell funeral goods or funeral services to the public, it is an unfair or deceptive act or practice for a funeral provider to fail to furnish accurate price information disclosing the cost to the purchaser for each of the specific funeral goods and funeral services used in connection with the disposition of deceased human bodies, including at least the price of embalming, transportation of remains, use of facilities, caskets, outer burial containers, immediate burials, or direct cremations, to persons inquiring about the purchase of funerals. Any funeral provider who complies with the preventive requirements in paragraph (b) of this section is not engaged in the unfair or deceptive acts or practices defined here.

(b) *Preventive requirements.* To prevent these unfair or deceptive acts or practices, as well as the unfair or deceptive acts or practices defined in §453.4(b)(1), funeral providers must:

(1) *Telephone price disclosure.* Tell persons who ask by telephone about the funeral provider's offerings or prices any accurate information from the price lists described in paragraphs (b)(2) through (4) of this section and any other readily available information that reasonably answers the question.

(2) *Casket price list.* (i) Give a printed or typewritten price list to people who inquire in person about the offerings or prices of caskets or alternative containers. The funeral provider must offer the list upon beginning discussion of, but in any event before showing caskets. The list must contain at least the retail prices of all caskets and alternative containers offered which do not require special ordering, enough information to identify each, and the effective date for the price list. In lieu of a written list, other formats, such as notebooks, brochures, or charts may be used if they contain the same information as would the printed or typewritten list, and display it in a clear and conspicuous manner. Provided, however, that funeral providers do not have to make a casket price list available if the funeral providers place on the general price list, specified in paragraph (b)(4) of this section, the information required by this paragraph.

(ii) Place on the list, however produced, the name of the funeral provider's place of business and a caption describing the list as a "casket price list."

(3) *Outer burial container price list.* (i) Give a printed or typewritten price list to persons who inquire in person about outer burial container offerings or prices. The funeral provider must offer the list upon beginning discussion of, but in any event before showing the containers. The list must contain at least the retail prices of all outer burial containers offered which do not require special ordering, enough information to identify each container, and the effective date for the prices listed. In lieu of a written list, the funeral provider may use other formats, such as notebooks, brochures, or charts, if they contain the same information as the printed or typewritten list, and display it in a clear and conspicuous manner. Provided, however, that funeral providers do not have to make an outer burial container price list available if the funeral providers place on the general price list, specified in paragraph (b)(4) of this section, the information required by this paragraph.

(ii) Place on the list, however produced, the name of the funeral provider's place of business and a caption describing the list as an "outer burial container price list."

(4) *General price list.* (i)(A) Give a printed or typewritten price list for retention to persons who inquire in person about the funeral goods, funeral services or prices of funeral goods or services offered by the funeral provider. The funeral provider must give the list upon beginning discussion of any of the following:

(*1*) The prices of funeral goods or funeral services;

(*2*) The overall type of funeral service or disposition; or

(*3*) Specific funeral goods or funeral services offered by the funeral provider.

(B) The requirement in paragraph (b)(4)(i)(A) of this section applies whether the discussion takes place in the funeral home or elsewhere. Provided, however, that when the deceased is removed for transportation to the funeral home, an in-person request at that time for authorization to embalm, required by § 453.5(a)(2), does not, by itself, trigger the requirement to offer the general price list if the provider in seeking prior embalming approval discloses that embalming is not required by law except in certain special cases, if any. Any other discussion during that time about prices or the selection of funeral goods or services triggers the requirement under paragraph (b)(4)(i)(A) of this section to give consumers a general price list.

(C) The list required in paragraph (b)(4)(i)(A) of this section must contain at least the following information:

(*1*) The name, address, and telephone number of the funeral provider's place of business;

(*2*) A caption describing the list as a "general price list"; and

(*3*) The effective date for the price list;

(ii) Include on the price list, in any order, the retail prices (expressed either as the flat fee, or as the price per hour, mile or other unit of computation) and the other information specified below for at least each of the following items, if offered for sale:

(A) Forwarding of remains to another funeral home, together with a list of the services provided for any quoted price;

(B) Receiving remains from another funeral home, together with a list of the services provided for any quoted price;

(C) The price range for the direct cremations offered by the funeral provider, together with:

(*1*) A separate price for a direct cremation where the purchaser provides the container;

(*2*) Separate prices for each direct cremation offered including an alternative container; and

(*3*) A description of the services and container (where applicable), included in each price;

(D) The price range for the immediate burials offered by the funeral provider, together with:

(*1*) A separate price for an immediate burial where the purchaser provides the casket;

(*2*) Separate prices for each immediate burial offered including a casket or alternative container; and

(*3*) A description of the services and container (where applicable) included in that price;

(E) Transfer of remains to funeral home;

(F) Embalming;

(G) Other preparation of the body;

(H) Use of facilities and staff for viewing;

(I) Use of facilities and staff for funeral ceremony;

(J) Use of facilities and staff for memorial service;

(K) Use of equipment and staff for graveside service;

(L) Hearse; and

(M) Limousine.

(iii) Include on the price list, in any order, the following information:

(A) Either of the following:

(*1*) The price range for the caskets offered by the funeral provider, together with the statement: "A complete price list will be provided at the funeral home."; or

(*2*) The prices of individual caskets, disclosed in the manner specified by paragraph (b)(2)(i) of this section; and

(B) Either of the following:

(*1*) The price range for the outer burial containers offered by the funeral provider, together with the statement: "A complete price list will be provided at the funeral home."; or

(*2*) The prices of individual outer burial containers, disclosed in the manner specified by paragraph (b)(3)(i) of this section; and

(C) Either of the following:

(*1*) The price for the basic services of funeral director and staff, together with a list of the principal basic services provided for any quoted price and, if the charge cannot be declined by the purchaser, the statement: "This fee for our basic services will be added to the total cost of the funeral arrangements you select. (This fee is already included in our charges for direct cremations, immediate burials, and forwarding or receiving remains.)". If the charge cannot be declined by the purchaser, the quoted price shall include all charges for the recovery of unallocated funeral provider overhead, and funeral providers may include in the required disclosure the phrase "and overhead" after the word "services"; or

(*2*) The following statement: "Please note that a fee of (*specify dollar amount*) for the use of our basic services is included in the price of our caskets. This same fee shall be added to the total cost of your funeral arrangements if you provide the casket. Our services include (specify)." The fee shall include all charges for the recovery of unallocated funeral provider overhead, and funeral providers may include in the required disclosure the phrase "and overhead" after the word "services." The statement must be placed on the general price list together with the casket price range, required by paragraph (b)(4)(iii)(A)(*1*) of this section, or together with the prices of individual caskets, required by (b)(4)(iii)(A)(*2*) of this section.

(iv) The services fee permitted by § 453.2(b)(4)(iii)(C)(*1*) or (C)(*2*) is the only funeral provider fee for services, facilities or unallocated overhead permitted by this part to be non-declinable, unless otherwise required by law.

(5) *Statement of funeral goods and services selected.* (i) Give an itemized written statement for retention to each person who arranges a funeral or other disposition of human remains, at the conclusion of the discussion of arrangements. The statement must list at least the following information:

(A) The funeral goods and funeral services selected by that person and the prices to be paid for each of them;

(B) Specifically itemized cash advance items. (These prices must be given to the extent then known or reasonably ascertainable. If the prices are not known or reasonably ascertainable, a good faith estimate shall be given and a written statement of the actual charges shall be provided before the final bill is paid.); and

(C) The total cost of the goods and services selected.

(ii) The information required by this paragraph (b)(5) may be included on any contract, statement, or other document which the funeral provider would otherwise provide at the conclusion of discussion of arrangements.

(6) *Other pricing methods.* Funeral providers may give persons any other price information, in any other format, in addition to that required by § 453.2(b)(2), (3), and (4) so long as the statement required by § 453.2(b)(5) is given when required by the rule.

§ 453.3 Misrepresentations.

(a) *Embalming provisions*—(1) *Deceptive acts or practices.* In selling or offering to sell funeral goods or funeral services to the public, it is a deceptive act or practice for a funeral provider to:

(i) Represent that state or local law requires that a deceased person be embalmed when such is not the case;

(ii) Fail to disclose that embalming is not required by law except in certain special cases, if any.

(2) *Preventive requirements.* To prevent these deceptive acts or practices, as well as the unfair or deceptive acts or practices defined in §§ 453.4(b)(1) and 453.5(2), funeral providers must:

(i) Not represent that a deceased person is required to be embalmed for:

(A) Direct cremation;

(B) Immediate burial; or

(C) A closed casket funeral without viewing or visitation when refrigeration is available and when state or local law does not require embalming; and

(ii) Place the following disclosure on the general price list, required by § 453.2(b)(4), in immediate conjunction with the price shown for embalming: "Except in certain special cases, embalming is not required by law. Embalming may be necessary, however, if you select certain funeral arrangements, such as a funeral with viewing. If you do not want embalming, you usually have the right to choose an arrangement that does not require you to pay for it, such as direct cremation or immediate burial." The phrase "except in certain special cases" need not be included in this disclosure if state or local law in the area(s) where the provider does business does not require embalming under any circumstances.

(b) *Casket for cremation provisions*—(1) *Deceptive acts or practices.* In selling or offering to sell funeral goods or funeral services to the public, it is a deceptive act or practice for a funeral provider to:

(i) Represent that state or local law requires a casket for direct cremations;

(ii) Represent that a casket is required for direct cremations.

(2) *Preventive requirements.* To prevent these deceptive acts or practices, as well as the unfair or deceptive acts or practices defined in § 453.4(a)(1), funeral providers must place the following disclosure in immediate conjunction with the price range shown for direct cremations: "If you want to arrange a direct cremation, you can use an alternative container. Alternative containers encase the body and can be made of materials like fiberboard or composition materials (with or without an outside covering). The containers we provide are (specify containers)." This disclosure only has to be placed on the general price list if the funeral provider arranges direct cremations.

(c) *Outer burial container provisions*—(1) *Deceptive acts or practices.* In selling or offering to sell funeral goods and funeral services to the public, it is a deceptive act or practice for a funeral provider to:

(i) Represent that state or local laws or regulations, or particular cemeteries, require outer burial containers when such is not the case;

(ii) Fail to disclose to persons arranging funerals that state law does not require the purchase of an outer burial container.

(2) *Preventive requirement.* To prevent these deceptive acts or practices, funeral providers must place the following disclosure on the outer burial container price list, required by § 453.2(b)(3)(i), or, if the prices of outer burial containers are listed on the general price list, required by § 453.2(b)(4), in immediate conjunction with those prices: "In most areas of the country, state or local law does not require that you buy a container to surround the casket in the grave. However, many cemeteries require that you have such a container so that the grave will not sink in. Either a grave liner or a burial vault will satisfy these requirements." The phrase "in most areas of the country" need not be included in this disclosure if state or local law in the area(s) where the provider does business does not require a container to surround the casket in the grave.

(d) *General provisions on legal and cemetery requirements*—(1) *Deceptive acts or practices.* In selling or offering to sell funeral goods or funeral services to the public, it is a deceptive act or practice for funeral providers to represent that federal, state, or local laws, or particular cemeteries or crematories, require the purchase of any funeral goods or funeral services when such is not the case.

(2) *Preventive requirements.* To prevent these deceptive acts or practices, as well as the deceptive acts or practices identified in §§ 453.3(a)(1), 453.3(b)(1), and 453.3(c)(1), funeral providers must identify and briefly describe in writing on the statement of funeral goods and services selected (required by § 453.2(b)(5)) any legal, cemetery, or crematory requirement which the funeral provider represents to persons as compelling the purchase of funeral goods or funeral services for the funeral which that person is arranging.

(e) *Provisions on preservative and protective value claims.* In selling or offering to sell funeral goods or funeral services to the public, it is a deceptive act or practice for a funeral provider to:

(1) Represent that funeral goods or funeral services will delay the natural decomposition of human remains for a long-term or indefinite time;

(2) Represent that funeral goods have protective features or will protect the body from gravesite substances, when such is not the case.

(f) *Cash advance provisions*—(1) *Deceptive acts or practices.* In selling or offering to sell funeral goods or funeral services to the public, it is a deceptive act or practice for a funeral provider to:

(i) Represent that the price charged for a cash advance item is the same as the cost to the funeral provider for the item when such is not the case;

(ii) Fail to disclose to persons arranging funerals that the price being charged for a cash advance item is not the same as the cost to the funeral provider for the item when such is the case.

(2) *Preventive requirements.* To prevent these deceptive acts or practices, funeral providers must place the following sentence in the itemized statement of funeral goods and services selected, in immediate conjunction with the list of itemized cash advance items required by §453.2(b)(5)(i)(B): "We charge you for our services in obtaining: (specify cash advance items)," if the funeral provider makes a charge upon, or receives and retains a rebate, commission or trade or volume discount upon a cash advance item.

§453.4 Required purchase of funeral goods or funeral services.

(a) *Casket for cremation provisions*—(1) *Unfair or deceptive acts or practices.* In selling or offering to sell funeral goods or funeral services to the public, it is an unfair or deceptive act or practice for a funeral provider, or a crematory, to require that a casket be purchased for direct cremation.

(2) *Preventive requirement.* To prevent this unfair or deceptive act or practice, funeral providers must make an alternative container available for direct cremations, if they arrange direct cremations.

(b) *Other required purchases of funeral goods or funeral services*—(1) *Unfair or deceptive acts or practices.* In selling or offering to sell funeral goods or funeral services, it is an unfair or deceptive act or practice for a funeral provider to:

(i) Condition the furnishing of any funeral good or funeral service to a person arranging a funeral upon the purchase of any other funeral good or funeral service, except as required by law or as otherwise permitted by this part;

(ii) Charge any fee as a condition to furnishing any funeral goods or funeral services to a person arranging a funeral, other than the fees for: (1) Services of funeral director and staff, permitted by §453.2(b)(4)(iii)(C); (2) other funeral services and funeral goods selected by the purchaser; and (3) other funeral goods or services required to be purchased, as explained on the itemized statement in accordance with §453.3(d)(2).

(2) *Preventive requirements.* (i) To prevent these unfair or deceptive acts or practices, funeral providers must:

(A) Place the following disclosure in the general price list, immediately above the prices required by §453.2(b)(4)(ii) and (iii): "The goods and services shown below are those we can provide to our customers. You may choose only the items you desire. If legal or other requirements mean you must buy any items you did not specifically ask for, we will explain the reason in writing on the statement we provide describing the funeral goods and services you selected." Provided, however, that if the charge for "services of funeral director and staff" cannot be declined by the purchaser, the statement shall include the sentence: "However, any funeral arrangements you select will include a charge for our basic services" between the second and third sentences of the statement specified above herein. The statement may include the phrase "and overhead" after the word "services" if the fee includes a charge for the recovery of unallocated funeral provider overhead;

(B) Place the following disclosure in the statement of funeral goods and services selected, required by §453.2(b)(5)(i): "Charges are only for those items that you selected or that are required. If we are required by law or by a cemetery or crematory to use any items, we will explain the reasons in writing below."

(ii) A funeral provider shall not violate this section by failing to comply with a request for a combination of goods or services which would be impossible, impractical, or excessively burdensome to provide.

§453.5 Services provided without prior approval.

(a) *Unfair or deceptive acts or practices.* In selling or offering to sell funeral goods or funeral services to the public, it is an unfair or deceptive act or practice for any provider to embalm a deceased human body for a fee unless:

(1) State or local law or regulation requires embalming in the particular circumstances regardless of any funeral choice which the family might make; or

(2) Prior approval for embalming (expressly so described) has been obtained from a family member or other authorized person; or

(3) The funeral provider is unable to contact a family member or other authorized person after exercising due diligence, has no reason to believe the family does not want embalming performed, and obtains subsequent approval for embalming already performed (expressly so described). In seeking approval, the funeral provider must disclose that a fee will be charged if the family selects a funeral which requires embalming, such as a funeral with viewing, and that no fee will be charged if the family selects a service which does not require embalming, such as direct cremation or immediate burial.

(b) *Preventive requirement.* To prevent these unfair or deceptive acts or practices, funeral providers must include on the itemized statement of funeral goods and services selected, required by § 453.2(b)(5), the statement: "If you selected a funeral that may require embalming, such as a funeral with viewing, you may have to pay for embalming. You do not have to pay for embalming you did not approve if you selected arrangements such as a direct cremation or immediate burial. If we charged for embalming, we will explain why below."

§ 453.6 Retention of documents.

To prevent the unfair or deceptive acts or practices specified in §§ 453.2 and 453.3 of this rule, funeral providers must retain and make available for inspection by Commission officials true and accurate copies of the price lists specified in §§ 453.2(b) (2) through (4), as applicable, for at least one year after the date of their last distribution to customers, and a copy of each statement of funeral goods and services selected, as required by § 453.2(b)(5), for at least one year from the date of the arrangements conference.

§ 453.7 Comprehension of disclosures.

To prevent the unfair or deceptive acts or practices specified in §§ 453.2 through 453.5, funeral providers must make all disclosures required by those sections in a clear and conspicuous manner. Providers shall not include in the casket, outer burial container, and general price lists, required by §§ 453.2(b)(2)–(4), any statement or information that alters or contradicts the information required by this part to be included in those lists.

§ 453.8 Declaration of intent.

(a) Except as otherwise provided in § 453.2(a), it is a violation of this rule to engage in any unfair or deceptive acts or practices specified in this rule, or to fail to comply with any of the preventive requirements specified in this rule;

(b) The provisions of this rule are separate and severable from one another. If any provision is determined to be invalid, it is the Commission's intention that the remaining provisions shall continue in effect.

(c) This rule shall not apply to the business of insurance or to acts in the conduct thereof.

§ 453.9 State exemptions.

If, upon application to the Commission by an appropriate state agency, the Commission determines that:

(a) There is a state requirement in effect which applies to any transaction to which this rule applies; and

(b) That state requirement affords an overall level of protection to consumers which is as great as, or greater than, the protection afforded by this rule; then the Commission's rule will not be in effect in that state to the extent specified by the Commission in its determination, for as long as the State administers and enforces effectively the state requirement.

PART 455—USED MOTOR VEHICLE TRADE REGULATION RULE

Sec.

FIGURE 6 TO PART 455—BACK OF BUYERS GUIDE (SPANISH)

AUTHORITY: 15 U.S.C. 2309; 15 U.S.C. 41–58.

SOURCE: 49 FR 45725, Nov. 19, 1984, unless otherwise noted.

§455.1 General duties of a used vehicle dealer; definitions.

(a) It is a deceptive act or practice for any used vehicle dealer, when that dealer sells or offers for sale a used vehicle in or affecting commerce as *commerce* is defined in the Federal Trade Commission Act:

(1) To misrepresent the mechanical condition of a used vehicle;

(2) To misrepresent the terms of any warranty offered in connection with the sale of a used vehicle; and

(3) To represent that a used vehicle is sold with a warranty when the vehicle is sold without any warranty.

(b) It is an unfair act or practice for any used vehicle dealer, when that dealer sells or offers for sale a used vehicle in or affecting commerce as *commerce* is defined in the Federal Trade Commission Act:

(1) To fail to disclose, prior to sale, that a used vehicle is sold without any warranty; and

(2) To fail to make available, prior to sale, the terms of any written warranty offered in connection with the sale of a used vehicle.

(c) The Commission has adopted this Rule in order to prevent the unfair and deceptive acts or practices defined in paragraphs (a) and (b). It is a violation of this Rule for any used vehicle dealer to fail to comply with the requirements set forth in §§455.2 through 455.5 of this part. If a used vehicle dealer complies with the requirements of §§455.2 through 455.5 of this part, the dealer does not violate this Rule.

(d) The following definitions shall apply for purposes of this part:

(1) *Vehicle* means any motorized vehicle, other than a motorcycle, with a gross vehicle weight rating (GVWR) of less than 8500 lbs., a curb weight of less than 6,000 lbs., and a frontal area of less than 46 sq. ft.

(2) *Used vehicle* means any vehicle driven more than the limited use necessary in moving or road testing a new vehicle prior to delivery to a consumer, but does not include any vehicle sold only for scrap or parts (title documents surrendered to the State and a salvage certificate issued).

(3) *Dealer* means any person or business which sells or offers for sale a used vehicle after selling or offering for sale five (5) or more used vehicles in the previous twelve months, but does not include a bank or financial institution, a business selling a used vehicle to an employee of that business, or a lessor selling a leased vehicle by or to that vehicle's lessee or to an employee of the lessee.

(4) *Consumer* means any person who is not a used vehicle dealer.

(5) *Warranty* means any undertaking in writing, in connection with the sale by a dealer of a used vehicle, to refund, repair, replace, maintain or take other action with respect to such used vehicle and provided at no extra charge beyond the price of the used vehicle.

(6) *Implied warranty* means an implied warranty arising under State law (as modified by the Magnuson-Moss Act) in connection with the sale by a dealer of a used vehicle.

(7) *Service contract* means a contract in writing for any period of time or any specific mileage to refund, repair, replace, or maintain a used vehicle and provided at an extra charge beyond the price of the used vehicle, unless offering such contract is "the business of insurance" and such business is regulated by State law.

(8) *You* means any dealer, or any agent or employee of a dealer, except where the term appears on the window form required by §455.2(a).

[49 FR 45725, Nov. 19, 1984, as amended at 81 FR 81678, Nov. 18, 2016]

§455.2 Consumer sales—window form.

(a) *General duty*. Before you offer a used vehicle for sale to a consumer, you must prepare, fill in as applicable and display on that vehicle the applicable "Buyers Guide" illustrated by Figures 1–2 at the end of this part. Dealers may use remaining stocks of the version of the Buyers Guide in effect prior to the effective date of this Rule for up to one year after that effective date (*i.e.*, until January 27, 2018). Dealers who opt to use their existing stock and choose to disclose the applicability of a non-dealer warranty, must add the following as applicable below the "Full/Limited Warranty" disclosure: "Manufacturer's Warranty still applies. The manufacturer's original warranty has not expired on the vehicle;" "Manufacturer's Used Vehicle Warranty Applies;" or "Other Used Vehicle Warranty Applies," followed by the statement, "Ask the dealer for a copy of the warranty document and an explanation of warranty coverage, exclusions, and repair obligations."

(1) The Buyers Guide shall be displayed prominently and conspicuously in any location on a vehicle and in such a fashion that both sides are readily readable. You may remove the form temporarily from the vehicle during any test drive, but you must return it as soon as the test drive is over.

(2) The capitalization, punctuation and wording of all items, headings, and text on the form must be exactly as required by this Rule. The entire form must be printed in 100% black ink on a white stock no smaller than 11 inches high by 7¼ inches wide in the type styles, sizes and format indicated. When filling out the form, follow the directions in paragraphs (b) through (f) of this section and § 455.4.

(b) *Warranties*—(1) *No Implied Warranty—"As Is"/No Dealer Warranty.* (i) If you offer the vehicle without any implied warranty, *i.e.*, "as is," mark the box appearing in Figure 1. If you offer the vehicle with implied warranties only, substitute the IMPLIED WARRANTIES ONLY disclosure specified in paragraph (b)(1)(ii) of this section, and mark the IMPLIED WARRANTIES ONLY box illustrated by Figure 2. If you first offer the vehicle "as is" or with implied warranties only but then sell it with a warranty, cross out the "As Is—No Dealer Warranty" or "Implied Warranties Only" disclosure, and fill in the warranty terms in accordance with paragraph (b)(2) of this section.

(ii) If your State law limits or prohibits "as is" sales of vehicles, that State law overrides this part and this rule does not give you the right to sell "as is." In such States, the heading "As Is—No Dealer Warranty" and the paragraph immediately accompanying that phrase must be deleted from the form, and the following heading and paragraph must be substituted as illustrated in the Buyers Guide in Figure 2. If you sell vehicles in States that permit "as is" sales, but you choose to offer implied warranties only, you must also use the following disclosure instead of "As Is—No Dealer Warranty" as illustrated by the Buyers Guide in Figure 2. *See* § 455.5 for the Spanish version of this disclosure.

IMPLIED WARRANTIES ONLY

The dealer doesn't make any promises to fix things that need repair when you buy the vehicle or afterward. But *implied warranties* under your state's laws may give you some rights to have the dealer take care of serious problems that were not apparent when you bought the vehicle.

(2) *Full/Limited Warranty.* If you offer the vehicle with a warranty, briefly describe the warranty terms in the space provided. This description must include the following warranty information:

(i) Whether the warranty offered is "Full" or "Limited." Mark the box next to the appropriate designation. A "Full" warranty is defined by the Federal Minimum Standards for Warranty set forth in section 104 of the Magnuson-Moss Act, 15 U.S.C. 2304 (1975). The Magnuson-Moss Act does not apply to vehicles manufactured before July 4, 1975. Therefore, if you choose not to designate "Full" or "Limited" for such vehicles, cross out both designations, leaving only "Warranty."

(ii) Which of the specific systems are covered (for example, "engine, transmission, differential"). You cannot use shorthand, such as "drive train" or "power train" for covered systems.

(iii) The duration (for example, "30 days or 1,000 miles, whichever occurs first").

(iv) The percentage of the repair cost paid by you (for example, "The dealer will pay 100% of the labor and 100% of the parts.")

(v) You may, but are not required to, disclose that a warranty from a source other than the dealer applies to the vehicle. If you choose to disclose the applicability of a non-dealer warranty, mark the applicable box or boxes beneath "NON-DEALER WARRANTIES FOR THIS VEHICLE" to indicate: "MANUFACTURER'S WARRANTY STILL APPLIES. The manufacturer's original warranty has not expired on some components of the vehicle," "MANUFACTURER'S USED VEHICLE WARRANTY APPLIES," and/or "OTHER USED VEHICLE WARRANTY APPLIES."

If, following negotiations, you and the buyer agree to changes in the warranty coverage, mark the changes on the form, as appropriate. If you first offer the vehicle with a warranty, but then sell it without one, cross out the offered warranty and mark either the "As Is—No Dealer Warranty" box or the "Implied Warranties Only" box, as appropriate.

(3) *Service contracts.* If you make a service contract available on the vehicle, you must add the following heading and paragraph below the Non-Dealer Warranties Section and mark the box labeled "Service Contract," unless offering such service contract is "the business of insurance" and such business is regulated by State law. *See* §455.5 for the Spanish version of this disclosure.

☐ SERVICE CONTRACT. A service contract on this vehicle is available for an extra charge. Ask for details about coverage, deductible, price, and exclusions. If you buy a service contract within 90 days of your purchase of this vehicle, *implied warranties* under your state's laws may give you additional rights.

(c) *Name and Address.* Put the name and address of your dealership in the space provided. If you do not have a dealership, use the name and address of your place of business (for example, your service station) or your own name and home address.

(d) *Make, Model, Model Year, VIN.* Put the vehicle's make (for example, "Chevrolet"), model (for example, "Corvette"), model year, and Vehicle Identification Number (VIN) in the spaces provided. You may write the dealer stock number in the space provided or you may leave this space blank.

(e) *Complaints.* In the space provided, put the name and telephone number of the person who should be contacted if any complaints arise after sale.

(f) Optional Signature Line. In the space provided for the name of the individual to be contacted in the event of complaints after sale, you may include a signature line for a buyer's signature. If you opt to include a signature line, you must include a disclosure in immediate proximity to the signature line stating: "I hereby acknowledge receipt of the Buyers Guide at the closing of this sale." You may pre-print this language on the form if you choose.

[49 FR 45725, Nov. 19, 1984, as amended at 60 FR 62205, Dec. 5, 1995; 77 FR 73914, Dec. 12, 2012; 81 FR 81678, Nov. 18, 2016]

§455.3 Window form.

(a) *Form given to buyer.* Give the buyer of a used vehicle sold by you the window form displayed under §455.2 containing all of the disclosures required by the Rule and reflecting the warranty coverage agreed upon. If you prefer, you may give the buyer a copy of the original, so long as that copy accurately reflects all of the disclosures required by the Rule and the warranty coverage agreed upon.

(b) *Incorporated into contract.* The information on the final version of the window form is incorporated into the contract of sale for each used vehicle you sell to a consumer. Information on the window form overrides any contrary provisions in the contract of sale. To inform the consumer of these facts, include the following language conspicuously in each consumer contract of sale:

The information you see on the window form for this vehicle is part of this contract. Information on the window form overrides any contrary provisions in the contract of sale.

§455.4 Contrary statements.

You may not make any statements, oral or written, or take other actions which alter or contradict the disclosures required by §§455.2 and 455.3. You may negotiate over warranty coverage, as provided in §455.2(b) of this part, as long as the final warranty terms are identified in the contract of sale and summarized on the copy of the window form you give to the buyer.

§455.5 Spanish language sales.

(a) If you conduct a sale in Spanish, the window form required by §455.2 and the contract disclosures required by §455.3 must be in that language. You may display on a vehicle both an English language window form and a

Spanish language translation of that form. Use the translation and layout for Spanish language sales in Figures 4, 5, and 6.

(b) Use the following language for the "Implied Warranties Only" disclosure when required by § 455.2(b)(1) as illustrated by Figure 5:

SOLO GARANTÍAS IMPLÍCITAS

El concesionario no hace ninguna promesa de reparar lo que sea necesario cuando compre el vehículo o posteriormente. Sin embargo, las *garantías implícitas* según las leyes estatales podrían darle algunos derechos para hacer que el concesionario se encargue de ciertos problemas que no fueran evidentes cuando compró el vehículo.

(c) Use the following language for the "Service Contract" disclosure required by § 455.2(b)(3) as illustrated by Figures 4 and 5:

CONTRATO DE MANTENIMIENTO. Con un cargo adicional, puede obtener un contrato de mantenimiento para este vehículo. Pregunte acerca de los detalles de la cobertura, los deducibles, el precio y las exclusiones. Si compra un contrato de mantenimiento dentro de los 90 días desde el momento en que compró el vehículo, las *garantías implícitas* según las leyes de su estado podrían darle derechos adicionales.

(d) Use the following language if you choose to use the Optional Signature Line provided by § 455.2(f):

Por este medio confirmo que he recibido copia de la Guía del Comprador al momento de la compraventa.

[81 FR 81679, Nov. 18, 2016]

§ 455.6 State exemptions.

(a) If, upon application to the Commission by an appropriate State agency, the Commission determines, that—

(1) There is a State requirement in effect which applies to any transaction to which this rule applies; and

(2) That State requirement affords an overall level of protection to consumers which is as great as, or greater than, the protection afforded by this Rule; then the Commission's Rule will not be in effect in that State to the extent specified by the Commission in its determination, for as long as the State administers and enforces effectively the State requirement.

(b) Applications for exemption under subsection (a) should be directed to the Secretary of the Commission. When appropriate, proceedings will be commenced in order to make a determination described in paragraph (a) of this section, and will be conducted in accordance with subpart C of part 1 of the Commission's Rules of Practice.

§ 455.7 Severability.

The provisions of this part are separate and severable from one another. If any provision is determined to be invalid, it is the Commission's intention that the remaining provisions shall continue in effect.

FIGURE 1 TO PART 455—"AS IS" – NO DEALER WARRANTY BUYERS GUIDE (ENGLISH)

FIGURE 1 TO PART 455 – "AS IS" - NO DEALER WARRANTY Buyers Guide (English)

BUYERS GUIDE

IMPORTANT: Spoken promises are difficult to enforce. Ask the dealer to put all promises in writing. Keep this form.

VEHICLE MAKE MODEL YEAR VEHICLE IDENTIFICATION NUMBER (VIN)

WARRANTIES FOR THIS VEHICLE:

☐ **AS IS - NO DEALER WARRANTY**

THE DEALER DOES NOT PROVIDE A WARRANTY FOR ANY REPAIRS AFTER SALE.

☐ **DEALER WARRANTY**

☐ FULL WARRANTY.

☐ LIMITED WARRANTY. The dealer will pay ____% of the labor and ____% of the parts for the covered systems that fail during the warranty period. Ask the dealer for a copy of the warranty, and for any documents that explain warranty coverage, exclusions, and the dealer's repair obligations. *Implied warranties* under your state's laws may give you additional rights.

SYSTEMS COVERED: **DURATION:**

NON-DEALER WARRANTIES FOR THIS VEHICLE:

☐ MANUFACTURER'S WARRANTY STILL APPLIES. The manufacturer's original warranty has not expired on some components of the vehicle.

☐ MANUFACTURER'S USED VEHICLE WARRANTY APPLIES.

☐ OTHER USED VEHICLE WARRANTY APPLIES.

Ask the dealer for a copy of the warranty document and an explanation of warranty coverage, exclusions, and repair obligations.

☐ SERVICE CONTRACT. A service contract on this vehicle is available for an extra charge. Ask for details about coverage, deductible, price, and exclusions. If you buy a service contract within 90 days of your purchase of this vehicle, *implied warranties* under your state's laws may give you additional rights.

ASK THE DEALER IF YOUR MECHANIC CAN INSPECT THE VEHICLE ON OR OFF THE LOT.

OBTAIN A VEHICLE HISTORY REPORT AND CHECK FOR OPEN SAFETY RECALLS. For information on how to obtain a vehicle history report, visit ftc.gov/usedcars. To check for open safety recalls, visit safercar.gov. You will need the vehicle identification number (VIN) shown above to make the best use of the resources on these sites.

SEE OTHER SIDE for important additional information, including a list of major defects that may occur in used motor vehicles.

Si el concesionario gestiona la venta en español, pídale una copia de la Guía del Comprador en español.

504 x 684 pt box, 1 pt stroke
26 pt bold caps centered
1 pt rule
8.5 pt bold & regular, caps & lc
0.5 pt rule
6 pt regular caps
12 pt bold caps
2 pt rule
22 pt box, 1 pt stroke
24 pt bold caps
8.5 pt regular, caps & lc
1 pt dashed rule
22 pt box, 1 pt stroke
24 pt bold caps
8 pt boxes, 1 pt stroke
8.5 pt regular, italic, caps & lc
10.2 pt leading
9 pt bold caps, 2 columns
12 pt bold caps
2 pt rule
8 pt boxes, 1 pt stroke
8.5 pt regular, caps & lc
10.2 pt leading
1 pt rule
8 pt box, 1 pt stroke
8.5 pt regular, italic, caps & lc
10.2 pt leading
2 pt rule
9 pt regular, bold, caps & lc
10.8 pt leading

* Typeface is Arial, text is flush left unless otherwise noted.

[81 FR 81679, Nov. 18, 2016]

FIGURE 2 TO PART 455—IMPLIED WARRANTIES ONLY BUYERS GUIDE (ENGLISH)

FIGURE 2 TO PART 455 – IMPLIED WARRANTIES ONLY Buyers Guide (English)

BUYERS GUIDE

IMPORTANT: Spoken promises are difficult to enforce. Ask the dealer to put all promises in writing. Keep this form.

VEHICLE MAKE MODEL YEAR VEHICLE IDENTIFICATION NUMBER (VIN)

WARRANTIES FOR THIS VEHICLE:

☐ **IMPLIED WARRANTIES ONLY**

The dealer doesn't make any promises to fix things that need repair when you buy the vehicle or afterward. But *implied warranties* under your state's laws may give you some rights to have the dealer take care of serious problems that were not apparent when you bought the vehicle.

☐ **DEALER WARRANTY**

☐ FULL WARRANTY.

☐ LIMITED WARRANTY. The dealer will pay ____% of the labor and ____% of the parts for the covered systems that fail during the warranty period. Ask the dealer for a copy of the warranty, and for any documents that explain warranty coverage, exclusions, and the dealer's repair obligations. *Implied warranties* under your state's laws may give you additional rights.

SYSTEMS COVERED: **DURATION:**

NON-DEALER WARRANTIES FOR THIS VEHICLE:

☐ MANUFACTURER'S WARRANTY STILL APPLIES. The manufacturer's original warranty has not expired on some components of the vehicle.

☐ MANUFACTURER'S USED VEHICLE WARRANTY APPLIES.

☐ OTHER USED VEHICLE WARRANTY APPLIES.

Ask the dealer for a copy of the warranty document and an explanation of warranty coverage, exclusions, and repair obligations.

☐ SERVICE CONTRACT. A service contract on this vehicle is available for an extra charge. Ask for details about coverage, deductible, price, and exclusions. If you buy a service contract within 90 days of your purchase of this vehicle, *implied warranties* under your state's laws may give you additional rights.

ASK THE DEALER IF YOUR MECHANIC CAN INSPECT THE VEHICLE ON OR OFF THE LOT.

OBTAIN A VEHICLE HISTORY REPORT AND CHECK FOR OPEN SAFETY RECALLS. For information on how to obtain a vehicle history report, visit ftc.gov/usedcars. To check for open safety recalls, visit safercar.gov. You will need the vehicle identification number (VIN) shown above to make the best use of the resources on these sites.

SEE OTHER SIDE for important additional information, including a list of major defects that may occur in used motor vehicles.

Si el concesionario gestiona la venta en español, pídale una copia de la Guía del Comprador en español.

504 x 684 pt box, 1 pt stroke
26 pt bold caps centered
1 pt rule
8.5 pt bold & regular, caps & lc
0.5 pt rule
6 pt regular caps
12 pt bold caps
2 pt rule
22 pt box, 1 pt stroke
24 pt bold caps
8.5 pt regular, italic, caps & lc
10.2 pt leading
1 pt dashed rule
22 pt box, 1 pt stroke
24 pt bold caps
8 pt boxes, 1 pt stroke
8.5 pt regular, italic, caps & lc
10.2 pt leading
9 pt bold caps, 2 columns
12 pt bold caps
2 pt rule
8 pt boxes, 1 pt stroke
8.5 pt regular, caps & lc
10.2 pt leading
1 pt rule
8 pt box, 1 pt stroke
8.5 pt regular, italic, caps & lc
10.2 pt leading
2 pt rule
9 pt regular, bold, caps & lc
10.8 pt leading

* Typeface is Arial, text is flush left unless otherwise noted.

[81 FR 81679, Nov. 18, 2016]

FIGURE 3 TO PART 455—BACK OF BUYERS GUIDE (ENGLISH)

FIGURE 3 TO PART 455 – Back of Buyers Guide (English)

504 x 684 pt box, 1 pt stroke

2 pt rule

Here is a list of some major defects that may occur in used vehicles.

7 pt regular, cap & lc

144 pt columns, left, center, right
7 pt bold, 2 pt before para,
7 pt regular, 15 pt left ind,
-10 pt first line ind
8.4 pt leading

Frame & Body
Frame-cracks, corrective welds, or rusted through
Dog tracks—bent or twisted frame

Engine
Oil leakage, excluding normal seepage
Cracked block or head
Belts missing or inoperable
Knocks or misses related to camshaft lifters and push rods
Abnormal exhaust discharge

Transmission & Drive Shaft
Improper fluid level or leakage, excluding normal seepage
Cracked or damaged case which is visible
Abnormal noise or vibration caused by faulty transmission or drive shaft
Improper shifting or functioning in any gear
Manual clutch slips or chatters

Differential
Improper fluid level or leakeage, excluding normal seepage
Cracked of damaged housing which is visible
Abnormal noise or vibration caused by faulty differential

Cooling System
Leakage including radiator
Improperly functioning water pump

Electrical System
Battery leakage
Improperly functioning alternator, generator, battery, or starter

Fuel System
Visible leakage

Inoperable Accessories
Gauges or warning devices
Air conditioner
Heater & Defroster

Brake System
Failure warning light broken
Pedal not firm under pressure (DOT spec.)
Not enough pedal reserve (DOT spec.)
Does not stop vehicle in straight line (DOT spec.)
Hoses damaged
Drum or rotor too thin (Mfgr. Specs)
Lining or pad thickness less than 1/32 inch
Power unit not operating or leaking
Structural or mechanical parts damaged

Air Bags

Steering System
Too much free play at steering wheel (DOT specs.)
Free play in linkage more than 1/4 inch
Steering gear binds or jams
Front wheels aligned improperly (DOT specs.)
Power unit belts cracked or slipping
Power unit fluid level improper

Suspension System
Ball joint seals damaged
Structural parts bent or damaged
Stabilizer bar disconnected
Spring broken
Shock absorber mounting loose
Rubber bushings damaged or missing
Radius rod damaged or missing
Shock absorber leaking or functioning improperly

Tires
Tread depth less than 2/32 inch
Sizes mismatched
Visible damage

Wheels
Visible cracks, damage or repairs
Mounting bolts loose or missing

Exhaust System
Leakage
Catalytic Converter

2 pt rule

DEALER NAME

ADDRESS

TELEPHONE EMAIL

FOR COMPLAINTS AFTER SALE, CONTACT:

0.5 pt rules
8 pt regular, caps
25 pts between rules

2 pt rule

IMPORTANT: The information on this form is part of any contract to buy this vehicle. Removing this label before consumer purchase (except for purpose of test-driving) violates federal law (16 C.F.R. 455).

9 pt bold & regular, caps & lc
10.8 pt leading

* Typeface is Arial, text is flush left unless otherwise noted.

[81 FR 81679, Nov. 18, 2016]

FIGURE 4 TO PART 455—"AS IS" – NO DEALER WARRANTY BUYERS GUIDE (SPANISH)

FIGURE 4 TO PART 455 – "AS IS"- NO DEALER WARRANTY Buyers Guide

(Spanish)

GUÍA DEL COMPRADOR

IMPORTANTE: Las promesas verbales son difíciles de hacer cumplir. Solicite al concesionario que ponga todas las promesas por escrito. Conserve este formulario.

MARCA DEL VEHÍCULO MODELO AÑO NÚMERO DE IDENTIFICACIÓN DEL VEHÍCULO (VIN)

GARANTÍAS PARA ESTE VEHÍCULO:

☐ **COMO ESTÁ - SIN GARANTÍA DEL CONCESIONARIO**

EL CONCESIONARIO NO PAGARÁ NINGUNA REPARACIÓN. El concesionario no provee una garantía para reparaciones hechas después del momento de la venta.

☐ **GARANTÍA DEL CONCESIONARIO**

☐ GARANTÍA COMPLETA.

☐ GARANTÍA LIMITADA. El concesionario pagará el ______% de la mano de obra y el ______% de las partes de los sistemas cubiertos que fallen durante el período de garantía. Pídale al concesionario una copia de la garantía y de cualquier documento que le explique la cobertura, las exclusiones y las obligaciones de reparación del concesionario. Las *garantías implícitas*, según las leyes de su estado, podrían darle derechos adicionales.

SISTEMAS CUBIERTOS: **DURACIÓN:**

GARANTÍAS QUE NO PERTENECEN AL CONCESIONARIO:

☐ LA GARANTÍA DEL FABRICANTE TODAVÍA APLICA. La garantía original del fabricante no ha expirado para algunos de los componentes del vehículo.

☐ SE APLICA LA GARANTÍA DEL FABRICANTE PARA VEHÍCULOS USADOS.

☐ SE APLICA OTRA GARANTÍA PARA VEHÍCULOS USADOS.

Pídale al concesionario una copia del documento de garantía y una explicación de la cobertura, las exclusiones y las obligaciones de reparación.

☐ CONTRATO DE MANTENIMIENTO. Con un cargo adicional, puede obtener un contrato de mantenimiento para este vehículo. Pregunte acerca de los detalles de la cobertura, los deducibles, el precio y las exclusiones. Si compra un contrato de mantenimiento dentro de los 90 días desde el momento en que compró el vehículo, las *garantías implícitas* según las leyes de su estado podrían darle derechos adicionales.

PREGÚNTELE AL CONCESIONARIO SI SU MECÁNICO PUEDE INSPECCIONAR EL VEHÍCULO DENTRO O FUERA DEL CONCESIONARIO.

OBTENGA UN INFORME DEL HISTORIAL DEL VEHÍCULO Y VERIFIQUE SI EXISTEN RETIROS POR DEFECTOS DE SEGURIDAD PENDIENTES. Para información sobre cómo obtener un Informe del Historial del Vehículo, visite el sitio ftc.gov/carrosusados. Para verificar si existen retiros por defectos de seguridad pendientes, visite safercar.gov. Para aprovechar al máximo los recursos de estos sitios necesitará el número de identificación de vehículo (VIN) mostrado anteriormente.

CONSULTE EL DORSO para obtener más información, incluyendo una lista de defectos importantes que pueden ocurrir en vehículos de motor usados.

504 x 684 pt box, 1 pt stroke
26 pt bold caps centered
1 pt rule
8.5 pt bold & regular, caps & lc
10.2 pt leading
0.5 pt rule
6 pt regular caps
12 pt bold caps
2 pt rule
22 pt box, 1 pt stroke
24 pt bold caps
24 pt leading
8.5 pt regular, caps & lc
10.2 pt leading
1 pt dashed rule
22 pt box, 1 pt stroke
24 pt bold caps
8 pt boxes, 1 pt stroke
8.5 pt regular, italic, caps & lc
10.2 pt leading
9 pt bold caps, 2 columns
12 pt bold caps
2 pt rule
8 pt boxes, 1 pt stroke
8.5 pt regular, caps & lc
10.2 pt leading
1 pt rule
8 pt box, 1 pt stroke
8.5 pt regular, italic, caps & lc
10.2 pt leading
2 pt rule
9 pt regular, bold, caps & lc
10.8 pt leading

* Typeface is Arial, text is flush left unless otherwise noted.

[81 FR 81679, Nov. 18, 2016]

FIGURE 5 TO PART 455—IMPLIED WARRANTIES ONLY BUYERS GUIDE (SPANISH)

FIGURE 5 TO PART 455 – IMPLIED WARRANTIES ONLY Buyers Guide (Spanish)

GUÍA DEL COMPRADOR

IMPORTANTE: Las promesas verbales son difíciles de hacer cumplir. Solicite al concesionario que ponga todas las promesas por escrito. Conserve este formulario.

MARCA DEL VEHÍCULO MODELO AÑO NÚMERO DE IDENTIFICACIÓN DEL VEHICULO (VIN)

GARANTÍAS PARA ESTE VEHÍCULO:

☐ SOLO GARANTÍAS IMPLÍCITAS

El concesionario no hace ninguna promesa de reparar lo que sea necesario cuando compre el vehículo o posteriormente. Sin embargo, las *garantías implícitas* según las leyes estatales podrían darle algunos derechos para hacer que el concesionario se encargue de ciertos problemas que no fueran evidentes cuando compró el vehículo.

- -

☐ GARANTÍA DEL CONCESIONARIO

☐ GARANTÍA COMPLETA.

☐ GARANTÍA LIMITADA. El concesionario pagará el ______% de la mano de obra y el ______% de las partes de los sistemas cubiertos que fallen durante el período de garantía. Pídale al concesionario una copia de la garantía y de cualquier documento que le explique la cobertura, las exclusiones y las obligaciones de reparación del concesionario. Las *garantías implícitas*, según las leyes de su estado, podrían darle derechos adicionales.

SISTEMAS CUBIERTOS: **DURACIÓN:**

GARANTÍAS QUE NO PERTENECEN AL CONCESIONARIO:

☐ LA GARANTÍA DEL FABRICANTE TODAVÍA APLICA. La garantía original del fabricante no ha expirado para algunos de los componentes del vehículo.

☐ SE APLICA LA GARANTÍA DEL FABRICANTE PARA VEHÍCULOS USADOS.

☐ SE APLICA OTRA GARANTÍA PARA VEHÍCULOS USADOS.

Pídale al concesionario una copia del documento de garantía y una explicación de la cobertura, las exclusiones y las obligaciones de reparación.

☐ CONTRATO DE MANTENIMIENTO. Con un cargo adicional, puede obtener un contrato de mantenimiento para este vehículo. Pregunte acerca de los detalles de la cobertura, los deducibles, el precio y las exclusiones. Si compra un contrato de mantenimiento dentro de los 90 días desde el momento en que compró el vehículo, las *garantías implícitas* según las leyes de su estado podrían darle derechos adicionales.

PREGÚNTELE AL CONCESIONARIO SI SU MECÁNICO PUEDE INSPECCIONAR EL VEHÍCULO DENTRO O FUERA DEL CONCESIONARIO.

OBTENGA UN INFORME DEL HISTORIAL DEL VEHÍCULO Y VERIFIQUE SI EXISTEN RETIROS POR DEFECTOS DE SEGURIDAD PENDIENTES. Para información sobre cómo obtener un Informe del Historial del Vehículo, visite el sitio ftc.gov/carrosusados. Para verificar si existen retiros por defectos de seguridad pendientes, visite safercar.gov. Para aprovechar al máximo los recursos de estos sitios necesitará el número de identificación de vehículo (VIN) mostrado anteriormente.

CONSULTE EL DORSO para obtener más información, incluyendo una lista de defectos importantes que pueden ocurrir en vehículos de motor usados.

504 x 684 pt box, 1 pt stroke
26 pt bold caps centered
1 pt rule
8.5 pt bold & regular, caps & lc
10.2 pt leading
0.5 pt rule
6 pt regular caps
12 pt bold caps
2 pt rule
22 pt box, 1 pt stroke
24 pt bold caps
8.5 pt regular, italic, caps & lc
10.2 pt leading
1 pt dashed rule
22 pt box, 1 pt stroke
24 pt bold caps
8 pt boxes, 1 pt stroke
8.5 pt regular, italic, caps & lc
10.2 pt leading
9 pt bold caps, 2 columns
12 pt bold caps
2 pt rule
8 pt boxes, 1 pt stroke
8.5 pt regular, caps & lc
10.2 pt leading
1 pt rule
8 pt box, 1 pt stroke
8.5 pt regular, italic, caps & lc
10.2 pt leading
2 pt rule
9 pt regular, bold, caps & lc
10.8 pt leading

* Typeface is Arial, text is flush left unless otherwise noted.

[81 FR 81679, Nov. 18, 2016]

FIGURE 6 TO PART 455—BACK OF BUYERS GUIDE (SPANISH)

FIGURE 6 TO PART 455 – Back of Buyers Guide (Spanish)

504 x 684 pt box, 1 pt stroke

2 pt rule

8 pt regular, cap & lc

A continuación podrá encontrar una lista de los defectos principales que podrían ocurrir en vehículos usados.

144 pt columns, left, center, right
7 pt bold, 2 pt before para,
7 pt regular, 15 pt left ind,
-10 pt first line ind
8.4 pt leading

Chasis y carrocería
Grietas en el chasis, soldaduras correctivas u oxidadas
Descuadrado: chasis doblado o torcido

Motor
Pérdidas de aceite, excepto las filtraciones normales
Bloque o cárter con grietas
Correas ausentes o fuera de servicio
Golpes o fallas relacionados con levantadores de levas o bielas
Descarga del escape fuera de lo normal

Transmisión y eje motor
Nivel inadecuado de fluido o pérdidas excepto filtraciones normales
Grietas o daños visibles en la caja.
Ruidos o vibraciones fuera de lo normal ocasionadas por la transmisión o el eje motor
Cambios o funcionamiento inadecuados en cualquier velocidad
Patinados o vibraciones del embrague manual

Diferencial
Nivel inadecuado de fluido o pérdidas excepto filtraciones normales
Grietas o daños visibles en el cárter del diferencial
Ruidos o vibraciones fuera de lo normal ocasionadas por fallas en el diferencial.

Sistema de enfriamiento
Pérdidas, incluidas las del radiador
Funcionamiento inadecuado de la bomba de agua

Sistema eléctrico
Pérdidas en la batería
Funcionamiento inadecuado del alternador, generador, batería o arrancador

Sistema de combustible
Pérdidas visibles

Accesorios fuera de servicio
Indicadores o dispositivos de advertencia
Aire acondicionado
Calefaccion y Desempañador

Sistema de frenos
Luz de advertencia de fallas rota
Falta de firmeza cuando se presiona el pedal (según especificaciones del Departamento de Transporte [DOT])
Distancia insuficiente del pedal (según especificaciones del DOT)
El vehículo no se detiene en línea recta (según especificaciones del DOT)
Mangueras dañadas
Tambor o rotor muy delgados (según especificaciones del fabricante)
Grosor de la placa o del revestimiento inferior que 1/32 pulgadas
Unidad de potencia fuera de servicio o con pérdidas
Partes estructurales o mecánicas dañadas

Bolsas de aire

Sistema de dirección
Demasiado juego en el volante (según especificaciones del DOT)
Juego mayor a 1/4 de pulgada en el varillaje
El mecanismo de dirección se traba
Alineación inadecuada de las ruedas frontales (según especificaciones del DOT)
Grietas o deslizamientos en las correas de la unidad de potencia
Nivel inadecuado de fluidos de la unidad de potencia

Sistema de suspensión
Juntas de rótula dañadas
Partes estructurales dobladas o dañadas
Barra estabilizadora desconectada
Resorte roto
Cojinete del amortiguador suelto
Cojinetes de caucho dañados o ausentes
Biela dañada o ausente
Amortiguador con pérdidas o con funcionamiento inadecuado

Neumáticos
Profundidad de las ranuras menor que 2/32 de pulgada
Tamaños que no corresponden
Daños visibles

Ruedas
Grietas, daños o reparaciones visibles
Tornillos de sujeción sueltos o ausentes

Sistema de escape
Pérdidas
Convertidor catalítico

2 pt rule

0.5 pt rules
8 pt regular, caps
25 pts between rules

NOMBRE DEL CONCESIONARIO

DIRECCIÓN DEL CONCESIONARIO

TELÉFONO CORREO ELECTRÓNICO

PARA QUEJAS DESPUÉS DE LA VENTA COMUNÍQUESE CON:

2 pt rule
9 pt bold & regular, caps & lc
10.8 pt leading

IMPORTANTE: La información de este formulario es parte de cualquier contrato para comprar este vehículo. Quitar esta etiqueta antes de la compra del consumidor (excepto a los fines de realizar una prueba de conducción) es una infracción a la ley federal (16 C. F. R. 455).

* Typeface is Arial, text is flush left unless otherwise noted.

[81 FR 81679, Nov. 18, 2016]

PART 456—OPHTHALMIC PRACTICE RULES (EYEGLASS RULE)

Sec.

AUTHORITY: 15 U.S.C. 57a; 5 U.S.C. 552.

SOURCE: 57 FR 18822, May 1, 1992, unless otherwise noted.

§ 456.1 Definitions.

(a) A *patient* is any person who has had an eye examination.

(b) An *eye examination* is the process of determining the refractive condition of a person's eyes or the presence of any visual anomaly by the use of objective or subjective tests.

(c) *Ophthalmic goods* are eyeglasses, or any component of eyeglasses, and contact lenses.

(d) *Ophthalmic services* are the measuring, fitting, and adjusting of ophthalmic goods subsequent to an eye examination.

(e) An *ophthalmologist* is any Doctor of Medicine or Osteopathy who performs eye examinations.

(f) An *optometrist* is any Doctor of Optometry.

(g) A *prescription* is the written specifications for lenses for eyeglasses which are derived from an eye examination, including all of the information specified by state law, if any, necessary to obtain lenses for eyeglasses.

§ 456.2 Separation of examination and dispensing.

It is an unfair act or practice for an ophthalmologist or optometrist to:

(a) Fail to provide to the patient one copy of the patient's prescription immediately after the eye examination is completed. Provided: An ophthalmologist or optometrist may refuse to give the patient a copy of the patient's prescription until the patient has paid for the eye examination, but only if that ophthalmologist or optometrist would have required immediate payment from that patient had the examination revealed that no ophthalmic goods were required;

(b) Condition the availability of an eye examination to any person on a requirement that the patient agree to purchase any ophthalmic goods from the ophthalmologist or optometrist;

(c) Charge the patient any fee in addition to the ophthalmologist's or optometrist's examination fee as a condition to releasing the prescription to the patient. Provided: An ophthalmologist or optometrist may charge an additional fee for verifying ophthalmic goods dispensed by another seller when the additional fee is imposed at the time the verification is performed; or

(d) Place on the prescription, or require the patient to sign, or deliver to the patient a form or notice waiving or disclaiming the liability or responsibility of the ophthalmologist or optometrist for the accuracy of the eye examination or the accuracy of the ophthalmic goods and services dispensed by another seller.

§ 456.3 Federal or State employees.

This rule does not apply to ophthalmologists or optometrists employed by any Federal, State or local government entity.

§ 456.4 Declaration of Commission Intent.

In prohibiting the use of waivers and disclaimers of liability in § 456.2(d), it is not the Commission's intent to impose liability on an ophthalmologist or optometrist for the ophthalmic goods and services dispensed by another seller pursuant to the ophthalmologist's or optometrist's prescription.

§ 456.5 Rules applicable to prescriptions for contact lenses and related issues.

Rules applicable to prescriptions for contact lenses and related issues may be found at 16 CFR part 315 (Contact Lens Rule).

[69 FR 40511, July 2, 2004]

PART 460—LABELING AND ADVERTISING OF HOME INSULATION

460.24 Stayed or invalid parts.

APPENDIX TO PART 460—EXEMPTIONS

AUTHORITY: 38 Stat. 717, as amended (15 U.S.C. 41 *et seq.*).

SOURCE: 44 FR 50242, Aug. 27, 1979, unless otherwise noted.

§460.1 What this regulation does.

This regulation deals with home insulation labels, fact sheets, ads, and other promotional materials in or affecting commerce, as "commerce" is defined in the Federal Trade Commission Act. If you are covered by this regulation, breaking any of its rules is an unfair and deceptive act or practice or an unfair method of competition under section 5 of that Act. You can be fined heavily (up to $11,000 plus an adjustment for inflation, under §1.98 of this chapter) each time you break a rule.

[70 FR 31274, May 31, 2005]

§460.2 What is home insulation.

Insulation is any material mainly used to slow down heat flow. It may be mineral or organic, fibrous, cellular, or reflective (aluminum foil). It may be in rigid, semirigid, flexible, or loose-fill form. Home insulation is for use in old or new homes, condominiums, cooperatives, apartments, modular homes, or mobile homes. It does not include pipe insulation. It does not include any kind of duct insulation except for duct wrap.

§460.3 Who is covered.

You are covered by this regulation if you are a member of the home insulation industry. This includes individuals, firms, partnerships, and corporations. It includes manufacturers, distributors, franchisors, installers, retailers, utility companies, and trade associations. Advertisers and advertising agencies are also covered. So are labs doing tests for industry members. If you sell new homes to consumers, you are covered.

§460.4 When the rules apply.

You must follow these rules each time you import, manufacture, distribute, sell, install, promote, or label home insulation. You must follow them each time you prepare, approve, place, or pay for home insulation labels, fact sheets, ads, or other promotional materials for consumer use. You must also follow them each time you supply anyone covered by this regulation with written information that is to be used in labels, fact sheets, ads, or other promotional materials for consumer use. Testing labs must follow the rules unless the industry members tells them, in writing, that labels, fact sheets, ads, or other promotional materials for home insulation will not be based on the test results.

§460.5 R-value tests.

R-value measures resistance to heat flow. R-values given in labels, fact sheets, ads, or other promotional materials must be based on tests done under the methods listed below. They were designed by the American Society of Testing and Materials (ASTM). The test methods are:

(a) All types of insulation except aluminum foil must be tested with ASTM C 177–04, "Standard Test Method for Steady-State Heat Flux Measurements and Thermal Transmission Properties by Means of the Guarded-Hot-Plate Apparatus;" ASTM C 518–04, "Standard Test Method for Steady-State Thermal Transmission Properties by Means of the Heat Flow Meter Apparatus;" ASTM C 1363–97, "Standard Test Method for the Thermal Performance of Building Assemblies by Means of a Hot Box Apparatus" or ASTM C 1114–00, "Standard Test Method for Steady-State Thermal Transmission Properties by Means of the Thin-Heater Apparatus." The tests must be done at a mean temperature of 75 [degrees] Fahrenheit and with a temperature differential of 50 [degrees] Fahrenheit plus or minus 10 degrees Fahrenheit. The tests must be done on the insulation material alone (excluding any airspace). R-values ("thermal resistance") based upon heat flux measurements according to ASTM C 177–04 or ASTM C 518–04 must be reported only in accordance with the requirements and restrictions of ASTM C 1045–01, "Standard Practice for Calculating Thermal Transmission Properties from Steady-State Conditions."

(1) For polyurethane, polyisocyanurate, and extruded polystyrene, the tests must be done on samples that fully reflect the effect of

aging on the product's R-value. To age the sample, follow the procedure in paragraph 4.6.4 of GSA Specification HH–I–530A, or another reliable procedure.

(2) For loose-fill cellulose, the tests must be done at the settled density determined under paragraph 8 of ASTM C 739–03, "Standard Specification for Cellulosic Fiber Loose-Fill Thermal Insulation."

(3) For loose-fill mineral wool, self-supported, spray-applied cellulose, and stabilized cellulose, the tests must be done on samples that fully reflect the effect of settling on the product's R-value.

(4) For self-supported spray-applied cellulose, the tests must be done at the density determined pursuant to ASTM C 1149–02, "Standard Specification for Self-Supported Spray Applied Cellulosic Thermal Insulation."

(5) For loose-fill insulations, the initial installed thickness for the product must be determined pursuant to ASTM C 1374–03, "Standard Test Method for Determination of Installed Thickness of Pneumatically Applied Loose-Fill Building Insulation," for R-values of 13, 19, 22, 30, 38, 49 and any other R-values provided on the product's label pursuant to §460.12.

(b) Single sheet systems of aluminum foil must be tested with ASTM E 408–71 (Reapproved 2002), "Standard Test Methods for Total Normal Emittance of Surfaces Using Inspection-Meter Techniques," or ASTM C 1371–04a, "Standard Test Method for Determination of Emittance of Materials Near Room Temperature Using Portable Emissometers." This tests the emissivity of the foil—its power to radiate heat. To get the R-value for a specific emissivity level, air space, and direction of heat flow, use the tables in the most recent edition of the American Society of Heating, Refrigerating, and Air-Conditioning Engineers' (ASHRAE) Fundamentals Handbook, if the product is intended for applications that meet the conditions specified in the tables. You must use the R-value shown for 50[degrees] Fahrenheit, with a temperature differential of 30[degrees] Fahrenheit.

(c) Aluminum foil systems with more than one sheet, and single sheet systems of aluminum foil that are intended for applications that do not meet the conditions specified in the tables in the most recent edition of the ASHRAE Fundamentals Handbook, must be tested with ASTM C 1363–97, "Standard Test Method for the Thermal Performance of Building Assemblies by Means of a Hot Box Apparatus," in a test panel constructed according to ASTM C 1224–03, "Standard Specification for Reflective Insulation for Building Applications," and under the test conditions specified in ASTM C 1224–03. To get the R-value from the results of those tests, use the formula specified in ASTM C 1224–03.

(d) For insulation materials with foil facings, you must test the R-value of the material alone (excluding any air spaces) under the methods listed in paragraph (a) of this section. You can also determine the R-value of the material in conjunction with an air space. You can use one of two methods to do this:

(1) You can test the system, with its air space, under ASTM C 1363–97, "Standard Test Method for the Thermal Performance of Building Assemblies by Means of a Hot Box Apparatus," which is incorporated by reference in paragraph (a) of this section. If you do this, you must follow the rules in paragraph (a) of this section on temperature, aging and settled density.

(2) You can add up the tested R-value of the material and the R-value of the air space. To get the R-value for the air space, you must follow the rules in paragraph (b) of this section.

(e) The standards listed above are incorporated by reference into this section. These incorporations by reference were approved by the Director of the Federal Register in accordance with 5 U.S.C. 552(a) and 1 CFR part 51. Copies may be inspected at the Federal Trade Commission, Consumer Response Center, Room 130, 600 Pennsylvania Avenue, NW., Washington, DC 20580, or at the National Archives and Records Administration (NARA). For information on the availability of this material at NARA, call (202) 741–6030, or go to: *http://www.archives.gov/federal_register/code_of_federal_regulations/ibr_locations.html*. Copies of materials and standards incorporated by reference may be obtained from the issuing organizations listed in this section.

(1) The American Society of Testing and Materials, 100 Barr Harbor Drive, P.O. Box C700, West Conshocken, PA 19428–2959.

(i) ASTM C 177–04, "Standard Test Method for Steady-State Heat Flux Measurements and Thermal Transmission Properties by Means of the Guarded-Hot-Plate Apparatus."

(ii) ASTM C 518–04, "Standard Test Method for Steady-State Thermal Transmission Properties by Means of the Heat Flow Meter Apparatus."

(iii) ASTM C 739–03, "Standard Specification for Cellulosic Fiber Loose-Fill Thermal Insulation."

(iv) ASTM C 1045–01, "Standard Practice for Calculating Thermal Transmission Properties from Steady-State Conditions."

(v) ASTM C 1114–00, "Standard Test Method for Steady-State Thermal Transmission Properties by Means of the Thin-Heater Apparatus."

(vi) ASTM C 1149–02, "Standard Specification for Self-Supported Spray Applied Cellulosic Thermal Insulation."

(vii) ASTM C 1224–03, "Standard Specification for Reflective Insulation for Building Applications."

(viii) ASTM C 1363–97, "Standard Test Method for the Thermal Performance of Building Assemblies by Means of a Hot Box Apparatus."

(ix) ASTM C 1371–04a, "Standard Test Method for Determination of Emittance of Materials Near Room Temperature Using Portable Emissometers."

(x) ASTM C 1374–03, "Standard Test Method for Determination of Installed Thickness of Pneumatically Applied Loose-Fill Building Insulation."

(xi) ASTM E 408–71 (Reapproved 2002), "Standard Test Methods for Total Normal Emittance of Surfaces Using Inspection-Meter Techniques."

(2) U.S. General Services Administration (GSA), 1800 F Street, NW., Washington, DC 20405.

(i) GSA Specification HH–I–530A, Federal Specification, Insulation Board, Thermal (Urethane), November 22, 1971.

(ii) [Reserved]

[70 FR 31274, May 31, 2005]

§ 460.6 "Representative thickness" testing.

All tests except aluminum foil tests must be done at a representative thickness for every thickness shown in a label, fact sheet, ad, or other promotional material. "Representative thickness" means a thickness at which the R-value per unit will vary no more than plus or minus 2% with increases in thickness. However, if the thickness shown in your label, fact sheet, ad, or promotional material is less than the representative thickness, then you can test the insulation at the thickness shown.

§ 460.7 Which test version to use.

Use the version of the ASTM test method that was in effect when this regulation was promulgated. If ASTM changes a test method, the new version will automatically replace the old one in these rules 90 days after ASTM first publishes the change. However, the Commission's staff or a person affected by the change can petition the Commission during the 90-day period not to adopt the change or to reopen the proceeding to consider it further.

§ 460.8 R-value tolerances.

If you are a manufacturer of home insulation, no individual specimen of the insulation you sell can have an R-value more than 10% below the R-value shown in a label, fact sheet, ad, or other promotional material for that insulation. If you are not a manufacturer, you can rely on the R-value data given to you by the manufacturer, unless you know or should know that the data is false or not based on the proper tests.

[70 FR 31275, May 31, 2005]

§ 460.9 What test records you must keep.

Manufacturers and testing labs must keep records of each item of information in the "Report" section of the ASTM test method that is used for a test. They must also keep the following records:

(a) The name and address of the testing lab that did each test.

(b) The date of each test.

(c) For manufacturers, the date each test report was received from a lab. For labs, the date each test report was sent to a manufacturer.

(d) For extruded polystyrene, polyurethane, and polyisocyanurate, the age (in days) of the specimen that was tested.

(e) For aluminum foil, the emissivity level that was found in the test.

Manufacturers who own their own testing labs need not keep records of the information in paragraph (c) of this section.

Keep these records for at least three years. If the documents show proof for your claims, the three years will begin again each time you make the claim. Federal Trade Commission staff members can check these records at any time, but they must give you reasonable notice first.

§460.10 How statements must be made.

All statements called for by this regulation must be made clearly and conspicuously. Among other things, you must follow the Commission's enforcement policy statement for clear and conspicuous disclosures in foreign language advertising and sales materials, 16 CFR 14.9.

[61 FR 13666, Mar. 28, 1996]

§460.11 Rounding off R-values.

R-values shown in labels, fact sheets, ads, or other promotional materials must be rounded to the nearest tenth. However, R-values of 10 or more may be rounded to the nearest whole number.

§460.12 Labels.

If you are a manufacturer, you must label all packages of your insulation. The labels must contain:

(a) The type of insulation.

(b) A chart showing these items:

(1) For batts and blankets of any type: the R-value, length, width, thickness, and square feet of insulation in the package.

(2) For all loose-fill insulation: the minimum settled thickness, initial installed thickness, maximum net coverage area, number of bags per 1,000 square feet, and minimum weight per square foot at R-values of 13, 19, 22, 30, 38, and 49. You must also give this information for any additional R-values you list on the chart. Labels for these products must state the minimum net weight of the insulation in the package. You must also provide information about the blowing machine and machine settings used to derive the initial installed thickness information.

(3) For boardstock: the R-value, length, width, and thickness of the boards in the package, and the square feet of insulation in the package.

(4) For aluminum foil: the number of foil sheets; the number and thickness of the air spaces; and the R-value provided by that system when the direction of heat flow is up, down, and horizontal. You can show the R-value for only one direction of heat flow if you clearly and conspicuously state that the foil can only be used in that application.

(5) For insulation materials with foil facings, you must follow the rule that applies to the material itself. For example, if you manufacture boardstock with a foil facing, follow paragraph (b)(3) of this section. You can also show the R-value of the insulation when it is installed in conjunction with an air space. This is its "system R-value." If you do this, you must clearly and conspicuously state the conditions under which the system R-value can be attained.

(6) For air duct insulation: the R-value, length, width, thickness, and square feet of insulation in the package.

(c) The following statement: "R means resistance to heat flow. The higher the R-value, the greater the insulating power."

(d) If installation instructions are included on the label or with the package, add this statement: "To get the marked R-value, it is essential that this insulation be installed properly. If you do it yourself, follow the instructions carefully."

(e) If no instructions are included, add this statement: "To get the marked R-value, it is essential that this insulation be installed properly. If you do it yourself, get instructions and follow them carefully. Instructions do not come with this package."

[70 FR 31276, May 31, 2005]

§ 460.13 Fact sheets.

If you are a manufacturer, you must give retailers and installers fact sheets for the insulation products you sell to them. Each sheet must contain what is listed here. You can add any disclosures that are required by federal laws, regulations, rules, or orders. You can add any disclosures that are required by State or local laws, rules, and orders, unless they are inconsistent with the provisions of this regulation. Do not add anything else.

Each fact sheet must contain these items:

(a) The name and address of the manufacturer. It can also include a logo or other symbol that the manufacturer uses.

(b) A heading: "This is _______ insulation." Fill in the blank with the type and form of your insulation.

(c) The heading must be followed by a chart:

(1) If § 460.12(b) requires a chart for your product's label, you must use that chart. For foamed-in-place insulations, you must show the R-value of your product at 3½ inches. You can also show R-values at other thicknesses.

(2) You can put the charts for similar products on the same fact sheet. For example, if you sell insulation boards or batts in three different thicknesses, you can put the label charts for all three products on one fact sheet. If you sell loose-fill insulation in two different bag sizes, you can put both coverage charts on one fact sheet, as long as you state which coverage chart applies to each bag size.

(d) For air duct insulation, the chart must be followed by this statement:

"The R-value of this insulation varies depending on how much it is compressed during installation."

(e) After the chart and any statement dealing with the specific type of insulation, ALL fact sheets must carry this statement, boxed, in 12-point type:

READ THIS BEFORE YOU BUY

What You Should Know About R-values

The chart shows the R-value of this insulation. R means resistance to heat flow. The higher the R-value, the greater the insulating power. Compare insulation R-values before you buy.

There are other factors to consider. The amount of insulation you need depends mainly on the climate you live in. Also, your fuel savings from insulation will depend upon the climate, the type and size of your house, the amount of insulation already in your house, and your fuel use patterns and family size. If you buy too much insulation, it will cost you more than what you'll save on fuel.

To get the marked R-value, it is essential that this insulation be installed properly.

[44 FR 50242, Aug. 27, 1979, as amended at 45 FR 68928, Oct. 17, 1980; 70 FR 31276, May 31, 2005]

§ 460.14 How retailers must handle fact sheets.

If you sell insulation to do-it-yourself customers, you must have fact sheets for the insulation products you sell. You must make the fact sheets available to your customers. You can decide how to do this, as long as your insulation customers are likely to notice them. For example, you can put them in a display, and let customers take copies of them. You can keep them in a binder at a counter or service desk, and have a sign telling customers where the fact sheets are. You need not make the fact sheets available to customers if you display insulation packages on the sales floor where your insulation customers are likely to notice them and each individual insulation package offered for sale contains all package label and fact sheet disclosures required by §§ 460.12 and 460.13.

[70 FR 31276, May 31, 2005]

§ 460.15 How installers must handle fact sheets.

If you are an installer, you must have fact sheets for the insulation products you sell. Before customers agree to buy insulation from you, you must show them the fact sheet(s) for the type(s) of insulation they want. You can decide how to do this. For example, you can give each customer a copy of the fact sheet(s). You can keep the fact sheets in a binder, and show customers the binder before they agree to buy.

§ 460.16 What new home sellers must tell new home buyers.

If you are a new home seller, you must put the following information in every sales contract: The type, thickness, and R-value of the insulation that will be installed in each part of the house. There is an exception to this rule. If the buyer signs a sales contract before you know what type of insulation will be put in the house, or if there is a change in the contract, you can give the buyer a receipt stating this information as soon as you find out.

§ 460.17 What installers must tell their customers.

If you are an installer, you must give your customers a contract or receipt for the insulation you install. For all insulation except loose-fill and aluminum foil, the receipt must show the coverage area, thickness, and R-value of the insulation you installed. The receipt must be dated and signed by the installer. To figure out the R-value of the insulation, use the data that the manufacturer gives you. If you put insulation in more than one part of the house, put the data for each part on the receipt. You can do this on one receipt, as long as you do not add up the coverage areas or R-values for different parts of the house. Do not multiply the R-value for one inch by the number of inches you installed. For loose-fill, the receipt must show the coverage area, initial installed thickness, minimum settled thickness, R-value, and the number of bags used. For aluminum foil, the receipt must show the number and thickness of the air spaces, the direction of heat flow, and the R-value.

[70 FR 31276, May 31, 2005]

§ 460.18 Insulation ads.

(a) If your ad gives an R-value, you must give the type of insulation and the thickness needed to get that R-value. Also, add this statement explaining R-values: "The higher the R-value, the greater the insulating power. Ask your seller for the fact sheet on R-values."

(b) If your ad gives a price, you must give the type of insulation, the R-value at a specific thickness, the statement explaining R-values in paragraph (a) of this section, and the coverage area for that thickness. If you give the price per square foot, you do not have to give the coverage area.

(c) If your ad gives the thickness of your insulation, you must give its R-value at that thickness and the statement explaining R-values in paragraph (a) of this section.

(d) If your ad compares one type of insulation to another, the comparison must be based on the same coverage areas. You must give the R-value at a specific thickness for each insulation, and the statement explaining R-values in paragraph (a) of this section. If you give the price of each insulation, you must also give the coverage area for the price and thickness shown. However, if you give the price per square foot, you do not have to give the coverage area.

(e) The affirmative disclosure requirements in § 460.18 do not apply to ads on television or radio.

[44 FR 50242, Aug. 27, 1979, as amended at 51 FR 39651, Oct. 30, 1986; 70 FR 31276, May 31, 2005]

§ 460.19 Savings claims.

(a) If you say or imply in your ads, labels, or other promotional materials that insulation can cut fuel bills or fuel use, you must have a reasonable basis for the claim. For example, if you say that insulation can "slash" or "lower" fuel bills, or that insulation "saves money," you must have a reasonable basis for the claim. Also, if you say that insulation can "cut fuel use in half," or "lower fuel bills by 30%," you must have a reasonable basis for the claim.

(b) If you say or imply in your ads, labels, or other promotional materials that insulation can cut fuel bills or fuel use, you must make this statement about savings: "Savings vary. Find out why in the seller's fact sheet on R-values. Higher R-values mean greater insulating power."

(c) If you say or imply that a combination of products can cut fuel bills or use, you must have a reasonable basis for the claim. You must make the statement about savings in paragraph (b) of this section. Also, you must list the combination of products used. They may be two or more types of insulation; one or more types of insulation and one or more other insulating products, like storm windows or siding; or insulation for two or more parts of the house, like the attic and walls. You must say how much of the savings came from each product or location. If you cannot give exact or approximate figures, you must give a ranking. For instance, if your ad says that insulation and storm doors combined to cut fuel use by 50%, you must say which one saved more.

(d) If your ad or other promotional material is covered by § 460.18 (a), (b), (c), or (d), and also makes a savings claim, you must follow the rules in §§ 460.18 and 460.19. However, you need not make the statement explaining R-value in § 460.18(a).

(e) Manufacturers are liable if they do not have a reasonable basis for their savings claims before the claim is made. If you are not a manufacturer, you are liable only if you know or should know that the manufacturer does not have a reasonable basis for the claim.

(f) Keep records of all data on savings claims for at least three years. For the records showing proof for claims, the three years will begin again each time you make the claim. Federal Trade Commission staff members can check these records at any time, but they must give you reasonable notice first.

(g) The affirmative disclosure requirements in § 460.19 do not apply to ads on television or radio.

[44 FR 50242, Aug. 27, 1979, as amended at 51 FR 39651, Oct. 30, 1986; 70 FR 31276, May 31, 2005]

§ 460.20 R-value per inch claims.

In labels, fact sheets, ads, or other promotional materials, do not give the R-value for one inch or the "R-value per inch" of your product. There are two exceptions:

(a) If an outstanding FTC Cease and Desist Order applies to you but differs from the rules given here, you can petition to amend the order.

(b) You can do this if actual test results prove that the R-values per inch of your product does not drop as it gets thicker. You can list a range of R-value per inch. If you do, you must say exactly how much the R-value drops with greater thickness. You must also add this statement: "The R-value per inch of this insulation varies with thickness. The thicker the insulation, the lower the R-value per inch."

[44 FR 50242, Aug. 27, 1979, as amended at 70 FR 31276, May 31, 2005]

§ 460.21 Government claims.

Do not say or imply that a government agency uses, certifies, recommends, or otherwise favors your product unless it is true. Do not say or imply that your insulation complies with a governmental standard or specification unless it is true.

§ 460.22 Tax claims.

Do not say or imply that your product qualifies for a tax benefit unless it is true.

§ 460.23 Other laws, rules, and orders.

(a) If an outstanding FTC Cease and Desist Order applies to you but differs from the rules given here, you can petition to amend to order.

(b) State and local laws and regulations that are inconsistent with, or frustrate the purposes of, the provisions of this regulation are preempted. However, a State or local government may petition the Commission, for good cause, to permit the enforcement of any part of a State or local law or regulation that would be preempted by this section.

(c) The Commission's three-day cooling-off rule stays in force.

[44 FR 50242, Aug. 27, 1979, as amended at 70 FR 31276, May 31, 2005]

§ 460.24 Stayed or invalid parts.

If any part of this regulation is stayed or held invalid, the rest of it will stay in force.

Appendix to Part 460—Exemptions

Section 18(g)(2) of the Federal Trade Commission Act, 15 U.S.C. 57a(g)(2), authorizes the Commission to exempt a person or class of persons from all or part of a trade regulation rule if the Commission finds that application of the rule is not necessary to prevent the unfair or deceptive acts or practices to which the rule relates. In response to petitions from industry representatives, the Commission has granted exemptions from specific requirements of 16 CFR part 460 to certain classes of sellers. Some of these exemptions are conditioned upon the performance of alternative actions. The exemptions are limited to specific sections of part 460. All other requirements of part 460 apply to these sellers. The exemptions are summarized below. For an explanation of the scope and application of the exemptions, see the formal Commission decisions in the FEDERAL REGISTER cited at the end of each exemption.

(a) Manufacturers of perlite insulation products that have an inverse relationship between R-value and density or weight per square foot are exempted from the requirements in §§460.12(b)(2) and 460.13(c)(1) that they disclose minimum weight per square foot for R-values listed on labels and fact sheets. This exemption is conditioned upon the alternative disclosure in labels and fact sheets of the maximum weight per square foot for each R-value required to be listed. 46 FR 22179 (1981).

(b) Manufacturers of rigid, flat-roof insulation products used in flat, built-up roofs are exempted from the requirements in §460.12 that they label these home insulation products. 46 FR 22180 (1981).

(c) New home sellers are exempted from:

(1) the requirement in §460.18(a) that they disclose the type and thickness of the insulation when they make a representation in an advertisement or other promotional material about the R-value of the insulation in a new home;

(2) the requirement that they disclose in an advertisement or other promotional material the R-value explanatory statement specified in §460.18(a) or the savings explanatory statement specified in §460.19(b), conditioned upon the new home sellers alternatively disclosing the appropriate explanatory statement in the sales contract along with the disclosures required by §460.16;

(3) the requirement that they make the disclosures specified in §460.19(c) if they claim that insulation, along with other products in a new home, will cut fuel bills or fuel use; and

(4) the requirement that they include the reference to fact sheets when they must disclose the R-value explanatory statement or the savings claim explanatory statement under §460.18(a) or §460.19(b), respectively.

The exemptions for new home sellers also apply to home insulation sellers other than new home sellers when they participate with a new home seller to advertise and promote the sale of new homes, provided that the primary thrust of the advertisement or other promotional material is the promotion of new homes, and not the promotion of the insulation product. 48 FR 31192 (1983).

[61 FR 13666, Mar. 28, 1996]

SUBCHAPTER E—RULES, REGULATIONS, STATEMENT OF GENERAL POLICY OR INTERPRETATION AND EXEMPTIONS UNDER THE FAIR PACKAGING AND LABELING ACT

PART 500—REGULATIONS UNDER SECTION 4 OF THE FAIR PACKAGING AND LABELING ACT

AUTHORITY: 15 U.S.C. 1453, 1454, 1455.

SOURCE: 59 FR 1872, Jan. 12, 1994, unless otherwise noted.

§ 500.1 Scope of the regulations of this part.

The regulations in this part establish requirements for labeling of consumer commodities as hereinafter defined with respect to identity of the commodity; the name and place of business of the manufacturer, packer, or distributor; the net quantity of contents; and net quantity of servings, uses, or applications represented to be present.

§ 500.2 Terms defined.

As used in this part, unless the context otherwise specifically requires:

(a) The term *Act* means the "Fair Packaging and Labeling Act" (Pub. L. 89–755, approved Nov. 3, 1966; 80 Stat. 1296 *et seq.;* 15 U.S.C. 1451 *et seq.*, as amended by Public Law 102–329, August 3, 1992).

(b) The term *regulation* or *regulations* means regulations promulgated by the Commission pursuant to sections 4, 5, and 6 of the Act (15 U.S.C. 1453, 1454, 1455).

(c) The term *consumer commodity* or *commodity* means any article, product, or commodity of any kind or class which is customarily produced or distributed for sale through retail sales agencies or instrumentalities for consumption by individuals, or use by individuals for purposes of personal care or in the performance of services ordinarily rendered within the household, and which usually is consumed or expended in the course of such consumption or use. For purposes of the regulations in this part the term *consumer commodity* does not include any food, drug, device or cosmetic as defined by section 201 of the Federal Food, Drug, and Cosmetic Act (21 U.S.C. 321); any meat or meat product, poultry or poultry product, or tobacco or tobacco product; any commodity subject to packaging or labeling requirements imposed by the Administrator of the Environmental Protection Agency pursuant to the Federal Insecticide, Fungicide, and Rodenticide Act (7 U.S.C. 136 *et seq.*); any commodity subject to the provisions of the eighth paragraph under the heading "Bureau of Animal Industry" of the Virus-Serum-Toxin Act (21 U.S.C. 151–157); any beverage subject to or complying with packaging or labeling requirements imposed under the Federal Alcohol Administration Act (27 U.S.C. 201 *et seq.*); any commodity subject to the provisions of the Federal Seed Act (7 U.S.C. 1551–1610).

(d) The term *package* means any container or wrapping in which any consumer commodity is enclosed for use in the delivery or display of that commodity to retail purchasers. For purposes of the regulations in this part the term *package* does not include shipping containers or wrappings used solely for the transportation of any consumer commodity in bulk or in quantity to manufacturers, packers, or processors, or to wholesale or retail distributors thereof unless used in retail display; shipping containers or outer wrappings used by retailers to ship or deliver any commodity to retail customers if such containers and wrappings bear no printed matter pertaining to any particular commodity; or containers subject to the provisions of the Act of August 3, 1912 (37 Stat. 250, as amended; 15 U.S.C. 231–233), the Act of March 4, 1915 (38 Stat. 1186, as amended; 15 U.S.C. 234–236); or transparent wrappers or containers which do not bear written, printed, or graphic matter obscuring any part of the label information required by this part.

(e) The term *label* means any written, printed, or graphic matter affixed to or appearing upon any consumer commodity or affixed to or appearing upon a package containing any consumer commodity; except that:

(1) An inspector's tag or other nonpromotional matter affixed to or appearing upon a consumer commodity shall not be deemed to be a label requiring the repetition of label information required by this part, and

(2) For the purposes of the regulations in this part the term *label* does not include written, printed, or graphic matter affixed to or appearing upon commodities, or affixed to or appearing upon containers or wrappers for commodities sold or distributed to industrial or institutional users.

(f) The term *person* includes any firm, corporation or associations.

(g) The term *commerce* means:

(1) Commerce between any State, the District of Columbia, the Commonwealth of Puerto Rico, or any territory or possession of the United States, and any place outside thereof, and

(2) Commerce within the District of Columbia or within any territory or possession of the United States, not organized with a legislature, but shall not include exports to foreign countries.

(h) The term *principal display panel* means that part of a label that is most likely to be displayed, presented, shown, or examined under normal and customary conditions of display for retail sale. The principal display panel must be large enough to accommodate all the mandatory label information required to be placed thereon by this part without obscuring designs, vignettes, or crowding. This definition does not preclude utilization of alternate principal display panels on a label of a package, but alternate principal display panels must duplicate the information required to be placed on the principal display panel by this part. This definition does not preclude utilization of the container closure as the surface bearing the principal display panel if that label location is the one most likely to be displayed, presented, shown, or examined under normal and customary conditions of display for retail sale. The principal display panel of a label appearing on a cylindrical surface is that 40 percent of the circumference which is more likely to be displayed, presented, shown, or examined under normal and customary conditions of display for retail sale. The principal display panel of a consumer commodity marketed in a decorative type container, or a container having a capacity of ¼ ounce (7.4 mL) or less, may be considered to be a tear-away tag or tape affixed to the container and bearing the mandatory label information as required by this part, but the type size of the net quantity of contents statement shall be governed by the dimensions of the container itself.

The principal display panel of a consumer commodity marketed on a display card to which the immediate container of the commodity is affixed may be considered to be the display panel of the card, and the type size of the net quantity of contents statement is governed by the dimensions of the display card.

(i) The term *random package* means a package which is one of a lot, shipment, or delivery of packages of the same consumer commodity with varying weights, that is, packages with no fixed weight pattern.

(j) The term *SI metric* refers to units belonging to the International System of Units (abbreviated "SI" from the French, *Le Systeme International d'Unites*), as interpreted or modified for use in the United States by the Secretary of Commerce. They include the SI units (together with their multiples and submultiples) as well as other metric units (e.g., the liter) that are accepted for use with the SI units because of their practical importance.

(k) The term *customary inch/pound* refers to units belonging to the system of units used in the United States based on or derived from the ounce, pound, and ton for weight; the inch, foot, yard, and mile for length; the fluid ounce, pint, quart, and gallon for volume; and dry pint, dry quart, peck, and bushel for dry measure.

(l) The term *"e" mark* refers to the symbol "e" used in connection with the quantity declarations on labels of some consumer commodities marketed primarily in the European Community (EC). The "e" mark constitutes a representation by the packer or importer that the package to which it is applied has been filled in accordance with the average system of quantity specified by the EC. The average system is a method of declaring package fill in the EC and other countries of the world, including the United States.

§ 500.3 Prohibited acts, coverage, general labeling requirements, exemption procedures.

(a) No person engaged in the packaging or labeling of any consumer commodity for distribution in commerce, and no person (other than a common carrier for hire, or a freight forwarder for hire) engaged in the distribution in commerce of any packaged or labeled consumer commodity, shall distribute or cause to be distributed in commerce any such commodity if such commodity is contained in a package, or if there is affixed to that commodity a label, which does not conform to the provisions of the Act and of the regulations in this part.

(b) Persons engaged in business as wholesale or retail distributors of consumer commodities shall be subject to the Act and the regulations in this part to the extent that such persons are engaged in the packaging or labeling of consumer commodities, or prescribe or specify by any means the manner in which such consumer commodities are packaged or labeled.

(c) Each packaged or labeled consumer commodity, unless it has been exempted through proceedings under section 5(b) of the Act (15 U.S.C. 1454(b)), shall, upon being prepared for distribution in commerce or for sale at retail, and before being distributed in commerce or offered for sale at retail, be labeled in accordance with the requirements of the Act and the regulations in this part.

(d) Each packaged or labeled consumer commodity, unless it has been exempted through proceedings under section 5(b) of the Act, shall bear a label specifying the identity of the commodity; the name and place of business of the manufacturer, packer, or distributor; the net quantity of contents; and the net quantity per serving, use or application, where there is a label representation as to the number of servings, uses, or applications obtainable from the commodity. Many products exempted through proceedings under section 5(b) of the Act and section 500.3(e) of this chapter or excluded under part 503 of this chapter nonetheless fall within the purview of the weights-and-measures laws of the individual states.

(e) Regulations will be promulgated by the Commission exempting particular consumer commodities from one or more of the requirements of section 4 of the Act and the regulations thereunder to the extent and under such conditions as are consistent with the declared policy of the Act whenever the Commission finds that, because of the nature, form, or quantity of the particular consumer commodity, or for other good and sufficient reasons, full compliance with all the requirements otherwise applicable is impracticable or is not necessary for the adequate protection of consumers. Proceedings for the promulgation of such exempting regulations may be commenced by the Commission upon its own initiative or pursuant to petition filed with the Secretary by any interested person or group stating reasonable grounds for the proposed exemption, pursuant to §1.15 of this chapter of the Commission's general procedures.

[59 FR 1872, Jan. 12, 1994, as amended at 80 FR 71689, Nov. 17, 2015]

§ 500.4 Statement of identity.

(a) The principal display panel of a consumer commodity shall bear a specification of the identity of the commodity.

(b) Such specification of identity shall comprise a principal feature of the principal display panel, shall be in such type size and so positioned as to render it easily read and understood by the consumer, and shall be in lines generally parallel to the base on which the package or commodity rests as it is designed to be displayed.

(c) Such specification of identity shall be in terms of:

(1) The name now or hereafter specified in or required by any applicable Federal law or regulation; or in the absence thereof,

(2) The common or usual name of the commodity; or in the absence thereof,

(3) The generic name or in other appropriately descriptive terms such as a specification which includes a statement of function.

(d) The specification of identity shall not be false, misleading, or deceptive in any respect. Ingredients or components which are not present in the commodity in a substantial or significantly effective amount may not be mentioned in the specification of identity; except that a component present in a formulation in substantial and effective amounts, but not present in the final product due to conversion or transformation into a different entity (which different entity is present in the final product), may be mentioned in the specification of identity.

§ 500.5 Name and place of business of manufacturer, packer or distributor.

(a) The label of a consumer commodity shall specify conspicuously the name and place of business of the manufacturer, packer, or distributor. Where the consumer commodity is not manufactured by the person whose name appears on the label, the name shall be qualified by a phrase that reveals the connection such person has with such commodity; such as "Manufactured for _____," "Distributed by _____," or any other wording that expresses the facts.

(b) The requirement for declaration of the manufacturer, packer, or distributor shall in the case of a corporation be deemed to be satisfied only by the actual corporate name, which may be preceded or followed by the name of the particular division of the corporation. In the case of an individual, partnership, or association, the name under which the business is conducted shall be used.

(c) The statement of the place of business shall include the street address, city, state, and zip code; however, the street address may be omitted if it is listed in a readily accessible, widely published, and publicly available resource, including but not limited to a printed directory, electronic database, or Web site.

(d) If a person manufactures, packs, or distributes a consumer commodity at a place other than his principal place of business, the label may state the principal place of business in lieu of the actual place where such consumer commodity was manufactured or packed or is to be distributed, unless such statement would be misleading.

(e) Standard abbreviations may be used in complying with the requirements of this section.

[59 FR 1872, Jan. 12, 1994, as amended at 80 FR 71689, Nov. 17, 2015]

§ 500.6 Net quantity of contents declaration, location.

(a) The label of a consumer commodity shall bear a declaration of the net quantity of contents separately and accurately stated on the principal display panel.

(b) The declaration of net quantity shall appear as a distinct item on the principal display panel, shall be separated (by at least a space equal to the height of the lettering used in the declaration) from other printed label information appearing above or below the declaration and, shall not include any term qualifying a unit of weight or mass, measure, or count such as "jumbo quart," "giant liter," "full gallon," "when packed," "minimum," or words of similar import. The declaration of net quantity shall be separated (by at least a space equal to twice the width of the letter "N" of the style of type used in the net quantity statement) from other printed label information appearing to the left or right of the declaration. However, the "e" mark shall not be considered to be a qualifying word or phrase and may be used as part of the statement of the net quantity of contents where warranted. When used, the "e" mark shall be at least 3 millimeters (approximately ⅛ in) in height. The declaration of net quantity of contents shall be placed on the principal display panel within the bottom 30 percent of the area of the label panel in lines generally parallel to the base on which the package or commodity rests as it is designed to be displayed: *Provided*, that:

(1) On consumer commodities having a principal display panel of 5 square inches (32.2 cm^2) or less, the requirement for placement within the bottom 30 percent of the area of the label panel shall not apply when the declaration of net quantity of contents meets the other requirements of this part, and

(2) The requirements as to separation, location, and type size, specified in this part are waived with respect to variety and combination packages as defined in this part.

§ 500.7 Net quantity of contents, method of expression.

The net quantity of contents shall be expressed in terms of weight or mass, measure, numerical count, or a combination of numerical count and weight or mass, size, or measure so as to give accurate information regarding the net quantity of contents thereof, and thereby facilitate value comparisons by consumers. The net quantity of contents statement shall be in terms of fluid measure if the commodity is liquid, or in terms of weight or mass if the commodity is solid, semi-solid, or viscous, or a mixture of solid and liquid. If there is a firmly established general consumer usage and trade custom of declaring the contents of a liquid by weight or mass, or a solid, semi-solid, or viscous product by fluid measure, numerical count, and/or size, or (as in the case of lawn and plant care products) by cubic measure, it may be used, when such declaration provides sufficient information to facilitate value comparisons by consumers. The declaration may appear in more than one line of print or type.

§ 500.8 Units of weight or mass and measure.

(a) Statements of weight or mass shall be in terms of both avoirdupois pound and ounce and SI metric kilograms, grams, or milligrams. (Examples of avoirdupois/metric declarations: "Net Wt 15 oz (425 g)" or "Net Wt 1½ lbs (680 g)" or " 2.5 oz (70.8 g)"; examples of metric/avoirdupois declarations: "Net Mass 425 g (15 oz)" or "Net Mass 680 g (1½ lbs)" or "100 g e (3.5 oz).")

(b) Statements of fluid measure shall be in terms of both the U.S. gallon of 231 cubic inches and quart, pint, and fluid ounce subdivisions thereof and SI metric liters or milliliters and shall (except in the case of petroleum products, for which the declaration shall express the volume at 60 °Fahrenheit (15.6 °Celsius)) express the volume at 68 °Fahrenheit (20 °Celsius). (Examples of gallon/metric declarations: "Net 12 fl oz (354 mL)" or "Net Contents 1 gal (3.78 L)" or "8 fl oz (236 mL)"; examples of metric/gallon declarations: "Net 500 mL (1.05 pt)" or "Net Contents 1 L (1.05 qt).")

(c) Statements of linear measure shall be in terms of both yards, feet, and inches and SI metric meters, centimeters, or millimeters.

(d) Statements of measure of area shall be in terms of both square yards, square feet, and square inches and SI metric square meters, square decimeters, square centimeters, or square millimeters.

(e) Statements of dry measure shall be in terms of both the U.S. bushel of 2,150.42 cubic inches and peck, dry quart, and dry pint subdivisions thereof and SI metric liters or milliliters.

(f) Statements of cubic measure shall be in terms of both cubic yard, cubic foot, and cubic inch and SI metric cubic meters, cubic decimeters, or cubic centimeters.

§ 500.9 Units of weight or mass, how expressed.

(a) The term *net weight* or *net mass* may be used in stating the net quantity of contents in terms of weight or mass. However, where the term "net weight" or "net mass" is not used, the quantity of contents shall always disclose the net quantity of contents. For example: "453 g (1 lb)" or "Net Wt 1 lb (453 g)" or "Net Mass 453 g (1 lb)".

(b) With the exception of random packages, the statement of net quantity of contents in terms of avoirdupois weight shall be expressed as follows:

(1) If less than 1 pound, in terms of ounces. (Examples: "Net Weight 12 oz. (340 g)" or "Net Mass 340 g (12 oz)".)

(2) If at least 1 pound but less than 4 pounds, in whole pounds, with any remainder in ounces or common or decimal fractions of the pound, except that it shall be optional to include an immediately adjacent additional expression of net quantity in terms of ounces.

(*Examples:* "Net Wt. 1 lb. 8 oz. (680 g)" or "Net Wt. 1.5 lb./24 oz. (680 g)" or "24 oz. (1½ lb.) 680 g".)

(3) If 4 pounds or more, in terms of whole pounds, with any remainder in terms of ounces or common or decimal fractions of the pound, except that it shall be optional to include an immediately adjacent additional expression of net quantity in terms of ounces. (Examples: "Net Weight 5 pounds 4 ounces (2.38 kg)" or "Net Mass 2.38 kg (5 lbs 4 oz)" or "Net Wt. 5¼ lbs. (2.38 kg)" or "Net Mass 2.38 kg (5¼ lbs.)" or "Net Wt. 5.25 lbs. (2.38 kg) or "Net Mass 2.38 kg (5.25 lbs)".)

(c) If the net quantity of contents declaration appears on a random package it may, when the net weight exceeds 1 pound, be expressed in terms of pounds and decimal fractions of the pound carried out to not more than three decimal places. When the net weight does not exceed 1 pound, the declaration on the random package may be in terms of decimal fractions of the pound in lieu of ounces. (Examples: "Net Wt. 0.75 lb." and "Net Weight 1.05 pounds.") Such decimal declaration shall be exempt from the type size and placement requirements of section 4(a) of the Act if the accurate statement of net weight is presented prominently and conspicuously on the principal display panel of the package. The net quantity of contents declaration on a random package is not required to, but may include a statement in terms of the SI metric system carried out to not more than 3 decimal places.

(d) It is sufficient to distinguish avoirdupois ounce from fluid ounce through association of terms. (Examples: "Net Wt. 6 oz." vs. "6 fl. oz." or "Net Contents 6 fl. oz.")

§ 500.10 Units of fluid measure, how expressed.

(a) Use of the terms "net" or "net contents" is optional.

(b) Declaration of net quantity of contents in terms of fluid measure shall be identified as such in each instance and the statement of U.S. gallon of 231 cubic inches and quart, pint, and fluid ounce subdivisions thereof shall be expressed as follows:

(1) If less than 1 pint, in terms of fluid ounces. (Example: "Net Contents 8 fl. oz. (236 mL)" or "Net Contents 236 mL (8 fl. oz.)".)

(2) If at least 1 pint but less than 1 gallon, in terms of the largest whole unit (quarts, quarts and pints or pints, as appropriate), with any remainder in terms of fluid ounces or common or decimal fractions of the pint or quart, except that it shall be optional to include an immediately adjacent additional expression of net quantity in terms of fluid ounces. (Examples: "1 qt. (946 mL)" or "Net contents 1 qt. 1 pt. 8 oz./56 fl. oz. (1.65 L)", but not in terms of quart and ounce such as "1 quart 24 ounces (1.65 L)".)

(3) If 1 gallon or more, in terms of the largest whole unit (gallons followed by common or decimal fractions of a gallon or by the next smaller whole unit or units viz, quarts and pints) with any remainder in terms of fluid ounces or

common or decimal fractions of the pint or quart, except that it shall be optional to include an immediately adjacent additional expression of net quantity in terms of fluid ounces.

(*Examples:* "Net contents 2½ gal. (9.46 L)", "Contents 2.5 gal. (9.46 L)", or "Net contents 2 gallons 2 quarts (9.46 L)" but not as "2 gallons 4 pints (9.46 L)".)

§ 500.11 Measurement of commodity length, how expressed.

Declaration of net quantity in terms of yards, feet, and inches shall be expressed as follows:

(a) If less than 1 foot, in terms of inches and fractions thereof.

(b) If 1 foot or more, in terms of the largest whole unit (a yard or foot) with any remainder in terms of inches or common or decimal fractions of the foot or yard, except that it shall be optional to express the length in the preceding manner followed by a statement of the length in terms of inches.

§ 500.12 Measurement of commodities by length and width, how expressed.

For bidimensional commodities (including roll-type commodities) measured in terms of commodity length and width, the declaration of net quantity of contents shall be expressed in the following manner:

(a) The declaration of net quantity for bidimensional commodities having a width of more than 4 inches (10.1 cm) shall:

(1) When the commodity has an area of less than 1 square foot (929 cm^2) be expressed in terms of length and width in linear measure. The customary inch/pound statement is to be expressed in inches and fractions thereof.

(2) When the commodity has an area of 1 square foot (929 cm^2) or more, but less than 4 square feet (37.1 dm^2), be expressed in terms of area, followed by the length and width. The customary inch/pound statement of area is to be expressed in square inches with length and width expressed in the largest whole unit (yard or foot) with any remainder in inches or common or decimal fractions of the yard or foot except that a dimension of less than 2 feet (60.9 cm) may be stated in inches. Commodities consisting of usable individual units (e.g., paper napkins) while requiring a declaration of unit area need not declare the total area of all such individual units.

(3) When the commodity has an area of 4 square feet (37.1 dm^2) or more, be expressed in terms of area, followed by the length and width. The customary inch/pound statement of area is to be expressed in square feet with the length and width expressed in the largest whole units (yards or feet) with any remainder in terms of inches or common or decimal fractions of the foot or yard except that a dimension of less than 2 feet (60.96 cm) may be stated in inches.

(4) For any commodity for which the quantity of contents is required by paragraph (a) (2) or (3) of this section to include a declaration of the linear dimensions, the quantity of contents, in addition to being declared in the manner prescribed by the appropriate provisions of this regulation, may also include, after the customary inch/pound statement of the linear dimensions of the largest unit of measurement, a parenthetical declaration of the linear dimensions of said commodity in terms of inches.

(*Example:* "25 sq. ft. (12 in. × 8.33 yd.) (12 in. × 300 in.) 42.32 m^2 (30.4 cm × 7.62 m)".)

(b) For bidimensional commodities having a width of 4 inches (10.16 cm) or less, the declaration of net quantity shall be expressed in terms of width and length in linear measure. The customary inch/pound statement of width shall be expressed in terms of linear inches and fractions thereof, and length shall be expressed in the largest whole unit (yard or foot) with any remainder in terms of the common or decimal fractions of the yard or foot, except that it shall be optional to express the length in the largest whole unit followed by a statement of length in inches or to express the length in inches followed by a statement of length in the largest whole unit.

(*Example:* "2 inches × 10 yards (5.08 cm × 9.14 m)", "2 inches × 10 yards (360 inches) 5.08 cm × 9.14 m", or "2 inches × 360 inches (10 yards) 5.08 cm × 9.14 m".)

§ 500.13 Measurement of commodities by area measure only, how expressed.

For commodities measured in terms of area measure only declaration of net quantity in terms of square yards, square feet, and square inches shall be expressed in the following manner:

(a) If less than 1 square foot (929 cm^2), in terms of square inches and fractions thereof.

(b) If at least 1 square foot (929 cm^2) but less than 4 square feet (37.1 dm^2), in terms of square feet with any remainder in terms of square inches or common or decimal fractions of the square foot.

(c) If 4 square feet (37.1 dm^2) or more, in terms of the largest appropriate whole unit (square yards, square yards and square feet, or square feet) with any remainder in terms of square inches or common or decimal fractions of the square foot or square yard.

§ 500.14 Statements of cubic measure and dry measure.

Statements of cubic measure and dry measure shall be expressed in terms most appropriate to the providing of accurate information as to the net quantity of contents, and to the facilitating of value comparisons by consumers. When the content declaration on a commodity sold in compressed form is stated in terms of cubic measure there may also be a statement indicating the amount of material from which the final product was compressed. Such statement shall not exceed the actual amount of material that can be recovered.

§ 500.15 Units of count, more than one ply.

If the commodity is in distinct usable units made up of one or more components or ply, the statement of net quantity of contents shall (in addition to complying with the requirements of linear and area measurement declaration for each unit as specified in § 500.12) include the number of ply and the total number of usable units.

(*Example:* "100 2-ply facial tissues, 8½ inches × 10 inches" (21.5 × 25.4 cm).)

For the purposes of this section, roll type commodities (e.g. paper towels), irrespective of perforations, shall not be considered to be usable units, and shall be labeled in terms of total area measurement and the number of ply. Such area measurement, however, shall be supplemented by a count statement and the dimensions of a single unit.

§ 500.16 Measurement of container type commodities, how expressed.

Notwithstanding other provisions of this part 500 of the regulations pertaining to the expression of net quantity of contents by measurement, commodities designed and sold at retail to be used as containers for other materials or objects, such as bags, cups, boxes, and pans, shall be labeled in accordance with the following paragraphs:

(a) The declaration of net quantity for container commodities shall be expressed as follows:

(1) For bag type commodities, in terms of count followed by linear dimensions of the bag (whether packaged in a perforated roll or otherwise) Net quantity of contents in terms of feet and inches shall be expressed as follows:

(i) When the unit bag is characterized by two dimensions because of the absence of a gusset, the width and length will be expressed in inches, except that a dimension of 2 feet or more will be expressed in feet with any remainder in terms of inches or common or decimal fractions of the foot.

(*Example:* "25 bags, 17 in. × 20 in. (43.1 × 50.8 cm)" or "200 bags, 20 in. × 2 ft. 6 in. (50.8 × 76.2 cm)", or "50 bags, 20 in. × 2½ ft. (50.8 × 76.2 cm)".)

(ii) When the unit bag is gussetted, the dimensions will be expressed as width, depth and length in terms of inches except that any dimensions of 2 feet or more will be expressed in feet with any remainder in terms of inches or the common or decimal fractions of the foot.

(*Examples:* "25 bags, 17 in. × 4 in. × 20 in. (43 × 10 × 50 cm)", or "200 bags, 20 in. × 12 in. × 2½ ft. (50.8 × 30.4 × 76.2 cm)".)

(2) For other square, oblong, rectangular or similarly shaped containers, in terms of count followed by length, width, and depth except depth need not

be listed when less than 2 inches (5.08 cm).

(*Example:* "2 cake pans, 8 in. × 8 in. (20.3 × 20.3 cm)", or "roasting pan, 12 in. × 8 in. × 3 in. (30.4 × 20.3 × 7.62 cm)".)

(3) For circular or other generally round shaped containers, except cups, and the like, in terms of count followed by diameter and depth except depth need not be listed when less than 2 inches (5.08 cm).

(*Example:* "4 pie pans, 8 in. diameter (20.3 cm)" or "2 cake pans, 8 in. diameter × 4 in. (20.3 × 10.1 cm)".)

(b) When the functional use of the container is related by label reference in standard terms of measure to the capability of holding a specific quantity of substance or class of substances such references shall be a part of the net quantity statement and shall specify capacity as follows:

(1) Liquid measure for containers which are intended to be used for liquids, semi-solids, viscous materials or mixtures of solids and liquids. The customary inch/pound statement of capacity shall be stated in terms of the largest whole U.S. gallon of 231 cubic inches, quart, pint, or ounce with any remainder in terms of the common or decimal fraction of that unit.

(*Example:* Freezer Boxes: "4 boxes, 1 qt. capacity, 6 in. × 6 in. × 4 in. (946 mL capacity, 15.2 × 15.2 × 10.1 cm)".)

(2) Dry measure for containers which are intended to be used for solids. The customary inch/pound statement of capacity shall be stated in terms of the largest whole U.S. bushel of 2,150.42 cubic inches, peck, dry quart, or dry pint with any remainder in terms of the common or decimal fraction of that unit.

(*Example:* Leaf Bags: "8 bags, 6 bushel capacity, 4 feet × 5 feet (211 L capacity—1.21 m × 1.52 m)".)

(3) Where containers are used as liners for other more permanent containers, in the same terms as are normally used to express the capacity of the more permanent container.

(*Example:* Garbage Can Liners: "10 liners, 2 ft. 6 in. × 3 ft. 1 in., fits up to 30 gallon cans (76.2 × 93.9 cm, fits up to 113 L cans".)

(c) Notwithstanding the above requirements, the net quantity statement for containers such as cups will be listed in terms of count and liquid capacity per unit.

(*Example:* "24 cups, 6 fl. oz. capacity (177 mL)".)

(d) For purposes of this section, the use of the terms "capacity," "diameter," and "fluid" is optional.

§ 500.17 Fractions.

(a) SI metric declarations of net quantity of contents of any consumer commodity may contain only decimal fractions. Other declarations of net quantity of contents may contain common or decimal fractions. A common fraction shall be in terms of halves, quarters, eighths, sixteenths, or thirty-seconds; except that:

(1) If there exists a firmly established general consumer usage and trade custom of employing different common fractions in the net quantity declaration of a particular commodity, they may be employed, and

(2) If linear measurements are required in terms of yards or feet, common fractions may be in terms of thirds. A common fraction shall be reduced to its lowest terms; a decimal fraction shall not be carried out to more than three places.

(b) If a statement includes small fractions, smaller variations in the actual size or weight of the commodity will be permitted as provided in § 500.25, than in cases where the larger fractions or whole numbers are used.

§ 500.18 SI metric prefixes.

The following chart indicates SI prefixes that may be used on a broad range of consumer commodity labels:

Prefix	Symbol	Multiplying factor [1]
Kilo-	k	$\times 10^3$
Deca-	da	$\times 10$
Deci-	d	$\times 10^{-1}$
Centi-	c	$\times 10^{-2}$
Milli-	m	$\times 10^{-3}$
Micro-	μ	$\times 10^{-6}$

[1] 10^2=100; 10^3=1000; 10^{-1}=0.1; 10^{-2}=0.01.

Thus, 2 kg=2 × 1000 g=2000 g, and 3 cm=3 × 0.01 m=0.03 m.

§ 500.19 Conversion of SI metric quantities to inch/pound quantities and inch/pound quantities to SI metric quantities.

(a) For calculating the conversion of SI metric quantities to and from customary inch/pound quantities, the conversion chart published in the following handbook shall be employed: National Institute of Standards and Technology (NIST) Handbook 133, Checking the Net Contents of Packaged Goods, Appendix E—General Tables of Units of Measurements, 2015 Edition, adopted November 2014. This incorporation by reference was approved by the Director of the Federal Register in accordance with 5 U.S.C. 552(a) and 1 CFR part 51. You may obtain a copy of NIST Handbook 133 at the National Institute of Standards and Technology's Web site, *http://www.nist.gov/pml/wmd/pubs/hb133.cfm.* You may inspect a copy at FTC Library, (202) 326–2395, Federal Trade Commission, Room H–630, 600 Pennsylvania Avenue NW., Washington, DC 20580, or at the National Archives and Records Administration (NARA). For information on the availability of this material at NARA, call 202–741–6030, or go to: *http://www.archives.gov/federal-register/cfr/ibr-locations.html.*

(b) The SI metric quantity declaration should be shown in three digits except where the quantity is below 100 grams, milliliters, centimeters, square centimeters or cubic centimeters, where it can be shown in two figures. In either case, any final zero appearing to the right of a decimal point need not be shown.

(*Examples:* "1 lb (453 g)" not "1 lb (453.592 g)"; "Net Wt. 2 oz (56 g)" or "Net Wt 2 oz (56.6 g)" not "Net Wt. 2 oz (56.69 g)".)

[59 FR 1872, Jan. 12, 1994, as amended at 80 FR 71689, Nov. 17, 2015]

§ 500.20 Conspicuousness.

The statement of net quantity of contents shall appear in conspicuous and easily legible boldface type or print in distinct contrast (by typography, layout, color, embossing, or molding) to other matter on the package; except that a statement of net quantity blown, embossed, or molded on a glass or plastic surface is permissible when all label information is so formed on the surface.

§ 500.21 Type size in relationship to the area of the principal display panel.

(a) The statement of net quantity of contents shall be in letters and numerals in a type size established in relationship to the area of the principal display panel of the package or commodity and shall be uniform for all packages or commodities of substantially the same size. For this purpose, "area of the principal display panel" means the area of the side or surface that bears the principal display panel, exclusive of tops, bottoms, flanges at tops and bottoms of cans, and shoulders and necks of bottles and jars. This area shall be:

(1) In the case of a rectangular package or commodity where one entire side properly can be considered to be a principal display panel side, the product of the height times the width of that side;

(2) In the case of a cylindrical or nearly cylindrical container or commodity, 40 percent of the product of the height of the container or commodity times the circumference; and

(3) In the case of any otherwise shaped container or commodity, 40 percent of the total surface of the container or commodity: *Provided*, however, that where such container or commodity presents an obvious "principal display panel" such as the top of a triangular or oval shaped container, the area shall consist of the entire top surface.

(b) With area of principal display panel defined as above, the type size in relationship to area of that panel shall comply with the following specifications:

(1) Not less than 1⁄16 inch (1.5 mm) in height on packages the principal display panel of which has an area of 5 square inches or (32.2 cm^2) less.

(2) Not less than 1⁄8 inch (3.1 mm) in height on packages the principal display panel of which has an area of more than 5 (32.2 cm^2) but not more than 25 square inches (161 cm^2).

(3) Not less than 3⁄16 inch (4.7 mm) in height on packages the principal display panel of which has an area of more

than 25 (161 cm²) but not more than 100 square inches (6.45 dm²).

(4) Not less than ¼ inch (6.35 mm) in height on packages the principal display panel of which has an area of more than 100 square inches (6.45 dm²), except not less than ½ (12.7 mm) inch in height if the area is more than 400 square inches (25.8 dm²).

(c) Where the statement of net quantity of contents is blown, embossed, or molded on a glass or plastic surface rather than by printing, typing, or coloring, the lettering sizes specified in paragraph (b) of this section shall be increased by 1⁄16 of an inch (1.5 mm).

(d) Letter heights pertain to upper case or capital letters. When upper and lower case or all lower case letters are used, it is the lower case letter "o" or its equivalent that shall meet the minimum standards.

(e) The ratio of height to width of a letter shall not exceed a differential of 3 units to 1 unit (no more than 3 times as high as it is wide).

(f) When fractions are used, each component shall meet one-half the minimum height standards.

(g) The type size requirements specified in this section do not apply to the "e" mark. (See § 500.6(b).)

(h) When upper and lower case or all lowercase letters are used in SI metric symbols, it is the uppercase "L," lowercase "d," or their equivalent in the print or type used that shall meet the minimum height requirement. Other letters and exponents must be presented in the same type style and in proportion to the type size used. However, no letter shall be less than 1.6 mm (1⁄16 inch) in height.

§ 500.22 Abbreviations.

The following abbreviations and none other may be employed in the required net quantity declaration:

Inch—in.
Feet or foot—ft.
Fluid—fl.
Liquid—liq.
Ounce—oz.
Gallon—gal.
Pint—pt.
Pound—lb.
Quart—qt.
Square—sq.
Weight—wt.
Yard—yd.
Avoirdupois—avdp.
Cubic—cu.

NOTE: Periods and plural forms shall be optional. Exponents are permitted.

[80 FR 71689, Nov. 17, 2015]

§ 500.23 Expression of net quantity of contents in SI Metric units.

(a) The selected multiple or submultiple prefixes for SI metric units shall result in numerical values between 1 and 1000, except that centimeters or millimeters may be used where a length declaration is less than 100 centimeters. For example, "1.96 kg" instead of "1960 g" and "750 mL" instead of "0.75 L".

(b) The following symbols for SI metric units and none others may be employed in the required net quantity declaration:

centimeter—cm
cubic centimeter—cm³
cubic decimeter—dm³
meter—m
milligram—mg
liter—L or l
milliliter—mL or ml
square decimeter—dm²
cubic meter—m³
kilogram—kg
micrometer—μm
gram—g
millimeter—mm
square meter—m²
square centimeter—cm²

NOTE: Symbols, except for liter, are not capitalized. Periods should not be used after the symbol. Symbols are always written in the singular form.

§ 500.24 Supplemental statements.

Nothing contained in the regulations in this part shall prohibit supplemental statements, at locations other than the principal display panel, describing in non-deceptive terms the net quantity of contents: *Provided* that such supplemental statements of net quantity of contents shall not include any term qualifying a unit of weight or mass, measure, or count that tends to exaggerate the amount of commodity contained in the package. (Examples of prohibited language are: "Giant Quart," "Jumbo Liter," "Full Gallon," "When Packed," "Minimum," or words of similar import.) Required combination declarations of net quantity of contents (for example, a combination of net weight or mass plus numerical count, numerical count plus dimensions of the commodity, etc.) are not regarded as supplemental net quantity statements and shall be located on the principal display panel. Dilution directions or other similar directions for use are not regarded as supplemental net quantity statements and may be located on the principal display panel. Size characterizations in compliance with standards promulgated under section 5(c)(1) of the Act may appear on the principal display panel.

§500.25 Net quantity, average quantity, permitted variations.

(a) The statement of net quantity of contents shall accurately reveal the quantity of the commodity in the container exclusive of wrappers and other material packed therewith: *Provided*, that in the case of a commodity packed in a container designed to deliver the commodity under pressure, the statement shall declare the net quantity of the contents that will be expelled when the instructions for use are followed. The propellant is included in the net quantity statement.

(b) Variations from the stated weight or mass or measure shall be permitted when caused by ordinary and customary exposure, after the commodity is introduced into interstate commerce, to conditions which normally occur in good distribution practice and which unavoidably result in change of weight or mass or measure.

(c) Variations from the stated weight or mass, measure, or numerical count shall be permitted when caused by unavoidable deviations in weighing, measuring, or counting the contents of individual packages which occur in good packaging practice: *Provided*, that such variations shall not be permitted to such extent that the average of the quantities in the packages comprising a shipment or other delivery of the commodity is below the quantity stated, and no unreasonable shortage in any package will be permitted even though overages in other packages in the same shipment or delivery compensate for such shortage. Variations from stated quantity of contents shall not be unreasonably large.

§500.26 Representations of servings, uses, applications.

(a) The label of any packaged consumer commodity which bears a representation as to the number of servings, uses, or applications of such commodity contained in such package shall bear in immediate conjunction therewith, and in letters the same size as those used for such representations, a statement of the net quantity (in terms of weight or mass, measure, or numerical count) of each such serving, use, or application: *Provided*, that such statement may be expressed in terms that differ from terms used in the required statement of net contents (e.g., cupsful, tablespoonful, etc.), when such differing terms describe a constant quantity. Such statement may not be misleading in any particular.

(b) Representations as to the total amount of object or objects to which the commodity may be applied or upon which or in which the commodity may be used, will not be considered to be representations as to servings, uses, or applications, if such amount is expressed in terms of standard units of weight or mass, measure, size, or count.

(c) If there exists a voluntary product standard promulgated pursuant to the procedures found in 15 CFR part 10, by the Department of Commerce, quantitatively defining the meaning of the terms *serving*, *use*, or *application* with respect to a particular consumer commodity, then any label representation as to the number of servings, uses, or applications in such packaged consumer commodity shall correspond with such quantitative definition. (Copies of published standards will be available upon request from the National Institute of Standards and Technology, Department of Commerce, Washington, DC 20899.)

§500.27 Multiunit packages.

(a) A multiunit package is a package intended for retail sale, containing two or more individual packaged or labeled units of an identical commodity in the same quantity. The declaration of net quantity of contents of a multiunit package shall be expressed as follows:

(1) The number of individual packaged or labeled units;

(2) The quantity of each individual packaged or labeled unit; and

(3) The total quantity of the multiunit package.

Examples: Soap bars: "6 Bars, Net Wt. 3.4 ozs. (96.3 g) each, Total Net Wt. 1 lb. 4.4 oz. (578 g)" Facial Tissues: "10 Packs, each 25 two-ply tissues, 9.7 in. × 8.2 in. (24.6 × 20.8 cm), Total 250 Tissues."

(b) The individual packages or labeled units of a multiunit package, when intended for individual sale separate from the multiunit package, shall be labeled in compliance with the regulations under this part 500 applicable to that package.

(c) A multiunit package containing unlabeled individual packages which are not intended for retail sale separate from the multiunit package may contain, in lieu of the requirements of Paragraph (a) of this section, a declaration of quantity of contents expressing the total quantity of the multiunit package without regard for inner packaging. For such multiunit packages it shall be optional to include a statement of the number of individual packages when such a statement is not otherwise required by the regulations.

Examples: Deodorant Cakes: "5 Cakes, Net Wt. 4 ozs. (113 g) each, Total Net Wt. 1.25 lb. (566 g)" or "5 Cakes, Total Net Wt. 1 lb. 4 ozs. (566 g)";

Soap Packets: "10 Packets, Net Wt. 2 ozs. (56.6 g) each, total Net Wt 1.25 lb. (566 g)" or "Net Wt 1 lb. 4 ozs. (566 g)" or "10 Packets, Total Net Wt. 1 lb. 4 ozs. (566 g)."

§ 500.28 Variety packages.

(a) A variety package is a package intended for retail sale, containing two or more individual packages or units of similar but not identical commodities. Commodities which are generically the same but which differ in weight or mass, measure, volume, appearance or quality are considered similar but not identical. The declaration of net quantity for a variety package will be expressed as follows:

(1) The number of units for each identical commodity followed by the weight or mass, volume, or measure of that commodity: and

(2) The total quantity by weight or mass, volume, measure, and count, as appropriate, of the variety package. The statement of total quantity shall appear as the last item in the declaration of net quantity and shall not be of greater prominence than other terms used.

Examples:

(i) "2 sponges 4½ ins. × 4 ins. × ¾ in. (11.4 cm × 10.1 cm × 1.9 cm); 1 sponge 4½ ins. × 8 ins. × ¾ in. (11.4 cm × 20.3 cm × 1.9 cm); 4 sponges 2½ ins. × 4 ins. × ½ in. (6.3 cm × 10.1 cm × 1.2 cm)

Total: 7 sponges".

(ii) "2 soap bars Net Wt. 3.2 ozs. (90 g) each; 1 soap bar Net Wt. 5.0 ozs. (141 g).

Total: 3 bars Net Wt. 11.4 ozs. (323 g)."

(iii) Liquid Shoe Polish: "1 Brown 3 fl. ozs. (88 mL); 1 Black 3 fl. ozs. (88 mL); 1 White 5 fl. ozs. (147 mL).

Total: 11 fl. ozs. (325 mL)."

(iv) Picnic Ware: "34 spoons; 33 forks; 33 knives.

Total: 100 pieces."

(b) When the individual units in a variety package are either packaged or labeled and are intended for retail sale as individual units, each unit shall be labeled in compliance with the applicable regulations under this part 500.

§ 500.29 Combination packages.

(a) A combination package is a package intended for retail sale, containing two or more individual packages or units of dissimilar commodities. The declaration of net quantity for a combination package will contain an expression of weight or mass, volume, measure or count or a combination, thereof, as appropriate for each individual package or unit: *Provided*, that the quantity statements for identical packages or units shall be combined.

Examples

(1) Lighter fluid and flints: "2 cans—each 8 fl. ozs. (236 mL); 1 package—8 flints."

(2) Sponges & Cleaner: "2 sponges each 4 in. × 6 in. × 1 in. (10.1 × 15.2 × 2.5 cm); 1 box cleaner—Net Wt. 6 ozs. (170 g)"

(3) Picnic Pack: "20 spoons, 10 knives and 10 forks, 10 2-ply napkins 10 ins. × 10 ins. (25.4 × 25.4 cm) 10 cups—6 fl. ozs. (177 mL)".

(b) When the individual units in a combination package are either packaged or labeled and are intended for retail sale as individual units, each unit shall be in compliance with the applicable regulations under this part 500.

PART 501—EXEMPTIONS FROM REQUIREMENTS AND PROHIBITIONS UNDER PART 500

AUTHORITY: Secs. 5, 6, 80 Stat. 1298, 1299, 1300; 15 U.S.C. 1454, 1455.

§ 501.1 Camera film.

Camera film packaged and labeled for retail sale is exempt from the net quantity statement requirements of part 500 of this chapter which specify how measurement of commodities should be expressed, provided:

(a) The net quantity of contents on packages of movie film and bulk still film is expressed in terms of the number of lineal feet of usable film contained therein.

(b) The net quantity of contents on packages of still film is expressed in terms of the number of exposures the contents will provide. The length and width measurements of the individual exposures, expressed in millimeters or inches, are authorized as an optional statement. (Example: "36 exposures, 36 × 24 mm. or 12 exposures, 2¼ × 2¼ inches".)

[35 FR 75, Jan. 3, 1970]

§ 501.2 Christmas tree ornaments.

Christmas tree ornaments packaged and labeled for retail sale are exempt from the net quantity statement requirements of part 500 of this chapter which specify how the net quantity statement should be expressed, provided:

(a) The quantity of contents is expressed in terms of numerical count of the ornaments, and

(b) The ornaments are so packaged that the ornaments are clearly visible to the retail purchaser at the time of purchase.

[35 FR 9108, June 12, 1970]

§ 501.3 Replacement bags for vacuum cleaners.

Replacement bags for vacuum cleaners, packaged and labeled for retail sale are exempt from the requirements of § 500.15a of this chapter which specifies how measurement of container type commodities should be expressed, provided:

(a) The quantity of contents is expressed in terms of numerical count of the bags;

(b) A statement appears on the principal display panel of the package accurately identifying the make and model of the vacuum cleaner or cleaners in which the replacement bag is intended to effectively function;

(c) The name and place of business of the manufacturer, packer, or distributor of the replacement bags, in addition to the requirements of § 500.5 of this chapter, appears on the principal display panel of the package.

[35 FR 10510, June 27, 1970]

§ 501.4 Chamois.

Chamois packaged or labeled for retail sale is exempt from the requirements of § 500.13 of this chapter which specifies how measurement of commodities by area measure should be expressed: *Provided:*

(a) The quantity of contents for full skins is expressed in terms of square feet with any remainder in terms of the common or decimal fraction of the square foot.

(b) The quantity of contents for cut skins of any configuration is expressed in terms of square inches and fractions thereof. Where the area of a cut skin is at least one square foot or more, the statement of square inches shall be followed in parentheses by a declaration in square feet with any remainder in terms of square inches or common or decimal fractions of the square foot.

[35 FR 19572, Dec. 24, 1970]

§ 501.5 Paper table covers, bedsheets, pillowcases.

Table covers, bedsheets, and pillowcases, fabricated from paper, are exempt from the requirements of § 500.12 of this chapter which specifies the expression of measurement of bidimensional commodities: *Provided,* That such commodities shall clearly present their actual length and width in terms of inches.

[35 FR 19077, Dec. 17, 1970]

§ 501.6 Cellulose sponges, irregular dimensions.

Variety packages of cellulose sponges of irregular dimensions, are exempted from the requirements of § 500.25 of this chapter, provided:

(a) Such sponges are packaged in transparent packages which afford visual inspection of the varied sizes, shapes, and irregular dimensions; and

(b) The quantity of contents declaration is expressed as a combination of count accompanied by the term *irregular dimensions.*

Example: "10 Assorted Sponges—Irregular dimensions."

[35 FR 18510, Dec. 5, 1970]

§ 501.7 Candles.

Tapered candles and irregularly shaped decorative candles which are either hand dipped or molded are exempt from the requirements of § 500.7 of this chapter which specifies that the net quantity of contents shall be expressed in terms of count and measure (e.g., length and diameter), to the extent that diameter of such candles need not be expressed. The requirements of § 500.7 of this chapter for these candles will be met by an expression of count and length or height in inches.

[36 FR 5690, Mar. 26, 1971]

§ 501.8 Solder.

Solder and brazing alloys containing precious metals when packaged and labeled for retail sale are exempt from the net quantity statement requirements of part 500 of this chapter which specify that all statements of weight shall be in terms of avoirdupois pound and ounce provided the net quantity declaration is stated in terms of the troy pound and ounce and the term *troy* is used in each declaration.

[37 FR 4429, Mar. 3, 1972]

PART 502—REGULATIONS UNDER SECTION 5(C) OF THE FAIR PACKAGING AND LABELING ACT

AUTHORITY: 15 U.S.C. 1454, 1455.

SOURCE: 36 FR 12286, June 30, 1971, unless otherwise noted.

SCOPE

§ 502.1 Scope of the regulations in this part.

The regulations in this part establish requirements for labeling of consumer commodities with respect to use of package size characterizations, retail sale price representations, and common name and ingredient listing. Additionally, the regulations in this part establish criteria to prevent nonfunctional-slack-fill of packages containing consumer commodities.

DEFINITIONS

§ 502.2 Terms defined.

As used in this part, unless the context otherwise specifically requires:

(a) The terms *Act, regulation* or *regulations, consumer commodity, package, label, person, commerce, principal display panel,* and *random package* have the same meaning as those terms are defined under part 500 of this chapter.

(b) The term *packager* and *labeler* means any person engaged in the packaging or labeling of any consumer commodity for distribution in commerce or any person, other than a common carrier for hire, a contract carrier for hire, or a freight forwarder for hire, engaged in the distribution in commerce of any packaged or labeled consumer commodity; except persons engaged in business as wholesale or retail distributors of consumer commodities are not included unless such persons (1) are engaged in the packaging or labeling of such commodities, or (2) prescribe or specify by any means the manner in which such commodities are packaged or labeled.

(c) The terms *ordinary and customary* and *regular* when used with the term *price* means the price at which a consumer commodity has been openly and actively sold in the most recent and regular course of business in a particular market or trade area for a reasonably substantial period of time, i.e., a 30-day period. For consumer commodities which fluctuate in price, the ordinary and customary price shall be the lowest price at which any substantial sales were made during the aforesaid 30-day period.

GENERAL REQUIREMENTS

§502.3 Prohibited acts.

(a) No person engaged in the packaging or labeling of any consumer commodity for distribution in commerce, and no person (other than a common carrier for hire, a contract carrier for hire, or a freight forwarder for hire) engaged in the distribution in commerce of any packaged or labeled consumer commodity, shall distribute or cause to be distributed in commerce any such commodity if such commodity is contained in a package, or if there is affixed to that commodity a label, which does not conform to the provisions of the Act and of the regulations in this part.

(b) Persons engaged in business as wholesale or retail distributors of consumer commodities shall be subject to the Act and the regulations in this part to the extent that such persons are engaged in the packaging or labeling of consumer commodities, or prescribe or specify by any means the manner in which such consumer commodities are packaged or labeled.

CHARACTERIZATION OF PACKAGE SIZE

§§502.4–502.99 [Reserved]

RETAIL SALE PRICE REPRESENTATIONS

§§502.100—502.102 [Reserved]

COMMON NAME AND INGREDIENT LISTING

§§502.200–502.299 [Reserved]

NONFUNCTIONAL-SLACK-FILL

§§502.300–502.399 [Reserved]

PART 503—STATEMENTS OF GENERAL POLICY OR INTERPRETATION

AUTHORITY: Secs. 4, 6, 10, 80 Stat. 1297, 1999, 1300, 1301; 15 U.S.C. 1453, 1455, 1456.

§503.1 Interpretations.

The regulations in parts 500, 501, and 502 of this chapter are necessarily general in application and requests for formal rulings, statements of policy or interpretations shall be addressed to the Secretary of the Commission for consideration. Statements of policy or interpretations binding on the Commission will be published in the FEDERAL REGISTER. However, technical questions not involving policy consideration may be answered by the staff.

[36 FR 23058, Dec. 3, 1971]

§ 503.2 Status of specific items under the Fair Packaging and Labeling Act.

Recent questions submitted to the Commission concerning whether certain articles, products or commodities are included under the definition of the term *consumer commodity*, as contained in section 10(a) of the Fair Packaging and Labeling Act, have been considered in the light of the Commission's interpretation of that term as set forth in § 503.5 of this part as follows:

(a) The Commission is of the opinion that the following commodities or classes of commodities are not "consumer commodities" within the meaning of the Act.

Antifreeze.
Artificial flowers and parts.
Automotive accessories.
Automotive chemical products.
Automotive replacement parts.
Bicycle tires and tubes.
Books.
Brushes (bristle, nylon, etc.).
Brooms and mops.
Cameras.
Chinaware.
Christmas light sets.
Cigarette lighters.
Clothespins (wooden, plastic).
Compacts and mirrors.
Diaries and calendars.
Flower seeds.
Footwear.
Garden tools.
Gift ties and tapes.
Glasses and glassware.
Gloves (work type).
Greeting cards.
Hand tools.
Handicraft and sewing thread.
Hardware.
Household cooking utensils.
Inks.
Jewelry.
Luggage.
Magnetic recording tape.
Metal pails.
Motor oil (automobile).
Mouse and rat traps.
Musical instruments.
Paintings and wall plaques.
Photo albums.
Pictures.
Plastic table cloths, plastic placement and plastic shelf paper.
Rubber gloves (household).
Safety flares.
Safety pins.
School supplies.
Sewing accessories.
Silverware, stainless steelware and pewterware.
Small arms ammunition.
Smoking pipes.
Souvenirs.
Sporting goods.
Toys.
Typewriter ribbons.
Woodenware.

(b) The Commission is of the opinion that the following commodities or classes of commodities are "consumer commodities" within the meaning of the Act:

Adhesives and sealants.
Aluminum foil cooking utensils.
Aluminum wrap.
Camera supplies.
Candles.
Christmas decorations.
Cordage.
Disposable diapers.
Dry cell batteries.
Light bulbs.
Liquified petroleum gas for other than heating and cooking.
Lubricants for home use.
Photographic chemicals.
Pressure sensitive tapes, excluding gift tapes.
Solder.
Solvents and cleaning fluids for home use.
Sponges and chamois.
Waxes for home use.

[35 FR 6185, Apr. 16, 1970]

§ 503.3 Name and place of business of manufacturer, packer, or distributor.

To clarify the identity of a manufacturer, packer, or distributor for the purpose of § 500.5 of this chapter, the following represents the opinions of the Commission.

(a) A manufacturer of a bulk product who supplies the product to a contract packager and permits his bulk product to be packaged by the contract packager remains the manufacturer of the commodity, if the contract packager does not perform any act other than package filling and labeling.

(b)(1) A manufacturer of a bulk product who supplies the bulk to a contract packager but permits the packager to modify the bulk commodity by the addition of any substance which changes the identity of the bulk, ceases to be the manufacturer of the consumer commodity. At that point, if the manufacturer of the bulk elects to use his name on the label of the consumer commodity, his name should be qualified to show "Distributed by __________", or "Manufactured for __________".

(2) The identity of a bulk substance received by a contract packager is changed if the packager, for example, adds a propellant as in the case of an aerosol, or adds a solvent as in the case of a paint, or blends two or more components, or changes the physical state as in the case of a liquid being changed to a gel or a semisolid being changed to a solid.

(c) A person or firm who supplies a formula and/or specifications to a contract packager but who takes no part in the actual production of the consumer commodity is not the manufacturer of the consumer commodity for the purpose of § 500.5(a) of this chapter. This is true whether the person or firm who supplies the formula or specifications, or both, also supplies the raw materials which are to be reacted, mixed, or otherwise modified to produce the consumer commodity.

(d) A corporation which wholly owns a manufacturing subsidiary which retains its separate corporate identity, is not the manufacturer of the consumer commodities manufactured by the wholly owned subsidiary, but must qualify its name if it elects to use its name on the label. Such qualification may be "Manufactured for __________", "Distributed by __________", or "Manufactured by __________ (XYZ, Inc., City, State, Zip Code, a subsidiary of ABC, Inc.)".

[34 FR 4956, Mar. 7, 1969, as amended at 34 FR 11199, July 3, 1969]

§ 503.4 Net quantity of contents, numerical count.

To clarify the requirement for declaration of net quantity in terms of count for the purpose of §§ 500.6 and 500.7 of this chapter, the following interpretation is rendered.

(a) When a consumer commodity is properly measured in terms of count only, or in terms of count and weight, volume, area, or dimension, the regulations are interpreted not to require the declaration of the net content as "one", provided the statement of identity clearly expresses the fact that only one unit is contained in the package. Thus the unit synthetic sponge, the unit light bulb, and the unit dry cell battery do not require a net quantity statement of "one sponge," "one light bulb," or "one dry cell battery." However, there still exists the necessity to provide a net quantity statement to specify weight, volume, area, or dimensions when such are required. For example, the synthetic sponge which is packaged, requires dimensions such as "5 in. × 3 in. × 1 in." A multicomponent package or a package containing two or more units of the same commodity shall bear the net quantity statement in terms of count, and weight, volume, area, or dimensions as required. This interpretation does not preclude the option to enumerate a unit count on a single packaged commodity if so desired.

(b) [Reserved]

[34 FR 18087, Nov. 8, 1969]

§ 503.5 Interpretation of the definition of "consumer commodity" as contained in section 10(a) of the Fair Packaging and Labeling Act.

(a) Section 10(a) of the Fair Packaging and Labeling Act defines the term *consumer commodity* in four classifications. These are:

(1) Any food, drug, device, or cosmetic;

(2) And any other article, product, or commodity of any kind or class which is customarily produced or distributed for sale through retail sales agencies or instrumentalities.

(i) For consumption by individuals and which usually is consumed or expended in the course of such consumption.

(ii) For use by individuals for purposes of personal care and which usually is consumed or expended in the course of such use.

(iii) For use by individuals in the performance of services ordinarily rendered within the household and which usually is consumed or expended in the course of such use.

(b) Section 10(a) then expressly excludes

(1) Meats, poultry, and tobacco,

(2) Economic poisons and biologics for animals,

(3) Prescription drugs,

(4) Alcoholic beverages, and

(5) Agricultural and vegetable seeds.

(c) Pursuant to sections 5 and 7 of the Fair Packaging and Labeling Act, the authority to promulgate regulations and to enforce the Act as to any food, drug, device, or cosmetic has been delegated to the Secretary of Health, Education, and Welfare and as to any other "consumer commodity" to the Federal Trade Commission.

(d) As to these articles, products, or commodities subject to regulation by the Federal Trade Commission, the legislative history of the Act demonstrates the intent of Congress, for the reasons stated therein, to place the following categories outside the scope of the definition of "consumer commodity":

(1) Durable articles or commodities;

(2) Textiles or items of apparel;

(3) Any household appliance, equipment, or furnishing, including feather and down-filled products, synthetic-filled bed pillows, mattress pads and patchwork quilts, comforters and decorative curtains;

(4) Bottled gas for heating or cooking purposes;

(5) Paints and kindred products;

(6) Flowers, fertilizer, and fertilizer materials, plants or shrubs, garden and lawn supplies;

(7) Pet care supplies;

(8) Stationery and writing supplies, gift wraps, fountain pens, mechanical pencils, and kindred products.

(e) The articles, products, or commodities that are within the terms of section 10(a) of the Act and subject to regulation by the Federal Trade Commission are either expendable commodities for consumption by individuals, expendable commodities used for personal care, or expendable commodities used for household services. The primary terms in section 10(a) for defining these categories are:

(1) Consumption by individuals;

(2) Use by individuals;

(3) Personal care by individuals;

(4) Performances of services ordinarily rendered within the household by individuals;

(5) Consumed or expended.

(f) These terms are defined as follows:

(1) *Consumption by individuals.* This term as it is used in section 10(a) means the using up of an article, product, or commodity by an individual.

(2) *Use by individuals.* This term as it is used in section 10(a) means the employment or application of an article, product, or commodity by an individual.

(3) *Personal care by individuals.* This term as it is used in section 10(a) means that activity of an individual which is concerned with protecting, enhancing, and providing for the general cleanliness, health, or appearance of the individual.

(4) *Performance of services ordinarily rendered within the household by individuals.* These terms as they are used in section 10(a) mean: The term *household* refers to the interior and exterior of dwellings or residences occupied by individuals, including the surrounding premises. The term *performance of services ordinarily rendered within the household* means the doing of any activity by an individual within the above-described area which is normally done in connection with the maintenance and occupation of the above-described area as a habitation for individuals.

(5) *Consumed or expended.* These terms as they are used in section 10(a) mean (i) the immediate destruction or extinction of an article, product, or commodity, or of the part used; or (ii) the substantial diminution in the quantity, quality or utility of an article, product, or commodity which results from usage upon one or several occasions over a comparatively short period of time.

(g) The foregoing definition serves to amplify the definition of "consumer commodity" supplied by Congress in section 10(a) of the Act. As questions arise as to whether specific articles, products, or commodities are included in the above definition, the Commission will consider, among other things, the Congressional policy declared in section 2 of the Act, namely, that packages and labels should enable consumers to obtain accurate information as to the quantity of contents and should facilitate value comparisons. That is, in making its determinations of inclusions and exclusions under this definition, the Commission will consider the requirements of both the Act and the pertinent regulations and in that connection will regard as one criterion the extent to which the disclosures required on "consumer commodities" are material to a consumer's selection of a particular article, product, or commodity. Interpretative rulings in such instances will be made public, and can be expected to further contribute to the development of clearer delineation of the scope of the term "consumer commodity".

(h) With respect to articles, products, or commodities included within the definition of "consumer commodities", the Commission will consider requests for exemptions in accordance with section 5(b) of the Act and § 500.3(e) of this chapter, and will make public its rulings on all such requests.

[34 FR 12945, Aug. 9, 1969]

§ 503.6 Packagers' duty to withhold availability of packages imprinted with retail sale price representations.

To clarify the requirements, under part 502 of this chapter, that a packager or labeler will not make packages marked with retail sale price representations available in any circumstance where he knows or should have reason to know that it will be used as an instrumentality for deception or for frustration of value comparison, the following represents the opinions of the Commission:

(a) Details of a plan to provide special packaging or special package sizes bearing retail sale price representations should contain the condition that customers will not be provided with such packages unless they resell the package at a price which fully passes on to the purchasers the represented savings or sale price advantage.

(b) A packager or labeler who, in good faith, takes reasonable and prudent measures to verify the performance of his customers will be deemed to have satisfied his obligation under the regulations. If the packager has taken such steps, the fact that a particular customer has failed to resell the packages at a price which fully passes on to the purchaser the represented savings or sale price advantage shall not alone place a seller in violation of the regulations.

(c) Any packager or labeler who determines that a customer does not intend to fulfill or has not fulfilled the conditions of an offer should immediately refrain from further sale under that offer to the customer. In situations where proper fulfillment of the conditions of an offer are in question, the Commission will resolve the issue after appropriate investigation of the facts submitted.

[36 FR 23058, Dec. 3, 1971]

SUBCHAPTER F—THE FAIR CREDIT REPORTING ACT

PART 600 [RESERVED]

PART 602—FAIR AND ACCURATE CREDIT TRANSACTIONS ACT OF 2003

AUTHORITY: 15 U.S.C. 1681s; sec. 3, Pub. L. 108–159; 117 Stat. 1953.

§ 602.1 Effective dates.

(a)–(b) [Reserved]

(c) The applicable provisions of the Fair and Accurate Credit Transactions Act of 2003 (FACT Act), Pub. L. 108–159, 117 Stat. 1952, shall be effective in accordance with the following schedule:

(1) *Provisions effective December 31, 2003.*

(i) Sections 151(a)(2), 212(e), 214(c), 311(b), and 711, concerning the relation to state laws; and

(ii) Each of the provisions of the FACT Act that authorizes an agency to issue a regulation or to take other action to implement the applicable provision of the FACT Act or the applicable provision of the Fair Credit Reporting Act, as amended by the FACT Act, but only with respect to that agency's authority to propose and adopt the implementing regulation or to take such other action.

(2) *Provisions effective March 31, 2004.*

(i) Section 111, concerning the definitions;

(ii) Section 156, concerning the statute of limitations

(iii) Sections 312(d), (e), and (f), concerning the furnisher liability exception, liability and enforcement, and rule of construction, respectively;

(iv) Section 313(a), concerning action regarding complaints;

(v) Section 611, concerning communications for certain employee investigations; and

(vi) Section 811, concerning clerical amendments.

(3) *Provisions effective December 1, 2004.*

(i) Section 112, concerning fraud alerts and active duty alerts;

(ii) Section 114, concerning procedures for the identification of possible instances of identity theft;

(iii) Section 115, concerning truncation of the social security number in a consumer report;

(iv) Section 151(a)(1), concerning the summary of rights of identity theft victims;

(v) Section 152, concerning blocking of information resulting from identity theft;

(vi) Section 153, concerning the coordination of identity theft complaint investigations;

(vii) Section 154, concerning the prevention of repollution of consumer reports;

(viii) Section 155, concerning notice by debt collectors with respect to fraudulent information;

(ix) Section 211(c), concerning a summary of rights of consumers;

(x) Section 212(a)–(d), concerning the disclosure of credit scores;

(xi) Section 213(c), concerning duration of elections;

(xii) Section 217(a), concerning the duty to provide notice to a consumer;

(xiii) Section 311(a), concerning the risk-based pricing notice;

(xiv) Section 312(a)–(c), concerning procedures to enhance the accuracy and integrity of information furnished to consumer reporting agencies;

(xv) Section 314, concerning improved disclosure of the results of reinvestigation;

(xvi) Section 315, concerning reconciling addresses;

(xvii) Section 316, concerning notice of dispute through reseller; and

(xviii) Section 317, concerning the duty to conduct a reasonable reinvestigation.

[69 FR 29063, May 20, 2004]

PART 603—DEFINITIONS

AUTHORITY: Pub. L. 108–159, sec. 111; 15 U.S.C. 1681a.

SOURCE: 77 FR 22203, Apr. 13, 2012, unless otherwise noted.

§ 603.1 Cross-reference.

The rules formerly at 16 CFR part 603 have been republished by the Consumer Financial Protection Bureau at 12 CFR

1022.3, "Fair Credit Reporting (Regulation V)."

PART 604—FAIR CREDIT REPORTING ACT RULES

AUTHORITY: Pub. L. 108–159, secs. 3, 111, 112, 114, 151, 153, 211, 212, 213, 214, 216, 311, 315; 15 U.S.C. 1681s.

§604.1 Severability.

All parts and subparts of this subchapter are separate and severable from one another. If any part or subpart is stayed or determined to be invalid, the Commission intends that the remaining parts and subparts shall continue in effect.

[69 FR 29063, May 20, 2004]

PART 610—FREE ANNUAL FILE DISCLOSURES

AUTHORITY: 15 U.S.C. 1681a, g, and h; sec. 211(a) and (d), Pub. L. 108–159, 117 Stat. 1968 and 1972 (15 U.S.C. 1681j); Pub. L. 111–24.

SOURCE: 77 FR 22203, Apr. 13, 2012, unless otherwise noted.

§610.1 Cross-reference.

The rules formerly at 16 CFR part 610 have been republished by the Consumer Financial Protection Bureau at 12 CFR 1022.130, "Fair Credit Reporting (Regulation V)."

PART 611—PROHIBITION AGAINST CIRCUMVENTING TREATMENT AS A NATIONWIDE CONSUMER REPORTING AGENCY

AUTHORITY: Pub. L. 108–159, sec. 211(b); 15 U.S.C. 1681x.

SOURCE: 77 FR 22203, Apr. 13, 2012, unless otherwise noted.

§611.1 Cross-reference.

The rules formerly at 16 CFR part 611 have been republished by the Consumer Financial Protection Bureau at 12 CFR 1022.140, "Fair Credit Reporting (Regulation V)."

PART 613—DURATION OF ACTIVE DUTY ALERTS

AUTHORITY: Pub. L. 108–159, sec. 112(a); 15 U.S.C. 1681c–1.

SOURCE: 77 FR 22203, Apr. 13, 2012, unless otherwise noted.

§613.1 Cross-reference.

The rules formerly at 16 CFR part 613 have been republished by the Consumer Financial Protection Bureau at 12 CFR 1022.121, "Fair Credit Reporting (Regulation V)."

PART 614—APPROPRIATE PROOF OF IDENTITY

AUTHORITY: Pub. L. 108–159, sec. 112(b).

SOURCE: 77 FR 22204, Apr. 13, 2012, unless otherwise noted.

§614.1 Cross-reference.

The rules formerly at 16 CFR part 614 have been republished by the Consumer Financial Protection Bureau at 12 CFR 1022.123, "Fair Credit Reporting (Regulation V)."

PART 640—DUTIES OF CREDITORS REGARDING RISK-BASED PRICING

AUTHORITY: Pub. L. 108–159, sec. 311; 15 U.S.C. 1681m(h).

SOURCE: 75 FR 2769, Jan. 15, 2010, unless otherwise noted.

§640.1 Scope.

(a) *Coverage*—(1) *In general*. This part applies to any person that both—

(i) Uses a consumer report in connection with an application for, or a grant, extension, or other provision of, credit to a consumer that is primarily for personal, family, or household purposes; and

(ii) Based in whole or in part on the consumer report, grants, extends, or otherwise provides credit to the consumer on material terms that are materially less favorable than the most favorable material terms available to a substantial proportion of consumers from or through that person.

(2) *Business credit excluded.* This part does not apply to an application for, or a grant, extension, or other provision of, credit to a consumer or to any other applicant primarily for a business purpose.

(b) *Relation to Board of Governors of the Federal Reserve System rules.* The rules in this part were developed jointly with the Board of Governors of the Federal Reserve System (Board) and are substantively identical to the Board's risk-based pricing rules in 12 CFR part 222. Both rules apply to the covered person described in paragraph (a) of this section. Compliance with either the Board's rules or the Commission's rules satisfies the requirements of the statute (15 U.S.C. 1681m(h)).

(c) *Enforcement.* The provisions of this part will be enforced in accordance with the enforcement authority set forth in sections 621(a) and (b) of the FCRA.

§ 640.2 Definitions.

For purposes of this part, the following definitions apply:

(a) *Adverse action* has the same meaning as in 15 U.S.C. 1681a(k)(1)(A).

(b) *Annual percentage rate* has the same meaning as in 12 CFR 226.14(b) with respect to an open-end credit plan and as in 12 CFR 226.22 with respect to closed-end credit.

(c) *Closed-end credit* has the same meaning as in 12 CFR 226.2(a)(10).

(d) *Consumer* has the same meaning as in 15 U.S.C. 1681a(c).

(e) *Consummation* has the same meaning as in 12 CFR 226.2(a)(13).

(f) *Consumer report* has the same meaning as in 15 U.S.C. 1681a(d).

(g) *Consumer reporting agency* has the same meaning as in 15 U.S.C. 1681a(f).

(h) *Credit* has the same meaning as in 15 U.S.C. 1681a(r)(5).

(i) *Creditor* has the same meaning as in 15 U.S.C. 1681a(r)(5).

(j) *Credit card* has the same meaning as in 15 U.S.C. 1681a(r)(2).

(k) *Credit card issuer* has the same meaning as in 15 U.S.C. 1681a(r)(1)(A).

(l) *Credit score* has the same meaning as in 15 U.S.C. 1681g(f)(2)(A).

(m) *Firm offer of credit* has the same meaning as in 15 U.S.C. 1681a(l).

(n) *Material terms* means—

(1) (i) Except as otherwise provided in paragraphs (n)(1)(ii) and (n)(3) of this section, in the case of credit extended under an open-end credit plan, the annual percentage rate required to be disclosed under 12 CFR 226.6(a)(1)(ii) or 12 CFR 226.6(b)(2)(i), excluding any temporary initial rate that is lower than the rate that will apply after the temporary rate expires, any penalty rate that will apply upon the occurrence of one or more specific events, such as a late payment or an extension of credit that exceeds the credit limit, and any fixed annual percentage rate option for a home equity line of credit;

(ii) In the case of a credit card (other than a credit card that is used to access a home equity line of credit or a charge card), the annual percentage rate required to be disclosed under 12 CFR 226.6(b)(2)(i) that applies to purchases ("purchase annual percentage rate") and no other annual percentage rate, or in the case of a credit card that has no purchase annual percentage rate, the annual percentage rate that varies based on information in a consumer report and that has the most significant financial impact on consumers;

(2) In the case of closed-end credit, the annual percentage rate required to be disclosed under 12 CFR 226.17(c) and 226.18(e); and

(3) In the case of credit for which there is no annual percentage rate, the financial term that varies based on information in a consumer report and that has the most significant financial impact on consumers, such as a deposit required in connection with credit extended by a telephone company or utility or an annual membership fee for a charge card.

(o) *Materially less favorable* means, when applied to material terms, that the terms granted, extended, or otherwise provided to a consumer differ from the terms granted, extended, or otherwise provided to another consumer from or through the same person such that the cost of credit to the first consumer would be significantly greater than the cost of credit granted, extended, or otherwise provided to the other consumer. For purposes of this definition, factors relevant to determining the significance of a difference in cost include the type of credit product, the term of the credit extension, if any, and the extent of the difference between the material terms granted, extended, or otherwise provided to the two consumers.

(p) *Open-end credit plan* has the same meaning as in 15 U.S.C. 1602(i), as interpreted by the Board in Regulation Z and the Official Staff Commentary to Regulation Z.

(q) *Person* has the same meaning as in 15 U.S.C. 1681a(b).

§ 640.3 General requirements for risk-based pricing notices.

(a) *In general.* Except as otherwise provided in this part, a person must provide to a consumer a notice ("risk-based pricing notice") in the form and manner required by this part if the person both—

(1) Uses a consumer report in connection with an application for, or a grant, extension, or other provision of, credit to that consumer that is primarily for personal, family, or household purposes; and

(2) Based in whole or in part on the consumer report, grants, extends, or otherwise provides credit to that consumer on material terms that are materially less favorable than the most favorable material terms available to a substantial proportion of consumers from or through that person.

(b) *Determining which consumers must receive a notice.* A person may determine whether paragraph (a) of this section applies by directly comparing the material terms offered to each consumer and the material terms offered to other consumers for a specific type of credit product. For purposes of this section, a "specific type of credit product" means one or more credit products with similar features that are designed for similar purposes. Examples of a specific type of credit product include student loans, unsecured credit cards, secured credit cards, new automobile loans, used automobile loans, fixed-rate mortgage loans, and variable-rate mortgage loans. As an alternative to making this direct comparison, a person may make the determination by using one of the following methods:

(1) *Credit score proxy method*—(i) *In general.* A person that sets the material terms of credit granted, extended, or otherwise provided to a consumer, based in whole or in part on a credit score, may comply with the requirements of paragraph (a) of this section by—

(A) Determining the credit score (hereafter referred to as the "cutoff score") that represents the point at which approximately 40 percent of the consumers to whom it grants, extends, or provides credit have higher credit scores and approximately 60 percent of the consumers to whom it grants, extends, or provides credit have lower credit scores; and

(B) Providing a risk-based pricing notice to each consumer to whom it grants, extends, or provides credit whose credit score is lower than the cutoff score.

(ii) *Alternative to the 40/60 cutoff score determination.* In the case of credit that has been granted, extended, or provided on the most favorable material terms to more than 40 percent of consumers, a person may, at its option, set its cutoff score at a point at which the approximate percentage of consumers who historically have been granted, extended, or provided credit on material terms other than the most favorable terms would receive risk-based pricing notices under this section.

(iii) *Determining the cutoff score*—(A) *Sampling approach.* A person that currently uses risk-based pricing with respect to the credit products it offers must calculate the cutoff score by considering the credit scores of all or a representative sample of the consumers to whom it has granted, extended, or provided credit for a specific type of credit product.

(B) *Secondary source approach in limited circumstances.* A person that is a new entrant into the credit business, introduces new credit products, or starts to use risk-based pricing with respect to the credit products it currently offers may initially determine the cutoff score based on information derived from appropriate market research or relevant third-party sources for a specific type of credit product, such as research or data from companies that develop credit scores. A person that acquires a credit portfolio as a result of a merger or acquisition may determine the cutoff score based on information from the party which it acquired, with which it merged, or from which it acquired the portfolio.

(C) *Recalculation of cutoff scores.* A person using the credit score proxy method must recalculate its cutoff score(s) no less than every two years in the manner described in paragraph (b)(1)(iii)(A) of this section. A person using the credit score proxy method using market research, third-party data, or information from a party which it acquired, with which it merged, or from which it acquired the portfolio as permitted by paragraph (b)(1)(iii)(B) of this section generally must calculate a cutoff score(s) based on the scores of its own consumers in the manner described in paragraph (b)(1)(iii)(A) of this section within one year after it begins using a cutoff score derived from market research, third-party data, or information from a party which it acquired, with which it merged, or from which it acquired the portfolio. If such a person does not grant, extend, or provide credit to new consumers during that one-year period such that it lacks sufficient data with which to recalculate a cutoff score based on the credit scores of its own consumers, the person may continue to use a cutoff score derived from market research, third-party data, or information from a party which it acquired, with which it merged, or from which it acquired the portfolio as provided in paragraph (b)(1)(iii)(B) until it obtains sufficient data on which to base the recalculation. However, the person must recalculate its cutoff score(s) in the manner described in paragraph (b)(1)(iii)(A) of this section within two years, if it has granted, extended, or provided credit to some new consumers during that two-year period.

(D) *Use of two or more credit scores.* A person that generally uses two or more credit scores in setting the material terms of credit granted, extended, or provided to a consumer must determine the cutoff score using the same method the person uses to evaluate multiple scores when making credit decisions. These evaluation methods may include, but are not limited to, selecting the low, median, high, most recent, or average credit score of each consumer to whom it grants, extends, or provides credit. If a person that uses two or more credit scores does not consistently use the same method for evaluating multiple credit scores (*e.g.*, if the person sometimes chooses the median score and other times calculates the average score), the person must determine the cutoff score using a reasonable means. In such cases, use of any one of the methods that the person regularly uses or the average credit score of each consumer to whom it grants, extends, or provides credit is deemed to be a reasonable means of calculating the cutoff score.

(iv) *Credit score not available.* For purposes of this section, a person using the credit score proxy method who grants, extends, or provides credit to a consumer for whom a credit score is not available must assume that the consumer receives credit on material terms that are materially less favorable than the most favorable credit terms offered to a substantial proportion of consumers from or through that person and must provide a risk-based pricing notice to the consumer.

(v) *Examples.* (A) A credit card issuer engages in risk-based pricing and the annual percentage rates it offers to consumers are based in whole or in part on a credit score. The credit card issuer takes a representative sample of the credit scores of consumers to whom it issued credit cards within the preceding three months. The credit card issuer determines that approximately 40 percent of the sampled consumers have a credit score at or above 720 (on a scale of 350 to 850) and approximately 60 percent of the sampled consumers have a credit score below 720. Thus, the card issuer selects 720 as its cutoff score. A consumer applies to the credit card issuer for a credit card. The card issuer obtains a credit score for the consumer. The consumer's credit score is 700. Since the consumer's 700 credit score falls below the 720 cutoff score, the credit card issuer must provide a risk-based pricing notice to the consumer.

(B) A credit card issuer engages in risk-based pricing, and the annual percentage rates it offers to consumers are based in whole or in part on a credit score. The credit card issuer takes a representative sample of the consumers to whom it issued credit cards over the preceding six months. The credit card issuer determines that approximately 80 percent of the sampled consumers received credit at its lowest annual percentage rate, and 20 percent received credit at a higher annual percentage rate. Approximately 80 percent of the sampled consumers have a credit score at or above 750 (on a scale of 350 to 850), and 20 percent have a credit score below 750. Thus, the card issuer selects 750 as its cutoff score. A consumer applies to the credit card issuer for a credit card. The card issuer obtains a credit score for the consumer. The consumer's credit score is 740. Since the consumer's 740 credit score falls below the 750 cutoff score, the credit card issuer must provide a risk-based pricing notice to the consumer.

(C) An auto lender engages in risk-based pricing, obtains credit scores from one of the nationwide consumer reporting agencies, and uses the credit score proxy method to determine which consumers must receive a risk-based pricing notice. A consumer applies to the auto lender for credit to finance the purchase of an automobile. A credit score about that consumer is not available from the consumer reporting agency from which the lender obtains credit scores. The lender nevertheless grants, extends, or provides credit to the consumer. The lender must provide a risk-based pricing notice to the consumer.

(2) *Tiered pricing method*—(i) *In general.* A person that sets the material terms of credit granted, extended, or provided to a consumer by placing the consumer within one of a discrete number of pricing tiers for a specific type of credit product, based in whole or in part on a consumer report, may comply with the requirements of paragraph (a) of this section by providing a risk-based pricing notice to each consumer who is not placed within the top pricing tier or tiers, as described below.

(ii) *Four or fewer pricing tiers.* If a person using the tiered pricing method has four or fewer pricing tiers, the person complies with the requirements of paragraph (a) of this section by providing a risk-based pricing notice to each consumer to whom it grants, extends, or provides credit who does not qualify for the top tier (that is, the lowest-priced tier). For example, a person that uses a tiered pricing structure with annual percentage rates of 8, 10, 12, and 14 percent would provide the risk-based pricing notice to each consumer to whom it grants, extends, or provides credit at annual percentage rates of 10, 12, and 14 percent.

(iii) *Five or more pricing tiers.* If a person using the tiered pricing method has five or more pricing tiers, the person complies with the requirements of paragraph (a) of this section by providing a risk-based pricing notice to each consumer to whom it grants, extends, or provides credit who does not qualify for the top two tiers (that is, the two lowest-priced tiers) and any other tier that, together with the top tiers, comprise no less than the top 30 percent but no more than the top 40 percent of the total number of tiers. Each consumer placed within the remaining tiers must receive a risk-based pricing notice. For example, if a person has nine pricing tiers, the top three tiers (that is, the three lowest-priced tiers) comprise no less than the top 30 percent but no more than the top 40 percent of the tiers. Therefore, a person using this method would provide a risk-based pricing notice to each consumer to whom it grants, extends, or provides credit who is placed within the bottom six tiers.

(c) *Application to credit card issuers*—(1) *In general.* A credit card issuer subject to the requirements of paragraph (a) of this section may use one of the methods set forth in paragraph (b) of this section to identify consumers to whom it must provide a risk-based pricing notice. Alternatively, a credit card issuer may satisfy its obligations under paragraph (a) of this section by providing a risk-based pricing notice to a consumer when—

(i) A consumer applies for a credit card either in connection with an application program, such as a direct-mail offer or a take-one application, or in response to a solicitation under 12 CFR 226.5a, and more than a single possible purchase annual percentage rate may apply under the program or solicitation; and

(ii) Based in whole or in part on a consumer report, the credit card issuer provides a credit card to the consumer with an annual percentage rate referenced in § 640.2(n)(1)(ii) that is greater than the lowest annual percentage rate referenced in § 640.2(n)(1)(ii) available in connection with the application or solicitation.

(2) *No requirement to compare different offers.* A credit card issuer is not subject to the requirements of paragraph (a) of this section and is not required to provide a risk-based pricing notice to a consumer if—

(i) The consumer applies for a credit card for which the card issuer provides a single annual percentage rate referenced in § 640.2(n)(1)(ii), excluding a temporary initial rate that is lower than the rate that will apply after the temporary rate expires and a penalty rate that will apply upon the occurrence of one or more specific events, such as a late payment or an extension of credit that exceeds the credit limit; or

(ii) The credit card issuer offers the consumer the lowest annual percentage rate referenced in § 640.2(n)(1)(ii) available under the credit card offer for which the consumer applied, even if a lower annual percentage rate referenced in § 640.2(n)(1)(ii) is available under a different credit card offer issued by the card issuer.

(3) *Examples.* (i) A credit card issuer sends a solicitation to the consumer that discloses several possible purchase annual percentage rates that may apply, such as 10, 12, or 14 percent, or a range of purchase annual percentage rates from 10 to 14 percent. The consumer applies for a credit card in response to the solicitation. The card issuer provides a credit card to the consumer with a purchase annual percentage rate of 12 percent based in whole or in part on a consumer report. Unless an exception applies under § 640.5, the card issuer may satisfy its obligations under paragraph (a) of this section by providing a risk-based pricing notice to the consumer because the consumer received credit at a purchase annual percentage rate greater than the lowest purchase annual percentage rate available under that solicitation.

(ii) The same facts as in the example in paragraph (c)(3)(i) of this section, except that the card issuer provides a credit card to the consumer at a purchase annual percentage rate of 10 percent. The card issuer is not required to provide a risk-based pricing notice to the consumer even if, under a different credit card solicitation, that consumer or other consumers might qualify for a purchase annual percentage rate of 8 percent.

(d) *Account review*—(1) *In general.* Except as otherwise provided in this part, a person is subject to the requirements of paragraph (a) of this section and must provide a risk-based pricing notice to a consumer in the form and manner required by this part if the person—

(i) Uses a consumer report in connection with a review of credit that has been extended to the consumer; and

(ii) Based in whole or in part on the consumer report, increases the annual percentage rate (the annual percentage rate referenced in § 640.2(n)(1)(ii) in the case of a credit card).

(2) *Example.* A credit card issuer periodically obtains consumer reports for the purpose of reviewing the terms of credit it has extended to consumers in connection with credit cards. As a result of this review, the credit card issuer increases the purchase annual percentage rate applicable to a consumer's credit card based in whole or in part on information in a consumer report. The credit card issuer is subject to the requirements of paragraph (a) of this section and must provide a risk-based pricing notice to the consumer.

§ 640.4 Content, form, and timing of risk-based pricing notices.

(a) *Content of the notice*—(1) *In general.* The risk-based pricing notice required by § 640.3(a) or (c) must include:

(i) A statement that a consumer report (or credit report) includes information about the consumer's credit history and the type of information included in that history;

(ii) A statement that the terms offered, such as the annual percentage rate, have been set based on information from a consumer report;

(iii) A statement that the terms offered may be less favorable than the terms offered to consumers with better credit histories;

(iv) A statement that the consumer is encouraged to verify the accuracy of the information contained in the consumer report and has the right to dispute any inaccurate information in the report;

(v) The identity of each consumer reporting agency that furnished a consumer report used in the credit decision;

(vi) A statement that federal law gives the consumer the right to obtain a copy of a consumer report from the consumer reporting agency or agencies identified in the notice without charge for 60 days after receipt of the notice;

(vii) A statement informing the consumer how to obtain a consumer report from the consumer reporting agency or agencies identified in the notice and providing contact information (including a toll-free telephone number, where applicable) specified by the consumer reporting agency or agencies;

(viii) A statement directing consumers to the Web sites of the Federal Reserve Board and Federal Trade Commission to obtain more information about consumer reports; and

(ix) If a credit score of the consumer to whom a person grants, extends, or otherwise provides credit is used in setting the material terms of credit:

(A) A statement that a credit score is a number that takes into account information in a consumer report, that the consumer's credit score was used to set the terms of credit offered, and that a credit score can change over time to reflect changes in the consumer's credit history;

(B) The credit score used by the person in making the credit decision;

(C) The range of possible credit scores under the model used to generate the credit score;

(D) All of the key factors that adversely affected the credit score, which shall not exceed four key factors, except that if one of the key factors is the number of enquiries made with respect to the consumer report, the number of key factors shall not exceed five;

(E) The date on which the credit score was created; and

(F) The name of the consumer reporting agency or other person that provided the credit score.

(2) *Account review.* The risk-based pricing notice required by § 640.3(d) must include:

(i) A statement that a consumer report (or credit report) includes information about the consumer's credit history and the type of information included in that credit history;

(ii) A statement that the person has conducted a review of the account using information from a consumer report;

(iii) A statement that as a result of the review, the annual percentage rate on the account has been increased based on information from a consumer report;

(iv) A statement that the consumer is encouraged to verify the accuracy of the information contained in the consumer report and has the right to dispute any inaccurate information in the report;

(v) The identity of each consumer reporting agency that furnished a consumer report used in the account review;

(vi) A statement that federal law gives the consumer the right to obtain a copy of a consumer report from the consumer reporting agency or agencies identified in the notice without charge for 60 days after receipt of the notice;

(vii) A statement informing the consumer how to obtain a consumer report from the consumer reporting agency or agencies identified in the notice and providing contact information (including a toll-free telephone number, where applicable) specified by the consumer reporting agency or agencies;

(viii) A statement directing consumers to the Web sites of the Federal Reserve Board and Federal Trade Commission to obtain more information about consumer reports; and

(ix) If a credit score of the consumer whose extension of credit is under review is used in increasing the annual percentage rate:

(A) A statement that a credit score is a number that takes into account information in a consumer report, that the consumer's credit score was used to set the terms of credit offered, and that a credit score can change over time to reflect changes in the consumer's credit history;

(B) The credit score used by the person in making the credit decision;

(C) The range of possible credit scores under the model used to generate the credit score;

(D) All of the key factors that adversely affected the credit score, which shall not exceed four key factors, except that if one of the key factors is the number of enquiries made with respect to the consumer report, the number of key factors shall not exceed five;

(E) The date on which the credit score was created; and

(F) The name of the consumer reporting agency or other person that provided the credit score.

(b) *Form of the notice*—(1) *In general.* The risk-based pricing notice required by § 640.3(a), (c), or (d) must be:

(i) Clear and conspicuous; and

(ii) Provided to the consumer in oral, written, or electronic form.

(2) *Model forms.* Model forms of the risk-based pricing notice required by § 640.3(a) and (c) are contained in appendices B–1 and B–6 of this part. Appropriate use of Model form B–1 or B–6 is deemed to comply with the requirements of § 640.3(a) and (c). Model forms of the risk-based pricing notice required by § 640.3(d) are contained in appendices B–2 and B–7 of this part. Appropriate use of Model form B–2 or B–7 is deemed to comply with the requirements of § 640.3(d). Use of the model forms is optional.

(c) *Timing*—(1) *General.* Except as provided in paragraph (c)(3) of this section, a risk-based pricing notice must be provided to the consumer—

(i) In the case of a grant, extension, or other provision of closed-end credit, before consummation of the transaction, but not earlier than the time the decision to approve an application for, or a grant, extension, or other provision of, credit, is communicated to the consumer by the person required to provide the notice;

(ii) In the case of credit granted, extended, or provided under an open-end credit plan, before the first transaction is made under the plan, but not earlier than the time the decision to approve an application for, or a grant, extension, or other provision of, credit is communicated to the consumer by the person required to provide the notice; or

(iii) In the case of a review of credit that has been extended to the consumer, at the time the decision to increase the annual percentage rate (annual percentage rate referenced in § 640.2(n)(1)(ii) in the case of a credit card) based on a consumer report is communicated to the consumer by the person required to provide the notice, or if no notice of the increase in the annual percentage rate is provided to the consumer prior to the effective date of the change in the annual percentage rate (to the extent permitted by law), no later than five days after the effective date of the change in the annual percentage rate.

(2) *Application to certain automobile lending transactions.* When a person to whom a credit obligation is initially payable grants, extends, or provides credit to a consumer for the purpose of financing the purchase of an automobile from an auto dealer or other party that is not affiliated with the person, any requirement to provide a risk-based pricing notice pursuant to this part is satisfied if the person:

(i) Provides a notice described in §§ 640.3(a), 640.5(e), or 640.5(f) to the consumer within the time periods set forth in paragraph (c)(1)(i) of this section, § 640.5(e)(3), or § 640.5(f)(4), as applicable; or

(ii) Arranges to have the auto dealer or other party provide a notice described in §§ 640.3(a), 640.5(e), or 640.5(f) to the consumer on its behalf within the time periods set forth in paragraph (c)(1)(i) of this section, § 640.5(e)(3), or § 640.5(f)(4), as applicable, and maintains reasonable policies and procedures to verify that the auto dealer or other party provides such notice to the consumer within the applicable time periods. If the person arranges to have the auto dealer or other party provide a notice described in § 640.5(e), the person's obligation is satisfied if the consumer receives a notice containing a credit score obtained by the dealer or other party, even if a different credit score is obtained and used by the person on whose behalf the notice is provided.

(3) *Timing requirements for contemporaneous purchase credit.* When credit under an open-end credit plan is granted, extended, or provided to a consumer in person or by telephone for the purpose of financing the contemporaneous purchase of goods or services, any risk-based pricing notice required to be provided pursuant to this part (or the disclosures permitted under § 640.5(e) or (f)) may be provided at the earlier of:

(i) The time of the first mailing by the person to the consumer after the decision is made to approve the grant, extension, or other provision of open-end credit, such as in a mailing containing the account agreement or a credit card; or

(ii) Within 30 days after the decision to approve the grant, extension, or other provision of credit.

(d) *Multiple credit scores*—(1) *In general.* When a person obtains or creates two or more credit scores and uses one of those credit scores in setting the material terms of credit, for example, by using the low, middle, high, or most recent score, the notices described in paragraphs (a)(1) and (2) of this section must include that credit score and information relating to that credit score required by paragraphs (a)(1)(ix) and (a)(2)(ix). When a person obtains or creates two or more credit scores and uses multiple credit scores in setting the material terms of credit by, for example, computing the average of all the credit scores obtained or created, the notices described in paragraphs (a)(1) and (2) of this section must include one of those credit scores and information relating to credit scores required by paragraphs (a)(1)(ix) and (a)(2)(ix). The notice may, at the person's option, include more than one credit score, along with the additional information specified in paragraphs (a)(1)(ix) and (a)(2)(ix) of this section for each credit score disclosed.

(2) *Examples.* (i) A person that uses consumer reports to set the material terms of credit cards granted, extended, or provided to consumers regularly requests credit scores from several consumer reporting agencies and uses the low score when determining the material terms it will offer to the consumer. That person must disclose the low score in the notices described in paragraphs (a)(1) and (2) of this section.

(ii) A person that uses consumer reports to set the material terms of automobile loans granted, extended, or provided to consumers regularly requests credit scores from several consumer reporting agencies, each of which it uses in an underwriting program in order to determine the material terms it will offer to the consumer. That person may choose one of these scores to include in the notices described in paragraph (a)(1) and (2) of this section.

[75 FR 2769, Jan. 15, 2010, as amended at 76 FR 41621, July 15, 2011]

§ 640.5 Exceptions.

(a) *Application for specific terms*—(1) *In general.* A person is not required to provide a risk-based pricing notice to the consumer under § 640.3(a) or (c) if the consumer applies for specific material terms and is granted those terms, unless those terms were specified by the person using a consumer report after the consumer applied for or requested credit and after the person obtained the consumer report. For purposes of this section, "specific material terms" means a single material term, or set of material terms, such as an annual percentage rate of 10 percent, and not a range of alternatives, such as an annual percentage rate that may be 8, 10, or 12 percent, or between 8 and 12 percent.

(2) *Example.* A consumer receives a firm offer of credit from a credit card issuer. The terms of the firm offer are based in whole or in part on information from a consumer report that the credit card issuer obtained under the FCRA's firm offer of credit provisions. The solicitation offers the consumer a credit card with a single purchase annual percentage rate of 12 percent. The consumer applies for and receives a credit card with an annual percentage rate of 12 percent. Other customers

with the same credit card have a purchase annual percentage rate of 10 percent. The exception applies because the consumer applied for specific material terms and was granted those terms. Although the credit card issuer specified the annual percentage rate in the firm offer of credit based in whole or in part on a consumer report, the credit card issuer specified that material term *before*, not *after*, the consumer applied for or requested credit.

(b) *Adverse action notice.* A person is not required to provide a risk-based pricing notice to the consumer under § 640.3(a), (c), or (d) if the person provides an adverse action notice to the consumer under section 615(a) of the FCRA.

(c) *Prescreened solicitations*—(1) *In general.* A person is not required to provide a risk-based pricing notice to the consumer under § 640.3(a) or (c) if the person:

(i) Obtains a consumer report that is a prescreened list as described in section 604(c)(2) of the FCRA; and

(ii) Uses the consumer report for the purpose of making a firm offer of credit to the consumer.

(2) *More favorable material terms.* This exception applies to any firm offer of credit offered by a person to a consumer, even if the person makes other firm offers of credit to other consumers on more favorable material terms.

(3) *Example.* A credit card issuer obtains two prescreened lists from a consumer reporting agency. One list includes consumers with high credit scores. The other list includes consumers with low credit scores. The issuer mails a firm offer of credit to the high credit score consumers with a single purchase annual percentage rate of 10 percent. The issuer also mails a firm offer of credit to the low credit score consumers with a single purchase annual percentage rate of 14 percent. The credit card issuer is not required to provide a risk-based pricing notice to the low credit score consumers who receive the 14 percent offer because use of a consumer report to make a firm offer of credit does not trigger the risk-based pricing notice requirement.

(d) *Loans secured by residential real property—credit score disclosure*—(1) *In general.* A person is not required to provide a risk-based pricing notice to a consumer under § 640.3(a) or (c) if:

(i) The consumer requests from the person an extension of credit that is or will be secured by one to four units of residential real property; and

(ii) The person provides to each consumer described in paragraph (d)(1)(i) of this section a notice that contains the following—

(A) A statement that a consumer report (or credit report) is a record of the consumer's credit history and includes information about whether the consumer pays his or her obligations on time and how much the consumer owes to creditors;

(B) A statement that a credit score is a number that takes into account information in a consumer report and that a credit score can change over time to reflect changes in the consumer's credit history;

(C) A statement that the consumer's credit score can affect whether the consumer can obtain credit and what the cost of that credit will be;

(D) The information required to be disclosed to the consumer pursuant to section 609(g) of the FCRA;

(E) The distribution of credit scores among consumers who are scored under the same scoring model that is used to generate the consumer's credit score using the same scale as that of the credit score that is provided to the consumer, presented in the form of a bar graph containing a minimum of six bars that illustrates the percentage of consumers with credit scores within the range of scores reflected in each bar or by other clear and readily understandable graphical means, or a clear and readily understandable statement informing the consumer how his or her credit score compares to the scores of other consumers. Use of a graph or statement obtained from the person providing the credit score that meets the requirements of this paragraph (d)(1)(ii)(E) is deemed to comply with this requirement;

(F) A statement that the consumer is encouraged to verify the accuracy of the information contained in the consumer report and has the right to dispute any inaccurate information in the report;

(G) A statement that federal law gives the consumer the right to obtain copies of his or her consumer reports directly from the consumer reporting agencies, including a free report from each of the nationwide consumer reporting agencies once during any 12-month period;

(H) Contact information for the centralized source from which consumers may obtain their free annual consumer reports; and

(I) A statement directing consumers to the web sites of the Board and Federal Trade Commission to obtain more information about consumer reports.

(2) *Form of the notice.* The notice described in paragraph (d)(1)(ii) of this section must be:

(i) Clear and conspicuous;

(ii) Provided on or with the notice required by section 609(g) of the FCRA;

(iii) Segregated from other information provided to the consumer, except for the notice required by section 609(g) of the FCRA; and

(iv) Provided to the consumer in writing and in a form that the consumer may keep.

(3) *Timing.* The notice described in paragraph (d)(1)(ii) of this section must be provided to the consumer at the time the disclosure required by section 609(g) of the FCRA is provided to the consumer, but in any event at or before consummation in the case of closed-end credit or before the first transaction is made under an open-end credit plan.

(4) *Multiple credit scores*—(i) *In general.* When a person obtains two or more credit scores from consumer reporting agencies and uses one of those credit scores in setting the material terms of credit granted, extended, or otherwise provided to a consumer, for example, by using the low, middle, high, or most recent score, the notice described in paragraph (d)(1)(ii) of this section must include that credit score and the other information required by that paragraph. When a person obtains two or more credit scores from consumer reporting agencies and uses multiple credit scores in setting the material terms of credit granted, extended, or otherwise provided to a consumer, for example, by computing the average of all the credit scores obtained, the notice described in paragraph (d)(1)(ii) of this section must include one of those credit scores and the other information required by that paragraph. The notice may, at the person's option, include more than one credit score, along with the additional information specified in paragraph (d)(1)(ii) of this section for each credit score disclosed.

(ii) *Examples.* (A) A person that uses consumer reports to set the material terms of mortgage credit granted, extended, or provided to consumers regularly requests credit scores from several consumer reporting agencies and uses the low score when determining the material terms it will offer to the consumer. That person must disclose the low score in the notice described in paragraph (d)(1)(ii) of this section.

(B) A person that uses consumer reports to set the material terms of mortgage credit granted, extended, or provided to consumers regularly requests credit scores from several consumer reporting agencies, each of which it uses in an underwriting program in order to determine the material terms it will offer to the consumer. That person may choose one of these scores to include in the notice described in paragraph (d)(1)(ii) of this section.

(5) *Model form.* A model form of the notice described in paragraph (d)(1)(ii) of this section consolidated with the notice required by section 609(g) of the FCRA is contained in 16 CFR Part 698, Appendix B. Appropriate use of Model Form B–3 is deemed to comply with the requirements of § 640.5(d). Use of the model form is optional.

(e) *Other extensions of credit—credit score disclosure*—(1) *In general.* A person is not required to provide a risk-based pricing notice to a consumer under § 640.3(a) or (c) if:

(i) The consumer requests from the person an extension of credit other than credit that is or will be secured by one to four units of residential real property; and

(ii) The person provides to each consumer described in paragraph (e)(1)(i) of this section a notice that contains the following—

(A) A statement that a consumer report (or credit report) is a record of the consumer's credit history and includes information about whether the consumer pays his or her obligations on time and how much the consumer owes to creditors;

(B) A statement that a credit score is a number that takes into account information in a consumer report and that a credit score can change over time to reflect changes in the consumer's credit history;

(C) A statement that the consumer's credit score can affect whether the consumer can obtain credit and what the cost of that credit will be;

(D) The current credit score of the consumer or the most recent credit score of the consumer that was previously calculated by the consumer reporting agency for a purpose related to the extension of credit;

(E) The range of possible credit scores under the model used to generate the credit score;

(F) The distribution of credit scores among consumers who are scored under the same scoring model that is used to generate the consumer's credit score using the same scale as that of the credit score that is provided to the consumer, presented in the form of a bar graph containing a minimum of six bars that illustrates the percentage of consumers with credit scores within the range of scores reflected in each bar, or by other clear and readily understandable graphical means, or a clear and readily understandable statement informing the consumer how his or her credit score compares to the scores of other consumers. Use of a graph or statement obtained from the person providing the credit score that meets the requirements of this paragraph (e)(1)(ii)(F) is deemed to comply with this requirement;

(G) The date on which the credit score was created;

(H) The name of the consumer reporting agency or other person that provided the credit score;

(I) A statement that the consumer is encouraged to verify the accuracy of the information contained in the consumer report and has the right to dispute any inaccurate information in the report;

(J) A statement that federal law gives the consumer the right to obtain copies of his or her consumer reports directly from the consumer reporting agencies, including a free report from each of the nationwide consumer reporting agencies once during any 12-month period;

(K) Contact information for the centralized source from which consumers may obtain their free annual consumer reports; and

(L) A statement directing consumers to the web sites of the Federal Reserve Board and Federal Trade Commission to obtain more information about consumer reports.

(2) *Form of the notice.* The notice described in paragraph (e)(1)(ii) of this section must be:

(i) Clear and conspicuous;

(ii) Segregated from other information provided to the consumer; and

(iii) Provided to the consumer in writing and in a form that the consumer may keep.

(3) *Timing.* The notice described in paragraph (e)(1)(ii) of this section must be provided to the consumer as soon as reasonably practicable after the credit score has been obtained, but in any event at or before consummation in the case of closed-end credit or before the first transaction is made under an open-end credit plan.

(4) *Multiple credit scores*—(i) *In General.* When a person obtains two or more credit scores from consumer reporting agencies and uses one of those credit scores in setting the material terms of credit granted, extended, or otherwise provided to a consumer, for example, by using the low, middle, high, or most recent score, the notice described in paragraph (e)(1)(ii) of this section must include that credit score and the other information required by that paragraph. When a person obtains two or more credit scores from consumer reporting agencies and uses multiple credit scores in setting the material terms of credit granted, extended, or otherwise provided to a consumer, for example, by computing the average of all the credit scores obtained, the notice described in paragraph (e)(1)(ii) of this section must include one of those credit scores and the other information required by that paragraph. The notice may, at the person's option, include more than one credit score, along with the additional information

specified in paragraph (e)(1)(ii) of this section for each credit score disclosed.

(ii) *Examples.* The manner in which multiple credit scores are to be disclosed under this section are substantially identical to the manner set forth in the examples contained in paragraph (d)(4)(ii) of this section.

(5) *Model form.* A model form of the notice described in paragraph (e)(1)(ii) of this section is contained in 16 CFR part B, appendix B. Appropriate use of Model Form B–4 is deemed to comply with the requirements of §640.5(e). Use of the model form is optional.

(f) *Credit score not available*—(1) *In general.* A person is not required to provide a risk-based pricing notice to a consumer under §640.3(a) or (c) if the person:

(i) Regularly obtains credit scores from a consumer reporting agency and provides credit score disclosures to consumers in accordance with paragraphs (d) or (e) of this section, but a credit score is not available from the consumer reporting agency from which the person regularly obtains credit scores for a consumer to whom the person grants, extends, or provides credit;

(ii) Does not obtain a credit score from another consumer reporting agency in connection with granting, extending, or providing credit to the consumer; and

(iii) Provides to the consumer a notice that contains the following—

(A) A statement that a consumer report (or credit report) includes information about the consumer's credit history and the type of information included in that history;

(B) A statement that a credit score is a number that takes into account information in a consumer report and that a credit score can change over time in response to changes in the consumer's credit history;

(C) A statement that credit scores are important because consumers with higher credit scores generally obtain more favorable credit terms;

(D) A statement that not having a credit score can affect whether the consumer can obtain credit and what the cost of that credit will be;

(E) A statement that a credit score about the consumer was not available from a consumer reporting agency, which must be identified by name, generally due to insufficient information regarding the consumer's credit history;

(F) A statement that the consumer is encouraged to verify the accuracy of the information contained in the consumer report and has the right to dispute any inaccurate information in the consumer report;

(G) A statement that federal law gives the consumer the right to obtain copies of his or her consumer reports directly from the consumer reporting agencies, including a free consumer report from each of the nationwide consumer reporting agencies once during any 12-month period;

(H) The contact information for the centralized source from which consumers may obtain their free annual consumer reports; and

(I) A statement directing consumers to the web sites of the Board and Federal Trade Commission to obtain more information about consumer reports.

(2) *Example.* A person that uses consumer reports to set the material terms of non-mortgage credit granted, extended, or provided to consumers regularly requests credit scores from a particular consumer reporting agency and provides those credit scores and additional information to consumers to satisfy the requirements of paragraph (e) of this section. That consumer reporting agency provides to the person a consumer report on a particular consumer that contains one trade line, but does not provide the person with a credit score on that consumer. If the person does not obtain a credit score from another consumer reporting agency and, based in whole or in part on information in a consumer report, grants, extends, or provides credit to the consumer, the person may provide the notice described in paragraph (f)(1)(iii) of this section. If, however, the person obtains a credit score from another consumer reporting agency, the person may not rely upon the exception in paragraph (f) of this section, but may satisfy the requirements of paragraph (e) of this section.

(3) *Form of the notice.* The notice described in paragraph (f)(1)(iii) of this section must be:

(i) Clear and conspicuous;

(ii) Segregated from other information provided to the consumer; and

(iii) Provided to the consumer in writing and in a form that the consumer may keep.

(4) *Timing.* The notice described in paragraph (f)(1)(iii) of this section must be provided to the consumer as soon as reasonably practicable after the person has requested the credit score, but in any event not later than consummation of a transaction in the case of closed-end credit or when the first transaction is made under an open-end credit plan.

(5) *Model form.* A model form of the notice described in paragraph (f)(1)(iii) of this section is contained in 16 CFR part 698, appendix B. Appropriate use of Model Form B–5 is deemed to comply with the requirements of § 640.5(f). Use of the model form is optional.

§ 640.6 Rules of construction.

For purposes of this part, the following rules of construction apply:

(a) *One notice per credit extension.* A consumer is entitled to no more than one risk-based pricing notice under § 640.3(a) or (c), or one notice under § 640.5(d), (e), or (f), for each grant, extension, or other provision of credit. Notwithstanding the foregoing, even if a consumer has previously received a risk-based pricing notice in connection with a grant, extension, or other provision of credit, another risk-based pricing notice is required if the conditions set forth in § 640.3(d) have been met.

(b) *Multi-party transactions*—(1) *Initial creditor.* The person to whom a credit obligation is initially payable must provide the risk-based pricing notice described in § 640.3(a) or (c), or satisfy the requirements for and provide the notice required under one of the exceptions in § 640.5(d), (e), or (f), even if that person immediately assigns the credit agreement to a third party and is not the source of funding for the credit.

(2) *Purchasers or assignees.* A purchaser or assignee of a credit contract with a consumer is not subject to the requirements of this part and is not required to provide the risk-based pricing notice described in § 640.3(a) or (c), or satisfy the requirements for and provide the notice required under one of the exceptions in § 640.5(d), (e), or (f).

(3) *Examples.* (i) A consumer obtains credit to finance the purchase of an automobile. If the auto dealer is the person to whom the loan obligation is initially payable, such as where the auto dealer is the original creditor under a retail installment sales contract, the auto dealer must provide the risk-based pricing notice to the consumer (or satisfy the requirements for and provide the notice required under one of the exceptions noted above), even if the auto dealer immediately assigns the loan to a bank or finance company. The bank or finance company, which is an assignee, has no duty to provide a risk-based pricing notice to the consumer.

(ii) A consumer obtains credit to finance the purchase of an automobile. If a bank or finance company is the person to whom the loan obligation is initially payable, the bank or finance company must provide the risk-based pricing notice to the consumer (or satisfy the requirements for and provide the notice required under one of the exceptions noted above) based on the terms offered by that bank or finance company only. The auto dealer has no duty to provide a risk-based pricing notice to the consumer. However, the bank or finance company may comply with this rule if the auto dealer has agreed to provide notices to consumers before consummation pursuant to an arrangement with the bank or finance company, as permitted under § 640.4(c).

(c) *Multiple consumers*—(1) *Risk-based pricing notices.* In a transaction involving two or more consumers who are granted, extended, or otherwise provided credit, a person must provide a notice to each consumer to satisfy the requirements of § 640.3(a) or (c). Whether the consumers have the same address or not, the person must provide a separate notice to each consumer if a notice includes a credit score(s). Each separate notice that includes a credit score(s) must contain only the credit score(s) of the consumer to whom the notice is provided, and not the credit score(s) of the other consumer. If the consumers have the same address, and the notice does not include a credit score(s), a person may satisfy the requirements by providing a single notice addressed to both consumers.

(2) *Credit score disclosure notices.* In a transaction involving two or more consumers who are granted, extended, or otherwise provided credit, a person must provide a separate notice to each consumer to satisfy the exceptions in § 640.5(d), (e), or (f). Whether the consumers have the same address or not, the person must provide a separate notice to each consumer. Each separate notice must contain only the credit score(s) of the consumer to whom the notice is provided, and not the credit score(s) of the other consumer.

(3) *Examples.* (i) Two consumers jointly apply for credit with a creditor. The creditor obtains credit scores on both consumers. Based in part on the credit scores, the creditor grants credit to the consumers on material terms that are materially less favorable than the most favorable terms available to other consumers from the creditor. The creditor provides risk-based pricing notices to satisfy its obligations under this subpart. The creditor must provide a separate risk-based pricing notice to each consumer whether the consumers have the same address or not. Each risk-based pricing notice must contain only the credit score(s) of the consumer to whom the notice is provided.

(ii) Two consumers jointly apply for credit with a creditor. The two consumers reside at the same address. The creditor obtains credit scores on each of the two consumer applicants. The creditor grants credit to the consumers. The creditor provides credit score disclosure notices to satisfy its obligations under this part. Even though the two consumers reside at the same address, the creditor must provide a separate credit score disclosure notice to each of the consumers. Each notice must contain only the credit score of the consumer to whom the notice is provided.

[75 FR 2769, Jan. 15, 2010, as amended at 76 FR 41622, July 15, 2011]

PART 641—DUTIES OF USERS OF CONSUMER REPORTS REGARDING ADDRESS DISCREPANCIES

AUTHORITY: Public Law 108–159, sec. 315; 15 U.S.C. 1681c(h).

SOURCE: 74 FR 22644, May 14, 2009, unless otherwise noted.

§ 641.1 Duties of users of consumer reports regarding address discrepancies.

(a) *Scope.* This section applies to users of consumer reports that are subject to administrative enforcement of the FCRA by the Federal Trade Commission pursuant to 15 U.S.C. 1681s(a)(1) (users).

(b) *Definition.* For purposes of this section, a *notice of address discrepancy* means a notice sent to a user by a consumer reporting agency described in 15 U.S.C. 1681a(p) pursuant to 15 U.S.C. 1681c(h)(1), that informs the user of a substantial difference between the address for the consumer that the user provided to request the consumer report and the address(es) in the agency's file for the consumer.

(c) *Reasonable belief*—(1) *Requirement to form a reasonable belief.* A user must develop and implement reasonable policies and procedures designed to enable the user to form a reasonable belief that a consumer report relates to the consumer about whom it has requested the report, when the user receives a notice of address discrepancy.

(2) *Examples of reasonable policies and procedures.* (i) Comparing the information in the consumer report provided by the consumer reporting agency with information the user:

(A) Obtains and uses to verify the consumer's identity in accordance with the requirements of the Customer Identification Program (CIP) rules implementing 31 U.S.C. 5318(l) (31 CFR 103.121);

(B) Maintains in its own records, such as applications, change of address notifications, other customer account records, or retained CIP documentation; or

(C) Obtains from third-party sources; or

(ii) Verifying the information in the consumer report provided by the consumer reporting agency with the consumer.

(d) *Consumer's address*—(1) *Requirement to furnish consumer's address to a consumer reporting agency.* A user must develop and implement reasonable policies and procedures for furnishing an address for the consumer that the user has reasonably confirmed is accurate to the consumer reporting agency described in 15 U.S.C. 1681a(p) from whom it received the notice of address discrepancy when the user:

(i) Can form a reasonable belief that the consumer report relates to the consumer about whom the user requested the report;

(ii) Establishes a continuing relationship with the consumer; and

(iii) Regularly and in the ordinary course of business furnishes information to the consumer reporting agency from which the notice of address discrepancy relating to the consumer was obtained.

(2) *Examples of confirmation methods.* The user may reasonably confirm an address is accurate by:

(i) Verifying the address with the consumer about whom it has requested the report;

(ii) Reviewing its own records to verify the address of the consumer;

(iii) Verifying the address through third-party sources; or

(iv) Using other reasonable means.

(3) *Timing.* The policies and procedures developed in accordance with paragraph (d)(1) of this section must provide that the user will furnish the consumer's address that the user has reasonably confirmed is accurate to the consumer reporting agency described in 15 U.S.C. 1681a(p) as part of the information it regularly furnishes for the reporting period in which it establishes a relationship with the consumer.

PART 642—PRESCREEN OPT-OUT NOTICE

Sec.

AUTHORITY: Pub. L. 108–159, sec. 213(a); 15 U.S.C. 1681m(d).

SOURCE: 70 FR 5032, Jan. 31, 2005, unless otherwise noted.

§ 642.1 Purpose and scope.

(a) *Purpose.* This part implements section 213(a) of the Fair and Accurate Credit Transactions Act of 2003, which requires the Federal Trade Commission to establish the format, type size, and manner of the notices to consumers, required by section 615(d) of the Fair Credit Reporting Act ("FCRA"), regarding the right to prohibit ("opt out" of) the use of information in a consumer report to send them solicitations of credit or insurance.

(b) *Scope.* This part applies to any person who uses a consumer report on any consumer in connection with any credit or insurance transaction that is not initiated by the consumer, and that is provided to that person under section 604(c)(1)(B) of the FCRA (15 U.S.C. 1681b(c)(1)(B)).

§ 642.2 Definitions.

As used in this part:

(a) *Simple and easy to understand* means:

(1) A layered format as described in § 642.3 of this part;

(2) Plain language designed to be understood by ordinary consumers; and

(3) Use of clear and concise sentences, paragraphs, and sections.

(i) *Examples.* For purposes of this part, examples of factors to be considered in determining whether a statement is in plain language and uses clear and concise sentences, paragraphs, and sections include:

(A) Use of short explanatory sentences;

(B) Use of definite, concrete, everyday words;

(C) Use of active voice;

(D) Avoidance of multiple negatives;

(E) Avoidance of legal and technical business terminology;

(F) Avoidance of explanations that are imprecise and reasonably subject to different interpretations; and

(G) Use of language that is not misleading.

(ii) [Reserved]

(b) *Principal promotional document* means the document designed to be seen first by the consumer, such as the cover letter.

§ 642.3 Prescreen opt-out notice.

Any person who uses a consumer report on any consumer in connection with any credit or insurance transaction that is not initiated by the consumer, and that is provided to that person under section 604(c)(1)(B) of the

FCRA (15 U.S.C. 1681b(c)(1)(B)), shall, with each written solicitation made to the consumer about the transaction, provide the consumer with the following statement, consisting of a short portion and a long portion, which shall be in the same language as the offer of credit or insurance:

(a) *Short notice.* The short notice shall be a clear and conspicuous, and simple and easy to understand statement as follows:

(1) *Content.* The short notice shall state that the consumer has the right to opt out of receiving prescreened solicitations, and shall provide the toll-free number the consumer can call to exercise that right. The short notice also shall direct the consumer to the existence and location of the long notice, and shall state the heading for the long notice. The short notice shall not contain any other information.

(2) *Form.* The short notice shall be:

(i) In a type size that is larger than the type size of the principal text on the same page, but in no event smaller than 12-point type, or if provided by electronic means, then reasonable steps shall be taken to ensure that the type size is larger than the type size of the principal text on the same page;

(ii) On the front side of the first page of the principal promotional document in the solicitation, or, if provided electronically, on the same page and in close proximity to the principal marketing message;

(iii) Located on the page and in a format so that the statement is distinct from other text, such as inside a border; and

(iv) In a type style that is distinct from the principal type style used on the same page, such as bolded, italicized, underlined, and/or in a color that contrasts with the color of the principal text on the page, if the solicitation is in more than one color.

(b) *Long notice.* The long notice shall be a clear and conspicuous, and simple and easy to understand statement as follows:

(1) *Content.* The long notice shall state the information required by section 615(d) of the Fair Credit Reporting Act (15 U.S.C. 1681m(d)). The long notice shall not include any other information that interferes with, detracts from, contradicts, or otherwise undermines the purpose of the notice.

(2) *Form.* The long notice shall:

(i) Appear in the solicitation;

(ii) Be in a type size that is no smaller than the type size of the principal text on the same page, and, for solicitations provided other than by electronic means, the type size shall in no event be smaller than 8-point type;

(iii) Begin with a heading in capital letters and underlined, and identifying the long notice as the "PRESCREEN & OPT-OUT NOTICE";

(iv) Be in a type style that is distinct from the principal type style used on the same page, such as bolded, italicized, underlined, and/or in a color that contrasts with the color of the principal text on the page, if the solicitation is in more than one color; and

(v) Be set apart from other text on the page, such as by including a blank line above and below the statement, and by indenting both the left and right margins from other text on the page.

§ 642.4 Effective date.

This part is effective on August 1, 2005.

PART 660—DUTIES OF FURNISHERS OF INFORMATION TO CONSUMER REPORTING AGENCIES

AUTHORITY: 15 U.S.C. 1681s-2(a)(8) and 1681s-2(e); Sec. 312, Pub. L. 108–159, 117 Stat. 1989.

SOURCE: 74 FR 31525, July 1, 2009, unless otherwise noted.

§ 660.1 Scope.

This part applies to furnishers of information to consumer reporting agencies that are subject to administrative enforcement of the FCRA by the Federal Trade Commission pursuant to 15

U.S.C. 1681s(a)(1) (referred to as "furnishers").

§ 660.2 Definitions.

For purposes of this part and appendix A of this part, the following definitions apply:

(a) *Accuracy* means that information that a furnisher provides to a consumer reporting agency about an account or other relationship with the consumer correctly:

(1) Reflects the terms of and liability for the account or other relationship;

(2) Reflects the consumer's performance and other conduct with respect to the account or other relationship; and

(3) Identifies the appropriate consumer.

(b) *Direct dispute* means a dispute submitted directly to a furnisher (including a furnisher that is a debt collector) by a consumer concerning the accuracy of any information contained in a consumer report and pertaining to an account or other relationship that the furnisher has or had with the consumer.

(c) *Furnisher* means an entity that furnishes information relating to consumers to one or more consumer reporting agencies for inclusion in a consumer report. An entity is not a furnisher when it:

(1) Provides information to a consumer reporting agency solely to obtain a consumer report in accordance with sections 604(a) and (f) of the Fair Credit Reporting Act;

(2) Is acting as a "consumer reporting agency" as defined in section 603(f) of the Fair Credit Reporting Act;

(3) Is a consumer to whom the furnished information pertains; or

(4) Is a neighbor, friend, or associate of the consumer, or another individual with whom the consumer is acquainted or who may have knowledge about the consumer, and who provides information about the consumer's character, general reputation, personal characteristics, or mode of living in response to a specific request from a consumer reporting agency.

(d) *Identity theft* has the same meaning as in 16 CFR 603.2(a).

(e) *Integrity* means that information that a furnisher provides to a consumer reporting agency about an account or other relationship with the consumer:

(1) Is substantiated by the furnisher's records at the time it is furnished;

(2) Is furnished in a form and manner that is designed to minimize the likelihood that the information may be incorrectly reflected in a consumer report; and

(3) Includes the information in the furnisher's possession about the account or other relationship that the Commission has:

(i) Determined that the absence of which would likely be materially misleading in evaluating a consumer's creditworthiness, credit standing, credit capacity, character, general reputation, personal characteristics, or mode of living; and (ii) Listed in section I.(b)(2)(iii) of Appendix A of this part.

§ 660.3 Reasonable policies and procedures concerning the accuracy and integrity of furnished information.

(a) *Policies and procedures.* Each furnisher must establish and implement reasonable written policies and procedures regarding the accuracy and integrity of the information relating to consumers that it furnishes to a consumer reporting agency. The policies and procedures must be appropriate to the nature, size, complexity, and scope of each furnisher's activities.

(b) *Guidelines.* Each furnisher must consider the guidelines in Appendix A of this part in developing its policies and procedures required by this section, and incorporate those guidelines that are appropriate.

(c) *Reviewing and updating policies and procedures.* Each furnisher must review its policies and procedures required by this section periodically and update them as necessary to ensure their continued effectiveness.

§ 660.4 Direct disputes.

(a) *General rule.* Except as otherwise provided in this section, a furnisher must conduct a reasonable investigation of a direct dispute if it relates to:

(1) The consumer's liability for a credit account or other debt with the furnisher, such as direct disputes relating to whether there is or has been identity theft or fraud against the consumer, whether there is individual or

joint liability on an account, or whether the consumer is an authorized user of a credit account;

(2) The terms of a credit account or other debt with the furnisher, such as direct disputes relating to the type of account, principal balance, scheduled payment amount on an account, or the amount of the credit limit on an open-end account;

(3) The consumer's performance or other conduct concerning an account or other relationship with the furnisher, such as direct disputes relating to the current payment status, high balance, date a payment was made, the amount of a payment made, or the date an account was opened or closed; or

(4) Any other information contained in a consumer report regarding an account or other relationship with the furnisher that bears on the consumer's creditworthiness, credit standing, credit capacity, character, general reputation, personal characteristics, or mode of living.

(b) *Exceptions.* The requirements of paragraph (a) of this section do not apply to a furnisher if:

(1) The direct dispute relates to:

(i) The consumer's identifying information (other than a direct dispute relating to a consumer's liability for a credit account or other debt with the furnisher, as provided in paragraph (a)(1) of this section) such as name(s), date of birth, Social Security number, telephone number(s), or address(es);

(ii) The identity of past or present employers;

(iii) Inquiries or requests for a consumer report;

(iv) Information derived from public records, such as judgments, bankruptcies, liens, and other legal matters (unless provided by a furnisher with an account or other relationship with the consumer);

(v) Information related to fraud alerts or active duty alerts; or

(vi) Information provided to a consumer reporting agency by another furnisher; or

(2) The furnisher has a reasonable belief that the direct dispute is submitted by, is prepared on behalf of the consumer by, or is submitted on a form supplied to the consumer by, a credit repair organization, as defined in 15 U.S.C. 1679a(3), or an entity that would be a credit repair organization, but for 15 U.S.C. 1679a(3)(B)(i).

(c) *Direct dispute address.* A furnisher is required to investigate a direct dispute only if a consumer submits a dispute notice to the furnisher at:

(1) The address of a furnisher provided by a furnisher and set forth on a consumer report relating to the consumer;

(2) An address clearly and conspicuously specified by the furnisher for submitting direct disputes that is provided to the consumer in writing or electronically (if the consumer has agreed to the electronic delivery of information from the furnisher); or

(3) Any business address of the furnisher if the furnisher has not so specified and provided an address for submitting direct disputes under paragraphs (c)(1) or (2) of this section.

(d) *Direct dispute notice contents.* A dispute notice must include:

(1) Sufficient information to identify the account or other relationship that is in dispute, such as an account number and the name, address, and telephone number of the consumer, if applicable;

(2) The specific information that the consumer is disputing and an explanation of the basis for the dispute; and

(3) All supporting documentation or other information reasonably required by the furnisher to substantiate the basis of the dispute. This documentation may include, for example: a copy of the relevant portion of the consumer report that contains the allegedly inaccurate information; a police report; a fraud or identity theft affidavit; a court order; or account statements.

(e) *Duty of furnisher after receiving a direct dispute notice.* After receiving a dispute notice from a consumer pursuant to paragraphs (c) and (d) of this section, the furnisher must:

(1) Conduct a reasonable investigation with respect to the disputed information;

(2) Review all relevant information provided by the consumer with the dispute notice;

(3) Complete its investigation of the dispute and report the results of the investigation to the consumer before the expiration of the period under section

611(a)(1) of the Fair Credit Reporting Act (15 U.S.C. 1681i(a)(1)) within which a consumer reporting agency would be required to complete its action if the consumer had elected to dispute the information under that section; and

(4) If the investigation finds that the information reported was inaccurate, promptly notify each consumer reporting agency to which the furnisher provided inaccurate information of that determination and provide to the consumer reporting agency any correction to that information that is necessary to make the information provided by the furnisher accurate.

(f) *Frivolous or irrelevant disputes.* (1) A furnisher is not required to investigate a direct dispute if the furnisher has reasonably determined that the dispute is frivolous or irrelevant. A dispute qualifies as frivolous or irrelevant if:

(i) The consumer did not provide sufficient information to investigate the disputed information as required by paragraph (d) of this section;

(ii) The direct dispute is substantially the same as a dispute previously submitted by or on behalf of the consumer, either directly to the furnisher or through a consumer reporting agency, with respect to which the furnisher has already satisfied the applicable requirements of the Act or this section; provided, however, that a direct dispute is not substantially the same as a dispute previously submitted if the dispute includes information listed in paragraph (d) of this section that had not previously been provided to the furnisher; or

(iii) The furnisher is not required to investigate the direct dispute because one or more of the exceptions listed in paragraph (b) of this section applies.

(2) *Notice of determination.* Upon making a determination that a dispute is frivolous or irrelevant, the furnisher must notify the consumer of the determination not later than five business days after making the determination, by mail or, if authorized by the consumer for that purpose, by any other means available to the furnisher.

(3) *Contents of notice of determination that a dispute is frivolous or irrelevant.* A notice of determination that a dispute is frivolous or irrelevant must include the reasons for such determination and identify any information required to investigate the disputed information, which notice may consist of a standardized form describing the general nature of such information.

APPENDIX A TO PART 660—INTERAGENCY GUIDELINES CONCERNING THE ACCURACY AND INTEGRITY OF INFORMATION FURNISHED TO CONSUMER REPORTING AGENCIES

The Commission encourages voluntary furnishing of information to consumer reporting agencies. Section 660.3 of this part requires each furnisher to establish and implement reasonable written policies and procedures concerning the accuracy and integrity of the information it furnishes to consumer reporting agencies. Under §660.3(b), a furnisher must consider the guidelines set forth below in developing its policies and procedures. In establishing these policies and procedures, a furnisher may include any of its existing policies and procedures that are relevant and appropriate. Section 660.3(c) requires each furnisher to review its policies and procedures periodically and update them as necessary to ensure their continued effectiveness.

I. NATURE, SCOPE, AND OBJECTIVES OF POLICIES AND PROCEDURES

(a) *Nature and Scope.* Section 660.3(a) of this part requires that a furnisher's policies and procedures be appropriate to the nature, size, complexity, and scope of the furnisher's activities. In developing its policies and procedures, a furnisher should consider, for example:

(1) The types of business activities in which the furnisher engages;

(2) The nature and frequency of the information the furnisher provides to consumer reporting agencies; and

(3) The technology used by the furnisher to furnish information to consumer reporting agencies.

(b) *Objectives.* A furnisher's policies and procedures should be reasonably designed to promote the following objectives:

(1) To furnish information about accounts or other relationships with a consumer that is accurate, such that the furnished information:

(i) Identifies the appropriate consumer;

(ii) Reflects the terms of and liability for those accounts or other relationships; and

(iii) Reflects the consumer's performance and other conduct with respect to the account or other relationship;

(2) To furnish information about accounts or other relationships with a consumer that has integrity, such that the furnished information:

(i) Is substantiated by the furnisher's records at the time it is furnished;

(ii) Is furnished in a form and manner that is designed to minimize the likelihood that the information may be incorrectly reflected in a consumer report; thus, the furnished information should:

(A) Include appropriate identifying information about the consumer to whom it pertains; and

(B) Be furnished in a standardized and clearly understandable form and manner and with a date specifying the time period to which the information pertains; and

(iii) Includes the credit limit, if applicable and in the furnisher's possession;

(3) To conduct reasonable investigations of consumer disputes and take appropriate actions based on the outcome of such investigations; and

(4) To update the information it furnishes as necessary to reflect the current status of the consumer's account or other relationship, including, for example:

(i) Any transfer of an account (*e.g.*, by sale or assignment for collection) to a third party; and

(ii) Any cure of the consumer's failure to abide by the terms of the account or other relationship.

II. ESTABLISHING AND IMPLEMENTING POLICIES AND PROCEDURES

In establishing and implementing its policies and procedures, a furnisher should:

(a) Identify practices or activities of the furnisher that can compromise the accuracy or integrity of information furnished to consumer reporting agencies, such as by:

(1) Reviewing its existing practices and activities, including the technological means and other methods it uses to furnish information to consumer reporting agencies and the frequency and timing of its furnishing of information;

(2) Reviewing its historical records relating to accuracy or integrity or to disputes; reviewing other information relating to the accuracy or integrity of information provided by the furnisher to consumer reporting agencies; and considering the types of errors, omissions, or other problems that may have affected the accuracy or integrity of information it has furnished about consumers to consumer reporting agencies;

(3) Considering any feedback received from consumer reporting agencies, consumers, or other appropriate parties;

(4) Obtaining feedback from the furnisher's staff; and

(5) Considering the potential impact of the furnisher's policies and procedures on consumers.

(b) Evaluate the effectiveness of existing policies and procedures of the furnisher regarding the accuracy and integrity of information furnished to consumer reporting agencies; consider whether new, additional, or different policies and procedures are necessary; and consider whether implementation of existing policies and procedures should be modified to enhance the accuracy and integrity of information about consumers furnished to consumer reporting agencies.

(c) Evaluate the effectiveness of specific methods (including technological means) the furnisher uses to provide information to consumer reporting agencies; how those methods may affect the accuracy and integrity of the information it provides to consumer reporting agencies; and whether new, additional, or different methods (including technological means) should be used to provide information to consumer reporting agencies to enhance the accuracy and integrity of that information.

III. SPECIFIC COMPONENTS OF POLICIES AND PROCEDURES

In developing its policies and procedures, a furnisher should address the following, as appropriate:

(a) Establishing and implementing a system for furnishing information about consumers to consumer reporting agencies that is appropriate to the nature, size, complexity, and scope of the furnisher's business operations.

(b) Using standard data reporting formats and standard procedures for compiling and furnishing data, where feasible, such as the electronic transmission of information about consumers to consumer reporting agencies.

(c) Maintaining records for a reasonable period of time, not less than any applicable recordkeeping requirement, in order to substantiate the accuracy of any information about consumers it furnishes that is subject to a direct dispute.

(d) Establishing and implementing appropriate internal controls regarding the accuracy and integrity of information about consumers furnished to consumer reporting agencies, such as by implementing standard procedures and verifying random samples of information provided to consumer reporting agencies.

(e) Training staff that participates in activities related to the furnishing of information about consumers to consumer reporting agencies to implement the policies and procedures.

(f) Providing for appropriate and effective oversight of relevant service providers whose activities may affect the accuracy or integrity of information about consumers furnished to consumer reporting agencies to ensure compliance with the policies and procedures.

(g) Furnishing information about consumers to consumer reporting agencies following mergers, portfolio acquisitions or sales, or other acquisitions or transfers of accounts or other obligations in a manner that prevents re-aging of information, duplicative reporting, or other problems that may similarly affect the accuracy or integrity of the information furnished.

(h) Deleting, updating, and correcting information in the furnisher's records, as appropriate, to avoid furnishing inaccurate information.

(i) Conducting reasonable investigations of disputes.

(j) Designing technological and other means of communication with consumer reporting agencies to prevent duplicative reporting of accounts, erroneous association of information with the wrong consumer(s), and other occurrences that may compromise the accuracy or integrity of information provided to consumer reporting agencies.

(k) Providing consumer reporting agencies with sufficient identifying information in the furnisher's possession about each consumer about whom information is furnished to enable the consumer reporting agency properly to identify the consumer.

(l) Conducting a periodic evaluation of its own practices, consumer reporting agency practices of which the furnisher is aware, investigations of disputed information, corrections of inaccurate information, means of communication, and other factors that may affect the accuracy or integrity of information furnished to consumer reporting agencies.

(m) Complying with applicable requirements under the Fair Credit Reporting Act and its implementing regulations.

PART 680—AFFILIATE MARKETING

Sec.

AUTHORITY: Sec. 214(b), Pub. L. 108-159; 15 U.S.C. 1681s-3

SOURCE: 72 FR 61455, Oct. 30, 2007, unless otherwise noted.

§ 680.1 Purpose and scope.

(a) *Purpose.* The purpose of this part is to implement section 214 of the Fair and Accu-rate Credit Transactions Act of 2003, which (by adding section 624 to Fair Credit Reporting Act) regulates the use, for marketing solicitation purposes, of consumer information provided by persons affiliated with the person making the solicitation.

(b) *Scope.* This part applies to any person over which the Federal Trade Commission has jurisdiction that uses information from its affiliates for the purpose of marketing solicitations, or provides information to its affiliates for that purpose.

§ 680.2 Examples.

The examples in this part are not exclusive. Compliance with an example, to the extent applicable, constitutes compliance with this part. Examples in a paragraph illustrate only the issue described in the paragraph and do not illustrate any other issue that may arise in this part.

§ 680.3 Definitions.

As used in this part:

(a) *Act.* The term "Act" means the Fair Credit Reporting Act (15 U.S.C. 1681 *et seq.*).

(b) *Affiliate.* The term "affiliate" means any company that is related by common ownership or common corporate control with another company.

(c) *Clear and conspicuous.* The term "clear and conspicuous" means reasonably under-standable and designed to call attention to the nature and significance of the information presented.

(d) *Common ownership or common corporate control.* The term "common ownership or common corporate control" means a relationship between two companies under which:

(1) One company has, with respect to the other company:

(i) Ownership, control, or the power to vote 25 percent or more of the outstanding shares of any class of voting security of a company, directly or indirectly, or acting through one or more other persons;

(ii) Control in any manner over the election of a majority of the directors, trustees, or general partners (or individuals exercising similar functions) of a company; or

(iii) The power to exercise, directly or indirectly, a controlling influence over the management or policies of a company, as the Commission determines; or

(2) Any person has, with respect to both companies, a relationship described in paragraphs (d)(1)(i) through (d)(1)(iii) of this section.

(e) *Company.* The term "company" means any corporation, limited liability company, business trust, general or limited partnership, association, or similar organization.

(f) *Concise*—(1) *In general.* The term "concise" means a reasonably brief expression or statement.

(2) *Combination with other required disclosures.* A notice required by this part may be concise even if it is combined with other disclosures required or authorized by federal or state law.

(g) *Consumer.* The term "consumer" means an individual.

(h) *Eligibility information.* The term "eligibility information" means any information the communication of which would be a consumer report if the exclusions from the definition of "consumer report" in section 603(d)(2)(A) of the Act did not apply. Eligibility information does not include aggregate or blind data that does not contain personal identifiers such as account numbers, names, or addresses.

(i) *Person.* The term "person" means any individual, partnership, corporation, trust, estate, cooperative, association, government or governmental subdivision or agency, or other entity.

(j) *Pre-existing business relationship*—(1) *In general.* The term "pre-existing business relationship" means a relationship between a person, or a person's licensed agent, and a consumer based on—

(i) A financial contract between the person and the consumer which is in force on the date on which the consumer is sent a solicitation covered by this part;

(ii) The purchase, rental, or lease by the consumer of the persons' goods or services, or a financial transaction (including holding an active account or a policy in force or having another continuing relationship) between the consumer and the person, during the 18-month period immediately preceding the date on which the consumer is sent a solicitation covered by this part; or

(iii) An inquiry or application by the consumer regarding a product or service offered by that person during the three-month period immediately preceding the date on which the consumer is sent a solicitation covered by this part.

(2) *Examples of pre-existing business relationships.* (i) If a consumer has an existing loan account with a creditor, the creditor has a pre-existing business relationship with the consumer and can use eligibility information it receives from its affiliates to make solicitations to the consumer about its products or services.

(ii) If a consumer obtained a mortgage from a mortgage lender, but refinanced the mortgage loan with a different lender when the mortgage loan came due, the first mortgage lender has a pre-existing business relationship with the consumer and can use eligibility information it receives from its affiliates to make solicitations to the consumer about its products or services for 18 months after the date the outstanding balance of the loan is paid and the loan is closed.

(iii) If a consumer obtains a mortgage, the mortgage lender has a pre-existing business relationship with the consumer. If the mortgage lender sells the consumer's entire loan to an investor, the mortgage lender has a pre-existing business relationship with the consumer and can use eligibility information it receives from its affiliates to make solicitations to the consumer about its products or services for 18 months after the date it sells the loan, and the investor has a pre-existing business relationship with the consumer upon purchasing the loan. If, however, the mortgage lender sells a fractional interest in the consumer's loan to an investor but also retains an ownership interest in the loan, the mortgage lender continues to have a pre-existing business relationship with the consumer, but the investor does not have a pre-existing business relationship with the consumer. If the mortgage lender retains ownership of the loan, but sells ownership of the servicing rights to the consumer's loan, the mortgage lender continues to have a pre-existing business relationship with the consumer. The purchaser of the servicing rights also has a pre-existing business relationship with the consumer as of the date it purchases ownership of the servicing rights, but only if it collects payments from or otherwise deals directly with the consumer on a continuing basis.

(iv) If a consumer applies to a creditor for a product or service that it offers, but does not obtain a product or service from or enter into a financial contract or transaction with the creditor, the creditor has a pre-existing business relationship with the consumer and can therefore use eligibility information it receives from an affiliate to make solicitations to the consumer about its products or services for three months after the date of the application.

(v) If a consumer makes a telephone inquiry to a creditor about its products or services and provides contact information to the creditor, but does not obtain a product or service from or enter into a financial contract or transaction with the creditor, the creditor has a pre-existing business relationship with the consumer and can therefore use eligibility information it receives from an affiliate to make solicitations to the consumer about its products or services for three months after the date of the inquiry.

(vi) If a consumer makes an inquiry to a creditor by e-mail about its products or services, but does not obtain a product or service from or enter into a financial contract or transaction with the creditor, the creditor has a pre-existing business relationship with the consumer and can therefore use eligibility information it receives from an affiliate to make solicitations to the consumer about its products or services for three months after the date of the inquiry.

(vii) If a consumer has an existing relationship with a creditor that is part of a group of affiliated companies, makes a telephone call to the centralized call center for the group of affiliated companies to inquire about products or services offered by the insurance affiliate, and provides contact information to the call center, the call constitutes an inquiry to the insurance affiliate that offers those products or services. The insurance affiliate has a pre-existing business relationship with the consumer and can therefore use eligibility information it receives from its affiliated creditor to make solicitations to the consumer about its products or services for three months after the date of the inquiry.

(3) *Examples where no pre-existing business relationship is created.* (i) If a consumer makes a telephone call to a centralized call center for a group of affiliated companies to inquire about the consumer's existing account with a creditor, the call does not constitute an inquiry to any affiliate other than the creditor that holds the consumer's account and does not establish a pre-existing business relationship between the consumer and any affiliate of the account-holding creditor.

(ii) If a consumer who has a loan account with a creditor makes a telephone call to an af-filiate of the creditor to ask about the affiliate's retail locations and hours, but does not make an inquiry about the affiliate's products or services, the call does not constitute an inquiry and does not establish a pre-existing business relationship between the consumer and the affiliate. Also, the affiliate's capture of the consumer's telephone number does not constitute an inquiry and does not establish a pre-existing business relationship between the consumer and the affiliate.

(iii) If a consumer makes a telephone call to a creditor in response to an advertisement that offers a free promotional item to consumers who call a toll-free number, but the advertisement does not indicate that creditor's products or services will be marketed to consumers who call in response, the call does not create a pre-existing business relationship between the consumer and the creditor because the consumer has not made an inquiry about a product or service offered by the creditor, but has merely responded to an offer for a free promotional item.

(k) *Solicitation*—(1) *In general.* The term "solicitation" means the marketing of a product or service initiated by a person to a particular consumer that is—

(i) Based on eligibility information communicated to that person by its affiliate as described in this part; and

(ii) Intended to encourage the consumer to purchase or obtain such product or service.

(2) *Exclusion of marketing directed at the general public.* A solicitation does not include marketing communications that are directed at the general public. For example, television, general circulation magazine, and billboard advertisements do not constitute solicitations, even if those communications are intended to encourage consumers to purchase products and services from the person initiating the communications.

(3) *Examples of solicitations.* A solicitation would include, for example, a telemarketing call, direct mail, e-mail, or other form of marketing communication directed to a particular consumer that is based on eligibility information received from an affiliate.

(l) *You* means a person described in §680.1(b).

§§680.4–680.20 [Reserved]

§680.21 Affiliate marketing opt-out and exceptions.

(a) *Initial notice and opt-out requirement*—(1) *In general.* You may not use eligibility information about a consumer that you receive from an affiliate to make a solicitation for marketing purposes to the consumer, unless—

(i) It is clearly and conspicuously disclosed to the consumer in writing or, if the consumer agrees, electronically, in a concise notice that you may use eligibility information about that consumer received from an affiliate to make solicitations for marketing purposes to the consumer;

(ii) The consumer is provided a reasonable opportunity and a reasonable and simple method to "opt out," or prohibit you from using eligibility information to make solicitations for marketing purposes to the consumer; and

(iii) The consumer has not opted out.

(2) *Example.* A consumer has a homeowner's insurance policy with an insurance company. The insurance company furnishes eligibility information about the consumer to its affiliated creditor. Based on that eligibility information, the creditor wants to make a solicitation to the consumer about its home equity loan products. The creditor does not have a pre-existing business relationship with the consumer and none of the other exceptions apply. The creditor is prohibited from using eligibility information received from its insurance affiliate to make solicitations to the consumer about its home equity loan products unless the consumer is given a notice and opportunity to opt out and the consumer does not opt out.

(3) *Affiliates who may provide the notice.* The notice required by this paragraph (a) must be provided:

(i) By an affiliate that has or has previously had a pre-existing business relationship with the consumer; or

(ii) As part of a joint notice from two or more members of an affiliated group of companies, provided that at least one of the affiliates on the joint notice has or has previously had a pre-existing business relationship with the consumer.

(b) *Making solicitations*—(1) *In general.* For purposes of this part, you make a solicitation for marketing purposes if—

(i) You receive eligibility information from an affiliate;

(ii) You use that eligibility information to do one or more of the following:

(A) Identify the consumer or type of consumer to receive a solicitation;

(B) Establish criteria used to select the consumer to receive a solicitation; or

(C) Decide which of your products or services to market to the consumer or tailor your solicitation to that consumer; and

(iii) As a result of your use of the eligibility information, the consumer is provided a solicitation.

(2) *Receiving eligibility information from an affiliate, including through a common database.* You may receive eligibility information from an affiliate in various ways, including when the affiliate places that information into a common database that you may access.

(3) *Receipt or use of eligibility information by your service provider.* Except as provided in paragraph (b)(5) of this section, you receive or use an affiliate's eligibility information if a service provider acting on your behalf (whether an affiliate or a nonaffiliated third party) receives or uses that information in

the manner described in paragraphs (b)(1)(i) or (b)(1)(ii) of this section. All relevant facts and circumstances will determine whether a person is acting as your service provider when it receives or uses an affiliate's eligibility information in connection with marketing your products and services.

(4) *Use by an affiliate of its own eligibility information.* Unless you have used eligibility information that you receive from an affiliate in the manner described in paragraph (b)(1)(ii) of this section, you do not make a solicitation subject to this part if your affiliate:

(i) Uses its own eligibility information that it obtained in connection with a pre-existing business relationship it has or had with the consumer to market your products or services to the consumer; or

(ii) Directs its service provider to use the affiliate's own eligibility information that it obtained in connection with a pre-existing business relationship it has or had with the consumer to market your products or services to the consumer, and you do not communicate directly with the service provider regarding that use.

(5) *Use of eligibility information by a service provider*—(i) *In general.* You do not make a solicitation subject to this part if a service provider (including an affiliated or third-party service provider that maintains or accesses a common database that you may access) receives eligibility information from your affiliate that your affiliate obtained in connection with a pre-existing business relationship it has or had with the consumer and uses that eligibility information to market your products or services to the consumer, so long as—

(A) Your affiliate controls access to and use of its eligibility information by the service provider (including the right to establish the specific terms and conditions under which the service provider may use such information to market your products or services);

(B) Your affiliate establishes specific terms and conditions under which the service provider may access and use the affiliate's eligibility information to market your products and services (or those of affiliates generally) to the consumer, such as the identity of the affiliated companies whose products or services may be marketed to the consumer by the service provider, the types of products or services of affiliated companies that may be marketed, and the number of times the consumer may receive marketing materials, and periodically evaluates the service provider's compliance with those terms and conditions;

(C) Your affiliate requires the service provider to implement reasonable policies and procedures designed to ensure that the service provider uses the affiliate's eligibility information in accordance with the terms and conditions established by the affiliate relating to the marketing of your products or services;

(D) Your affiliate is identified on or with the marketing materials provided to the consumer; and

(E) You do not directly use your affiliate's eligibility information in the manner described in paragraph (b)(1)(ii) of this section.

(ii) *Writing requirements.* (A) The requirements of paragraphs (b)(5)(i)(A) and (C) of this section must be set forth in a written agreement between your affiliate and the service provider; and

(B) The specific terms and conditions established by your affiliate as provided in paragraph (b)(5)(i)(B) of this section must be set forth in writing.

(6) *Examples of making solicitations.* (i) A consumer has a loan account with a creditor, which is affiliated with an insurance company. The insurance company receives eligibility information about the consumer from the creditor. The insurance company uses that eligibility information to identify the consumer to receive a solicitation about insurance products, and, as a result, the insurance company provides a solicitation to the consumer about its insurance products. Pursuant to paragraph (b)(1) of this section, the insurance company has made a solicitation to the consumer.

(ii) The same facts as in the example in paragraph (b)(6)(i) of this section, except that after using the eligibility information to identify the consumer to receive a solicitation about insurance products, the insurance company asks the creditor to send the solicitation to the consumer and the creditor does so. Pursuant to paragraph (b)(1) of this section, the insurance company has made a solicitation to the consumer because it used eligibility information about the consumer that it received from an affiliate to identify the consumer to receive a solicitation about its products or services, and, as a result, a solicitation was provided to the consumer about the insurance company's products.

(iii) The same facts as in the example in paragraph (b)(6)(i) of this section, except that eligibility information about consumers that have loan accounts with the creditor is placed into a common database that all members of the affiliated group of companies may independently access and use. Without using the creditor's eligibility information, the insurance company develops selection criteria and provides those criteria, marketing materials, and related instructions to the creditor. The creditor reviews eligibility information about its own consumers using the selection criteria provided by the insurance company to determine which consumers should receive the insurance company's marketing materials and sends marketing materials about the insurance company's products to those consumers. Even though the insurance company has received eligibility information through the common database as provided in paragraph (b)(2) of this section, it did not use that information to identify consumers or establish selection criteria; instead, the creditor used its own eligibility information. Therefore, pursuant to paragraph (b)(4)(i) of this section, the insurance company has not made a solicitation to the consumer.

(iv) The same facts as in the example in paragraph (b)(6)(iii) of this section, except that the creditor provides the insurance company's criteria to the creditor's service provider and directs the service provider to use the creditor's eligibility information to identify creditor consumers who meet the criteria and to send the insurance company's marketing materials to those consumers. The insurance company does not communicate directly with the service provider regarding the use of the creditor's information to market its products to the creditor's consumers. Pursuant to paragraph (b)(4)(ii) of this section, the insurance company has not made a solicitation to the consumer.

(v) An affiliated group of companies includes a creditor, an insurance company, and a service provider. Each affiliate in the group places information about its consumers into a common database. The service provider has access to all information in the common database. The creditor controls access to and use of its eligibility information by the service provider. This control is set forth in a written agreement between the creditor and the service provider. The written agreement also requires the service provider to establish reasonable policies and procedures designed to ensure that the service provider uses the creditor's eligibility information in accordance with specific terms and conditions established by the creditor relating to the marketing of the products and services of all affiliates, including the insurance company. In a separate written communication, the creditor specifies the terms and conditions under which the service provider may use the creditor's eligibility information to market the insurance company's products and services to the creditor's consumers. The specific terms and conditions are: a list of affiliated companies (including the insurance company) whose products or services may be marketed to the creditor's consumers by the service provider; the specific products or types of products that may be marketed to the creditor's consumers by the service provider; the categories of eligibility information that may be used by the service provider in marketing products or services to the creditor's consumers; the types or categories of the creditor's consumers to whom the service provider may market products or services of creditor affiliates; the number and/or types of marketing communications that the service provider may send to the creditor's consumers; and the length of time during which the service provider may market the prod-ucts or services of the creditor's affiliates to its consumers. The creditor periodically evaluates the service provider's compliance with these terms and conditions. The insurance company asks the service provider to market insurance products to certain consumers who have loan accounts with the creditor. Without using the creditor's eligibility information, the insurance company develops selection criteria and provides those criteria, marketing materials, and related instructions to the service provider. The service provider uses the creditor's eligibility information from the common database to identify the creditor's consumers to whom insurance products will be marketed. When the insurance company's marketing materials are provided to the identified consumers, the name of the creditor is displayed on the insurance marketing materials, an introductory letter that accompanies the marketing materials, an account statement that accompanies the marketing materials, or the envelope containing the marketing materials. The requirements of paragraph (b)(5) of this section have been satisfied, and the insurance company has not made a solicitation to the consumer.

(vi) The same facts as in the example in paragraph (b)(6)(v) of this section, except that the terms and conditions permit the service provider to use the creditor's eligibility information to market the products and services of other affiliates to the creditor's consumers whenever the service provider deems it appropriate to do so. The service provider uses the creditor's eligibility information in accordance with the discretion af-forded to it by the terms and conditions. Because the terms and conditions are not specific, the requirements of paragraph (b)(5) of this section have not been satisfied.

(c) *Exceptions.* The provisions of this part do not apply to you if you use eligibility information that you receive from an affiliate:

(1) To make a solicitation for marketing purposes to a consumer with whom you have a pre-existing business relationship;

(2) To facilitate communications to an individual for whose benefit you provide employee benefit or other services pursuant to a contract with an employer related to and arising out of the current employment relationship or status of the individual as a participant or beneficiary of an employee benefit plan;

(3) To perform services on behalf of an affiliate, except that this paragraph shall not be construed as permitting you to send solicitations on behalf of an affiliate if the affiliate would not be permitted to send the solicitation as a result of the election of the consumer to opt out under this part;

(4) In response to a communication about your products or services initiated by the consumer;

(5) In response to an authorization or request by the consumer to receive solicitations; or

(6) If your compliance with this part would prevent you from complying with any provision of State insurance laws pertaining to unfair discrimination in any State in which you are lawfully doing business.

(d) *Examples of exceptions*—(1) *Example of the pre-existing business relationship exception.* A consumer has a loan account with a creditor. The consumer also has a relationship with the creditor's securities affiliate for management of the consumer's securities portfolio. The creditor receives eligibility information about the consumer from its securities affiliate and uses that information to make a solicitation to the consumer about the creditor's wealth management services. The creditor may make this solicitation even if the consumer has not been given a notice and opportunity to opt out because the creditor has a pre-existing business relationship with the consumer.

(2) *Examples of service provider exception.* (i) A consumer has an insurance policy issued by an insurance company. The insurance company furnishes eligibility information about the consumer to an affiliated creditor. Based on that eligibility information, the creditor wants to make a solicitation to the consumer about its credit products. The creditor does not have a pre-existing business relationship with the consumer and none of the other exceptions in para-graph (c) of this section apply. The consumer has been given an opt-out notice and has elected to opt out of receiving such solicitations. The creditor asks a service provider to send the

solicitation to the consumer on its behalf. The service provider may not send the solicitation on behalf of the creditor because, as a result of the consumer's opt-out election, the creditor is not permitted to make the solicitation.

(ii) The same facts as in paragraph (d)(2)(i) of this section, except the consumer has been given an opt-out notice, but has not elected to opt out. The creditor asks a service provider to send the solicitation to the consumer on its behalf. The service provider may send the solicitation on behalf of the creditor because, as a result of the consumer's not opting out, the creditor is permitted to make the solicitation.

(3) *Examples of consumer-initiated communications.* (i) A consumer who has a consumer loan account with a finance company initiates a communication with the creditor's mortgage lending affiliate to request information about a mortgage. The mortgage lender affiliate may use eligibility information about the consumer it obtains from the finance company or any other affiliate to make solicitations regarding mortgage products in response to the consumer-initiated communication.

(ii) A consumer who has a loan account with a creditor contacts the creditor to request information about how to save and invest for a child's college education without specifying the type of product in which the consumer may be interested. Information about a range of different products or services offered by the creditor and one or more affiliates of the creditor may be responsive to that communication. Such products or services may include the following: mutual funds offered by the creditor's mutual fund affil-iate; section 529 plans offered by the creditor, its mutual fund affiliate, or another securities affiliate; or trust services offered by a different creditor in the affiliated group. Any affiliate offering investment products or services that would be responsive to the consumer's request for information about saving and investing for a child's college education may use eligibility information to make solicitations to the consumer in response to this communication.

(iii) A credit card issuer makes a marketing call to the consumer without using eligibility information received from an affiliate. The issuer leaves a voice-mail message that invites the consumer to call a toll-free number to apply for the issuer's credit card. If the consumer calls the toll-free number to inquire about the credit card, the call is a consumer-initiated communication about a product or service and the credit card issuer may now use eligibility information it receives from its affiliates to make solicitations to the consumer.

(iv) A consumer calls a creditor to ask about retail locations and hours, but does not request information about products or services. The creditor may not use eligibility information it receives from an affiliate to make solicitations to the consumer about its products or services because the consumer-initiated communication does not relate to the creditor's products or services. Thus, the use of eligibility information received from an affiliate would not be responsive to the communication and the exception does not apply.

(v) A consumer calls a creditor to ask about office locations and hours. The customer service representative asks the consumer if there is a particular product or service about which the consumer is seeking information. The consumer responds that the consumer wants to stop in and find out about second mortgage loans. The customer service representative offers to provide that information by telephone and mail additional information and application materials to the consumer. The consumer agrees and provides or confirms contact information for receipt of the materials to be mailed. The creditor may use eligibility information it receives from an affiliate to make solicitations to the consumer about mortgage loan products because such solicitations respond to the consumer-initiated communication about products or services.

(4) *Examples of consumer authorization or request for solicitations.* (i) A consumer who obtains a mortgage from a mortgage lender authorizes or requests information about homeowner's insurance offered by the mortgage lender's insurance affiliate. Such authorization

or request, whether given to the mortgage lender or to the insurance affiliate, would permit the insurance affiliate to use eligibility information about the consumer it obtains from the mortgage lender or any other affiliate to make solicitations to the consumer about homeowner's insurance.

(ii) A consumer completes an online application to apply for a credit card from a department store. The store's online application contains a blank check box that the consumer may check to authorize or request information from the store's affiliates. The consumer checks the box. The consumer has authorized or requested solicitations from store's affiliates.

(iii) A consumer completes an online application to apply for a credit card from a department store. The store's online application contains a pre-selected check box indicating that the consumer authorizes or requests information from the store's affiliates. The consumer does not deselect the check box. The consumer has not authorized or requested solicitations from the store's affiliates.

(iv) The terms and conditions of a credit account agreement contain preprinted boilerplate language stating that by applying to open an account the consumer authorizes or requests to receive solicitations from the creditor's affiliates. The consumer has not authorized or requested solicitations from the creditor's affiliates.

(e) *Relation to affiliate-sharing notice and opt-out.* Nothing in this part limits the responsibility of a person to comply with the notice and opt-out provisions of section 603(d)(2)(A)(iii) of the Act where applicable.

§ 680.22 Scope and duration of opt-out.

(a) *Scope of opt-out*—(1) *In general.* Except as otherwise provided in this section, the consumer's election to opt out prohibits any affiliate covered by the opt-out notice from using eligibility information received from another affiliate as described in the notice to make solicitations to the consumer.

(2) *Continuing relationship*—(i) *In general.* If the consumer establishes a continuing relationship with you or your affiliate, an opt-out notice may apply to eligibility information obtained in connection with—

(A) A single continuing relationship or multiple continuing relationships that the consumer establishes with you or your affiliates, including continuing relationships established subsequent to delivery of the opt-out notice, so long as the notice adequately describes the continuing relationships covered by the opt-out; or

(B) Any other transaction between the consumer and you or your affiliates as described in the notice.

(ii) *Examples of continuing relationships.* A consumer has a continuing relationship with you or your affiliate if the consumer—

(A) Opens a credit account with you or your affiliate;

(B) Obtains a loan for which you or your affiliate owns the servicing rights;

(C) Purchases an insurance product from you or your affiliate;

(D) Holds an investment product through you or your affiliate, such as when you act or your affiliate acts as a custodian for securities or for assets in an individual retirement arrangement;

(E) Enters into an agreement or understanding with you or your affiliate whereby you or your affiliate undertakes to arrange or broker a home mortgage loan for the consumer;

(F) Enters into a lease of personal property with you or your affiliate; or

(G) Obtains financial, investment, or economic advisory services from you or your affiliate for a fee.

(3) *No continuing relationship*—(i) *In general.* If there is no continuing relationship between a consumer and you or your affiliate, and you or your affiliate obtain eligibility information about a consumer in connection with a transaction with the consumer, such as an isolated transaction or a credit application that is denied, an opt-out notice provided to the consumer only applies to eligibility information obtained in connection with that transaction.

(ii) *Examples of isolated transactions.* An isolated transaction occurs if—

(A) The consumer uses your or your affiliate's ATM to withdraw cash from an account at a financial institution; or

(B) You or your affiliate sells the consumer a money order, airline tickets, travel insurance, or traveler's checks in isolated transactions.

(4) *Menu of alternatives.* A consumer may be given the opportunity to choose from a menu of alternatives when electing to prohibit solicitations, such as by electing to prohibit solicitations from certain types of affiliates covered by the opt-out notice but not other types of affiliates covered by the notice, electing to prohibit solicitations based on certain types of eligibility information but not other types of eligibility information, or electing to prohibit solicitations by certain methods of delivery but not other methods of delivery. However, one of the alternatives must allow the consumer to prohibit all solicitations from all of the affiliates that are covered by the notice.

(5) *Special rule for a notice following termination of all continuing relationships*—(i) *In general.* A consumer must be given a new opt-out notice if, after all continuing relationships with you or your affiliate(s) are terminated, the consumer subsequently establishes another continuing relationship with you or your affiliate(s) and the consumer's eligibility information is to be used to make a solicitation. The new opt-out notice must apply, at a minimum, to eligibility information obtained in connection with the new continuing relationship. Consistent with paragraph (b) of this section, the consumer's decision not to opt out after receiving the new opt-out notice would not override a prior opt-out election by the consumer that applies to eligibility information obtained in connection with a terminated relationship, regardless of whether the new opt-out notice applies to eligibility information obtained in connection with the terminated relationship.

(ii) *Example.* A consumer has an automobile loan account with a creditor that is part of an affiliated group. The consumer pays off the loan. After paying off the loan, the consumer subsequently obtains a second mortgage loan from the creditor. The consumer must be given a new notice and opportunity to opt out before the creditor's affiliates may make solicitations to the consumer using eligibility information obtained by the creditor in connection with the new mortgage relationship, regardless of whether the consumer opted out in connection with the automobile loan account.

(b) *Duration of opt-out.* The election of a consumer to opt out must be effective for a period of at least five years (the "opt-out period") beginning when the consumer's opt-out election is received and implemented, unless the consumer subsequently revokes the opt-out in writing or, if the consumer agrees, electronically. An opt-out period of more than five years may be established, including an opt-out period that does not expire unless revoked by the consumer.

(c) *Time of opt-out.* A consumer may opt out at any time.

§ 680.23 Contents of opt-out notice; consolidated and equivalent notices.

(a) *Contents of opt-out notice*—(1) *In general.* A notice must be clear, conspicuous, and concise, and must accurately disclose:

(i) The name of the affiliate(s) providing the notice. If the notice is provided jointly by multiple affiliates and each affiliate shares a common name, such as "ABC," then the notice may indicate that it is being provided by multiple companies with the ABC name or multiple companies in the ABC group or family of companies, for example, by stating that the notice is provided by "all of the ABC companies," "the ABC banking, credit card, insurance, and securities companies," or by listing the name of each affiliate providing the notice. But if the affiliates providing the joint notice do not all share a common name, then the notice must either separately identify each affiliate by name or identify each of the common names used by those affiliates, for example, by stating that the notice is provided by "all of the ABC and XYZ companies" or by "the ABC banking and credit card companies and the XYZ insurance companies;"

(ii) A list of the affiliates or types of affiliates whose use of eligibility information is covered by the notice, which may include companies that become affiliates after the notice is provided to the consumer. If each affiliate covered by the notice shares a common name, such as "ABC," then the notice may indicate that it applies to multiple companies with the ABC name or multiple companies in the ABC group or family of companies, for example, by stating that the notice is provided by "all of the ABC companies," "the ABC banking, credit card, insurance, and securities companies," or by listing the name of each affiliate providing the notice. But if the affiliates covered by the notice do not all share a common name, then the notice must either separately identify each covered affiliate by name or identify each of the common names used by those affiliates, for example, by stating that the notice applies to "all of the ABC and XYZ companies" or to "the ABC banking and credit card companies and the XYZ insurance companies;"

(iii) A general description of the types of eligibility information that may be used to make solicitations to the consumer;

(iv) That the consumer may elect to limit the use of eligibility information to make solicitations to the consumer;

(v) That the consumer's election will apply for the specified period of time stated in the notice and, if applicable, that the consumer will be allowed to renew the election once that period expires;

(vi) If the notice is provided to consumers who may have previously opted out, such as if a notice is provided to consumers annually, that the consumer who has chosen to limit solicitations does not need to act again until the consumer receives a renewal notice; and

(vii) A reasonable and simple method for the consumer to opt out.

(2) *Joint relationships.* (i) If two or more consumers jointly obtain a product or service, a single opt-out notice may be provided to the joint consumers. Any of the joint consumers may exercise the right to opt out.

(ii) The opt-out notice must explain how an opt-out direction by a joint consumer will be treated. An opt-out direction by a joint consumer may be treated as applying to all of the associated joint consumers, or each joint consumer may be permitted to opt out separately. If each joint consumer is permitted to opt out separately, one of the joint consumers must be permitted to opt out on behalf of all of the joint consumers and the joint consumers must be permitted to exercise their separate rights to opt out in a single response.

(iii) It is impermissible to require all joint consumers to opt out before implementing any opt-out direction.

(3) *Alternative contents.* If the consumer is afforded a broader right to opt out of receiving marketing than is required by this part, the requirements of this section may be satisfied by providing the consumer with a clear, conspicuous, and concise notice that accurately discloses the consumer's opt-out rights.

(4) *Model notices.* Model notices are provided in Appendix C of Part 698 of this chapter.

(b) *Coordinated and consolidated notices.* A notice required by this part may be coordinated and consolidated with any other notice or disclosure required to be issued under any other provision of law by the entity providing the notice, including but not limited to the notice de-scribed in section 603(d)(2)(A)(iii) of the Act and the Gramm-Leach-Bliley Act privacy notice.

(c) *Equivalent notices.* A notice or other disclosure that is equivalent to the notice required by this part, and that is provided to a consumer together with disclosures required by any other provision of law, satisfies the requirements of this section.

§ 680.24 Reasonable opportunity to opt out.

(a) *In general.* You must not use eligibility information about a consumer that you receive from an affiliate to make a solicitation to the consumer about your products or services, unless the consumer is provided a reasonable opportunity to opt out, as required by § 680.21(a)(1)(ii) of this part.

(b) *Examples of a reasonable opportunity to opt out.* The consumer is given a reasonable opportunity to opt out if:

(1) *By mail.* The opt-out notice is mailed to the consumer. The consumer

is given 30 days from the date the notice is mailed to elect to opt out by any reasonable means.

(2) *By electronic means.* (i) The opt-out notice is provided electronically to the consumer, such as by posting the notice at an Internet Web site at which the consumer has obtained a product or service. The consumer acknowledges receipt of the electronic notice. The consumer is given 30 days after the date the consumer acknowledges receipt to elect to opt out by any reasonable means.

(ii) The opt-out notice is provided to the consumer by e-mail where the consumer has agreed to receive disclosures by e-mail from the person sending the notice. The consumer is given 30 days after the e-mail is sent to elect to opt out by any reasonable means.

(3) *At the time of an electronic transaction.* The opt-out notice is provided to the consumer at the time of an electronic transaction, such as a transaction conducted on an Internet Web site. The consumer is required to decide, as a necessary part of proceeding with the transaction, whether to opt out before completing the transaction. There is a simple process that the consumer may use to opt out at that time using the same mechanism through which the transaction is conducted.

(4) *At the time of an in-person transaction.* The opt-out notice is provided to the consumer in writing at the time of an in-person transaction. The consumer is required to decide, as a necessary part of proceeding with the transaction, whether to opt out before completing the transaction, and is not permitted to complete the transaction without making a choice. There is a simple process that the consumer may use during the course of the in-person transaction to opt out, such as completing a form that requires consumers to write a "yes" or "no" to indicate their opt-out preference or that requires the consumer to check one of two blank check boxes—one that allows consumers to indicate that they want to opt out and one that allows consumers to indicate that they do not want to opt out.

(5) *By including in a privacy notice.* The opt-out notice is included in a Gramm-Leach-Bliley Act privacy notice. The consumer is allowed to exercise the opt-out within a reasonable period of time and in the same manner as the opt-out under that privacy notice.

§ 680.25 Reasonable and simple methods of opting out.

(a) *In general.* You must not use eligibility information about a consumer that you receive from an affiliate to make a solicitation to the consumer about your products or services, unless the consumer is provided a reasonable and simple method to opt out, as required by § 680.21(a)(1)(ii) of this part.

(b) *Examples*—(1) *Reasonable and simple opt-out methods.* Reasonable and simple methods for exercising the opt-out right include—

(i) Designating a check-off box in a prominent position on the opt-out form;

(ii) Including a reply form and a self-addressed envelope together with the opt-out notice;

(iii) Providing an electronic means to opt out, such as a form that can be electronically mailed or processed at an Internet Web site, if the consumer agrees to the electronic delivery of information;

(iv) Providing a toll-free telephone number that consumers may call to opt out; or

(v) Allowing consumers to exercise all of their opt-out rights described in a consolidated opt-out notice that includes the privacy opt-out under the Gramm-Leach-Bliley Act, 15 U.S.C. 6801 *et seq.*, the affiliate sharing opt-out under the Act, and the affiliate marketing opt-out under the Act, by a single method, such as by calling a single toll-free telephone number.

(2) *Opt-out methods that are not reasonable and simple.* Reasonable and simple methods for exercising an opt-out right *do not* include—

(i) Requiring the consumer to write his or her own letter;

(ii) Requiring the consumer to call or write to obtain a form for opting out, rather than including the form with the opt-out notice;

(iii) Requiring the consumer who receives the opt-out notice in electronic form only, such as through posting at an Internet Web site, to opt out solely by paper mail or by visiting a different

Web site without providing a link to that site.

(c) *Specific opt-out means.* Each consumer may be required to opt out through a specific means, as long as that means is reasonable and simple for that consumer.

§ 680.26 Delivery of opt-out notices.

(a) *In general.* The opt-out notice must be provided so that each consumer can reasonably be expected to receive actual notice. For opt-out notices provided electronically, the notice may be provided in compliance with either the electronic disclosure provisions in this part or the provisions in section 101 of the Electronic Signatures in Global and National Commerce Act, 15 U.S.C. 7001 *et seq.*

(b) *Examples of reasonable expectation of actual notice.* A consumer may reasonably be expected to receive actual notice if the affiliate providing the notice:

(1) Hand-delivers a printed copy of the notice to the consumer;

(2) Mails a printed copy of the notice to the last known mailing address of the consumer;

(3) Provides a notice by e-mail to a consumer who has agreed to receive electronic disclosures by e-mail from the affiliate providing the notice; or

(4) Posts the notice on the Internet Web site at which the consumer obtained a product or service electronically and requires the consumer to acknowledge receipt of the notice.

(c) *Examples of no reasonable expectation of actual notice.* A consumer may *not* reasonably be expected to receive actual notice if the affiliate providing the notice:

(1) Only posts the notice on a sign in a branch or office or generally publishes the notice in a newspaper;

(2) Sends the notice via e-mail to a consumer who has not agreed to receive electronic disclosures by e-mail from the affiliate providing the notice; or

(3) Posts the notice on an Internet Web site without requiring the consumer to acknowledge receipt of the notice.

§ 680.27 Renewal of opt-out.

(a) *Renewal notice and opt-out requirement*—(1) *In general.* After the opt-out period expires, you may not make solicitations based on eligibility information you receive from an affiliate to a consumer who previously opted out, unless:

(i) The consumer has been given a renewal notice that complies with the requirements of this section and §§ 680.24 through 680.26 of this part, and a reasonable opportunity and a reasonable and simple method to renew the opt-out, and the consumer does not renew the opt-out; or

(ii) An exception in § 680.21(c) of this part applies.

(2) *Renewal period.* Each opt-out renewal must be effective for a period of at least five years as provided in § 680.22(b) of this part.

(3) *Affiliates who may provide the notice.* The notice required by this paragraph must be provided:

(i) By the affiliate that provided the previous opt-out notice, or its successor; or

(ii) As part of a joint renewal notice from two or more members of an affiliated group of companies, or their successors, that jointly provided the previous opt-out notice.

(b) *Contents of renewal notice.* The renewal notice must be clear, conspicuous, and concise, and must accurately disclose:

(1) The name of the affiliate(s) providing the notice. If the notice is provided jointly by multiple affiliates and each affiliate shares a common name, such as "ABC," then the notice may indicate that it is being provided by multiple companies with the ABC name or multiple companies in the ABC group or family of companies, for example, by stating that the notice is provided by "all of the ABC companies," "the ABC banking, credit card, insurance, and securities companies," or by listing the name of each affiliate providing the notice. But if the affiliates providing the joint notice do not all share a common name, then the notice must either separately identify each affiliate by name or identify each of the common names used by those affiliates, for example, by stating that the notice is provided by "all of the

ABC and XYZ companies" or by "the ABC banking and credit card companies and the XYZ insurance companies;"

(2) A list of the affiliates or types of affiliates whose use of eligibility information is covered by the notice, which may include companies that become affiliates after the notice is provided to the consumer. If each affiliate covered by the notice shares a common name, such as "ABC," then the notice may indicate that it applies to multiple companies with the ABC name or multiple companies in the ABC group or family of companies, for example, by stating that the notice is provided by "all of the ABC companies," "the ABC banking, credit card, insurance, and securities companies," or by listing the name of each affiliate providing the notice. But if the affiliates covered by the notice do not all share a common name, then the notice must either separately identify each covered affiliate by name or identify each of the common names used by those affiliates, for example, by stating that the notice applies to "all of the ABC and XYZ companies" or to "the ABC banking and credit card companies and the XYZ insurance companies;"

(3) A general description of the types of eligibility information that may be used to make solicitations to the consumer;

(4) That the consumer previously elected to limit the use of certain information to make solicitations to the consumer;

(5) That the consumer's election has expired or is about to expire;

(6) That the consumer may elect to renew the consumer's previous election;

(7) If applicable, that the consumer's election to renew will apply for the specified period of time stated in the notice and that the consumer will be allowed to renew the election once that period expires; and

(8) A reasonable and simple method for the consumer to opt out.

(c) *Timing of the renewal notice*—(1) *In general.* A renewal notice may be provided to the consumer either—

(i) A reasonable period of time before the expiration of the opt-out period; or

(ii) Any time after the expiration of the opt-out period but before solicitations that would have been prohibited by the expired opt-out are made to the consumer.

(2) *Combination with annual privacy notice.* If you provide an annual privacy notice under the Gramm-Leach-Bliley Act, 15 U.S.C. 6801 *et seq.*, providing a renewal notice with the last annual privacy notice provided to the consumer before expiration of the opt-out period is a reasonable period of time before expiration of the opt-out in all cases.

(d) *No effect on opt-out period.* An opt-out period may not be shortened by sending a renewal notice to the consumer before expiration of the opt-out period, even if the consumer does not renew the opt out.

§ 680.28 Effective date, compliance date, and prospective application.

(a) *Effective date.* This part is effective January 1, 2008.

(b) *Mandatory compliance date.* Compliance with this part is required not later than October 1, 2008.

(c) *Prospective application.* The provisions of this part shall not prohibit you from using eligibility information that you receive from an affiliate to make solicitations to a consumer if you receive such information prior to October 1, 2008. For purposes of this section, you are deemed to receive eligibility information when such information is placed into a common database and is accessible by you.

PART 681—IDENTITY THEFT RULES

AUTHORITY: 15 U.S.C. 1681m(e); 15 U.S.C. 1681m(e)(4); 15 U.S.C. 1681c(h).

SOURCE: 72 FR 63771, Nov. 9, 2007, unless otherwise noted.

§ 681.1 Duties regarding the detection, prevention, and mitigation of identity theft.

(a) *Scope.* This section applies to financial institutions and creditors that are subject to administrative enforcement of the FCRA by the Federal Trade Commission pursuant to 15 U.S.C. 1681s(a)(1).

(b) *Definitions.* For purposes of this section, and Appendix A, the following definitions apply:

(1) *Account* means a continuing relationship established by a person with a financial institution or creditor to obtain a product or service for personal, family, household or business purposes. Account includes:

(i) An extension of credit, such as the purchase of property or services involving a deferred payment; and

(ii) A deposit account.

(2) The term *board of directors* includes:

(i) In the case of a branch or agency of a foreign bank, the managing official in charge of the branch or agency; and

(ii) In the case of any other creditor that does not have a board of directors, a designated employee at the level of senior management.

(3) *Covered account* means:

(i) An account that a financial institution or creditor offers or maintains, primarily for personal, family, or household purposes, that involves or is designed to permit multiple payments or transactions, such as a credit card account, mortgage loan, automobile loan, margin account, cell phone account, utility account, checking account, or savings account; and

(ii) Any other account that the financial institution or creditor offers or maintains for which there is a reasonably foreseeable risk to customers or to the safety and soundness of the financial institution or creditor from identity theft, including financial, operational, compliance, reputation, or litigation risks.

(4) *Credit* has the same meaning as in 15 U.S.C. 1681a(r)(5).

(5) *Creditor* has the same meaning as in 15 U.S.C. 1681m(e)(4).

(6) *Customer* means a person that has a covered account with a financial institution or creditor.

(7) *Financial institution* has the same meaning as in 15 U.S.C. 1681a(t).

(8) *Identity theft* has the same meaning as in 16 CFR 603.2(a).

(9) *Red Flag* means a pattern, practice, or specific activity that indicates the possible existence of identity theft.

(10) *Service provider* means a person that provides a service directly to the financial institution or creditor.

(c) *Periodic Identification of Covered Accounts.* Each financial institution or creditor must periodically determine whether it offers or maintains covered accounts. As a part of this determination, a financial institution or creditor must conduct a risk assessment to determine whether it offers or maintains covered accounts described in paragraph (b)(3)(ii) of this section, taking into consideration:

(1) The methods it provides to open its accounts;

(2) The methods it provides to access its accounts; and

(3) Its previous experiences with identity theft.

(d) *Establishment of an Identity Theft Prevention Program*—(1) *Program requirement.* Each financial institution or creditor that offers or maintains one or more covered accounts must develop and implement a written Identity Theft Prevention Program (Program) that is designed to detect, prevent, and mitigate identity theft in connection with the opening of a covered account or any existing covered account. The Program must be appropriate to the size and complexity of the financial institution or creditor and the nature and scope of its activities.

(2) *Elements of the Program.* The Program must include reasonable policies and procedures to:

(i) Identify relevant Red Flags for the covered accounts that the financial institution or creditor offers or maintains, and incorporate those Red Flags into its Program;

(ii) Detect Red Flags that have been incorporated into the Program of the financial institution or creditor;

(iii) Respond appropriately to any Red Flags that are detected pursuant to paragraph (d)(2)(ii) of this section to prevent and mitigate identity theft; and

(iv) Ensure the Program (including the Red Flags determined to be relevant) is updated periodically, to reflect changes in risks to customers and to the safety and soundness of the financial institution or creditor from identity theft.

(e) *Administration of the Program.* Each financial institution or creditor that is required to implement a Program must provide for the continued administration of the Program and must:

(1) Obtain approval of the initial written Program from either its board of directors or an appropriate committee of the board of directors;

(2) Involve the board of directors, an appropriate committee thereof, or a designated employee at the level of senior management in the oversight, development, implementation and administration of the Program;

(3) Train staff, as necessary, to effectively implement the Program; and

(4) Exercise appropriate and effective oversight of service provider arrangements.

(f) *Guidelines.* Each financial institution or creditor that is required to implement a Program must consider the guidelines in appendix A of this part and include in its Program those guidelines that are appropriate.

[74 FR 22645, May 14, 2009, as amended at 77 FR 72715, Dec. 6, 2012]

§ 681.2 Duties of card issuers regarding changes of address.

(a) *Scope.* This section applies to a person described in § 681.1(a) that issues a debit or credit card (card issuer).

(b) *Definitions.* For purposes of this section:

(1) *Cardholder* means a consumer who has been issued a credit or debit card.

(2) *Clear and conspicuous* means reasonably understandable and designed to call attention to the nature and significance of the information presented.

(c) *Address validation requirements.* A card issuer must establish and implement reasonable policies and procedures to assess the validity of a change of address if it receives notification of a change of address for a consumer's debit or credit card account and, within a short period of time afterwards (during at least the first 30 days after it receives such notification), the card issuer receives a request for an additional or replacement card for the same account. Under these circumstances, the card issuer may not issue an additional or replacement card, until, in accordance with its reasonable policies and procedures and for the purpose of assessing the validity of the change of address, the card issuer:

(1)(i) Notifies the cardholder of the request:

(A) At the cardholder's former address; or

(B) By any other means of communication that the card issuer and the cardholder have previously agreed to use; and

(ii) Provides to the cardholder a reasonable means of promptly reporting incorrect address changes; or

(2) Otherwise assesses the validity of the change of address in accordance with the policies and procedures the card issuer has established pursuant to § 681.1 of this part.

(d) *Alternative timing of address validation.* A card issuer may satisfy the requirements of paragraph (c) of this section if it validates an address pursuant to the methods in paragraph (c)(1) or (c)(2) of this section when it receives an address change notification, before it receives a request for an additional or replacement card.

(e) *Form of notice.* Any written or electronic notice that the card issuer provides under this paragraph must be clear and conspicuous and provided separately from its regular correspondence with the cardholder.

[74 FR 22645, May 14, 2009]

APPENDIX A TO PART 681—INTERAGENCY GUIDELINES ON IDENTITY THEFT DETECTION, PREVENTION, AND MITIGATION

Section 681.1 of this part requires each financial institution and creditor that offers or maintains one or more covered accounts, as defined in § 681.1(b)(3) of this part, to develop and provide for the continued administration of a written Program to detect, prevent, and mitigate identity theft in connection with the opening of a covered account or any existing covered account. These guidelines are intended to assist financial institutions and creditors in the formulation and maintenance of a Program that satisfies the requirements of § 681.1 of this part.

I. The Program

In designing its Program, a financial institution or creditor may incorporate, as appropriate, its existing policies, procedures, and other arrangements that control reasonably foreseeable risks to customers or to the safety and soundness of the financial institution or creditor from identity theft.

II. Identifying Relevant Red Flags

(a) *Risk Factors.* A financial institution or creditor should consider the following factors in identifying relevant Red Flags for covered accounts, as appropriate:

(1) The types of covered accounts it offers or maintains;

(2) The methods it provides to open its covered accounts;

(3) The methods it provides to access its covered accounts; and

(4) Its previous experiences with identity theft.

(b) *Sources of Red Flags.* Financial institutions and creditors should incorporate relevant Red Flags from sources such as:

(1) Incidents of identity theft that the financial institution or creditor has experienced;

(2) Methods of identity theft that the financial institution or creditor has identified that reflect changes in identity theft risks; and

(3) Applicable supervisory guidance.

(c) *Categories of Red Flags.* The Program should include relevant Red Flags from the following categories, as appropriate. Examples of Red Flags from each of these categories are appended as supplement A to this appendix A.

(1) Alerts, notifications, or other warnings received from consumer reporting agencies or service providers, such as fraud detection services;

(2) The presentation of suspicious documents;

(3) The presentation of suspicious personal identifying information, such as a suspicious address change;

(4) The unusual use of, or other suspicious activity related to, a covered account; and

(5) Notice from customers, victims of identity theft, law enforcement authorities, or other persons regarding possible identity theft in connection with covered accounts held by the financial institution or creditor.

III. Detecting Red Flags

The Program's policies and procedures should address the detection of Red Flags in connection with the opening of covered accounts and existing covered accounts, such as by:

(a) Obtaining identifying information about, and verifying the identity of, a person opening a covered account, for example, using the policies and procedures regarding identification and verification set forth in the Customer Identification Program rules implementing 31 U.S.C. 5318(l) (31 CFR 103.121); and

(b) Authenticating customers, monitoring transactions, and verifying the validity of change of address requests, in the case of existing covered accounts.

IV. Preventing and Mitigating Identity Theft

The Program's policies and procedures should provide for appropriate responses to the Red Flags the financial institution or creditor has detected that are commensurate with the degree of risk posed. In determining an appropriate response, a financial institution or creditor should consider aggravating factors that may heighten the risk of identity theft, such as a data security incident that results in unauthorized access to a customer's account records held by the financial institution, creditor, or third party, or notice that a customer has provided information related to a covered account held by the financial institution or creditor to someone fraudulently claiming to represent the financial institution or creditor or to a fraudulent website. Appropriate responses may include the following:

(a) Monitoring a covered account for evidence of identity theft;

(b) Contacting the customer;

(c) Changing any passwords, security codes, or other security devices that permit access to a covered account;

(d) Reopening a covered account with a new account number;

(e) Not opening a new covered account;

(f) Closing an existing covered account;

(g) Not attempting to collect on a covered account or not selling a covered account to a debt collector;

(h) Notifying law enforcement; or

(i) Determining that no response is warranted under the particular circumstances.

V. Updating the Program

Financial institutions and creditors should update the Program (including the Red Flags determined to be relevant) periodically, to reflect changes in risks to customers or to the safety and soundness of the financial institution or creditor from identity theft, based on factors such as:

(a) The experiences of the financial institution or creditor with identity theft;

(b) Changes in methods of identity theft;

(c) Changes in methods to detect, prevent, and mitigate identity theft;

(d) Changes in the types of accounts that the financial institution or creditor offers or maintains; and

(e) Changes in the business arrangements of the financial institution or creditor, including mergers, acquisitions, alliances, joint ventures, and service provider arrangements.

VI. Methods for Administering the Program

(a) *Oversight of Program.* Oversight by the board of directors, an appropriate committee of the board, or a designated employee at the level of senior management should include:

(1) Assigning specific responsibility for the Program's implementation;

(2) Reviewing reports prepared by staff regarding compliance by the financial institution or creditor with §681.1 of this part; and

(3) Approving material changes to the Program as necessary to address changing identity theft risks.

(b) *Reports.* (1) *In general.* Staff of the financial institution or creditor responsible for development, implementation, and administration of its Program should report to the board of directors, an appropriate committee of the board, or a designated employee at the level of senior management, at least annually, on compliance by the financial institution or creditor with §681.1 of this part.

(2) *Contents of report.* The report should address material matters related to the Program and evaluate issues such as: The effectiveness of the policies and procedures of the financial institution or creditor in addressing the risk of identity theft in connection with the opening of covered accounts and with respect to existing covered accounts; service provider arrangements; significant incidents involving identity theft and management's response; and recommendations for material changes to the Program.

(c) *Oversight of service provider arrangements.* Whenever a financial institution or creditor engages a service provider to perform an activity in connection with one or more covered accounts the financial institution or creditor should take steps to ensure that the activity of the service provider is conducted in accordance with reasonable policies and procedures designed to detect, prevent, and mitigate the risk of identity theft. For example, a financial institution or creditor could require the service provider by contract to have policies and procedures to detect relevant Red Flags that may arise in the performance of the service provider's activities, and either report the Red Flags to the financial institution or creditor, or to take appropriate steps to prevent or mitigate identity theft.

VII. Other Applicable Legal Requirements

Financial institutions and creditors should be mindful of other related legal requirements that may be applicable, such as:

(a) For financial institutions and creditors that are subject to 31 U.S.C. 5318(g), filing a Suspicious Activity Report in accordance with applicable law and regulation;

(b) Implementing any requirements under 15 U.S.C. 1681c–1(h) regarding the circumstances under which credit may be extended when the financial institution or creditor detects a fraud or active duty alert;

(c) Implementing any requirements for furnishers of information to consumer reporting agencies under 15 U.S.C. 1681s–2, for example, to correct or update inaccurate or incomplete information, and to not report information that the furnisher has reasonable cause to believe is inaccurate; and

(d) Complying with the prohibitions in 15 U.S.C. 1681m on the sale, transfer, and placement for collection of certain debts resulting from identity theft.

Supplement A to Appendix A

In addition to incorporating Red Flags from the sources recommended in section II.b. of the Guidelines in appendix A of this part, each financial institution or creditor may consider incorporating into its Program, whether singly or in combination, Red Flags from the following illustrative examples in connection with covered accounts:

Alerts, Notifications or Warnings from a Consumer Reporting Agency

1. A fraud or active duty alert is included with a consumer report.

2. A consumer reporting agency provides a notice of credit freeze in response to a request for a consumer report.

3. A consumer reporting agency provides a notice of address discrepancy, as defined in §641.1(b) of this part.

4. A consumer report indicates a pattern of activity that is inconsistent with the history and usual pattern of activity of an applicant or customer, such as:

a. A recent and significant increase in the volume of inquiries;

b. An unusual number of recently established credit relationships;

c. A material change in the use of credit, especially with respect to recently established credit relationships; or

d. An account that was closed for cause or identified for abuse of account privileges by a financial institution or creditor.

Suspicious Documents

5. Documents provided for identification appear to have been altered or forged.

6. The photograph or physical description on the identification is not consistent with the appearance of the applicant or customer presenting the identification.

7. Other information on the identification is not consistent with information provided by the person opening a new covered account or customer presenting the identification.

8. Other information on the identification is not consistent with readily accessible information that is on file with the financial

institution or creditor, such as a signature card or a recent check.

9. An application appears to have been altered or forged, or gives the appearance of having been destroyed and reassembled.

Suspicious Personal Identifying Information

10. Personal identifying information provided is inconsistent when compared against external information sources used by the financial institution or creditor. For example:

a. The address does not match any address in the consumer report; or

b. The Social Security Number (SSN) has not been issued, or is listed on the Social Security Administration's Death Master File.

11. Personal identifying information provided by the customer is not consistent with other personal identifying information provided by the customer. For example, there is a lack of correlation between the SSN range and date of birth.

12. Personal identifying information provided is associated with known fraudulent activity as indicated by internal or third-party sources used by the financial institution or creditor. For example:

a. The address on an application is the same as the address provided on a fraudulent application; or

b. The phone number on an application is the same as the number provided on a fraudulent application.

13. Personal identifying information provided is of a type commonly associated with fraudulent activity as indicated by internal or third-party sources used by the financial institution or creditor. For example:

a. The address on an application is fictitious, a mail drop, or a prison; or

b. The phone number is invalid, or is associated with a pager or answering service.

14. The SSN provided is the same as that submitted by other persons opening an account or other customers.

15. The address or telephone number provided is the same as or similar to the address or telephone number submitted by an unusually large number of other persons opening accounts or by other customers.

16. The person opening the covered account or the customer fails to provide all required personal identifying information on an application or in response to notification that the application is incomplete.

17. Personal identifying information provided is not consistent with personal identifying information that is on file with the financial institution or creditor.

18. For financial institutions and creditors that use challenge questions, the person opening the covered account or the customer cannot provide authenticating information beyond that which generally would be available from a wallet or consumer report.

Unusual Use of, or Suspicious Activity Related to, the Covered Account

19. Shortly following the notice of a change of address for a covered account, the institution or creditor receives a request for a new, additional, or replacement card or a cell phone, or for the addition of authorized users on the account.

20. A new revolving credit account is used in a manner commonly associated with known patterns of fraud. For example:

a. The majority of available credit is used for cash advances or merchandise that is easily convertible to cash (e.g., electronics equipment or jewelry); or

b. The customer fails to make the first payment or makes an initial payment but no subsequent payments.

21. A covered account is used in a manner that is not consistent with established patterns of activity on the account. There is, for example:

a. Nonpayment when there is no history of late or missed payments;

b. A material increase in the use of available credit;

c. A material change in purchasing or spending patterns;

d. A material change in electronic fund transfer patterns in connection with a deposit account; or

e. A material change in telephone call patterns in connection with a cellular phone account.

22. A covered account that has been inactive for a reasonably lengthy period of time is used (taking into consideration the type of account, the expected pattern of usage and other relevant factors).

23. Mail sent to the customer is returned repeatedly as undeliverable although transactions continue to be conducted in connection with the customer's covered account.

24. The financial institution or creditor is notified that the customer is not receiving paper account statements.

25. The financial institution or creditor is notified of unauthorized charges or transactions in connection with a customer's covered account.

Notice from Customers, Victims of Identity Theft, Law Enforcement Authorities, or Other Persons Regarding Possible Identity Theft in Connection With Covered Accounts Held by the Financial Institution or Creditor

26. The financial institution or creditor is notified by a customer, a victim of identity theft, a law enforcement authority, or any other person that it has opened a fraudulent account for a person engaged in identity theft.

[72 FR 63771, Nov. 9, 2007, as amended at 74 FR 22646, May 14, 2009]

PART 682—DISPOSAL OF CONSUMER REPORT INFORMATION AND RECORDS

Sec.

AUTHORITY: Pub. L. 108–159, sec. 216.

SOURCE: 69 FR 68697, Nov. 24, 2004, unless otherwise noted.

§ 682.1 Definitions.

(a) *In general.* Except as modified by this part or unless the context otherwise requires, the terms used in this part have the same meaning as set forth in the Fair Credit Reporting Act, 15 U.S.C. 1681 *et seq.*

(b) "*Consumer information*" means any record about an individual, whether in paper, electronic, or other form, that is a consumer report or is derived from a consumer report. Consumer information also means a compilation of such records. Consumer information does not include information that does not identify individuals, such as aggregate information or blind data.

(c) "*Dispose,*" "*disposing,*" or "*disposal*" means:

(1) The discarding or abandonment of consumer information, or

(2) The sale, donation, or transfer of any medium, including computer equipment, upon which consumer information is stored.

§ 682.2 Purpose and scope.

(a) *Purpose.* This part ("rule") implements section 216 of the Fair and Accurate Credit Transactions Act of 2003, which is designed to reduce the risk of consumer fraud and related harms, including identity theft, created by improper disposal of consumer information.

(b) *Scope.* This rule applies to any person over which the Federal Trade Commission has jurisdiction, that, for a business purpose, maintains or otherwise possesses consumer information.

§ 682.3 Proper disposal of consumer information.

(a) *Standard.* Any person who maintains or otherwise possesses consumer information for a business purpose must properly dispose of such information by taking reasonable measures to protect against unauthorized access to or use of the information in connection with its disposal.

(b) *Examples.* Reasonable measures to protect against unauthorized access to or use of consumer information in connection with its disposal include the following examples. These examples are illustrative only and are not exclusive or exhaustive methods for complying with the rule in this part.

(1) Implementing and monitoring compliance with policies and procedures that require the burning, pulverizing, or shredding of papers containing consumer information so that the information cannot practicably be read or reconstructed.

(2) Implementing and monitoring compliance with policies and procedures that require the destruction or erasure of electronic media containing consumer information so that the information cannot practicably be read or reconstructed.

(3) After due diligence, entering into and monitoring compliance with a contract with another party engaged in the business of record destruction to dispose of material, specifically identified as consumer information, in a manner consistent with this rule. In this context, due diligence could include reviewing an independent audit of the disposal company's operations and/or its compliance with this rule, obtaining information about the disposal company from several references or other reliable sources, requiring that the disposal company be certified by a recognized trade association or similar third party, reviewing and evaluating the disposal company's information security policies or procedures, or taking other appropriate measures to determine the competency and integrity of the potential disposal company.

(4) For persons or entities who maintain or otherwise possess consumer information through their provision of services directly to a person subject to

this part, implementing and monitoring compliance with policies and procedures that protect against unauthorized or unintentional disposal of consumer information, and disposing of such information in accordance with examples (b)(1) and (2) of this section.

(5) For persons subject to the Gramm-Leach-Bliley Act, 15 U.S.C. 6081 *et seq.*, and the Federal Trade Commission's Standards for Safeguarding Customer Information, 16 CFR part 314 ("Safeguards Rule"), incorporating the proper disposal of consumer information as required by this rule into the information security program required by the Safeguards Rule.

§ 682.4 Relation to other laws.

Nothing in the rule in this part shall be construed:

(a) To require a person to maintain or destroy any record pertaining to a consumer that is not imposed under other law; or

(b) To alter or affect any requirement imposed under any other provision of law to maintain or destroy such a record.

§ 682.5 Effective date.

The rule in this part is effective on June 1, 2005.

PART 698—MODEL FORMS AND DISCLOSURES

AUTHORITY: 15 U.S.C. 1681e, 1681g, 1681j, 1681m, 1681s, and 1681s–3; Public Law 108–159, sections 211(d), 214(b), and 311; 117 Stat. 1952.

SOURCE: 69 FR 35500, June 24, 2004, unless otherwise noted.

§ 698.1 Authority and purpose.

(a) *Authority.* This part is issued by the Commission pursuant to the provisions of the Fair Credit Reporting Act (15 U.S.C. 1681 *et seq.*), as amended by the Consumer Credit Reporting Reform Act of 1996 (Title II, Subtitle D, Chapter 1, of the Omnibus Consolidated Appropriations Act for Fiscal Year 1997), Public Law 104–208, 110 Stat. 3009–426 (Sept. 30, 1996), and the Fair and Accurate Credit Transactions Act of 2003, Public Law 108–159, 117 Stat. 1952 (Dec. 4, 2003).

(b) *Purpose.* The purpose of this part is to comply with sections 607(d), 609(c), 609(d), 612(a), 615(d), 615(h) and 624 of the Fair Credit Reporting Act, as amended by the Fair and Accurate Credit Transactions Act of 2003, and sections 211(d) and 214(b) of the Fair and Accurate Credit Transactions Act of 2003.

[69 FR 69784, Nov. 30, 2004, as amended at 70 FR 5032, Jan. 31, 2005; 72 FR 61463, Oct. 30, 2007; 75 FR 2776, Jan. 15, 2010]

§ 698.2 Legal effect.

These model forms and disclosures prescribed by the FTC do not constitute a trade regulation rule. The issuance of the model forms and disclosures set forth below carries out the directive in the statute that the FTC prescribe these forms and disclosures. Use or distribution of these model forms and disclosures will constitute compliance with any section or subsection of the FCRA requiring that such forms and disclosures be used by or supplied to any person.

[69 FR 69784, Nov. 30, 2004]

§ 698.3 Definitions.

As used in this part, unless otherwise provided:

(a) *Substantially similar* means that all information in the Commission's prescribed model is included in the document that is distributed, and that the document distributed is formatted in a way consistent with the format prescribed by the Commission. The document that is distributed shall not include anything that interferes with, detracts from, or otherwise undermines the information contained in the Commission's prescribed model.

[69 FR 69784, Nov. 30, 2004]

APPENDIX A TO PART 698—MODEL PRESCREEN OPT-OUT NOTICES

In order to comply with part 642 of this title, the following model notices may be used:

(a) *English language model notice*—(1) *Short notice.*

Here's a Line About Credit

J.S. Name
12345 Friendly Street
City, ST 12345

Dear Ms. Name,

Back in the last century, we saw how technology was changing the way people do things. So we set out to create a the last century, we saw how technology was changing the way people do things. Back in the last century, we saw how technology was changing the way people do things. So we set out to create a the last century, we saw how technology was changing the way people do things.

Back in the last century, we saw how technology was changing the way people do things. So we set out to create a smart kind of credit card. Back in the last century, we saw how technology was changing the way. Back in the last century, we saw how technology was changing the way people do things. So we set out to create a the last century, we saw how technology was changing the way people do things.

Back in the last century, we saw how technology was changing the way people do things. So we set out to create a smart kind of credit card. Back in the last century, we saw how technology was changing the way peop. So we set out to create a smart kind of credit card. Back in the last century, we saw how technology was changing the way people do things. So we set out to create a smart kind of credit a smart kind of credit card.

So we set out to create a smart kind of credit card. Back in the last century, we saw how technology was changing the way people. Back in the last century, we saw how technology was changing the way people do things. So we set out to create a smart kind of credit card.

We saw how technology was changing the way people do things. So we set out to create a smart kind of credit card. Back in the last century, we saw how technology.

Sincerely,

John W. Doe
President, Credit Card Company

PFOR 00 MON
FIXED ABC

■

BALANCE TR
FOR 00 MONTHS

■

NO MONTHS FEE

■

INTERNET SECURITY
SECURITY

■

ONLINE FRAUD PRO
GUARANTEE

■

YOUR BALANCE
PAY YOUR BILL

■

FEE-FREE REWARDS
PROGRAM

You can choose to stop receiving "prescreened" offers of [credit or insurance] from this and other companies by calling toll-free [toll-free number]. See <u>PRESCREEN & OPT-OUT NOTICE</u> on other side [or other location] for more information about prescreened offers.

(2) *Long notice.*

Back in the last century, we saw how technology was changing the way people do things. So we set out to create a smart kind of credit card. Back in the last century, we saw how technology was changing the way. Back in the last century, we saw how technology was changing the way people do things. So we set out to create a the last century, we saw how technology was changing the way people do things.

HEADER

Percent Rate for	Other ABCs	Variable info material	Grace or repases Are placed here	Computing the balast	Annual Fee	Usual Place Finance Charge
Back in the last century, we saw how technology was changing the way people do things. So we set out to create a smart kind of credit card.	Back in the last century, we saw how technology was changing the way people do things. So we set out to create a smart kind of credit card. Back in the last century, we saw how technology was changing the way.	Back in the last century, we saw how technology was changing the way people do things. So we set out to create a smart kind of credit card.	Back in the last century, we saw how technology was changing.	Back in the last century, we saw how technology was changing the way people do things. So we set out to create a smart kind of credit card.	Back long ago.	Back in the last century, we saw how technology.

Back in the last century, we saw how technology was changing the way people do things. So we set out to create a smart kind of credit card. Back in the last century, we saw how technology was changing the way. Back in the last century, we saw how technology was changing the way people do things. So we set out to create a smart kind of credit card. Back in the last century, we saw how technology was changing the way. Back in the last century, we saw how technology was changing the way people do things. So we set out to create a smart kind of credit card. Back in the last century, we saw how technology was changing the way.

Back in the last century, we saw how technology was changing the way people do things. So we set out to create a smart kind of credit card. Back in the last century, we saw how technology was changing the way. Back in the last century, we saw how technology was changing the way people do things. So we set out to create a smart kind of credit card. Back in the last century, we saw how technology was changing the way. Back in the last century, we saw how technology was changing the way people do things. So we set out to create a smart kind of credit card. Back in the last century, we saw how technology was changing the way. Back in the last century, we saw how technology was changing the way people do things. So we set out to create a smart kind of credit card. Back in the last century, we saw how technology was changing the way. Back in the last century, we saw how technology was changing the way people do things. So we set out to create a smart kind of credit card. Back in the last century, we saw how technology was changing the way.

Back in the last century, we saw how technology was changing the way. Back in the last century, we saw how technology was changing the way people do things. So we set out to create a smart kind of credit card. Back in the last century, we saw how technology was changing the way.

Back in the last century, we saw how technology was changing the way. Back in the last century, we saw how technology was changing the way people do things. So we set out to create a smart kind of credit card. Back in the last century, we saw how technology was changing the way.

TERMS AND CONDITIONS

Back in the last century, we saw how technology was changing the way people do things. So we set out to create a smart kind of credit card. Back in the last century, we saw how technology was changing the way. Back in the last century, we saw how technology was changing the way people do things. So we set out to create a smart kind of credit card. Back in the last century, we saw how technology was changing the way. Back in the last century, we saw how technology was changing the way people do things. So we set out to create a smart kind of credit card. Back in the last century, we saw how technology was changing the way. Back in the last century, we saw how technology was changing the way people do things. So we set out to create a smart kind of credit card. Back in the last century, we saw how technology was changing the way. Back in the last century, we saw how technology was changing the way people do things. So we set out to create a smart kind of credit card. Back in the last century, we saw how technology was changing the way. Back in the last century, we saw how technology was changing the way people do things. So we set out to create a smart kind of credit card. Back in the last century, we saw how technology was changing the way. Back in the last century, we saw how technology was changing the way people do things. So we set out to create a smart kind of credit card. Back in the last century, we saw how technology was changing the way. Back in the last century, we saw how technology was changing the way people do things. So we set out to create a smart kind of credit card. Back in the last century, we saw how technology was changing the way. Back in the last century, we saw how technology was changing the way people do things. So we set out to create a smart kind of credit card. Back in the last century, we saw how technology was changing the way. Back in the last century, we saw how technology was changing the way people do things. So we set out to create a smart kind of credit card. Back in the last century, we saw how technology was changing the way. Back in the last century, we saw how technology was changing the way people do things. So we set out to create a smart kind of credit card. Back in the last century, we saw how technology was changing the way. Back in the last century, we saw how technology was changing the way people do things. Back in the last century, we saw how technology was changing the way. Back in the last century, we saw y, we saw how technology was changing the way. Back in the last century, we saw how technology was changing the way people do things.

Act Notice: the a smart kind of credit card. Back in the last century, we saw how technology was changing the way people do things. So we set out to create a smart kind of credit card. Back in the last century, we saw how technology was changing the way. Back in the last century, we saw.

<u>PRESCREEN & OPT-OUT NOTICE</u>: This "prescreened" offer of [credit or insurance] is based on information in your credit report indicating that you meet certain criteria. This offer is not guaranteed if you do not meet our criteria [including providing acceptable property as collateral]. If you do not want to receive prescreened offers of [credit or insurance] from this and other companies, call the consumer reporting agencies [or name of consumer reporting agency] toll-free, [toll-free number]; or write: [consumer reporting agency name and mailing address].

Notice to Some Residents: te a smart kind of credit card. Back in the last century, we saw how technology was changing the way. Back in the last century, we saw how technology was changing the way people do things. So we set out to create a smart kind of credit card. Back in the last century, we saw how technology was changing the way. Back in the last century. So we set out to create a smart kind of credit card. Back in the last century, we saw how technology was changing the way.

(b) *Spanish language model notice*—(1) *Short notice.*

Aquí están líneas crédito

J.S. Nombre
1234 Calle Amistosa
Ciudad, ST 12345

Estimada Señora Nombre:

En el siglo pasado vimos como la tecnología estaba cambiando la manera en que la gente hace las cosas. Así que creamos una tarjeta de crédito inteligente, vimos como la tecnología estaba cambiando la manera en que la gente hace las cosas. En el siglo pasado vimos como la tecnología estaba cambiando la manera en que la gente hace las cosas. Así que creamos una tarjeta de crédito inteligente. Vimos como la tecnología estaba cambiando la manera en que la gente hace las cosas.

Así que creamos una tarjeta de crédito inteligente. Vimos como la tecnología estaba cambiando la manera en que la gente hace las cosas. En el siglo pasado vimos como la tecnología estaba cambiando la manera en que la gente hace las cosas. Así que creamos una tarjeta de crédito inteligente, vimos como la tecnología estaba cambiando la manera en que la gente hace las cosas.

Vimos como la tecnología estaba cambiando la manera en que la gente hace las cosas. En el siglo pasado vimos como la tecnología estaba cambiando la manera en que la gente hace las cosas. Así que creamos una tárjeta de crédito inteligente, vimos como la tecnología estaba cambiando la manera en que la gente hace las cosas. En el siglo pasado vimos como la tecnología estaba cambiando la manera en que la gente hace las cosas.

Así que creamos una tarjeta de crédito inteligente. Vimos como la tecnología estaba cambiando la manera en que la gente hace las cosas. En el siglo pasado vimos como la tecnología estaba cambiando la manera en que la gente hace las cosas. Así que creamos una tarjeta de crédito inteligente. Vimos como la tecnología estaba cambiando la manera en que la gente hace las cosas.

Sinceramente,

John W. Doe
Presidente, Compañía

PFOR 00 MON FIJO ABC

■

TRANSFERENCIA DE BALANCE POR MESES

■

SIN CUOTA MENSUAL

■

PAGO ELECTRÓNICO SEGURO

■

PROTECCIÓN CONTRA FRAUDE EN LÍNEA GARANTIZADO

■

SU BALANCE PAGA SU CUENTA

■

PROGRAMA DE RECOMPENSAS SIN CUENTA

Usted puede elegir no recibir más "ofertas de [crédito o seguro] pre-investigadas" de esta y otras compañías llamando sin cargos al [número sin cargo]. Ver la <u>NOTIFICACIÓN DE PRE-INVESTIGACIÓN Y EXCLUSIÓN VOLUNTARIA</u> al otro lado de esta página [o en otro lugar] para más información sobre ofertas pre-investigadas.

(2) *Long notice.*

En el siglo pasado vimos como la tecnología estaba cambiando la manera en que la gente hace las cosas. Así que creamos una tarjeta de crédito inteligente, vimos como la tecnología estaba cambiando la manera en que la gente hace las cosas. En el siglo pasado vimos como la tecnología estaba cambiando la manera en que la gente hace las cosas. Así que creamos una tarjeta de crédito inteligente.

AQUÍ ESTÁN

Protección Contra Fraude	Programa de Recompensas	Su Balance Paga	Sin Cuota Mensual	Protección Contra Fraude	Recompensas Sin Cuenta	Sin Cuota Mensual
En el siglo pasado vimos como la tecnología estaba cambiando la manera en que la gente hace las cosas.	Vimos como la tecnología estaba cambiando la manera en que la gente hace las cosas. Vimos como la tecnología estaba cambiando la manera en que la gente hace las cosas.	En el siglo pasado vimos como la tecnología estaba cambiando la manera en que la gente hace las cosas. En el siglo pasado vimos como la gente hace las cosas. Así que cremos.	Así que creamos una tarjeta de crédito inteligente.	En el siglo pasado vimos como la tecnología estaba cambiando la manera en que la gente hace las cosas.	Así que cremos.	Vimos como la tecnología estaba cambiando la manera en que la gente hace las cosas.

En el siglo pasado vimos como la tecnología estaba cambiando la manera en que la gente hace las cosas. Así que creamos una tarjeta de crédito inteligente, vimos como la tecnología estaba cambiando la manera en que la gente hace las cosas. En el siglo pasado vimos como la tecnología estaba cambiando la manera en que la gente hace las cosas. Así que creamos una tarjeta de crédito inteligente. Vimos como la tecnología estaba cambiando la manera en que la gente hace las cosas. Así que creamos una tarjeta de crédito inteligente. Vimos como la tecnología estaba cambiando la manera en que la gente hace las cosas.

Así que creamos una tarjeta de crédito inteligente, vimos como la tecnología estaba cambiando la manera en que la gente hace las cosas. En el siglo pasado vimos como la tecnología estaba cambiando la manera en que la gente hace las cosas. Así que creamos una tarjeta de crédito inteligente. Vimos como la tecnología estaba cambiando la manera en que la gente hace las cosas. Así que creamos una tarjeta de crédito inteligente. Vimos como la tecnología estaba cambiando la manera en que la gente hace las cosas. En el siglo pasado vimos como la tecnología estaba cambiando la manera en que la gente hace las cosas. Así que creamos una tarjeta de crédito inteligente, vimos como la tecnología estaba cambiando la manera en que la gente hace las cosas.

Vimos como la tecnología estaba cambiando la manera en que la gente hace las cosas. En el siglo pasado vimos como la tecnología estaba cambiando la manera en que la gente hace las cosas. Así que creamos una tarjeta de crédito inteligente, vimos como la tecnología estaba cambiando la manera en que la gente hace las cosas. En el siglo pasado vimos como la tecnología estaba cambiando la manera en que la gente hace las cosas. Así que creamos una tarjeta de crédito inteligente. Vimos como la tecnología estaba cambiando la manera en que la gente hace las cosas. En el siglo pasado vimos como la tecnología estaba cambiando la manera en que la gente hace las cosas. En el siglo pasado vimos como la tecnología estaba cambiando la manera en que la gente hace las cosas.

TERMINOS Y CONDICIONA

En el siglo pasado vimos como la tecnología estaba cambiando la manera en que la gente hace las cosas. Así que creamos una tarjeta de crédito inteligente, vimos como la tecnología estaba cambiando la manera en que la gente hace las cosas. En el siglo pasado vimos como la tecnología estaba cambiando la manera en que la gente hace las cosas. Así que creamos una tarjeta de crédito inteligente. Vimos como la tecnología estaba cambiando la manera en que la gente hace las cosas.

Así que creamos una tarjeta de crédito inteligente. Vimos como la tecnología estaba cambiando la manera en que la gente hace las cosas. En el siglo pasado vimos como la tecnología estaba cambiando la manera en que la gente hace las cosas. Así que creamos una tarjeta de crédito inteligente, vimos como la tecnología estaba cambiando la manera en que la gente hace las cosas.

Vimos como la tecnología estaba cambiando la manera en que la gente hace las cosas. En el siglo pasado vimos como la tecnología estaba cambiando la manera en que la gente hace las cosas. Así que creamos una tarjeta de crédito inteligente, vimos como la tecnología estaba cambiando la manera en que la gente hace las cosas. En el siglo pasado vimos como la tecnología estaba cambiando la manera en que la gente hace las cosas.

Así que creamos una tarjeta de crédito inteligente. Vimos como la tecnología estaba cambiando la manera en que la gente hace las cosas. En el siglo pasado vimos como la tecnología estaba cambiando la manera en que la gente hace las cosas. Así que creamos una tarjeta de crédito inteligente. Vimos como la tecnología estaba cambiando la manera en que la gente hace las cosas.

En el siglo pasado vimos como la tecnología estaba cambiando la manera en que la gente hace las cosas. Así que creamos una tarjeta de crédito inteligente, vimos como la tecnología estaba cambiando la manera en que la gente hace las cosas. En el siglo pasado vimos como la tecnología estaba cambiando la manera en que la gente hace las cosas. Así que creamos una tarjeta de crédito inteligente. Vimos como la tecnología estaba cambiando la manera en que la gente hace las cosas. Así que creamos una tarjeta de crédito inteligente. Vimos como la tecnología estaba cambiando la manera en que la gente hace las cosas. En el siglo pasado vimos como la tecnología estaba cambiando la manera en que la gente hace las cosas. Así que creamos una tarjeta de crédito inteligente. Vimos como la tecnología estaba cambiando la manera en que la gente hace las cosas. Vimos como la tecnología estaba cambiando la manera en que la gente hace las cosas. Vimos como la tecnología estaba cambiando la manera en que la gente hace las cosas.

NOTIFICACIÓN DE PRE-INVESTIGACIÓN Y EXCLUSIÓN VOLUNTARIA: Esta oferta de [crédito o seguro] está basada en información contenida en su informe de crédito que indica que usted cumple con ciertos criterios [incluyendo la condición de tener propiedades aceptables como colateral]. Si usted no cumple con nuestros criterios, esta oferta no está garantizada. Si usted no desea recibir ofertas de [crédito o seguro] pre-investigadas de ésta y otras compañías, llame a las agencias de información del consumidor [o nombre de la agencia de información del consumidor] sin cargos, [número sin cargo]; o escriba a: [nombre de la agencia de información del consumidor y dirección de correo].

En el siglo pasado vimos como: la tecnología estaba cambiando la manera en que la gente hace las cosas. Así que creamos una tarjeta de crédito inteligente. Vimos como la tecnología estaba cambiando la manera en que la gente hace las cosas. Vimos como la tecnología estaba cambiando la manera en que la gente hace las cosas. Vimos como la tecnología estaba cambiando la manera en que la gente hace las cosas. Vimos como la tecnología estaba cambiando la manera en que la gente hace las cosas.

[70 FR 5033, Jan. 31, 2005]

APPENDIX B TO PART 698—MODEL FORMS FOR RISK-BASED PRICING AND CREDIT SCORE DISCLOSURE EXCEPTION NOTICES

1. This appendix contains four model forms for risk-based pricing notices and three model forms for use in connection with the credit score disclosure exceptions. Each of the model forms is designated for use in a particular set of circumstances as indicated by the title of that model form.

2. Model form B–1 is for use in complying with the general risk-based pricing notice requirements in §640.3 if a credit score is not used in setting the material terms of credit. Model form B–2 is for risk-based pricing notices given in connection with account review if a credit score is not used in increasing the annual percentage rate. Model form B–3 is for use in connection with the credit score disclosure exception for loans secured by residential real property. Model form B–4 is for use in connection with the credit score disclosure exception for loans that are not secured by residential real property. Model form B–5 is for use in connection with the credit score disclosure exception when no credit score is available for a consumer. Model form B–6 is for use in complying with the general risk-based pricing notice requirements in §640.3 if a credit score is used in setting the material terms of credit. Model form B–7 is for risk-based pricing notices given in connection with account review if a credit score is used in increasing the annual percentage rate. All forms contained in this appendix are models; their use is optional.

3. A person may change the forms by rearranging the format or by making technical modifications to the language of the forms, in each case without modifying the substance of the disclosures. Any such rearrangement or modification of the language of the model forms may not be so extensive as to materially affect the substance, clarity, comprehensibility, or meaningful sequence of the forms. Persons making revisions with that effect will lose the benefit of the safe harbor for appropriate use of Appendix B model forms. A person is not required to conduct consumer testing when rearranging the format of the model forms.

a. Acceptable changes include, for example:

i. Corrections or updates to telephone numbers, mailing addresses, or web site addresses that may change over time.

ii. The addition of graphics or icons, such as the person's corporate logo.

iii. Alteration of the shading or color contained in the model forms.

iv. Use of a different form of graphical presentation to depict the distribution of credit scores.

v. Substitution of the words "credit" and "creditor" or "finance" and "finance company" for the terms "loan" and "lender."

vi. Including pre-printed lists of the sources of consumer reports or consumer reporting agencies in a "check-the-box" format.

vii. Including the name of the consumer, transaction identification numbers, a date, and other information that will assist in identifying the transaction to which the form pertains.

viii. Including the name of an agent, such as an auto dealer or other party, when providing the "Name of the Entity Providing the Notice."

b. Unacceptable changes include, for example:

i. Providing model forms on register receipts or interspersed with other disclosures.

ii. Eliminating empty lines and extra spaces between sentences within the same section.

4. Optional language in model forms B–6 and B–7 may be used to direct the consumer to the entity (which may be a consumer reporting agency or the creditor itself, for a proprietary score that meets the definition of a credit score) that provided the credit score for any questions about the credit score, along with the entity's contact information. Creditors may use or not use the additional language without losing the safe harbor, since the language is optional.

B–1 Model form for risk-based pricing notice.

B–2 Model form for account review risk-based pricing notice.

B–3 Model form for credit score disclosure exception for credit secured by one to four units of residential real property.

B–4 Model form for credit score disclosure exception for loans not secured by residential real property.

B–5 Model form for credit score disclosure exception for loans where credit score is not available.

B–6 Model form for risk-based pricing notice with credit score information

B–7 Model form for account review risk-based pricing notice with credit score information

B-1. Model form for risk-based pricing notice

[Name of Entity Providing the Notice]
Your Credit Report[s] and the Price You Pay for Credit

What is a credit report?	A credit report is a record of your credit history. It includes information about whether you pay your bills on time and how much you owe to creditors.
How did we use your credit report[s]?	We used information from your credit report[s] to set the terms of the credit we are offering you, such as the [Annual Percentage Rate/down payment]. The terms offered to you may be less favorable than the terms offered to consumers who have better credit histories.
What if there are mistakes in your credit report[s]?	You have a right to dispute any inaccurate information in your credit report[s]. If you find mistakes on your credit report[s], contact **[insert name of CRA(s)]**, which [is/are] the [consumer reporting agency/consumer reporting agencies] from which we obtained your credit report[s]. It is a good idea to check your credit report[s] to make sure the information [it contains/they contain] is accurate.
How can you obtain a copy of your credit report[s]?	Under federal law, you have the right to obtain a copy of your credit report[s] without charge for 60 days after you receive this notice. To obtain your free report[s], contact **[insert name of CRA(s)]**: *By telephone:* Call toll-free: 1-877-xxx-xxxx *By mail:* Mail your written request to: **[Insert address]** *On the web:* Visit **[insert web site address]**
How can you get more information about credit reports?	For more information about credit reports and your rights under federal law, visit the Federal Reserve Board's web site at www.federalreserve.gov, or the Federal Trade Commission's web site at www.ftc.gov.

B-2. Model form for account review risk-based pricing notice

[Name of Entity Providing the Notice]
Your Credit Report[s] and the Pricing of Your Account

What is a credit report?	A credit report is a record of your credit history. It includes information about whether you pay your bills on time and how much you owe to creditors.
How did we use your credit report[s]?	We have used information from your credit report[s] to review the terms of your account with us. Based on our review of your credit report[s], we have increased the annual percentage rate on your account.
What if there are mistakes in your credit report[s]?	You have a right to dispute any inaccurate information in your credit report[s]. If you find mistakes on your credit report[s], contact **[insert name of CRA(s)]**, which [is/are] [a consumer reporting agency/consumer reporting agencies] from which we obtained your credit report[s]. It is a good idea to check your credit report[s] to make sure the information [it contains/they contain] is accurate.
How can you obtain a copy of your credit report[s]?	Under federal law, you have the right to obtain a copy of your credit report[s] without charge for 60 days after you receive this notice. To obtain your free report[s], contact **[insert name of CRA(s)]**: *By telephone:* Call toll-free: 1-877-xxx-xxxx *By mail:* Mail your written request to: **[Insert address]** *On the web:* Visit **[insert web site address]**
How can you get more information about credit reports?	For more information about credit reports and your rights under federal law, visit the Federal Reserve Board's web site at www.federalreserve.gov, or the Federal Trade Commission's web site at www.ftc.gov.

B-3. Model form for credit score disclosure exception for loans secured by one to four units of residential real property

[Name of Entity Providing the Notice]
Your Credit Score and the Price You Pay for Credit

Your Credit Score	
Your credit score	**[Insert credit score]** Source: **[Insert source]** Date: **[Insert date score was created]**

Understanding Your Credit Score	
What you should know about credit scores	Your credit score is a number that reflects the information in your credit report. Your credit report is a record of your credit history. It includes information about whether you pay your bills on time and how much you owe to creditors. Your credit score can change, depending on how your credit history changes.
How we use your credit score	Your credit score can affect whether you can get a loan and how much you will have to pay for that loan.
The range of scores	Scores range from a low of **[Insert bottom number in the range]** to a high of **[Insert top number in the range]**. Generally, the higher your score, the more likely you are to be offered better credit terms.
How your score compares to the scores of other consumers	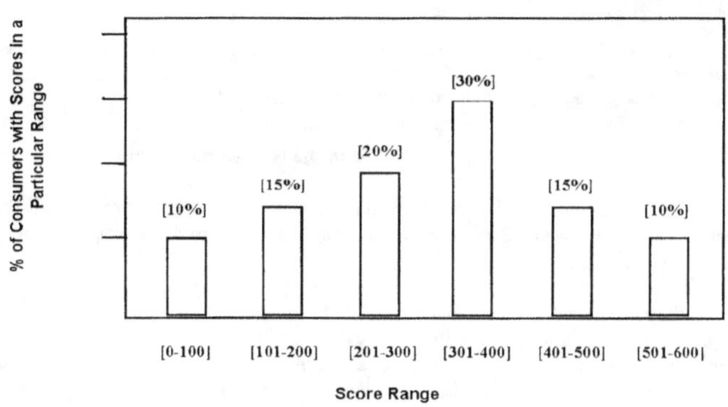 **[or]** [Your credit score ranks higher than [X] percent of U.S. consumers.]

Understanding Your Credit Score (continued)	
Key factors that adversely affected your credit score	**[Insert first factor]** **[Insert second factor]** **[Insert third factor]** **[Insert fourth factor]** **[Insert fifth factor, if applicable]**

Checking Your Credit Report		
What if there are mistakes in your credit report?	You have a right to dispute any inaccurate information in your credit report. If you find mistakes on your credit report, contact the consumer reporting agency. It is a good idea to check your credit report to make sure the information it contains is accurate.	
How can you obtain a copy of your credit report?	Under federal law, you have the right to obtain a free copy of your credit report from each of the nationwide consumer reporting agencies once a year. To order your free annual credit report—	
	By telephone:	Call toll-free: 1-877-322-8228
	On the web:	Visit www.annualcreditreport.com
	By mail:	Mail your completed Annual Credit Report Request Form (which you can obtain from the Federal Trade Commission's web site at http://www.ftc.gov/ bcp/conline/include/requestformfinal.pdf) to: Annual Credit Report Request Service P.O. Box 105281 Atlanta, GA 30348-5281
How can you get more information?	For more information about credit reports and your rights under federal law, visit the Federal Reserve Board's web site at www.federalreserve.gov, or the Federal Trade Commission's web site at www.ftc.gov.	

Notice to the Home Loan Applicant

In connection with your application for a home loan, the lender must disclose to you the score that a consumer reporting agency distributed to users and the lender used in connection with your home loan, and the key factors affecting your credit scores.

The credit score is a computer generated summary calculated at the time of the request and based on information that a consumer reporting agency or lender has on file. The scores are based on data about your credit history and payment patterns. Credit scores are important because they are used to assist the lender in determining whether you will obtain a loan. They may also be used to determine what interest rate you may be offered on the mortgage. Credit scores can change over time, depending on your conduct, how your credit history and payment patterns change, and how credit scoring technologies change.

Because the score is based on information in your credit history, it is very important that you review the credit-related information that is being furnished to make sure it is accurate. Credit records may vary from one company to another.

If you have questions about your credit score or the credit information that is furnished to you, contact the consumer reporting agency at the address and telephone number provided with this notice, or contact the lender, if the lender developed or generated the credit score. The consumer reporting agency plays no part in the decision to take any action on the loan application and is unable to provide you with specific reasons for the decision on a loan application.

If you have questions concerning the terms of the loan, contact the lender.

B-4. Model form for credit score disclosure exception for loans not secured by residential real property

[Name of Entity Providing the Notice]
Your Credit Score and the Price You Pay for Credit

Your Credit Score	
Your credit score	**[Insert credit score]** Source: **[Insert source]** Date: **[Insert date score was created]**

Understanding Your Credit Score	
What you should know about credit scores	Your credit score is a number that reflects the information in your credit report. Your credit report is a record of your credit history. It includes information about whether you pay your bills on time and how much you owe to creditors. Your credit score can change, depending on how your credit history changes.
How we use your credit score	Your credit score can affect whether you can get a loan and how much you will have to pay for that loan.
The range of scores	Scores range from a low of **[Insert bottom number in the range]** to a high of **[Insert top number in the range]**. Generally, the higher your score, the more likely you are to be offered better credit terms.
How your score compares to the scores of other consumers	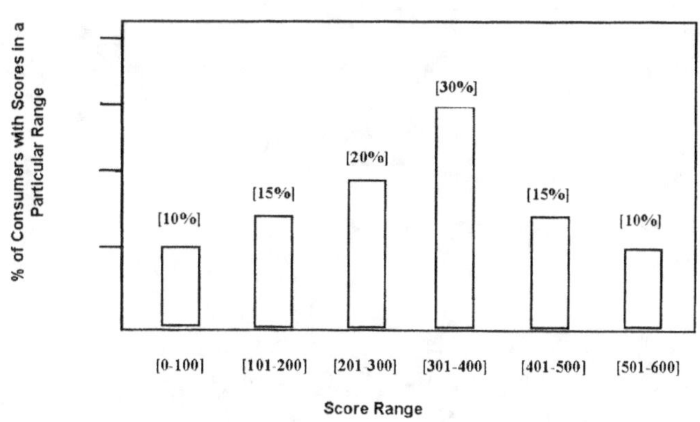 **[or]** [Your credit score ranks higher than [X] percent of U.S. consumers.]

<table>
<tr><th colspan="2">Checking Your Credit Report</th></tr>
<tr><td>What if there are mistakes in your credit report?</td><td>You have a right to dispute any inaccurate information in your credit report. If you find mistakes on your credit report, contact the consumer reporting agency.

It is a good idea to check your credit report to make sure the information it contains is accurate.</td></tr>
<tr><td>How can you obtain a copy of your credit report?</td><td>Under federal law, you have the right to obtain a free copy of your credit report from each of the nationwide consumer reporting agencies once a year.

To order your free annual credit report—

By telephone: Call toll-free: 1-877-322-8228

On the web: Visit www.annualcreditreport.com

By mail: Mail your completed Annual Credit Report Request Form (which you can obtain from the Federal Trade Commission's web site at http://www.ftc.gov/ bcp/conline/include/requestformfinal.pdf) to:

Annual Credit Report Request Service
P.O. Box 105281
Atlanta, GA 30348-5281</td></tr>
<tr><td>How can you get more information?</td><td>For more information about credit reports and your rights under federal law, visit the Federal Reserve Board's web site at www.federalreserve.gov, or the Federal Trade Commission's web site at www.ftc.gov.</td></tr>
</table>

B-5. Model form for loans where credit score is not available

[Name of Entity Providing the Notice]
Credit Scores and the Price You Pay for Credit

Your Credit Score	
Your credit score	Your credit score is not available from [**Insert name of CRA**], which is a consumer reporting agency, because they may not have enough information about your credit history to calculate a score.
What you should know about credit scores	A credit score is a number that reflects the information in a credit report. A credit report is a record of your credit history. It includes information about whether you pay your bills on time and how much you owe to creditors. A credit score can change, depending on how a consumer's credit history changes.
Why credit scores are important	Credit scores are important because consumers who have higher credit scores generally will get more favorable credit terms. Not having a credit score can affect whether you can get a loan and how much you will have to pay for that loan.
Checking Your Credit Report	
What if there are mistakes in your credit report?	You have a right to dispute any inaccurate information in your credit report. If you find mistakes on your credit report, contact the consumer reporting agency. It is a good idea to check your credit report to make sure the information it contains is accurate.
How can you obtain a copy of your credit report?	Under federal law, you have the right to obtain a free copy of your credit report from each of the nationwide consumer reporting agencies once a year. To order your free annual credit report— *By telephone:* Call toll-free: 1-877-322-8228 *On the web:* Visit www.annualcreditreport.com *By mail:* Mail your completed Annual Credit Report Request Form (which you can obtain from the Federal Trade Commission's web site at http://www.ftc.gov/bcp/conline/include/requestformfinal.pdf) to: Annual Credit Report Request Service P.O. Box 105281 Atlanta, GA 30348-5281
How can you get more information?	For more information about credit reports and your rights under federal law, visit the Federal Reserve Board's web site at www.federalreserve.gov, or the Federal Trade Commission's web site at www.ftc.gov.

H-6. Model form for risk-based pricing notice with credit score information

[Name of Entity Providing the Notice]
Your Credit Report[s] and the Price You Pay for Credit

What is a credit report?	A credit report is a record of your credit history. It includes information about whether you pay your bills on time and how much you owe to creditors.
How did we use your credit report[s]?	We used information from your credit report[s] to set the terms of the credit we are offering you, such as the [Annual Percentage Rate/down payment]. The terms offered to you may be less favorable than the terms offered to consumers who have better credit histories.
What if there are mistakes in your credit report[s]?	You have a right to dispute any inaccurate information in your credit report[s]. If you find mistakes on your credit report[s], contact **[insert name of CRA(s)]**, which [is/are] the [consumer reporting agency/consumer reporting agencies] from which we obtained your credit report[s]. It is a good idea to check your credit report[s] to make sure the information [it contains/they contain] is accurate.
How can you obtain a copy of your credit report[s]?	Under federal law, you have the right to obtain a copy of your credit report[s] without charge for 60 days after you receive this notice. To obtain your free report[s], contact **[insert name of CRA(s)]**: *By telephone:* Call toll-free: 1-877-xxx-xxxx *By mail:* Mail your written request to: **[Insert address]** *On the web:* Visit **[insert web site address]**
How can you get more information about credit reports?	For more information about credit reports and your rights under federal law, visit the Federal Reserve Board's web site at www.federalreserve.gov, or the Federal Trade Commission's web site at www.ftc.gov.

Your Credit Score and Understanding Your Credit Score

Your credit score	**[Insert credit score]** Source: **[Insert source]** Date: **[Insert date score was created]**
What you should know about credit scores	Your credit score is a number that reflects the information in your credit report. We used your credit score to set the terms of credit we are offering you. Your credit score can change, depending on how your credit history changes.
The range of scores	Scores range from a low of **[Insert bottom number in the range]** to a high of **[Insert top number in the range]**.
Key factors that adversely affected your credit score	**[Insert first factor]** **[Insert second factor]** **[Insert third factor]** **[Insert fourth factor]** **[Insert number of enquiries as a key factor, if applicable]**
[How can you get more information about your credit score?]	[If you have any questions regarding your credit score, you should contact [entity that provided the credit score] at: Address: ____________________ ____________________ [Toll-free] Telephone number:____________________]

H-7. Model form for account review risk-based pricing notice with credit score information

[Name of Entity Providing the Notice]
Your Credit Report[s] and the Pricing of Your Account

What is a credit report?	A credit report is a record of your credit history. It includes information about whether you pay your bills on time and how much you owe to creditors.
How did we use your credit report[s]?	We have used information from your credit report[s] to review the terms of your account with us. Based on our review of your credit report[s], we have increased the annual percentage rate on your account.
What if there are mistakes in your credit report[s]?	You have a right to dispute any inaccurate information in your credit report[s]. If you find mistakes on your credit report[s], contact **[insert name of CRA(s)]**, which [is/are] [a consumer reporting agency/consumer reporting agencies] from which we obtained your credit report[s]. It is a good idea to check your credit report[s] to make sure the information [it contains/they contain] is accurate.
How can you obtain a copy of your credit report[s]?	Under federal law, you have the right to obtain a copy of your credit report[s] without charge for 60 days after you receive this notice. To obtain your free report[s], contact **[insert name of CRA(s)]**: *By telephone:* Call toll-free: 1-877-xxx-xxxx *By mail:* Mail your written request to: **[Insert address]** *On the web:* Visit **[insert web site address]**
How can you get more information about credit reports?	For more information about credit reports and your rights under federal law, visit the Federal Reserve Board's web site at www.federalreserve.gov, or the Federal Trade Commission's web site at www.ftc.gov.

Your Credit Score and Understanding Your Credit Score

Your credit score	**[Insert credit score]** Source: **[Insert source]** Date: **[Insert date score was created]**
What you should know about credit scores	Your credit score is a number that reflects the information in your credit report. We used your credit score to set the terms of credit we are offering you. Your credit score can change, depending on how your credit history changes.
The range of scores	Scores range from a low of **[Insert bottom number in the range]** to a high of **[Insert top number in the range]**.
Key factors that adversely affected your credit score	**[Insert first factor]** **[Insert second factor]** **[Insert third factor]** **[Insert fourth factor]** **[Insert number of enquiries as a key factor, if applicable]**
[How can you get more information about your credit score?]	[If you have any questions regarding your credit score, you should contact [entity that provided the credit score] at: Address: ____________________ ____________________ [Toll-free] Telephone number:____________________]

[75 FR 2776, Jan. 15, 2010, as amended at 76 FR 41622, July 15, 2011]

APPENDIX C TO PART 698—MODEL FORMS FOR AFFILIATE MARKETING OPT-OUT NOTICES

A. Although use of the model forms is not required, use of the model forms in this appendix (as applicable) complies with the requirement in section 624 of the Act for clear, conspicuous, and concise notices.

B. Certain changes may be made to the language or format of the model forms without losing the protection from liability afforded by use of the model forms. These changes may not be so extensive as to affect the substance, clarity, or meaningful sequence of the language in the model forms. Persons making such extensive revisions will lose the safe harbor that this appendix provides. Acceptable changes include, for example:

1. Rearranging the order of the references to "your income," "your account history," and "your credit score."

2. Substituting other types of information for "income," "account history," or "credit score" for accuracy, such as "payment history," "credit history," "payoff status," or "claims history."

3. Substituting a clearer and more accurate description of the affiliates providing or covered by the notice for phrases such as "the [ABC] group of companies," including without limitation a statement that the entity providing the notice recently purchased the consumer's account.

4. Substituting other types of affiliates covered by the notice for "credit card," "insurance," or "securities" affiliates.

5. Omitting items that are not accurate or applicable. For example, if a person does not limit the duration of the opt-out period, the notice may omit information about the renewal notice.

6. Adding a statement informing consumers how much time they have to opt out before shared eligibility information may be used to make solicitations to them.

7. Adding a statement that the consumer may exercise the right to opt out at any time.

8. Adding the following statement, if accurate: "If you previously opted out, you do not need to do so again."

9. Providing a place on the form for the consumer to fill in identifying information, such as his or her name and address.

10. Adding disclosures regarding the treatment of opt-outs by joint consumers to comply with §680.23(a)(2) of part 680.

C-1 Model Form for Initial Opt-out notice (Single-Affiliate Notice)
C-2 Model Form for Initial Opt-out notice (Joint Notice)
C-3 Model Form for Renewal Notice (Single-Affiliate Notice)
C-4 Model Form for Renewal Notice (Joint Notice)
C-5 Model Form for Voluntary "No Marketing" Notice

C-1 MODEL FORM FOR INITIAL OPT-OUT NOTICE (SINGLE-AFFILIATE NOTICE)

[YOUR CHOICE TO LIMIT MARKETING]/[MARKETING OPT-OUT]

— [Name of Affiliate] is providing this notice.
— [Optional: Federal law gives you the right to limit some but not all marketing from our affiliates. Federal law also requires us to give you this notice to tell you about your choice to limit marketing from our affiliates.]
— You may limit our affiliates in the [ABC] group of companies, such as our [credit card, insurance, and securities] affiliates, from marketing their products or services to you based on your personal information that we collect and share with them. This information includes your [income], your [account history with us], and your [credit score].
— Your choice to limit marketing offers from our affiliates will apply [until you tell us to change your choice]/[for x years from when you tell us your choice]/[for at least 5 years from when you tell us your choice]. [Include if the opt-out period expires.] Once that period expires, you will receive a renewal notice that will allow you to continue to limit marketing offers from our affiliates for [another x years]/[at least another 5 years].
— [Include, if applicable, in a subsequent notice, including an annual notice, for consumers who may have previously opted out.] If you have already made a choice to limit marketing offers from our affiliates, you do not need to act again until you receive the renewal notice.

TO LIMIT MARKETING OFFERS, CONTACT US [include all that apply]:

— BY TELEPHONE: 1-877-###-####
— ON THE WEB: *www.—.com*
— BY MAIL: check the box and complete the form below, and send the form to:

[Company name]
[Company address]

____ Do not allow your affiliates to use my personal information to market to me.

C-2 MODEL FORM FOR INITIAL OPT-OUT NOTICE (JOINT NOTICE)

[YOUR CHOICE TO LIMIT MARKETING]/[MARKETING OPT-OUT]

— The [ABC group of companies] is providing this notice.
— [Optional: Federal law gives you the right to limit some but not all marketing from the [ABC] companies. Federal law also requires us to give you this notice to tell you about your choice to limit marketing from the [ABC] companies.]
— You may limit the [ABC companies], such as the [ABC credit card, insurance, and securities] affiliates, from marketing their products or services to you based on your personal information that they receive from other [ABC] companies. This information includes your [income], your [account history], and your [credit score].
— Your choice to limit marketing offers from the [ABC] companies will apply [until you tell us to change your choice]/[for x years from when you tell us your choice]/[for at least 5 years from when you tell us your choice]. [Include if the opt-out period expires.] Once that period expires, you will receive a renewal notice that will allow you to continue to limit marketing offers from the [ABC] companies for [another x years]/[at least another 5 years].
— [Include, if applicable, in a subsequent notice, including an annual notice, for consumers who may have previously opted out.] If you have already made a choice to limit marketing offers from the [ABC] companies, you do not need to act again until you receive the renewal notice.

TO LIMIT MARKETING OFFERS, CONTACT US [include all that apply]:

— BY TELEPHONE: 1-877-###-####
— ON THE WEB: *www.—.com*
— BY MAIL: check the box and complete the form below, and send the form to:

[Company name]
[Company address]

____ Do not allow any company [in the ABC group of companies] to use my personal information to market to me.

C-3 MODEL FORM FOR RENEWAL NOTICE (SINGLE-AFFILIATE NOTICE)

[RENEWING YOUR CHOICE TO LIMIT MARKETING]/[RENEWING YOUR MARKETING OPT-OUT]

— [Name of Affiliate] is providing this notice.
— [Optional: Federal law gives you the right to limit some but not all marketing from

our affiliates. Federal law also requires us to give you this notice to tell you about your choice to limit marketing from our affiliates.]

— You previously chose to limit our affiliates in the [ABC] group of companies, such as our [credit card, insurance, and securities] affiliates, from marketing their products or services to you based on your personal information that we share with them. This information includes your [income], your [account history with us], and your [credit score].

— Your choice has expired or is about to expire.

TO RENEW YOUR CHOICE TO LIMIT MARKETING FOR [X] MORE YEARS, CONTACT US [include all that apply]:

— BY TELEPHONE: 1-877-###-####

— ON THE WEB: *www.—.com*

— BY MAIL: check the box and complete the form below, and send the form to:

[Company name]

[Company address]

___ Renew my choice to limit marketing for [x] more years.

C-4 MODEL FORM FOR RENEWAL NOTICE (JOINT NOTICE)

[RENEWING YOUR CHOICE TO LIMIT MARKETING]/[RENEWING YOUR MARKETING OPT-OUT]

— The [ABC group of companies] is providing this notice.

— [Optional: Federal law gives you the right to limit some but not all marketing from the [ABC] companies. Federal law also requires us to give you this notice to tell you about your choice to limit marketing from the [ABC] companies.]

— You previously chose to limit the [ABC companies], such as the [ABC credit card, insurance, and securities] affiliates, from marketing their products or services to you based on your personal information that they receive from other [ABC] companies. This information includes your [income], your [account history], and your [credit score].

— Your choice has expired or is about to expire.

TO RENEW YOUR CHOICE TO LIMIT MARKETING FOR [X] MORE YEARS, CONTACT US [include all that apply]:

— BY TELEPHONE: 1-877-###-####

— ON THE WEB: *www.—.com*

— BY MAIL: check the box and complete the form below, and send the form to:

[Company name]

[Company address]

___ Renew my choice to limit marketing for [x] more years.

C-5—MODEL FORM FOR VOLUNTARY "NO MARKETING" NOTICE

YOUR CHOICE TO STOP MARKETING

- [Name of Affiliate] is providing this notice.
- You may choose to stop all marketing from us and our affiliates.
- [Your choice to stop marketing from us and our affiliates will apply until you tell us to change your choice.]

To stop all marketing, contact us [include all that apply]:

- By telephone: 1-877-###-####
- On the Web: *www.—.com*
- By mail: Check the box and complete the form below, and send the form to:

[Company name]

[Company address]

__Do not market to me.

[72 FR 61463, Oct. 30, 2007, as amended at 74 FR 22646, May 14, 2009; 74 FR 32410, July 8, 2009]

APPENDIX D TO PART 698—STANDARDIZED FORM FOR REQUESTING ANNUAL FILE DISCLOSURES.

REQUEST FOR FREE CREDIT REPORT

Note to Consumers: **You have the right to obtain a free copy of your credit report once every 12 months (also known as an "annual file disclosure"), from each of the nationwide consumer reporting agencies. Your report may contain information on where you work and live, the credit accounts that have been opened in your name, if you've paid your bills on time, and whether you have been sued, arrested, or have filed for bankruptcy. Businesses use this information in making decisions about whether to offer you credit, insurance, or employment, and on what terms.**

Use this form to request your credit report from any, or all, of the nationwide consumer reporting agencies.

The following information is required to process your request:

Your Full Name: ______________________________

Your Street Address: ______________________________

Your City, State & Zip Code: ______________________________

Your Telephone Numbers (with area code): Day: ____________________
Evening: ____________________

Your Social Security number: ______________ Your Date of Birth______________

Place a check next to each credit report you want.

_____ I want a credit report from each of the nationwide consumer reporting agencies

OR

_____ I want a credit report from:

_____ [name of nationwide consumer reporting agency]
_____ [name of nationwide consumer reporting agency]
_____ [name of nationwide consumer reporting agency]

Please check how you would like to receive your report. (Note: because of the need to accurately identify you before we send you your credit report, we may not be able to offer every delivery method to every consumer. We will try to honor your preference.)

_____ [available delivery method]
_____ [available delivery method]
_____ [available delivery method]

_____ Check here if, for security purposes, you want your copy of your credit report to include only the last four digits of your Social Security number (SSN), rather than your entire SSN.

For more information on obtaining your free credit report, visit [insert appropriate website address], call [insert appropriate telephone number], or write to [insert appropriate address].

Mail this form to:
[insert appropriate address]

Your report(s) will be sent within 15 days after we receive your request.

APPENDIX E TO PART 698—SUMMARY OF CONSUMER IDENTITY THEFT RIGHTS

The prescribed form for this summary is a disclosure that is substantially similar to the Commission's model summary with all information clearly and prominently displayed. A summary should accurately reflect changes to those items that may change over time (such as telephone numbers) to remain in compliance. Translations of this summary will be in compliance with the Commission's prescribed model, provided that the translation is accurate and that it is provided in a language used by the recipient consumer.

Para informacion en espanol, visite www.consumer.gov/idtheft o escribe a la FTC, Consumer Response Center, Room 130-B, 600 Pennsylvania Avenue, N.W. Washington, D.C., 20580.

Remedying the Effects of Identity Theft

You are receiving this information because you have notified a consumer reporting agency that you believe that you are a victim of identity theft. Identity theft occurs when someone uses your name, Social Security number, date of birth, or other identifying information, without authority, to commit fraud. For example, someone may have committed identity theft by using your personal information to open a credit card account or get a loan in your name. For more information, visit www.consumer.gov/idtheft or write to: FTC, Consumer Response Center, Room 130-B, 600 Pennsylvania Avenue, N.W. Washington, D.C., 20580.

The Fair Credit Reporting Act (FCRA) gives you specific rights when you are, or believe that you are, the victim of identity theft. Here is a brief summary of the rights designed to help you recover from identity theft.

1. **You have the right to ask that nationwide consumer reporting agencies place "fraud alerts" in your file** to let potential creditors and others know that you may be a victim of identity theft. A fraud alert can make it more difficult for someone to get credit in your name because it tells creditors to follow certain procedures to protect you. It also may delay your ability to obtain credit. You may place a fraud alert in your file by calling just one of the three nationwide consumer reporting agencies. As soon as that agency processes your fraud alert, it will notify the other two, which then also must place fraud alerts in your file.

   - Equifax: 1-800-XXX-XXXX; www.equifax.com
   - Experian: 1-800-XXX-XXXX; www.experian.com
   - TransUnion: 1-800-XXX-XXXX; www.transunion.com

   An initial fraud alert stays in your file for at least 90 days. An extended alert stays in your file for seven years. To place either of these alerts, a consumer reporting agency will require you to provide appropriate proof of your identity, which may include your Social Security number. If you ask for an extended alert, you will have to provide an *identity theft report.* An *identity theft report* includes a copy of a report you have filed with a federal, state, or local law enforcement agency, and additional information a consumer reporting agency may require you to submit. For more detailed information about the *identity theft report*, visit www.consumer.gov/idtheft.

2. **You have the right to free copies of the information in your file (your "file disclosure").** An initial fraud alert entitles you to a copy of all the information in your file at each of the three nationwide agencies, and an extended alert entitles you to two free file disclosures in a 12-month period following the placing of the alert. These additional disclosures may help you detect signs of fraud, for example, whether fraudulent accounts have been opened in your name or whether someone has reported a change in your address. Once a year, you also have the right to a free copy of the information in your file

at any consumer reporting agency, if you believe it has inaccurate information due to fraud, such as identity theft. You also have the ability to obtain additional free file disclosures under other provisions of the FCRA. See www.ftc.gov/credit.

3. **You have the right to obtain documents relating to fraudulent transactions made or accounts opened using your personal information.** A creditor or other business must give you copies of applications and other business records relating to transactions and accounts that resulted from the theft of your identity, if you ask for them in writing. A business may ask you for proof of your identity, a police report, and an affidavit before giving you the documents. It also may specify an address for you to send your request. Under certain circumstances, a business can refuse to provide you with these documents. See www.consumer.gov/idtheft.

4. **You have the right to obtain information from a debt collector.** If you ask, a debt collector must provide you with certain information about the debt you believe was incurred in your name by an identity thief – like the name of the creditor and the amount of the debt.

5. **If you believe information in your file results from identity theft, you have the right to ask that a consumer reporting agency block that information from your file.** An identity thief may run up bills in your name and not pay them. Information about the unpaid bills may appear on your consumer report. Should you decide to ask a consumer reporting agency to block the reporting of this information, you must identify the information to block, and provide the consumer reporting agency with proof of your identity and a copy of your *identity theft report*. The consumer reporting agency can refuse or cancel your request for a block if, for example, you don't provide the necessary documentation, or where the block results from an error or a material misrepresentation of fact made by you. If the agency declines or rescinds the block, it must notify you. Once a debt resulting from identity theft has been blocked, a person or business with notice of the block may not sell, transfer, or place the debt for collection.

6. **You also may prevent businesses from reporting information about you to consumer reporting agencies if you believe the information is a result of identity theft.** To do so, you must send your request to the address specified by the business that reports the information to the consumer reporting agency. The business will expect you to identify what information you do not want reported and to provide an *identity theft report*.

To learn more about identity theft and how to deal with its consequences, visit www.consumer.gov/idtheft, or write to the FTC. You may have additional rights under state law. For more information, contact your local consumer protection agency or your state attorney general.

In addition to the new rights and procedures to help consumers deal with the effects of identity theft, the FCRA has many other important consumer protections. They are described in more detail at www.ftc.gov/credit.

[69 FR 69784, Nov. 30, 2004]

APPENDIX F TO PART 698—GENERAL SUMMARY OF CONSUMER RIGHTS

The prescribed form for this summary is a disclosure that is substantially similar to the Commission's model summary with all information clearly and prominently displayed. The list of federal regulators that is included in the Commission's prescribed summary may be provided separately so long as this is done in a clear and conspicuous way. A summary should accurately reflect changes to those items that may change over time (e.g., dollar amounts, or telephone numbers and addresses of federal agencies) to remain in compliance. Translations of this summary will be in compliance with the Commission's prescribed model, provided that the translation is accurate and that it is provided in a language used by the recipient consumer.

Para informacion en espanol, visite www.ftc.gov/credit o escribe a la FTC Consumer Response Center, Room 130-A 600 Pennsylvania Ave. N.W., Washington, D.C. 20580.

A Summary of Your Rights Under the Fair Credit Reporting Act

The federal Fair Credit Reporting Act (FCRA) promotes the accuracy, fairness, and privacy of information in the files of consumer reporting agencies. There are many types of consumer reporting agencies, including credit bureaus and specialty agencies (such as agencies that sell information about check writing histories, medical records, and rental history records). Here is a summary of your major rights under the FCRA. **For more information, including information about additional rights, go to www.ftc.gov/credit or write to: Consumer Response Center, Room 130-A, Federal Trade Commission, 600 Pennsylvania Ave. N.W., Washington, D.C. 20580.**

- **You must be told if information in your file has been used against you.** Anyone who uses a credit report or another type of consumer report to deny your application for credit, insurance, or employment – or to take another adverse action against you – must tell you, and must give you the name, address, and phone number of the agency that provided the information.
- **You have the right to know what is in your file.** You may request and obtain all the information about you in the files of a consumer reporting agency (your "file disclosure"). You will be required to provide proper identification, which may include your Social Security number. In many cases, the disclosure will be free. You are entitled to a free file disclosure if:
  - a person has taken adverse action against you because of information in your credit report;
  - you are the victim of identify theft and place a fraud alert in your file;
  - your file contains inaccurate information as a result of fraud;
  - you are on public assistance;
  - you are unemployed but expect to apply for employment within 60 days.

  In addition, by September 2005 all consumers will be entitled to one free disclosure every 12 months upon request from each nationwide credit bureau and from nationwide specialty consumer reporting agencies. See www.ftc.gov/credit for additional information.
- **You have the right to ask for a credit score.** Credit scores are numerical summaries of your credit-worthiness based on information from credit bureaus. You may request a credit score from consumer reporting agencies that create scores or distribute scores used in residential real property loans, but you will have to pay for it. In some mortgage transactions, you will receive credit score information for free from the mortgage lender.
- **You have the right to dispute incomplete or inaccurate information.** If you identify information in your file that is incomplete or inaccurate, and report it to the consumer reporting agency, the agency must investigate unless your dispute is frivolous. See www.ftc.gov/credit for an explanation of dispute procedures.
- **Consumer reporting agencies must correct or delete inaccurate, incomplete, or unverifiable information.** Inaccurate, incomplete or unverifiable information must be removed or corrected, usually within 30 days. However, a consumer reporting agency may continue to report information it has verified as accurate.

- **Consumer reporting agencies may not report outdated negative information.** In most cases, a consumer reporting agency may not report negative information that is more than seven years old, or bankruptcies that are more than 10 years old.
- **Access to your file is limited.** A consumer reporting agency may provide information about you only to people with a valid need -- usually to consider an application with a creditor, insurer, employer, landlord, or other business. The FCRA specifies those with a valid need for access.
- **You must give your consent for reports to be provided to employers.** A consumer reporting agency may not give out information about you to your employer, or a potential employer, without your written consent given to the employer. Written consent generally is not required in the trucking industry. For more information, go to www.ftc.gov/credit.
- **You may limit "prescreened" offers of credit and insurance you get based on information in your credit report.** Unsolicited "prescreened" offers for credit and insurance must include a toll-free phone number you can call if you choose to remove your name and address from the lists these offers are based on. You may opt-out with the nationwide credit bureaus at 1-800-XXX-XXXX.
- **You may seek damages from violators.** If a consumer reporting agency, or, in some cases, a user of consumer reports or a furnisher of information to a consumer reporting agency violates the FCRA, you may be able to sue in state or federal court.
- **Identity theft victims and active duty military personnel have additional rights.** For more information, visit www.ftc.gov/credit.

States may enforce the FCRA, and many states have their own consumer reporting laws. In some cases, you may have more rights under state law. For more information, contact your state or local consumer protection agency or your state Attorney General. Federal enforcers are:

TYPE OF BUSINESS:	CONTACT:
Consumer reporting agencies, creditors and others not listed below	Federal Trade Commission: Consumer Response Center - FCRA Washington, DC 20580 1-877-382-4357
National banks, federal branches/agencies of foreign banks (word "National" or initials "N.A." appear in or after bank's name)	Office of the Comptroller of the Currency Compliance Management, Mail Stop 6-6 Washington, DC 20219 800-613-6743
Federal Reserve System member banks (except national banks, and federal branches/agencies of foreign banks)	Federal Reserve Board Division of Consumer & Community Affairs Washington, DC 20551 202-452-3693
Savings associations and federally chartered savings banks (word "Federal" or initials "F.S.B." appear in federal institution's name)	Office of Thrift Supervision Consumer Complaints Washington, DC 20552 800-842-6929
Federal credit unions (words "Federal Credit Union" appear in institution's name)	National Credit Union Administration 1775 Duke Street Alexandria, VA 22314 703-519-4600
State-chartered banks that are not members of the Federal Reserve System	Federal Deposit Insurance Corporation Consumer Response Center, 2345 Grand Avenue, Suite 100 Kansas City, Missouri 64108-2638 1-877-275-3342
Air, surface, or rail common carriers regulated by former Civil Aeronautics Board or Interstate Commerce Commission	Department of Transportation , Office of Financial Management Washington, DC 20590 202-366-1306
Activities subject to the Packers and Stockyards Act, 1921	Department of Agriculture Office of Deputy Administrator - GIPSA Washington, DC 20250 202-720-7051

[69 FR 69787, Nov. 30, 2004]

Appendix G to Part 698—Notice of Furnisher Responsibilities

The prescribed form for this disclosure is a separate document that is substantially similar to the Commission's model notice with all information clearly and prominently displayed. Consumer reporting agencies may limit the disclosure to only those items that they know are relevant to the furnisher that will receive the notice.

All furnishers subject to the Federal Trade Commission's jurisdiction must comply with all applicable regulations, including regulations promulgated after this notice was prescribed in 2004. Information about applicable regulations currently in effect can be found at the Commission's Web site, www.ftc.gov/credit. Furnishers who are not subject to the Commission's jurisdiction should consult with their regulators to find any relevant regulations.

NOTICE TO FURNISHERS OF INFORMATION: OBLIGATIONS OF FURNISHERS UNDER THE FCRA

The federal Fair Credit Reporting Act (FCRA), 15 U.S.C. 1681-1681y, imposes responsibilities on all persons who furnish information to consumer reporting agencies (CRAs). These responsibilities are found in Section 623 of the FCRA, 15 U.S.C. 1681s-2. State law may impose additional requirements on furnishers. All furnishers of information to CRAs should become familiar with the applicable laws and may want to consult with their counsel to ensure that they are in compliance. The text of the FCRA is set forth in full at the Website of the Federal Trade Commission (FTC): www.ftc.gov/credit. A list of the sections of the FCRA cross-referenced to the U.S. Code is at the end of this document.

Section 623 imposes the following duties upon furnishers:

Accuracy Guidelines

The banking and credit union regulators and the FTC will promulgate guidelines and regulations dealing with the accuracy of information provided to CRAs by furnishers. The regulations and guidelines issued by the FTC will be available at www.ftc.gov/credit when they are issued. Section 623(e).

General Prohibition on Reporting Inaccurate Information

The FCRA prohibits information furnishers from providing information to a CRA that they know or have reasonable cause to believe is inaccurate. However, the furnisher is not subject to this general prohibition if it clearly and conspicuously specifies an address to which consumers may write to notify the furnisher that certain information is inaccurate. Sections 623(a)(1)(A) and (a)(1)(C).

Duty to Correct and Update Information

If at any time a person who regularly and in the ordinary course of business furnishes information to one or more CRAs determines that the information provided is not complete or accurate, the furnisher must promptly provide complete and accurate information to the CRA. In addition, the furnisher must notify all CRAs that received the information of any corrections, and must thereafter report only the complete and accurate information. Section 623(a)(2).

Duties After Notice of Dispute from Consumer

If a consumer notifies a furnisher, at an address specified for the furnisher for such notices, that specific information is inaccurate, and the information is, in fact, inaccurate, the furnisher must thereafter report the correct information to CRAs. Section 623(a)(1)(B).

If a consumer notifies a furnisher that the consumer disputes the completeness or accuracy of any information reported by the furnisher, the furnisher may not subsequently report that information to a CRA without providing notice of the dispute. Section 623(a)(3).

The federal banking and credit union regulators and the FTC will issue regulations that will identify when an information furnisher must investigate a dispute made directly to the furnisher by a consumer. Once these regulations are issued, furnishers must comply with them and complete an investigation within 30 days (or 45 days, if the consumer later provides relevant additional information) unless the dispute is frivolous or irrelevant or comes from a "credit repair organization." The FTC regulations will be available at www.ftc.gov/credit. Section 623(a)(8).

Duties After Notice of Dispute from Consumer Reporting Agency

If a CRA notifies a furnisher that a consumer disputes the completeness or accuracy of information provided by the furnisher, the furnisher has a duty to follow certain procedures. The furnisher must:

- Conduct an investigation and review all relevant information provided by the CRA, including information given to the CRA by the consumer. Sections 623(b)(1)(A) and (b)(1)(B).
- Report the results to the CRA that referred the dispute, and, if the investigation establishes that the information was, in fact, incomplete or inaccurate, report the results to all CRAs to which the furnisher provided the information that compile and maintain files on a nationwide basis. Section 623(b)(1)(C) and (b)(1)(D).
- Complete the above steps within 30 days from the date the CRA receives the dispute (or 45 days, if the consumer later provides relevant additional information to the CRA). Section 623(b)(2).
- Promptly modify or delete the information, or block its reporting. Section 623(b)(1)(E).

Duty to Report Voluntary Closing of Credit Accounts

If a consumer voluntarily closes a credit account, any person who regularly and in the ordinary course of business furnishes information to one or more CRAs must report this fact when it provides information to CRAs for the time period in which the account was closed. Section 623(a)(4).

Duty to Report Dates of Delinquencies

If a furnisher reports information concerning a delinquent account placed for collection, charged to profit or loss, or subject to any similar action, the furnisher must, within 90 days after reporting the information, provide the CRA with the month and the year of the commencement of the delinquency that immediately preceded the action, so that the agency will know how long to keep the information in the consumer's file. Section 623(a)(5).

Any person, such as a debt collector, that has acquired or is responsible for collecting delinquent accounts and that reports information to CRAs may comply with the requirements of Section 623(a)(5) (until there is a consumer dispute) by reporting the same delinquency date previously reported by the creditor. If the creditor did not report this date, they may comply with the FCRA by establishing reasonable procedures to obtain and report delinquency dates, or, if a delinquency date cannot be reasonably obtained, by following reasonable procedures to ensure that the date reported precedes the date when the account was placed for collection, charged to profit or loss, or subjected to any similar action. Section 623(a)(5).

Duties of Financial Institutions When Reporting Negative Information

Financial institutions that furnish information to "nationwide" consumer reporting agencies, as defined in Section 603(p), must notify consumers in writing if they may furnish or have furnished negative information to a CRA. Section 623(a)(7). The Federal Reserve Board has prescribed model disclosures, 12 CFR Part 222, App. B.

Duties When Furnishing Medical Information

A furnisher whose primary business is providing medical services, products, or devices (and such furnisher's agents or assignees) is a medical information furnisher for the purposes of the FCRA and must notify all CRAs to which it reports of this fact. Section 623(a)(9). This notice will enable CRAs to comply with their duties under Section 604(g) when reporting medical information.

Duties When ID Theft Occurs

All furnishers must have in place reasonable procedures to respond to notifications from CRAs that information furnished is the result of identity theft, and to prevent refurnishing the information in the future. A furnisher may not furnish information that a consumer has identified as resulting from identity theft unless the furnisher subsequently knows or is informed by the consumer that the information is correct. Section 623(a)(6). If a furnisher learns that it has furnished inaccurate information due to identity theft, it must notify each consumer reporting agency of the correct information and must thereafter report only complete and accurate information. Section 623(a)(2). When any furnisher of information is notified pursuant to the procedures set forth in Section 605B that a debt has resulted from identity theft, the furnisher may not sell, transfer, or place for collection the debt except in certain limited circumstances. Section 615(f).

The FTC's Web site, www.ftc.gov/credit, has more information about the FCRA, including publications for businesses and the full text of the FCRA.

Citations for FCRA sections in the U.S. Code, 15 U.S.C. § 1681 et seq.:

Section 602	15 U.S.C. 1681	Section 615	15 U.S.C. 1681m
Section 603	15 U.S.C. 1681a	Section 616	15 U.S.C. 1681n
Section 604	15 U.S.C. 1681b	Section 617	15 U.S.C. 1681o
Section 605	15 U.S.C. 1681c	Section 618	15 U.S.C. 1681p
Section 605A	15 U.S.C. 1681cA	Section 619	15 U.S.C. 1681q
Section 605B	15 U.S.C. 1681cB	Section 620	15 U.S.C. 1681r
Section 606	15 U.S.C. 1681d	Section 621	15 U.S.C. 1681s
Section 607	15 U.S.C. 1681e	Section 622	15 U.S.C. 1681s-1
Section 608	15 U.S.C. 1681f	Section 623	15 U.S.C. 1681s-2
Section 609	15 U.S.C. 1681g	Section 624	15 U.S.C. 1681t
Section 610	15 U.S.C. 1681h	Section 625	15 U.S.C. 1681u
Section 611	15 U.S.C. 1681i	Section 626	15 U.S.C. 1681v
Section 612	15 U.S.C. 1681j	Section 627	15 U.S.C. 1681w
Section 613	15 U.S.C. 1681k	Section 628	15 U.S.C. 1681x
Section 614	15 U.S.C. 1681*l*	Section 629	15 U.S.C. 1681y

[69 FR 69790, Nov. 30, 2004]

APPENDIX H TO PART 698—NOTICE OF USER RESPONSIBILITIES

The prescribed form for this disclosure is a separate document that is substantially similar to the Commission's notice with all information clearly and prominently displayed. Consumer reporting agencies may limit the disclosure to only those items that they know are relevant to the user that will receive the notice.

All users subject to the Federal Trade Commission's jurisdiction must comply with all applicable regulations, including regulations promulgated after this notice was prescribed in 2004. Information about applicable regulations currently in effect can be found at the Commission's Web site, www.ftc.gov/credit. Persons not subject to the Commission's jurisdiction should consult with their regulators to find any relevant regulations.

NOTICE TO USERS OF CONSUMER REPORTS: OBLIGATIONS OF USERS UNDER THE FCRA

The Fair Credit Reporting Act (FCRA),15 U.S.C. 1681-1681y, requires that this notice be provided to inform users of consumer reports of their legal obligations. State law may impose additional requirements. The text of the FCRA is set forth in full at the Federal Trade Commission's Website at www.ftc.gov/credit. At the end of this document is a list of United States Code citations for the FCRA. Other information about user duties is also available at the Commission's Web site. **Users must consult the relevant provisions of the FCRA for details about their obligations under the FCRA.**

The first section of this summary sets forth the responsibilities imposed by the FCRA on all users of consumer reports. The subsequent sections discuss the duties of users of reports that contain specific types of information, or that are used for certain purposes, and the legal consequences of violations. If you are a furnisher of information to a consumer reporting agency (CRA), you have additional obligations and will receive a separate notice from the CRA describing your duties as a furnisher.

I. OBLIGATIONS OF ALL USERS OF CONSUMER REPORTS

A. Users Must Have a Permissible Purpose

Congress has limited the use of consumer reports to protect consumers' privacy. All users must have a permissible purpose under the FCRA to obtain a consumer report. Section 604 contains a list of the permissible purposes under the law. These are:

- As ordered by a court or a federal grand jury subpoena. Section 604(a)(1)
- As instructed by the consumer in writing. Section 604(a)(2)
- For the extension of credit as a result of an application from a consumer, or the review or collection of a consumer's account. Section 604(a)(3)(A)
- For employment purposes, including hiring and promotion decisions, where the consumer has given written permission. Sections 604(a)(3)(B) and 604(b)

- For the underwriting of insurance as a result of an application from a consumer. Section 604(a)(3)(C)
- When there is a legitimate business need, in connection with a business transaction that is initiated by the consumer. Section 604(a)(3)(F)(i)
- To review a consumer's account to determine whether the consumer continues to meet the terms of the account. Section 604(a)(3)(F)(ii)
- To determine a consumer's eligibility for a license or other benefit granted by a governmental instrumentality required by law to consider an applicant's financial responsibility or status. Section 604(a)(3)(D)
- For use by a potential investor or servicer, or current insurer, in a valuation or assessment of the credit or prepayment risks associated with an existing credit obligation. Section 604(a)(3)(E)
- For use by state and local officials in connection with the determination of child support payments, or modifications and enforcement thereof. Sections 604(a)(4) and 604(a)(5)

In addition, creditors and insurers may obtain certain consumer report information for the purpose of making "prescreened" unsolicited offers of credit or insurance. Section 604(c). The particular obligations of users of "prescreened" information are described in Section VII below.

B. Users Must Provide Certifications

Section 604(f) prohibits any person from obtaining a consumer report from a consumer reporting agency (CRA) unless the person has certified to the CRA the permissible purpose(s) for which the report is being obtained and certifies that the report will not be used for any other purpose.

C. Users Must Notify Consumers When Adverse Actions Are Taken

The term "adverse action" is defined very broadly by Section 603. "Adverse actions" include all business, credit, and employment actions affecting consumers that can be considered to have a negative impact as defined by Section 603(k) of the FCRA – such as denying or canceling credit or insurance, or denying employment or promotion. No adverse action occurs in a credit transaction where the creditor makes a counteroffer that is accepted by the consumer.

1. Adverse Actions Based on Information Obtained From a CRA

If a user takes any type of adverse action as defined by the FCRA that is based at least in part on information contained in a consumer report, Section 615(a) requires the user to notify the consumer. The notification may be done in writing, orally, or by electronic means. It must include the following:

- The name, address, and telephone number of the CRA (including a toll-free telephone number, if it is a nationwide CRA) that provided the report.
- A statement that the CRA did not make the adverse decision and is not able to explain why the decision was made.
- A statement setting forth the consumer's right to obtain a free disclosure of the consumer's file from the CRA if the consumer makes a request within 60 days.
- A statement setting forth the consumer's right to dispute directly with the CRA the accuracy or completeness of any information provided by the CRA.

2. Adverse Actions Based on Information Obtained From Third Parties Who Are Not Consumer Reporting Agencies

If a person denies (or increases the charge for) credit for personal, family, or household purposes based either wholly or partly upon information from a person other than a CRA, and the information is the type of consumer information covered by the FCRA, Section 615(b)(1) requires that the user clearly and accurately disclose to the consumer his or her right to be told the nature of the information that was relied upon if the consumer makes a written request within 60 days of notification. The user must provide the disclosure within a reasonable period of time following the consumer's written request.

3. Adverse Actions Based on Information Obtained From Affiliates

If a person takes an adverse action involving insurance, employment, or a credit transaction initiated by the consumer, based on information of the type covered by the FCRA, and this information was obtained from an entity affiliated with the user of the information by common ownership or control, Section 615(b)(2) requires the user to notify the consumer of the adverse action. The notice must inform the consumer that he or she may obtain a disclosure of the nature of the information relied upon by making a written request within 60 days of receiving the adverse action notice. If the consumer makes such a request, the user must disclose the nature of the information not later than 30 days after receiving the request. If consumer report information is shared among affiliates and then used for an adverse action, the user must make an adverse action disclosure as set forth in I.C.1 above.

D. Users Have Obligations When Fraud and Active Duty Military Alerts are in Files

When a consumer has placed a fraud alert, including one relating to identity theft, or an active duty military alert with a nationwide consumer reporting agency as defined in Section 603(p) and resellers, Section 605A(h) imposes limitations on users of reports obtained from the consumer reporting agency in certain circumstances, including the establishment of a new credit plan and the issuance of additional credit cards. For initial fraud alerts and active duty alerts, the user must have reasonable policies and procedures in place to form a belief that the user knows the identity of the applicant or contact the consumer at a telephone number specified by the consumer; in the case of extended fraud alerts, the user must contact the consumer in accordance with the contact information provided in the consumer's alert.

E. Users Have Obligations When Notified of an Address Discrepancy

Section 605(h) requires nationwide CRAs, as defined in Section 603(p), to notify users that request reports when the address for a consumer provided by the user in requesting the report is substantially different from the addresses in the consumer's file. When this occurs, users must comply with regulations specifying the procedures to be followed, which will be issued by the Federal Trade Commission and the banking and credit union regulators. The Federal Trade Commission's regulations will be available at www.ftc.gov/credit.

F. Users Have Obligations When Disposing of Records

Section 628 requires that all users of consumer report information have in place procedures to properly dispose of records containing this information. The Federal Trade Commission, the Securities and Exchange Commission, and the banking and credit union regulators have issued regulations covering disposal. The Federal Trade Commission's regulations may be found at www.ftc.gov/credit.

II. CREDITORS MUST MAKE ADDITIONAL DISCLOSURES

If a person uses a consumer report in connection with an application for, or a grant, extension, or provision of, credit to a consumer on material terms that are materially less favorable than the most favorable terms available to a substantial proportion of consumers from or through that person, based in whole or in part on a consumer report, the person must provide a risk-based pricing notice to the consumer in accordance with regulations to be jointly prescribed by the Federal Trade Commission and the Federal Reserve Board.

Section 609(g) requires a disclosure by all persons that make or arrange loans secured by residential real property (one to four units) and that use credit scores. These persons must provide credit scores and other information about credit scores to applicants, including the disclosure set forth in Section 609(g)(1)(D) ("Notice to the Home Loan Applicant").

III. OBLIGATIONS OF USERS WHEN CONSUMER REPORTS ARE OBTAINED FOR EMPLOYMENT PURPOSES

A. Employment Other Than in the Trucking Industry

If information from a CRA is used for employment purposes, the user has specific duties, which are set forth in Section 604(b) of the FCRA. The user must:

- Make a clear and conspicuous written disclosure to the consumer before the report is obtained, in a document that consists solely of the disclosure, that a consumer report may be obtained.
- Obtain from the consumer prior written authorization. Authorization to access reports during the term of employment may be obtained at the time of employment.
- Certify to the CRA that the above steps have been followed, that the information being obtained will not be used in violation of any federal or state equal opportunity law or regulation, and that, if any adverse action is to be taken based on the consumer report, a copy of the report and a summary of the consumer's rights will be provided to the consumer.
- **Before** taking an adverse action, the user must provide a copy of the report to the consumer as well as the summary of consumer's rights. (The user should receive this summary from the CRA.) A Section 615(a) adverse action notice should be sent after the adverse action is taken.

An adverse action notice also is required in employment situations if credit information (other than transactions and experience data) obtained from an affiliate is used to deny employment. Section 615(b)(2)

The procedures for investigative consumer reports and employee misconduct investigations are set forth below.

B. Employment in the Trucking Industry

Special rules apply for truck drivers where the only interaction between the consumer and the potential employer is by mail, telephone, or computer. In this case, the consumer may provide consent orally or electronically, and an adverse action may be made orally, in writing, or electronically. The consumer may obtain a copy of any report relied upon by the trucking company by contacting the company.

IV. OBLIGATIONS WHEN INVESTIGATIVE CONSUMER REPORTS ARE USED

Investigative consumer reports are a special type of consumer report in which information about a consumer's character, general reputation, personal characteristics, and mode of living is obtained through personal interviews by an entity or person that is a consumer reporting agency. Consumers who are the subjects of such reports are given special rights under the FCRA. If a user intends to obtain an investigative consumer report, Section 606 requires the following:

- The user must disclose to the consumer that an investigative consumer report may be obtained. This must be done in a written disclosure that is mailed, or otherwise delivered, to the consumer at some time before or not later than three days after the date on which the report was first requested. The disclosure must include a statement informing the consumer of his or her right to request additional disclosures of the nature and scope of the investigation as described below, and the summary of consumer rights required by Section 609 of the FCRA. (The summary of consumer rights will be provided by the CRA that conducts the investigation.)
- The user must certify to the CRA that the disclosures set forth above have been made and that the user will make the disclosure described below.
- Upon the written request of a consumer made within a reasonable period of time after the disclosures required above, the user must make a complete disclosure of the nature and scope of the investigation. This must be made in a written statement that is mailed, or otherwise delivered, to the consumer no later than five days after the date on which the request was received from the consumer or the report was first requested, whichever is later in time.

V. SPECIAL PROCEDURES FOR EMPLOYEE INVESTIGATIONS

Section 603(x) provides special procedures for investigations of suspected misconduct by an employee or for compliance with Federal, state or local laws and regulations or the rules of a self-regulatory organization, and compliance with written policies of the employer. These investigations are not treated as consumer reports so long as the employer or its agent complies with the procedures set forth in Section 603(x), and a summary describing the nature and scope of the inquiry is made to the employee if an adverse action is taken based on the investigation.

VI. OBLIGATIONS OF USERS OF MEDICAL INFORMATION

Section 604(g) limits the use of medical information obtained from consumer reporting agencies (other than payment information that appears in a coded form that does not identify the medical provider). If the information is to be used for an insurance transaction, the consumer must give consent to the user of the report or the information must be coded. If the report is to be used for employment purposes – or in connection with a credit transaction (except as provided in regulations issued by the banking and credit union regulators) – the consumer must provide specific written consent and the medical information must be relevant. Any user who receives medical information shall not disclose the information to any other person (except where necessary to carry out the purpose for which the information was disclosed, or as permitted by statute, regulation, or order).

VII. OBLIGATIONS OF USERS OF "PRESCREENED" LISTS

The FCRA permits creditors and insurers to obtain limited consumer report information for use in connection with unsolicited offers of credit or insurance under certain circumstances. Sections 603(l), 604(c), 604(e), and 615(d). This practice is known as "prescreening" and typically involves obtaining from a CRA a list of consumers who meet certain preestablished criteria. If any person intends to use prescreened lists, that person must (1) before the offer is made, establish the criteria that will be relied upon to make the offer and to grant credit or insurance, and (2) maintain such criteria on file for a three-year period beginning on the date on which the offer is made to each consumer. In addition, any user must provide with each written solicitation a clear and conspicuous statement that:

- Information contained in a consumer's CRA file was used in connection with the transaction.
- The consumer received the offer because he or she satisfied the criteria for credit worthiness or insurability used to screen for the offer.
- Credit or insurance may not be extended if, after the consumer responds, it is determined that the consumer does not meet the criteria used for screening or any applicable criteria bearing on credit worthiness or insurability, or the consumer does not furnish required collateral.
- The consumer may prohibit the use of information in his or her file in connection with future prescreened offers of credit or insurance by contacting the notification system established by the CRA that provided the report. The statement must include the address and toll-free telephone number of the appropriate notification system.

In addition, once the Federal Trade Commission by rule has established the format, type size, and manner of the disclosure required by Section 615(d), users must be in compliance with the rule. The FTC's regulations will be at www.ftc.gov/credit.

VIII. OBLIGATIONS OF RESELLERS

A. Disclosure and Certification Requirements

Section 607(e) requires any person who obtains a consumer report for resale to take the following steps:

- Disclose the identity of the end-user to the source CRA.
- Identify to the source CRA each permissible purpose for which the report will be furnished to the end-user.
- Establish and follow reasonable procedures to ensure that reports are resold only for permissible purposes, including procedures to obtain:
  (1) the identity of all end-users;
  (2) certifications from all users of each purpose for which reports will be used; and
  (3) certifications that reports will not be used for any purpose other than the purpose(s) specified to the reseller. Resellers must make reasonable efforts to verify this information before selling the report.

B. Reinvestigations by Resellers

Under Section 611(f), if a consumer disputes the accuracy or completeness of information in a report prepared by a reseller, the reseller must determine whether this is a result of an action or omission on its part and, if so, correct or delete the information. If not, the reseller must send the dispute to the source CRA for reinvestigation. When any CRA notifies the reseller of the results of an investigation, the reseller must immediately convey the information to the consumer.

C. Fraud Alerts and Resellers

Section 605A(f) requires resellers who receive fraud alerts or active duty alerts from another consumer reporting agency to include these in their reports.

IX. LIABILITY FOR VIOLATIONS OF THE FCRA

Failure to comply with the FCRA can result in state government or federal government enforcement actions, as well as private lawsuits. Sections 616, 617, and 621. In addition, any person who knowingly and willfully obtains a consumer report under false pretenses may face criminal prosecution. Section 619.

The FTC's Web site, www.ftc.gov/credit, has more information about the FCRA including publications for businesses and the full text of the FCRA.

Citations for FCRA sections in the U.S. Code, 15 U.S.C. § 1681 et seq.:

Section 602	15 U.S.C. 1681
Section 603	15 U.S.C. 1681a
Section 604	15 U.S.C. 1681b
Section 605	15 U.S.C. 1681c
Section 605A	15 U.S.C. 1681cA
Section 605B	15 U.S.C. 1681cB
Section 606	15 U.S.C. 1681d
Section 607	15 U.S.C. 1681e
Section 608	15 U.S.C. 1681f
Section 609	15 U.S.C. 1681g
Section 610	15 U.S.C. 1681h
Section 611	15 U.S.C. 1681i
Section 612	15 U.S.C. 1681j
Section 613	15 U.S.C. 1681k
Section 614	15 U.S.C. 1681*l*
Section 615	15 U.S.C. 1681m
Section 616	15 U.S.C. 1681n
Section 617	15 U.S.C. 1681o
Section 618	15 U.S.C. 1681p
Section 619	15 U.S.C. 1681q
Section 620	15 U.S.C. 1681r
Section 621	15 U.S.C. 1681s
Section 622	15 U.S.C. 1681s-1
Section 623	15 U.S.C. 1681s-2
Section 624	15 U.S.C. 1681t
Section 625	15 U.S.C. 1681u
Section 626	15 U.S.C. 1681v
Section 627	15 U.S.C. 1681w
Section 628	15 U.S.C. 1681x
Section 629	15 U.S.C. 1681y

[69 FR 69795, Nov. 30, 2004]

SUBCHAPTER G—RULES, REGULATIONS, STATEMENTS AND INTERPRETATIONS UNDER THE MAGNUSON-MOSS WARRANTY ACT

PART 700—INTERPRETATIONS OF MAGNUSON-MOSS WARRANTY ACT

AUTHORITY: Magnuson-Moss Warranty Act, Pub. L. 93–637, 15 U.S.C. 2301.

SOURCE: 42 FR 36114, July 13, 1977, unless otherwise noted.

§ 700.1 Products covered.

(a) The Act applies to written warranties on tangible personal property which is normally used for personal, family, or household purposes. This definition includes property which is intended to be attached to or installed in any real property without regard to whether it is so attached or installed. This means that a product is a "consumer product" if the use of that type of product is not uncommon. The percentage of sales or the use to which a product is put by any individual buyer is not determinative. For example, products such as automobiles and typewriters which are used for both personal and commercial purposes come within the definition of consumer product. Where it is unclear whether a particular product is covered under the definition of consumer product, any ambiguity will be resolved in favor of coverage.

(b) Agricultural products such as farm machinery, structures and implements used in the business or occupation of farming are not covered by the Act where their personal, family, or household use is uncommon. However, those agricultural products normally used for personal or household gardening (for example, to produce goods for personal consumption, and not for resale) are consumer products under the Act.

(c) The definition of "Consumer product" limits the applicability of the Act to personal property, "including any such property intended to be attached to or installed in any real property without regard to whether it is so attached or installed." This provision brings under the Act separate items of equipment attached to real property, such as air conditioners, furnaces, and water heaters.

(d) The coverage of separate items of equipment attached to real property includes, but is not limited to, appliances and other thermal, mechanical, and electrical equipment. (It does not extend to the wiring, plumbing, ducts, and other items which are integral component parts of the structure.) State law would classify many such products as fixtures to, and therefore a part of, realty. The statutory definition is designed to bring such products under the Act regardless of whether they may be considered fixtures under state law.

(e) The coverage of building materials which are not separate items of equipment is based on the nature of the purchase transaction. An analysis of the transaction will determine whether the goods are real or personal property. The numerous products which go into the construction of a consumer dwelling are all consumer products when sold "over the counter," as by hardware and building supply retailers. This is also true where a consumer contracts for the purchase of such materials in connection with the improvement, repair, or modification of a home (for example, paneling, dropped ceilings, siding, roofing, storm windows, remodeling). However, where such products are at the time of sale integrated into the structure of a dwelling they are not consumer products as they cannot be practically distinguished from realty. Thus, for example, the beams, wallboard, wiring, plumbing, windows, roofing, and other structural components of a dwelling are not consumer products when they are sold as part of real estate covered by a written warranty.

(f) In the case where a consumer contracts with a builder to construct a home, a substantial addition to a home, or other realty (such as a garage or an in-ground swimming pool) the building materials to be used are not consumer products. Although the materials are separately identifiable at the time the contract is made, it is the intention of the parties to contract for the construction of realty which will integrate the component materials. Of course, as noted above, any separate items of equipment to be attached to such realty are consumer products under the Act.

(g) Certain provisions of the Act apply only to products actually costing the consumer more than a specified amount. Section 103, 15 U.S.C. 2303, applies to consumer products actually costing the consumer more than $10, excluding tax. The $10 minimum will be interpreted to include multiple-packaged items which may individually sell for less than $10, but which have been packaged in a manner that does not permit breaking the package to purchase an item or items at a price less than $10. Thus, a written warranty on a dozen items packaged and priced for resale at $12 must be designated, even though identical items may be offered in smaller quantities at under $10. This interpretation applies in the same manner to the minimum dollar limits in section 102, 15 U.S.C. 2302, and rules promulgated under that section.

(h) Warranties on replacement parts and components used to repair consumer products are covered; warranties on services are not covered. Therefore, warranties which apply solely to a repairer's workmanship in performing repairs are not subject to the Act. Where a written agreement warrants both the parts provided to effect a repair and the workmanship in making that repair, the warranty must comply with the Act and the rules thereunder.

(i) The Act covers written warranties on consumer products "distributed in commerce" as that term is defined in section 101(13), 15 U.S.C. 2301(13). Thus, by its terms the Act arguably applies to products exported to foreign jurisdictions. However, the public interest would not be served by the use of Commission resources to enforce the Act with respect to such products. Moreover, the legislative intent to apply the requirements of the Act to such products is not sufficiently clear to justify such an extraordinary result. The Commission does not contemplate the enforcement of the Act with respect to consumer products exported to foreign jurisdictions. Products exported for sale at military post exchanges remain subject to the same enforcement standards as products sold within the United States, its territories and possessions.

[42 FR 36114, July 13, 1977, as amended at 80 FR 42721, July 20, 2015]

§ 700.2 Date of manufacture.

Section 112 of the Act, 15 U.S.C. 2312, provides that the Act shall apply only to those consumer products manufactured after July 4, 1975. When a consumer purchases repair of a consumer product the date of manufacture of any replacement parts used is the measuring date for determining coverage under the Act. The date of manufacture of the consumer product being repaired is in this instance not relevant. Where a consumer purchases or obtains on an exchange basis a rebuilt consumer product, the date that the rebuilding process is completed determines the Act's applicability.

[42 FR 36114, July 13, 1977; 42 FR 38341, July 28, 1977, as amended at 80 FR 42721, July 20, 2015]

§ 700.3 Written warranty.

(a) The Act imposes specific duties and liabilities on suppliers who offer written warranties on consumer products. Certain representations, such as energy efficiency ratings for electrical appliances, care labeling of wearing apparel, and other product information disclosures may be express warranties under the Uniform Commercial Code.

However, these disclosures alone are not written warranties under this Act. Section 101(6), 15 U.S.C. 2301(6), provides that a written affirmation of fact or a written promise of a specified level of performance must relate to a specified period of time in order to be considered a "written warranty."[1] A product information disclosure without a specified time period to which the disclosure relates is therefore not a written warranty. In addition, section 111(d), 15 U.S.C. 2311(d), exempts from the Act (except section 102(c), 15 U.S.C. 2302(c)) any written warranty the making or content of which is required by federal law. The Commission encourages the disclosure of product information which is not deceptive and which may benefit consumers, and will not construe the Act to impede information disclosure in product advertising or labeling.

(b) Certain terms, or conditions, of sale of a consumer product may not be "written warranties" as that term is defined in section 101(6), 15 U.S.C. 2301(6), and should not be offered or described in a manner that may deceive consumers as to their enforceability under the Act. For example, a seller of consumer products may give consumers an unconditional right to revoke acceptance of goods within a certain number of days after delivery without regard to defects or failure to meet a specified level of performance. Or a seller may permit consumers to return products for any reason for credit toward purchase of another item. Such terms of sale taken alone are not written warranties under the Act. Therefore, suppliers should avoid any characterization of such terms of sale as warranties. The use of such terms as "free trial period" and "trade-in credit policy" in this regard would be appropriate. Furthermore, such terms of sale should be stated separately from any written warranty. Of course, the offering and performance of such terms of sale remain subject to section 5 of the Federal Trade Commission Act, 15 U.S.C. 45.

(c) The Magnuson-Moss Warranty Act generally applies to written warranties covering consumer products. Many consumer products are covered by warranties which are neither intended for, nor enforceable by, consumers. A common example is a warranty given by a component supplier to a manufacturer of consumer products. (The manufacturer may, in turn, warrant these components to consumers.) The component supplier's warranty is generally given solely to the product manufacturer, and is neither intended to be conveyed to the consumer nor brought to the consumer's attention in connection with the sale. Such warranties are not subject to the Act, since a written warranty under section 101(6) of the Act, 15 U.S.C. 2301(6), must become "part of the basis of the bargain between a supplier and a buyer for purposes other than resale." However, the Act applies to a component supplier's warranty in writing which is given to the consumer. An example is a supplier's written warranty to the consumer covering a refrigerator that is sold installed in a boat or recreational vehicle. The supplier of the refrigerator relies on the boat or vehicle assembler to convey the written agreement to the consumer. In this case, the supplier's written warranty is to a consumer, and is covered by the Act.

[42 FR 36114, July 13, 1977, as amended at 80 FR 42721, July 20, 2015]

§ 700.4 Parties "actually making" a written warranty.

Section 110(f) of the Act, 15 U.S.C. 2310(f), provides that only the supplier "actually making" a written warranty is liable for purposes of FTC and private enforcement of the Act. A supplier who does no more than distribute or sell a consumer product covered by a written warranty offered by another person or business and which identifies that person or business as the warrantor is not liable for failure of the written warranty to comply with the Act or rules thereunder. However,

[1] A "written warranty" is also created by a written affirmation of fact or a written promise that the product is defect free, or by a written undertaking of remedial action within the meaning of section 101(6)(B), 15 U.S.C. 2301(6)(B).

other actions and written and oral representations of such a supplier in connection with the offer or sale of a warranted product may obligate that supplier under the Act. If under State law the supplier is deemed to have "adopted" the written affirmation of fact, promise, or undertaking, the supplier is also obligated under the Act. Suppliers are advised to consult State law to determine those actions and representations which may make them co-warrantors, and therefore obligated under the warranty of the other person or business.

[42 FR 36114, July 13, 1977, as amended at 80 FR 42721, July 20, 2015]

§ 700.5 Expressions of general policy.

(a) Under section 103(b), 15 U.S.C. 2303(b), statements or representations of general policy concerning customer satisfaction which are not subject to any specific limitation need not be designated as full or limited warranties, and are exempt from the requirements of sections 102, 103, and 104 of the Act, 15 U.S.C. 2302–2304, and rules thereunder. However, such statements remain subject to the enforcement provisions of section 110 of the Act, 15 U.S.C. 2310, and to section 5 of the Federal Trade Commission Act, 15 U.S.C. 45.

(b) The section 103(b), 15 U.S.C. 2303(b), exemption applies only to general policies, not to those which are limited to specific consumer products manufactured or sold by the supplier offering such a policy. In addition, to qualify for an exemption under section 103(b), 15 U.S.C. 2303(b), such policies may not be subject to any specific limitations. For example, policies which have an express limitation of duration or a limitation of the amount to be refunded are not exempted. This does not preclude the imposition of reasonable limitations based on the circumstances in each instance a consumer seeks to invoke such an agreement. For instance, a warrantor may refuse to honor such an expression of policy where a consumer has used a product for 10 years without previously expressing any dissatisfaction with the product. Such a refusal would not be a specific limitation under this provision.

[42 FR 36114, July 13, 1977, as amended at 80 FR 42721, July 20, 2015]

§ 700.6 Designation of warranties.

(a) Section 103 of the Act, 15 U.S.C. 2303, provides that written warranties on consumer products manufactured after July 4, 1975, and actually costing the consumer more than $10, excluding tax, must be designated either "Full (statement of duration) Warranty" or "Limited Warranty". Warrantors may include a statement of duration in a limited warranty designation. The designation or designations should appear clearly and conspicuously as a caption, or prominent title, clearly separated from the text of the warranty. The full (statement of duration) warranty and limited warranty are the exclusive designations permitted under the Act, unless a specific exception is created by rule.

(b) Based on section 104(b)(4), 15 U.S.C. 2304(b)(4), the duties under subsection (a) of section 104, 15 U.S.C. 2304, extend from the warrantor to each person who is a consumer with respect to the consumer product. Section 101(3), 15 U.S.C. 2301(3), defines a consumer as a buyer (other than for purposes of resale) of any consumer product, any person to whom such product is transferred during the duration of an implied or written warranty (or service contract) applicable to the product. Therefore, a full warranty may not expressly restrict the warranty rights of a transferee during its stated duration. However, where the duration of a full warranty is defined solely in terms of first purchaser ownership there can be no violation of section 104(b)(4), 15 U.S.C. 2304(b)(4), since the duration of the warranty expires, by definition, at the time of transfer. No rights of a subsequent transferee are cut off as there is no transfer of ownership "during the duration of (any) warranty." Thus, these provisions do not preclude the offering of a full warranty with its duration determined exclusively by the period during which the first purchaser owns the product, or uses it in conjunction with another product. For example, an automotive battery or muffler warranty may be designated as "full warranty for as long as you own your car." Because this type of warranty leads the consumer to believe that proof of purchase is not needed so long as he or she owns the product a duty to furnish documentary proof may not be reasonably imposed on the consumer under this type of warranty. The burden is on the warrantor to prove that a particular claimant under this type of warranty is not the original purchaser or owner of the product. Warrantors or their designated agents may, however, ask consumers to state or affirm that they are the first purchaser of the product.

[42 FR 36114, July 13, 1977, as amended at 80 FR 42721, July 20, 2015]

§ 700.7 Use of warranty registration cards.

(a) Under section 104(b)(1) of the Act, 15 U.S.C. 2304(b)(1), a warrantor offering a full warranty may not impose on consumers any duty other than notification of a defect as a condition of securing remedy of the defect or malfunction, unless such additional duty can be demonstrated by the warrantor to be reasonable. Warrantors have in the past stipulated the return of a "warranty registration" or similar card. By "warranty registration card" the Commission means a card which must be returned by the consumer shortly after purchase of the product and which is stipulated or implied in the warranty to be a condition precedent to warranty coverage and performance.

(b) A requirement that the consumer return a warranty registration card or a similar notice as a condition of performance under a full warranty is an unreasonable duty. Thus, a provision such as, "This warranty is void unless the warranty registration card is returned to the warrantor" is not permissible in a full warranty, nor is it permissible to imply such a condition in a full warranty.

(c) This does not prohibit the use of such registration cards where a warrantor suggests use of the card as one possible means of proof of the date the product was purchased. For example, it is permissible to provide in a full warranty that a consumer may fill out and return a card to place on file proof of the date the product was purchased. Any such suggestion to the consumer must include notice that failure to return the card will not affect rights under the warranty, so long as the consumer can show in a reasonable manner the date the product was purchased. Nor does this interpretation prohibit a seller from obtaining from purchasers at the time of sale information requested by the warrantor.

[42 FR 36114, July 13, 1977, as amended at 80 FR 42721, July 20, 2015]

§ 700.8 Warrantor's decision as final.

A warrantor shall not indicate in any written warranty or service contract either directly or indirectly that the decision of the warrantor, service contractor, or any designated third party is final or binding in any dispute concerning the warranty or service contract. Nor shall a warrantor or service contractor state that it alone shall determine what is a defect under the agreement. Such statements are deceptive since section 110(d) of the Act, 15 U.S.C. 2310(d), gives state and federal courts jurisdiction over suits for breach of warranty and service contract.

[42 FR 36114, July 13, 1977, as amended at 80 FR 42721, July 20, 2015]

§ 700.9 Duty to install under a full warranty.

Under section 104(a)(1) of the Act, 15 U.S.C. 2304(a)(1), the remedy under a full warranty must be provided to the consumer without charge. If the warranted product has utility only when installed, a full warranty must provide such installation without charge regardless of whether or not the consumer originally paid for installation by the warrantor or his agent. However, this does not preclude the warrantor from imposing on the consumer a duty to remove, return, or reinstall where such duty can be demonstrated by the warrantor to meet the standard of reasonableness under section 104(b)(1), 15 U.S.C. 2304(b)(1).

[42 FR 36114, July 13, 1977, as amended at 80 FR 42721, July 20, 2015]

§ 700.10 Prohibited tying.

(a) Section 102(c), 15 U.S.C. 2302(c), prohibits tying arrangements that condition coverage under a written warranty on the consumer's use of an article or service identified by brand, trade, or corporate name unless that article or service is provided without charge to the consumer.

(b) Under a limited warranty that provides only for replacement of defective parts and no portion of labor charges, section 102(c), 15 U.S.C. 2302(c), prohibits a condition that the consumer use only service (labor) identified by the warrantor to install the replacement parts. A warrantor or his designated representative may not provide parts under the warranty in a manner which impedes or precludes the choice by the consumer of the person or business to perform necessary labor to install such parts.

(c) No warrantor may condition the continued validity of a warranty on the use of only authorized repair service and/or authorized replacement parts for non-warranty service and maintenance (other than an article of service provided without charge under the warranty or unless the warrantor has obtained a waiver pursuant to section 102(c) of the Act, 15 U.S.C. 2302(c)). For example, provisions such as, "This warranty is void if service is performed by anyone other than an authorized 'ABC' dealer and all replacement parts must be genuine 'ABC' parts," and the like, are prohibited where the service or parts are not covered by the warranty. These provisions violate the Act in two ways. First, they violate the section 102(c), 15 U.S.C. 2302(c), ban against tying arrangements. Second, such provisions are deceptive under section 110 of the Act, 15 U.S.C. 2310, because a warrantor cannot, as a matter of law, avoid liability under a written warranty where a defect is unrelated to the use by a consumer of "unauthorized" articles or service. In addition, warranty language that implies to a consumer acting reasonably in the circumstances that warranty coverage requires the consumer's purchase of an article or service identified by brand, trade or corporate name is similarly deceptive. For example, a provision in the warranty such as, "use only an authorized 'ABC' dealer" or "use only 'ABC' replacement parts," is prohibited where the service or parts are not provided free of charge pursuant to the warranty. This does not preclude a warrantor from expressly excluding liability for defects or damage caused by "unauthorized" articles or service; nor does it preclude the warrantor from denying liability where the warrantor can demonstrate that the defect or damage was so caused.

[42 FR 36114, July 13, 1977, as amended at 80 FR 42721, July 20, 2015]

§ 700.11 Written warranty, service contract, and insurance distinguished for purposes of compliance under the Act.

(a) The Act recognizes two types of agreements which may provide similar coverage of consumer products, the written warranty, and the service contract. In addition, other agreements may meet the statutory definitions of either "written warranty" or "service contract," but are sold and regulated under state law as contracts of insurance. One example is the automobile breakdown insurance policies sold in many jurisdictions and regulated by the state as a form of casualty insurance. The McCarran-Ferguson Act, 15 U.S.C. 1011 *et seq.*, provides that most federal laws (including the Magnuson-Moss Warranty Act) shall not be construed to invalidate, impair, or supersede any law enacted by any State for the purpose of regulating the business of insurance. While three specific laws are subject to a separate proviso, the Magnuson-Moss Warranty Act is not one of them. Thus, to the extent the Magnuson-Moss Warranty Act's service contract provisions apply to the business of insurance, they are effective so long as they do not invalidate, impair, or supersede a State law enacted for the purpose of regulating the business of insurance.

(b) "Written warranty" and "service contract" are defined in sections 101(6) and 101(8) of the Act, 15 U.S.C. 2301(6) and 15 U.S.C. 2301(8), respectively. This means that it must be conveyed at the time of sale of the consumer product and the consumer must not give any consideration beyond the purchase price of the consumer product in order to benefit from the agreement. It is not a requirement of the Act that an agreement obligate a supplier of the consumer product to a written warranty, but merely that it be part of the basis of the bargain between a supplier and a consumer. This contemplates written warranties by third-party non-suppliers.

(c) A service contract under the Act must meet the definitions of section 101(8), 15 U.S.C. 2301(8). An agreement which would meet the definition of written warranty in section 101(6)(A) or (B), 15 U.S.C. 2301(6)(A) or (B), but for its failure to satisfy the basis of the bargain test is a service contract. For example, an agreement which calls for some consideration in addition to the purchase price of the consumer product, or which is entered into at some date after the purchase of the consumer product to which it applies, is a service contract. An agreement which relates only to the performance of maintenance and/or inspection services and which is not an undertaking, promise, or affirmation with respect to a specified level of performance, or that the product is free of defects in materials or workmanship, is a service contract. An agreement to perform periodic cleaning and inspection of a product over a specified period of time, even when offered at the time of sale and without charge to the consumer, is an example of such a service contract.

[42 FR 36114, July 13, 1977, as amended at 80 FR 42722, July 20, 2015]

§ 700.12 Effective date of 16 CFR parts 701 and 702.

The Statement of Basis and Purpose of the final rules promulgated on December 31, 1975, provides that parts 701 and 702 of this chapter will become effective one year after the date of promulgation, December 31, 1976. The Commission intends this to mean that these rules apply only to written warranties on products manufactured after December 31, 1976.

PART 701—DISCLOSURE OF WRITTEN CONSUMER PRODUCT WARRANTY TERMS AND CONDITIONS

Sec.

AUTHORITY: 15 U.S.C. 2302 and 2309.

SOURCE: 40 FR 60188, Dec. 31, 1975, unless otherwise noted.

§ 701.1 Definitions.

(a) *The Act* means the Magnuson-Moss Warranty Federal Trade Commission Improvement Act, 15 U.S.C. 2301, *et seq.*

(b) *Consumer product* means any tangible personal property which is distributed in commerce and which is normally used for personal, family, or household purposes (including any such property intended to be attached to or installed in any real property without regard to whether it is so attached or installed. Products which are purchased solely for commercial or industrial use are excluded solely for purposes of this part.

(c) *Written warranty* means:

(1) Any written affirmation of fact or written promise made in connection with the sale of a consumer product by a supplier to a buyer which relates to the nature of the material or workmanship and affirms or promises that such material or workmanship is defect free or will meet a specified level of performance over a specified period of time, or

(2) Any undertaking in writing in connection with the sale by a supplier of a consumer product to refund, repair, replace, or take other remedial action with respect to such product in the event that such product fails to meet the specifications set forth in the undertaking, which written affirmation, promise or undertaking becomes part of the basis of the bargain between a supplier and a buyer for purposes other than resale of such product.

(d) *Implied warranty* means an implied warranty arising under State law (as modified by sections 104(a) and 108 of the Act, 15 U.S.C. 2304(a) and 2308), in connection with the sale by a supplier of a consumer product.

(e) *Remedy* means whichever of the following actions the warrantor elects:

(1) Repair,

(2) Replacement, or

(3) Refund; except that the warrantor may not elect refund unless:

(i) The warrantor is unable to provide replacement and repair is not commercially practicable or cannot be timely made, or

(ii) The consumer is willing to accept such refund.

(f) *Supplier* means any person engaged in the business of making a consumer product directly or indirectly available to consumers.

(g) *Manufacturer* means any person engaged in the business of making a consumer product.

(h) *Warrantor* means any supplier, manufacturer, or other person who gives or offers to give a written warranty.

(i) *Consumer* means a buyer (other than for purposes of resale or use in the ordinary course of the buyer's business) of any consumer product, any person to whom such product is transferred during the duration of an implied or written warranty applicable to the product, and any other such person who is entitled by the terms of such warranty or under applicable State law to enforce against the warrantor the obligations of the warranty.

(j) *On the face of the warranty* means:

(1) Where the warranty is a single sheet with printing on both sides of the sheet or where the warranty is comprised of more than one sheet, the page on which the warranty text begins;

(2) Where the warranty is included as part of a larger document, such as a use and care manual, the page in such document on which the warranty text begins;

(3) Where the warranty is on an Internet Web site or displayed electronically, in close proximity to the location where the warranty text begins.

[40 FR 60188, Dec. 31, 1975, as amended at 80 FR 42722, July 20, 2015; 81 FR 63669, Sept. 15, 2016]

§ 701.2 Scope.

The regulations in this part establish requirements for warrantors for disclosing the terms and conditions of written warranties on consumer products actually costing the consumer more than $15.00.

§ 701.3 Written warranty terms.

(a) Any warrantor warranting to a consumer by means of a written warranty a consumer product actually costing the consumer more than $15.00 shall clearly and conspicuously disclose in a single document in simple and readily understood language, the following items of information:

(1) The identity of the party or parties to whom the written warranty is extended, if the enforceability of the written warranty is limited to the original consumer purchaser or is otherwise limited to persons other than every consumer owner during the term of the warranty;

(2) A clear description and identification of products, or parts, or characteristics, or components or properties covered by and where necessary for clarification, excluded from the warranty;

(3) A statement of what the warrantor will do in the event of a defect, malfunction or failure to conform with the written warranty, including the items or services the warrantor will pay for or provide, and, where necessary for clarification, those which the warrantor will not pay for or provide;

(4) The point in time or event on which the warranty term commences, if different from the purchase date, and the time period or other measurement of warranty duration;

(5) A step-by-step explanation of the procedure which the consumer should follow in order to obtain performance of any warranty obligation, including the persons or class of persons authorized to perform warranty obligations. This includes the name(s) of the warrantor(s), together with: The mailing address(es) of the warrantor(s), and/or the name or title and the address of any employee or department of the warrantor responsible for the performance of warranty obligations, and/or a telephone number which consumers may use without charge to obtain information on warranty performance;

(6) Information respecting the availability of any informal dispute settlement mechanism elected by the warrantor in compliance with part 703 of this subchapter;

(7) Any limitations on the duration of implied warranties, disclosed on the face of the warranty as provided in section 108 of the Act, 15 U.S.C. 2308, accompanied by the following statement:

Some States do not allow limitations on how long an implied warranty lasts, so the above limitation may not apply to you.

(8) Any exclusions of or limitations on relief such as incidental or consequential damages, accompanied by the following statement, which may be combined with the statement required in paragraph (a)(7) of this section:

Some States do not allow the exclusion or limitation of incidental or consequential damages, so the above limitation or exclusion may not apply to you.

(9) A statement in the following language:

This warranty gives you specific legal rights, and you may also have other rights which vary from State to State.

(b) Paragraphs (a) (1) through (9) of this section shall not be applicable with respect to statements of general policy on emblems, seals or insignias issued by third parties promising replacement or refund if a consumer product is defective, which statements contain no representation or assurance of the quality or performance characteristics of the product; *Provided* That: (1) The disclosures required by paragraphs (a) (1) through (9) of this section are published by such third parties in each issue of a publication with a general circulation, and (2) such disclosures are provided free of charge to any consumer upon written request.

[40 FR 60188, Dec. 31, 1975, as amended at 80 FR 42722, July 20, 2015]

§ 701.4 Owner registration cards.

When a warrantor employs any card such as an owner's registration card, a warranty registration card, or the like, and the return of such card is a condition precedent to warranty coverage and performance, the warrantor shall disclose this fact in the warranty. If the return of such card reasonably appears to be a condition precedent to warranty coverage and performance, but is not such a condition, that fact shall be disclosed in the warranty.

PART 702—PRE-SALE AVAILABILITY OF WRITTEN WARRANTY TERMS

AUTHORITY: 15 U.S.C. 2302 and 2309.

SOURCE: 40 FR 60189, Dec. 31, 1975, unless otherwise noted.

§ 702.1 Definitions.

(a) *The Act* means the Magnuson-Moss Warranty Federal Trade Commission Improvement Act, 15 U.S.C. 2301, *et seq.*

(b) *Consumer product* means any tangible personal property which is distributed in commerce and which is normally used for personal, family, or household purposes (including any such property intended to be attached to or installed in any real property without regard to whether it is so attached or installed). Products which are purchased solely for commercial or industrial use are excluded solely for purposes of this part.

(c) *Written warranty* means—

(1) Any written affirmation of fact or written promise made in connection with the sale of a consumer product by a supplier to a buyer which relates to the nature of the material or workmanship and affirms or promises that such material or workmanship is defect free or will meet a specified level of performance over a specified period of time, or

(2) Any undertaking in writing in connection with the sale by a supplier of a consumer product to refund, repair, replace or take other remedial action with respect to such product in the event that such product fails to meet the specifications set forth in the undertaking,

which written affirmation, promise, or undertaking becomes part of the basis of the bargain between a supplier and a buyer for purposes other than resale of such product.

(d) *Warrantor* means any supplier, manufacturer, or other person who gives or offers to give a written warranty.

(e) *Seller* means any person who sells or offers for sale for purposes other than resale or use in the ordinary course of the buyer's business any consumer product.

(f) *Supplier* means any person engaged in the business of making a consumer product directly or indirectly available to consumers.

(g) *Manufacturer* means any person engaged in the business of making a consumer product.

[40 FR 60189, Dec. 31, 1975, as amended at 52 FR 7574, Mar. 12, 1987; 81 FR 63669, Sept. 15, 2016]

§ 702.2 Scope.

The regulations in this part establish requirements for sellers and warrantors for making the terms of any written warranty on a consumer product available to the consumer prior to sale.

§ 702.3 Pre-sale availability of written warranty terms.

The following requirements apply to consumer products actually costing the consumer more than $15.00:

(a) *Duties of seller.* Except as provided in paragraphs (c) through (d) of this section, the seller of a consumer product with a written warranty shall make a text of the warranty readily available for examination by the prospective buyer by:

(1) Displaying it in close proximity to the warranted product (including through electronic or other means, if the warrantor has elected the option described in paragraph (b)(2) of this section), or

(2) Furnishing it upon request prior to sale (including through electronic or other means, if the warrantor has elected the option described in paragraph (b)(2) of this section) and placing signs reasonably calculated to elicit the prospective buyer's attention in prominent locations in the store or department advising such prospective buyers of the availability of warranties upon request.

(b) *Duties of the warrantor.* (1) A warrantor who gives a written warranty warranting to a consumer a consumer product actually costing the consumer more than $15.00 shall:

(i) Provide sellers with warranty materials necessary for such sellers to comply with the requirements set forth in paragraph (a) of this section, by the use of one or more of the following means:

(A) Providing a copy of the written warranty with every warranted consumer product;

(B) Providing a tag, sign, sticker, label, decal or other attachment to the product, which contains the full text of the written warranty;

(C) Printing on or otherwise attaching the text of the written warranty to the package, carton, or other container if that package, carton or other container is normally used for display purposes. If the warrantor elects this option a copy of the written warranty must also accompany the warranted product; or

(D) Providing a notice, sign, or poster disclosing the text of a consumer product warranty. If the warrantor elects this option, a copy of the written warranty must also accompany each warranted product.

(ii) Provide catalog, mail order, and door-to-door sellers with copies of written warranties necessary for such sellers to comply with the requirements set forth in paragraphs (c) and (d) of this section.

(2) As an alternative method of compliance with paragraph (b)(1) of this section, a warrantor may provide the warranty terms in an accessible digital format on the warrantor's Internet Web site. If the warrantor elects this option, the warrantor must:

(i) Provide information to the consumer that will inform the consumer how to obtain warranty terms by indicating, in a clear and conspicuous manner, in the product manual or on the product or product packaging:

(A) The Internet Web site of the warrantor where such warranty terms can be reviewed, and

(B) The phone number, the postal mailing address of the warrantor, or other reasonable non-Internet based means for the consumer to request a copy of the warranty terms;

(ii) Provide a hard copy of the warranty terms promptly and free of charge upon request by a consumer or seller made pursuant to paragraph (b)(2)(i)(B) of this section;

(iii) Ensure that warranty terms are posted in a clear and conspicuous manner and remain accessible to the consumer on the Internet Web site of the warrantor; and

(iv) Provide information with the consumer product or on the Internet Web site of the warrantor sufficient to allow the consumer to readily identify on such Internet Web sites the warranty terms that apply to the specific warranted product.

(3) Paragraph (a)(1) of this section shall not be applicable with respect to statements of general policy on emblems, seals or insignias issued by third parties promising replacement or refund if a consumer product is defective, which statements contain no representation or assurance of the quality or performance characteristics of the product; provided that

(i) The disclosures required by §701.3(a)(1) through (9) of this chapter are published by such third parties in each issue of a publication with a general circulation, and

(ii) Such disclosures are provided free of charge to any consumer upon written request.

(c) *Catalog and mail order sales.* (1) For purposes of this paragraph:

(i) Catalog or mail order sales means any offer for sale, or any solicitation for an order for a consumer product with a written warranty, which includes instructions for ordering the product which do not require a personal visit to the seller's establishment.

(ii) Close conjunction means on the page containing the description of the warranted product, or on the page facing that page.

(2) Any seller who offers for sale to consumers consumer products with written warranties by means of a catalog or mail order solicitation shall clearly and conspicuously disclose in such catalog or solicitation in close conjunction to the description of the warranted product, or in an information section of the catalog or solicitation clearly referenced, including a page number, in close conjunction to the description of the warranted product, either:

(i) The full text of the written warranty; or

(ii) The address of the Internet Web site of the warrantor where such warranty terms can be reviewed (if such Internet Web site exists), as well as that the written warranty can be obtained free upon specific request, and the address or phone number where such warranty can be requested. If this option is elected, such seller shall promptly provide a copy of any written warranty requested by the consumer (and may provide such copy through electronic or other means, if the warrantor has elected the option described in paragraph (b)(2) of this section).

(d) *Door-to-door sales.* (1) For purposes of this paragraph:

(i) Door-to-door sale means a sale of consumer products in which the seller or his representative personally solicits the sale, including those in response to or following an invitation by a buyer, and the buyer's agreement to offer to purchase is made at a place other than the place of business of the seller.

(ii) Prospective buyer means an individual solicited by a door-to-door seller to buy a consumer product who indicates sufficient interest in that consumer product or maintains sufficient contact with the seller for the seller reasonably to conclude that the person solicited is considering purchasing the product.

(2) Any seller who offers for sale to consumers consumer products with written warranties by means of door-to-door sales shall, prior to the consummation of the sale, disclose the fact that the sales representative has copies of the warranties for the warranted products being offered for sale, which may be inspected by the prospective buyer at any time during the sales presentation. Such disclosure shall be made orally and shall be included in any written materials shown to prospective buyers. If the warrantor has elected the option described in paragraph (b)(2) of this section, the sales representative may provide a copy of the warranty through electronic or other means.

[81 FR 63669, Sept. 15, 2016]

PART 703—INFORMAL DISPUTE SETTLEMENT PROCEDURES

AUTHORITY: 15 U.S.C. 2309 and 2310.

SOURCE: 40 FR 60215, Dec. 31, 1975, unless otherwise noted.

§ 703.1 Definitions.

(a) *The Act* means the Magnuson-Moss Warranty—Federal Trade Commission Improvement Act, 15 U.S.C. 2301, *et seq.*

(b) *Consumer product* means any tangible personal property which is distributed in commerce and which is normally used for personal, family, or household purposes (including any such property intended to be attached to or installed in any real property without regard to whether it is so attached or installed).

(c) *Written warranty* means:

(1) Any written affirmation of fact or written promise made in connection with the sale of a consumer product by a supplier to a buyer which relates to the nature of the material or workmanship and affirms or promises that such material or workmanship is defect free or will meet a specified level of performance over a specified period of time, or

(2) Any undertaking in writing in connection with the sale by a supplier of a consumer product to refund, repair, replace, or take other remedial action with respect to such product in the event that such product fails to meet the specifications set forth in the undertaking, which written affirmation, promise or undertaking becomes part of the basis of the bargain between a supplier and a buyer for purposes other than resale of such product.

(d) *Warrantor* means any person who gives or offers to give a written warranty which incorporates an informal dispute settlement mechanism.

(e) *Mechanism* means an informal dispute settlement procedure which is incorporated into the terms of a written warranty to which any provision of Title I of the Act applies, as provided in section 110 of the Act, 15 U.S.C. 2310.

(f) *Members* means the person or persons within a Mechanism actually deciding disputes.

(g) *Consumer* means a buyer (other than for purposes of resale) of any consumer product, any person to whom such product is transferred during the duration of a written warranty applicable to the product, and any other person who is entitled by the terms of such warranty or under applicable state law to enforce against the warrantor the obligations of the warranty.

(h) *On the face of the warranty* means:

(1) If the warranty is a single sheet with printing on both sides of the sheet, or if the warranty is comprised of more than one sheet, the page on which the warranty text begins;

(2) If the warranty is included as part of a longer document, such as a use and care manual, the page in such document on which the warranty text begins.

[40 FR 60215, Dec. 31, 1975, as amended at 80 FR 42722, July 20, 2015]

§ 703.2 Duties of warrantor.

(a) The warrantor shall not incorporate into the terms of a written warranty a Mechanism that fails to comply with the requirements contained in §§ 703.3 through 703.8 of this part. This paragraph (a) shall not prohibit a warrantor from incorporating into the terms of a written warranty the step-by-step procedure which the consumer should take in order to obtain performance of any obligation under the warranty as described in section 102(a)(7) of the Act, 15 U.S.C. 2302(a)(7), and required by part 701 of this subchapter.

(b) The warrantor shall disclose clearly and conspicuously at least the following information on the face of the written warranty:

(1) A statement of the availability of the informal dispute settlement mechanism;

(2) The name and address of the Mechanism, or the name and a telephone number of the Mechanism which consumers may use without charge;

(3) A statement of any requirement that the consumer resort to the Mechanism before exercising rights or seeking remedies created by Title I of the Act; together with the disclosure that if a consumer chooses to seek redress by pursuing rights and remedies not created by Title I of the Act, resort to the Mechanism would not be required by any provision of the Act; and

(4) A statement, if applicable, indicating where further information on the Mechanism can be found in materials accompanying the product, as provided in § 703.2(c) of this section.

(c) The warrantor shall include in the written warranty or in a separate section of materials accompanying the product, the following information:

(1) Either

(i) A form addressed to the Mechanism containing spaces requesting the information which the Mechanism may require for prompt resolution of warranty disputes; or

(ii) A telephone number of the Mechanism which consumers may use without charge;

(2) The name and address of the Mechanism;

(3) A brief description of Mechanism procedures;

(4) The time limits adhered to by the Mechanism; and

(5) The types of information which the Mechanism may require for prompt resolution of warranty disputes.

(d) The warrantor shall take steps reasonably calculated to make consumers aware of the Mechanism's existence at the time consumers experience warranty disputes. Nothing contained in paragraphs (b), (c), or (d) of this section shall limit the warrantor's option to encourage consumers to seek redress directly from the warrantor as long as the warrantor does not expressly require consumers to seek redress directly from the warrantor. The warrantor shall proceed fairly and expeditiously to attempt to resolve all disputes submitted directly to the warrantor.

(e) Whenever a dispute is submitted directly to the warrantor, the warrantor shall, within a reasonable time, decide whether, and to what extent, it will satisfy the consumer, and inform the consumer of its decision. In its notification to the consumer of its decision, the warrantor shall include the information required in § 703.2 (b) and (c) of this section.

(f) The warrantor shall:

(1) Respond fully and promptly to reasonable requests by the Mechanism for information relating to disputes;

(2) Upon notification of any decision of the Mechanism that would require action on the part of the warrantor, immediately notify the Mechanism whether, and to what extent, warrantor will abide by the decision; and

(3) Perform any obligations it has agreed to.

(g) The warrantor shall act in good faith in determining whether, and to what extent, it will abide by a Mechanism decision.

(h) The warrantor shall comply with any reasonable requirements imposed by the Mechanism to fairly and expeditiously resolve warranty disputes.

[40 FR 60215, Dec. 31, 1975, as amended at 80 FR 42722, July 20, 2015]

MINIMUM REQUIREMENTS OF THE MECHANISM

§ 703.3 Mechanism organization.

(a) The Mechanism shall be funded and competently staffed at a level sufficient to ensure fair and expeditious resolution of all disputes, and shall not charge consumers any fee for use of the Mechanism.

(b) The warrantor and the sponsor of the Mechanism (if other than the warrantor) shall take all steps necessary to ensure that the Mechanism, and its members and staff, are sufficiently insulated from the warrantor and the sponsor, so that the decisions of the members and the performance of the staff are not influenced by either the warrantor or the sponsor. Necessary steps shall include, at a minimum, committing funds in advance, basing personnel decisions solely on merit, and not assigning conflicting warrantor or sponsor duties to Mechanism staff persons.

(c) The Mechanism shall impose any other reasonable requirements necessary to ensure that the members and staff act fairly and expeditiously in each dispute.

§ 703.4 Qualification of members.

(a) No member deciding a dispute shall be:

(1) A party to the dispute, or an employee or agent of a party other than for purposes of deciding disputes; or

(2) A person who is or may become a party in any legal action, including but not limited to class actions, relating to the product or complaint in dispute, or an employee or agent of such person other than for purposes of deciding disputes. For purposes of this paragraph (a) a person shall not be considered a "party" solely because he or she acquires or owns an interest in a party solely for investment, and the acquisition or ownership of an interest which is offered to the general public shall be prima facie evidence of its acquisition or ownership solely for investment.

(b) When one or two members are deciding a dispute, all shall be persons having no direct involvement in the manufacture, distribution, sale or service of any product. When three or more members are deciding a dispute, at least two-thirds shall be persons having no direct involvement in the manufacture, distribution, sale or service of any product. "Direct involvement" shall not include acquiring or owning an interest solely for investment, and the acquisition or ownership of an interest which is offered to the general public shall be prima facie evidence of its acquisition or ownership solely for investment. Nothing contained in this section shall prevent the members from consulting with any persons knowledgeable in the technical, commercial or other areas relating to the product which is the subject of the dispute.

(c) Members shall be persons interested in the fair and expeditious settlement of consumer disputes.

§ 703.5 Operation of the Mechanism.

(a) The Mechanism shall establish written operating procedures which shall include at least those items specified in paragraphs (b) through (j) of this section. Copies of the written procedures shall be made available to any person upon request.

(b) Upon notification of a dispute, the Mechanism shall immediately inform both the warrantor and the consumer of receipt of the dispute.

(c) The Mechanism shall investigate, gather and organize all information necessary for a fair and expeditious decision in each dispute. When any evidence gathered by or submitted to the Mechanism raises issues relating to the number of repair attempts, the length of repair periods, the possibility of unreasonable use of the product, or any other issues relevant in light of Title I of the Act (or rules thereunder), including issues relating to consequential damages, or any other remedy under the Act (or rules thereunder), the Mechanism shall investigate these issues. When information which will or may be used in the decision, submitted by one party, or a consultant under § 703.4(b) of this part, or any other source tends to contradict facts submitted by the other party, the Mechanism shall clearly, accurately, and completely disclose to both parties the contradictory information (and its source) and shall provide both parties an opportunity to explain or rebut the information and to submit additional materials. The Mechanism shall not require any information not reasonably necessary to decide the dispute.

(d) If the dispute has not been settled, the Mechanism shall, as expeditiously as possible but at least within 40 days of notification of the dispute, except as provided in paragraph (e) of this section:

(1) Render a fair decision based on the information gathered as described in paragraph (c) of this section, and on any information submitted at an oral presentation which conforms to the requirements of paragraph (f) of this section (A decision shall include any remedies appropriate under the circumstances, including repair, replacement, refund, reimbursement for expenses, compensation for damages, and any other remedies available under the written warranty or the Act (or rules thereunder); and a decision shall state a specified reasonable time for performance);

(2) Disclose to the warrantor its decision and the reasons therefor;

(3) If the decision would require action on the part of the warrantor, determine whether, and to what extent,

warrantor will abide by its decision; and

(4) Disclose to the consumer its decision, the reasons therefor, warrantor's intended actions (if the decision would require action on the part of the warrantor), and the information described in paragraph (g) of this section. For purposes of paragraph (d) of this section a dispute shall be deemed settled when the Mechanism has ascertained from the consumer that:

(i) The dispute has been settled to the consumer's satisfaction; and

(ii) The settlement contains a specified reasonable time for performance.

(e) The Mechanism may delay the performance of its duties under paragraph (d) of this section beyond the 40 day time limit:

(1) Where the period of delay is due solely to failure of a consumer to provide promptly his or her name and address, brand name and model number of the product involved, and a statement as to the nature of the defect or other complaint; or

(2) For a 7 day period in those cases where the consumer has made no attempt to seek redress directly from the warrantor.

(f) The Mechanism may allow an oral presentation by a party to a dispute (or a party's representative) only if:

(1) Both warrantor and consumer expressly agree to the presentation;

(2) Prior to agreement the Mechanism fully discloses to the consumer the following information:

(i) That the presentation by either party will take place only if both parties so agree, but that if they agree, and one party fails to appear at the agreed upon time and place, the presentation by the other party may still be allowed;

(ii) That the members will decide the dispute whether or not an oral presentation is made;

(iii) The proposed date, time and place for the presentation; and

(iv) A brief description of what will occur at the presentation including, if applicable, parties' rights to bring witnesses and/or counsel; and

(3) Each party has the right to be present during the other party's oral presentation. Nothing contained in this paragraph (b) of this section shall preclude the Mechanism from allowing an oral presentation by one party, if the other party fails to appear at the agreed upon time and place, as long as all of the requirements of this paragraph have been satisfied.

(g) The Mechanism shall inform the consumer, at the time of disclosure required in paragraph (d) of this section that:

(1) If he or she is dissatisfied with its decision or warrantor's intended actions, or eventual performance, legal remedies, including use of small claims court, may be pursued;

(2) The Mechanism's decision is admissible in evidence as provided in section 110(a)(3) of the Act, 15 U.S.C. 2310(a)(3); and

(3) The consumer may obtain, at reasonable cost, copies of all Mechanism records relating to the consumer's dispute.

(h) If the warrantor has agreed to perform any obligations, either as part of a settlement agreed to after notification to the Mechanism of the dispute or as a result of a decision under paragraph (d) of this section, the Mechanism shall ascertain from the consumer within 10 working days of the date for performance whether performance has occurred.

(i) A requirement that a consumer resort to the Mechanism prior to commencement of an action under section 110(d) of the Act, 15 U.S.C. 2310(d), shall be satisfied 40 days after notification to the Mechanism of the dispute or when the Mechanism completes all of its duties under paragraph (d) of this section, whichever occurs sooner. Except that, if the Mechanism delays performance of its paragraph (d) of this section duties as allowed by paragraph (e) of this section, the requirement that the consumer initially resort to the Mechanism shall not be satisfied until the period of delay allowed by paragraph (e) of this section has ended.

(j) Decisions of the Mechanism shall not be legally binding on any person. However, the warrantor shall act in good faith, as provided in § 703.2(g) of this part. In any civil action arising out of a warranty obligation and relating to a matter considered by the Mechanism, any decision of the Mechanism shall be admissible in evidence, as provided in section 110(a)(3) of the Act, 15 U.S.C. 2310(a)(3).

[40 FR 60215, Dec. 31, 1975, as amended at 80 FR 42722, July 20, 2015]

§ 703.6 Recordkeeping.

(a) The Mechanism shall maintain records on each dispute referred to it which shall include:

(1) Name, address and telephone number of the consumer;

(2) Name, address, telephone number and contact person of the warrantor;

(3) Brand name and model number of the product involved;

(4) The date of receipt of the dispute and the date of disclosure to the consumer of the decision;

(5) All letters or other written documents submitted by either party;

(6) All other evidence collected by the Mechanism relating to the dispute, including summaries of relevant and material portions of telephone calls and meetings between the Mechanism and any other person (including consultants described in § 703.4(b) of this part);

(7) A summary of any relevant and material information presented by either party at an oral presentation;

(8) The decision of the members including information as to date, time and place of meeting, and the identity of members voting; or information on any other resolution;

(9) A copy of the disclosure to the parties of the decision;

(10) A statement of the warrantor's intended action(s);

(11) Copies of follow-up letters (or summaries of relevant and material portions of follow-up telephone calls) to the consumer, and responses thereto; and

(12) Any other documents and communications (or summaries of relevant and material portions of oral communications) relating to the dispute.

(b) The Mechanism shall maintain an index of each warrantor's disputes grouped under brand name and subgrouped under product model.

(c) The Mechanism shall maintain an index for each warrantor as will show:

(1) All disputes in which the warrantor has promised some performance (either by settlement or in response to a Mechanism decision) and has failed to comply; and

(2) All disputes in which the warrantor has refused to abide by a Mechanism decision.

(d) The Mechanism shall maintain an index as will show all disputes delayed beyond 40 days.

(e) The Mechanism shall compile semi-annually and maintain statistics which show the number and percent of disputes in each of the following categories:

(1) Resolved by staff of the Mechanism and warrantor has complied;

(2) Resolved by staff of the Mechanism, time for compliance has occurred, and warrantor has not complied;

(3) Resolved by staff of the Mechanism and time for compliance has not yet occurred;

(4) Decided by members and warrantor has complied;

(5) Decided by members, time for compliance has occurred, and warrantor has not complied;

(6) Decided by members and time for compliance has not yet occurred;

(7) Decided by members adverse to the consumer;

(8) No jurisdiction;

(9) Decision delayed beyond 40 days under § 703.5(e)(1) of this part;

(10) Decision delayed beyond 40 days under § 703.5(e)(2) of this part;

(11) Decision delayed beyond 40 days for any other reason; and

(12) Pending decision.

(f) The Mechanism shall retain all records specified in paragraphs (a) through (e) of this section for at least 4 years after final disposition of the dispute.

§ 703.7 Audits.

(a) The Mechanism shall have an audit conducted at least annually, to determine whether the Mechanism and its implementation are in compliance with this part. All records of the Mechanism required to be kept under § 703.6 of this part shall be available for audit.

(b) Each audit provided for in paragraph (a) of this section shall include at a minimum the following:

(1) Evaluation of warrantors' efforts to make consumers aware of the Mechanism's existence as required in § 703.2(d) of this part;

(2) Review of the indexes maintained pursuant to § 703.6 (b), (c), and (d) of this part; and

(3) Analysis of a random sample of disputes handled by the Mechanism to determine the following:

(i) Adequacy of the Mechanism's complaint and other forms, investigation, mediation and follow-up efforts, and other aspects of complaint handling; and

(ii) Accuracy of the Mechanism's statistical compilations under § 703.6(e) of this part. (For purposes of this subparagraph "analysis" shall include oral or written contact with the consumers involved in each of the disputes in the random sample.)

(c) A report of each audit under this section shall be submitted to the Federal Trade Commission, and shall be made available to any person at reasonable cost. The Mechanism may direct its auditor to delete names of parties to disputes, and identity of products involved, from the audit report.

(d) Auditors shall be selected by the Mechanism. No auditor may be involved with the Mechanism as a warrantor, sponsor or member, or employee or agent thereof, other than for purposes of the audit.

§ 703.8 Openness of records and proceedings.

(a) The statistical summaries specified in § 703.6(e) of this part shall be available to any person for inspection and copying.

(b) Except as provided under paragraphs (a) and (e) of this section, and paragraph (c) of § 703.7 of this part, all records of the Mechanism may be kept confidential, or made available only on such terms and conditions, or in such form, as the Mechanism shall permit.

(c) The policy of the Mechanism with respect to records made available at the Mechanism's option shall be set out in the procedures under § 703.5(a) of this part; the policy shall be applied uniformly to all requests for access to or copies of such records.

(d) Meetings of the members to hear and decide disputes shall be open to observers on reasonable and nondiscriminatory terms. The identity of the parties and products involved in disputes need not be disclosed at meetings.

(e) Upon request the Mechanism shall provide to either party to a dispute:

(1) Access to all records relating to the dispute; and

(2) Copies of any records relating to the dispute, at reasonable cost.

(f) The Mechanism shall make available to any person upon request, information relating to the qualifications of Mechanism staff and members.

SUBCHAPTER H—RULES, REGULATIONS, STATEMENTS AND INTERPRETATIONS UNDER THE HART-SCOTT-RODINO ANTITRUST IMPROVEMENTS ACT OF 1976

PART 801—COVERAGE RULES

AUTHORITY: 15 U.S.C. 18a(d).

SOURCE: 43 FR 33537, July 31, 1978, unless otherwise noted.

§ 801.1 Definitions.

When used in the act and these rules—

(a)(1) *Person.* Except as provided in paragraphs (a) and (b) of § 801.12, the term *person* means an ultimate parent entity and all entities which it controls directly or indirectly.

Examples: 1. In the case of corporations, "person" encompasses the entire corporate structure, including all parent corporations, subsidiaries and divisions (whether consolidated or unconsolidated, and whether incorporated or unincorporated), and all related corporations under common control with any of the foregoing.

2. Corporations A and B are each directly controlled by the same foreign state. They are not included within the same "person," although the corporations are under common control, because the foreign state which controls them is not an "entity" (see § 801.1(a)(2)). Corporations A and B* are the ultimate parent entities within persons "A", and "B" which include any entities each may control.

3. Since a natural person is an entity (see § 801.1(a)(2)), a natural person and a corporation which he or she controls are part of the same "person." If that natural person controls two otherwise separate corporations, both corporations and the natural person are all part of the same "person."

4. See the example to § 801.2(a).

(2) *Entity.* The term *entity* means any natural person, corporation, company, partnership, joint venture, association, joint-stock company, trust, estate of a deceased natural person, foundation, fund, institution, society, union, or club, whether incorporated or not, wherever located and of whatever citizenship, or any receiver, trustee in bankruptcy or similar official or any liquidating agent for any of the foregoing, in his or her capacity as such; or any joint venture or other corporation which has not been formed but the acquisition of the voting securities or other interest in which, if already formed, would require notification under the act and these rules:

Provided, however, that the term entity shall not include any foreign state, foreign government, or agency thereof (other than a corporation or unincorporated entity engaged in commerce), nor the United States, any of the States thereof, or any political subdivision or agency of either (other than a corporation or unincorporated entity engaged in commerce).

(3) *Ultimate parent entity.* The term *ultimate parent entity* means an entity

---

*Throughout the examples to the rules, persons are designated ("A", "B," etc.) with quotation marks, and entities are designated (A, B, etc.) without quotation marks.

which is not controlled by any other entity.

Examples: 1. If corporation A holds 100 percent of the stock of subsidiary B, and B holds 75 percent of the stock of its subsidiary C, corporation A is the ultimate parent entity, since it controls subsidiary B directly and subsidiary C indirectly, and since it is the entity within the person which is not controlled by any other entity.

2. If corporation A is controlled by natural person D, natural person D is the ultimate parent entity.

3. P and Q are the ultimate parent entities within persons "P" and "Q." If P and Q each own 50 percent of the voting securities of R, then P and Q are both ultimate parents of R, and R is part of both persons "P" and "Q."

(b) *Control.* The term *control* (as used in the terms *control(s), controlling, controlled by* and *under common control with*) means:

(1) *Either.* (i) Holding 50 percent or more of the outstanding voting securities of an issuer or

(ii) In the case of an unincorporated entity, having the right to 50 percent or more of the profits of the entity, or having the right in the event of dissolution to 50 percent or more of the assets of the entity; or

(2) Having the contractual power presently to designate 50 percent or more of the directors of a for-profit or not-for-profit corporation, or 50 percent or more of the trustees in the case of trusts that are irrevocable and/or in which the settlor does not retain a reversionary interest.

Examples: 1. Corporation A holds 100 percent of the stock of corporation B, 75 percent of the stock of corporation C, 50 percent of the stock of corporation D, and 30 percent of the stock of corporation E. Corporation A controls corporations B, C and D, but not corporation E. Corporation A is the ultimate parent entity of a person comprised of corporations A, B, C and D, and each of these corporations (but not corporation E) is "included within the person."

2. A statutory limited partnership agreement provides as follows: The general partner "A" is entitled to 50 percent of the partnership profits, "B" is entitled to 40 percent of the profits and "C" is entitled to 10 percent of the profits. Upon dissolution, "B" is entitled to 75 percent of the partnership assets and "C" is entitled to 25 percent of those assets. All limited and general partners are entitled to vote on the following matters: the dissolution of the partnership, the transfer of assets not in the ordinary course of business, any change in the nature of the business, and the removal of the general partner. The interest of each partner is evidenced by an ownership certificate that is transferable under the terms of the partnership agreement and is subject to the Securities Act of 1933. For purposes of these rules, control of this partnership is determined by paragraph (1)(ii) of this section. Although partnership interests may be securities and have some voting rights attached to them, they do not entitle the owner of that interest to vote for a corporate "director" as required by §801.1(f)(1). Thus control of a partnership is not determined on the basis of either paragraph (1)(i) or (2) of this section. Consequently, "A" is deemed to control the partnership because of its right to 50 percent of the partnership's profits. "B" is also deemed to control the partnership because it is entitled to 75 percent of the partnership's assets upon dissolution.

3. "A" is a nonprofit charitable foundation that has formed a partnership joint venture with "B," a nonprofit university, to establish C, a nonprofit hospital corporation that does not issue voting securities. Pursuant to its charter "A" and "B" are each entitled to appoint three of C's six directors. "A" and "B" would each be deemed to control C, pursuant to §801.1(b)(2) because each is deemed to have the contractual power presently to designate 50 percent or more of the directors of a not-for-profit corporation.

4. "A" is entitled to 50 percent of the profits of partnership B and 50 percent of the profits of partnership C. B and C form a partnership E with "D" in which each entity has a right to one-third of the profits. When E acquires company X, "A" must report the transaction (assuming it is otherwise reportable). Pursuant to §801.1(b)(1)(ii), E is deemed to be controlled by "A," even though "A" ultimately will receive only one-third of the profits of E. Because B and C are considered as part of "A," the rules attribute all profits to which B and C are entitled (two-thirds of the profits of E in this example) to "A."

5. A is the settlor of an irrevocable trust in which it does not retain a reversionary interest in the corpus of the trust. A is entitled under the trust indenture to designate four of the eight trustees of the trust. A controls the trust pursuant to §801.1(b)(2) and is deemed to hold the assets that constitute the corpus of the trust. Note that the right to designate 50 percent or more of the trustees of a business trust that has equity holders entitled to profits or assets upon dissolution of the business trust does not constitute control. Such business trusts are treated as unincorporated entities and control is determined pursuant to §801.1(b)(1)(ii).

(c) *Hold.* (1) Subject to the provisions of paragraphs (c) (2) through (8) of this section, the term *hold* (as used in the terms *hold(s)*, *holding*, *holder* and *held*) means beneficial ownership, whether direct, or indirect through fiduciaries, agents, controlled entities or other means.

Example: If a stockbroker has stock in "street name" for the account of a natural person, only the natural person (who has beneficial ownership) and not the stockbroker (which may have record title) "holds" that stock.

(2) The holdings of spouses and their minor children shall be holdings of each of them.

(3) Except for a common trust fund or collective investment fund within the meaning of 12 CFR 9.18(a) (both of which are hereafter referred to in this paragraph as "collective investment funds"), and any revocable trust or an irrevocable trust in which the settlor retains a reversionary interest in the corpus, a trust, including a pension trust, shall hold all assets and voting securities constituting the corpus of the trust.

Example: Under this paragraph the trust—and not the trustee—"holds" the voting securities and assets constituting the corpus of any irrevocable trust (in which the settlor retains no reversionary interest, and which is not a collective investment fund). Therefore, the trustee need not aggregate its holdings of any other assets or voting securities with the holdings of the trust for purposes of determining whether the requirements of the act apply to an acquisition by the trust. Similarly, the trustee, if making an acquisition for its own account, need not aggregate its holdings with those of any trusts for which it serves as trustee. (However, the trustee must aggregate any collective investment funds which it administers; see paragraph (c)(6) of this section.)

(4) The assets and voting securities constituting the corpus of a revocable trust or the corpus of an irrevocable trust in which the settlor(s) retain(s) a reversionary interest in the corpus shall be holdings of the settlor(s) of such trust.

(5) Except as provided in paragraph (c)(4) of this section, beneficiaries of a trust, including a pension trust or a collective investment fund, shall not hold any assets or voting securities constituting the corpus of such trust.

(6) A bank or trust company which administers one or more collective investment funds shall hold all assets and voting securities constituting the corpus of each such fund.

Example: Suppose A, a bank or trust company, administers collective investment funds W, X, Y and Z. Whenever person "A" is to make an acquisition, whether of not on behalf of one or more of the funds, it must aggregate the holdings of W, X, Y and Z in determining whether the requirements of the act apply to the acquisition.

(7) An insurance company shall hold all assets and voting securities held for the benefit of any general account of, or any separate account administered by, such company.

(8) A person holds all assets and voting securities held by the entities included within it; in addition to its own holding, an entity holds all assets and voting securities held by the entities which it controls directly or indirectly.

(d)(1) *Affiliate.* An entity is an affiliate of a person if it is controlled, directly or indirectly, by the ultimate parent entity of such person.

(2) *Associate.* For purposes of Items 6 and 7 of the Form, an associate of an acquiring person shall be an entity that is not an affiliate of such person but:

(A) Has the right, directly or indirectly, to manage the operations or investment decisions of an acquiring entity (a "managing entity"); or

(B) Has its operations or investment decisions, directly or indirectly, managed by the acquiring person; or

(C) Directly or indirectly controls, is controlled by, or is under common control with a managing entity; or

(D) Directly or indirectly manages, is managed by, or is under common operational or investment decision management with a managing entity.

Examples: 1. ABC Investment Group has organized a number of investment partnerships. Each of the partnerships is its own ultimate parent, but ABC makes the investment decisions for all of the partnerships. One of the partnerships intends to make a reportable acquisition. For purposes of Items 6(c) and 7, each of the other investment partnerships, and ABC Investment Group itself are associates of the partnership that is the acquiring person. In response to Item 6(c)(i), the acquiring person will disclose any of its 5 percent or greater minority holdings that generate revenues in any of the same NAICS codes as the acquired entity(s) in the reportable transaction. In Item 6(c)(ii) it would report any 5 percent or greater minority holdings of its associates in the acquired entity(s) and in any entities that generate revenues in any of the same NAICS codes as the acquired entity(s). In Item 7, the acquiring person will indicate whether there are any NAICS code overlaps between the acquired entity(s) in the reportable transaction, on the one hand, and the acquiring person and all of its associates, on the other.

2. XYZ Corporation is its own ultimate parent and intends to make a reportable acquisition. Pursuant to a management contract, Fund MNO has the right to manage the investments of XYZ Corporation. For the HSR filing by XYZ Corporation, Fund MNO is an associate of XYZ, as is any other entity that either controls, or is controlled by, or manages or is managed by Fund MNO or is under common control or common investment management with Fund MNO.

3. EFG Investment Group has the contractual power to determine the investments of PRS Corporation, which is its own ultimate parent. Natural person Mr. X, who is not an employee of EFG Investment Group, has been contracted by EFG Investment Group as its investment manager. When PRS Corporation makes an acquisition, its associates include (i) EFG Investment Group, (ii) any entity over which EFG Investment Group has investment authority, (iii) any entity that controls, or is controlled by, EFG Investment Group, (iv) Natural person Mr. X, (v) any entity over which Natural person Mr. X has investment management authority, and (vi) any entity which is controlled by Natural person Mr. X, directly or indirectly.

4. CORP1 controls GP1 and GP2, the sole general partners of private equity funds LP1 and LP2 respectively. LP1 controls GP3, the sole general partner of MLP1, a newly formed master limited partnership which is its own ultimate parent entity. LP2 controls GP4, the sole general partner of MLP2, another master limited partnership that is its own ultimate parent entity and which owns and operates a natural gas pipeline. In addition, GP4 holds 25 percent of the voting securities of CORP2, which also owns and operates a natural gas pipeline.

MLP1 is acquiring 100 percent of the membership interests of LLC1, also the owner and operator of a natural gas pipeline. MLP2, CORP2 and LLC1 all derive revenues in the same NAICS code (Pipeline Transportation of Natural Gas). All of the entities under common investment management of CORP1, including GP4 and MLP2, are associates of MLP1, the acquiring person.

In Item 7 of its HSR filing, MLP1 would identify MLP2 as an associate that has an overlap in pipeline transportation of natural gas with LLC1, the acquired person. Because GP4 does not control CORP2 it would not be listed in Item 7, however, GP4 would be listed in Item 6(c)(ii) as an associate that holds 25 percent of the voting securities of CORP2. In this example, even though there is no direct overlap between the acquiring person (MLP1) and the acquired person (LLC1), there is an overlap reported for an associate (MLP2) of the acquiring person in Item 7. 5. LLC is the investment manager for and ultimate parent entity of general partnerships GP1 and GP2. GP1 is the general partner of LP1, a limited partnership that holds 30 percent of the voting securities of CORP1. GP2 is the general partner of LP2, which holds 55 percent of the voting securities of CORP1. GP2 also directly holds 2 percent of the voting securities of CORP1. LP1 is acquiring 100 percent of the voting securities of CORP2. CORP1 and CORP2 both derive revenues in the same NAICS code (Industrial Gas Manufacturing).

All of the entities under common investment management of the managing entity LLC, including GP1, GP2, LP2 and CORP1 are associates of LP1. In Item 6(c)(i) of its HSR filing, LP1 would report its own holding of 30 percent of the voting securities of CORP1. It would not report the 55 percent holding of LP2 in Item 6(c)(ii) because it is greater than 50 percent. It also would not report GP2's 2 percent holding because it is less than 5 percent. In Item 7, LP1 would identify both LP2 and CORP1 as associates that derive revenues in the same NAICS code as CORP2.

6. LLC is the investment manager for GP1 and GP2 which are the general partners of limited partnerships LP1 and LP2, respectively. LLC holds no equity interests in either general partnership but manages their investments and the investments of the limited partnerships by contract. LP1 is newly formed and its own ultimate parent entity. It plans to acquire 100 percent of the voting securities of CORP1, which derives revenues in the NAICS code for Consumer Lending. LP2 controls CORP2, which derives revenues in the same NAICS code. All of the entities under the common management of LLC, including LP2 and CORP2, are associates of LP1. For purposes of Item 7, LP1 would report LP2 and CORP2 as associates that derive revenues in the NAICS code that overlaps with CORP1. Even though the investment manager (LLC) holds no equity interest in GP1 or GP2, the contractual arrangement with them makes them associates of LP1 through common management.

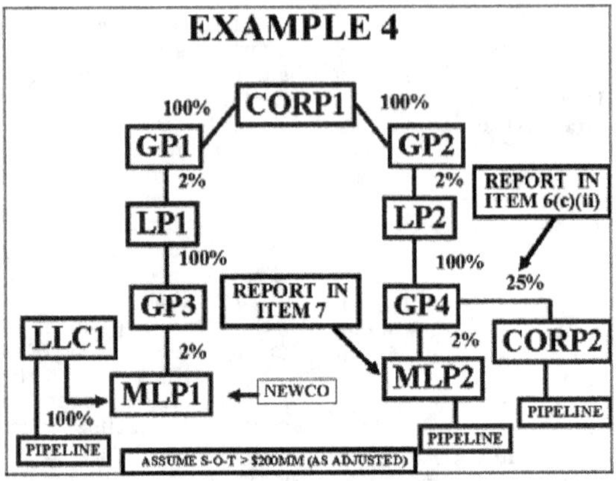

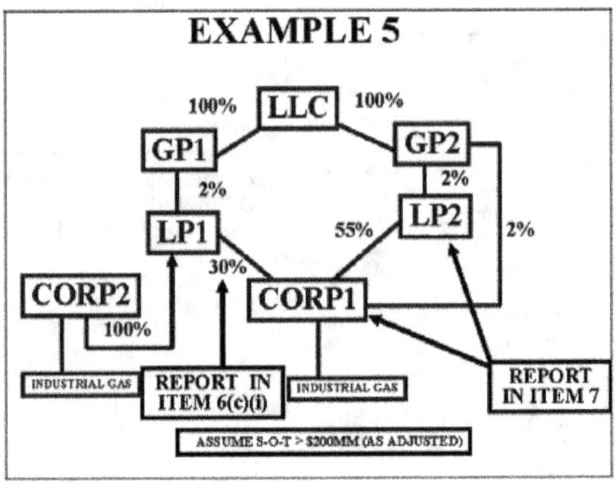

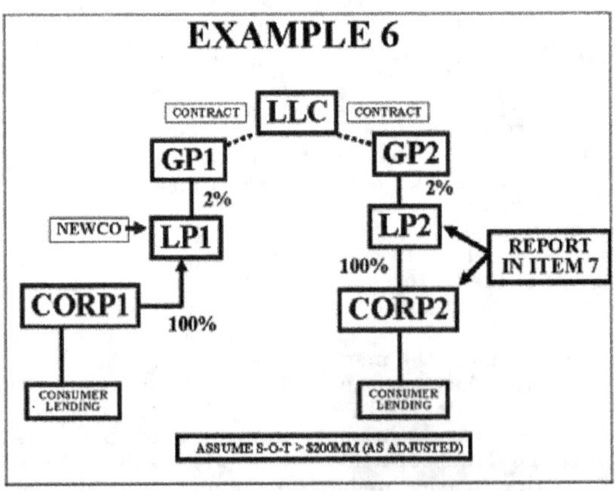

7. Corporation A is its own ultimate parent entity and is making an acquisition of Corporation B. Although Corporation A is operationally managed by its officers and its investments, including the acquisition of Corporation B, are managed by its directors, neither the officers nor directors are considered associates of A.

8. Limited partnership A is an investment partnership that is making an acquisition. LLC B has no equity interest in A, but has a contract to manage its investments for a fee. LLC B has an investment committee comprised of twelve of its employees that makes the actual investment decisions. LLC B is an associate of A but none of the twelve employees are associates of A, as LLC B is a managing entity and the twelve individuals are merely its employees. Contrast this with example 3 where a managing entity, EFG, is itself managed by another entity, Mr. X, who is thus an associate.

9. GP is the general partner of FUND. GP has contracted with LLC to act as an investment advisor with respect to FUND's investments. In this role, LLC acts as a consultant who makes recommendations to GP on what portfolio companies FUND should invest in. The recommendations are non-binding and GP is the only entity that has the authority to exercise investment discretion over FUND's acquisitions of interests in portfolio companies. In this example, GP is an associate of FUND, while LLC is not.

10. GP A is the general partner and investment manager of FUND A1. Mr. X is a principal in the A family of private equity funds and has the contractual right to veto certain proposed actions of GP A and FUND A1, for example, divestitures of stock that would result in a change of control in a portfolio company. His contractual right to veto certain proposed actions does not constitute managing operations. Mr. X does not have the authority under the contract to veto proposed investments of FUND A1 directed by GP A or to direct GP A to authorize investments by FUND A1. In this example, GP A is an associate of FUND A1, while Mr. X is not.

11. LLC is the general partner of LP and has entered into a management contract to exercise investment discretion over LP's investments in portfolio companies as well as to provide certain other administrative services for LP. Mr. Y is the managing member of LLC and as such is the person who actually makes the investment decisions on behalf of LLC. Mr. Y has no management contract with either LLC or LP. In this example, LLC is an associate of LP, while Mr. Y is not. Compare with Example 7 where officers and directors of a corporation are not associates of the corporation.

12. GP is the general partner of LP and has entered into a management contract to exercise investment discretion over LP's investments in portfolio companies. GP has entered into a contract with CORP, under which CORP will manage building maintenance and certain back office functions (e.g., maintenance of phones and computers, accounting, IT and human resources) for LP. GP is an associate of LP because it manages LP's investments. However, the management services provided by CORP do not constitute operational management, therefore, CORP is not an associate of LP.

(e)(1)(i) *United States person.* The term *United States person* means a person the ultimate parent entity of which—

(A) Is incorporated in the United States, is organized under the laws of the United States or has its principal offices within the United States; or

(B) If a natural person, either is a citizen of the United States or resides in the United States.

(ii) *United States issuer.* The term *United States issuer* means an issuer which is incorporated in the United States, is organized under the laws of the United States or has its principal offices within the United States.

(2)(i) *Foreign person.* The term *foreign person* means a person the ultimate parent entity of which—

(A) Is not incorporated in the United States, is not organized under the laws of the United States and does not have its principal offices within the United States; or

(B) If a natural person, neither is a citizen of the United States nor resides in the United States.

(ii) *Foreign issuer.* The term *foreign issuer* means an issuer which is not incorporated in the United States, is not organized under the laws of the United States and does not have its principal offices within the United States.

(f)(1)(i) *Voting securities.* The term voting securities means any securities which at present or upon conversion entitle the owner or holder thereof to vote for the election of directors of the issuer, or of an entity included within the same person as the issuer.

(ii) *Non-corporate interest.* The term "non-corporate interest" means an interest in any unincorporated entity which gives the holder the right to any profits of the entity or in the event of dissolution of that entity the right to any of its assets after payment of its debts. These unincorporated entities include, but are not limited to, general partnerships, limited partnerships, limited liability partnerships, limited liability companies, cooperatives and business trusts; but these unincorporated entities do not include trusts that are irrevocable and/or in which the settlor does not retain a reversionary interest and any interest in such a trust is not a non-corporate interest as defined by this rule.

(2) *Convertible voting security.* The term *convertible voting security* means a voting security which presently does not entitle its owner or holder to vote for directors of any entity.

(3) *Conversion.* The term *conversion* means the exercise of a right inherent in the ownership or holding of particular voting securities to exchange such securities for securities which presently entitle the owner or holder to vote for directors of the issuer or of any entity included within the same person as the issuer.

Examples: 1. The acquisition of convertible debentures which are convertible into common stock is an acquisition of "voting securities." However, § 802.31 exempts the acquisition of such securities from the requirements of the act, provided that they have no present voting rights.

2. Options and warrants are also "voting securities" for purposes of the act, because they can be exchanged for securities with present voting rights. Section 802.31 exempts the acquisition of options and warrants as well, since they do not themselves have present voting rights and hence are convertible voting securities. Notification may be required prior to exercising options and warrants, however.

3. Assume that X has issued preferred shares which presently entitle the holder to vote for directors of X, and that these shares are convertible into common shares of X. Because the preferred shares confer a present right to vote for directors of X, they are "voting securities." (See § 801.1(f)(1).) They are not "convertible voting securities," however, because the definition of that term excludes securities which confer a present right to vote for directors of any entity. (See § 801.1(f)(2).) Thus, an acquisition of these preferred shares issued by X would not be exempt as an acquisition of "convertible voting securities." (See § 802.31.) If the criteria in section 7A(a) are met, an acquisition of X's preferred shares would be subject to the reporting and waiting period requirements of the Act. Moreover, the conversion of these preferred shares into common shares of X would also be potentially reportable, since the holder would be exercising a right to exchange particular voting securities for different voting securities having a present right to vote for directors of the issuer. Because this exchange would be a "conversion," § 801.30 would apply. (See § 801.30(a)(6).)

(g)(1) *Tender offer.* The term *tender offer* means any offer to purchase voting securities which is a tender offer within the meaning of section 14 of the Securities Exchange Act of 1934, 15 U.S.C. 78n.

(2) *Cash tender offer.* The term *cash tender offer* means a tender offer in which cash is the only consideration offered to the holders of the voting securities to be acquired.

(3) *Non-cash tender offer.* The term *non-cash tender offer* means any tender offer which is not a cash tender offer.

(h) *Notification threshold.* The term "notification threshold" means:

(1) An aggregate total amount of voting securities of the acquired person valued at greater than $50 million (as adjusted) but less than $100 million (as adjusted);

(2) An aggregate total amount of voting securities of the acquired person valued at $100 million (as adjusted) or greater but less than $500 million (as adjusted);

(3) An aggregate total amount of voting securities of the acquired person valued at $500 million (as adjusted) or greater;

(4) Twenty-five percent of the outstanding voting securities of an issuer if valued at greater than $1 billion (as adjusted); or

(5) Fifty percent of the outstanding voting securities of an issuer if valued at greater than $50 million (as adjusted).

(i)(1) *Solely for the purpose of investment.* Voting securities are held or acquired "solely for the purpose of investment" if the person holding or acquiring such voting securities has no intention of participating in the formulation, determination, or direction of the basic business decisions of the issuer.

Example: If a person holds stock "solely for the purpose of investment" and thereafter decides to influence or participate in management of the issuer of that stock, the stock is no longer held "solely for the purpose of investment."

(2) *Investment assets.* The term *investment assets* means cash, deposits in financial institutions, other money market instruments, and instruments evidencing government obligations.

(j) *Engaged in manufacturing.* A person is engaged in manufacturing if it produces and derives annual sales or revenues in excess of $1 million from products within industries in Sectors 31–33 as coded by the North American Industry Classification System (2002 Edition) published by the Executive Office of the President, Office of Management and Budget.

(k) *United States.* The term *United States* shall include the several States, the territories, possessions, and commonwealths of the United States, and the District of Columbia.

(l) *Commerce.* The term *commerce* shall have the meaning ascribed to that term in section 1 of the Clayton Act, 15 U.S.C. 12, or section 4 of the Federal Trade Commission Act, 15 U.S.C. 44.

(m) *The act.* References to "the act" refer to Section 7A of the Clayton Act, 15 U.S.C. 18a, as added by section 201 of the Hart-Scott-Rodino Antitrust Improvements Act of 1976, Pub. L. 94–435, 90 Stat. 1390, and as amended by Pub. L. 106–553, 114 Stat. 2762. References to "Section 7A( )" refer to subsections of Section 7A of the Clayton Act. References to "this section" refer to the section of these rules in which the term appears.

(n) *(as adjusted).* The parenthetical "(as adjusted)" refers to the adjusted values published in the FEDERAL REGISTER notice titled "Revised Jurisdictional Threshold for Section 7A of the Clayton Act." This FEDERAL REGISTER notice will be published in January of each year and the values contained therein will be effective as of the effective date published in the FEDERAL REGISTER notice and will remain effective until superseded in the next calendar year. The notice will also be available at *http://www.ftc.gov.* Such adjusted values will be calculated in accordance with Section 7A(a)(2)(A) and will be rounded up to the next highest $100,000.

(o) *All commercially significant rights.* For purposes of paragraph (g) of §801.2, the term all commercially significant rights means the exclusive rights to a patent that allow only the recipient of the exclusive patent rights to use the patent in a particular therapeutic area (or specific indication within a therapeutic area).

(p) *Limited manufacturing rights.* For purposes of paragraph (o) of this section and paragraph (g) of §801.2, the term limited manufacturing rights means the rights retained by a patent holder to manufacture the product(s) covered by a patent when all other exclusive rights to the patent within a therapeutic area (or specific indication within a therapeutic area) have been transferred to the recipient of the patent rights. The retained right to manufacture is limited in that it is retained by the patent holder solely to provide the recipient of the patent rights with product(s) covered by the patent (which either the patent holder alone or both the patent holder and the recipient may manufacture).

(q) *Co-rights.* For purposes of paragraph (o) of this section and paragraph (g) of §801.2, the term co-rights means shared rights retained by the patent holder to assist the recipient of the exclusive patent rights in developing and commercializing the product covered by the patent. These co-rights include, but are not limited to, co-development, co-promotion, co-marketing and co-commercialization.

[43 FR 33537, July 31, 1978, as amended at 48 FR 34429, July 29, 1983; 52 FR 20063, May 29, 1987; 66 FR 8687, Feb. 1, 2001; 66 FR 23565, May 9, 2001; 68 FR 2430, Jan. 17, 2003; 70 FR 4990, Jan. 31, 2005; 70 FR 11510, Mar. 8, 2005; 70 FR 73372, Dec. 12, 2005; 70 FR 77313, Dec. 30, 2005; 76 FR 42479, July 19, 2011; 78 FR 68712, Nov. 15, 2013; 83 FR 32770, July 16, 2018]

§801.2 Acquiring and acquired persons.

(a) Any person which, as a result of an acquisition, will hold voting securities or assets, either directly or indirectly, or through fiduciaries, agents, or other entities acting on behalf of such person, is an acquiring person.

Example: Assume that corporations A and B, which are each ultimate parent entitles of their respective "persons," created a joint venture, corporation V, and that each holds half of V's shares. Therefore, A and B each control V (see §801.1(b)), and V is included within two persons, "A" and "B." Under this section, if V is to acquire corporation X, both "A" and "B" are acquiring persons.

(b) Except as provided in paragraphs (a) and (b) of §801.12, the person(s) within which the entity whose assets or voting securities are being acquired is included, is an acquired person.

Examples: 1. Assume that person "Q" will acquire voting securities of corporation X held by "P" and that X is not included within person "P." Under this section, the acquired person is the person within which X is included, and is not "P."

2. In the example to paragraph (a) of this section, if V were to be acquired by X, then both "A" and "B" would be acquired persons.

(c) For purposes of the act and these rules, a person may be an acquiring person and an acquired person with respect to separate acquisitions which comprise a single transaction.

(d)(1)(i) Mergers and consolidations are transactions subject to the act and shall be treated as acquisitions of voting securities.

(ii) In a merger, the person which, after consummation, will include the corporation in existence prior to consummation which is designated as the surviving corporation in the plan, agreement, or certificate of merger required to be filed with State authorities to effectuate the transaction shall be deemed to have made an acquisition of voting securities.

(2)(i) Any person party to a merger or consolidation is an acquiring person if, as a result of the transaction, such person will hold any assets or voting securities which it did not hold prior to the transaction.

(ii) Any person party to a merger or consolidation is an acquired person if, as a result of the transaction, the assets or voting securities of any entity included within such person will be held by any other person.

(iii) All persons party to a transaction as a result of which all parties will lose their separate pre-acquisition identities or will become wholly owned subsidiaries of a newly formed entity shall be both acquiring and acquired persons. This includes any combination of corporations and unincorporated entities consolidating into any newly formed entity. In such transactions, each consolidating entity is deemed to be acquiring all of the voting securities (in the case of a corporation) or interests (in the case of an unincorporated entity) of each of the others.

Examples: 1. Corporation A (the ultimate parent entity included within person "A") proposes to acquire Y, a wholly-owned subsidiary of B (the ultimate parent entity included within person "B"). The transaction is to be carried out by merging Y into X, a wholly-owned subsidiary of A, with X surviving, and by distributing the assets of X to B, the only shareholder of Y. The assets of X consist solely of cash and the voting securities of C, an entity unrelated to "A" or "B". Since X is designated the surviving corporation in the plan or agreement of merger or consolidation and since X will be included in "A" after consummation of the transaction, "A" will be deemed to have made an acquisition of voting securities. In this acquisition, "A" is an acquiring person because it will hold assets or voting securities it did not hold prior to the transaction, and "B" is an acquired person because the assets or the voting securities of an entity previously included within it will be held by A as a result of the acquisition. B will hold the cash and voting securities of C as a result of the transaction, but since § 801.21 applies, this acquisition is not reportable. "A" is therefore an acquiring person only, and "B" is an acquired person only. "B" may, however, have a separate reporting obligation as an acquiring person in a separate transaction involving the voting securities of C.

2. In the above example, suppose the consideration for Y consists of $8 million worth of the voting securities of A. With regard to the transfer of this consideration, "B" is an acquiring person because it will hold voting securities it did not previously hold, and "A" is an acquired person because its voting securities will be held by B. Since these voting securities are worth less than $50 million (as adjusted), the acquisition of these securities is not reportable. "A" will therefore report as an acquiring person only and "B" as an acquired person only.

3. In the above example, suppose that, as consideration for Y, A transfers to B a manufacturing plant valued in excess of $50 million (as adjusted). "B" is thus an acquiring person and "A" an acquired person in a reportable acquisition of assets. "A" and "B" will each report as both an acquiring and an acquired person in this transaction because each occupies each role in a reportable acquisition.

4. Corporations A (the ultimate parent entity in person "A") and B (the ultimate parent entity in person "B") propose to consolidate into C, a newly formed corporation. All shareholders of A and B will receive shares of C, and both A and B will lose their separate pre-acquisition identities. "A" and "B" are both acquiring and acquired persons because they are parties to a transaction in which all parties lose their separate pre-acquisition identities

5. Partnership A and Corporation B form a new LLC in which they combine their businesses. A and B cease to exist and partners of A and shareholders of B receive membership interests in the new LLC. For purposes of determining reportability, A is deemed to be acquiring 100 percent of the voting securities

of B and B is deemed to be acquiring 100 percent of the interests of A. Pursuant to § 803.9(b) of this chapter, even if such a transaction consists of two reportable acquisitions, only one filing fee is required.

(e) Whenever voting securities or assets are to be acquired from an acquiring person in connection with an acquisition, the acquisition of voting securities or assets shall be separately subject to the act.

(f)(1)(i) In an acquisition of non-corporate interests which results in an acquiring person controlling the entity, that person is deemed to hold all of the assets of the entity as a result of the acquisition. The acquiring person is the person acquiring control of the entity and the acquired person is the pre-acquisition ultimate parent entity of the entity.

(ii) The value of an acquisition described in paragraph (f)(1)(i) of this section is determined in accordance with § 801.10(d).

(2) Any contribution of assets or voting securities to an existing unincorporated entity or to any successor thereof is deemed an acquisition of such voting securities or assets by the ultimate parent entity of that entity and is not subject to § 801.50.

Examples: 1. A, B and C each hold 33⅓ percent of the interests in Partnership X. D contributes assets valued in excess of $50 million (as adjusted) to X and as a result D receives 40 percent of the interests in X and A, B and C are each reduced to 20 percent. Partnership X is deemed to be acquiring the assets from D, in a transaction which may be reportable. This is not treated as a formation of a new partnership. Because no person will control Partnership X, no additional filing is required by any of the four partners.

2. LLC X is its own ultimate parent entity. A contributes a manufacturing plant valued in excess of $200 million (as adjusted) to X which issues new interests to A resulting in A having a 50% interest in X. A is acquiring non-corporate interests which confer control of X and therefore will file as an acquiring person. Because A held the plant prior to the transaction and continues to hold it through its acquisition of control of LLC X after the transaction is completed no acquisition of the plant has occurred and LLC X is therefore not an acquiring person.

(3) Any person who acquires control of an existing not-for-profit corporation which has no outstanding voting securities is deemed to be acquiring all of the assets of that corporation.

Example: A becomes the sole corporate member of not-for-profit corporation B and accordingly has the right to designate all of the directors of B. A is deemed to be acquiring all of the assets of B as a result.

(g) Transfers of patent rights within NAICS Industry Group 3254.

(1) This paragraph applies only to patents covering products whose manufacture and sale would generate revenues in NAICS Industry Group 3254, including:

325411 Medical and Botanical Manufacturing
325412 Pharmaceutical Preparation Manufacturing
325413 In-Vitro Diagnostic Substance Manufacturing
325414 Biological Product (except Diagnostic) Manufacturing

(2) The transfer of patent rights covered by this paragraph constitutes an asset acquisition; and

(3) Patent rights are transferred if and only if all commercially significant rights to a patent, as defined in § 801.1(o), for any therapeutic area (or specific indication within a therapeutic area) are transferred to another entity. All commercially significant rights are transferred even if the patent holder retains limited manufacturing rights, as defined in § 801.1(p), or co-rights, as defined in § 801.1(q).

Examples: Although these examples refer to licenses, which are typically used to effect the transfer of pharmaceutical patent rights to a recipient of those rights, other methods of transferring patent rights, by assignment or grant, among others, are similarly covered by these rules and examples.

1. B holds a patent relating to an active pharmaceutical ingredient for cardiovascular use. A will obtain a license from B that grants A the exclusive right to all of B's patent rights except that both A and B can manufacture the active pharmaceutical ingredient to be sold by A under the exclusive license agreement. B retains limited manufacturing rights as defined in § 801.1(p) because it retains the right to manufacture the product covered by the patent for cardiovascular use solely to provide the product to A. A is still receiving all commercially significant rights to the

patent, and the transfer of these rights via the license constitutes an asset acquisition. Further, even if B retained all rights to manufacture (so that A could not manufacture), B would still retain limited manufacturing rights, and A would still receive all commercially significant rights to the patent. Thus, the transfer of these rights via the license would also constitute an asset acquisition.

2. B holds a patent for an in-vitro diagnostic substance relating to arthritis. B will grant A an exclusive license to all of B's patent rights for all veterinary indications. B retains all patent rights for all human indications. The exclusive license to all commercially significant rights for all veterinary indications is an asset acquisition because A is receiving all rights to the patent for a therapeutic area.

3. B holds a patent relating to a biological product. B will grant A an exclusive license to all of B's patent rights in all therapeutic areas. A and B are also entering into a co-development and co-commercialization agreement under which B will assist A in developing, marketing and promoting the product to physicians. B cannot separately use the patent in the same therapeutic area as A under the co-development and co-commercialization agreement. A will book all sales of the product and will pay B a portion of the profits resulting from those sales. Despite B's retention of these co-rights, A is still receiving all commercially significant rights. The licensing agreement is an asset acquisition. This would be an asset acquisition even if B also retained limited manufacturing rights.

4. B holds a patent relating to an active pharmaceutical ingredient and a bulk compound that contains that active pharmaceutical ingredient. B will grant A an exclusive license to use the bulk compound to manufacture and sell a finished product in the neurological therapeutic area. B cannot manufacture the active pharmaceutical ingredient or bulk compound for any other finished products in the neurological area, but it can manufacture either for use by another party in a different therapeutic area. Despite B's retention of manufacturing rights of the active pharmaceutical ingredient and bulk compound for therapeutic areas other than neurology, A is still receiving all commercially significant rights in a therapeutic area and the licensing agreement is the acquisition of an asset.

5. B holds a patent related to a pharmaceutical product that has been approved by the FDA. B will enter into an exclusive distribution agreement with A that will give A the right to distribute the product in the U.S. B will manufacture the product for A and will receive a portion of all revenues from the sale of the product. A receives no exclusive patent rights under the distribution agreement. A has not obtained all commercially significant rights to the patent because it is only handling the logistics of selling and distributing the product on B's behalf. Therefore, the exclusive distribution agreement is not an asset acquisition.

[43 FR 33537, July 31, 1978, as amended at 48 FR 34431, July 29, 1983; 66 FR 8688, Feb. 1, 2001; 70 FR 4990, Jan. 31, 2005; 70 FR 11510, Mar. 8, 2005; 78 FR 68713, Nov. 15, 2013]

§ 801.3 Activities in or affecting commerce.

Section 7A(a)(1) is satisfied if any entity included within the acquiring person, or any entity included within the acquired person, is engaged in commerce or in any activity affecting commerce.

Examples: 1. A foreign subsidiary of a U.S. corporation seeks to acquire a foreign business. The acquiring person includes the U.S. parent corporation. If the U.S. corporation, or the foreign subsidiary, or any entity controlled by either one of them, is engaged in commerce or in any activity affecting commerce, section 7A(a)(1) is satisfied. Note, however, that §§ 802.50–802.52 may exempt certain acquisitions of foreign businesses or assets.

2. Even if none of the entities within the acquiring person is engaged in commerce or in any activity affecting commerce, the acquisition nevertheless satisfies section 7A(a)(1) if any entity included within the acquired person is so engaged.

[43 FR 33537, July 31, 1978; 43 FR 36054, Aug. 15, 1978]

§ 801.4 Secondary acquisitions.

(a) Whenever as the result of an acquisition (the "primary acquisition") an acquiring person controls an entity which holds voting securities of an issuer that entity does not control, then the acquiring person's acquisition of the issuer's voting securities is a secondary acquisition and is separately subject to the act and these rules.

(b) *Exemptions*. (1) No secondary acquisition shall be exempt from the requirements of the act solely because the related primary acquisition is exempt from the requirements of the act.

(2) A secondary acquisition may itself be exempt from the requirements of the act under section 7A(c) or these rules.

Examples: 1. Assume that acquiring person "A" proposes to acquire all the voting securities of corporation B. This section provides that the acquisition of voting securities of issuers held but not controlled by B or by any entity which B controls are secondary acquisitions by "A." Thus, if B holds more than $50 million (as adjusted) of the voting securities of corporation X (but does not control X), and "A" and "X" satisfy Sections 7A (a)(1) and (a)(2), "A" must file notification separately with respect to its secondary acquisition of voting securities of X. "X" must file notification within fifteen days (or in the case of a cash tender offer, 10 days) after "A" files, pursuant to §801.30.

2. If in the previous example "A" acquires only 50 percent of the voting securities of B, the result would remain the same. Since "A" would be acquiring control of B, all of B's holdings in X would be attributable to "A."

3. In the previous examples, if "A's" acquisition of the voting securities of B is exempt, "A" may still be required to file notification with respect to its secondary acquisition of the voting securities of X, unless that acquisition is itself exempt.

4. In the previous examples, assume A's acquisition of B is accomplished by merging B into A's subsidiary, S, and S is designated the surviving corporation. B's voting securities are cancelled, and B's shareholders are to receive cash in return. Since S is designated the surviving corporation and A will control S and also hold assets or voting securities it did not hold previously, "A" is an acquiring person in an acquisition of voting securities by virtue of §§801.2 (d)(1)(ii) and (d)(2)(i). A will be deemed to have acquired control of B, and A's resulting acquisition of the voting securities of X is a secondary acquisition. Since cash, the only consideration paid for the voting securities of B, is not considered an asset of the person from which it is acquired, by virtue of §801.2(d)(2) "A" is an acquiring person only. The acquisition of the minority holding of B in X is therefore a secondary acquisition by "A," but since "B" is an acquired person only, "B" is not deemed to make any secondary acquisition in this transaction.

5. In previous Example 4, suppose the consideration paid by A for the acquisition of B is in excess of $50 million (as adjusted) worth of the voting securities of A. By virtue of §801.2(d)(2), "A" and "B" are each both acquiring and acquired persons. A will still be deemed to have acquired control of B, and therefore the resulting acquisition of the voting securities of X is a secondary acquisition. Although "B" is now also an acquiring person, unless B gains control of A in the transaction, B still makes no secondary acquisitions of stock held by A. If the consideration paid by A is the voting securities of one of A's subsidiaries and B thereby gains control of that subsidiary, B will make secondary acquisitions of any minority holdings of that subsidiary.

6. Assume that A and B propose through consolidation to create a new corporation, C, and that both A and B will lose their corporate identities as a result. Since no participating corporation in existence prior to consummation is the designated surviving corporation, "A" and "B" are each both acquiring and acquired persons by virtue of §801.2(d)(2)(iii). The acquisition of the minority holdings of entities within each are therefore potential secondary acquisitions by the other.

(c) Where the primary acquisition is—

(1) A cash tender offer, the waiting period procedures established for cash tender offers pursuant to sections 7A(a) and 7A(e) of the act shall be applicable to both the primary acquisition and the secondary acquisition;

(2) A non-cash tender offer, the waiting period procedures established for tender offers pursuant to section 7A(e)(2) of the act shall be applicable to both the primary acquisition and the secondary acquisition.

[43 FR 33537, July 31, 1978, as amended at 48 FR 34432, July 29, 1983; 52 FR 7080, Mar. 6, 1987; 66 FR 8688, Feb. 1, 2001; 67 FR 11902, Mar. 18, 2002; 70 FR 4990, Jan. 31, 2005; 70 FR 11511, Mar. 8, 2005]

§801.10 Value of voting securities, non-corporate interests and assets to be acquired.

Except as provided in §801.13, the value of voting securities and assets to be acquired shall be determined as follows:

(a) *Voting securities*. (1) If the security is traded on a national securities exchange or is authorized to be quoted in an interdealer quotation system of a national securities association registered with the U.S. Securities and Exchange Commission—

(i) And the acquisition price has been determined, the value shall be the market price or the acquisition price, whichever is greater; or if

(ii) The acquisition price has not been determined, the value shall be the market price.

(2) If paragraph (a)(1) of this section is inapplicable—

(i) But the acquisition price has been determined, the value shall be the acquisition price; or if

(ii) The acquisition price has not been determined, the value shall be the fair market value.

(b) *Assets.* The value of assets to be acquired shall be the fair market value of the assets, or, if determined and greater than the fair market value, the acquisition price.

(c) For purposes of this section and § 801.13(a)(2):

(1) *Market price.* (i) For acquisitions subject to § 801.30, the market price shall be the lowest closing quotation, or, in an interdealer quotation system, the lowest closing bid price, within the 45 calendar days prior to the receipt of the notice required by § 803.5(a) or prior to the consummation of the acquisition.

(ii) For acquisitions not subject to § 801.30, the market price shall be the lowest closing quotation, or, in an interdealer quotation system, the lowest closing bid price, within the 45 or fewer calendar days which are prior to the consummation of the acquisition but not earlier than the day prior to the execution of the contract, agreement in principle or letter of intent to merge or acquire.

(iii) When the security was not traded within the period specified by this paragraph, the last closing quotation or closing bid price preceding such period shall be used. If such closing quotations are available in more than one market, the person filing notification may select any such quotation.

(2) *Acquisition price.* The acquisition price shall include the value of all consideration for such voting securities, non-corporate interests or assets to be acquired.

(3) *Fair market value.* The fair market value shall be determined in good faith by the board of directors of the ultimate parent entity included within the acquiring person, or, if unincorporated, by officials exercising similar functions; or by an entity delegated that function by such board or officials. Such determination must be made as of any day within 60 calendar days prior to the filing of the notification required by the act, or, if such notification has not been filed, within 60 calendar days prior to the consummation of the acquisition.

Example: Corporation A, the ultimate parent entity in person "A," contracts to acquire assets of corporation B, and the contract provides that the acquisition price is not to be determined until after the acquisition is effected. Under paragraph (b) of this section, for purposes of the act, the value of the assets is to be the fair market value of the assets. Under paragraph (c)(3), the board of directors of corporation A must in good faith determine the fair market value. That determination will control for 60 days whether "A" and "B" must observe the requirements of the act; that is, "A" and "B" must either file notification or consummate the acquisition within that time. If "A" and "B" neither file nor consummate within 60 days, the parties would no longer be entitled to rely on the determination of fair market value, and, if in doubt about whether required to observe the requirements of the act, would have to make a second determination of fair market value.

(d) *Value of interests in an unincorporated entity.* In an acquisition of non-corporate interests that confers control of either an existing or a newly-formed unincorporated entity, the value of the non-corporate interests held as a result of the acquisition is the sum of the acquisition price of the interests to be acquired (provided the acquisition price has been determined), and the fair market value of any of the interests in the same unincorporated entity held by the acquiring person prior to the acquisition; or, if the acquisition price has not been determined, the fair market value of interests held as a result of the acquisition.

[43 FR 33537, July 31, 1978, as amended at 66 FR 8688, Feb. 1, 2001; 70 FR 11511, Mar. 8, 2005; 76 FR 42482, July 19, 2011]

§801.11 Annual net sales and total assets.

(a) The annual net sales and total assets of a person shall include all net sales and all assets held, whether foreign or domestic, except as provided in paragraphs (d) and (e) of this section.

(b) Except for the total assets of a corporation or unincorporated entity at the time of its formation which shall be determined pursuant to Sec. 801.40(d) or 801.50(c) the annual net sales and total assets of a person shall be as stated on the financial statements specified in paragraph (c) of this section: *Provided:*

(1) That the annual net sales and total assets of each entity included within such person are consolidated therein. If the annual net sales and total assets of any entity included within the person are not consolidated in such statements, the annual net sales and total assets of the person filing notification shall be recomputed to include the nonduplicative annual net sales and nonduplicative total assets of each such entity; and

(2) That such statements, and any restatements pursuant to paragraph (b)(1) of this section (insofar as possible), have been prepared in accordance with the accounting principles normally used by such person, and are of a date not more than 15 months prior to the date of filing of the notification required by the act, or the date of consummation of the acquisition.

Example: Person "A" is composed of entity A, subsidiaries B1 and B2 which A controls, subsidiaries C1 and C2 which B1 controls, and subsidiary C3 which B2 controls. Suppose that A's most recent financial statement consolidates the annual net sales and total assets of B1, C1, and C2, but not B2 or C3. In order to determine whether person "A" meets the criteria of Section 7A(a)(2)(B), as either an acquiring or an acquired person, A must recompute its annual net sales and total assets to reflect consolidation of the nonduplicative annual net sales and nonduplicative total assets of B2 and C3.

(c) Subject to the provisions of paragraph (b) of this section:

(1) The annual net sales of a person shall be as stated on the last regularly prepared annual statement of income and expense of that person; and

(2) The total assets of a person shall be as stated on the last regularly prepared balance sheet of that person.

Example: Suppose "A" sells assets to "B" on January 1. "A's" next regularly prepared balance sheet, dated February 1, reflects that sale. On March 1, "A" proposes to sell more assets to "B." "A's" total assets on March 1 are "A's" total assets as stated on its February 1 balance sheet.

(d) No assets of any natural person or of any estate of a deceased natural person, other than investment assets, voting securities and other income-producing property, shall be included in determining the total assets of a person.

(e) Subject to the limitations of paragraph (d) of this section, the total assets of:

(1) An acquiring person that does not have the regularly prepared balance sheet described in paragraph (c)(2) of this section shall be, for acquisitions of each acquired person:

(i) All assets held by the acquiring person at the time of the acquisition,

(ii) Less all cash that will be used by the acquiring person as consideration in an acquisition of assets from, or in an acquisition of voting securities issued by, or in an acquisition of non-corporate interests of, that acquired person (or an entity within that acquired person) and less all cash that will be used for expenses incidental to the acquisition, and less all securities of the acquired person (or an entity within that acquired person); and

(2) An acquired person that does not have the regularly prepared balance sheet described in paragraph (c)(2) of this section shall be either

(i) All assets held by the acquired person at the time of the acquisition, or

(ii) Where applicable, its assets as determined in accordance with §801.40(d).

Examples: For examples 1–4, assume that A is a newly-formed company which is not controlled by any other entity. Assume also that A has no sales and does not have the balance sheet described in paragraph (c)(2) of this section.

1. A will borrow $105 million in cash and will purchase assets from B for $100 million. In order to establish whether A's acquisition of B's assets is reportable, A's total assets are determined by subtracting the $100 million that it will use to acquire B's assets

from the $105 million that A will have at the time of the acquisition. Therefore, A has total assets of less than $10 million (as adjusted) and does not meet any size-of-person test of Section 7A(a)(2).

2. Assume that A will acquire assets from B and that, at the time it acquires B's assets, A will have $85 million in cash and a factory valued at $60 million. A will exchange the factory and $80 million cash for B's assets. To determine A's total assets, A should subtract from the $85 million cash the $80 million that will be used to acquire assets from B and add the remainder to the value of the factory. Thus, A has total assets of $65 million. Even though A will use the factory as part of the consideration for the acquisition, the value of the factory must still be included in A's total assets. Note that A and B may also have to report the acquisition by B of A's non-cash assets (i.e., the factory). For that acquisition, the value of the cash A will use to buy B's assets is not excluded from A's total assets. Thus, in the acquisition by B, A's total assets are $145 million.

3. Assume that company A will make a $150 million acquisition and that it must pay a loan origination fee of $5 million. A borrows $161 million. A does not meet the size-of-person test in Section 7A(a)(2) because its total assets are less than $10 million (as adjusted). $150 million is excluded because it will be consideration for the acquisition and $5 million is excluded because it is an expense incidental to the acquisition. Therefore, A is only a $6 million person. Note that if A were making an acquisition valued at over $200 million (as adjusted), the acquisition would be reportable without regard to the sizes of the persons involved.

4. Assume that "A" borrows $195 million to acquire $100 million of assets from "B" and $60 million of voting securities of "C." The balance of the loan will be used for working capital. To determine its size for purposes of its acquisition from "B," "A" subtracts the $100 million that it will use for that acquisition. Therefore, A has total assets of $95 million for purposes of its acquisition from "B." To determine its size with respect to its acquisition from "C," "A" subtracts the $60 million that will be paid for "C's" voting securities. Thus, for purposes of its acquisition from "C", "A" has total assets of $135 million. In the first acquisition "A" meets the $10 million (as adjusted) size-of-person test and in the second acquisition "A" meets the $100 million (as adjusted) size-of-person test of Section 7A(a)(2).

[43 FR 33537, July 31, 1978, as amended at 48 FR 34429, July 29, 1983; 52 FR 7080, Mar. 6, 1987; 66 FR 8688, Feb. 1, 2001; 70 FR 4990, Jan. 31, 2005; 70 FR 11511, Mar. 8, 2005; 70 FR 73372, Dec. 12, 2005]

§ 801.12 Calculating percentage of voting securities.

(a) *Voting securities.* Whenever the act or these rules require calculation of the percentage of voting securities to be held or acquired, the issuer whose voting securities are being acquired shall be deemed the "acquired persons."

Example: Person "A" is composed of corporation A1 and subsidiary A2; person "B" is composed of corporation B1 and subsidiary B2. Assume that A2 proposes to sell assets to B1 in exchange for common stock of B2. Under this paragraph, for purposes of calculating the percentage of voting securities to be held, the "acquired person" is B2. For all other purposes, the acquired person is "B." (For all purposes, the "acquiring persons" are "A" and "B.")

(b) *Percentage of voting securities.* (1) Whenever the act or these rules require calculation of the percentage of voting securities of an issuer to be held or acquired, the percentage shall be the sum of the separate ratios for each class of voting securities, expressed as a percentage. The ratio for each class of voting securities equals:

(i)(A) The number of votes for directors of the issuer which the holder of a class of voting securities is presently entitled to cast, and as a result of the acquisition, will become entitled to cast, divided by,

(B) The total number of votes for directors of the issuer which presently may be cast by that class, and which will be entitled to be cast by that class after the acquisition, multiplied by,

(ii)(A) The number of directors that class is entitled to elect, divided by (B) the total number of directors.

Examples: In each of the following examples company X has two classes of voting securities, class A, consisting of 1000 shares with each share having one vote, and class B, consisting of 100 shares with each share having one vote. The class A shares elect four of the ten directors and the class B shares elect six of the ten directors.

In this situation, § 801.12(b) requires calculations of the percentage of voting securities held to be made according to the following formula:

Number of votes of class A held divided by Total votes of class A times Directors elected by class A stock divided by Total number of directors

Plus

Number of votes of class B held divided by Total votes of class B times Directors elected by class B stock divided by Total number of directors

1. Assume that company Y holds all 100 shares of class B stock and no shares of class A stock. By virtue of its class B holdings, Y has all 100 of the votes which may be cast by class B stock and can elect six of company X's ten directors. Applying the formula which results from the rule, Y calculates that it holds 100/100 × 6/10 or 60 percent of the voting securities of company X because of its holdings of class B stock and no additional percentage derived from holdings of class A stock. Consequently, Y holds a total of 60 percent of the voting securities of company X.

2. Assume that company Y holds 500 shares of class A stock and no shares of class B stock. By virtue of its class A holdings, Y has 500 of the 1000 votes which may be cast by class A to elect four of company X's ten directors. Applying the formula, Y calculates that it holds 500/1000 × 4/10 or 20 percent of the voting securities of company X from its holdings of class A stock and no additional percentage derived from holdings of class B stock. Consequently, Y holds a total of 20 percent of the voting securities of company X.

3. Assume that company Y holds 500 shares of class A stock and 60 shares of class B stock. Y calculates that it holds 20 percent of the voting securities of company X because of its holdings of class A stock (see example 2). Additionally, as a result of its class B holdings Y has 60 of the 100 votes which may be cast by class B stock to elect six of company X's ten directors. Applying the formula, Y calculates that it holds 60/100 × 6/10 or 36 percent of the voting securities of company X because of its holdings of class B stock. Since the formula requires that a person that holds different classes of voting securities of the same issuer add together the separate percentages calculated for each class, Y holds a total of 56 percent (20 percent plus 36 percent) of the voting securities of company X.

(2) Authorized but unissued voting securities and treasury voting securities shall not be considered securities presently entitled to vote for directors of the issuer.

(3) For purposes of determining the number of outstanding voting securities of an issuer, a person may rely upon the most recent information set forth in filings with the U.S. Securities and Exchange Commission, unless such person knows or has reason to believe that the information contained therein is inaccurate.

Examples: 1. In the example to paragraph (a), to determine the percentage of B2's voting securities which will be held by "A" after the transaction, all voting securities of B2 held by "A," the "acquiring person" (including A2 and all other entities included in person "A"), must be aggregated. If "A" holds convertible securities of B2 which meet the definition of voting securities in § 801.1(f), these securities are to be disregarded in calculating the percentage of voting securities held by "A."

2. Under this formula, any votes obtained by means of proxies from other persons are also disregarded in calculating the percentage of voting securities to be held or acquired.

[43 FR 33537, July 31, 1978; 43 FR 36054, Aug. 15, 1978, as amended at 52 FR 7081, Mar. 6, 1987; 66 FR 8689, Feb. 1, 2001]

§ 801.13 Aggregation of voting securities, assets and non-corporate interests.

(a) *Voting securities.* (1) Subject to the provisions of § 801.15, and paragraph (a)(3) of this section, all voting securities of the issuer which will be held by the acquiring person after the consummation of an acquisition shall be deemed voting securities held as a result of the acquisition. The value of such voting securities shall be the sum of the value of the voting securities to be acquired, determined in accordance with § 801.10(a), and the value of the voting securities held by the acquiring person prior to the acquisition, determined in accordance with paragraph (a)(2) of this section.

(2) The value of voting securities of an issuer held prior to an acquisition shall be—

(i) If the security is traded on a national securities exchange or is authorized to be quoted in an interdealer quotation system of a national securities association registered with the United States Securities and Exchange Commission, the market price calculated in accordance with § 801.10(c)(1); or

(ii) If paragraph (a)(2)(i) of this section is not applicable, the fair market value determined in accordance with § 801.10(c)(3).

Examples: 1. Assume that acquiring person "A" holds in excess of $50 million (as adjusted) of the voting securities of X, and is to acquire another $1 million of the same voting securities. Since under paragraph (a) of this section all voting securities "A" will hold after the acquisition are held "as a result of" the acquisition, "A" will hold in excess of $50 million (as adjusted) of the voting securities of X as a result of the acquisition. "A" must therefore observe the requirements of the act before making the acquisition, unless the present acquisition is exempt under Section 7A(c), § 802.21 or any other rule.

2. See § 801.15 and the examples to that rule.

3. See § 801.20 and the examples to that rule.

4. On January 1, company A acquired in excess of $50 million (as adjusted) of voting securities of company B. "A" and "B" filed notification and observed the waiting period for that acquisition. Company A plans to acquire $1 million of assets from company B on May 1 of the same year. Under § 801.13(a)(3), "A" and "B" do not aggregate the value of the earlier acquired voting securities to determine whether the acquisition is subject to the act. Therefore, the value of the acquisition is $1 million and it is not reportable.

(3) Voting securities held by the acquiring person prior to an acquisition shall not be deemed voting securities held as a result of that subsequent acquisition if:

(i) The acquiring person is, in the subsequent acquisition, acquiring only assets; and

(ii) The acquisition of the previously acquired voting securities was subject to the filing and waiting requirements of the act (and such requirements were observed) or was exempt pursuant to § 802.21.

(b) *Assets.* (1) All assets to be acquired from the acquired person shall be assets held as a result of the acquisition. The value of such assets shall be determined in accordance with § 801.10(b).

(2) If the acquiring person signs a letter of intent or agreement in principle to acquire assets from an acquired person, and within the previous 180 days the acquiring person has

(i) Signed a letter of intent or agreement in principle to acquire assets from the same acquired person, which is still in effect but has not been consummated, or has acquired assets from the same acquired person which it still holds; and

(ii) The previous acquisition (whether consummated or still contemplated) was not subject to the requirements of the Act; then for purposes of the size-of-transaction test of Section 7A(a)(2), both the acquiring and the acquired persons shall treat the assets that were the subject of the earlier letter of intent or agreement in principal as though they are being acquired as part of the present acquisition. The value of any assets which are subject to this paragraph is determined in accordance with § 801.10(b).

Examples: 1. On day 1, A enters into an agreement with B to acquire assets valued at $45 million. On day 90, A and B sign a letter of intent pursuant to which A will acquire additional assets from B, valued at $45 million. The original transaction has not closed, however, the agreement is still in effect. For purposes of the size-of-transaction test in Section 7A(a)(2), A must aggregate the value of both of its acquisitions and file prior to acquiring the assets if the aggregate value exceeds $50 million (as adjusted).

2. On March 30, A enters into a letter of intent to acquire assets of B valued at $45 million. On January 31, earlier the same year, A closed on an acquisition of assets of B valued at $45 million. For purposes of the size-of-transaction test in Section 7A(a)(2), A must aggregate the value of both of its acquisitions and file prior to acquiring the assets of B if the aggregate value exceeds $50 million (as adjusted).

3. On day 1, A enters into an agreement with B to acquire assets valued in excess of $50 million (as adjusted). A and B file notification and observe the waiting period. On day 60, A signs a letter of intent to acquire an additional $40 million of assets from B. Because the earlier acquisition was subject to the requirements of the Act, A does not aggregate the two acquisitions of assets and is free to acquire the additional assets of B without filing an additional notification.

4. On day 1, A consummates an acquisition of assets of B valued at $45 million. On day 60, A consummates a sale of the same assets to an unrelated third party. On day 120, A enters into an agreement to acquire additional assets of B valued at $45 million. Because A no longer holds the assets from the previous acquisition, no aggregation of the two asset acquisitions is required and A may acquire all of the additional assets without filing notification.

(c)(1) *Non-corporate interests.* In an acquisition of non-corporate interests, any previously acquired non-corporate interests in the same unincorporated entity is aggregated with the newly acquired interests. The value of such an acquisition is determined in accordance with § 801.10(d) of these rules.

(2) *Other assets or voting securities of the same acquired person.* An acquisition

of non-corporate interests which does not confer control of the unincorporated entity is not aggregated with any other assets or voting securities which have been or are currently being acquired from the same acquired person.

Examples: 1. A currently has the right to 30 percent of the profits in LLC. B has the right to the remaining 70 percent. A acquires an additional 30 percent interest in LLC from B for $90 million in cash. As a result of the acquisition, A is deemed to now have a 60 percent interest in LLC. The current acquisition is valued at $90 million, the acquisition price. The value of the 30 percent interest that A already holds is the fair market value of that interest. The value for size-of-transaction purposes is the sum of the two.

2. A acquires the following from B: (1) All of the assets of a subsidiary of B; (2) all of the voting securities of another subsidiary of B; and (3) a 30 percent interest in an LLC which is currently wholly-owned by B. In determining the size-of-transaction, A aggregates the value of the voting securities and assets of the subsidiaries that it is acquiring from B, but does not include the value of the 30 percent interest in the LLC, pursuant to §801.13(c)(2).

[43 FR 33537, July 31, 1978, as amended at 52 FR 7081, Mar. 6, 1987; 66 FR 8689, Feb. 1, 2001; 70 FR 4991, Jan. 31, 2005; 70 FR 11513, Mar. 8, 2005]

§801.14 Aggregate total amount of voting securities and assets.

For purposes of Section 7A(a)(2) and §801.1(h), the aggregate total amount of voting securities and assets shall be the sum of:

(a) The value of all voting securities of the acquired person which the acquiring person would hold as a result of the acquisition, determined in accordance with §801.13(a); and

(b) The value of all assets of the acquired person which the acquiring person would hold as a result of the acquisition, determined in accordance with §801.13(b).

Examples: 1. Acquiring person "A" previously acquired less than $50 million (as adjusted) of the voting securities (not convertible voting securities) of corporation X. "A" now intends to acquire additional assets of X. Under paragraph (a) of this section, "A" looks to §801.13(a) and determines that the voting securities are to be held "as a result of" the acquisition. Section 801.13(a) also provides that "A" must determine the present value of the previously acquired securities. Under paragraph (b) of this section, "A" looks to §801.13(b)(1) and determines that the assets to be acquired will be held "as a result of" the acquisition, and are valued under §801.10(b). Therefore, if the voting securities have a present value which when combined with the value of the assets would exceed $50 million (as adjusted), the asset acquisition is subject to the requirements of the act since, as a result of it, "A" would hold an aggregate total amount of the voting securities and assets of "X" in excess of $50 million (as adjusted) .

2. In the previous example, assume that the assets acquisition occurred first, and that the acquisition of the voting securities is to occur within 180 days of the first acquisition. "A" now looks to §801.13(b)(2) and determines that because the second acquisition is of voting securities and not assets, the asset and voting securities acquisitions are not treated as one transaction. Therefore, the second acquisition would not be subject to the requirements of the act since the value of the securities to be acquired does not exceed the $50 million (as adjusted) size-of-transaction test.

(c) The value of all non-corporate interests of the acquired person which the acquiring person would hold as a result of the acquisition, determined in accordance with §801.13(c).

[43 FR 33537, July 31, 1978, as amended at 66 FR 8689, Feb. 1, 2001; 67 FR 11902, Mar. 18, 2002; 70 FR 4991, Jan. 31, 2005; 70 FR 73372, Dec. 12, 2005]

§801.15 Aggregation of voting securities, non-corporate interests and assets the acquisition of which was exempt.

Notwithstanding §801.13, for purposes of determining the aggregate total amount of voting securities, non-corporate interests and assets of the acquired person held by the acquiring person under Section 7A(a)(2) and §801.1(h), none of the following will be held as a result of an acquisition:

(a) Assets, non-corporate interests or voting securities the acquisition of which was exempt at the time of acquisition (or would have been exempt, had the act and these rules been in effect), or the present acquisition of which is exempt, under—

(1) Sections 7A(c)(1), (3), (5), (6), (7), (8), and (11)(B);

(2) Sections 802.1, 802.2, 802.5, 802.6(b)(1), 802.8, 802.30, 802.31, 802.35, 802.52, 802.53, 802.63, and 802.70 of this chapter;

(b) Assets, non-corporate interests or voting securities the acquisition of which was exempt at the time of acquisition (or would have been exempt, had the Act and these rules been in effect), or the present acquisition of which is exempt, under Section 7A(c)(9) and §§ 802.3, 802.4, and 802.64 of this chapter unless the limitations contained in Section 7A(c)(9) or those sections do not apply or as a result of the acquisition would be exceeded, in which case the assets or voting securities so acquired will be held; and

(c) Voting securities the acquisition of which was exempt at the time of acquisition (or would have been exempt, had the Act and these rules been in effect), or the present acquisition of which is exempt, under section 7A(c)(11)(A) unless additional voting securities of the same issuer have been or are being acquired; and

(d) Assets or voting securities the acquisition of which was exempt at the time of acquisition (or would have been exempt, had the Act and these rules been in effect), or the present acquisition of which is exempt, under §§ 802.50(a), 802.51(a), 802.51(b) of this chapter unless the limitations, in aggregate for §§ 802.50(a), 802.51(a), 802.51(b) , do not apply or as a result of the acquisition would be exceeded, in which case the assets or voting securities so acquired will be held.

Examples: 1. Assume that acquiring person "A" is simultaneously to acquire in excess of $50 million (as adjusted) of the convertible voting securities of X and less than $50 million (as adjusted) of the voting common stock of X. Although the acquisition of the convertible voting securities is exempt under § 802.31, since the overall value of the securities to be acquired is greater than $50 million (as adjusted), "A" must determine whether it is obliged to file notification and observe a waiting period before acquiring the securities. Because § 802.31 is one of the exemptions listed in paragraph (a)(2) of this section, "A" would not hold the convertible voting securities as a result of the acquisition. Therefore, since as a result of the acquisition "A" would hold only the common stock, the size-of-transaction tests of Section 7A(a)(2) would not be satisfied, and "A" need not observe the requirements of the act before acquiring the common stock. (Note, however, that the value of the convertible voting securities would be reflected in "A's" next regularly prepared balance sheet, for purposes of § 801.11).

2. In the previous example, the rule was applied to voting securities the present acquisition of which is exempt. Assume instead that "A" had acquired the convertible voting securities prior to its acquisition of the common stock. "A" still would not hold the convertible voting securities as a result of the acquisition of the common stock, because the rule states that voting securities the previous acquisition of which was exempt also fall within the rule. Thus, the size-of-transaction tests of Section 7A(a)(2) would again not be satisfied, and "A" need not observe the requirements of the act before acquiring the common stock.

3. In example 2, assume instead that "A" acquired the convertible voting securities in 1975, before the act and rules went into effect. Since the rule applies to voting securities the acquisition of which would have been exempt had the act and rules been in effect, the result again would be identical. If the rules had been in effect in 1975, the acquisition of the convertible voting securities would have been exempt under § 802.31.

4. Assume that acquiring person "B," a United States person, acquired from corporation "X" two manufacturing plants located abroad, and assume that the acquisition price was in excess of $50 million (as adjusted). In the most recent year, sales into the United States attributable to the plants were less than $50 million (as adjusted), and thus the acquisition was exempt under § 802.50(a)(2). Within 180 days of that acquisition, "B" seeks to acquire a third plant from "X," to which United States sales were attributable in the most recent year. Since under § 801.13(b)(2), as a result of the acquisition, "B" would hold all three plants of "X,"if the $50 million (as adjusted) limitation in § 802.50(a)(2) would be exceeded, under paragraph (b) of this section, "B" would hold the previously acquired assets for purposes of the second acquisition. Therefore, as a result of the second acquisition, "B" would hold assets of "X" exceeding $50 million (as adjusted) in value, would not qualify for the exemption in § 802.50(a)(2), and must observe the requirements of the act and file notification for the acquisition of all three plants before acquiring the third plant

5. "A" acquires producing oil reserves valued at $400 million from "B." Two months later, "A" agrees to acquire oil and gas rights valued at $75 million from "B." Paragraph (b) of this section and § 801.13(b)(2) require aggregating the previously exempt acquisition of oil reserves with the second acquisition. If the two acquisitions, when aggregated, exceed the $500 million limitation on the exemption for oil and gas reserves in § 802.3(a), "A" and "B" will be required to file notification for the latter acquisition, including within the filings the earlier acquisition. Since, in this example, the total value of the assets in the two acquisitions, when

aggregated, is less than $500 million, both acquisitions are exempt from the notification requirements. In determining whether the value of the assets in the two acquisitions exceeds $500 million, "A" need not determine the current fair market value of the oil reserves acquired in the first transaction, since these assets are now within the person of "A." Instead, "A" is directed by §801.13(b)(2)(ii) to use the value of the oil reserves at the time of their prior acquisition in accordance with §801.10(b).

6. "X" acquired 55 percent of the voting securities of M, an entity controlled by "Z," six months ago and now proposes to acquire 50 percent of the voting stock of N, another entity controlled by "Z." M's assets consist of $150 million worth of producing coal reserves plus less than $50 million (as adjusted) worth of non-exempt assets and N's assets consist of a producing coal mine worth $100 million together with non-exempt assets with a fair market value of less than $50 million (as adjusted). "X's" acquisition of the voting securities of M was exempt under §802.4(a) because M held exempt assets pursuant to §802.3(b) and less than $50 million (as adjusted) of non-exempt assets. Because "X" acquired control of M in the earlier transaction, M is now within the person of "X," and the assets of M need not be aggregated with those of N to determine if the subsequent acquisition of N will exceed the limitation for coal reserves or for non-exempt assets. Since the assets of N alone do not exceed these limitations, "X's" acquisition of N also is not reportable.

7. In previous Example 6, assume that "X" acquired 30 percent of the voting securities of M and proposes to acquire 40 percent of the voting securities of N, another entity controlled by "Z." Assume also that M's assets at the time of "X's" acquisition of M's voting securities consisted of $90 million worth of producing coal reserves and non-exempt assets with a fair market value of less than $50 million (as adjusted), and that N's assets currently consist of $60 million worth of producing coal reserves and non-exempt assets with a fair market value which when aggregated with M's non-exempt assets would exceed $50 million (as adjusted). Since "X" acquired a minority interest in M and intends to acquire a minority interest in N, and since M and N are controlled by "Z," the assets of M and N must be aggregated, pursuant to Secs. 801.15(b) and 801.13, to determine whether the acquisition of N's voting securities is exempt. "X" is required to determine the current fair market value of M's assets. If the fair market value of M's coal reserves is unchanged, the aggregated exempt assets do not exceed the limitation for coal reserves. However, if the present fair market value of N's non-exempt assets also is unchanged, the present fair market value of the non-exempt assets of M and N when aggregated is greater than $50 million. Thus the acquisition of the voting securities of N is not exempt. If "X" proposed to acquire 50 percent or more of the voting securities of both M and N in the same acquisition, the assets of M and N must be aggregated to determine if the acquisition of the voting securities of both issuers is exempt. Since the fair market value of the aggregated non-exempt assets exceeds $50 million (as adjusted), the acquisition would not be exempt.

8. "A" acquired 49 percent of the voting securities of M and 45 percent of the voting securities of N. Both M and N are controlled by "B." At the time of the acquisition, M held rights to producing coal reserves worth $90 million and N held a producing coal mine worth $90 million. This acquisition was exempt since the aggregated holdings fell below the $200 million limitation for coal in §802.3(b) of this chapter. A year later, "A" proposes to acquire an additional 10 percent of the voting securities of both M and N. In the intervening year, M has acquired coal reserves so that its holdings are now valued at $140 million, and the value of N's assets remained unchanged. "A's" second acquisition would not be exempt. "A" is required to determine the value of the exempt assets and any non-exempt assets held by any issuer whose voting securities it intends to acquire before each proposed acquisition (unless "A" already owns 50 percent or more of the voting securities of the issuer) to determine if the value of those holdings of the issuer falls below the limitation of the applicable exemption. Here, the holdings of M and N now exceed the $200 million exemption for acquisitions of coal reserves in §802.3 of this chapter, and thus do not qualify for the exemption of voting securities provided by §802.4(a) of this chapter.

9. A acquires assets of B located outside of the U.S. with sales into the U.S. of $45 million. It also acquires voting securities of B's foreign subsidiary X which has sales into the U.S. of $45 million. Both the assets and the voting securities of X are exempt under §§802.50 and 802.51 respectively when analyzed separately. However, because §801.15(d) requires that the sales into the U.S. for both the assets and the voting securities be aggregated to determine whether the $50 million (as adjusted) limitation has been exceeded, both are held as a result of the acquisition because the aggregate sales into the U.S. total in excess of $50 million (as adjusted).

[43 FR 33537, July 31, 1978, as amended at 52 FR 7081, Mar. 6, 1987; 61 FR 13684, Mar. 28, 1996; 66 FR 8689, Feb. 1, 2001; 67 FR 11902, Mar. 18, 2002; 70 FR 11512, Mar. 8, 2005; 76 FR 42482, July 19, 2011]

§ 801.20 Acquisitions subsequent to exceeding threshold.

Acquisitions meeting the criteria of section 7A(a), and not otherwise exempted by section 7A(c) or § 802.21 or any other of these rules, are subject to the requirements of the act even though:

(a) Earlier acquisitions of assets or voting securities may have been subject to the requirements of the act;

(b) The acquiring person's holdings initially may have met or exceeded a notification threshold before the effective date of these rules; or

(c) The acquiring person's holdings initially may have met or exceeded a notification threshold by reason of increases in market values or events other than acquisitions.

[43 FR 33537, July 31, 1978, as amended at 66 FR 8690, Feb. 1, 2001; 70 FR 4992, Jan. 31, 2005]

§ 801.21 Securities and cash not considered assets when acquired.

For purposes of determining the aggregate total amount of assets under Section 7A(a)(2)(A), Section 7A(a)(2)(B)(i), Sec. 801.13(b), and Sec. 802.4:

(a) Cash shall not be considered an asset of the person from which it is acquired; and

(b) Neither voting or nonvoting securities nor obligations referred to in section 7A(c)(2) shall be considered assets of another person from which they are acquired.

Examples: 1. Assume that acquiring person "A" acquires voting securities of issuer X from "B," a person unrelated to X. Under this paragraph, the acquisition is treated only as one of voting securities, requiring "A" and "X" to comply with the requirements of the act, rather than one in which "A" acquires the assets of "B," requiring "A" and "B" to comply. See also example 2 to § 801.30. Note that for purposes of section 7A(a)(2)—that is, for the next regularly prepared balance sheet of "A" referred to in § 801.11—the voting securities of X must be reflected after their acquisition; see § 801.11(c)(2).

2. In the previous example, if "A" acquires nonvoting securities of X from "B," then under this section the acquisition would be treated only as one of nonvoting securities of X (and would be exempt under section 7A(c)(2)), rather than one in which "A" acquires assets of "B," requiring "A" and "B" to comply. Again, the nonvoting securities of X would have to be reflected in "A's" next regularly prepared balance sheet for purposes of section 7A(a)(2).

3. In example 1, assume that "B" receives only cash from "A" in exchange for the voting securities of X. Under this section, "B's" acquisition of cash is *not* an acquisition of the "assets" of "A," and "B" is not required to file notification as an acquiring person.

[43 FR 33537, July 31, 1978, as amended at 66 FR 8690, Feb. 1, 2001; 68 FR 2430, Jan. 17, 2003; 70 FR 4992, Jan. 31, 2005]

§ 801.30 Tender offers and acquisitions of voting securities and non-corporate interests from third parties.

(a) This section applies to:

(1) Acquisitions on a national securities exchange or through an interdealer quotation system registered with the United States Securities and Exchange Commission;

(2) Acquisitions described by § 801.31;

(3) Tender offers;

(4) Secondary acquisitions;

(5) All acquisitions (other than mergers and consolidations) in which voting securities or non-corporate interests are to be acquired from a holder or holders other than the issuer or unincorporated entity or an entity included within the same person as the issuer or unincorporated entity;

(6) Conversions; and

(7) Acquisitions of voting securities resulting from the exercise of options or warrants which are—

(i) Issued by the issuer whose voting securities are to be acquired (or by any entity included within the same person as the issuer); and

(ii) The subject of a currently effective registration statement filed with the United States Securities and Exchange Commission under the Securities Act of 1933.

(b) For acquisitions described by paragraph (a) of this section:

(1) The waiting period required under the act shall commence upon the filing of notification by the acquiring person as provided in § 803.10(a); and

(2) The acquired person shall file the notification required by the act, in accordance with these rules, no later than 5 p.m. Eastern Time on the 15th (or, in the case of cash tender offers, the 10th) calendar day following the date of receipt, as defined by § 803.10(a), by the Federal Trade Commission and

Assistant Attorney General of the notification filed by the acquiring person. Should the 15th (or, in the case of cash tender offers, the 10th) calendar day fall on a weekend day or federal holiday, the notification shall be filed no later than 5 p.m. Eastern Time on the next following business day.

Examples: 1. Acquiring person "A" proposes to acquire from corporation B the voting securities of B's wholly owned subsidiary, corporation S. Since "A" is acquiring the shares of S from its parent, this section does not apply, and the waiting period does not begin until both "A" and "B" file notification.

2. Acquiring person "A" proposes to acquire in excess of $50 million (as adjusted) of the voting securities of corporation X on a securities exchange. The waiting period begins when "A" files notification. "X" must file notification within 15 calendar days thereafter. The seller of the X shares is not subject to any obligations under the act.

3. Suppose that acquiring person "A" proposes to acquire 50 percent of the voting securities of corporation B which in turn owns 30 percent of the voting securities of corporation C. Thus "A's" acquisition of C's voting securities is a secondary acquisition (see § 801.4) to which this section applies because "A" is acquiring C's voting securities from a third party (B). Therefore, the waiting period with respect to "A's" acquisition of C's voting securities begins when "A" files its separate Notification and Report Form with respect to C, and "C" must file within 15 days (or in the case of a cash tender offer, 10 days) thereafter. "A's" primary and secondary acquisitions of the voting securities of B and C are subject to separate waiting periods; see § 801.4.

[43 FR 33537, July 31, 1978; 43 FR 36054, Aug. 15, 1978, as amended at 52 FR 7082, Mar. 6, 1987; 66 FR 8690, Feb. 1, 2001; 70 FR 4992, Jan. 31, 2005; 76 FR 42482, July 19, 2011]

§ 801.31 Acquisitions of voting securities by offerees in tender offers.

Whenever an offeree in a noncash tender offer is required to, and does, file notification with respect to an acquisition described in § 801.2(e):

(a) The waiting period with respect to such acquisition shall begin upon filing of notification by the offeree, pursuant to §§ 801.30 and 803.10(a)(1);

(b) The person within which the issuer of the shares to be acquired by the offeree is included shall file notification as required by § 801.30(b);

(c) Any request for additional information or documentary material pursuant to section 7A(e) and § 803.20 shall extend the waiting period in accordance with § 803.20(c); and

(d) The voting securities to be acquired by the offeree may be placed into escrow, for the benefit of the offeree, pending expiration or termination of the waiting period with respect to the acquisition of such securities; *Provided however,* That no person may vote any voting securities placed into escrow pursuant to this paragraph.

Example: Assume that "A," which has annual net sales exceeding $100 million (as adjusted), makes a tender offer for voting securities of corporation X. The consideration for the tender offer is to be voting securities of A. "S," a shareholder of X with total assets exceeding $10 million (as adjusted), wishes to tender its holdings of X and in exchange would receive shares of A valued in excess of $50 million (as adjusted). Under this section, "S's" acquisition of the shares of A would be an acquisition separately subject to the requirements of the act. Before "S" may acquire the voting securities of A, "S" must first file notification and observe a waiting period—which is separate from any waiting period that may apply with respect to "A" and "X." Since § 801.30 applies, the waiting period applicable to "A" and "S" begins upon filing by "S," and "A" must file with respect to "S's" acquisition within 15 days pursuant to § 801.30(b). Should the waiting period with respect to "A" and "X" expire or be terminated prior to the waiting period with respect to "S" and "A," "S" may wish to tender its X-shares and place the A-shares into a nonvoting escrow until the expiration or termination of the latter waiting period.

[43 FR 33537, July 31, 1978, as amended at 66 FR 8690, Feb. 1, 2001; 70 FR 4992, Jan. 31, 2005]

§ 801.32 Conversion and acquisition.

A conversion is an acquisition within the meaning of the act.

Example: Assume that acquiring person "A" wishes to convert convertible voting securities of issuer X, and is to receive common stock of X valued in excess of $50 million (as adjusted). If "A" and "X" satisfy the criteria of Section 7A(a)(1) and Section 7A(a)(2)(B)(ii), then "A" and "X" must file notification and observe the waiting period before "A" completes the acquisition of the X common stock, unless exempted by Section 7A(c) or the regulations in this part. Since § 801.30 applies, the waiting period begins upon notification by "A," and "X" must file notification within 15 days.

[43 FR 33537, July 31, 1978, as amended at 66 FR 8690, Feb. 1, 2001; 70 FR 4992, Jan. 31, 2005]

§ 801.33 Consummation of an acquisition by acceptance of tendered shares of payment.

The acceptance for payment of any shares tendered in a tender offer is the consummation of an acquisition of those shares within the meaning of the act.

[48 FR 34433, July 29, 1983]

§ 801.40 Formation of joint venture or other corporations.

(a) In the formation of a joint venture or other corporation (other than in connection with a merger or consolidation), even though the persons contributing to the formation of a joint venture or other corporation and the joint venture or other corporation itself may, in the formation transaction, be both acquiring and acquired persons within the meaning of § 801.2, the contributors shall be deemed acquiring persons only, and the joint venture or other corporation shall be deemed the acquired person only.

(b) Unless exempted by the act or any of these rules, upon the formation of a joint venture or other corporation, in a transaction meeting the criteria of Section 7A(a)(1) and 7A(a)(2)(A) (other than in connection with a merger or consolidation), an acquiring person shall be subject to the requirements of the act.

(c) Unless exempted by the act or any of these rules, upon the formation of a joint venture or other corporation, in a transaction meeting the criteria of Section 7A(a)(1) and the criteria of Section 7A(a)(2)(B)(i) (other than in connection with a merger or consolidation), an acquiring person shall be subject to the requirements of the act if:

(1)(i) The acquiring person has annual net sales or total assets of $100 million (as adjusted) or more;

(ii) The joint venture or other corporation will have total assets of $10 million (as adjusted) or more; and

(iii) At least one other acquiring person has annual net sales or total assets of $10 million (as adjusted) or more; or

(2)(i) The acquiring person has annual net sales or total assets of $10 million (as adjusted) or more;

(ii) The joint venture or other corporation will have total assets of $100 million (as adjusted) or more; and

(iii) At least one other acquiring person has annual net sales or total assets of $10 million (as adjusted) or more.

(d) For purposes of paragraphs (b) and (c) of this section and determining whether any exemptions provided by the act and these rules apply to its formation, the assets of the joint venture or other corporation shall include:

(1) All assets which any person contributing to the formation of the joint venture or other corporation has agreed to transfer or for which agreements have been secured for the joint venture or other corporation to obtain at any time, whether or not such person is subject to the requirements of the act; and

(2) Any amount of credit or any obligations of the joint venture or other corporation which any person contributing to the formation has agreed to extend or guarantee, at any time.

(e) The commerce criterion of Section 7A(a)(1) is satisfied if either the activities of any acquiring person are in or affect commerce, or the person filing notification should reasonably believe that the activities of the joint venture or other corporation will be in or will affect commerce.

Examples: 1. Persons "A," "B," and "C" agree to create new corporation "N," a joint venture. "A," "B," and "C" will each hold one third of the shares of "N." "A" has more than $100 million (as adjusted) in annual net sales. "B" has more than $10 million (as adjusted) in total assets but less than $100 million (as adjusted) in annual net sales and total assets. Both "C's" total assets and its annual net sales are less than $10 million (as adjusted). "A," "B," and "C" are each engaged in commerce. "A," "B," and "C" have agreed to make an aggregate initial contribution to the new entity of $18 million in assets and each to make additional contributions of $21 million in each of the next three years. Under paragraph (d) of this section, the assets of the new corporation are $207 million. Under paragraph (c) of this section, "A" and "B" must file notification. Note that "A" and "B" also meet the criterion of Section 7A(a)(2)(B)(i) since they will be acquiring one third of the voting securities of the new entity for in excess of $50 million (as adjusted). N need not file notification; see § 802.41.

2. In the preceding example "A" has over $10 million (as adjusted) but less than $100 million (as adjusted) in sales and assets, "B"

and "C" have less than $10 million (as adjusted) in sales and assets. "N" has total assets of $500 million. Assume that "A" will acquire 50 percent of the voting securities of "N" and "B" and "C" will each acquire 25 percent. Since "A" will acquire in excess of $200 million (as adjusted) in voting securities of "N", the size-of-person test in §801.40(c) is inapplicable and "A" is required to file notification.

[43 FR 33537, July 31, 1978, as amended at 48 FR 34434, July 29, 1983; 52 FR 7082, Mar. 6, 1987; 66 FR 8690, Feb. 1, 2001; 70 FR 4992, Jan. 31, 2005]

§801.50 Formation of unincorporated entities.

(a) In the formation of an unincorporated entity (other than in connection with a consolidation), even though the persons contributing to the formation of the unincorporated entity and the unincorporated entity itself may, in the formation transaction, be both acquiring and acquired persons within the meaning of §801.2, the contributors shall be deemed acquiring persons only and the unincorporated entity shall be deemed the acquired person only.

(b) Unless exempted by the Act or any of these rules, upon the formation of an unincorporated entity, in a transaction meeting the criteria of Section 7A(a)(1) and 7A(a)(2)(A) (other than in connection with a consolidation), a person is subject to the requirements of the Act if it acquires control of the newly-formed entity. Unless exempted by the Act or any of these rules, upon the formation of an unincorporated entity, in a transaction meeting the criteria of Section 7A(a)(1), the criteria of Section 7A(a)(2)(B)(i) (other than in connection with a consolidation), a person is subject to the requirements of the Act if:

(1)(i) The acquiring person has annual net sales or total assets of $100 million (as adjusted) or more;

(ii) The newly-formed entity has total assets of $10 million (as adjusted) or more; and

(iii) The acquiring person acquires control of the newly-formed entity; or

(2)(i) The acquiring person has annual net sales or total assets of $10 million (as adjusted) or more;

(ii) The newly-formed entity has total assets of $100 million (as adjusted) or more; and

(iii) The acquiring person acquires control of the newly-formed entity.

(c) For purposes of paragraph (b) of this section, the total assets of the newly-formed entity is determined in accordance with §801.40(d).

(d) Any person acquiring control of the newly-formed entity determines the value of its acquisition in accordance with §801.10(d).

(e) The commerce criterion of Section 7A(a)(1) is satisfied if either the Activities of any acquiring person are in or affect commerce, or the person filing notification should reasonably believe that the Activities of the newly-formed entity will be in or will affect commerce.

Example: A and B form a new partnership (LP) in which each will acquire a 50 percent interest. A contributes a plant valued at $250 million and $100 million in cash. B contributes $350 million in cash. Because each is acquiring non-corporate interests, valued in excess of $50 million (as adjusted) which confer control of LP both A and B are acquiring persons in the formation. Each must now determine if the exemption in §802.4 is applicable to their acquisitions of non-corporate interests in LP. For A, LP's exempt assets consist of all of the cash contributed by A and B (pursuant to §801.21) and A's contribution of the plant (pursuant to §802.30(c)). Because all of the assets of LP are exempt with regard to A, A's acquisition of non-corporate interests in LP is exempt under §802.4. For B, LP's exempt assets include only the cash contributions by A and B. The plant contributed by A, valued at $250 million is not exempt under §802.30(c) with regard to B. Because LP has non-exempt assets in excess of $50 million (as adjusted) with regard to B, B's acquisition of non-corporate interests in LP is not exempt under §802.4. B must now value its acquisition of non-corporate interests pursuant to §801.10(d) and because the value of the non-corporate interests is the same as B's contribution to the formation ($350 million), the value exceeds $200 million (as adjusted) and B must file notification prior to acquiring non-corporate interests in LP. See additional examples following §§802.30(c) and 802.4.

[70 FR 11512, Mar. 8, 2005]

§801.90 Transactions or devices for avoidance.

Any transaction(s) or other device(s) entered into or employed for the purpose of avoiding the obligation to comply with the requirements of the act shall be disregarded, and the obligation to comply shall be determined by applying the act and these rules to the substance of the transaction.

Examples: 1. Suppose corporations A and B wish to form a joint venture. A and B contemplate a total investment of over $100 million (as adjusted) in the joint venture; persons "A" and "B" each have total assets in excess of $100 million (as adjusted). Instead of filing notification pursuant to §801.40, A creates a new subsidiary, A1, which issues half of its authorized shares to A. Assume that A1 has total assets of $3000. "A" then sells 50 percent of its A1 stock to "B" for $1500. Thereafter, "A" and "B" each contribute in excess of $50 million (as adjusted) to A1 in exchange for the remaining authorized A1 stock (one-fourth each to "A" and "B"). A's creation of A1 was exempt under Sec. 802.30; its $1500 sale of A1 stock to "B" did not meet the size-of-transaction filing threshold in Section 7A(a)(2)(B); and the second acquisition of stock in A1 by "A" and "B" was exempt under §802.30 and Sections 7A(c)(3) and (10). Since this scheme appears to be for the purpose of avoiding the requirements of the act, the sequence of transactions will be disregarded. The transactions will be viewed as the formation of a joint venture corporation by "A" and "B" having over $10 million (as adjusted) in assets. Such a transaction would be covered by §801.40 and "A" and "B" must file notification and observe the waiting period.

2. Suppose "A" wholly owns and operates a chain of twenty retail hardware stores, each of which is separately incorporated and has assets of less than $10 million. The aggregate fair market value of the assets of the twenty store corporations is in excess of $50 million (as adjusted). "A" proposes to sell the stores to "B" for in excess of $50 million (as adjusted). For various reasons it is decided that "B" will buy the stock of each of the store corporations from "A." Instead of filing notification and observing the waiting period as contemplated by the act, "A" and "B" enter into a series of five stock purchase-sale agreements for $12 million each. Under the terms of each contract, the stock of four stores will pass from "A" to "B". The five agreements are to be consummated on five successive days. Because after each of these transactions the store corporations are no longer part of the acquired person (§801.13(a) does not apply because control has passed, see §801.2), and because $12 million is below the size-of-transaction filing threshold of Section 7A(a)(2)(B), none of the contemplated acquisitions would be subject to the requirements of the act. However, if the stock of all of the store corporations were to be purchased in one transaction, no exemption would be applicable, and the act's requirements would have to be met. Because it appears that the purpose of making five separate contracts is to avoid the requirements of the act, this section would ignore the form of the separate transactions and consider the substance to be one transaction requiring compliance with the act.

[43 FR 33537, July 31, 1978, as amended at 66 FR 8691, Feb. 1, 2001; 67 FR 11903, Mar. 18, 2002; 70 FR 4992, Jan. 31, 2005]

PART 802—EXEMPTION RULES

Sec.

AUTHORITY: 15 U.S.C. 18a(d).

SOURCE: 43 FR 33544, July 31, 1978, unless otherwise noted.

§802.1 Acquisitions of goods in the ordinary course of business.

Pursuant to section 7A(c)(1) of the Clayton Act (the "Act"), acquisitions of goods transferred in the ordinary course of business are exempt from the notification requirements of the Act. This section identifies certain acquisitions of goods that are exempt as transfers in the ordinary course of business. This section also identifies certain acquisitions of goods that are not in the ordinary course of business and, therefore, do not qualify for the exemption.

(a) *Operating unit*. An acquisition of all or substantially all the assets of an operating unit is not an acquisition in the ordinary course of business. *Operating unit* means assets that are operated by the acquired person as a business undertaking in a particular location or for particular products or services, even though those assets may not be organized as a separate legal entity.

(b) *New goods*. An acquisition of new goods is in the ordinary course of business, except when the goods are acquired as part of an acquisition described in paragraph (a) of this section.

(c) *Current supplies*. An acquisition of current supplies is in the ordinary course of business, except when acquired as part of an acquisition described in paragraph (a) of this section. The term "current supplies" includes the following kinds of new or used assets:

(1) Goods acquired and held solely for the purpose of resale or leasing to an entity not within the acquiring person (e.g., inventory),

(2) Goods acquired for consumption in the acquiring person's business (e.g., office supplies, maintenance supplies or electricity), and

(3) Goods acquired to be incorporated in the final product (e.g., raw materials and components).

(d) *Used durable goods*. A good is "durable" if it is designed to be used repeatedly and has a useful life greater than one year. An acquisition of used durable goods is an acquisition in the ordinary course of business if the goods are not acquired as part of an acquisition described in paragraph (a) of this section and any of the following criteria are met:

(1) The goods are acquired and held solely for the purpose of resale or leasing to an entity not within the acquiring person; or

(2) The goods are acquired from an acquired person who acquired and has held the goods solely for resale or leasing to an entity not within the acquired person; or

(3) The acquired person has replaced, by acquisition or lease, all or substantially all of the productive capacity of the goods being sold within six months of that sale, or the acquired person has in good faith executed a contract to replace within six months after the sale, by acquisition or lease, all or substantially all of the productive capacity of the goods being sold; or

(4) The goods have been used by the acquired person solely to provide management and administrative support services for its business operations, and the acquired person has in good faith executed a contract to obtain substantially similar services as were provided by the goods being sold. Management and administrative support services include services such as accounting, legal, purchasing, payroll, billing and repair and maintenance of the acquired person's own equipment. Manufacturing, research and development, testing and distribution (i.e., warehousing and transportation) are not considered management and administrative support services.

Examples: 1. Greengrocer Inc. intends to sell to "A" all of the assets of one of the 12 grocery stores that it owns and operates throughout the metropolitan area of City X. Each of Greengrocer's stores constitutes an operating unit, i.e., a business undertaking in a particular location. Thus "A's" acquisition is not exempt as an acquisition in the ordinary course of business. However, the acquisition will not be subject to the notification requirements if the acquisition price or fair market value of the store's assets does not exceed $50 million (as adjusted).

2. "A," a manufacturer of airplane engines, agrees to pay in excess of $50 million (as adjusted) to "B," a manufacturer of airplane parts, for certain new engine components to be used in the manufacture of airplane engines. The acquisition is exempt under

§ 802.1(b) as new goods as well as under § 802.1(c)(3) as current supplies.

3. "A," a power generation company, proposes to purchase from "B," a coal company, in excess of $50 million (as adjusted) of coal under a long-term contract for use in its facilities to supply electric power to a regional public utility and steam to several industrial sites. This transaction is exempt under § 802.1(c)(2) as an acquisition of current supplies. However, if "A" proposed to purchase coal reserves rather than enter into a contract to acquire output of a coal mine, the acquisition would not be exempt as an acquisition of goods in the ordinary course of business. The acquisition may still be exempt pursuant to § 802.3(b) as an acquisition of reserves of coal if the requirements of that section are met.

4. "A," a national producer of canned fruit, preserves, jams and jellies, agrees to purchase from "B" for in excess of $50 million (as adjusted) a total of 20,000 acres of orchards and vineyards in several locations throughout the U.S. "A" plans to harvest the fruit from the acreage for use in its canning operations. The acquisition is not exempt under this section because orchards and vineyards are real property, not "goods." If, on the other hand, "A" had contracted to acquire from "B" the fruit and grapes harvested from the orchards and vineyards, the acquisition would qualify for the exemption as an acquisition of current supplies under paragraph (c)(3) of this section. Although the transfer of orchards and vineyards is not exempt under this section, the acquisition could be exempt under § 802.2(g) as an acquisition of agricultural property.

5. "A," a railcar leasing company, will purchase in excess of $50 million (as adjusted) of new railcars from a railcar manufacturer in order to expand its existing fleet of cars available for lease. The transaction is exempt under § 802.1(b) as an acquisition of new goods and § 802.1(c), as an acquisition of current supplies. If "A" subsequently sells the railcars to "C," a commercial railroad company, that acquisition would be exempt under § 802.1(d)(2), provided that "A" acquired and held the railcars solely for resale or leasing to an entity not within itself.

6. "A," a major oil company, proposes to sell two of its used oil tankers for in excess of $50 million (as adjusted) to "B," a dealer who purchases oil tankers from the major U.S. oil companies. "B's" acquisition of the used oil tankers is exempt under § 802.1(d)(1) provided that "B" is actually acquiring beneficial ownership of the used tankers and is not acting as an agent of the seller or purchaser.

7. "A," a cruise ship operator, plans to sell for in excess of $50 million (as adjusted) one of its cruise ships to "B," another cruise ship operator. "A" has, in good faith, executed a contract to acquire a new cruise ship with substantially the same capacity from a manufacturer. The contract specifies that "A" will receive the new cruise ship within one month after the scheduled date of the sale of its used cruise ship to "B." Since "B" is acquiring a used durable good that "A" has contracted to replace within six months of the sale, the acquisition is exempt under § 802.1(d)(3).

8. "A," a luxury cruise ship operator, proposes to sell to "B," a credit company engaged in the ordinary course of its business in lease financing transactions, its fleet of six passenger ships under a 10-year sale/leaseback arrangement. That acquisition is exempt pursuant to § 802.1(d)(1), used durable goods acquired for leasing purposes. The acquisition is also exempt under § 802.63(a) as a bona fide credit transaction entered into in the ordinary course of "B's" business. "B" now proposes to sell the ships, subject to the current lease financing arrangement, to "C," another lease financing company. This transaction is exempt under §§ 802.1(d)(1) and 802.1(d)(2).

9. Three months ago "A," a manufacturing company, acquired several new machines that will replace equipment on one of its production lines. "A's" capacity to produce the same products increased modestly when the integration of the new equipment was completed. "B," a manufacturing company that produces products similar to those produced by "A," has entered into a contract to acquire for in excess of $50 million (as adjusted) the machinery that "A" replaced. Delivery of the equipment by "A" to "B" is scheduled to occur within thirty days. Since "A" purchased new machinery to replace the productive capacity of the used equipment, which it sold within six months of the purchase of the new equipment, the acquisition by "B" is exempt under § 802.1(d)(3).

10. "A" will sell to "B" for in excess of $50 million (as adjusted) all of the equipment "A" uses exclusively to perform its billing requirements. "B" will use the equipment to provide "A's" billing needs pursuant to a contract which "A" and "B" executed 30 days ago in conjunction with the equipment purchase agreement. Although the assets "B" will acquire make up essentially all of the assets of one of "A's" management and administrative support services divisions, the acquisition qualifies for the exemption under § 802.1(d)(4) because a company's internal management and administrative support services, however organized, are not an operating unit as defined by § 802.1(a). Management and administrative support services are not a "business undertaking" as that term is used in § 802.1(a). Rather, they provide support and benefit to the company's operating units and support the company's business operations. However, if the assets being sold also derived revenues from providing billing services for third parties, then

the transfer of these assets would not be exempt under § 802.1(d)(4), since the equipment is not being used solely to provide management and administrative support services to "A".

11. "A," a manufacturer of pharmaceutical products, and "B" have entered into a contract under which "B" will provide all of "A's" research and development needs. Pursuant to the contract, "B" will also purchase all of the equipment that "A" formerly used to perform its own research and development activities. The sale of the equipment is not an exempt transaction under § 802.1(d)(3) because "A" is not replacing the productive capacity of the equipment being sold. The sale is also not exempt under § 802.1(d)(4), because functions such as research and development and testing are not management and administrative support services of a company but are integral to the design, development or production of the company's products.

12. "A," an automobile manufacturer, is discontinuing its manufacture of metal seat frames for its cars. "A" enters into a contract with "B," a manufacturer of various fabricated metal products, to sell its seat frame production lines and to purchase from "B" all of its metal seat frame needs for the next five years. This transfer of productive capacity by "A" is not exempt pursuant to § 802.1(d)(3), since "A" is not replacing the productive capacity of the equipment being sold. The acquisition is also not exempt under § 802.1(d)(4). "A's" sale of production lines is not the transfer of goods that provide management and administrative services to support the business operations of"A"; this manufacturing equipment is an integral part of "A's" production operations.

[61 FR 13684, Mar. 28, 1996, as amended at 66 FR 8691, Feb. 1, 2001; 70 FR 4993, Jan. 31, 2005; 83 FR 32770, July 16, 2018]

§ 802.2 Certain acquisitions of real property assets.

(a) *New facilities.* An acquisition of a new facility shall be exempt from the requirements of the act. A new facility is a structure that has not produced income and was either constructed by the acquired person for sale or held at all times by the acquired person solely for resale. The new facility may include realty, equipment or other assets incidental to the ownership of the new facility. In an acquisition that includes a new facility, the transfer of any other assets shall be subject to the requirements of the act and these rules as if they were being acquired in a separate acquisition.

(b) *Used facilities.* An acquisition of a used facility shall be exempt from the requirements of the act if the facility is acquired from a lessor that has held title to the facility for financing purposes in the ordinary course of the lessor's business by a lessee that has had sole and continuous possession and use of the facility since it was first built as a new facility. The used facility may include realty, equipment or other assets associated with the operation of the facility. In an acquisition that includes a used facility that meets the requirements of this paragraph, the transfer of any other assets shall be subject to the requirements of the act and these rules as if they were acquired in a separate transaction.

(c) *Unproductive real property.* An acquisition of unproductive real property shall be exempt from the requirements of the act. In an acquisition that includes unproductive real property, the transfer of any assets that are not unproductive real property shall be subject to the requirements of the act and these rules as if they were being acquired in a separate acquisition.

(1) Subject to the limitations of (c)(2), unproductive real property is any real property, including raw land, structures or other improvements (but excluding equipment), associated production and exploration assets as defined in § 802.3(c), natural resources and assets incidental to the ownership of the real property, that has not generated total revenues in excess of $5 million during the thirty-six (36) months preceding the acquisition.

(2) Unproductive real property does not include the following:

(i) Manufacturing or non-manufacturing facilities that have not yet begun operation;

(ii) Manufacturing or non-manufacturing facilities that were in operation at any time during the twelve (12) months preceding the acquisition; and

(iii) Real property that is either adjacent to or used in conjunction with real property that is not unproductive real property and is included in the acquisition.

(d) *Office and residential property.* (1) An acquisition of office or residential property shall be exempt from the requirements of the act. In an acquisition that includes office or residential property, the transfer of any assets that are not office or residential property shall be subject to the requirements of the act and these rules as if such assets were being transferred in a separate acquisition.

(2) Office and residential property is real property that is used primarily for office or residential purposes. In determining whether real property is used primarily for office or residential purposes, all real property, the acquisition of which is exempt under another provision of the act and these rules, shall be excluded from the determination. Office and residential property includes:

(i) Office buildings,

(ii) Residences,

(iii) Common areas on the property, including parking and recreational facilities, and

(iv) Assets incidental to the ownership of such property, including cash, prepaid taxes or insurance, rental receivables and the like.

(3) If the acquisition includes the purchase of a business conducted on the office and residential property, the transfer of that business, including the space in which the business is conducted, shall be subject to the requirements of the act and these rules as if such business were being transferred in a separate acquisition.

(e) *Hotels and motels.* (1) An acquisition of a hotel or motel, its improvements such as golf, swimming, tennis, restaurant, health club or parking facilities (but excluding ski facilities), and assets incidental to the ownership and operation of the hotel or motel (e.g., prepaid taxes or insurance, management contracts and licenses to use trademarks associated with the hotel or motel being acquired) shall be exempt from the requirements of the act. In an acquisition that includes a hotel or motel, the transfer of any assets that are not a hotel or motel, its improvements such as golf, swimming, tennis, restaurant, health club or parking facilities (but excluding ski facilities) and assets incidental to the ownership of the hotel or motel, shall be subject to the requirements of the act and these rules as if they were being acquired in a separate acquisition.

(2) Notwithstanding paragraph (1) of the section, an acquisition of a hotel or motel that includes a gambling casino shall be subject to the requirements of the act and these rules.

(f) *Recreational land.* An acquisition of recreational land shall be exempt from the requirements of the act. Recreational land is real property used primarily as a golf course or a swimming or tennis club facility, and assets incidental to the ownership of such property. In an acquisition that includes recreational land, the transfer of any property or assets that are not recreational land shall be subject to the requirements of the act and these rules as if they were being acquired in a separate acquisition.

(g) *Agricultural property.* An acquisition of agricultural property and assets incidental to the ownership of such property shall be exempt from the requirements of the Act. Agricultural property is real property that primarily generates revenues from the production of crops, fruits, vegetables, livestock, poultry, milk and eggs (certain activities within NAICS sector 11).

(1) Agricultural property does not include either:

(i) Processing facilities such as poultry and livestock slaughtering, processing and packing facilities; or

(ii) Any real property and assets either adjacent to or used in conjunction with processing facilities that are included in the acquisition; or

(iii) Timberland or other real property that generates revenues from activities within NAICS subsector 113 (Forestry and logging) or NAICS industry group 1153 (Support activities for forestry and logging).

(2) In an acquisition that includes agricultural property, the transfer of any assets that are not agricultural property or assets incidental to the ownership of such property (cash, prepaid taxes or insurance, rentals receivable and the like) shall be subject to the requirements of the act and these rules as if such assets were being transferred in a separate acquisition.

(h) *Retail rental space; warehouses.* An acquisition of retail rental space (including shopping centers) or warehouses and assets incidental to the ownership of retail rental space or warehouses shall be exempt from the requirements of the act, except when the retail rental space or warehouse is to be acquired in an acquisition of a business conducted on the real property. In an acquisition that includes retail rental space or warehouses, the transfer of any assets that are neither retail rental space nor warehouses shall be subject to the requirements of the act and these rules as if such assets were being transferred in a separate acquisition.

Examples. 1. "A," a major automobile manufacturer, builds a new automobile plant in anticipation of increased demand for its cars. The market does not improve and "A" never occupies the facility. "A" then sells the facility, which is fully equipped and ready for operation, to "B," another automobile manufacturer. The acquisition of this plant, including any equipment and assets associated with its operation, is not exempt as an acquisition of a new facility, even though the facility has not produced any income, since "A" did not construct the facility for sale or hold it at all times solely for resale. Also, the acquisition is not exempt as an acquisition of unproductive property, because manufacturing facilities that have not yet begun operations are explicitly excluded from that exemption.

2. "B," a subsidiary of "A," a financial institution, acquired a newly constructed power plant, which it leased to "X" pursuant to a lease financing arrangement. "A's" acquisition of the plant through B was exempt under § 802.63(a) as a bona fide credit transaction entered into in the ordinary course of "A's" business. "X" operated the plant as sole lessee for the next eight years and now proposes to exercise an option to buy the plant for in excess of $50 million (as adjusted). "X's" acquisition of the plant is exempt pursuant to § 802.2(b). The plant is being acquired from B, the lessor, which held title to the plant for financing purposes, and the purchaser, "X," has had sole and continuous possession and use of the plant since its construction.

3. "A" proposes to acquire a tract of wilderness land from "B" for consideration in excess of $50 million (as adjusted). Copper deposits valued in excess of $50 million (as adjusted) and timber reserves valued in excess of $50 million (as adjusted) are situated on the land and will be conveyed as part of this transaction. During the last three fiscal years preceding the sale, the property generated $50,000 from the sale of a small amount of timber cut from the reserves two years ago. "A's" acquisition of the wilderness land from "B" is exempt as an acquisition of unproductive real property because the property did not generate revenues exceeding $5 million during the thirty-six months preceding the acquisition. The copper deposits and timber reserves are by definition unproductive real property and, thus, are not separately subject to the notification requirements.

4. "A" proposes to purchase from "B" for in excess of $200 million (as adjusted) an old steel mill that is not currently operating to add to "A's" existing steel production capacity. The mill has not generated revenues during the 36 months preceding the acquisition but contains equipment valued in excess of $50 million (as adjusted) that "A" plans to refurbish for use in its operations. "A's" acquisition of the mill and the land on which it is located is exempt as unproductive real property. However, the transfer of the equipment and any assets other than the unproductive property is not exempt and is separately subject to the notification requirements of the act.

5. "A" proposes to purchase two downtown lots, Parcels 1 and 2, from "B" for in excess of $50 million (as adjusted). Parcel 1, located in the southwest section, contains no structures or improvements. A hotel is located in the northeast section on Parcel 2, and it has generated $9 million in revenues during the past three years. The purchase of Parcel 1 is exempt if it qualifies as unproductive real property, i.e., it has not generated annual revenues in excess of $5 million in the three fiscal years prior to the acquisition. Parcel 2 is not unproductive real property, but its acquisition is exempt under § 802.2(e) as the acquisition of a hotel.

6. "A" plans to purchase from "B," a manufacturer, a newly-constructed building that "B" had intended to equip for use in its manufacturing operations. "B" was unable to secure financing to purchase the necessary equipment and "A", also a manufacturer, will be required to invest in excess of $50 million (as adjusted) in order to equip the building for use in its production operations. This building is not a new facility under § 802.2 (a), because it was not constructed or held by "B" for sale or resale. However, the acquisition of the building qualifies for exemption as unproductive real property pursuant to § 802.2(c)(1). The building is not yet a manufacturing facility since it does not contain equipment and requires significant capital investment before it can be used as a manufacturing facility.

7. "A" proposes to purchase from "B," for in excess of $50 million (as adjusted), a 100 acre parcel of land that includes a currently operating factory occupying 10 acres. The other 90 adjoining acres are vacant and unimproved and are used by "B" for storage of supplies and equipment. The factory and the unimproved acreage have an aggregate fair market value of in excess of $50 million (as adjusted). The transaction is not exempt under § 802.2(c) because the vacant property is adjacent to property occupied by the operating factory. Moreover, if the 90 acres were

not adjacent to the 10 acres occupied by the factory, the transaction would not be exempt because the 90 acres are being used in conjunction with the factory being acquired and thus are not unproductive property.

8. "X" proposes to buy a five-story building from "Y." The ground floor of this building houses a department store, and "X" currently leases the third floor to operate a medical laboratory. The remaining three floors are used for offices. "X" is not acquiring the business of the department store. Because the ground floor is rental retail space, the acquisition of which is exempt under § 802.2(h), this part of the building is excluded from the determination of whether the building is used primarily for office purposes. The laboratory is therefore the only non-office use, and, since it makes up 25 percent of the remainder of the building, the building is used 75 percent for offices. Thus the building qualifies as an office building and its acquisition is therefore exempt under § 802.2(d).

9. "A" intends to acquire three shopping centers from "B" for a total of in excess of $200 million (as adjusted). The anchor stores in two of the shopping centers are department stores, the businesses of which "A" is buying from "B" as part of the overall transaction. The acquisition of the shopping centers is an acquisition of retail rental space that is exempt under § 802.2(h). However, "A's" acquisition of the department store businesses, including the portion of the shopping centers that the two department stores being purchased occupy, are separately subject to the notification requirements. If the value of these assets exceeds $50 million (as adjusted), "A" must comply with the requirements of the act for this part of the transaction.

10. "A" wishes to purchase from "B" a parcel of land for in excess of $50 million (as adjusted). The parcel contains a race track and a golf course. The golf course qualifies as recreational land pursuant to § 802.2(f), but the race track is not included in the exemption. Therefore, if the value of the race track is more than $50 million (as adjusted), "A" will have to file notification for the purchase of the race track.

11. "A" intends to purchase a poultry farm from "B." The acquisition of the poultry farm is a transfer of agricultural property that is exempt pursuant to § 802.2(g). If, however, "B" has a poultry slaughtering and processing facility on his farm that is included in the acquisition, "A's" acquisition of the farm is not exempt as an acquisition of agricultural property because agricultural property does not include property or assets adjacent to or used in conjunction with a processing facility that is included in an acquisition.

12. "A" proposes to purchase the prescription drug wholesale distribution business of "B" for in excess of $50 million (as adjusted). The business includes six regional warehouses used for "B's" national wholesale drug distribution business. Since "A" is acquiring the warehouses in connection with the acquisition of "B's" prescription drug wholesale distribution business, the acquisition of the warehouses is not exempt.

[61 FR 13686, Mar. 28, 1996, as amended at 66 FR 8692, Feb. 1, 2001; 66 FR 23565, May 9, 2001; 67 FR 11903, Mar. 18, 2002; 70 FR 4993, Jan. 31, 2005; 70 FR 11513, Mar. 8, 2005]

§ 802.3 Acquisitions of carbon-based mineral reserves.

(a) An acquisition of reserves of oil, natural gas, shale or tar sands, or rights to reserves of oil, natural gas, shale or tar sands together with associated exploration or production assets shall be exempt from the requirements of the act if the value of the reserves, the rights and the associated exploration or production assets to be held as a result of the acquisition does not exceed $500 million. In an acquisition that includes reserves of oil, natural gas, shale or tar sands, or rights to reserves of oil, natural gas, shale or tar sands and associated exploration or production assets, the transfer of any other assets shall be subject to the requirements of the act and these rules as if they were being acquired in a separate acquisition.

(b) An acquisition of reserves of coal, or rights to reserves of coal and associated exploration or production assets, shall be exempt from the requirements of the act if the value of the reserves, the rights and the associated exploration or production assets to be held as a result of the acquisition does not exceed $200 million. In an acquisition that includes reserves of coal, rights to reserves of coal and associated exploration or production assets, the transfer of any other assets shall be subject to the requirements of the act and these rules as if they were being acquired in a separate acquisition.

(c) Associated exploration or production assets means equipment, machinery, fixtures and other assets that are integral and exclusive to current or future exploration or production activities associated with the carbon-based mineral reserves that are being acquired. Associated exploration or production assets do not include the following:

(1) Any pipeline and pipeline system or processing facility which transports or processes oil and gas after it passes through the meters of a producing field located within reserves that are being acquired; and

(2) Any pipeline or pipeline system that receives gas directly from gas wells for transportation to a natural gas processing facility or other destination.

Examples: 1. "A" proposes to purchase from "B" for $550 million gas reserves that are not yet in production and have not generated any income. "A" will also acquire from "B" for $280 million producing oil reserves and associated assets such as wells, compressors, pumps and other equipment. The acquisition of the gas reserves is exempt as a transfer of unproductive property under §802.2(c). The acquisition of the oil reserves and associated assets is exempt pursuant to §802.3(a), since the value of the reserves and associated assets does not exceed the $500 million limitation.

2. "A," an oil company, proposes to acquire for $180 million oil reserves currently in production along with field pipelines and treating and metering facilities which serve such reserves exclusively. The acquisition of the reserves and the associated assets are exempt. "A" will also acquire from "B" for in excess of $50 million (as adjusted) a natural gas processing plant and its associated gathering pipeline system. This acquisition is not exempt since §802.3(c) excludes these assets from the exemption in §802.3 for transfers of associated exploration or production assets.

3. "A," an oil company, proposes to acquire a coal mine currently in operation and associated production assets for $90 million from "B," an oil company. "A" will also purchase from "B" producing oil reserves valued at $100 million and an oil refinery valued at $13 million. The acquisition of the coal mine and the oil reserves is exempt pursuant to §802.3. Although §802.3(c) excludes the refinery from the exemption in §802.3 for transfers of associated exploration and production assets, "A's" acquisition of the refinery is not subject to the notification requirements of the act because its value does not exceed $50 million (as adjusted).

4. "X" proposes to acquire from "Z" coal reserves which, together with associated exploration assets, are valued at $230 million. Since the value of the reserves and the assets exceeds the $200 million limitation in §802.3(b), this transaction is not exempt under §802.3. However, if the coal reserves qualify as unproductive property under the requirements of §802.2(c), their acquisition, along with the acquisition of their associated assets, would be exempt.

[61 FR 13688, Mar. 28, 1996, as amended at 66 FR 8692, Feb. 1, 2001; 70 FR 4994, Jan. 31, 2005]

§802.4 Acquisitions of voting securities of issuers or non-corporate interests in unincorporated entities holding certain assets the acquisition of which is exempt.

(a) An acquisition of voting securities of an issuer or non-corporate interests in an unincorporated entity whose assets together with those of all entities it controls consist or will consist of assets whose acquisition is exempt from the requirements of the Act pursuant to section 7A(c) of the Act, this part 802, or pursuant to §801.21, is exempt from the reporting requirements if the acquired issuer or unincorporated entity and all entities it controls do not hold non-exempt assets with an aggregate fair market value of more than $50 million (as adjusted). The value of voting or non-voting securities of any other issuer or interests in any unincorporated entity not included within the acquired issuer or unincorporated entity does not count toward the $50 million (as adjusted) limitation for non-exempt assets.

(b) For purposes of paragraph (a) of this section, the assets of all issuers and unincorporated entities that are being acquired from the same acquired person are included in determining if the limitation for non-exempt assets is exceeded.

(c) In connection with paragraph (a) of this section and §801.15 (b), the value of the assets of an issuer whose voting securities or an unincorporated entity whose non-corporate interests are being acquired pursuant to this section shall be the fair market value, determined in accordance with §801.10(c).

Examples: 1. "A," a real estate investment company, proposes to purchase 100 percent of the voting securities of C, a wholly-owned subsidiary of "B," a construction company. C's assets are a newly constructed, never occupied hotel, including fixtures, furnishings and insurance policies. The acquisition of the hotel would be exempt under §802.2(a) as a new facility and under §802.2(d). Therefore, the acquisition of the voting securities of C is exempt pursuant to §802.4(a) since C holds assets whose direct purchase would be exempt under § 802.2 and does not hold non-exempt assets exceeding $50 million (as adjusted) in value.

2. "A" proposes to acquire 60 percent of the voting securities of C from "B." C's assets consist of a portfolio of mortgages valued at $55 million and a small manufacturing plant valued at $26 million. The manufacturing plant is an operating unit for purposes of § 802.1(a). Since the acquisition of the mortgages would be exempt pursuant to Section 7A(c)(2) of the act and since the value of the non-exempt manufacturing plant is less than $50 million (as adjusted), this acquisition is exempt under § 802.4(a).

3. "A" proposes to acquire from "B" 100 percent of the voting securities of each of three issuers, M, N and O, simultaneously. M's assets consist of oil reserves worth $160 million and coal reserves worth $40 million. N has assets consisting of $130 million of gas reserves and $100 million of coal reserves. O's assets are oil shale reserves worth $140 million and a coal mine worth $80 million. Since "A" is simultaneously acquiring the voting securities of three issuers from the same acquired person, it must aggregate the assets of the issuers to determine if any of the limitations in § 802.3 is exceeded. As a result of aggregating the assets of M, N and O, "A's" holdings of oil and gas reserves are below the $500 limitation for such assets in § 802.3(a). However, the aggregated holdings exceed the $200 million limitation for coal reserves in § 802.3(b). "A's" acquisition therefore is not exempt, and it must report the entire transaction.

[61 FR 13688, Mar. 28, 1996, as amended at 66 FR 8693, Feb. 1, 2001; 70 FR 4994, Jan. 31, 2005; 70 FR 11513, Mar. 8, 2005; 76 FR 42482, July 19, 2011]

§ 802.5 Acquisitions of investment rental property assets.

(a) Acquisitions of investment rental property assets shall be exempt from the requirements of the act.

(b) Investment rental property assets. "Investment rental property assets" means real property that will not be rented to entities included within the acquiring person except for the sole purpose of maintaining, managing or supervising the operation of the real property, and will be held solely for rental or investment purposes. In an acquisition that includes investment rental property assets, the transfer of any property or assets that are not investment rental property assets shall be subject to the requirements of the act and these rules as if they were being acquired in a separate transaction. Investment rental property assets include:

(1) Property currently rented,

(2) Property held for rent but not currently rented,

(3) Common areas on the property, and

(4) Assets incidental to the ownership of property, which may include cash, prepaid taxes or insurance, rental receivables and the like.

Example: 1. "X", a corporation, proposes to purchase a sports/entertainment complex which it will rent to professional sports teams and promoters of special events for concerts, ice shows, sporting events and other entertainment activities. "X" will provide office space in the complex for "Y", a management company which will maintain and manage the facility for "X." This acquisition is an exempt acquisition of investment rental property assets since "X" intends to rent the facility to third parties and is providing space within the facility to a management company solely to maintain, manage or supervise the operation of the facility on its behalf. If, however, "X" controls Z, a concert promoter to whom it also intends to rent the complex, the acquisition would not be exempt under § 802.5, since the property would not meet the requirements of § 802.5(b)(1).

2. "X" intends to buy from "Y" a development commonly referred to as an industrial park. The industrial park contains a warehouse/distribution center, a retail tire and automobile parts store, an office building, and a small factory. The industrial park also contains several parcels of vacant land. If "X" intends to acquire this industrial park as investment rental property, the acquisition will be exempt pursuant to § 802.5. If, however, "X" intends to use the factory for its own manufacturing operations, this exemption would be unavailable. The exemptions in § 802.2 for warehouses, rental retail space, office buildings, and undeveloped land may still apply and, if the value of the factory is $50 million (as adjusted) or less, the entire transaction may be exempted by that section.

[61 FR 13688, Mar. 28, 1996, as amended at 66 FR 8693, Feb. 1, 2001; 70 FR 4994, Jan. 31, 2005]

§ 802.6 Federal agency approval.

(a) For the purposes of section 7A (c)(6) and (c)(8), the term *information and documentary material* includes one copy of all documents, application forms, and all written submissions of any type whatsoever. In lieu of providing all such information and documentary material, or any portion thereof, one copy of an index describing such information and documentary material may be provided, together with a certification that any such information or documentary material not provided will be provided within 10 calendar days upon request by the Federal Trade Commission or Assistant Attorney General, or a delegated official of either. Any material submitted pursuant to this section shall be submitted to the offices specified in §803.10(c).

(b)(1) A mixed transaction is one that has some portion that is exempt under Section 7A (c)(6), (c)(7) or (c)(8) because it requires regulatory agency premerger competitive review and approval, and another portion that does not require such review.

(2) The portion of a mixed transaction that does not require advance competitive review and approval by a regulatory agency is subject to the act and these rules as if it were being acquired in a separate acquisition.

Example: Bank "A" acquires Bank "B", which owns a financial subsidiary engaged in securities underwriting. "A"'s acquisition of "B" requires agency approval by the Office of the Comptroller of the Currency, the Board of Governors of the Federal Reserve System or Federal Deposit Insurance Corporation (depending on whether "A" is a national bank, state member bank, or state non-member bank under section 18(c) of the FDI Act), and therefore is exempt from filing under Section 7A (c)(7). However, the acquisition of the financial subsidiary is subject to HSR reporting requirements, and "A" and "B" each must make a filing for that portion of the transaction and observe the waiting period if the act's thresholds are met.

[43 FR 33544, July 31, 1978, as amended at 48 FR 34435, July 29, 1983; 66 FR 8693, Feb. 1, 2001; 67 FR 11903, Mar. 18, 2002]

§ 802.8 Certain supervisory acquisitions.

(a) A merger, consolidation, purchase of assets, or acquisition requiring agency approval under sections 403 or 408(e) of the National Housing Act, 12 U.S.C. 1726, 1730a(e), or under section 5 of the Home Owners' Loan Act of 1933, 12 U.S.C. 1464, shall be exempt from the requirements of the act, including specifically the filing requirement of Section 7A(c)(8), if the agency whose approval is required finds that approval of such merger, consolidation, purchase of assets, or acquisition is necessary to prevent the probable failure of one of the institutions involved.

(b)(1) A merger, consolidation, purchase of assets, or acquisition which requires agency approval under 12 U.S.C. 1817(j) or 12 U.S.C. 1730(q) shall be exempt from the requirements of the act if copies of all information and documentary materials filed with any such agency are contemporaneously filed with the Federal Trade Commission and the Assistant Attorney General at least 30 days prior to consummation of the proposed acquisition.

(2) A transaction described in paragraph (b)(1) of this section shall be exempt from the requirements of the act, including specifically the filing requirement, if the agency whose approval is required finds that approval of such transaction is necessary to prevent the probable failure of one of the institutions involved.

[43 FR 33544, July 31, 1978, as amended at 48 FR 34436, July 29, 1983; 67 FR 11903, Mar. 18, 2002]

§ 802.9 Acquisition solely for the purpose of investment.

An acquisition of voting securities shall be exempt from the requirements of the act pursuant to section 7A(c)(9) if made solely for the purpose of investment and if, as a result of the acquisition, the acquiring person would hold ten percent or less of the outstanding voting securities of the issuer, regardless of the dollar value of voting securities so acquired or held.

Examples: 1. Suppose that acquiring person "A" acquires 6 percent of the voting securities of issuer X, valued in excess of $50 million (as adjusted). If the acquisition is solely for the purpose of investment, it is exempt under Section 7A(c)(9).

2. After the acquisition in example 1, "A" decides to acquire an additional 7 percent of the voting securities of X. Regardless of "A"'s intentions, the acquisition is not exempt under section 7A(c)(9).

3. After the acquisition in example 1, acquiring person "A" decides to participate in the management of issuer X. Any subsequent

acquisitions of X stock by "A" would not be exempt under section 7A(c)(9).

[43 FR 33544, July 31, 1978, as amended at 66 FR 8693, Feb. 1, 2001; 70 FR 4994, Jan. 31, 2005]

§ 802.10 Stock dividends and splits; reorganizations.

(a) The acquisition of voting securities pursuant to a stock split or pro rata stock dividend is exempt from the requirements of the Act under section 7A(c)(10).

(b) An acquisition of non-corporate interests or voting securities as a result of the conversion of a corporation or unincorporated entity into a new entity is exempt from the requirements of the Act if:

(1) No new assets will be contributed to the new entity as a result of the conversion; and

(2) Either:

(i) As a result of the transaction the acquiring person does not increase its per centum holdings in the new entity relative to its per centum holdings in the original entity; or

(ii) The acquiring person controlled the original entity.

Examples: 1. Partners A and B hold 60 percent and 40 percent respectively of the partnership interests in C. C is converted to a corporation in which A and B hold 60 percent and 40 percent respectively of the voting securities. No new assets are contributed. The conversion to a corporation is exempt from notification for both A and B.

2. Shareholder A holds 55% and B holds 45% of the voting securities of corporation C. C is converted to a limited liability company in which A holds 60% and B holds 40% of the membership interests. No new assets are contributed. The conversion to a limited liability company is exempt from notification because A controlled the corporation. If however, B holds 55% and A holds 45% in the new limited liability company, the conversion is not exempt for B and may require notification because control changes.

3. Shareholders A, B and C each hold one third of the voting securities of corporation X. Pursuant to a reorganization agreement, A and B each contribute new assets to X and C contributes cash. X is then being reincorporated in a new state. Each of A, B and C receive one third of the voting securities of newly reincorporated C. The reincorporation is not exempt from notification and may be reportable for A, B and C because of the contribution of new assets.

[70 FR 11513, Mar. 8, 2005]

§ 802.20 [Reserved]

§ 802.21 Acquisitions of voting securities not meeting or exceeding greater notification threshold (as adjusted).

(a) An acquisition of voting securities shall be exempt from the requirements of the act if:

(1) The acquiring person and all other persons required by the act and these rules to file notification filed notification with respect to an earlier acquisition of voting securities of the same issuer;

(2) The waiting period with respect to the earlier acquisition has expired, or been terminated pursuant to § 803.11, and the acquisition will be consummated within 5 years of such expiration or termination; and

(3) The acquisition will not increase the holdings of the acquiring person to meet or exceed a notification threshold (as adjusted) greater than the greatest notification threshold met or exceeded in the earlier acquisition.

Examples: 1. In 2004, Corporation A acquired $53 million of the voting securities of corporation B and both "A" and "B" filed notification as required, indicating the $50 million threshold. Within five years of the expiration of the original waiting period, "A" acquires additional voting securities of B but not in an amount sufficient to meet or exceed $100 million (as adjusted) or 50 percent of the voting securities of B. No additional notification is required.

2. In 2004, Corporation A acquired $53 million of the voting securities of corporation B and both "A" and "B" filed notification as required, indicating the $50 million threshold. Suppose that in year three following the expiration of the waiting period, the $50 million notification threshold has been adjusted to $56 million pursuant to Section 7A(a)(2)(a) of the Act. "A" now intends to acquire an additional $5 million of the voting securities of B. "A" is not required to file another notification even though it now holds voting securities in excess of the $56 million notification threshold (which is greater than the $50 million notification threshold indicated in its filing), because it has not met or exceeded a notification threshold (as adjusted) greater than the notification threshold exceeded in the earlier acquisition (i.e. $100 million (as adjusted) or 50% notification thresholds).

3. Same facts as in Example 2 above except now the five year period has expired. Suppose that, the $50 million notification threshold has been adjusted to $57 million

pursuant to Section 7A(a)(2)(a) of the Act. "A" now holds $58 million of voting securities of B. Because § 802.21(a)(2) is no longer satisfied, the acquisition of any additional voting securities of B will require a new filing because "A" will hold voting securities valued in excess of the $57 million notification threshold. If, however, the $50 million notification threshold had been adjusted to $60 million at the end of the five-year period, A could acquire up to that threshold without a new filing.

4. This section also allows a person to recross any of the threshold notification levels that were in effect at the time of filing notification any number of times within five years of the expiration of the waiting period following notification. Thus, if in Example 1, "A" had disposed of some voting securities so that it held less than $50 million of the voting securities of B, and thereafter had increased its holdings to more than $50 million but less than $100 million or 50 percent of B, notification would not be required if the increase occurred within 5 years of the expiration of the original waiting period.

5. A files notification at the $50 million notification threshold and acquires $51 million of the voting securities of B in the year following expiration of the waiting period. The next greater notification threshold at the time of filing was $100 million. In year three, the $100 million notification threshold has been adjusted to $106 million. A can now acquire up to, but not meet or exceed, voting securities of B valued at $106 million. As the original $100 million threshold is adjusted upward in years four and five, A can acquire up to those new thresholds as the adjustments are effected.

6. A files notification at the $50 million threshold in January of year one. In February of year one, the $50 million threshold is adjusted to $52 million. A only needs to acquire in excess of $50 million of voting securities of B, not in excess of $52 million, to have exceeded the threshold which was filed for in the year following expiration of the waiting period (see § 803.7). It may then acquire up to the next greater notification threshold (as adjusted) during the five years following expiration of the waiting period.

(b) [Reserved]

[43 FR 33544, July 31, 1978, as amended at 66 FR 8693, Feb. 1, 2001; 67 FR 11906, Mar. 18, 2002; 70 FR 4995, Jan. 31, 2005; 76 FR 42482, July 19, 2011]

§ 802.23 Amended or renewed tender offers.

Whenever a tender offer is amended or renewed after notification has been filed by the offeror, no new notification shall be required, and the running of the waiting period shall be unaffected, except as follows:

(a) If the number of voting securities to be acquired pursuant to the offer is increased such that a greater notification threshold would be met or exceeded, only the acquiring person need again file notification, but a new waiting period must be observed;

(b) If a noncash tender offer is amended to become a cash tender offer, (1) one copy of the amended tender offer shall be filed in the manner prescribed by § 803.10(c) with the Federal Trade Commission and Assistant Attorney General, and (2) subject to the provisions of § 803.10(b)(1), the waiting period shall expire on the 15th day after the date of receipt (determined in accordance with § 803.10(c)) of the amended tender offer, or on the 30th day after filing notification, whichever is earlier; or

(c) If a cash tender offer is amended to become a noncash tender offer, (1) one copy of the amended tender offer shall be filed in the manner prescribed by § 803.10(c) with the Federal Trade Commission and Assistant Attorney General, and (2) subject to the provisions of § 803.10(b)(1), the waiting period shall expire on the 15th day after the date of receipt (as determined in accordance with § 803.10(c)) of the amended tender offer, or on the 30th day after filing notification, whichever is later.

Examples: 1. Assume that corporation A makes a tender offer for 20 percent of the voting securities of corporation B and that "A" files notification. Under this section, if A subsequently amends its tender offer only as to the amount of consideration offered, the waiting period so commenced is not affected, and no new notification need be filed.

2. In the previous example, assume that A makes an amended tender offer for 27 percent of the voting securities of B, valued at greater than $1 billion. Since a new notification threshold will be crossed, this section requires that "A" must again file notification and observe a new waiting period. Paragraph (a) of this section, however, provides that "B" need not file notification again.

3. Assume that "A" makes a tender offer for shares of corporation B. "A" includes its voting securities as part of the consideration. "A" files notification. Five days later, "A" changes its tender offer to a cash tender offer, and on the same day files copies of its amended tender offer with the offices designated in § 803.10(c). Under paragraph (b) of

this section, the waiting period expires (unless extended or terminated) 15 days after the receipt of the amended offer (on the 20th day after filing notification), since that occurs earlier than the expiration of the original waiting period (which would occur on the 30th day after filing).

4. Assume that "A" makes a cash tender offer for shares of corporation B and files notification. Six days later, "A" amends the tender offer and adds voting securities as consideration, and on the same day files copies of the amended tender offer with the offices designated in § 803.10(c). Under paragraph (c) of this section, the waiting period expires (unless extended or terminated) on the 30th day following the date of filing of notification (determined under § 803.10(c)), since that occurs later than the 15th day after receipt of the amended tender offer (which would occur on the 21st day).

[43 FR 33544, July 31, 1978; 43 FR 36054, Aug. 15, 1978, as amended at 66 FR 8694, Feb. 1, 2001]

§ 802.30 Intraperson transactions.

(a) An acquisition (other than the formation of a corporation or unincorporated entity under § 801.40 or § 801.50 of this chapter) in which the acquiring and at least one of the acquired persons are, the same person by reason of § 801.1(b)(1) of this chapter, or in the case of a not-for-profit corporation which has no outstanding voting securities, by reason of § 801.1(b)(2) of this chapter, is exempt from the requirements of the Act.

Examples to paragraph (a): 1. A and B each have the right to 50% of the profits of partnership X. A also holds 100% of the voting securities of corporation Y. A pays B in excess of $50 million in cash (as adjusted) and transfers certain assets of X to Y. Because A is the acquiring person through its control of Y, pursuant to § 801.1(b)(1)(i), and one of the acquired persons through its control of X pursuant to § 801.1(b)(1)(ii), the acquisition of assets is exempt under § 802.30(a).

2. A and B each have the right to 50% of the profits of partnership X. A contributes assets to X valued in excess of $50 million (as adjusted). B contributes cash to X. Because B is an acquiring person but not an acquired person, its acquisition of the assets contributed to X by A is not exempt under § 802.30(a). However, A is both an acquiring and acquired person, and its acquisition of the assets it is contributing to X is exempt under § 802.30(a).

(b) The formation of any wholly owned entity is exempt from the requirements of the Act.

(c) For purposes of applying § 802.4(a) to an acquisition that may be reportable under § 801.40 or § 801.50, assets, voting securities, or non-corporate interests contributed by the acquiring person to a new entity upon its formation are assets, voting securities, or non- corporate interests whose acquisition by that acquiring person is exempt from the requirements of the Act.

Examples to paragraph (c): 1. A and B form a new partnership to which A contributes a manufacturing plant valued at $102 million and acquires a 51% interest in the partnership. B contributes $98 million in cash and acquires a 49% interest. B is not acquiring non-corporate interests which confer control of the partnership and therefore is not making a reportable acquisition. A is acquiring non-corporate interests which confer control of the partnership, however, the manufacturing plant it is contributing to the formation is exempt under § 802.30(c) and the cash contributed by B is excluded under § 801.21, therefore, the acquisition of non-corporate interests by A is exempt under § 802.4.

2. A and B form a new corporation to which A contributes a plant valued at $120 million and acquires 60% of the voting securities of the new corporation. B contributes a plant valued at $80 million and acquires 40% of the voting securities of the new corporation. While the assets contributed to the formation are exempted by § 802.30(c) for each of A and B, the new corporation holds more than $50 million (as adjusted) in non-exempt assets (the plant contributed by the other person) with respect to both acquisitions. A is now acquiring voting securities of an issuer which holds $80 million in non-exempt assets (the plant contributed by B), and B is acquiring voting securities of an issuer which holds $120 million in non-exempt assets (the plant contributed by A). Therefore neither acquisition of voting securities is exempt under § 802.4. Note that in contrast to the formation of the partnership in Example 1, B is not required to acquire a controlling interest in the corporation in order to have a reportable transaction.

3. A and B form a 50/50 partnership. A contributes a plant valued at $100 million and B contributes a plant valued at $40 million and $60 million in cash. Because with respect to A, the new partnership has non-exempt assets of $40 million (the plant contributed by B), A's acquisition of non-corporate interests is exempt under § 802.4. With respect to B, the new partnership holds in excess of $50 million (as adjusted) in non-exempt assets (the plant contributed by A), therefore B's

acquisition of non-corporate interests would not be exempt under §802.4.

[70 FR 11513, Mar. 8, 2005, as amended at 83 FR 32771, July 16, 2018]

§802.31 Acquisitions of convertible voting securities.

Acquisitions of convertible voting securities shall be exempt from the requirements of the act.

Example: This section applies regardless of the dollar value of the convertible voting securities held or to be acquired. Note, however, that subsequent conversions of convertible voting securities may be subject to the requirements of the act. See §801.32.

[43 FR 33544, July 31, 1978, as amended at 66 FR 8694, Feb. 1, 2001]

§802.35 Acquisitions by employee trusts.

An acquisition of voting securities shall be exempt from the notification requirements of the act if:

(a) The securities are acquired by a trust that meets the qualifications of section 401 of the Internal Revenue Code;

(b) The trust is controlled by a person that employs the beneficiaries and,

(c) The voting securities acquired are those of that person or an entity within that person.

Examples: 1. Company A establishes a trust for its employees that meets the qualifications of section 401 of the Internal Revenue Code. Company A has the power to designate the trustee of the trust. That trust then acquires 30% of the voting securities of Company A for in excess of $50 million (as adjusted). Later, the trust acquires 20% of the stock of Company B, a wholly-owned subsidiary of Company A, for in excess of $50 million (as adjusted). Neither acquisition is reportable.

2. Assume that in the example above, "A" has total assets of $100 million (as adjusted). "C" also has total assets of $100 million (as adjusted) and is not controlled by Company A. The trust controlled by Company A plans to acquire 40 percent of the voting securities of Company C for in excess of $50 million (as adjusted). Since Company C is not included within "A," "A" must observe the requirements of the act before the trust makes the acquisition of Company C's shares.

[52 FR 7082, Mar. 6, 1987, as amended at 66 FR 8694, Feb. 1, 2001; 70 FR 4995, Jan. 31, 2005]

§802.40 Exempt formation of corporations or unincorporated entities.

The formation of an entity is exempt from the requirements of the Act if the entity will be not-for-profit within the meaning of sections 501(c)(1)–(4), (6)–(15), (17)–(20) or (d) of the Internal Revenue Code.

[70 FR 11514, Mar. 8, 2005]

§802.41 Corporations or unincorporated entities at time of formation.

Whenever any person(s) contributing to the formation of an entity are subject to the requirements of the Act by reason of §801.40 or §801.50 of this chapter, the new entity need not file the notification required by the Act and §803.1 of this chapter.

Examples: 1. Corporations A and B, each having sales of in excess of $100 million (as adjusted), each propose to contribute in excess of $50 million (as adjusted) in assets in exchange for 50 percent of the voting securities of a new corporation, N. Under this section, the new corporation need not file notification, although both A and B must do so and observe the waiting period prior to receiving any voting securities of N.

2. In addition to the facts in Example 1 of this section, A and B have agreed that upon creation N will purchase 100 percent of the voting securities of corporation C for in excess of $50 million (as adjusted). Because N's purchase of C is not a transaction in connection with N's formation, and because in any event C is not a contributor to the formation of N, "A," "B" and "C" must file with respect to the proposed acquisition of C and must observe the waiting period.

[43 FR 33544, July 31, 1978, as amended at 52 FR 7082, Mar. 6, 1987; 70 FR 4995, Jan. 31, 2005; 70 FR 11514, Mar. 8, 2005; 83 FR 32771, July 16, 2018]

§802.42 Partial exemption for acquisitions in connection with the formation of certain joint ventures or other corporations.

(a) Whenever one or more of the contributors in the formation of a joint venture or other corporation which otherwise would be subject to the requirements of the act by reason of §801.40 are exempt from these requirements under section 7A(c)(8), any other contributor in the formation which is subject to the act and not exempt under section 7A(c)(8) need not file a

Notification and Report Form, provided that no less than 30 days prior to the date of consummation any such contributor claiming this exemption has submitted an affidavit to the Federal Trade Commission and to the Assistant Attorney General stating its good faith intention to make the proposed acquisition and asserting the applicability of this exemption.

(b) Persons relieved of the requirement to file a Notification and Report Form pursuant to paragraph (a) of this section remain subject to all other provisions of the act and these rules.

[48 FR 34436, July 29, 1983]

§ 802.50 Acquisitions of foreign assets.

(a) The acquisition of assets located outside the United States shall be exempt from the requirements of the act unless the foreign assets the acquiring person would hold as a result of the acquisition generated sales in or into the U.S. exceeding $50 million (as adjusted) during the acquired person's most recent fiscal year.

(b) Where the foreign assets being acquired exceed the threshold in paragraph (a) of this section, the acquisition nevertheless shall be exempt where:

(1) Both acquiring and acquired persons are foreign;

(2) The aggregate sales of the acquiring and acquired persons in or into the United States are less than $110 million (as adjusted) in their respective most recent fiscal years;

(3) The aggregate total assets of the acquiring and acquired persons located in the United States (other than investment assets, voting or nonvoting securities of another person, and assets included pursuant to § 801.40(d)(2) of this chapter) are less than $110 million (as adjusted); and

(4) The transaction does not meet the criteria of Section 7A(a)(2)(A).

Example to § 802.50: 1. Assume that "A" and "B" are both U.S. persons. "A" proposes selling to "B" a manufacturing plant located abroad. Sales in or into the United States attributable to the plant totaled $13 million in the most recent fiscal year. The transaction is exempt under this paragraph (a) of this section.

2. Sixty days after the transaction in example 1, "A" proposes to sell to "B" a second manufacturing plant located abroad; sales in or into the United States attributable to this plant, when combined with the sales into the United States of the first plant, totaled in excess of $50 million (as adjusted) in the most recent fiscal year. Since "B" would be acquiring the second plant within 180 days of the first plant, both plants would be considered assets of "A" held by "B" as a result of the second acquisition (see § 801.13(b)(2) of this chapter). Since the total sales in or into the United States exceed $50 million (as adjusted), the acquisition of the second plant would not be exempt under this paragraph (a) of this section.

3. Assume that "A" and "B" are foreign persons with aggregate sales in or into the United States of in excess of $110 million (as adjusted). If "A" acquires only foreign assets of "B," and if those assets generated $50 million (as adjusted) or less in sales in or into the United States, the transaction is exempt.

4. Assume that "A" and "B" are foreign persons with aggregate sales in or into the United States and assets located in the United Sates of less than $110 million (as adjusted). If "A" acquires only foreign assets of "B," and those assets generated in excess of $50 million (as adjusted) in sales in or into the United States during the most recent fiscal year, the transaction is exempt from reporting if the assets are valued at $200 million (as adjusted) or less, but is reportable if valued at greater than $200 million (as adjusted).

[67 FR 11903, Mar. 18, 2002, as amended at 70 FR 4995, Jan. 31, 2005]

§ 802.51 Acquisitions of voting securities of a foreign issuer.

(a) *By U.S. persons.* (1) The acquisition of voting securities of a foreign issuer by a U.S. person shall be exempt from the requirements of the act unless the issuer (including all entities controlled by the issuer) either: holds assets located in the United States (other than investment assets, voting or nonvoting securities of another person, and assets included pursuant to § 801.40(d)(2) of this chapter) having an aggregate total value of over $50 million (as adjusted); or made aggregate sales in or into the United States of over $50 million (as adjusted) in its most recent fiscal year.

(2) If interests in multiple foreign issuers are being acquired from the same acquired person, the assets located in the United States and sales in or into the United States of all the

issuers must be aggregated to determine whether either $50 million (as adjusted) limitation is exceeded.

(b) *By foreign persons.* (1) The acquisition of voting securities of a foreign issuer by a foreign person shall be exempt from the requirements of the act unless the acquisition will confer control of the issuer and the issuer (including all entities controlled by the issuer) either: holds assets located in the United States (other than investment assets, voting or nonvoting securities of another person, and assets included pursuant to § 801.40(d)(2) of this chapter) having an aggregate total value of over $50 million (as adjusted); or made aggregate sales in or into the United States of over $50 million (as adjusted) in its most recent fiscal year.

(2) If controlling interests in multiple foreign issuers are being acquired from the same acquired person, the assets located in the United States and sales in or into the United States of all the issuers must be aggregated to determine whether either $50 million (as adjusted) limitation is exceeded.

(c) Where a foreign issuer whose securities are being acquired exceeds the threshold in paragraph (b)(1) of this section, the acquisition nevertheless shall be exempt where:

(1) Both acquiring and acquired persons are foreign;

(2) The aggregate sales of the acquiring and acquired persons in or into the United States are less than $110 million (as adjusted) in their respective most recent fiscal years;

(3) The aggregate total assets of the acquiring and acquired persons located in the United States (other than investment assets, voting or nonvoting securities of another person, and assets included pursuant to § 801.40(d)(2) of this chapter) are less than $110 million (as adjusted); and

(4) The transaction does not meet the criteria of Section 7A(a)(2)(A).

Example to § 802.51 1. "A," a U.S. person, is to acquire the voting securities of C, a foreign issuer. C has no assets in the United States, but made aggregate sales into the United States of in excess of 50 million (as adjusted) in the most recent fiscal year. The transaction is not exempt under this section.

2. Assume that "A" and "B" are foreign persons with aggregate sales in or into the United States in excess of $110 million (as adjusted), and that "A" is acquiring 100% of the voting securities of "B." Included within "B" is U.S. issuer C, whose total U.S. assets are valued in excess of $50 million (as adjusted). Since "A" will be acquiring control of an issuer, C, with total U.S. assets of more than $50 million (as adjusted), and the parties' aggregate sales in or into the U.S. in the relevant time period exceed $110 million (as adjusted), the acquisition is not exempt under this section.

3. "A," a foreign person, intends to acquire 100 percent of the voting securities of two wholly owned subsidiaries of "B" for a total of in excess of $50 million (as adjusted). BSUB1 is a foreign issuer with less than $50 million (as adjusted) in sales into the U.S. in its most recent fiscal year and with assets of less than $50 million (as adjusted) located in the U.S. Less than $50 million (as adjusted) of the acquisition price has been allocated to BSUB1. BSUB2 is a U.S. issuer with more than $50 million (as adjusted) in U.S. sales and more than $50 million (as adjusted) in assets located in the U.S. Less than $50 million (as adjusted) of the acquisition price is allocated to BSUB2. Since BSUB1 does not exceed the $50 million (as adjusted) limitation for U.S. sales or assets in § 802.51(b), its voting securities are not held as a result of the acquisition (see § 801.15(b) of this chapter). Since the acquisition price for BSUB2 alone would not result in "A" holding in excess of $50 million (as adjusted) of voting securities of the acquired person, the transaction is non-reportable in its entirety. Note that the U.S. sales and assets of BSUB1 are not aggregated with those of BSUB2 for purposes of determining whether the limitations in paragraph (b) of this section are exceeded. If BSUB2 were also a foreign issuer, such aggregation would be required under paragraph (b)(2) of this section, and the transaction in its entirety would be reportable.

[67 FR 11904, Mar. 18, 2002; 67 FR 13716, Mar. 26, 2002, as amended at 70 FR 4996, Jan. 31, 2005]

§ 802.52 Acquisitions by or from foreign governmental entities.

An acquisition shall be exempt from the requirements of the act if:

(a) The ultimate parent entity of either the acquiring person or the acquired person is controlled by a foreign state, foreign government, or agency thereof; and

(b) The acquisition is of assets located within that foreign state or of voting securities or non-corporate interests of an entity organized under the laws of that state.

Example: The government of foreign country X has decided to sell assets of its wholly owned corporation, B, all of which are located in foreign country X. The buyer is "A," a U.S. person. Regardless of the aggregate sales in or into the United States attributable to the assets of B, the transaction is exempt under this section. (If such aggregate sales were $50 million (as adjusted) or less, the transaction would also be exempt under § 802.50).

[43 FR 33544, July 31, 1978, as amended at 67 FR 11904, Mar. 18, 2002; 70 FR 4996, Jan. 31, 2005; 76 FR 42482, July 19, 2011]

§ 802.53 Certain foreign banking transactions.

An acquisition which requires the consent or approval of the Board of Governors of the Federal Reserve System under section 25 or section 25(a) of the Federal Reserve Act, 12 U.S.C. 601, 615, shall be exempt from the requirements of the act if copies of all information and documentary material filed with the Board of Governors are contemporaneously filed with the Federal Trade Commission and Assistant Attorney General at least 30 days prior to consummation of the acquisition. In lieu of such information and documentary material or any portion thereof, an index describing such material may be provided in the manner authorized by § 802.6(a).

[43 FR 33544, July 31, 1978, as amended at 48 FR 34435, July 29, 1983]

§ 802.60 Acquisitions by securities underwriters.

An acquisition of voting securities by a person acting as a securities underwriter, in the ordinary course of business, and in the process of underwriting, shall be exempt from the requirements of the act.

§ 802.63 Certain acquisitions by creditors and insurers.

(a) *Creditors.* An acquisition of collateral or receivables, or an acquisition in foreclosure, or upon default, or in connection with the establishment of a lease financing, or in connection with a bona fide debt work-out shall be exempt from the requirements of the act if made by a creditor in a bona fide credit transaction entered into in the ordinary course of the creditor's business.

(b) *Insurers.* An acquisition pursuant to a condition in a contract of insurance relating to fidelity, surety, or casualty obligations shall be exempt from the requirements of the act if made by an insurer in the ordinary course of business.

Examples: 1. A bank makes a loan and takes actual or constructive possession of collateral in any form. Since the bank is not the beneficial owner of the collateral, the bank's receipt of it is not an acquisition which is subject to the requirements of the act. However, if upon default the bank becomes the beneficial owner of the collateral, that acquisition is exempt under this section.

2. This section exempts only the acquisition by the creditor or insurer, and not the subsequent disposition of the assets or voting securities. If a creditor or insurer sells voting securities or assets that have come into its possession in a transaction which is exempt under this section, the requirements of the act may apply to that disposition.

§ 802.64 Acquisitions of voting securities by certain institutional investors.

(a) *Institutional investor.* For purposes of this section, the term *institutional investor* means any entity of the following type:

(1) A bank within the meaning of 15 U.S.C. 80b–2(a)(2);

(2) Savings bank;

(3) Savings and loan or building and loan company or association;

(4) Trust company;

(5) Insurance company;

(6) Investment company registered with the U.S. Securities and Exchange Commission under the Investment Company Act of 1940 (15 U.S.C. 80a–1 *et seq.*);

(7) Finance company;

(8) Broker-dealer within the meaning of 15 U.S.C. 78c(a)(4) or (a)(5);

(9) Small Business Investment Company or Minority Enterprise Small Business Investment Company regulated by the U.S. Small Business Administration pursuant to 15 U.S.C. 662;

(10) A stock bonus, pension, or profit-sharing trust qualified under section 401 of the Internal Revenue Code;

(11) Bank holding company within the meaning of 12 U.S.C. 1841;

(12) An entity which is controlled directly or indirectly by an institutional investor and the activities of which are in the ordinary course of business of the institutional investor;

(13) An entity which may supply incidental services to entities which it controls directly or indirectly but which performs no operating functions, and which is otherwise engaged only in holding controlling interests in institutional investors; or

(14) A nonprofit entity within the meaning of sections 501(c) (1) through (4), (6) through (15), (17) through (20), or (d) of the Internal Revenue Code.

(b) *Exemption.* An acquisition of voting securities shall be exempt from the requirements of the act, except as provided in paragraph (c) of this section, if:

(1) Made directly by an institutional investor;

(2) Made in the ordinary course of business;

(3) Made solely for the purpose of investment; and

(4) As a result of the acquisition the acquiring person would hold fifteen percent or less of the outstanding voting securities of the issuer.

(c) *Exception to exemption.* Notwithstanding paragraph (b) of this section:

(1) No acquisition of voting securities of an institutional investor of the same type as any entity included within the acquiring person shall be exempt under this section; and

(2) No acquisition by an institutional investor shall be exempt under this section if any entity included within the acquiring person which is not an institutional investor holds any voting securities of the issuer whose voting securities are to be acquired.

Examples: 1. Assume that A and its subsidiary, B, are both institutional investors as defined in paragraph (a) of this section, that X is not, and that the conditions set forth in paragraphs (b)(2), (3) and (4) of this section are satisfied. Either A or B may acquire voting securities of X worth in excess of $50 million (as adjusted) as long as the aggregate amount held by person "A" as a result of the acquisition does not exceed 15 percent of X's outstanding voting securities. If the aggregate holdings would exceed 15 percent, "A" may acquire no more than $50 million (as adjusted) worth of voting securities without being subject to the requirements of the act.

2. In example 1, assume that B plans to make the acquisition, but that corporation B's parent, corporation A, is not an institutional investor and is engaged in manufacturing. Subparagraph (c)(2) provides that acquisitions by B can never be exempt under this section if A owns any amount of X's voting securities.

3. In example 1, the exemption does not apply if X is also an institutional investor of the same type as either A or B.

4. Assume that H is a holding company which controls a life insurance company, a casualty insurer and a finance company. The life insurance company controls a data processing company which performs services for the two insurers. Any acquisition by any of these entities could qualify for exemption under this section.

5. In example 4, if H also controls a manufacturing entity, H is not an institutional investor, and only the acquisitions made by the two insurance companies, the finance company and the data processing company can qualify for the exemption under this section.

[43 FR 33544, July 31, 1978, as amended at 66 FR 8694, Feb. 1, 2001; 70 FR 4996, Jan. 31, 2005]

§ 802.65 Exempt acquisition of non-corporate interests in financing transactions.

An acquisition of non-corporate interests that confers control of a new or existing unincorporated entity is exempt from the notification requirements of the Act if:

(a) The acquiring person is contributing only cash to the unincorporated entity;

(b) For the purpose of providing financing; and

(c) The terms of the financing agreement are such that the acquiring person will no longer control the entity after it realizes its preferred return.

[70 FR 11514, Mar. 8, 2005]

§ 802.70 Acquisitions subject to order.

An acquisition shall be exempt from the requirements of the act if the voting securities or assets are to be acquired from an entity pursuant to and in accordance with:

(a) An order of the Federal Trade Commission or of any Federal court in an action brought by the Federal Trade Commission or the Department of Justice;

(b) An Agreement Containing Consent Order that has been accepted by the Commission for public comment, pursuant to the Commission's Rules of Practice; or

(c) A proposal for a consent judgment that has been submitted to a Federal court by the Federal Trade Commission or the Department of Justice and that is subject to public comment.

[63 FR 34594, June 25, 1998]

§ 802.71 Acquisitions by gift, intestate succession or devise, or by irrevocable trust.

Acquisitions resulting from a gift, intestate succession, testamentary disposition or transfer by a settlor to an irrevocable trust shall be exempt from the requirements of the act.

§ 802.80 Transitional rule for transactions investigated by the agencies.

§§ 801.2 and 801.50 shall not apply to any transaction that has been the subject of investigation by either the Federal Trade Commission or the Antitrust Division of the Department of Justice in which, prior to the effective date of that section, the reviewing agency obtained documentary material and information under compulsory process from all parties that would be required to submit a Notification and Report Form for Certain Mergers and Acquisitions under Section 801.50 but for this transitional rule.

[70 FR 11514, Mar. 8, 2005]

PART 803—TRANSMITTAL RULES

AUTHORITY: 15 U.S.C. 18a(d).

SOURCE: 43 FR 33548, July 31, 1978, unless otherwise noted.

§ 803.1 Notification and Report Form.

(a) The notification required by the act shall be the Notification and Report Form set forth in the appendix to this part, as amended from time to time. All acquiring and acquired persons required to file notification by the act and these rules shall do so by completing and filing the Notification and Report Form, in accordance with the instructions thereon and these rules. The current version of the Form can be obtained at *http://www.ftc.gov.*

(b) Any person filing notification may, in addition to the submissions required by this section, submit any other information or documentary material which such person believes will be helpful to the Federal Trade Commission and Assistant Attorney General in assessing the impact of the acquisition upon competition.

[43 FR 33548, July 31, 1978, as amended at 66 FR 8695, Feb. 1, 2001; 71 FR 35998, June 23, 2006; 81 FR 60259, Sept. 1, 2016]

§ 803.2 Instructions applicable to Notification and Report Form.

(a) The notification required by the act shall be filed by the preacquisition ultimate parent entity, or by any entity included within the person authorized by such preacquisition ultimate parent entity to file notification on its behalf. In the case of a natural person required by the act to file notification, such notification may be filed by his or her legal representative: *Provided however,* That notwithstanding §§ 801.1(c)(2) and 801.2, only one notification shall be filed by or on behalf of a natural person, spouse and minor children with respect to an acquisition as a result of which more than one such natural person will hold voting securities of the same issuer.

Example: Jane Doe, her husband and minor child collectively hold more than 50 percent of the shares of family corporation F. Therefore, Jane Doe (or her husband or minor child) is the "ultimate parent entity" of a "person" composed to herself (or her husband or minor child) and F; see paragraphs (a)(3), (b) and (c)(2) of § 801.1. If corporation F is to acquire corporation X, under this paragraph only one notification is to be filed by Jane Doe, her husband and minor child collectively.

(b) Except as provided in paragraph (b)(2) of this section and paragraph (c) of this section:

(1) Items 5–8 of the Notification and Report Form must be completed—

(i) By acquiring persons, with respect to all entities included within the acquiring person;

(ii) By acquired persons, in the case of an acquisition of assets, only with respect to the assets to be acquired;

(iii) By acquired persons, in the case of an acquisition of voting securities, with respect to only the issuer whose voting securities are being acquired, and all entities controlled by such issuer; and

(iv) By acquired persons, in the case of an acquisition of non-corporate interests, with respect to the unincorporated entity whose non-corporate interests are being acquired, and all entities controlled by such unincorporated entity; and

(v) By persons which are both acquiring and acquired persons, separately in the manner that would be required of acquiring and acquired persons under this paragraph, if different.

(2) For purposes of item 7 of the Notification and Report Form, the acquiring person shall regard the acquired person in the manner described in paragraphs (b)(1)(ii), (iii) and (iv) of this section.

Example: Person "A" is comprised of entities separately engaged in grocery retailing, auto rental, and coal mining. Person "B" is comprised of entities separately engaged in wholesale magazine distribution, auto rental and book publishing. "A" proposes to purchase 100 percent of the voting securities of "B"'s book publishing subsidiary. For purposes of item 5, under clause (b)(1)(i), "A" reports the activities of all its entities; under clause (b)(1)(iii), "B" reports only the operations of its book publishing subsidiary. For purposes of items 7 and 8, under paragraph (b)(2) of this section, "A" must regard "B" as consisting only of its book publishing subsidiary and must disregard the fact that "A" and "B" are both engaged in the auto rental business.

(c) In response to items 5, 7, and 8 of the Notification and Report Form—Information need not be supplied with respect to assets or voting securities to be acquired, the acquisition of which is exempt from the requirements of the act.

(d) The term *dollar revenues*, as used in the Notification and Report Form, means value of shipments for manufacturing operations, and sales, receipts, revenues, or other appropriate dollar value measure for operations other than manufacturing, f.o.b. the plant or establishment less returns, after discounts and allowances and excluding freight charges and excise taxes. Dollar revenues including delivery may be supplied if delivery is an integral part of the sales price. Dollar revenues include interplant transfers.

(e) For documents required by item 4(b) of the Notification and Report Form, a person filing the notification may, instead of submitting a document, provide a cite to an operative Internet address directly linking to the document, if the linked document is complete and payment is not required to access the document. If an Internet address becomes inoperative during the waiting period, or the document is otherwise rendered inaccessible or incomplete, upon notification by the Commission or Assistant Attorney General, the parties must make the document available to the agencies by either referencing an operative Internet address where the complete document may be accessed or by providing paper copies to the agencies as provided in § 803.10(c)(1) by 5 p.m. on the next regular business day. Failure to make the document available, by the Internet or by providing paper copies, by 5 p.m. on the next regular business day, will result in notice of a deficient filing pursuant to § 803.10(c)(2).

(f) Filings made via DVD must comply with all format requirements set forth at the Premerger Notification Office pages at *http://www.ftc.gov*. The use of any format not specified as acceptable, or any other failure to comply with the applicable format requirements, shall render the entire filing deficient within the meaning of § 803.10(c)(2).

[43 FR 33548, July 31, 1978, as amended at 48 FR 34438, July 29, 1983; 66 FR 8695, Feb. 1, 2001; 66 FR 23565, May 9, 2001; 70 FR 11514, Mar. 8, 2005; 70 FR 73372, Dec. 12, 2005; 71 FR 35998, June 23, 2006; 76 FR 42483, July 19, 2011; 81 FR 60259, Sept. 1, 2016]

§ 803.3 Statement of reasons for noncompliance.

A complete response shall be supplied to each item on the Notification and Report Form and to any request for additional information pursuant to section 7A(e) and § 803.20. Whenever the person filing notification is unable to supply a complete response, that person shall provide, for each item for which less than a complete response has been supplied, a statement of reasons for noncompliance. The statement of reasons for noncompliance shall contain all information upon which a person relies in explanation of its noncompliance and shall include at least the following:

(a) Why the person is unable to supply a complete response;

(b) What information, and what specific documents or categories of documents, would have been required for a complete response;

(c) Who, if anyone, has the required information, and specific documents or categories of documents; and a description of all efforts made to obtain such information and documents, including the names of persons who searched for required information and documents, and where the search was conducted. If no such efforts were made, provide an explanation of the reasons why, and a description of all efforts necessary to obtain required information and documents;

(d) Where noncompliance is based on a claim of privilege, a statement of the claim of privilege and all facts relied on in support thereof, including the identity of each document, its author, the author's title/position, addressee, the addressee's title/position, date, subject matter, all recipients of the original and of any copies, the recipients' titles/positions, the document's present location, and who has control of it.

[48 FR 34439, July 29, 1983, as amended at 81 FR 60259, Sept. 1, 2016]

§ 803.4 Foreign persons refusing to file notification.

(a) In an acquisition to which § 801.30 does not apply, and in which no assets (other than investment assets) located in the United States and no voting securities of a United States issuer will be acquired directly or indirectly, if a foreign acquired person refuses to file notification, then any other person which is a party to the acquisition may file notification on behalf of the foreign person. Such notification shall constitute the notification required of the foreign person by the act and these rules.

(b) Any person filing on behalf of the foreign person pursuant to this section must state in the affidavit required by § 803.5(b) that such foreign person has refused to file notification and must explain all efforts made by the person filing on behalf of the foreign person to obtain compliance with the act and these rules by such foreign person.

(c) Any notification filed on behalf of a foreign person pursuant to this section must contain all information and documentary material reasonably available to the person filing on behalf of the foreign person which such foreign person would be required to provide. Whenever information or documentary material is not reasonably available, the person filing on behalf of the foreign person shall so indicate on the Notification and Report Form, and need not supply the statement of reasons for noncompliance required by § 803.3.

(d) Any foreign person on whose behalf notification has been filed by another person pursuant to this section shall be a "person filing notification" for purposes of the act and these rules. Nothing in this section shall exempt a foreign person from the requirements of the act or these rules with respect to a request for additional information or an extension of the waiting period pursuant to section 7A(e) and these rules.

§ 803.5 Affidavits required.

(a)(1) *Section 801.30 acquisitions.* For acquisitions to which § 801.30 applies, the notification required by the Act from each acquiring person shall contain an affidavit, attached to the front of the notification, or with the DVD submission, attesting that the issuer or unincorporated entity whose voting securities or non-corporate interests are to be acquired has received written notice delivered to an officer (or a person exercising similar functions in the case of an entity without officers) by email, certified or registered mail, wire, or hand delivery, at its principal executive offices, of:

(i) The identity of the acquiring person;

(ii) The fact that the acquiring person intends to acquire voting securities or non-corporate interests of the issuer or unincorporated entity;

(iii) The specific classes of voting securities or non-corporate interests of the issuer or unincorporated entity sought to be acquired; and if known, the number of voting securities or non-corporate interests of each such class that would be held by the acquiring person as a result of the acquisition or, if the number of voting securities is not known in the case of an issuer, the specific notification threshold that the acquiring person intends to meet or exceed; and, if designated by the acquiring person, a higher threshold for additional voting securities it may hold in the year following the expiration of the waiting period;

(iv) The fact that the acquisition may be subject to the act, and that the acquiring person will file notification under the act with the Federal Trade Commission and Assistant Attorney General;

(v) The anticipated date of receipt of such notification under § 803.10(c); and

(vi) The fact that the person within which the issuer or unincorporated entity is included may be required to file notification under the act.

Example to paragraph (a)(1)(vi): 1. Company A intends to acquire voting securities of Company B. "A" sends, via email, a notice letter to a general email account, *information@CompanyB.com.* "A" has not provided sufficient notice. Alternatively, "A" sends, via email, a notice letter to "B's" President, Jane Doe, at *Jane.Doe@CompanyB.com.* "A" has provided email notice to a specific officer of "B."

(2) The affidavit required by this paragraph must also state the good faith intention of the person filing notification to make the acquisition, and, in the case of a tender offer, that the intention to make the tender offer has been publicly announced.

Examples to paragraph (a)(2) 1. This paragraph permits the tender offeror to file notification at any time after the intention to make the tender offer has been publicly announced.

In examples 2–5 assume that one percent of B's shares are valued at $15 million.

2. "A" holds 100,000 shares of the voting securities of Company B. "A" has a good faith intention to acquire an additional 900,000 shares of Company B's voting securities. "A" states in its notice to B, inter alia, that as a result of the acquisition it will hold 1,000,000 shares. If 1,000,000 shares of Company B represent 20 percent of Company B's outstanding voting securities, the statement will be deemed by the enforcement agencies a notification for the $100 million threshold (as adjusted).

3. Company A intends to acquire voting securities of Company B. "A" does not know exactly how many shares it will acquire, but it knows it will definitely acquire in excess of $50 million (as adjusted) worth and may acquire 50 percent of Company B's shares. "A"'s notice to the acquired person would meet the requirements of Sec. 803.5(a)(1)(iii) if it states, inter alia, either: "Company A has a present good faith intention to acquire in excess of $50 million (as adjusted) of the outstanding voting securities of Company B, and depending on market conditions, may acquire more of the voting securities of Company B and thus designates the 50 percent threshold," or "Company A has a present good faith intention to acquire in excess of $50 million (as adjusted) of the outstanding voting securities of Company B, and depending on market conditions may acquire 50 percent or more of the voting securities of Company B." The Commission would deem either of these statements as intending to give notice for the 50 percent threshold.

4. "A" states, inter alia, that, "depending on market conditions, it may acquire 100 percent of the shares of B." "A"'s notice does not comply with § 803.5 because it does not state an intent to meet or exceed any notification threshold. "A"'s filing will be considered deficient within the meaning of § 803.10(c)(2).

5. "A" states, inter alia, that it has commenced a tender offer for "up to 55 percent of the outstanding voting securities of Company B." "A"'s notice does not comply with

§ 803.5 because use of the term "up to" does not state an intent to meet or exceed any notification threshold. The filing will therefore be considered deficient within the meaning of § 803.10 (c)(2).

(3) The affidavit required by this paragraph must have attached to it a copy of the written notice received by the acquired person pursuant to paragraph (a)(1) of this section. For DVD filings, the written notice (in a form specified in the instructions) must be included on the DVD.

(b) *Non-section 801.30 acquisitions.* For acquisitions to which § 801.30 does not apply, the notification required by the act shall contain an affidavit, attached to the front of the notification, or with the DVD submission, attesting that a contract, agreement in principle or letter of intent to merge or acquire has been executed, and further attesting to the good faith intention of the person filing notification to complete the transaction.

[43 FR 33548, July 31, 1978, as amended at 48 FR 34439, July 29, 1983; 52 FR 7082, Mar. 6, 1987; 66 FR 8695, Feb. 1, 2001; 70 FR 4996, Jan. 31, 2005; 71 FR 35998, June 23, 2006; 76 FR 42483, July 19, 2011; 81 FR 60259, Sept. 1, 2016; 83 FR 32771, July 16, 2018]

§ 803.6 Certification.

(a) The notification required by the act shall be certified:

(1) In the case of a partnership, by any general partner thereof;

(2) In the case of a corporation, by any officer or director thereof;

(3) In the case of a person lacking officers, directors, or partners, by any individual exercising similar functions;

(4) In the case of a natural person, by such natural person or his or her legal representative;

(5) In the case of the estate of a deceased natural person, by any duly authorized legal representative of such estate.

(b) Additional information or documentary material submitted in response to a request pursuant to section 7A(e) and § 803.20 shall be accompanied by a certification in the format appearing at the end of the Notification and Report Form, completed in accordance with paragraph (a) of this section by the person or individual to whom it was directed.

(c) In all cases, the certifying individual must possess actual authority to make the certification on behalf of the person filing notification.

[43 FR 33548, July 31, 1978, as amended at 48 FR 34429, July 29, 1983]

§ 803.7 Expiration of notification.

(a) *One year after waiting period expired.* Notification with respect to an acquisition shall expire 1 year following the expiration of the waiting period. If the acquiring person's holdings do not, within such time period, meet or exceed the notification threshold with respect to which the notification was filed, the requirements of the act must thereafter be observed with respect to any notification threshold not met or exceeded.

Example: "A" files notification that in excess of $100 million (as adjusted) of the voting securities of corporation B are to be acquired. One year after the expiration of the waiting period, "A" has acquired less than $100 million (as adjusted) of B's voting securities. Although § 802.21 will permit "A" to purchase any amount of B's voting securities short of $100 million (as adjusted) within 5 years from the expiration of the waiting period, A's holdings may not meet or exceed the $100 million (as adjusted) notification threshold without "A" and "B" again filing notification and observing a waiting period.

(b) *Upon failure to comply with request for additional information.* An acquiring person's notification and, in the case of an acquisition to which § 801.30 does not apply, an acquired person's notification, shall expire eighteen months following the date of receipt of such person's notification if a request for additional information or documentary material remains outstanding to such person (or entities included therein, officers, directors, partners, agents or employees thereof), without a certification as required by § 803.6(b), on such date. If either person's notification expires pursuant to this paragraph, both parties must file a new notification in order to carry out the transaction.

Example: A files notification on January 15 of Year 1 to acquire voting securities of B. On February 15 of Year 1, prior to expiration of the waiting period, requests for additional information or documentary material are issued to A and B. Before A supplies the information and documentary material requested, business conditions change, and A and B decide not to go forward with the transaction. A does not withdraw its filing and takes the position that it will comply with the request for additional information and documentary material if and when the proposed transaction is ever revived. A's notification expires July 15 of Year 2, eighteen months following the date of receipt of its notification. If A and B wish to revive their transaction, both parties must file a new notification and observe the waiting period in order to carry out the transaction.

[70 FR 73372, Dec. 12, 2005]

§803.8 Foreign language documents.

(a) Whenever at the time of filing a Notification and Report Form there is an English language outline, summary, extract or verbatim translation of any information or of all or portions of any documentary materials in a foreign language required to be submitted by the act or these rules, all such English language versions shall be filed along with the foreign language information or materials.

(b) Documentary materials or information in a foreign language required to be submitted in responses to a request for additional information or documentary material shall be submitted with verbatim English language translations, or all existing English language versions, or both, as specified in such request.

[48 FR 34440, July 29, 1983]

§803.9 Filing fee.

(a) Each acquiring person shall pay the filing fee required by the act to the Federal Trade Commission, except as provided in paragraphs (b), (c) and (f) of this section. No additional fee is to be submitted to the Antitrust Division of the Department of Justice.

Examples: 1. "A" wishes to acquire voting securities issued by B, where the greater of the acquisition price and the market price is in excess of $50 million (as adjusted) but less than $100 million (as adjusted) pursuant to §801.10. When "A" files notification for the transaction, it must indicate the $50 million (as adjusted) threshold and pay a filing fee of $45,000 because the aggregate total amount of the acquisition is less than $100 million (as adjusted), but greater than $50 million (as adjusted).

2. "A" acquires less than $50 million (as adjusted) of assets from "B." The parties meet the size of person criteria of Section 7A(a)(2)(B), but the transaction is not reportable because it does not exceed the $50 million (as adjusted) size of transaction threshold of that provision. Two months later "A" acquires additional assets from "B" valued at between $50 million (as adjusted) and $100 million (as adjusted). Pursuant to the aggregation requirements of §801.13(b)(2)(ii), the aggregate total amount of "B's" assets that "A" will hold as a result of the second acquisition is in excess of $100 million (as adjusted). Accordingly, when "A" files notification for the second transaction, "A" must indicate the $100 million (as adjusted) threshold and pay a filing fee of $125,000 because the aggregate total amount of the acquisition is less than $500 million (as adjusted), but not less than $100 million (as adjusted).

3. "A" acquires in excess of $50 million (as adjusted) of voting securities issued by B after submitting its notification and $45,000 filing fee and indicates the $50 million (as adjusted) threshold. Two years later, "A" files to acquire additional voting securities issued by B valued at $50 million (as adjusted) because it will exceed the next higher reporting threshold (*see* §§801.1(h)). Assuming the second transaction is reportable and the value of its initial holdings is unchanged (*see* §§801.13(a)(2) and 801.10(c)), the provisions of §801.13(a)(1) require that "A" report that the value of the second transaction is in excess of $100 million (as adjusted) because "A" must aggregate previously acquired securities in calculating the value of B's voting securities that it will hold as a result of the second acquisition. "A" should pay a filing fee of $125,000.

4. "A" signs a contract with a stated purchase price in excess of $100 million (as adjusted), subject to adjustments, to acquire all of the assets of "B." If the amount of adjustments can be reasonably estimated, the acquisition price—as adjusted to reflect that estimate—is determined. If the amount of adjustments cannot be reasonably estimated, the acquisition price is undetermined. In either case the board or its delegee must also determine in good faith the fair market value. (§801.10(b) states that the value of an asset acquisition is to be the fair market value or the acquisition price, if determined and greater than fair market value.) "A" files notification and submits a $45,000 filing fee. "A"'s decision to pay that fee may be justified on either of two bases, and "A" should submit an attachment to the Notification and Report Form explaining the valuation. First, "A" may have concluded that the acquisition price can be reasonably estimated to be less than $100 million (as adjusted), because of anticipated adjustments—e.g., based on due diligence by "A's" accounting firm indicating that one third of the inventory is not saleable. If fair market value is also determined in good faith to be less than $100 million (as adjusted), the

$45,000 fee is appropriate. Alternatively, "A" may conclude that because the adjustments cannot reasonably be estimated, acquisition price is undetermined. If so, "A" would base the valuation on the good faith determination of fair market value. The acquiring party's execution of the Certification also attests to the good faith valuation of the value of the transaction.

5. "A" contracts to acquire all of the assets of "B" for in excess of $500 million (as adjusted). The assets include hotels, office buildings, and rental retail property, all of which are exempted by § 802.2. Section 802.2 directs that these assets are exempt from the requirements of the act and that reporting requirements for the transaction should be determined by analyzing the remainder of the acquisition as if it were a separate transaction. Furthermore, § 801.15(a)(2) states that those exempt assets are never held as a result of the acquisition. Accordingly, the aggregate amount of the transaction is in excess of $100 million (as adjusted), but less than $500 million (as adjusted). "A" will be liable for a filing fee of $125,000, rather than $280,000, because the value of the transaction is not less than $100 million (as adjusted) but less than $500 million (as adjusted). Note, however, that "A" must include an attachment in its Notification and Report Form setting out both the in excess of $500 million (as adjusted) total purchase price and the basis for its determination that the aggregate total amount of the acquisition under the rules is between $100 million (as adjusted) and $500 million (as adjusted) rather than in excess of $500 million (as adjusted), in accordance with the Instructions to the Form.

6. "A" acquires coal reserves from "B" valued at $150 million. No notification or filing fee is required because the acquisition is exempted by § 802.3(b). Three months later, A proposes to acquire additional coal reserves from "B" valued at $500 million (as adjusted). This transaction is subject to the notification requirements of the act because the value of the acquisition exceeds the $200 million limitation on the exemption in § 802.3(b). As a result of § 801.13(b)(2)(ii), the prior $150 million acquisition must be added because the additional $500 million (as adjusted) of coal reserves were acquired from the same person within 180 days of the initial acquisition. Because aggregating the two acquisitions exceeds the $200 million exemption limitation, § 801.15(b) directs that "A" will also hold the previously exempt $150 million acquisition; thus, the aggregate amount held as a result of the $500 million (as adjusted) acquisition exceeds $500 million (as adjusted). Accordingly, "A" must file notification to acquire the coal reserves valued in excess of $500 million (as adjusted) and pay a filing fee of $280,000.

7. "A" intends to acquire 20 percent of the voting securities of B, a non-publicly traded issuer. The agreed upon acquisition price is $99 million subject to post-closing adjustments of up to plus or minus $2 million. "A" estimates that the adjustments will be minus $1 million. In this example, since "A" is able in good faith to reasonably estimate the adjustments to the agreed-on price, the acquisition price is deemed to be determined and the appropriate filing fee threshold is $50 million. Even if the post-closing adjustments cause the final price actually paid to exceed $100 million, "A" would be deemed to hold $98 million in B voting securities as a result of this acquisition. Note, however, since the potential acquisition price subject to adjustments could have exceeded the $100 million threshold (e.g., "straddles two filing fee thresholds"), an explanation of why the lower threshold was indicated should be attached. Also note that any additional acquisition by "A" of B voting stock (if the value of the stock currently held by "A" is $100 million or more) will cause "A" to cross the $100 million threshold and another filing and the appropriate fee will be required.

8. "A" intends to make a cash tender offer for a minimum of 50 percent plus one share of the voting securities of B, a non-publicly traded issuer, but will accept up to 100 percent of the shares if they are tendered. There are 12 million shares of B voting stock outstanding and the tender offer price is $10 per share. In this instance, since there is no cap on the number of shares that can be tendered, the value of the transaction will be the value of 100 percent of B's voting securities, and "A" must pay the $125,000 fee for the $100 million filing fee threshold. Note that if the tender offer had been for a maximum of 50 percent plus one share the value of the transaction would be $60 million, and the appropriate fee would be $45,000, based on the $50 million filing fee threshold. This would be true even if the tender offer were to be followed by a merger which would be exempt under Section 7A(c)(3),

(b) For a transaction described by § 801.2(d)(2)(iii), the parties shall pay only one filing fee. In accordance with § 801.2(d)(2)(iii), both parties to a consolidation are acquiring and acquired persons and must submit a Notification and Report Form where the transaction meets the reporting requirements of that act; however, only one filing fee is required in connection with such a transaction, and is payable by either party to the transaction. The filing fee is based on the greater of the two sizes of transaction in the consolidation.

(c) For a reportable transaction in which the acquiring entity has two ultimate parent entities, both ultimate parent entities are acquiring persons; however, if the responses for both ultimate parent entities would be the same for item 5 of the Notification and Report Form, only one filing fee is required in connection with the transaction.

(d) *Manner of payment.* Fees may be paid by United States postal money order, bank money order, bank cashier's check, certified check or by electronic wire transfer (EWT). The fee must be paid in U.S. currency.

(1) Fees paid by money order or check shall be made payable to the "Federal Trade Commission," omitting the name or title of any official of the Commission, and shall be submitted to the Premerger Notification Office of the Federal Trade Commission along with the Notification and Report Form.

(2) Fees paid by EWT shall be deposited to the Treasury's account at the New York Federal Reserve Bank. Specific instructions for making EWT payments are contained in the Instructions to the Notification and Report Form.

(e) *Refunds.* Except as provided in this paragraph, no filing fee received by the Commission will be returned to the payer and no part of the filing fee shall be refunded. The filing fee shall be refunded only if the Commission's staff determines, based on the information and representations contained in the filing person's notification, that premerger notification was not required by the act. Once the Commission's staff has determined that the notification was required, the filing fee shall not be refunded even if it appears at the time of consummation that the transaction does not meet the reporting requirements established in the act.

(f) For a transaction described by paragraph (c) of §803.12, the parties shall pay no additional filing fee.

[66 FR 8695, Feb. 1, 2001, as amended at 68 FR 2431, Jan. 17, 2003; 70 FR 4997, Jan. 31, 2005; 78 FR 41296, July 10, 2013]

§803.10 Running of time.

(a) *Beginning of waiting period.* The waiting period required by the act shall begin on the date of receipt of the notification required by the act, in the manner provided by these rules (or, if such notification is not completed, the notification to the extent completed and a statement of the reasons for such noncompliance in accordance with §803.3) from:

(1) In the case of acquisitions to which §801.30 applies, the acquiring person;

(2) In the case of the formation of a corporation covered by Sec. 801.40 or an unincorporated entity covered by Sec. 801.50, all persons contributing to the formation of the joint venture or other corporation that are required by the act and these rules to file notification;

(3) In the case of all other acquisitions, all persons required by the act and these rules to file notification.

(b) *Expiration of waiting period.* (1) Subject to paragraph (b)(3) of this section, for purposes of Section 7A(b)(1)(B), the waiting period shall expire at 11:59 p.m. Eastern Time on the 30th (or in the case of a cash tender offer or of an acquisition covered by 11 U.S.C. 363(b), the 15th) calendar day (or if §802.23 applies, such other day as that section may provide) following the beginning of the waiting period as determined under paragraph (a) of this section, unless extended pursuant to Section 7A(e) and §803.20, or Section 7A(g)(2), or unless terminated pursuant to Section 7A(b)(2) and §803.11.

(2) Unless further extended pursuant to Section 7A(g)(2), or terminated pursuant to Section 7A(b)(2) and §803.11, any waiting period which has been extended pursuant to Section 7A(e)(2) and §803.20 shall, subject to paragraph (b)(3) of this section, expire at 11:59 p.m. Eastern Time—

(i) On the 30th (or, in the case of a cash tender offer or of an acquisition covered by 11 U.S.C. 363(b), the 10th) day following the date of receipt of all additional information or documentary material requested from all persons to whom such requests have been directed (or, if a request is not fully complied with, the information and documentary material submitted and a statement of the reasons for such noncompliance in accordance with § 803.3), by the Federal Trade Commission or Assistant Attorney General, whichever requested additional information or documentary material, at the office designated in paragraph (c) of this section, or

(ii) As provided in paragraph (b)(1) of this section, whichever is later.

(3) If any waiting period would expire on a Saturday, Sunday, or legal public holiday (as defined in 5 U.S.C. 6103(a)) the waiting period shall be extended to 11:59 p.m. Eastern Time of the next regular business day.

(c)(1) *Date of receipt and means of delivery.* For purposes of this section, these procedures shall apply.

(i) For paper copy filings and DVD filings, the date of receipt shall be the date on which delivery is effected to the designated offices (Premerger Notification Office, Federal Trade Commission, Room 5301, 400 7th Street SW., Washington, DC 20024, and Director of Civil Enforcement, Office of Operations, Antitrust Division, Department of Justice, 950 Pennsylvania Avenue NW., Room #3335, Washington, DC 20530) during normal business hours. Delivery should be effected directly to the designated offices, either by hand or by certified or registered mail (including FedEx and UPS). In the event one or both of the delivery sites are unavailable, the FTC and DOJ may designate alternate sites for delivery of the filing. Notification of the alternate delivery sites will normally be made through a press release and, if possible, on the *http://www.ftc.gov* Web site.

(ii) Delivery effected after 5 p.m. eastern time on a business day, or at any time on any day other than a business day, shall be deemed effected on the next following business day. If delivery of all required filings to all offices required to receive such filings is not effected on the same date, the date of receipt shall be the latest of the dates on which delivery is effected.

Example: In an acquisition other than a tender offer, assume that requests for additional information are issued to both the acquiring and acquired persons on the 26th day of the waiting period. One person submits the additional information on the 35th day, while the other responds on the 44th day. Under this section, the waiting period expires thirty days following the last receipt of additional information, that is, it expires on the 74th day (unless that day is a Saturday, Sunday or legal public holiday).

(2) *Deficient filings.* If notification or a response to a request for additional information or documentary material received by the Commission or Assistant Attorney General does not comply with these rules, the Commission or the Assistant Attorney General shall promptly notify the person filing such notification or response of the deficiencies in such filing, and the date of receipt shall be the date on which a filing which complies with these rules is received.

[43 FR 33548, July 31, 1978; 43 FR 36054, Aug. 15, 1978, as amended at 52 FR 7083, Mar. 6, 1987; 66 FR 8696, Feb. 1, 2001; 70 FR 11514, Mar. 8, 2005; 71 FR 35998, June 23, 2006; 79 FR 25663, May 6, 2014; 81 FR 60260, Sept. 1, 2016]

§ 803.11 Termination of waiting period.

(a) Except as provided in paragraph (c) of this section, no waiting period shall be terminated pursuant to section 7A(b)(2) unless—

(1) All notifications required to be filed with respect to the acquisition by the act and these rules (or, if such notification is not completed, the notification to the extent completed and a statement of the reasons for such noncompliance in accordance with § 803.3) have been received,

(2) It has been determined that no additional information or documentary material pursuant to section 7A(e) and § 803.20 will be requested, or, if such additional information or documentary material has been requested, it (or, if a request is not fully complied with, the information and documentary material submitted and a statement of the reasons for such noncompliance in accordance with § 803.3) has been received, and

(3) The Federal Trade Commission and the Assistant Attorney General have concluded that neither intends to take any further action within the waiting period.

(b) Any request for additional information or documentary material pursuant to section 7A(e) and § 803.20 shall constitute a denial of all pending requests for termination of the waiting period.

(c) The Federal Trade Commission and the Assistant Attorney General may, in their discretion, terminate a waiting period upon the written request of any person filing notification or, notwithstanding paragraph (a) of this section, sua sponte. A request for termination of the waiting period shall be sent to the offices designated in § 803.10(c). Termination shall be effective upon notice to any requesting person by either email or telephone, and such notice shall be given as soon as possible. Such notice shall be made to each person which has filed notification, and notice of termination shall be published in the FEDERAL REGISTER in accordance with section 7A(b)(2) of the Clayton Act (the "act"). The Federal Trade Commission and the Assistant Attorney General also may use other means to make the termination public, prior to publication in the FEDERAL REGISTER in a manner that will make the information equally accessible to all members of the public.

[43 FR 33548, July 31, 1978, as amended at 54 FR 21427, May 18, 1989; 83 FR 32771, July 16, 2018]

§ 803.12 Withdraw and refile notification.

(a) *Voluntary*. An acquiring person, and in the case of an acquisition to which § 801.30 does not apply, an acquired person, may withdraw its notification by notifying the Federal Trade Commission and the Antitrust Division in writing by email or mail of such withdrawal.

(b) *Upon public announcement of termination*. An acquiring person's notification or, in the case of an acquisition to which § 801.30 of this chapter does not apply, an acquiring or an acquired person's notification, will be deemed to have been withdrawn if any filing that publicly announces the expiration, termination or withdrawal of a tender offer or the termination of an agreement or letter of intent is made by the acquiring person or the acquired person with the U.S. Securities and Exchange Commission ("SEC") under the Securities Exchange Act of 1934 (15 U.S.C. 78a *et seq.*) and rules promulgated under that act. The acquiring person or acquired person must notify the Federal Trade Commission and the Antitrust Division in writing by email or mail that such filing has been made with the SEC and the withdrawal shall be deemed effective on the date of the SEC filing. Withdrawal of the HSR notification(s) shall occur even if statements are made in the SEC filing indicating a desire to recommence the tender offer or enter into a new or amended agreement or letter of intent. This paragraph is inapplicable if the initial 15-day or 30-day waiting period has expired without issuance of a request for additional information or documentary material and without an agreement in place with the Agencies to delay closing of the transaction ("a timing agreement"); or early termination of that waiting period has been granted, without a timing agreement in place; or if a request for additional information or documentary material has been issued and the Agencies have either granted early termination or allowed the extended waiting period to expire following certification of compliance without a timing agreement in place.

(c) *Resubmission without a new filing fee*. (1) An acquiring person whose notification has been voluntarily withdrawn pursuant to paragraph (a) of this section, or an acquiring person whose notification is deemed to have been automatically withdrawn under paragraph (b) of this section, may resubmit its notification, thereby initiating a new waiting period for the same transaction without an additional filing fee pursuant to § 803.9(f). This procedure may be used only one time, and only under the following circumstances:

(i) The notification is withdrawn prior to the expiration or early termination of the waiting period and prior to the issuance of a request for additional information pursuant to § 803.20 and section 7A(e) of the act;

(ii) The proposed acquisition does not change in any material way;

(iii) The resubmitted notification is recertified, and the submission, as it relates to Items 4(a), 4(b), 4(c), and 4(d) of the Notification and Report Form, is updated to the date of the resubmission;

(iv) A new executed affidavit is provided with the resubmitted HSR filing; and

(v) The resubmitted notification is refiled prior to the close of the second business day after withdrawal.

(2) If the acquired person, in the case of an acquisition to which § 801.30 of this chapter does not apply, withdraws its notification under paragraph (a) of this section or if its notification is automatically withdrawn under paragraph (b) of this section, no resubmission is available under this paragraph.

Examples: 1. A commences a tender offer to acquire 100% of B's voting securities and files a Schedule TO with the SEC and a premerger notification filing with the Federal Trade Commission and the Antitrust Division ("the Agencies"). Subsequently, A decides to withdraw the tender offer and files an amended Schedule TO announcing the withdrawal. A states in its amended filing, designated as a Schedule TO–T/A on EDGAR, the SEC's Electronic Data Gathering, Analysis, and Retrieval system, which announces the tender offer withdrawal that it reserves the right to recommence the tender offer, should circumstances change. A's premerger notification filing is deemed to have been withdrawn on the date of the filing of the Schedule TO–T/A with the SEC.

2. A commences a tender offer for at least 75% of B's voting securities and files a Schedule TO with the SEC stating that the tender offer will expire after 30 days. A also files a premerger notification filing with the Agencies and a request for additional information or documentary material ("Second Request") is issued. At the end of the 30 day effective period of the tender offer sufficient shares have not been tendered and the tender offer expires. A files a closing Schedule TO–T/A with the SEC announcing the expiration of the tender offer. A's premerger notification filing is deemed to have been withdrawn on the date of the filing of the Schedule TO–T/A with the SEC.

3. A commences a tender offer for 100% of B's voting securities and files a Schedule TO with the SEC stating that shareholders tendering their shares will receive $2.00 per share. During the effective period of the tender offer, A increases the amount it will pay per share to $2.25 and files a Schedule TO–T/A with the SEC announcing the increased share price. A's premerger notification filing is not deemed to have been withdrawn on the date of the filing of the Schedule TO–T/A with the SEC because it is not notifying the SEC that the tender offer has expired or is being withdrawn.

4. A commences a tender offer for 100% of B's voting securities and files a Schedule TO with the SEC. During the effective period of the tender offer, A and B enter into a merger agreement and A files a Schedule TO–T/A with the SEC announcing the withdrawal of the tender offer. A's premerger notification filing is deemed to have been withdrawn on the date of the filing of the Schedule TO–T/A with the SEC. A can, however, refile within two business days on the merger agreement, commencing a new waiting period, without paying an additional filing fee, if it meets the requirements of § 803.12(c).

5. A and B enter into a merger agreement conditioned on successful completion of due diligence. A and B file premerger notification filings with the Agencies and also Form 8–Ks with the SEC announcing they have entered into an agreement to merge. Subsequent findings in the course of due diligence cause A and B to terminate the merger agreement and A files an additional Form 8–K announcing the termination of an agreement. A states that it may seek to enter into a new or amended merger agreement with B. A's premerger notification filing is deemed to have been withdrawn on the date of the filing of the Form 8–K announcing the termination of the merger agreement. A can, however, refile within two business days on a new merger agreement, commencing a new waiting period, without paying an additional filing fee, if it meets the requirements of § 803.12(c).

6. A and B enter into a merger agreement and file premerger notification filings with the Agencies and Form 8–Ks with the SEC. Second requests are issued. A and B subsequently certify compliance with the second request, starting the extended waiting period. Prior to the expiration of the extended waiting period, the parties enter into an agreement with the agency conducting the investigation to delay closing of the transaction, allowing the consummation of the acquisition only after 30-days' notice (a "timing agreement"), and the extended waiting period expires. During the pendency of the timing agreement, A and B terminate the merger agreement and A files a Form 8–K with the SEC announcing the termination of an agreement. A's premerger notification filing is deemed withdrawn on the date of the SEC filing as a result of that filing, even though the extended waiting period has expired and the parties are still within the one year period following that expiration under § 803.7(a). Note that had the extended waiting period expired and no timing agreement had been entered into, a filing with the SEC announcing the termination of the agreement would not result in the withdrawal of A's premerger notification filing.

7. A and B enter into a merger agreement and file premerger notification filings with the Agencies and Form 8–Ks with the SEC. The agencies complete their review and

early termination of the initial 30-day waiting period is granted. Prior to the expiration of the one year period following the grant of early termination, A and B terminate the merger agreement and A files a Form 8-K with the SEC announcing the termination of an agreement. A's premerger notification filing is not deemed withdrawn as a result of the SEC filing because the initial 30-day premerger notification waiting period had been granted early termination. Therefore, the parties still have the full one year period prior to the expiration of the notification under § 803.7(a) to consummate the transaction should it be recommenced.

[78 FR 41296, July 10, 2013, as amended at 83 FR 32771, July 16, 2018]

§ 803.20 Requests for additional information or documentary material.

(a)(1) *Persons and individuals subject to request.* Pursuant to section 7A(e)(1), the submission of additional information or documentary material relevant to the acquisition may be required from one or more persons required to file notification, and, with respect to each such person, from one or more entities included therein, or from one or more officers, directors, partners, agents, or employees thereof, if so required by the same request.

Example: A request for additional information may require a corporation and, in addition, a named officer or employee to provide certain information or documents, if both the corporation and the officer or employee are named in the same request. See subparagraph (b)(3) of this section.

(2) All the information and documentary material required to be submitted pursuant to a request under paragraph (a)(1) of this section shall be supplied to the Commission or to the Assistant Attorney General, whichever made such request, at such location as may be designated in the request, or, if no such location is designated, at the office designated in § 803.10(c). If such request is not fully complied with, a statement of reasons for noncompliance pursuant to § 803.3 shall be provided for each item or portion of such request which is not fully complied with.

(b)(1) *Who may require submission.* A request for additional information or documentary material with respect to an acquisition may be issued by the Federal Trade Commission or its designee, or by the Assistant Attorney General or his or her designee, but not by both to the same person, any entities included therein, or any officers, directors, partners, agents, or employees of that person.

(2) *When request effective.* A request for additional information or documentary material shall be effective—

(i) In the case of a written request, upon receipt of the request by the ultimate parent entity of the person to which the request is directed (or, if another entity included within the person filed notification pursuant to § 803.2(a), then by such entity), within the original 30-day (or, in the case of a cash tender offer or of an acquisition covered by 11 U.S.C. 363(b), 15-day) waiting period (or, if § 802.23 applies, such other period as that section provides); or

(ii) In the case of a written request, upon notice of the issuance of such request to the person to which it is directed within the original 30-day (or, in the case of a cash tender offer or of an acquisition covered by 11 U.S.C. 363(b), 15-day) waiting period (or, if § 802.23 applies, such other period as that section provides), provided that written confirmation of the request is emailed or mailed to the person to which the request is directed within the original 30-day (or, in the case of a cash tender offer or of an acquisition covered by 11 U.S.C. 363(b), 15-day) waiting period (or, if § 802.23 applies, such other period as that section provides). Notice to the person to which the request is directed may be given by email, telephone or in person. The person filing notification shall keep a designated individual reasonably available during normal business hours throughout the waiting period at the email or telephone number supplied in the Notification and Report Form. Notice of a request for additional information or documentary material need be given by email or telephone only to that individual or to the individual designated in accordance with paragraph (b)(2)(iii) of this section. The written confirmation of the request shall be emailed or mailed to the ultimate parent entity of the person filing notification, or if another entity within the person filed notification pursuant to § 803.2(a), then to such entity.

(iii) When the individual designated in accordance with paragraph (b)(2)(ii) of this section is not located in the United States, the person filing notification shall designate an additional individual located within the United States to be reasonably available during normal business hours throughout the waiting period through a telephone number supplied on the certification page of the Notification and Report Form. This individual shall be designated for the limited purpose of receiving notification of the issuance of requests for additional information or documentary material in accordance with the procedure described in paragraph (b)(2)(ii) of this section.

(3) *Requests to natural persons.* A request addressed to an individual, requiring that he or she submit additional information or documentary material, shall be transmitted to the person filing notification of which the individual is an ultimate parent entity, officer, director, partner, agent or employee, and shall be effective as to that individual when effective as to the person filing notification pursuant to paragraph (b)(2) of this section. A written copy of the request shall also be delivered to the individual by email, by hand, or by registered or certified mail at his or her home or business address.

Example: A designee of the Federal Trade Commission sends, by email, a written request for additional information to the CEO of corporation W, the ultimate parent entity within a person that filed notification. The request is effective under paragraph (b)(2)(i) of this section. If the email also addressed a request for documentary material to the Secretary of corporation W, a named individual, under this paragraph (b)(3), the request would likewise be effective as to the individual upon receipt of the email by corporation W. In the latter case, the Federal Trade Commission also would send a copy of the request to the Secretary of the corporation at his or her home or business address, or email.

(c) *Waiting period extended.* (1) During the time period when a request for additional information or documentary material remains outstanding to any person other than either:

(i) In the case of a tender offer, the person whose voting securities are sought to be acquired by the tender offeror (or any officer, director, partner, agent or employee thereof), or

(ii) In the case of an acquisition covered by 11 U.S.C. 363(b), the acquired person, the waiting period shall remain in effect, even though the waiting period would have expired (see § 803.10(b)) if no such request had been made.

(2) A request for additional information or documentary material to any person other than either:

(i) In the case of a tender offer, the person whose voting securities are being acquired pursuant to the tender offer (or any officer, director, partner, agent or employee thereof), or

(ii) In the case of an acquisition covered by 11 U.S.C. 363(b), the acquired person, shall in every instance extend the waiting period for a period of 30 (or, in the case of a cash tender offer or of an acquisition covered by 11 U.S.C. 363(b), 10) calendar days from the date of receipt (as determined under § 803.10) of the additional information or documentary material requested.

Example: Acquiring person "A" makes a non-cash tender offer for voting securities of corporation "X", and files notification. Under § 801.30, the waiting period begins upon filing by "A," and "X" must file within 15 days thereafter (10 days if it were a cash tender offer). Assume that before the end of the waiting period, the Assistant Attorney General issues a request for additional information to "A" and "X." Since the transaction is a non-cash tender offer, the waiting period is extended for 30 days (10 days if it were a cash tender offer) beyond the date on which "A" responds. Note that under § 803.21, even though the waiting period is not affected by the second request to "X" or by "X" supplying the requested information, "X" is obliged to respond to the request within a reasonable time. Nevertheless, the Federal Trade Commission and Assistant Attorney General could, notwithstanding the pendency of the request for additional information, terminate the waiting period sua sponte pursuant to § 803.11(c).

(d)(1) *Identification of requests.* Every request for additional information or documentary material shall be clearly identified as such, whether communicated in person, by telephone or in writing, and shall clearly identify the person, entity or entities, or individual(s) to which it is addressed.

(2) *Request for clarification.* No request for clarification or amplification of a

response to any item on the Notification and Report Form, whether communicated in person, by telephone or in writing, shall be considered a request for additional information or documentary material within the meaning of section 7A(e) and this section.

[43 FR 33548, July 31, 1978, as amended at 48 FR 34441, July 29, 1983; 66 FR 8697, Feb. 1, 2001; 68 FR 2431, Jan. 17, 2003; 83 FR 32772, July 16, 2018]

§803.21 Additional information shall be supplied within reasonable time.

All additional information or documentary material requested pursuant to section 7A(e) and §803.20 (or, if such request is not fully complied with, the information or documentary material submitted and a statement of the reasons for such noncompliance in accordance with §803.3) shall be supplied within a reasonable time.

§803.30 Formal and informal interpretations of requirements under the Act and the rules.

(a) The Commission staff may consider requests for formal or informal interpretations as to the obligations under the act and these rules of any party to an acquisition. A request for a formal interpretation shall be made in writing to the offices designated in §803.10(c), and shall state: (1) all facts which the applicant believes to be material, (2) the reasons why the requirements of the act are or may be applicable and (3) the question(s) that the applicant wishes resolved. The Commission staff may, in its discretion, render a formal or informal response to any request, however made, or may decline to render such advice.

(b) In the sole discretion of the staff, any request for interpretation may be referred to the Commission.

(c) Formal interpretations by the Commission staff or by the Commission shall be rendered with the concurrence of the Assistant Attorney General or his or her designee.

(d) Any formal interpretation shall be without prejudice to the right of either the Commission or the Assistant Attorney General to rescind any such interpretation rendered pursuant to this section. In the event of such rescission, the party which requested the interpretation shall be so notified in writing.

(e) The Commission shall publish a summary of formal interpretations by the Commission, and any rescissions thereof, in the FEDERAL REGISTER.

§803.90 Separability.

If any provision of the rules in this subchapter (H) (including the Notification and Report Form) or the application of any such provision to any person or circumstances is held invalid, neither the other provisions of the rules nor the application of such provision to other persons or circumstances shall be affected thereby.

APPENDIX A TO PART 803—NOTIFICATION AND REPORT FORM FOR CERTAIN MERGERS AND ACQUISITIONS

NOTIFICATION AND REPORT FORM FOR CERTAIN MERGERS AND ACQUISITIONS

☐☐☐☐☐☐☐☐
TRANSACTION NUMBER ASSIGNED

FEE INFORMATION *(For Payer Only)*

TAXPAYER IDENTIFICATION NUMBER ______
OR SOCIAL SECURITY NUMBER FOR NATURAL PERSONS

AMOUNT PAID $ ______

NAME OF PAYER *(if different from PERSON FILING)* ______

WIRE TRANSFER ☐ or CERTIFIED CHECK / MONEY ORDER ATTACHED ☐

WIRE TRANSFER CONFIRMATION NO. ______

FROM (NAME OF INSTITUTION) ______

IS THIS A CORRECTIVE FILING? ☐ YES ☐ NO | CASH TENDER OFFER? ☐ YES ☐ NO | BANKRUPTCY? ☐ YES ☐ NO

DO YOU REQUEST EARLY TERMINATION OF THE WAITING PERIOD? ☐ YES ☐ NO
(Grants of early termination are published in the Federal Register and on the FTC web site, www.ftc.gov)

(voluntary) IS THIS ACQUISITION SUBJECT TO NON-US FILING REQUIREMENTS? ☐ YES ☐ NO
IF YES, list jurisdictions:

ITEM 1

1(a) PERSON FILING

NAME
HEADQUARTERS ADDRESS
ADDRESS LINE 2
CITY, STATE, COUNTRY
ZIP CODE
WEB SITE

1(b) PERSON FILING NOTIFICATION IS ☐ an acquiring person ☐ an acquired person ☐ both

1(c) PUT AN "X" IN THE APPROPRIATE BOX TO DESCRIBE THE PERSON FILING NOTIFICATION
☐ Corporation ☐ Unincorporated Entity ☐ Natural Person ☐ Other *(Specify)* ______

1(d) DATA FURNISHED BY
☐ calendar year ☐ fiscal year *(specify period):* ______ (month/year) to ______ (month/year)

1(e) PUT AN "X" IN THE APPROPRIATE BOX BELOW AND GIVE THE NAME AND ADDRESS OF THE ENTITY FILING NOTIFICATION, IF DIFFERENT THAN THE ULTIMATE PARENT ENTITY

☐ Not Applicable | ☐ This report is being filed on behalf of a foreign person pursuant to § 803.4. | ☐ This report is being filed on behalf of the ultimate parent entity by another entity within the same person authorized by it to file pursuant to § 803.2(a).

NAME
ADDRESS
CITY, STATE, COUNTRY
ZIP CODE

1(f) NAME AND ADDRESS OF ENTITY MAKING ACQUISITION OR WHOSE ASSETS, VOTING SECURITIES OR NON-CORPORATE INTERESTS ARE BEING ACQUIRED, IF DIFFERENT FROM THE ULTIMATE PARENT ENTITY IDENTIFIED IN ITEM 1(a)

NAME
ADDRESS
CITY, STATE, COUNTRY
ZIP CODE

☐ Not Applicable

PERCENT OF VOTING SECURITIES OR NON-CORPORATE INTERESTS THAT THE UPE HOLDS DIRECTLY OR INDIRECTLY IN THE ACQUIRING OR ACQUIRED ENTITY IDENTIFIED IN ITEM 1(f) %

1(g) IDENTIFICATION OF PERSONS TO CONTACT REGARDING THIS REPORT

CONTACT PERSON 1		CONTACT PERSON 2	
FIRM NAME		FIRM NAME	
BUSINESS ADDRESS		BUSINESS ADDRESS	
CITY, STATE, COUNTRY		CITY, STATE, COUNTRY	
ZIP CODE		ZIP CODE	
TELEPHONE NUMBER		TELEPHONE NUMBER	
FAX NUMBER		FAX NUMBER	
E-MAIL ADDRESS		E-MAIL ADDRESS	

1(h) IDENTIFICATION OF AN INDIVIDUAL LOCATED IN THE UNITED STATES DESIGNATED FOR THE LIMITED PURPOSE OF RECEIVING NOTICE OF ISSUANCE OF A REQUEST FOR ADDITIONAL INFORMATION OR DOCUMENTS (See § 803.20(b)(2)(iii))

NAME
FIRM NAME
BUSINESS ADDRESS
CITY, STATE, COUNTRY
ZIP CODE
TELEPHONE NUMBER
FAX NUMBER
E-MAIL ADDRESS

ITEM 2

2(a) LIST NAMES OF ULTIMATE PARENT ENTITIES OF ALL ACQUIRING PERSONS

NAME	NON-REPORTABLE
	☐

LIST NAMES OF ULTIMATE PARENT ENTITIES OF ALL ACQUIRED PERSONS

NAME	NON-REPORTABLE
	☐

2(b) THIS ACQUISITION IS *(put an "X" in all the boxes that apply)*

☐ an acquisition of assets
☐ a merger (see § 801.2)
☐ an acquisition subject to § 801.2 (e)
☐ a formation of a joint venture or other corporation or unincorporated entity (see § 801.40 or § 801.50)
☐ an acquisition subject to § 801.30 *(specify type)*
☐ a consolidation (see § 801.2)
☐ an acquisition of voting securities
☐ a secondary acquisition
☐ an acquisition subject to § 801.31
☐ an acquisition of non-corporate interests
☐ other *(specify)*

2(c) INDICATE THE HIGHEST NOTIFICATION THRESHOLD IN § 801.1(h) FOR WHICH THIS FORM IS BEING FILED
(acquiring person only in an acquisition of voting securities)

☐ $50 million (as adjusted) ☐ $100 million (as adjusted) ☐ $500 million (as adjusted) ☐ 25% (see Instructions) (as adjusted) ☐ 50% ☐ N/A

2(d)(i) VALUE OF VOTING SECURITIES ALREADY HELD ($MM) $	(v) VALUE OF NON-CORPORATE INTERESTS ALREADY HELD ($MM) $	
(ii) PERCENTAGE OF VOTING SECURITIES ALREADY HELD %	(vi) PERCENTAGE OF NON-CORPORATE INTERESTS ALREADY HELD %	
(iii) TOTAL VALUE OF VOTING SECURITIES TO BE HELD AS A RESULT OF THE ACQUISITION ($MM) $	(vii) TOTAL VALUE OF NON-CORPORATE INTERESTS TO BE HELD AS A RESULT OF THE ACQUISITION ($MM) $	(ix) VALUE OF ASSETS TO BE HELD AS A RESULT OF THE ACQUISITION ($MM) $
(iv) TOTAL PERCENTAGE OF VOTING SECURITIES TO BE HELD AS A RESULT OF THE ACQUISITION %	(viii) TOTAL PERCENTAGE OF NON-CORPORATE INTERESTS TO BE HELD AS A RESULT OF THE ACQUISITION %	(x) AGGREGATE TOTAL VALUE ($MM) $

ITEM 3

3(a) DESCRIPTION OF ACQUISITION

ACQUIRING UPE(S)		ACQUIRED UPE(S)	
NAME		NAME	
ADDRESS		ADDRESS	
ADDRESS LINE 2		ADDRESS LINE 2	
CITY, STATE		CITY, STATE	
ZIP CODE, COUNTRY		ZIP CODE, COUNTRY	

ACQUIRING ENTITY(S)		ACQUIRED ENTITY(S)	
NAME		NAME	
ADDRESS		ADDRESS	
ADDRESS LINE 2		ADDRESS LINE 2	
CITY, STATE		CITY, STATE	
ZIP CODE, COUNTRY		ZIP CODE, COUNTRY	

TRANSACTION DESCRIPTION

3(b) SUBMIT A COPY OF THE MOST RECENT VERSION OF THE CONTRACT OR AGREEMENT *(or letter of intent to merge or acquire)*

(IF SUBMITTING PAPER, DO NOT ATTACH THE DOCUMENT TO THIS PAGE) ATTACHMENT NUMBER

ITEM 4

PERSONS FILING NOTIFICATION MAY PROVIDE BELOW AN OPTIONAL INDEX OF DOCUMENTS REQUIRED TO BE SUBMITTED BY ITEM 4 *(See Item by Item instructions)*. THESE DOCUMENTS SHOULD NOT BE ATTACHED TO THIS PAGE.

4(a) ENTITIES WITHIN THE PERSON FILING NOTIFICATION THAT FILE ANNUAL REPORTS WITH THE SECURITIES AND EXCHANGE COMMISSION ☐ None

	CENTRAL INDEX KEY NUMBER	

4(b) ANNUAL REPORTS AND ANNUAL AUDIT REPORTS ☐ None

	ATTACHMENT OR REFERENCE NUMBER

4(c) STUDIES, SURVEYS, ANALYSES, AND REPORTS ☐ None

	ATTACHMENT OR REFERENCE NUMBER	

4(d) ADDITIONAL DOCUMENTS ☐ None

	ATTACHMENT OR REFERENCE NUMBER	

ITEM 5

5(a) DOLLAR REVENUES BY NON-MANUFACTURING INDUSTRY CODE AND BY MANUFACTURED PRODUCT CODE

Check None at the bottom of the page and provide explanation if you are not reporting revenue

6-DIGIT INDUSTRY CODE AND/OR 10-DIGIT PRODUCT CODE	DESCRIPTION	YEAR TOTAL DOLLAR REVENUES ($MM)	
	Attachment:		
			☐ Overlap

NONE ☐ *(PROVIDE EXPLANATION)*

5(b) COMPLETE ONLY IF ACQUISITION IS IN THE FORMATION OF A JOINT VENTURE CORPORATION OR UNINCORPORATED ENTITY	☐ Not Applicable

5(b)(i) CONTRIBUTIONS THAT EACH PERSON FORMING THE JOINT VENTURE CORPORATION OR UNINCORPORATED ENTITY HAS AGREED TO MAKE

Attachment:

5(b)(ii) DESCRIPTION OF CONSIDERATION THAT EACH PERSON FORMING THE JOINT VENTURE CORPORATION OR UNINCORPORATED ENTITY WILL RECEIVE

Attachment:

5(b)(iii) DESCRIPTION OF THE BUSINESS IN WHICH THE JOINT VENTURE CORPORATION OR UNINCORPORATED ENTITY WILL ENGAGE

Attachment:

5(b)(iv) SOURCE OF DOLLAR REVENUES BY 6-DIGIT INDUSTRY CODE (non-manufacturing) AND BY 10-DIGIT PRODUCT CODE (manufactured)

Attachment:

CODE	DESCRIPTION

ITEM 6

6(a) ENTITIES WITHIN PERSON FILING NOTIFICATION Attachment:

NAME	CITY	STATE	COUNTRY

6(b) HOLDERS OF PERSON FILING NOTIFICATION Attachment:

ISSUER/ UNINCORPORATED ENTITY	SHAREHOLDER/ INTEREST HOLDER	HQ ADDRESS	% HELD

6(c)(i) HOLDINGS OF PERSON FILING NOTIFICATION Attachment:

UPE OF FILING PERSON	ISSUER/ UNINCORPORATED ENTITY	% HELD

6(c)(ii) HOLDINGS OF ASSOCIATES *(ACQUIRING PERSON ONLY)* Attachment:

TOP LEVEL ASSOCIATE	ISSUER/ UNINCORPORATED ENTITY	% HELD

ITEM 7

OVERLAP DOLLAR REVENUES

7(a) 6-DIGIT NAICS INDUSTRY CODE AND DESCRIPTION ☐ None

CODE	DESCRIPTION	PERSON / ASSOCIATE / BOTH

7(b)(i) LIST THE NAME OF EACH PERSON THAT ALSO DERIVED DOLLAR REVENUES

UPE OF OTHER FILING PERSON	ENTITY THAT OVERLAPS (IF DIFFERENT)

7(b)(ii) LIST THE NAME OF EACH ASSOCIATE OF THE ACQUIRING PERSON THAT ALSO DERIVED DOLLAR REVENUES (*ACQUIRING PERSON ONLY)*

TOP LEVEL ASSOCIATE	ENTITY THAT OVERLAPS (IF DIFFERENT)

7(c) GEOGRAPHIC MARKET INFORMATION FOR EACH PERSON THAT ALSO DERIVED DOLLAR REVENUES

CODE	GEOGRAPHIC MARKET INFORMATION

7(d) GEOGRAPHIC MARKET INFORMATION FOR ASSOCIATES OF THE ACQUIRING PERSON (*ACQUIRING PERSON ONLY)*

CODE	GEOGRAPHIC MARKET INFORMATION

ITEM 8

PRIOR ACQUISITIONS *(ACQUIRING PERSON ONLY)*

NAICS Code	
Acquired Entity	
Former HQ Address	
Acquisition Type	☐ Securities ☐ Assets ☐ Non Corporate Interests Date of Acquisition:
Notes	

CERTIFICATION

This **NOTIFICATION AND REPORT FORM,** together with any and all appendices and attachments thereto, was prepared and assembled under my supervision in accordance with instructions issued by the Federal Trade Commission. Subject to the recognition that, where so indicated, reasonable estimates have been made because books and records do not provide the required data, the information is, to the best of my knowledge, true, correct, and complete in accordance with the statute and rules.

NAME (Please print or type)	TITLE
SIGNATURE	DATE

Subscribed and sworn to before me at the

City of____________________, State of______________________________________ [SEAL]

this______________day of_________________________, the year _____________________

Signature ____

My Commission expires ___________________________________

16 C.F.R. Part 803 - Appendix NOTIFICATION AND REPORT FORM FOR CERTAIN MERGERS AND ACQUISITIONS	Approved by OMB 3084-0005

Attach the Affidavit required by § 803.5 to the Form.

THE INFORMATION REQUIRED TO BE SUPPLIED ON THESE ANSWER SHEETS IS SPECIFIED IN THE INSTRUCTIONS

THIS FORM IS REQUIRED BY LAW and must be filed separately by each person which, by reason of a merger, consolidation or acquisition, is subject to §7A of the Clayton Act, 15 U.S.C. §18a, as added by Section 201 of the Hart-Scott-Rodino Antitrust Improvements Act of 1976, Pub. L. No. 94-435, 90 Stat. 1390, and rules promulgated thereunder (hereinafter referred to as "the rules" or by section number). The statute and rules are set forth in the *Federal Register* at 43 FR 33450; the rules may also be found at 16 CFR Parts 801-03. Failure to file this **Notification and Report Form**, and to observe the required waiting period before consummating the acquisition in accordance with the applicable provisions of 15 U.S.C. §18a and the rules, subjects any "person," as defined in the rules, or any individuals responsible for noncompliance, to liability for a penalty for each day during which such person is in violation of 15 U.S.C. §18a. The maximum daily civil penalty amount is listed in 16 C.F.R. §1.98(a).

Pursuant to the Hart-Scott-Rodino Act, information and documentary material filed in or with this Form is confidential. It is exempt from disclosure under the Freedom of Information Act, and may be made public only in an administrative or judicial proceeding, or disclosed to Congress or to a duly authorized committee or subcommittee of Congress.

DISCLOSURE NOTICE - Public reporting burden for this report is estimated to vary from 8 to 160 hours per response, with an average of 37 hours per response, including time for reviewing instructions, searching existing data sources, gathering and maintaining the data needed, and completing and reviewing the collection of information. Send comments regarding the burden estimate or any other aspect of this report, including suggestions for reducing this burden to:

> Premerger Notification Office, Federal Trade Commission, 400 7th St. SW, Room # 5301, Washington, DC 20024
> and
> Office of Information and Regulatory Affairs, Office of Management and Budget, Washington, DC 20503

Under the **Paperwork Reduction Act**, as amended, an agency may not conduct or sponsor, and a person is not required to respond to, a collection of information unless it displays a currently valid OMB control number. That number is 3084-0005, which also appears above.

Privacy Act Statement--Section 18a(a) of Title 15 of the U.S. Code authorizes the collection of this information. Our authority to collect Social Security numbers is 31 U.S.C. 7701. The primary use of information submitted on this Form is to determine whether the reported merger or acquisition may violate the antitrust laws. Taxpayer information is collected, used, and may be shared with other agencies and contractors for payment processing, debt collection and reporting purposes. Furnishing the information on the Form is voluntary. Consummation of an acquisition required to be reported by the statute cited above without having provided this information may, however, render a person liable to civil penalties up to the amount listed in 16 C.F.R. §1.98(a) per day. We also may be unable to process the Form unless you provide all of the requested information.

This page may be omitted when submitting the Form.

[82 FR 32124, July 12, 2017]

APPENDIX B TO PART 803—INSTRUCTIONS TO THE NOTIFICATION AND REPORT FORM FOR CERTAIN MERGERS AND ACQUISITIONS

ANTITRUST IMPROVEMENTS ACT NOTIFICATION AND REPORT FORM for Certain Mergers and Acquisitions

INSTRUCTIONS OMB: 3084-0005

GENERAL

The Notification and Report Form ("the Form") is required to be submitted pursuant to § 803.1(a) of the premerger notification rules, 16 CFR Parts 801-803 ("the Rules"). These instructions specify the information that must be provided in response to the items on the Form.

Information
The central office for information and assistance concerning the Form and the Rules is:

Premerger Notification Office
Federal Trade Commission, Room #5301
400 7th Street, S.W.
Washington, D.C. 20024
Phone: (202) 326-3100
E-mail: HSRhelp@ftc.gov

Copies of the Form, Instructions and Rules as well as information to assist in completing the Form are available at the PNO website.

Definitions
The definitions used in this Form are set forth in the Rules. See Statute, Rules and Formal Interpretations for copies of the Hart-Scott-Rodino Act ("the Act"), the Rules, and the Federal Register Notices issuing the Rules and Rule amendments ("Statements of Basis and Purpose").

The term "documentary attachments" refers only to materials submitted in response to Item 3(b), Item 4 and to submissions pursuant to § 803.1(b) of the Rules.

The terms "person filing" or "filing person" mean the ultimate parent entity ("UPE"). (See § 801.1(a)(3)). The terms are used herein interchangeably.

Filing
Parties should file the completed Form, together with all documentary attachments, with the Premerger Notification Office ("PNO") of the Federal Trade Commission ("FTC") and the Premerger Unit of the Antitrust Division of the Department of Justice ("DOJ") (together, "the Agencies"). Filers have the option of submitting a DVD filing or a paper filing. Filings should be submitted to:

Premerger Notification Office
Federal Trade Commission, Room #5301
400 7th Street, S.W.
Washington, D.C. 20024

and

Department of Justice
Antitrust Division
Premerger and Division Statistics Unit
450 Fifth Street, N.W., Suite 1100
Washington, D.C. 20530

If one or both delivery sites are unavailable, the Agencies may announce alternate sites for delivery through the media and, if possible, at the PNO website.

If submitting a DVD filing

1) Provide the FTC with:

   TWO (2) DVDs, each containing the Form, affidavit, certification and all documentary attachments, along with the original hard copies of the cover letter, certification and affidavit.

2) Provide DOJ with:

   TWO (2) DVDs containing the same content as above, along with **THREE** (3) hard copies of the cover letter.

The Form must be a searchable PDF document. All other files must be in searchable PDF or MS Excel spreadsheet format and saved in color, if applicable. This includes the affidavit and certification.

Label each DVD with the name of the person filing, the name of a contact person and that person's phone number. Leave space on the DVD for the Agencies to write the assigned transaction number and date of receipt.

If the DVD or files contain viruses, passwords, or are not readable, the filing will not be accepted and the waiting period will not start.

For further instructions on DVD filing and specific DVD requirements, go to HSR Resources on the PNO website.

If submitting a paper filing

1) Provide the FTC with:

   ONE (1) original and **ONE** (1) copy of the Form, certification page and affidavit, along with an original cover letter and **ONE** (1) set of documentary attachments.

2) Provide DOJ with:

   TWO (2) copies of the Form, certification page and affidavit, along with **THREE** (3) copies of the cover letter, and **ONE** (1) set of documentary attachments.

Affidavits
Affidavit(s) are required by § 803.5 and must attest to the good faith of the persons filing to complete the transaction. Affidavits must be notarized or use the language found in 28 U.S.C. § 1746 relating to unsworn declarations under penalty of perjury. If an entity is filing on behalf of the acquiring or acquired person, the affidavit must still attest to the good faith of the UPE.

In non-§ 801.30 transactions, the affidavit(s) (submitted by both persons filing) must attest that a contract, agreement in principle or letter of intent to merge or acquire has been executed, and further attest to the good faith intention of the person filing notification to complete the transaction. (See § 803.5(b)).

In § 801.30 transactions, the affidavit (submitted only by the acquiring person) must attest:

1) that the issuer whose voting securities or the unincorporated entity whose non-corporate interests are to be acquired has received notice, as described below, from the acquiring person;

2) in the case of a tender offer, that the intention to make the tender offer has been publicly announced; and

3) the good faith intention of the person filing notification to complete the transaction.

Acquiring persons in § 801.30 transactions are required to submit a copy of the notice received by the acquired person pursuant to § 803.5(a)(3) along with the filing. This notice must include:

1) the identity of the acquiring person and the fact that the acquiring person intends to acquire voting securities of the issuer or non-corporate interests of the unincorporated entity;

2) the specific notification threshold that the acquiring person intends to meet or exceed in an acquisition of voting securities;

3) the fact that the acquisition may be subject to the Act, and that the acquiring person will file notification under the Act;

4) the anticipated date of receipt of such notification by the Agencies; and

5) the fact that the person within which the issuer or unincorporated entity is included may be required to file notification under the Act. (See § 803.5(a)).

Responses
Enter the name of the person filing notification in Item 1(a) on page 1 of the Form, and enter the same name and the date on which the Form is completed at the top of each page of the Form.

If there is insufficient room on the Form for a response to a particular item, attach "additional pages" behind that item on the Form. Filers must submit a complete set of additional pages within each copy of the Form.

Each additional page should identify, at the top of the page, the name of the person filing notification, the date on which the Form is completed and the item to which it is addressed.

Voluntary submissions pursuant to § 803.1(b) should be identified as V-1, V-2, etc.

If unable to answer any item fully, provide such information as is available and a statement of reasons for non-compliance as required by § 803.3. If exact answers to any item cannot be given, enter best estimates and indicate the source or basis of such estimates. Add an endnote with the notation "est." to any item where data are estimated.

All financial information should be expressed in millions of dollars rounded to the nearest one-tenth of a million dollars.

Limited Response
The acquired person should limit its response in Items 5-7:

1) in the case of an acquisition of assets, to the assets being acquired;

2) in the case of an acquisition of voting securities, to the issuer(s) whose voting securities are being acquired and all entities controlled by such acquired entities; and

3) in the case of an acquisition of non-corporate interests, to the unincorporated entity(s) whose non-corporate interests are being acquired and all entities controlled by such acquired entities.

Separate responses may be required where a person is both acquiring and acquired. (See § 803.2(b)).

Information need not be supplied regarding assets, voting securities or non-corporate interests currently being acquired when their acquisition is exempt under the Act or Rules. (See § 803.2(c)).

Year
All references to "year" refer to calendar year. If data are not available on a calendar year basis, supply the requested data for the fiscal year reporting period that most nearly corresponds to the calendar year specified. References to "most recent year" mean the most recent calendar or fiscal year for which the requested information is available.

North American Industry Classification System (NAICS) Data
The Form requests "dollar revenues" categorized by NAICS codes for non-manufactured and manufactured products with respect to operations conducted within the United States, and for products manufactured outside of the United States and sold into the United States. (See § 803.2(d)). Filing persons must submit data at the 6-digit NAICS national industry code level to reflect non-manufacturing dollar revenues. To the extent that dollar revenues are derived from manufacturing operations (NAICS Sectors 31-33), filing persons must only submit data at the 10-digit NAICS product code levels, not the 6-digit level. (See Item 5 below).

In reporting information by 6-digit NAICS industry code, refer to the 2012 *North American Industry Classification System - United States* published by the Executive Office of the President, Office of Management and Budget. In reporting information by 10-digit NAICS product code, refer to the 2012 *Numerical List of Manufactured and Mineral Products* published by the Bureau of the Census. Information regarding NAICS is available at www.census.gov. This site also provides assistance in choosing the proper code(s) for reporting in Item 5 of the Form.

Filers should continue to use 6- and 10-digit 2012 NAICS codes when filling out Items 5, 7, and 8 of the Form. The U.S. Census Bureau is transitioning to a new classification system and the PNO will wait until that system is fully functional before switching. Please monitor the PNO's website for further announcements on this topic.

Thresholds
Filing fee and notification thresholds are adjusted annually pursuant to 15 U.S.C. § 18A(a)(2)(A) based on the change in gross national product, in accordance with 15 U.S.C. § 19(a)(5). The current threshold values can be found at Current Filing Thresholds.

END OF GENERAL SECTION

Online Style Sheet for the Form

Online Tips for the Form

THE FORM - ITEM BY ITEM

Fee Information
The fee for filing the Form is based on the aggregate total value of assets, voting securities and controlling non-corporate interests to be held as a result of the acquisition:

Value of assets, voting securities and controlling non-corporate interests to be held	Fee Amount
greater than $50 million (as adjusted) but less than $100 million (as adjusted)	$45,000
$100 million (as adjusted) or greater but less than $500 million (as adjusted)	$125,000
$500 million or greater (as adjusted)	$280,000

For current thresholds and fee information, see the PNO website.

Amount Paid
Indicate the amount of the filing fee paid. This amount should be net of any banking or financial institution charges.

Payer Identification
Provide the payer's name and 9-digit Taxpayer Identification Number (TIN). If the payer is a natural person with no TIN, provide the natural person's social security number.

Method of Payment
The preferred method of payment is by electronic wire transfer (EWT). For EWT payments, provide the EWT confirmation number and the name of the financial institution from which the EWT is being sent. If the EWT confirmation number is not available at the time of filing, provide this information to the PNO within two business days of filing.

In order for the FTC to track payment, the payer must provide information required by the Fedwire Instructions to the financial institution initiating the EWT. A template of the Fedwire Instructions is available at the PNO website on the Filing Fee Information page.

There are now specific, limited criteria for paying by certified check. Please see the Filing Fee Information page for details.

Corrective Filings
Put an X in the appropriate box to indicate whether the notification is a corrective filing (i.e., an acquisition that has already taken place without filing, in violation of the statute). See Procedures for Submitting Post-Consummation Filings for more information on how to proceed in the case of a corrective filing.

Cash Tender Offer
Put an X in the appropriate box to indicate whether the acquisition is a cash tender offer.

Bankruptcy
Put an X in the appropriate box to indicate whether the acquired person's filing is being made by a trustee in bankruptcy or by a debtor-in-possession for a transaction that is subject to Section 363(b) of the Bankruptcy Code (11 U.S.C. § 363).

Early Termination
Put an X in the "yes" box to request early termination of the waiting period. Notification of each grant of early termination will be published in the Federal Register, as required by 15 U.S.C. § 18A(b)(2), and on the PNO website. Note that if either party in any transaction requests early termination, it may be granted and published.

Transactions Subject to International Antitrust Notification
If, to the knowledge or belief of the filing person at the time of filing, a non-U.S. antitrust or competition authority has been or will be notified of the proposed transaction, list the name of each such authority. Response to this item is voluntary.

Index of Hyperlinks in these Instructions:

PNO website: https://www.ftc.gov/enforcement/premerger-notification-program

Statute, Rules and Formal Interpretations: https://www.ftc.gov/enforcement/premerger-notification-program/statute-rules-formal-interpretations

HSR Resources: https://www.ftc.gov/enforcement/premerger-notification-program/hsr-resources

Current Filing Thresholds: https://www.ftc.gov/enforcement/premerger-notification-program/current-thresholds

Online Style Sheet for the Form: https://www.ftc.gov/enforcement/premerger-notification-program/form-instructions/style-sheet

Online Tips for the Form: https://www.ftc.gov/system/files/attachments/form-instructions/hsr_form_tip_sheet_1.0.5.pdf

Filing Fee Information: https://www.ftc.gov/enforcement/premerger-notification-program/filing-fee-information

Procedures for Submitting Post-Consummation Filings: https://www.ftc.gov/enforcement/premerger-notification-program/post-consummation-filings-hsr-violations

Online Tips for Item 4(c): https://www.ftc.gov/sites/default/files/attachments/hsr-resources/4ctipsheet.pdf

Online Tips for Item 4(d): https://www.ftc.gov/enforcement/premerger-notification-program/hsr-resources/pno-guidance-item-4d

Online Tips for Item 5: https://www.ftc.gov/enforcement/premerger-notification-program/hsr-resources/reporting-revenues-item-5

Online Tips for Item 6: https://www.ftc.gov/enforcement/premerger-notification-program/hsr-resources/tips-completing-item-6-hsr-form

Online Tips for Item 7: https://www.ftc.gov/enforcement/premerger-notification-program/hsr-resources/tips-completing-item-7-hsr-form

Instructions to FTC Form **C4** (rev. 02/04/2018) III

ITEM 1

Item 1(a)
Provide the name, headquarters address and website (if one exists) of the person filing notification. The name of the person filing is the name of the UPE. (See § 801.1(a)(3)).

Item 1(b)
Indicate whether the person filing notification is an acquiring person, an acquired person, or both an acquiring and acquired person. (See § 801.2).

Item 1(c)
Put an X in the appropriate box to indicate whether the person in Item 1(a) is a corporation, unincorporated entity, natural person, or other (specify). (See § 801.1).

Item 1(d)
Put an X in the appropriate box to indicate whether data furnished in Item 5 is by calendar year or fiscal year. If fiscal year, specify the time period.

Item 1(e)
Put an X in the appropriate box to indicate if the Form is being filed on behalf of the UPE by another entity within the same person authorized by it to file notification on its behalf pursuant to § 803.2(a), or if the Form is being filed pursuant to § 803.4 on behalf of a foreign person. Then provide the name and mailing address of the entity filing notification on behalf of the filing person named in Item 1(a) of the Form.

Item 1(f)
For the acquiring person, if an entity other than the UPE listed in Item 1(a) is making the acquisition, provide the name and mailing address of that entity and the percentage of its voting securities or non-corporate interests held directly or indirectly by the person named in Item 1(a) above.

For the acquired person, if the assets, voting securities or non-corporate interests of an entity other than the UPE listed in Item 1(a) are being acquired, provide the name and mailing address of that entity and the percentage of its voting securities or non-corporate interests held directly or indirectly by the person named in Item 1(a) above.

Item 1(g)
Provide the name and title, firm name, address, telephone number, and e-mail address of the primary and secondary individuals to contact regarding the Form. A second contact person is required. (See § 803.20(b)(2)(ii)).

Item 1(h)
Foreign filing persons must provide the name, firm name, address, telephone number, and e-mail address of an individual located in the United States designated for the limited purpose of receiving notice of the issuance of a request for additional information or documentary material. (See § 803.20(b)(2)(iii)).

Note: The Form has fields for fax numbers in Item 1. Providing fax numbers is no longer necessary. The fields will be deleted during the next update of the HSR Form.

END OF ITEM 1

ITEM 2

Item 2(a)
Provide the names of all UPEs of acquiring and acquired persons that are parties to the transaction, whether or not they are required to file notification. If a person is not required to file, check the non-reportable box.

Item 2(b)
Put an X in all the boxes that apply to the transaction.

Item 2(c)
This item should only be completed by the acquiring person where voting securities are being acquired. If more than voting securities are being acquired, respond to this item only regarding voting securities. Put an X in the box to indicate the highest applicable threshold for which notification is being filed: $50 million (as adjusted), $100 million (as adjusted), $500 million (as adjusted), 25% (if the value of voting securities to be held is greater than $1 billion, as adjusted), or 50%. (See § 801.1(h)).

Note that the 50% notification threshold is the highest threshold and should be used for any acquisition of 50% or more of the voting securities of an issuer, regardless of the value of the voting securities. For instance, an acquisition of 100% of the voting securities of an issuer, valued in excess of $500 million (as adjusted) would cross the 50% notification threshold, not the $500 million (as adjusted) threshold.

Item 2(d)
Provide the requested information on assets, voting securities and non-corporate interests. If a combination of assets, voting securities and/or non-corporate interests are being acquired and allocation is not possible, note such information in an endnote.

For determining percentage of voting securities, evaluate total voting power per § 801.12.

For determining percentage of non-corporate interests, evaluate the economic interests per § 801.1(b)(1)(ii).

Item 2(d)(i)
State the value of voting securities already held. (See § 801.10).

Item 2(d)(ii)
State the percentage of voting securities already held. (See § 801.12).

Item 2(d)(iii)
State the total value of voting securities to be held as a result of the acquisition. (See § 801.10).

Item 2(d)(iv)
State the total percentage of voting securities to be held as a result of the acquisition. (See § 801.12).

Item 2(d)(v)
State the value of non-corporate interests already held. (See § 801.10).

Item 2(d)(vi)
State the percentage of non-corporate interests already held. (See § 801.1(b)(1)(ii)).

Item 2(d)(vii)
State the total value of non-corporate interests to be held as a result of the acquisition. (See § 801.10).

ITEM 2 cont.

Item 2(d)(viii)
State the total percentage of non-corporate interests to be held as a result of the acquisition. (See §§ 801.10 and 801.1(b)(1)(ii)).

Item 2(d)(ix)
State the value of assets to be held as a result of the acquisition. (See § 801.10).

Item 2(d)(x)
State the aggregate total value of assets, voting securities and non-corporate interests of the acquired person to be held as a result of the acquisition. (See §§ 801.10, 801.12, 801.13 and 801.14).

END OF ITEM 2

Most Common Mistakes When Completing the HSR Form

- Noncompliant affidavit
- Missing contact information in Item 1(g)
- Failure to describe target in Item 3(a)
- Incomplete privilege log
- Failure to properly identify authors and recipients of Item 4c/4d documents
- Failure to properly round revenues in Item 5 to nearest tenth of a million and failure to list in ascending order
- Failure to provide required geographic information (e.g., state, county, and city or town) in Item 7(c)(iv)(b)
- Failure to provide the total number of states and territories in response to Item 7(c)

ITEM 3

Item 3(a)
At the top of Item 3(a), list the name and mailing address of each acquiring and acquired person, and acquiring and acquired entity, whether or not required to file notification. It is not necessary to list every subsidiary wholly-owned owned by an acquired entity.

In the Transaction Description section, briefly describe the transaction, indicating whether assets, voting securities or non-corporate interests (or some combination) are to be acquired. Describe the business operation(s) being acquired. If assets, describe the assets and whether they comprise a business operation. Also, indicate what consideration will be received by each party and the scheduled consummation date of the transaction.

If any attached transaction documents use coded names to refer to the parties, please provide an index identifying the codes.

If there are additional filings, such as shareholder backside filings, associated with the transaction, identify those. Also, identify any special circumstances that apply to the filing, such as whether part of the transaction is exempt under one of the exemptions found in Part 802.

Item 3(b)
Furnish copies of all documents that constitute the agreement(s) among the acquiring person(s) and the person(s) whose assets, voting securities or non-corporate interests are to be acquired. Also furnish agreements not to compete and other agreements between the parties. Do not submit schedules and the like unless they contain agreements not to compete, other agreements between the parties, or other important terms of the transaction. For purposes of Item 3(b), responsive documents must be submitted; identifying an internet address or providing a link is not sufficient.

Documents that constitute the agreement(s) (e.g., a Letter of Intent, Merger Agreement, Purchase and Sale Agreement) must be executed, while agreements not to compete may be provided in draft form if that is the most recent version.

If parties are filing on an executed Letter of Intent, they may also submit a draft of the definitive agreement, if one exists.

Note that transactions subject to § 801.30 and bankruptcies under 11 U.S.C. § 363 do not require an executed agreement or letter of intent. For bankruptcies, provide the order from the bankruptcy court.

END OF ITEM 3

ITEM 4

Item 4(a)
Provide the names of all entities within the person filing notification, including the UPE, that file annual reports (Form 10-K or Form 20-F) with the United States Securities and Exchange Commission, and provide the Central Index Key (CIK) number for each entity.

Item 4(b)
Provide the most recent annual reports and/or annual audit reports (or, if audited is unavailable, unaudited) of the person filing notification.

The acquiring person should also provide the most recent reports of the acquiring entity(s) and any controlled entity whose dollar revenues contribute to an overlap reported in Item 7.

The acquired person should also provide the most recent reports of the acquired entity(s).

Natural persons need only provide the most recent reports for the highest level entity(s) they control. Do not provide personal balance sheets or tax returns.

If the most recent reports do not show sales or assets sufficient to meet the size of person test, and the size of person test is relevant given the size of the transaction, the filing person must stipulate in Item 4(b) that it meets the test.

Note that the person filing notification may incorporate a document by reference to an internet address directly linking to the document. (See § 803.2(e)).

Items 4(c) and 4(d)
For each document responsive to Items 4(c) and 4(d), provide the:

1) document's title;
2) date of preparation; and
3) name and title of each individual who prepared the document.

If a specific date is not available, indicate the month and year the document was prepared.

If a large group of people prepared the document, list all the authors and their titles, identifying the principal authors.

Alternatively, it is acceptable to indicate that the document was prepared under the supervision of the lead author and to provide the name and title of that author. If a third party prepared the document, the date of preparation and the name of the third party will suffice.

Numbering
Number each document provided in response to Items 4(c) and 4(d). Number 4(c) documents 4(c)-1, 4(c)-2, 4(c)-3, etc. Likewise, number 4(d) documents 4(d)-1, 4(d)-2, 4(d)-3, etc., regardless of the three sub-categories within Item 4(d). If providing only one document, identify it as 4(c)-1 or 4(d)-1.

When submitting a document responsive to both 4(c) and 4(d), list it only once, under 4(c) or 4(d). If a document is responsive to both 4(c) and 4(d), do not cross-reference.

Privilege
Note that if the filing person withholds or redacts portions of any document responsive to Items 4(c) and 4(d) based on a claim of privilege, the person must provide a statement of reasons for non-compliance (a "privilege log") detailing the claim of privilege for each withheld or redacted document. (See § 803.3(d)).

For each document, include the:

1) title of the document;
2) its author;
3) author's title/position;
4) addressee;
5) addressee's title/position;
6) date;
7) subject matter;
8) all recipients of the original and any copies;
9) recipients' titles/positions;
10) document's present location; and
11) who has control over it.

Additionally, the filing person must state the factual basis supporting the privilege claim in sufficient detail to enable staff to assess the validity of the claim for each document without disclosing the protected information.

If a privileged document was circulated to a group, such as the Board or an investment committee, the name of the group is sufficient, but the filing person should be prepared to disclose the names and titles/positions of the individual group members, if requested. If the claim of privilege is based on advice from inside and/or outside counsel, the name of the inside and/or outside counsel providing the advice (and the law firm, if applicable) must be provided. If several lawyers participated in providing advice, identifying lead counsel is sufficient. In identifying who controls a document, the name of the law firm is sufficient.

When creating a privilege log, use a separate numbering system for withheld documents, such as P-1, P-2, etc. Redacted documents should also be listed in a separate log that complies with § 803.3(d).

Item 4(c)
Provide all studies, surveys, analyses and reports which were prepared by or for any officer(s) or director(s) (or, in the case of unincorporated entities, individuals exercising similar functions) for the purpose of evaluating or analyzing the acquisition with respect to market shares, competition, competitors, markets, potential for sales growth or expansion into product or geographic markets.

Item 4(d)
Item 4(d)(i)
Provide all Confidential Information Memoranda prepared by or for any officer(s) or director(s) (or, in the case of unincorporated entities, individuals exercising similar functions) of the UPE of the acquiring or acquired person or of the acquiring or acquired entity(s) that specifically relate to the sale of the acquired entity(s)

ITEM 4 cont.

or assets. If no such Confidential Information Memorandum exists, submit any document(s) given to any officer(s) or director(s) of the buyer meant to serve the function of a Confidential Information Memorandum. This does not include ordinary course documents and/or financial data shared in the course of due diligence, except to the extent that such materials served the purpose of a Confidential Information Memorandum when no such Confidential Information Memorandum exists. Documents responsive to this item are limited to those produced up to one year before the date of filing.

Item 4(d)(ii)
Provide all studies, surveys, analyses and reports prepared by investment bankers, consultants or other third party advisors ("third party advisors") for any officer(s) or director(s) (or, in the case of unincorporated entities, individuals exercising similar functions) of the UPE of the acquiring or acquired person or of the acquiring or acquired entity(s) for the purpose of evaluating or analyzing market shares, competition, competitors, markets, potential for sales growth or expansion into product or geographic markets that specifically relate to the sale of the acquired entity(s) or assets. This item requires only materials developed by third party advisors during an engagement or for the purpose of seeking an engagement. Documents responsive to this item are limited to those produced up to one year before the date of filing.

Item 4(d)(iii)
Provide all studies, surveys, analyses and reports evaluating or analyzing synergies and/or efficiencies prepared by or for any officer(s) or director(s) (or, in the case of unincorporated entities, individuals exercising similar functions) for the purpose of evaluating or analyzing the acquisition. Financial models without stated assumptions need not be provided in response to this item.

END OF ITEM 4

Tip for Item 4
If there is insufficient room on the Form for a response, attach "additional pages" behind that item on the Form. (See Responses on page II).

Online Tips for Item 4(c)

Online Tips for Item 4(d)

ITEMS 5 THROUGH 7

Limited response for acquired person. For Items 5 through 7, the acquired person should limit its response in the case of an acquisition of:

1) assets, to the assets to be acquired;

2) voting securities, to the issuer(s) whose voting securities are being acquired and all entities controlled by such issuer; and/or

3) non-corporate interests, to the unincorporated entity(s) being acquired and all entities controlled by such unincorporated entity(s).

A person filing as both acquiring and acquired persons may be required to provide a separate response to Items 5 through 7 in each capacity so that it can properly limit its response as an acquired person. (See §§ 803.2(b) and (c)).

ITEM 5

This item requests revenue information by NAICS code regarding dollar revenues. (See NAICS Data section on page II). All persons must submit data on non-manufacturing dollar revenues at the 6-digit NAICS industry code level. To the extent that dollar revenues are derived from manufacturing operations (NAICS Sectors 31-33), only submit data at the 10-digit product code level (NAICS-based codes).

List all NAICS codes in ascending order.

Persons filing notification should include the total dollar revenues for all entities included within the person filing notification at the time the Form is prepared. If no dollar revenues are reported, check the "None" box and provide a brief explanation.

Item 5(a)
Provide 6-digit NAICS industry data concerning the aggregate U.S. operations of the person filing notification for the most recent year in all non-manufacturing NAICS Sectors in which the person engaged. If the dollar revenues for a non-manufacturing NAICS code totaled less than one million dollars in the most recent year, that code may be omitted from Item 5(a).

Provide 10-digit NAICS product code data for each product code within all manufacturing NAICS Sectors (31-33) in which the person engaged in the U.S., including dollar revenues for each product manufactured outside the U.S. but sold into the U.S. Sales of any manufactured product should be reported in a manufacturing code only, even if sold through a separate warehouse or retail establishment.

If such data have not been compiled for the most recent year, estimates of dollar revenues by 6-digit NAICS industry codes and 10-digit NAICS product codes may be provided.

Check the Overlap box for a NAICS code if both parties to the transaction generate dollar revenues in that NAICS code. If there is only a 6-digit overlap in a manufacturing code in Item 7, do not check the Overlap box for a related 10-digit code in Item 5.

ITEM 5 cont.

Item 5(b)
Complete only if the acquisition is the formation of a joint venture corporation or unincorporated entity. (See §§ 801.40 and 801.50). If the acquisition is not the formation of a joint venture, check the "Not Applicable" box.

Item 5(b)(i)
List the contributions that each person forming the joint venture corporation or unincorporated entity has agreed to make, specifying when each contribution is to be made and the value of the contribution as agreed by the contributors.

Item 5(b)(ii)
Describe fully the consideration that each person forming the joint venture corporation or unincorporated entity will receive in exchange for its contribution(s).

Item 5(b)(iii)
Describe generally the business in which the joint venture corporation or unincorporated entity will engage, including its principal types of products or activities, and the geographic areas in which it will do business.

Item 5(b)(iv)
Identify each 6-digit NAICS industry code in which the joint venture corporation or unincorporated entity will derive dollar revenues. If the joint venture corporation or unincorporated entity will be engaged in manufacturing, also specify each 10-digit NAICS product code in which it will derive dollar revenues.

END OF ITEM 5

Tip for Item 5
Remember, all financial information should be expressed in millions of dollars, rounded to the nearest one-tenth of a million dollars.

Online Tips for Item 5

ITEM 6

An acquired person does not complete Item 6 if the transaction involves only the acquisition of assets. If the transaction involves a mix of assets along with voting securities and/or non-corporate interests, the acquired person must complete Item 6 as related to the voting securities and non-corporate interests.

Item 6(a)
Subsidiaries of filing person. List the name, city and state/country of all U.S. entities, and all foreign entities that have sales in or into the U.S., that are included within the person filing notification. Entities with total assets of less than $10 million may be omitted. Alternatively, the filing person may report all entities within it.

Item 6(b)
Minority shareholders. For the acquired entity(s) and for the acquiring entity(s) and its UPE or, in the case of natural persons, the top-level corporate or unincorporated entity(s) within that UPE, list the name and headquarters mailing address of each shareholder that holds 5% or more but less than 50% of the outstanding voting securities or non-corporate interests of the entity, and the percentage of voting securities or non-corporate interests held by that person. (See § 801.1(c))

For limited partnerships, only the general partner(s), regardless of percentage held, should be listed.

Item 6(c)
Minority holdings. Item 6(c) requires the disclosure of holdings of 5% or more but less than 50%, of any entity(s) that derives dollar revenues in any 6-digit NAICS code reported by the other person filing notification. Holdings in those entities that have total assets of less than $10 million may be omitted.

The acquiring person may rely on its regularly prepared financials that list its investments, and those of its associates that list their investments, to respond to Items 6(c)(i) and (ii), provided the financials are no more than three months old.

If NAICS codes are unavailable, holdings in entities that have operations in the same industry, based on the knowledge or belief of the acquiring person, should be listed. In responding to Items 6(c)(i) and 6(c)(ii), it is permissible for the acquiring person to list all entities in which it or its associate(s) holds 5% or more but less than 50% of the voting securities of any issuer or non-corporate interests of any unincorporated entity. Holdings in those entities that have total assets of less than $10 million may be omitted.

Item 6(c)(i)
Minority holdings of filing person. If the person filing notification holds 5% or more but less than 50% of the voting securities of any issuer or non-corporate interests of any unincorporated entity, list the issuer and percentage of voting securities held, or in the case of an unincorporated entity, list the unincorporated entity and the percentage of non-corporate interests held.

The acquiring person should limit its response, based on its knowledge or belief, to entities that derived dollar revenues in the most recent year from operations in industries within any 6-digit NAICS industry code in which the acquired entity(s) or assets also derived dollar revenues in the most recent year.

The acquired person should limit its response, based on its knowledge or belief, to entities that derive dollar revenues in the

ITEM 6 cont.

same 6-digit NAICS industry code as the acquiring person.

Item 6(c)(ii)
Minority holdings of associates.
This item should only be completed by the acquiring person. Based on the knowledge or belief of the acquiring person, for each associate (see § 801.1(d)(2)) of the acquiring person holding:

1) 5% or more but less than 50% of the voting securities or non-corporate interests of the acquired entity(s); and/or

2) 5% or more but less than 50% of the voting securities of any issuer or non-corporate interests of any unincorporated entity that derived dollar revenues in the most recent year from operations in industries within any 6-digit NAICS industry code in which the acquired entity(s) or assets also derived dollar revenues in the most recent year;

list the associate, the issuer or unincorporated entity and the percentage held.

END OF ITEM 6

Tip for Item 6(c)
Remember, if NAICS codes are unavailable, holdings in entities that have operations in the same industry, based on the knowledge or belief of the acquiring person, should be listed.

Online Tips for Item 6

ITEM 7

If, to the knowledge or belief of the person filing notification, the acquiring person, or any associate (see § 801.1(d)(2)) of the acquiring person, derived any amount of dollar revenues (even if omitted from Item 5) in the most recent year from operations:

1) in industries within any 6-digit NAICS industry code in which any acquired entity that is a party to the acquisition also derived any amount of dollar revenues in the most recent year; or

2) in which a joint venture corporation or unincorporated entity will derive dollar revenues;

then for each such 6-digit NAICS industry code follow the instructions below for this section.

Note that if the acquired entity is a joint venture, the only overlaps that should be reported are those between the assets to be held by the joint venture and any assets of the acquiring person or its associates not contributed to the joint venture.

Also, if the acquiring person reports an associate overlap only, the acquired person does not need to respond to Item 7.

Item 7(a)
Industry Code Overlap Information
Provide the 6-digit NAICS industry code and description for the industry, and indicate whether the overlap is from the person, an associate or both.

Item 7(b)
Item 7(b)(i)
If the UPE of the other person(s) filing notification derived dollar revenues in the same 6-digit industry code(s) listed in Item 7(a), list the name of that UPE and the name of the entity(s) within that UPE that actually derived those dollar revenues, if different from the entity(s) listed in Item 3(a).

Item 7(b)(ii)
This item should only be completed by the acquiring person. List the name of each associate of the acquiring person that also derived dollar revenues through a controlled operating company(s) in the 6-digit industry and, if different, the name of the entity(s) that actually derived those dollar revenues.

Item 7(c)
Geographic Market Information
Use the 2-digit postal codes for states and territories and provide the total number of states and territories at the end of the response.

Note that except in the case of those NAICS industries in the Sectors and Subsectors mentioned in Item 7(c)(iv)(b), the person filing notification may respond with the word "national" if business is conducted in all 50 states.

Item 7(c)(i)
NAICS Sectors 31-33
For each 6-digit NAICS industry code within NAICS Sectors 31-33 (manufacturing industries) listed in Item 7(a), list the relevant geographic information in which, to the knowledge or belief of the person filing the notification, the products in that 6-digit NAICS industry code produced by the person filing notification are sold without a significant change in their form (whether they are sold by the person filing notification or by others to whom such products have been sold or resold). Except for industries covered

ITEM 7 cont.

by Item 7(c)(iv)(b), the relevant geographic information is all states or, if desired, portions thereof.

Item 7(c)(ii)
NAICS Sector 42
For each 6-digit NAICS industry code within NAICS Sector 42 (wholesale trade) listed in Item 7(a), list the states or, if desired, portions thereof in which the customers of the person filing notification are located.

Item 7(c)(iii)
NAICS Industry Group 5241
For each 6-digit NAICS industry code within NAICS Industry Group 5241 (insurance carriers) listed in Item 7(a), list the state(s) in which the person filing notification is licensed to write insurance.

Item 7(c)(iv)(a)
Other NAICS Sectors
For each 6-digit NAICS industry code listed in item 7(a) within the NAICS Sectors or Subsectors below, list the states or, if desired, portions thereof in which the person filing notification conducts such operations.

11	agriculture, forestry, fishing and hunting
21	mining
22	utilities
23	construction
48-49	transportation and warehousing
511	publishing industries
515	broadcasting
517	telecommunications
71	arts, entertainment and recreation

Item 7(c)(iv)(b)
For each 6-digit NAICS industry code listed in item 7(a) within the NAICS Sectors or Subsectors below, provide the address, arranged by state, county and city or town, of each establishment from which dollar revenues were derived in the most recent year by the person filing notification.

2123	nonmetallic mineral mining and quarrying
32512	industrial gases
32732	concrete
32733	concrete products
44-45	retail trade, except 442 (furniture and home furnishings stores), and 443 (electronics and appliance stores)
512	motion picture and sound recording industries
521	monetary authorities - central bank
522	credit intermediation and related activities
532	rental and leasing services
62	health care and social assistance
72	accommodations and food services, except 7212 (recreational vehicle parks and recreational camps), and 7213 (rooming and boarding houses)
811	repair and maintenance, except 8114 (personal and household goods repair and maintenance)
812	personal and laundry services

Item 7(c)(iv)(c)
For each 6-digit NAICS industry code listed in item 7(a) within the NAICS Sectors or Subsectors below, list the states or, if desired, portions thereof in which the person filing notification conducts such operations.

442	furniture and home furnishings stores
443	electronics and appliance stores
516	internet publishing & broadcasting
518	internet service providers
519	other information services
523	securities, commodity contracts and other financial investments and related activities
5242	insurance agencies and brokerages, and other insurance related activities
525	funds, trusts and other financial vehicles
53	real estate and rental and leasing
54	professional, scientific and technical services
55	management of companies and enterprises
56	administrative and support and waste management and remediation services
61	educational services
7212	recreational vehicle parks and recreational camps
7213	rooming and boarding houses
813	religious, grantmaking, civic, professional, and similar organizations
8114	personal and household goods repair and maintenance

Item 7(d)
This item should only be completed by the acquiring person.
Use the geographic markets listed in Items 7(c)(i) through 7(c)(iv) to respond to this item, providing the information for associates of the acquiring person. Provide separate responses for each associate of the acquiring person and, if different, the controlled operating company(s) that actually derived the dollar revenues.

END OF ITEM 7

Online Tips for Item 7

ITEM 8

This item should only be completed by the acquiring person. Determine each 6-digit NAICS industry code listed in Item 7(a), in which the acquiring person derived dollar revenues of $1 million or more in the most recent year and in which either:

1) the acquired entity derived dollar revenues of $1 million or more in the recent year (or in the case of the formation of a joint venture corporation or unincorporated entity, the joint venture corporation or unincorporated entity reasonably can be expected to derive dollar revenues of $1 million or more); or

2) in the case of acquired assets, to which dollar revenues of $1 million or more were attributable in the most recent year.

For each such 6-digit NAICS industry code, list all acquisitions of entities or assets deriving dollar revenues in that 6-digit NAICS industry code made by the acquiring person in the five years prior to the date of the instant filing, even if the transaction was non-reportable. List only acquisitions of 50% or more of the voting securities of an issuer or 50% or more of non-corporate interests of an unincorporated entity that had annual net sales or total assets greater than $10 million in the year prior to the acquisition, and any acquisitions of assets valued at or above the statutory size-of-transaction test at the time of their acquisition.

This item pertains only to acquisitions of U.S. entities/assets and foreign entities/assets with sales in or into the U.S., i.e., with dollar revenues that would be reported in Item 5.

For each such acquisition, supply:

1) the 6-digit NAICS industry code (by number and description) identified above in which the acquired entity derived dollar revenues;

2) the name of the entity from which the assets, voting securities or non-corporate interests were acquired;

3) the headquarters address of that entity prior to the acquisition;

4) whether assets, voting securities or non-corporate interests were acquired; and

5) the consummation date of the acquisition.

END OF ITEM 8

CERTIFICATION

See § 803.6 for requirements.

The certification must be notarized or use the language found in 28 U.S.C. § 1746 relating to unsworn declarations under penalty of perjury.

PRIVACY ACT STATEMENT

Section 18a(a) of Title 15 of the U.S. Code authorizes the collection of this information. Our authority to collect Social Security numbers is 31 U.S.C. § 7701. The primary use of information submitted on this Form is to determine whether the reported merger or acquisition may violate the antitrust laws. Taxpayer information is collected, used, and may be shared with other agencies and contractors for payment processing, debt collection and reporting purposes. Furnishing the information on the Form is voluntary. Consummation of an acquisition required to be reported by the statute cited above without having provided this information may, however, render a person liable to civil penalties up to the amount listed in 16 C.F.R. §1.98(a) per day.

We also may be unable to process the Form unless you provide all of the requested information.

DISCLOSURE NOTICE

Public reporting burden for this report is estimated to vary from 8 to 160 hours per response, with an average of 37 hours per response, including time for reviewing instructions, searching existing data sources, gathering and maintaining the data needed, and completing and reviewing the collection of information. Send comments regarding the burden estimate or any other aspect of this report, including suggestions for reducing this burden to:

Premerger Notification Office
Federal Trade Commission, Room #5301
400 7th Street, S.W.
Washington, D.C. 20024

and

Office of Information and Regulatory Affairs
Office of Management and Budget
Washington, D.C. 20503

Under the Paperwork Reduction Act, as amended, an agency may not conduct or sponsor, and a person is not required to respond to, a collection of information unless it displays a currently valid OMB control number. The operative OMB control number, 3084-0005, appears within the Notification and Report Form and these Instructions.

END OF FORM INSTRUCTIONS

Instructions to FTC Form **C4** (rev. 02/04/2018) XI

[83 FR 32772, July 16, 2018; 83 FR 45555, Sept. 10, 2018]

SUBCHAPTER I—FAIR DEBT COLLECTION PRACTICES ACT

PART 901—PROCEDURES FOR STATE APPLICATION FOR EXEMPTION FROM THE PROVISIONS OF THE ACT

AUTHORITY: Pub. L. 95–109, 91 Stat. 874, 15 U.S.C. 1692o; 5 U.S.C. 552.

SOURCE: 77 FR 22204, Apr. 13, 2012, unless otherwise noted.

§ 901.1 Cross-reference.

The rules formerly at 16 CFR part 901 have been republished by the Consumer Financial Protection Bureau at 12 CFR part 1006, "Fair Debt Collection Practices Act (Regulation F)."

PARTS 902–999 [RESERVED]

FINDING AIDS

A list of CFR titles, subtitles, chapters, subchapters and parts and an alphabetical list of agencies publishing in the CFR are included in the CFR Index and Finding Aids volume to the Code of Federal Regulations which is published separately and revised annually.

Table of CFR Titles and Chapters

(Revised as of January 1, 2019)

Title 1—General Provisions

I	Administrative Committee of the Federal Register (Parts 1—49)
II	Office of the Federal Register (Parts 50—299)
III	Administrative Conference of the United States (Parts 300—399)
IV	Miscellaneous Agencies (Parts 400—599)
VI	National Capital Planning Commission (Parts 600—699)

Title 2—Grants and Agreements

	SUBTITLE A—OFFICE OF MANAGEMENT AND BUDGET GUIDANCE FOR GRANTS AND AGREEMENTS
I	Office of Management and Budget Governmentwide Guidance for Grants and Agreements (Parts 2—199)
II	Office of Management and Budget Guidance (Parts 200—299)
	SUBTITLE B—FEDERAL AGENCY REGULATIONS FOR GRANTS AND AGREEMENTS
III	Department of Health and Human Services (Parts 300—399)
IV	Department of Agriculture (Parts 400—499)
VI	Department of State (Parts 600—699)
VII	Agency for International Development (Parts 700—799)
VIII	Department of Veterans Affairs (Parts 800—899)
IX	Department of Energy (Parts 900—999)
X	Department of the Treasury (Parts 1000—1099)
XI	Department of Defense (Parts 1100—1199)
XII	Department of Transportation (Parts 1200—1299)
XIII	Department of Commerce (Parts 1300—1399)
XIV	Department of the Interior (Parts 1400—1499)
XV	Environmental Protection Agency (Parts 1500—1599)
XVIII	National Aeronautics and Space Administration (Parts 1800—1899)
XX	United States Nuclear Regulatory Commission (Parts 2000—2099)
XXII	Corporation for National and Community Service (Parts 2200—2299)
XXIII	Social Security Administration (Parts 2300—2399)
XXIV	Department of Housing and Urban Development (Parts 2400—2499)
XXV	National Science Foundation (Parts 2500—2599)
XXVI	National Archives and Records Administration (Parts 2600—2699)

Title 2—Grants and Agreements—Continued

Chap.	
XXVII	Small Business Administration (Parts 2700—2799)
XXVIII	Department of Justice (Parts 2800—2899)
XXIX	Department of Labor (Parts 2900—2999)
XXX	Department of Homeland Security (Parts 3000—3099)
XXXI	Institute of Museum and Library Services (Parts 3100—3199)
XXXII	National Endowment for the Arts (Parts 3200—3299)
XXXIII	National Endowment for the Humanities (Parts 3300—3399)
XXXIV	Department of Education (Parts 3400—3499)
XXXV	Export-Import Bank of the United States (Parts 3500—3599)
XXXVI	Office of National Drug Control Policy, Executive Office of the President (Parts 3600—3699)
XXXVII	Peace Corps (Parts 3700—3799)
LVIII	Election Assistance Commission (Parts 5800—5899)
LIX	Gulf Coast Ecosystem Restoration Council (Parts 5900—5999)

Title 3—The President

I	Executive Office of the President (Parts 100—199)

Title 4—Accounts

I	Government Accountability Office (Parts 1—199)

Title 5—Administrative Personnel

I	Office of Personnel Management (Parts 1—1199)
II	Merit Systems Protection Board (Parts 1200—1299)
III	Office of Management and Budget (Parts 1300—1399)
IV	Office of Personnel Management and Office of the Director of National Intelligence (Parts 1400—1499)
V	The International Organizations Employees Loyalty Board (Parts 1500—1599)
VI	Federal Retirement Thrift Investment Board (Parts 1600—1699)
VIII	Office of Special Counsel (Parts 1800—1899)
IX	Appalachian Regional Commission (Parts 1900—1999)
XI	Armed Forces Retirement Home (Parts 2100—2199)
XIV	Federal Labor Relations Authority, General Counsel of the Federal Labor Relations Authority and Federal Service Impasses Panel (Parts 2400—2499)
XVI	Office of Government Ethics (Parts 2600—2699)
XXI	Department of the Treasury (Parts 3100—3199)
XXII	Federal Deposit Insurance Corporation (Parts 3200—3299)
XXIII	Department of Energy (Parts 3300—3399)
XXIV	Federal Energy Regulatory Commission (Parts 3400—3499)
XXV	Department of the Interior (Parts 3500—3599)
XXVI	Department of Defense (Parts 3600—3699)

Title 5—Administrative Personnel—Continued

Chap.	
XXVIII	Department of Justice (Parts 3800—3899)
XXIX	Federal Communications Commission (Parts 3900—3999)
XXX	Farm Credit System Insurance Corporation (Parts 4000—4099)
XXXI	Farm Credit Administration (Parts 4100—4199)
XXXIII	Overseas Private Investment Corporation (Parts 4300—4399)
XXXIV	Securities and Exchange Commission (Parts 4400—4499)
XXXV	Office of Personnel Management (Parts 4500—4599)
XXXVI	Department of Homeland Security (Parts 4600—4699)
XXXVII	Federal Election Commission (Parts 4700—4799)
XL	Interstate Commerce Commission (Parts 5000—5099)
XLI	Commodity Futures Trading Commission (Parts 5100—5199)
XLII	Department of Labor (Parts 5200—5299)
XLIII	National Science Foundation (Parts 5300—5399)
XLV	Department of Health and Human Services (Parts 5500—5599)
XLVI	Postal Rate Commission (Parts 5600—5699)
XLVII	Federal Trade Commission (Parts 5700—5799)
XLVIII	Nuclear Regulatory Commission (Parts 5800—5899)
XLIX	Federal Labor Relations Authority (Parts 5900—5999)
L	Department of Transportation (Parts 6000—6099)
LII	Export-Import Bank of the United States (Parts 6200—6299)
LIII	Department of Education (Parts 6300—6399)
LIV	Environmental Protection Agency (Parts 6400—6499)
LV	National Endowment for the Arts (Parts 6500—6599)
LVI	National Endowment for the Humanities (Parts 6600—6699)
LVII	General Services Administration (Parts 6700—6799)
LVIII	Board of Governors of the Federal Reserve System (Parts 6800—6899)
LIX	National Aeronautics and Space Administration (Parts 6900—6999)
LX	United States Postal Service (Parts 7000—7099)
LXI	National Labor Relations Board (Parts 7100—7199)
LXII	Equal Employment Opportunity Commission (Parts 7200—7299)
LXIII	Inter-American Foundation (Parts 7300—7399)
LXIV	Merit Systems Protection Board (Parts 7400—7499)
LXV	Department of Housing and Urban Development (Parts 7500—7599)
LXVI	National Archives and Records Administration (Parts 7600—7699)
LXVII	Institute of Museum and Library Services (Parts 7700—7799)
LXVIII	Commission on Civil Rights (Parts 7800—7899)
LXIX	Tennessee Valley Authority (Parts 7900—7999)
LXX	Court Services and Offender Supervision Agency for the District of Columbia (Parts 8000—8099)
LXXI	Consumer Product Safety Commission (Parts 8100—8199)
LXXIII	Department of Agriculture (Parts 8300—8399)

Title 5—Administrative Personnel—Continued

Chap.	
LXXIV	Federal Mine Safety and Health Review Commission (Parts 8400—8499)
LXXVI	Federal Retirement Thrift Investment Board (Parts 8600—8699)
LXXVII	Office of Management and Budget (Parts 8700—8799)
LXXX	Federal Housing Finance Agency (Parts 9000—9099)
LXXXIII	Special Inspector General for Afghanistan Reconstruction (Parts 9300—9399)
LXXXIV	Bureau of Consumer Financial Protection (Parts 9400—9499)
LXXXVI	National Credit Union Administration (Parts 9600—9699)
XCVII	Department of Homeland Security Human Resources Management System (Department of Homeland Security—Office of Personnel Management) (Parts 9700—9799)
XCVIII	Council of the Inspectors General on Integrity and Efficiency (Parts 9800—9899)
XCIX	Military Compensation and Retirement Modernization Commission (Parts 9900—9999)
C	National Council on Disability (Parts 10000—10049)
CI	National Mediation Board (Part 10101)

Title 6—Domestic Security

I	Department of Homeland Security, Office of the Secretary (Parts 1—199)
X	Privacy and Civil Liberties Oversight Board (Parts 1000—1099)

Title 7—Agriculture

	SUBTITLE A—OFFICE OF THE SECRETARY OF AGRICULTURE (PARTS 0—26)
	SUBTITLE B—REGULATIONS OF THE DEPARTMENT OF AGRICULTURE
I	Agricultural Marketing Service (Standards, Inspections, Marketing Practices), Department of Agriculture (Parts 27—209)
II	Food and Nutrition Service, Department of Agriculture (Parts 210—299)
III	Animal and Plant Health Inspection Service, Department of Agriculture (Parts 300—399)
IV	Federal Crop Insurance Corporation, Department of Agriculture (Parts 400—499)
V	Agricultural Research Service, Department of Agriculture (Parts 500—599)
VI	Natural Resources Conservation Service, Department of Agriculture (Parts 600—699)
VII	Farm Service Agency, Department of Agriculture (Parts 700—799)
VIII	Grain Inspection, Packers and Stockyards Administration (Federal Grain Inspection Service), Department of Agriculture (Parts 800—899)

Title 7—Agriculture—Continued

Chap.	
IX	Agricultural Marketing Service (Marketing Agreements and Orders; Fruits, Vegetables, Nuts), Department of Agriculture (Parts 900—999)
X	Agricultural Marketing Service (Marketing Agreements and Orders; Milk), Department of Agriculture (Parts 1000—1199)
XI	Agricultural Marketing Service (Marketing Agreements and Orders; Miscellaneous Commodities), Department of Agriculture (Parts 1200—1299)
XIV	Commodity Credit Corporation, Department of Agriculture (Parts 1400—1499)
XV	Foreign Agricultural Service, Department of Agriculture (Parts 1500—1599)
XVI	Rural Telephone Bank, Department of Agriculture (Parts 1600—1699)
XVII	Rural Utilities Service, Department of Agriculture (Parts 1700—1799)
XVIII	Rural Housing Service, Rural Business-Cooperative Service, Rural Utilities Service, and Farm Service Agency, Department of Agriculture (Parts 1800—2099)
XX	Local Television Loan Guarantee Board (Parts 2200—2299)
XXV	Office of Advocacy and Outreach, Department of Agriculture (Parts 2500—2599)
XXVI	Office of Inspector General, Department of Agriculture (Parts 2600—2699)
XXVII	Office of Information Resources Management, Department of Agriculture (Parts 2700—2799)
XXVIII	Office of Operations, Department of Agriculture (Parts 2800—2899)
XXIX	Office of Energy Policy and New Uses, Department of Agriculture (Parts 2900—2999)
XXX	Office of the Chief Financial Officer, Department of Agriculture (Parts 3000—3099)
XXXI	Office of Environmental Quality, Department of Agriculture (Parts 3100—3199)
XXXII	Office of Procurement and Property Management, Department of Agriculture (Parts 3200—3299)
XXXIII	Office of Transportation, Department of Agriculture (Parts 3300—3399)
XXXIV	National Institute of Food and Agriculture (Parts 3400—3499)
XXXV	Rural Housing Service, Department of Agriculture (Parts 3500—3599)
XXXVI	National Agricultural Statistics Service, Department of Agriculture (Parts 3600—3699)
XXXVII	Economic Research Service, Department of Agriculture (Parts 3700—3799)
XXXVIII	World Agricultural Outlook Board, Department of Agriculture (Parts 3800—3899)
XLI	[Reserved]
XLII	Rural Business-Cooperative Service and Rural Utilities Service, Department of Agriculture (Parts 4200—4299)

Title 8—Aliens and Nationality

Chap.

I Department of Homeland Security (Immigration and Naturalization) (Parts 1—499)

V Executive Office for Immigration Review, Department of Justice (Parts 1000—1399)

Title 9—Animals and Animal Products

I Animal and Plant Health Inspection Service, Department of Agriculture (Parts 1—199)

II Grain Inspection, Packers and Stockyards Administration (Packers and Stockyards Programs), Department of Agriculture (Parts 200—299)

III Food Safety and Inspection Service, Department of Agriculture (Parts 300—599)

Title 10—Energy

I Nuclear Regulatory Commission (Parts 0—199)

II Department of Energy (Parts 200—699)

III Department of Energy (Parts 700—999)

X Department of Energy (General Provisions) (Parts 1000—1099)

XIII Nuclear Waste Technical Review Board (Parts 1300—1399)

XVII Defense Nuclear Facilities Safety Board (Parts 1700—1799)

XVIII Northeast Interstate Low-Level Radioactive Waste Commission (Parts 1800—1899)

Title 11—Federal Elections

I Federal Election Commission (Parts 1—9099)

II Election Assistance Commission (Parts 9400—9499)

Title 12—Banks and Banking

I Comptroller of the Currency, Department of the Treasury (Parts 1—199)

II Federal Reserve System (Parts 200—299)

III Federal Deposit Insurance Corporation (Parts 300—399)

IV Export-Import Bank of the United States (Parts 400—499)

V (Parts 500—599) [Reserved]

VI Farm Credit Administration (Parts 600—699)

VII National Credit Union Administration (Parts 700—799)

VIII Federal Financing Bank (Parts 800—899)

IX Federal Housing Finance Board (Parts 900—999)

X Bureau of Consumer Financial Protection (Parts 1000—1099)

XI Federal Financial Institutions Examination Council (Parts 1100—1199)

XII Federal Housing Finance Agency (Parts 1200—1299)

XIII Financial Stability Oversight Council (Parts 1300—1399)

Title 12—Banks and Banking—Continued

Title 13—Business Credit and Assistance

Title 14—Aeronautics and Space

Title 15—Commerce and Foreign Trade

Title 15—Commerce and Foreign Trade—Continued

Title 16—Commercial Practices

Title 17—Commodity and Securities Exchanges

Title 18—Conservation of Power and Water Resources

Title 19—Customs Duties

Title 20—Employees' Benefits

Title 20—Employees' Benefits—Continued

Chap.	
IV	Employees' Compensation Appeals Board, Department of Labor (Parts 500—599)
V	Employment and Training Administration, Department of Labor (Parts 600—699)
VI	Office of Workers' Compensation Programs, Department of Labor (Parts 700—799)
VII	Benefits Review Board, Department of Labor (Parts 800—899)
VIII	Joint Board for the Enrollment of Actuaries (Parts 900—999)
IX	Office of the Assistant Secretary for Veterans' Employment and Training Service, Department of Labor (Parts 1000—1099)

Title 21—Food and Drugs

I	Food and Drug Administration, Department of Health and Human Services (Parts 1—1299)
II	Drug Enforcement Administration, Department of Justice (Parts 1300—1399)
III	Office of National Drug Control Policy (Parts 1400—1499)

Title 22—Foreign Relations

I	Department of State (Parts 1—199)
II	Agency for International Development (Parts 200—299)
III	Peace Corps (Parts 300—399)
IV	International Joint Commission, United States and Canada (Parts 400—499)
V	Broadcasting Board of Governors (Parts 500—599)
VII	Overseas Private Investment Corporation (Parts 700—799)
IX	Foreign Service Grievance Board (Parts 900—999)
X	Inter-American Foundation (Parts 1000—1099)
XI	International Boundary and Water Commission, United States and Mexico, United States Section (Parts 1100—1199)
XII	United States International Development Cooperation Agency (Parts 1200—1299)
XIII	Millennium Challenge Corporation (Parts 1300—1399)
XIV	Foreign Service Labor Relations Board; Federal Labor Relations Authority; General Counsel of the Federal Labor Relations Authority; and the Foreign Service Impasse Disputes Panel (Parts 1400—1499)
XV	African Development Foundation (Parts 1500—1599)
XVI	Japan-United States Friendship Commission (Parts 1600—1699)
XVII	United States Institute of Peace (Parts 1700—1799)

Title 23—Highways

I	Federal Highway Administration, Department of Transportation (Parts 1—999)

Title 23—Highways—Continued

Chap.

II National Highway Traffic Safety Administration and Federal Highway Administration, Department of Transportation (Parts 1200—1299)

III National Highway Traffic Safety Administration, Department of Transportation (Parts 1300—1399)

Title 24—Housing and Urban Development

SUBTITLE A—OFFICE OF THE SECRETARY, DEPARTMENT OF HOUSING AND URBAN DEVELOPMENT (PARTS 0—99)

SUBTITLE B—REGULATIONS RELATING TO HOUSING AND URBAN DEVELOPMENT

I Office of Assistant Secretary for Equal Opportunity, Department of Housing and Urban Development (Parts 100—199)

II Office of Assistant Secretary for Housing-Federal Housing Commissioner, Department of Housing and Urban Development (Parts 200—299)

III Government National Mortgage Association, Department of Housing and Urban Development (Parts 300—399)

IV Office of Housing and Office of Multifamily Housing Assistance Restructuring, Department of Housing and Urban Development (Parts 400—499)

V Office of Assistant Secretary for Community Planning and Development, Department of Housing and Urban Development (Parts 500—599)

VI Office of Assistant Secretary for Community Planning and Development, Department of Housing and Urban Development (Parts 600—699) [Reserved]

VII Office of the Secretary, Department of Housing and Urban Development (Housing Assistance Programs and Public and Indian Housing Programs) (Parts 700—799)

VIII Office of the Assistant Secretary for Housing—Federal Housing Commissioner, Department of Housing and Urban Development (Section 8 Housing Assistance Programs, Section 202 Direct Loan Program, Section 202 Supportive Housing for the Elderly Program and Section 811 Supportive Housing for Persons With Disabilities Program) (Parts 800—899)

IX Office of Assistant Secretary for Public and Indian Housing, Department of Housing and Urban Development (Parts 900—1699)

XII Office of Inspector General, Department of Housing and Urban Development (Parts 2000—2099)

XV Emergency Mortgage Insurance and Loan Programs, Department of Housing and Urban Development (Parts 2700—2799) [Reserved]

XX Office of Assistant Secretary for Housing—Federal Housing Commissioner, Department of Housing and Urban Development (Parts 3200—3899)

XXIV Board of Directors of the HOPE for Homeowners Program (Parts 4000—4099) [Reserved]

XXV Neighborhood Reinvestment Corporation (Parts 4100—4199)

Title 25—Indians

Chap.

I Bureau of Indian Affairs, Department of the Interior (Parts 1—299)

II Indian Arts and Crafts Board, Department of the Interior (Parts 300—399)

III National Indian Gaming Commission, Department of the Interior (Parts 500—599)

IV Office of Navajo and Hopi Indian Relocation (Parts 700—899)

V Bureau of Indian Affairs, Department of the Interior, and Indian Health Service, Department of Health and Human Services (Part 900—999)

VI Office of the Assistant Secretary, Indian Affairs, Department of the Interior (Parts 1000—1199)

VII Office of the Special Trustee for American Indians, Department of the Interior (Parts 1200—1299)

Title 26—Internal Revenue

I Internal Revenue Service, Department of the Treasury (Parts 1—End)

Title 27—Alcohol, Tobacco Products and Firearms

I Alcohol and Tobacco Tax and Trade Bureau, Department of the Treasury (Parts 1—399)

II Bureau of Alcohol, Tobacco, Firearms, and Explosives, Department of Justice (Parts 400—699)

Title 28—Judicial Administration

I Department of Justice (Parts 0—299)

III Federal Prison Industries, Inc., Department of Justice (Parts 300—399)

V Bureau of Prisons, Department of Justice (Parts 500—599)

VI Offices of Independent Counsel, Department of Justice (Parts 600—699)

VII Office of Independent Counsel (Parts 700—799)

VIII Court Services and Offender Supervision Agency for the District of Columbia (Parts 800—899)

IX National Crime Prevention and Privacy Compact Council (Parts 900—999)

XI Department of Justice and Department of State (Parts 1100—1199)

Title 29—Labor

SUBTITLE A—OFFICE OF THE SECRETARY OF LABOR (PARTS 0—99)

SUBTITLE B—REGULATIONS RELATING TO LABOR

I National Labor Relations Board (Parts 100—199)

Title 29—Labor—Continued

Chap.	
II	Office of Labor-Management Standards, Department of Labor (Parts 200—299)
III	National Railroad Adjustment Board (Parts 300—399)
IV	Office of Labor-Management Standards, Department of Labor (Parts 400—499)
V	Wage and Hour Division, Department of Labor (Parts 500—899)
IX	Construction Industry Collective Bargaining Commission (Parts 900—999)
X	National Mediation Board (Parts 1200—1299)
XII	Federal Mediation and Conciliation Service (Parts 1400—1499)
XIV	Equal Employment Opportunity Commission (Parts 1600—1699)
XVII	Occupational Safety and Health Administration, Department of Labor (Parts 1900—1999)
XX	Occupational Safety and Health Review Commission (Parts 2200—2499)
XXV	Employee Benefits Security Administration, Department of Labor (Parts 2500—2599)
XXVII	Federal Mine Safety and Health Review Commission (Parts 2700—2799)
XL	Pension Benefit Guaranty Corporation (Parts 4000—4999)

Title 30—Mineral Resources

I	Mine Safety and Health Administration, Department of Labor (Parts 1—199)
II	Bureau of Safety and Environmental Enforcement, Department of the Interior (Parts 200—299)
IV	Geological Survey, Department of the Interior (Parts 400—499)
V	Bureau of Ocean Energy Management, Department of the Interior (Parts 500—599)
VII	Office of Surface Mining Reclamation and Enforcement, Department of the Interior (Parts 700—999)
XII	Office of Natural Resources Revenue, Department of the Interior (Parts 1200—1299)

Title 31—Money and Finance: Treasury

	SUBTITLE A—OFFICE OF THE SECRETARY OF THE TREASURY (PARTS 0—50)
	SUBTITLE B—REGULATIONS RELATING TO MONEY AND FINANCE
I	Monetary Offices, Department of the Treasury (Parts 51—199)
II	Fiscal Service, Department of the Treasury (Parts 200—399)
IV	Secret Service, Department of the Treasury (Parts 400—499)
V	Office of Foreign Assets Control, Department of the Treasury (Parts 500—599)
VI	Bureau of Engraving and Printing, Department of the Treasury (Parts 600—699)
VII	Federal Law Enforcement Training Center, Department of the Treasury (Parts 700—799)

Title 31—Money and Finance: Treasury—Continued

Title 32—National Defense

Title 33—Navigation and Navigable Waters

Title 34—Education

Title 34—Education—Continued

Chap.

IV Office of Career, Technical and Adult Education, Department of Education (Parts 400—499)

V Office of Bilingual Education and Minority Languages Affairs, Department of Education (Parts 500—599) [Reserved]

VI Office of Postsecondary Education, Department of Education (Parts 600—699)

VII Office of Educational Research and Improvement, Department of Education (Parts 700—799) [Reserved]

SUBTITLE C—REGULATIONS RELATING TO EDUCATION

XI (Parts 1100—1199) [Reserved]

XII National Council on Disability (Parts 1200—1299)

Title 35 [Reserved]

Title 36—Parks, Forests, and Public Property

I National Park Service, Department of the Interior (Parts 1—199)

II Forest Service, Department of Agriculture (Parts 200—299)

III Corps of Engineers, Department of the Army (Parts 300—399)

IV American Battle Monuments Commission (Parts 400—499)

V Smithsonian Institution (Parts 500—599)

VI [Reserved]

VII Library of Congress (Parts 700—799)

VIII Advisory Council on Historic Preservation (Parts 800—899)

IX Pennsylvania Avenue Development Corporation (Parts 900—999)

X Presidio Trust (Parts 1000—1099)

XI Architectural and Transportation Barriers Compliance Board (Parts 1100—1199)

XII National Archives and Records Administration (Parts 1200—1299)

XV Oklahoma City National Memorial Trust (Parts 1500—1599)

XVI Morris K. Udall Scholarship and Excellence in National Environmental Policy Foundation (Parts 1600—1699)

Title 37—Patents, Trademarks, and Copyrights

I United States Patent and Trademark Office, Department of Commerce (Parts 1—199)

II U.S. Copyright Office, Library of Congress (Parts 200—299)

III Copyright Royalty Board, Library of Congress (Parts 300—399)

IV National Institute of Standards and Technology, Department of Commerce (Parts 400—599)

Title 38—Pensions, Bonuses, and Veterans' Relief

I Department of Veterans Affairs (Parts 0—199)

II Armed Forces Retirement Home (Parts 200—299)

Title 39—Postal Service

Chap.

I United States Postal Service (Parts 1—999)

III Postal Regulatory Commission (Parts 3000—3099)

Title 40—Protection of Environment

I Environmental Protection Agency (Parts 1—1099)

IV Environmental Protection Agency and Department of Justice (Parts 1400—1499)

V Council on Environmental Quality (Parts 1500—1599)

VI Chemical Safety and Hazard Investigation Board (Parts 1600—1699)

VII Environmental Protection Agency and Department of Defense; Uniform National Discharge Standards for Vessels of the Armed Forces (Parts 1700—1799)

VIII Gulf Coast Ecosystem Restoration Council (Parts 1800—1899)

Title 41—Public Contracts and Property Management

SUBTITLE A—FEDERAL PROCUREMENT REGULATIONS SYSTEM [NOTE]

SUBTITLE B—OTHER PROVISIONS RELATING TO PUBLIC CONTRACTS

50 Public Contracts, Department of Labor (Parts 50–1—50–999)

51 Committee for Purchase From People Who Are Blind or Severely Disabled (Parts 51–1—51–99)

60 Office of Federal Contract Compliance Programs, Equal Employment Opportunity, Department of Labor (Parts 60–1—60–999)

61 Office of the Assistant Secretary for Veterans' Employment and Training Service, Department of Labor (Parts 61–1—61–999)

62—100 [Reserved]

SUBTITLE C—FEDERAL PROPERTY MANAGEMENT REGULATIONS SYSTEM

101 Federal Property Management Regulations (Parts 101–1—101–99)

102 Federal Management Regulation (Parts 102–1—102–299)

103—104 [Reserved]

105 General Services Administration (Parts 105–1—105–999)

109 Department of Energy Property Management Regulations (Parts 109–1—109–99)

114 Department of the Interior (Parts 114–1—114–99)

115 Environmental Protection Agency (Parts 115–1—115–99)

128 Department of Justice (Parts 128–1—128–99)

129—200 [Reserved]

SUBTITLE D—OTHER PROVISIONS RELATING TO PROPERTY MANAGEMENT [RESERVED]

SUBTITLE E—FEDERAL INFORMATION RESOURCES MANAGEMENT REGULATIONS SYSTEM [RESERVED]

SUBTITLE F—FEDERAL TRAVEL REGULATION SYSTEM

300 General (Parts 300–1—300–99)

301 Temporary Duty (TDY) Travel Allowances (Parts 301–1—301–99)

Title 41—Public Contracts and Property Management—Continued

Chap.

302	Relocation Allowances (Parts 302–1—302–99)
303	Payment of Expenses Connected with the Death of Certain Employees (Part 303–1—303–99)
304	Payment of Travel Expenses from a Non-Federal Source (Parts 304–1—304–99)

Title 42—Public Health

I	Public Health Service, Department of Health and Human Services (Parts 1—199)
II—III	[Reserved]
IV	Centers for Medicare & Medicaid Services, Department of Health and Human Services (Parts 400—699)
V	Office of Inspector General-Health Care, Department of Health and Human Services (Parts 1000—1099)

Title 43—Public Lands: Interior

	SUBTITLE A—OFFICE OF THE SECRETARY OF THE INTERIOR (PARTS 1—199)
	SUBTITLE B—REGULATIONS RELATING TO PUBLIC LANDS
I	Bureau of Reclamation, Department of the Interior (Parts 400—999)
II	Bureau of Land Management, Department of the Interior (Parts 1000—9999)
III	Utah Reclamation Mitigation and Conservation Commission (Parts 10000—10099)

Title 44—Emergency Management and Assistance

I	Federal Emergency Management Agency, Department of Homeland Security (Parts 0—399)
IV	Department of Commerce and Department of Transportation (Parts 400—499)

Title 45—Public Welfare

	SUBTITLE A—DEPARTMENT OF HEALTH AND HUMAN SERVICES (PARTS 1—199)
	SUBTITLE B—REGULATIONS RELATING TO PUBLIC WELFARE
II	Office of Family Assistance (Assistance Programs), Administration for Children and Families, Department of Health and Human Services (Parts 200—299)
III	Office of Child Support Enforcement (Child Support Enforcement Program), Administration for Children and Families, Department of Health and Human Services (Parts 300—399)
IV	Office of Refugee Resettlement, Administration for Children and Families, Department of Health and Human Services (Parts 400—499)

Title 45—Public Welfare—Continued

Title 46—Shipping

Title 47—Telecommunication

Title 48—Federal Acquisition Regulations System

Chap.

1 Federal Acquisition Regulation (Parts 1—99)

2 Defense Acquisition Regulations System, Department of Defense (Parts 200—299)

3 Department of Health and Human Services (Parts 300—399)

4 Department of Agriculture (Parts 400—499)

5 General Services Administration (Parts 500—599)

6 Department of State (Parts 600—699)

7 Agency for International Development (Parts 700—799)

8 Department of Veterans Affairs (Parts 800—899)

9 Department of Energy (Parts 900—999)

10 Department of the Treasury (Parts 1000—1099)

12 Department of Transportation (Parts 1200—1299)

13 Department of Commerce (Parts 1300—1399)

14 Department of the Interior (Parts 1400—1499)

15 Environmental Protection Agency (Parts 1500—1599)

16 Office of Personnel Management, Federal Employees Health Benefits Acquisition Regulation (Parts 1600—1699)

17 Office of Personnel Management (Parts 1700—1799)

18 National Aeronautics and Space Administration (Parts 1800—1899)

19 Broadcasting Board of Governors (Parts 1900—1999)

20 Nuclear Regulatory Commission (Parts 2000—2099)

21 Office of Personnel Management, Federal Employees Group Life Insurance Federal Acquisition Regulation (Parts 2100—2199)

23 Social Security Administration (Parts 2300—2399)

24 Department of Housing and Urban Development (Parts 2400—2499)

25 National Science Foundation (Parts 2500—2599)

28 Department of Justice (Parts 2800—2899)

29 Department of Labor (Parts 2900—2999)

30 Department of Homeland Security, Homeland Security Acquisition Regulation (HSAR) (Parts 3000—3099)

34 Department of Education Acquisition Regulation (Parts 3400—3499)

51 Department of the Army Acquisition Regulations (Parts 5100—5199)

52 Department of the Navy Acquisition Regulations (Parts 5200—5299)

53 Department of the Air Force Federal Acquisition Regulation Supplement (Parts 5300—5399) [Reserved]

54 Defense Logistics Agency, Department of Defense (Parts 5400—5499)

57 African Development Foundation (Parts 5700—5799)

61 Civilian Board of Contract Appeals, General Services Administration (Parts 6100—6199)

99 Cost Accounting Standards Board, Office of Federal Procurement Policy, Office of Management and Budget (Parts 9900—9999)

Title 49—Transportation

Chap.

SUBTITLE A—OFFICE OF THE SECRETARY OF TRANSPORTATION (PARTS 1—99)

SUBTITLE B—OTHER REGULATIONS RELATING TO TRANSPORTATION

I Pipeline and Hazardous Materials Safety Administration, Department of Transportation (Parts 100—199)

II Federal Railroad Administration, Department of Transportation (Parts 200—299)

III Federal Motor Carrier Safety Administration, Department of Transportation (Parts 300—399)

IV Coast Guard, Department of Homeland Security (Parts 400—499)

V National Highway Traffic Safety Administration, Department of Transportation (Parts 500—599)

VI Federal Transit Administration, Department of Transportation (Parts 600—699)

VII National Railroad Passenger Corporation (AMTRAK) (Parts 700—799)

VIII National Transportation Safety Board (Parts 800—999)

X Surface Transportation Board (Parts 1000—1399)

XI Research and Innovative Technology Administration, Department of Transportation (Parts 1400—1499) [Reserved]

XII Transportation Security Administration, Department of Homeland Security (Parts 1500—1699)

Title 50—Wildlife and Fisheries

I United States Fish and Wildlife Service, Department of the Interior (Parts 1—199)

II National Marine Fisheries Service, National Oceanic and Atmospheric Administration, Department of Commerce (Parts 200—299)

III International Fishing and Related Activities (Parts 300—399)

IV Joint Regulations (United States Fish and Wildlife Service, Department of the Interior and National Marine Fisheries Service, National Oceanic and Atmospheric Administration, Department of Commerce); Endangered Species Committee Regulations (Parts 400—499)

V Marine Mammal Commission (Parts 500—599)

VI Fishery Conservation and Management, National Oceanic and Atmospheric Administration, Department of Commerce (Parts 600—699)

Alphabetical List of Agencies Appearing in the CFR

(Revised as of January 1, 2019)

Agency	CFR Title, Subtitle or Chapter
Administrative Conference of the United States	1, III
Advisory Council on Historic Preservation	36, VIII
Advocacy and Outreach, Office of	7, XXV
Afghanistan Reconstruction, Special Inspector General for	5, LXXXIII
African Development Foundation	22, XV
Federal Acquisition Regulation	48, 57
Agency for International Development	2, VII; 22, II
Federal Acquisition Regulation	48, 7
Agricultural Marketing Service	7, I, IX, X, XI
Agricultural Research Service	7, V
Agriculture, Department of	2, IV; 5, LXXIII
Advocacy and Outreach, Office of	7, XXV
Agricultural Marketing Service	7, I, IX, X, XI
Agricultural Research Service	7, V
Animal and Plant Health Inspection Service	7, III; 9, I
Chief Financial Officer, Office of	7, XXX
Commodity Credit Corporation	7, XIV
Economic Research Service	7, XXXVII
Energy Policy and New Uses, Office of	2, IX; 7, XXIX
Environmental Quality, Office of	7, XXXI
Farm Service Agency	7, VII, XVIII
Federal Acquisition Regulation	48, 4
Federal Crop Insurance Corporation	7, IV
Food and Nutrition Service	7, II
Food Safety and Inspection Service	9, III
Foreign Agricultural Service	7, XV
Forest Service	36, II
Grain Inspection, Packers and Stockyards Administration	7, VIII; 9, II
Information Resources Management, Office of	7, XXVII
Inspector General, Office of	7, XXVI
National Agricultural Library	7, XLI
National Agricultural Statistics Service	7, XXXVI
National Institute of Food and Agriculture	7, XXXIV
Natural Resources Conservation Service	7, VI
Operations, Office of	7, XXVIII
Procurement and Property Management, Office of	7, XXXII
Rural Business-Cooperative Service	7, XVIII, XLII
Rural Development Administration	7, XLII
Rural Housing Service	7, XVIII, XXXV
Rural Telephone Bank	7, XVI
Rural Utilities Service	7, XVII, XVIII, XLII
Secretary of Agriculture, Office of	7, Subtitle A
Transportation, Office of	7, XXXIII
World Agricultural Outlook Board	7, XXXVIII
Air Force, Department of	32, VII
Federal Acquisition Regulation Supplement	48, 53
Air Transportation Stabilization Board	14, VI
Alcohol and Tobacco Tax and Trade Bureau	27, I
Alcohol, Tobacco, Firearms, and Explosives, Bureau of	27, II
AMTRAK	49, VII
American Battle Monuments Commission	36, IV
American Indians, Office of the Special Trustee	25, VII
Animal and Plant Health Inspection Service	7, III; 9, I

Agency	CFR Title, Subtitle or Chapter
Appalachian Regional Commission	5, IX
Architectural and Transportation Barriers Compliance Board	36, XI
Arctic Research Commission	45, XXIII
Armed Forces Retirement Home	5, XI
Army, Department of	32, V
Engineers, Corps of	33, II; 36, III
Federal Acquisition Regulation	48, 51
Bilingual Education and Minority Languages Affairs, Office of	34, V
Blind or Severely Disabled, Committee for Purchase from People Who Are	41, 51
Broadcasting Board of Governors	22, V
Federal Acquisition Regulation	48, 19
Career, Technical, and Adult Education, Office of	34, IV
Census Bureau	15, I
Centers for Medicare & Medicaid Services	42, IV
Central Intelligence Agency	32, XIX
Chemical Safety and Hazardous Investigation Board	40, VI
Chief Financial Officer, Office of	7, XXX
Child Support Enforcement, Office of	45, III
Children and Families, Administration for	45, II, III, IV, X, XIII
Civil Rights, Commission on	5, LXVIII; 45, VII
Civil Rights, Office for	34, I
Council of the Inspectors General on Integrity and Efficiency	5, XCVIII
Court Services and Offender Supervision Agency for the District of Columbia	5, LXX
Coast Guard	33, I; 46, I; 49, IV
Coast Guard (Great Lakes Pilotage)	46, III
Commerce, Department of	2, XIII; 44, IV; 50, VI
Census Bureau	15, I
Economic Analysis, Bureau of	15, VIII
Economic Development Administration	13, III
Emergency Management and Assistance	44, IV
Federal Acquisition Regulation	48, 13
Foreign-Trade Zones Board	15, IV
Industry and Security, Bureau of	15, VII
International Trade Administration	15, III; 19, III
National Institute of Standards and Technology	15, II; 37, IV
National Marine Fisheries Service	50, II, IV
National Oceanic and Atmospheric Administration	15, IX; 50, II, III, IV, VI
National Technical Information Service	15, XI
National Telecommunications and Information Administration	15, XXIII; 47, III, IV
National Weather Service	15, IX
Patent and Trademark Office, United States	37, I
Secretary of Commerce, Office of	15, Subtitle A
Commercial Space Transportation	14, III
Commodity Credit Corporation	7, XIV
Commodity Futures Trading Commission	5, XLI; 17, I
Community Planning and Development, Office of Assistant Secretary for	24, V, VI
Community Services, Office of	45, X
Comptroller of the Currency	12, I
Construction Industry Collective Bargaining Commission	29, IX
Consumer Financial Protection Bureau	5, LXXXIV; 12, X
Consumer Product Safety Commission	5, LXXI; 16, II
Copyright Royalty Board	37, III
Corporation for National and Community Service	2, XXII; 45, XII, XXV
Cost Accounting Standards Board	48, 99
Council on Environmental Quality	40, V
Court Services and Offender Supervision Agency for the District of Columbia	5, LXX; 28, VIII
Customs and Border Protection	19, I
Defense Contract Audit Agency	32, I
Defense, Department of	2, XI; 5, XXVI; 32, Subtitle A; 40, VII
Advanced Research Projects Agency	32, I
Air Force Department	32, VII

Agency	CFR Title, Subtitle or Chapter
Army Department	32, V; 33, II; 36, III; 48, 51
Defense Acquisition Regulations System	48, 2
Defense Intelligence Agency	32, I
Defense Logistics Agency	32, I, XII; 48, 54
Engineers, Corps of	33, II; 36, III
National Imagery and Mapping Agency	32, I
Navy Department	32, VI; 48, 52
Secretary of Defense, Office of	2, XI; 32, I
Defense Contract Audit Agency	32, I
Defense Intelligence Agency	32, I
Defense Logistics Agency	32, XII; 48, 54
Defense Nuclear Facilities Safety Board	10, XVII
Delaware River Basin Commission	18, III
Denali Commission	45, IX
Disability, National Council on	5, C; 34, XII
District of Columbia, Court Services and Offender Supervision Agency for the	5, LXX; 28, VIII
Drug Enforcement Administration	21, II
East-West Foreign Trade Board	15, XIII
Economic Analysis, Bureau of	15, VIII
Economic Development Administration	13, III
Economic Research Service	7, XXXVII
Education, Department of	2, XXXIV; 5, LIII
Bilingual Education and Minority Languages Affairs, Office of	34, V
Career, Technical, and Adult Education, Office of	34, IV
Civil Rights, Office for	34, I
Educational Research and Improvement, Office of	34, VII
Elementary and Secondary Education, Office of	34, II
Federal Acquisition Regulation	48, 34
Postsecondary Education, Office of	34, VI
Secretary of Education, Office of	34, Subtitle A
Special Education and Rehabilitative Services, Office of	34, III
Educational Research and Improvement, Office of	34, VII
Election Assistance Commission	2, LVIII; 11, II
Elementary and Secondary Education, Office of	34, II
Emergency Oil and Gas Guaranteed Loan Board	13, V
Emergency Steel Guarantee Loan Board	13, IV
Employee Benefits Security Administration	29, XXV
Employees' Compensation Appeals Board	20, IV
Employees Loyalty Board	5, V
Employment and Training Administration	20, V
Employment Policy, National Commission for	1, IV
Employment Standards Administration	20, VI
Endangered Species Committee	50, IV
Energy, Department of	2, IX; 5, XXIII; 10, II, III, X
Federal Acquisition Regulation	48, 9
Federal Energy Regulatory Commission	5, XXIV; 18, I
Property Management Regulations	41, 109
Energy, Office of	7, XXIX
Engineers, Corps of	33, II; 36, III
Engraving and Printing, Bureau of	31, VI
Environmental Protection Agency	2, XV; 5, LIV; 40, I, IV, VII
Federal Acquisition Regulation	48, 15
Property Management Regulations	41, 115
Environmental Quality, Office of	7, XXXI
Equal Employment Opportunity Commission	5, LXII; 29, XIV
Equal Opportunity, Office of Assistant Secretary for	24, I
Executive Office of the President	3, I
Environmental Quality, Council on	40, V
Management and Budget, Office of	2, Subtitle A; 5, III, LXXVII; 14, VI; 48, 99
National Drug Control Policy, Office of	2, XXXVI; 21, III
National Security Council	32, XXI; 47, 2

Agency	CFR Title, Subtitle or Chapter
Contract Appeals, Board of	48, 61
Federal Acquisition Regulation	48, 5
Federal Management Regulation	41, 102
Federal Property Management Regulations	41, 101
Federal Travel Regulation System	41, Subtitle F
General	41, 300
Payment From a Non-Federal Source for Travel Expenses	41, 304
Payment of Expenses Connected With the Death of Certain Employees	41, 303
Relocation Allowances	41, 302
Temporary Duty (TDY) Travel Allowances	41, 301
Geological Survey	30, IV
Government Accountability Office	4, I
Government Ethics, Office of	5, XVI
Government National Mortgage Association	24, III
Grain Inspection, Packers and Stockyards Administration	7, VIII; 9, II
Gulf Coast Ecosystem Restoration Council	2, LIX; 40, VIII
Harry S. Truman Scholarship Foundation	45, XVIII
Health and Human Services, Department of	2, III; 5, XLV; 45, Subtitle A
Centers for Medicare & Medicaid Services	42, IV
Child Support Enforcement, Office of	45, III
Children and Families, Administration for	45, II, III, IV, X, XIII
Community Services, Office of	45, X
Family Assistance, Office of	45, II
Federal Acquisition Regulation	48, 3
Food and Drug Administration	21, I
Indian Health Service	25, V
Inspector General (Health Care), Office of	42, V
Public Health Service	42, I
Refugee Resettlement, Office of	45, IV
Homeland Security, Department of	2, XXX; 5, XXXVI; 6, I; 8, I
Coast Guard	33, I; 46, I; 49, IV
Coast Guard (Great Lakes Pilotage)	46, III
Customs and Border Protection	19, I
Federal Emergency Management Agency	44, I
Human Resources Management and Labor Relations Systems	5, XCVII
Immigration and Customs Enforcement Bureau	19, IV
Transportation Security Administration	49, XII
HOPE for Homeowners Program, Board of Directors of	24, XXIV
Housing and Urban Development, Department of	2, XXIV; 5, LXV; 24, Subtitle B
Community Planning and Development, Office of Assistant Secretary for	24, V, VI
Equal Opportunity, Office of Assistant Secretary for	24, I
Federal Acquisition Regulation	48, 24
Federal Housing Enterprise Oversight, Office of	12, XVII
Government National Mortgage Association	24, III
Housing—Federal Housing Commissioner, Office of Assistant Secretary for	24, II, VIII, X, XX
Housing, Office of, and Multifamily Housing Assistance Restructuring, Office of	24, IV
Inspector General, Office of	24, XII
Public and Indian Housing, Office of Assistant Secretary for	24, IX
Secretary, Office of	24, Subtitle A, VII
Housing—Federal Housing Commissioner, Office of Assistant Secretary for	24, II, VIII, X, XX
Housing, Office of, and Multifamily Housing Assistance Restructuring, Office of	24, IV
Immigration and Customs Enforcement Bureau	19, IV
Immigration Review, Executive Office for	8, V
Independent Counsel, Office of	28, VII
Independent Counsel, Offices of	28, VI
Indian Affairs, Bureau of	25, I, V
Indian Affairs, Office of the Assistant Secretary	25, VI

Agency	CFR Title, Subtitle or Chapter
Federal Procurement Regulations System	41, 50
Labor-Management Standards, Office of	29, II, IV
Mine Safety and Health Administration	30, I
Occupational Safety and Health Administration	29, XVII
Public Contracts	41, 50
Secretary of Labor, Office of	29, Subtitle A
Veterans' Employment and Training Service, Office of the Assistant Secretary for	41, 61; 20, IX
Wage and Hour Division	29, V
Workers' Compensation Programs, Office of	20, I, VII
Labor-Management Standards, Office of	29, II, IV
Land Management, Bureau of	43, II
Legal Services Corporation	45, XVI
Libraries and Information Science, National Commission on	45, XVII
Library of Congress	36, VII
Copyright Royalty Board	37, III
U.S. Copyright Office	37, II
Local Television Loan Guarantee Board	7, XX
Management and Budget, Office of	5, III, LXXVII; 14, VI; 48, 99
Marine Mammal Commission	50, V
Maritime Administration	46, II
Merit Systems Protection Board	5, II, LXIV
Micronesian Status Negotiations, Office for	32, XXVII
Military Compensation and Retirement Modernization Commission	5, XCIX
Millennium Challenge Corporation	22, XIII
Mine Safety and Health Administration	30, I
Minority Business Development Agency	15, XIV
Miscellaneous Agencies	1, IV
Monetary Offices	31, I
Morris K. Udall Scholarship and Excellence in National Environmental Policy Foundation	36, XVI
Museum and Library Services, Institute of	2, XXXI
National Aeronautics and Space Administration	2, XVIII; 5, LIX; 14, V
Federal Acquisition Regulation	48, 18
National Agricultural Library	7, XLI
National Agricultural Statistics Service	7, XXXVI
National and Community Service, Corporation for	2, XXII; 45, XII, XXV
National Archives and Records Administration	2, XXVI; 5, LXVI; 36, XII
Information Security Oversight Office	32, XX
National Capital Planning Commission	1, IV, VI
National Counterintelligence Center	32, XVIII
National Credit Union Administration	5, LXXXVI; 12, VII
National Crime Prevention and Privacy Compact Council	28, IX
National Drug Control Policy, Office of	2, XXXVI; 21, III
National Endowment for the Arts	2, XXXII
National Endowment for the Humanities	2, XXXIII
National Foundation on the Arts and the Humanities	45, XI
National Geospatial-Intelligence Agency	32, I
National Highway Traffic Safety Administration	23, II, III; 47, VI; 49, V
National Imagery and Mapping Agency	32, I
National Indian Gaming Commission	25, III
National Institute of Food and Agriculture	7, XXXIV
National Institute of Standards and Technology	15, II; 37, IV
National Intelligence, Office of Director of	5, IV; 32, XVII
National Labor Relations Board	5, LXI; 29, I
National Marine Fisheries Service	50, II, IV
National Mediation Board	5, CI; 29, X
National Oceanic and Atmospheric Administration	15, IX; 50, II, III, IV, VI
National Park Service	36, I
National Railroad Adjustment Board	29, III
National Railroad Passenger Corporation (AMTRAK)	49, VII
National Science Foundation	2, XXV; 5, XLIII; 45, VI
Federal Acquisition Regulation	48, 25
National Security Council	32, XXI

Agency	CFR Title, Subtitle or Chapter
National Security Council and Office of Science and Technology Policy	47, II
National Technical Information Service	15, XI
National Telecommunications and Information Administration	15, XXIII; 47, III, IV, V
National Transportation Safety Board	49, VIII
Natural Resources Conservation Service	7, VI
Natural Resource Revenue, Office of	30, XII
Navajo and Hopi Indian Relocation, Office of	25, IV
Navy, Department of	32, VI
Federal Acquisition Regulation	48, 52
Neighborhood Reinvestment Corporation	24, XXV
Northeast Interstate Low-Level Radioactive Waste Commission	10, XVIII
Nuclear Regulatory Commission	2, XX; 5, XLVIII; 10, I
Federal Acquisition Regulation	48, 20
Occupational Safety and Health Administration	29, XVII
Occupational Safety and Health Review Commission	29, XX
Ocean Energy Management, Bureau of	30, V
Oklahoma City National Memorial Trust	36, XV
Operations Office	7, XXVIII
Overseas Private Investment Corporation	5, XXXIII; 22, VII
Patent and Trademark Office, United States	37, I
Payment From a Non-Federal Source for Travel Expenses	41, 304
Payment of Expenses Connected With the Death of Certain Employees	41, 303
Peace Corps	2, XXXVII; 22, III
Pennsylvania Avenue Development Corporation	36, IX
Pension Benefit Guaranty Corporation	29, XL
Personnel Management, Office of	5, I, XXXV; 5, IV; 45, VIII
Human Resources Management and Labor Relations Systems, Department of Homeland Security	5, XCVII
Federal Acquisition Regulation	48, 17
Federal Employees Group Life Insurance Federal Acquisition Regulation	48, 21
Federal Employees Health Benefits Acquisition Regulation	48, 16
Pipeline and Hazardous Materials Safety Administration	49, I
Postal Regulatory Commission	5, XLVI; 39, III
Postal Service, United States	5, LX; 39, I
Postsecondary Education, Office of	34, VI
President's Commission on White House Fellowships	1, IV
Presidential Documents	3
Presidio Trust	36, X
Prisons, Bureau of	28, V
Privacy and Civil Liberties Oversight Board	6, X
Procurement and Property Management, Office of	7, XXXII
Public Contracts, Department of Labor	41, 50
Public and Indian Housing, Office of Assistant Secretary for	24, IX
Public Health Service	42, I
Railroad Retirement Board	20, II
Reclamation, Bureau of	43, I
Refugee Resettlement, Office of	45, IV
Relocation Allowances	41, 302
Research and Innovative Technology Administration	49, XI
Rural Business-Cooperative Service	7, XVIII, XLII
Rural Development Administration	7, XLII
Rural Housing Service	7, XVIII, XXXV
Rural Telephone Bank	7, XVI
Rural Utilities Service	7, XVII, XVIII, XLII
Safety and Environmental Enforcement, Bureau of	30, II
Saint Lawrence Seaway Development Corporation	33, IV
Science and Technology Policy, Office of	32, XXIV
Science and Technology Policy, Office of, and National Security Council	47, II
Secret Service	31, IV
Securities and Exchange Commission	5, XXXIV; 17, II

List of CFR Sections Affected

All changes in this volume of the Code of Federal Regulations (CFR) that were made by documents published in the FEDERAL REGISTER since January 1, 2014 are enumerated in the following list. Entries indicate the nature of the changes effected. Page numbers refer to FEDERAL REGISTER pages. The user should consult the entries for chapters, parts and subparts as well as sections for revisions.

For changes to this volume of the CFR prior to this listing, consult the annual edition of the monthly List of CFR Sections Affected (LSA). The LSA is available at *www.govinfo.gov*. For changes to this volume of the CFR prior to 2001, see the "List of CFR Sections Affected, 1949–1963, 1964–1972, 1973–1985, and 1986–2000" published in 11 separate volumes. The "List of CFR Sections Affected 1986–2000" is available at *www.govinfo.gov*.

2014

16 CFR

79 FR Page

Chapter I

1.98 Revised 13540
4.8 (a)(2), (3), (4), (b) introductory text, (2) through (6), (c) through (f) and (k) revised; (b)(7) added 15683
20 Revised 40628
240 Revised 58252
300 Authority citation revised 32163
300.1 (a) and (j) revised 32163
300.3 (a)(1) revised 32163
300.8 (d) revised 32163
300.19 Revised 32163
300.20 Revised 32163
300.20a Added 32163
300.24 (b) revised 32164
300.25 (d) and (f) revised 32164
300.32 Revised 32164
300.33 (c) revised 32164
301.0 Revised 30456
301.1 (a)(4) revised; (a)(6), (7) and (8) removed; new (a)(6) added 30458
301.2 (b) and (c) revised 30458
301.19 (l)(1) through (7) removed 30458
301.20 (a) revised 30458
301.27 Revised 30458
301.28 Removed 30458
301.29 (a) revised 30458
301.30 Removed 30458
301.31 (b) revised 30458

16 CFR—Continued

79 FR Page

Chapter I—Continued

301.35 (b) revised 30458
301.39 Revised 30458
301.40 Removed 30458
301.41 (a)(4) revised; (a)(7) removed 30458
301.47 Revised 30458
301.48 Heading and (b) revised 30458
303.1 (h) revised 18770
303.7 Introductory text revised 18770
303.12 (a) revised 18770
303.17 (b) revised 18771
303.21 (a)(3) and (b) revised 18771
303.31 Revised 18771
303.33 (d) and (f) revised 18771
303.35 Revised 18771
303.36 (a) introductory text, (2) and (b) revised 18771
303.37 Revised 18771
303.38 (b) and (c) revised 18772
303.41 (a) revised 18774
303.42 (a) revised 18774
303.44 Revised 18774
303.45 Revised 18774
305.3 (y) revised 19466
305.5 (d) revised; (e) removed 19467
305.7 (a) and (b) revised; eff. 4-6-15 77870
305.8 (a)(1), (3) and (b)(1) revised; (a)(4) added 19467
305.12 (g) and (h) removed; (i) redesignated as new (g); (f) and new (g) revised; eff. 4-6-15 77870

16 CFR—Continued

79 FR Page

Chapter I—Continued

305.17 (h) removed 19467
305 Appendixes G1, G3, H and I revised 46986
Appendix L amended 46987
Appendix H corrected 52549
Appendixes I and L corrected 52550
Appendixes G1 through G8 revised; eff. 4-6-15 77872
Appendix L amended; eff. 4-6-15 77874
310.8 (c) and (d) revised 51478
424 Authority citation revised 70056
424.1 Amended 70056
424.2 (d) amended 70056
425 Policy statement 44271
435 Revised 55619
803.10 (c)(1) introductory text and (i) revised 25663
803 Appendix amended 25663

2015

16 CFR

80 FR Page

Chapter I

2.7 (l) revised 15160
2.10 (a)(5) and (c) revised 15160
3.14 (a) revised 25941
3.22 (a) amended; (b) revised 15160
3.23 (b) revised 15160
3.26 Revised 15161
3.32 (a) and (b) revised 15161
3.33 (c)(2) revised 15162
3.35 (b)(2) revised 15162
3.41 (f) revised 15162
3.42 (c)(2) revised 15162
3.45 (e) amended; (f) revised 15162
3.46 (c)(4) revised 15162
3.52 (a)(2) revised 15162
3.83 (a) revised 25941
4.2 (c) through (f) revised 25941
4.3 (c) and (d) revised 25942
4.4 Revised 25942
(a)(3) correctly amended 60797
4.9 (a)(1), (2), (3), (4) introductory text, (i) and (10)(viii) revised 15162
(b)(10)(viii) correctly revised 16961

16 CFR—Continued

80 FR Page

Chapter I—Continued

4.11 (a)(1)(i)(A) and (F) revised 15163
4.13 (m) revised 15163
305.3 (j) and (r) revised; (z) added; eff. in part 11-2-17 67298
305.7 (d) revised 67299
305.8 (a)(4) revised; eff. 11-2-17 67299
305.11 (d) revised; eff. 11-2-16 67299
305.15 (c) through (f) redesignated as (e) through (h); new (c) and (d) added; (b), new (f)(1), (4) and (6) revised; eff. 11-2-17 67299
305.17 (f)(4) and (5) revised 16260
305.20 (a)(1)(i) and (ii) introductory text revised; eff. 11-2-17 67300
305 Appendix L amended 16260
Appendix L amended; eff. 11-2-17 67300
310.2 (aa) through (ee) redesignated as (dd) through (hh); (f) through (z) redesignated as (h) through (bb); new (f), (g) and (cc) added; eff. 2-12-16 77558
310.3 (a)(3)(ii)(A) through (G) redesignated as (a)(3)(ii)(B) through (H); new (a)(3)(ii)(A) added; eff. 2-12-16 77558
310.4 (a)(3), (b)(1)(ii), (iii)(B) and (3)(vi) revised; (a)(7)(ii)(B) and (8) amended; (a)(9) and (10) added; eff. in part 2-12-16 and 6-13-16 77559
310.6 (b)(5), (6) and (7) revised; eff. 2-12-16 77559
(b)(5)(ii) and (6)(ii) added; eff. 6-13-16 77559
310.8 (c) revised; eff. 2-12-16 77560
429.0 (a) introductory text revised 1332
500.3 (d) revised 71689
500.5 (c) revised 71689
500.19 (a) revised 71689
500.22 Revised 71689
502 Authority citation revised 71689
502.100 Removed 71689
502.101 Removed 71689
502.102 Removed 71689

16 CFR—Continued

80 FR Page

Chapter I—Continued

700.1 (g) and (i) amended 42721
700.2 Amended 42721
700.3 (a), (b) and (c) amended; (a) footnote 1 revised 42721
700.4 Amended 42721
700.5 (a) revised; (b) amended 42721
700.6 (a) and (b) amended 42721
700.7 (a) amended 42721
700.8 Amended 42721
700.9 Amended 42721
700.10 Heading, (a) and (c) revised; (b) amended 42721
700.11 (a), (b) and (c) amended 42722
701.1 (d) revised 42722
701.3 (a)(7) revised 42722
703.1 (e) revised 42722
703.2 (a) amended 42722
703.5 (g)(2) revised; (i) and (j) amended 42722

2016

16 CFR

81 FR Page

Chapter I

1.98 (Subpart L) Revised; interim 42478
1.100 (a) amended 2742
1.110—1.119 (Subpart P) Added 2742
1.120—1.124 (Subpart Q) Added 2742
4.9 (b)(10)(ix) revised 93805
4.10 (a)(3) revised 93805
4.11 (a)(1)(i)(A), (D)(*1*), (ii)(B)(*1*), (C), (iii)(A), (2) and (3)(i)(A)(*2*) revised 93805
304.3 Revised 70938
305.3 (x) revised; eff. 9-17-18 63646
305.7 (g) revised 7202
(a), (b) and (d) revised; eff. 6-12-17 63646
305.8 Amended; (a)(5) added; eff. 6-12-17 63646
305.10 (b) revised 7202
305.11 (f)(9)(viii) removed; (f)(9)(ix) and (x) redesignated as new (f)(9)(viii) and (ix); (f)(5), (6), (9)(ii) and new (viii) revised 7202
(a) and (f) revised; eff. 6-12-17 63646
305.12 (f)(2), (3) and (g) revised; (f)(14) added; eff. 6-12-17 63648
305.13 (a) revised; eff. 9-17-18 63649
(a)(1) introductory text, (xii) and (5) corrected 74917
305.14 Revised; eff. 6-12-17 63650
305 Appendixes F1 and F2 revised; Appendix L amended 7202

16 CFR—Continued

81 FR Page

Chapter I—Continued

Appendixes A1 through A8 revised; eff. 6-12-17 63650
Appendix A9 added; Appendixes B1, B2 and B3 revised; eff. 6-12-17 63653
Appendixes D1 through D4 revised; eff. 6-12-17 63654
Appendix D5 removed; Appendix H revised; eff. 6-12-17 63656
Appendix L amended; eff. 9-17-18 63656
Appendix L corrected 74917
306 Policy statement 86914
306.0 (b), (i), (j) and (l) revised; (o) added 2062
306.5 Revised 2063
306.6 (b) revised 2063
306.10 (a) and (f) revised 2063
306.12 (a)(4) through (9) redesignated as (a)(5) through (10); new (a)(4) added; (f) amended 2063
306.13 Added 2064
310.8 (c) and (d) revised 59845
436.8 (a)(1), (5)(i) and (ii) amended 31501
455.1 (d)(7) revised; eff. 1-27-17 81678
455.2 (a) introductory text, (2) and (b) revised; eff. 1-27-17 81678
455.5 Revised; eff. 1-27-17 81679
455 Figures 1 through 6 added; eff. 1-27-17 81679
701.1 (g), (h) and (i) redesignated as (h), (i) and (j); new (g) added; new (h) and (j) revised 63669
702.1 (d) revised; (g) added 63669
702.3 Revised 63669
803.1 (a) revised 60259
803.2 (e) and (f) revised 60259
803.3 (d) revised 60259
803.5 (a)(1) introductory text, (3) and (b) revised 60259
803.10 (c)(1)(i) revised; (c)(1)(ii) and (iii) removed; (c)(1)(iv) redesignated as new (c)(1)(ii) 60260
803 Appendix amended 60260

2017

16 CFR

82 FR Page

Chapter I

1.98 Revised 8137
1.125—1.129 (Subpart Q) Added 30966
1.130 (Subpart R) Added 30966
4.8 (b)(2)(iii), (6)(i), (7), (e)(2)(i)(C) and (i) revised 21686

16 CFR—Continued

82 FR Page

2018

16 CFR

83 FR Page

16 CFR—Continued

83 FR Page

○

www.ingramcontent.com/pod-product-compliance
Lightning Source LLC
LaVergne TN
LVHW052203200926
848481LV00001B/21